THE Visual Basic 5 Programmer's Reference

Windows 95/NT

VENTANA

THE
Visual
Basic 5
Programmer's
Reference

Windows 95/NT

Wayne S. Freeze

The Visual Basic 5 Programmer's Reference
Copyright © 1997 by Wayne Freeze

All rights reserved. This book may not be duplicated in any way without the expressed written consent of the publisher, except in the form of brief excerpts or quotations for the purposes of review. The information contained herein is for the personal use of the reader and may not be incorporated in any commercial programs, other books, databases, or any kind of software without written consent of the publisher or author. Making copies of this book or any portion for any purpose other than your own is a violation of United States copyright laws.

Library of Congress Cataloging-in-Publication Data

Freeze, Wayne S.
    The Visual Basic 5 programmer's reference/ Wayne S. Freeze. –1st ed.,
        p.   cm.
    ISBN 1-56604-714-5
    1. Microsoft Visual BASIC. 2. BASIC (Computer program language) I. Title.
QA76.73.B3F76 1997
005.26'8—dc21

                                                    CIP

First Edition 9 8 7 6 5 4 3 2 1

Printed in the United States of America

Ventana Communications Group
P.O. Box 13964
Research Triangle Park, NC 27709-3964
919.544.9404
FAX 919.544.9472
http://www.vmedia.com

Ventana Communications Group is a division of International Thomson Publishing.

Limits of Liability & Disclaimer of Warranty
The author and publisher of this book have used their best efforts in preparing the book and the programs contained in it. These efforts include the development, research, and testing of the theories and programs to determine their effectiveness. The author and publisher make no warranty of any kind, expressed or implied, with regard to these programs or the documentation contained in this book.
    The author and publisher shall not be liable in the event of incidental or consequential damages in connection with, or arising out of, the furnishing, performance or use of the programs, associated instructions and/or claims of productivity gains.

Trademarks
Trademarked names appear throughout this book and on the accompanying compact disk, if applicable. Rather than list the names and entities that own the trademarks or insert a trademark symbol with each mention of the trademarked name, the publisher states that it is using the names only for editorial purposes and to the benefit of the trademark owner with no intention of infringing upon that trademark.

President
Michael E. Moran

**Director of Acquisitions
and Development**
Robert Kern

Editorial Operations Manager
Kerry L. B. Foster

Production Manager
Jaimie Livingston

Brand Manager
Jamie Jaeger Fiocco

Art Director
Marcia Webb

Creative Services Manager
Diane Lennox

Acquisitions Editor
Neweleen A. Trebnik

Project Editor
Jennifer Huntley Mario

Development Editor
Michelle Corbin Nichols

Copy Editor
Marie Dobson

CD-ROM Specialist
Ginny Phelps

Technical Reviewer
Russ Mullen

Desktop Publisher
Scott Hosa

Proofreader
Alicia Farris

Cover Illustrator
Lisa Gill

About the Author

Born and raised in Baltimore, Maryland, **Wayne S. Freeze** currently splits his time between writing computer books and software, and working as a consultant for the University of Maryland at College Park. He has written two other books about Visual Basic and is the author of a popular shareware program called Car Collector, also written in Visual Basic.

His experience with personal computers began 20 years ago when he built one of the original personal computer systems, the Altair 8800, from a kit. With 4K BASIC in ROM and 1K of RAM, it wasn't very practical, but it was a lot of fun. Since then, he has used nearly every major type of personal computer built and currently has five different machines scattered around the house.

Wayne has been with the University of Maryland since 1979 and recently, he was the Technical Support Manager for the University of Maryland at College Park's Administrative Computer Center. He was responsible for the systems programming staff who installed and maintained the MVS/ESA operating system on the IBM mainframe and he advised the university's management on computer technology.

His hobbies include collecting cars ranging in size from a 1:144 scale stock car driven by Terry Labonte to a 1:1 Porsche Turbo driven only when there is no rain in sight. He can also be found at air shows photographing World War II fighters and someday hopes to get his pilot's license. In his spare time, he enjoys reading science fiction, watching stock car races, and going for long drives in the country. Now that he has started writing computer books, his spare time is mainly limited to his favorite activity: playing with his two children.

Wayne currently resides in Beltsville, Maryland, with his lovely wife, Jill, who helps him with his writing by deleting all those unnecessary commas and making sure that everything he writes makes sense. Her second computer book is expected out shortly. Wayne's son, Christopher, is four and has figured out how to crash Windows 95 on demand and is working on learning how to install his own software. Wayne's two-year-old daughter, Samantha, specializes in being cute and making sure his lap is never empty.

Acknowledgments

To Bill Adler, Jr., here's book number three. I'm still in shock. Add the two Jill is working on and the one that I should be working on, that makes six. Think we can double this by this time next year? I'm willing to try, especially now that I'm only working half time.

To my friends at Ventana, especially Neweleen, Michelle, and Jennifer. Thanks for all your help and patience in writing this book. How the original estimate of 600 pages turned into this monster, I still don't know.

To Shaun, Kyle, Ian, Michelle, Wanda, Walter, Bob, Veronica, Scott, Elwyn, Rick, and the rest of my friends who would stop by and ask how I'm doing, thanks for your support. It means more than you know.

To Bucky and Goose, see you in Mickey land real soon.

To Mom and Dad, I'm sure you don't understand some of the decisions I've made recently. To be honest, I'm not totally sure of it myself. But I believe that everything will be better in the long run.

To Chris and Sam, I love it when you scream "Daddy's book! Daddy's book!" in the bookstore (and anywhere else you may find it). Maybe we can have some ice cream after I finish just one more page and I'll try to fix your computer real soon.

To Jill, you did it. By the time this book hits the shelves your first book should be there. I've always known that you could do it and now so does the whole world. It's been fun working across the table from you. Now go find something to eat so you can get back to work. And remember this always, I love you.

Dedication

To Jill, Christopher, Samantha, and our new life.

Contents

Jump Table   xv

Introduction   lxxxv

Alphabetical Sections

A	1	N	635
B	27	O	640
C	34	P	683
D	127	Q	785
E	277	R	791
F	290	S	878
G	367	T	976
H	376	U	1052
I	386	V	1120
K	419	W	1133
L	420	Y	1150
M	496		

Appendix   1151

Jump Tables

Class	Element	Edition (see Legend)	Page
Abs	Function	CCE, LE, PE, EE	1
AmbientProperties	Object	CCE, LE, PE, EE	1
Animation	Control	LE, PE, EE	3
AnimationControl.Close			5
AnimationControl.Drag [DragAction]			5
AnimationControl.Move Left [, Top [, Width [, Height]]]			6
AnimationControl.OLEDrag			6
AnimationControl.Open [AVIFile]			6
AnimationControl.Play [Repeat [, StartFrame [, EndFrame]]]			6
AnimationControl.SetFocus			6
AnimationControl.ShowWhatsThis			6
AnimationControl.Stop			7
AnimationControl.ZOrder [position]			7
EventsPrivate Sub AnimationControl _Click([index As Integer])			7
Private Sub AnimationControl _DragDrop([index As Integer ,] source as Control, x as Single, y as Single)			7
Private Sub AnimationControl _DragOver([index As Integer ,] source as Control, x as Single, y as Single, state as Integer)			8
Private Sub AnimationControl _GotFocus ([index As Integer])			9
Private Sub AnimationControl _LostFocus ([index As Integer])			9
Private Sub AnimationControl _MouseDown([index As Integer ,] button as Integer, shift as Single, x as Single, y as Single)			9
Private Sub AnimationControl _MouseMove ([index As Integer ,] button as Integer, shift as Single, x as Single, y as Single)			10
Private Sub AnimationControl _MouseUp([index As Integer ,] button as Integer, shift as Single, x as Single, y as Single)			11

Class	Element	Edition (see Legend)	Page
Animation (con't)	Control	LE, PE, EE	3
Private Sub AnimationControl _OLECompleteDrag([index As Integer ,] effect as Long)			11
Private Sub AnimationControl _OLEDragDrop([index As Integer ,] data as DataObject, effect as Long, button as Integer, shift as Single, x as Single, y as Single)			12
Private Sub AnimationControl _OLEDragOver([index As Integer ,] data as DataObject, effect as Long, button as Integer, shift as Single, x as Single, y as Single, state as Integer)			13
Private Sub AnimationControl _OLEGiveFeedback ([index As Integer ,] effect as Long)			14
Private Sub AnimationControl _OLESetData([index As Integer ,] data as DataObject, DataFormat as Integer)			15
Private Sub AnimationControl _OLEStartDrag ([index As Integer ,] data as DataObject, AllowedEffects as Long)			15
App	Object	CCE, LE, PE, EE	16
App.LogEvent (logBuffer, eventType)			19
App.StartLogging logTarget, logMode			19
AppActivate	Statement	CCE, LE, PE, EE	20
Array	Function	CCE, LE, PE, EE	20
Asc	Function	CCE, LE, PE, EE	21
AscB	Function	CCE, LE, PE, EE	22
AscW	Function	CCE, LE, PE, EE	22
AsyncProperty	Object	CCE, LE, PE, EE	23
Atn	Function	CCE, LE, PE, EE	24
Axis	Object	PE, EE	24
AxisGrid	Object	PE, EE	25
AxisScale	Object	PE, EE	25
AxisTitle	Object	PE, EE	26
Backdrop	Object	PE, EE	27
Beep	Statement	CCE, LE, PE, EE	27
Boolean	Data Type	CCE, LE, PE, EE	28
Brush	Object	PE, EE	28
Button	Object	CCE, LE, PE, EE	29
Buttons	Collection	CCE, LE, PE, EE	31
ButtonsCollection.Add ([index] , [key] , [caption] , [style] , [image])			32
ButtonsCollection.Clear			33
ButtonsCollection.Remove reference			33

Class	Element	Edition (see Legend)	Page
Byte	Data Type	CCE, LE, PE, EE	33
Call	Statement	CCE, LE, PE, EE	34
CategoryScale	Object	PE, EE	35
CBool	Function	CCE, LE, PE, EE	35
CByte	Function	CCE, LE, PE, EE	36
CCur	Function	CCE, LE, PE, EE	37
CDate	Function	CCE, LE, PE, EE	37
CDbl	Function	CCE, LE, PE, EE	38
CDec	Function	CCE, LE, PE, EE	39
ChDir	Statement	CCE, LE, PE, EE	40
ChDrive	Statement	CCE, LE, PE, EE	41
CheckBox	Control	CCE, LE, PE, EE	42
CheckBoxControl.Drag [DragAction]			47
CheckBoxControl.Move Left [, Top [, Width [, Height]]]			47
CheckBoxControl.OLEDrag			47
CheckBoxControl.Refresh			47
CheckBoxControl.SetFocus			48
CheckBoxControl.ShowWhatsThis			48
CheckBoxControl.ZOrder [position]			48
Private Sub CheckBoxControl__Click([index As Integer])			48
Private Sub CheckBoxControl_DragDrop([index As Integer ,] source As Control, x As Single, y As Single)			48
Private Sub CheckBoxControl_DragOver([index As Integer ,] source As Control, x As Single, y As Single, state As Integer)			49
Private Sub CheckBoxControl_GotFocus ([index As Integer])			50
Private Sub CheckBoxControl_KeyDown ([index As Integer ,] keycode As Integer, shift As Single)			50
Private Sub CheckBoxControl_KeyPress([index As Integer ,] keychar As Integer)			50
Private Sub CheckBoxControl_KeyUp ([index As Integer ,] keycode As Integer, shift As Single)			50
Private Sub CheckBoxControl_LostFocus ([index As Integer])			51

Legend

CCE .... Control Creation Edition
LE .... Learning Edition
VBA .... Visual Basic for Applications
EE .... Enterprise Edition
PE .... Professional Edition

Class	Element	Edition (see Legend)	Page
CheckBox (con't)	Control	CCE, LE, PE, EE	42
Private Sub CheckBoxControl_MouseDown([index As Integer ,] button As Integer, shift As Single, x As Single, y As Single)			51
Private Sub CheckBoxControl_MouseMove ([index As Integer ,] button As Integer, shift As Single, x As Single, y As Single)			52
Private Sub CheckBoxControl_MouseUp([index As Integer ,] button As Integer, shift As Single, x As Single, y As Single)			53
Private Sub CheckBoxControl_OLECompleteDrag([index As Integer ,] effect As Long)			53
Private Sub CheckBoxControl_OLEDragDrop([index As Integer ,] data As DataObject, effect As Long, button As Integer, shift As Single, x As Single, y As Single)			54
Private Sub CheckBoxControl_OLEDragOver([index As Integer ,] data As DataObject, effect As Long, button As Integer, shift As Single, x As Single, y As Single, state As Integer)			55
Private Sub CheckBoxControl_OLEGiveFeedback ([index As Integer ,] effect As Long)			56
Private Sub CheckBoxControl_OLESetData([index As Integer ,] data As DataObject, DataFormat As Integer)			57
Private Sub CheckBoxControl_OLEStartDrag ([index As Integer ,] data As DataObject, AllowedEffects As Long)			57
Choose	Function	CCE, LE, PE, EE	58
Chr	Function	CCE, LE, PE, EE	59
ChrB	Function	CCE, LE, PE, EE	60
ChrW	Function	CCE, LE, PE, EE	60
CInt	Function	CCE, LE, PE, EE	61
Clipboard	Object	CCE, LE, PE, EE	62
Clipboard.Clear			62
Object = Clipboard.GetData ([format])			62
exists = Clipboard.GetFormat ([format])			63
object = Clipboard.GetText ([format])			63
Clipboard.SetData (data [, format])			64
Clipboard.SetText (data [, format])			64
CLng	Function	CCE, LE, PE, EE	65
Close	Statement	CCE, LE, PE, EE	66
Collection	Object	CCE, LE, PE, EE	67
CollectionObject.Add item, key, [before I , after]			67
CollectionObject.Clear			67
Item = CollectionObject.Item (index)			67
CollectionObject.Remove index			68
Column	Object	CCE, LE, PE, EE	68
text = ColumnObject.CellText (bookmark)			70
value = ColumnObject.CellValue (bookmark)			70

Class	Element	Edition (see Legend)	Page
Column Header	Object	CCE, LE, PE, EE	70
Column Headers	Collection	CCE, LE, PE, EE	71
ColumnHeaderObject = ColumnHeaders.Add ([index] , [key] , [text] , [width] , [alignment])			71
ColumnHeaders.Clear			72
Item = ColumnHeaders.Item (index)			72
ColumnHeaders.Remove index			72
Columns	Collection	PE, EE	73
column = ColumnsCollection.Add index			73
column = ColumnsCollection.Item (index)			73
ColumnsCollection.Remove index			73
ComboBox	Control	CCE, LE, PE, EE	74
ComboBoxControl.AddItem item [, index]			79
ComboBoxControl.Clear			79
ComboBoxControl.Drag [DragAction]			80
ComboBoxControl.Move Left [, Top [, Width [, Height]]]			80
ComboBoxControl.OLEDrag			80
ComboBoxControl.Refresh			80
ComboBoxControl.RemoveItem index			80
ComboBoxControl.SetFocus			81
ComboBoxControl.ShowWhatsThis			81
ComboBoxControl.ZOrder [position]			81
Private Sub ComboBoxControl_Change([index As Integer])			81
Private Sub ComboBoxControl_Click([index As Integer])			81
Private Sub ComboBoxControl_DblClick([index As Integer])			82
Private Sub ComboBoxControl_DragDrop([index As Integer ,] source As Control, x As Single, y As Single)			82
Private Sub ComboBoxControl_DragOver([index As Integer ,] source As Control, x As Single, y As Single, state As Integer)			82
Private Sub ComboBoxControl_GotFocus ([index As Integer])			83
Private Sub ComboBoxControl_KeyDown ([index As Integer ,] keycode As Integer, shift As Single)			83
Private Sub ComboBoxControl_KeyPress([index As Integer ,] keychar As Integer)			84

Legend

CCE .... Control Creation Edition
LE .... Learning Edition
VBA .... Visual Basic for Applications
EE .... Enterprise Edition
PE .... Professional Edition

Class	Element	Edition (see Legend)	Page
ComboBox (con't)	Control	CCE, LE, PE, EE	74
Private Sub ComboBoxControl_KeyUp ([index As Integer ,] keycode As Integer, shift As Single)			84
Private Sub ComboBoxControl_LostFocus ([index As Integer])			85
Private Sub ComboBoxControl_OLECompleteDrag([index As Integer ,] effect As Long)			85
Private Sub ComboBoxControl_OLEDragDrop([index As Integer ,] data As DataObject, effect As Long, button As Integer, shift As Single, x As Single, y As Single)			85
Private Sub ComboBoxControl_OLEDragOver([index As Integer ,] data As DataObject, effect As Long, button As Integer, shift As Single, x As Single, y As Single, state As Integer)			87
Private Sub ComboBoxControl_OLEGiveFeedback ([index As Integer ,] effect As Long)			88
Private Sub ComboBoxControl_OLESetData([index As Integer ,] data As DataObject, DataFormat As Integer)			89
Private Sub ComboBoxControl_OLEStartDrag ([index As Integer ,] data As DataObject, AllowedEffects As Long)			89
Private Sub ComboBoxControl_Scroll ([index As Integer])			90
Command	Function	CCE, LE, PE, EE	90
CommandButton	Control	CCE, LE, PE, EE	91
CommandButtonControl.Drag [DragAction]			95
CommandButtonControl.Move Left [, Top [, Width [, Height]]]			96
CommandButtonControl.OLEDrag			96
CommandButtonControl.Refresh			96
CommandButtonControl.SetFocus			96
CommandButtonControl.ShowWhatsThis			96
CommandButtonControl.ZOrder [position]			96
Private Sub CommandButtonControl_Click([index As Integer])			97
Private Sub CommandButtonControl_DragDrop([index As Integer ,] source As Control, x As Single, y As Single)			97
Private Sub CommandButtonControl_DragOver([index As Integer ,] source As Control, x As Single, y As Single, state As Integer)			97
Private Sub CommandButtonControl_GotFocus ([index As Integer])			98
Private Sub CommandButtonControl_KeyDown ([index As Integer ,] keycode As Integer, shift As Single)			98
Private Sub CommandButtonControl_KeyPress([index As Integer ,] keychar As Integer)			99
Private Sub CommandButtonControl_KeyUp ([index As Integer ,] keycode As Integer, shift As Single)			99
Private Sub CommandButtonControl_LostFocus ([index As Integer])			100
Private Sub CommandButtonControl_MouseDown([index As Integer ,] button As Integer, shift As Single, x As Single, y As Single)			100
Private Sub CommandButtonControl_MouseMove ([index As Integer ,] button As Integer, shift As Single, x As Single, y As Single)			101
Private Sub CommandButtonControl_MouseUp([index As Integer ,] button As Integer, shift As Single, x As Single, y As Single)			101
Private Sub CommandButtonControl_OLECompleteDrag([index As Integer ,] effect As Long)			102
Private Sub CommandButtonControl_OLEDragDrop([index As Integer ,] data As DataObject, effect As Long, button As Integer, shift As Single, x As Single, y As Single)			103
Private Sub CommandButtonControl_OLEDragOver([index As Integer ,] data As DataObject, effect As Long, button As Integer, shift As Single, x As Single, y As Single, state As Integer)			104

Class	Element	Edition (see Legend)	Page
CommandButton (con't)	Control	CCE, LE, PE, EE	91
Private Sub CommandButtonControl_OLEGiveFeedback ([index As Integer ,] effect As Long)			105
Private Sub CommandButtonControl_OLESetData([index As Integer ,] data As DataObject, DataFormat As Integer)			106
Private Sub CommandButtonControl_OLEStartDrag ([index As Integer ,] data As DataObject, AllowedEffects As Long)			106
CommonDialog	Control	CCE, LE, PE, EE	107
CommonDialogControl.AboutBox			112
CommonDialogControl.ShowColor			112
CommonDialogControl.ShowFont			112
CommonDialogControl.ShowHelp			112
CommonDialogControl.ShowOpen			112
CommonDialogControl.ShowPrinter			112
CommonDialogControl.ShowSave			112
Connection	Object	PE, EE	113
ConnectionObject.Cancel			114
ConnectionObject.Close			114
querydef = ConnectionObject.CreateQueryDef ([name] [, [sql]])			114
ConnectionObject.Execute source [, options]			114
recordset = ConnectionObject.OpenRecordset (source [, type [, options] [, lockedits]])			114
Connections	Collection	PE, EE	116
ConnectionsCollection.Refresh			116
Const	Statement	CCE, LE, PE, EE	116
ContainedControls	Collection	CCE, LE, PE, EE	117
Container	Object	PE, EE	117
Containers	Collection	PE, EE	118
ContainersCollection.Refresh			118
Control	Object	CCE, LE, PE, EE	119

Legend

CCE .... Control Creation Edition
LE .... Learning Edition
VBA .... Visual Basic for Applications
EE .... Enterprise Edition
PE .... Professional Edition

Class	Element	Edition (see Legend)	Page
Controls	Collection	CCE, LE, PE, EE	119
ControlsCollection.Clear			119
Item = ControlsCollection.Item (index)			119
ControlCollection.Remove index			119
Coor	Object	CCE, LE, PE, EE	120
CoorObject.Set xvalue, yvalue			120
Cos	Function	CCE, LE, PE, EE	120
CreateObject	Function	CCE, LE, PE, EE	121
CSng	Function	CCE, LE, PE, EE	122
CStr	Function	CCE, LE, PE, EE	122
CurDir	Statement	CCE, LE, PE, EE	123
Currency	Data Type	CCE, LE, PE, EE	124
CVar	Function	CCE, LE, PE, EE	124
CVDate	Function	CCE, LE, PE, EE	125
CVErr	Function	CCE, LE, PE, EE	126
Data	Control	CCE, LE, PE, EE	127
DataControl.Drag [DragAction]			132
DataControl.Move Left [, Top [, Width [, Height]]]			132
DataControl.OLEDrag			133
DataControl.Refresh			133
DataControl.ShowWhatsThis			133
DataControl.UpdateControls			133
DataControl.UpdateRecord			133
DataControl.ZOrder [position]			133
Private Sub DataControl__DragDrop([index As Integer ,] source As Control, x As Single, y As Single)			134
Private Sub DataControl__DragOver([index As Integer ,] source As Control, x As Single, y As Single, state As Integer)			134
Private Sub DataControl__Error ([index As Integer ,] errcode As Integer, resp As Single)			135
Private Sub DataControl__MouseDown([index As Integer ,] button As Integer, shift As Single, x As Single, y As Single)			135
Private Sub DataControl__MouseMove ([index As Integer ,] button As Integer, shift As Single, x As Single, y As Single)			136
Private Sub DataControl__MouseUp([index As Integer ,] button As Integer, shift As Single, x As Single, y As Single)			137
Private Sub DataControl__OLECompleteDrag([index As Integer ,] effect As Long)			137
Private Sub DataControl__OLEDragDrop([index As Integer ,] data As DataObject, effect As Long, button As Integer, shift As Single, x As Single, y As Single)			138

Class	Element	Edition (see Legend)	Page
Data (con't)	Control	CCE, LE, PE, EE	127
	Private Sub DataControl_OLEDragOver([index As Integer ,] data As DataObject, effect As Long, button As Integer, shift As Single, x As Single, y As Single, state As Integer)		139
	Private Sub DataControl_OLEGiveFeedback ([index As Integer ,] effect As Long)		140
	Private Sub DataControl_OLESetData([index As Integer ,] data As DataObject, DataFormat As Integer)		141
	Private Sub DataControl_OLEStartDrag ([index As Integer ,] data As DataObject, AllowedEffects As Long)		141
	Private Sub DataControl_Reposition ([index As Integer])		142
	Private Sub DataControl_Resize ([index As Integer])		142
	Private Sub DataControl_Validate ([index As Integer ,] action As Integer, save As Single)		142
Database	Object	PE, EE	144
	DatabaseObject.Close		145
	property = DatabaseObject.CreateProperty ([name] [, [type] [, [value] [, DDL]]])		145
	querydef = DatabaseObject.CreateQueryDef ([name] [, [sql]])		146
	relation = DatabaseObject.CreateRelation ([name] [, [table] [, [foreign] [, attr]]])		146
	tabledef = DatabaseObject.CreateTableDef ([name] [, [attr] [, [source] [, connect]]])		147
	DatabaseObject.Execute source [, options]		147
	DatabaseObject.MakeReplica replica, description [, options]		148
	DatabaseObject.NewPassword oldpwd, newpwd		148
	recordset = DatabaseObject.OpenRecordset (source [, type [, options] [, lockedits]])		148
	DatabaseObject.PopulatePartial dbname		149
	DatabaseObject.Synchronize dbname [, exchange]		150
Databases	Collection	PE, EE	150
	DatabasesCollection.Refresh		150
DataBinding	Object	PE, EE	151
DataBindings	Collection	PE, EE	151
DataGrid	Object	PE, EE	152
	DataGridObject.DeleteColumnLabels labelindex, count		152
	DataGridObject.DeleteColumns column, count		152
	DataGridObject.DeleteRowLabels labelindex, count		152

Legend

CCE .... Control Creation Edition
LE .... Learning Edition
VBA .... Visual Basic for Applications
EE .... Enterprise Edition
PE .... Professional Edition

Class	Element	Edition (see Legend)	Page
DataGrid (con't)	Object	PE, EE	152
DataGridObject.DeleteRows row, count			153
DataGridObject.GetData row, column, datapoint, nullflag			153
DataGridObject.InitializeLabels			153
DataGridObject.InsertColumnLabels labelindex, count			153
DataGridObject.InsertColumns column, count			153
DataGridObject.InsertRowLabels labelindex, count			153
DataGridObject.InsertRows row, count			154
DataGridObject.MoveData top, left, bottom, right, overoffset, downoffset			154
DataGridObject.RandomDataFill			154
DataGridObject.RandomFillColumns column, count			154
DataGridObject.RandomFillRows row, count			154
DataGridObject.SetData row, column, datapoint, nullflag			155
DataGridObject.SetSize rowlabelcount, columnlabelcount, datarowcount, datacolumncount			155
DataObject	Object	CCE, LE, PE, EE	155
DataObjectObject.Clear			155
value = DataObjectObject.GetData format			155
bvalue = DataObjectObject.GetFormat format			156
DataObjectObject.SetData [data] [, format]			156
DataObjectFiles	Collection	CCE, LE, PE, EE	157
DataObjectFilesCollection.Add filename, [index]			157
DataObjectFilesCollection.Clear			158
DataObjectFilesCollection.Remove index			158
DataPoint	Object	PE, EE	158
DataPointObject.ResetCustom			158
DataPointObject.Select			158
DataPointLabel	Object	PE, EE	159
DataPointObject.ResetCustomLabel			160
DataPointObject.Select			160
DataPoints	Collection	PE, EE	160
Date	Data Type	CCE, LE, PE, EE	161
Date	Function	CCE, LE, PE, EE	161
Date	Statement	CCE, LE, PE, EE	162

Class	Element	Edition (see Legend)	Page
DateAdd	Function	CCE, LE, PE, EE	162
DateDiff	Function	CCE, LE, PE, EE	163
DatePart	Function	CCE, LE, PE, EE	165
DateValue	Function	CCE, LE, PE, EE	167
Day	Function	CCE, LE, PE, EE	168
DBCombo	Control	PE, EE	168
DBComboControl.AboutBox			173
DBComboControl.Drag [DragAction]			173
DBComboControl.Move Left [, Top [, Width [, Height]]]			173
DBComboControl.OLEDrag			173
DBComboControl.ReFill			173
DBComboControl.Refresh			174
DBComboControl.SetFocus			174
DBComboControl.ShowWhatsThis			174
DBComboControl.ZOrder [position]			174
Private Sub DBComboControl__Click([index As Integer])			174
Private Sub DBComboControl__DblClick([index As Integer])			174
Private Sub DBComboControl__DragDrop([index As Integer ,] source As Control, x As Single, y As Single)			175
Private Sub DBComboControl__DragOver([index As Integer ,] source As Control, x As Single, y As Single, state As Integer)			175
Private Sub DBComboControl__GotFocus ([index As Integer])			176
Private Sub DBComboControl__KeyDown ([index As Integer ,] keycode As Integer, shift As Single)			176
Private Sub DBComboControl__KeyPress([index As Integer ,] keychar As Integer)			177
Private Sub DBComboControl__KeyUp ([index As Integer ,] keycode As Integer, shift As Single)			177
Private Sub DBComboControl_LostFocus ([index As Integer])			177
Private Sub DBComboBoxControl_MouseDown([index As Integer ,] button As Integer, shift As Single, x As Single, y As Single)			177
Private Sub DBComboControl_MouseMove ([index As Integer ,] button As Integer, shift As Single, x As Single, y As Single)			178
Private Sub DBComboBoxControl_MouseUp([index As Integer ,] button As Integer, shift As Single, x As Single, y As Single)			179
Private Sub DBComboControl_OLECompleteDrag([index As Integer ,] effect As Long)			180

Legend

CCE .... Control Creation Edition
LE .... Learning Edition
VBA .... Visual Basic for Applications
EE .... Enterprise Edition
PE .... Professional Edition

Class	Element	Edition (see Legend)	Page
DBCombo (con't)	Control	PE, EE	168
	Private Sub DBComboControl_OLEDragDrop([index As Integer ,] data As DataObject, effect As Long, button As Integer, shift As Single, x As Single, y As Single)		180
	Private Sub DBComboControl_OLEDragOver([index As Integer ,] data As DataObject, effect As Long, button As Integer, shift As Single, x As Single, y As Single, state As Integer)		182
	Private Sub DBComboControl_OLEGiveFeedback ([index As Integer ,] effect As Long)		183
	Private Sub DBComboControl_OLESetData([index As Integer ,] data As DataObject, DataFormat As Integer)		183
	Private Sub DBComboControl_OLEStartDrag ([index As Integer ,] data As DataObject, AllowedEffects As Long)		184
DBGrid	Control	PE, EE	185
	DBGridControl.ClearFields		191
	DBGridControl.ClearSelCols		191
	column = DBGridControl.ColContaining coord		191
	DBGridControl.Drag [DragAction]		192
	bookmark = DBGridControl.GetBookmark value		192
	DBGridControl.HoldFields		192
	DBGridControl.Move Left [, Top [, Width [, Height]]]		192
	DBGridControl.ReBind		192
	DBGridControl.Refresh		193
	bookmark = DBGridControl.RowBookmark value		193
	row = DBGridControl.RowContaining coord		193
	ycoord = DBGridControl.RowTop value		193
	DBGridControl.Scroll colvalue, rowvalue		193
	DBGridControl.SetFocus		193
	DBGridControl.ShowWhatsThis		193
	split = DBGridControl.SplitContaining x, y		194
	DBGridControl.ZOrder [position]		194
	Private Sub DBGridControl_AfterColEdit ([index As Integer ,] colindex)		194
	Private Sub DBGridControl_AfterColUpdate ([index As Integer ,] colindex)		194
	Private Sub DBGridControl_AfterDelete ([index As Integer])		195
	Private Sub DBGridControl_AfterInsert ([index As Integer])		195
	Private Sub DBGridControl_AfterUpdate ([index As Integer])		195
	Private Sub DBGridControl_BeforeColEdit ([index As Integer ,] ByVal colindex As Integer, ByVal keyascii As Integer, cancel As Boolean)		195
	Private Sub DBGridControl_BeforeColUpdate ([index As Integer ,] colindex As Integer, currentvalue As Integer, cancel As Boolean)		195
	Private Sub DBGridControl_BeforeDelete ([index As Integer ,] cancel)		196
	Private Sub DBGridControl_BeforeInsert ([index As Integer ,] cancel As Boolean)		196
	Private Sub DBGridControl_BeforeUpdate ([index As Integer ,] cancel As Boolean)		196
	Private Sub DBGridControl_ButtonClick ([index As Integer ,] ByVal colindex As Integer)		196

Class	Element	Edition (see Legend)	Page
DBGrid (con't)	Control	PE, EE	185
	Private Sub DBGridControl_Change([index As Integer])		197
	Private Sub DBGridControl_Click([index As Integer])		197
	Private Sub DBGridControl_ColEdit ([index As Integer ,] ByVal colindex As Integer)		197
	Private Sub DBGridControl_ColResize ([index As Integer ,] colindex As Integer, cancel As Boolean)		197
	Private Sub DBGridControl_DblClick([index As Integer])		198
	Private Sub DBGridControl_DragDrop([index As Integer ,] source As Control, x As Single, y As Single)		198
	Private Sub DBGridControl_DragOver([index As Integer ,] source As Control, x As Single, y As Single, state As Integer)		198
	Private Sub DBGridControl_Error ([index As Integer ,] errcode As Integer, resp As Single)		199
	Private Sub DBGridControl_GotFocus ([index As Integer])		199
	Private Sub DBGridControl_HeadClick ([index As Integer ,] colindex As Integer)		200
	Private Sub DBGridControl_KeyDown ([index As Integer ,] keycode As Integer, shift As Single)		200
	Private Sub DBGridControl_KeyPress([index As Integer ,] keychar As Integer)		200
	Private Sub DBGridControl_KeyUp ([index As Integer ,] keycode As Integer, shift As Single)		201
	Private Sub DBGridControl_LostFocus ([index As Integer])		201
	Private Sub DBGridBoxControl_MouseDown([index As Integer ,] button As Integer, shift As Single, x As Single, y As Single)		201
	Private Sub DBGridControl_MouseMove ([index As Integer ,] button As Integer, shift As Single, x As Single, y As Single)		202
	Private Sub DBGridBoxControl_MouseUp([index As Integer ,] button As Integer, shift As Single, x As Single, y As Single)		203
	Private Sub DBGridControl_OnAddNew ([index As Integer])		204
	Private Sub DBGridControl_RowColChange ([index As Integer ,] row As Integer, col As Integer)		204
	Private Sub DBGridControl_RowResize ([index As Integer ,] rowindex As Integer, cancel As Boolean)		204
	Private Sub DBGridControl_Scroll ([index As Integer ,] cancel As Boolean)		204
	Private Sub DBGridControl_SelChange ([index As Integer ,] cancel As Boolean)		205
	Private Sub DBGridControl_SplitChange ([index As Integer])		205
	Private Sub DBGridControl_UnboundAddData ([index As Integer ,] rowbuf As RowBuffer , bookmark As Variant)		205
	Private Sub DBGridControl_UnboundDeleteRow ([index As Integer ,] bookmark As Variant)		205
	Private Sub DBGridControl_UnboundGetRelative-Bookmark ([index As Integer ,] start As Variant, ByVal offset As Long, new As Variant, pos As Long)		206
	Private Sub DBGridControl_UnboundReadData ([index As Integer ,] row As RowBuffer, start As Variant, readprior As Boolean)		206
	Private Sub DBGridControl_UnboundWriteData ([index As Integer ,] row As RowBuffer, start As Variant)		206

Legend

CCE .... Control Creation Edition
LE .... Learning Edition
VBA .... Visual Basic for Applications
EE .... Enterprise Edition
PE .... Professional Edition

Class	Element	Edition (see Legend)	Page
DBEngine	Object	PE, EE	207
	DBEngine.BeginTrans		207
	DBEngine.CommitTrans [dbFlushOSCacheWrites]		207
	DBEngine.CompactDatabase olddb, newdb [, locale [, options [, password]]]		208
	DBEngine.CompactDatabase dbname, locale , options		209
	DBEngine.CreateWorkspace name, user, password, options		210
	DBEngine.Idle [dbRefreshCache]		210
	connection = DBEngine.OpenConnection name [, options [, readonly [, connect]]]		210
	database = DBEngine.OpenDatabase name [, options [, readonly [, connect]]]		211
	DBEngine.RegisterDatabase name [, driver [, silent [, keywords]]]		212
	DBEngine.RepairDatabase name		212
	DBEngine.RollBack		212
	DBEngine.SetOption option, value		213
DBList	Control	PE, EE	214
	DBListControl.AboutBox		218
	DBListControl.Drag [DragAction]		218
	DBListControl.Move Left [, Top [, Width [, Height]]]		218
	DBListControl.OLEDrag		219
	DBListControl.ReFill		219
	DBListControl.Refresh		219
	DBListControl.SetFocus		219
	DBListControl.ShowWhatsThis		219
	DBListControl.ZOrder [position]		219
	Private Sub DBListControl _Click([index As Integer])		220
	Private Sub DBListControl _DblClick([index As Integer])		220
	Private Sub DBListControl _DragDrop([index As Integer ,] source As Control, x As Single, y As Single)		220
	Private Sub DBListControl _DragOver([index As Integer ,] source As Control, x As Single, y As Single, state As Integer)		221
	Private Sub DBListControl _GotFocus ([index As Integer])		221
	Private Sub DBListControl _KeyDown ([index As Integer ,] keycode As Integer, shift As Single)		222
	Private Sub DBListControl _KeyPress([index As Integer ,] keychar As Integer)		222
	Private Sub DBListControl _KeyUp ([index As Integer ,] keycode As Integer, shift As Single)		222
	Private Sub DBListControl _LostFocus ([index As Integer])		223
	Private Sub DBListBoxControl _MouseDown([index As Integer ,] button As Integer, shift As Single, x As Single, y As Single)		223
	Private Sub DBListControl _MouseMove ([index As Integer ,] button As Integer, shift As Single, x As Single, y As Single)		224
	Private Sub DBListBoxControl _MouseUp([index As Integer ,] button As Integer, shift As Single, x As Single, y As Single)		225
	Private Sub DBListControl _OLECompleteDrag([index As Integer ,] effect As Long)		225

Class	Element	Edition (see Legend)	Page
DBList (con't)	Control	PE, EE	214
	Private Sub DBListControl _OLEDragDrop([index As Integer ,] data As DataObject, effect As Long, button As Integer, shift As Single, x As Single, y As Single)		226
	Private Sub DBListControl _OLEDragOver([index As Integer ,] data As DataObject, effect As Long, button As Integer, shift As Single, x As Single, y As Single, state As Integer)		227
	Private Sub DBListControl _OLEGiveFeedback ([index As Integer ,] effect As Long)		228
	Private Sub DBListControl _OLESetData([index As Integer ,] data As DataObject, DataFormat As Integer)		229
	Private Sub DBListControl _OLEStartDrag ([index As Integer ,] data As DataObject, AllowedEffects As Long)		229
DDB	Function	CCE, LE, PE, EE	230
Debug	Object	CCE, LE, PE, EE	231
	Debug.Assert bvalue		231
	Debug.Print [printexpr [{ ,	; } printexpr] . . .]		231
Decimal	Data Type	CCE, LE, PE, EE	232
Declare	Statement	CCE, LE, PE, EE	233
DefBool	Statement	CCE, LE, PE, EE	234
DefByte	Statement	CCE, LE, PE, EE	234
DefCur	Statement	CCE, LE, PE, EE	235
DefDate	Statement	CCE, LE, PE, EE	235
DefDbl	Statement	CCE, LE, PE, EE	235
DefInt	Statement	CCE, LE, PE, EE	236
DefLng	Statement	CCE, LE, PE, EE	236
DefObj	Statement	CCE, LE, PE, EE	236
DefSng	Statement	CCE, LE, PE, EE	237
DefStr	Statement	CCE, LE, PE, EE	237
DefVar	Statement	CCE, LE, PE, EE	237
DeleteSetting	Statement	CCE, LE, PE, EE	238

Legend

CCE .... Control Creation Edition
LE .... Learning Edition
VBA .... Visual Basic for Applications
EE .... Enterprise Edition
PE .... Professional Edition

Class	Element	Edition (see Legend)	Page
Dim	Statement	CCE, LE, PE, EE	238
Dir	Function	CCE, LE, PE, EE	240
DirListBox	Control	CCE, LE, PE, EE	241
DirListBoxControl.Drag [DragAction]			245
DirListBoxControl.Move Left [, Top [, Width [, Height]]]			245
DirListBoxControl.OLEDrag			245
DirListBoxControl.Refresh			246
DirListBoxControl.SetFocus			246
DirListBoxControl.ShowWhatsThis			246
DirListBoxControl.ZOrder [position]			246
Private Sub DirListBoxControl _Change ([index As Integer])			246
Private Sub DirListBoxControl _Click([index As Integer])			246
Private Sub DirListBoxControl _DragDrop([index As Integer ,] source As Control, x As Single, y As Single)			247
Private Sub DirListBoxControl _DragOver([index As Integer ,] source As Control, x As Single, y As Single, state As Integer)			247
Private Sub DirListBoxControl _GotFocus ([index As Integer])			248
Private Sub DirListBoxControl _KeyDown ([index As Integer ,] keycode As Integer, shift As Single)			248
Private Sub DirListBoxControl _KeyPress([index As Integer ,] keychar As Integer)			249
Private Sub DirListBoxControl _KeyUp ([index As Integer ,] keycode As Integer, shift As Single)			249
Private Sub DirListBoxControl _LostFocus ([index As Integer])			249
Private Sub DirListBoxControl _MouseDown([index As Integer ,] button As Integer, shift As Single, x As Single, y As Single)			249
Private Sub DirListBoxControl _MouseMove ([index As Integer ,] button As Integer, shift As Single, x As Single, y As Single)			250
Private Sub DirListBoxControl _MouseUp([index As Integer ,] button As Integer, shift As Single, x As Single, y As Single)			251
Private Sub DirListBoxControl _OLECompleteDrag([index As Integer ,] effect As Long)			252
Private Sub DirListBoxControl _OLEDragDrop([index As Integer ,] data As DataObject, effect As Long, button As Integer, shift As Single, x As Single, y As Single)			252
Private Sub DirListBoxControl _OLEDragOver([index As Integer ,] data As DataObject, effect As Long, button As Integer, shift As Single, x As Single, y As Single, state As Integer)			253
Private Sub DirListBoxControl _OLEGiveFeedback ([index As Integer ,] effect As Long)			255
Private Sub DirListBoxControl _OLESetData([index As Integer ,] data As DataObject, DataFormat As Integer)			255
Private Sub DirListBoxControl _OLEStartDrag ([index As Integer ,] data As DataObject, AllowedEffects As Long)			256
Private Sub DirListBoxControl _Scroll ([index As Integer])			256
Do	Statement	CCE, LE, PE, EE	257
Document	Object	PE, EE	258
property = DocumentObject.CreateProperty ([name] [, [type] [, [value] [, DDL]]])			260

Class	Element	Edition (see Legend)	Page
Documents	Collection	PE, EE	261
DocumentObject.Refresh			261
DoEvents	Function	CCE, LE, PE, EE	261
Double	Data Type	CCE, LE, PE, EE	262
DriveListBox	Control	CCE, LE, PE, EE	262
DriveListBoxControl.Drag [DragAction]			266
DriveListBoxControl.Move Left [, Top [, Width [, Height]]]			266
DriveListBoxControl.OLEDrag			267
DriveListBoxControl.Refresh			267
DriveListBoxControl.SetFocus			267
DriveListBoxControl.ShowWhatsThis			267
DriveListBoxControl.ZOrder [position]			267
Private Sub DriveListBoxControl _Change ([index As Integer])			267
Private Sub DriveListBoxControl _DragDrop([index As Integer ,] source As Control, x As Single, y As Single)			268
Private Sub DriveListBoxControl _DragOver([index As Integer ,] source As Control, x As Single, y As Single, state As Integer)			268
Private Sub DriveListBoxControl _GotFocus ([index As Integer])			269
Private Sub DriveListBoxControl _KeyDown ([index As Integer ,] keycode As Integer, shift As Single)			269
Private Sub DriveListBoxControl _KeyPress([index As Integer ,] keychar As Integer)			270
Private Sub ComoBoxControl _KeyUp ([index As Integer ,] keycode As Integer, shift As Single)			270
Private Sub DriveListBoxControl _LostFocus ([index As Integer])			270
Private Sub DriveListBoxControl _OLECompleteDrag([index As Integer ,] effect As Long)			271
Private Sub DriveListBoxControl _OLEDragDrop([index As Integer ,] data As DataObject, effect As Long, button As Integer, shift As Single, x As Single, y As Single)			271
Private Sub DriveListBoxControl _OLEDragOver([index As Integer ,] data As DataObject, effect As Long, button As Integer, shift As Single, x As Single, y As Single, state As Integer)			272
Private Sub DriveListBoxControl _OLEGiveFeedback ([index As Integer ,] effect As Long)			274
Private Sub DriveListBoxControl _OLESetData([index As Integer ,] data As DataObject, DataFormat As Integer)			274
Private Sub DriveListBoxControl _OLEStartDrag ([index As Integer ,] data As DataObject, AllowedEffects As Long)			275
Private Sub DriveListBoxControl _Scroll ([index As Integer])			275

Legend

CCE .... Control Creation Edition
LE .... Learning Edition
VBA .... Visual Basic for Applications
EE .... Enterprise Edition
PE .... Professional Edition

Class	Element	Edition (see Legend)	Page
End	Statement	CCE, LE, PE, EE	277
Enum	Statement	CCE, LE, PE, EE	277
Environ	Function	CCE, LE, PE, EE	278
EOF	Function	CCE, LE, PE, EE	279
Erase	Statement	CCE, LE, PE, EE	280
Err	Object	CCE, LE, PE, EE	281
Err.Clear			282
Err.Raise number [, source [, description [, helpfile [, helpcontex]]]]			283
Error	Function	CCE, LE, PE, EE	283
Error	Object	CCE, LE, PE, EE	284
Error	Statement	CCE, LE, PE, EE	285
Errors	Collection	CCE, LE, PE, EE	285
Errors.Refresh			285
Event	Statement	CCE, LE, PE, EE	286
Exit	Statement	CCE, LE, PE, EE	287
Exp	Function	CCE, LE, PE, EE	287
Extender	Object	CCE, LE, PE, EE	288
Field	Object	EE	290
FieldObject.AppendChunk source			292
property = FieldObject.CreateProperty ([name] [, [type] [, [value] [, DDL]]])			292
value = FieldObject.GetChunk (offset, number)			293
Fields	Collection		293
FieldsCollection.Append object			293
FieldsCollection.Delete objectname			294
FieldsCollection.Refresh			294
FileAttr	Function		294
FileCopy	Statement		295
FileDateTime	Function		296
FileLen	Function		296

Class	Element	Edition (see Legend)	Page
FileListBox	Control		302
	FileListControl.Drag [DragAction]		302
	FileListControl.Move Left [, Top [, Width [, Height]]]		302
	FileListControl.OLEDrag		302
	FileListControl.Refresh		303
	FileListControl.SetFocus		303
	FileListControl.ShowWhatsThis		303
	FileListControl.ZOrder [position]		303
	Private Sub FileListControl_Click([index As Integer])		303
	Private Sub FileListControl_DblClick([index As Integer])		303
	Private Sub FileListControl_DragDrop([index As Integer ,] source As Control, x As Single, y As Single)		304
	Private Sub FileListControl_DragOver([index As Integer ,] source As Control, x As Single, y As Single, state As Integer)		304
	Private Sub FileListControl_GotFocus ([index As Integer])		305
	Private Sub FileListControl_KeyDown ([index As Integer ,] keycode As Integer, shift As Single)		305
	Private Sub FileListControl_KeyPress([index As Integer ,] keychar As Integer)		306
	Private Sub ComoBoxControl_KeyUp ([index As Integer ,] keycode As Integer, shift As Single)		306
	Private Sub FileListControl_LostFocus ([index As Integer])		306
	Private Sub FileListControl_OLECompleteDrag([index As Integer ,] effect As Long)		307
	Private Sub FileListControl_OLEDragDrop([index As Integer ,] data As DataObject, effect As Long, button As Integer, shift As Single, x As Single, y As Single)		307
	Private Sub FileListControl_OLEDragOver([index As Integer ,] data As DataObject, effect As Long, button As Integer, shift As Single, x As Single, y As Single, state As Integer)		308
	Private Sub FileListControl_OLEGiveFeedback ([index As Integer ,] effect As Long)		310
	Private Sub FileListControl_OLESetData([index As Integer ,] data As DataObject, DataFormat As Integer)		310
	Private Sub FileListControl_OLEStartDrag ([index As Integer ,] data As DataObject, AllowedEffects As Long)		311
	Private Sub FileListControl_PathChange([index As Integer])		311
	Private Sub FileListControl_PatternChange ([index As Integer])		311
	Private Sub FileListControl_Scroll ([index As Integer])		312
Fill	Object		313
Fix	Function		313

Legend

CCE .... Control Creation Edition
LE .... Learning Edition
VBA .... Visual Basic for Applications
EE .... Enterprise Edition
PE .... Professional Edition

Class	Element	Edition (see Legend)	Page
Font	Object		314
For . . . Next	Statement		315
For Each . . . Next	Statement		316
Form	Object		317
	FormObject.Circle [Step] (x , y), radius [, color [, start [, stop [, aspect]]]]		325
	FormObject.Cls		326
	FormObject.Hide		326
	FormObject.Line [Step] (x1 , y1), [Step] (x2 , y2) [, B	BF]		326
	FormObject.Move Left [, Top [, Width [, Height]]]		327
	FormObject.OLEDrag		327
	FormObject.PaintPicture picture, x1 , y1, [width1] , [height1] ,[x2] , [y2] , [width2] , [height2] , [rasterop]		327
	color = FormObject.Point (x , y)		328
	FormObject.PopupMenu menu, flags, x, y, menuitem		328
	FormObject.PrintForm		329
	FormObject.Point [Step] (x , y), color		329
	FormObject.Refresh		330
	FormObject.Scale [(x1 , y1)—(x2 , y2)]		330
	result = FormObject.ScaleX (width , fromscale , toscale)		330
	result = FormObject.ScaleY (height , fromscale , toscale)		330
	FormObject.SetFocus		331
	FormObject.Show [style [, owner]]		331
	height = FormObject.TextHeight (string)		331
	width = FormObject.TextWidth (string)		332
	FormObject.WhatsThisMode		332
	FormObject.ZOrder [position]		332
	Private Sub FormObject_Activate ( )		332
	Private Sub FormObject_Click( )		332
	Private Sub FormObject_DblClick( )		332
	Private Sub FormObject_Deactivate ( )		333
	Private Sub FormObject_DragDrop (source As Control, x As Single, y As Single)		333
	Private Sub FormObject_DragOver (source As Control, x As Single, y As Single, state As Integer)		333
	Private Sub FormObject_GotFocus ( )		334
	Private Sub FormObject_Initialize ( )		334
	Private Sub FormObject_KeyDown (keycode As Integer, shift As Single)		334
	Private Sub FormObject_KeyPress (keychar As Integer)		335

Class	Element	Edition (see Legend)	Page
Form (con't)	Object		335
	Private Sub FormObject_KeyUp (keycode As Integer, shift As Single)		335
	Private Sub FormObject_LinkClose ( )		335
	Private Sub FormObject_LinkError (errcode As Integer)		335
	Private Sub FormObject_LinkExecute (cmd As String, cancel As Integer)		336
	Private Sub FormObject_LinkOpen (cancel As Integer)		336
	Private Sub FormObject_Load ( )		336
	Private Sub FormObject_LostFocus ( )		337
	Private Sub FormObject_MouseDown (button As Integer, shift As Single, x As Single, y As Single)		337
	Private Sub FormObject_MouseMove (button As Integer, shift As Single, x As Single, y As Single)		337
	Private Sub FormObject_MouseUp (button As Integer, shift As Single, x As Single, y As Single)		338
	Private Sub FormObject_OLECompleteDrag(effect As Long)		339
	Private Sub FormObject_OLEDragDrop (data As DataObject, effect As Long, button As Integer, shift As Single, x As Single, y As Single)		339
	Private Sub FormObject_OLEDragOver (data As DataObject, effect As Long, button As Integer, shift As Single, x As Single, y As Single, state As Integer)		340
	Private Sub FormObject_OLEGiveFeedback (effect As Long)		342
	Private Sub FormObject_OLESetData (data As DataObject, DataFormat As Integer)		342
	Private Sub FormObject_OLEStartDrag (data As DataObject, AllowedEffects As Long)		343
	Private Sub FormObject_Paint ( )		343
	Private Sub FormObject_QueryUnload (cancel As Integer, unloadmode As Long)		343
	Private Sub FormObject_Resize ( )		344
	Private Sub FormObject_Terminate ( )		344
	Private Sub FormObject_Unload (cancel As Integer)		344
Format	Function		345
Forms	Collection		349
	formobject = Forms.Point (item)		349
Frame	Control		350
	FrameControl.Drag [DragAction]		353
	FrameControl.Move Left [, Top [, Width [, Height]]]		354

Legend

CCE .... Control Creation Edition
LE .... Learning Edition
VBA .... Visual Basic for Applications
EE .... Enterprise Edition
PE .... Professional Edition

Class	Element	Edition (see Legend)	Page
Frame (con't)	Control		354
FrameControl.OLEDrag			354
FrameControl.Refresh			354
FrameControl.ShowWhatsThis			354
FrameControl.ZOrder [position]			354
Private Sub FrameControl_Click([index As Integer])			354
Private Sub FrameControl_DblClick([index As Integer])			355
Private Sub FrameControl_DragDrop([index As Integer ,] source As Control, x As Single, y As Single)			355
Private Sub FrameControl_DragOver([index As Integer ,] source As Control, x As Single, y As Single, state As Integer)			355
Private Sub FrameControl_MouseDown([index As Integer ,] button As Integer, shift As Single, x As Single, y As Single)			356
Private Sub FrameControl_MouseMove ([index As Integer ,] button As Integer, shift As Single, x As Single, y As Single)			357
Private Sub FrameControl_MouseUp([index As Integer ,] button As Integer, shift As Single, x As Single, y As Single)			358
Private Sub FrameControl_OLECompleteDrag([index As Integer ,] effect As Long)			358
Private Sub FrameControl_OLEDragDrop([index As Integer ,] data As DataObject, effect As Long, button As Integer, shift As Single, x As Single, y As Single)			359
Private Sub FrameControl_OLEDragOver([index As Integer ,] data As DataObject, effect As Long, button As Integer, shift As Single, x As Single, y As Single, state As Integer)			360
Private Sub FrameControl_OLEGiveFeedback ([index As Integer ,] effect As Long)			361
Private Sub FrameControl_OLESetData([index As Integer ,] data As DataObject, DataFormat As Integer)			362
Private Sub FrameControl_OLEStartDrag ([index As Integer ,] data As DataObject, AllowedEffects As Long)			362
FreeFile	Statement		363
FV	Function		366
Get	Statement	CCE, LE, PE, EE	367
GetAllSettings	Function	CCE, LE, PE, EE	368
GetAttr	Function	CCE, LE, PE, EE	369
GetObject	Function	CCE, LE, PE, EE	370
GetSetting	Function	CCE, LE, PE, EE	370
GoSub	Statement	CCE, LE, PE, EE	372
GoTo	Statement	CCE, LE, PE, EE	373
Group	Object	PE, EE	374
user = GroupObject.CreateUser (name, pid, password)			374

Class	Element	Edition (see Legend)	Page
Groups	Collection	PE, EE	375
GroupsCollection.Append object			375
ListItemsCollection.Delete name			375
ListItemsCollection.Refresh			375
Hex	Function	CCE, LE, PE, EE	376
Hour	Function	CCE, LE, PE, EE	376
HScrollBar	Control	CCE, LE, PE, EE	377
HScrollBarControl.Drag [DragAction]			380
HScrollBarControl.Move Left [, Top [, Width [, Height]]]			380
HScrollBarControl.Refresh			380
HScrollBarControl.SetFocus			380
HScrollBarControl.ShowWhatsThis			380
HScrollBarControl.ZOrder [position]			380
Private Sub HScrollBarControl _Change([index As Integer])			381
Private Sub HScrollBarControl _DragDrop([index As Integer ,] source as Control, x as Single, y as Single)			381
Private Sub HScrollBarControl _DragOver([index As Integer ,] source as Control, x as Single, y as Single, state as Integer)			381
Private Sub HScrollBarControl _GotFocus ([index As Integer])			382
Private Sub HScrollBarControl _KeyDown ([index As Integer ,] keycode as Integer, shift as Single)			382
Private Sub HScrollBarControl _KeyPress([index As Integer ,] keychar as Integer)			383
Private Sub ComoBoxControl _KeyUp ([index As Integer ,] keycode as Integer, shift as Single)			383
Private Sub HScrollBarControl _LostFocus ([index As Integer])			384
Private Sub HScrollBarControl _Scroll ([index As Integer])			384
Hyperlink	Object	CCE, LE, PE, EE	385
HyperlinkObject.GoBack			385
HyperlinkObject.GoForward			385
HyperlinkObject.NavigateTo target [, location [, frame]]			385
If . . . Then . . . Else	Statement	CCE, LE, PE, EE	386
IIf	Function	CCE, LE, PE, EE	387

Legend

CCE .... Control Creation Edition
LE .... Learning Edition
VBA .... Visual Basic for Applications
EE .... Enterprise Edition
PE .... Professional Edition

Class	Element	Edition (see Legend)	Page
Image	Control	CCE, LE, PE, EE	387
ImageControl.Drag [DragAction]			390
ImageControl.Move Left [, Top [, Width [, Height]]]			391
ImageControl.OLEDrag			391
ImageControl.Refresh			391
ImageControl.ShowWhatsThis			391
ImageControl.ZOrder [position]			391
Private Sub ImageControl _Click([index As Integer])			392
Private Sub ImageControl _DblClick([index As Integer])			392
Private Sub ImageControl _DragDrop([index As Integer ,] source Panel Control, x As Single, y As Single)			392
Private Sub ImageControl _DragOver([index As Integer ,] source As Control, x As Single, y As Single, state As Integer)			392
Private Sub ImageControl _MouseDown([index As Integer ,] button As Integer, shift As Single, x As Single, y As Single)			393
Private Sub ImageControl _MouseMove ([index As Integer ,] button As Integer, shift As Single, x As Single, y As Single)			394
Private Sub ImageControl _MouseUp([index As Integer ,] button As Integer, shift As Single, x As Single, y As Single)			395
Private Sub ImageControl _OLECompleteDrag([index As Integer ,] effect As Long)			396
Private Sub ImageControl _OLEDragDrop([index As Integer ,] data As DataObject, effect As Long, button As Integer, shift As Single, x As Single, y As Single)			396
Private Sub ImageControl _OLEDragOver([index As Integer ,] data As DataObject, effect As Long, button As Integer, shift As Single, x As Single, y As Single, state As Integer)			397
Private Sub ImageControl _OLEGiveFeedback ([index As Integer ,] effect As Long)			399
Private Sub ImageControl _OLESetData([index As Integer ,] data As DataObject, DataFormat As Integer)			399
Private Sub ImageControl _OLEStartDrag ([index As Integer ,] data As DataObject, AllowedEffects As Long)			400
ImageList	Control	CCE, LE, PE, EE	401
picture = ImageListControl.Overlay image1, image2			401
IMEStatus	Function	CCE, LE, PE, EE	402
Implements	Statement	CCE, LE, PE, EE	403
Index	Object	PE, EE	403
field = IndexObject.CreateField ([name [, type [, size]]])			404
property = IndexObject.CreateProperty ([name] [, [type] [, [value] [, DDL]]])			405
Indexes	Collection	PE, EE	406
IndexesCollection.Append object			406
IndexesCollection.Delete objectname			406
IndexesCollection.Refresh			406

Class	Element	Edition (see Legend)	Page
Input	Function	CCE, LE, PE, EE	406
Input	Statement	CCE, LE, PE, EE	407
InputB	Function	CCE, LE, PE, EE	408
InputBox	Function	CCE, LE, PE, EE	408
InStr	Function	CCE, LE, PE, EE	409
InStrB	Function	CCE, LE, PE, EE	410
Int	Function	CCE, LE, PE, EE	411
Integer	Data Type	CCE, LE, PE, EE	411
IPmt	Function	CCE, LE, PE, EE	412
IRR	Function	CCE, LE, PE, EE	412
IsArray	Function	CCE, LE, PE, EE	413
IsDate	Function	CCE, LE, PE, EE	414
IsEmpty	Function	CCE, LE, PE, EE	414
IsError	Function	CCE, LE, PE, EE	415
IsMissing	Function	CCE, LE, PE, EE	416
IsNull	Function	CCE, LE, PE, EE	417
IsNumeric	Function	CCE, LE, PE, EE	417
IsObject	Function	CCE, LE, PE, EE	418
Kill	Statement	CCE, LE, PE, EE	419
Label	Control	CCE, LE, PE, EE	420
LabelControl.Drag [DragAction]			425
LabelControl.LinkExecute command			425
LabelControl.LinkPoke			425
LabelControl.LinkRequest			425
LabelControl.LinkSend			425
LabelControl.Move Left [, Top [, Width [, Height]]]			425

Legend

CCE .... Control Creation Edition
LE .... Learning Edition
VBA .... Visual Basic for Applications
EE .... Enterprise Edition
PE .... Professional Edition

Class	Element	Edition (see Legend)	Page
Label (con't)	Control	CCE, LE, PE, EE	420
LabelControl.OLEDrag			426
LabelControl.Refresh			426
LabelControl.ShowWhatsThis			426
LabelControl.ZOrder [position]			426
Private Sub LabelControl__Change ([index As Integer])			426
Private Sub LabelControl__Click([index As Integer])			426
Private Sub LabelControl__DblClick([index As Integer])			427
Private Sub LabelControl__DragDrop([index As Integer ,] source As Control, x As Single, y As Single)			427
Private Sub LabelControl__DragOver([index As Integer ,] source As Control, x As Single, y As Single, state As Integer)			427
Private Sub LabelControl_LinkClose ([index As Integer ,])			428
Private Sub LabelControl _LinkError ([index As Integer ,] errcode As Integer)			428
Private Sub LabelControl _LinkExecute ([index As Integer ,] cmd As String, cancel As Integer)			429
Private Sub LabelControl _LinkOpen ([index As Integer ,] cancel As Integer)			429
Private Sub LabelControl_MouseDown([index As Integer ,] button As Integer, shift As Single, x As Single, y As Single)			429
Private Sub LabelControl_MouseMove ([index As Integer ,] button As Integer, shift As Single, x As Single, y As Single)			430
Private Sub LabelControl_MouseUp([index As Integer ,] button As Integer, shift As Single, x As Single, y As Single)			431
Private Sub LabelControl_OLECompleteDrag([index As Integer ,] effect As Long)			431
Private Sub LabelControl_OLEDragDrop([index As Integer ,] data As DataObject, effect As Long, button As Integer, shift As Single, x As Single, y As Single)			432
Private Sub LabelControl_OLEDragOver([index As Integer ,] data As DataObject, effect As Long, button As Integer, shift As Single, x As Single, y As Single, state As Integer)			433
Private Sub LabelControl_OLEGiveFeedback ([index As Integer ,] effect As Long)			434
Private Sub LabelControl_OLESetData([index As Integer ,] data As DataObject, DataFormat As Integer)			435
Private Sub LabelControl_OLEStartDrag ([index As Integer ,] data As DataObject, AllowedEffects As Long)			436
Label	Object	PE, EE	436
Labels	Collection	PE, EE	437
LBound	Function	CCE, LE, PE, EE	437
LCase	Function	CCE, LE, PE, EE	438
LCoor	Object	PE, EE	438
LCoorObject.Set xvalue, yvalue			438
Left	Function	CCE, LE, PE, EE	439
LeftB	Function	CCE, LE, PE, EE	439
Legend	Object	PE, EE	440
LegendObject.Select			440

Class	Element	Edition (see Legend)	Page
Len	Function	CCE, LE, PE, EE	440
LenB	Function	CCE, LE, PE, EE	441
Let	Statement	CCE, LE, PE, EE	441
Light	Object	PE, EE	442
LightObject.Set xvalue, yvalue			442
LightSource	Object	PE, EE	442
LightSourceObject.Set xvalue, yvalue, zvalue, intensity			442
LightSources	Collection	PE, EE	443
LightSourcesCollection.Add xvalue, yvalue, zvalue, intensity			443
LightSourcesCollection.Remove index			443
Line	Control	CCE, LE, PE, EE	443
LineControl.Refresh			445
LineControl.ZOrder [position]			445
Line Input #	Statement	CCE, LE, PE, EE	445
ListBox	Control	CCE, LE, PE, EE	446
ListBoxControl.AddItem item [, index]			451
ListBoxControl.Clear			452
ListBoxControl.Drag [DragAction]			452
ListBoxControl.Move Left [, Top [, Width [, Height]]]			452
ListBoxControl.OLEDrag			452
ListBoxControl.Refresh			453
ListBoxControl.SetFocus			453
ListBoxControl.ShowWhatsThis			453
ListBoxControl.ZOrder [position]			453
Private Sub ListBoxControl_Click([index As Integer])			453
Private Sub ListBoxControl_DblClick([index As Integer])			453
Private Sub ListBoxControl_DragDrop([index As Integer ,] source As Control, x As Single, y As Single)			454
Private Sub ListBoxControl_DragOver([index As Integer ,] source As Control, x As Single, y As Single, state As Integer)			454

Legend

CCE .... Control Creation Edition
LE .... Learning Edition
VBA .... Visual Basic for Applications
EE .... Enterprise Edition
PE .... Professional Edition

Class	Element	Edition (see Legend)	Page
ListBox (con't)	Control	CCE, LE, PE, EE	446
Private Sub ListBoxControl_GotFocus ([index As Integer])			455
Private Sub ListBoxControl_KeyDown ([index As Integer ,] keycode As Integer, shift As Single)			455
Private Sub ListBoxControl_KeyPress([index As Integer ,] keychar As Integer)			456
Private Sub ListBoxControl_KeyUp ([index As Integer ,] keycode As Integer, shift As Single)			456
Private Sub ListBoxControl_LostFocus ([index As Integer])			456
Private Sub ListBoxBoxControl_MouseDown([index As Integer ,] button As Integer, shift As Single, x As Single, y As Single)			456
Private Sub ListBoxControl_MouseMove ([index As Integer ,] button As Integer, shift As Single, x As Single, y As Single)			457
Private Sub ListBoxBoxControl_MouseUp([index As Integer ,] button As Integer, shift As Single, x As Single, y As Single)			458
Private Sub ListBoxControl_OLECompleteDrag([index As Integer ,] effect As Long)			459
Private Sub ListBoxControl_OLEDragDrop([index As Integer ,] data As DataObject, effect As Long, button As Integer, shift As Single, x As Single, y As Single)			459
Private Sub ListBoxControl_OLEDragOver([index As Integer ,] data As DataObject, effect As Long, button As Integer, shift As Single, x As Single, y As Single, state As Integer)			460
Private Sub ListBoxControl_OLEGiveFeedback ([index As Integer ,] effect As Long)			462
Private Sub ListBoxControl_OLESetData([index As Integer ,] data As DataObject, DataFormat As Integer)			462
Private Sub ListBoxControl_OLEStartDrag ([index As Integer ,] data As DataObject, AllowedEffects As Long)			463
ListImage	Object	PE, EE	464
ListImageObject.Draw hDC [, x, y [, style]]			464
icon = ListImageObject.ExtractIcon			465
ListImages	Collection	PE, EE	465
ListImagesCollection.Add [index], [key], picture			465
ListImagesCollection.Clear			465
ListImagesCollection.Remove index			465
ListItem	Object	PE, EE	466
image = ListItemObject.CreateDragImage			466
BValue = ListItemObject.EnsureVisible			467
ListItems	Collection	PE, EE	467
ListItemsCollection.Add [index [, key [, text [, icon [, smallicon]]]]]			467
ListItemsCollection.Clear			467
ListItemsCollection.Remove index			467
ListView	Control	PE, EE	468
ListViewControl.Drag [DragAction]			473
result = ListViewControl.FindItem (string [, where [, index [, match]]])			473
result = ListViewControl.GetFirstVisible			474
result = ListViewControl.HitTest (x As Single, y As Single)			474

Class	Element	Edition (see Legend)	Page
	ListViewControl.Move Left [, Top [, Width [, Height]]]		474
	ListViewControl.OLEDrag		474
	ListViewControl.Refresh		474
	ListViewControl.SetFocus		474
	ListViewControl.ShowWhatsThis		474
	ListViewControl.StartLabelEdit		475
	ListViewControl.ZOrder [position]		475
	Private Sub ListViewControl_AfterLabelEdit([index As Integer ,] cancel As Integer, NewString As String)		475
	Private Sub ListViewControl_BeforeLabelEdit([index As Integer ,] cancel As Integer)		475
	Private Sub ListViewControl_Click([index As Integer])		476
	Private Sub ListViewControl_ColumnClick([index As Integer ,] ColumnHeader As ColumnHeader)		476
	Private Sub ListViewControl_DblClick([index As Integer])		476
	Private Sub ListViewControl_DragDrop([index As Integer ,] source As Control, x As Single, y As Single)		476
	Private Sub ListViewControl_DragOver([index As Integer ,] source As Control, x As Single, y As Single, state As Integer)		477
	Private Sub ListViewControl_GotFocus ([index As Integer])		478
	Private Sub ListViewControl_ItemClick([index As Integer ,] Item As ListItem)		478
	Private Sub ListViewControl_KeyDown ([index As Integer ,] keycode As Integer, shift As Single)		478
	Private Sub ListViewControl_KeyPress([index As Integer ,] keychar As Integer)		479
	Private Sub ListViewControl_KeyUp ([index As Integer ,] keycode As Integer, shift As Single)		479
	Private Sub ListViewControl_LostFocus ([index As Integer])		479
	Private Sub ListViewBoxControl_MouseDown([index As Integer ,] button As Integer, shift As Single, x As Single, y As Single)		480
	Private Sub ListViewControl_MouseMove ([index As Integer ,] button As Integer, shift As Single, x As Single, y As Single)		480
	Private Sub ListViewBoxControl_MouseUp([index As Integer ,] button As Integer, shift As Single, x As Single, y As Single)		481
	Private Sub ListViewControl_OLECompleteDrag([index As Integer ,] effect As Long)		482
	Private Sub ListViewControl_OLEDragDrop([index As Integer ,] data As DataObject, effect As Long, button As Integer, shift As Single, x As Single, y As Single)		482
	Private Sub ListViewControl_OLEDragOver([index As Integer ,] data As DataObject, effect As Long, button As Integer, shift As Single, x As Single, y As Single, state As Integer)		483
	Private Sub ListViewControl_OLEGiveFeedback ([index As Integer ,] effect As Long)		485
	Private Sub ListViewControl_OLESetData([index As Integer ,] data As DataObject, DataFormat As Integer)		485

Legend

CCE .... Control Creation Edition
LE .... Learning Edition
VBA .... Visual Basic for Applications
EE .... Enterprise Edition
PE .... Professional Edition

Class	Element	Edition (see Legend)	Page
	Private Sub ListViewControl_OLEStartDrag ([index As Integer ,] data As DataObject, AllowedEffects As Long)		486
Load	Statement	CCE, LE, PE, EE	488
LoadPicture	Function	CCE, LE, PE, EE	488
LoadResData	Function	CCE, LE, PE, EE	489
LoadResPicture	Function	CCE, LE, PE, EE	490
LoadResString	Function	CCE, LE, PE, EE	490
Loc	Function	CCE, LE, PE, EE	491
Location	Object	PE, EE	491
Lock	Statement	CCE, LE, PE, EE	492
LOF	Function	CCE, LE, PE, EE	493
Log	Function	CCE, LE, PE, EE	494
Long	Data Type	CCE, LE, PE, EE	494
LSet	Statement	CCE, LE, PE, EE	494
LTrim	Function	CCE, LE, PE, EE	495
MAPIMessages	Control	CCE, LE, PE, EE	496
	MAPIMessagesControl.Compose		499
	MAPIMessagesControl.Copy		499
	MAPIMessagesControl.Delete object		499
	MAPIMessagesControl.Fetch		500
	MAPIMessagesControl.Forward		500
	MAPIMessagesControl.Reply		500
	MAPIMessagesControl.ReplyAll		500
	MAPIMessagesControl.ResolveName		500
	MAPIMessagesControl.Save		500
	MAPIMessagesControl.Send dialog		500
	MAPIMessagesControl.Send [details]		501
MAPISession	Control	CCE, LE, PE, EE	501
	MAPISessionControl.SignOff		502
	MAPISessionControl.SignOn		502
Masked Edit	Control	CCE, LE, PE, EE	502
	MaskedEditControl.Drag [DragAction]		508
	MaskedEditControl.Move Left [, Top [, Width [, Height]]]		508

Class	Element	Edition (see Legend)	Page
	MaskedEditControl.OLEDrag		508
	MaskedEditControl.Refresh		509
	MaskedEditControl.SetFocus		509
	MaskedEditControl.ShowWhatsThis		509
	MaskedEditControl.ZOrder [position]		509
	Private Sub MaskedEditControl_Change ([index As Integer])		509
	Private Sub MaskedEditControl_DragDrop([index As Integer ,] source As Control, x As Single, y As Single)		509
	Private Sub MaskedEditControl_DragOver([index As Integer ,] source As Control, x As Single, y As Single, state As Integer)		510
	Private Sub MaskedEditControl_GotFocus ([index As Integer])		511
	Private Sub MaskedEditControl_KeyDown ([index As Integer ,] keycode As Integer, shift As Single)		511
	Private Sub MaskedEditControl_KeyPress([index As Integer ,] keychar As Integer)		511
	Private Sub MaskedEditControl_KeyUp ([index As Integer ,] keycode As Integer, shift As Single)		511
	Private Sub MaskedEditControl_LostFocus ([index As Integer])		512
	Private Sub MaskedEditBoxControl_MouseDown([index As Integer ,] button As Integer, shift As Single, x As Single, y As Single)		512
	Private Sub MaskedEditControl_MouseMove ([index As Integer ,] button As Integer, shift As Single, x As Single, y As Single)		513
	Private Sub MaskedEditBoxControl_MouseUp([index As Integer ,] button As Integer, shift As Single, x As Single, y As Single)		514
	Private Sub MaskedEditControl_OLECompleteDrag([index As Integer ,] effect As Long)		514
	Private Sub MaskedEditControl_OLEDragDrop([index As Integer ,] data As DataObject, effect As Long, button As Integer, shift As Single, x As Single, y As Single)		515
	Private Sub MaskedEditControl_OLEDragOver([index As Integer ,] data As DataObject, effect As Long, button As Integer, shift As Single, x As Single, y As Single, state As Integer)		516
	Private Sub MaskedEditControl_OLEGiveFeedback ([index As Integer ,] effect As Long)		517
	Private Sub MaskedEditControl_OLESetData([index As Integer ,] data As DataObject, DataFormat As Integer)		518
	Private Sub MaskedEditControl_OLEStartDrag ([index As Integer ,] data As DataObject, AllowedEffects As Long)		519
MDIForm	Object	CCE, LE, PE, EE	520
	MDIFormObject.Arrange arrange		523
	MDIFormObject.Hide		524
	MDIFormObject.Move Left [, Top [, Width [, Height]]]		524
	MDIFormObject.OLEDrag		524
	MDIFormObject.PopupMenu menu, flags, x, y, menuitem		524

Legend

CCE .... Control Creation Edition
LE .... Learning Edition
VBA .... Visual Basic for Applications
EE .... Enterprise Edition
PE .... Professional Edition

Class	Element	Edition (see Legend)	Page
	MDIFormObject.SetFocus		525
	MDIFormObject.Show [style [, owner]]		525
	MDIFormObject.WhatsThisMode		525
	MDIFormObject.ZOrder [position]		525
	Private Sub MDIFormObject_Activate ( )		525
	Private Sub MDIFormObject_Click( )		525
	Private Sub MDIFormObject_DblClick( )		526
	Private Sub MDIFormObject_Deactivate ( )		526
	Private Sub MDIFormObject_DragDrop (source As Control, x As Single, y As Single)		526
	Private Sub MDIFormObject_DragOver (source As Control, x As Single, y As Single, state As Integer)		526
	Private Sub MDIFormObject_Initialize ( )		527
	Private Sub MDIFormObject_LinkClose ( )		527
	Private Sub MDIFormObject_LinkError (errcode As Integer)		528
	Private Sub MDIFormObject_LinkExecute (cmd As String, cancel As Integer)		528
	Private Sub MDIFormObject_LinkOpen (cancel As Integer)		528
	Private Sub MDIFormObject_Load ( )		528
	Private Sub MDIFormObject_MouseDown (button As Integer, shift As Single, x As Single, y As Single)		529
	Private Sub MDIFormObject_MouseMove (button As Integer, shift As Single, x As Single, y As Single)		529
	Private Sub MDIFormObject_MouseUp (button As Integer, shift As Single, x As Single, y As Single)		530
	Private Sub MDIFormObject_OLECompleteDrag(effect As Long)		531
	Private Sub MDIFormObject_OLEDragDrop (data As DataObject, effect As Long, button As Integer, shift As Single, x As Single, y As Single)		531
	Private Sub MDIFormObject_OLEDragOver (data As DataObject, effect As Long, button As Integer, shift As Single, x As Single, y As Single, state As Integer)		532
	Private Sub MDIFormObject_OLEGiveFeedback (effect As Long)		534
	Private Sub MDIFormObject_OLESetData (data As DataObject, DataFormat As Integer)		534
	Private Sub MDIFormObject_OLEStartDrag (data As DataObject, AllowedEffects As Long)		535
	Private Sub MDIFormObject_QueryUnload (cancel As Integer, unloadmode As Long)		535
	Private Sub MDIFormObject_Resize ( )		536
	Private Sub MDIFormObject_Terminate ( )		536
	Private Sub MDIFormObject_Unload (cancel As Integer)		536
Menu	Control	CCE, LE, PE, EE	537
	Private Sub MenuControl_Click([index As Integer])		538
Microsoft Internet Transfer Control	Control	CCE, LE, PE, EE	539
	INetControl.Cancel		541
	INetControl.Execute [url [, operation [, data [, headers]]]]		541

Class	Element	Edition (see Legend)	Page
	value = INetControl.GetChunk size [, datatype]		542
	value = INetControl.GetHeader [header]		542
	value = INetControl.OpenURL url [, datatype]		542
	Private Sub MaskedEditControl_StateChanged ([index As Integer ,] ByVal state As Integer)		543
Mid	Function	CCE, LE, PE, EE	544
Mid	Statement	CCE, LE, PE, EE	544
MidB	Function	CCE, LE, PE, EE	545
MidB	Statement	CCE, LE, PE, EE	545
Minute	Function	CCE, LE, PE, EE	546
MIRR	Function	CCE, LE, PE, EE	546
MkDir	Statement	CCE, LE, PE, EE	547
Month	Function	CCE, LE, PE, EE	548
MSChart	Control	CCE, LE, PE, EE	548
	MSChartControl.About		554
	MSChartControl.Drag [DragAction]		554
	MSChartControl.EditCopy		554
	MSChartControl.EditPaste		554
	MSChartControl.GetSelectedPart parttype, index1, index2, index3, index4		554
	MSChartControl.Layout		555
	MSChartControl.Move Left [, Top [, Width [, Height]]]		555
	MSChartControl.Refresh		555
	MSChartControl.SelectPart parttype, index1, index2, index3, index4		555
	MSChartControl.SetFocus		556
	MSChartControl.ShowWhatsThis		556
	MSChartControl.ToDefaults		556
	MSChartControl.TwipsToChartPart x, y, parttype, index1, index2, index3, index4		556
	MSChartControl.ZOrder [position]		557

Legend

CCE .... Control Creation Edition
LE .... Learning Edition
VBA .... Visual Basic for Applications
EE .... Enterprise Edition
PE .... Professional Edition

Class	Element	Edition (see Legend)	Page
	Private Sub MSChartControl_AxisActivated ([index As Integer ,] axisId As Integer, axisIndex As Integer, mouseFlag As Integer, cancel As Integer)		558
	Private Sub MSChartControl_AxisLabelActivated ([index As Integer ,] axisId As Integer, axisIndex As Integer, labelSetIndex As Integer, labelIndex As Integer, mouseFlag As Integer, cancel As Integer)		558
	Private Sub MSChartControl_AxisLabelSelected ([index As Integer ,] axisId As Integer, axisIndex As Integer, labelSetIndex As Integer, labelIndex As Integer, mouseFlag As Integer, cancel As Integer)		559
	Private Sub MSChartControl_AxisLabelUpdated ([index As Integer ,] axisId As Integer, axisIndex As Integer, labelSetIndex As Integer, labelIndex As Integer, updateFlag As Integer)		560
	Private Sub MSChartControl_AxisSelected ([index As Integer ,] axisId As Integer, axisIndex As Integer, mouseFlag As Integer, cancel As Integer)		560
	Private Sub MSChartControl_AxisTitleActivated ([index As Integer ,] axisId As Integer, axisIndex As Integer, mouseFlag As Integer, cancel As Integer)		561
	Private Sub MSChartControl_AxisTitleSelected ([index As Integer ,] axisId As Integer, axisIndex As Integer, mouseFlag As Integer, cancel As Integer)		562
	Private Sub MSChartControl_AxisTitleUpdated ([index As Integer ,] axisId As Integer, axisIndex As Integer, updateFlag As Integer)		562
	Private Sub MSChartControl_AxisUpdated ([index As Integer ,] axisId As Integer, axisIndex As Integer, updateFlag As Integer)		563
	Private Sub MSChartControl_ChartActivated ([index As Integer ,] mouseFlag As Integer, cancel As Integer)		564
	Private Sub MSChartControl_ChartSelected ([index As Integer ,] cancel As Integer)		564
	Private Sub MSChartControl_ChartUpdated ([index As Integer ,] updateFlag As Integer)		564
	Private Sub MSChartControl_Click([index As Integer])		565
	Private Sub MSChartControl_DataUpdated ([index As Integer ,] row As Integer, column As Integer, labelRow As Integer, labelColumn As Integer, labelSetIndex As Integer, updateFlag As Integer)		565
	Private Sub MSChartControl_DblClick([index As Integer])		566
	Private Sub MSChartControl_DonePainting ([index As Integer])		566
	Private Sub MSChartControl_DragDrop([index As Integer ,] source As Control, x As Single, y As Single)		566
	Private Sub MSChartControl_DragOver([index As Integer ,] source As Control, x As Single, y As Single, state As Integer)		566
	Private Sub MSChartControl_FootnoteActivated ([index As Integer ,] mouseFlag As Integer, cancel As Integer)		567
	Private Sub MSChartControl_FootnoteSelected ([index As Integer ,] mouseFlag As Integer, cancel As Integer)		568
	Private Sub MSChartControl_FootnoteUpdated ([index As Integer ,] updateFlag As Integer)		568
	Private Sub MSChartControl_GotFocus ([index As Integer])		568
	Private Sub MSChartControl_KeyDown ([index As Integer ,] keycode As Integer, shift As Single)		569
	Private Sub MSChartControl_KeyPress([index As Integer ,] keychar As Integer)		569
	Private Sub MSChartControl_KeyUp ([index As Integer ,] keycode As Integer, shift As Single)		569
	Private Sub MSChartControl_LegendActivated ([index As Integer ,] mouseFlag As Integer, cancel As Integer)		570
	Private Sub MSChartControl_LegendSelected ([index As Integer ,] cancel As Integer)		570
	Private Sub MSChartControl_LegendUpdated ([index As Integer ,] updateFlag As Integer)		571
	Private Sub MSChartControl_LostFocus ([index As Integer])		571
	Private Sub MSChartBoxControl_MouseDown([index As Integer ,] button As Integer, shift As Single, x As Single, y As Single)		571

Class	Element	Edition (see Legend)	Page
	Private Sub MSChartControl_MouseMove ([index As Integer ,] button As Integer, shift As Single, x As Single, y As Single)		572
	Private Sub MSChartBoxControl_MouseUp([index As Integer ,] button As Integer, shift As Single, x As Single, y As Single)		573
	Private Sub MSChartControl_PlotActivated ([index As Integer ,] mouseFlag As Integer, cancel As Integer)		574
	Private Sub MSChartControl_PlotSelected ([index As Integer ,] cancel As Integer)		574
	Private Sub MSChartControl_PlotUpdated ([index As Integer ,] updateFlag As Integer)		574
	Private Sub MSChartControl_PointActivated ([index As Integer ,] series As Integer, dataPoint As Integer, mouseFlag As Integer, cancel As Integer)		575
	Private Sub MSChartControl_PointLabelActivated ([index As Integer ,] series As Integer, dataPoint As Integer, mouseFlag As Integer, cancel As Integer)		575
	Private Sub MSChartControl_PointLabelSelected ([index As Integer ,] series As Integer, dataPoint As Integer, cancel As Integer)		576
	Private Sub MSChartControl_PointLabelUpdated ([index As Integer ,] series As Integer, dataPoint As Integer, updateFlag As Integer)		576
	Private Sub MSChartControl_PointSelected ([index As Integer ,] series As Integer, dataPoint As Integer, cancel As Integer)		577
	Private Sub MSChartControl_PointUpdated ([index As Integer ,] series As Integer, dataPoint As Integer, updateFlag As Integer)		577
	Private Sub MSChartControl_SeriesActivated ([index As Integer ,] series As Integer, mouseFlag As Integer, cancel As Integer)		578
	Private Sub MSChartControl_SeriesSelected ([index As Integer ,] series As Integer, dataPoint As Integer, cancel As Integer)		578
	Private Sub MSChartControl_SeriesUpdated ([index As Integer ,] series As Integer, dataPoint As Integer, updateFlag As Integer)		578
	Private Sub MSChartControl_TitleActivated ([index As Integer ,] mouseFlag As Integer, cancel As Integer)		579
	Private Sub MSChartControl_TitleSelected ([index As Integer ,] cancel As Integer)		579
	Private Sub MSChartControl_TitleUpdated ([index As Integer ,] updateFlag As Integer)		580
MSComm	Control	CCE, LE, PE, EE	581
	Private Sub MSCommControl_OnComm ([index As Integer])		584
MSFlexGrid	Control	PE, EE	585
	MSFlexGridControl.AddItem item, [row]		597
	MSFlexGridControl.Clear		597
	MSFlexGridControl.Drag [DragAction]		597
	MSFlexGridControl.Move Left [, Top [, Width [, Height]]]		597
	MSFlexGridControl.OLEDrag		597
	MSFlexGridControl.Refresh		597
	MSFlexGridControl.RemoveItem [rowvalue]		598
	MSFlexGridControl.SetFocus		598

Legend

CCE .... Control Creation Edition
LE .... Learning Edition
VBA .... Visual Basic for Applications
EE .... Enterprise Edition
PE .... Professional Edition

• The Visual Basic 5 Programmer's Reference

Class	Element	Edition (see Legend)	Page
	MSFlexGridControl.ShowWhatsThis		598
	MSFlexGridControl.ZOrder [position]		598
	Private Sub MSFlexGridControl_Click([index As Integer])		598
	Private Sub MSFlexGridControl_Compare ([index As Integer ,] row1 As Long, row2 As Long, comp As Integer)		598
	Private Sub MSFlexGridControl_DblClick([index As Integer])		599
	Private Sub MSFlexGridControl_DragDrop([index As Integer ,] source As Control, x As Single, y As Single)		599
	Private Sub MSFlexGridControl_DragOver([index As Integer ,] source As Control, x As Single, y As Single, state As Integer)		599
	Private Sub MSFlexGridControl_EnterCell ([index As Integer])		600
	Private Sub MSFlexGridControl_GotFocus ([index As Integer])		600
	Private Sub MSFlexGridControl_KeyDown ([index As Integer ,] keycode As Integer, shift As Single)		600
	Private Sub MSFlexGridControl_KeyPress([index As Integer ,] keychar As Integer)		601
	Private Sub MSFlexGridControl_KeyUp ([index As Integer ,] keycode As Integer, shift As Single)		601
	Private Sub MSFlexGridControl_LeaveCell ([index As Integer])		602
	Private Sub MSFlexGridControl_LostFocus ([index As Integer])		602
	Private Sub MSFlexGridBoxControl_MouseDown([index As Integer ,] button As Integer, shift As Single, x As Single, y As Single)		602
	Private Sub MSFlexGridControl_MouseMove ([index As Integer ,] button As Integer, shift As Single, x As Single, y As Single)		603
	Private Sub MSFlexGridBoxControl_MouseUp([index As Integer ,] button As Integer, shift As Single, x As Single, y As Single)		604
	Private Sub MSFlexGridControl_OLECompleteDrag(effect As Long)		604
	Private Sub MSFlexGridControl_OLEDragDrop (data As DataObject, effect As Long, button As Integer, shift As Single, x As Single, y As Single)		605
	Private Sub MSFlexGridControl_OLEDragOver (data As DataObject, effect As Long, button As Integer, shift As Single, x As Single, y As Single, state As Integer)		606
	Private Sub MSFlexGridControl_OLEGiveFeedback (effect As Long)		607
	Private Sub MSFlexGridControl_OLESetData (data As DataObject, DataFormat As Integer)		608
	Private Sub MSFlexGridControl_OLEStartDrag (data As DataObject, AllowedEffects As Long)		608
	Private Sub MSFlexGridControl_RowColChange ([index As Integer])		609
	Private Sub MSFlexGridControl_Scroll ([index As Integer])		609
	Private Sub MSFlexGridControl_SelChange ([index As Integer])		609
MsgBox		Function	CCE, LE, PE, EE	610
Multimedia MCI Control		Control	PE, EE	612
	MMControl.Drag [DragAction]		619
	MMControl.Move Left [, Top [, Width [, Height]]]		620
	MMControl.OLEDrag		620
	MMControl.Refresh		620
	MMControl.SetFocus		620
	MMControl.ShowWhatsThis		620

Class	Element	Edition (see Legend)	Page
	MMControl.ZOrder [position]		620
	Private Sub MMControl_BackClick([index As Integer ,] cancel As Integer)		621
	Private Sub MMControl_BackCompleted([index As Integer ,] ErrorCode As Long)		621
	Private Sub MMControl_BackGotFocus ([index As Integer])		621
	Private Sub MMControl_BackLostFocus ([index As Integer])		621
	Private Sub MMControl_Done ([index As Integer ,] NotifyCode)		622
	Private Sub MMControl_DragDrop([index As Integer ,] source As Control, x As Single, y As Single)		622
	Private Sub MMControl_DragOver([index As Integer ,] source As Control, x As Single, y As Single, state As Integer)		623
	Private Sub MMControl_EjectClick([index As Integer ,] cancel As Integer)		623
	Private Sub MMControl_EjectCompleted([index As Integer ,] ErrorCode As Long)		624
	Private Sub MMControl_EjectGotFocus ([index As Integer])		624
	Private Sub MMControl_EjectLostFocus ([index As Integer])		624
	Private Sub MMControl_GotFocus ([index As Integer])		624
	Private Sub MMControl_LostFocus ([index As Integer])		624
	Private Sub MMControl_NextClick([index As Integer ,] cancel As Integer)		624
	Private Sub MMControl_NextCompleted ([index As Integer ,] ErrorCode As Long)		625
	Private Sub MMControl_NextGotFocus ([index As Integer])		625
	Private Sub MMControl_NextLostFocus ([index As Integer])		625
	Private Sub MMControl_OLECompleteDrag(effect As Long)		625
	Private Sub MMControl_OLEDragDrop (data As DataObject, effect As Long, button As Integer, shift As Single, x As Single, y As Single)		626
	Private Sub MMControl_OLEDragOver (data As DataObject, effect As Long, button As Integer, shift As Single, x As Single, y As Single, state As Integer)		627
	Private Sub MMControl_OLEGiveFeedback (effect As Long)		628
	Private Sub MMControl_OLESetData (data As DataObject, DataFormat As Integer)		628
	Private Sub MMControl_OLEStartDrag (data As DataObject, AllowedEffects As Long)		629
	Private Sub MMControl_PauseClick([index As Integer ,] cancel As Integer)		629
	Private Sub MMControl_PauseCompleted([index As Integer ,] ErrorCode As Long)		630
	Private Sub MMControl_PauseGotFocus ([index As Integer])		630
	Private Sub MMControl_PauseLostFocus ([index As Integer])		630
	Private Sub MMControl_PlayClick([index As Integer ,] cancel As Integer)		630

Legend

CCE .... Control Creation Edition
LE .... Learning Edition
VBA .... Visual Basic for Applications
EE .... Enterprise Edition
PE .... Professional Edition

Class	Element	Edition (see Legend)	Page
	Private Sub MMControl_PlayCompleted([index As Integer ,] ErrorCode As Long)		630
	Private Sub MMControl_PlayGotFocus ([index As Integer])		631
	Private Sub MMControl_PlayLostFocus ([index As Integer])		631
	Private Sub MMControl_PrevClick([index As Integer ,] cancel As Integer)		631
	Private Sub MMControl_PrevCompleted([index As Integer ,] ErrorCode As Long)		631
	Private Sub MMControl_PrevGotFocus ([index As Integer])		631
	Private Sub MMControl_PrevLostFocus ([index As Integer])		631
	Private Sub MMControl_RecordClick([index As Integer ,] cancel As Integer)		632
	Private Sub MMControl_RecordCompleted([index As Integer ,] ErrorCode As Long)		632
	Private Sub MMControl_RecordGotFocus ([index As Integer])		632
	Private Sub MMControl_RecordLostFocus ([index As Integer])		632
	Private Sub MMControl_StatusUpdate ([index As Integer])		632
	Private Sub MMControl_StepClick([index As Integer ,] cancel As Integer)		633
	Private Sub MMControl_StepCompleted([index As Integer ,] ErrorCode As Long)		633
	Private Sub MMControl_StepGotFocus ([index As Integer])		633
	Private Sub MMControl_StepLostFocus ([index As Integer])		633
	Private Sub MMControl_StopClick([index As Integer ,] cancel As Integer)		633
	Private Sub MMControl_StopCompleted([index As Integer ,] ErrorCode As Long)		634
	Private Sub MMControl_StopGotFocus ([index As Integer])		634
	Private Sub MMControl_StopLostFocus ([index As Integer])		634
Name	Statement	CCE, LE, PE, EE	635
Node	Object	CCE, LE, PE, EE	635
	image = NodeObject.CreateDragImage		636
	bvalue = NodeObject.EnsureVisible		637
Nodes	Collection	CCE, LE, PE, EE	637
	NodesCollection.Add item, key, [before | , after]		637
	NodesCollection.Clear		637
	NodesCollection.Remove index		637
Now	Function	CCE, LE, PE, EE	638
NPer	Function	CCE, LE, PE, EE	638
NPV	Function	CCE, LE, PE, EE	639
Object	Data Type	CCE, LE, PE, EE	640
Oct	Function	CCE, LE, PE, EE	640

Class	Element	Edition (see Legend)	Page
OLE Container	Control	CCE, LE, PE, EE	641
	OLEContainerControl.Close		648
	OLEContainerControl.Copy		648
	OLEContainerControl.CreateEmbed sourcedoc, [class]		648
	OLEContainerControl.CreateLink sourcedoc, [sourceitem]		648
	OLEContainerControl.Delete		648
	OLEContainerControl.DoVerb verb		649
	OLEContainerControl.Drag [DragAction]		649
	OLEContainerControl.FetchVerbs		649
	OLEContainerControl.InsertObjDlg		649
	OLEContainerControl.Move Left [, Top [, Width [, Height]]]		650
	OLEContainerControl.Paste		650
	OLEContainerControl.PasteSpecialDlg		650
	OLEContainerControl.ReadFromFile filenum		650
	OLEContainerControl.Refresh		650
	OLEContainerControl.SaveToFile filenum		650
	OLEContainerControl.SaveToOle1File filenum		650
	OLEContainerControl.SetFocus		651
	OLEContainerControl.ShowWhatsThis		651
	OLEContainerControl.Update		651
	OLEContainerControl.ZOrder [position]		651
	Private Sub OLEContainerControl_Click([index As Integer])		651
	Private Sub OLEContainerControl_DblClick([index As Integer])		652
	Private Sub OLEContainerControl_DragDrop([index As Integer,] source As Control, x As Single, y As Single)		652
	Private Sub OLEContainerControl_DragOver([index As Integer,] source As Control, x As Single, y As Single, state As Integer)		652
	Private Sub OLEContainerControl_GotFocus ([index As Integer])		653
	Private Sub OLEContainerControl_KeyDown ([index As Integer,] keycode As Integer, shift As Single)		653
	Private Sub OLEContainerControl_KeyPress([index As Integer,] keychar As Integer)		654
	Private Sub OLEContainerControl_KeyUp ([index As Integer,] keycode As Integer, shift As Single)		654
	Private Sub OLEContainerControl_LostFocus ([index As Integer])		655

Legend

CCE .... Control Creation Edition
LE .... Learning Edition
VBA .... Visual Basic for Applications
EE .... Enterprise Edition
PE .... Professional Edition

Class	Element	Edition (see Legend)	Page
	Private Sub OLEContainerControl_MouseDown([index As Integer,] button As Integer, shift As Single, x As Single, y As Single)		655
	Private Sub OLEContainerControl_MouseMove ([index As Integer,] button As Integer, shift As Single, x As Single, y As Single)		656
	Private Sub OLEContainerControl_MouseUp([index As Integer,] button As Integer, shift As Single, x As Single, y As Single)		656
	Private Sub OLEContainerControl_ObjectMove ([index As Integer,] left As Single, top As Single, width As Single, height As Single)		657
	Private Sub OLEContainerControl_Resize ([index As Integer,] width As Single, height As Single)		657
	Private Sub OLEContainerControl_Updated ([index As Integer,] code As Integer)		658
On Error	Statement	CCE, LE, PE, EE	658
On GoSub	Statement	CCE, LE, PE, EE	659
On GoTo	Statement	CCE, LE, PE, EE	660
Open	Statement	CCE, LE, PE, EE	661
Operators		CCE, LE, PE, EE	662
	Arithmetic Operators		662
	Comparison Operators		663
	Logical Operators		663
	Miscellaneous Operators		663
Option Base	Statement	CCE, LE, PE, EE	664
Option Compare	Statement	CCE, LE, PE, EE	664
Option Explicit	Statement	CCE, LE, PE, EE	665
Option Private	Statement	CCE, LE, PE, EE	665
OptionButton	Control	CCE, LE, PE, EE	665
	OptionButtonControl.Drag [DragAction]		670
	OptionButtonControl.Move Left [, Top [, Width [, Height]]]		671
	OptionButtonControl.OLEDrag		671
	OptionButtonControl.Refresh		671
	OptionButtonControl.SetFocus		671
	OptionButtonControl.ShowWhatsThis		671
	OptionButtonControl.ZOrder [position]		671
	Private Sub OptionButtonControl_Click([index As Integer])		672
	Private Sub OptionButtonControl_DragDrop([index As Integer,] source As Control, x As Single, y As Single)		672
	Private Sub OptionButtonControl_DragOver([index As Integer,] source As Control, x As Single, y As Single, state As Integer)		672
	Private Sub OptionButtonControl_GotFocus ([index As Integer])		673
	Private Sub OptionButtonControl_KeyDown ([index As Integer,] keycode As Integer, shift As Single)		674
	Private Sub OptionButtonControl_KeyPress([index As Integer,] keychar As Integer)		674

Class	Element	Edition (see Legend)	Page
	Private Sub OptionButtonControl_KeyUp ([index As Integer,] keycode As Integer, shift As Single)		674
	Private Sub OptionButtonControl_LostFocus ([index As Integer])		675
	Private Sub OptionButtonControl_MouseDown([index As Integer,] button As Integer, shift As Single, x As Single, y As Single)		675
	Private Sub OptionButtonControl_MouseMove ([index As Integer,] button As Integer, shift As Single, x As Single, y As Single)		676
	Private Sub OptionButtonControl_MouseUp([index As Integer,] button As Integer, shift As Single, x As Single, y As Single)		677
	Private Sub OptionButtonControl_OLECompleteDrag([index As Integer,] effect As Long)		677
	Private Sub OptionButtonControl_OLEDragDrop([index As Integer,] data As DataObject, effect As Long, button As Integer, shift As Single, x As Single, y As Single)		678
	Private Sub OptionButtonControl_OLEDragOver([index As Integer,] data As DataObject, effect As Long, button As Integer, shift As Single, x As Single, y As Single, state As Integer)		679
	Private Sub OptionButtonControl_OLEGiveFeedback ([index As Integer,] effect As Long)		680
	Private Sub OptionButtonControl_OLESetData([index As Integer,] data As DataObject, DataFormat As Integer)		681
	Private Sub OptionButtonControl_OLEStartDrag ([index As Integer,] data As DataObject, AllowedEffects As Long)		682
Panel	Object	PE, EE	683
Panels	Collection	PE, EE	684
	panel = PanelsCollection.Add ([index [, key [, text [, style [, picture]]]])		685
	PanelsObject.Clear		685
	PanelsObject.Remove index		685
Parameter	Object	PE, EE	685
Parameters	Collection	PE, EE	686
	ParametersCollection.Refresh		687
Pen	Object	PE, EE	687
Picture	Object	LE, CCE, PE, EE	688
	PictureObject.Render hdc, xdest, ydest, destwidth, destheight, xsrc, ysrc, srcwidth, srcheight, wbounds		689
PictureBox	Control	CCE, LE, PE, EE	690
	PictureBoxControl.Circle [Step] (x , y), radius [, color [, start [, stop [, aspect]]]]		698
	PictureBoxControl.Cls		698
	PictureBoxControl.Drag [DragAction]		698
	PictureBoxControl.Line [Step] (x1 , y1), [Step] (x2 , y2) [, B	BF]		699

Legend

CCE .... Control Creation Edition
LE .... Learning Edition
VBA .... Visual Basic for Applications
EE .... Enterprise Edition
PE .... Professional Edition

Class	Element	Edition (see Legend)	Page
	PictureBoxControl.LinkExecute command		699
	PictureBoxControl.LinkPoke		699
	PictureBoxControl.LinkRequest		699
	PictureBoxControl.LinkSend		699
	PictureBoxControl.Move Left [, Top [, Width [, Height]]]		699
	PictureBoxControl.OLEDrag		700
	PictureBoxControl.PaintPicture picture, x1 , y1, [width1] ,[height1] ,[x2] , [y2] , [width2] , [height2] , [rasterop]		700
	color = PictureBoxControl.Point (x , y)		701
	PictureBoxControl.PSet [Step] (x , y), [color]		701
	PictureBoxControl.Refresh		702
	PictureBoxControl.Scale [(x1 , y1)—(x2 , y2)]		702
	result = PictureBoxControl.ScaleX (width , fromscale , toscale)		702
	result = PictureBoxControl.ScaleY (height , fromscale , toscale)		702
	PictureBoxControl.SetFocus		703
	PictureBoxControl.ShowWhatsThis		703
	height = PictureBoxControl.TextHeight (string)		703
	width = PictureBoxControl.TextWidth (string)		703
	PictureBoxControl.ZOrder [position]		704
	Private Sub PictureBoxControl__Change ([index As Integer])		704
	Private Sub PictureBoxControl__Click([index As Integer])		704
	Private Sub PictureBoxControl_DblClick([index As Integer])		704
	Private Sub PictureBoxControl_DragDrop([index As Integer ,] source Panel Control, x As Single, y As Single)		705
	Private Sub PictureBoxControl_DragOver([index As Integer ,] source As Control, x As Single, y As Single, state As Integer)		705
	Private Sub PicturetBoxControl_GotFocus ([index As Integer])		706
	Private Sub PictureBoxControl_KeyDown ([index As Integer ,] keycode As Integer, shift As Single)		706
	Private Sub PictureBoxControl_KeyPress([index As Integer ,] keychar As Integer)		707
	Private Sub PictureBoxControl_KeyUp ([index As Integer ,] keycode As Integer, shift As Single)		707
	Private Sub PictureBoxControl_LinkClose ([index As Integer ,])		707
	Private Sub PictureBoxControl_LinkError ([index As Integer ,] errcode As Integer)		707
	Private Sub PictureBoxControl_LinkNotify ([index As Integer])		708
	Private Sub PictureBoxControl _LinkOpen ([index As Integer ,] cancel As Integer)		708
	Private Sub PictureBoxControl_LostFocus ([index As Integer])		708
	Private Sub PictureBoxControl_MouseDown([index As Integer ,] button As Integer, shift As Single, x As Single, y As Single)		708
	Private Sub PictureBoxControl_MouseMove ([index As Integer ,] button As Integer, shift As Single, x As Single, y As Single)		709
	Private Sub PictureBoxControl_MouseUp([index As Integer ,] button As Integer, shift As Single, x As Single, y As Single)		710
	Private Sub PictureBoxControl_OLECompleteDrag([index As Integer ,] effect As Long)		711

Class	Element	Edition (see Legend)	Page
	Private Sub PictureBoxControl_OLEDragDrop([index As Integer ,] data As DataObject, effect As Long, button As Integer, shift As Single, x As Single, y As Single)		711
	Private Sub PictureBoxControl_OLEDragOver([index As Integer ,] data As DataObject, effect As Long, button As Integer, shift As Single, x As Single, y As Single, state As Integer)		712
	Private Sub PictureBoxControl_OLEGiveFeedback ([index As Integer ,] effect As Long)		714
	Private Sub PictureBoxControl_OLESetData([index As Integer ,] data As DataObject, DataFormat As Integer)		714
	Private Sub PictureBoxControl_OLEStartDrag ([index As Integer ,] data As DataObject, AllowedEffects As Long)		715
	Private Sub PictureBoxControl_Paint ([index As Integer])		715
	Private Sub PictureBoxControl_Resize ([index As Integer])		716
PictureClip	Control	PE, EE	716
Plot	Object	PE, EE	718
PlotBase	Object	PE, EE	720
Pmt	Function	CCE, LE, PE, EE	720
PPmt	Function	CCE, LE, PE, EE	721
Print	Statement	CCE, LE, PE, EE	722
Printer	Object	CCE, LE, PE, EE	722
	PrinterObject.Circle [Step] (x , y), radius [, color [, start [, stop [, aspect]]]]		728
	PrinterObject.EndDoc		729
	PrinterObject.KillDoc		729
	PrinterObject.Line [Step] (x1 , y1), [Step] (x2 , y2) [, B	BF]		729
	PrinterObject.NewPage		730
	PrinterObject.PaintPicture picture, x1 , y1, [width1] , [height1] ,[x2] , [y2] , [width2] , [height2] , [rasterop]		730
	PrinterObject.PSet [Step] (x , y), [color]		731
	PrinterObject.Scale [(x1 , y1) - (x2 , y2)]		731
	result = PrinterObject.ScaleX (width , fromscale , toscale)		732
	result = PrinterObject.ScaleY (height , fromscale , toscale)		732
	height = PrinterObject.TextHeight (string)		733
	width = PrinterObject.TextWidth (string)		733
Printers	Collection	PE, EE	734

Legend

CCE .... Control Creation Edition
LE .... Learning Edition
VBA .... Visual Basic for Applications
EE .... Enterprise Edition
PE .... Professional Edition

Class	Element	Edition (see Legend)	Page
Private	Statement	CCE, LE, PE, EE	734
ProgressBar	Control	PE, EE	736
ProgressBarControl.Drag [DragAction]			740
ProgressBarControl.Move Left [, Top [, Width [, Height]]]			740
ProgressBarControl.OLEDrag			740
ProgressBarControl.ShowWhatsThis			740
ProgressBarControl.ZOrder [position]			740
Private Sub ProgressBarControl_Click([index As Integer])			741
Private Sub ProgressBarControl_DragDrop([index As Integer ,] source As Control, x As Single, y As Single)			741
Private Sub ProgressBarControl_DragOver([index As Integer ,] source As Control, x As Single, y As Single, state As Integer)			741
Private Sub ProgressBarControl_MouseDown([index As Integer ,] button As Integer, shift As Single, x As Single, y As Single)			742
Private Sub ProgressBarControl_MouseMove ([index As Integer ,] button As Integer, shift As Single, x As Single, y As Single)			743
Private Sub ProgressBarControl_MouseUp([index As Integer ,] button As Integer, shift As Single, x As Single, y As Single)			744
Private Sub ProgressBarControl_OLECompleteDrag([index As Integer ,] effect As Long)			744
Private Sub ProgressBarControl_OLEDragDrop([index As Integer ,] data As DataObject, effect As Long, button As Integer, shift As Single, x As Single, y As Single)			745
Private Sub ProgressBarControl_OLEDragOver([index As Integer ,] data As DataObject, effect As Long, button As Integer, shift As Single, x As Single, y As Single, state As Integer)			746
Private Sub ProgressBarControl_OLEGiveFeedback ([index As Integer ,] effect As Long)			747
Private Sub ProgressBarControl_OLESetData([index As Integer ,] data As DataObject, DataFormat As Integer)			748
Private Sub ProgressBarControl_OLEStartDrag ([index As Integer ,] data As DataObject, AllowedEffects As Long)			749
Properties	Collection	PE, EE	750
PropertiesCollection.Append object			750
PropertiesCollection.Delete objectname			750
PropertiesCollection.Refresh			750
Property	Object	PE, EE	750
Property Get	Statement	CCE, LE, PE, EE	751
Property Let	Statement	CCE, LE, PE, EE	754
Property Set	Statement	CCE, LE, PE, EE	756
PropertyBag	Object	CCE, LE, PE, EE	757
value = PropertyBag.ReadProperty name, [, default]			757
PropertBag.WriteProperty name, value [, default]			757
PropertyPage	Object	CCE, LE, PE, EE	758
PropertyPageObject.Circle [Step] (x , y), radius [, color [, start [, stop [, aspect]]]]			763

Class	Element Edition (see Legend)	Page
	PropertyPageObject.Cls	764
	PropertyPageObject.Line [Step] (x1 , y1), [Step] (x2 , y2) [, B	BF]	764
	PropertyPageObject.OLEDrag	765
	PropertyPageObject.PaintPicture picture, x1 , y1, [width1] , [height1] ,[x2] , [y2] , [width2] , [height2] , [rasterop]	765
	color = PropertyPageObject.Point (x , y)	766
	PropertyPageObject.PopupMenu menu, flags, x, y, menuitem	766
	PropertyPageObject.PSet [Step] (x , y), [color]	767
	PropertyPageObject.Refresh	767
	PropertyPageObject.Scale [(x1 , y1)—(x2 , y2)]	767
	result = PropertyPageObject.ScaleX (width , fromscale , toscale)	768
	result = PropertyPageObject.ScaleY (height , fromscale , toscale)	768
	PropertyPageObject.SetFocus	769
	height = PropertyPageObject.TextHeight (string)	769
	width = PropertyPageObject.TextWidth (string)	769
	Private Sub PropertyPage_Activate ( )	770
	Private Sub PropertyPage_ApplyChanges ( )	770
	Private Sub PropertyPageObject_Click( )	770
	Private Sub PropertyPageObject_DblClick( )	770
	Private Sub PropertyPageObject_Deactivate ( )	770
	Private Sub PropertyPageObject_DragDrop (source As Control, x As Single, y As Single)	770
	Private Sub PropertyPageObject_DragOver (source As Control, x As Single, y As Single, state As Integer)	771
	Private Sub PropertyPageObject_EditProperty (name As String)	772
	Private Sub PropertyPageObject_GotFocus ( )	772
	Private Sub PropertyPageObject_Initialize ( )	772
	Private Sub PropertyPageObject_KeyDown (keycode As Integer, shift As Single)	772
	Private Sub PropertyPageObject_KeyPress (keychar As Integer)	773
	Private Sub PropertyPageObject_KeyUp (keycode As Integer, shift As Single)	773
	Private Sub PropertyPageObject_Load ( )	773
	Private Sub PropertyPageObject_LostFocus ( )	774
	Private Sub PropertyPageObject_MouseDown (button As Integer, shift As Single, x As Single, y As Single)	774

Legend

CCE .... Control Creation Edition
LE .... Learning Edition
VBA .... Visual Basic for Applications
EE .... Enterprise Edition
PE .... Professional Edition

Class	Element	Edition (see Legend)	Page
	Private Sub PropertyPageObject_MouseMove (button As Integer, shift As Single, x As Single, y As Single)		774
	Private Sub PropertyPageObject_MouseUp (button As Integer, shift As Single, x As Single, y As Single)		775
	Private Sub PropertyPageObject_OLECompleteDrag(effect As Long)		776
	Private Sub PropertyPageObject_OLEDragDrop (data As DataObject, effect As Long, button As Integer, shift As Single, x As Single, y As Single)		776
	Private Sub PropertyPageObject_OLEDragOver (data As DataObject, effect As Long, button As Integer, shift As Single, x As Single, y As Single, state As Integer)		778
	Private Sub PropertyPageObject_OLEGiveFeedback (effect As Long)		779
	Private Sub PropertyPageObject_OLESetData (data As DataObject, DataFormat As Integer)		779
	Private Sub PropertyPageObject_OLEStartDrag (data As DataObject, AllowedEffects As Long)		780
	Private Sub PropertyPageObject_Paint ( )		780
	Private Sub PropertyPageObject_SelectionChanged ( )		781
	Private Sub PropertyPageObject_Terminate ( )		781
	Private Sub PropertyPageObject_Unload (cancel As Integer)		781
Public	Statement	CCE, LE, PE, EE	781
Put	Statement	CCE, LE, PE, EE	783
PV	Function	CCE, LE, PE, EE	784
QBColor	Function	CCE, LE, PE, EE	785
QueryDef	Object	PE, EE	785
	QueryDefObject.Cancel		787
	QueryDefObject.Close		787
	property = QueryDefObject.CreateProperty ([name] [, [type] [, [value] [, DDL]]])		787
	QueryDefObject.Execute source [, options]		788
	recordset = QueryDefObject.OpenRecordset (type [, options] [, lockedits]])		788
QueryDefs	Collection	PE, EE	789
	QueryDefsCollection.Append object		789
	QueryDefsCollection.Delete objectname		790
	QueryDefsCollection.Refresh		790
RaiseEvent	Statement	CCE, LE, PE, EE	791
Randomize	Statement	CCE, LE, PE, EE	791
Rate	Function	CCE, LE, PE, EE	792
rdoColumn	Object	EE	793
	rdoColumnObject.AppendChunk source		795
	size = rdoColumnObject.ColumnSize ( )		795

Class	Element	Edition (see Legend)	Page
	value = rdoColumnObject.GetChunk (number)		795
	Private Sub rdoColumnObject.DataChanged ( )		795
	Private Sub rdoColumnObject.WillChangeData (NewValue As Variant, Cancel As Boolean)		795
rdoColumns	Collection	EE	795
	rdoColumnsCollection.Refresh		796
rdoConnection	Object	EE	796
	rdoConnectionObject.BeginTrans		797
	rdoConnectionObject.Cancel		797
	rdoConnectionObject.Close		797
	rdoConnectionObject.CommitTrans		798
	rdoConnectionObject.CreateQuery name [, SQLQuery]		798
	rdoConnectionObject.EstablishConnection [prompt [, readonly [, options]]]		798
	rdoConnectionObject.Execute source [, options]		799
	results = rdoConnectionObject.OpenResultset (name [, type [, locktype [, options]]])		799
	rdoConnectionObject.RollbackTrans		800
	Private Sub rdoConnectionObject.BeforeConnect (ConnectString As String, Prompt As Variant)		800
	Private Sub rdoConnectionObject. Connect (ErrorOccured As Boolean)		801
	Private Sub rdoConnectionObject. Disconnect ( )		801
	Private Sub rdoConnectionObject. QueryComplete (Query As rdoQuery, ErrorOccured As Boolean)		801
	rdoConnectionObject.QueryTimeout (Query As rdoQuery, Cancel As Boolean)		801
	rdoConnectionObject.WillExecute (Query As rdoQuery, Cancel As Boolean)		801
rdoConnections	Collection	EE	802
	rdoConnectionsCollection.Add connection		802
	rdoConnectionsCollection.Remove connection		802
rdoEngine	Object	EE	802
	environ = rdoEngine.rdoCreateEnvironment (name, user, password)		803
	rdoEngine.RegisterDataSource name, driver, silent, attributes		803
	Private Sub rdoEngine_InfoMessage ( )		804
rdoEnvironment	Object	PE, EE	804

Legend

CCE .... Control Creation Edition
LE .... Learning Edition
VBA .... Visual Basic for Applications

EE .... Enterprise Edition
PE .... Professional Edition

Class	Element	Edition (see Legend)	Page
	rdoEnvironmentObject.BeginTrans		805
	rdoEnvironmentObject.Close		805
	rdoEnvironmentObject.CommitTrans		805
	connection = rdoEnvironmentObject.OpenConnection (dsname [, prompt [, readonly [, connect [, options]]]])		805
	rdoEnvironmentObject.RollbackTrans		806
	Private Sub rdoEnvironment_BeginTrans ( )		806
	Private Sub rdoEnvironment_CommitTrans ( )		806
	Private Sub rdoEnvironment_RollbackTrans ( )		806
rdoEnvironments	Collection	EE	806
	rdoEnvironmentsCollection.Add environment		806
	rdoEnvironmentsCollection.Remove connection		806
rdoError	Object	EE	807
rdoErrors	Collection	EE	807
	rdoErrorsCollection.Clear		808
rdoParameter	Object	EE	808
	rdoColumnObject.AppendChunk source		809
rdoParameters	Collection	EE	809
rdoQuery	Object	EE	809
	rdoQueryObject.Cancel		811
	rdoQueryObject.Close		811
	rdoQueryObject.Execute source [, options]		812
	results = rdoConnectionObject.OpenResultset ([, type [, locktype [, options]]])		812
rdoResultset	Object	EE	813
	rdoResultsetObject.AddNew		816
	rdoResultsetObject.BatchUpdate [singlerow [, force]]		816
	rdoResultsetObject.Cancel		816
	rdoResultsetObject.CancelBatch		817
	rdoResultsetObject.CancelUpdate		817
	rdoResultsetObject.Close		817
	rdoResultsetObject.Delete		817
	rdoResultsetObject.Edit		817
	rows = rdoResultsetObject.GetClipString (NumRows [, ColumnDelim [, RowDelim [, NullExp]]])		817
	rows = rdoResultsetObject.GetRows (NumRows)		818
	Return = rdoResultsetObject.MoreResults		818

Jump Tables • lxiii

Class	Element	Edition (see Legend)	Page
	rdoResultsetObject.Move rows [, start]		818
	rdoResultsetObject.MoveFirst		818
	rdoResultsetObject.MoveLast [option]		818
	rdoResultsetObject.MoveNext		819
	rdoResultsetObject.MovePrevious		819
	rdoResultsetObject.Requery [option]		819
	rdoResultsetObject.Update		819
	Private Sub rdoResultsetObject.Associate ( )		819
	Private Sub rdoResultsetObject.Dissociate ( )		819
	Private Sub rdoResultsetObject.ResultsChanged ( )		820
	Private Sub rdoResultsetObject.RowCurrentyChange ( )		820
	Private Sub rdoResultsetObject.RowStatusChanged ( )		820
	Private Sub rdoResultsetObject.WillAssociate (connection As rdoConnection, Cancel As Boolean)		820
	Private Sub rdoResultsetObject.WillDissociate (Cancel As Boolean)		820
	Private Sub rdoResultsetObject.WillUpdateRows (returncode As Long)		820
rdoResultsets	Collection	EE	821
rdoTable	Object	EE	821
	results = rdoTableObject.OpenResultset ([, type [, locktype [, options]]])		822
rdoTables	Collection	EE	823
	rdoTablesCollection.Refresh		823
Recordset	Object	PE, EE	823
	RecordsetObject.AddNew		827
	RecordsetObject.Cancel		827
	RecordsetObject.CancelUpdate		827
	RecordsetObject.Close		827
	querydef = RecordsetObject.CopyQueryDef		827
	rdoRecordsetObject.Delete		828
	RecordsetObject.Edit		828
	RecordsetObject.FillCache [rows] [, start]		828

Legend

CCE .... Control Creation Edition
LE .... Learning Edition
VBA .... Visual Basic for Applications
EE .... Enterprise Edition
PE .... Professional Edition

Class	Element	Edition (see Legend)	Page
	RecordsetObject.FindFirst [criteria]		828
	RecordsetObject.FindLast [criteria]		829
	RecordsetObject.FindNext [criteria]		829
	RecordsetObject.FindPrevious [criteria]		829
	rows = RecordsetObject.GetRows (NumRows)		829
	RecordsetObject.Move rows [, start]		830
	RecordsetObject.MoveFirst		830
	RecordsetObject.MoveLast [option]		830
	RecordsetObject.MoveNext		830
	RecordsetObject.MovePrevious		830
	Return = rdoRecordsetObject.NextRecordset		830
	results = RecordsetObject.OpenRecordset ([type [, options [, locktype]]])		831
	RecordsetObject.Requery [option]		832
	RecordsetObject.Seek comparison [, key [, key . . . [, key]]])		832
	RecordsetObject.Update [type] [, force]		833
Recordsets		Collection	EE	833
	RecordsetsCollection.Refresh		833
Rect		Object	PE, EE	834
ReDim		Statement	CCE, LE, PE, EE	834
Relation		Object	PE, EE	835
	field = RelationObject.CreateField ([name [, type [, size]]])		836
Relations		Collection	PE, EE	836
	RelationsCollection.Append object		837
	RelationsCollection.Delete objectname		837
	RelationsCollection.Refresh		837
Rem		Statement	CCE, LE, PE, EE	837
RemoteData		Control	EE	838
	RemoteDataControl.BeginTrans		845
	RemoteDataControl.Cancel		845
	RemoteDataControl.CommitTrans		845
	RemoteDataControl.Drag [DragAction]		845
	RemoteDataControl.Move Left [, Top [, Width [, Height]]]		845
	RemoteDataControl.Refresh		845
	rdoEnvironmentObject.RollbackTrans		846

Class	Element	Edition (see Legend)	Page
	RemoteDataControl.ShowWhatsThis		846
	RemoteDataControl.UpdateControls		846
	RemoteDataControl.UpdateRow		846
	RemoteDataControl.ZOrder [position]		846
	Private Sub RemoteDataControl_DragDrop([index As Integer ,] source As Control, x As Single, y As Single)		847
	Private Sub RemoteDataControl_DragOver([index As Integer ,] source As Control, x As Single, y As Single, state As Integer)		847
	Private Sub RemoteDataControl_Error ([index As Integer ,] number As Integer, description As String, scode As Long, source As String, helpfile As String, helpcontext As Long, resp As Single)		848
	Private Sub RemoteDataControl_MouseDown([index As Integer ,] button As Integer, shift As Single, x As Single, y As Single)		848
	Private Sub CheckBoxControl_MouseMove ([index As Integer ,] button As Integer, shift As Single, x As Single, y As Single)		849
	Private Sub RemoteDataControl_MouseUp([index As Integer ,] button As Integer, shift As Single, x As Single, y As Single)		850
	Private Sub RemoteDataControl_QueryCompleted ([index As Integer])		851
	Private Sub RemoteDataControl_Reposition ([index As Integer])		851
	Private Sub RemoteDataControl_Resize ([index As Integer])		851
	Private Sub RemoteDataControl_Validate ([index As Integer ,] action As Integer, save As Integer)		851
Reset	Statement	CCE, LE, PE, EE	852
Resume	Statement	CCE, LE, PE, EE	853
RGB	Function	CCE, LE, PE, EE	853
RichTextBox	Control	PE, EE	854
	RichTextBoxControl.Drag [DragAction]		860
	return = RichTextBoxControl.Find (string [, start [, stop [, options]]])		860
	return = RichTextBoxControl.GetLineFromChar (position)		861
	RichTextBoxControl.LoadFile fname, ftype		861
	RichTextBoxControl.Move Left [, Top [, Width [, Height]]]		861
	RichTextBoxControl.OLEDrag		862
	RichTextBoxControl.Refresh		862
	RichTextBoxControl.SaveFile fname, ftype		862
	RichTextBoxControl.SelPrint hdc		862
	RichTextBoxControl.SetFocus		862

Legend

CCE .... Control Creation Edition
LE .... Learning Edition
VBA .... Visual Basic for Applications
EE .... Enterprise Edition
PE .... Professional Edition

Class	Element	Edition (see Legend)	Page
	RichTextBoxControl.ShowWhatsThis		863
	RichTextBoxControl.Span charset, forward, negate		863
	RichTextBoxControl.Upto charset, forward, negate		863
	RichTextBoxControl.ZOrder [position]		863
	Private Sub RichTextBoxControl_Change ([index As Integer])		864
	Private Sub RichTextBoxControl_Click([index As Integer])		864
	Private Sub RichTextBoxControl_DblClick([index As Integer])		864
	Private Sub RichTextBoxControl_DragDrop([index As Integer ,] source As Control, x As Single, y As Single)		864
	Private Sub RichTextBoxControl_DragOver([index As Integer ,] source As Control, x As Single, y As Single, state As Integer)		865
	Private Sub RichTextBoxControl_GotFocus ([index As Integer])		865
	Private Sub RichTextBoxControl_KeyDown ([index As Integer ,] keycode As Integer, shift As Single)		866
	Private Sub RichTextBoxControl_KeyPress([index As Integer ,] keychar As Integer)		866
	Private Sub RichTextBoxControl_KeyUp ([index As Integer ,] keycode As Integer, shift As Single)		866
	Private Sub RichTextBoxControl_LostFocus ([index As Integer])		867
	Private Sub RichTextBoxBoxControl_MouseDown([index As Integer ,] button As Integer, shift As Single, x As Single, y As Single)		867
	Private Sub RichTextBoxControl_MouseMove ([index As Integer ,] button As Integer, shift As Single, x As Single, y As Single)		868
	Private Sub RichTextBoxBoxControl_MouseUp([index As Integer ,] button As Integer, shift As Single, x As Single, y As Single)		868
	Private Sub RichTextBoxControl_OLECompleteDrag([index As Integer ,] effect As Long)		869
	Private Sub RichTextBoxControl_OLEDragDrop([index As Integer ,] data As DataObject, effect As Long, button As Integer, shift As Single, x As Single, y As Single)		870
	Private Sub RichTextBoxControl_OLEDragOver([index As Integer ,] data As DataObject, effect As Long, button As Integer, shift As Single, x As Single, y As Single, state As Integer)		871
	Private Sub RichTextBoxControl_OLEGiveFeedback ([index As Integer ,] effect As Long)		872
	Private Sub RichTextBoxControl_OLESetData([index As Integer ,] data As DataObject, DataFormat As Integer)		873
	Private Sub RichTextBoxControl_OLEStartDrag ([index As Integer ,] data As DataObject, AllowedEffects As Long)		873
	Private Sub RichTextBoxControl_OLEStartDrag ([index As Integer ,] data As DataObject, AllowedEffects As Long)		874
Right		Function	CCE, LE, PE, EE	874
RightB		Function	CCE, LE, PE, EE	875
RmDir		Statement	CCE, LE, PE, EE	875
Rnd		Function	CCE, LE, PE, EE	876
RowBuffer		Object	PE, EE	876
RSet		Statement	CCE, LE, PE, EE	877
RTrim		Function	CCE, LE, PE, EE	877
SavePicture		Statement	CCE, LE, PE, EE	878

Class	Element	Edition (see Legend)	Page
SaveSetting	Statement	CCE, LE, PE, EE	878
Screen	Object	CCE, LE, PE, EE	879
Second	Function	CCE, LE, PE, EE	881
Seek	Function	CCE, LE, PE, EE	881
Seek	Statement	CCE, LE, PE, EE	882
SelBookmarks	Collection	CCE, LE, PE, EE	883
SelBookmarksCollection.Add bookmark			883
SelBookmarksCollection.Clear			883
SelBookmarksCollection.Remove index			883
Select Case	Statement	CCE, LE, PE, EE	884
SendKeys	Statement	CCE, LE, PE, EE	885
Series	Object	PE, EE	886
SeriesObject.Select			888
SeriesCollection	Collection	PE, EE	888
count = SeriesCollection.Count			888
SeriesMarker	Object	PE, EE	888
SeriesPosition	Object	PE, EE	889
Set	Function	CCE, LE, PE, EE	889
SetAttr	Function	CCE, LE, PE, EE	890
Sgn	Function	CCE, LE, PE, EE	891
Shadow	Object	PE, EE	892
Shape	Control	CCE, LE, PE, EE	892
ShapeControl.Move Left [, Top [, Width [, Height]]]			895
ShapeControl.Refresh			895
ShapeControl.ZOrder [position]			895
Shell	Statement	CCE, LE, PE, EE	895

Legend

CCE .... Control Creation Edition
LE .... Learning Edition
VBA .... Visual Basic for Applications
EE .... Enterprise Edition
PE .... Professional Edition

Class	Element	Edition (see Legend)	Page
Sin	Function	CCE, LE, PE, EE	896
Single	Data Type	CCE, LE, PE, EE	897
Slider	Control	PE, EE	897
SliderControl.ClearSel			901
SliderControl.Drag [DragAction]			901
SliderControl.Move Left [, Top [, Width [, Height]]]			902
SliderControl.OLEDrag			902
SliderControl.Refresh			902
SliderControl.SetFocus			902
SliderControl.ShowWhatsThis			902
SliderControl.ZOrder [position]			902
Private Sub SliderControl_Change ([index As Integer])			903
Private Sub SliderControl_Click([index As Integer])			903
Private Sub SliderControl_DragDrop([index As Integer ,] source As Control, x As Single, y As Single)			903
Private Sub SliderControl_DragOver([index As Integer ,] source As Control, x As Single, y As Single, state As Integer)			903
Private Sub SliderControl_GotFocus ([index As Integer])			904
Private Sub SliderControl_KeyDown ([index As Integer ,] keycode As Integer, shift As Single)			904
Private Sub SliderControl_KeyPress([index As Integer ,] keychar As Integer)			905
Private Sub SliderControl_KeyUp ([index As Integer ,] keycode As Integer, shift As Single)			905
Private Sub SliderControl_MouseDown([index As Integer ,] button As Integer, shift As Single, x As Single, y As Single)			906
Private Sub SliderControl_MouseMove ([index As Integer ,] button As Integer, shift As Single, x As Single, y As Single)			906
Private Sub SliderControl_MouseUp([index As Integer ,] button As Integer, shift As Single, x As Single, y As Single)			907
Private Sub SliderControl_OLECompleteDrag([index As Integer ,] effect As Long)			908
Private Sub SliderControl_OLEDragDrop([index As Integer ,] data As DataObject, effect As Long, button As Integer, shift As Single, x As Single, y As Single)			908
Private Sub SliderControl_OLEDragOver([index As Integer ,] data As DataObject, effect As Long, button As Integer, shift As Single, x As Single, y As Single, state As Integer)			909
Private Sub SliderControl_OLEGiveFeedback ([index As Integer ,] effect As Long)			911
Private Sub SliderControl_OLESetData([index As Integer ,] data As DataObject, DataFormat As Integer)			911
Private Sub SliderControl_OLEStartDrag ([index As Integer ,] data As DataObject, AllowedEffects As Long)			912
Private Sub SliderControl_Scroll ([index As Integer])			912
SLN	Function	CCE, LE, PE, EE	913
Space	Function	CCE, LE, PE, EE	914
Split	Object	PE, EE	914
SplitObject.ClearSelCols			916

Class	Element	Edition (see Legend)	Page
Splits	Collection	PE, EE	916
split = SplitsCollection.Add index			916
split = SplitsCollection.Item (index)			916
SplitsCollection.Remove index			917
Sqr	Function	CCE, LE, PE, EE	917
SSTab	Control	PE, EE	917
SSTabControl.Drag [DragAction]			921
SSTabControl.Move Left [, Top [, Width [, Height]]]			922
SSTabControl.OLEDrag			922
SSTabControl.SetFocus			922
SSTabControl.ShowWhatsThis			922
SSTabControl.ZOrder [position]			922
Private Sub SSTabControl_Click([index As Integer ,] oldtab As Integer)			922
Private Sub SSTabControl_DblClick([index As Integer])			923
Private Sub SSTabControl_DragDrop([index As Integer ,] source As Control, x As Single, y As Single)			923
Private Sub SSTabControl_DragOver([index As Integer ,] source As Control, x As Single, y As Single, state As Integer)			923
Private Sub SSTabControl_GotFocus ([index As Integer])			924
Private Sub SSTabControl_KeyDown ([index As Integer ,] keycode As Integer, shift As Single)			924
Private Sub SSTabControl_KeyPress([index As Integer ,] keychar As Integer)			925
Private Sub SSTabControl_KeyUp ([index As Integer ,] keycode As Integer, shift As Single)			925
Private Sub SSTabControl_LostFocus ([index As Integer])			925
Private Sub TextBoxBoxControl_MouseDown([index As Integer ,] button As Integer, shift As Single, x As Single, y As Single)			926
Private Sub SSTabControl_MouseMove ([index As Integer ,] button As Integer, shift As Single, x As Single, y As Single)			926
Private Sub TextBoxBoxControl_MouseUp([index As Integer ,] button As Integer, shift As Single, x As Single, y As Single)			927
Private Sub SSTabControl_OLECompleteDrag([index As Integer ,] effect As Long)			928
Private Sub SSTabControl_OLEDragDrop([index As Integer ,] data As DataObject, effect As Long, button As Integer, shift As Single, x As Single, y As Single)			928
Private Sub SSTabControl_OLEDragOver([index As Integer ,] data As DataObject, effect As Long, button As Integer, shift As Single, x As Single, y As Single, state As Integer)			929
Private Sub SSTabControl_OLEGiveFeedback ([index As Integer ,] effect As Long)			931

Legend

CCE .... Control Creation Edition
LE .... Learning Edition
VBA .... Visual Basic for Applications
EE .... Enterprise Edition
PE .... Professional Edition

Class	Element	Edition (see Legend)	Page
	Private Sub SSTabControl_OLESetData([index As Integer ,] data As DataObject, DataFormat As Integer)		931
	Private Sub SSTabControl_OLEStartDrag ([index As Integer ,] data As DataObject, AllowedEffects As Long)		932
Static	Statement	CCE, LE, PE, EE	932
StatLine	Object	PE, EE	934
StatusBar	Control	PE, EE	934
	StatusBarControl.Drag [DragAction]		938
	StatusBarControl.Move Left [, Top [, Width [, Height]]]		938
	StatusBarControl.OLEDrag		938
	StatusBarControl.Refresh		938
	StatusBarControl.ShowWhatsThis		938
	StatusBarControl.ZOrder [position]		938
	Private Sub StatusBarControl_Click([index As Integer])		939
	Private Sub StatusBarControl_DblClick([index As Integer])		939
	Private Sub StatusBarControl_DragDrop([index As Integer ,] source As Control, x As Single, y As Single)		939
	Private Sub StatusBarControl_DragOver([index As Integer ,] source As Control, x As Single, y As Single, state As Integer)		940
	Private Sub StatusBarBoxControl_MouseDown([index As Integer ,] button As Integer, shift As Single, x As Single, y As Single)		940
	Private Sub StatusBarControl_MouseMove ([index As Integer ,] button As Integer, shift As Single, x As Single, y As Single)		941
	Private Sub StatusBarBoxControl_MouseUp([index As Integer ,] button As Integer, shift As Single, x As Single, y As Single)		942
	Private Sub StatusBarControl_OLECompleteDrag([index As Integer ,] effect As Long)		943
	Private Sub StatusBarControl_OLEDragDrop([index As Integer ,] data As DataObject, effect As Long, button As Integer, shift As Single, x As Single, y As Single)		943
	Private Sub StatusBarControl_OLEDragOver([index As Integer ,] data As DataObject, effect As Long, button As Integer, shift As Single, x As Single, y As Single, state As Integer)		944
	Private Sub StatusBarControl_OLEGiveFeedback ([index As Integer ,] effect As Long)		946
	Private Sub StatusBarControl_OLESetData([index As Integer ,] data As DataObject, DataFormat As Integer)		946
	Private Sub StatusBarControl_OLEStartDrag ([index As Integer ,] data As DataObject, AllowedEffects As Long)		947
	Private Sub StatusBarControl_PanelClick([index As Integer ,] ByVal panel As Panel)		947
	Private Sub StatusBarControl_PanelDblClick([index As Integer ,] ByVal panel As Panel)		948
Stop	Statement	CCE, LE, PE, EE	948
Str	Function	CCE, LE, PE, EE	949
StrComp	Function	CCE, LE, PE, EE	949
StrConv	Function	CCE, LE, PE, EE	950
Single	Data Type	CCE, LE, PE, EE	951
String	Function	CCE, LE, PE, EE	952

Class	Element	Edition (see Legend)	Page
Sub	Statement	CCE, LE, PE, EE	952
Switch	Function	CCE, LE, PE, EE	954
SYD	Function	CCE, LE, PE, EE	954
SysInfo	Control	PE, EE	955
	Private Sub SysInfoControl_ConfigChangeCancelled ([index As Integer])		957
	Private Sub SysInfoControl_ConfigChanged ([index As Integer ,] ByVal oldconfignum As Long, ByVal newconfignum As Long)		957
	Private Sub SysInfoControl_DeviceArrival ([index As Integer ,] ByVal devicetype As Long, ByVal deviceid As Long, ByVal devicetype As Long, ByVal devicename As String, ByVal devicedata As Long)		957
	Private Sub SysInfoControl_DeviceOtherEvent ([index As Integer ,] ByVal devicetype As Long, ByVal eventname As String, ByVal datapointer As Long)		958
	Private Sub SysInfoControl_DeviceQueryRemove ([index As Integer ,] ByVal devicetype As Long, ByVal deviceid As Long, ByVal devicetype As Long, ByVal devicename As String, ByVal devicedata As Long, cancel As Boolean)		959
	Private Sub SysInfoControl_DeviceQueryRemoveFailed ([index As Integer ,] ByVal devicetype As Long, ByVal deviceid As Long, ByVal devicetype As Long, ByVal devicename As String, ByVal devicedata As Long)		960
	Private Sub SysInfoControl_DeviceRemoveComplete ([index As Integer ,] ByVal devicetype As Long, ByVal deviceid As Long, ByVal devicetype As Long, ByVal devicename As String, ByVal devicedata As Long)		961
	Private Sub SysInfoControl_DeviceRemovePending ([index As Integer ,] ByVal devicetype As Long, ByVal deviceid As Long, ByVal devicetype As Long, ByVal devicename As String, ByVal devicedata As Long)		963
	Private Sub SysInfoControl_DevModeChange ([index As Integer ,] ByVal devicename As String)		964
	Private Sub SysInfoControl_DisplayChanged ([index As Integer])		964
	Private Sub SysInfoControl_PowerQuerySuspend ([index As Integer ,] cancel As Boolean)		964
	Private Sub SysInfoControl_PowerResume ([index As Integer])		964
	Private Sub SysInfoControl_PowerStatusChanged ([index As Integer])		965
	Private Sub SysInfoControl_PowerSuspend ([index As Integer])		965
	Private Sub SysInfoControl_QueryChangeConfig ([index As Integer ,] cancel As Boolean)		965
	Private Sub SysInfoControl_SettingChanged ([index As Integer ,] ByVal item As Integer)		965
	Private Sub SysInfoControl_SysColorsChanged ([index As Integer])		965
	Private Sub SysInfoControl_TimeChanged ([index As Integer])		966
Tab	Object	PE, EE	967
TableDef	Object	PE, EE	967

Legend

CCE .... Control Creation Edition
LE .... Learning Edition
VBA .... Visual Basic for Applications
EE .... Enterprise Edition
PE .... Professional Edition

Class	Element	Edition (see Legend)	Page
	field = TableDefObject.CreateField ([name [, type [, size]]])		969
	index = TableDefObject.CreateIndex ([name])		969
	property = TableDefObject.CreateProperty ([name] [, [type] [, [value] [, DDL]]])		970
	recordset = TableDefObject.OpenRecordset (type [, options] [, lockedits])		970
	TableDefObject.RefreshLink		971
TableDefs	Collection	PE, EE	972
	TableDefsCollection.Append object		972
	TableDefsCollection.Delete objectname		972
	TableDefsCollection.Refresh		972
Tabs	Collection	PE, EE	972
	Tab = TabsCollection.Add ([index [, key [, caption [, image]]]])		973
	TabsCollection.Clear		973
	TabsCollection.Remove index		973
TabStrip	Control	PE, EE	973
	TabStripControl.Drag [DragAction]		977
	TabStripControl.Move Left [, Top [, Width [, Height]]]		977
	TabStripControl.OLEDrag		977
	TabStripControl.Refresh		977
	TabStripControl.SetFocus		978
	TabStripControl.ShowWhatsThis		978
	TabStripControl.ZOrder [position]		978
	Private Sub TabStripControl_BeforeClick ([index As Integer ,] cancel As Integer)		978
	Private Sub TabStripControl_Click([index As Integer])		978
	Private Sub TabStripControl_DragDrop([index As Integer ,] source As Control, x As Single, y As Single)		979
	Private Sub TabStripControl_DragOver([index As Integer ,] source As Control, x As Single, y As Single, state As Integer)		979
	Private Sub TabStripControl_GotFocus ([index As Integer])		980
	Private Sub TabStripControl_KeyDown ([index As Integer ,] keycode As Integer, shift As Single)		980
	Private Sub TabStripControl_KeyPress([index As Integer ,] keychar As Integer)		981
	Private Sub TabStripControl_KeyUp ([index As Integer ,] keycode As Integer, shift As Single)		981
	Private Sub TabStripControl_LostFocus ([index As Integer])		981
	Private Sub TabStripBoxControl_MouseDown([index As Integer ,] button As Integer, shift As Single, x As Single, y As Single)		981
	Private Sub TabStripControl_MouseMove ([index As Integer ,] button As Integer, shift As Single, x As Single, y As Single)		982
	Private Sub TabStripBoxControl_MouseUp([index As Integer ,] button As Integer, shift As Single, x As Single, y As Single)		983
	Private Sub TabStripControl_OLECompleteDrag([index As Integer ,] effect As Long)		984

Class	Element	Edition (see Legend)	Page
	Private Sub TabStripControl_OLEDragDrop([index As Integer ,] data As DataObject, effect As Long, button As Integer, shift As Single, x As Single, y As Single)		984
	Private Sub TabStripControl_OLEDragOver([index As Integer ,] data As DataObject, effect As Long, button As Integer, shift As Single, x As Single, y As Single, state As Integer)		985
	Private Sub TabStripControl_OLEGiveFeedback ([index As Integer ,] effect As Long)		987
	Private Sub TabStripControl_OLESetData([index As Integer ,] data As DataObject, DataFormat As Integer)		987
	Private Sub TabStripControl_OLEStartDrag ([index As Integer ,] data As DataObject, AllowedEffects As Long)		988
Tan	Function	CCE, LE, PE, EE	988
TextBox	Control	CCE, LE, PE, EE	989
	TextBoxControl.Drag [DragAction]		995
	TextBoxControl.LinkExecute command		995
	TextBoxControl.LinkPoke		995
	TextBoxControl.LinkRequest		995
	TextBoxControl.LinkSend		995
	TextBoxControl.Move Left [, Top [, Width [, Height]]]		995
	TextBoxControl.OLEDrag		996
	TextBoxControl.Refresh		996
	TextBoxControl.SetFocus		996
	TextBoxControl.ShowWhatsThis		996
	TextBoxControl.ZOrder [position]		996
	Private Sub TextBoxControl_Change ([index As Integer])		996
	Private Sub TextBoxControl_Click([index As Integer])		997
	Private Sub TextBoxControl_DblClick([index As Integer])		997
	Private Sub TextBoxControl_DragDrop([index As Integer ,] source As Control, x As Single, y As Single)		997
	Private Sub TextBoxControl_DragOver([index As Integer ,] source As Control, x As Single, y As Single, state As Integer)		997
	Private Sub TextBoxControl_GotFocus ([index As Integer])		998
	Private Sub TextBoxControl_KeyDown ([index As Integer ,] keycode As Integer, shift As Single)		998
	Private Sub TextBoxControl_KeyPress([index As Integer ,] keychar As Integer)		999
	Private Sub TextBoxControl_KeyUp ([index As Integer ,] keycode As Integer, shift As Single)		999
	Private Sub TextBoxControl_LinkClose ([index As Integer ,])		1000

Legend

CCE .... Control Creation Edition
LE .... Learning Edition
VBA .... Visual Basic for Applications
EE .... Enterprise Edition
PE .... Professional Edition

Class	Element	Edition (see Legend)	Page
	Private Sub TextBoxControl_LinkError ([index As Integer ,] errcode As Integer)		1000
	Private Sub TextBoxControl_LinkExecute ([index As Integer ,] cmd As String, cancel As Integer)		1000
	Private Sub TextBoxControl_LinkOpen ([index As Integer ,] cancel As Integer)		1001
	Private Sub TextBoxControl_LostFocus ([index As Integer])		1001
	Private Sub TextBoxBoxControl_MouseDown([index As Integer ,] button As Integer, shift As Single, x As Single, y As Single)		1001
	Private Sub TextBoxControl_MouseMove ([index As Integer ,] button As Integer, shift As Single, x As Single, y As Single)		1002
	Private Sub TextBoxBoxControl_MouseUp([index As Integer ,] button As Integer, shift As Single, x As Single, y As Single)		1002
	Private Sub TextBoxControl_OLECompleteDrag([index As Integer ,] effect As Long)		1003
	Private Sub TextBoxControl_OLEDragDrop([index As Integer ,] data As DataObject, effect As Long, button As Integer, shift As Single, x As Single, y As Single)		1004
	Private Sub TextBoxControl_OLEDragOver([index As Integer ,] data As DataObject, effect As Long, button As Integer, shift As Single, x As Single, y As Single, state As Integer)		1005
	Private Sub TextBoxControl_OLEGiveFeedback ([index As Integer ,] effect As Long)		1006
	Private Sub TextBoxControl_OLESetData([index As Integer ,] data As DataObject, DataFormat As Integer)		1007
	Private Sub TextBoxControl_OLEStartDrag ([index As Integer ,] data As DataObject, AllowedEffects As Long)		1007
TextLayout	Object	PE, EE	1008
Tick	Object	PE, EE	1009
Time	Function	CCE, LE, PE, EE	1009
Time	Statement	CCE, LE, PE, EE	1010
Timer	Control	PE, EE	1011
	Private Sub TimerControl_Timer ([index As Integer])		1011
Timer	Function	CCE, LE, PE, EE	1012
TimeValue	Function	CCE, LE, PE, EE	1012
TimeValue	Function	CCE, LE, PE, EE	1013
Title	Object	PE, EE	1014
	TitleObject.Select		1014
Toolbar	Control	PE, EE	1014
	ToolbarControl.Customize		1018
	ToolbarControl.Drag [DragAction]		1018
	ToolbarControl.Move Left [, Top [, Width [, Height]]]		1019
	ToolbarControl.OLEDrag		1019
	ToolbarControl.Refresh		1019
	ToolbarControl.RestoreToolbar key, subkey, value		1019
	ToolbarControl.SaveToolbar key, subkey, value		1019

Class	Element	Edition (see Legend)	Page
	ToolbarControl.ShowWhatsThis		1020
	ToolbarControl.ZOrder [position]		1020
	Private Sub ToolbarControl_ButtonClick([index As Integer ,] ByVal button As Button)		1020
	Private Sub ToolbarControl_Change ([index As Integer])		1020
	Private Sub ToolbarControl_Click([index As Integer])		1021
	Private Sub ToolbarControl_DblClick([index As Integer])		1021
	Private Sub ToolbarControl_DragDrop([index As Integer ,] source As Control, x As Single, y As Single)		1021
	Private Sub ToolbarControl_DragOver([index As Integer ,] source As Control, x As Single, y As Single, state As Integer)		1021
	Private Sub ToolbarBoxControl_MouseDown([index As Integer ,] button As Integer, shift As Single, x As Single, y As Single)		1022
	Private Sub ToolbarControl_MouseMove ([index As Integer ,] button As Integer, shift As Single, x As Single, y As Single)		1023
	Private Sub ToolbarBoxControl_MouseUp([index As Integer ,] button As Integer, shift As Single, x As Single, y As Single)		1024
	Private Sub ToolbarControl_OLECompleteDrag([index As Integer ,] effect As Long)		1024
	Private Sub ToolbarControl_OLEDragDrop([index As Integer ,] data As DataObject, effect As Long, button As Integer, shift As Single, x As Single, y As Single)		1025
	Private Sub ToolbarControl_OLEDragOver([index As Integer ,] data As DataObject, effect As Long, button As Integer, shift As Single, x As Single, y As Single, state As Integer)		1026
	Private Sub ToolbarControl_OLEGiveFeedback ([index As Integer ,] effect As Long)		1027
	Private Sub ToolbarControl_OLESetData([index As Integer ,] data As DataObject, DataFormat As Integer)		1028
	Private Sub ToolbarControl_OLEStartDrag ([index As Integer ,] data As DataObject, AllowedEffects As Long)		1029
TreeView	Control	PE, EE	1029
	TreeViewControl.Drag [DragAction]		1034
	result = TreeViewControl.GetVisibleCount		1034
	result = TreeViewControl.GetFirstVisible		1034
	result = TreeViewControl.HitTest (x As Single, y As Single)		1034
	TreeViewControl.Move Left [, Top [, Width [, Height]]]		1035
	TreeViewControl.OLEDrag		1035
	TreeViewControl.Refresh		1035
	TreeViewControl.SetFocus		1035
	TreeViewControl.ShowWhatsThis		1035
	TreeViewControl.StartLabelEdit		1035

Legend

CCE .... Control Creation Edition
LE .... Learning Edition
VBA .... Visual Basic for Applications
EE .... Enterprise Edition
PE .... Professional Edition

Class	Element	Edition (see Legend)	Page
	TreeViewControl.ZOrder [position]		1035
	Private Sub TreeViewControl _AfterLabelEdit([index As Integer ,] cancel As Integer, NewString As String)		1036
	Private Sub TreeViewControl_BeforeLabelEdit([index As Integer ,] cancel As Integer)		1036
	Private Sub TreeViewControl_Click([index As Integer])		1036
	Private Sub TreeViewControl_Collapse ([index As Integer ,] ByVal node As Node)		1037
	Private Sub TreeViewControl_DblClick([index As Integer])		1037
	Private Sub TreeViewControl_DragDrop([index As Integer ,] source As Control, x As Single, y As Single)		1037
	Private Sub TreeViewControl_DragOver([index As Integer ,] source As Control, x As Single, y As Single, state As Integer)		1038
	Private Sub TreeViewControl_Expand([index As Integer ,] ByVal node As Node)		1038
	Private Sub TreeViewControl_GotFocus ([index As Integer])		1039
	Private Sub TreeViewControl_KeyDown ([index As Integer ,] keycode As Integer, shift As Single)		1039
	Private Sub TreeViewControl_KeyPress([index As Integer ,] keychar As Integer)		1039
	Private Sub TreeViewControl_KeyUp ([index As Integer ,] keycode As Integer, shift As Single)		1040
	Private Sub TreeViewControl_LostFocus ([index As Integer])		1040
	Private Sub TreeViewBoxControl_MouseDown([index As Integer ,] button As Integer, shift As Single, x As Single, y As Single)		1040
	Private Sub TreeViewControl_MouseMove ([index As Integer ,] button As Integer, shift As Single, x As Single, y As Single)		1041
	Private Sub TreeViewBoxControl_MouseUp([index As Integer ,] button As Integer, shift As Single, x As Single, y As Single)		1042
	Private Sub TreeViewControl_NodeClick([index As Integer ,] ByVal node As Node)		1043
	Private Sub TreeViewControl_OLECompleteDrag([index As Integer ,] effect As Long)		1043
	Private Sub TreeViewControl_OLEDragDrop([index As Integer ,] data As DataObject, effect As Long, button As Integer, shift As Single, x As Single, y As Single)		1043
	Private Sub TreeViewControl_OLEDragOver([index As Integer ,] data As DataObject, effect As Long, button As Integer, shift As Single, x As Single, y As Single, state As Integer)		1044
	Private Sub TreeViewControl_OLEGiveFeedback ([index As Integer ,] effect As Long)		1046
	Private Sub TreeViewControl_OLESetData([index As Integer ,] data As DataObject, DataFormat As Integer)		1046
	Private Sub TreeViewControl_OLEStartDrag ([index As Integer ,] data As DataObject, AllowedEffects As Long)		1047
Trim	Function	CCE, LE, PE, EE	1049
Type	Statement	CCE, LE, PE, EE	1049
TypeName	Function	CCE, LE, PE, EE	1050
UBound	Function	CCE, LE, PE, EE	1052
UCase	Function	CCE, LE, PE, EE	1052
Unload	Statement	CCE, LE, PE, EE	1053
Unlock	Statement	CCE, LE, PE, EE	1053
UpDown	Control	CCE, LE, PE, EE	1054

Class	Element	Edition (see Legend)	Page
	UpDownControl.Drag [DragAction]		1058
	UpDownControl.Move Left [, Top [, Width [, Height]]]		1058
	UpDownControl.OLEDrag		1058
	UpDownControl.SetFocus		1058
	UpDownControl.ShowWhatsThis		1058
	UpDownControl.ZOrder [position]		1058
	Private Sub UpDownControl _Change([index As Integer])		1059
	Private Sub UpDownControl _DownClick ([index As Integer])		1059
	Private Sub UpDownControl _DragDrop([index As Integer,] source As Control, x As Single, y As Single)		1059
	Private Sub UpDownControl _DragOver([index As Integer,] source As Control, x As Single, y As Single, state As Integer)		1060
	Private Sub UpDownControl _GotFocus ([index As Integer])		1061
	Private Sub UpDownControl _LostFocus ([index As Integer])		1061
	Private Sub UpDownControl_OLEDragDrop([index As Integer,] data As DataObject, effect As Long, button As Integer, shift As Single, x As Single, y As Single)		1061
	Private Sub LabelControl_OLEDragDrop([index As Integer,] data As DataObject, effect As Long, button As Integer, shift As Single, x As Single, y As Single)		1062
	Private Sub LabelControl_OLEDragOver([index As Integer,] data As DataObject, effect As Long, button As Integer, shift As Single, x As Single, y As Single, state As Integer)		1063
	Private Sub LabelControl_OLEGiveFeedback ([index As Integer,] effect As Long)		1065
	Private Sub LabelControl_OLESetData([index As Integer,] data As DataObject, DataFormat As Integer)		1065
	Private Sub LabelControl_OLEStartDrag ([index As Integer,] data As DataObject, AllowedEffects As Long)		1066
	Private Sub UpDownControl_UpClick ([index As Integer])		1066
User	Object	PE, EE	1067
	Group = UserObject.CreateGroup ([name] [, pid])		1067
	UserObject.NewPassword oldpass, newpass		1067
Users	Collection	PE, EE	1068
	UsersCollection.Append object		1068
	UsersCollection.Delete name		1068
	UsersCollection.Refresh		1068
UserControl	Object	CCE, LE, PE, EE	1068

Legend

CCE .... Control Creation Edition
LE .... Learning Edition
VBA .... Visual Basic for Applications
EE .... Enterprise Edition
PE .... Professional Edition

Class	Element	Edition (see Legend)	Page
	UserControlObject.AsyncRead target, type, [propertyname]		1075
	UserControlObject.CancelAsyncRead [propertyname]		1076
	status = UserControlObject.CanPropertyChange (propertyname)		1076
	UserControlObject.Circle [Step] (x, y), radius [, color [, start [, stop [, aspect]]]]		1076
	UserControlObject.Cls		1077
	UserControlObject.Line [Step] (x1, y1), [Step] (x2, y2) [, B	BF]		1077
	UserControlObject.OLEDrag		1077
	UserControlObject.PaintPicture picture, x1, y1, [width1], [height1], [x2], [y2], [width2], [height2], [rasterop]		1077
	color = UserControlObject.Point (x, y)		1078
	UserControlObject.PopupMenu menu, flags, x, y, menuitem		1079
	UserControlObject.PropertyChanged propertyname		1079
	UserControlObject.PSet [Step] (x, y), color		1080
	UserControlObject.Refresh		1080
	UserControlObject.Scale [((x1, y1)—(x2, y2)]		1080
	result = UserControlObject.ScaleX (width, fromscale, toscale)		1080
	result = UserControlObject.ScaleY (height, fromscale, toscale)		1081
	UserControlObject.SetFocus		1081
	UserControlObject.Size width, height		1081
	height = UserControlObject.TextHeight (string)		1082
	width = UserControlObject.TextWidth (string)		1082
	Private Sub UserControlObject_AccessKeyPress (keychar As Integer)		1082
	Private Sub UserControlObject_AmbientChanged (propertyname As String)		1082
	Private Sub UserControlObject_AsyncReadComplete (propertyvalue As AsyncProperty)		1082
	Private Sub UserControlObject_Click( )		1083
	Private Sub UserControlObject_DblClick( )		1083
	Private Sub UserControlObject_DragDrop (source As Control, x As Single, y As Single)		1083
	Private Sub UserControlObject_DragOver (source As Control, x As Single, y As Single, state As Integer)		1084
	Private Sub UserControlObject_EnterFocus ( )		1084
	Private Sub UserControlObject_ExitFocus ( )		1085
	Private Sub UserControlObject_GotFocus ( )		1085
	Private Sub UserControlObject_Hide ( )		1085
	Private Sub UserControlObject _Initialize ( )		1085
	Private Sub UserControlObject _InitProperties ( )		1085
	Private Sub UserControlObject _KeyDown (keycode As Integer, shift As Single)		1085
	Private Sub UserControlObject _KeyPress (keychar As Integer)		1086
	Private Sub UserControlObject _KeyUp (keycode As Integer, shift As Single)		1086

Class	Element	Edition (see Legend)	Page
	Private Sub UserControlObject _LostFocus ( )		1087
	Private Sub UserControlObject _MouseDown (button As Integer, shift As Single, x As Single, y As Single)		1087
	Private Sub UserControlObject _MouseMove (button As Integer, shift As Single, x As Single, y As Single)		1087
	Private Sub UserControlObject _MouseUp (button As Integer, shift As Single, x As Single, y As Single)		1088
	Private Sub UserControlObject_OLECompleteDrag(effect As Long)		1089
	Private Sub UserControlObject_OLEDragDrop (data As DataObject, effect As Long, button As Integer, shift As Single, x As Single, y As Single)		1089
	Private Sub UserControlObject_OLEDragOver (data As DataObject, effect As Long, button As Integer, shift As Single, x As Single, y As Single, state As Integer)		1091
	Private Sub UserControlObject_OLEGiveFeedback (effect As Long)		1092
	Private Sub UserControlObject_OLESetData (data As DataObject, DataFormat As Integer)		1092
	Private Sub UserControlObject_OLEStartDrag (data As DataObject, AllowedEffects As Long)		1093
	Private Sub UserControlObject_Paint ( )		1093
	Private Sub UserControlObject_ReadProperties (pb As PropertyBag)		1094
	Private Sub UserControlObject_Resize ( )		1094
	Private Sub UserControlObject_Show ( )		1094
	Private Sub UserControlObject_Terminate ( )		1094
	Private Sub UserControlObject_WriteProperties (pb As PropertyBag)		1094
UserDocument	Object	CCE, LE, PE, EE	1094
	UserDocumentObject.AsyncRead target, type, [propertyname]		1101
	UserDocumentObject.CancelAsyncRead [propertyname]		1101
	UserDocumentObject.Circle [Step] (x, y), radius [, color [, start [, stop [, aspect]]]]		1102
	UserDocumentObject.Cls		1102
	UserDocumentObject.Line [Step] (x1, y1), [Step] (x2, y2) [, B|BF]		1102
	UserDocumentObject.OLEDrag		1103
	UserDocumentObject.PaintPicture picture, x1, y1, [width1], [height1], [x2], [y2], [width2], [height2], [rasterop]		1103
	color = UserDocumentObject.Point (x, y)		1104
	UserDocumentObject.PopupMenu menu, flags, x, y, menuitem		1104
	UserDocumentObject.PrintForm		1105
	UserDocumentObject.PropertyChanged propertyname		1105

Legend

CCE .... Control Creation Edition
LE .... Learning Edition
VBA .... Visual Basic for Applications
EE .... Enterprise Edition
PE .... Professional Edition

Class	Element	Edition (see Legend)	Page
	UserDocumentObject.PSet [Step] (x, y), color		1105
	UserDocumentObject.Refresh		1106
	UserDocumentObject.Scale [(x1, y1)—(x2, y2)]		1106
	result = UserDocumentObject.ScaleX (width, fromscale, toscale)		1106
	result = UserDocumentObject.ScaleY (height, fromscale, toscale)		1107
	UserDocumentObject.SetFocus		1107
	UserDocumentObject.SetViewport left, top		1107
	height = UserDocumentObject.TextHeight (string)		1107
	width = UserDocumentObject.TextWidth (string)		1108
	Private Sub UserDocumentObject_AsyncReadComplete (propertyvalue As AsyncProperty)		1108
	Private Sub UserDocumentObject_Click( )		1108
	Private Sub UserDocumentObject_DblClick( )		1108
	Private Sub UserDocumentObject_DragDrop (source As Control, x As Single, y As Single)		1108
	Private Sub UserDocumentObject_DragOver (source As Control, x As Single, y As Single, state As Integer)		1109
	Private Sub UserDocumentObject_EnterFocus ( )		1110
	Private Sub UserDocumentObject_ExitFocus ( )		1110
	Private Sub UserDocumentObject_GotFocus ( )		1110
	Private Sub UserDocumentObject_Hide ( )		1110
	Private Sub UserDocumentObject_Initialize ( )		1110
	Private Sub UserDocumentObject_InitProperties ( )		1110
	Private Sub UserDocumentObject_KeyDown (keycode As Integer, shift As Single)		1110
	Private Sub UserDocumentObject _KeyPress (keychar As Integer)		1111
	Private Sub UserDocumentObject_KeyUp (keycode As Integer, shift As Single)		1111
	Private Sub UserDocumentObject_LostFocus ( )		1112
	Private Sub UserDocumentObject _MouseDown (button As Integer, shift As Single, x As Single, y As Single)		1112
	Private Sub UserDocumentObject_MouseMove (button As Integer, shift As Single, x As Single, y As Single)		1112
	Private Sub UserDocumentObject_MouseUp (button As Integer, shift As Single, x As Single, y As Single)		1113
	Private Sub UserDocumentObject_OLECompleteDrag(effect As Long)		1114
	Private Sub UserDocumentObject_OLEDragDrop (data As DataObject, effect As Long, button As Integer, shift As Single, x As Single, y As Single)		1114
	Private Sub UserDocumentObject_OLEDragOver (data As DataObject, effect As Long, button As Integer, shift As Single, x As Single, y As Single, state As Integer)		1116
	Private Sub UserDocumentObject_OLEGiveFeedback (effect As Long)		1117
	Private Sub UserDocumentObject_OLESetData (data As DataObject, DataFormat As Integer)		1117
	Private Sub UserDocumentObject_OLEStartDrag (data As DataObject, AllowedEffects As Long)		1118
	Private Sub UserDocumentObject_Paint ( )		1118

Class	Element	Edition (see Legend)	Page
	Private Sub UserDocumentObject_ReadProperties (pb As PropertyBag)		1119
	Private Sub UserDocumentObject_Resize ( )		1119
	Private Sub UserDocumentObject_Scroll ( )		1119
	Private Sub UserDocumentObject_Show ( )		1119
	Private Sub UserDocumentObject_Terminate ( )		1119
	Private Sub UserDocumentObject_WriteProperties (pb As PropertyBag)		1119
Val	Function	CCE, LE, PE, EE	1120
ValueScale	Object	PE, EE	1121
Variant	Data Type	CCE, LE, PE, EE	1121
VarType	Function	CCE, LE, PE, EE	1122
View3D	Object	PE, EE	1123
	View3DObject.Set elevation, rotation		1123
VScrollBar	Control	CCE, LE, PE, EE	1123
	VScrollBarControl.Drag [DragAction]		1126
	VScrollBarControl.Move Left [, Top [, Width [, Height]]]		1126
	VScrollBarControl.Refresh		1127
	VScrollBarControl.SetFocus		1127
	VScrollBarControl.ShowWhatsThis		1127
	VScrollBarControl.ZOrder [position]		1127
	Private Sub VScrollBarControl _Change([index As Integer])		1127
	Private Sub VScrollBarControl _DragDrop([index As Integer ,] source As Control, x As Single, y As Single)		1128
	Private Sub VScrollBarControl _DragOver([index As Integer ,] source As Control, x As Single, y As Single, state As Integer)		1128
	Private Sub VScrollBarControl _GotFocus ([index As Integer])		1129
	Private Sub VScrollBarControl _KeyDown ([index As Integer ,] keycode As Integer, shift As Single)		1129
	Private Sub VScrollBarControl _KeyPress([index As Integer ,] keychar As Integer)		1130
	Private Sub ComoBoxControl _KeyUp ([index As Integer ,] keycode As Integer, shift As Single)		1130
	Private Sub VScrollBarControl _LostFocus ([index As Integer])		1130
	Private Sub VScrollBarControl _Scroll ([index As Integer])		1131

Legend

CCE .... Control Creation Edition   EE .... Enterprise Edition
LE .... Learning Edition   PE .... Professional Edition
VBA .... Visual Basic for Applications

Class	Element	Edition (see Legend)	Page
VtColor	Object	PE, EE	1131
VtColorObject.Set red, green, blue			1132
VtFont	Object	PE, EE	1132
Wall	Object	PE, EE	1133
Weekday	Function	CCE, LE, PE, EE	1133
Weighting	Object	PE, EE	1134
WeightingObject.Set basis, style			1135
While	Statement	CCE, LE, PE, EE	1135
Width	Statement	CCE, LE, PE, EE	1136
Winsock	Control	CCE, LE, PE, EE	1136
WinsockControl.Accept requestid			1138
WinsockControl.Bind localport, localip			1138
WinsockControl.Close			1138
WinsockControl.GetData data [, datatype [, len]]			1138
WinsockControl.Listen			1139
WinsockControl.PeekData data [, datatype [, len]]			1139
WinsockControl.SendData data			1140
Private Sub WinsockControl_Close ([index As Integer])			1140
Private Sub WinsockControl_Connect ([index As Integer])			1140
Private Sub WinsockControl_ConnectionRequest ([index As Integer ,] requestid As Long)			1140
Private Sub WinsockControl_DataArrival ([index As Integer ,] bytestotal As Long)			1140
Private Sub WinsockControl_Error ([index As Integer ,] number As Integer, description As String, scode As Long, source As String, HelpFile As String, HelpContext As Long, CancelDisplay As Boolean)			1140
Private Sub WinsockControl_SendComplete ([index As Integer])			1142
Private Sub WinsockControl_SendProgress ([index As Integer ,] BytesSent As Long, BytesRemaining As Long)			1142
With	Statement	CCE, LE, PE, EE	1143
Workspace	Object	PE, EE	1143
WorkspaceObject.BeginTrans			1144
WorkspaceObject.Close			1144
WorkspaceObject.CommitTrans [dbFlushOSCacheWrites]			1144
Database = WorkspaceObject.CreateDatabase (dbname, locale, options)			1144
Group = WorkspaceObject.CreateGroup ([name] [, pid])			1146
User = WorkspaceObject.CreateUser ([name] [, [pid] [,password]])			1146
connection = WorkspaceObject.OpenConnection name [, options [, readonly [, connect]]]			1146

Class	Element	Edition (see Legend)	Page
	database = WorkspaceObject.OpenDatabase name [, options [, readonly [, connect]]]		1146
	WorkspaceObject.RollBack		1147
Workspaces	Collection	PE, EE	1147
	WorkspacesCollection.Append object		1147
	WorkspacesCollection.Delete name		1148
	WorkspacesCollection.Refresh		1148
Write	Statement	CCE, LE, PE, EE	1148
Year	Function	CCE, LE, PE, EE	1150

Legend

CCE .... Control Creation Edition
LE .... Learning Edition
VBA .... Visual Basic for Applications
EE .... Enterprise Edition
PE .... Professional Edition

Introduction

After writing two books about using Visual Basic with the Internet and creating a relatively complex Visual Basic application, I jumped at the chance to write a Visual Basic reference. I wanted to create the kind of reference that an experienced programmer would use. I got tired flipping around through the help files and manuals and not finding the information I needed or worse, finding too much information that wasn't useful.

What you hold in your hands is the result of much time and effort to pull all of this information together. I wanted a reference that would be comprehensive, informative, and concise. I didn't want a reference that would try to teach someone how to program. I didn't want another copy of the help files. I wanted something that would show me all of the properties in a control and what they were used for. I wanted to find it quickly and easily and without a lot of extra commentary.

Also, you will notice that I repeat some information rather than put it in a common element. Since I expect people to use this book as a reference and not read the book cover to cover, I felt that it was worthwhile to place all the information you need for a control in one location. This saves you time and effort since you don't have to go searching for the information you really want.

Who Needs This Book?

This book covers all flavors of Microsoft Visual Basic, ranging from the Learning Edition, through the Control Creation Edition and Professional Edition, to the Enterprise Edition. So while I wrote this reference with the experienced programmer in mind, nearly anyone who programs in Visual Basic can benefit from it. While the material in this book can be easily used by all levels of Visual Basic programmers, beginning programmers may want to supplement this book with a book that discusses how to write a Visual Basic program.

How This Book Is Organized

This book is organized in alphabetical order by element. An element is either a statement, function, control, or object name. Each element contains the sections listed below:

- **Syntax**—contains an element's formal syntax (applies to statements and functions only).
- **Usage**—contains a short description of the element and how it is used.
- **Arguments**—contains a list of the arguments that are contained the element with a short description of how they are used. If an element contains no arguments, then this section is omitted (this applies to statements and functions only). This section may also include a list of constants associated with the argument.
- **Properties**—contains a list of properties associated with the element. If no properties are present, then this section is omitted (this applies to controls and objects only). This section may also include a list of constants associated with the property.
- **Methods**—contains a list of methods associated with the element. If no methods are present, then this section is omitted (this applies to controls and objects only). The method's syntax is listed including any arguments. This will be followed by a **Usage** section that contains a short description of the method and how it is used. If any arguments are present in the method, an **Arguments** section that describes each of the arguments will follow. Each argument may be followed by a list of associated constants.
- **Events**—contains a list of events associated with the element. If no events are present, then this section is omitted (this applies to controls and objects only). The event's syntax is listed including any arguments. This will be followed by a **Usage** section that contains a short description of the event and how it is used. If any arguments are present in the event, an **Arguments** section that describes each of the arguments will follow. Each argument may be followed by a list of associated constants.
- **Examples**—contains one or more examples that illustrate how to use the element.
- **See Also**—contains a list of elements that are similar to or related to the element.

I've added useful tips or warnings throughout the book about various features of Visual Basic. Also present at the beginning of the book is a series of Jump Tables. These tables are useful when you want to locate information in the book and you're not sure where to start or when you want to use a comprehensive cross-reference.

Conventions

To make the book easier to read, all Visual Basic keywords are displayed in bold. If an element like a function or an event contains a list of arguments, the argument names are listed in italics. Also, any Visual Basic constant is also listed in italics.

I also use three sets of symbols while describing the syntax of a function, statement, method, or event. The first set of symbols are the brackets "[" and "]". Anything inside brackets is optional.

Next are braces "{" and "}" and the vertical bar "|". The braces are used to present a list of choices from which you may select exactly one item. Each item in the list is separated by a vertical bar.

The ellipsis "…" is used to indicate that the preceding syntax element may be repeated as many times as desired.

These conventions are used in the following example:

Print # *filenum,* [*printexpr* [{ , | ; } *printexpr*] . . .] [{ , | ; }]

First **Print #** is in bold, since it is a Visual Basic keyword. The arguments *filenum* and *printexpr* are italics. The expression { , | ; } means that you must select either the comma "," or the semicolon ";". The expression [{ , | ; }] means that you can select the comma "," or the semicolon ";" or nothing. The expression [{ , | ; } *printexpr*] . . . means that you can repeat the expression [{ , | ; } *printexpr*] one or more times.

Updates & Feedback

The good folks at Ventana are committed to ensuring that you have the most up-to-date information available. As updates become available, simply go to Ventana's Web site at http://www.vmedia.com/updates.html to retrieve them. I also love hearing from my readers, so you can visit my Web site at http://www.JustPC.com or send me email at WFreeze@JustPC.com.

Abs

FUNCTION

CCE, LE, PE, EE

Syntax
: *RValue* = **Abs** (*Number*)

Usage
: The **Abs** function returns the absolute value of the expression. **Abs** (2) will return 2. **Abs** (-2) will also return 2.

Arguments
: - *RValue*—the absolute value of **Number**.
: - *Number*—an **Integer**, **Long**, **Single**, or **Double**.

Examples
:
```
Private Sub Command1_Click()
If IsNumeric(Text1.Text) Then
   MsgBox "The absolute value of " & Text1.Text & " is " &
   Format(Abs(CDbl(Text1.Text)))
Else
   MsgBox "Invalid number."
End If
End Sub
```

This routine displays the absolute value of the number in the Text1 text box.

See Also
: **Sgn** (function)

AmbientProperties

OBJECT

CCE, LE, PE, EE

Usage
: The **AmbientProperties** object holds suggested values for controls contained within a container. The **Ambient** property in a **UserControl** object references this object. If the object that contains the **UserControl** object changes any of its properties that affect the **AmbientProperties** that the **UserControl** sees, then the **UserControl's AmbientEvent** is called.

> **Tip**
>
> *Use this object to determine how an embedded control should act to maintain a consistent look and feel. For instance the container can provide default values for **Font**, **BackColor**, and **ForeColor** that a control should use to blend in with the rest of the controls in the container.*

Properties
: - **Ambient.BackColor**—a **Long** value that contains the suggested value for the background color of the contained control. This property is read only at run time.
: - **Ambient.DisplayAsDefault**—a **Boolean** value that when **True** means that the control is the default control. When **False**, it means that the control is not the default control or that the container does not support this property. (You can only make button-type controls a default control.) This property is read only at run time.
: - **Ambient.DisplayName**—a **String** value that contains the name that the control should display for itself. An empty string means that the container does not support this property. This property is read only at run time.

- **Ambient.Font**—a **Font** object that contains suggested font information that you want the control to use. This property is read only at run time.
- **Ambient.ForeColor**—a **Long** value that contains the suggested value for the foreground color of the contained control. This property is read only at run time.
- **Ambient.LocaleID**—a **Long** value that contains the suggested values for language and country of the user. The default value for **LocaleID** is the current System LocaleID if the container does not support this property. This property is read only at run time.
- **Ambient.MessageReflect**—a **Boolean** value that is **True** if the container supports message reflection, **False** otherwise. This property is read only at run time.
- **Ambient.Palette**—a **Picture** object that contains a suggested palette for the control. This property is read only at run time.
- **Ambient.RightToLeft**—a **Boolean** value that is **True** if you want the text and controls displayed right to left in a bi-directional system, **False** if you want the text and controls displayed left to right or if the control does not support this property. This property is read only at run time.
- **Ambient.ScaleUnits**—a **String** value that contains the name of the coordinate units used by the container. The default value is an empty string. This property is read only at run time.
- **Ambient.ShowGrabHandles**—a **Boolean** value when **True** suggests that the control should show grab handles if needed. When **False**, the container does not support this property or the control should not show grab handles. This property is read only at run time.
- **Ambient.ShowHatchings**—a **Boolean** value when **True** suggests that the control should show hatching around the control or the container does not support this property. **False**, the control should not show hatching. This property is read only at run time.
- **Ambient.SupportsMnemonics**—a **Boolean** value when **True** indicates that the control supports handle access keys. **False**, if the container does not support this property or the container does not handle access keys. This property is read only at run time.
- **Ambient.TextAlign**—an **Integer** value that contains the suggested value for text alignment. If the control does not implement this property, then the default value is **General** alignment. This property is read only at run time.
- **Ambient.UIDead**—a **Boolean** value when **True** indicates that the control should respond to user input such as clicking the mouse or pressing keys on the keyboard. **False** means that the control does not support this property or that the control should handle user input as normal. This property is read only at run time.
- **Ambient.UserMode**—a **Boolean** value when **True** indicates that a form user is using the control. **False** means that a form designer is using the control. This property is read only at run time.

Examples
```
Private Sub Label1_Click()
MsgBox Ambient.DisplayName
End Sub
```

The routine is part of an ActiveX control that is called by another main program. The display area of the control is a label that will respond to the click event. When the user clicks on the area of the control on the main program, the control will display the name that it was given in the main program.

See Also   **UserControl** (control): **Ambient** property, **AmbientChanged** event

Animation

CONTROL

LE, PE, EE

Usage The **Animation** control is an ActiveX control found in Microsoft Windows Common Controls -2 (COMCT232.OCX) which you use to play .avi files. The .avi file must either be uncompressed or compressed using Run-Length Encoding. The .avi file must not contain any sound information. A file with an improper .avi format or one that contains sound information will generate an error number 35752. If your .avi file contains sound, then use the Multimedia MCI control.

> **Tip**
>
> Visual Basic comes with an assortment of standard .avi files in the graphics\avis subdirectory, including some animations commonly seen in such Windows operations as File Copy and File Delete.

Properties
- *AnimationControl*.**AutoPlay**—a **Boolean** value that when **True**, the control will start playing the .avi file when the .avi file is loaded and will play it again when the control has reached the end of the file. When **False**, the control will wait until the **Play** method is used or will stop automatically replaying the .avi file if the **AutoPlay** property was initially set to **True**.
- *AnimationControl*.**BackColor**—a **Long** that contains the suggested value for the background color of the control. Visual Basic rounds this property to the nearest 8-bit color in the standard palette, since the control can only display 8-bit colors.
- *AnimationControl*.**BackStyle**—a **Boolean** value that when **True**, the background color specified in the .avi file will be used for the entire background of the control (Opaque). When **False**, the color specified in the **BackColor** property is visible (Transparent). This property is read only at run time.
- *AnimationControl*.**Center**—a **Boolean** value that when **True**, the .avi will be displayed in the center of the control. When **False**, the .avi will be displayed starting at location (0,0) within the control.

> **Note**
>
> If the .avi frames are larger than the size of the control, then the edges of the .avi will not be shown.

- *AnimationControl*.**Container**—an object used to set or return the container of the control at run time. You cannot set this property at design time.
- *AnimationControl*.**DragIcon**—an object that contains the picture value of an icon. At design time, you can specify an icon file that has a file type of .ico.

> **Tip**
>
> You can create this value by copying the value from another control's **DragIcon** value, a form's icon, or by using the **LoadPicture** function.

- *AnimationControl*.**Enabled**—a **Boolean** value that when **True**, the control will respond to events. When **False**, the control will not respond to events.
- *AnimationControl*.**ForeColor**—a **Long** that contains the value for the foreground color of the control.
- *AnimationControl*.**Height**—a **Single** that contains the height of the control in twips.
- *AnimationControl*.**HelpContextID**—a **Long** that contains a help file context ID number references an entry in the help file. When the user presses the F1 key while this control is active, the corresponding entry in the help file will automatically display. A value of zero means that no context number was specified.

> **Note**
>
> You must compile a help file using the Windows Help Compiler available in the Professional and Enterprise editions of Visual Basic.

- *AnimationControl*.**hWnd**—a **Long** that contains a Windows handle to the control.

> **Tip**
>
> The **hWnd** property is most useful when making calls to Windows API functions. Since this value can change during execution, do not save the value into a variable for later use.

- *AnimationControl*.**Index**—an **Integer** that uniquely identifies a control in a control array.
- *AnimationControl*.**Left**—a **Single** that contains the distance measured in twips between the left edge of the control and the left edge of the control's container.
- *AnimationControl*.**Name**—a **String** that contains the name of the control that references the control in a Visual Basic program. This property is read only at run-time.
- *AnimationControl*.**Object**—an object that contains a reference to the *AnimationControl* object.
- *AnimationControl*.**OLEDropMode**—an **Integer** value (see Table A-1) that describes how the control will respond to OLE drop operations.

OLEDropMode Name	Value	Description
vbOLEDropNone	0	The control does not accept OLE drops. The cursor is changed to the No Drop cursor (default value).
vbOLEDropManual	1	The control responds to OLE drops under the program's control (manual).
vbOLEDropAutomatic	2	The control automatically accepts OLE drops if it recognizes the format of the data object.

Table A-1: OLEDropMode *values*.

- *AnimationControl*.**Parent**—an object that contains a reference to the Form, Frame, or other container that contains the **Animation** control.

- *AnimationControl*.**TabIndex**—an **Integer** that determines the order that a user will tab through the objects on a form.
- *AnimationControl*.**TabStop**—a **Boolean** value that when **True**, allows the user to tab to this object. When **False**, this control will be skipped to the next control in the **TabIndex** order.
- *AnimationControl*.**Tag**—a **String** that can hold programmer-specific information. This property is not used by Visual Basic.
- *AnimationControl*.**ToolTipText**—a **String** that holds a text value that Visual Basic can display as a ToolTip box. The ToolTip box displays whenever the cursor is held over the control for about one second.
- *AnimationControl*.**Top**—a **Single** that contains the distance measured in twips between the top edge of the control and the top edge of the control's container.
- *AnimationControl*.**Visible**—a **Boolean** value that when **True**, the control is visible. When **False**, the control is not visible.

Tip

You can use this property to hide the control until the program is ready to display it.

- *AnimationControl*.**WhatsThisHelpID**—a **Long** that contains a help file context ID number that references an entry in the help file. This is used to provide a What's This PopUp help display in response to the What's This button in the upper right corner of the window.
- *AnimationControl*.**Width**—a **Single** that contains the width of the control in twips.

Methods

AnimationControl.Close

Usage — This method closes the currently open .avi file. You should execute the **Stop** method to stop the .avi file from playing or set the AutoPlay to **False** to stop the .avi file from repeating.

AnimationControl.Drag [*DragAction*]

Usage — This method begins, ends, or cancels a drag operation.

Arguments — *DragAction*—an **Integer** that contains a value selected from Table A-2 below.

DragAction Name	Value	Description
vbCancel	0	Cancels any drag operation in progress.
vbBeginDrag	1	Begins a drag operation (default).
vbEndDrag	2	Ends a drag operation and drops *object*.

Table A-2: **DragAction** *values.*

AnimationControl.Move Left [, Top [, Width [, Height]]]

Usage This method changes the position and the size of the **Animation** control. The **ScaleMode** of the **Form** or other container object that holds the animation control will determine the units that specify the coordinates.

Arguments
- *Left*—a **Single** that specifies the new position of the left edge of the control.
- *Top*—a **Single** that specifies the new position of the top edge of the control.
- *Width*—a **Single** that specifies the new width of the control.
- *Height*—a **Single** that specifies the new height of the control.

AnimationControl.OLEDrag

Usage This method begins an OLEDrag and drop operation. Invoking this method will trigger the **OLEStartDrag** event.

AnimationControl.Open [AVIFile]

Usage This method loads an animation file. If **AutoPlay** is **True**, then the file will begin playing immediately. Otherwise, the **Play** method is required to begin playing the animation.

Arguments
- *AVIFile*—a **String** containing the path and file name containing the animation you want to display.

AnimationControl.Play [Repeat [, StartFrame [, EndFrame]]]

Usage This method starts playing an .avi file that was loaded with the **Open** method.

Arguments
- *Repeat*—an **Integer** specifying the number of times the .avi file will be displayed. If -1 is specified, then the .avi file will be displayed indefinitely. (-1 is the default value for this argument.)
- *StartFrame*—an **Integer** that specifies the starting frame in the .avi clip. Values can range from 0 to 65535.
- *EndFrame*—an **Integer** that specifies the ending frame in the .avi clip. Values can range from 0 to 65535.

AnimationControl.SetFocus

Usage This method transfers the focus from the form or control that currently has the focus to this control. To receive the focus, this control must be enabled and visible.

AnimationControl.ShowWhatsThis

Usage This method displays the ShowWhatsThis help information for this control.

AnimationControl.Stop

Usage This method stops playing an animation file that was started with the **Play** method. Using this method to stop an .avi file that was started by setting the **AutoPlay** property to **True** will generate the error code 35759.

AnimationControl.ZOrder [position]

Usage This method specifies the position of the animation control relative to the other objects on the form.

Note

There are three layers of objects on a form; the back layer is the drawing space which contains the results of the graphical methods, the middle layer contains graphical objects and Labels, the top layer contains nongraphical controls such as the CommandButton. The **ZOrder** method only affects how the objects are arranged within a single layer.

Arguments ▪ *position*—an **Integer** that specifies the relative position of this object. A value of 0 means that the control is positioned at the head of the list, a value of 1 means that Visual Basic will place the control at the end of the list.

EventsPrivate Sub AnimationControl _Click([index As Integer])

Usage This event occurs when the user clicks a mouse button while the cursor is positioned over this control.

Tip

If you need to identify which mouse button was pressed, use the **MouseUp** and **MouseDown** events.

Arguments ▪ *index*—an **Integer** that uniquely identifies a control in a control array. This argument is not present if the control is not part of a control array.

Private Sub AnimationControl _DragDrop([index As Integer ,] source as Control, x as Single, y as Single)

Usage This event occurs when a drag-and-drop operation is completed by using the Drag method with a *DragAction* value of *vbEndDrag* (2).

Tip

When using drag-and-drop operations, use the **DragOver** event to determine what the cursor should look like while the cursor moves over the control.

Arguments
- *index*—an **Integer** that uniquely identifies a control in a control array. This argument is not present if the control is not part of a control array.
- *source*—a control object that is the control that is being dragged.

> **Tip**
>
> *You can access a property or method from the source control using **source.property** or **source.method**. You can determine the type of object or control using the **TypeOf** operator.*

- *x*—a **Single** that contains the horizontal location of the mouse pointer.
- *y*—a **Single** that contains the vertical location of the mouse pointer.

Private Sub *AnimationControl* _DragOver([*index* As Integer ,] *source* as Control, *x* as Single, *y* as Single, *state* as Integer)

Usage This event occurs while a drag operation is in progress and the cursor is moved over the control.

> **Tip**
>
> *When using drag-and-drop operations, use the **DragOver** event to determine what the cursor should look like while the cursor moves over the control. When state is 0, you can change the cursor to a no drop cursor (vbNoDrop) or highlight the field that the cursor is near. When state is 1, you can undo the changes you made when the state was 0.*

Arguments
- *index*—an **Integer** that uniquely identifies a control in a control array. This argument is not present if the control is not part of a control array.
- *source*—a control object that is the control that is being dragged.

> **Tip**
>
> *You can access a property or method from the source control using source.property or source.method. You can determine the type of object or control using the **TypeOf** operator.*

- *x*—a **Single** that contains the horizontal location of the mouse pointer.
- *y*—a **Single** that contains the vertical location of the mouse pointer.
- *state*—an **Integer** value (see Table A-3) that indicates the state of the object being dragged.

state Name	Value	Description
vbEnter	0	The dragged object is entering range of the control.
vbLeave	1	The dragged object is leaving range of the control.
vbOver	2	The dragged object has moved from one position over the control to another.

Table A-3: state values.

Private Sub *AnimationControl*_GotFocus ([*index* As Integer])

Usage   This event occurs when the control is given focus.

Tip

You can use this routine to display help or other information in a status bar.

Arguments   • *index*—an **Integer** that uniquely identifies a control in a control array. This argument is not present if the control is not part of a control array.

Private Sub *AnimationControl*_LostFocus ([*index* As Integer])

Usage   This event occurs when the control loses focus.

Tip

This routine is useful in performing data verification.

Arguments   • *index*—an **Integer** that uniquely identifies a control in a control array. This argument is not present if the control is not part of a control array.

Private Sub *AnimationControl*_MouseDown([*index* As Integer ,] *button* as Integer, *shift* as Single, *x* as Single, *y* as Single)

Usage   This event occurs when a mouse button is pressed while the cursor is over the control.

Arguments
• *index*—an **Integer** that uniquely identifies a control in a control array. This argument is not present if the control is not part of a control array.

• *button*—an **Integer** value (see Table A-4) that contains information about the mouse buttons that were pressed. Only one button will be indicated when this event occurs.

button Name	Value	Description
vbLeftButton	1	The left button was pressed.
vbRightButton	2	The right button was pressed.
vbMiddleButton	4	The middle button was pressed.

Table A-4: **button** *values.*

- *shift*—an **Integer** value (see Table A-5) that contains information about the Shift and Alt keys that were pushed when the mouse button was pressed. Visual Basic can add these values together if more than one key was down. For instance, a value of 5 would mean that the Shift and Alt keys were both down when the mouse button was pressed.

shift Name	Value	Description
vbShiftMask	1	The Shift key was pressed.
vbCtrlMask	2	The Ctrl key was pressed.
vbAltMask	4	The Alt key was pressed.

Table A-5: shift *values*.

- *x*—a **Single** that contains the horizontal location of the mouse pointer.
- *y*—a **Single** that contains the vertical location of the mouse pointer.

Private Sub *AnimationControl* _MouseMove ([*index* As Integer ,] *button* as Integer, *shift* as Single, *x* as Single, *y* as Single)

Usage   This event occurs while the cursor is moved over the control.

Arguments
- *index*—an **Integer** that uniquely identifies a control in a control array. This argument is not present if the control is not part of a control array.
- *button*—an **Integer** value (see Table A-6) that contains information about the mouse buttons that were pressed. Visual Basic can add these values together if more than one button was pushed. For instance, a value of 3 means that both the left and right buttons were pressed. A value of 0 means that no buttons were pressed.

button Name	Value	Description
vbLeftButton	1	The left button was pressed.
vbRightButton	2	The right button was pressed.
vbMiddleButton	4	The middle button was pressed.

Table A-6: button *values*.

- *shift*—an **Integer** value (see Table A-7) that contains information about the Shift and Alt keys that were pushed when the mouse button was pressed. For instance, a value of 5 means that the Shift and Alt keys were both down when the mouse button was pressed. A value of 0 means that none of these keys were pressed.

shift Name	Value	Description
vbShiftMask	1	The Shift key was pressed.
vbCtrlMask	2	The Ctrl key was pressed.
vbAltMask	4	The Alt key was pressed.

Table A-7: shift v*alues*.

- *x*—a **Single** that contains the horizontal location of the mouse pointer.
- *y*—a **Single** that contains the vertical location of the mouse pointer.

Private Sub *AnimationControl*_MouseUp([*index* As Integer ,] *button* as Integer, *shift* as Single, *x* as Single, *y* as Single)

Usage This event occurs when a mouse button is released while the cursor is over the control.

Arguments
- *index*—an **Integer** that uniquely identifies a control in a control array. This argument is not present if the control is not part of a control array.
- *button*—an **Integer** value (see Table A-8) that contains information about the mouse buttons that were released. Only one of these values will be present.

button Name	Value	Description
vbLeftButton	1	The left button was released.
vbRightButton	2	The right button was released.
vbMiddleButton	4	The middle button was released.

Table A-8: button *values.*

- *shift*—an **Integer** value (see Table A-9) that contains information about the Shift and Alt keys that were pushed when the mouse button was released. Visual Basic can add these values together if more than one key was down. For instance, a value of 5 means that the Shift and Alt keys were both down when the mouse button was released. A value of 0 means that none of these keys were pressed.

shift Name	Value	Description
vbShiftMask	1	The Shift key was pressed.
vbCtrlMask	2	The Ctrl key was pressed.
vbAltMask	4	The Alt key was pressed.

Table A-9: shift *values.*

- *x*—a **Single** that contains the horizontal location of the mouse pointer.
- *y*—a **Single** that contains the vertical location of the mouse pointer.

Private Sub *AnimationControl*_OLECompleteDrag([*index* As Integer ,] *effect* as Long)

Usage This event tells the source control the results of an OLE drag-and-drop operation. This is the final event to occur in the series of actions that make up an OLE drag-and-drop operation.

Arguments
- *index*—an **Integer** that uniquely identifies a control in a control array. This argument is not present if the control is not part of a control array.

- *effect*—a **Long** value (see Table A-10) that returns the status of the OLE drag-and-drop operation.

effect Name	Value	Description
vbDropEffectNone	0	The operation was canceled or the target control can't accept the drop operation.
vbDropEffectCopy	1	The operation copied data from the source control to the target control. The original data is unchanged.
vbDropEffectMove	2	The operation results in a link from the original data to the target control.

Table A-10: effect *values*.

Private Sub *AnimationControl* _OLEDragDrop([*index* As Integer ,] *data* as DataObject, *effect* as Long, *button* as Integer, *shift* as Single, *x* as Single, *y* as Single)

Usage   This event tells the source control the results of an OLE drag-and-drop operation. This is the final event to occur in the series of actions that make up an OLE drag-and-drop operation.

Arguments
- *index*—an **Integer** that uniquely identifies a control in a control array. This argument is not present if the control is not part of a control array.
- *data*—a **DataObject** that contains the formats that the source control will provide. If the data is not contained in the **DataObject**, then Visual Basic can retrieve it with the **GetData** method.
- *effect*—a **Long** value (see Table A-11) that returns the status of the OLE drag-and-drop operation.

effect Name	Value	Description
vbDropEffectNone	0	The operation was canceled or the target control can't accept the drop operation.
vbDropEffectCopy	1	The operation copied data from the source control to the target control. The original data is unchanged.
vbDropEffectMove	2	The operation results in a link from the original data to the target control.

Table A-11: effect *values*.

- *button*—an **Integer** value (see Table A-12) that contains information about the mouse buttons that were pressed. Visual Basic can add these values together if more than one button was pushed. For instance, a value of 3 means that both the left and right buttons were pressed. A value of 0 means that no buttons were pressed.

button Name	Value	Description
vbLeftButton	1	The left button was pressed.
vbRightButton	2	The right button was pressed.
vbMiddleButton	4	The middle button was pressed.

Table A-12: button values.

- *shift*—an **Integer** value (see Table A-13) that contains information about the Shift and Alt keys that were pushed when the mouse button was released. Visual Basic can add these values together if more than one key was down. For instance, a value of 5 means that the Shift and Alt keys were both down when the mouse button was released. A value of 0 means that none of these keys were pressed.

shift Name	Value	Description
vbShiftMask	1	The Shift key was pressed.
vbCtrlMask	2	The Ctrl key was pressed.
vbAltMask	4	The Alt key was pressed.

Table A-13: shift values.

- *x*—a **Single** that contains the horizontal location of the mouse pointer.
- *y*—a **Single** that contains the vertical location of the mouse pointer.

Private Sub *AnimationControl* _OLEDragOver([*index* As Integer ,] *data* as DataObject, *effect* as Long, *button* as Integer, *shift* as Single, *x* as Single, *y* as Single, *state* as Integer)

Usage   This event happens when an OLE drag-and-drop operation is in progress.

Arguments
- *index*—an **Integer** that uniquely identifies a control in a control array. This argument is not present if the control is not part of a control array.
- *data*—a **DataObject** that contains the formats that the source control will provide. If the data is not contained in the **DataObject**, then Visual Basic can retrieve it with the **GetData** method.
- *effect*—a **Long** value (see Table A-14) that returns the status of the OLE drag-and-drop operation.

effect Name	Value	Description
vbDropEffectNone	0	The operation was canceled or the target control can't accept the drop operation.
vbDropEffectCopy	1	The operation copied data from the source control to the target control. The original data is unchanged.
vbDropEffectMove	2	The operation results in a link from the original data to the target control.

Table A-14: effect values.

- *button*—an **Integer** value (see Table A-15) that contains information about the mouse buttons that were pressed. Visual Basic can add these values together if more than one button was pushed. For instance, a value of 3 means that both the left and right buttons were pressed. A value of 0 means that no buttons were pressed.

button Name	Value	Description
vbLeftButton	1	The left button was pressed.
vbRightButton	2	The right button was pressed.
vbMiddleButton	4	The middle button was pressed.

Table A-15: button *values*.

- *shift*—an **Integer** value (see Table A-16) that contains information about the Shift and Alt keys that were pushed when the mouse button was released. Visual Basic can add these values together if more than one key was down. For instance, a value of 5 means that the Shift and Alt keys were both down when the mouse button was released. A value of 0 means that none of these keys were pressed.

shift Name	Value	Description
vbShiftMask	1	The Shift key was pressed.
vbCtrlMask	2	The Ctrl key was pressed.
vbAltMask	4	The Alt key was pressed.

Table A-16: shift *values*.

- *x*—a **Single** that contains the horizontal location of the mouse pointer.
- *y*—a **Single** that contains the vertical location of the mouse pointer.
- *state*—an **Integer** value (see Table A-17) that indicates the state of the object being dragged.

state Name	Value	Description
vbEnter	0	The dragged object is entering range of the control.
vbLeave	1	The dragged object is leaving range of the control.
vbOver	2	The dragged object has moved from one position over the control to another.

Table A-17: state *values*.

Private Sub *AnimationControl* _OLEGiveFeedback ([*index* As Integer ,] *effect* as Long)

Usage   This event tells the source control what is happening while the OLE drag-and-drop operation is in progress. This event occurs after the **OLEDragOver** event.

Tip

You may want to use this event to change the cursor to reflect what can happen in the remote object.

Arguments
- *index*—an **Integer** that uniquely identifies a control in a control array. This argument is not present if the control is not part of a control array.
- *effect*—a **Long** value (see Table A-18) that returns the status of the OLE drag-and-drop operation.

effect Name	Value	Description
vbDropEffectNone	0	The operation was canceled or the target control can't accept the drop operation.
vbDropEffectCopy	1	The operation copied data from the source control to the target control. The original data is unchanged.
vbDropEffectMove	2	The operation results in a link from the original data to the target control.
vbDropEffectScroll	&H80000000	The target control is about to scroll or is scrolling. This value may be added to the other *shift* values.

Table A-18: effect *values*.

Private Sub *AnimationControl*_OLESetData([*index* As Integer ,] *data* as DataObject, *DataFormat* as Integer)

Usage
This event happens in response to the target object performing a **GetData** method on *data*. This routine will respond by using the **SetData** method with the desired data using the **DataObject** *data*.

Arguments
- *index*—an **Integer** that uniquely identifies a control in a control array. This argument is not present if the control is not part of a control array.
- *data*—a **DataObject** that will contain the data to be returned to the target object.
- *format*—an **Integer** value (see Table A-19) that contains the format of the data.

format Name	Value	Description
vbCFText	1	Text (.txt files)
vbCFBitmap	2	Bitmap (.bmp files)
vbCFMetafile	3	Metafile (.wmf files)
vbCFEDIB	8	Device-independent bitmap (DIB)
vbCFPallette	9	Color palette
vbCFEMetafile	14	Enhanced metafile (.emf files)
vbCFFiles	15	List of files
vbCFRTF	-16639	Rich Text Format (.rtf files)

Table A-19: format *values*.

Private Sub *AnimationControl*_OLEStartDrag ([*index* As Integer ,] *data* as DataObject, *AllowedEffects* as Long)

Usage
This event starts an OLE drag-and-drop operation.

Arguments
- *index*—an **Integer** that uniquely identifies a control in a control array. This argument is not present if the control is not part of a control array.

- *data*—a **DataObject** that will contain the formats that the source object is willing to provide to the target object. It may optionally contain the data you want to transfer.
- *AllowedEffects*—a **Long** value (see Table A-20) that contains the effects that the target object can request from the source object. Visual Basic can add the *AllowedEffects* together if the source object supports more than one effect. Note that the target object can always use the *vbDropEffectNone* effect.

AllowedEffects Name	Value	Description
vbDropEffectNone	0	The target can't copy the data.
vbDropEffectCopy	1	The target can copy the data and the source will keep the data unchanged.
vbDropEffectMove	2	The target can copy the data and the source will delete the data.

Table A-20: AllowedEffects *values*.

Examples
```
Private Sub Command1_Click()
If Animation1.AutoPlay = False Then
    Animation1.AutoPlay = True
    Animation1.Open "graphics\avis\filecopy.avi"
Else
    Animation1.AutoPlay = False
End If
End Sub
```

This routine will load and begin playing an animation if the animation control is idle. Otherwise it will stop the currently playing animation.

See Also **DataObject**(object), **Form**(object): **ScaleMode** property, **Multimedia MCI**(control)

App

OBJECT

CCE, LE, PE, EE

Usage The **App** object holds various properties and methods that are global to the application.

Properties
- **App.Comments**—a **String** that contains comments about the running application. This property is read only at run time. You can set this property in the Project Properties dialog box.
  - **App.CompanyName**—a **String** that contains the name of the company that developed the running application. This property is read only at run time. You can set this property in the Project Properties dialog box.
    - **App.EXEName**—a **String** that contains the name of the running application without the file extension. If the program is running in the development environment, then this property will hold the name of the project. This property is read only at run time.

- **App.FileDescription**—a **String** that contains file description information about the running application. This property is read only at run time. You can set this property in the Project Properties dialog box.
- **App.HelpFile**—a **String** that contains the path and filename of the default help file you want to use in conjunction with the HelpContextID property. The HelpFile property will also be used when the user hits the F1 key.
- **App.hInstance**—a **Long** that contains the handle to the instance of the running application. This property is read only at run time.
- **App.LegalCopyright**—a **String** that contains the copyright information for the running application. This property is read only at run time. You can set this property in the Project Properties dialog box.
- **App.LegalTrademarks**—a **String** that contains the trademark information for the running application. This property is read only at run time. You can set this property in the Project Properties dialog box.
- **App.LogMode**—a **Long** value (see Table A-21) that determines how the logging information generated by the **LogEvent** method is written to the log file specified by the **LogPath** property. Visual Basic can add the **LogMode** values *vbLogOverWrite* and *vbLogThreadID* together or with any one of the *vbLogOn*, *vbLogOff*, *vbLogToFile*, or *vbLogToNT* values.

LogMode Name	LogMode Value	LogMode Description
vbLogOn	0	Win95: messages are logged to the file specified by the **LogPath** property. WinNT: messages are logged to the NT application event log.
vbLogOff	1	Turns off logging. All messages are ignored and discarded.
vbLogToFile	2	Sends messages to the file specified by the **LogPath** property.
vbLogToNT	3	Win95: same as vbLogOff. WinNT: messages are logged to the NT application event log.
vbLogOverWrite	0x10	Recreates the log file each time the application is started. Has no effect if logging to the NT application event log.
vbLogThreadID	0x20	The thread ID is written in front of the log message.

Table A-21: LogMode *values.*

- **App.LogPath**—a **String** that the path and filename of a file used for application event logging. If an empty string is specified, then the messages are written to the NT application event log (if running on NT) or ignored and discarded (if running on Windows 95).
- **App.Major**—an **Integer** that contains the major revision level of the application. It may range in value from 0 to 9999. This property is read only at run time. You can set this property in the Project Properties dialog box.
- **App.Minor**—an **Integer** that contains the minor revision level of the application. It may range in value from 0 to 9999. This property is read only at run time. You can set this property in the Project Properties dialog box.
- **App.nonModalAllowed**—a **Boolean** when **True** means that a form can be shown non-modally. **False** means that the form must be shown modally. This property is read only at run time.
- **App.OLERequestPendingMsgText**—a **String** that replaces the default Server Busy dialog box with an alternate message box containing your message text and an OK button.

- **App.OLERequestPendingMsgTitle**—a **String** that is used as the caption in the alternate message box created when a value is specified for **OLERequestPendingMsgText**. If this property is set to the empty string (the default value), then the value of **App.Title** will be used.
- **App.OLERequestPendingTimeout**—a **Long** that contains the number of milliseconds that must pass while waiting for an OLE request to complete before a mouse movement or keyboard input can trigger a busy message. The default value is 5000 milliseconds (5 seconds).
- **App.OLEServerBusyMsgText**—a **String** that replaces the default Server Busy dialog box with an alternate message box containing your message text and an OK button.
- **App.OLEServerBusyMsgTitle**—a **String** that is used as the caption in the alternate message box created when a value is specified for **OLEServerBusyMsgText**. If this property is set to the empty string (the default value), then the value of **App.Title** will be used.
- **App.OLEServerBusyRaiseError**—a **Boolean** value when **True** indicates that when the amount of time specified in **OLEServerBusyTimeout** has passed, an error event will occur. **False** means that the Server Busy dialog box (or a message box constructed with the **OLEServerBusyMsgText**) will be displayed.
- **App.OLEServerBusyTimeout**—a **Long** that contains the number of milliseconds that an OLE request will be retried before a mouse movement or keyboard input can trigger a busy message. The default value is 10,000 milliseconds (10 seconds).
- **App.PrevInstance**—a **Boolean** value that is **True** when there is another copy of the current application already running; **False** if this is the only copy of the application currently running.
- **App.ProductName**—a **String** that contains the name of the product. This property is read only at run time. You can set this property in the Project Properties dialog box.
- **App.Revision**—an **Integer** that contains the revision number of the application. It may range in value from 0 to 9999. This property is read only at run time. You can set this property in the Project Properties dialog box.
- **App.StartMode**—an **Integer** value (see Table A-22) that determines whether to start a Visual Basic program as a normal program or as an ActiveX component in the development environment. When the program is compiled and run stand-alone, the **StartMode** property is determined by how the program is actually started. You can set this property in the Project Options dialog box.

StartMode Name	StartMode Value	StartMode Description
vbSModeStandalone	0	The application will be started as a normal program (default).
vbSModeAutomation	1	The application will be started as an ActiveX component.

Table A-22: StartMode *values.*

Tip

If you set **StartMode** *to* vbSModeAutomation *and there are no public classes in the project, you must end the program with an* End *statement. Otherwise, the form will close but the program will continue to run.*

- **App.TaskVisible**—a **Boolean** value when **True**, the application will appear in the Windows task list. When **False**, the application won't appear in the task list. To create an entry in the Windows task bar, see the **ShowTaskInTaskbar** property of the Form object.
- **App.ThreadID**—a **Long** value, that contains the Win32 thread ID of the current task.
- **App.Title**—a **String** that contains the title of the application. This property is displayed in the Windows task list and can be up to 40 characters in length. You can set this property in the Project Properties dialog box.
- **App.UnattendedApp**—a **Boolean** value when **True** means that the application doesn't have a user interface. **False** means that the application does have a user interface.

Methods

App.LogEvent (*logBuffer, eventType*)

Usage — This method uses the information in the **LogPath** and **LogMode** properties to log information in the application log file.

Arguments
- *logBuffer*—a **String** containing the information to be written to the log file.
- *eventType*—a **Long** value (see Table A-23) that contains the type of event that is being logged.

eventType Name	Value	Description
EVENTLOG_ERROR_TYPE	1	An error log entry.
EVENTLOG_WARNING_TYPE	2	A warning log entry.
EVENTLOG_INFORMATION_TYPE	4	An information log entry.

Table A-23: eventType *values*.

App.StartLogging *logTarget, logMode*

Usage — This method uses the information in the **LogPath** and **LogMode** properties to log information in the application log file.

Arguments
- *logTarget*—a **String** containing the path and filename for the log file. This will set the value in the **LogPath** property.
- *logMode*—a **Long** value that determines how the logging information is written to the log file. This will set the value in the **LogPath** property. (See the **LogMode** property for more details.)

Examples
```
Private Sub Command1_Click()
MsgBox "The application title is " & App.Title
End Sub
```

Pressing the command button will display a message box with the application title from the Project Description listed on the Project Properties menu.

See Also — **Form**(object): **ShowTaskInTaskbar** property

AppActivate

STATEMENT

CCE, LE, PE, EE

Syntax **AppActivate** *Title* [, *Wait*]

Usage The **AppActivate** statement changes the focus to the active application specified by *Title*. If *Title* does not match the title of any existing applications exactly, then it will activate the application whose title matches the most leading characters in *Title*.
  The **Shell** function is useful to launch an application. Then once the application is activated, you can use the **SendKeys** statement to simulate sending a sequence of key strokes to the application.

Arguments
- *Title*—a **String** containing the title bar of a running application, or a **Variant** containing the Task ID value returned by the **Shell** function.
- *Wait*—an optional **Boolean** expression that when **True** means that the calling application waits until it has the focus before activating the application. **False** means that the specified application is immediately activated even if the current application does not have the focus.

Examples
```
Private Sub Command1_Click()
Dim TaskID As Variant
TaskID = Shell("C:\Program Files\MSOffice\WINWORD\WINWORD.EXE", vbNormalNoFocus)
MsgBox "Ready to activate Word?"
AppActivate TaskID
End Sub
```

This routine will use the Shell command to start Microsoft Word in a normal window, but without giving Word the focus. Then it displays a message box. After pressing OK on the message box, the routine will then use the AppActivate statement to transfer the focus to the Word program.

See Also **SendKeys** (statement), **Shell** (function)

Array

FUNCTION

CCE, LE, PE, EE

Syntax *RValue* = Array ([*Value1*] [, *Value2*] [, *ValueN*]...)

Usage The **Array** function returns a variable of type **Variant** that contains an array with the specified values. If no values are included, then the array of zero elements will be created. The lower bound of the array is always zero no matter what the value is specified in Option Base.

> **Tip**
>
> *An array created by the **Array** function is stored differently in memory than an array that was defined with the **Dim** statement; however, the same syntax is used to access the elements in both.*

Arguments
- *RValue*—a **Variant** that contains the array.
- *Value1*—any Visual Basic data type except for fixed-length strings and user defined types.

- *Value2*—any Visual Basic data type except for fixed-length strings and user defined types.
- *ValueN*—any Visual Basic data type except for fixed-length strings and user defined types. May be repeated as needed.

Examples
```
Private Sub Command1_Click()
Dim i As Integer
Dim Names As Variant
Names = Array("hello", "Jill", "Chris", "Sam")
For i = 0 To 3
    MsgBox Names(i)
Next i
End Sub
```

This routine will create an array structure using the **Array** function and a **Variant** variable. Then it will display each element of the array using the message box statement.

See Also **Option Base** (statement), **Variant** (data type)

Asc

FUNCTION

CCE, LE, PE, EE

Syntax *RValue* = Asc(*String*)

Usage The **Asc** function returns an **Integer** value that contains the numeric value of the first character of the string. On non-DBCS systems this value can range from 0 to 255, while on DBCS systems this value can range from -32,767 to 32,768. A run time error "5" (invalid procedure call or argument) will occur if the string *String* is empty.

This function was useful in the past for converting characters from lowercase to uppercase (Chr(Asc("b"))—32) = "B") or for storing numeric data in a string to save space. Specialized functions such as **UCase** and **LCase** and the **Byte** data type have made these types of uses unnecessary, but there is always someone that may still want to access the numeric equivalent of a character in a string.

Arguments
- *RValue*—an **Integer** that contains the value of the first character of the string.
- *String*—a **String** with at least one character.

Examples
```
Private Sub Command1_Click()
Dim s As String
s = "ABC"
MsgBox "The ASCII value of " & Mid(s, 2, 1) & " is " & Format(Asc(Mid(s, 2, 1)))
End Sub
```

This routine will display the ASCII value of the second character of the string s, which should be 66, since the second character of the string is "B."

See Also **AscB** (function), **AscW** (function), **Byte** (data type), **Chr** (function), **Mid** (function), **String** (data type), **UCase** (function)

AscB

FUNCTION

CCE, LE, PE, EE

Syntax   RValue = AscB(ByteArray)

Usage   The **AscB** function returns an **Integer** value that contains the numeric value of the first character of the **Byte** array. This value will be in the range of 0 to 255.

Arguments
- *RValue*—an **Integer** that contains the value of the first character of the string.
- *ByteArray*—a Byte array containing the data you want to convert.

Examples
```
Private Sub Command1_Click()
Dim s(4) As Byte
s(1) = AscB("A")
s(2) = AscB("B")
s(3) = AscB("C")
MsgBox "The ASCII value of " & Chr(s(2)) & " is " & Format(s(2))
End Sub
```

This routine will display the ASCII value of the second character of the string *s*, which should be 66, since the second character of the Byte array is "B."

See Also   **Asc** (function), **AscW** (function), **Byte** (data type), **Chr** (function)

AscW

FUNCTION

CCE, LE, PE, EE

Syntax   RValue = AscW(**String**)

Usage   The **AscW** function returns an **Integer** value that contains the unicode character code of the first character in **String**. If the system does not support unicode characters, then this function will behave the same as the **Asc** function. A run time error "5"(Invalid procedure call or argument) will occur if the string **String** is empty.

Arguments
- *RValue*—an **Integer** that contains the value of the first character of the string.
- *String*—a **String** containing unicode characters.

Examples
```
Private Sub Command1_Click()
Dim s As String
s = "ABC"
MsgBox "The Unicode value of " & Mid(s, 2, 1) & " is " & Format(AscW(Mid(s, 2,
   1)))
End Sub
```

This routine will display the ASCII value of the second character of the string *s*, which should be 66, since the second character of the Byte array is "B."

See Also   **Asc** (function), **AscB** (function), **Chr** (function), **Mid** (function), **String** (data type)

AsyncProperty

OBJECT

CCE, LE, PE, EE

Usage   The **AsyncProperty** is an object that is passed to the **AsyncReadComplete** event and is used to hold the results of an **AsyncRead** method.

Properties
- **AsyncType**—an **Integer** value (see Table A-24) that describes the type of data stored in the Value property.

AsyncType Name	AsyncType Value	AsyncType Description
vbAsyncTypePicture	0	A picture object (default value).
vbAsyncTypeFile	1	The data is in a Visual Basic file.
vbAsyncTypeByteArray	2	The data is in a Byte array.

Table A-24: AsyncType values.

- **PropertyName**—a **String** that contains the name of the property associated with the Value that was specified in the **AsyncRead** method.
- **Value**—a **Variant** that contains the data retrieved by the **AsyncRead** method.

Examples
```
Private Sub Command1_Click()
   AsyncRead "c:\config.sys", vbAsyncTypeByteArray
End Sub
Private Sub UserControl_AsyncReadComplete(AsyncProp As AsyncProperty)
   Dim i As Integer
   Text1.Text = ""
   For i = 0 To 512
      Text1.Text = Text1.Text & Chr(AsyncProp.Value(i))
   Next i
End Sub
```

In this example, a user control contains both a command button and a text box. Pressing the Command button starts an asynchronous read operation that will transfer the contents of the file "c:\config.sys" to a Byte array. The **AsyncReadComplete** event is triggered when the asynchronous read is complete and will copy the contents of the array into the text box.

See Also   UserControl (control)

Atn

FUNCTION

CCE, LE, PE, EE

Syntax   *RValue* = Atn (*Number*)

Usage   The **Atn** function will return the arctangent of *Number*.

> **Tip**
>
> *Arctangent is the inverse trigonometric function of **Tangent**. This is different from **Cotangent**, which is the simple inverse of the **Tangent** (1/Tangent).*

Arguments
- *RValue*—a Double that returns the arctangent of *Number*.
- *Number*—a Double expression that computes the arctangent.

Examples
```
Private Sub Command1_Click()
If IsNumeric(Text1.Text) Then
    Text2.Text = Format(Atn(CDbl(Text1.Text)))
End If
End Sub
```

This routine will compute the arctangent of the value in the Text1 text box and display the results in the Text2 text box.

See Also   **Cos** (function), **Sin** (function), **Tan** (function)

Axis

OBJECT

PE, EE

Usage   The **Axis** object is used by the **MSChart** control to contain information about an axis on the chart.

Properties
- *AxisObject*.**AxisGrid**—an object reference to an **AxisGrid** object containing information about the area surrounding a chart axis.
- *AxisObject*.**AxisScale**—an object reference to an **AxisScale** object that describes how chart values are drawn on the axis.
- *AxisObject*.**AxisTitle**—an object reference to an **AxisTitle** object containing the title for the axis.
- *AxisObject*.**AxisGrid**—an object reference to an **AxisGrid** object containing information about the area surrounding a chart axis.
- *AxisObject*.**CategoryScale**—an object reference to a **CategoryScale** object containing scale information for the axis.
- *AxisObject*.**Intersection**—an object reference to an **Intersection** object containing information how this axis intersects another axis.
- *AxisObject*.**LevelCount**—an **Integer** containing the number of labels on the axis.
- *AxisObject*.**Labels**—an object reference to a **Labels** collection containing the labels that will be displayed on the axis.

- *AxisObject*.**Pen**—an object reference to a **Pen** object that describes the lines and colors of the axis.
- *AxisObject*.**Tick**—an object reference to a **Tick** object containing information about the tick marks displayed along the axis.
- *AxisObject*.**ValueScale**—an object reference to a **ValueScale** object containing information scale used to display the values on the axis.

See Also   **MSChart** (control)

AxisGrid
OBJECT

PE, EE

Usage   The **AxisGrid** object is used by the **Axis** object of the **MSChart** control to hold information about the planar area surrounding an axis.

Properties
- *AxisGridObject*.**MajorPen**—an object reference to a **Pen** object that describes the major axis grid lines.
- *AxisGridObject*.**MinorPen**—an object reference to a **Pen** object that describes the minor axis grid lines.

See Also   **Axis** (object), **MSChart** (control)

AxisScale
OBJECT

PE, EE

Usage   The **AxisScale** object is used by the **Axis** object of the **MSChart** control to describe how values are plotted on the axis.

Properties
- *AxisScaleObject*.**Hide**—a **Boolean** when **True** means that the axis scale, line, ticks, and title information are hidden on the chart.
- *AxisScaleObject*.**LogBase**—an **Integer** value containing the log base used to plot values along the chart axis. This value can range from 2 to 100. If not specified, this value will default to 10.
- *AxisScaleObject*.**PercentBasis**—an **Integer** value describing the percentage used to plot percentage axis values (see Table A-25).

PercentBasis Name	Description
vtChPercentAxisBasisMaxChart	The largest value in the chart is considered to be 100 percent and all other values are displayed as percentages of that.
vtChPercentAxisBasisMaxRow	The largest value in the row is considered to be 100 percent and all other values are displayed as percentages of that.
vtChPercentAxisBasisMaxColumn	The largest value in the series is considered to be 100 percent and all other values are displayed as percentages of that.
vtChPercentAxisBasisSumChart	All of the values in the chart are added together and that sum is considered to be 100 percent and all other values are displayed as percentages of that.

PercentBasis Name	Description
vtChPercentAxisBasisSumRow	All of the values in the row are added together and that sum is considered to be 100 percent and all other values are displayed as percentages of that.
vtChPercentAxisBasisSumColumn	All of the values in the series are added together and that sum is considered to be 100 percent and all other values are displayed as percentages of that.

Table A-25: PercentBasis *values.*

- *AxisScaleObject.***ScaleType**—an **Integer** value describing the method used to plot values along the axis (see Table A-26).

ScaleType Name	Description
vtChScaleTypeLinear	The axis values are plotted linearly from the minimum to the maximum chart value.
vtChScaleTypeLogarithmic	The axis values are plotted logarithmically using **LogBase**.
vtChScaleTypePercent	The axis values are plotted linearly from based on the percentage values.

Table A-26: ScaleType *values.*

See Also **Axis** (object), **MSChart** (control)

AxisTitle

OBJECT

PE, EE

Usage The **AxisTitle** object is used by the **Axis** object of the **MSChart** control to describe the title of an axis.

Properties
- *AxisTitleObject.***Backdrop**—an object reference to a **Backdrop** object describing the appearance of the title's background.
- *AxisTitleObject.***Font**—an object reference to a **Font** object that describes the text font and size used to display the title.
- *AxisTitleObject.***Text**—a **String** containing the text to be displayed as the axis title.
- *AxisTitleObject.***TextLayout**—an object reference to a **TextLayout** object describing how the title is positioned.
- *AxisTitleObject.***TextLength**—an **Integer** containing the length of the **Text** property.
- *AxisScaleObject.***Visible**—a **Boolean** when **True** means that the title is displayed on the chart. **False** means that the title is not displayed.
- *AxisTitleObject.***VtFont**—an object reference to a **VtFont** object describing the font used to display the title.

See Also **Axis** (object), **MSChart** (control)

Backdrop

OBJECT

PE, EE

Usage The **Backdrop** object is used by the **MSChart** control to contain information about the shadow or pattern displayed behind a chart element.

Properties
- *BackdropObject*.**Fill**—an object reference to a **Fill** object containing information about the type and appearance of the backdrop.
- *BackdropObject*.**Frame**—an object reference to a **Frame** object that describes the appearance of the frame around the backdrop.
- *BackdropObject*.**Shadow**—an object reference to a **Shadow** object describing how a shadow will appear on the chart.

See Also **MSChart** (control)

Beep

STATEMENT

CCE, LE, PE, EE

Syntax Beep

Usage The **Beep** statement makes a sound through the computer's speaker. Beeps will be generated using a sound card if one is available. More sophisticated sounds can be generated using the Multimedia MCI control.

> **Tip**
>
> *Executing two or more **Beep** statements too close together will result in a single beep, so it is important to add a little delay between beeps. This can be done using the **Timer** control or with a loop similar to that in the example below.*

Examples
```
Private Sub Command1_Click()
Dim i As Integer
Dim w As Integer
For i = 1 To 5
    Beep
    w = Second(Now)
    Do While w = Second(Now)
        DoEvents
    Loop
Next i
End Sub
```

Pressing the Command button starts a **For Next** loop that will sound five beeps. Inside the loop, I generate the beep and then I wait until the current second changes. In order not to tie up the system, I call the DoEvents function inside the loop. Once I've finished waiting, I will start the for loop over again.

See Also **Multimedia MCI** (control), **Timer** (control)

Boolean

DATA TYPE

CCE, LE, PE, EE

Usage   The **Boolean** data type has only two values, **True** and **False**. A single **Boolean** variable occupies 16 bits of storage or 2 bytes.

See Also   **Do** (statement), **If** (statement), **While** (statement)

Brush

OBJECT

PE, EE

Usage   The **Brush** object is used by the **MSChart** control to describe the chart element.

Properties
- *BrushObject*.**Fill**—an object reference to a **VtColor** object containing the color used to fill the chart element.
- *BrushObject*.**Index**—an **Integer** containing the hatch (see Table B-1) if **Style** is set to *vtBrushStyleHatched* is selected or the pattern (see Table B-2) if **Style** is set to *vtBrushStylePattern* is selected.

Hatch Name	Description
vtBrushHatchHorizontal	Horizontal lines are drawn.
vtBrushHatchVertical	Vertical lines are drawn.
vtBrushHatchDownDiagonal	Down diagonal (upper left to lower right) hatch lines are drawn.
vtBrushHatchUpDiagonal	Up diagonal (lower left to upper right) hatch lines are drawn.
VtBrushHatchCross	Horizontal and vertical lines are drawn in a cross hatch pattern.
VtBrushHatchDiagonalCross	Up and down diagonal lines are drawn in a cross hatch pattern.

Table B-1: Hatch *values.*

Pattern Name	Description
vtBrushPattern94percent	94 percent pattern color.
VtBrushPattern88percent	88 percent pattern color.
VtBrushPattern75percent	75 percent pattern color.
VtBrushPattern50percent	50 percent pattern color.
VtBrushPattern25percent	25 percent pattern color.
VtBrushPatternBoldHorizontal	Bold horizontal lines.
VtBrushPatternBoldVertical	Bold vertical lines.
VtBrushPatternBoldDownDiagonal	Bold down diagonal (upper left to lower right) lines.
VtBrushPatternBoldUpDiagonal	Bold up diagonal (lower left to upper right) lines.
VtBrushPatternChecks	Checks pattern.
VtBrushPatternWeave	Weave pattern.
VtBrushPatternHorizontal	Horizontal lines.
VtBrushPatternVertical	Vertical lines.
VtBrushPatternDownDiagonal	Down diagonal (upper left to lower right) lines.
VtBrushPatternUpDiagonal	Up diagonal (lower left to upper right) lines.

Pattern Name	Description
VtBrushPatternGrid	Grid pattern.
VtBrushPatternTrellis	Trellis pattern.
VtBrushPatternInvertedTrellis	Inverted trellis pattern.

Table B-2: Pattern *values.*

- *BrushObject.***PatternColor**—an object reference to a **VtColor** object describing the pattern color used to fill the chart element.
- *BrushObject.***Style**—an **Integer** value describing the method used to plot values along the axis (see Table B-3).

Style Name	Description
vtBrushStyleNull	No brush style. The background shows through.
vtBrushStyleSolid	A solid color is used.
vtBrushStylePattern	A bitmapped patterned brush is used.
vtBrushStyleHatched	A hatched brush is used.

Table B-3: Style *values.*

See Also   **MSChart** (control)

Button

OBJECT

CCE, LE, PE, EE

Usage   The **Button** object is used with the **Toolbar** ActiveX control which is found in Microsoft Windows Common Controls (MSCOMCTL.OCX). The **Button** object contains detailed information about each individual button on the **toolbar**.

Buttons can be displayed with icons or a text caption, or both. Buttons can be arranged into Button Groups where only one button can be pressed at a time. Normally buttons will pop up after being pressed, but you can also choose a Check button which stays in after being pressed. Pressing a Check button a second time will pop the button back out.

> **Tip**
>
> *Since it is often desirable to use other controls on a toolbar like a ComboBox control, you can use Place Holder buttons to reserve space on the toolbar and use Toolbar events to move or resize the control whenever the button is resized.*

Properties
- *ButtonObject.***Caption**—a **String** that contains text that will be displayed inside the button. The width of the button will be adjusted, if necessary, to hold all of the text in the caption. If the button is wider than the text, the text will be centered inside the button. The height will also be adjusted so that the text is visible below the icon if included.
- *ButtonObject.***Description**—a **String** that contains text that describes the button. It will be displayed if the user invokes the Customize Toolbar dialog box.

- *ButtonObject*.**Enabled**—a **Boolean** value that when **True** the button will respond to events. When **False**, the button will not respond to events.
- *ButtonObject*.**Height**—a **Single** that contains the height of the button.
- *ButtonObject*.**Image**—a **Variant** that contains a reference to the **ListImage** in an **ImageList**. This value may be an **Integer** which points to the Index of the **ListImage** or a **String** that contains the **Key** associated with the **ListImage**. The default value is 0, which means do not display an image. The **ImageList** is defined in the **Toolbar** control.
- *ButtonObject*.**Index**—an **Integer** that uniquely identifies a **Button** in a **Toolbar** control.
- *ButtonObject*.**Key**—a **String** that uniquely identifies a button in a **Toolbar** control.
- *ButtonObject*.**Left**—a **Single** that specifies the distance between the left edge of the toolbar and the left edge of the button.

Tip

*Do not change the value of the **Left** property directly. This value is computed based on the order and size of the buttons displayed on the toolbar.*

- *ButtonObject*.**MixedState**—a **Boolean** value that when **True**, the button is in an indeterminate state. When **False**, the button is in a normal state.

Tip

*This is most useful to indicate a situation that is not merely **True** or **False**. For example this could be used to display a selected block of text that is left justified in some places and centered in others. Pressing the button allows the program to underline the entire block of text thus resolving the mixed state.*

- *ButtonObject*.**Style**—an **Integer** value (see Table B-4) that contains the style of button displayed on the toolbar.

Style Name	Value	Description
tbrDefault	0	The **Button** is displayed as a regular button (default value).
tbrCheck	1	The **Button** is displayed as a Check button.
tbrButtonGroup	2	The **Button** is part of a Button Group. The Button Group is delimited by Button Separators.
tbrSeparator	3	The **Button** separates other buttons on the toolbar or marks the beginning or end of a Button Group. Its width is fixed at 8 pixels.
tbrPlaceholder	4	The **Button** is similar in appearance and function to a Separator button, but its width can vary.

Table B-4: Style *values*.

Tip

Button Groups are useful when only one button out of the group can be pressed at one time. A Button Group is delimited by Separator buttons on each side of the group.

- *ButtonObject*.**Tag**—a **String** that holds programmer specific information. This property is not used by Visual Basic.
- *ButtonObject*.**ToolTipText**—a **String** that holds a text value that Visual Basic can display as a ToolTip box. The ToolTip box displays whenever the cursor is held over the control for about one second.
- *ButtonObject*.**Top**—a **Single** that specifies the distance between the top of the toolbar and the top of the button.

> **Tip**
>
> *Do not change the value of the **Top** property directly. This value is computed based on the order and size of the buttons displayed on the toolbar.*

- *ButtonObject*.**Value**—an **Integer** value (see Table B-5) that contains the state of the button.

Value Name	Value	Description
tbrUnpressed	0	The Button is not pressed or checked (default value).
tbrPressed	1	The Button is pressed or checked.

Table B-5: Value *values.*

- *ButtonObject*.**Visible**—a **Boolean** value that when **True**, the button is visible on the toolbar. When **False**, the button is not visible on the toolbar. If the button is not visible, it will not occupy space on the toolbar.
- *ButtonObject*.**Width**—a **Single** that contains the width of the button.

Examples
```
Private Sub Toolbar1_ButtonClick(ByVal Button As ComctlLib.Button)
Text1.Text = Button.Description
End Sub
```

This routine is called each time a button on the toolbar is pushed and will display the description of the button that was pushed.

See Also **Buttons** (collection), **ComboBox** (control), **ImageList** (control), **Toolbar** (control)

Buttons

COLLECTION

CCE, LE, PE, EE

Usage The **Buttons** collection is used by the **Toolbar** ActiveX control found in Microsoft Windows Common Controls -2 (COMCT232.OCX). Essentially the **Buttons** collection holds all of the individual **Button** objects in the **Toolbar** control. Properties and methods are available to maintain the collection.

Properties
- *ButtonsCollection*.**Count**—a **Integer** value that contains the number of **Buttons** in the collection. This property is read only.

- *ButtonsCollection.**Item** (reference)*—retrieves a **Button** object from the **Buttons** collection that is identified by *reference*. If *reference* is an **Integer**, then the **Button** object with the same value for its **Index** property will be returned. If *reference* is a **String**, then the **Button** object with the same value for its **Key** property will be returned. If the *reference* is not found, then a run-time error "'35601' Element not found" will be displayed and the program will stop running.

> **Tip**
>
> *Key values are case-sensitive when used as a value for* reference, *so it is wise to adopt a standard where all key values are either uppercase or lowercase and then you can use either the **UCase** function or the **LCase** function before using the value as the reference.*

Methods

ButtonsCollection.Add ([index] , [key] , [caption] , [style] , [image])

Usage
: This method adds buttons to the **Button** collection of a toolbar at run time.

Arguments
: - *index*—an **Integer** that specifies the position in the button collection where the button will be inserted. If no value is specified, this **Button** will be added to the end of the collection.
  - *key*—a **String** that specifies a unique name for the button. If no value is specified, then the **Button** can't be accessed using a value for **Key**.
  - *caption*—a **String** that contains the text that will be displayed at the bottom of the button. If no value is specified then no text will be displayed on the button.
  - *style*—an **Integer** value (see Table B-6) that contains the style of button displayed on the toolbar.

Style Name	Value	Description
tbrDefault	0	The **Button** is displayed as a regular button (default value).
tbrCheck	1	The **Button** is displayed as a Check button.
tbrButtonGroup	2	The **Button** is part of a Button Group. The Button Group is delimited by Button Separators.
tbrSeparator	3	The **Button** separates other buttons on the toolbar or marks the beginning or end of a Button Group. Its width is fixed at 8 pixels.
tbrPlaceholder	4	The **Button** is similar in appearance and function to a Separator button, but its width can vary.

Table B-6: Style values.

- *image*—a **Variant** that contains a reference to the **ListImage** in an **ImageList**. This value may be an **Integer** which points to the **Index** of the **ListImage** or a **String** that contains the **Key** associated with the **ListImage**. The default value is 0—Do not display an image. The **ImageList** is defined in the **Toolbar** control.

ButtonsCollection.Clear

Usage This method removes all of the **Button** objects from the **Button** collection.

ButtonsCollection.Remove *reference*

Usage This method removes a single **Button** object from the **Buttons** collection.

Arguments *reference*—a **Variant** that identifies a **Button** object in the **Buttons** collection. If *reference* is an **Integer**, then the **Button** object with the same value for its **Index** property will be removed. If *reference* is a **String**, then the **Button** object with the same value for its **Key** property will be removed. If the *reference* is not found, then a run-time error "'35601' Element not found" will be displayed and the program will stop running.

See Also **Button** (object), **ImageList** (control), **Toolbar** (control)

Byte

DATA TYPE

CCE, LE, PE, EE

Usage The **Byte** data type holds integer values in the range from 0 to 255. A single **Byte** variable only occupies 8 bits of storage or 1 byte.

See Also **Asc** (function), **AscB** (function), **CByte** (function), **CInt** (function), **CLng** (function), **CStr** (function), **Dim** (statement), **Format** (function), **Integer** (data type), **IsNumeric** (function)

Call

STATEMENT

CCE, LE, PE, EE

Syntax `Call` *subroutine* [(*arg* [, *arg* [, . . . *arg*]])]
subroutine [*arg* [, *arg* [, . . . *arg*]]]

Usage The **Call** statement invokes a subroutine with an optional list of arguments. There are three basic types of subroutines that can be invoked by the **Call** statement:

- **Sub**—A subroutine that is included in your Visual Basic program and begins with the **Sub** statement.
- **Function**—A subroutine, similar to the first type, but that begins with the **Function** statement. Even though functions return a value, when the functions are invoked by the **Call** statement, the return value is discarded.
- **DLL**—A subroutine that exists in DLL libraries. Before they can be used, the DLL subroutines must be defined to Visual Basic using a **Define** statement.

Two different forms of the syntax are available. The first form begins with the **Call** keyword, followed by the name of the subroutine, followed by the optional list of arguments. In this form, the list of arguments must be enclosed in a set of parentheses.

The second form of the **Call** statement omits the **Call** keyword and begins with the name of the subroutine, followed by an optional list of arguments. In this form of the **Call** statement, there must be no parentheses between the subroutine name and the first argument.

Arguments can be nearly anything as long as they are compatible with the argument's definition in the subroutine header.

Arguments *arg*—a variable or an expression that will be passed to the subroutine, function, or DLL subroutine. Arg may be proceeded by **ByRef** or **ByVal** for arguments that are passed to a DLL subroutine. Arrays are passed by specifying the name of the array followed by an empty set of parentheses.

Examples
```
Private Declare Function MessageBox Lib "user32" Alias "MessageBoxA" (ByVal hwnd
    As Long, ByVal lpText As String, ByVal lpCaption As String, ByVal wType As
    Long) As Long

Private Sub MySub(Arg As String)
MsgBox Arg
End Sub

Private Function MyFunc(Arg As String) As String
MsgBox Arg
MyFunc = "Okay"
End Function

Private Sub Command1_Click()
Call MySub("Call MySub")
MySub "MySub"
Call MyFunc("Call MyFunc")
MyFunc "MyFunc"
```

```
Call MessageBox(Me.hwnd, "Call WinAPI function", App.Title, vbOKOnly)
MessageBox Me.hwnd, "WinAPI function", App.Title, vbOKOnly
End Sub
```

This program shows you the different ways that you can call a subroutine. The first two statements in the Command1_Click routine show how a normal subroutine can be called. The next two statements show how a function can be called as a subroutine. Finally, the last two statements show how to call a Windows API function.

See Also   **Declare** (statement), **Function** (statement), **Sub** (statement)

CategoryScale

OBJECT

PE, EE

Usage   The **CategoryScale** object is used by the **MSChart** control to contain information about the scale on a category axis.

Properties
- *CategoryScaleObject*.**Auto**—a **Boolean** value when **True** means that the axis is automatically scaled based on the data charted on the axis. **False** means that the values in **DivisionsPerLabel** and **DivisionsPerTick** are used.
- *CategoryScaleObject*.**DivisionsPerLabel**—an **Integer** containing the number of divisions to be skipped between labels. Setting this property will set the **Auto** property to **False**.
- *CategoryScaleObject*.**DivisionsPerTick**—an **Integer** containing the number of divisions to be skipped between tick marks. Setting this property will set the **Auto** property to **False**.
- *CategoryScaleObject*.**LabelTicks**—a **Boolean** when **True** means that labels are centered on a tick mark. **False** means that the labels are centered between two tick marks.

See Also   **MSChart** (control)

CBool

FUNCTION

CCE, LE, PE, EE

Syntax   *BValue* = **CBool** (*Value*)

Usage   The **CBool** function converts a string or numeric value to a **Boolean** value. Any string value other than **True** or **False** will result in a run-time error '13' Type mismatch. Any numeric value other than 0 will return **True**. Only a numeric value of 0 will return **False**.

> **Tip**
>
> *To prevent run-time errors, use the **On Error** statement to prevent the error from stopping the program, and test the **Err** object to see if an error occurred.*

Arguments
- *BValue*—a **Boolean** that contains the result of converting *value* to a Boolean value.
- *Value*—a numeric or string value to be converted to a **Boolean** value.

Examples
```
Private Sub Command1_Click()
On Error Resume Next
Text2.Text = Format(CBool(Text1.Text))
If Err.Number > 0 Then
   Text2.Text = Err.Description
End If
End Sub
```

This routine converts the value in Text1.Text to a **Boolean** value and then uses the **Format** function to convert the **Boolean** value into a form that can be shown in a **TextBox**. Note that I checked the **Err** object to ensure that the conversion process worked properly.

See Also **Boolean** (data type), **Err** (object), **Format** (function), **On Error** (statement)

CByte

FUNCTION

CCE, LE, PE, EE

Syntax *BValue* = **CByte** (*Value*)

Usage The **CByte** function converts a string or numeric value to a **Byte** value in the range of 0 to 255. Any **String** value that does not contain a valid numeric value will generate a run-time error '13' type mismatch. Any value outside of the range of 0 to 255 will also generate a run-time error '6' overflow.

> **Tip**
>
> *To prevent run-time errors, use the **On Error** statement to prevent the error from stopping the program, and test the **Err** object to see if an error occurred. Also using the **IsNumeric** function will help to prevent conversion errors.*

Arguments
- *BValue*—a **Byte** that contains the result of converting *value* to a **Byte** value.
- *Value*—a numeric value or **String** value to be converted to a **Byte** value.

Examples
```
Private Sub Command1_Click()
On Error Resume Next
Text2.Text = Format(CByte(Text1.Text))
If Err.Number > 0 Then
   Text2.Text = Err.Description
End If
End Sub
```

This routine converts the value in Text1.Text to a **Byte** value and then uses the **Format** function to convert the **Byte** value into a form that can be shown in a **TextBox**. Note that I checked the **Err** object to ensure that the conversion process worked properly.

See Also **Byte** (data type), **Err** (object), **Format** (function), **IsNumeric** (function), **On Error** (statement)

CCur

FUNCTION

CCE, LE, PE, EE

Syntax *CValue* = **CCur** (*Value*)

Usage The **CCur** function converts a string or numeric value to a **Currency** value in the range of -922,337,203,685,477.5808 to 922,337,203,685,477.5807. Any **String** value that does not contain a valid numeric value will generate a run-time error '13' Type mismatch. Any value that is outside of the range of acceptable values will generate a run-time error '6' Overflow.

Also if *value* contains more than four decimal places, the result in *CValue* will be rounded to the nearest fourth decimal place value.

> **Tip**
>
> *To prevent run-time errors, use the **On Error** statement to prevent the error from stopping the program, and test the **Err** object to see if an error occurred. Also using the **IsNumeric** function will help to prevent conversion errors.*

Arguments
- *CValue*—a **Currency** variable that contains the result of converting *value* to a **Currency** value.
- *Value*—a numeric or string value to be converted to a **Currency** value.

Examples
```
Private Sub Command1_Click()
On Error Resume Next
Text2.Text = Format(CCur (Text1.Text))
If Err.Number > 0 Then
    Text2.Text = Err.Description
End If
End Sub
```

This routine converts the value in Text1.Text to a **Currency** value and then uses the **Format** function to convert the **Currency** value into a form that can be shown in a **TextBox**. Note that I checked the **Err** object to ensure that the conversion process worked properly.

See Also **Currency** (data type), **Error** (object), **Format** (function), **IsNumeric** (function), **On Error** (statement)

CDate

FUNCTION

CCE, LE, PE, EE

Syntax *DValue* = **CDate** (*Value*)

Usage The **CDate** function converts a string or numeric value to a **Date** value in the range of 1 January 100 to 31 December 9999. Also, any **String** value that does not contain a valid date value will generate a Run-time error '13' Type mismatch.

The **CDate** will also handle time values, either alone or in combination with a date value.

> **Tip**
>
> To prevent run-time errors, use the **On Error** statement to prevent the error from stopping the program, and test the **Err** object to see if an error occurred. Also using the **IsDate** function will help to prevent conversion errors.

Arguments
- *DValue*—a **Date** variable that contains the result of converting *value* to a **Date** value.
- *Value*—a numeric or string value to be converted to a **Date** value.

Examples
```
Private Sub Command1_Click()
On Error Resume Next
Text2.Text = Format(CDate (Text1.Text))
If Err.Number > 0 Then
    Text2.Text = Err.Description
End If
End Sub
```

This routine converts the value in Text1.Text to a **Date** value and then uses the **Format** function to convert the **Date** value into a form that can be shown in a **TextBox**. Note that I checked the **Err** object to ensure that the conversion process worked properly.

See Also **Date** (data type), **Error** (object), **Format** (function), **IsDate** (function), **On Error** (statement)

CDbl

FUNCTION

CCE, LE, PE, EE

Syntax *DValue* = **CDbl** (*Value*)

Usage Sets value to a **Double** value in the range -1.79769313486232E308 to -4.94065645841247E-324 for negative values and 4.94065645841247E-324 to 1.79769313486232E308 for positive values. Any **String** value that does not contain a valid numeric value will generate a Run-time error '13' Type mismatch. Any value that is outside of the range of acceptable values will generate a run-time error '6' Overflow.

> **Tip**
>
> To prevent run-time errors, use the **On Error** statement to prevent the error from stopping the program, and test the **Err** object to see if an error occurred. Also using the **IsNumeric** function will help to prevent conversion errors.

Arguments
- *DValue*—a **Double** variable that contains the result of converting *value* to a **Double** value.
- *Value*—a numeric or string value to be converted to a **Double** value.

Examples
```
Private Sub Command1_Click()
On Error Resume Next
Text2.Text = Format(CDbl (Text1.Text))
If Err.Number > 0 Then
```

```
        Text2.Text = Err.Description
    End If
End Sub
```

This routine converts the value in Text1.Text to a **Double** value and then uses the **Format** function to convert the **Double** value into a form that can be shown in a **TextBox**. Note that I checked the **Err** object to ensure that the conversion process worked properly.

See Also **Double** (data type), **Error** (object), **Format** (function), **IsNumeric** (function), **On Error** (statement)

CDec

FUNCTION

CCE, LE, PE, EE

Syntax *DValue* = **CDec** (*Value*)

Usage The **CDec** function converts a string or numeric value to a **Decimal** value in the range +/- 9,228,162,514,264,337,593,543,950,335 for zero-scaled numbers, that is, numbers with no decimal places. For numbers with 28 decimal places, the range is +/- .9228162514264337593543950335. The smallest possible nonzero number is 0.0000000000000000000000000001. Any string value that does not contain a valid numeric value will generate a Run-time error '13' Type mismatch. Any value that is outside of the range of acceptable values will generate a run-time error '6' Overflow.

Note that you cannot declare a variable of type **Decimal**. You must declare the variable to be **Variant** and use the **CDec** function to create the **Decimal** variable. Once this has been done, you can use it just like you had declared a variable of type **Decimal**.

Tip

*To prevent run-time errors, use the **On Error** statement to prevent the error from stopping the program, and test the **Err** object to see if an error occurred. Also using the **IsNumeric** function will help to prevent conversion errors.*

Arguments
- *DValue*—a **Variant** variable that contains the result of converting *value* to a **Decimal** value.
- *Value*—a numeric or string value to be converted to a **Decimal** value.

Examples
```
Private Sub Command1_Click()
On Error Resume Next
Text2.Text = Format(CDec (Text1.Text))
If Err.Number > 0 Then
    Text2.Text = Err.Description
End If
End Sub
```

This routine converts the value in Text1.Text to a **Decimal** value and then uses the **Format** function to convert the **Decimal** value into a form that can be shown in a **TextBox**. Note that I checked the **Err** object to ensure that the conversion process worked properly.

See Also **Decimal** (data type), **Error** (object), **Format** (function), **IsNumeric** (function), **On Error** (statement), **Variant** (data type)

ChDir

STATEMENT

CCE, LE, PE, EE

Syntax ChDir *path*

Usage The **ChDir** statement changes the current directory.

To find the current directory use the **CurDir** function. If you omit the drive name from *path*, the default drive will be assumed. To change the default drive, use the **ChDrive** function. Directories can be created and deleted using the **MkDir** and the **RmDir** statements. The **CommonDialog** control, the **DirListBox** control, the **DriveListBox** control, and the **FileListBox** control can be used to create several different sets of graphical displays of files and directories. The **Dir** function can be used to retrieve the names of files.

If the directory path in *path* is not valid, a Run-time error '76' path not found will be displayed.

> **Tip**
>
> To prevent run-time errors, use the **On Error** statement to prevent the error from stopping the program, and test the **Err** object to see if an error occurred.

Arguments
- *path*—a **String** expression that contains the new directory path.

Examples
```
Private Sub Command1_Click()
On Error Resume Next
If Len(Text1.Text) > 0 Then
    ChDir Text1.Text
End If
If Err.Number = 0 Then
    Text2.Text = CurDir("c:")
Else
    Text2.Text = Err.Description
End If
End Sub
```

This routine uses the **ChDir** function to switch the current directory to the value specified in Text1.Text. I then check the **Err** object to see if an error occurred and display either the error information or the new current directory.

See Also **ChDrive** (function), **CommonDialog** (control), **CurDir** (function), **Dir** (function), **DirListBox** (control), **DriveListBox** (control), **FileListBox** (control), **MkDir** (statement), **RmDir** (statement).

ChDrive

STATEMENT

CCE, LE, PE, EE

Syntax   **ChDrive** *drive*

Usage   The **ChDrive** statement changes the current drive. If the length of *drive* is greater than one, only the first character in the string is significant. To find the current drive use the **CurDir** function. The current drive will be in the first character in the string.

To change the current directory, use the **ChDir** function. Directories can be created and deleted using the **MkDir** and the **RmDir** statements. The **CommonDialog** control, the **DirListBox** control, the **DriveListBox** control, the **FileListBox** control can be used to create several different sets of graphical displays of files and directories. The **Dir** function can be used to retrieve the names of files.

If the drive in *drive* is not valid, a Run-time error '68' device unavailable will be displayed.

> **Tip**
>
> *To prevent run-time errors, use the **On Error** statement to prevent the error from stopping the program and test the **Err** object to see if an error occurred.*

Arguments   • *drive*—a **String** expression that contains the new directory path.

Examples
```
Private Sub Command1_Click()
On Error Resume Next
If Len(Text1.Text) > 0 Then
    ChDrive Text1.Text
End If
If Err.Number = 0 Then
    Text2.Text = CurDir("c:")
Else
    Text2.Text = Err.Description
End If
End Sub
```

This routine uses the **ChDrive** function to switch the current directory to the value specified in Text1.Text. I then check the **Err** object to see if an error occurred and display either the error information or the new current directory.

See Also   **ChDir** (function), **CommonDialog** (control), **CurDir** (function), **Dir** (function), **DirListBox** (control), **DriveListBox** (control), **FileListBox** (control), **MkDir** (statement), **RmDir** (statement)

CheckBox

CONTROL

CCE, LE, PE, EE

Usage The **CheckBox** control is an intrinsic control which provides the user with a Yes/No choice. Text can be displayed next to the box by using the **Caption** property. The value of the control can be checked by using the **Value** property.

An **OptionButton** is similar to a **CheckBox** in that it allows a user to make a Yes/No choice. However an **OptionButton** only allows one choice in a group to be Yes or **True**, the rest of the buttons must be **False**. A **CheckBox** does not have this restriction.

Properties
- *CheckBoxControl*.**Alignment**—an **Integer** value (see Table C-1) that describes the placement of the check box and the caption within the space occupied by the control.

Alignment Name	Value	Description
vbLeftJustify	0	The check box shown on the left side of the control, while the caption is shown to the right of the check box (default value).
vbRightJustify	1	The check box is shown on the right side of the control, while the caption is shown to the left of the check box.

Table C-1: **Alignment** *values.*

- *CheckBoxControl*.**Appearance**—an **Integer** value (see Table C-2) that describes how the check box will appear on the form:

AppearanceValue	Description
0	The check box is displayed without the 3D effects.
1	The check box is displayed with 3D effects (default value).

Table C-2: **Appearance** *values.*

- *CheckBoxControl*.**BackColor**—a **Long** that contains the suggested value for the background color of the control. The **BackColor** and **ForeColor** must both be solid to display text. If you choose a color that is dithered, it will be changed to the nearest solid color.
- *CheckBoxControl*.**Caption**—a **String** value that is displayed next to the check box. You can include an access key for this control by inserting an ampersand (&) in front of the character you want to use. The selected character will then appear with an underline. Then if the user presses the Alt key with the underlined character, the control will gain the focus.
- *CheckBoxControl*.**Container**—an object that can be used to set or return the container of the control at run time. This property cannot be set at design time.
- *CheckBoxControl*.**DataChanged**—a **Boolean** that applies only to data bound controls. When **True**, it means that the data contained in this control was changed either by the user or by some means other than retrieving data from the current record. When **False**, it means the data in the control is unchanged from the current record. Simply reading the next record is not sufficient to set the **DataChanged** property to **True**.

When the **Data** control moves to the next record, it will automatically invoke the **Edit** and **Update** methods to post the changes to the database.

CheckBox • 43

- *CheckBoxControl*.**DataField**—a **String** value that associates the control with a field in a **RecordSet** object in a **Data** control.
- *CheckBoxControl*.**DisabledPicture**—a picture object (a bitmap, icon, or metafile) that will be shown on top of the control when the control's **Enabled** property is **False** and the **Style** property is set to *vbButtonGraphical*.

> **Tip**
>
> *This value can be created using the* **LoadPicture** *function.*

- *CheckBoxControl*.**DownPicture**—a picture object (a bitmap, icon, or metafile) that will be displayed on top of the control when the control is pressed. This will replace the standard picture displayed when the control is not pressed. This feature requires that the **Style** property be set to *vbButtonGraphical*.

> **Tip**
>
> *This value can be created using the* **LoadPicture** *function.*

- *CheckBoxControl*.**DragIcon**—an object that contains the picture value of an icon. At design time, you can specify an icon file that has a file type of .ICO.

> **Tip**
>
> *This value can be created by copying the value from another control's* **DragIcon** *value, a form's icon, or by using the* **LoadPicture** *function.*

- *CheckBoxControl*.**DragMode**—an **Integer** value (see Table C-3) specifying how the control will respond to a drag request:

> **Tip**
>
> *Setting* **DragMode** *to vbAutomatic will automatically begin a drag operation when the user clicks on the control. However, the control will not respond to the usual mouse events (***Click***,* ***DblClick***, ***MouseDown***,* ***MouseMove***,* ***MouseUp***).*

DragMode Name	Value	Description
vbManual	0	The Drag method must be used to begin a drag drop operation (default value).
vbAutomatic	1	The source control will automatically begin a drag-and-drop operation when the user clicks on the control.

Table C-3: **DragMode** *values.*

- *CheckBoxControl*.**Enabled**—a **Boolean** value when **True** means that the control will respond to events. When **False**, the control will not respond to events.
- *CheckBoxControl*.**Font**—an object that contains information about the character font used by this object.

> **Tip**
>
> The **Font** object should be used in place of the other **Font** properties, since it offers more functionality than the individual properties.

- *CheckBoxControl*.**FontBold**—a **Boolean** when **True**, means that the characters display in bold. **False** means that the characters display normally.
- *CheckBoxControl*.**FontItalic**—a **Boolean** when **True**, means that the characters display in italics. **False** means that the characters display normally.
- *CheckBoxControl*.**FontName**—a **String** that specifies the name of the font that should be used to display the characters in this control.
- *CheckBoxControl*.**FontSize**—a **Single** that specifies the point size that should be used to display the characters in the control.
- *CheckBoxControl*.**FontStrikethru**—a **Boolean** when **True**, means that the characters display with a line through the center. **False** means that the characters display normally.
- *CheckBoxControl*.**FontUnderlined**—a **Boolean** when **True**, means that the characters display with a line beneath them. **False** means that the characters display normally.
- *CheckBoxControl*.**ForeColor**—a **Long** that contains the suggested value for the foreground color of the contained control. This property is read only at run time.
- *CheckBoxControl*.**Height**—a **Single** that contains the height of the control.
- *CheckBoxControl*.**HelpContextID**—a **Long** that contains a help file context ID number which references an entry in the help file. When the user presses the F1 key while this control is active, the corresponding entry in the help file will automatically be displayed. A value of zero means that no context number was specified.

> **Tip**
>
> A help file must be compiled using the Windows Help Compiler available in the Professional and Enterprise editions of Visual Basic.

- *CheckBoxControl*.**hWnd**—a **Long** that contains a Windows handle to the control.

> **Tip**
>
> The **hWnd** property is most useful when making calls to Windows API functions. Since this value can change during execution, do not save the value into a variable for later use.

- *CheckBoxControl*.**Index**—an **Integer** that uniquely identifies a control in a control array.
- *CheckBoxControl*.**Left**—a **Single** that contains the distance measured in twips between the left edge of the control and the left edge of the control's container.

CheckBox

- *CheckBoxControl*.**MaskColor**—a **Long** that identifies a color that will be used as a mask or transparent color for bitmaps displayed within the control. This is useful for bitmap images that do not specify transparency information like icons and metafiles. The **UseMaskColor** property must be **True** for this property to take effect.
- *CheckBoxControl*.**MouseIcon**—a picture object (a bitmap, icon, or metafile) that will be used as a cursor when the **MousePointer** property is set to 99. Note that Visual Basic does not support color cursors from a .CUR file. A color icon from a .ICO file should be used instead.
- *CheckBoxControl*.**MousePointer**—an **Integer** value (see Table C-4) that contains the value of the cursor that should be displayed when the cursor is moved over this control. Use *vbCustom* to display the custom icon stored in the **MouseIcon** property.

Cursor Name	Value	Description
vbDefault	0	Shape determined by the object (default value)
vbArrow	1	Arrow
vbCrosshair	2	Crosshair
vbIbeam	3	I beam
vbIconPointer	4	Square inside a square
vbSizePointer	5	Four sided arrow (north, south, east, west)
vbSizeNESW	6	Two sided arrow (northeast, southwest)
vbSizeNS	7	Two sided arrow (north, south)
vbSizeNWSE	8	Two sided arrow (northwest, southeast)
vbSizeWE	9	Two sided arrow (west, east)
vbUpArrow	10	Single sided arrow pointing north
vbHourglass	11	Hourglass
vbNoDrop	12	No Drop
vbArrowHourglass	13	An arrow and an Hourglass
vbArrowQuestion	14	An arrow and a question mark
vbSizeAll	15	Size all
vbCustom	99	Custom icon from the **MouseIcon** property of this control

Table C-4: **Cursor** *values.*

- *CheckBoxControl*.**Name**—a **String** that contains the name of the control that will be used to reference the control in a Visual Basic program. This property is read only at run time.
- *CheckBoxControl*.**OLEDropMode**—an **Integer** value (see Table C-5) that describes how the control will respond to OLE drop operations.

OLEDropMode Name	Value	Description
vbOLEDropNone	0	The control does not accept OLE drops. The cursor is changed to the No Drop cursor (default value).
vbOLEDropManual	1	The control responds to OLE drops under the program's control (manual).
vbOLEDropAutomatic	2	The control automatically accepts OLE drops if it recognizes the format of the data object.

Table C-5: **OLEDropMode** *values.*

- *CheckBoxControl*.**Parent**—an object that contains a reference to the **Form**, **Frame**, or other container that contains the **CheckBox** control.

- *CheckBoxControl*.**Picture**—a picture object (a bitmap, icon, metafile, GIF, or JPEG) that will be displayed on the control. You can also use the **LoadPicture** function at run time to load a bitmap, icon, or metafile. Note that **Style** must be set to *vbButtonGraphical* for the image to be shown.
- *CheckBoxControl*.**RightToLeft**—a **Boolean** value when **True** means that the text is displayed from right to left. When **False** means that the text is displayed from left to right. A bi-directional version of Windows is required to set this property to **True**.
- *CheckBoxControl*.**Style**—an **Integer** value (see Table C-6) that contains the style used to display the control.

Style Name	Value	Description
vbButtonStandard	0	The control is displayed as a check box next to a caption (default value).
vbButtonGraphic	1	The control is displayed like a command button, which can be toggled on and off.

Table C-6: **Style** *values.*

- *CheckBoxControl*.**TabIndex**—an Integer that determines the order that a user will tab through the objects on a form.
- *CheckBoxControl*.**TabStop**—a **Boolean** value when **True** means that the user can tab to this object. When **False**, means that this control will be skipped to the next control in the **TabIndex** order.
- *CheckBoxControl*.**Tag**—a **String** that can hold programmer specific information. This property is not used by Visual Basic.
- *CheckBoxControl*.**ToolTipText**—a **String** that holds a text value that can be displayed as a **ToolTip** box that is displayed whenever the cursor is held over the control for about one second.
- *CheckBoxControl*.**Top**—a **Single** that contains the distance measured in twips between the top edge of the control and the top edge of the control's container.
- *CheckBoxControl*.**UseMaskColor**—a **Boolean** value when **True** means you should use the color specified in the **MaskColor** property to create a transparent background for the picture objects contained in the control. When **False**, the picture objects will not be displayed with a transparent background.
- *CheckBoxControl*.**Value**—an **Integer** value (see Table C-7) that contains the check box's status.

Value Name	Value	Description
vbUnchecked	0	The check box is not marked.
vbChecked	1	The check box is marked.
vbGrayed	2	The check box is grayed out.

Table C-7: **Value** *values.*

Tip

Setting the check box to vbGrayed *is useful when you need to show that the value represents an indeterminate state. For example, then you could use a check box to indicate that the selected text in a RichTextBox is either bold or normal. However, if the selected text contains both bold and normal text, you could set the value of the check box to* vbGrayed.

CheckBox • 47

- *CheckBoxControl*.**Visible**—a **Boolean** value when **True** means that the control is visible. When **False** means that the control is not visible.

> **Tip**
>
> *This property can hide the control until the program is ready to display it.*

- *CheckBoxControl*.**WhatsThisHelpID**—a **Long** that contains a help file context ID number which references an entry in the help file. This provides a What's This PopUp help display in response to the What's This button in the upper right corner of the window.
- *CheckBoxControl*.**Width**—a **Single** that contains the width of the control.

Methods

CheckBoxControl.Drag [*DragAction*]

Usage This method begins, ends, or cancels a drag operation.

Arguments • *DragAction*—an **Integer** that contains a value selected from Table C-8 below.

DragAction Name	Value	Description
vbCancel	0	Cancels any drag operation in progress.
vbBeginDrag	1	Begins a drag operation (default).
vbEndDrag	2	Ends a drag operation and drops *object*.

Table C-8: DragAction *values.*

CheckBoxControl.Move *Left* [, *Top* [, *Width* [, *Height*]]]

Usage This method changes the position and the size of the **CheckBox** control. The **ScaleMode** of the **Form** or other container object that holds the **CheckBox** control will determine the units used to specify the coordinates.

Arguments
- *Left*—a **Single** that specifies the new position of the left edge of the control.
- *Top*—a **Single** that specifies the new position of the top edge of the control.
- *Width*—a **Single** that specifies the new width of the control.
- *Height*—a **Single** that specifies the new height of the control.

CheckBoxControl.OLEDrag

Usage This method begins an **OLEDrag** and drop operation. Invoking this method will trigger the **OLEStartDrag** event.

CheckBoxControl.Refresh

Usage This method redraws the contents of the control.

CheckBoxControl.SetFocus

Usage   This method transfers the focus from the form or control that currently has the focus to this control. To receive the focus, this control must be enabled and visible.

CheckBoxControl.ShowWhatsThis

Usage   This method displays the ShowWhatsThis help information for this control.

CheckBoxControl.ZOrder [position]

Usage   This method specifies the position of the **CheckBox** control relative to the other objects on the form.

Tip

*Note that there are three layers of objects on a form: the back layer is the drawing space which contains the results of the graphical methods; the middle layer contains graphical objects and **Labels**; and the top layer contains nongraphical controls such as the **CommandButton**. The **ZOrder** method only affects how the objects are arranged within a single layer.*

Arguments   ▪ *position*—an **Integer** that specifies the relative position of this object. A value of 0 means that the control is positioned at the head of the list; a value of 1 means that the control will be placed at the end of the list.

Events

Private Sub CheckBoxControl__Click([index As Integer])

Usage   This event occurs when the user clicks a mouse button while the cursor is positioned over this control.

Tip

*If you need to identify which mouse button was pressed, use the **MouseUp** and **MouseDown** events.*

Arguments   ▪ *index*—an **Integer** that uniquely identifies a control in a control array. This argument is not present if the control is not part of a control array.

Private Sub CheckBoxControl_DragDrop([index As Integer ,] source As Control, x As Single, y As Single)

Usage   This event occurs when a drag-and-drop operation is completed by using the **Drag** method with a *DragAction* value of *vbEndDrag* (2).

Tip

*When using drag-and-drop operations, use the **DragOver** event to determine what the cursor should look like while the cursor moves over the control.*

Arguments	▪ *index*—an **Integer** that uniquely identifies a control in a control array. This argument is not present if the control is not part of a control array.
	▪ *source*—a control object that is the control that is being dragged.

> **Tip**
>
> *You can access a property or method from the source control by using* source.*property or* source.*method. You can determine the type of object or control by using the* **TypeOf** *operator.*

▪ *x*—a **Single** that contains the horizontal location of the mouse pointer.

▪ *y*—a **Single** that contains the vertical location of the mouse pointer.

Private Sub *CheckBoxControl*_DragOver([*index* As Integer ,] *source* As Control, *x* As Single, *y* As Single, *state* As Integer)

Usage	This event occurs while a drag operation is in progress and the cursor is moved over the control.

> **Tip**
>
> *When using drag-and-drop operations, use the* **DragOver** *event to determine what the cursor should look like while the cursor moves over the control. When* state *is 0, you can change the cursor to a No Drop (vbNoDrop) cursor or highlight the field that the cursor is near. When* state *is 1, you can undo the changes you made when the* state *was 0.*

Arguments	▪ *index*—an **Integer** that uniquely identifies a control in a control array. This argument is not present if the control is not part of a control array.
	▪ *source*—a control object that is the control that is being dragged.

> **Tip**
>
> *You can access a property or method from the source control by using* source.*property or* source.*method. You can determine the type of object or control by using the* **TypeOf** *operator.*

▪ *x*—a **Single** that contains the horizontal location of the mouse pointer.

▪ *y*—a **Single** that contains the vertical location of the mouse pointer.

▪ *state*—an **Integer** value (see Table C-9) that indicates the state of the object being dragged.

state Name	Value	Description
vbEnter	0	The dragged object is entering range of the control.
vbLeave	1	The dragged object is leaving range of the control.
vbOver	2	The dragged object has moved from one position over the control to another.

Table C-9: state *values.*

Private Sub *CheckBoxControl*_GotFocus ([*index* As Integer])

Usage This event occurs when the control is given focus.

> **Tip**
>
> *You can use this routine to display help or other information in a status bar.*

Arguments • *index*—an **Integer** that uniquely identifies a control in a control array. This argument is not present if the control is not part of a control array.

Private Sub *CheckBoxControl*_KeyDown ([*index* As Integer ,] *keycode* As Integer, *shift* As Single)

Usage This event occurs when a key is pressed while the control has the focus.

Arguments • *index*—an **Integer** that uniquely identifies a control in a control array. This argument is not present if the control is not part of a control array.
• *keycode*—an **Integer** that contains information about which key was pressed.
• *shift*—an **Integer** value (see Table C-10) that contains information about the Shift and Alt keys that were pushed when the mouse button was pressed. These values can be added together if more than one key was down. For instance, a value of 5 would mean that the Shift and Alt keys were both down when the mouse button was pressed.

shift Name	Value	Description
vbShiftMask	1	The Shift key was pressed.
vbCtrlMask	2	The Ctrl key was pressed.
vbAltMask	4	The Alt key was pressed.

Table C-10: shift *values.*

Private Sub *CheckBoxControl*_KeyPress([*index* As Integer ,] *keychar* As Integer)

Usage This event occurs whenever a key is pressed while the control has the focus.

Arguments • *index*—an **Integer** that uniquely identifies a control in a control array. This argument is not present if the control is not part of a control array.
• *keychar*—an **Integer** that contains the ASCII character that was pressed.

Private Sub *CheckBoxControl*_KeyUp ([*index* As Integer ,] *keycode* As Integer, *shift* As Single)

Usage This event occurs when a key is released while the control has the focus.

CheckBox

Arguments
- *index*—an **Integer** that uniquely identifies a control in a control array. This argument is not present if the control is not part of a control array.
- *keycode*—an **Integer** that contains information about which key was released.
- *shift*—an **Integer** value (see Table C-11) that contains information about the Shift and Alt keys that were pushed when the mouse button was pressed. These values can be added together if more than one key was down. For instance, a value of 5 would mean that the Shift and Alt keys were both down when the mouse button was pressed.

shift Name	Value	Description
vbShiftMask	1	The Shift key was pressed.
vbCtrlMask	2	The Ctrl key was pressed.
vbAltMask	4	The Alt key was pressed.

Table C-11: shift *values*.

Private Sub *CheckBoxControl*_LostFocus ([*index* As Integer])

Usage   This event occurs when the control loses focus.

Tip

This routine is useful to performing data verification.

Arguments
- *index*—an **Integer** that uniquely identifies a control in a control array. This argument is not present if the control is not part of a control array.

Private Sub *CheckBoxControl*_MouseDown([*index* As Integer ,] *button* As Integer, *shift* As Single, *x* As Single, *y* As Single)

Usage   This event occurs when a mouse button is pressed while the cursor is over the control.

Arguments
- *index*—an **Integer** that uniquely identifies a control in a control array. This argument is not present if the control is not part of a control array.
- *button*—an **Integer** value (see Table C-12) that contains information about the mouse buttons that were pressed. Only one button will be indicated when this event occurs.

button Name	Value	Description
vbLeftButton	1	The left button was pressed.
vbRightButton	2	The right button was pressed.
vbMiddleButton	4	The middle button was pressed.

Table C-12: button *values*.

- *shift*—an **Integer** value (see Table C-13) that contains information about the Shift and Alt keys that were pushed when the mouse button was pressed. These values can be added together if more than one key was down. For instance, a value of 5 would mean that the Shift and Alt keys were both down when the mouse button was pressed.

shift Name	Value	Description
vbShiftMask	1	The Shift key was pressed.
vbCtrlMask	2	The Ctrl key was pressed.
vbAltMask	4	The Alt key was pressed.

Table C-13: shift *values*.

- *x*—a **Single** that contains the horizontal location of the mouse pointer.
- *y*—a **Single** that contains the vertical location of the mouse pointer.

Private Sub *CheckBoxControl*_MouseMove ([*index* As Integer ,] *button* As Integer, *shift* As Single, *x* As Single, *y* As Single)

Usage — This event occurs while the cursor is moved over the control.

Arguments
- *index*—an **Integer** that uniquely identifies a control in a control array. This argument is not present if the control is not part of a control array.
- *button*—an **Integer** value (see Table C-14) that contains information about the mouse buttons that were pressed. These values can be added together if more than one button was pushed. For instance, a value of 3 means that both the left and right buttons were pressed. A value of 0 means that no buttons were pressed.

button Name	Value	Description
vbLeftButton	1	The left button was pressed.
vbRightButton	2	The right button was pressed.
vbMiddleButton	4	The middle button was pressed.

Table C-14: button *values*.

- *shift*—an **Integer** value (see Table C-15) that contains information about the Shift and Alt keys that were pushed when the mouse button was pressed. For instance, a value of 5 would mean that the Shift and Alt keys were both down when the mouse button was pressed. A value of 0 means that none of these keys were pressed.

shift Name	Value	Description
vbShiftMask	1	The Shift key was pressed.
vbCtrlMask	2	The Ctrl key was pressed.
vbAltMask	4	The Alt key was pressed.

Table C-15: shift *values*.

- *x*—a **Single** that contains the horizontal location of the mouse pointer.
- *y*—a **Single** that contains the vertical location of the mouse pointer.

Private Sub *CheckBoxControl*_MouseUp([*index* As Integer ,] *button* As Integer, *shift* As Single, *x* As Single, *y* As Single)

Usage   This event occurs when a mouse button is released while the cursor is over the control.

Arguments
- *index*—an **Integer** that uniquely identifies a control in a control array. This argument is not present if the control is not part of a control array.
- *button*—an **Integer** value (see Table C-16) that contains information about the mouse buttons that were released. Only one of these values will be present.

button Name	Value	Description
vbLeftButton	1	The left button was released.
vbRightButton	2	The right button was released.
vbMiddleButton	4	The middle button was released.

Table C-16: button *values*.

- *shift*—an **Integer** value (see Table C-17) that contains information about the Shift and Alt keys that were pushed when the mouse button was released. These values can be added together if more than one key was down. For instance, a value of 5 would mean that the Shift and Alt keys were both down when the mouse button was released. A value of 0 means that none of these keys were pressed.

shift Name	Value	Description
vbShiftMask	1	The Shift key was pressed.
vbCtrlMask	2	The Ctrl key was pressed.
vbAltMask	4	The Alt key was pressed.

Table C-17: shift *values*.

- *x*—a **Single** that contains the horizontal location of the mouse pointer.
- *y*—a **Single** that contains the vertical location of the mouse pointer.

Private Sub *CheckBoxControl*_OLECompleteDrag([*index* As Integer ,] *effect* As Long)

Usage   This event tells the source control the results of an OLE drag-and-drop operation. This is the final event to occur in the series of actions that make up an OLE drag-and-drop operation.

Arguments
- *index*—an **Integer** that uniquely identifies a control in a control array. This argument is not present if the control is not part of a control array.
- *effect*—a **Long** (see Table C-18) that returns the status of the OLE drag-and-drop operation.

effect Name	Value	Description
vbDropEffectNone	0	The operation was canceled or the target control can't accept the drop operation.
vbDropEffectCopy	1	The operation copied data from the source control to the target control. The original data is unchanged.
vbDropEffectMove	2	The operation results in a link from the original data to the target control.

Table C-18: effect *values*.

Private Sub *CheckBoxControl*_OLEDragDrop([*index* As Integer ,] *data* As DataObject, *effect* As Long, *button* As Integer, *shift* As Single, *x* As Single, *y* As Single)

Usage
This event tells the source control the results of an OLE drag-and-drop operation. This is the final event to occur in the series of actions that make up an OLE drag-and-drop operation.

Arguments
- *index*—an **Integer** that uniquely identifies a control in a control array. This argument is not present if the control is not part of a control array.
- *data*—a **DataObject** that contains the formats that the source control will provide. If the data is not contained in the **DataObject**, then it can be retrieved with the **GetData** method.
- *effect*—a **Long** (see Table C-19) that returns the status of the OLE drag-and-drop operation.

effect Name	Value	Description
vbDropEffectNone	0	The operation was canceled or the target control can't accept the drop operation.
vbDropEffectCopy	1	The operation copied data from the source control to the target control. The original data is unchanged.
vbDropEffectMove	2	The operation results in a link from the original data to the target control.

Table C-19: effect *values*.

- *button*—an **Integer** value (see Table C-20) that contains information about the mouse buttons that were pressed. These values can be added together if more than one button was pushed. For instance, a value of 3 means that both the left and right buttons were pressed. A value of 0 means that no buttons were pressed.

button Name	Value	Description
vbLeftButton	1	The left button was pressed.
vbRightButton	2	The right button was pressed.
vbMiddleButton	4	The middle button was pressed.

Table C-20: button *values*.

- *shift*—an **Integer** value (see Table C-21) that contains information about the Shift and Alt keys that were pushed when the mouse button was released. These values can be added together if more than one key was down. For instance, a value of 5 would mean that the Shift and Alt keys were both down when the mouse button was released. A value of 0 means that none of these keys were pressed.

shift Name	Value	Description
vbShiftMask	1	The Shift key was pressed.
vbCtrlMask	2	The Ctrl key was pressed.
vbAltMask	4	The Alt key was pressed.

Table C-21: shift *values*.

- *x*—a **Single** that contains the horizontal location of the mouse pointer.
- *y*—a **Single** that contains the vertical location of the mouse pointer.

Private Sub *CheckBoxControl*_OLEDragOver([*index* As Integer ,] *data* As DataObject, *effect* As Long, *button* As Integer, *shift* As Single, *x* As Single, *y* As Single, *state* As Integer)

Usage   This event happens when an OLE drag-and-drop operation is in progress.

Arguments
- *index*—an **Integer** that uniquely identifies a control in a control array. This argument is not present if the control is not part of a control array.
- *data*—a **DataObject** that contains the formats that the source control will provide. If the data is not contained in the **DataObject**, then it can be retrieved with the **GetData** method.
- *effect*—a **Long** (see Table C-22) that returns the status of the OLE drag-and-drop operation.

effect Name	Value	Description
vbDropEffectNone	0	The operation was canceled or the target control can't accept the drop operation.
vbDropEffectCopy	1	The operation copied data from the source control to the target control. The original data is unchanged.
vbDropEffectMove	2	The operation results in a link from the original data to the target control.

Table C-22: effect *values*.

- *button*—an **Integer** value (see Table C-23) that contains information about the mouse buttons that were pressed. These values can be added together if more than one button was pushed. For instance, a value of 3 means that both the left and right buttons were pressed. A value of 0 means that no buttons were pressed.

button Name	Value	Description
vbLeftButton	1	The left button was pressed.
vbRightButton	2	The right button was pressed.
vbMiddleButton	4	The middle button was pressed.

Table C-23: button *values*.

- *shift*—an **Integer** value (see Table C-24) that contains information about the Shift and Alt keys that were pushed when the mouse button was released. These values can be added together if more than one key was down. For instance, a value of 5 would mean that the Shift and Alt keys were both down when the mouse button was released. A value of 0 means that none of these keys were pressed.

shift Name	Value	Description
vbShiftMask	1	The Shift key was pressed.
vbCtrlMask	2	The Ctrl key was pressed.
vbAltMask	4	The Alt key was pressed.

Table C-24: shift *values*.

- *x*—a **Single** that contains the horizontal location of the mouse pointer.
- *y*—a **Single** that contains the vertical location of the mouse pointer.
- *state*—an **Integer** value (see Table C-25) that indicates the state of the object being dragged.

state Name	Value	Description
vbEnter	0	The dragged object is entering range of the control.
vbLeave	1	The dragged object is leaving range of the control.
vbOver	2	The dragged object has moved from one position over the control to another.

Table C-25: state *values*.

Private Sub *CheckBoxControl*_OLEGiveFeedback ([*index* As Integer ,] *effect* As Long)

Usage This event tells the source control what is happening while the OLE drag-and-drop operation is in progress. This event occurs after the **OLEDragOver** event.

Tip

You may want to use this event to change the cursor to reflect what can happen in the remote object.

Arguments
- *index*—an **Integer** that uniquely identifies a control in a control array. This argument is not present if the control is not part of a control array.
- *effect*—a **Long** (see Table C-26) that returns the status of the OLE drag-and-drop operation.

effect Name	Value	Description
vbDropEffectNone	0	The operation was canceled or the target control can't accept the drop operation.
vbDropEffectCopy	1	The operation copied data from the source control to the target control. The original data is unchanged.
vbDropEffectMove	2	The operation results in a link from the original data to the target control.
vbDropEffectScroll	&H80000000	The target control is about to scroll or is scrolling. This value may be added to the other *shift* values.

Table C-26: effect *values.*

Private Sub *CheckBoxControl*_OLESetData([*index* As Integer ,] *data* As DataObject, *DataFormat* As Integer)

Usage — This event happens in response to the target object performing a **GetData** method on *data*. This routine will respond by using the **SetData** method with the desired data using the **DataObject** *data*.

Arguments
- *index*—an **Integer** that uniquely identifies a control in a control array. This argument is not present if the control is not part of a control array.
- *data*—a **DataObject** that will contain the data to be returned to the target object.
- *format*—an **Integer** value (see Table C-27) that contains the format of the data.

format Name	Value	Description
vbCFText	1	Text (.TXT files)
vbCFBitmap	2	Bitmap (.BMP files)
vbCFMetafile	3	Metafile (.WMF files)
vbCFEDIB	8	Device independent bitmap (DIB)
vbCFPallette	9	Color palette
vbCFEMetafile	14	Enhanced metafile (.EMF files)
vbCFFiles	15	List of files
vbCFRTF	-16639	Rich Text Format (.RTF files)

Table C-27: format *values.*

Private Sub *CheckBoxControl*_OLEStartDrag ([*index* As Integer ,] *data* As DataObject, *AllowedEffects* As Long)

Usage — This event starts an OLE drag-and-drop operation.

Arguments
- *index*—an **Integer** that uniquely identifies a control in a control array. This argument is not present if the control is not part of a control array.

- *data*—a **DataObject** that will contain the formats that the source object is willing to provide to the target object. It may optionally contain the data to be transferred.
- *AllowedEffects*—a **Long** value (see Table C-28) that contains the effects that the target object can request from the source object. The *AllowedEffects* can be added together if the source object supports more than one effect. Note that the target object can always use the *vbDropEffectNone* effect.

AllowedEffects Name	Value	Description
vbDropEffectNone	0	The target can't copy the data.
vbDropEffectCopy	1	The target can copy the data and the source will keep the data unchanged.
vbDropEffectMove	2	The target can copy the data and the source will delete the data.

Table C-28: AllowedEffects *values.*

Examples
```
Private Sub Check1_Click()
MsgBox "The value of the checkbox is " & Format(Check1.Value)
End Sub
```

This routine will display the value of the check box each time it is clicked.

See Also **Data** (control), **LoadPicture** (function), **OptionButton** (control)

Choose

FUNCTION

CCE, LE, PE, EE

Syntax *Value* = **Choose** [(*choice*, *val1* [, *val2* [, . . . *valN*]])]

Usage The **Choose** function returns a single value pointed to by *choice* from a list of values. This is similar to the **Switch** function that also returns a value from a list of values.

Arguments
- *Value*—a **Variant** that contains the result of choosing one of the *arg* values or **Null** if *choice* is not valid.
  - *choice*—a **Single** that selects one of the arguments.
  - *val1*—a **Variant** value that will be returned if the value of *choice* is 1.
  - *Val2*—a **Variant** value that will be returned if the value of *choice* is 2.
  - *valN*—a **Variant** value that will be returned if the value of *choice* is N.

Examples
```
Private Sub Command1_Click()
Dim v As Variant
If IsNumeric(Text1.Text) Then
    v = Choose(CSng(Text1.Text), "A", "B", "C", "D", "E", "F", "G", "H")
```

```
        Else
            v = "Non-numeric choice"
        End If
        If IsNull(v) Then
            v = "Choice out of range"
        End If
        MsgBox v
        End Sub
```

This routine uses the value from the Text1 TextBox to select a value from a list of values. Note that I took the time to ensure that the value of *choice* was a valid number and that the returned choice is not **Null**, before I displayed the result.

See Also   **Switch** (function), **Variant** (data type)

Chr

FUNCTION

CCE, LE, PE, EE

Syntax   *CharValue* = **Chr[$]**(*CharCode*)

Usage   The **Chr** function returns a single **String** character whose numeric value is *CharCode*. The dollar sign ($) is optional and indicates that the return value is a **String** rather than a **Variant**. This function performs the inverse operation of the **Asc** function. A run-time error '5' invalid procedure call or argument will occur if the value of *CharCode* represents an illegal character.

Arguments
- *CharValue*—a **Variant** that contains the result of choosing one of the *arg* values or **Null** if *choice* is not valid. If the **Asc$** is used instead of **Asc**, *CharValue* will be a **String**.
- *CharCode*—a **Long** value that contains the numeric character code value.

Examples
```
        Private Sub Command1_Click()
        On Error Resume Next
        If IsNumeric(Text1.Text) Then
            Text2.Text = Chr(CLng(Text1.Text))
        Else
            Text2.Text = "Value is not numeric"
        End If
        If Err.Number > 0 Then
            Text2.Text = Err.Description
        End If
        End Sub
```

This routine attempts to convert the numeric value in the Text1 TextBox into its displayable character equivalent. Error checking is included to ensure that the program doesn't abort at run time.

See Also   **Asc** (function), **String** (data type), **Variant** (data type)

ChrB
FUNCTION

CCE, LE, PE, EE

Syntax   *CharValue* = **ChrB[$]**(*CharCode*)

Usage   The **ChrB** function returns a single **String** character whose numeric value is *CharCode*. The dollar sign ($) is optional and indicates that the return value is a **String** rather than a **Variant**. This function performs the inverse operation of the **AscB** function. A run-time error '5' invalid procedure call or argument will occur if the value of *CharCode* represents an illegal character.

Arguments
- *CharValue*—a **Variant** that contains the result of choosing one of the *arg* values or **Null** if *choice* is not valid. If the **AscB$** is used instead of **AscB**, *CharValue* will be a **String**.
- *CharCode*—a **Byte** value that contains the numeric character code value.

Examples
```
Private Sub Command1_Click()
On Error Resume Next
If IsNumeric(Text1.Text) Then
   Text2.Text = ChrB(CByte(Text1.Text))
   MsgBox Len(Text2.Text)
Else
   Text2.Text = "Value is not numeric"
End If
If Err.Number <> 0 Then
   Text2.Text = Err.Description
End If
End Sub
```

This routine attempts to convert the numeric value in the Text1 TextBox into its displayable character equivalent. Error checking is included to ensure that the program doesn't abort at run time.

See Also   **AscB** (function), **Byte** (data type), **String** (data type), **Variant** (data type)

ChrW
FUNCTION

CCE, LE, PE, EE

Syntax   *CharValue* = **ChrW[$]**(*CharCode*)

Usage   The **ChrW** function returns a single **String** character whose numeric value is *CharCode*. The dollar sign ($) is optional and indicates that the return value is a **String** rather than a **Variant**. This function performs the inverse operation of the **AscW** function. A run-time error '5' invalid procedure call or argument will occur if the value of *CharCode* represents an illegal character.
    Unlike the **Chr** function, the **ChrW** uses unicode characters. If the system does not support unicode characters, then this function will behave the same as the **Chr** function.

Arguments
- *CharValue*—a **Variant** that contains the result of choosing one of the *arg* values or **Null** if *choice* is not valid. If the **AscW$** is used instead of **AscW**, *CharValue* will be a **String**.
- *CharCode*—a **Long** value that contains the numeric character code value.

Examples
```
Private Sub Command1_Click()
On Error Resume Next
If IsNumeric(Text1.Text) Then
    Text2.Text = ChrW(CLng(Text1.Text))
Else
    Text2.Text = "Value is not numeric"
End If
If Err.Number > 0 Then
    Text2.Text = Err.Description
End If
End Sub
```

This routine attempts to convert the numeric value in the Text1 TextBox into its displayable character equivalent. Error checking is included to ensure that the program doesn't abort at run time.

See Also **Asc** (function), **String** (data type), **Variant** (data type)

CInt

FUNCTION

CCE, LE, PE, EE

Syntax *IValue* = **CInt** (*Value*)

Usage The **CInt** function converts a **String** or numeric value to an **Integer** value in the range -32,768 to 32,767. Any fractional values will be rounded to the nearest integer value. Any **String** value that does not contain a valid numeric value will generate a run-time error '13' type mismatch. Any value that is outside of the range of acceptable values will generate a run-time error '6' overflow.

> **Tip**
>
> To prevent run-time errors, use the **On Error** statement to prevent the error from stopping the program, and test the **Err** object to see if an error occurred. Also using the **IsNumeric** function will help to prevent conversion errors.

Arguments
- *IValue*—an integer variable that contains the result of converting *value* to an integer value.
- *Value*—a numeric or string value to be converted to an integer value.

Examples
```
Private Sub Command1_Click()
On Error Resume Next
Text2.Text = Format(CInt (Text1.Text))
If Err.Number > 0 Then
   Text2.Text = Err.Description
End If
End Sub
```

This routine converts the value in Text1.Text to an integer value and then uses the **Format** function to convert the **Integer** value into a form that can be shown in a **TextBox**. Note that I checked the **Err** object to ensure that the conversion process worked properly.

See Also **Error** (object), **Format** (function), **Integer** (data type), **IsNumeric** (function), **On Error** (statement)

Clipboard

OBJECT

CCE, LE, PE, EE

Usage The **Clipboard** object contains a set of methods to store, retrieve, and manipulate information on the Windows clipboard. The clipboard can contain multiple pieces of information, one for each available format.

> **Tip**
>
> *Since information can be stored in multiple formats, a graphic image could be stored as a device independent bitmap format, and the title of the image could be stored as a text format.*

> **Tip**
>
> *The Windows clipboard is shared among all applications. This permits you to write programs that copy text to the clipboard in one application and paste it into another application. Some controls, such as the **TextBox** control will automatically take advantage of the clipboard without any explicit code.*

Methods **Clipboard.Clear**

Usage This method clears the clipboard before a copy operation.

Object = Clipboard.GetData ([*format*])

Usage This method retrieves graphic information from the clipboard. If *format* is omitted then the method will attempt to determine the appropriate format.

Arguments
- *object*—a picture object that will hold the information from the clipboard.
- *format*—an **Integer** that contains a value selected from Table C-29 below.

format Name	Value	Description
vbCFBitmap	2	Retrieves a bitmap image from the clipboard.
vbCFMetafile	3	Retrieves a metafile from the clipboard.
vbCCFDIB	8	Retrieves a device independent bitmap from the clipboard.
vbCFPallette	9	Retrieves a color palette from the clipboard.

Table C-29: format *values.*

exists = Clipboard.GetFormat ([format])

Usage This method determines if there is information stored on the clipboard in the specified format.

Arguments
- *exists*—a **Boolean** value when **True** means that the specified information is available on the clipboard. When **False** means that the specified information is not available on the clipboard.
- *format*—an **Integer** that contains a value selected from Table C-30 below.

format Name	Value	Description
vbCFText	1	Text information is on the clipboard.
vbCFBitmap	2	A bitmap image is on the clipboard.
vbCFMetafile	3	A metafile is on the clipboard.
vbCCFDIB	8	A device independent bitmap is on the clipboard.
vbCFPallette	9	A color palette is on the clipboard.
vbCFEMetafile	14	An enhanced metafile is on the clipboard.
vbCFLink	&HFFFFBF00	DDE conversion information is on the clipboard.
vbCFRTF	&HFFFFBF01	A Rich Text File document is on the clipboard.

Table C-30: format *values.*

object = Clipboard.GetText ([format])

Usage This method retrieves text formatted information from the clipboard.

Arguments
- *object*—a **String** that contains the information from the clipboard.
- *format*—an **Integer** that contains a value selected from Table C-31 below.

format Name	Value	Description
vbCFText	1	Retrieves text from the clipboard.
vbCFLink	&HFFFFBF00	Retrieves DDE conversion information from the clipboard.
vbCFRTF	&HFFFFBF01	Retrieves a Rich Text File document from the clipboard.

Table C-31: format *values.*

Clipboard.SetData (data [, format])

Usage This method stores graphic information onto the clipboard. If *format* is omitted then the method will attempt to determine the appropriate format.

Tip

The value for data *can come from either the* **LoadPicture** *function, or the* **Picture** *property of the* **Form**, **Image**, *or a* **PictureBox** *control.*

Arguments
- *data*—a picture object that will hold the information from the clipboard.
- *format*—an **Integer** that contains a value selected from Table C-32 below. This argument is optional and if omitted, the value will be determined from the type of graphic image in *data*.

format Name	Value	Description
vbCFBitmap	2	Retrieves a bitmap image from the clipboard.
vbCFMetafile	3	Retrieves a metafile from the clipboard.
vbCCFDIB	8	Retrieves a device independent bitmap from the clipboard.
vbCFPallette	9	Retrieves a color palette from the clipboard.

Table C-32: format *values.*

Clipboard.SetText (*data* [, *format*])

Usage This method retrieves text formatted information from the clipboard.

Tip

The value for data *can come from many different places, but most likely you will want to copy the data from either a* **RichTextBox** *or a* **TextBox** *control.*

Arguments
- *data*—a **String** that contains the information from the clipboard.
- *format*—an **Integer** that contains a value selected from Table C-33 below. This argument is optional and will default to *vbCFText*.

format Name	Value	Description
vbCFText	1	Retrieves text from the clipboard.
vbCFLink	&HFFFFBF00	Retrieves DDE conversion information from the clipboard.
vbCFRTF	&HFFFFBF01	Retrieves a Rich Text File document from the clipboard.

Table C-33: format *values.*

Examples
```
Private Sub Command1_Click()
If Clipboard.GetFormat(vbCFText) Then
    Text1.Text = Clipboard.GetText(vbCFText)
Else
    Text1.Text = " There is no text on the clipboard."
End If
End Sub
```

This routine checks to see if there is text information available on the clipboard, and if there is text information, it will display it.

See Also **Form** (control), **Image** (control), **LoadPicture** (function), **PictureBox** (control), **RichTextBox** (control), **TextBox** (control)

CLng

FUNCTION

CCE, LE, PE, EE

Syntax *LValue* = **CLng** (*Value*)

Usage The **CLng** function converts a **String** or numeric value to a **Long** value in the range -2,147,483,648 to 2,147,483,647. Any **String** value that does not contain a valid numeric value will generate a run-time error '13' type mismatch. Any value that is outside of the range of acceptable values will generate a run-time error '6' overflow. Values to the right of the decimal point will be rounded to the nearest whole number.

> **Tip**
>
> *To prevent run-time errors, use the **On Error** statement to prevent the error from stopping the program, and test the **Err** object to see if an error occurred. Also using the **IsNumeric** function will help to prevent conversion errors.*

Arguments
- *LValue*—a **Long** variable that contains the result of converting *value* to a **Long** value.
- *Value*—a numeric or string value to be converted to a **Long** value.

Examples
```
Private Sub Command1_Click()
On Error Resume Next
Text2.Text = Format(CLng (Text1.Text))
If Err.Number > 0 Then
    Text2.Text = Err.Description
End If
End Sub
```

This routine converts the value in Text1.Text to a **Long** value and then uses the **Format** function to convert the **Long** value into a form that can be shown in a **TextBox**. Note that I checked the **Err** object to ensure that the conversion process worked properly.

See Also **Error** (object), **Format** (function), **IsNumeric** (function), **Long** (data type), **On Error** (statement)

Close

STATEMENT

CCE, LE, PE, EE

Syntax Close [[#] *file* [, [#] *file* [, . . . [#] *file*]]]

Usage The **Close** statement performs the cleanup work necessary when a file is no longer needed. This includes writing buffers to disk (when the file was originally opened in output or append mode), deallocating buffers, and so on. If no arguments are included with the **Close** statement, then all open files will be closed. This is similar to the **Reset** statement.

> **Tip**
>
> *You should always close a file when you are finished with it. Otherwise the contents of the file may be in an unpredictable state if the program crashes. Executing an **End** statement will always close any open files before it stops the program.*

Arguments
- *file*—an **Integer** expression that contains the file number that was used in the **Open** statement.

Examples
```
Private Sub Command1_Click()
Dim s As String
On Error Resume Next
Text2.Text = ""
Open Text1.Text For Input As #1
If Err.Number <> 0 Then
    MsgBox "Can't open the input file: " & Err.Description
Else
    Do While Not EOF(1)
        Input #1, s
        Text2.Text = Text2.Text & s & vbCrLf
    Loop
    Close #1
End If
End Sub
```

This routine opens the file specified in Text1.Text, displays the contents in Text2.Text, and then closes the file.

See Also **End** (statement), **Open** (statement), **Reset** (statement)

Collection

OBJECT

CCE, LE, PE, EE

Usage The **Collection** object contains a set of methods to store and retrieve items in a set. The items need not be of the same data type. Items can be retrieved by specifying their relative position within the collection or by a unique key value.

Tip

*To loop through each item in the collection, use the **For Each** statement.*

Tip

*If you examine some other Visual Basic controls such as **TreeView**, you will see extensive use of the **Collection** object.*

Properties
- *CollectionObject*.**Count**—a **Long** value that contains the number of items in the collection.

Methods

CollectionObject.**Add** *item, key,* [*before* | , *after*]

Usage This method adds an item to the collection specified by *CollectionObject*.

Arguments
- *item*—an expression that contains an object to be added to the collection.
- *key*—a **String** that contains a unique value that can be used to reference the value of *item*.
- *before*—either a numeric value that represents the relative position or a **String** value that contains a key value of the object that will immediately precede this object in the collection. This argument cannot be used if a value for *after* is specified.
- *after*—either a numeric value that represents the relative position or a **String** value that contains a key value of the object that will immediately follow this object in the collection. This argument cannot be used if a value for *before* is specified.

CollectionObject.**Clear**

Usage This method removes all of the objects in the collection.

Item = *CollectionObject*.**Item** (*index*)

Usage This method retrieves an item specified by *index* from the collection specified by *CollectionObject*. This is the default method for this object, so the method name **Item** can be omitted.

Arguments
- *item*—a variable that will contain the object from the collection.
- *index*—either a numeric value that represents the relative position or a **String** value that contains a key value of the object to be retrieved from the collection.

CollectionObject.**Remove** *index*

Usage   This method deletes an item specified by *index* from the collection specified by *CollectionObject*.

Arguments   *index*—either a numeric value that represents the relative position or a **String** value that contains a key value of the object to be deleted from the collection.

Examples
```
Dim TheCollection As New Collection

Private Sub Command1_Click()
TheCollection.Add Text2.Text, Text1.Text
End Sub

Private Sub Command2_Click()
Dim o
Text3.Text = ""
For Each o In TheCollection
    Text3.Text = Text3.Text & o.Item & vbCrLf
Next
End Sub
```

This program declares a variable as **New Collection** to create a new collection object. Then it uses a command button to add new objects to the collection. Finally another command button displays the contents of the collection using the **For Each** statement.

See Also   **For Each** (statement), **TreeView** (control)

Column

OBJECT

CCE, LE, PE, EE

Usage   The **Column** object contains a set of properties and methods that describe a column of items in the **DBGrid** control.

Properties   *ColumnObject*.**Alignment**—an **Integer** value (see Table C-34) containing how a particular column of information is arranged.

Alignment Name	Value	Description
dbgLeft	0	The data in the column is left justified (default).
dbgRight	1	The data in the column is right justified.
dbgCenter	2	The data in the column is centered.
dbgGeneral	3	The data in the column is left aligned when it contains text and right aligned when it contains numbers.

Table C-34: Alignment *values*.

- *ColumnObject*.**AllowSizing**—a **Boolean** value when **True** means the user will be allowed resize the column. **False** means the user will not be allowed to resize the column (default).
- *ColumnObject*.**Button**—a **Boolean** value when **True** a button will be displayed in the current call. **False** means the user will not be allowed to resize the column (default). When the user clicks on the button the **ButtonClick** event will be triggered.
- *ColumnObject*.**Caption**—a **String** value containing the text that will be displayed in the column's heading.
- *ColumnObject*.**ColIndex**—an **Integer** value containing the relative position of the column in the collection.
- *ColumnObject*.**DataChanged**—a **Boolean** that applies only to data bound controls. When **True**, means that the data contained in this control was changed either by the user or by some means other than retrieving data from the current record. **False** means the data in the control is unchanged from the current record.

  Simply reading the next record is not sufficient to set the **DataChanged** property to **True**. When the **Data** control moves to the next record, it will automatically invoke the **Edit** and **Update** methods to post the changes to the database.
- *ColumnObject*.**DataField**—a **String** value that associates the control with a field in a **RecordSet** object in a **Data** control.
- *ColumnObject*.**DefaultValue**—a **Variant** value containing the default value for the **Column** object in an unbound **DBGrid**.
- *ColumnObject*.**DividerStyle**—an **Integer** value (see Table C-35) describing the border that will be drawn on the right edge of the column.

DividerStyle Name	Value	Description
dbgNoDividers	0	No divider is used.
dbgBlackLine	1	A black line is used.
dbgDarkGrayLine	2	A dark gray line is used.
dbgRaised	3	A raised line is used.
dbgInset	4	An inset line is used.
dbgUserForeColor	5	The line using the **ForeColor** property is used.
dbgLightGrayLine	6	A light gray line is used.

Table C-35: DividerStyle *values*.

- *ColumnObject*.**Left**—a **Single** that contains the distance, measured in twips between the left edge of the column and the left edge of the grid.
- *ColumnObject*.**Locked**—a **Boolean** when **True** means that the user can't enter or change any values in the column. **False** means that information in the column can be updated.
- *ColumnObject*.**NumberFormat**—a **String** containing the information about how to format a value in a cell. The formats are the same as used with the **Format** function.
- *ColumnHeader*.**Text**—a **String** value containing the text that will be displayed in the current row.
- *ColumnObject*.**Top**—a **Single** value containing the distance between the top edge of the **ListView** control and the top edge of the column. This property is read only at run time.
- *ColumnObject*.**Value**—a **Variant** value containing the underlying data value for the current row.

- *ColumnObject*.**Visible**—a **Boolean** value when **True** means that the column is visible. **False** means that the column is not visible.
- *ColumnObject*.**Width**—a **Single** that contains the width of the column.
- *ColumnObject*.**WrapText**—a **Boolean** value when **True** means that the text will be wrapped to the next line at a word boundary before the cell's edge. **False** means that the text will be truncated at the end of the cell's edge.

Methods

text = ColumnObject.CellText (bookmark)

Usage   This method returns a value similar to the **Text** property, but for the specified row.

Arguments
- *text*—a **String** containing the text that will be displayed in the specified row.
- *bookmark*—a **Variant** specifying the bookmark for the desired row.

value = ColumnObject.CellValue (bookmark)

Usage   This method returns a value similar to the **Text** property, but for the specified row.

Arguments
- *value*—a **Variant** containing the underlying value for the specified row.
- *bookmark*—a **Variant** specifying the bookmark for the desired row.

See Also   **Columns** (collection), **DBGrid** (control)

Column Header

OBJECT

CCE, LE, PE, EE

Usage   The **Column Header** object contains a set of properties that describe a column of items in the **ListView** object. The column header object is only available when the **ListView** is displaying items in the Report mode.

Properties
- *ColumnHeaderObject*.**Alignment**—an **Integer** value (see Table C-36) containing how a particular column of information is arranged.

Alignment Name	Value	Description
lvwColumnLeft	0	The information in the column is left justified (default).
lvwColumnRight	1	The information in the column is right justified.
lvwColumnCenter	2	The information in the column is centered.

Table C-36: Alignment *values.*

- *ColumnHeaderObject*.**Index**—an **Long** value containing the relative position of the column header in the column headers collection. This property is read only at run time.

- *ColumnHeader*.**Key**—a **String** value containing a unique value that can be used to identify a particular column in the column headers collection.
- *ColumnHeader*.**Left**—a **Single** value containing the distance between the left edge of the **ListView** control and the left edge of the column. This property is read only at run time.
- *ColumnHeader*.**SubItemIndex**—an **Integer** value that can be used by the **ListItem** object to add information to the proper column.
- *ColumnHeader*.**Tag**—a **String** that can hold programmer specific information. This property is not used by Visual Basic.
- *ColumnHeader*.**Text**—a **String** value containing title information that will be displayed in the column header.
- *ColumnHeader*.**Top**—a **Single** value containing the distance between the top edge of the **ListView** control and the top edge of the column. This property is read only at run time.
- *ColumnHeader*.**Width**—a **Single** value containing the width of the column.

Examples
```
Private Sub Form_Load()
ListView1.View = lvwReport
ListView1.ColumnHeaders.Add , "name", "Name"
ListView1.ColumnHeaders("name").Width = 2000
ListView1.ColumnHeaders.Add , "nick", "Nickname"
ListView1.ColumnHeaders("nick").Width = 2000
ListView1.ColumnHeaders.Add , "email", "E-Mail"
ListView1.ColumnHeaders("email").Width = 2000
End Sub
```

This routine selects the report view format for the ListView1 control and then adds three columns, Name, Nickname, and E-Mail address. It also sets the width of each column to 2000 twips.

See Also   **Column Headers** (collection), **ListItem** (object), **ListItems** (collection) **ListView** (control)

Column Headers

COLLECTION

CCE, LE, PE, EE

Usage   The **Column Headers** collection contains a set of methods to store and retrieve information about the column headers in a **ListView** control.

Properties   *ColumnHeaders*.**Count**—a **Long** value that contains the number of items in the collection.

Methods   *ColumnHeaderObject* = *ColumnHeaders*.**Add** ([*index*] , [*key*] , [*text*] , [*width*] , [*alignment*])

Usage   This method adds an item to the collection specified by *ColumnHeaders*.

Arguments
- *ColumnHeaderObject*—a reference to the **Column Header** object created by this method.
  - *index*—an **Integer** that uniquely identifies the column header being added.

- *key*—a **String** that contains a unique value that can be used to reference the value of the column header.
- *text*—a **String** value that will be displayed as the title of the column.
- *width*—a **Single** value containing the width of the column.
- *alignment*—an **Integer** value (see Table C-37) that determines how to arrange a particular column of information.

Alignment Name	Value	Description
lvwColumnLeft	0	The information in the column is left justified (default).
lvwColumnRight	1	The information in the column is right justified.
lvwColumnCenter	2	The information in the column is centered.

Table C-37: Alignment *values*.

ColumnHeaders.Clear

Usage This method removes all of the column headers in the column headers collection.

Item = ColumnHeaders.Item (index)

Usage This method retrieves an item specified by *index* from the column headers collection. This is the default method for this object, so the method name **Item** can be omitted.

Arguments
- *item*—a variable that will contain the object from the collection.
- *index*—either a numeric value that represents the relative position or a **String** value that contains a key value of the object to be retrieved from the column headers collection.

ColumnHeaders.Remove index

Usage This method deletes an item specified by *index* from the column headers.

Arguments
- *index*—either a numeric value that represents the relative position or a **String** value that contains a key value of the object to be deleted from the collection.

Examples
```
Private Sub Form_Load()
ListView1.View = lvwReport
ListView1.ColumnHeaders.Add , "name", "Name"
ListView1.ColumnHeaders("name").Width = 2000
ListView1.ColumnHeaders.Add , "nick", "Nickname"
ListView1.ColumnHeaders("nick").Width = 2000
ListView1.ColumnHeaders.Add , "email", "E-Mail"
ListView1.ColumnHeaders("email").Width = 2000
End Sub
```

This routine selects the report view format for the ListView1 control and then adds three columns, Name, Nickname, and E-Mail address. It also sets the width of each column to 2000 twips.

See Also **Column Header** (object), **ListItem** (object), **ListItems** (collection), **ListView** (control)

Columns

COLLECTION

PE, EE

Usage The **Columns** collection contains the set of **Column** objects in the **DBGrid** control.

Properties *ColumnsCollection*.**Count**—an **Integer** containing the number of **Column** objects in the collection.

Methods

column = ColumnsCollection.Add index

Usage This method adds a new **Column** to the collection.

Arguments *column*—a reference to the new **Column** object.
index—an **Integer** containing where the **Column** is to be added to the collection.

Tip

*Use the **Count** property to add a new **Column** object to the end of the collection.*

column = ColumnsCollection.Item (index)

Usage This method returns a **Column** object.

Arguments *column*—a reference to a **Column** object.
index—an **Integer** containing the index value of the desired **Column**.

Tip

*The first element of the collection is zero, while the last element is **Count** -1.*

ColumnsCollection.Remove index

Usage This method removes the specified object from the collection.

Arguments *index*—an **Integer** value specifying the item to be removed from the collection.

See Also **Column** (object), **DBGrid** (object)

ComboBox

CONTROL

CCE, LE, PE, EE

Usage The **ComboBox** control is an intrinsic control that combines the functions of the **TextBox** control and the **ListBox** control. Data can be entered into the text area of the combo box, or it can be selected from the drop-down list.

Properties
- *ComboBoxControl*.**Appearance**—an **Integer** value (see Table C-38) that determines how the combo box will appear on the form.

AppearanceValue	Description
0	The combo box is displayed without the 3D effects.
1	The combo box is displayed with 3D effects (default value).

Table C-38: **Appearance** *values.*

- *ComboBoxControl*.**BackColor**—a **Long** that contains the suggested value for the background color of the control. The **BackColor** and **ForeColor** must both be solid to display text. If you choose a color that is dithered, it will be changed to the nearest solid color.
- *ComboBoxControl*.**Container**—an object that can be used to set or return the container of the control at run time. This property cannot be set at design time.
- *ComboBoxControl*.**DataChanged**—a **Boolean** that applies only to data bound controls. When **True**, it means that the data contained in this control was changed either by the user or by some means other than retrieving data from the current record. When **False**, it means the data in the control is unchanged from the current record. Simply reading the next record is not sufficient to set the **DataChanged** property to **True**.
  When the **Data** control moves to the next record, it will automatically invoke the **Edit** and **Update** methods to post the changes to the database.
- *ComboBoxControl*.**DataField**—a **String** value that associates the control with a field in a **RecordSet** object in a **Data** control.
- *ComboBoxControl*.**DragIcon**—an object that contains the picture value of an icon. At design time, you can specify an icon file that has a file type of .ICO.

Tip

This value can be created by copying the value from another control's **DragIcon** *value, a form's icon, or by using the* **LoadPicture** *function.*

- *ComboBoxControl*.**DragMode**—an **Integer** value (see Table C-39) specifying how the control will respond to a drag request.

Tip

Setting **DragMode** *to vbAutomatic will automatically begin a drag operation when the user clicks on the control. However, the control will not respond to the usual mouse events (***Click***,* **DblClick***).*

DragMode Name	Value	Description
vbManual	0	The Drag method must be used to begin a drag drop operation (default value).
vbAutomatic	1	The source control will automatically begin a drag drop operation when the user clicks on the control.

Table C-39: **DragMode** *values.*

- *ComboBoxControl.***Enabled**—a **Boolean** value when **True** means that the control will respond to events. When **False**, the control will not respond to events.
- *ComboBoxControl.***Font**—an object that contains information about the character font used by this object.

Tip

The **Font** *object should be used in place of the other* **Font** *properties, since it offers more functionality than the individual properties.*

- *ComboBoxControl.***FontBold**—a **Boolean** when **True**, means that the characters display in bold. **False** means that the characters display normally.
- *ComboBoxControl.***FontItalic**—a **Boolean** when **True**, means that the characters display in italics. **False** means that the characters display normally.
- *ComboBoxControl.***FontName**—a **String** that specifies the name of the font that should be used to display the characters in this control.
- *ComboBoxControl.***FontSize**—a **Single** that specifies the point size that should be used to display the characters in the control.
- *ComboBoxControl.***FontStrikethru**—a **Boolean** when **True**, means that the characters display with a line through the center. **False** means that the characters display normally.
- *ComboBoxControl.***FontUnderlined**—a **Boolean** when **True**, means that the characters display with a line beneath them. **False** means that the characters display normally.
- *ComboBoxControl.***ForeColor**—a **Long** that contains the suggested value for the foreground color of the contained control. This property is read only at run time.
- *ComboBoxControl.***Height**—a **Single** that contains the height of the control.
- *ComboBoxControl.***HelpContextID**—a **Long** that contains a help file context ID number which references an entry in the help file. When the user presses the F1 key while this control is active, the corresponding entry in the help file will automatically be displayed. A value of zero means that no context number was specified.

Tip

A help file must be compiled using the Windows Help Compiler available in the Professional and Enterprise editions of Visual Basic.

- *ComboBoxControl*.**hWnd**—a **Long** that contains a Windows handle to the control.

> **Tip**
>
> The **hWnd** property is most useful when making calls to Windows API functions. Since this value can change during execution, do not save the value into a variable for later use.

- *ComboBoxControl*.**Index**—an **Integer** that uniquely identifies a control in a control array.
- *ComboBoxControl*.**IntegralHeight**—a **Boolean** value when **True** means that the drop-down list will resize itself so that it will only show complete items. When **False** the drop-down list will show partial items.
- *ComboBoxControl*.**ItemData**(*index*)—an array of **Long** values where each value pointed to by *index* corresponds to an entry in an array of strings in the **List** property. The first element in this array has an index value of zero.
- *ComboBoxControl*.**Left**—a **Single** that contains the distance measured in twips between the left edge of the control and the left edge of the control's container.
- *ComboBoxControl*.**List**(*index*)—an array of **String** values displayed in the drop-down part of the **ComboBox**. The number of elements in this array can be found in the **ListCount** property.

> **Tip**
>
> The first element of the **List** array is zero, while the last array element is **ListCount** -1.

- *ComboBoxControl*.**ListCount**—an **Integer** value containing the number of elements in the **List**.
- *ComboBoxControl*.**ListIndex**—an **Integer** value containing the index of the selected item from the drop-down box. If no value was selected, **ListIndex** will be set to -1.
- *ComboBoxControl*.**Locked**—a **Boolean** value when **True** means that the user can't type a value in the text box part of the control. When **False**, the user can type a value into the text box part of the control.
- *ComboBoxControl*.**MouseIcon**—a picture object (a bitmap, icon, or metafile) that will be used as a cursor when the **MousePointer** property is set to 99. Note that Visual Basic does not support color cursors from a .CUR file. A color icon from a .ICO file should be used instead.
- *ComboBoxControl*.**MousePointer**—an **Integer** value (see Table C-40) that contains the value of the cursor that should be displayed when the cursor is moved over this control. Use *vbCustom* to display the custom icon stored in the **MouseIcon** property.

Cursor Name	Value	Description
vbDefault	0	Shape determined by the object (default value)
vbArrow	1	Arrow
vbCrosshair	2	Crosshair
vbIbeam	3	I beam
vbIconPointer	4	Square inside a square
vbSizePointer	5	Four sided arrow (north, south, east, west)
vbSizeNESW	6	Two sided arrow (northeast, southwest)

ComboBox

Cursor Name	Value	Description
vbSizeNS	7	Two sided arrow (north, south)
vbSizeNWSE	8	Two sided arrow (northwest, southeast)
vbSizeWE	9	Two sided arrow (west, east)
vbUpArrow	10	Single sided arrow pointing north
vbHourglass	11	Hourglass
vbNoDrop	12	No Drop
vbArrowHourglass	13	An arrow and an Hourglass
vbArrowQuestion	14	An arrow and a question mark
vbSizeAll	15	Size all
vbCustom	99	Custom icon from the **MouseIcon** property of this control

Table C-40: **Cursor** values.

- *ComboBoxControl*.**Name**—a **String** that contains the name of the control that will be used to reference the control in a Visual Basic program. This property is read only at run time.
- *ComboBoxControl*.**NewIndex**—an **Integer** value corresponding to the index of the last item added to the control. This property will have a value of -1 if there are no items in **List** or the most recent action was to delete an item from **List**.
- *ComboBoxControl*.**OLEDragMode**—an **Integer** value (see Table C-41) that describes how the control will respond to OLE drag operations.

Note

*When the **DragMode** is **True**, the standard Visual Basic drag-and-drop functions will override the OLE drag-and-drop functions.*

OLEDragMode Name	Value	Description
vbOLEDragManual	0	All drag requests will be handled by the programmer (default value).
vbOLEDragAutomatic	1	The control responds to all OLE drag request automatically.

Table C-41: **OLEDragMode** values.

- *ComboBoxControl*.**OLEDropMode**—an **Integer** value (see Table C-42) that describes how the control will respond to OLE drop operations.

OLEDropMode Name	Value	Description
vbOLEDropNone	0	The control does not accept OLE drops. The cursor is changed to the No Drop cursor (default value).
vbOLEDropManual	1	The control responds to OLE drops under the program's control (manual).
vbOLEDropAutomatic	2	The control automatically accepts OLE drops if it recognizes the format of the data object.

Table C-42: **OLEDropMode** values.

- *ComboBoxControl*.**Parent**—an object that contains a reference to the **Form**, **Frame,** or other container that contains the **ComboBox** control.
- *ComboBoxControl*.**RightToLeft**—a **Boolean** value when **True** means that the text is displayed from right to left. When **False** means that the text is displayed from left to right. A bi-directional version of Windows is required to set this property to **True**.
- *ComboBoxControl*.**SelLength**—a **Long** value containing the number of characters selected from the text box part of the control.
- *ComboBoxControl*.**SelStart**—a **Long** value containing the starting position of the selected text in the text box part of the control.
- *ComboBoxControl*.**SelText**—a **String** value containing the selected text.

Tip

*The **SelLength**, **SelStart**, **SelText** properties work together to allow a programmer to insert or delete text. Setting **SelLength** to zero, specifying a value for **SelStart**, and then assigning a value to **SelText** will insert the new text into the text box. Assigning an empty string to **SelText** will delete the marked text.*

- *ComboBoxControl*.**Sorted**—a **Boolean** value when **True** means that the contents of the **List** property will be automatically sorted as new objects are added. When **False**, the contents are not automatically sorted.

Note

*Using the **AddItem** method while specifying a value for the index will override the automatic sort and may leave the contents of **List** in the wrong order.*

- *ComboBoxControl*.**Style**—an **Integer** value (see Table C-43) that contains the style used to display the control.

Style Name	Value	Description
vbComboDropDown	0	The control contains a text box where the user can type and a drop-down box where the user can select a value (default value).
vbComboSimple	1	The control contains a text box where the user can type and a list that doesn't drop down.
vbComboDropDownList	2	The control only allows the user to select a value from the drop-down list.

Table C-43: Style *Values.*

- *ComboBoxControl*.**TabIndex**—an **Integer** that determines the order that a user will tab through the objects on a form.
- *ComboBoxControl*.**TabStop**—a **Boolean** value when **True** means that the user can tab to this object. When **False**, it means that this control will be skipped to the next control in the **TabIndex** order.

- *ComboBoxControl*.**Tag**—a **String** that can hold programmer specific information. This property is not used by Visual Basic.
- *ComboBoxControl*.**Text**—a **String** that sets or returns the value from the text box part of the control.
- *ComboBoxControl*.**ToolTipText**—a **String** that holds a text value that can be displayed as a **ToolTip** box that is displayed whenever the cursor is held over the control for about one second.
- *ComboBoxControl*.**Top**—a **Single** that contains the distance measured in twips between the top edge of the control and the top edge of the control's container.
- *ComboBoxControl*.**TopIndex**—an **Integer** that sets or returns the first value displayed in the drop-down window. The default value is zero.
- *ComboBoxControl*.**Visible**—a **Boolean** value when **True** means that the control is visible. When **False** means that the control is not visible.

Tip

This property can hide the control until the program is ready to display it.

- *ComboBoxControl*.**WhatsThisHelpID**—a **Long** that contains a help file context ID number which references an entry in the help file. This provides a What's This PopUp help display in response to the What's This button in the upper right corner of the window.
- *ComboBoxControl*.**Width**—a **Single** that contains the width of the control.

Methods

ComboBoxControl.AddItem *item* [, *index*]

Usage This method inserts a new value into a **ComboBox**.

Warning

This method will not work if the control is bound to a **Data** *control.*

Arguments
- *item*—a **String** that contains the value to be added to the drop-down list.
- *index*—an **Integer** that specifies the position in the drop-down list where the item will be added. This value must be in the range of zero to **ListCount**, where zero is the first item in the list and **ListCount** will add the item to the end of the list. If omitted, the item will be added to the end of the list.

Note

Specifying a value for index, while the **Sorted** *property is set to* **True**, *may cause unpredictable results.*

ComboBoxControl.Clear

Usage This method clears all of the items in the drop-down list.

ComboBoxControl.Drag [DragAction]

Usage This method begins, ends, or cancels a drag operation.

Arguments ▪ *DragAction*—an **Integer** that contains a value selected from Table C-44 below.

DragAction Name	Value	Description
vbCancel	0	Cancels any drag operation in progress.
vbBeginDrag	1	Begins a drag operation (default).
vbEndDrag	2	Ends a drag operation and drops *object*.

Table C-44: DragAction *values.*

ComboBoxControl.Move Left [, Top [, Width [, Height]]]

Usage This method changes the position and the size of the **ComboBox** control. The **ScaleMode** of the **Form** or other container object that holds the **ComboBox** control will determine the units used to specify the coordinates.

Arguments ▪ *Left*—a **Single** that specifies the new position of the left edge of the control.
▪ *Top*—a **Single** that specifies the new position of the top edge of the control.
▪ *Width*—a **Single** that specifies the new width of the control.
▪ *Height*—a **Single** that specifies the new height of the control.

ComboBoxControl.OLEDrag

Usage This method begins an **OLEDrag** and drop operation. Invoking this method will trigger the **OLEStartDrag** event.

ComboBoxControl.Refresh

Usage This method redraws the contents of the control.

ComboBoxControl.RemoveItem *index*

Usage This method removes an item from a **ComboBox**.

Tip
This method will not work if the control is bound to a **Data** *control.*

Arguments ▪ *index*—an **Integer** that specifies the item in the drop-down list that will be deleted. This value must be in the range of zero to **ListCount -1**, where zero is the first item in the list and **ListCount** -1 is the last item in the list.

ComboBoxControl.SetFocus

Usage This method transfers the focus from the form or control that currently has the focus to this control. To receive the focus, this control must be enabled and visible.

ComboBoxControl.ShowWhatsThis

Usage This method displays the ShowWhatsThis help information for this control.

ComboBoxControl.ZOrder [*position*]

Usage This method specifies the position of the **ComboBox** control relative to the other objects on the form.

> **Tip**
>
> *Note that there are three layers of objects on a form: the back layer is the drawing space which contains the results of the graphical methods, the middle layer contains graphical objects and **Labels**, and the top layer contains nongraphical controls such as the **CommandButton**. The **ZOrder** method only affects how the objects are arranged within a single layer.*

Arguments • *position*—an **Integer** that specifies the relative position of this object. A value of 0 means that the control is positioned at the head of the list, a value of 1 means that the control will be placed at the end of the list.

Events

Private Sub ComboBoxControl_Change([*index* As Integer])

Usage This event occurs when the text in the text box part of the control is changed. This event will only happen when the **Style** property is set to *vbComboDropDown* or *vbComboSimple*.

Arguments • *index*—an **Integer** that uniquely identifies a control in a control array. This argument is not present if the control is not part of a control array.

Private Sub ComboBoxControl_Click([*index* As Integer])

Usage This event occurs when the user clicks a mouse button to select an item in the drop-down list or selects an item from the drop-down list using the keyboard.

Arguments • *index*—an **Integer** that uniquely identifies a control in a control array. This argument is not present if the control is not part of a control array.

Private Sub ComboBoxControl_DblClick([*index* As Integer])

Usage   This event occurs when the user double clicks a mouse button to select an item in the drop-down list or selects an item from the drop-down list using the keyboard. This applies only when **Style** is set to *vbComboSimple*.

Arguments   • *index*—an **Integer** that uniquely identifies a control in a control array. This argument is not present if the control is not part of a control array.

Private Sub ComboBoxControl_DragDrop([*index* As Integer ,] *source* As Control, *x* As Single, *y* As Single)

Usage   This event occurs when a drag-and-drop operation is completed by using the **Drag** method with an *DragAction* value of *vbEndDrag*.

> **Tip**
>
> *When using drag-and-drop operations, use the **DragOver** event to determine what the cursor should look like while the cursor moves over the control.*

Arguments   • *index*—an **Integer** that uniquely identifies a control in a control array. This argument is not present if the control is not part of a control array.
• *source*—a control object that is the control that is being dragged.

> **Tip**
>
> *You can access a property or method from the source control by using* source.property *or* source.method. *You can determine the type of object or control by using the **TypeOf** operator.*

• *x*—a **Single** that contains the horizontal location of the mouse pointer.
• *y*—a **Single** that contains the vertical location of the mouse pointer.

Private Sub ComboBoxControl_DragOver([*index* As Integer ,] *source* As Control, *x* As Single, *y* As Single, *state* As Integer)

Usage   This event occurs while a drag operation is in progress and the cursor is moved over the control.

> **Tip**
>
> *When using drag-and-drop operations, use the **DragOver** event to determine what the cursor should look like while the cursor moves over the control. When* state *is 0, you can change the cursor to a No Drop (vbNoDrop) cursor or highlight the field that the cursor is near. When* state *is 1, you can undo the changes you made when the* state *was 0.*

ComboBox

Arguments
- *index*—an **Integer** that uniquely identifies a control in a control array. This argument is not present if the control is not part of a control array.
- *source*—a control object that is the control that is being dragged.

Tip
You can access a property or method from the source control by using **source**.*property or* **source**.*method. You can determine the type of object or control by using the* **TypeOf** *operator.*

- *x*—a **Single** that contains the horizontal location of the mouse pointer.
- *y*—a **Single** that contains the vertical location of the mouse pointer.
- *state*—an **Integer** value (see Table C-45) that indicates the state of the object being dragged.

state Name	Value	Description
vbEnter	0	The dragged object is entering range of the control.
vbLeave	1	The dragged object is leaving range of the control.
vbOver	2	The dragged object has moved from one position over the control to another.

Table C-45: state *values.*

Private Sub *ComboBoxControl*_GotFocus ([*index* As Integer])

Usage This event occurs when the control is given focus.

Tip
You can use this routine to display help or other information in a status bar.

Arguments
- *index*—an **Integer** that uniquely identifies a control in a control array. This argument is not present if the control is not part of a control array.

Private Sub *ComboBoxControl*_KeyDown ([*index* As Integer ,] *keycode* As Integer, *shift* As Single)

Usage This event occurs when a key is pressed while the control has the focus.

Arguments
- *index*—an **Integer** that uniquely identifies a control in a control array. This argument is not present if the control is not part of a control array.
- *keycode*—an **Integer** that contains information about which key was pressed.

- *shift*—an **Integer** value (see Table C-46) that contains information about the Shift and Alt keys that were pushed when the mouse button was pressed. These values can be added together if more than one key was down. For instance, a value of 5 would mean that the Shift and Alt keys were both down when the mouse button was pressed.

shift Name	Value	Description
vbShiftMask	1	The Shift key was pressed.
vbCtrlMask	2	The Ctrl key was pressed.
vbAltMask	4	The Alt key was pressed.

Table C-46: shift *values.*

Private Sub *ComboBoxControl*_KeyPress([*index* As Integer ,] *keychar* As Integer)

Usage This event occurs whenever a key is pressed while the control has the focus.

Arguments
- *index*—an **Integer** that uniquely identifies a control in a control array. This argument is not present if the control is not part of a control array.
- *keychar*—an **Integer** that contains the ASCII character that was pressed.

Private Sub *ComboBoxControl*_KeyUp ([*index* As Integer ,] *keycode* As Integer, *shift* As Single)

Usage This event occurs when a key is released while the control has the focus.

Arguments
- *index*—an **Integer** that uniquely identifies a control in a control array. This argument is not present if the control is not part of a control array.
- *keycode*—an **Integer** that contains information about which key was released.
- *shift*—an **Integer** value (see Table C-47) that contains information about the Shift and Alt keys that were pushed when the mouse button was pressed. These values can be added together if more than one key was down. For instance, a value of 5 would mean that the Shift and Alt keys were both down when the mouse button was pressed.

shift Name	Value	Description
vbShiftMask	1	The Shift key was pressed.
vbCtrlMask	2	The Ctrl key was pressed.
vbAltMask	4	The Alt key was pressed.

Table C-47: shift *values.*

Private Sub *ComboBoxControl*_LostFocus ([*index* As Integer])

Usage   This event occurs when the control loses focus.

Tip

This routine is useful to performing data verification.

Arguments
- *index*—an **Integer** that uniquely identifies a control in a control array. This argument is not present if the control is not part of a control array.

Private Sub *ComboBoxControl*_OLECompleteDrag([*index* As Integer ,] *effect* As Long)

Usage   This event tells the source control the results of an OLE drag-and-drop operation. This is the final event to occur in the series of actions that make up an OLE drag-and-drop operation.

Arguments
- *index*—an **Integer** that uniquely identifies a control in a control array. This argument is not present if the control is not part of a control array.
- *effect*—a **Long** (see Table C-48) that returns the status of the OLE drag-and-drop operation.

effect Name	Value	Description
vbDropEffectNone	0	The operation was canceled or the target control can't accept the drop operation.
vbDropEffectCopy	1	The operation copied data from the source control to the target control. The original data is unchanged.
vbDropEffectMove	2	The operation results in a link from the original data to the target control.

Table C-48: effect *values*.

Private Sub *ComboBoxControl*_OLEDragDrop([*index* As Integer ,] *data* As DataObject, *effect* As Long, *button* As Integer, *shift* As Single, *x* As Single, *y* As Single)

Usage   This event tells the source control the results of an OLE drag-and-drop operation. This is the final event to occur in the series of actions that make up an OLE drag-and-drop operation.

Arguments
- *index*—an **Integer** that uniquely identifies a control in a control array. This argument is not present if the control is not part of a control array.

- *data*—a **DataObject** that contains the formats that the source control will provide. If the data is not contained in the **DataObject**, then it can be retrieved with the **GetData** method.
- *effect*—a **Long** (see Table C-49) that returns the status of the OLE drag-and-drop operation.

effect Name	Value	Description
vbDropEffectNone	0	The operation was canceled or the target control can't accept the drop operation.
vbDropEffectCopy	1	The operation copied data from the source control to the target control. The original data is unchanged.
vbDropEffectMove	2	The operation results in a link from the original data to the target control.

Table C-49: effect *values*.

- *button*—an **Integer** value (see Table C-50) that contains information about the mouse buttons that were pressed. These values can be added together if more than one button was pushed. For instance, a value of 3 means that both the left and right buttons were pressed. A value of 0 means that no buttons were pressed.

button Name	Value	Description
vbLeftButton	1	The left button was pressed.
vbRightButton	2	The right button was pressed.
vbMiddleButton	4	The middle button was pressed.

Table C-50: button *values*.

- *shift*—an **Integer** value (see Table C-51) that contains information about the Shift and Alt keys that were pushed when the mouse button was released. These values can be added together if more than one key was down. For instance, a value of 5 would mean that the Shift and Alt keys were both down when the mouse button was released. A value of 0 means that none of these keys were pressed.

shift Name	Value	Description
vbShiftMask	1	The Shift key was pressed.
vbCtrlMask	2	The Ctrl key was pressed.
vbAltMask	4	The Alt key was pressed.

Table C-51: shift *values*.

- *x*—a **Single** that contains the horizontal location of the mouse pointer.
- *y*—a **Single** that contains the vertical location of the mouse pointer.

Private Sub *ComboBoxControl*_OLEDragOver([*index* As Integer ,] *data* As DataObject, *effect* As Long, *button* As Integer, *shift* As Single, *x* As Single, *y* As Single, *state* As Integer)

Usage — This event happens when an OLE drag-and-drop operation is in progress.

Arguments
- *index*—an **Integer** that uniquely identifies a control in a control array. This argument is not present if the control is not part of a control array.
- *data*—a **DataObject** that contains the formats that the source control will provide. If the data is not contained in the **DataObject**, then it can be retrieved with the **GetData** method.
- *effect*—a **Long** (see Table C-52) that returns the status of the OLE drag-and-drop operation.

effect Name	Value	Description
vbDropEffectNone	0	The operation was canceled or the target control can't accept the drop operation.
vbDropEffectCopy	1	The operation copied data from the source control to the target control. The original data is unchanged.
vbDropEffectMove	2	The operation results in a link from the original data to the target control.

Table C-52: effect *values*.

- *button*—an **Integer** value (see Table C-53) that contains information about the mouse buttons that were pressed. These values can be added together if more than one button was pushed. For instance, a value of 3 means that both the left and right buttons were pressed. A value of 0 means that no buttons were pressed.

button Name	Value	Description
vbLeftButton	1	The left button was pressed.
vbRightButton	2	The right button was pressed.
vbMiddleButton	4	The middle button was pressed.

Table C-53: button *values*.

- *shift*—an **Integer** value (see Table C-54) that contains information about the Shift and Alt keys that were pushed when the mouse button was released. These values can be added together if more than one key was down. For instance, a value of 5 would mean that the Shift and Alt keys were both down when the mouse button was released. A value of 0 means that none of these keys were pressed.

shift Name	Value	Description
vbShiftMask	1	The Shift key was pressed.
vbCtrlMask	2	The Ctrl key was pressed.
vbAltMask	4	The Alt key was pressed.

Table C-54: shift *values*.

- *x*—a **Single** that contains the horizontal location of the mouse pointer.
- *y*—a **Single** that contains the vertical location of the mouse pointer.
- *state*—an **Integer** value (see Table C-55) that indicates the state of the object being dragged.

state Name	Value	Description
vbEnter	0	The dragged object is entering range of the control.
vbLeave	1	The dragged object is leaving range of the control
vbOver	2	The dragged object has moved from one position over the control to another.

Table C-55: state *values.*

Private Sub *ComboBoxControl*_OLEGiveFeedback ([*index* As Integer ,] *effect* As Long)

Usage This event tells the source control what is happening while the OLE drag-and-drop operation is in progress. This event occurs after the **OLEDragOver** event.

Tip

You may want to use this event to change the cursor to reflect what can happen in the remote object.

Arguments
- *index*—an **Integer** that uniquely identifies a control in a control array. This argument is not present if the control is not part of a control array.
- *effect*—a **Long** (see Table C-56) that returns the status of the OLE drag-and-drop operation.

effect Name	Value	Description
vbDropEffectNone	0	The operation was canceled or the target control can't accept the drop operation.
vbDropEffectCopy	1	The operation copied data from the source control to the target control. The original data is unchanged.
vbDropEffectMove	2	The operation results in a link from the original data to the target control.
vbDropEffectScroll	&H80000000	The target control is about to scroll or is scrolling. This value may be added to the other *shift* values.

Table C-56: effect *values.*

Private Sub *ComboBoxControl*_OLESetData([*index* As Integer ,] *data* As DataObject, *DataFormat* As Integer)

Usage   This event happens in response to the target object performing a **GetData** method on *data*. This routine will respond by using the **SetData** method with the desired data using the **DataObject** *data*.

Arguments
- *index*—an **Integer** that uniquely identifies a control in a control array. This argument is not present if the control is not part of a control array.
- *data*—a **DataObject** that will contain the data to be returned to the target object.
- *format*—an **Integer** value (see Table C-57) that contains the format of the data.

format Name	Value	Description
vbCFText	1	Text (.TXT files)
vbCFBitmap	2	Bitmap (.BMP files)
vbCFMetafile	3	Metafile (.WMF files)
vbCFEDIB	8	Device independent bitmap (DIB)
vbCFPallette	9	Color palette
vbCFEMetafile	14	Enhanced metafile (.EMF files)
vbCFFiles	15	List of files
vbCFRTF	-16639	Rich Text Format (.RTF files)

Table C-57: format *values.*

Private Sub *ComboBoxControl*_OLEStartDrag ([*index* As Integer ,] *data* As DataObject, *AllowedEffects* As Long)

Usage   This event start an OLE drag-and-drop operation.

Arguments
- *index*—an **Integer** that uniquely identifies a control in a control array. This argument is not present if the control is not part of a control array.
- *data*—a **DataObject** that will contain the formats that the source object is willing to provide to the target object. It may optionally contain the data to be transferred.
- *AllowedEffects*—a **Long** (see Table C-58) that contains the effects that the target object can request from the source object. The *AllowedEffects* can be added together if the source object supports more than one effect. Note that the target object can always use the *vbDropEffectNone* effect.

AllowedEffects Name	Value	Description
vbDropEffectNone	0	The target can't copy the data.
vbDropEffectCopy	1	The target can copy the data and the source will keep the data unchanged.
vbDropEffectMove	2	The target can copy the data and the source will delete the data.

Table C-58: AllowedEffects *values.*

Private Sub *ComboBoxControl*_Scroll ([*index* As Integer])

Usage This event is called each time the scroll bar is repositioned in the drop-down box.

Arguments *index*—an **Integer** that uniquely identifies a control in a control array. This argument is not present if the control is not part of a control array.

Examples
```
Private Sub Combo1_Click()
MsgBox Combo1.List(Combo1.ListIndex)
End Sub

Private Sub Form_Load()
Combo1.AddItem "One"
Combo1.AddItem "Two"
Combo1.AddItem "Three"
End Sub
```

This program initializes a combo box with three values and then displays a message box whenever the user clicks on one of the items from the drop-down menu.

See Also **ListBox** (control), **TextBox** (control)

Command

FUNCTION

CCE, LE, PE, EE

Syntax *SValue* = **Command** ( )

Usage The **Command** function returns the argument string from the command line. To simulate this information while in the Visual Basic development environment, simply enter the information in the Program Properties menu.

> **Tip**
>
> *Command line arguments are useful for specifying a file that should be processed or for enabling debugging code in your program. Also you could use it to set a different default value for a global variable while you execute a program once.*

Arguments *SValue*—a **String** that contains the command line argument.

Examples
```
Private Sub Form_Load()
MsgBox Command()
End Sub
```

This routine displays the command line argument when the program starts.

See Also **String** (data type)

CommandButton

CONTROL

CCE, LE, PE, EE

Usage The **CommandButton** control is an intrinsic control which provides the programmer with a push button that can be used to trigger new events.

Properties
- *CommandButtonControl*.**Appearance**—an **Integer** value (see Table C-59) that determines how the control button will appear on the form.

AppearanceValue	Description
0	The control button is displayed without the 3D effects.
1	The control button is displayed with 3D effects (default value).

Table C-59: **Appearance** *values.*

- *CommandButtonControl*.**BackColor**—a **Long** that contains the suggested value for the background color of the control. The **BackColor** and **ForeColor** must both be solid to display text. If you choose a color that is dithered, it will be changed to the nearest solid color.
- *CommandButtonControl*.**Caption**—a **String** value that is displayed inside the control button. You can include an access key for this control by inserting an ampersand (&) in front of the character you want to use. The selected character will then appear with an underline. Then if the user presses the Alt key with the underlined character, the control will gain the focus.
- *CommandButtonControl*.**Container**—an object that can be used to set or return the container of the control at run time. This property cannot be set at design time.
- *CommandButtonControl*.**Default**—a **Boolean** that determines which button on a form is executed when the form itself has the focus. Only one button can be set as default (**True**). Setting the **Default** property to **True** will set the rest of the command button's **Default** properties to **False** at design time.
- *CommandButtonControl*.**DisabledPicture**—a picture object (a bitmap, icon, or metafile) that will be shown on top of the control when the control's **Enabled** property is **False** and the **Style** property is set to *vbButtonGraphical*.

> **Tip**
>
> *This value can be created using the* **LoadPicture** *function.*

- *CommandButtonControl*.**DownPicture**—a picture object (a bitmap, icon, or metafile) that will be displayed on top of the control when the control is pressed. This will replace the standard picture displayed when the control is not pressed. This feature requires that the **Style** property be set to *vbButtonGraphical*.

> **Tip**
>
> *This value can be created using the* **LoadPicture** *function.*

- *CommandButtonControl*.**DragIcon**—an object that contains the picture value of an icon. At design time, you can specify an icon file that has a file type of .ICO.

> **Tip**
>
> *This value can be created by copying the value from another control's **DragIcon** value, a form's icon, or by using the **LoadPicture** function.*

- *CommandButtonControl*.**DragMode**—an **Integer** value (see Table C-60) specifying how the control will respond to a drag request.

> **Tip**
>
> *Setting **DragMode** to vbAutomatic will automatically begin a drag operation when the user clicks on the control. However, the control will not respond to the usual mouse events (**Click**, **DblClick**, **MouseDown**, **MouseMove**, **MouseUp**).*

DragMode Name	Value	Description
vbManual	0	The Drag method must be used to begin a drag-and-drop operation (default value).
vbAutomatic	1	The source control will automatically begin a drag-and-drop operation when the user clicks on the control.

Table C-60: **DragMode** *values.*

- *CommandButtonControl*.**Enabled**—a **Boolean** value when **True** means that the control will respond to events. When **False**, the control will not respond to events.
- *CommandButtonControl*.**Font**—an object that contains information about the character font used by this object.

> **Tip**
>
> *The **Font** object should be used in place of the other **Font** properties, since it offers more functionality than the individual properties.*

- *CommandButtonControl*.**FontBold**—a **Boolean** when **True**, means that the characters display in bold. **False** means that the characters display normally.
- *CommandButtonControl*.**FontItalic**—a **Boolean** when **True**, means that the characters display in italics. **False** means that the characters display normally.
- *CommandButtonControl*.**FontName**—a **String** that specifies the name of the font that should be used to display the characters in this control.
- *CommandButtonControl*.**FontSize**—a **Single** that specifies the point size that should be used to display the characters in the control.
- *CommandButtonControl*.**FontStrikethru**—a **Boolean** when **True**, means that the characters display with a line through the center. **False** means that the characters display normally.

- *CommandButtonControl*.**FontUnderlined**—a **Boolean** when **True**, means that the characters display with a line beneath them. **False** means that the characters display normally.
- *CommandButtonControl*.**Height**—a **Single** that contains the height of the control.
- *CommandButtonControl*.**HelpContextID**—a **Long** that contains a help file context ID number which references an entry in the help file. When the user presses the F1 key while this control is active, the corresponding entry in the help file will automatically be displayed. A value of zero means that no context number was specified.

> **Tip**
>
> *A help file must be compiled using the Windows Help Compiler available in the Professional and Enterprise editions of Visual Basic.*

- *CommandButtonControl*.**hWnd**—a **Long** that contains a Windows handle to the control.

> **Tip**
>
> *The **hWnd** property is most useful when making calls to Windows API functions. Since this value can change during execution, do not save the value into a variable for later use.*

- *CommandButtonControl*.**Index**—an **Integer** that uniquely identifies a control in a control array.
- *CommandButtonControl*.**Left**—a **Single** that contains the distance measured in twips between the left edge of the control and the left edge of the control's container.
- *CommandButtonControl*.**MaskColor**—a **Long** that identifies a color that will be used as a mask or transparent color for bitmaps displayed within the control. This is useful for bitmap images that do not specify transparency information like icons and metafiles. The **UseMaskColor** property must be **True** for this property to take effect.
- *CommandButtonControl*.**MouseIcon**—a picture object (a bitmap, icon, or metafile) that will be used as a cursor when the **MousePointer** property is set to 99. Note that Visual Basic does not support color cursors from a .CUR file. A color icon from a .ICO file should be used instead.
- *CommandButtonControl*.**MousePointer**—an **Integer** value (see Table C-61) that contains the value of the cursor that should be displayed when the cursor is moved over this control. Use *vbCustom* to display the custom icon stored in the **MouseIcon** property.

Cursor Name	Value	Description
vbDefault	0	Shape determined by the object (default value)
vbArrow	1	Arrow
vbCrosshair	2	Crosshair
vbIbeam	3	I beam
vbIconPointer	4	Square inside a square
vbSizePointer	5	Four sided arrow (north, south, east, west)
vbSizeNESW	6	Two sided arrow (northeast, southwest)
vbSizeNS	7	Two sided arrow (north, south)
vbSizeNWSE	8	Two sided arrow (northwest, southeast)
vbSizeWE	9	Two sided arrow (west, east)

Cursor Name	Value	Description
vbUpArrow	10	Single sided arrow pointing north
vbHourglass	11	Hourglass
vbNoDrop	12	No Drop
vbArrowHourglass	13	An arrow and an Hourglass
vbArrowQuestion	14	An arrow and a question mark
vbSizeAll	15	Size all
vbCustom	99	Custom icon from the **MouseIcon** property of this control

Table C-61: **Cursor** *values.*

- *CommandButtonControl.***Name**—a **String** that contains the name of the control that will be used to reference the control in a Visual Basic program. This property is read only at run time.
- *CommandButtonControl.***OLEDropMode**—an **Integer** value (see Table C-62) that describes how the control will respond to OLE drop operations.

OLEDropMode Name	Value	Description
vbOLEDropNone	0	The control does not accept OLE drops. The cursor is changed to the No Drop cursor (default value).
vbOLEDropManual	1	The control responds to OLE drops under the program's control (manual).
vbOLEDropAutomatic	2	The control automatically accepts OLE drops if it recognizes the format of the data object.

Table C-62: **OLEDropMode** *values.*

- *CommandButtonControl.***Parent**—an object that contains a reference to the **Form**, **Frame**, or other container that contains the **CommandButton** control.
- *CommandButtonControl.***Picture**—a picture object (a bitmap, icon, metafile, GIF, or JPEG) that will be displayed on the control. You can also use the **LoadPicture** function at run time to load a bitmap, icon, or metafile. Note that **Style** must be set to *vbButtonGraphical* for the image to be shown.
- *CommandButtonControl.***RightToLeft**—a **Boolean** value when **True** means that the text is displayed from right to left. When **False** means that the text is displayed from left to right. A bi-directional version of Windows is required to set this property to **True**.
- *CommandButtonControl.***Style**—an **Integer** value (see Table C-63) that contains the style used to display the control.

Style Name	Value	Description
vbButtonStandard	0	The control is displayed as a check box next to a caption (default value).
vbButtonGraphic	1	The control is displayed like a command button, which can be toggled up and down.

Table C-63: **Style** *values.*

- *CommandButtonControl*.**TabIndex**—an **Integer** that determines the order that a user will tab through the objects on a form.
- *CommandButtonControl*.**TabStop**—a **Boolean** value when **True** means that the user can tab to this object. When **False**, means that this control will be skipped to the next control in the **TabIndex** order.
- *CommandButtonControl*.**Tag**—a **String** that can hold programmer specific information. This property is not used by Visual Basic.
- *CommandButtonControl*.**ToolTipText**—a **String** that holds a text value that can be displayed as a **ToolTip** box that is displayed whenever the cursor is held over the control for about one second.
- *CommandButtonControl*.**Top**—a **Single** that contains the distance measured in twips between the top edge of the control and the top edge of the control's container.
- *CommandButtonControl*.**UseMaskColor**—a **Boolean** value when **True** means should use the color specified in the **MaskColor** property to create a transparent background for the picture objects contained in the control. When **False**, the picture objects will not be displayed with a transparent background.
- *CommandButtonControl*.**Value**—a **Boolean** value when **True**, means that the button was pushed. When **False** means that the button has not been pushed. It is possible to trigger the click event by setting this property to **True**.
- *CommandButtonControl*.**Visible**—a **Boolean** value when **True** means that the control is visible. When **False** means that the control is not visible.

Tip

This property can hide the control until the program is ready to display it.

- *CommandButtonControl*.**WhatsThisHelpID**—a **Long** that contains a help file context ID number which references an entry in the help file. This provides a What's This PopUp help display in response to the What's This button in the upper right corner of the window.
- *CommandButtonControl*.**Width**—a **Single** that contains the width of the control.

Methods

CommandButtonControl.Drag [*DragAction*]

Usage This method begins, ends, or cancels a drag operation.

Arguments
- *DragAction*—an **Integer** that contains a value selected from Table C-64 below.

DragAction Name	Value	Description
vbCancel	0	Cancels any drag operation in progress.
vbBeginDrag	1	Begins a drag operation (default).
vbEndDrag	2	Ends a drag operation and drops *object*.

Table C-64: DragAction *values.*

CommandButtonControl.Move Left [, Top [, Width [, Height]]]

Usage This method changes the position and the size of the **CommandButton** control. The **ScaleMode** of the **Form** or other container object that holds the **CommandButton** control will determine the units used to specify the coordinates.

Arguments
- *Left*—a **Single** that specifies the new position of the left edge of the control.
- *Top*—a **Single** that specifies the new position of the top edge of the control.
- *Width*—a **Single** that specifies the new width of the control.
- *Height*—a **Single** that specifies the new height of the control.

CommandButtonControl.OLEDrag

Usage This method begins an **OLEDrag** and drop operation. Invoking this method will trigger the **OLEStartDrag** event.

CommandButtonControl.Refresh

Usage This method redraws the contents of the control.

CommandButtonControl.SetFocus

Usage This method transfers the focus from the form or control that currently has the focus to this control. To receive the focus, this control must be enabled and visible.

CommandButtonControl.ShowWhatsThis

Usage This method displays the ShowWhatsThis help information for this control.

CommandButtonControl.ZOrder [position]

Usage This method specifies the position of the **CommandButton** control relative to the other objects on the form.

> **Tip**
>
> *Note that there are three layers of objects on a form: the back layer is the drawing space which contains the results of the graphical methods; the middle layer contains graphical objects and **Labels**; and the top layer contains nongraphical controls such as the **CommandButton**. The ZOrder method only affects how the objects are arranged within a single layer.*

Arguments
- *position*—an **Integer** that specifies the relative position of this object. A value of 0 means that the control is positioned at the head of the list, a value of 1 means that the control will be placed at the end of the list.

Events

Private Sub *CommandButtonControl*_Click([*index* As Integer])

Usage — This event occurs when the user clicks a mouse button while the cursor is positioned over this control.

Tip
*If you need to identify which mouse button was pressed, use the **MouseUp** and **MouseDown** events.*

Arguments — *index*—an **Integer** that uniquely identifies a control in a control array. This argument is not present if the control is not part of a control array.

Private Sub *CommandButtonControl*_DragDrop([*index* As Integer ,] *source* As Control, *x* As Single, *y* As Single)

Usage — This event occurs when a drag-and-drop operation is completed by using the **Drag** method with an *DragAction* value of *vbEndDrag* (2).

Tip
*When using drag-and-drop operations, use the **DragOver** event to determine what the cursor should look like while the cursor moves over the control.*

Arguments
- *index*—an **Integer** that uniquely identifies a control in a control array. This argument is not present if the control is not part of a control array.
- *source*—a control object that is the control that is being dragged.

Tip
You can access a property or method from the source control by using source.*property or* source.*method. You can determine the type of object or control by using the **TypeOf** operator.*

- *x*—a **Single** that contains the horizontal location of the mouse pointer.
- *y*—a **Single** that contains the vertical location of the mouse pointer.

Private Sub *CommandButtonControl*_DragOver([*index* As Integer ,] *source* As Control, *x* As Single, *y* As Single, *state* As Integer)

Usage — This event occurs while a drag operation is in progress and the cursor is moved over the control.

Tip
*When using drag-and-drop operations, use the **DragOver** event to determine what the cursor should look like while the cursor moves over the control. When* state *is 0, you can change the cursor to a No Drop (vbNoDrop) cursor or highlight the field that the cursor is near. When* state *is 1, you can undo the changes you made when the* state *was 0.*

Arguments
- *index*—an **Integer** that uniquely identifies a control in a control array. This argument is not present if the control is not part of a control array.
- *source*—a control object that is the control that is being dragged.

> **Tip**
> *You can access a property or method from the source control by using* source.*property or* source.*method. You can determine the type of object or control by using the* **TypeOf** *operator.*

- *x*—a **Single** that contains the horizontal location of the mouse pointer.
- *y*—a **Single** that contains the vertical location of the mouse pointer.
- *state*—an **Integer** value (see Table C-65) that indicates the state of the object being dragged.

state Name	Value	Description
vbEnter	0	The dragged object is entering range of the control.
vbLeave	1	The dragged object is leaving range of the control.
vbOver	2	The dragged object has moved from one position over the control to another.

Table C-65: state *values*.

Private Sub CommandButtonControl_GotFocus ([*index* As Integer])

Usage This event occurs when the control is given focus.

> **Tip**
> *You can use this routine to display help or other information in a status bar.*

Arguments
- *index*—an **Integer** that uniquely identifies a control in a control array. This argument is not present if the control is not part of a control array.

Private Sub CommandButtonControl_KeyDown ([*index* As Integer ,] *keycode* As Integer, *shift* As Single)

Usage This event occurs when a key is pressed while the control has the focus.

Arguments
- *index*—an **Integer** that uniquely identifies a control in a control array. This argument is not present if the control is not part of a control array.
- *keycode*—an **Integer** that contains information about which key was pressed.

- *shift*—an **Integer** value (see Table C-66) that contains information about the Shift and Alt keys that were pushed when the mouse button was pressed. These values can be added together if more than one key was down. For instance, a value of 5 would mean that the Shift and Alt keys were both down when the mouse button was pressed.

shift Name	Value	Description
vbShiftMask	1	The Shift key was pressed.
vbCtrlMask	2	The Ctrl key was pressed.
vbAltMask	4	The Alt key was pressed.

Table C-66: shift *values.*

Private Sub *CommandButtonControl*_KeyPress([*index* As Integer ,] *keychar* As Integer)

Usage   This event occurs whenever a key is pressed while the control has the focus.

Arguments
- *index*—an **Integer** that uniquely identifies a control in a control array. This argument is not present if the control is not part of a control array.
- *keychar*—an **Integer** that contains the ASCII character that was pressed.

Private Sub *CommandButtonControl*_KeyUp ([*index* As Integer ,] *keycode* As Integer, *shift* As Single)

Usage   This event occurs when a key is released while the control has the focus.

Arguments
- *index*—an **Integer** that uniquely identifies a control in a control array. This argument is not present if the control is not part of a control array.
- *keycode*—an **Integer** that contains information about which key was released.
- *shift*—an **Integer** value (see Table C-67) that contains information about the Shift and Alt keys that were pushed when the mouse button was pressed. These values can be added together if more than one key was down. For instance, a value of 5 would mean that the Shift and Alt keys were both down when the mouse button was pressed.

shift Name	Value	Description
vbShiftMask	1	The Shift key was pressed.
vbCtrlMask	2	The Ctrl key was pressed.
vbAltMask	4	The Alt key was pressed.

Table C-67: shift *values.*

Private Sub *CommandButtonControl*_LostFocus ([*index* As Integer])

Usage This event occurs when the control loses focus.

Tip

This routine is useful to performing data verification.

Arguments • *index*—an **Integer** that uniquely identifies a control in a control array. This argument is not present if the control is not part of a control array.

Private Sub *CommandButtonControl*_MouseDown([*index* As Integer ,] *button* As Integer, *shift* As Single, *x* As Single, *y* As Single)

Usage This event occurs when a mouse button was pressed while the cursor is over the control.

Arguments • *index*—an **Integer** that uniquely identifies a control in a control array. This argument is not present if the control is not part of a control array.

• *button*—an **Integer** value (see Table C-68) that contains information about the mouse buttons that were pressed. Only one button will be indicated when this event occurs.

button Name	Value	Description
vbLeftButton	1	The left button was pressed.
vbRightButton	2	The right button was pressed.
vbMiddleButton	4	The middle button was pressed.

Table C-68: button *values.*

• *shift*—an **Integer** value (see Table C-69) that contains information about the Shift and Alt keys that were pushed when the mouse button was pressed. These values can be added together if more than one key was down. For instance, a value of 5 would mean that the Shift and Alt keys were both down when the mouse button was pressed.

shift Name	Value	Description
vbShiftMask	1	The Shift key was pressed.
vbCtrlMask	2	The Ctrl key was pressed.
vbAltMask	4	The Alt key was pressed.

Table C-69: shift *values.*

• *x*—a **Single** that contains the horizontal location of the mouse pointer.
• *y*—a **Single** that contains the vertical location of the mouse pointer.

Private Sub *CommandButtonControl*_MouseMove ([*index* As Integer ,] *button* As Integer, *shift* As Single, *x* As Single, *y* As Single)

Usage   This event occurs while the cursor is moved over the control.

Arguments
- *index*—an **Integer** that uniquely identifies a control in a control array. This argument is not present if the control is not part of a control array.
- *button*—an **Integer** value (see Table C-70) that contains information about the mouse buttons that were pressed. These values can be added together if more than one button was pushed. For instance, a value of 3 means that both the left and right buttons were pressed. A value of 0 means that no buttons were pressed.

button Name	Value	Description
vbLeftButton	1	The left button was pressed.
vbRightButton	2	The right button was pressed.
vbMiddleButton	4	The middle button was pressed.

Table C-70: button *values.*

- *shift*—an **Integer** value (see Table C-71) that contains information about the Shift and Alt keys that were pushed when the mouse button was pressed. For instance, a value of 5 would mean that the Shift and Alt keys were both down when the mouse button was pressed. A value of 0 means that none of these keys were pressed.

shift Name	Value	Description
vbShiftMask	1	The Shift key was pressed.
vbCtrlMask	2	The Ctrl key was pressed.
vbAltMask	4	The Alt key was pressed.

Table C-71: shift *values.*

- *x*—a **Single** that contains the horizontal location of the mouse pointer.
- *y*—a **Single** that contains the vertical location of the mouse pointer.

Private Sub *CommandButtonControl*_MouseUp([*index* As Integer ,] *button* As Integer, *shift* As Single, *x* As Single, *y* As Single)

Usage   This event occurs when a mouse button is released while the cursor is over the control.

Arguments
- *index*—an **Integer** that uniquely identifies a control in a control array. This argument is not present if the control is not part of a control array.
- *button*—an **Integer** value (see Table C-72) that contains information about the mouse buttons that were released. Only one of these values will be present.

button Name	Value	Description
vbLeftButton	1	The left button was released.
vbRightButton	2	The right button was released.
vbMiddleButton	4	The middle button was released.

Table C-72: button *values*.

- *shift*—an **Integer** value (see Table C-73) that contains information about the Shift and Alt keys that were pushed when the mouse button was released. These values can be added together if more than one key was down. For instance, a value of 5 would mean that the Shift and Alt keys were both down when the mouse button was released. A value of 0 means that none of these keys were pressed.

shift Name	Value	Description
vbShiftMask	1	The Shift key was pressed.
vbCtrlMask	2	The Ctrl key was pressed.
vbAltMask	4	The Alt key was pressed.

Table C-73: shift *values*.

- *x*—a **Single** that contains the horizontal location of the mouse pointer.
- *y*—a **Single** that contains the vertical location of the mouse pointer.

Private Sub *CommandButtonControl*_OLECompleteDrag([*index* As Integer ,] *effect* As Long)

Usage This event tells the source control the results of an OLE drag-and-drop operation. This is the final event to occur in the series of actions that make up an OLE drag-and-drop operation.

Arguments
- *index*—an **Integer** that uniquely identifies a control in a control array. This argument is not present if the control is not part of a control array.
- *effect*—a **Long** (see Table C-74) that returns the status of the OLE drag-and-drop operation.

effect Name	Value	Description
vbDropEffectNone	0	The operation was canceled or the target control can't accept the drop operation.
vbDropEffectCopy	1	The operation copied data from the source control to the target control. The original data is unchanged.
vbDropEffectMove	2	The operation results in a link from the original data to the target control.

Table C-74: effect *values*.

Private Sub *CommandButtonControl*_OLEDragDrop([*index* As Integer ,] *data* As DataObject, *effect* As Long, *button* As Integer, *shift* As Single, *x* As Single, *y* As Single)

Usage — This event tells the source control the results of an OLE drag-and-drop operation. This is the final event to occur in the series of actions that make up an OLE drag-and-drop operation.

Arguments
- *index*—an **Integer** that uniquely identifies a control in a control array. This argument is not present if the control is not part of a control array.
- *data*—a **DataObject** that contains the formats that the source control will provide. If the data is not contained in the **DataObject**, then it can be retrieved with the **GetData** method.
- *effect*—a **Long** (see Table C-75) that returns the status of the OLE drag-and-drop operation.

effect Name	Value	Description
vbDropEffectNone	0	The operation was canceled or the target control can't accept the drop operation.
vbDropEffectCopy	1	The operation copied data from the source control to the target control. The original data is unchanged.
vbDropEffectMove	2	The operation results in a link from the original data to the target control.

Table C-75: effect *values*.

- *button*—an **Integer** value (see Table C-76) that contains information about the mouse buttons that were pressed. These values can be added together if more than one button was pushed. For instance, a value of 3 means that both the left and right buttons were pressed. A value of 0 means that no buttons were pressed.

button Name	Value	Description
vbLeftButton	1	The left button was pressed.
vbRightButton	2	The right button was pressed.
vbMiddleButton	4	The middle button was pressed.

Table C-76: button *values*.

- *shift*—an **Integer** value (see Table C-77) that contains information about the Shift and Alt keys that were pushed when the mouse button was released. These values can be added together if more than one key was down. For instance, a value of 5 would mean that the Shift and Alt keys were both down when the mouse button was released. A value of 0 means that none of these keys were pressed.

shift Name	Value	Description
vbShiftMask	1	The Shift key was pressed.
vbCtrlMask	2	The Ctrl key was pressed.
vbAltMask	4	The Alt key was pressed.

Table C-77: shift values.

- x—a **Single** that contains the horizontal location of the mouse pointer.
- y—a **Single** that contains the vertical location of the mouse pointer.

Private Sub CommandButtonControl_OLEDragOver([index As Integer ,] data As DataObject, effect As Long, button As Integer, shift As Single, x As Single, y As Single, state As Integer)

Usage This event happens when an OLE drag-and-drop operation is in progress.

Arguments
- *index*—an **Integer** that uniquely identifies a control in a control array. This argument is not present if the control is not part of a control array.
- *data*—a **DataObject** that contains the formats that the source control will provide. If the data is not contained in the **DataObject**, then it can be retrieved with the **GetData** method.
- *effect*—a **Long** (see Table C-78) that returns the status of the OLE drag-and-drop operation.

effect Name	Value	Description
vbDropEffectNone	0	The operation was canceled or the target control can't accept the drop operation.
vbDropEffectCopy	1	The operation copied data from the source control to the target control. The original data is unchanged.
vbDropEffectMove	2	The operation results in a link from the original data to the target control.

Table C-78: effect values.

- *button*—an **Integer** value (see Table C-79) that contains information about the mouse buttons that were pressed. These values can be added together if more than one button was pushed. For instance, a value of 3 means that both the left and right buttons were pressed. A value of 0 means that no buttons were pressed.

button Name	Value	Description
vbLeftButton	1	The left button was pressed.
vbRightButton	2	The right button was pressed.
vbMiddleButton	4	The middle button was pressed.

Table C-79: button values.

CommandButton • 105

- *shift*—an **Integer** value (see Table C-80) that contains information about the Shift and Alt keys that were pushed when the mouse button was released. These values can be added together if more than one key was down. For instance, a value of 5 would mean that the Shift and Alt keys were both down when the mouse button was released. A value of 0 means that none of these keys were pressed.

shift Name	Value	Description
vbShiftMask	1	The Shift key was pressed.
vbCtrlMask	2	The Ctrl key was pressed.
vbAltMask	4	The Alt key was pressed.

Table C-80: shift *values.*

- *x*—a **Single** that contains the horizontal location of the mouse pointer.
- *y*—a **Single** that contains the vertical location of the mouse pointer.
- *state*—an **Integer** value (see Table C-81) that indicates the state of the object being dragged.

state Name	Value	Description
vbEnter	0	The dragged object is entering range of the control.
vbLeave	1	The dragged object is leaving range of the control.
vbOver	2	The dragged object has moved from one position over the control to another.

Table C-81: state *values.*

Private Sub *CommandButtonControl*_OLEGiveFeedback ([*index* As Integer ,] *effect* As Long)

Usage   This event tells the source control what is happening while the OLE drag-and-drop operation is in progress. This event occurs after the **OLEDragOver** event.

Tip

You may want to use this event to change the cursor to reflect what can happen in the remote object.

Arguments
- *index*—an **Integer** that uniquely identifies a control in a control array. This argument is not present if the control is not part of a control array.
- *effect*—a **Long** (see Table C-82) that returns the status of the OLE drag-and-drop operation.

effect Name	Value	Description
vbDropEffectNone	0	The operation was canceled or the target control can't accept the drop operation.
vbDropEffectCopy	1	The operation copied data from the source control to the target control. The original data is unchanged.

effect Name	Value	Description
vbDropEffectMove	2	The operation results in a link from the original data to the target control.
vbDropEffectScroll	&H80000000	The target control is about to scroll or is scrolling. This value may be added to the other *shift* values.

Table C-82: effect *values*.

Private Sub *CommandButtonControl*_OLESetData([*index* As Integer ,] *data* As DataObject, *DataFormat* As Integer)

Usage   This event happens in response to the target object performing a **GetData** method on *data*. This routine will respond by using the **SetData** method with the desired data using the **DataObject** *data*.

Arguments
- *index*—an **Integer** that uniquely identifies a control in a control array. This argument is not present if the control is not part of a control array.
- *data*—a **DataObject** that will contain the data to be returned to the target object.
- *format*—an **Integer** value (see Table C-83) that contains the format of the data.

format Name	Value	Description
vbCFText	1	Text (.TXT files)
vbCFBitmap	2	Bitmap (.BMP files)
vbCFMetafile	3	Metafile (.WMF files)
vbCFEDIB	8	Device independent bitmap (DIB)
vbCFPallette	9	Color palette
vbCFEMetafile	14	Enhanced metafile (.EMF files)
vbCFFiles	15	List of files
vbCFRTF	-16639	Rich Text Format (.RTF files)

Table C-83: format *values*.

Private Sub *CommandButtonControl*_OLEStartDrag ([*index* As Integer ,] *data* As DataObject, *AllowedEffects* As Long)

Usage   This event starts an OLE drag-and-drop operation.

Arguments
- *index*—an **Integer** that uniquely identifies a control in a control array. This argument is not present if the control is not part of a control array.
- *data*—a **DataObject** that will contain the formats that the source object is willing to provide to the target object. It may optionally contain the data to be transferred.

- *AllowedEffects*—a **Long** (see Table C-84) that contains the effects that the target object can request from the source object. The *AllowedEffects* can be added together if the source object supports more than one effect. Note that the target object can always use the *vbDropEffectNone* effect.

AllowedEffects Name	Value	Description
vbDropEffectNone	0	The target can't copy the data.
vbDropEffectCopy	1	The target can copy the data and the source will keep the data unchanged.
vbDropEffectMove	2	The target can copy the data and the source will delete the data.

Table C-84: AllowedEffects *values.*

Examples
```
Private Sub Command1_Click()
MsgBox "Command button was pressed"
End Sub
```

This routine will display a message each time the Command1 button is pushed.

See Also   **Data** (control), **LoadPicture** (function), **OptionButton** (control)

CommonDialog

CONTROL

CCE, LE, PE, EE

Usage   The **CommonDialog** control is an intrinsic control which provides the programmer with standard dialog boxes for opening files, saving files, showing colors, showing fonts, showing printers, and using the help facility.

Properties
- *CommonDialogControl.***Action**—an **Integer** value (see Table C-85) that selects the type of dialog box displayed by the control. This property exists to maintain compatibility with previous versions of Visual Basic. See the **ShowColor**, **ShowFont**, **ShowHelp**, **ShowOpen**, **ShowPrinter**, and **ShowSave** methods.

Action Value	Description
0	No action.
1	Displays the Open File dialog box.
2	Displays the Save File dialog box.
3	Displays the Color dialog box.
4	Displays the Font dialog box.
5	Displays the Printer dialog box.
6	Displays a Windows help file.

Table C-85: Action *values.*

- *CommonDialogControl*.**CancelError**—a **Boolean** value that when **True** will cause an error 32755 (*cdlCancel*) to occur when the user hits the Cancel button on the dialog box. When **False** no error will be generated when the user hits the Cancel botton.
- *CommonDialogControl*.**Color**—a **Long** value that sets a color value for the dialog box. For the dialog box to return a value for this property, the *cdlCCRGBInit* flag must be set for the Color dialog box or *cdlCFEffects* flag must be set for the Font dialog box.
- *CommonDialogControl*.**Copies**—an **Integer** value that sets or returns the number of copies value from the Printer dialog box. If the *cdlPDUseDevModeCopies* flag is set the Printer dialog box will always return 1.
- *CommonDialogControl*.**DefaultExt**—a **String** value that sets or returns the default value for the file extension (i.e., .TXT for text files, .DOC for Word files, etc.) in the Open File and Save File dialog boxes.
- *CommonDialogControl*.**DialogTitle**—a **String** value that sets or returns the title displayed in the Open File and Save File dialog boxes. The default value for the Open File dialog box is Open, while the default value for the Save File dialog box is Save As. This property is ignored for all other dialog boxes.
- *CommonDialogControl*.**FileName**—a **String** value that sets or returns the filename and path in the Open File and Save File dialog boxes.

> **Tip**
>
> *You can set the filename to provide a default value before displaying the dialog box.*

- *CommonDialogControl*.**FileTitle**—a **String** value that sets or returns the filename only for the Open File and Save File dialog boxes. File path information is not included. If the *cdlOFNNoValidate* flag is set, then this property will not return a value after the dialog box is displayed.
- *CommonDialogControl*.**Filter**—a **String** value that sets or returns the values that will be displayed in the Files of Type text box on an Open or Save window. This string is composed of a series of descriptions and filters. A description which is shown to the user usually takes the form of a title followed by the file types associated by that title in parentheses. A filter which is not shown to the user is composed of a set of file types that will be used to select the files shown to the user. Filters and descriptions are separated by a vertical bar ("|") also known as the pipe character without spaces on either side of the vertical bar. The following example shows how to construct a **Filter** string.
  ```
  Text files (*.txt;*.prn)|*.txt;*.prn| files (*.vb*)|*.vb* Visual Basic
  ```
- *CommonDialogControl*.**FilterIndex**—an **Integer** value that specifies the filter that should be displayed. The first description and filter pair is selected with a value of one. If no value is specified, the default value will be one.
- *CommonDialogControl*.**Flags**—a **Long** value (see Tables C-86, C-87, and C-88) that sets or returns a set of options that enables or disables various options for each of the five different functions. In most cases, the options can be added together to select multiple options.

> **Note**
>
> *You must set the Flags property to cdlCFScreenFonts, cdlCFPrinterFonts, or cdlCFBoth when using the Font dialog box or a message saying no fonts selected will be displayed.*

Color Flags Name	Value	Description
cdlCCRGBInit	&H1	The initial color is specified in Color; otherwise black will be used as the default color.
cdlCCIFullOpen	&H2	The entire dialog box will be displayed, including the Define Custom Colors button.
cdlCCPreventFullOpen	&H4	Disable the Define Custom Colors button.
cdlCCHelpButton	&H8	Display a help button.

Table C-86: **Color Flags** *values.*

Font Flags Name	Value	Description
cdlCFScreenFonts	&H1	Display only screen fonts.
cdlCFPrinterFonts	&H2	Display only printer fonts supported by the printer specified in **hDC**.
cdlCFBoth	&H3	Display both screen fonts and printer fonts.
cdlCFHelpButton	&H4	Display a help button.
cdlCFEffects	&H100	Enable strikethrough, underline, and color effects.
cdlCFApply	&H200	Display an Apply button.
cdlCFANSIOnly	&H400	Prevent a user from selecting a character font that consists of only symbols.
cdlCFNoVectorFonts	&H800	The dialog box doesn't allow vector fonts.
cdlCFNoSimulations	&H1000	The dialog box doesn't allow GDI font simulations.
cdlCFLimitSize	&H2000	The font size is limited by the values in the Min and Max properties.
cdlCFFixedPitchOnly	&H4000	Display fixed pitch fonts only.
cdlCFWYSIWYG	&H8000	Display only fonts that will work on the screen and the printer. Note the *cdlCFBoth* and *cdlCFScalableOnly* flags should also be set.
cdlCFForceFontExist	&H10000	Generate an error message if the font doesn't exist.
cdlCFScalableOnly	&H20000	Display only scalable fonts.
cdlCFTTOnly	&H40000	The user can only select a True Type font.
cdlCFNoFaceSel	&H80000	No font name was selected.
cdlCFNoStyleSel	&H100000	No style was selected.
cdlCFNoSizeSel	&H200000	No size was selected.

Table C-87: **Font Flags** *values.*

Printer Flags Name	Value	Description
cdlPDSelection	&H1	Set the Print Range to Selection from the default of All.
cdlPDPageNums	&H2	Set the Print Range to PageNums from the default of All.
cdlPDNoSelection	&H4	Disable the Print Range box by forcing it to select all.
cdlPDNoPageNums	&H8	Disable the PageNums selection.
cdlPDCollate	&H10	Set or return the state of Collate.
cdlPDPrintToFile	&H20	Set or return the state of the PrintToFile check box.
cdlPDPrintSetup	&H40	Display the Print Setup rather than the Printer dialog box.
cdlPDNoWarning	&H80	No warning message is displayed if there is not a default printer.

Printer Flags Name	Value	Description
cdlPDReturnDC	&H100	Return a device context for the printer in the **hDC** property.
cdlPDReturnIC	&H200	Return an information context for the printer in the **hDC** property.
cdlPDReturnDefault	&H400	Return the default printer name.
cdlPDHelpButton	&H800	Enable the help button.
cdlPDUseDevModeCopies	&H40000	If the driver supports multiple copies, then the Copies field is enabled, otherwise it is disabled.
cdlPDDisablePrintToFile	&H80000	Disable the Print To File check box.
cdlPDHidePrintToFile	&H100000	Hide the Print To File check box.

Table C-88: **Printer Flags** *values.*

- *CommonDialogControl.***FontBold**—a **Boolean** when **True**, means that the characters display in bold. **False** means that the characters display normally.
- *CommonDialogControl.***FontItalic**—a **Boolean** when **True**, means that the characters display in italics. **False** means that the characters display normally.
- *CommonDialogControl.***FontName**—a **String** that specifies the name of the font that should be used to display the characters in this control.
- *CommonDialogControl.***FontSize**—a **Single** that specifies the point size that should be used to display the characters in the control.
- *CommonDialogControl.***FontStrikethru**—a **Boolean** when **True**, means that the characters display with a line through the center. **False** means that the characters display normally.
- *CommonDialogControl.***FontUnderlined**—a **Boolean** when **True**, means that the characters display with a line beneath them. **False** means that the characters display normally.
- *CommonDialogControl.***FromPage**—an **Integer** that contains the starting page for the document to be printed.
- *CommonDialogControl.***hDC**—a **Long** that contains a handle to the device context to an object.
- *CommonDialogControl.***HelpCommand**—an **Integer** value (see Table C-89) that contains a command that will be passed to the Windows Help system.

Help Command Name	Value	Description
cdlHelpContext	&H1	Display help for the help context specified in the HelpContext property.
cdlHelpQuit	&H2	Tell the help system to close the current help file.
cdlHelpContents	&H3	Display the help contents topic. Note this help command has been superceded by the help finder command with hex value &HB.
cdlHelpHelpOnHelp	&H4	Display help for the help system.
cdlHelpSetContents	&H5	Display the help information in the **HelpContext** property when the user hits the F1 key.

Help Command Name	Value	Description
cdlHelpSetIndex	&H5	Use the value in **HelpContext** as the current index for the help file if more than one index exists in the help file.
cdlHelpContextPopup	&H8	Display the help information in a pop-up window.
cdlHelpForceFile	&H9	Ensure that Windows displays the correct help file. If an incorrect help file is displayed, the help system opens the correct one.
	&HB	Display the help finder. While this is the recommended replacement for the *cdlHelpContents* help command, no keyword value is supplied with Visual Basic.
cdlHelpKey	&H101	Display help for the keyword specified in **HelpKey**.
cdlHelpCommand	&H102	Execute a help macro command.
cdlHelpPartialKey	&H105	Use the partial key specified in **HelpKey** to search the help index file. If only one match is found, then the help topic is displayed; otherwise the search form is shown.

Table C-89: **Help Command** *values.*

- *CommonDialogControl*.**HelpFile**—a **String** that contains the name of the help file.
- *CommonDialogControl*.**HelpKey**—a **String** containing a keyword that accesses an entry in the help file's index.
- *CommonDialogControl*.**Index**—an **Integer** that uniquely identifies a control in a control array.
- *CommonDialogControl*.**InitDir**—a **String** that contains the initial directory used in the Open and Save As dialog boxes.
- *CommonDialogControl*.**Left**—a **Single** that contains the distance measured in twips between the left edge of the control and the left edge of the control's container.
- *CommonDialogControl*.**Min**—an **Integer** that sets either the minimum point size for the font dialog box or the minimum page number that can be selected in the Printer dialog box.
- *CommonDialogControl*.**Max**—an **Integer** that sets either the maximum point size for the font dialog box or the maximum page number that can be selected in the Printer dialog box.
- *ComboBoxControl*.**Name**—a **String** that contains the name of the control that will be used to reference the control in a Visual Basic program. This property is read only at run time.
- *ComboBoxControl*.**Object**—an object that contains a reference to the *ComboBoxControl* object.
- *ComboBoxControl*.**Parent**—an object that contains a reference to the **Form**, **Frame,** or other container that contains this control.
- *ComboBoxControl*.**PrinterDefault**—a **Boolean** when **True** any changes in the Printer dialog box are saved as the default system printer. When **False** the changes don't affect the default system printer.
- *CommonDialogControl*.**Top**—a **Single** that contains the distance measured in twips between the top edge of the control and the top edge of the control's container.
- *CommonDialogControl*.**ToPage**—an **Integer** that contains the ending page for the document to be printed.

Methods

CommonDialogControl.AboutBox

Usage   This method displays an About box for this common dialog control.

CommonDialogControl.ShowColor

Usage   This method displays the Color dialog box.

CommonDialogControl.ShowFont

Usage   This method display the Font dialog box.

CommonDialogControl.ShowHelp

Usage   This method starts the help system.

CommonDialogControl.ShowOpen

Usage   This method displays the Open File dialog box.

CommonDialogControl.ShowPrinter

Usage   This method displays the Printer dialog box.

CommonDialogControl.ShowSave

Usage   This method displays the Save As dialog box.

Examples
```
Private Sub Command2_Click()
On Error Resume Next
CommonDialog1.CancelError = True
CommonDialog1.Flags = cdlCFEffects Or cdlCFForceFontExist Or cdlCFScreenFonts
CommonDialog1.FontBold = Label1.Font.Bold
CommonDialog1.FontItalic = Label1.Font.Italic
CommonDialog1.FontName = Label1.Font.Name
CommonDialog1.FontSize = Label.Font.Size
CommonDialog1.FontStrikethru = Label1.Font.Strikethrough
CommonDialog1.FontUnderline = Label1.Font.Underline
CommonDialog1.ShowFont
If Err.Number = 32755 Then
   MsgBox "Operation canceled!"
```

```
    Else
        Label1.Font.Name = CommonDialog1.FontName
        Label1.Font.Size = CommonDialog1.FontSize
        Label1.Font.Bold = CommonDialog1.FontBold
        Label1.Font.Italic = CommonDialog1.FontItalic
        Label1.Font.Underline = CommonDialog1.FontUnderline
        Label1.FontStrikethru = CommonDialog1.FontStrikethru
        Label1.ForeColor = CommonDialog1.Color
    End If
End Sub
```

This routine shows you how to display the Font dialog box and change the font properties of another object on a form. First I set the font related properties with the values from Label1. Then I use the **ShowFont** method to display the dialog box. After the method I check the **Err** object to see if the user hit the Cancel button. If they did, I display a message box. Otherwise I change the font properties and exit the routine.

See Also **ChDir** (statement), **Font** (object)

Connection

OBJECT

PE, EE

Usage The **Connection** object is used by the Data Access Objects to contain information about a connection to an ODBC database.

Properties
- *ConnectionObject*.**Connect**—a **String** value containing the type of database and any necessary connection information.
- *ConnectionObject*.**Database**—a reference to the underlying database object used to support the control.
- *ConnectionObject*.**Name**—a **String** containing the name of the **Connection** object.
- *ConnectionObject*.**QueryDefs**—a collection of **QueryDef** objects.
- *ConnectionObject*.**QueryTimeout**—an **Integer** value containing the number of seconds before an ODBC connection times out.
- *ConnectionObject*.**RecordsAffected**—a **Long** value containing the number of records affected by the last **Execute** method.
- *ConnectionObject*.**Recordsets**—a collection of **Recordset** objects.
- *ConnectionObject*.**StillExecuting**—a **Boolean** when **True** means that the **Execute** or **OpenConnection** method is still executing asynchronously. **False** means that no methods are currently executing.
- *ConnectionObject*.**Transactions**—a **Boolean** when **True** means that the connection supports transactions using the **BeginTrans**, **CommitTrans**, or **RollBack** methods. **False** means that transactions are not supported.
- *ConnectionObject*.**Updatable**—a **Boolean** when **True** means that the information in the database may be updated. **False** means that database is read only.

Methods

ConnectionObject.Cancel

Usage This method stops the asynchronous execution of the **Execute** or **OpenConnection** method.

ConnectionObject.Close

Usage This method closes a connection object. If there are any open **Recordset** objects, they will be closed before the **Connection** object is closed.

querydef = ConnectionObject.CreateQueryDef ([name] [, [sql]])

Usage This method creates a **QueryDef** object.

Arguments
- *querydef*—an object variable that will contain the new **QueryDef** object.
- *name*—a **String** containing the name of the **QueryDef** object. Must begin with a letter and can be followed by letters, numbers, or an underscore ("_"). You can create a temporary **QueryDef** object by using an empty string form *name*.
- *sql*—a **String** containing an SQL query. If omitted, the query string can be set directly in the object.

ConnectionObject.Execute source [, options]

Usage This method runs an SQL statement on a **Database** object.

Arguments
- *source*—a **String** containing the name of a **QueryDef** object or an SQL query statement.
- *options*—a **Long** containing one or more of the attributes in Table C-90 below.

options Name	Description
dbDenyWrite	Write access is denied to other users.
dbInconsistent	Allow inconsistent updates in Microsoft Jet databases.
dbConsistent	Allow only consistent updates in Microsoft Jet databases.
dbSQLPassThrough	Pass SQL query through Microsoft Jet workspace to remote ODBC database.
dbFileOnError	Perform a rollback if an error is encountered.
dbSeeChanges	Return error if another user is updating data you are using.

Table C-90: options values.

recordset = ConnectionObject.OpenRecordset (source [, type [, options] [, lockedits]])

Usage This method creates a new **RecordSet** object and appends it to the **RecordSets** collection.

Arguments *recordset*—an object variable that will contain the new **TableDef** object.

- *source*—a **String** value containing the table name, query name, or an SQL statement that contains the source for the new record set. For table type record set, only a table name can be used.
- *type*—a constant from Table C-91 below.

type Name	Description
dbOpenTable	Table type record set.
dbOpenDynamic	Open a dynamic type record set (ODBC databases only).
dbOpenDynaset	Open a dynaset type record set.
dbOpenSnapshot	Open a snapshot type record set.
dbOpenForwardOnly	Open a forward-only type record set.

Table C-91: type values.

- *options*—a **Long** containing one or more of the options in Table C-92 below.

options Name	Description
dbAppendOnly	Add new records, but can't delete or edit existing records.
dbConsistent	Allow only consistent updates in Microsoft Jet databases (can't be used with *dbConsistent*).
dbDenyRead	Read access is denied to other users.
dbDenyWrite	Write access is denied to other users.
dbExecDirect	Skip SQLPrepare and run SQLExecDirect for ODBC queries only.
dbInconsistent	Allow inconsistent updates in Microsoft Jet databases (can't be used with *dbConsistent*).
dbReadOnly	User can't change records in the database (can't be used if *dbReadOnly* is specified in *lockedits*).
dbRunAsync	Run ODBC query asynchronously.
dbSeeChanges	Return error if another user is updating data you are using.
dbSQLPassThrough	Pass SQL query through Microsoft Jet workspace to remote ODBC database.

Table C-92: options values.

- *lockedits*—a **Long** containing one or more of the attributes in Table C-93 below.

lockedits Name	Description
dbOptimistic	Lock the page containing the record you are editing when you use the Update method.
dbOptimisticBatch	Enable batch optimistic updating.
dbOptimisticValue	Enable optimistic updating based on row values.
dbPessimistic	Lock the page containing the record you are editing as soon you use the **Edit** method.
dbReadOnly	User can't change records in the database (can't be used if *dbReadOnly* is specified in *options*).

Table C-93: lockedits values.

See Also   **Connections** (collection), **Database** (object), **QueryDef** (object)

Connections

COLLECTION

PE, EE

Usage: The **Connections** collection is used by Data Access Objects (DAO) to contain information about open connections to ODBC databases.

Properties: *ConnectionsCollection*.**Count**—an **Integer** containing the number of **Connection** objects in the collection.

Methods: ***ConnectionsCollection*.Refresh**

> Usage: This method gets a current copy of the documents in the collection. This is important in a multi-user environment where more than one user may be making changes in the **Connections** collection.

See Also: **Connection** (object), **Database** (object)

Const

STATEMENT

CCE, LE, PE, EE

Syntax: [**Public** | **Private**] **Const** *name* [**As** *type*] = *expr* [, *name* [**As** *type*] = *expr*] . . .

Usage: The **Const** statement defines values that can be referenced in your program by name. By default, constants are private and can only be used within the routine or module. Public constants can be referenced outside the module, except in class modules where the constants can't be made public.

Constants can be declared to be a specific type or the best type based on the value of the expression that will be used. The expression can be any valid expression for the specific data type.

Multiple constants may be defined in a single statement. While the public or private keyword will apply to all of the constants in the statement, the value of type is unique to each name and must be explicitly specified for each constant, if needed.

Arguments:
- *name*—the name that contains the value of the constant.
- *type*—a valid Visual Basic type: **Byte**, **Boolean**, **Currency**, **Date**, **Double**, **Integer**, **Long**, **Single**, **String**, **Variant**.
- *expr*—any valid expression.

Examples:
```
Const MaxSize = 32
Dim MyArray(MaxSize) As Integer

Private Sub Command1_Click()
Dim i As Integer
```

```
For i = 0 To MaxSize
    MyArray(i) = 0
Next i
End Sub
```

This program declares and initializes an integer array. The size of the array depends on the value of the constant MaxSize. Note that the constant is also used inside the program rather than using the **LBound** and **UBound** functions.

See Also **Byte** (data type), **Boolean** (data type), **Currency** (data type), **Date** (data type), **Dim** (statement), **Double** (data type), **Integer** (data type), **LBound** (function), **Long** (data type), **Single** (data type), **String** (data type), **Variant** (data type), **UBound** (function)

ContainedControls

COLLECTION

CCE, LE, PE, EE

Usage The **ContainedControls** collection is used by the **UserControl** to keep track of the controls that are contained in the user control.

Properties
- *ContainedControlsCollection*.**Count**—an **Integer** containing the number of controls in the collection.
- *ContainedControlsCollection*.**Item** (*index*)—returns an object from the collection specified by *index*. Index can range in value from zero to **Count -1**.

See Also **UserControl** (object)

Container

OBJECT

PE, EE

Usage The **Container** object is used by the Data Access Objects to contain information about **Document** objects.

Properties
- *ContainerObject*.**AllPermissions**—a **Long** containing the permissions (see Table C-94) that apply to the current **UserName** including those that are inherited from membership in various **Workgroups**.

AllPermissions Name	Description
dbSecReadDef	Read table definitions, including column and index definitions.
dbSecWriteDef	Update or delete table definitions, including column and index definitions.
dbSecRetrieveData	Retrieve information from the document object.
dbSecInsertData	Add records.
dbSecReplaceData	Update records.
dbSecDeleteData	Delete records.

Table C-94: AllPermissions values.

- *ContainerObject*.**Inherit**—a **Boolean** when **True** means that a new **Document** object will inherit the default **Permissions** property setting. **False** means that the new document will not inherit any permissions.
- *ContainerObject*.**Name**—a **String** containing the name of the **Container** object.
- *ContainerObject*.**Owner**—a **String** value containing the owner of the document.
- *ContainerObject*.**Permissions**—a **Long** containing the permissions (see Table C-95) that apply to the current **UserName**. Does not include those that are inherited from membership in various **Workgroups**.

Permissions Name	Description
dbSecReadDef	Read table definitions, including column and index definitions.
dbSecWriteDef	Update or delete table definitions, including column and index definitions.
dbSecRetrieveData	Retrieve information from the document object.
dbSecInsertData	Add records.
dbSecReplaceData	Update records.
dbSecDeleteData	Delete records.

Table C-95: Permissions values.

- *ContainerObject*.**Properties**—a collection of **Property** objects.
- *ContainerObject*.**UserName**—a **String** value containing the name of a user or group of users that are associated with the **Permissions** and **AllPermissions** properties.

See Also **Containers** (collection), **Database** (object), **Document** (object)

Containers

COLLECTION

PE, EE

Usage The **Containers** collection is used by Data Access Objects (DAO) to contain information about the collection of **Container** objects.

Properties
- *ContainersCollection*.**Count**—an **Integer** containing the number of **Container** objects in the collection.

Methods *ContainersCollection*.**Refresh**

Usage This method gets a current copy of the documents in the collection. This is important in a multi-user environment where more than one user may be making changes in the **Containers** collection.

See Also **Database** (object)

Control

OBJECT

CCE, LE, PE, EE

Usage The **Control** object is the class name used for all controls. It has no properties or methods and can be treated like a regular object.

Examples
```
Private Sub Command1_Click()
Dim MyControl As Control
Set MyControl = Text1
MyControl.Text = "MyControl"
End Sub
```

This routine declares a variable of type control and then assigns a reference of the Text1 text box to it. Then it uses the Text property to assign the value of "MyControl" to the text box.

See Also **Dim** (statement), **Set** (statement)

Controls

COLLECTION

CCE, LE, PE, EE

Usage The **Controls** collection contains a set of methods to store and retrieve information about the column headers in a **ListView** control.

Properties ▪ *ControlCollection*.**Count**—a **Long** value that contains the number of items in the collection.

Methods

ControlsCollection.Clear

Usage This method removes all of the controls from the control collection.

Item = *ControlsCollection*.Item (*index*)

Usage This method retrieves an item specified by *index* from the controls collection. This is the default method for this object, so the method name **Item** can be omitted.

Arguments
- *item*—a variable that will contain a reference to the control from the collection.
- *index*—either a numeric value that represents the relative position or a **String** value that contains the name of the control to be retrieved from the controls collection.

ControlCollection.Remove *index*

Usage This method deletes an item specified by *index* from the controls collection.

Arguments
- *index*—either a numeric value that represents the relative position or a **String** value that contains the name of the control to be retrieved from the controls collection.

Examples
```
Private Sub Form_Load()
    ListView1.View = lvwReport
    ListView1.ColumnHeaders.Add , "name", "Name"
    ListView1.ColumnHeaders("name").Width = 2000
    ListView1.ColumnHeaders.Add , "nick", "Nickname"
    ListView1.ColumnHeaders("nick").Width = 2000
    ListView1.ColumnHeaders.Add , "email", "E-Mail"
    ListView1.ColumnHeaders("email").Width = 2000
End Sub
```

This routine selects the report view format for the ListView1 control and then adds three columns, Name, Nickname, and E-Mail address. It also sets the width of each column to 2000 twips.

See Also **Control** (object), **Form** (object)

Coor
OBJECT

CCE, LE, PE, EE

Usage The **Coor** object contains a pair of **Single** coordinate values.

Properties
- *CoorObject*.**X**—a **Single** value that contains the X coordinate.
- *CoorObject*.**Y**—a **Single** value that contains the X coordinate.

Methods *CoorObject*.**Set** *xvalue, yvalue*

    Usage This method is used to assign a value to the coordinates.

    Arguments
- *xvalue*—a **Single** expression that contain the x coordinate value.
- *yvalue*—a **Single** expression that contain the y coordinate value.

See Also **LCoor** (object), **MSChart** (control)

Cos
FUNCTION

CCE, LE, PE, EE

Syntax *RValue* = **Cos** (*Number*)

Usage The **Cos** function will return the cosine of *Number* specified in radians.

> **Tip**
>
> *There are two pi radians in a circle, and there are 360 degrees in a circle. Pi is approximately equal to 3.1415926535897932384. To convert radians to degrees, multiply by 180/pi. To convert degrees to radians, multiply by pi/180.*

Arguments
- *RValue*—a **Double** that contains the cosine of *Number*.
- *Number*—a **Double** expression that is passed to the **Cos** function. This value is specified in radians.

Examples
```
Private Sub Command1_Click()
If IsNumeric(Text1.Text) Then
    Text2.Text = Format(Cos(CDbl(Text1.Text)))
End If
End Sub
```

This routine will compute the cosine of the value in the Text1 text box and display the results in the Text2 text box.

See Also   **Atn** (function), **Sin** (function), **Tan** (function)

CreateObject

FUNCTION

CCE, LE, PE, EE

Syntax   *RValue* = **CreateObject**(*Class*)

Usage   The **CreateObject** will dynamically create an instance of an ActiveX control.

Arguments
- *class*—a **String** which contains the application name and object type within the application.

Examples
```
Private Sub Command1_Click()
Dim myobj As Object
Set myobj = CreateObject("excel.application")
myobj.Visible = True
MsgBox "Close Excel?"
myobj.quit
End Sub
```

This routine declares a variable of type object and assigns a pointer to a newly created instance of Excel's application object. It then makes Excel visible and prompts the user to close Excel. Finally, it uses the Quit method of the Excel.Application object to close the window.

See Also   **GetObject** (function)

CSng

FUNCTION

CCE, LE, PE, EE

Syntax BValue = **CSng** (Value)

Usage The **CSng** function converts a string or numeric value to a single precision, floating point value in the range -3.402823E38 to -1.401298E-45 for negative values and 1.401298E-45 to 3.402823E38 for positive values. Any **String** value that does not contain a valid numeric value will generate a run-time error '13' type mismatch. Any value that is outside of the range of acceptable values will generate a run-time error '6' overflow.

Tip

*To prevent run-time errors, use the **On Error** statement to prevent the error from stopping the program, and test the **Err** object to see if an error occurred. Also using the **IsNumeric** function will help to prevent conversion errors.*

Arguments
- *SValue*—a **Single** that contains the result of converting *value* to a single value.
- *Value*—a numeric or **String** value to be converted to a **Single** value.

Examples
```
Private Sub Command1_Click()
On Error Resume Next
Text2.Text = Format(CSng(Text1.Text))
If Err.Number > 0 Then
    Text2.Text = Err.Description
End If
End Sub
```

This routine converts the value in Text1.Text to a **Single** value and then uses the **Format** function to convert the **Single** value into a form that can be shown in a text box. Note that I checked the **Err** object to ensure that the conversion process worked properly.

See Also **Err** (object), **Format** (function), **On Error** (statement), **Single** (data type)

CStr

FUNCTION

CCE, LE, PE, EE

Syntax SValue = **CStr** (Value)

Usage The **CStr** function converts nearly any variable type into a string. Numeric values are converted into a string value that can be displayed.

Tip

*Use the **Format** function to convert numeric and date values into displayable string values.*

Arguments
- *SValue*—a **String** variable that contains the result of converting *value* to a **String** value.
- *Value*—a numeric or **String** value (see Table C-96) to be converted to a **String** value.

Value	SValue
Boolean	True or False will be returned.
Date	A string containing the data in short date format will be returned.
Null	An error will occur.
Empty	An empty string will be returned.
Other numeric	A string containing the number will be returned.

Table C-96: Return values for value.

Examples
```
Private Sub Command1_Click()
On Error Resume Next
Text2.Text = CStr (CDbl(Text1.Text))
If Err.Number > 0 Then
    Text2.Text = Err.Description
End If
End Sub
```

This routine converts the value in Text1.Text to a **Double** value and then uses the **CStr** function to convert the **Double** value back into a string. Note that I checked the **Err** object to ensure that the conversion process worked properly.

See Also   **Double** (data type), **Error** (object), **Format** (function), **On Error** (statement)

CurDir

STATEMENT

CCE, LE, PE, EE

Syntax   *path* = **CurDir[$]** [(*drive*)]

Usage   The **CurDir** function returns the current directory for the specified drive. If *drive* is not specified, then the current directory for the current drive will be returned. If the $ is specified, the return value will be a **String**; otherwise a **Variant** will be returned.

If the directory path in *path* is not valid, a run-time error '76' path not found will be displayed.

> **Tip**
>
> *To prevent run-time errors, use the **On Error** statement to prevent the error from stopping the program, and test the **Err** object to see if an error occurred.*

Arguments
- *path*—a **Variant** or **String** expression that will contain the current directory path.
- *drive*—a **String** expression that contains the valid drive.

Examples
```
Private Sub Command1_Click()
On Error Resume Next
If Len(Text1.Text) > 0 Then
    ChDir Text1.Text
End If
If Err.Number = 0 Then
    Text2.Text = CurDir("c:")
Else
    Text2.Text = Err.Description
End If
End Sub
```

This routine uses the **ChDir** function to switch the current directory to the value specified in Text1.Text. I then check the **Err** object to see if an error occurred and display either the error information or the new current directory using the **CurDir** function.

See Also   **ChDir** (function), **ChDrive** (function), **Dir** (function), **DirListBox** (control), **DriveListBox** (control), **FileListBox** (control), **MkDir** (statement), **RmDir** (statement)

Currency

DATA TYPE

CCE, LE, PE, EE

Usage   The **Currency** data type holds integer values in the range -922,337,203,685,477.5808 to 922,337,203,685,477.5807. A single **Currency** variable only occupies 64 bits of storage or 8 bytes. The actual value is stored as an integer value with four digits to the right of the decimal point and as many as fifteen digits to the left.

> **Tip**
>
> *This data type is useful when doing monetary calculations, since the decimal values are represented exactly rather than approximated as in **Single** and **Double** values.*

See Also   **CCur** (function), **CInt** (function), **CLng** (function), **CStr** (function), **Double** (data type), **Dim** (statement), **Format** (function), **Integer** (data type), **IsNumeric** (function), **Single** (data type)

CVar

FUNCTION

CCE, LE, PE, EE

Syntax   *VValue* = **CVar** (*Value*)

Usage   The **CVar** function converts a **String** or numeric value into a **Variant** value. Numeric values are converted to a **Double** value in the range -1.79769313486232E308 to -4.94065645841247E-324 for negative values and 4.94065645841247E-324 to 1.79769313486232E308 for positive values, while **String** values are simply stored in the **Variant**.

Arguments
- *VValue*—a **Variant** variable that contains the result of converting *value* to a **Variant** value.
- *Value*—a numeric or **String** value to be converted to a **Variant** value.

Examples
```
Private Sub Command1_Click()
On Error Resume Next
Text2.Text = Format(CDbl (Text1.Text))
If Err.Number > 0 Then
    Text2.Text = Err.Description
End If
End Sub
```

This routine converts the value in Text1.Text to a **Double** value and then uses the **Format** function to convert the **Double** value into a form that can be shown in a **TextBox**. Note that I checked the **Err** object to ensure that the conversion process worked properly.

See Also **Double** (data type), **Error** (object), **Format** (function), **IsNumeric** (function), **On Error** (statement), **Variant** (data type)

CVDate

FUNCTION

CCE, LE, PE, EE

Syntax *DValue* = **CVDate** (*Value*)

Usage The **CVDate** function converts a **String** or numeric value to a **Variant** value with a subtype of date, in the range of 1 January 100 to 31 December 9999. Also any **String** value that does not contain a valid date value will generate a run-time error '13' Type mismatch. The **CVDate** will also handle time values, either alone or in combination with a date value.

> **Note**
>
> *This function exists to maintain compatibility with previous versions of Visual Basic. You should use the **CDate** routine and **Date** variables instead.*

> **Tip**
>
> *To prevent run-time errors, use the **On Error** statement to prevent the error from stopping the program, and test the **Err** object to see if an error occurred. Also using the **IsDate** function will help to prevent conversion errors.*

Arguments
- *DValue*—a **Variant** variable that contains the result of converting *value* to a **Variant** value.
- *Value*—a numeric or **String** value to be converted to a **Variant** value.

Examples
```
Private Sub Command1_Click()
On Error Resume Next
Text2.Text = Format(CVDate (Text1.Text))
If Err.Number > 0 Then
   Text2.Text = Err.Description
End If
End Sub
```

This routine converts the value in Text1.Text to a **Variant** value and then uses the **Format** function to convert the **Variant** value into a form that can be shown in a **TextBox**. Note that I checked the **Err** object to ensure that the conversion process worked properly.

See Also   **Date** (data type), **Error** (object), **Format** (function), **IsDate** (function), **On Error** (statement), **Variant** (data type)

CVErr

FUNCTION

CCE, LE, PE, EE

Syntax   *EValue* = **CVErr** (*Value*)

Usage   The **CVErr** function returns a **Variant** of subtype error that contains the error number contained in *Value*.

Arguments
- *EValue*—a **Variant** variable that contains the result of converting *value* to a **Variant** value.
- *Value*—a numeric value that will indicate the error number.

Examples
```
Private Sub Command1_Click()
On Error Resume Next
Text2.Text = CStr(CVErr(Text1.Text))
If Err.Number = 13 Then
   Text2.Text = Err.Description
End If
End Sub
```

This routine converts the value in Text1.Text to a **Variant** value and then uses the **CStr** function to convert the **Variant** value into a form that can be shown in a **TextBox**. Note that I checked the **Err** object to ensure that the conversion process worked properly.

See Also   **CSrt** (function), **Date** (data type), **Error** (object), **On Error** (statement), **Variant** (data type)

Data

CONTROL

CCE, LE, PE, EE

Usage　The **Data** control is an intrinsic control which provides access to databases. This control includes facilities for inserting new records into the database, and updating and deleting existing records. It also provides you with the ability to move through the database and have other, data aware controls (like the **CheckBox**, **ComboBox**, **Image**, **Label**, **ListBox**, **MaskedEdit**, **Picture**, **RichTextBox**, and **TextBox** controls) automatically update the information they display. Other controls like **DBCombo**, **DBGrid**, **DBList**, and **MSFlexGrid** will also work with the **Data** control to provide access to a database.

Properties
- *DataControl*.**Align**—an **Integer** value (see Table D-1) that describes the placement of the **Data** control.

Align Name	Value	Description
vbAlignNone	0	The **Data** control's position is set at design time or by the program (default value for objects on a non-**MDIForm**).
vbAlignTop	1	The **Data** control is placed at the top of the form and its width is set to **ScaleWidth**. It will automatically be resized when the form is resized (default value for objects on an MDI Form).
vbAlignBottom	2	The **Data** control is placed at the bottom of the form and its width is set to **ScaleWidth**. It will automatically be resized when the form is resized.
vbAlignLeft	3	The **Data** control is placed at the left edge of the form and its width is set to **ScaleWidth**. It is not resized when the form is resized.
vbAlignRight	4	The **Data** control is placed at the right edge of the form and its width is set to **ScaleWidth**. It is not resized when the form is resized.

Table D-1: Align *values.*

- *DataControl*.**Appearance**—an **Integer** value (see Table D-2) that specifies how the **Data** control will appear on the form.

Appearance Value	Description
0	The **Data** control displays without the 3D effects.
1	The **Data** control displays with 3D effects (default value).

Table D-2: Appearance *values.*

- *DataControl*.**BackColor**—a **Long** that contains the suggested value for the background color of the control. The **BackColor** and **ForeColor** must both be solid to display text. If you choose a color that is dithered, it will change to the nearest solid color.
- *DataControl*.**BOFAction**—an **Integer** value (see Table D-3) containing the action to take when the beginning of file is encountered.

BOFAction Name	Value	Description
vbBOFActionMoveFirst	0	The first record is kept as the current record.
vbEOFActionBOF	1	Encountering the BOF will trigger the **Validate** event, followed by a **Reposition** event. The Move Previous button on the control will be disabled.

Table D-3: BOFAction *values*.

- *DataControl.***Caption**—a **String** value that displays inside data control. You can include an access key for this control by inserting an ampersand (&) in front of the character you want to use. The selected character will then appear with an underline. Then, if the user presses the Alt key with the underlined character, the control will gain the focus.
- *DataControl.***Connect**—a **String** value containing the type of database and any necessary connection information.
- *DataControl.***Database**—a reference to the underlying database object used to support the control.

> **Note**
>
> *This property is useful mostly with the Professional and Enterprise editions of Visual Basic where you can manipulate the database object directly.*

- *DataControl.***DatabaseName**—a **String** value that contains the path and file name for a Microsoft Jet database file (.MDB) or other database file.
- *DataControl.***DefaultCursorType**—an **Integer** constant (see Table D-4) that is used by ODBC database only to identify the type of database cursor.

DefaultCursorType Name	Value	Description
vbUseDefaultCursor	0	The ODBC driver will choose the type of cursor (default).
vbUseODBCCursor	1	The ODBC cursor library will be used. This option offers better performance on small tables but rather poor performance on large tables.
vbUseServerSideCursor	2	The server's cursor is used. This option offers better performance on large tables but may place a higher load on the network.

Table D-4: DefaultCursorType *values*.

- *DataControl.***DefaultType**—an **Integer** value (see Table D-5) describing the type of database engine you want to use.

DefaultType Name	Value	Description
vbUseODBC	1	The ODBC database driver is used directly.
vbUseJet	2	The Microsoft Jet database engine is used (default).

Table D-5: DefaultType *values*.

- *DataControl*.**DragIcon**—an object that contains the picture value of an icon. At design time, you can specify an icon file that has a file type of .ICO.

> **Tip**
>
> *This value can be created by copying the value from another control's **DragIcon** value, a form's icon, or by using the **LoadPicture** function.*

- *DataControl*.**DragMode**—an **Integer** value (see Table D-6) specifying how the control will respond to a drag request.

> **Tip**
>
> *Setting **DragMode** to vbAutomatic will automatically begin a drag operation when the user clicks on the control. However, the control will not respond to the usual mouse events (**Click**, **DblClick**, **MouseDown**, **MouseMove**, **MouseUp**).*

DragMode Name	Value	Description
vbManual	0	The **Drag** method must be used to begin a drag-and-drop operation (default value).
vbAutomatic	1	The source control will automatically begin a drag-and-drop operation when the user clicks on the control.

Table D-6: **DragMode** *values.*

- *DataControl*.**Enabled**—a **Boolean** value when **True** means that the control will respond to events. When **False**, the control will not respond to events.
- *DataControl*.**EOFAction**—an **Integer** value (see Table D-7) containing the action to take when the end of file is encountered.

EOFAction Name	Value	Description
vbEOFActionMoveFirst	0	The last record is kept as the current record.
vbEOFActionEOF	1	Encountering the EOF will trigger the **Validate** event, followed by a **Reposition** event. The Move Next button on the control will be disabled.
vbEOFActionAddNew	2	Encountering the EOF will trigger the **Validate** event on the current record, followed by an **AddNew**, followed by a **Reposition** event.

Table D-7: EOFAction *values.*

- *DataControl*.**Exclusive**—a **Boolean** when **True** means that the database is opened in single-user (exclusive) mode. When **False** means that other users can access the database (default).
- *DataControl*.**Font**—an object that contains information about the character font used by this object.

> **Tip**
>
> *The **Font** object should be used in place of the other **Font** properties, since it offers more functionality than the individual properties.*

130 • The Visual Basic 5 Programmer's Reference

- *DataControl*.**FontBold**—a **Boolean** when **True** means that the characters display in bold. **False** means that the characters display normally.
- *DataControl*.**FontItalic**—a **Boolean** when **True** means that the characters display in italics. **False** means that the characters display normally.
- *DataControl*.**FontName**—a **String** that specifies the name of the font that should be used to display the characters in this control.
- *DataControl*.**FontSize**—a **Single** that specifies the point size that should be used to display the characters in the control.
- *DataControl*.**FontStrikethru**—a **Boolean** when **True** means that the characters display with a line through the center. **False** means that the characters display normally.
- *DataControl*.**FontUnderlined**—a **Boolean** when **True** means that the characters display with a line beneath them. **False** means that the characters display normally.
- *DataControl*.**ForeColor**—a **Long** that contains the suggested value for the foreground color of the contained control. This property is read only at run time.
- *DataControl*.**Height**—a **Single** that contains the height of the control.
- *DataControl*.**Index**—an **Integer** that uniquely identifies a control in a control array.
- *DataControl*.**Left**—a **Single** that contains the distance measured in twips between the left edge of the control and the left edge of the control's container.
- *DataControl*.**MouseIcon**—a **Picture** object (a bitmap, icon, or metafile) that will be used as a cursor when the **MousePointer** property is set to 99. Note that Visual Basic does not support color cursors from a .CUR file. Use a color icon from an .ICO file instead.
- *DataControl*.**MousePointer**—an **Integer** value (see Table D-8) that contains the value of the cursor to display when the cursor is moved over this control. Use *vbCustom* to display the custom icon stored in the **MouseIcon** property.

Cursor Name	Value	Description
vbDefault	0	Shape determined by the object (default value)
vbArrow	1	Arrow
vbCrosshair	2	Crosshair
vbIbeam	3	I beam
vbIconPointer	4	Square inside a square
vbSizePointer	5	Four sided arrow (north, south, east, west)
vbSizeNESW	6	Two sided arrow (northeast, southwest)
vbSizeNS	7	Two sided arrow (north, south)
vbSizeNWSE	8	Two sided arrow (northwest, southeast)
vbSizeWE	9	Two sided arrow (west, east)
vbUpArrow	10	Single sided arrow pointing north
vbHourglass	11	Hourglass
vbNoDrop	12	No Drop
vbArrowHourglass	13	An arrow and an hourglass
vbArrowQuestion	14	An arrow and a question mark
vbSizeAll	15	Size all
vbCustom	99	Custom icon from the **MouseIcon** property of this control

Table D-8: Cursor *values.*

- *DataControl*.**Name**—a **String** that contains the name of the control that will be used to reference the control in a Visual Basic program. This property is read only at run time.
- *DataControl*.**OLEDropMode**—an **Integer** value (see Table D-9) that describes how the control will respond to OLE drop operations.

OLEDropMode Name	Value	Description
vbOLEDropNone	0	The control does not accept OLE drops. The cursor is changed to the No Drop cursor (default value).
vbOLEDropManual	1	The control responds to OLE drops under the program's control (manual).
vbOLEDropAutomatic	2	The control automatically accepts OLE drops if it recognizes the format of the data object.

Table D-9: OLEDropMode values.

- *DataControl*.**Options**—an **Integer** value (see Table D-10) containing options that apply to the **Recordset**. To specify multiple options, simply add them together.

Options Name	Value	Description
dbDenyWrite	1	Other users can't update the data in the record set.
dbDenyRead	2	Other users can't read the data in a table type record set.
dbReadOnly	4	You can't update the data in the record set.
dbAppendOnly	8	You can add new records to the record set, but you can't read them.
dbInconsistent	16	You can change any value in the record set, even if it means that it wouldn't be part of the record set.
dbConsistent	32	You can change any value in the record, unless it would violate the select condition.
dbSQLPassThrough	64	The SQL statement in the **RecordSource** statement is sent to the ODBC server.
dbForwardOnly	256	You can only scroll forward in the record set.
dbSeeChanges	512	Generate an error if someone else is changing the data you are editing.

Table D-10: Options values.

- *DataControl*.**Parent**—an object that contains a reference to the **Form**, **Frame**, or other container that contains the **Data** control.
- *DataControl*.**Picture**—a **Boolean** value when **True** means that the database is opened in read-only mode. When **False** means that the database is opened with read-write access (default).
- *DataControl*.**Recordset**—returns or sets a reference to the **Recordset** object used by the **Data** control.
- *DataControl*.**RecordsetType**—an **Integer** value (see Table D-11) that contains the type of record set.

RecordsetType Name	Value	Description
vbRSTypeTable	0	Table-type record set
vbRSTypeDynaset	1	Dynaset type record set (default)
vbRSTypeSnapshot	2	Snapshot type record set

Table D-11: RecordsetType values.

- *DataControl*.**RecordSource**—a **String** value containing the underlying table, SQL statement, or **QueryDef** object.
- *DataControl*.**RightToLeft**—a **Boolean** value when **True** means that the text displays from right to left. When **False** means that the text displays from left to right. A bi-directional version of Windows is required to set this property to **True**.
- *DataControl*.**Tag**—a **String** that can hold programmer specific information. This property is not used by Visual Basic.
- *DataControl*.**ToolTipText**—a **String** that holds a text value that can be displayed as a **ToolTip** box that displays whenever the cursor is held over the control for about one second.
- *DataControl*.**Top**—a **Single** that contains the distance measured in twips between the top edge of the control and the top edge of the control's container.
- *DataControl*.**Visible**—a **Boolean** value when **True** means that the control is visible. When **False** means that the control is not visible.

> **Tip**
>
> *This property hides the control until the program is ready to display it.*

- *DataControl*.**WhatsThisHelpID**—a **Long** that contains a help file context ID number that references an entry in the help file. This provides a What's This PopUp help display in response to the What's This button in the upper right corner of the window.
- *DataControl*.**Width**—a **Single** that contains the width of the control.

Methods

DataControl.**Drag** [*DragAction*]

Usage This method begins, ends, or cancels a drag operation.

Arguments *DragAction*—an **Integer** that contains a value selected from Table D-12 below.

DragAction Name	Value	Description
vbCancel	0	Cancels any drag operation in progress.
vbBeginDrag	1	Begins a drag operation (default).
vbEndDrag	2	Ends a drag operation and drops *object*.

Table D-12: DragAction *values*.

DataControl.**Move** *Left* [, *Top* [, *Width* [, *Height*]]]

Usage This method changes the position and the size of the **Data** control. The **ScaleMode** of the **Form** or other container object that holds the control will determine the units used to specify the coordinates.

Arguments
- *Left*—a **Single** that specifies the new position of the left edge of the control.
- *Top*—a **Single** that specifies the new position of the top edge of the control.
- *Width*—a **Single** that specifies the new width of the control.
- *Height*—a **Single** that specifies the new height of the control.

DataControl.OLEDrag

Usage   This method begins an **OLEDrag** and drop operation. Invoking this method will trigger the **OLEStartDrag** event.

DataControl.Refresh

Usage   This method gets a fresh copy of the data in the record set.

DataControl.ShowWhatsThis

Usage   This method displays the ShowWhatsThis help information for this control.

DataControl.UpdateControls

Usage   This method retrieves the current record from the record set object and updates the fields in the bound data controls.

Tip

When the user wants to cancel their changes to the bound data controls, use this method to restore the old values from the database. It has the added advantage of not triggering any events.

DataControl.UpdateRecord

Usage   This method updates the database with the current values of the data bound controls.

Tip

When the user wants to save their changes to the bound data controls, use this method to save the changes. It has the added advantage of not triggering any events.

DataControl.ZOrder [position]

Usage   This method specifies the position of the control relative to the other objects on the form.

Tip

*Note that there are three layers of objects on a form: the back layer is the drawing space which contains the results of the graphical methods, the middle layer contains graphical objects and **Labels**, and the top layer contains nongraphical controls such as the **Data** control. The **ZOrder** method only affects how the objects are arranged within a single layer.*

Arguments   ▪ *position*—an **Integer** that specifies the relative position of this object. A value of 0 means that the control is positioned at the head of the list, a value of 1 means that the control will be placed at the end of the list.

Events

Private Sub *DataControl*_DragDrop([*index* As Integer ,] *source* As Control, *x* As Single, *y* As Single)

Usage — This event occurs when a drag-and-drop operation is completed by using the **Drag** method with a *DragAction* value of *vbEndDrag* (2).

Tip

*When using drag-and-drop operations, use the **DragOver** event to determine what the cursor should look like while the cursor moves over the control.*

Arguments
- *index*—an **Integer** that uniquely identifies a control in a control array. This argument is not present if the control is not part of a control array.
- *source*—a control object that is the control that is being dragged.

Tip

You can access a property or method from the source control by using source.property *or* source.method. *You can determine the type of object or control by using the **TypeOf** operator.*

- *x*—a **Single** that contains the horizontal location of the mouse pointer.
- *y*—a **Single** that contains the vertical location of the mouse pointer.

Private Sub *DataControl*_DragOver([*index* As Integer ,] *source* As Control, *x* As Single, *y* As Single, *state* As Integer)

Usage — This event occurs while a drag operation is in progress and the cursor is moved over the control.

Tip

*When using drag-and-drop operations, use the **DragOver** event to determine what the cursor should look like while the cursor moves over the control. When* state *is 0, you can change the cursor to a No Drop (vbNoDrop) cursor or highlight the field that the cursor is near. When* state *is 1, you can undo the changes you made when the* state *was 0.*

Arguments
- *index*—an **Integer** that uniquely identifies a control in a control array. This argument is not present if the control is not part of a control array.
- *source*—a control object that is the control that is being dragged.

Tip

You can access a property or method from the source control by using source.property *or* source.method. *You can determine the type of object or control by using the **TypeOf** operator.*

- *x*—a **Single** that contains the horizontal location of the mouse pointer.
- *y*—a **Single** that contains the vertical location of the mouse pointer.

- *state*—an **Integer** value (see Table D-13) that indicates the state of the object being dragged.

state Name	Value	Description
vbEnter	0	The dragged object is entering range of the control.
vbLeave	1	The dragged object is leaving range of the control.
vbOver	2	The dragged object has moved from one position over the control to another.

Table D-13: state *values.*

Private Sub *DataControl*_Error ([*index* As Integer ,] *errcode* As Integer, *resp* As Single)

Usage   This event occurs when a data error occurs while your code is not running. This could happen because a user clicked the **Data** control, the **Data** control automatically loading a record set after Form_Load occurred or if a custom control performs a **MoveNext**, **AddNew**, or a **Delete**.

Arguments
- *errcode*—an **Integer** containing the error code.
- *resp*—an **Integer** value (see Table D-14) that contains the program's response to the error.

resp Name	Value	Description
vbDataErrContinue	0	Continue processing.
vbDataErrDisplay	1	Display error message (default).

Table D-14: resp *values.*

Private Sub *DataControl*_MouseDown([*index* As Integer ,] *button* As Integer, *shift* As Single, *x* As Single, *y* As Single)

Usage   This event occurs when a mouse button was pressed while the cursor is over the control.

Arguments
- *index*—an **Integer** that uniquely identifies a control in a control array. This argument is not present if the control is not part of a control array.
- *button*—an **Integer** value (see Table D-15) that contains information about the mouse buttons that were pressed. Only one button will be indicated when this event occurs.

button Name	Value	Description
vbLeftButton	1	The left button was pressed.
vbRightButton	2	The right button was pressed.
vbMiddleButton	4	The middle button was pressed.

Table D-15: button *values.*

- *shift*—an **Integer** value (see Table D-16) that contains information about the Shift and Alt keys that were pushed when the mouse button was pressed. These values can be added together if more than one key was down. For instance, a value of 5 would mean that the Shift and Alt keys were both down when the mouse button was pressed.

shift Name	Value	Description
vbShiftMask	1	The Shift key was pressed.
vbCtrlMask	2	The Ctrlkey was pressed.
vbAltMask	4	The Alt key was pressed.

Table D-16: shift *values.*

- *x*—a **Single** that contains the horizontal location of the mouse pointer.
- *y*—a **Single** that contains the vertical location of the mouse pointer.

Private Sub *DataControl__MouseMove* ([*index* As Integer ,] *button* As Integer, *shift* As Single, *x* As Single, *y* As Single)

Usage This event occurs while the cursor is moved over the control.

Arguments
- *index*—an **Integer** that uniquely identifies a control in a control array. This argument is not present if the control is not part of a control array.
- *button*—an **Integer** value (see Table D-17) that contains information about the mouse buttons that were pressed. These values can be added together if more than one button was pushed. For instance, a value of 3 means that both the left and right buttons were pressed. A value of 0 means that no buttons were pressed.

button Name	Value	Description
vbLeftButton	1	The left button was pressed.
vbRightButton	2	The right button was pressed.
vbMiddleButton	4	The middle button was pressed.

Table D-17: button *values.*

- *shift*—an **Integer** value (see Table D-18) that contains information about the Shift and Alt keys that were pushed when the mouse button was pressed. These values can be added together if more than one key was down. For instance, a value of 5 would mean that the Shift and Alt keys were both down when the mouse button was pressed. A value of 0 means that none of these keys were pressed.

shift Name	Value	Description
vbShiftMask	1	The Shift key was pressed.
vbCtrlMask	2	The Ctrl key was pressed.
vbAltMask	4	The Alt key was pressed.

Table D-18: shift *values.*

- *x*—a **Single** that contains the horizontal location of the mouse pointer.
- *y*—a **Single** that contains the vertical location of the mouse pointer.

Private Sub *DataControl*_MouseUp([*index* As Integer ,] *button* As Integer, *shift* As Single, *x* As Single, *y* As Single)

Usage — This event occurs when a mouse button is released while the cursor is over the control.

Arguments
- *index*—an **Integer** that uniquely identifies a control in a control array. This argument is not present if the control is not part of a control array.
- *button*—an **Integer** value (see Table D-19) that contains information about the mouse buttons that were released. Only one of these values will be present.

button Name	Value	Description
vbLeftButton	1	The left button was released.
vbRightButton	2	The right button was released.
vbMiddleButton	4	The middle button was released.

Table D-19: button *values*.

- *shift*—an **Integer** value (see Table D-20) that contains information about the Shift and Alt keys that were pushed when the mouse button was released. These values can be added together if more than one key was down. For instance, a value of 5 would mean that the Shift and Alt keys were both down when the mouse button was released. A value of 0 means that none of these keys were pressed.

shift Name	Value	Description
vbShiftMask	1	The Shift key was pressed.
vbCtrlMask	2	The Ctrl key was pressed.
vbAltMask	4	The Alt key was pressed.

Table D-20: shift *values*.

- *x*—a **Single** that contains the horizontal location of the mouse pointer.
- *y*—a **Single** that contains the vertical location of the mouse pointer.

Private Sub *DataControl*_OLECompleteDrag([*index* As Integer ,] *effect* As Long)

Usage — This event tells the source control the results of an OLE drag-and-drop operation. This is the final event to occur in the series of actions that make up an OLE drag-and-drop operation.

Arguments
- *index*—an **Integer** that uniquely identifies a control in a control array. This argument is not present if the control is not part of a control array.
- *effect*—a **Long** (see Table D-21) that returns the status of the OLE drag-and-drop operation.

effect Name	Value	Description
vbDropEffectNone	0	The operation was canceled or the target control can't accept the drop operation.
vbDropEffectCopy	1	The operation copied data from the source control to the target control. The original data is unchanged.
vbDropEffectMove	2	The operation results in a link from the original data to the target control.

Table D-21: effect *values.*

Private Sub *DataControl*_OLEDragDrop([*index* As Integer ,] *data* As DataObject, *effect* As Long, *button* As Integer, *shift* As Single, *x* As Single, *y* As Single)

Usage   This event tells the source control the results of an OLE drag-and-drop operation. This is the final event to occur in the series of actions that make up an OLE drag-and-drop operation.

Arguments
- *index*—an **Integer** that uniquely identifies a control in a control array. This argument is not present if the control is not part of a control array.
- *data*—a **DataObject** that contains the formats that the source control will provide. If the data is not contained in the **DataObject**, then it can be retrieved with the **GetData** method.
- *effect*—a **Long** (see Table D-22) that returns the status of the OLE drag-and-drop operation.

effect Name	Value	Description
vbDropEffectNone	0	The operation was canceled or the target control can't accept the drop operation.
vbDropEffectCopy	1	The operation copied data from the source control to the target control. The original data is unchanged.
vbDropEffectMove	2	The operation results in a link from the original data to the target control.

Table D-22: effect *values.*

- *button*—an **Integer** (see Table D-23) that contains information about the mouse buttons that were pressed. These values can be added together if more than one button was pushed. For instance, a value of 3 means that both the left and right buttons were pressed. A value of 0 means that no buttons were pressed.

button Name	Value	Description
vbLeftButton	1	The left button was pressed.
vbRightButton	2	The right button was pressed.
vbMiddleButton	4	The middle button was pressed.

Table D-23: button values.

- *shift*—an **Integer** value (see Table D-24) that contains information about the Shift and Alt keys that were pushed when the mouse button was released. These values can be added together if more than one key was down. For instance, a value of 5 would mean that the Shift and Alt keys were both down when the mouse button was released. A value of 0 means that none of these keys were pressed.

shift Name	Value	Description
vbShiftMask	1	The Shift key was pressed.
vbCtrlMask	2	The Ctrl key was pressed.
vbAltMask	4	The Alt key was pressed.

Table D-24: shift values.

- *x*—a **Single** that contains the horizontal location of the mouse pointer.
- *y*—a **Single** that contains the vertical location of the mouse pointer.

Private Sub *DataControl*_OLEDragOver([*index* As Integer ,] *data* As DataObject, *effect* As Long, *button* As Integer, *shift* As Single, *x* As Single, *y* As Single, *state* As Integer)

Usage   This event happens when an OLE drag-and-drop operation is in progress.

Arguments
- *index*—an **Integer** that uniquely identifies a control in a control array. This argument is not present if the control is not part of a control array.
- *data*—a **DataObject** that contains the formats that the source control will provide. If the data is not contained in the **DataObject**, then it can be retrieved with the **GetData** method.
- *effect*—a **Long** (see Table D-25) that returns the status of the OLE drag-and-drop operation.

effect Name	Value	Description
vbDropEffectNone	0	The operation was canceled or the target control can't accept the drop operation.
vbDropEffectCopy	1	The operation copied data from the source control to the target control. The original data is unchanged.
vbDropEffectMove	2	The operation results in a link from the original data to the target control.

Table D-25: effect values.

- *button*—an **Integer** value (see Table D-26) that contains information about the mouse buttons that were pressed. These values can be added together if more than one button was pushed. For instance, a value of 3 means that both the left and right buttons were pressed. A value of 0 means that no buttons were pressed.

button Name	Value	Description
vbLeftButton	1	The left button was pressed.
vbRightButton	2	The right button was pressed.
vbMiddleButton	4	The middle button was pressed.

Table D-26: button *Values*

- *shift*—an **Integer** value (see Table D-27) that contains information about the Shift and Alt keys that were pushed when the mouse button was released. These values can be added together if more than one key was down. For instance, a value of 5 would mean that the Shift and Alt keys were both down when the mouse button was released. A value of 0 means that none of these keys were pressed.

shift Name	Value	Description
vbShiftMask	1	The Shift key was pressed.
vbCtrlMask	2	The Ctrl key was pressed.
vbAltMask	4	The Alt key was pressed.

Table D-27: shift *values.*

- *x*—a **Single** that contains the horizontal location of the mouse pointer.
- *y*—a **Single** that contains the vertical location of the mouse pointer.
- *state*—an **Integer** value (see Table D-28) that indicates the state of the object being dragged.

state Name	Value	Description
vbEnter	0	The dragged object is entering range of the control.
vbLeave	1	The dragged object is leaving range of the control
vbOver	2	The dragged object has moved from one position over the control to another.

Table D-28: state *values.*

Private Sub *DataControl_OLEGiveFeedback* ([*index* As Integer ,] *effect* As Long)

Usage — This event tells the source control what is happening while the OLE drag-and-drop operation is in progress. This event occurs after the **OLEDragOver** event.

Tip

You may want to use this event to change the cursor to reflect what can happen in the remote object.

Arguments
- *index*—an **Integer** that uniquely identifies a control in a control array. This argument is not present if the control is not part of a control array.
- *effect*—a **Long** (see Table D-29) that returns the status of the OLE drag-and-drop operation.

effect Name	Value	Description
vbDropEffectNone	0	The operation was canceled or the target control can't accept the drop operation.
vbDropEffectCopy	1	The operation copied data from the source control to the target control. The original data is unchanged.
vbDropEffectMove	2	The operation results in a link from the original data to the target control.
vbDropEffectScroll	&H80000000	The target control is about to scroll or is scrolling. This value may be added to the other *shift* values.

Table D-29: effect *values.*

Private Sub *DataControl*_OLESetData([*index* As Integer ,] *data* As DataObject, *DataFormat* As Integer)

Usage
This event happens in response to the target object performing a **GetData** method on *data*. This routine will respond by using the **SetData** method with the desired data using the **DataObject** *data*.

Arguments
- *index*—an **Integer** that uniquely identifies a control in a control array. This argument is not present if the control is not part of a control array.
- *data*—a **DataObject** that will contain the data to be returned to the target object.
- *format*—an **Integer** value (see Table D-30) that contains the format of the data.

format Name	Value	Description
vbCFText	1	Text (.TXT files)
vbCFBitmap	2	Bitmap (.BMP files)
vbCFMetafile	3	Metafile (.WMF files)
vbCFEDIB	8	Device independent bitmap (DIB)
vbCFPallette	9	Color palette
vbCFEMetafile	14	Enhanced metafile (.EMF files)
vbCFFiles	15	List of files
vbCFRTF	-16639	Rich Text Format (.RTF files)

Table D-30: format *values.*

Private Sub *DataControl*_OLEStartDrag ([*index* As Integer ,] *data* As DataObject, *AllowedEffects* As Long)

Usage
This event starts an OLE drag-and-drop operation.

Arguments
- *index*—an **Integer** that uniquely identifies a control in a control array. This argument is not present if the control is not part of a control array.

- *data*—a **DataObject** that will contain the formats that the source object is willing to provide to the target object. It may optionally contain the data to be transferred.
- *AllowedEffects*—a **Long** (see Table D-31) that contains the effects that the target object can request from the source object. The *AllowedEffects* can be added together if the source object supports more than one effect. Note that the target object can always use the *vbDropEffectNone* effect.

AllowedEffects Name	Value	Description
vbDropEffectNone	0	The target can't copy the data.
vbDropEffectCopy	1	The target can copy the data and the source will keep the data unchanged.
vbDropEffectMove	2	The target can copy the data and the source will delete the data.

Table D-31: AllowedEffects *values*.

Private Sub *DataControl*_Reposition ([*index* As Integer])

Usage   This event occurs after a new record becomes the current record.

Tip

Use this event to perform any processing that may be required after a new record becomes the current record but before it is made available to the user.

Arguments   ▪ *index*—an **Integer** that uniquely identifies a control in a control array. This argument is not present if the control is not part of a control array.

Private Sub *DataControl*_Resize ([*index* As Integer])

Usage   This event occurs whenever the form is resized.

Tip

*This event isn't particularly useful, since you can resize the control whenever the form is resized, in the form's **Resize** event.*

Arguments   ▪ *index*—an **Integer** that uniquely identifies a control in a control array. This argument is not present if the control is not part of a control array.

Private Sub *DataControl*_Validate ([*index* As Integer ,] *action* As Integer, *save* As Single)

Usage   This event occurs before a new record becomes the current record, before the **Update** method (but not the **UpdateRecord** method), before a **Delete**, **Unload**, or **Close** operation.

Arguments *action*—an **Integer** value (see Table D-32) containing the action that triggers the event and the action to take when the **Validate** event finishes.

action Name	Value	Description
vbDataActionCancel	0	Cancel the command that triggers the **Validate** event.
vbDataActionMoveFirst	1	Move to the first record.
vbDataActionMovePrevious	2	Move to the previous record.
vbDataActionMoveNext	3	Move to the next record.
vbDataActionMoveLast	4	Move to the last record.
vbDataActionAddNew	5	Add a new record.
vbDataActionUpdate	6	Update the current record. (This is not the same as **UpdateRecord**.)
vbDataActionDelete	7	Delete the current record.
vbDataActionFind	8	Find a new record.
vbDataActionBookmark	9	Bookmark the current record.
vbDataActionClose	10	Close the record set.
vbDataActionUnload	11	Unload the form with the **Data** control.

Table D-32: action values.

save—a **Boolean** when **True** means that the data has changed and should be saved. When **False** means that the data has not changed and should not be saved.

Examples
```
Private Sub Data1_Reposition()
If Data1.Recordset.EditMode = dbEditAdd Then
   Data1.Caption = "Adding new record"
Else
   If Data1.Recordset.AbsolutePosition = -1 Then
      Data1.Recordset.AddNew
   Else
      Data1.Caption = "At record number: " &
Format(Data1.Recordset.AbsolutePosition)
   End If
End If
End Sub
```

This routine lets the user know when the database is in add mode or lets the user know the current record number. If there are no records in the database, then it will force the database into add mode.

See Also **CheckBox** (control), **ComboBox** (control), **Database** (object), **DBCombo** (control), **DBGrid** (control), **DBList** (control), **Image** (control), **Label** (control), **ListBox** (control), **MSFlexGrid** (control), **Picture** (control), **Recordset** (object), **TextBox** (control)

Database

OBJECT

PE, EE

Usage
: The **Database** object accesses the Microsoft Jet database engine directly or accesses other database systems using ODBC.

Properties
: - *DatabaseObject*.**CollatingOrder**—a **Long** value (see Table D-33) that describes the placement of the **Data** control.

CollatingOrder Name	Value	Description
dbSortArabic	1025	Arabic
dbSortChineseSimplified	2052	Simplified Chinese
dbSortChineseTraditional	1028	Traditional Chinese
dbSortCyrillic	1049	Cyrillic
dbSortCzech	1029	Czech
dbSortDutch	1043	Dutch
dbSortGeneral	1033	English, French, German, Portuguese, Italian, and Modern Spanish
dbSortGreek	1032	Greek
dbSortHebrew	1037	Hebrew
dbSortHungarian	1038	Hungarian
dbSortIcelandic	1039	Icelandic
dbSortJapanese	1041	Japanese
dbSortKorean	1042	Korean
dbSortNeutral	1024	Neutral
dbSortNorwDan	1030	Norwegian or Danish
dbSortPDXIntl	1033	Paradox International
dbSortPDXNor	1030	Paradox Norwegian
dbSortPDXSwe	1053	Paradox Swedish
dbSortPolish	1045	Polish
dbSortSlovenian	1060	Slovenian
dbSortSpanish	1034	Spanish
dbSortSwedFin	1053	Swedish or Finnish
dbSortThai	1054	Thai
dbSortTurkish	1055	Turkish
dbSortUndefined	-1	Undefined

Table D-33: CollatingOrder *values.*

- *DatabaseObject*.**Connect**—a **String** value containing the type of database and any necessary connection information.
- *DatabaseObject*.**Connection**—an object that contains database connection information. Used by ODBC databases only.
- *DatabaseObject*.**Containers**—an object that contains the collection of **Container** objects defined in the **Database** object.
- *DatabaseObject*.**DesignMasterId**—a 16-byte **String** value that contains the Globally Unique Identifier which identifies the Design Master. The Design Master contains information about system tables, system fields, and replication information.
- *DatabaseObject*.**Name**—a **String** value that contains the name of the **Database** object.

- *DatabaseObject*.**Properties**—a collection of **Property** objects.
- *DatabaseObject*.**QueryDefs**—a collection of **QueryDef** objects.
- *DatabaseObject*.**QueryTimeout**—an **Integer** value containing the number of seconds before an ODBC connection times out.
- *DatabaseObject*.**RecordsAffected**—a **Long** value containing the number of records affected by the last **Execute** method.
- *DatabaseObject*.**Recordsets**—a collection of **Recordset** objects.
- *DatabaseObject*.**Relations**—a collection of **Relation** objects.
- *DatabaseObject*.**Replicable**—an object created by using the **CreateProperty** method that when "T" means that the database can be replicated. When "F" means that the database can't be replicated. Once this value is set to "T," it can't be changed.
- *DatabaseObject*.**ReplicaID**—a 16-byte **String** value that contains the Globally Unique Identifier which identifies a database replica.
- *DatabaseObject*.**TableDefs**—a collection of **TableDef** objects.
- *DatabaseObject*.**Updatable**—a **Boolean** value when **True** means that the object can be updated. When **False** means that the object can't be updated.
- *DatabaseObject*.**Version**—a **String** value containing the version of the database engine.

Methods

DatabaseObject.Close

Usage This method closes a database object. If there are any open **Recordset** objects, they will be closed before the **Database** object is closed.

property = *DatabaseObject*.CreateProperty ([*name*] [, [*type*] [, [*value*] [, *DDL*]]])

Usage This method creates a user-defined **Property** object.

Arguments
- *property*—an object variable that will contain the new **Property** object.
- *name*—a **String** containing the name of the property. Must begin with a letter and can be followed by letters, numbers, or an underscore ("_").
- *type*—a value selected from Table D-34 below.

type Name	Description
dbBigInt	Big Integer
dbBinary	Binary
dbBoolean	Boolean
dbByte	Byte
dbChar	Character
dbCurrency	Currency
dbDate	Date
dbDecimal	Decimal
dbDouble	Double
dbFloat	Float

type Name	Description
dbGUID	Globally unique identifier *dbInteger*
dbLong	Long
dbLongBinary	Long binary
DbMemo	Memo
DbNumeric	Numeric
DbSingle	Single
DbText	Text
DbTime	Time
dbTimeStamp	Time stamp
DbVarBinary	Variable-length binary data (up to 255 bytes)

Table D-34: type values.

- *value*—a **Variant** containing the initial value for the property.
- *DDL*—a **Boolean** when **True** means that the user cannot change this property value without the *dbSecWriteDef* permission. When **False** this permission is not required to change the value.

querydef = *DatabaseObject*.CreateQueryDef ([*name*] [, [*sql*]])

Usage   This method creates a **QueryDef** object.

Arguments
- *querydef*—an object variable that will contain the new **QueryDef** object.
- *name*—a **String** containing the name of the **QueryDef** object. Must begin with a letter and can be followed by letters, numbers, or an underscore ("_"). You can create a temporary **QueryDef** object by using an empty string form *name*.
- *sql*—a **String** containing an SQL query. If omitted, the query string can be set directly in the object.

relation = *DatabaseObject*.CreateRelation ([*name*] [, [*table*] [, [*foreign*] [, *attr*]]])

Usage   This method creates a new **Relation** object.

Arguments
- *relation*—an object variable that will contain the new **Relation** object.
- *name*—a **String** containing the name of the relation. Must begin with a letter and can be followed by letters, numbers, or an underscore ("_").
- *table*—a **String** value containing the name of the primary table in the relationship.
- *foreign*—a **String** containing the name of the foreign table in the relationship.
- *attr*—a **Long** containing one or more of the attributes in Table D-35 below.

Database • 147

attr Name	Description
dbRelationUnique	One-to-one relationship.
dbRelationDontEnforce	No referential integrity (the relationship is not enforced).
dbRelationInherited	The relationship exists in a noncurrent database that contains the two tables.
dbRelationUpdateCascade	Cascade updates.
dbRelationDeleteCascade	Cascade deletes.

Table D-35: attr values.

tabledef = DatabaseObject.CreateTableDef ([name] [, [attr] [, [source] [, connect]]])

Usage   This method creates a new **TableDef** object.

Arguments
- *tabledef*—an object variable that will contain the new **TableDef** object.
- *name*—a **String** containing the name of the tabledef. Must begin with a letter and can be followed by letters, numbers, or an underscore ("_").
- *attr*—a **Long** containing one or more of the attributes in Table D-36 below.

attr Name	Description
dbAttachExclusive	A Microsoft Jet linked table opened for exclusive use.
dbAttachSavePWD	Save the userid and password for a remote linked table.
dbSystemObject	A Microsoft Jet system table.
dbHiddenObject	A Microsoft Jet hidden table.
dbAttachedTable	A linked table from a non-ODBC source (i.e., a Paradox table).
dbAttachedODBC	A linked table from an ODBC source.

Table D-36: attr values.

- *source*—a **String** value containing the name of the remote source table name. This value will become the **SourceTableName** property of the new **TableDef** object.
- *connect*—a **String** containing the ODBC connection information.

DatabaseObject.Execute source [, options]

Usage   This method runs an SQL statement on a **Database** object.

Arguments
- *source*—a **String** containing the name of a **QueryDef** object or an SQL query statement.
- *options*—a **Long** containing one or more of the attributes in Table D-37.

options Name	Description
dbDenyWrite	Write access is denied to other users.
dbInconsistent	Allow inconsistent updates in Microsoft Jet databases.
dbConsistent	Allow only consistent updates in Microsoft Jet databases.
dbSQLPassThrough	Pass SQL query through Microsoft Jet workspace to remote ODBC database.
dbFileOnError	Perform a rollback if an error is encountered.
dbSeeChanges	Return error if another user is updating data you are using.

Table D-37: options values.

DatabaseObject.MakeReplica replica, description [, options]

Usage   This method makes a replica copy of a database.

Arguments
- replica—a **String** containing the filename and path of the new replica database. This file must not already exist or an error will occur.
- description—a **String** containing a description for the new replica.
- options—a **Long** containing one or more of the attributes in Table D-38 below.

options Name	Description
dbRepMakePartial	Make a partial replica.
dbRepMakeReadOnly	Make the replica read-only.

Table D-38: options values.

DatabaseObject.NewPassword oldpwd, newpwd

Usage   This method will change the password on a **Database** object.

Arguments
- oldpwd—a **String** containing the old database password.
- newpwd—a **String** containing the new database password.

recordset = DatabaseObject.OpenRecordset (source [, type [, options] [, lockedits]])

Usage   This method creates a new **RecordSet** object and appends it to the **RecordSets** collection.

Arguments
- recordset—an object variable that will contain the new **TableDef** object.
- source—a **String** value containing the table name, query name, or an SQL statement that contains the source for the new record set. For table type record set, only a table name can be used.
- type—a constant from Table D-39 below.

type Name	Description
dbOpenTable	Table type record set.
dbOpenDynamic	Open a dynamic type record set (ODBC databases only).
dbOpenDynaset	Open a dynaset type record set.
dbOpenSnapshot	Open a snapshot type record set.
dbOpenForwardOnly	Open a forward-only type record set.

Table D-39: *type values.*

- *options*—a **Long** containing one or more of the options in Table D-40 below.

options Name	Description
dbAppendOnly	Add new records, but can't delete or edit existing records.
dbConsistent	Allow only consistent updates in Microsoft Jet databases (can't be used with *dbConsistent*).
dbDenyRead	Read access is denied to other users.
dbDenyWrite	Write access is denied to other users.
dbExecDirect	Skip SQLPrepare and run SQLExecDirect for ODBC queries only.
dbInconsistent	Allow inconsistent updates in Microsoft Jet databases (can't be used with *dbConsistent*).
dbReadOnly	User can't change records in the database (can't be used if *dbReadOnly* is specified in *lockedits*).
dbRunAsync	Run ODBC query asynchronously.
dbSeeChanges	Return error if another user is updating data you are using.
dbSQLPassThrough	Pass SQL query through Microsoft Jet workspace to remote ODBC database.

Table D-40: *options values.*

- *lockedits*—a **Long** containing one or more of the attributes in Table D-41 below.

lockedits Name	Description
dbOptimistic	Lock the page containing the record you are editing when you use the **Update** method.
dbOptimisticBatch	Enable batch optimistic updating.
dbOptimisticValue	Enable optimistic updating based on row values.
dbPessimistic	Lock the page containing the record you are editing as soon you use the **Edit** method.
dbReadOnly	User can't change records in the database (can't be used if *dbReadOnly* is specified in *options*).

Table D-41: *lockedits values.*

DatabaseObject.PopulatePartial *dbname*

Usage   This method synchronizes changes between a partial replica and a full replica.

Arguments   - *dbname*—a **String** containing the path and filename of the replica database.

*DatabaseObject.*Synchronize *dbname* [, *exchange*]

Usage This method synchronizes two replica databases.

Arguments
- *dbname*—a **String** containing the path and filename of a replica database.
- *exchange*—a **Long** containing one of the first three attributes in Table D-42 below, plus *dbRepSyncInternet*.

exchange Name	Description
dbRepExportChanges	Send changes to *dbname*.
dbRepImportChanges	Get changes from *dbname*.
dbRepImpExpChanges	Bi-directional exchange of information.
dbRepSyncInternet	Exchange information via the Internet (can be used with the any of the above values).

Table D-42: exchange values.

See Also **Database** (object), **Databases** (collection), **Property** (object), **Properties** (collection), **Recordset** (object), **Recordsets** (collection), **Relation** (object), **Relations** (collection), **TableDef** (object), **TableDefs** (collection).

Databases

COLLECTION

PE, EE

Usage The **Databases** collection is used by Data Access Objects (DAO) to contain information about open databases in a **Workspace** object.

Properties
- *DatabasesCollection.***Count**—an **Integer** containing the number of **Database** objects in the collection.

Methods *DatabasesCollection.*Refresh

Usage This method gets a current copy of the documents in the collection. This is important in a multi-user environment where more than one user may be making changes in the **Databases** collection.

See Also **Database** (object), **Workspace** (object)

DataBinding

OBJECT

PE, EE

Usage The **DataBinding** object binds multiple properties of a **UserControl** with a **Database** object. Each property must be marked as Bindable in the Procedure Attributes dialog box.

Properties
- *DataBindingObject*.**DataChanged**—a **Boolean** that applies only to data bound controls. When **True** means that the data contained in this control was changed either by the user or by some means other than retrieving data from the current record. When **False** means the data in the control is unchanged from the current record. Simply reading the next record is not sufficient to set the **DataChanged** property to **True**.

   When the **Data** control moves to the next record, it will automatically invoke the **Edit** and **Update** methods to post the changes to the database.

- *DataBindingObject*.**DataField**—a **String** value that associates the control with a field in a **RecordSet** object in a **Data** control.
- *DataBindingObject*.**DataSource**—a **String** containing the name of the **Data** control to which the property is bound.
- *DataBindingObject*.**IsBindable**—a **Boolean** value when **True** means that the property can be bound to a **Data** control and **False** otherwise.
- *DataBindingObject*.**IsDataSource**—a **Boolean** value when **True** means that the property is a data source and can be used attached to a **Data** control and **False** otherwise.
- *DataBindingObject*.**PropertyName**—a **String** containing the name of the property that is bound.

See Also **Data** (control), **DataBindings** (collection), **User Control** (object)

DataBindings

COLLECTION

PE, EE

Usage The **DataBindings** collection contains the set of the **DataBinding** objects available in a **User Control**.

Properties
- *DataBindingsCollection*.**Count**—an **Integer** containing the number of **DataBinding** objects in the collection.
- *DataBindingsCollection*.**Item** (*index*)—returns a specific member of the collection specified by *index*.

> **Tip**
>
> *The first element of the collection is zero, while the last element is **Count** -1.*

See Also **DataBinding** (object), **Workspace** (object)

DataGrid

OBJECT

PE, EE

Usage The **DataGrid** object contains information about the data displayed in a **MSChart** control.

Properties
- *DataGridObject*.**ColumnCount**—an **Integer** containing the number of columns in the current data grid.
- *DataGridObject*.**ColumnLabel** (*column, labelindex*)—a **String** containing a label displayed on a column. *Column* begins with **1** and ranges to **ColumnCount**. *Labelindex* begins with **1** and is used to identify a label when a column contains more than one label.
- *DataGridObject*.**ColumnLabelCount**—an **Integer** containing the number of labels in each column.
- *DataGridObject*.**CompositeColumnLabel** (*column*)—a **String** containing a multilevel label for the specified column. *Column* begins with **1** and ranges to **ColumnCount**.
- *DataGridObject*.**CompositeRowLabel** (*row*)—a **String** containing a multilevel label for the specified row. *Row* begins with **1** and ranges to **RowCount**.
- *DataGridObject*.**RowCount**—an **Integer** containing the number of rows in the current data grid.
- *DataGridObject*.**RowLabel** (*row, labelindex*)—a **String** containing a label displayed on a row. *Row* begins with **1** and ranges to **RowCount**. *Labelindex* begins with **1** and is used to identify a label when a row contains more than one label.
- *DataGridObject*.**RowLabelCount**—an **Integer** containing the number of labels in each row.

Methods *DataGridObject*.**DeleteColumnLabels** *labelindex, count*

    Usage This method deletes levels of labels from the columns.

    Arguments
- *labelindex*—an **Integer** containing the beginning label to be deleted from all columns.
- *count*—an **Integer** containing the number of labels to be deleted. This value must be greater than or equal to **1**.

DataGridObject.**DeleteColumns** *column, count*

    Usage This method deletes one or more columns of data and labels from the data grid.

    Arguments
- *column*—an **Integer** containing the first column to be deleted.
- *count*—an **Integer** containing the number of columns to be deleted. This value must be greater than or equal to **1**.

DataGridObject.**DeleteRowLabels** *labelindex, count*

    Usage This method deletes levels of labels from the rows.

    Arguments
- *labelindex*—an **Integer** containing the beginning label to be deleted from all rows.
- *count*—an **Integer** containing the number of labels to be deleted. This value must be greater than or equal to **1**.

DataGridObject.DeleteRows *row, count*

Usage This method deletes one or more rows of data and labels from the data grid.

Arguments
- *row*—an **Integer** containing the first row to be deleted.
- *count*—an **Integer** containing the number of rows to be deleted. This value must be greater than or equal to **1**.

DataGridObject.GetData *row, column, datapoint, nullflag*

Usage This method retrieves the data point from the specified row and column.

Arguments
- *row*—an **Integer** containing the row number.
- *column*—an **Integer** containing the column number.
- *datapoint*—a **Double** containing the value of the data point.
- *nullflag*—an **Integer** when zero means that the data contains valid data. A non-zero value means that the datapoint contains a Null value.

DataGridObject.InitializeLabels

Usage This method assigns the first label in each element of the grid a unique value.

DataGridObject.InsertColumnLabels *labelindex, count*

Usage This method increases the number of levels of labels in the columns.

Arguments
- *labelindex*—an **Integer** containing the beginning level of the labels to be inserted.
- *count*—an **Integer** containing the number of labels to be inserted. This value must be greater than or equal to **1**.

DataGridObject.InsertColumns *column, count*

Usage This method inserts one or more columns of data and labels into the data grid.

Arguments
- *column*—an **Integer** containing the first column to be inserted.
- *count*—an **Integer** containing the number of columns to be inserted. This value must be greater than or equal to **1**.

DataGridObject.InsertRowLabels *labelindex, count*

Usage This method increases the number of levels of labels in the rows.

Arguments
- *labelindex*—an **Integer** containing the beginning label to be inserted into all rows.
- *count*—an **Integer** containing the number of labels to be inserted. This value must be greater than or equal to **1**.

*DataGridObject.*InsertRows *row, count*

Usage This method inserts one or more rows of data and labels into the data grid.

Arguments
- *row*—an **Integer** containing the first row to be inserted.
- *count*—an **Integer** containing the number of rows to be inserted. This value must be greater than or equal to **1**.

*DataGridObject.*MoveData *top, left, bottom, right, overoffset, downoffset*

Usage This method moves data around in the grid.

Arguments
- *top*—an **Integer** containing the first row number to be moved.
- *left*—an **Integer** containing the first column number to be moved.
- *bottom*—an **Integer** containing the last row number to be moved.
- *right*—an **Integer** containing the last column number to be moved.
- *overoffset*—an **Integer** containing the number of positions to move the data. A positive number moves the data to the right, while a negative number moves it to the left.
- *downoffset*—an **Integer** containing the number of positions to move the data. A positive number moves the data to the bottom, while a negative number moves it to the top.

*DataGridObject.*RandomDataFill

Usage This method assigns each row and column in the grid with a random value.

*DataGridObject.*RandomFillColumns *column, count*

Usage This method assigns each specified column with random data.

Arguments
- *column*—an **Integer** containing the first column to be assigned random data.
- *count*—an **Integer** containing the number of columns to be assigned random data. This value must be greater than or equal to **1**.

*DataGridObject.*RandomFillRows *row, count*

Usage This method assigns each specified row with random data.

Arguments
- *row*—an **Integer** containing the first row to be assigned random data.
- *count*—an **Integer** containing the number of rows to be assigned random data. This value must be greater than or equal to **1**.

DataGridObject.SetData *row, column, datapoint, nullflag*

Usage This method assigns a value to the data point specified by row and column.

Arguments
- *row*—an **Integer** containing the row number.
- *column*—an **Integer** containing the column number.
- *datapoint*—a **Double** containing the value of the data point.
- *nullflag*—an **Integer** when zero means that the data contains valid data. A non-zero value means that the datapoint contains a Null value.

DataGridObject.SetSize *rowlabelcount, columnlabelcount, datarowcount, datacolumncount*

Usage This method sets the size of the data grid. It is an alternative to assigning values to each of the individual properties.

Arguments
- *rowlabelcount*—an **Integer** containing the number of row labels (**RowLabelCount**).
- *columnlabelcount*—an **Integer** containing the number of column labels (**ColumnLabelCount**).
- *datarowcount*—an **Integer** containing the number of rows (**RowCount**).
- *datacolumncount*—an **Integer** containing the number of columns (**ColumnCount**).

DataObject

OBJECT

CCE, LE, PE, EE

Usage The **DataObject** object uses a container to transfer data from a source control to a destination control. This mirrors the IDataObject interface, which allows OLE drag-and-drop and clipboard operations to be built.

Properties
- *DataObjectObject*.**Files**—a reference to a **DataObjectFiles** collection.

Methods

DataObjectObject.Clear

Usage This method erases **DataObject** object. It is available only to OLE Drag sources.

value = DataObjectObject.GetData *format*

Usage This method returns data from a **DataObject** object in the specified *format*.

Arguments
- *value*—a **Variant** that contains the data retrieved from the **DataObject**.
- *format*—an **Integer** value (see Table D-43) that contains the format of the data.

format Name	Value	Description
vbCFText	1	Text (.TXT files)
vbCFBitmap	2	Bitmap (.BMP files)
vbCFMetafile	3	Metafile (.WMF files)
vbCFEDIB	8	Device independent bitmap (DIB)
vbCFPalette	9	Color palette
vbCFEMetafile	14	Enhanced metafile (.EMF files)
vbCFFiles	15	List of files
vbCFRTF	-16639	Rich Text Format (.RTF files)

Table D-43: format *values*.

bvalue = DataObjectObject.GetFormat format

Usage
This method returns **True** when the **DataObject** contains data in the specified format.

Arguments
- *bvalue*—a **Boolean** value when **True** means that the **DataObject** contains data in the specified format and **False** otherwise.
- *format*—an **Integer** value (see Table D-44) that contains the format of the data.

format Name	Value	Description
vbCFText	1	Text (.TXT files)
vbCFBitmap	2	Bitmap (.BMP files)
vbCFMetafile	3	Metafile (.WMF files)
vbCFEDIB	8	Device independent bitmap (DIB)
vbCFPalette	9	Color palette
vbCFEMetafile	14	Enhanced metafile (.EMF files)
vbCFFiles	15	List of files
vbCFRTF	-16639	Rich Text Format (.RTF files)

Table D-44: format *values*.

DataObjectObject.SetData [data] [, format]

Usage
This method returns **True** when the **DataObject** contains data in the specified format.

Arguments
- *data*—a **Variant** value containing the data to be passed to **DataObject**. If omitted, then a value for *format* must be specified. This allows you to pass one copy of the data and allow it to be available in multiple formats.

format—an **Integer** value (see Table D-45) that contains the format of the data. If omitted, Visual Basic will attempt to determine the best value for *format* based on the value of *data*.

format Name	Value	Description
vbCFText	1	Text (.TXT files)
vbCFBitmap	2	Bitmap (.BMP files)
vbCFMetafile	3	Metafile (.WMF files)
vbCFEDIB	8	Device independent bitmap (DIB)
vbCFPalette	9	Color palette
vbCFEMetafile	14	Enhanced metafile (.EMF files)
vbCFFiles	15	List of files
vbCFRTF	-16639	Rich Text Format (.RTF files)

Table D-45: format *values*.

See Also **DataObjectFiles** (collection)

DataObjectFiles

COLLECTION

CCE, LE, PE, EE

Usage   The **DataObjectFiles** collection contains the set of the **DataBinding** objects available in a **User Control**.

Properties
- *DataObjectFilesCollection*.**Count**—an **Integer** containing the number of **DataBinding** objects in the collection.
- *DataObjectFilesCollection*.**Item** (*index*)—returns a specific member of the collection specified by *index*.

> **Tip**
> *The first element of the collection is zero, while the last element is* **Count** *-1.*

Methods *DataObjectFilesCollection*.**Add** *filename*, [*index*]

Usage   This method adds a new filename to the collection.

Arguments
- *filename*—a **String** expression containing the path and filename to be added to the collection.
- *index*—an **Integer** value specifying the position where the filename will be added to the collection.

DataObjectFilesCollection.Clear

Usage This method removes all of the objects from the collection.

DataObjectFilesCollection.Remove *index*

Usage This method removes all of the objects from the collection.

Arguments *index*—an **Integer** value specifying the item to be removed from the collection.

See Also **DataObject** (object)

DataPoint

OBJECT

PE, EE

Usage The **DataPoint** object contains information about a single data point used in the **MSChart** control.

Properties
- *DataPointObject*.**Brush**—an object reference to a **Brush** object describing how the **DataPoint** object is drawn.
- *DataPointObject*.**DataPointLabel**—an object reference to a **DataPointLabel** object containing a label associated with the **DataPoint** object.
- *DataPointObject*.**EdgePen**—an object reference to a **Pen** object describing how the edge of the **DataPoint** will be drawn.
- *DataPointObject*.**Marker**—an object reference to a **Marker** object that is used to identify the **DataPoint** on the chart.
- *DataPointObject*.**Offset**—a **Single** containing the distance between the **DataPoint** and its default position on the chart. This distance is measured in inches or centimeters depending on your default Windows setting.

Methods **DataPointObject.ResetCustom**

Usage This method resets any custom properties that may have been set to the default for the chart.

DataPointObject.Select

Usage This method selects a **DataPoint** object.

See Also **DataPointLabel** (object), **DataPoints** (collection), **MSChart** (control)

DataPointLabel

OBJECT

PE, EE

Usage The **DataPointLabel** object contains information about a label for a **DataPoint** object in the **MSChart** control.

Properties
- *DataPointLabelObject*.**Backdrop**—an object reference to a **Backdrop** object describing the appearance of the area behind the label.
- *DataPointLabelObject*.**Component**—an **Integer** (see Table D-46) describing the contents of the label.

Component Name	Description
vtChLabelComponentValue	The value of the data point appears in the label.
vtChLabelComponentPercent	The value of the data point is displayed as a percentage of the whole series.
vtChLabelComponentSeriesName	The name of the series from label associated with the column is displayed.
vtChLabelComponentPointName	The data point name is displayed.

Table D-46: Component *values.*

- *DataPointLabelObject*.**Custom**—a **Boolean** when **True** means that the value in **Text** is displayed as the data point's label. **False** means that the label is constructed according to the **Component** property.
- *DataPointLabelObject*.**Font**—an object reference to a **Font** object containing the font that will be used to display the label.
- *DataPointLabelObject*.**LineStyle**—an **Integer** (see Table D-47) describing the line used to connect the label to the data point.

LineStyle Name	Description
vtChLabelLineStyleNone	The label and data point are not connected.
vtChLabelLineStyleStraight	The label and data point are connected by a straight line.
vtChLabelLineStyleBent	The label and data point are connected by a bent line.

Table D-47: LineStyle *values.*

- *DataPointLabelObject*.**LocationType**—an **Integer** (see Table D-48) describing how the label is positioned relative to the data point.

LocationType Name	Description
vtChLabelLocationTypeAbovePoint	The label is positioned above the data point.
vtChLabelLocationTypeBase	The label is positioned at the base along the category axis below the data point.
vtChLabelLocationTypeBelowPoint	The label is positioned below the data point.
vtChLabelLocationTypeCenter	The label is centered on the data point.

LocationType Name	Description
vtChLabelLocationTypeInside	The label is positioned inside the pie slice.
VtChLabelLocationTypeLeft	The label is positioned to the left of the data point.
VtChLabelLocationTypeNone	The label is not displayed.
vtChLabelLocationTypeOutside	The label is positioned outside the pie slice.
VtChLabelLocationTypeRight	The label is positioned to the right of the data point.

Table D-48: LocationType *values.*

- *DataPointLabelObject*.**Offset**—an object reference to a **Coor** object containing the location of the **DataPointLabel.**
- *DataPointLabelObject*.**PercentFormat**—a **String** containing the format used to display a percentage in the label. Some typical formats are "0%", "0.0%", and "0.00%".
- *DataPointLabelObject*.**Text**—a **String** containing the text to be displayed as the data point's label.
- *DataPointLabelObject*.**TextLayout**—an object reference to a **TextLayout** object describing how the label is positioned.
- *DataPointLabelObject*.**TextLength**—an **Integer** containing the length of the **Text** property.
- *DataPointLabelObject*.**ValueFormat**—a **String** containing the format used to display a value in the label.
- *DataPointLabelObject*.**VtFont**—an object reference to a **VtFont** object used to display the label.

Methods *DataPointObject*.**ResetCustomLabel**

> Usage This method resets any custom properties that may have been set to the default for the chart.

DataPointObject.**Select**

> Usage This method selects a **DataPointLabel** object.

See Also **DataPoint** (object), **DataPoints** (collection), **MSChart** (control)

DataPoints

COLLECTION

PE, EE

Usage The **DataPoints** collection contains the set of the **DataPoints** in the **MSChart** control.

Properties
- *DataPointsCollection*.**Count**—a **Long** containing the number of **DataPoint** objects in the collection.
- *DataPointsCollection*.**Item** (*index*)—returns a specific member of the collection specified by *index*.

See Also **DataPoint** (object), **MSChart** (control)

Date

DATA TYPE

CCE, LE, PE, EE

Usage
The **Date** data type holds date values using the same IEEE 64-bit floating point number as the **Double** data type. Date values range from 1 January 100 to 31 December 9999 and are stored as the integer part of the floating point number. Time values range from 00:00:00 to 23:59:59 and are stored as the fractional part of the floating point number. Noon or 12:00:00 equals .5000, while midnight or 00:00:00 equals 0.

See Also
CDate (function), **Date** (function), **Date** (statement), **DateAdd** (function), **DateDiff** (function), **DatePart** (function), **DateValue** (function), **Day** (fuction), **DefDate** (statement), **Dim** (statement), **Double** (data type), **Format** (function), **Hour** (function), **IsDate** (function), **Minute** (function), **Month** (function), **Second** (fuction), **Time** (function), **Time** (statement), **Year** (function)

Date

FUNCTION

CCE, LE, PE, EE

Syntax
DValue = **Date**

Usage
The **Date** function returns the current date.

Arguments
DValue—a **Date** value containing the current date.

Examples
```
Private Sub Command1_Click()
Dim d As Date
d = Date
MsgBox "The current date is: " & Format(d)
Date = CDate("1-Jan-2001")
MsgBox "The new date is: " & Format(Date)
Date = d
MsgBox "The date has been restored to: " & Format(Date)
End Sub
```

This routine saves the current date into a local variable and displays it. Then it changes the current to 1 January 2001 using the **Date** statement. Next the **Date** function verifies the new date. Finally it restores the original date using the **Date** statement, and the **Date** function is again used to verify it.

See Also
CDate (function), **Date** (data type), **Date** (statement), **Now** (function), **Time** (function), **Time** (statement)

Date

STATEMENT

CCE, LE, PE, EE

Syntax **Date** = *DValue*

Usage The **Date** statement sets the computer's current date.

Arguments • *DValue*—a **Date** value containing the current date.

Examples
```
Private Sub Command1_Click()
Dim d As Date
d = Date
MsgBox "The current date is: " & Format(d)
Date = CDate("1-Jan-2001")
MsgBox "The new date is: " & Format(Date)
Date = d
MsgBox "The date has been restored to: " & Format(Date)
End Sub
```

This routine saves the current date into a local variable and displays it. Then it changes the current to 1 January 2001 using the **Date** statement. Next the **Date** function verifies the new date. Finally it restores the original date using the **Date** statement, and the **Date** function is again used to verify it.

See Also **CDate** (function), **Date** (data type), **Date** (function), **Now** (function), **Time** (function), **Time** (statement)

DateAdd

FUNCTION

CCE, LE, PE, EE

Syntax *DValue* = **DateAdd** (*interval, value, date*)

Usage The **DateAdd** function returns a value containing the result of adding *value* in the units specified by *interval* to *date*.

Arguments • *DValue*—a **Date** value containing the result of adding *value* in the units specified by *interval* to *date*.

• *interval*—a **String** value (see Table D-49) that will determine the type of information returned.

interval	Description
d	*value is* in days.
h	*value is* in hours.
m	*value is* in months.
n	*value is* in minutes.
q	*value is* in quarter years.

interval	Description
s	*value is* in seconds.
w	*value is* in weekdays.
ww	*value is* in weeks.
yyyy	*value is* in years.

Table D-49: interval characters.

- *date*—a **Date** value containing a date value.

Examples
```
Private Sub Command1_Click()
Text3.Text = Format(DateAdd(Trim(Left(Combo1.Text, 4)), CLng(Text1.Text),
    CDate(Text2.Text)))
End Sub

Private Sub Form_Load()
Combo1.Clear
Combo1.AddItem "d       Value is in days."
Combo1.AddItem "h       Value is in hours."
Combo1.AddItem "m       Value is in months."
Combo1.AddItem "n       Value is in minutes."
Combo1.AddItem "q       Value is in quarter years."
Combo1.AddItem "s       Value is in seconds."
Combo1.AddItem "w       Value is in weekdays."
Combo1.AddItem "ww      Value is in weeks."
Combo1.AddItem "yyyy    Value is in years"
Combo1.Text = Combo1.List(0)
End Sub
```

This program loads a combo box with all of the possible values for *interval* and adds the specified value to the date each time the Command1 command button is pressed.

See Also **CDate** (function), **Date** (data type), **DatePart** (function), **Day** (function), **Hour** (function), **IsDate** (function), **Minute** (function), **Now** (function), **Second** (function), **Time** (function), **Time** (statement)

DateDiff

FUNCTION

CCE, LE, PE, EE

Syntax *LValue* = **DateDiff** (*interval*, *date1*, *date2* [, *firstday* [, *firstweek*]])

Usage The **DateDiff** function returns a value containing the difference between *date1* and *date2* in the units specified by *interval*.

Arguments
- *LValue*—a **Long** value containing the difference between the two dates in units specified by *interval*.

- *interval*—a **String** value (see Table D-50) that will determine the type of information returned.

interval	Description
d	Return the difference in days.
h	Return the difference in hours.
m	Return the difference in months.
n	Return the difference in minutes.
q	Return the difference in quarter years.
s	Return the difference in seconds.
w	Return the difference in weekdays.
ww	Return the difference in weeks.
yyyy	Return the difference in years.

Table D-50: interval characters.

- *date1*—a **Date** value containing the first date value.
- *date2*—a **Date** value containing the second date value.
- *firstday*—an **Integer** value (see Table D-51) describing the date on which the first day of the week falls.

firstday Name	Value	Description
vbUseSystem	0	Use the system default.
vbSunday	1	Use Sunday as the first day of the week.
vbMonday	2	Use Monday as the first day of the week.
vbTuesday	3	Use Tuesday as the first day of the week.
vbWednesday	4	Use Wednesday as the first day of the week.
vbThursday	5	Use Thursday as the first day of the week.
vbFriday	6	Use Friday as the first day of the week.
vbSaturday	7	Use Saturday as the first day of the week.

Table D-51: firstday values.

- *firstweek*—an **Integer** value (see Table D-52) describing the first week of the year.

firstweek Name	Value	Description
vbUseSystem	0	Use the system default.
vbFirstJan1	1	Use the week where 1 January falls.
vbFirstFourDays	2	If the first week of the year has three or fewer days, then use the following week as the first week of the year.
vbFirstFullWeek	3	Start the year with the first full week.

Table D-52: firstweek values.

Examples

```
Private Sub Command1_Click()
Text3.Text = Format(DateDiff(Trim(Left(Combo1.Text, 4)), CDate(Text1.Text),
    CDate(Text2.Text)))
End Sub

Private Sub Form_Load()
Combo1.Clear
Combo1.AddItem "d       Return the difference in days."
Combo1.AddItem "h       Return the difference in hours."
Combo1.AddItem "m       Return the difference in months."
Combo1.AddItem "n       Return the difference in minutes."
Combo1.AddItem "q       Return the difference in quarter years."
Combo1.AddItem "s       Return the difference in seconds."
Combo1.AddItem "w       Return the difference in weekdays."
Combo1.AddItem "ww      Return the difference in weeks."
Combo1.AddItem "yyyy    Return the difference in years"
Combo1.Text = Combo1.List(0)
End Sub
```

This program loads a combo box with all of the possible values for *interval* and displays the selected information from the date in the Text1 text box each time the Command1 command button is pressed.

See Also

CDate (function), **Date** (data type), **DateAdd** (function), **DatePart** (function), **Day** (function), **Hour** (function), **IsDate** (function), **Minute** (function), **Now** (function), **Second** (function), **Time** (function), **Time** (statement)

DatePart

FUNCTION

CCE, LE, PE, EE

Syntax *DValue* = **DatePart** (*interval, date, firstday, firstweek*)

Usage The **DatePart** function returns a value containing information extracted from *date*.

Arguments
- *IValue*—an **Integer** value containing the information extracted from *date*.
- *interval*—a **String** value (see Table D-53) that will determine the type of information extracted by *date*.

interval	Description
d	Return the day of month (1-31).
h	Return the hour (1-23).
m	Return the month (1-12).
n	Return the minute (0-59).
q	Return the quarter of the year (1-4).

interval	Description
s	Return the second (0-59).
w	Return the day of week (1-7). The first day of the week is specified by *firstday*.
ww	Return the week of the year (1-54).
yyyy	Return the day of year (1-366).

Table D-53: *interval characters.*

- *date*—a **Date** value containing the date from which you wish to extract information.
- *firstday*—an **Integer** value (see Table D-54) describing the first day of the week.

firstday Name	Value	Description
vbUseSystem	0	Use the system default.
vbSunday	1	Use Sunday as the first day of the week.
vbMonday	2	Use Monday as the first day of the week.
vbTuesday	3	Use Tuesday as the first day of the week.
vbWednesday	4	Use Wednesday as the first day of the week.
vbThursday	5	Use Thursday as the first day of the week.
vbFriday	6	Use Friday as the first day of the week.
vbSaturday	7	Use Saturday as the first day of the week.

Table D-54: *firstday values.*

- *firstweek*—an **Integer** describing the first week of the year (see Table D-55).

firstweek Name	Value	Description
vbUseSystem	0	Use the system default.
vbFirstJan1	1	Use the week where 1 January falls.
vbFirstFourDays	2	If the first week of the year has three or fewer days, then use the following week as the first week of the year.
vbFirstFullWeek	3	Start the year with the first full week.

Table D-55: *firstweek values.*

Examples
```
Private Sub Command1_Click()
Text2.Text = Format(DatePart(Trim(Left(Combo1.Text, 4)), CDate(Text1.Text)))
End Sub

Private Sub Form_Load()
Combo1.Clear
Combo1.AddItem "d    Return the day of month (1-31)"
Combo1.AddItem "h    Return the hour (1-23)."
Combo1.AddItem "m    Return the month (1-12)."
Combo1.AddItem "n    Return the minute (0-59)."
Combo1.AddItem "q    Return the quarter of the year (1-4)."
Combo1.AddItem "s    Return the second (0-59)."
```

```
Combo1.AddItem "w      Return the day of week (1-7)."
Combo1.AddItem "ww     Return the week of the year. (1-54)."
Combo1.AddItem "yyyy   Return the day of year (1-366)"
Combo1.Text = Combo1.List(0)
End Sub
```

This program loads a combo box with all of the possible values for *interval* and displays the selected information from the date in the Text1 text box each time the Command1 command button is pressed.

See Also CDate (function), Date (data type), DateAdd (function), DateDiff (function), DateValue (function), Day (function), Hour (function), IsDate (function), Minute (function), Now (function), Second (function), Time (function), Time (statement)

DateValue

FUNCTION

CCE, LE, PE, EE

Syntax *DValue* = **DateValue** (*year, month, day*)

Usage The **DateValue** function returns a date value for given values for year, month, and day. If a value for a given day or month is outside its normal range, then that value is adjusted to be in the normal range, and the other values are adjusted accordingly. For example, assume a year of 1997, a month of May, and a day of -30. This would convert to the value 31 March 97, which is 31 days prior to 1 May 97.

> **Tip**
>
> *To compute a value that is 30 days prior to 5 May 1997, use 1997 for* year, *5 for* month, *and 5-30 for* day. *This will result in the date 5 April 1997.*

Arguments
- *DValue*—a **Date** value including the month, day, and year.
- *year*—an **Integer** value containing a year between 0 and 9999. Values between 0 and 29 are interpreted as 2000 to 2029. Values between 30 and 99 are interpreted as 1930 to 1999. Values between 100 and 9999 are not changed.
- *month*—an **Integer** value containing the month.
- *day*—an **Integer** value containing the day of the month.

Examples
```
Private Sub Command1_Click()
Text4.Text = DateSerial(CInt(Text3.Text), CInt(Text2.Text), CInt(Text1.Text))
End Sub
```

This routine takes the values from the Text1, Text2, and Text3 text boxes to compute a date displayed in the Text4 text box.

See Also CDate (function), Date (data type), Day (function), DateAdd (function), DateDiff (function), DatePart (function), Hour (function), IsDate (function), Minute (function), Now (function), Second (function), Time (function), Time (statement)

Day

FUNCTION

CCE, LE, PE, EE

- **Syntax** *DValue* = **Day** (*date*)

- **Usage** The **Day** function returns the day of the month from a numeric, **Date**, or **String** variable containing a valid date or time.

- **Arguments**
  - *DValue*—an **Integer** value in the range of 1 to 31 indicating the day of the month.
  - *dime*—a **Date**, **Long**, or **String** value that contains a valid time or date.

- **Examples**
  ```
  Private Sub Command1_Click()
  If IsDate(Text1.Text) Then
      Text2.Text = Day(Text1.Text)
  Else
      Text2.Text = "Illegal date."
  End If
  End Sub
  ```

  This routine verifies that the date or time in the Text1 text box is valid and then extracts the day of month value from the text box.

- **See Also** **CDate** (function), **Date** (data type), **Hour** (function), **IsDate** (function), **Minute** (function), **Now** (function), **Second** (function), **Time** (function), **Time** (statement)

DBCombo

CONTROL

PE, EE

- **Usage** The **DBCombo** control is an ActiveX control that works like a **ComboBox** but the data automatically comes from one database via a **Data** control and the results can optionally update a field in a second database via a second **Data** control.

- **Properties**
  - *DBComboControl*.**Appearance**—an **Integer** value that specifies how the combo box will appear on the form (see Table D-56).

AppearanceValue	Description
0	The **DBCombo** control displays without the 3D effects.
1	The **DBCombo** control displays with 3D effects (default value).

Table D-56: Appearance *values.*

- *DBComboControl*.**BackColor**—a **Long** that contains the suggested value for the background color of the control. The **BackColor** and **ForeColor** must both be solid to display text. If you choose a color that is dithered, it will be changed to the nearest solid color.
- *DBComboControl*.**BoundColumn**—a **String** containing the name of a database field in **RowSource** that passes back to **DataField**, once the selection is made.

- *DBComboControl.***BoundText**—a **String** containing the text value of the **BoundColumn** field.
- *DBComboControl.***Container**—an object that can be used to set or return the container of the control at run time. This property cannot be set at design time.
- *DBComboControl.***DataBindings**—a reference to the **DataBindings** collection containing the bindable properties available.
- *DBComboControl.***DataChanged**—a **Boolean** that applies only to data bound controls. When **True** means that the data contained in this control was changed either by the user or by some means other than retrieving data from the current record. When **False** means the data in the control is unchanged from the current record. Simply reading the next record is not sufficient to set the **DataChanged** property to **True**.
- *DBComboControl.***DataField**—a **String** value that associates the control with a field in a **RecordSet** object in a **Data** control.
- *DBComboControl.***DataSource**—a **String** containing the name of a **Data** control that will be updated once the selection is made.
- *DBComboControl.***DragIcon**—an object that contains the picture value of an icon. At design time, you can specify an icon file that has a file type of .ICO.

Tip

*This value can be created by copying the value from another control's **DragIcon** value, a form's icon, or by using the **LoadPicture** function.*

- *DBComboControl.***DragMode**—an **Integer** value (see Table D-57) specifying how the control will respond to a drag request.

Tip

*Setting **DragMode** to vbAutomatic will automatically begin a drag operation when the user clicks on the control. However, the control will not respond to the usual mouse events (**Click**, **DblClick**, **MouseDown**, **MouseMove**, **MouseUp**).*

DragMode Name	Value	Description
vbManual	0	The **Drag** method must be used to begin a drag-and-drop operation (default value).
vbAutomatic	1	The source control will automatically begin a drag-and-drop operation when the user clicks on the control.

*Table D-57: **DragMode** values.*

- *DBComboControl.***Enabled**—a **Boolean** value when **True** means that the control will respond to events. When **False**, the control will not respond to events.
- *DBComboControl.***Font**—an object that contains information about the character font used by this control.
- *DataControl.***ForeColor**—a **Long** that contains the suggested value for the foreground color of the contained control. This property is read only at run time.

- *DBComboControl*.**Height**—a **Single** that contains the height of the control.
- *DBComboControl*.**HelpContextID**—a **Long** that contains a help file context ID number which references an entry in the help file. When the user presses the F1 key while this control is active, the corresponding entry in the help file will automatically display. A value of zero means that no context number was specified.

> **Tip**
>
> A help file must be compiled using the Windows Help Compiler available in the Professional and Enterprise editions of Visual Basic.

- *DBComboControl*.**hWnd**—a **Long** that contains a Windows handle to the control.

> **Tip**
>
> The **hWnd** property is most useful when making calls to Windows API functions. Since this value can change during execution, do not save the value into a variable for later use.

- *DBComboControl*.**Index**—an **Integer** that uniquely identifies a control in a control array.
- *DBComboControl*.**IntegralHeight**—a **Boolean** value when **True** means that the drop-down list will resize itself so that it only shows complete items. When **False** the drop-down list shows partial items.
- *DBComboControl*.**Left**—a **Single** that contains the distance measured in twips between the left edge of the control and the left edge of the control's container.
- *DBComboControl*.**ListField**—a **String** containing the name of a field in a record set that will be used to populate the list box.
- *DBComboControl*.**Locked**—a **Boolean** value when **True** means that the user can't type a value in the text box part of the control. When **False**, the user can type a value into the text box part of the control.
- *DBComboControl*.**MatchedWithList**—a **Boolean** when **True** means that the value of the **BoundText** property matches one of the records in the list portion of the control.
- *DBComboControl*.**MatchEntry**—an **Integer** value (see Table D-58) that describes how the user's typing will be used to match entries in the list box.

MatchEntry Name	Value	Description
dblBasicMatching	0	Typing a letter jumps to the first entry in the list box with that value. Typing the same letter again will cycle through the values that begin with that letter.
dblExtendedMatching	1	Typing a letter jumps to the first entry in the list box with that value. Typing a second letter will try to match the first two letters. Typing additional letters will continue to refine this process.

Table D-58: MatchEntry values.

- *DBComboControl*.**MouseIcon**—a **Picture** object (a bitmap, icon, or metafile) that will be used as a cursor when the **MousePointer** property is set to 99. Note that Visual Basic does not support color cursors from a .CUR file. A color icon from an .ICO file should be used instead.
- *DBComboControl*.**MousePointer**—an **Integer** value (see Table D-59) that contains the value of the cursor that should be displayed when the cursor is moved over this control. Use *vbCustom* to display the custom icon stored in the **MouseIcon** property.

Cursor Name	Value	Description
vbDefault	0	Shape determined by the object (default value)
vbArrow	1	Arrow
vbCrosshair	2	Crosshair
vbIbeam	3	I beam
vbIconPointer	4	Square inside a square
vbSizePointer	5	Four sided arrow (north, south, east, west)
vbSizeNESW	6	Two sided arrow (northeast, southwest)
vbSizeNS	7	Two sided arrow (north, south)
vbSizeNWSE	8	Two sided arrow (northwest, southeast)
vbSizeWE	9	Two sided arrow (west, east)
vbUpArrow	10	Single sided arrow pointing north
vbHourglass	11	Hourglass
vbNoDrop	12	No Drop
vbArrowHourglass	13	An arrow and an hourglass
vbArrowQuestion	14	An arrow and a question mark
vbSizeAll	15	Size all
vbCustom	99	Custom icon from the **MouseIcon** property of this control

Table D-59: Cursor values.

- *DBComboControl*.**Name**—a **String** that contains the name of the control that will be used to reference the control in a Visual Basic program. This property is read only at run-time.
- *DBComboControl*.**Object**—an object that contains a reference to the *DBComboControl* object.
- *DBComboControl*.**OLEDragMode**—an **Integer** value (see Table D-60) that describes how the control will respond to OLE drag operations.

> **Note**
>
> When the **DragMode** is **True**, the standard Visual Basic drag-and-drop functions will override the OLE drag-and-drop functions.

OLEDragMode Name	Value	Description
vbOLEDragManual	0	All drag requests will be handled by the programmer (default value).
vbOLEDragAutomatic	1	The control responds to all OLE drag requests automatically.

Table D-60: OLEDragMode values.

- *DBComboControl.***OLEDropMode**—an **Integer** value (see Table D-61) that describes how the control will respond to OLE drop operations.

OLEDropMode Name	Value	Description
vbOLEDropNone	0	The control does not accept OLE drops. The cursor is changed to the No Drop cursor (default value).
vbOLEDropManual	1	The control responds to OLE drops under the program's control (manual).
vbOLEDropAutomatic	2	The control automatically accepts OLE drops if it recognizes the format of the data object.

Table D-61: OLEDropMode values.

- *DBComboControl.***Parent**—an object that contains a reference to the **Form**, **Frame**, or other container that contains this control.
- *DBComboControl.***RightToLeft**—a **Boolean** value when **True** means that the text displays from right to left. When **False** means that the text displays from left to right. A bi-directional version of Windows is required to set this property to **True**.
- *DBComboControl.***RowSource**—a **String** containing the name of the **Data** control that will be used to fill the text box.
- *DBComboControl.***SelectedItem**—a **Variant** value containing the bookmark for the selected database item.
- *DBComboControl.***SelLength**—a **Long** value containing the number of characters selected from the text box part of the control.
- *DBComboControl.***SelStart**—a **Long** value containing the starting position of the selected text in the text box part of the control.
- *DBComboControl.***SelText**—a **String** value containing the selected text.
- *DBComboControl.***TabIndex**—an Integer that determines the order that a user will tab through the objects on a form.
- *DBComboControl.***TabStop**—a **Boolean** value when **True** means that the user can tab to this object. When **False** means that this control will be skipped to the next control in the **TabIndex** order.
- *DBComboControl.***Tag**—a **String** that can hold programmer specific information. This property is not used by Visual Basic.
- *DBComboControl.***Text**—a **String** that sets or returns the value from the text box part of the control.
- *DBComboControl.***ToolTipText**—a **String** that holds a text value that can be displayed as a **ToolTip** box that displays whenever the cursor is held over the control for about one second.
- *DBComboControl.***Top**—a **Single** that contains the distance measured in twips between the top edge of the control and the top edge of the control's container.
- *DBComboControl.***Visible**—a **Boolean** value when **True** means that the control is visible. When **False** means that the control is not visible.

Tip

This property hides the control until the program is ready to display it.

- *DBComboControl*.**VisibleCount**—an **Integer** containing the number of items visible in the list box.
- *DBComboControl*.**VisibleItems**(*index*)—an array of bookmarks corresponding to the visible items in the list box.
- *DBComboControl*.**WhatsThisHelpID**—a **Long** that contains a help file context ID number that references an entry in the help file. This provides a What's This PopUp help display in response to the What's This button in the upper right corner of the window.
- *DBComboControl*.**Width**—a **Single** that contains the width of the control.

Methods

DBComboControl.**AboutBox**

Usage   This method displays an AboutBox for the control.

DBComboControl.**Drag** [*DragAction*]

Usage   This method begins, ends, or cancels a drag operation.

Arguments   *DragAction*—an **Integer** that contains a value selected from Table D-62 below.

DragAction Name	Value	Description
vbCancel	0	Cancels any drag operation in progress.
vbBeginDrag	1	Begins a drag operation (default).
vbEndDrag	2	Ends a drag operation and drops *object*.

Table D-62: DragAction *values*.

DBComboControl.**Move** *Left* [, *Top* [, *Width* [, *Height*]]]

Usage   This method changes the position and the size of the **DBCombo** control. The **ScaleMode** of the **Form** or other container object that holds the control will determine the units used to specify the coordinates.

Arguments
- *Left*—a **Single** that specifies the new position of the left edge of the control.
- *Top*—a **Single** that specifies the new position of the top edge of the control.
- *Width*—a **Single** that specifies the new width of the control.
- *Height*—a **Single** that specifies the new height of the control.

DBComboControl.**OLEDrag**

Usage   This method begins an **OLEDrag** and drop operation. Invoking this method will trigger the **OLEStartDrag** event.

DBComboControl.**ReFill**

Usage   This method gets a fresh copy of the contents of the list box and redraws its contents.

DBComboControl.Refresh

Usage This method redraws the contents of the control.

DBComboControl.SetFocus

Usage This method transfers the focus from the form or control that currently has the focus to this control. To receive the focus, this control must be enabled and visible.

DBComboControl.ShowWhatsThis

Usage This method displays the ShowWhatsThis help information for this control.

DBComboControl.ZOrder [*position*]

Usage This method specifies the position of the control relative to the other objects on the form.

> **Tip**
>
> *Note that there are three layers of objects on a form: the back layer is the drawing space which contains the results of the graphical methods, the middle layer contains graphical objects and* **Labels,** *and the top layer contains nongraphical controls such as the* **DBCombo** *control. The* **ZOrder** *method only affects how the objects are arranged within a single layer.*

Arguments *position*—an **Integer** that specifies the relative position of this object. A value of 0 means that the control is positioned at the head of the list, a value of 1 means that the control will be placed at the end of the list.

Events **Private Sub *DBComboControl*_Click([*index* As Integer])**

Usage This event occurs when the user clicks a mouse button to select an item in the drop-down list or selects an item from the drop-down list using the keyboard.

Arguments *index*—an **Integer** that uniquely identifies a control in a control array. This argument is not present if the control is not part of a control array.

Private Sub *DBComboControl*_DblClick([*index* As Integer])

Usage This event occurs when the user double-clicks a mouse button to select an item in the drop-down list or selects an item from the drop-down list using the keyboard. This applies only when **Style** is set to *vbComboSimple*.

Arguments *index*—an **Integer** that uniquely identifies a control in a control array. This argument is not present if the control is not part of a control array.

Private Sub *DBComboControl_DragDrop*([*index* As Integer ,] *source* As Control, *x* As Single, *y* As Single)

Usage   This event occurs when a drag-and-drop operation is completed by using the **Drag** method with a *DragAction* value of *vbEndDrag*.

Tip

*When using drag-and-drop operations, use the **DragOver** event to determine what the cursor should look like while the cursor moves over the control.*

Arguments
- *index*—an **Integer** that uniquely identifies a control in a control array. This argument is not present if the control is not part of a control array.
- *source*—a control object that is the control that is being dragged.

Tip

You can access a property or method from the source control by using source.property *or* source.method. *You can determine the type of object or control by using the **TypeOf** operator.*

- *x*—a **Single** that contains the horizontal location of the mouse pointer.
- *y*—a **Single** that contains the vertical location of the mouse pointer.

Private Sub *DBComboControl_DragOver*([*index* As Integer ,] *source* As Control, *x* As Single, *y* As Single, *state* As Integer)

Usage   This event occurs while a drag operation is in progress and the cursor is moved over the control.

Tip

*When using drag-and-drop operations, use the **DragOver** event to determine what the cursor should look like while the cursor moves over the control. When* state *is 0, you can change the cursor to a No Drop (vbNoDrop) cursor or highlight the field that the cursor is near. When* state *is 1, you can undo the changes you made when the* state *was 0.*

Arguments
- *index*—an **Integer** that uniquely identifies a control in a control array. This argument is not present if the control is not part of a control array.
- *source*—a control object that is the control that is being dragged.

Tip

You can access a property or method from the source control by using source.property *or* source.method. *You can determine the type of object or control by using the **TypeOf** operator.*

- *x*—a **Single** that contains the horizontal location of the mouse pointer.
- *y*—a **Single** that contains the vertical location of the mouse pointer.
- *state*—an **Integer** value (see Table D-63) that indicates the state of the object being dragged.

state Name	Value	Description
vbEnter	0	The dragged object is entering range of the control.
vbLeave	1	The dragged object is leaving range of the control.
vbOver	2	The dragged object has moved from one position over the control to another.

Table D-63: state *values*.

Private Sub *DBComboControl*__GotFocus ([*index* As Integer])

Usage This event occurs when the control is given focus.

Tip

You can use this routine to display help or other information in a status bar.

Arguments • *index*—an **Integer** that uniquely identifies a control in a control array. This argument is not present if the control is not part of a control array.

Private Sub *DBComboControl*__KeyDown ([*index* As Integer ,] *keycode* As Integer, *shift* As Single)

Usage This event occurs when a key is pressed while the control has the focus.

Arguments • *index*—an **Integer** that uniquely identifies a control in a control array. This argument is not present if the control is not part of a control array.
- *keycode*—an **Integer** that contains information about which key was pressed.
- *shift*—an **Integer** value (see Table D-64) that contains information about the Shift and Alt keys that were pushed when the mouse button was pressed. These values can be added together if more than one key was down. For instance, a value of 5 would mean that the Shift and Alt keys were both down when the mouse button was pressed.

shift Name	Value	Description
vbShiftMask	1	The Shift key was pressed.
vbCtrlMask	2	The Ctrlkey was pressed.
vbAltMask	4	The Alt key was pressed.

Table D-64: shift *values*.

Private Sub *DBComboControl__KeyPress*([*index* As Integer ,] *keychar* As Integer)

Usage This event occurs whenever a key is pressed while the control has the focus.

Arguments
- *index*—an **Integer** that uniquely identifies a control in a control array. This argument is not present if the control is not part of a control array.
- *keychar*—an **Integer** that contains the ASCII character that was pressed.

Private Sub *DBComboControl__KeyUp* ([*index* As Integer ,] *keycode* As Integer, *shift* As Single)

Usage This event occurs when a key is released while the control has the focus.

Arguments
- *index*—an **Integer** that uniquely identifies a control in a control array. This argument is not present if the control is not part of a control array.
- *keycode*—an **Integer** that contains information about which key was released.
- *shift*—an **Integer** value (see Table D-65) that contains information about the Shift and Alt keys that were pushed when the mouse button was pressed. These values can be added together if more than one key was down. For instance, a value of 5 would mean that the Shift and Alt keys were both down when the mouse button was pressed.

shift Name	Value	Description
vbShiftMask	1	The Shift key was pressed.
vbCtrlMask	2	The Ctrl key was pressed.
vbAltMask	4	The Alt key was pressed.

Table D-65: shift *values.*

Private Sub *DBComboControl_LostFocus* ([*index* As Integer])

Usage This event occurs when the control loses focus.

Tip

This routine is useful to performing data verification.

Arguments
- *index*—an **Integer** that uniquely identifies a control in a control array. This argument is not present if the control is not part of a control array.

Private Sub *DBComboBoxControl_MouseDown*([*index* As Integer ,] *button* As Integer, *shift* As Single, *x* As Single, *y* As Single)

Usage This event occurs when a mouse button was pressed while the cursor is over the control.

Arguments
- *index*—an **Integer** that uniquely identifies a control in a control array. This argument is not present if the control is not part of a control array.
- *button*—an **Integer** value (see Table D-66) that contains information about the mouse buttons that were pressed. Only one button will be indicated when this event occurs.

button Name	Value	Description
vbLeftButton	1	The left button was pressed.
vbRightButton	2	The right button was pressed.
vbMiddleButton	4	The middle button was pressed.

Table D-66: button *values.*

- *shift*—an **Integer** value (see Table D-67) that contains information about the Shift and Alt keys that were pushed when the mouse button was pressed. These values can be added together if more than one key was down. For instance, a value of 5 would mean that the Shift and Alt keys were both down when the mouse button was pressed.

shift Name	Value	Description
vbShiftMask	1	The Shift key was pressed.
vbCtrlMask	2	The Ctrlkey was pressed.
vbAltMask	4	The Alt key was pressed.

Table D-67: shift *values.*

- *x*—a **Single** that contains the horizontal location of the mouse pointer.
- *y*—a **Single** that contains the vertical location of the mouse pointer.

Private Sub *DBComboControl*_MouseMove ([*index* As Integer ,] *button* As Integer, *shift* As Single, *x* As Single, *y* As Single)

Usage — This event occurs while the cursor is moved over the control.

Arguments
- *index*—an **Integer** that uniquely identifies a control in a control array. This argument is not present if the control is not part of a control array.
- *button*—an **Integer** value (see Table D-68) that contains information about the mouse buttons that were pressed. These values can be added together if more than one button was pushed. For instance, a value of 3 means that both the left and right buttons were pressed. A value of 0 means that no buttons were pressed.

button Name	Value	Description
vbLeftButton	1	The left button was pressed.
vbRightButton	2	The right button was pressed.
vbMiddleButton	4	The middle button was pressed.

Table D-68: button *values*.

- *shift*—an **Integer** value (see Table D-69) that contains information about the Shift and Alt keys that were pushed when the mouse button was pressed. For instance, a value of 5 would mean that the Shift and Alt keys were both down when the mouse button was pressed. A value of 0 means that none of these keys were pressed.

shift Name	Value	Description
vbShiftMask	1	The Shift key was pressed.
vbCtrlMask	2	The Ctrl key was pressed.
vbAltMask	4	The Alt key was pressed.

Table D-69: shift *values*.

- *x*—a **Single** that contains the horizontal location of the mouse pointer.
- *y*—a **Single** that contains the vertical location of the mouse pointer.

Private Sub *DBComboBoxControl*_MouseUp([*index* As Integer ,] *button* As Integer, *shift* As Single, *x* As Single, *y* As Single)

Usage
: This event occurs when a mouse button is released while the cursor is over the control.

Arguments
: - *index*—an **Integer** that uniquely identifies a control in a control array. This argument is not present if the control is not part of a control array.
  - *button*—an **Integer** value (see Table D-70) that contains information about the mouse buttons that were released. Only one of these values will be present.

button Name	Value	Description
vbLeftButton	1	The left button was released.
vbRightButton	2	The right button was released.
vbMiddleButton	4	The middle button was released.

Table D-70: button *values*.

- *shift*—an **Integer** value (see Table D-71) that contains information about the Shift and Alt keys that were pushed when the mouse button was released. These values can be added together if more than one key was down. For instance, a value of 5 would mean that the Shift and Alt keys were both down when the mouse button was released. A value of 0 means that none of these keys were pressed.

shift Name	Value	Description
vbShiftMask	1	The Shift key was pressed.
vbCtrlMask	2	The Ctrl key was pressed.
vbAltMask	4	The Alt key was pressed.

Table D-71: shift *values*.

- *x*—a **Single** that contains the horizontal location of the mouse pointer.
- *y*—a **Single** that contains the vertical location of the mouse pointer.

Private Sub *DBComboControl_OLECompleteDrag*([*index* As Integer ,] *effect* As Long)

Usage — This event tells the source control the results of an OLE drag-and-drop operation. This is the final event to occur in the series of actions that make up an OLE drag-and-drop operation.

Arguments
- *index*—an **Integer** that uniquely identifies a control in a control array. This argument is not present if the control is not part of a control array.
- *effect*—a **Long** (see Table D-72) that returns the status of the OLE drag-and-drop operation.

effect Name	Value	Description
vbDropEffectNone	0	The operation was canceled or the target control can't accept the drop operation.
vbDropEffectCopy	1	The operation copied data from the source control to the target control. The original data is unchanged.
vbDropEffectMove	2	The operation results in a link from the original data to the target control.

Table D-72: effect *values*.

Private Sub *DBComboControl_OLEDragDrop*([*index* As Integer ,] *data* As DataObject, *effect* As Long, *button* As Integer, *shift* As Single, *x* As Single, *y* As Single)

Usage — This event tells the source control the results of an OLE drag-and-drop operation. This is the final event to occur in the series of actions that make up an OLE drag-and-drop operation.

Arguments
- *index*—an **Integer** that uniquely identifies a control in a control array. This argument is not present if the control is not part of a control array.
- *data*—a **DataObject** that contains the formats that the source control will provide. If the data is not contained in the **DataObject**, then it can be retrieved with the **GetData** method.
- *effect*—a **Long** (see Table D-73) that returns the status of the OLE drag-and-drop operation.

effect Name	Value	Description
vbDropEffectNone	0	The operation was canceled or the target control can't accept the drop operation.
vbDropEffectCopy	1	The operation copied data from the source control to the target control. The original data is unchanged.
vbDropEffectMove	2	The operation results in a link from the original data to the target control.

Table D-73: effect *values*.

- *button*—an **Integer** value (see Table D-74) that contains information about the mouse buttons that were pressed. These values can be added together if more than one button was pushed. For instance, a value of 3 means that both the left and right buttons were pressed. A value of 0 means that no buttons were pressed.

button Name	Value	Description
vbLeftButton	1	The left button was pressed.
vbRightButton	2	The right button was pressed.
vbMiddleButton	4	The middle button was pressed.

Table D-74: button *values*.

- *shift*—an **Integer** value (see Table D-75) that contains information about the Shift and Alt keys that were pushed when the mouse button was released. These values can be added together if more than one key was down. For instance, a value of 5 would mean that the Shift and Alt keys were both down when the mouse button was released. A value of 0 means that none of these keys were pressed.

shift Name	Value	Description
vbShiftMask	1	The Shift key was pressed.
vbCtrlMask	2	The Ctrl key was pressed.
vbAltMask	4	The Alt key was pressed.

Table D-75: shift *values*.

- *x*—a **Single** that contains the horizontal location of the mouse pointer.
- *y*—a **Single** that contains the vertical location of the mouse pointer.

```
Private Sub DBComboControl_OLEDragOver( [ index As Integer ,] data As
DataObject, effect As Long, button As Integer, shift As Single, x As Single,
y As Single, state As Integer )
```

Usage   This event happens when an OLE drag-and-drop operation is in progress.

Arguments
- *index*—an **Integer** that uniquely identifies a control in a control array. This argument is not present if the control is not part of a control array.
- *data*—a **DataObject** that contains the formats that the source control will provide. If the data is not contained in the **DataObject**, then it can be retrieved with the **GetData** method.
- *effect*—a **Long** (see Table D-76) that returns the status of the OLE drag-and-drop operation.

effect Name	Value	Description
vbDropEffectNone	0	The operation was canceled or the target control can't accept the drop operation.
vbDropEffectCopy	1	The operation copied data from the source control to the target control. The original data is unchanged.
vbDropEffectMove	2	The operation results in a link from the original data to the target control.

Table D-76: effect *values*.

- *button*—an **Integer** value (see Table D-77) that contains information about the mouse buttons that were pressed. These values can be added together if more than one button was pushed. For instance, a value of 3 means that both the left and right buttons were pressed. A value of 0 means that no buttons were pressed.

button Name	Value	Description
vbLeftButton	1	The left button was pressed.
vbRightButton	2	The right button was pressed.
vbMiddleButton	4	The middle button was pressed.

Table D-77: button *values*.

- *shift*—an **Integer** value (see Table D-78) that contains information about the Shift and Alt keys that were pushed when the mouse button was released. These values can be added together if more than one key was down. For instance, a value of 5 would mean that the Shift and Alt keys were both down when the mouse button was released. A value of 0 means that none of these keys were pressed.

shift Name	Value	Description
vbShiftMask	1	The Shift key was pressed.
vbCtrlMask	2	The Ctrl key was pressed.
vbAltMask	4	The Alt key was pressed.

Table D-78: shift *values*.

- *x*—a **Single** that contains the horizontal location of the mouse pointer.
- *y*—a **Single** that contains the vertical location of the mouse pointer.
- *state*—an **Integer** value (see Table D-79) that indicates the state of the object being dragged.

state Name	Value	Description
vbEnter	0	The dragged object is entering range of the control.
vbLeave	1	The dragged object is leaving range of the control.
vbOver	2	The dragged object has moved from one position over the control to another.

Table D-79: state *values*.

Private Sub *DBComboControl*_OLEGiveFeedback ([*index* As Integer ,] *effect* As Long)

Usage — This event tells the source control what is happening while the OLE drag-and-drop operation is in progress. This event occurs after the **OLEDragOver** event.

Tip

You may want to use this event to change the cursor to reflect what can happen in the remote object.

Arguments
- *index*—an **Integer** that uniquely identifies a control in a control array. This argument is not present if the control is not part of a control array.
- *effect*—a **Long** (see Table D-80) that returns the status of the OLE drag-and-drop operation.

effect Name	Value	Description
vbDropEffectNone	0	The operation was canceled or the target control can't accept the drop operation.
vbDropEffectCopy	1	The operation copied data from the source control to the target control. The original data is unchanged.
vbDropEffectMove	2	The operation results in a link from the original data to the target control.
vbDropEffectScroll	&H80000000	The target control is about to scroll or is scrolling. This value may be added to the other *shift* values.

Table D-80: effect *values*.

Private Sub *DBComboControl*_OLESetData([*index* As Integer ,] *data* As DataObject, *DataFormat* As Integer)

Usage — This event happens in response to the target object performing a **GetData** method on *data*. This routine will respond by using the **SetData** method with the desired data using the **DataObject** *data*.

184 • The Visual Basic 5 Programmer's Reference

Arguments
- *index*—an **Integer** that uniquely identifies a control in a control array. This argument is not present if the control is not part of a control array.
- *data*—a **DataObject** that will contain the data to be returned to the target object.
- *format*—an **Integer** value (see Table D-81) that contains the format of the data.

format Name	Value	Description
vbCFText	1	Text (.TXT files)
vbCFBitmap	2	Bitmap (.BMP files)
vbCFMetafile	3	Metafile (.WMF files)
vbCFEDIB	8	Device independent bitmap (DIB)
vbCFPallette	9	Color palette
vbCFEMetafile	14	Enhanced metafile (.EMF files)
vbCFFiles	15	List of files
vbCFRTF	-16639	Rich Text Format (.RTF files)

Table D-81: format *values.*

Private Sub *DBComboControl*_OLEStartDrag ([*index* As Integer ,] *data* As DataObject, *AllowedEffects* As Long)

Usage
This event starts an OLE drag-and-drop operation.

Arguments
- *index*—an **Integer** that uniquely identifies a control in a control array. This argument is not present if the control is not part of a control array.
- *data*—a **DataObject** that will contain the formats that the source object is willing to provide to the target object. It may optionally contain the data to be transferred.
- *AllowedEffects*—a **Long** (see Table D-82) that contains the effects that the target object can request from the source object. The *AllowedEffects* can be added together if the source object supports more than one effect. Note that the target object can always use the *vbDropEffectNone* effect.

AllowedEffects Name	Value	Description
vbDropEffectNone	0	The target can't copy the data.
vbDropEffectCopy	1	The target can copy the data and the source will keep the data unchanged.
vbDropEffectMove	2	The target can copy the data and the source will delete the data.

Table D-82: AllowedEffects *values.*

Examples
```
Private Sub Combo1_Click()
    MsgBox Combo1.List(Combo1.ListIndex)
End Sub
```

```
Private Sub Form_Load()
Combo1.AddItem "One"
Combo1.AddItem "Two"
Combo1.AddItem "Three"
End Sub
```

This program initializes a combo box with three values and then displays a message box whenever the user clicks on one of the items from the drop-down menu.

See Also   **ComboBox** (control), **ListBox** (control), **TextBox** (control)

DBGrid

CONTROL

PE, EE

Usage   The **DBGrid** control is an ActiveX control that works like a **ComboBox** but the data automatically comes from one database via a **Data** control and the results can optionally update a field in a second database via a second **Data** control.

Properties
- *DBGridControl*.**AddNewMode**—a read-only **Integer** value (see Table D-83) specifying how the current cell relates to the list row of the grid. If **AllowAddNew** is **False**, then **AddNewMode** will always return zero.

AddNewMode Name	Value	Description
dbgNoAddNew	0	Cell is not in the last row and no AddNew operations are in progress.
dbgAddNewCurrent	1	Cell is in the last row, but no AddNew operations are in progress.
dbgAddNewPending	2	Cell is in the next to last row because an AddNew operation was started.

Table D-83: AddNewMode values.

- *DBGridControl*.**Align**—an **Integer** value (see Table D-84) that describes the placement of the **DBGrid** control.

Align Name	Value	Description
vbAlignNone	0	The control's position is set at design time or by the program (default value for objects on a non-MDI Form).
vbAlignTop	1	The control is placed at the top of the form and its width is set to **ScaleWidth**. It will automatically be resized when the form is resized (default value for objects on an MDI Form).
vbAlignBottom	2	The control is placed at the bottom of the form and its width is set to **ScaleWidth**. It will automatically be resized when the form is resized.
vbAlignLeft	3	The control is placed at the left edge of the form and its width is set to **ScaleWidth**. It is not resized when the form is resized.
vbAlignRight	4	The control is placed at the right edge of the form and its width is set to **ScaleWidth**. It is not resized when the form is resized.

Table D-84: Align *values.*

- *DBGridControl*.**AllowAddNew**—a **Boolean** value when **True** the user will be allowed to add new records, and the last row of the grid will be blank. When **False** the user will not be permitted to add records, and the last row of the grid will contain the last row of data.
- *DBGridControl*.**AllowArrows**—a **Boolean** value when **True** the user will allowed to use arror keys to scroll through the grid. When **False** the user will not be allowed to use the cursor keys.
- *DBGridControl*.**AllowDelete**—a **Boolean** value when **True** the user will be allowed to delete records from the database. When **False** the user will not be allowed to delete records from the database.
- *DBGridControl*.**AllowRowSizing**—a **Boolean** value when **True** the user will be allowed to resize rows in the grid. When **False** the user will not be allowed to resize rows in the grid.
- *DBGridControl*.**AllowUpdate**—a **Boolean** value when **True** the user will be allowed to update records in the database. When **False** the user will not be allowed to update records in the database.
- *DBGridControl*.**Appearance**—an **Integer** value (see Table D-85) that specifies how the combo box will appear on the form.

Appearance Value	Description
0	The **DBGrid** control displays without the 3D effects.
1	The **DBGrid** control displays with 3D effects (default value).

Table D-85: Appearance *values.*

- *DBGridControl*.**ApproxCount**—a **Long** value containing the approximate number of rows in the grid. This optimizes the scroll bar.
- *DBGridControl*.**BackColor**—a **Long** that contains the suggested value for the background color of the control. The **BackColor** and **ForeColor** must both be solid to display text. If you choose a color that is dithered, it will be changed to the nearest solid color.
- *DBGridControl*.**BookMark** (*index*)—an array of bookmarks for each row in the grid. *Index* ranges from 0 to **RowCount** -1.
- *DBGridControl*.**BorderStyle**—an **Integer** value (see Table D-86) specifying how the border will be drawn. This value also indicates how the form can be resized and is read only at run time.

BorderStyle Name	Value	Description
vbBSNone	0	No border, control box menu, title bar, maximize and minimize buttons. Cannot be resized.
vbFixedSingle	1	Single line around the form. Form can only be resized by maximize and minimize buttons.

Table D-86: BorderStyle *values.*

- *DBGridControl*.**Col**—an **Integer** containing the current column. Can be set at run time to change the current column.
- *DBGridControl*.**ColumnHeaders**—a **Boolean** value when **True** means column headers display. When **False** means column headers do not display.

- *DBGridControl*.**Columns**—returns a **Columns** collection.
- *DBGridControl*.**Container**—an object that can be used to set or return the container of the control at run time. This property cannot be set at design time.
- *DBGridControl*.**CurrentCellModified**—a **Boolean** value when **True** means the current cell has been modified. When **False** means the current cell has not be modified.
- *DBGridControl*.**CurrentCellVisible**—a **Boolean** value when **True** means the current cell is visible. When **False** means the current cell is not visible.
- *DBGridControl*.**DataBinding**—a reference to the **DataBindings** collection containing the bindable properties available.
- *DBGridControl*.**DataChanged**—a **Boolean** that applies only to data bound controls. When **True** means that the data contained in this control was changed either by the user or by some means other than retrieving data from the current record. When **False** means the data in the control is unchanged from the current record. Simply reading the next record is not sufficient to set the **DataChanged** property to **True**.
- *DBGridControl*.**DataField**—a **String** value that associates the control with a field in a **RecordSet** object in a **Data** control.
- *DBGridControl*.**DataMode**—an **Integer** value (see Table D-87) specifying if the grid operates in bound mode or unbound mode.

DataMode Name	Value	Description
dbgBound	0	Grid runs in bound mode.
dbgUnbound	1	Grid runs in unbound mode.

Table D-87: **DataMode** values.

- *DBGridControl*.**DataSource**—a **String** containing the name of a **Data** control that will be updated once the selection is made.
- *DBGridControl*.**DefColWidth**—a **Single** specifying the default column width in the units specified in the container's **ScaleMode**.
- *DBGridControl*.**DragIcon**—an object that contains the picture value of an icon. At design time, you can specify an icon file that has a file type of .ICO.

> **Tip**
>
> *This value can be created by copying the value from another control's **DragIcon** value, a form's icon, or by using the **LoadPicture** function.*

- *DBGridControl*.**DragMode**—an **Integer** value (see Table D-88) specifying how the control will respond to a drag request.

> **Tip**
>
> *Setting **DragMode** to vbAutomatic will automatically begin a drag operation when the user clicks on the control. However, the control will not respond to the usual mouse events (**Click**, **DblClick**, **MouseDown**, **MouseMove**, **MouseUp**).*

DragMode Name	Value	Description
vbManual	0	The **Drag** method must be used to begin a drag-and-drop operation (default value).
vbAutomatic	1	The source control will automatically begin a drag-and-drop operation when the user clicks on the control.

Table D-88: **DragMode** *values.*

- *DBGridControl*.**EditActive**—a **Boolean** value when **True** means that the current cell is being edited. When **False**, the current cell is not being edited.
- *DBGridControl*.**Enabled**—a **Boolean** value when **True** means that the control will respond to events. When **False**, the control will not respond to events.
- *DBGridControl*.**ErrorText**—a **String** value containing the error message from the underlying data source.
- *DBGridControl*.**FirstRow**—a bookmark to the first visible row in the grid.
- *DBGridControl*.**Font**—an object that contains information about the character font used by this control.
- *DataControl*.**ForeColor**—a **Long** that contains the suggested value for the foreground color of the contained control. This property is read only at run time.
- *DBGridControl*.**HeadFont**—an object that contains information about the character font used by the headers.
- *DBGridControl*.**HeadLines**—a **Single** value ranging from 0 to 10 which corresponds to the number of lines displayed in the header. The default value is 1 line.
- *DBGridControl*.**Height**—a **Single** that contains the height of the control.
- *DBGridControl*.**HelpContextID**—a **Long** that contains a help file context ID number which references an entry in the help file. When the user presses the F1 key while this control is active, the corresponding entry in the help file will automatically display. A value of zero means that no context number was specified.

> **Tip**
>
> *A help file must be compiled using the Windows Help Compiler available in the Professional and Enterprise editions of Visual Basic.*

- *DBGridControl*.**hWnd**—a **Long** that contains a Windows handle to the control.

> **Tip**
>
> *The* **hWnd** *property is most useful when making calls to Windows API functions. Since this value can change during execution, do not save the value into a variable for later use.*

- *DBGridControl*.**hWndEditor**—a **Long** that contains a Windows handle to the editor window. A return value of zero means that the editor window does not currently exist.
- *DBGridControl*.**Index**—an **Integer** that uniquely identifies a control in a control array.

- *DBGridControl*.**Left**—a **Single** that contains the distance measured in twips between the left edge of the control and the left edge of the control's container.
- *DBGridControl*.**LeftCol**—an **Integer** value containing the leftmost visible column.
- *DBGridControl*.**MarqueeStyle**—an **Integer** value (see Table D-89) containing the Marquee style for the **DBGrid** or split object.

MarqueeStyle Name	Value	Description
dbgDottedCellBorder	0	The current cell will be highlighted by drawing a dotted border around the cell.
dbgSolidCellBorder	1	The current cell will be highlighted by drawing a solid line around the cell.
dbgHighlightCell	2	The current cell will be highlighted.
dbgHighlightRow	3	The current row will be highlighted by inverting the colors within the row.
dbgHighlightRowRaiseCell	4	The current row will be highlighted and the current cell will be raised.
dbgNoMarquee	5	No highlighting will be used.
dbgFloatingEditor	6	The current cell will be highlighted by a floating editor window (default).

Table D-89: MarqueeStyle *values.*

- *DBGridControl*.**MarqueeUnique**—a **Boolean** value when **True** the current cell displays with a marquee in the split only. When **False**, each split's current cell displays using a marquee.
- *DBGridControl*.**Name**—a **String** that contains the name of the control that will be used to reference the control in a Visual Basic program. This property is read only at run time.
- *DBGridControl*.**Object**—an object that contains a reference to the *DBGridControl* object.
- *DBGridControl*.**Parent**—an object that contains a reference to the **Form**, **Frame,** or other container that contains the **DBGrid** control.
- *DBGridControl*.**RecordSelectors**—a **Boolean** value when **True** means that the record selectors display. When **False** means that record selectors do not display.
- *DBGridControl*.**Row**—an **Integer** containing the current row. Can be set at run time to change the current row.
- *DBGridControl*.**RowDividerStyle**—an **Integer** value (see Table D-90) containing the row divider style for the **DBGrid** control.

RowDividerStyleValue	Description
0	No divider is used.
1	A black line displays between rows.
2	A dark gray line displays between rows (default).
3	A raised line displays between rows.
4	An inset line displays between rows.
5	A line is drawn using the **ForeColor** property.

Table D-90: RowDividerStyle *values.*

- *DBGridControl*.**RowHeight**—a **Single** specifying the default row height in the units specified in the container's **ScaleMode**.
- *DBGridControl*.**ScrollBars**—an **Integer** value (see Table D-91) containing the row divider style for the **DBGrid** control.

ScrollBars Name	Value	Description
vbSBNone	0	No scroll bars display (default).
vbHorizontal	1	A horizontal scroll bar displays.
vbVertical	2	A vertical scroll bar displays.
vbBoth	3	Both scroll bars display.

Table D-91: ScrollBars *values.*

- *DBGridControl*.**SelectedItem**—a **Variant** value containing the bookmark for the selected database item.
- *DBGridControl*.**SelEndCol**—an **Integer** value containing the ending column when a range of rows and columns are selected.
- *DBGridControl*.**SelEndRow**—an **Integer** value containing the ending row when a range of rows and columns are selected.
- *DBGridControl*.**SelLength**—a **Long** value containing the number of characters selected from the text box part of the control.
- *DBGridControl*.**SelStart**—a **Long** value containing the starting position of the selected text in the text box part of the control.
- *DBGridControl*.**SelStartCol**—an **Integer** value containing the starting column when a range of rows and columns are selected.
- *DBGridControl*.**SelStartRow**—an **Integer** value containing the starting row when a range of rows and columns are selected.
- *DBGridControl*.**SelText**—a **String** value containing the selected text.
- *DBGridControl*.**Split**—an **Integer** value containing the index of the current split.
- *DBGridControl*.**Splits**—returns a **Split** object containing information about the splits in the current grid.
- *DBGridControl*.**TabAcrossSplits**—a **Boolean** value when **True** means that the tab and arrow keys will move across a split boundary. When **False** means that they wrap or stop depending on the **TabAction** and **WrapCellPointer** properties.
- *DBGridControl*.**TabAction**—an **Integer** value (see Table D-92) describing how the tab key operates.

TabAction Name	Value	Description
dbgControlNavigation	0	Tab key moves to the next control (default).
dbgColumnNavigation	1	Tab key moves the current cell to the next or previous cell.
dbgGridNavigation	2	Same as *dbgColumnNavigation*, except that the **WrapCellPointer** property determines the action when the current cell reaches the edge of the split or grid.

Table D-92: TabAction *values.*

- *DBGridControl*.**TabIndex**—an **Integer** that determines the order that a user will tab through the objects on a form.
- *DBGridControl*.**TabStop**—a **Boolean** value when **True** means that the user can tab to this object. When **False** means that this control will be skipped to the next control in the **TabIndex** order.
- *DBGridControl*.**Tag**—a **String** that can hold programmer specific information. This property is not used by Visual Basic.
- *DBGridControl*.**Text**—a **String** that sets or returns the value from the text box part of the control.
- *DBGridControl*.**ToolTipText**—a **String** that holds a text value that can be displayed as a **ToolTip** box that displays whenever the cursor is held over the control for about one second.
- *DBGridControl*.**Top**—a **Single** that contains the distance measured in twips between the top edge of the control and the top edge of the control's container.
- *DBGridControl*.**Visible**—a **Boolean** value when **True** means that the control is visible. When **False** means that the control is not visible.

> **Tip**
>
> *This property hides the control until the program is ready to display it.*

- *DBGridControl*.**VisibleCols**—an **Integer** containing the number of columns visible in the grid.
- *DBGridControl*.**VisibleRows**—an **Integer** containing the number of rows visible in the grid.
- *DBGridControl*.**WhatsThisHelpID**—a **Long** that contains a help file context ID number references an entry in the help file. This provides a What's This PopUp help display in response to the What's This button in the upper right corner of the window.
- *DBGridControl*.**Width**—a **Single** that contains the width of the control.
- *DBGridControl*.**WrapCellPointer**—a **Boolean** value when **True** means that the cell pointer will go from the last row or column to the first row or column (or the reverse). When **False** means that cell pointer will stop at the edge of the grid.

Methods

DBGridControl.ClearFields

Usage This method restores the default grid layout.

DBGridControl.ClearSelCols

Usage This method deselects all selected columns in a split.

column = *DBGridControl*.ColContaining *coord*

Usage This method returns the column index based for a particular X-coordinate value.

Arguments
- *column*—an **Integer** containing the column index.
  - *coord*—a **Single** containing an X-coordinate in units of the control's container's **ScaleMode**.

DBGridControl.Drag [DragAction]

Usage This method begins, ends, or cancels a drag operation.

Arguments ▪ *DragAction*—an **Integer** that contains a value selected from Table D-93.

DragAction Name	Value	Description
vbCancel	0	Cancels any drag operation in progress.
vbBeginDrag	1	Begins a drag operation (default).
vbEndDrag	2	Ends a drag operation and drops *object*.

Table D-93: DragAction *values.*

bookmark = DBGridControl.GetBookmark value

Usage This method returns a bookmark for a row relative to the current row.

Arguments ▪ *bookmark*—a bookmark for the specified row.

▪ *value*—an **Integer** containing an offset from the current row. A value of 0 means the current row. A value of 1 means the row after the current row. A value of -1 means the row before the current row.

DBGridControl.HoldFields

Usage This method sets the current column and field layout as the custom layout. This can be undone by using the **ClearFields** method.

DBGridControl.Move Left [, Top [, Width [, Height]]]

Usage This method changes the position and the size of the **DBGrid** control. The **ScaleMode** of the **Form** or other container object that holds the control will determine the units used to specify the coordinates.

Arguments ▪ *Left*—a **Single** that specifies the new position of the left edge of the control.
▪ *Top*—a **Single** that specifies the new position of the top edge of the control.
▪ *Width*—a **Single** that specifies the new width of the control.
▪ *Height*—a **Single** that specifies the new height of the control.

DBGridControl.ReBind

Usage This method rebuilds the rows and columns in the control's grid. Changes to the column and row structure are restored after the process completes.

DBGridControl.Refresh

Usage   This method redraws the contents of the control.

bookmark = DBGridControl.RowBookmark *value*

Usage   This method returns a bookmark for a row.

Arguments   ▪ *bookmark*—a bookmark for the specified row.
▪ *value*—an **Integer** containing the row number.

row = DBGridControl.RowContaining *coord*

Usage   This method returns the row index based for a particular Y-coordinate value.

Arguments   ▪ *row*—an **Integer** containing the row index.
▪ *coord*—a **Single** containing a Y-coordinate in units of the control's container's **ScaleMode**.

ycoord = DBGridControl.RowTop *value*

Usage   This method returns the column index based for a particular Y-coordinate value.

Arguments   ▪ *ycoord*—a **Single** containing Y-coordinate of the top edge of the specified row.
▪ *value*—an **Integer** containing the row number.

DBGridControl.Scroll *colvalue, rowvalue*

Usage   This method scrolls the grid by the specified amounts. Positive values scroll toward the end of the grid. Negative values scroll toward the beginning of the grid.

Arguments   ▪ *colvalue*—a **Long** containing the number of columns to scroll.
▪ *rowvalue*—a **Long** containing the number of rows to scroll.

DBGridControl.SetFocus

Usage   This method transfers the focus from the form or control that currently has the focus to this control. To receive the focus, this control must be enabled and visible.

DBGridControl.ShowWhatsThis

Usage   This method displays the ShowWhatsThis help information for this control.

split = *DBGridControl*.**SplitContaining** *x, y*

Usage This method returns the index of the split based on a particular set of X- and Y-coordinates.

Arguments
- *split*—an **Integer** containing the index of the split.
- *X*—a **Single** containing an X-coordinate in units of the control's container's ScaleMode.
- *y*—a **Single** containing a Y-coordinate in units of the control's container's ScaleMode.

DBGridControl.**ZOrder** [*position*]

Usage This method specifies the position of the control relative to the other objects on the form.

> **Tip**
>
> *Note that there are three layers of objects on a form: the back layer is the drawing space which contains the results of the graphical methods, the middle layer contains graphical objects and* **Labels***, and the top layer contains nongraphical controls such as the* **DBGrid** *control. The* **ZOrder** *method only affects how the objects are arranged within a single layer.*

Arguments
- *position*—an **Integer** that specifies the relative position of this object. A value of 0 means that the control is positioned at the head of the list, a value of 1 means that the control will be placed at the end of the list.

Events **Private Sub** *DBGridControl*_**AfterColEdit** ([*index* **As Integer** ,] *colindex*)

Usage This event occurs after the user has finished editing a cell in the grid.

Arguments
- *index*—an **Integer** that uniquely identifies a control in a control array. This argument is not present if the control is not part of a control array.
- *colindex*—an **Integer** that contains the column that was edited.

Private Sub *DBGridControl*_**AfterColUpdate** ([*index* **As Integer** ,] *colindex*)

Usage This event occurs after the user has finished editing a cell in the grid and after the data was copied to the control's copy buffer.

Arguments
- *index*—an **Integer** that uniquely identifies a control in a control array. This argument is not present if the control is not part of a control array.
- *colindex*—an **Integer** that contains the column that was edited.

Private Sub *DBGridControl*_AfterDelete ([*index* As Integer])

- **Usage** This event occurs after the user has deleted a row from the grid.

- **Arguments** • *index*—an **Integer** that uniquely identifies a control in a control array. This argument is not present if the control is not part of a control array.

Private Sub *DBGridControl*_AfterInsert ([*index* As Integer])

- **Usage** This event occurs after the user has inserted a new row into the grid.

- **Arguments** • *index*—an **Integer** that uniquely identifies a control in a control array. This argument is not present if the control is not part of a control array.

Private Sub *DBGridControl*_AfterUpdate ([*index* As Integer])

- **Usage** This event occurs after the user has changed any of the values in a row, moved the current cell pointer to the another row, and the updated data has been written to the database.

- **Arguments** • *index*—an **Integer** that uniquely identifies a control in a control array. This argument is not present if the control is not part of a control array.

Private Sub *DBGridControl*_BeforeColEdit ([*index* As Integer ,] ByVal *colindex* As Integer, ByVal *keyascii* As Integer, *cancel* As Boolean)

- **Usage** This event occurs when a user begins to edit the current row by either typing a character or clicking on a cell with the mouse.

- **Arguments** • *index*—an **Integer** that uniquely identifies a control in a control array. This argument is not present if the control is not part of a control array.
  - *colindex*—an **Integer** that contains the column that was edited. This property is read-only.
  - *keyascii*—an **Integer** containing the character that was pressed to begin the edit or zero if the mouse was clicked on the cell. This property is read-only.
  - *cancel*—a **Boolean** value when **True** means that the cell should not be edited. When **False** means that the cell can be edited (default).

Private Sub *DBGridControl*_BeforeColUpdate ([*index* As Integer ,] *colindex* As Integer, *currentvalue* As Integer, *cancel* As Boolean)

- **Usage** This event occurs after the user has finished editing a cell, but before the new value is moved to the database copy buffer.

Arguments
- *index*—an **Integer** that uniquely identifies a control in a control array. This argument is not present if the control is not part of a control array.
- *colindex*—an **Integer** that contains the column that was updated.
- *currentvalue*—a **Variant** containing the value of the cell before it was changed.
- *cancel*—a **Boolean** value when **True** means that the cell should not be edited. When **False** means that the cell can be edited (default).

Private Sub *DBGridControl*_BeforeDelete ([*index* As Integer ,] *cancel*)

Usage   This event occurs before a row is deleted from the grid.

Arguments
- *index*—an **Integer** that uniquely identifies a control in a control array. This argument is not present if the control is not part of a control array.
- *cancel*—a **Boolean** value when **True** means that the cell should not be edited. When **False** means that the cell can be edited (default).

Private Sub *DBGridControl*_BeforeInsert ([*index* As Integer ,] *cancel* As Boolean)

Usage   This event occurs before a new row is inserted into the grid.

Arguments
- *index*—an **Integer** that uniquely identifies a control in a control array. This argument is not present if the control is not part of a control array.
- *cancel*—a **Boolean** value when **True** means that the row should not be inserted. When **False** means that the row can be inserted (default).

Private Sub *DBGridControl*_BeforeUpdate ([*index* As Integer ,] *cancel* As Boolean)

Usage   This event occurs after the user has changed any of the values in a row, moved the current cell pointer to the another row, but before the information is written to the database copy buffer and written to the database.

Arguments
- *index*—an **Integer** that uniquely identifies a control in a control array. This argument is not present if the control is not part of a control array.
- *cancel*—a **Boolean** value when **True** means that the row should not be updated. When **False** means that the row can be updated (default).

Private Sub *DBGridControl*_ButtonClick ([*index* As Integer ,] ByVal *colindex* As Integer)

Usage   This event occurs when the user clicks the current cell's built-in button. The button is enabled when the **Column** collection's **Button** property is **True**.

Arguments
- *index*—an **Integer** that uniquely identifies a control in a control array. This argument is not present if the control is not part of a control array.
- *colindex*—an **Integer** that contains the column that was edited.

Private Sub *DBGridControl*_Change([*index* As Integer])

Usage   This event occurs when a change is made to the grid.

Warning

*Unless you are careful, it is possible to make a change in the control that will trigger another **Change** event. Then it would change the control again, triggering the **Change** event again. This is called a **Cascading** event. This process will continue until the system grinds to a halt or the program aborts due to a lack of resources or memory. To prevent this, don't use this event or use a global flag to indicate when the event is active. Then add code inside the event to determine if the event is active, and exit the event without making any changes. Otherwise set the flag, perform the necessary processing, and finally reset the flag just before exiting the routine.*

Arguments
- *index*—an **Integer** that uniquely identifies a control in a control array. This argument is not present if the control is not part of a control array.

Private Sub *DBGridControl*_Click([*index* As Integer])

Usage   This event occurs when the user clicks a mouse button to select an item in the drop-down list or selects an item from the drop-down list using the keyboard.

Arguments
- *index*—an **Integer** that uniquely identifies a control in a control array. This argument is not present if the control is not part of a control array.

Private Sub *DBGridControl*_ColEdit ([*index* As Integer ,] ByVal *colindex* As Integer)

Usage   This event occurs after the **BeginColEdit** event assuming that the **BeginColEdit** event didn't set the *cancel* flag. Both events are in response to the user typing a character of clicking a mouse in a cell.

Arguments
- *index*—an **Integer** that uniquely identifies a control in a control array. This argument is not present if the control is not part of a control array.
- *colindex*—an **Integer** that contains the column that was edited. This property is read-only.

Private Sub *DBGridControl*_ColResize ([*index* As Integer ,] *colindex* As Integer, *cancel* As Boolean)

Usage   This event occurs after the size of a column has been changed.

Arguments
- *index*—an **Integer** that uniquely identifies a control in a control array. This argument is not present if the control is not part of a control array.
- *colindex*—an **Integer** that contains the column that was resized.
- *cancel*—a **Boolean** value when **True** means that the size of the cell should not changed. When **False** means that the size of the cell can be changed (default).

Private Sub *DBGridControl*_DblClick([*index* As Integer])

Usage This event occurs when the user double-clicks a mouse button to select an item in the drop-down list or selects an item from the drop-down list using the keyboard. This applies only when **Style** is set to *vbComboSimple*.

Arguments ▪ *index*—an **Integer** that uniquely identifies a control in a control array. This argument is not present if the control is not part of a control array.

Private Sub *DBGridControl*_DragDrop([*index* As Integer ,] *source* As Control, *x* As Single, *y* As Single)

Usage This event occurs when a drag-and-drop operation is completed by using the **Drag** method with a *DragAction* value of *vbEndDrag*.

> **Tip**
>
> *When using drag-and-drop operations, use the **DragOver** event to determine what the cursor should look like while the cursor moves over the control.*

Arguments ▪ *index*—an **Integer** that uniquely identifies a control in a control array. This argument is not present if the control is not part of a control array.

▪ *source*—a control object that is the control that is being dragged.

> **Tip**
>
> *You can access a property or method from the source control by using* source.property *or* source.method. *You can determine the type of object or control by using the **TypeOf** operator.*

▪ *x*—a **Single** that contains the horizontal location of the mouse pointer.

▪ *y*—a **Single** that contains the vertical location of the mouse pointer.

Private Sub *DBGridControl*_DragOver([*index* As Integer ,] *source* As Control, *x* As Single, *y* As Single, *state* As Integer)

Usage This event occurs while a drag operation is in progress and the cursor is moved over the control.

> **Tip**
>
> *When using drag-and-drop operations, use the **DragOver** event to determine what the cursor should look like while the cursor moves over the control. When* state *is 0, you can change the cursor to a No Drop (vbNoDrop) cursor or highlight the field that the cursor is near. When* state *is 1, you can undo the changes you made when the* state *was 0.*

Arguments ▪ *index*—an **Integer** that uniquely identifies a control in a control array. This argument is not present if the control is not part of a control array.

▪ *source*—a control object that is the control that is being dragged.

Tip

You can access a property or method from the source control by using source.*property or* source.*method. You can determine the type of object or control by using the* **TypeOf** *operator.*

- *x*—a **Single** that contains the horizontal location of the mouse pointer.
- *y*—a **Single** that contains the vertical location of the mouse pointer.
- *state*—an **Integer** value (see Table D-94) that indicates the state of the object being dragged.

state Name	Value	Description
vbEnter	0	The dragged object is entering range of the control.
vbLeave	1	The dragged object is leaving range of the control.
vbOver	2	The dragged object has moved from one position over the control to another.

Table D-94: state *values.*

Private Sub *DBGridControl*_Error ([*index* As Integer ,] *errcode* As Integer, *resp* As Single)

Usage — This event occurs when a data error occurs while your code is not running. This could happen because a user clicked the **DBGrid** control, the **DBGrid** control automatically loading a record set after Form_Load occured, or if a custom control performs a **MoveNext**, **AddNew**, or a **Delete**.

Arguments
- *errcode*—an **Integer** containing the error code.
- *resp*—an **Integer** value (see Table D-95) that contains the program's response to the error.

resp Name	Value	Description
vbDataErrContinue	0	Continue processing.
vbDataErrDisplay	1	Display error message (default).

Table D-95: resp *values.*

Private Sub *DBGridControl*_GotFocus ([*index* As Integer])

Usage — This event occurs when the control is given focus.

Tip

You can use this routine to display help or other information in a status bar.

Arguments
- *index*—an **Integer** that uniquely identifies a control in a control array. This argument is not present if the control is not part of a control array.

Private Sub *DBGridControl*_HeadClick ([*index* As Integer ,] *colindex* As Integer)

Usage This event occurs when the user clicks on a column header.

Arguments
- *index*—an **Integer** that uniquely identifies a control in a control array. This argument is not present if the control is not part of a control array.
- *colindex*—an **Integer** that contains the index of the column header.

Tip

This event changes the sort order of the data in the grid. For example, the first click on the header could sort in ascending order by this column. Then the second click on the same header could sort in descending order.

Private Sub *DBGridControl*_KeyDown ([*index* As Integer ,] *keycode* As Integer, *shift* As Single)

Usage This event occurs when a key is pressed while the control has the focus.

Arguments
- *index*—an **Integer** that uniquely identifies a control in a control array. This argument is not present if the control is not part of a control array.
- *keycode*—an **Integer** that contains information about which key was pressed.
- *shift*—an **Integer** value (see Table D-96) that contains information about the Shift and Alt keys that were pushed when the mouse button was pressed. These values can be added together if more than one key was down. For instance, a value of 5 would mean that the Shift and Alt keys were both down when the mouse button was pressed.

shift Name	Value	Description
vbShiftMask	1	The Shift key was pressed.
vbCtrlMask	2	The Ctrlkey was pressed.
vbAltMask	4	The Alt key was pressed.

Table D-96: shift *values.*

Private Sub *DBGridControl*_KeyPress([*index* As Integer ,] *keychar* As Integer)

Usage This event occurs whenever a key is pressed while the control has the focus.

Arguments
- *index*—an **Integer** that uniquely identifies a control in a control array. This argument is not present if the control is not part of a control array.
- *keychar*—an **Integer** that contains the ASCII character that was pressed.

Private Sub *DBGridControl*_KeyUp ([*index* As Integer ,] *keycode* As Integer, *shift* As Single)

- Usage: This event occurs when a key is released while the control has the focus.
- Arguments:
  - *index*—an **Integer** that uniquely identifies a control in a control array. This argument is not present if the control is not part of a control array.
  - *keycode*—an **Integer** that contains information about which key was released.
  - *shift*—an **Integer** value (see Table D-97) that contains information about the Shift and Alt keys that were pushed when the mouse button was pressed. These values can be added together if more than one key was down. For instance, a value of 5 would mean that the Shift and Alt keys were both down when the mouse button was pressed.

shift Name	Value	Description
vbShiftMask	1	The Shift key was pressed.
vbCtrlMask	2	The Ctrl key was pressed.
vbAltMask	4	The Alt key was pressed.

Table D-97: shift *values.*

Private Sub *DBGridControl*_LostFocus ([*index* As Integer])

- Usage: This event occurs when the control loses focus.

Tip

This routine is useful to performing data verification.

- Arguments:
  - *index*—an **Integer** that uniquely identifies a control in a control array. This argument is not present if the control is not part of a control array.

Private Sub *DBGridBoxControl*_MouseDown([*index* As Integer ,] *button* As Integer, *shift* As Single, *x* As Single, *y* As Single)

- Usage: This event occurs when a mouse button was pressed while the cursor is over the control.
- Arguments:
  - *index*—an **Integer** that uniquely identifies a control in a control array. This argument is not present if the control is not part of a control array.
  - *button*—an **Integer** value (see Table D-98) that contains information about the mouse buttons that were pressed. Only one button will be indicated when this event occurs.

button Name	Value	Description
vbLeftButton	1	The left button was pressed.
vbRightButton	2	The right button was pressed.
vbMiddleButton	4	The middle button was pressed.

Table D-98: button *values*.

- shift—an **Integer** value (see Table D-99) that contains information about the Shift and Alt keys that were pushed when the mouse button was pressed. These values can be added together if more than one key was down. For instance, a value of 5 would mean that the Shift and Alt keys were both down when the mouse button was pressed.

shift Name	Value	Description
vbShiftMask	1	The Shift key was pressed.
vbCtrlMask	2	The Ctrl key was pressed.
vbAltMask	4	The Alt key was pressed.

Table D-99: shift *values*.

- x—a **Single** that contains the horizontal location of the mouse pointer.
- y—a **Single** that contains the vertical location of the mouse pointer.

Private Sub *DBGridControl*_MouseMove ([*index* As Integer ,] *button* As Integer, *shift* As Single, *x* As Single, *y* As Single)

Usage   This event occurs while the cursor is moved over the control.

Arguments
- *index*—an **Integer** that uniquely identifies a control in a control array. This argument is not present if the control is not part of a control array.
- *button*—an **Integer** value (see Table D-100) that contains information about the mouse buttons that were pressed. These values can be added together if more than one button was pushed. For instance, a value of 3 means that both the left and right buttons were pressed. A value of 0 means that no buttons were pressed.

button Name	Value	Description
vbLeftButton	1	The left button was pressed.
vbRightButton	2	The right button was pressed.
vbMiddleButton	4	The middle button was pressed.

Table D-100: button *values*.

- *shift*—an **Integer** value (see Table D-101) that contains information about the Shift and Alt keys that were pushed when the mouse button was pressed. For instance, a value of 5 would mean that the Shift and Alt keys were both down when the mouse button was pressed. A value of 0 means that none of these keys were pressed.

shift Name	Value	Description
vbShiftMask	1	The Shift key was pressed.
vbCtrlMask	2	The Ctrl key was pressed.
vbAltMask	4	The Alt key was pressed.

Table D-101: shift *values*.

- *x*—a **Single** that contains the horizontal location of the mouse pointer.
- *y*—a **Single** that contains the vertical location of the mouse pointer.

Private Sub *DBGridBoxControl*_MouseUp([*index* As Integer ,] *button* As Integer, *shift* As Single, *x* As Single, *y* As Single)

Usage — This event occurs when a mouse button is released while the cursor is over the control.

Arguments
- *index*—an **Integer** that uniquely identifies a control in a control array. This argument is not present if the control is not part of a control array.
- *button*—an **Integer** value (see Table D-102) that contains information about the mouse buttons that were released. Only one of these values will be present.

button Name	Value	Description
vbLeftButton	1	The left button was released.
vbRightButton	2	The right button was released.
vbMiddleButton	4	The middle button was released.

Table D-102: button *values*.

- *shift*—an **Integer** value (see Table D-103) that contains information about the Shift and Alt keys that were pushed when the mouse button was released. These values can be added together if more than one key was down. For instance, a value of 5 would mean that the Shift and Alt keys were both down when the mouse button was released. A value of 0 means that none of these keys were pressed.

shift Name	Value	Description
vbShiftMask	1	The Shift key was pressed.
vbCtrlMask	2	The Ctrl key was pressed.
vbAltMask	4	The Alt key was pressed.

Table D-103: shift *values*.

- *x*—a **Single** that contains the horizontal location of the mouse pointer.
- *y*—a **Single** that contains the vertical location of the mouse pointer.

Private Sub *DBGridControl*_OnAddNew ([*index* As Integer])

Usage This event occurs after an **AddNew** operation has begun.

Arguments *index*—an **Integer** that uniquely identifies a control in a control array. This argument is not present if the control is not part of a control array.

Private Sub *DBGridControl*_RowColChange ([*index* As Integer ,] *row* As Integer, *col* As Integer)

Usage This event occurs whenever the current cell is moved from one location to another.

Arguments *index*—an **Integer** that uniquely identifies a control in a control array. This argument is not present if the control is not part of a control array.

row—an **Integer** that contains the number of the row before the current cell was changed.

col—an **Integer** that contains the number of the column before the current cell was changed.

Private Sub *DBGridControl*_RowResize ([*index* As Integer ,] *rowindex* As Integer, *cancel* As Boolean)

Usage This event occurs after the size of a row has been changed.

Arguments *index*—an **Integer** that uniquely identifies a control in a control array. This argument is not present if the control is not part of a control array.

rowindex—an **Integer** that contains the row that was resized.

cancel—a **Boolean** value when **True** means that the size of the cell should not changed. When **False** means that the size of the cell can be changed (default).

Private Sub *DBGridControl*_Scroll ([*index* As Integer ,] *cancel* As Boolean)

Usage This event is called each time the scroll bar is repositioned in the drop-down box.

Arguments *index*—an **Integer** that uniquely identifies a control in a control array. This argument is not present if the control is not part of a control array.

cancel—a **Boolean** value when **True** means that the scroll operation should be canceled. When **False** means that the scroll operation should not be canceled (default).

Private Sub *DBGridControl_*SelChange ([*index* As Integer ,] *cancel* As Boolean)

Usage   This event is called when the range of selected cells changes.

Arguments
- *index*—an **Integer** that uniquely identifies a control in a control array. This argument is not present if the control is not part of a control array.
- *cancel*—a **Boolean** value when **True** means that the currently selected cells should be retained. When **False** the newly selected cells should be kept (default).

Private Sub *DBGridControl_*SplitChange ([*index* As Integer])

Usage   This event is called whenever the current cell is moved from one split to another.

Arguments
- *index*—an **Integer** that uniquely identifies a control in a control array. This argument is not present if the control is not part of a control array.

Private Sub *DBGridControl_*UnboundAddData ([*index* As Integer ,] *rowbuf* As RowBuffer , *bookmark* As Variant)

Usage   This event is called in an unbound **DBGrid** when a new row is added. To cancel the add operation, set the **RowCount** property of the **RowBuffer** object to zero.

Arguments
- *index*—an **Integer** that uniquely identifies a control in a control array. This argument is not present if the control is not part of a control array.
- *rowbuf*—a **RowBuffer** object containing the new row of data.
- *bookmark*—a bookmark containing the database reference to the new row of data.

Private Sub *DBGridControl_*UnboundDeleteRow ([*index* As Integer ,] *bookmark* As Variant)

Usage   This event is called in an unbound **DBGrid** when an existing row is about to be deleted. This event may be canceled by setting *bookmark* to **Null**.

Arguments
- *index*—an **Integer** that uniquely identifies a control in a control array. This argument is not present if the control is not part of a control array.
- *bookmark*—a bookmark containing the database reference of the row to be deleted. Set this value to **Null** to cancel the operation.

Private Sub *DBGridControl*_UnboundGetRelative-Bookmark ([*index* As Integer ,] *start* As Variant, ByVal *offset* As Long, *new* As Variant, *pos* As Long)

Usage   This event computes the location of a new row in the database when the grid needs more data.

Arguments
- *index*—an **Integer** that uniquely identifies a control in a control array. This argument is not present if the control is not part of a control array.
- *start*—a **Variant** containing a bookmark.
- *offset*—a **Long** containing the offset from the bookmark specified in *start*. A positive number indicates a forward selection, while a negative number indicates a backward selection.
- *new*—a **Variant** containing a new bookmark that is computed by selecting the record, *offset* number of records away from the *start* bookmark.
- *pos*—a **Long** value containing the approximate ordinal value of the *new* bookmark. If the exact value can't be computed, the best approximate value should be used. If the best approximate value can't be computed, then this value can be ignored.

Private Sub *DBGridControl*_UnboundReadData ([*index* As Integer ,] *row* As RowBuffer, *start* As Variant, *readprior* As Boolean)

Usage   This event is called each time an unbound grid requires data.

Arguments
- *index*—an **Integer** that uniquely identifies a control in a control array. This argument is not present if the control is not part of a control array.
- *row*—a **RowBuffer** object that will contain the newly read records. The number of records to be read can be found in the **RowCount** property.
- *start*—a **Variant** containing the bookmark of the starting location to be retrieved.
- *readprior*—a **Boolean** when **True** means that the rows prior to the *start* are to be read. When **False** means that the rows after *start* are to be read.

Private Sub *DBGridControl*_UnboundWriteData ([*index* As Integer ,] *row* As RowBuffer, *start* As Variant)

Usage   This event is called each time an unbound grid needs to write a row to the database.

Arguments
- *index*—an **Integer** that uniquely identifies a control in a control array. This argument is not present if the control is not part of a control array.
- *row*—a **RowBuffer** object that will contain the row to be written.
- *start*—a **Variant** containing the bookmark of the location where the row is to be written.

See Also   **Data** (control), **MSFlexGrid** (control)

DBEngine

OBJECT

PE, EE

Usage
: The **DBEngine** object is the highest level object in the Data Access Object model. It provides multiple database workspaces in which the actual database work is performed.

Properties
: - *DBEngine*.**DefaultPassword**—a **String** containing the password associated with **DefaultUser**. Note that this value is case-sensitive and can be up to 14 characters long for Microsoft Jet databases and any size for an ODBC database. The default value for this property is the empty string ("").
  - *DBEngine*.**DefaultType**—a **Long** (see Table D-104) containing the type of workspace object created.

DefaultType Name	Description
dbUseJet	The workspace is connected to the Microsoft Jet database engine.
dbUseODBC	The workspace is connected to an ODBC database system.

Table D-104: DefaultType values.

  - *DBEngine*.**DefaultUser**—a **String** containing the username used to create the **WorkSpace**. Note that this value is not case sensitive and can be up to 20 characters long for Microsoft Jet databases and any size for an ODBC database. The default value for this property is "admin."
  - *DBEngine*.**IniPath**—a **String** containing the Windows Registry key where information about the Microsoft Jet database is kept. Typical keys are either "\HKEY_LOCAL_MACHINE\SOFTWARE\Microsoft\Jet\3.5\" or "\HKEY_LOCAL_USER\SOFTWARE\Microsoft\Jet\3.5\".
  - *DBEngine*.**LoginTimeout**—an **Integer** value containing the number of seconds that must pass before an error is returned during the login attempt to an ODBC database. The default value is 20 seconds.
  - *DBEngine*.**SystemDB**—a **String** containing the path where the workgroup information file is kept for the Microsoft Jet database engine. The default value is "system.mdb," and it can be found in the Windows Registry.
  - *DBEngine*.**Version**—a **String** value containing the version number of the database engine.

Methods
: ## DBEngine.BeginTrans

Usage
: This method marks the beginning of a transaction.

DBEngine.CommitTrans [*dbFlushOSCacheWrites*]

Usage
: This method marks the end of a transaction and saves the data into the database. After the commit has finished, the transaction can't be undone using the **RollBack** method.

Arguments • *dbFlushOSCacheWrites*—a **Long** value when present instructs the Microsoft Jet database engine to ensure that the operating system disk cache is flushed before returning to the user. This ensures that the transaction is posted to disk at a cost of slowing down the transaction a small amount.

DBEngine.CompactDatabase *olddb, newdb* [, *locale* [, *options* [, *password*]]]

Usage   This method copies and compresses a database file. At the same time you can also change some of the database options such as language and encryption.

Arguments • *olddb*—a **String** value containing the filename and path of the current database file.
• *newdb*—a **String** value containing the filename and path of the new database file.
• *locale*—a **String** value containing the language of the new database (see Table D-105) and/or the password for the new database. To specify the password, use the string ";pwd=password" where password is the new password. To specify both, concatenate the two strings together like, *dbLangNorwDan* & ";pwd=password."

Language Name	Description
dbLangArabic	Arabic
dbLangChineseSimplified	Simplified Chinese
dbLangChineseTraditional	Traditional Chinese
dbLangCyrillic	Cyrillic
dbLangCzech	Czech
dbLangDutch	Dutch
dbLangGeneral	English, French, German, Portuguese, Italian, and Modern Spanish
dbLangGreek	Greek
dbLangHebrew	Hebrew
dbLangHungarian	Hungarian
dbLangIcelandic	Icelandic
dbLangJapanese	Japanese
dbLangKorean	Korean
dbLangNordic	Nordic (Jet version 1.0 only)
dbLangNorwDan	Norwegian or Danish
dbLangPolish	Polish
dbLangSlovenian	Slovenian
dbLangSpanish	Spanish
dbLangSwedFin	Swedish or Finnish
dbLangThai	Thai
dbLangTurkish	Turkish

Table D-105: Language *values.*

- *options*—a **Variant** value containing the sum of the selected constants from Table D-106 below. If omitted, this argument will default to the values in the *olddb*.

options Name	Description
dbEncrypt	Encrypt the database.
dbDecrypt	Decrypt the database.
dbVersion10	Create a Version 1.0 compatible database.
dbVersion11	Create a Version 1.1 compatible database.
dbVersion20	Create a Version 2.0/2.5 compatible database.
dbVersion30	Create a Version 3.0/3.5 compatible database.

Table D-106: options *values*.

DBEngine.CompactDatabase *dbname, locale , options*

Usage   This method creates a new database.

Arguments
- *dbname*—a **String** value containing the filename and path of the new database file.
- *locale*—a **String** value containing the language of the new database (see Table D-107) and/or the password for the new database. To specify the password, use the string ";pwd=password" where password is the new password. To specify both, concatenate the two strings together like, *dbLangNorwDan* & ";pwd=password".

Language Name	Description
dbLangArabic	Arabic
dbLangChineseSimplified	Simplified Chinese
dbLangChineseTraditional	Traditional Chinese
dbLangCyrillic	Cyrillic
dbLangCzech	Czech
dbLangDutch	Dutch
dbLangGeneral	English, French, German, Portuguese, Italian, and Modern Spanish
dbLangGreek	Greek
dbLangHebrew	Hebrew
dbLangHungarian	Hungarian
dbLangIcelandic	Icelandic
dbLangJapanese	Japanese
dbLangKorean	Korean
dbLangNordic	Nordic (Jet version 1.0 only)
dbLangNorwDan	Norwegian or Danish
dbLangPolish	Polish
dbLangSlovenian	Slovenian
dbLangSpanish	Spanish
dbLangSwedFin	Swedish or Finnish
dbLangThai	Thai
dbLangTurkish	Turkish

Table D-107: Language *values*.

- *options*—a **Variant** value containing the sum of the selected constants from Table D-108 below. If omitted, this argument will default to the values in the *olddb*.

options Name	Description
dbEncrypt	Encrypt the database.
dbDecrypt	Decrypt the database.
dbVersion10	Create a Version 1.0 compatible database.
dbVersion11	Create a Version 1.1 compatible database.
dbVersion20	Create a Version 2.0/2.5 compatible database.
dbVersion30	Create a Version 3.0/3.5 compatible database.

Table D-108: options *values.*

DBEngine.CreateWorkspace *name, user, password, options*

Usage This method creates a new database.

Arguments
- *name*—a **String** value containing the name of the workspace. It must begin with a letter and can contain any combination of letters, numbers, or underscore characters ("_"). The length of the name can be up to 20 characters long.
- *user*—a **String** containing the username associated with the workspace.
- *password*—a **String** containing the password for the workspace. It can be up to 14 characters long and contain any ASCII character except for the null character (ASCII value of 0).
- *type*—an **Integer** value (see Table D-109) containing the type of workspace.

Type Name	Description
dbUseJet	The workspace is connected to the Microsoft Jet database engine.
dbUseODBC	The workspace is connected to an ODBC database system.

Table D-109: Type *values.*

DBEngine.Idle [*dbRefreshCache*]

Usage This method lets the Microsoft Jet engine catch up on tasks that it may not have time to complete while performing heavy processing.

Arguments
- *dbRefreshCache*—a constant when present instructs the Microsoft Jet database engine to flush the memory buffers to the database file and then reload them from disk.

connection = DBEngine.OpenConnection *name* [, *options* [, *readonly* [, *connect*]]]

Usage This method opens a connection to an ODBC database system.

Arguments
- *connection*—a connection object containing the opened connection.
- *name*—a **String** value containing ODBC connection information.

- *options*—an **Integer** value (see Table D-110) containing the options for the connection process.

options Name	Description
dbDriverNoPrompt	The connection information in *name* and *connect* are used to connect to the database. If sufficient information is not present, an error will occur.
dbDriverPrompt	The ODBC driver takes the information supplied in *name* and *connect* and displays it in the ODBC Data Sources dialog box.
dbDriverComplete	The ODBC driver uses the information supplied in *name* and *connect* to connect to the database. If there is insufficient information, the ODBC Data Sources dialog box will be displayed (default).
dbDriverCompleteRequired	This is similar to the *dbDriverComplete* option, but information supplied in *name* and *connect* can't be changed.
dbRunAsync	Connect to the database asynchronously. This option can be added to any of the other options.

Table D-110: options *values.*

- *readonly*—a **Boolean** value which is **True** for a read-only connection and **False** for a read/write connection (default).
- *connect*—a **String** value containing ODBC connection information.

database = **DBEngine.OpenDatabase** *name* [, *options* [, *readonly* [, *connect*]]]

Usage This method opens a Microsoft Jet database.

Arguments
- *database*—a database object containing the opened database.
- *name*—a **String** value containing the filename and path of the Microsoft Jet database or the ODBC data source.
- *options*—an **Integer** value (see Table D-111) containing options for the database.

options Name	Description
dbDriverNoPrompt	The connection information in *name* and *connect* are used to connect to the database. If sufficient information is not present, an error will occur.
dbDriverPrompt	The ODBC driver takes the information supplied in *name* and *connect* and displays it in the ODBC Data Sources dialog box.
dbDriverComplete	The ODBC driver uses the information supplied in *name* and *connect* to connect to the database. If there is insufficient information, the ODBC Data Sources dialog box will be displayed (default).
dbDriverCompleteRequired	This is similar to the *dbDriverComplete* option, but information supplied in *name* and *connect* can't be changed.

Table D-111: options *values.*

- *readonly*—a **Boolean** value which is **True** for a read-only connection and **False** for a read/write connection (default).
- *connect*—a **String** value containing connection information including passwords.

DBEngine.RegisterDatabase *name* [, *driver* [, *silent* [, *keywords*]]]

Usage   This method saves information about an ODBC database connection in the Windows Registry.

Arguments
- *name*—a **String** value containing the filename and path of the Microsoft Jet database or the ODBC data source. This will be used in **OpenDatabase** as the *name* parameter.
- *driver*—a **String** containing the name of the ODBC database driver.
- *silent*—a **Boolean** value which is **True** for a read-only connection and **False** for a read/write connection (default).
- *keywords*—a **String** value containing a list of keywords to be saved with the connection information.

DBEngine.RepairDatabase *name*

Usage   This method will attempt to repair a Microsoft Jet database that was marked as possibly corrupt. This can be caused by a power failure or system crash while the database engine attempts to write to the physical file.

Arguments
- *name*—a **String** value containing the filename and path of the Microsoft Jet database.

DBEngine.RollBack

Usage   This method abandons all of the changes to the database, so the database is at the same state as it was when the **BeginTrans** method was used.

Arguments
- *name*—a **String** containing the name of the property. Must begin with a letter and can be followed by letters, numbers, or an underscore ("_").
- *type*—a value selected from Table D-112 below.

type Name	Description
dbBigInt	Big Integer
dbBinary	Binary
dbBoolean	Boolean
dbByte	Byte
dbChar	Character
dbCurrency	Currency
dbDate	Date

type Name	Description
dbDecimal	Decimal
dbDouble	Double
dbFloat	Float
dbGUID	Globally unique identifier *dbInteger*
dbLong	Long
dbLongBinary	Long binary
dbMemo	Memo
dbNumeric	Numeric
dbSingle	Single
dbText	Text
dbTime	Time
dbTimeStamp	Time stamp
dbVarBinary	Variable length binary data (up to 255 bytes)

Table D-112: *type* values.

- *value*—a **Variant** containing the initial value for the property.
- *DDL*—a **Boolean** when **True** means that the user cannot change this property value without the *dbSecWriteDef* permission. When **False** this permission is not required to change the value.

DBEngine.SetOption *option, value*

Usage This method overrides the default values for the Microsoft Jet database engine while the DBEngine object is active.

Arguments • *option*—a **Long** value containing the option (see Table D-113) to be changed. Each option's description corresponds to the key value in the Windows Registry under the partial key "Jet\3.5\Engines\Jet 3.5\".

option Name	Description
dbPageTimeout	PageTimeout
dbSharedAsyncDelay	SharedAsyncDelay
dbExclusiveAsyncDelay	ExclusiveAsyncDelay
dbLockRetry	LockRetry
dbUserCommitSync	UserCommitSync
dbImplicitCommitSync	ImplicitCommitSync
dbMaxBufferSize	MaxBufferSize
dbMaxLocksPerFile	MaxLocksPerFile
dbLockDelay	LockDelay
dbRecycleLVs	RecycleLVs
dbFlushTransactionTimeout	FlushTransactionTimeout

Table D-113: option *values*.

- *value*—a **Variant** value corresponding to the option selected.

See Also **Database** (object), **Workspace** (object)

DBList

CONTROL

PE, EE

Usage   The **DBList** control is an ActiveX control that works like a **ListBox** but the data automatically comes from one database via a **Data** control and the results can optionally update a field in a second database via a second **Data** control.

Properties   ▪ *DBListControl*.**Appearance**—an **Integer** value (see Table D-114) that specifies how the combo box will appear on the form.

Appearance Value	Description
0	The **DBList** control displays without the 3D effects.
1	The **DBList** control displays with 3D effects (default value).

Table D-114: Appearance *values*.

▪ *DBListControl*.**BackColor**—a **Long** that contains the suggested value for the background color of the control. The **BackColor** and **ForeColor** must both be solid to display text. If you choose a color that is dithered, it will be changed to the nearest solid color.

▪ *DBListControl*.**BoundColumn**—a **String** containing the name of a database field in **RowSource** that passes back to **DataField**, once the selection is made.

▪ *DBListControl*.**BoundText**—a **String** containing the text value of the **BoundColumn** field.

▪ *DBListControl*.**Container**—an object that can be used to set or return the container of the control at run time. This property cannot be set at design time.

▪ *DBListControl*.**DataBindings**—a reference to the **DataBindings** collection containing the bindable properties available.

▪ *DBListControl*.**DataChanged**—a **Boolean** that applies only to data bound controls. When **True** means that the data contained in this control was changed either by the user or by some means other than retrieving data from the current record. When **False** means the data in the control is unchanged from the current record. Simply reading the next record is not sufficient to set the **DataChanged** property to **True**.

▪ *DBListControl*.**DataField**—a **String** value that associates the control with a field in a **RecordSet** object in a **Data** control.

▪ *DBListControl*.**DataSource**—a **String** containing the name of a **Data** control that will be updated once the selection is made.

▪ *DBListControl*.**DragIcon**—an object that contains the picture value of an icon. At design time, you can specify an icon file that has a file type of .ICO.

> **Tip**
>
> *This value can be created by copying the value from another control's **DragIcon** value, a form's icon, or by using the **LoadPicture** function.*

▪ *DBListControl*.**DragMode**—an **Integer** value (see Table D-115) specifying how the control will respond to a drag request.

> **Tip**
>
> Setting **DragMode** to vbAutomatic *will automatically begin a drag operation when the user clicks on the control. However, the control will not respond to the usual mouse events (***Click***, ***DblClick***, ***MouseDown***, ***MouseMove***, ***MouseUp***).*

DragMode Name	Value	Description
vbManual	0	The **Drag** method must be used to begin a drag-and-drop operation (default value).
vbAutomatic	1	The source control will automatically begin a drag-and-drop operation when the user clicks on the control.

Table D-115: DragMode *values.*

- *DBListControl.***Enabled**—a **Boolean** value when **True** means that the control will respond to events. When **False**, the control will not respond to events.
- *DBListControl.***Font**—an object that contains information about the character font used by this control.
- *DataControl.***ForeColor**—a **Long** that contains the suggested value for the foreground color of the contained control. This property is read only at run time.
- *DBListControl.***Height**—a **Single** that contains the height of the control.
- *DBListControl.***HelpContextID**—a **Long** that contains a help file context ID number which references an entry in the help file. When the user presses the F1 key while this control is active, the corresponding entry in the help file will automatically be displayed. A value of zero means that no context number was specified.

> **Tip**
>
> *A help file must be compiled using the Windows Help Compiler available in the Professional and Enterprise editions of Visual Basic.*

- *DBListControl.***hWnd**—a **Long** that contains a Windows handle to the control.

> **Tip**
>
> *The **hWnd** property is most useful when making calls to Windows API functions. Since this value can change during execution, do not save the value into a variable for later use.*

- *DBListControl.***Index**—an **Integer** that uniquely identifies a control in a control array.
- *DBListControl.***IntegralHeight**—a **Boolean** value when **True** means that the drop-down list will resize itself so that it will only show complete items. When **False** the drop-down list will show partial items.
- *DBListControl.***Left**—a **Single** that contains the distance measured in twips between the left edge of the control and the left edge of the control's container.

- *DBListControl*.**ListField**—a **String** containing the name of a field in a recordset that will be used to populate the list box.
- *DBListControl*.**Locked**—a **Boolean** value when **True** means that the user can't type a value in the text box part of the control. When **False**, the user can type a value into the text box part of the control.
- *DBListControl*.**MatchedWithList**—a **Boolean** when **True** means that the value of the **BoundText** property matches one of the records in the list portion of the control.
- *DBListControl*.**MatchEntry**—an **Integer** value (see Table D-116) that describes how the user's typing will be used to match entries in the list box.

MatchEntry Name	Value	Description
dblBasicMatching	0	Typing a letter jumps to the first entry in the list box with that value. Typing the same letter again will cycle through the values that begin with that letter.
dblExtendedMatching	1	Typing a letter jumps to the first entry in the list box with that value. Typing a second letter will try to match the first two letters. Typing additional letters will continue to refine this process.

Table D-116: MatchEntry *values.*

- *DBListControl*.**MouseIcon**—a **Picture** object (a bitmap, icon, or metafile) that will be used as a cursor when the **MousePointer** property is set to 99. Note that Visual Basic does not support color cursors from a .CUR file. Use a color icon from an .ICO file instead.
- *DBListControl*.**MousePointer**—an **Integer** value (see Table D-117) that contains the value of the cursor that should be displayed when the cursor is moved over this control. Use *vbCustom* to display the custom icon stored in the **MouseIcon** property.

Cursor Name	Value	Description
vbDefault	0	Shape determined by the object (default value)
vbArrow	1	Arrow
vbCrosshair	2	Crosshair
vbIbeam	3	I beam
vbIconPointer	4	Square inside a square
vbSizePointer	5	Four sided arrow (north, south, east, west)
vbSizeNESW	6	Two sided arrow (northeast, southwest)
vbSizeNS	7	Two sided arrow (north, south)
vbSizeNWSE	8	Two sided arrow (northwest, southeast)
vbSizeWE	9	Two sided arrow (west, east)
vbUpArrow	10	Single sided arrow pointing north
vbHourglass	11	Hourglass
vbNoDrop	12	No Drop
vbArrowHourglass	13	An arrow and an hourglass
vbArrowQuestion	14	An arrow and a question mark
vbSizeAll	15	Size all
vbCustom	99	Custom icon from the **MouseIcon** property of this control

Table D-117: Cursor *values.*

- *DBListControl*.**Name**—a **String** that contains the name of the control that will be used to reference the control in a Visual Basic program. This property is read only at run time.
- *DBListControl*.**Object**—an object that contains a reference to the *DBListControl* object.
- *DBListControl*.**OLEDragMode**—an **Integer** value (see Table D-118) that describes how the control will respond to OLE drag operations.

> **Note**
>
> When the **DragMode** is **True**, the standard Visual Basic drag-and-drop functions will override the OLE drag-and-drop functions.

OLEDragMode Name	Value	Description
vbOLEDragManual	0	All drag requests will be handled by the programmer (default value).
vbOLEDragAutomatic	1	The control responds to all OLE drag requests automatically.

Table D-118: OLEDragMode values.

- *DBListControl*.**OLEDropMode**—an **Integer** value (see Table D-119) that describes how the control will respond to OLE drop operations.

OLEDropMode Name	Value	Description
vbOLEDropNone	0	The control does not accept OLE drops. The cursor is changed to the No Drop cursor (default value).
vbOLEDropManual	1	The control responds to OLE drops under the program's control (manual).
vbOLEDropAutomatic	2	The control automatically accepts OLE drops if it recognizes the format of the data object.

Table D-119: OLEDropMode values.

- *DBListControl*.**Parent**—an object that contains a reference to the **Form**, **Frame,** or other container that contains this control.
- *DBListControl*.**RightToLeft**—a **Boolean** value when **True** means that the text displays from right to left. When **False** means that the text displays from left to right. A bi-directional version of Windows is required to set this property to **True**.
- *DBListControl*.**RowSource**—a **String** containing the name of the **Data** control that will be used to fill the text box.
- *DBListControl*.**SelectedItem**—a **Variant** value containing the bookmark for the selected database item.
- *DBListControl*.**TabIndex**—an **Integer** that determines the order that a user will tab through the objects on a form.
- *DBListControl*.**TabStop**—a **Boolean** value when **True** means that the user can tab to this object. When **False** means that this control will be skipped to the next control in the **TabIndex** order.
- *DBListControl*.**Tag**—a **String** that can hold programmer-specific information. This property is not used by Visual Basic.

- *DBListControl*.**Text**—a **String** that sets or returns the value from the text box part of the control.
- *DBListControl*.**ToolTipText**—a **String** that holds a text value that can be displayed as a **ToolTip** box that displays whenever the cursor is held over the control for about one second.
- *DBListControl*.**Top**—a **Single** that contains the distance measured in twips between the top edge of the control and the top edge of the control's container.
- *DBListControl*.**Visible**—a **Boolean** value when **True** means that the control is visible. When **False** means that the control is not visible.

> **Tip**
>
> This property hides the control until the program is ready to display it.

- *DBListControl*.**VisibleCount**—an **Integer** containing the number of items visible in the list box.
- *DBListControl*.**VisibleItems**(*index*)—an array of bookmarks corresponding to the visible items in the list box.
- *DBListControl*.**WhatsThisHelpID**—a **Long** that contains a help file context ID number references an entry in the help file. This provides a What's This PopUp help display in response to the What's This button in the upper right corner of the window.
- *DBListControl*.**Width**—a **Single** that contains the width of the control.

Methods

DBListControl.AboutBox

Usage This method displays an AboutBox for the control.

DBListControl.Drag [*DragAction*]

Usage This method begins, ends, or cancels a drag operation.

Arguments *DragAction*—an **Integer** that contains a value selected from Table D-120 below.

DragAction Name	Value	Description
vbCancel	0	Cancels any drag operation in progress.
vbBeginDrag	1	Begins a drag operation (default).
vbEndDrag	2	Ends a drag operation and drops *object*.

Table D-120: DragAction *values*.

DBListControl.Move *Left* [, *Top* [, *Width* [, *Height*]]]

Usage This method changes the position and the size of the **DBList** control. The **ScaleMode** of the **Form** or other container object that holds the **DBList** control will determine the units used to specify the coordinates.

Arguments
- *Left*—a **Single** that specifies the new position of the left edge of the control.
- *Top*—a **Single** that specifies the new position of the top edge of the control.
- *Width*—a **Single** that specifies the new width of the control.
- *Height*—a **Single** that specifies the new height of the control.

*DBListControl.*OLEDrag

Usage — This method begins an **OLEDrag** and drop operation. Invoking this method will trigger the **OLEStartDrag** event.

*DBListControl.*ReFill

Usage — This method gets a fresh copy of the contents of the list box and redraws its contents.

*DBListControl.*Refresh

Usage — This method redraws the contents of the control.

*DBListControl.*SetFocus

Usage — This method transfers the focus from the form or control that currently has the focus to this control. To receive the focus, this control must be enabled and visible.

*DBListControl.*ShowWhatsThis

Usage — This method displays the ShowWhatsThis help information for this control.

*DBListControl.*ZOrder [*position*]

Usage — This method specifies the position of the **DBList** control relative to the other objects on the form.

Tip

*Note that there are three layers of objects on a form: the back layer is the drawing space which contains the results of the graphical methods, the middle layer contains graphical objects and **Labels**, and the top layer contains nongraphical controls such as the **DBList** control. The **ZOrder** method only affects how the objects are arranged within a single layer.*

Arguments
- *position*—an **Integer** that specifies the relative position of this object. A value of 0 means that the control is positioned at the head of the list, a value of 1 means that the control will be placed at the end of the list.

Events **Private Sub *DBListControl* _Click([*index* As Integer])**

Usage   This event occurs when the user clicks a mouse button to select an item in the drop-down list or selects an item from the drop-down list using the keyboard.

Arguments
- *index*—an **Integer** that uniquely identifies a control in a control array. This argument is not present if the control is not part of a control array.

Private Sub *DBListControl* _DblClick([*index* As Integer])

Usage   This event occurs when the user double-clicks a mouse button to select an item in the drop-down list or selects an item from the drop-down list using the keyboard. This applies only when **Style** is set to *vbComboSimple*.

Arguments
- *index*—an **Integer** that uniquely identifies a control in a control array. This argument is not present if the control is not part of a control array.

Private Sub *DBListControl* _DragDrop([*index* As Integer ,] *source* As Control, *x* As Single, *y* As Single)

Usage   This event occurs when a drag-and-drop operation is completed by using the **Drag** method with a *DragAction* value of *vbEndDrag*.

Tip

When using drag-and-drop operations, use the **DragOver** event to determine what the cursor should look like while the cursor moves over the control.

Arguments
- *index*—an **Integer** that uniquely identifies a control in a control array. This argument is not present if the control is not part of a control array.
- *source*—a control object that is the control that is being dragged.

Tip

You can access a property or method from the source control by using source.*property* or source.*method*. You can determine the type of object or control by using the **TypeOf** operator.

- *x*—a **Single** that contains the horizontal location of the mouse pointer.
- *y*—a **Single** that contains the vertical location of the mouse pointer.

Private Sub *DBListControl*_DragOver([*index* As Integer ,] *source* As Control, *x* As Single, *y* As Single, *state* As Integer)

Usage   This event occurs while a drag operation is in progress and the cursor is moved over the control.

Tip

*When using drag-and-drop operations, use the **DragOver** event to determine what the cursor should look like while the cursor moves over the control. When state is 0, you can change the cursor to a No Drop (vbNoDrop) cursor or highlight the field that the cursor is near. When state is 1, you can undo the changes you made when the state was 0.*

Arguments
- *index*—an **Integer** that uniquely identifies a control in a control array. This argument is not present if the control is not part of a control array.
- *source*—a control object that is the control that is being dragged.

Tip

You can access a property or method from the source control by using source.*property or* source.*method. You can determine the type of object or control by using the **TypeOf** operator.*

- *x*—a **Single** that contains the horizontal location of the mouse pointer.
- *y*—a **Single** that contains the vertical location of the mouse pointer.
- *state*—an **Integer** value (see Table D-121) that indicates the state of the object being dragged.

state Name	Value	Description
vbEnter	0	The dragged object is entering range of the control.
vbLeave	1	The dragged object is leaving range of the control.
vbOver	2	The dragged object has moved from one position over the control to another.

Table D-121: state *values.*

Private Sub *DBListControl*_GotFocus ([*index* As Integer])

Usage   This event occurs when the control is given focus.

Tip

You can use this routine to display help or other information in a status bar.

Arguments
- *index*—an **Integer** that uniquely identifies a control in a control array. This argument is not present if the control is not part of a control array.

Private Sub *DBListControl*_KeyDown ([*index* As Integer ,] *keycode* As Integer, *shift* As Single)

Usage This event occurs when a key is pressed while the control has the focus.

Arguments
- *index*—an **Integer** that uniquely identifies a control in a control array. This argument is not present if the control is not part of a control array.
- *keycode*—an **Integer** that contains information about which key was pressed.
- *shift*—an **Integer** value (see Table D-122) that contains information about the Shift and Alt keys that were pushed when the mouse button was pressed. These values can be added together if more than one key was down. For instance, a value of 5 would mean that the Shift and Alt keys were both down when the mouse button was pressed.

shift Name	Value	Description
vbShiftMask	1	The Shift key was pressed.
vbCtrlMask	2	The Ctrl key was pressed.
vbAltMask	4	The Alt key was pressed.

Table D-122: shift *values.*

Private Sub *DBListControl*_KeyPress([*index* As Integer ,] *keychar* As Integer)

Usage This event occurs whenever a key is pressed while the control has the focus.

Arguments
- *index*—an **Integer** that uniquely identifies a control in a control array. This argument is not present if the control is not part of a control array.
- *keychar*—an **Integer** that contains the ASCII character that was pressed.

Private Sub *DBListControl*_KeyUp ([*index* As Integer ,] *keycode* As Integer, *shift* As Single)

Usage This event occurs when a key is released while the control has the focus.

Arguments
- *index*—an **Integer** that uniquely identifies a control in a control array. This argument is not present if the control is not part of a control array.
- *keycode*—an **Integer** that contains information about which key was released.
- *shift*—an **Integer** value (see Table D-123) that contains information about the Shift and Alt keys that were pushed when the mouse button was pressed. These values can be added together if more than one key was down. For instance, a value of 5 would mean that the Shift and Alt keys were both down when the mouse button was pressed.

shift Name	Value	Description
vbShiftMask	1	The Shift key was pressed.
vbCtrlMask	2	The Ctrl key was pressed.
vbAltMask	4	The Alt key was pressed.

Table D-123: shift *values*.

Private Sub *DBListControl*_LostFocus ([*index* As Integer])

Usage This event occurs when the control loses focus.

Tip

This routine is useful to performing data verification.

Arguments *index*—an **Integer** that uniquely identifies a control in a control array. This argument is not present if the control is not part of a control array.

Private Sub *DBListBoxControl*_MouseDown([*index* As Integer ,] *button* As Integer, *shift* As Single, *x* As Single, *y* As Single)

Usage This event occurs when a mouse button was pressed while the cursor was over the control.

Arguments *index*—an **Integer** that uniquely identifies a control in a control array. This argument is not present if the control is not part of a control array.

button—an **Integer** value (see Table D-124) that contains information about the mouse buttons that were pressed. Only one button will be indicated when this event occurs.

button Name	Value	Description
vbLeftButton	1	The left button was pressed.
vbRightButton	2	The right button was pressed.
vbMiddleButton	4	The middle button was pressed.

Table D-124: button *values*.

shift—an **Integer** value (see Table D-125) that contains information about the Shift and Alt keys that were pushed when the mouse button was pressed. These values can be added together if more than one key was down. For instance, a value of 5 would mean that the Shift and Alt keys were both down when the mouse button was pressed.

shift Name	Value	Description
vbShiftMask	1	The Shift key was pressed.
vbCtrlMask	2	The Ctrl key was pressed.
vbAltMask	4	The Alt key was pressed.

Table D-125: shift *values*.

- *x*—a **Single** that contains the horizontal location of the mouse pointer.
- *y*—a **Single** that contains the vertical location of the mouse pointer.

Private Sub *DBListControl* _MouseMove ([*index* As Integer ,] *button* As Integer, *shift* As Single, *x* As Single, *y* As Single)

Usage   This event occurs while the cursor is moved over the control.

Arguments
- *index*—an **Integer** that uniquely identifies a control in a control array. This argument is not present if the control is not part of a control array.
- *button*—an **Integer** value (see Table D-126) that contains information about the mouse buttons that were pressed. These values can be added together if more than one button was pushed. For instance, a value of 3 means that both the left and right buttons were pressed. A value of 0 means that no buttons were pressed.

button Name	Value	Description
vbLeftButton	1	The left button was pressed.
vbRightButton	2	The right button was pressed.
vbMiddleButton	4	The middle button was pressed.

Table D-126: button *values*.

- *shift*—an **Integer** value (see Table D-127) that contains information about the Shift and Alt keys that were pushed when the mouse button was pressed. For instance, a value of 5 would mean that the Shift and Alt keys were both down when the mouse button was pressed. A value of 0 means that none of these keys were pressed.

shift Name	Value	Description
vbShiftMask	1	The Shift key was pressed.
vbCtrlMask	2	The Ctrl key was pressed.
vbAltMask	4	The Alt key was pressed.

Table D-127: shift *values*.

- *x*—a **Single** that contains the horizontal location of the mouse pointer.
- *y*—a **Single** that contains the vertical location of the mouse pointer.

Private Sub *DBListBoxControl*_MouseUp([*index* As Integer ,] *button* As Integer, *shift* As Single, *x* As Single, *y* As Single)

Usage
: This event occurs when a mouse button is released while the cursor is over the control.

Arguments
: - *index*—an **Integer** that uniquely identifies a control in a control array. This argument is not present if the control is not part of a control array.
  - *button*—an **Integer** value (see Table D-128) that contains information about the mouse buttons that were released. Only one of these values will be present.

button Name	Value	Description
vbLeftButton	1	The left button was released.
vbRightButton	2	The right button was released.
vbMiddleButton	4	The middle button was released.

Table D-128: button *values.*

- *shift*—an **Integer** value (see Table D-129) that contains information about the Shift and Alt keys that were pushed when the mouse button was released. These values can be added together if more than one key was down. For instance, a value of 5 would mean that the Shift and Alt keys were both down when the mouse button was released. A value of 0 means that none of these keys were pressed.

shift Name	Value	Description
vbShiftMask	1	The Shift key was pressed.
vbCtrlMask	2	The Ctrl key was pressed.
vbAltMask	4	The Alt key was pressed.

Table D-129: shift *values.*

- *x*—a **Single** that contains the horizontal location of the mouse pointer.
- *y*—a **Single** that contains the vertical location of the mouse pointer.

Private Sub *DBListControl*_OLECompleteDrag([*index* As Integer ,] *effect* As Long)

Usage
: This event tells the source control the results of an OLE drag-and-drop operation. This is the final event to occur in the series of actions that make up an OLE drag-and-drop operation.

Arguments
: - *index*—an **Integer** that uniquely identifies a control in a control array. This argument is not present if the control is not part of a control array.
  - *effect*—a **Long** (see Table D-130) that returns the status of the OLE drag-and-drop operation.

effect Name	Value	Description
vbDropEffectNone	0	The operation was canceled or the target control can't accept the drop operation.
vbDropEffectCopy	1	The operation copied data from the source control to the target control. The original data is unchanged.
vbDropEffectMove	2	The operation results in a link from the original data to the target control.

Table D-130: effect *values*.

Private Sub *DBListControl*_OLEDragDrop([*index* As Integer ,] *data* As DataObject, *effect* As Long, *button* As Integer, *shift* As Single, *x* As Single, *y* As Single)

Usage This event tells the source control the results of an OLE drag-and-drop operation. This is the final event to occur in the series of actions that make up an OLE drag-and-drop operation.

Arguments
- *index*—an **Integer** that uniquely identifies a control in a control array. This argument is not present if the control is not part of a control array.
- *data*—a **DataObject** that contains the formats that the source control will provide. If the data is not contained in the **DataObject**, then it can be retrieved with the **GetData** method.
- *effect*—a **Long** (see Table D-131) that returns the status of the OLE drag-and-drop operation.

effect Name	Value	Description
vbDropEffectNone	0	The operation was canceled or the target control can't accept the drop operation.
vbDropEffectCopy	1	The operation copied data from the source control to the target control. The original data is unchanged.
vbDropEffectMove	2	The operation results in a link from the original data to the target control.

Table D-131: effect *values*.

- *button*—an **Integer** value (see Table D-132) that contains information about the mouse buttons that were pressed. These values can be added together if more than one button was pushed. For instance, a value of 3 means that both the left and right buttons were pressed. A value of 0 means that no buttons were pressed.

button Name	Value	Description
vbLeftButton	1	The left button was pressed.
vbRightButton	2	The right button was pressed.
vbMiddleButton	4	The middle button was pressed.

Table D-132: button *values*.

- *shift*—an **Integer** value (see Table D-133) that contains information about the Shift and Alt keys that were pushed when the mouse button was released. These values can be added together if more than one key was down. For instance, a value of 5 would mean that the Shift and Alt keys were both down when the mouse button was released. A value of 0 means that none of these keys were pressed.

shift Name	Value	Description
vbShiftMask	1	The Shift key was pressed.
vbCtrlMask	2	The Ctrl key was pressed.
vbAltMask	4	The Alt key was pressed.

Table D-133: shift *values*.

- *x*—a **Single** that contains the horizontal location of the mouse pointer.
- *y*—a **Single** that contains the vertical location of the mouse pointer.

Private Sub *DBListControl*_OLEDragOver([*index* As Integer ,] *data* As DataObject, *effect* As Long, *button* As Integer, *shift* As Single, *x* As Single, *y* As Single, *state* As Integer)

Usage   This event happens when an OLE drag-and-drop operation is in progress.

Arguments
- *index*—an **Integer** that uniquely identifies a control in a control array. This argument is not present if the control is not part of a control array.
- *data*—a **DataObject** that contains the formats that the source control will provide. If the data is not contained in the **DataObject**, then it can be retrieved with the **GetData** method.
- *effect*—a **Long** (see Table D-134) that returns the status of the OLE drag-and-drop operation.

effect Name	Value	Description
vbDropEffectNone	0	The operation was canceled or the target control can't accept the drop operation.
vbDropEffectCopy	1	The operation copied data from the source control to the target control. The original data is unchanged.
vbDropEffectMove	2	The operation results in a link from the original data to the target control.

Table D-134: effect *values*.

- *button*—an **Integer** value (see Table D-135) that contains information about the mouse buttons that were pressed. These values can be added together if more than one button was pushed. For instance, a value of 3 means that both the left and right buttons were pressed. A value of 0 means that no buttons were pressed.

button Name	Value	Description
vbLeftButton	1	The left button was pressed.
vbRightButton	2	The right button was pressed.
vbMiddleButton	4	The middle button was pressed.

Table D-135: button *values.*

- *shift*—an **Integer** value (see Table D-136) that contains information about the Shift and Alt keys that were pushed when the mouse button was released. These values can be added together if more than one key was down. For instance, a value of 5 would mean that the Shift and Alt keys were both down when the mouse button was released. A value of 0 means that none of these keys were pressed.

shift Name	Value	Description
vbShiftMask	1	The Shift key was pressed.
vbCtrlMask	2	The Ctrl key was pressed.
vbAltMask	4	The Alt key was pressed.

Table D-136: shift *values.*

- *x*—a **Single** that contains the horizontal location of the mouse pointer.
- *y*—a **Single** that contains the vertical location of the mouse pointer.
- *state*—an **Integer** value (see Table D-137) that indicates the state of the object being dragged.

state Name	Value	Description
vbEnter	0	The dragged object is entering range of the control.
vbLeave	1	The dragged object is leaving range of the control.
vbOver	2	The dragged object has moved from one position over the control to another.

Table D-137: state *values.*

Private Sub *DBListControl* _OLEGiveFeedback ([*index* As Integer ,] *effect* As Long)

Usage   This event tells the source control what is happening while the OLE drag-and-drop operation is in progress. This event occurs after the **OLEDragOver** event.

Tip

You may want to use this event to change the cursor to reflect what can happen in the remote object.

Arguments
- *index*—an **Integer** that uniquely identifies a control in a control array. This argument is not present if the control is not part of a control array.
- *effect*—a **Long** (see Table D-138) that returns the status of the OLE drag-and-drop operation.

effect Name	Value	Description
vbDropEffectNone	0	The operation was canceled or the target control can't accept the drop operation.
vbDropEffectCopy	1	The operation copied data from the source control to the target control. The original data is unchanged.
vbDropEffectMove	2	The operation results in a link from the original data to the target control.
vbDropEffectScroll	&H80000000	The target control is about to scroll or is scrolling. This value may be added to the other effect values.

Table D-138: effect *values.*

Private Sub *DBListControl* _OLESetData([*index* As Integer ,] *data* As DataObject, *DataFormat* As Integer)

Usage   This event happens in response to the target object performing a **GetData** method on *data*. This routine will respond by using the **SetData** method with the desired data using the **DataObject** *data*.

Arguments   • *index*—an **Integer** that uniquely identifies a control in a control array. This argument is not present if the control is not part of a control array.

• *data*—a **DataObject** that will contain the data to be returned to the target object.

• *format*—an **Integer** value (see Table D-139) that contains the format of the data.

format Name	Value	Description
vbCFText	1	Text (.TXT files)
vbCFBitmap	2	Bitmap (.BMP files)
vbCFMetafile	3	Metafile (.WMF files)
vbCFEDIB	8	Device independent bitmap (DIB)
vbCFPallette	9	Color palette
vbCFEMetafile	14	Enhanced metafile (.EMF files)
vbCFFiles	15	List of files
vbCFRTF	-16639	Rich Text Format (.RTF files)

Table D-139: format *values.*

Private Sub *DBListControl* _OLEStartDrag ([*index* As Integer ,] *data* As DataObject, *AllowedEffects* As Long)

Usage   This event starts an OLE drag-and-drop operation.

Arguments   • *index*—an **Integer** that uniquely identifies a control in a control array. This argument is not present if the control is not part of a control array.

• *data*—a **DataObject** that will contain the formats that the source object is willing to provide to the target object. It may optionally contain the data to be transferred.

- *AllowedEffects*—a **Long** (see Table D-140) that contains the effects that the target object can request from the source object. The *AllowedEffects* can be added together if the source object supports more than one effect. Note that the target object can always use the *vbDropEffectNone* effect.

AllowedEffects Name	Value	Description
vbDropEffectNone	0	The target can't copy the data.
vbDropEffectCopy	1	The target can copy the data and the source will keep the data unchanged.
vbDropEffectMove	2	The target can copy the data and the source will delete the data.

Table D-140: AllowedEffects *values*.

Examples
```
Private Sub Combo1_Click()
MsgBox Combo1.List(Combo1.ListIndex)
End Sub

Private Sub Form_Load()
Combo1.AddItem "One"
Combo1.AddItem "Two"
Combo1.AddItem "Three"
End Sub
```

This program initializes a combo box with three values and then displays a message box whenever the user clicks on one of the items from the drop-down menu.

See Also   **ListBox** (control), **TextBox** (control)

DDB

FUNCTION

CCE, LE, PE, EE

Syntax   depreciation = **DDB**(cost, salvage, life, period [, factor])

Usage   The **DDB** function returns the double declining balance depreciation for an asset.

Arguments
- *depreciation*—a **Double** value containing the depreciation.
- *cost*—a **Double** value containing the initial cost of the asset.
- *salvage*—a **Double** value containing the salvage value of the asset.
- *life*—an **Double** value specifying the useful life of the asset.
- *period*—a **Double** value specifying the period for which the depreciation is to be computed.
- *factor*—a **Variant** value specifying the rate of depreciation. If omitted, it will default to 2, which is double declining balance depreciation.

Examples
```
Private Sub Command1_Click()
Dim period As Double
Dim sum As Double
Dim temp As Double
For period = 1 To 5
   temp = DDB(1000, 100, 5, period)
   sum = sum + temp
   Debug.Print "Year "; period; " depreciation is ", Format(temp, "currency")
Next period
Debug.Print "Total depreciation is ", Format(sum, "currency")
End Sub
```

This routine computes the double declining balance depreciation for an asset that costs $1,000 with a salvage value of $100 over a five year period.

See Also FV (function), IPmt (function), IRR (function), MIRR (function), NPer (function), NPV (function), PMT (function), PPmt (function), PV (function), Rate (function), SLN (function), SYD (function)

Debug

OBJECT

CCE, LE, PE, EE

Usage The **Debug** object provides useful methods to help you debug your programs.

Methods **Debug.Assert** *bvalue*

Usage This method will suspend your program and enter debugging mode if *bvalue* is **False**. Note that the program must be running in the development environment for the **Assert** method to work.

Arguments *bvalue*—a **Boolean** value that when **False** will cause a Visual Basic program to enter debugging mode.

> **Note**
>
> *Unlike most boolean expressions, all pieces of* bvalue *will be evaluated, including cases like* expr1 *and* expr2, *where* expr1 *is* **False**. *Since* expr1 *is* **False**, *there is no need to evaluate* expr2, *and usually Visual Basic will not evaluate* expr2 *as part of its optimization process.*
>
> *All this means is that you can perform assert tests using functions and be sure that all of the functions are executed.*

Debug.Print [*printexpr* [{ , | ; } *printexpr*] . . .]

Usage This method displays information in the immediate pane of the debug window.

Arguments *printexpr*—any **Boolean**, numeric, or **String** expression, plus the functions listed below. If *printexpr* is omitted, then a blank line will be printed. A comma (",") positions the print cursor at the next print zone. A semicolon (";") positions the print cursor immediately after the expression that was just printed. Each print zone is 14 characters wide and begins with column 1. Note that the print zones are characters and not inches, so you may experience problems when using proportional character fonts.

- **Spc**(*chars*)—prints the specified number of spaces.
- **Tab** [(*col*)]—positions the print cursor at the specified print column. If the print column is less than the current position of the cursor, then the print cursor will be moved to the next line. If no argument is specified, the cursor will be positioned at the beginning of the next print zone.

Examples
```
Private Sub Command1_Click()
Debug.Print "Application:", App.Title
Debug.Print "Location:", App.Path
End Sub
```

This routine shows how the **Debug** object displays information about the application. The commas in each **Print** method allow the **App.Title** and **App.Path** values to be aligned in the debug immediate window.

See Also   Form (object)

Decimal

DATA TYPE

CCE, LE, PE, EE

Usage   The **Decimal** data type holds integer values in the range +/-79,228,162,514,264,337,593,543,950,335. These values can be scaled by placing a decimal point anywhere in the twenty-eight digits. A single **Decimal** variable occupies 96 bits or 12 bytes of storage.

Caution

Decimal values are not directly supported in Visual Basic. You must define a variable with a type of Variant and then use the CDec function to create a variable of type Decimal.

See Also   **CDec** (function), **Dim** (statement), **Format** (function), **IsNumeric** (function)

Declare

STATEMENT

CCE, LE, PE, EE

Syntax
[**Public** | **Private**] **Declare Function** name **Lib** lib [**Alias** alias] [([arg] [, arg] . . . [, arg])] [**As** type]

[**Public** | **Private**] **Declare Sub** name **Lib** lib [**Alias** alias] [([arg] [, arg] . . . [, arg])]

Usage
The **Declare** statement defines an external subroutine or function from a DLL to Visual Basic.

Arguments
- **Public**—an optional keyword indicating that the function can be called from any module in the program.
- **Private**—an optional keyword indicating that the function can only be called by other routines in the same module.
- *name*—an identifier containing the name of the function or subroutine that will be used in Visual Basic.
- *lib*—a **String** containing the path and filename of the DLL.
- *alias*—a **String** containing the real name of the function or subroutine. If not specified then the *name* will be used.
- *arg*—an argument that is passed to the function:

  [Optional] [ByVal | ByRef] [ParamArray] AName [( )] [As type]

Optional	An optional keyword meaning that the argument is optional and need not be passed to the function. Once an argument is declared to be optional, all arguments that follow must be declared as optional.
ByVal	An optional keyword meaning that the argument is passed by value to the event. Thus the event is free to change the contents of the argument and the calling object will not see the changes.
ByRef	An optional keyword meaning that the argument is passed by reference to the event. Any changes to the argument in the calling control will be seen by the calling object.
ParamArray	An optional keyword meaning that the function can receive an unspecified number of arguments of type **Variant** starting at this position. This must be the last argument in the function declaration and can't be used with **Optional**, **ByVal**, or **ByRef**.
AName	The formal argument being passed to the event.
[( )]	If present, indicates that the argument is an array.
type	A valid Visual Basic type: **Byte**, **Boolean**, **Currency**, **Date**, **Double**, **Integer**, **Long**, **Single**, **String**, **Object**, or **Variant**. If the argument is not **Optional**, then specific object types and user-defined types may be used.

- *type*—a valid Visual Basic type: **Byte**, **Boolean**, **Currency**, **Date**, **Double**, **Integer**, **Long**, **Single**, **String**, **Object**, or **Variant**.

Examples
```
Private Declare Function MessageBox Lib "user32" Alias "MessageBoxA" (ByVal hwnd _
    As Long, ByVal lpText As String, ByVal lpCaption As String, ByVal wType As _
    Long) As Long

Private Sub Command1_Click()
Call MessageBox(Me.hwnd, "Call WinAPI function", App.Title, vbOKOnly)
MessageBox Me.hwnd, "WinAPI function", App.Title, vbOKOnly
End Sub
```

This program uses the **Declare** statement to define the Windows API function MessageBoxA. Then the **Command1_Click** event calls the declared function to show that there is no difference between calling a declared function and a normal Visual Basic function.

See Also **Call** (statement), **Function** (statement), **Sub** (statement)

DefBool
STATEMENT

CCE, LE, PE, EE

Syntax **DefBool** *letter* [-*letter*] [, *letter* [-*letter*]] . . .

Usage The **DefBool** statement defines the default data type to be **Boolean** for all variables that begin with the specified letters. Either a single letter can be used or a range of letters (i.e., A-C, would include the letters A, B, and C). Once a letter has been used in a deftype statement, it cannot be reused or a compile-time error will occur. The default type of a variable can be overridden with the **Dim** statement.

See Also **Boolean** (data type), **CBool** (function), **DefByte** (statement), **DefCur** (statement), **DefDate** (statement), **DefDbl** (statement), **DefInt** (statement), **DefLng** (statement), **DefObj** (statement), **DefSng** (statement), **DefStr** (statement), **DefVar** (statement), **Dim** (statement)

DefByte
STATEMENT

CCE, LE, PE, EE

Syntax **DefByte** *letter* [-*letter*] [, *letter* [-*letter*]] . . .

Usage The **DefByte** statement defines the default data type to be **Byte** for all variables that begin with the specified letters. Either a single letter can be used or a range of letters (i.e., A-C, would include the letters A, B, and C). Once a letter has been used in a deftype statement, it cannot be reused or a compile-time error will occur. The default type of a variable can be overridden with the **Dim** statement.

See Also **Byte** (data type), **CByte** (function), **DefBool** (statement), **DefCur** (statement), **DefDate** (statement), **DefDbl** (statement), **DefInt** (statement), **DefLng** (statement), **DefObj** (statement), **DefSng** (statement), **DefStr** (statement), **DefVar** (statement), **Dim** (statement)

DefCur

STATEMENT

CCE, LE, PE, EE

Syntax   **DefCur** `letter [-letter] [,letter [-letter] ] . . .`

Usage   The **DefCur** statement defines the default data type to be **Currency** for all variables that begin with the specified letters. Either a single letter can be used or a range of letters (i.e., A-C, would include the letters A, B, and C). Once a letter has been used in a deftype statement, it cannot be reused or a compile time error will occur. The default type of a variable can be overridden with the **Dim** statement.

See Also   **Currency** (data type), **CCur** (function), **DefBool** (statement), **DefByte** (statement), **DefDate** (statement), **DefDbl** (statement), **DefInt** (statement), **DefLng** (statement), **DefObj** (statement), **DefSng** (statement), **DefStr** (statement), **DefVar** (statement), **Dim** (statement)

DefDate

STATEMENT

CCE, LE, PE, EE

Syntax   **DefDate** `letter [-letter] [,letter [-letter] ] . . .`

Usage   The **DefDate** statement defines the default data type to be **Date** for all variables that begin with the specified letters. Either a single letter can be used or a range of letters (i.e., A-C, would include the letters A, B, and C). Once a letter has been used in a deftype statement, it cannot be reused or a compile-time error will occur. The default type of a variable can be overridden with the **Dim** statement.

See Also   **Date** (data type), **CDate** (function), **DefBool** (statement), **DefByte** (statement), **DefCur** (statement), **DefDbl** (statement), **DefInt** (statement), **DefLng** (statement), **DefObj** (statement), **DefSng** (statement), **DefStr** (statement), **DefVar** (statement), **Dim** (statement), **IsDate** (function)

DefDbl

STATEMENT

CCE, LE, PE, EE

Syntax   **DefDbl** `letter [-letter] [,letter [-letter] ] . . .`

Usage   The **DefDbl** statement defines the default data type to be **Double** for all variables that begin with the specified letters. Either a single letter can be used or a range of letters (i.e., A-C, would include the letters A, B, and C). Once a letter has been used in a deftype statement, it cannot be reused or a compile-time error will occur. The default type of a variable can be overridden with the **Dim** statement.

See Also   **Double** (data type), **CDbl** (function), **DefBool** (statement), **DefByte** (statement), **DefCur** (statement), **DefDate** (statement), **DefInt** (statement), **DefLng** (statement), **DefObj** (statement), **DefSng** (statement), **DefStr** (statement), **DefVar** (statement), **Dim** (statement)

DefInt
STATEMENT
CCE, LE, PE, EE

Syntax **DefInt** *letter* [*-letter*] [, *letter* [*-letter*]] . . .

Usage The **DefInt** statement defines the default data type to be **Integer** for all variables that begin with the specified letters. Either a single letter can be used or a range of letters (i.e., A-C, would include the letters A, B, and C). Once a letter has been used in a deftype statement, it cannot be reused or a compile-time error will occur. The default type of a variable can be overridden with the **Dim** statement.

See Also **CInt** (function), **DefBool** (statement), **DefByte** (statement), **DefCur** (statement), **DefDate** (statement), **DebDbl** (statement), **DefLng** (statement), **DefObj** (statement), **DefSng** (statement), **DefStr** (statement), **DefVar** (statement), **Dim** (statement), **Integer** (data type)

DefLng
STATEMENT
CCE, LE, PE, EE

Syntax **DefLng** *letter* [*-letter*] [, *letter* [*-letter*]] . . .

Usage The **DefLng** statement defines the default data type to be **Long** for all variables that begin with the specified letters. Either a single letter can be used or a range of letters (i.e., A-C, would include the letters A, B, and C). Once a letter has been used in a deftype statement, it cannot be reused or a compile-time error will occur. The default type of a variable can be overridden with the **Dim** statement.

See Also **CLng** (function), **DefBool** (statement), **DefByte** (statement), **DefCur** (statement), **DefDate** (statement), **DebDbl** (statement), **DefInt** (statement), **DefObj** (statement), **DefSng** (statement), **DefStr** (statement), **DefVar** (statement), **Dim** (statement), **Long** (data type)

DefObj
STATEMENT
CCE, LE, PE, EE

Syntax **DefObj** *letter* [*-letter*] [, *letter* [*-letter*]] . . .

Usage The **DefObj** statement defines the default data type to be **Object** for all variables that begin with the specified letters. Either a single letter can be used or a range of letters (i.e., A-C, would include the letters A, B, and C). Once a letter has been used in a deftype statement, it cannot be reused or a compile-time error will occur. The default type of a variable can be overridden with the **Dim** statement.

See Also **DefBool** (statement), **DefByte** (statement), **DefCur** (statement), **DefDate** (statement), **DebDbl** (statement), **DefInt** (statement), **DefLng** (statement), **DefSng** (statement), **DefStr** (statement), **DefVar** (statement), **Dim** (statement), **Object** (data type)

DefSng

STATEMENT
CCE, LE, PE, EE

Syntax **DefSng** *letter* [*-letter*] [,*letter* [*-letter*]] . . .

Usage The **DefSng** statement defines the default data type to be **Single** for all variables that begin with the specified letters. Either a single letter can be used or a range of letters (i.e., A-C, would include the letters A, B, and C). Once a letter has been used in a deftype statement, it cannot be reused or a compile-time error will occur. The default type of a variable can be overridden with the **Dim** statement.

See Also **Single** (data type), **CSng** (function), **DefBool** (statement), **DefByte** (statement), **DefCur** (statement), **DefDate** (statement), **DebDbl** (statement), **DefInt** (statement), **DefLng** (statement), **DefObj** (statement), **DefStr** (statement), **DefVar** (statement), **Dim** (statement)

DefStr

STATEMENT
CCE, LE, PE, EE

Syntax **DefStr** *letter* [*-letter*] [,*letter* [*-letter*]] . . .

Usage The **DefStr** statement defines the default data type to be **String** for all variables that begin with the specified letters. Either a single letter can be used or a range of letters (i.e., A-C, would include the letters A, B, and C). Once a letter has been used in a deftype statement, it cannot be reused or a compile-time error will occur. The default type of a variable can be overridden with the **Dim** statement.

See Also **String** (data type), **CStr** (function), **DefBool** (statement), **DefByte** (statement), **DefCur** (statement), **DefDate** (statement), **DebDbl** (statement), **DefInt** (statement), **DefLng** (statement), **DefObj** (statement), **DefSng** (statement), **DefVar** (statement), **Dim** (statement)

DefVar

STATEMENT
CCE, LE, PE, EE

Syntax **DefVar** *letter* [*-letter*] [,*letter* [*-letter*]] . . .

Usage The **DefVar** statement defines the default data type to be **Variant** for all variables that begin with the specified letters. Either a single letter can be used or a range of letters (i.e., A-C, would include the letters A, B, and C). Once a letter has been used in a deftype statement, it cannot be reused or a compile-time error will occur. The default type of a variable can be overridden with the **Dim** statement.

See Also **DefBool** (statement), **DefByte** (statement), **DefCur** (statement), **DefDate** (statement), **DebDbl** (statement), **DefInt** (statement), **DefLng** (statement), **DefObj** (statement), **DefSng** (statement), **DefStr** (statement), **Dim** (statement), **Variant** (data type)

DeleteSetting

STATEMENT

CCE, LE, PE, EE

Syntax **DeleteSetting** *app* , *section* [, *key*]

Usage The **DeleteSetting** statement deletes the specified setting (if *key* is specified) or all settings for a particular *app* and *section* from the Windows Registry. This is useful if you want to restore default settings for a program or clean up after a program has been uninstalled.

> **Tip**
>
> *This function and the related functions* **GetSetting**, **GetAllSettings**, *and* **SaveSetting** *are useful to save information about the state from one run to the next.*

Arguments
- *app*—a **String** that identifies the application.
- *section*—a **String** that identifies a section within the application.
- *key*—a **String** that identifies a keyword within the section.

Examples
```
Private Sub Command1_Click()
On Error Resume Next
DeleteSetting "VBPR", "Settings", Text2.Text
If Err.Number <> 0 Then
    Text1.Text = "Delete error: " & Err.Description
End If
End Sub
```

This routine deletes a setting from the Windows Registry.

See Also **GetSetting** (statement), **GetAllSettings** (function), **SaveSetting** (statement)

Dim

STATEMENT

CCE, LE, PE, EE

Syntax **Dim** [**WithEvents**] *identifier[typechar]* [*arrayinfo*] [**As** [**New**] *type*] , [[**WithEvents**] *identifier[typechar]* [*arrayinfo*] [**As** [**New**] *type*]] . . .

Usage The **Dim** statement declares the variables used in your Visual Basic program. If **Option Explicit** is included in a module, then all of the variables used in your program must be declared before they can be used.

> **Tip**
>
> *Use* **Option Explicit** *in all modules, because this will force you to declare all variables before you use them. This will help you avoid the situation where you think you have one variable, but Visual Basic thinks you have two because you used two different spellings.*

Arguments
- **WithEvents**—an optional keyword used only in class modules that means *Variable* responds to events triggered by an ActiveX object.
- *identifier*—the Visual Basic identifier that will be used to reference this particular variable. It must begin with a letter which can be followed by any number of letters or numbers or the underscore character ("_"). Identifiers are not case-sensitive, though the case will be preserved for easier reading.
- *typechar*—one of the following characters can be included as the last character of a variable name to declare its type: "@" for **Currency**, "#" for **Double**, "%" for **Integer**, "&" for **Long**, "!" for **Single**, or "$" for **String**. The default type for variables without a typechar is **Variant** unless the type is specified using the **As** clause or by using one of the deftype statements.
- *arrayinfo*—optionally indicates an array. It can have zero to 60 dimensions. If no dimensions are specified, then the variable is considered a dynamic array and the subscripts must be set with the **ReDim** statement before it can be used. The subscripts are defined as the following:

([ubound | lbound **To** ubound] [, ubound | , lbound **To** ubound] . . .)]

ubound	The upper bound for an array.
lbound	The lower bound for an array's subscript. If omitted, the value from **Option Base** will be used. If there is no **Option Base** statement in the module zero will be used.

- **New**—an optional keyword that means that a new instance of the object is automatically created the first time it is used. It can't be used with either the **WithEvents** keyword or with a nonobject type.
- *type*—a valid Visual Basic type: **Byte**, **Boolean**, **Currency**, **Date**, **Double**, **Integer**, **Long**, **Single**, **String**, **Object**, or **Variant**. Specific objects can also be used and user-defined types defined with the **Type** statement may also be used.

Examples
```
Private Sub Command1_Click()
Dim x As String, y(-1 To 1)
MsgBox "x is of type " & TypeName(x)
MsgBox "y is of type " & TypeName(y)
End Sub
```

This routine declares two variables, a simple string called x and a variant array with one dimension whose subscripts range from -1 to +1. The message boxes use the **TypeName** function to confirm the types.

See Also
Byte (data type), **Boolean** (data type), **Currency** (data type), **Date** (data type), **Double** (data type), **Integer** (data type), **Long** (data type), **Object** (data type), **Option Base** (statement), **Option Explicit** (statement), **Private** (statement), **Public** (statement), **ReDim** (statement), **Single** (data type), **String** (data type), **Static** (statement), **Type** (statement), **TypeName** (function), **Variant** (data type)

Dir

FUNCTION

CCE, LE, PE, EE

Syntax   fname = **Dir[$]** [([path] [,attr])

Usage   The **Dir** function returns a single filename from a directory. The first call to the **Dir** function must include a value for *path*. Assuming that a file was found, any subsequent calls to **Dir** without parameters will return the next file that matches the criteria setup by the first call. When no more files are found, then an empty string will be returned. Any attempts to call **Dir** without specifying *path* after it returns an empty string will result in an error.

Arguments
- *fname*—a **String** value containing the name of a file. If an empty string is returned (length equals zero), then no file was found.
- *path*—a **String** value containing either the complete name of a file or a directory that should be examined for files. Wildcard characters may be used.
- *attr*—an **Integer** value (see Table D-141) that describes the file attributes that will be retrieved.

attr Name	Value	Description
vbNormal	0	Normal files
vbHidden	2	Hidden files
vbSystem	4	System files
vbVolume	8	Volume label—overrides other values of *attr*
vbDirectory	16	Directories

Table D-141: attr values.

Examples
```
Private Sub Command1_Click()
Dim d As String
Text1.Text = ""
d = Dir(Text2.Text)
Do While Len(d) > 0
    Text1.Text = Text1.Text & d & vbCrLf
    d = Dir
Loop
End Sub
```

This routine uses the **Dir** function to display all of the files in the directory specified by the Text2 text box in the Text1 text box. The first call to **Dir** specifies the path that I want to search. If a file is found, then I will add it to the Text2 text box and get the next file in the directory by using the **Dir** function without any parameters.

See Also   **ChDir** (function), **ChDrive** (function)

DirListBox

CONTROL
CCE, LE, PE, EE

Usage The **DirListBox** control is an intrinsic control that allows the user to select a directory.

Properties
- *DirListBoxControl*.**Appearance**—an **Integer** value (see Table D-142) that specifies how the file list box will appear on the form.

Appearance Value	Description
0	The directory list box displays without the 3D effects.
1	The directory list box displays with 3D effects (default value).

Table D-142: Appearance *values*.

- *DirListBoxControl*.**BackColor**—a **Long** that contains the suggested value for the background color of the control. The **BackColor** and **ForeColor** must both be solid to display text. If you choose a color that is dithered, it will be changed to the nearest solid color.
- *DirListBoxControl*.**Container**—an object that can be used to set or return the container of the control at run time. This property cannot be set at design time.
- *DirListBoxControl*.**DragIcon**—an object that contains the picture value of an icon. At design time, you can specify an icon file that has a file type of .ICO.

Tip

*This value can be created by copying the value from another control's **DragIcon** value, a form's icon, or by using the **LoadPicture** function.*

- *DirListBoxControl*.**DragMode**—an **Integer** value (see Table D-143) specifying how the control will respond to a drag request.

Tip

*Setting **DragMode** to* vbAutomatic *will automatically begin a drag operation when the user clicks on the control. However, the control will not respond to the usual mouse events (**Click**, **DblClick**).*

DragMode Name	Value	Description
vbManual	0	The **Drag** method must be used to begin a drag-and-drop operation (default value).
vbAutomatic	1	The source control will automatically begin a drag-and-drop operation when the user clicks on the control.

Table D-143: DragMode *values*.

- *DirListBoxControl*.**Enabled**—a **Boolean** value when **True** means that the control will respond to events. When **False**, the control will not respond to events.
- *DirListBoxControl*.**Font**—an object that contains information about the character font used by this object.

> **Tip**
>
> The **Font** object should be used in place of the other **Font** properties, since it offers more functionality than the individual properties.

- *DirListBoxControl*.**FontBold**—a **Boolean** when **True** means that the characters display in bold. **False** means that the characters display normally.
- *DirListBoxControl*.**FontItalic**—a **Boolean** when **True** means that the characters display in italics. **False** means that the characters display normally.
- *DirListBoxControl*.**FontName**—a **String** that specifies the name of the font that should be used to display the characters in this control.
- *DirListBoxControl*.**FontSize**—a **Single** that specifies the point size that should be used to display the characters in the control.
- *DirListBoxControl*.**FontStrikethru**—a **Boolean** when **True** means that the characters display with a line through the center. **False** means that the characters display normally.
- *DirListBoxControl*.**FontUnderlined**—a **Boolean** when **True** means that the characters display with a line beneath them. **False** means that the characters display normally.
- *DirListBoxControl*.**ForeColor**—a **Long** that contains the suggested value for the foreground color of the contained control. This property is read only at run time.
- *DirListBoxControl*.**Height**—a **Single** that contains the height of the control.
- *DirListBoxControl*.**HelpContextID**—a **Long** that contains a help file context ID number which references an entry in the help file. When the user presses the F1 key while this control is active, the corresponding entry in the help file automatically displays. A value of zero means that no context number was specified.

> **Tip**
>
> A help file must be compiled using the Windows Help Compiler available in the Professional and Enterprise editions of Visual Basic.

- *DirListBoxControl*.**hWnd**—a **Long** that contains a Windows handle to the control.

> **Tip**
>
> The **hWnd** property is most useful when making calls to Windows API functions. Since this value can change during execution, do not save the value into a variable for later use.

- *DirListBoxControl*.**Index**—an **Integer** that uniquely identifies a control in a control array.
- *DirListBoxControl*.**Left**—a **Single** that contains the distance measured in twips between the left edge of the control and the left edge of the control's container.
- *DirListBoxControl*.**List** (*index*)—an array of **String** values display in the drop-down part of the **DirListBox**. The number of elements in this array can be found in the **ListCount** property.

> **Tip**
>
> *The first element of the **List** array is zero, while the last array element is **ListCount** -1.*

- *DirListBoxControl*.**ListCount**—an **Integer** value containing the number of elements in the **List**.
- *DirListBoxControl*.**ListIndex**—an **Integer** value containing the index of the selected item from the drop-down box. If no value was selected, **ListIndex** will be set to -1.
- *DirListBoxControl*.**MouseIcon**—a **Picture** object (a bitmap, icon, or metafile) that will be used as a cursor when the **MousePointer** property is set to 99. Note that Visual Basic does not support color cursors from a .CUR file. A color icon from an .ICO file should be used instead.
- *DirListBoxControl*.**MousePointer**—an **Integer** value (see Table D-144) that contains the value of the cursor that should be displayed when the cursor is moved over this control. Use *vbCustom* to display the custom icon stored in the **MouseIcon** property.

Cursor Name	Value	Description
vbDefault	0	Shape determined by the object (default value)
vbArrow	1	Arrow
vbCrosshair	2	Crosshair
vbIbeam	3	I beam
vbIconPointer	4	Square inside a square
vbSizePointer	5	Four sided arrow (north, south, east, west)
vbSizeNESW	6	Two sided arrow (northeast, southwest)
vbSizeNS	7	Two sided arrow (north, south)
vbSizeNWSE	8	Two sided arrow (northwest, southeast)
vbSizeWE	9	Two sided arrow (west, east)
vbUpArrow	10	Single sided arrow pointing north
vbHourglass	11	Hourglass
vbNoDrop	12	No Drop
vbArrowHourglass	13	An arrow and an hourglass
vbArrowQuestion	14	An arrow and a question mark
vbSizeAll	15	Size all
vbCustom	99	Custom icon from the **MouseIcon** property of this control

Table D-144: Cursor *values.*

- *DirListBoxControl*.**Name**—a **String** that contains the name of the control that will be used to reference the control in a Visual Basic program. This property is read only at run time.

- *DirListControl*.**OLEDragMode**—an **Integer** value (see Table D-145) that describes how the control will respond to OLE drag operations.

> **Note**
>
> When the **DragMode** is **True**, the standard Visual Basic drag-and-drop functions will override the OLE drag-and-drop functions.

OLEDragMode Name	Value	Description
vbOLEDragManual	0	All drag requests will be handled by the programmer (default value).
vbOLEDragAutomatic	1	The control responds to all OLE drag requests automatically.

Table D-145: OLEDragMode values.

- *DirListBoxControl*.**OLEDropMode**—an **Integer** value (see Table D-146) that describes how the control will respond to OLE drop operations.

OLEDropMode Name	Value	Description
vbOLEDropNone	0	The control does not accept OLE drops. The cursor is changed to the No Drop cursor (default value).
vbOLEDropManual	1	The control responds to OLE drops under the program's control (manual).
vbOLEDropAutomatic	2	The control automatically accepts OLE drops if it recognizes the format of the data object.

Table D-146: OLEDropMode values.

- *DirListBoxControl*.**Parent**—an object that contains a reference to the **Form, Frame,** or other container that contains this control.
- *DirListBoxControl*.**Path**—a **String** containing the path to the directory to be displayed in the **DirListBox** control.

> **Tip**
>
> Use this property to set the **FileListBox** control **Path** property.

- *DirListBoxControl*.**TabIndex**—an Integer that determines the order that a user will tab through the objects on a form.
- *DirListBoxControl*.**TabStop**—a **Boolean** value when **True** means that the user can tab to this object. When **False** means that this control will be skipped to the next control in the **TabIndex** order.
- *DirListBoxControl*.**Tag**—a **String** that can hold programmer specific information. This property is not used by Visual Basic.
- *DirListBoxControl*.**ToolTipText**—a **String** that holds a text value that can be displayed as a **ToolTip** box that displays whenever the cursor is held over the control for about one second.

- *DirListBoxControl*.**Top**—a **Single** that contains the distance measured in twips between the top edge of the control and the top edge of the control's container.
- *DirListBoxControl*.**TopIndex**—an **Integer** that sets or returns the first value displayed in the drop-down window. The default value is zero.
- *DirListBoxControl*.**Visible**—a **Boolean** value when **True** means that the control is visible. When **False** means that the control is not visible.

Tip

This property hides the control until the program is ready to display it.

- *DirListBoxControl*.**WhatsThisHelpID**—a **Long** that contains a help file context ID number references an entry in the help file. This provides a What's This PopUp help display in response to the What's This button in the upper right corner of the window.
- *DirListBoxControl*.**Width**—a **Single** that contains the width of the control.

Methods

DirListBoxControl.Drag [*DragAction*]

Usage This method begins, ends, or cancels a drag operation.

Arguments *DragAction*—an **Integer** that contains a value selected from Table D-147.

DragAction Name	Value	Description
vbCancel	0	Cancels any drag operation in progress.
vbBeginDrag	1	Begins a drag operation (default).
vbEndDrag	2	Ends a drag operation and drops *object*.

Table D-147: DragAction *values.*

DirListBoxControl.Move *Left* [, *Top* [, *Width* [, *Height*]]]

Usage This method changes the position and the size of the **DriveListBox** control. The **ScaleMode** of the **Form** or other container object that holds the **DirListBox** control will determine the units used to specify the coordinates.

Arguments
- *Left*—a **Single** that specifies the new position of the left edge of the control.
- *Top*—a **Single** that specifies the new position of the top edge of the control.
- *Width*—a **Single** that specifies the new width of the control.
- *Height*—a **Single** that specifies the new height of the control.

DirListBoxControl.OLEDrag

Usage This method begins an **OLEDrag** and drop operation. Invoking this method will trigger the **OLEStartDrag** event.

DirListBoxControl.Refresh

Usage This method updates the contents of the drive list box.

DirListBoxControl.SetFocus

Usage This method transfers the focus from the form or control that currently has the focus to this control. To receive the focus, this control must be enabled and visible.

DirListBoxControl.ShowWhatsThis

Usage This method displays the ShowWhatsThis help information for this control.

DirListBoxControl.ZOrder [*position*]

Usage This method specifies the position of the file list control relative to the other objects on the form.

> **Tip**
>
> *Note that there are three layers of objects on a form: the back layer is the drawing space which contains the results of the graphical methods, the middle layer contains graphical objects and* **Labels***, and the top layer contains nongraphical controls such as the* **DirListBoxControl***. The* **ZOrder** *method only affects how the objects are arranged within a single layer.*

Arguments *position*—an **Integer** that specifies the relative position of this object. A value of 0 means that the control is positioned at the head of the list, a value of 1 means that the control will be placed at the end of the list.

Events

Private Sub *DirListBoxControl*_Change ([*index* As Integer])

Usage This event occurs when the user selects a different directory or the **Path** property is reset by your program.

Arguments *index*—an **Integer** that uniquely identifies a control in a control array. This argument is not present if the control is not part of a control array.

Private Sub *DirListBoxControl*_Click([*index* As Integer])

Usage This event occurs when the user clicks a mouse button to select an item in the drop-down list or selects an item from the drop-down list using the keyboard.

Arguments *index*—an **Integer** that uniquely identifies a control in a control array. This argument is not present if the control is not part of a control array.

Private Sub *DirListBoxControl* _DragDrop([*index* As Integer ,] *source* As Control, *x* As Single, *y* As Single)

Usage This event occurs when a drag-and-drop operation is completed by using the **Drag** method with a *DragAction* value of *vbEndDrag*.

Tip

*When using drag-and-drop operations, use the **DragOver** event to determine what the cursor should look like while the cursor moves over the control.*

Arguments
- *index*—an **Integer** that uniquely identifies a control in a control array. This argument is not present if the control is not part of a control array.
- *source*—a control object that is the control that is being dragged.

Tip

You can access a property or method from the source control by using source.property *or* source.method. *You can determine the type of object or control by using the **TypeOf** operator.*

- *x*—a **Single** that contains the horizontal location of the mouse pointer.
- *y*—a **Single** that contains the vertical location of the mouse pointer.

Private Sub *DirListBoxControl* _DragOver([*index* As Integer ,] *source* As Control, *x* As Single, *y* As Single, *state* As Integer)

Usage This event occurs while a drag operation is in progress and the cursor is moved over the control.

Tip

*When using drag-and-drop operations, use the **DragOver** event to determine what the cursor should look like while the cursor moves over the control. When* state *is 0, you can change the cursor to a No Drop (vbNoDrop) cursor or highlight the field that the cursor is near. When* state *is 1, you can undo the changes you made when the* state *was 0.*

Arguments
- *index*—an **Integer** that uniquely identifies a control in a control array. This argument is not present if the control is not part of a control array.
- *source*—a control object that is the control that is being dragged.

Tip

You can access a property or method from the source control by using source.property *or* source.method. *You can determine the type of object or control by using the **TypeOf** operator.*

- *x*—a **Single** that contains the horizontal location of the mouse pointer.
- *y*—a **Single** that contains the vertical location of the mouse pointer.
- *state*—an **Integer** value (see Table D-148) that indicates the state of the object being dragged.

state Name	Value	Description
vbEnter	0	The dragged object is entering range of the control.
vbLeave	1	The dragged object is leaving range of the control.
vbOver	2	The dragged object has moved from one position over the control to another.

Table D-148: state *values.*

Private Sub *DirListBoxControl*_GotFocus ([*index* As Integer])

Usage   This event occurs when the control is given focus.

Tip

You can use this routine to display help or other information in a status bar.

Arguments   *index*—an **Integer** that uniquely identifies a control in a control array. This argument is not present if the control is not part of a control array.

Private Sub *DirListBoxControl*_KeyDown ([*index* As Integer ,] *keycode* As Integer, *shift* As Single)

Usage   This event occurs when a key is pressed while the control has the focus.

Arguments
- *index*—an **Integer** that uniquely identifies a control in a control array. This argument is not present if the control is not part of a control array.
- *keycode*—an **Integer** that contains information about which key was pressed.
- *shift*—an **Integer** value (see Table D-149) that contains information about the Shift and Alt keys that were pushed when the mouse button was pressed. These values can be added together if more than one key was down. For instance, a value of 5 would mean that the Shift and Alt keys were both down when the mouse button was pressed.

shift Name	Value	Description
vbShiftMask	1	The Shift key was pressed.
vbCtrlMask	2	The Ctrl key was pressed.
vbAltMask	4	The Alt key was pressed.

Table D-149: shift *values.*

Private Sub *DirListBoxControl*_KeyPress([*index* As Integer ,] *keychar* As Integer)

Usage	This event occurs whenever a key is pressed while the control has the focus.
Arguments	• *index*—an **Integer** that uniquely identifies a control in a control array. This argument is not present if the control is not part of a control array.
	• *keychar*—an **Integer** that contains the ASCII character that was pressed.

Private Sub *DirListBoxControl*_KeyUp ([*index* As Integer ,] *keycode* As Integer, *shift* As Single)

Usage	This event occurs when a key is released while the control has the focus.
Arguments	• *index*—an **Integer** that uniquely identifies a control in a control array. This argument is not present if the control is not part of a control array.
	• *keycode*—an **Integer** that contains information about which key was released.
	• *shift*—an **Integer** value (see Table D-150) that contains information about the Shift and Alt keys that were pushed when the mouse button was pressed. These values can be added together if more than one key was down. For instance, a value of 5 would mean that the Shift and Alt keys were both down when the mouse button was pressed.

shift Name	Value	Description
vbShiftMask	1	The Shift key was pressed.
vbCtrlMask	2	The Ctrl key was pressed.
vbAltMask	4	The Alt key was pressed.

Table D-150: shift *values.*

Private Sub *DirListBoxControl*_LostFocus ([*index* As Integer])

Usage	This event occurs when the control loses focus.

Tip

This routine is useful to performing data verification.

Arguments	• *index*—an **Integer** that uniquely identifies a control in a control array. This argument is not present if the control is not part of a control array.

Private Sub *DirListBoxControl*_MouseDown([*index* As Integer ,] *button* As Integer, *shift* As Single, *x* As Single, *y* As Single)

Usage	This event occurs when a mouse button was pressed while the cursor is over the control.

Arguments
- *index*—an **Integer** that uniquely identifies a control in a control array. This argument is not present if the control is not part of a control array.
- *button*—an **Integer** value (see Table D-151) that contains information about the mouse buttons that were pressed. Only one button will be indicated when this event occurs.

button Name	Value	Description
vbLeftButton	1	The left button was pressed.
vbRightButton	2	The right button was pressed.
vbMiddleButton	4	The middle button was pressed.

Table D-151: button *values*.

- *shift*—an **Integer** value (see Table D-152) that contains information about the Shift and Alt keys that were pushed when the mouse button was pressed. These values can be added together if more than one key was down. For instance, a value of 5 would mean that the Shift and Alt keys were both down when the mouse button was pressed.

shift Name	Value	Description
vbShiftMask	1	The Shift key was pressed.
vbCtrlMask	2	The Ctrl key was pressed.
vbAltMask	4	The Alt key was pressed.

Table D-152: shift *values*.

- *x*—a **Single** that contains the horizontal location of the mouse pointer.
- *y*—a **Single** that contains the vertical location of the mouse pointer.

Private Sub *DirListBoxControl*_MouseMove ([*index* As Integer ,] *button* As Integer, *shift* As Single, *x* As Single, *y* As Single)

Usage This event occurs while the cursor is moved over the control.

Arguments
- *index*—an **Integer** that uniquely identifies a control in a control array. This argument is not present if the control is not part of a control array.
- *button*—an **Integer** value (see Table D-153) that contains information about the mouse buttons that were pressed. These values can be added together if more than one button was pushed. For instance, a value of 3 means that both the left and right buttons were pressed. A value of 0 means that no buttons were pressed.

button Name	Value	Description
vbLeftButton	1	The left button was pressed.
vbRightButton	2	The right button was pressed.
vbMiddleButton	4	The middle button was pressed.

Table D-153: button *values*.

- *shift*—an **Integer** value (see Table D-154) that contains information about the Shift and Alt keys that were pushed when the mouse button was pressed. For instance, a value of 5 would mean that the Shift and Alt keys were both down when the mouse button was pressed. A value of 0 means that none of these keys were pressed.

shift Name	Value	Description
vbShiftMask	1	The Shift key was pressed.
vbCtrlMask	2	The Ctrlkey was pressed.
vbAltMask	4	The Alt key was pressed.

Table D-154: shift *values*.

- *x*—a **Single** that contains the horizontal location of the mouse pointer.
- *y*—a **Single** that contains the vertical location of the mouse pointer.

Private Sub *DirListBoxControl* _MouseUp([*index* As Integer ,] *button* As Integer, *shift* As Single, *x* As Single, *y* As Single)

Usage   This event occurs when a mouse button is released while the cursor is over the control.

Arguments
- *index*—an **Integer** that uniquely identifies a control in a control array. This argument is not present if the control is not part of a control array.
- *button*—an **Integer** value (see Table D-155) that contains information about the mouse buttons that were released. Only one of these values will be present.

button Name	Value	Description
vbLeftButton	1	The left button was released.
vbRightButton	2	The right button was released.
vbMiddleButton	4	The middle button was released.

Table D-155: button *values*.

- *shift*—an **Integer** value (see Table D-156) that contains information about the Shift and Alt keys that were pushed when the mouse button was released. These values can be added together if more than one key was down. For instance, a value of 5 would mean that the Shift and Alt keys were both down when the mouse button was released. A value of 0 means that none of these keys were pressed.

shift Name	Value	Description
vbShiftMask	1	The Shift key was pressed.
vbCtrlMask	2	The Ctrl key was pressed.
vbAltMask	4	The Alt key was pressed.

Table D-156: shift *values*.

- *x*—a **Single** that contains the horizontal location of the mouse pointer.
- *y*—a **Single** that contains the vertical location of the mouse pointer.

Private Sub *DirListBoxControl*_OLECompleteDrag ([*index* As Integer ,] *effect* As Long)

Usage This event tells the source control the results of an OLE drag-and-drop operation. This is the final event to occur in the series of actions that make up an OLE drag-and-drop operation.

Arguments
- *index*—an **Integer** that uniquely identifies a control in a control array. This argument is not present if the control is not part of a control array.
- *effect*—a **Long** (see Table D-157) that returns the status of the OLE drag-and-drop operation.

effect Name	Value	Description
vbDropEffectNone	0	The operation was canceled or the target control can't accept the drop operation.
vbDropEffectCopy	1	The operation copied data from the source control to the target control. The original data is unchanged.
vbDropEffectMove	2	The operation results in a link from the original data to the target control.

Table D-157: effect *values*.

Private Sub *DirListBoxControl*_OLEDragDrop([*index* As Integer ,] *data* As DataObject, *effect* As Long, *button* As Integer, *shift* As Single, *x* As Single, *y* As Single)

Usage This event tells the source control the results of an OLE drag-and-drop operation. This is the final event to occur in the series of actions that make up an OLE drag-and-drop operation.

Arguments
- *index*—an **Integer** that uniquely identifies a control in a control array. This argument is not present if the control is not part of a control array.
- *data*—a **DataObject** that contains the formats that the source control will provide. If the data is not contained in the **DataObject**, then it can be retrieved with the **GetData** method.
- *effect*—a **Long** (see Table D-158) that returns the status of the OLE drag-and-drop operation.

effect Name	Value	Description
vbDropEffectNone	0	The operation was canceled or the target control can't accept the drop operation.
vbDropEffectCopy	1	The operation copied data from the source control to the target control. The original data is unchanged.
vbDropEffectMove	2	The operation results in a link from the original data to the target control.

Table D-158: effect *values*.

- *button*—an **Integer** value (see Table D-159) that contains information about the mouse buttons that were pressed. These values can be added together if more than one button was pushed. For instance, a value of 3 means that both the left and right buttons were pressed. A value of 0 means that no buttons were pressed.

button Name	Value	Description
vbLeftButton	1	The left button was pressed.
vbRightButton	2	The right button was pressed.
vbMiddleButton	4	The middle button was pressed.

Table D-159: button *values.*

- *shift*—an **Integer** value (see Table D-160) that contains information about the Shift and Alt keys that were pushed when the mouse button was released. These values can be added together if more than one key was down. For instance, a value of 5 would mean that the Shift and Alt keys were both down when the mouse button was released. A value of 0 means that none of these keys were pressed.

shift Name	Value	Description
vbShiftMask	1	The Shift key was pressed.
vbCtrlMask	2	The Ctrl key was pressed.
vbAltMask	4	The Alt key was pressed.

Table D-160: shift *values.*

- *x*—a **Single** that contains the horizontal location of the mouse pointer.
- *y*—a **Single** that contains the vertical location of the mouse pointer.

Private Sub *DirListBoxControl* _OLEDragOver([*index* As Integer ,] *data* As DataObject, *effect* As Long, *button* As Integer, *shift* As Single, *x* As Single, *y* As Single, *state* As Integer)

Usage: This event happens when an OLE drag-and-drop operation is in progress.

Arguments:
- *index*—an **Integer** that uniquely identifies a control in a control array. This argument is not present if the control is not part of a control array.
- *data*—a **DataObject** that contains the formats that the source control will provide. If the data is not contained in the **DataObject**, then it can be retrieved with the **GetData** method.
- *effect*—a **Long** (see Table D-161) that returns the status of the OLE drag-and-drop operation.

effect Name	Value	Description
vbDropEffectNone	0	The operation was canceled or the target control can't accept the drop operation.
vbDropEffectCopy	1	The operation copied data from the source control to the target control. The original data is unchanged.
vbDropEffectMove	2	The operation results in a link from the original data to the target control.

Table D-161: effect *values*.

- *button*—an **Integer** value (see Table D-162) that contains information about the mouse buttons that were pressed. These values can be added together if more than one button was pushed. For instance, a value of 3 means that both the left and right buttons were pressed. A value of 0 means that no buttons were pressed.

button Name	Value	Description
vbLeftButton	1	The left button was pressed.
vbRightButton	2	The right button was pressed.
vbMiddleButton	4	The middle button was pressed.

Table D-162: button *values*.

- *shift*—an **Integer** value (see Table D-163) that contains information about the Shift and Alt keys that were pushed when the mouse button was released. These values can be added together if more than one key was down. For instance, a value of 5 would mean that the Shift and Alt keys were both down when the mouse button was released. A value of 0 means that none of these keys were pressed.

shift Name	Value	Description
vbShiftMask	1	The Shift key was pressed.
vbCtrlMask	2	The Ctrl key was pressed.
vbAltMask	4	The Alt key was pressed.

Table D-163: shift *values*.

- *x*—a **Single** that contains the horizontal location of the mouse pointer.
- *y*—a **Single** that contains the vertical location of the mouse pointer.
- *state*—an **Integer** value (see Table D-164) that indicates the state of the object being dragged.

state Name	Value	Description
vbEnter	0	The dragged object is entering range of the control.
vbLeave	1	The dragged object is leaving range of the control.
vbOver	2	The dragged object has moved from one position over the control to another.

Table D-164: state *values*.

Private Sub *DirListBoxControl*_OLEGiveFeedback ([*index* As Integer ,] *effect* As Long)

Usage — This event tells the source control what is happening while the OLE drag-and-drop operation is in progress. This event occurs after the **OLEDragOver** event.

Tip

You may want to use this event to change the cursor to reflect what can happen in the remote object.

Arguments
- *index*—an **Integer** that uniquely identifies a control in a control array. This argument is not present if the control is not part of a control array.
- *effect*—a **Long** (see Table D-165) that returns the status of the OLE drag-and-drop operation.

effect Name	Value	Description
vbDropEffectNone	0	The operation was canceled or the target control can't accept the drop operation.
vbDropEffectCopy	1	The operation copied data from the source control to the target control. The original data is unchanged.
vbDropEffectMove	2	The operation results in a link from the original data to the target control.
vbDropEffectScroll	&H80000000	The target control is about to scroll or is scrolling. This value may be added to the other *effect* values.

Table D-165: effect *values.*

Private Sub *DirListBoxControl*_OLESetData([*index* As Integer ,] *data* As DataObject, *DataFormat* As Integer)

Usage — This event happens in response to the target object performing a **GetData** method on *data*. This routine will respond by using the **SetData** method with the desired data using the **DataObject** *data*.

Arguments
- *index*—an **Integer** that uniquely identifies a control in a control array. This argument is not present if the control is not part of a control array.
- *data*—a **DataObject** that will contain the data to be returned to the target object.
- *format*—an **Integer** value (see Table D-166) that contains the format of the data.

format Name	Value	Description
vbCFText	1	Text (.TXT files)
vbCFBitmap	2	Bitmap (.BMP files)
vbCFMetafile	3	Metafile (.WMF files)
vbCFEDIB	8	Device independent bitmap (DIB)
vbCFPallette	9	Color palette
vbCFEMetafile	14	Enhanced metafile (.EMF files)
vbCFFiles	15	List of files
vbCFRTF	-16639	Rich Text Format (.RTF files)

Table D-166: format *values.*

Private Sub *DirListBoxControl* _OLEStartDrag ([*index* As Integer ,] *data* As DataObject, *AllowedEffects* As Long)

Usage   This event starts an OLE drag-and-drop operation.

Arguments
- *index*—an **Integer** that uniquely identifies a control in a control array. This argument is not present if the control is not part of a control array.
- *data*—a **DataObject** that will contain the formats that the source object is willing to provide to the target object. It may optionally contain the data to be transferred.
- *AllowedEffects*—a **Long** that contains the effects (see Table D-167) that the target object can request from the source object. The *AllowedEffects* can be added together if the source object supports more than one effect. Note that the target object can always use the *vbDropEffectNone* effect.

AllowedEffects Name	Value	Description
vbDropEffectNone	0	The target can't copy the data.
vbDropEffectCopy	1	The target can copy the data and the source will keep the data unchanged.
vbDropEffectMove	2	The target can copy the data and the source will delete the data.

Table D-167: AllowedEffects *values*.

Private Sub *DirListBoxControl* _Scroll ([*index* As Integer])

Usage   This event is called each time the scroll bar is repositioned in the drop-down box.

Arguments
- *index*—an **Integer** that uniquely identifies a control in a control array. This argument is not present if the control is not part of a control array.

Examples
```
Private Sub Command1_Click()
Dim i As Integer
Text2.Text = ""
For i = 0 To File1.ListCount--1
    If File1.Selected(i) Then
        Text2.Text = Text2.Text & File1.List(i) & vbCrLf
    End If
Next i
End Sub

Private Sub Dir1_Change()
File1.Path = Dir1.Path
File1.Refresh
End Sub
```

```
Private Sub Drive1_Change()
Dir1.Path = Drive1.Drive
Dir1.Refresh
End Sub

Private Sub Text1_Change()
File1.Pattern = Text1.Text
End Sub
```

This program will cascade changes from the **DriveListBox** to the **DirListBox** and then to the **DriveListBox**. Changing the information in Text1 **TextBox** will change the **Pattern** property in the **DriveListBox**. After the user selects the files in the **DriveListBox**, and presses the OK button, the list of selected files is copied to the Text2 **TextBox**.

See Also   **CommonDialog** (control), **Dir** (function), **DriveListBox** (control), **FileListBox** (control)

Do

STATEMENT

CCE, LE, PE, EE

Syntax
```
Do
        [ list of statements ]
        [ Exit Do ]
        [ list of statements ]
Loop
Do { While | Until } condition
        [ list of statements ]
        [ Exit Do ]
        [ list of statements ]
Loop
Do
        [ list of statements ]
        [ Exit Do ]
        [ list of statements ]
Loop { While | Until } condition
```

Usage   There are three different forms for **Do . . . Loop** statements:
- The first form will execute the list of statements forever unless an **Exit Do** statement is executed.
- The second form of the **Do . . . Loop** statement adds a conditional statement that is executed before the loop is executed. If **While** *condition* is **True** or **Until** *condition* is **False** the statements inside the loop will be executed. When *condition* becomes **False** for **While** or **True** for **Until** the loop will stop executing.
- The third form of the **Do . . . Loop** statement includes the same **While** and **Until** clauses from the second form, but they are executed at the end of the loop. This means that no matter what the value of *condition* the loop will always be executed at least once.

> **Tip**
>
> The **While** and **Until** clauses are the logical **Not** of each other. Thus the **While Not** condition clause is identical to **Until** condition, and the **While** condition clause is identical to **Until Not** condition.

> **Tip**
>
> The **Do ... Loop** statement can be confusing with all its different forms and options. I prefer to use only the **Do While ... Loop** for most loops, except those loops where a **For Next** loop would be simpler.

Arguments
- *Variable*—a **Date, Double, Integer, Long,** or **Single** variable.
- *InitialValue*—an expression that contains the initial value for *Variable*.
- *FinalValue*—an expression that contains the final value for *Variable*.
- *Increment*—the value that would be added to *Variable* after each loop.

Examples
```
Private Sub Command1_Click()
Dim i As Integer
Dim l As Integer
Dim cl As Integer
l = Len(Text1.Text)
cl = 0

For i = 1 To l
    If Mid(Text1.Text, i, 1) = Left(Text2.Text, 1) Then
        cl = cl + 1
    End If
Next i
Text3.Text = Format(cl)
End Sub
```

This routine counts the number of times a letter occurs in the Text1 **TextBox**. It uses a **For ... Next** loop to look at each character in the text box and increments a counter each time one is found.

See Also **For** (statement), **While** (statement)

Document   OBJECT
PE, EE

Usage The **Document** object is used by Data Access Objects (DAO) to contain information about saved databases, tables, queries, or relationships depending on the **Container** object's parent.

Properties
- *DocumentObject*.**AllPermissions**—a **Long** containing the permissions (see Table D-168) that apply to the current **UserName** including those that are inherited from membership in various **Workgroups**.

AllPermissions Name	Description
dbSecReadDef	Read table definitions, including column and index definitions.
dbSecWriteDef	Update or delete table definitions, including column and index definitions.
dbSecRetrieveData	Retrieve information from the document object.
dbSecInsertData	Add records.
dbSecReplaceData	Update records.
dbSecDeleteData	Delete records.
dbSecDBAdmin	Can replicate the database and change its password.
dbSecDBCreate	Can create new databases.
dbSecDBExclusive	Has exclusive access to the database.
dbSecDBOpen	Can open the database.

Table D-168: AllPermissions values.

- *DocumentObject*.**Container**—a **String** containing the name of the document's **Container** object.
- *DocumentObject*.**DateCreated**—a **Date** value containing the date and time the object was created.
- *DocumentObject*.**KeepLocal**—an object created by using the **CreateProperty** method that sets or returns a value that will not be copied when the database is replicated. This property is the opposite of **Replicable**.
- *DocumentObject*.**LastUpdated**—a **Date** value containing the date and time the object was last updated.
- *DocumentObject*.**Name**—a **String** value containing the name of the object. This property is read-only.
- *DocumentObject*.**Owner**—a **String** value containing the owner of the document.
- *DocumentObject*.**Permissions**—a **Long** containing the permissions (see Table D-169) that apply to the current **UserName**. Does not include those that are inherited from membership in various **Workgroups**.

Permissions Name	Description
dbSecReadDef	Read table definitions, including column and index definitions.
dbSecWriteDef	Update or delete table definitions, including column and index definitions.
dbSecRetrieveData	Retrieve information from the document object.
dbSecInsertData	Add records.
dbSecReplaceData	Update records.
dbSecDeleteData	Delete records.
dbSecDBAdmin	Can replicate the database and change its password.
dbSecDBCreate	Can create new databases.
dbSecDBExclusive	Has exclusive access to the database.
dbSecDBOpen	Can open the database.

Table D-169: Permissions values.

- *DocumentObject*.**Replicable**—an object created by using the **CreateProperty** method that sets or returns a value that will be copied when the database is replicated. This property is the opposite of **KeepLocal**.
- *DocumentObject*.**UserName**—a **String** value containing the name of a user or group of users that are associated with the **Permissions** and **AllPermissions** properties.

Methods

property = DocumentObject.CreateProperty ([name] [, [type] [, [value] [, DDL]]])

Usage This method creates a user-defined property object.

Arguments
- *property*—an object variable that will contain the new property object.
- *name*—a **String** containing the name of the property. Must begin with a letter and can be followed by letters, numbers or an underscore ("_").
- *type*—a value selected from Table D-170 below.

type Name	Description
dbBigInt	Big Integer
dbBinary	Binary
dbBoolean	Boolean
dbByte	Byte
dbChar	Character
dbCurrency	Currency
dbDate	Date
dbDecimal	Decimal
dbDouble	Double
dbFloat	Float
dbGUID	Globally unique identifier *dbInteger* Integer
dbLong	Long
dbLongBinary	Long binary
DbMemo	Memo
DbNumeric	Numeric
DbSingle	Single
DbText	Text
DbTime	Time
dbTimeStamp	Time stamp
DbVarBinary	Variable length binary data (up to 255 bytes)

Table D-170: *type values.*

- *value*—a **Variant** containing the initial value for the property.
- *DDL*—a **Boolean** when **True** means that the user cannot change this property value without the *dbSecWriteDef* permission. When **False** this permission is not required to change the value.

See Also **Documents** (collection), **User** (object)

Documents

COLLECTION

PE, EE

Usage
: The **Documents** collection is used by Data Access Objects (DAO) to contain information about saved databases, tables, queries, or relationships depending on the **Container** object's parent.

Properties
: *DocumentsCollection*.**Count**—an **Integer** containing the number of **Document** objects in the collection.

Methods
: ***DocumentObject*.Refresh**

    Usage
    : This method gets a current copy of the documents in the collection. This is important in a multi-user environment where more than one user may be making changes in the **Documents** collection.

See Also
: **Document** (object), **User** (object)

DoEvents

FUNCTION

CCE, LE, PE, EE

Syntax
: *IValue* = **DoEvents( )**

Usage
: The **DoEvents** function temporarily yields control to Windows so that the operating system can process other events in your program. It should be placed in long running tasks, such as database loads, large reports, or loading large graphic displays.

> **Tip**
>
> *The **DoEvents** function was very important in the previous versions of Visual Basic that ran on older Windows platforms. With Windows 95 and NT, using **DoEvents** is less critical but still useful, since it frees other parts of your program to respond to events while still performing a long running task.*

Arguments
: *IValue*—an **Integer** that contains the number of open forms in the program depending on the edition of Visual Basic.

Examples
:
```
Private Sub Command1_Click()
Dim l As Long
For l = 1 To 499
    Debug.Print l
Next l
End Sub
```

```
Private Sub Command2_Click()
Dim i As Integer
Dim l As Long
For l = 1 To 499
    Debug.Print l
    i = DoEvents()
Next l
End Sub
```

These two routines are identical, except for the call to **DoEvents** in the second routine. Running the first prevents any other windows in Visual Basic from gaining the focus, while the second will allow you to easily switch windows.

See Also **Abs** (function), **Int** (function), **Sng** (function)

Double

DATA TYPE

CCE, LE, PE, EE

Usage The **Double** data type holds floating point values in the range -1.79769313486232E308 to -4.94065645841247E-324 for negative values and from 4.94065645841247E-324 to 1.79769313486232E308 for positive values. A single **Double** variable is formatted as an IEEE 64-bit floating point number that occupies 8 bytes of storage.

See Also **CDbl** (function), **CSng** (function), **DefDbl** (statement), **Dim** (statement), **Format** (function), **IsNumeric** (function), **Single** (data type)

DriveListBox

CONTROL

CCE, LE, PE, EE

Usage The **DriveListBox** control is an intrinsic control that allows the user to select a disk drive.

Properties
- *DriveListBoxControl*.**Appearance**—an **Integer** value (see Table D-171) that specifies how the file list box will appear on the form.

AppearanceValue	Description
0	The drive list box displays without the 3D effects.
1	The drive list box displays with 3D effects (default value).

Table D-171: Appearance values.

- *DriveListBoxControl*.**BackColor**—a **Long** that contains the suggested value for the background color of the control. The **BackColor** and **ForeColor** must both be solid to display text. If you choose a color that is dithered, it will be changed to the nearest solid color.
- *DriveListBoxControl*.**Container**—an object that sets or returns the container of the control at run time. This property cannot be set at design time.

- *DriveListBoxControl*.**DragIcon**—an object that contains the picture value of an icon. At design time, you can specify an icon file that has a file type of .ICO.

> **Tip**
>
> This value can be created by copying the value from another control's **DragIcon** value, a form's icon, or by using the **LoadPicture** function.

- *DriveListBoxControl*.**DragMode**—an **Integer** value (see Table D-172) specifying how the control will respond to a drag request.

> **Tip**
>
> Setting **DragMode** to vbAutomatic *will automatically begin a drag operation when the user clicks on the control. However, the control will not respond to the usual mouse events (***Click***, ***DblClick***).*

DragMode Name	Value	Description
vbManual	0	The **Drag** method must be used to begin a drag-and-drop operation (default value).
vbAutomatic	1	The source control will automatically begin a drag-and-drop operation when the user clicks on the control.

Table D-172: **DragMode** *values.*

- *DriveListBoxControl*.**Enabled**—a **Boolean** value when **True** means that the control will respond to events. When **False**, the control will not respond to events.
- *DriveListBoxControl*.**Font**—an object that contains information about the character font used by this object.

> **Tip**
>
> The **Font** *object should be used in place of the other* **Font** *properties, since it offers more functionality than the individual properties.*

- *DriveListBoxControl*.**FontBold**—a **Boolean** when **True** means that the characters display in bold. **False** means that the characters display normally.
- *DriveListBoxControl*.**FontItalic**—a **Boolean** when **True** means that the characters display in italics. **False** means that the characters display normally.
- *DriveListBoxControl*.**FontName**—a **String** that specifies the name of the font that should be used to display the characters in this control.
- *DriveListBoxControl*.**FontSize**—a **Single** that specifies the point size that should be used to display the characters in the control.
- *DriveListBoxControl*.**FontStrikethru**—a **Boolean** when **True** means that the characters display with a line through the center. **False** means that the characters display normally.

- *DriveListBoxControl*.**FontUnderlined**—a **Boolean** when **True** means that the characters display with a line beneath them. **False** means that the characters display normally.
- *DriveListBoxControl*.**ForeColor**—a **Long** that contains the suggested value for the foreground color of the contained control. This property is read only at run time.
- *DriveListBoxControl*.**Height**—a **Single** that contains the height of the control.
- *DriveListBoxControl*.**HelpContextID**—a **Long** that contains a help file context ID number which references an entry in the help file. When the user presses the F1 key while this control is active, the corresponding entry in the help file will automatically display. A value of zero means that no context number was specified.

Tip

A help file must be compiled using the Windows Help Compiler available in the Professional and Enterprise editions of Visual Basic.

- *DriveListBoxControl*.**hWnd**—a **Long** that contains a Windows handle to the control.

Tip

The **hWnd** *property is most useful when making calls to Windows API functions. Since this value can change during execution, do not save the value into a variable for later use.*

- *DriveListBoxControl*.**Index**—an **Integer** that uniquely identifies a control in a control array.
- *DriveListBoxControl*.**Left**—a **Single** that contains the distance measured in twips between the left edge of the control and the left edge of the control's container.
- *DriveListBoxControl*.**List** (*index*)—an array of **String** values display in the drop-down part of the **DriveListBox**. The number of elements in this array can be found in the **ListCount** property.

Tip

The first element of the **List** *array is zero, while the last array element is* **ListCount** *-1.*

- *DriveListBoxControl*.**ListCount**—an **Integer** value containing the number of elements in the **List**.
- *DriveListBoxControl*.**ListIndex**—an **Integer** value containing the index of the selected item from the drop-down box. If no value was selected, **ListIndex** will be set to -1.
- *DriveListBoxControl*.**MouseIcon**—a **Picture** object (a bitmap, icon, or metafile) that will be used as a cursor when the **MousePointer** property is set to 99. Note that Visual Basic does not support color cursors from a .CUR file. A color icon from an .ICO file should be used instead.
- *DriveListBoxControl*.**MousePointer**—an **Integer** value (see Table D-173) that contains the value of the cursor that should be displayed when the cursor is moved over this control. Use *vbCustom* to display the custom icon stored in the **MouseIcon** property.

Cursor Name	Value	Description
vbDefault	0	Shape determined by the object (default value)
vbArrow	1	Arrow
vbCrosshair	2	Crosshair
vbIbeam	3	I beam
vbIconPointer	4	Square inside a square
vbSizePointer	5	Four sided arrow (north, south, east, west)
vbSizeNESW	6	Two sided arrow (northeast, southwest)
vbSizeNS	7	Two sided arrow (north, south)
vbSizeNWSE	8	Two sided arrow (northwest, southeast)
vbSizeWE	9	Two sided arrow (west, east)
vbUpArrow	10	Single sided arrow pointing north
vbHourglass	11	Hourglass
vbNoDrop	12	No Drop
vbArrowHourglass	13	An arrow and an hourglass
vbArrowQuestion	14	An arrow and a question mark
vbSizeAll	15	Size all
vbCustom	99	Custom icon from the **MouseIcon** property of this control

Table D-173: Cursor *values.*

- *DriveListBoxControl.***Name**—a **String** that contains the name of the control that will be used to reference the control in a Visual Basic program. This property is read only at run time.
- *DriveListBoxControl.***OLEDropMode**—an **Integer** value (see Table D-174) that describes how the control will respond to OLE drop operations.

OLEDropMode Name	Value	Description
vbOLEDropNone	0	The control does not accept OLE drops. The cursor is changed to the No Drop cursor (default value).
vbOLEDropManual	1	The control responds to OLE drops under the program's control (manual).
vbOLEDropAutomatic	2	The control automatically accepts OLE drops if it recognizes the format of the data object.

Table D-174: OLEDropMode values.

- *DriveListBoxControl.***Parent**—an object that contains a reference to the **Form**, **Frame,** or other container that contains this control.
- *DriveListBoxControl.***TabIndex**—an **Integer** that determines the order that a user will tab through the objects on a form.
- *DriveListBoxControl.***TabStop**—a **Boolean** value when **True** means that the user can tab to this object. When **False** means that this control will be skipped to the next control in the **TabIndex** order.
- *DriveListBoxControl.***Tag**—a **String** that can hold programmer specific information. This property is not used by Visual Basic.

- *DriveListBoxControl*.**ToolTipText**—a **String** that holds a text value that can be displayed as a **ToolTip** box that displays whenever the cursor is held over the control for about one second.
- *DriveListBoxControl*.**Top**—a **Single** that contains the distance measured in twips between the top edge of the control and the top edge of the control's container.
- *DriveListBoxControl*.**TopIndex**—an **Integer** that sets or returns the first value displayed in the drop-down window. The default value is zero.
- *DriveListBoxControl*.**Visible**—a **Boolean** value when **True** means that the control is visible. When **False** means that the control is not visible.

> **Tip**
>
> *This property hides the control until the program is ready to display it.*

- *DriveListBoxControl*.**WhatsThisHelpID**—a **Long** that contains a help file context ID number references an entry in the help file. This provides a What's This PopUp help display in response to the What's This button in the upper right corner of the window.
- *DriveListBoxControl*.**Width**—a **Single** that contains the width of the control.

Methods

*DriveListBoxControl.*Drag [*DragAction*]

Usage This method begins, ends, or cancels a drag operation.

Arguments *DragAction*—an **Integer** that contains a value selected from Table D-175 below.

DragAction Name	Value	Description
vbCancel	0	Cancels any drag operation in progress.
vbBeginDrag	1	Begins a drag operation (default).
vbEndDrag	2	Ends a drag operation and drops *object*.

Table D-175: DragAction *values.*

*DriveListBoxControl.*Move *Left* [, *Top* [, *Width* [, *Height*]]]

Usage This method changes the position and the size of the **DriveListBox** control. The **ScaleMode** of the **Form** or other container object that holds the **DriveListBox** control will determine the units used to specify the coordinates.

Arguments
- *Left*—a **Single** that specifies the new position of the left edge of the control.
- *Top*—a **Single** that specifies the new position of the top edge of the control.
- *Width*—a **Single** that specifies the new width of the control.
- *Height*—a **Single** that specifies the new height of the control.

DriveListBoxControl.OLEDrag

Usage This method begins an **OLEDrag** and drop operation. Invoking this method will trigger the **OLEStartDrag** event.

DriveListBoxControl.Refresh

Usage This method updates the contents of the drive list box.

DriveListBoxControl.SetFocus

Usage This method transfers the focus from the form or control that currently has the focus to this control. To receive the focus, this control must be enabled and visible.

DriveListBoxControl.ShowWhatsThis

Usage This method displays the ShowWhatsThis help information for this control.

DriveListBoxControl.ZOrder [*position*]

Usage This method specifies the position of the file list control relative to the other objects on the form.

> **Tip**
>
> *Note that there are three layers of objects on a form: the back layer is the drawing space which contains the results of the graphical methods, the middle layer contains graphical objects and **Labels**, and the top layer contains nongraphical controls such as the **DriveListBox** Control. The **ZOrder** method only affects how the objects are arranged within a single layer.*

Arguments • *position*—an **Integer** that specifies the relative position of this object. A value of 0 means that the control is positioned at the head of the list, a value of 1 means that the control will be placed at the end of the list.

Events Private Sub *DriveListBoxControl*_Change ([*index* As Integer])

Usage This event occurs when the user selects a different drive or the **Drive** property is reset by your program.

Arguments • *index*—an **Integer** that uniquely identifies a control in a control array. This argument is not present if the control is not part of a control array.

Private Sub *DriveListBoxControl*_DragDrop([*index* As Integer ,] *source* As Control, *x* As Single, *y* As Single)

Usage   This event occurs when a drag-and-drop operation is completed by using the **Drag** method with a *DragAction* value of *vbEndDrag*.

Tip

*When using drag-and-drop operations, use the **DragOver** event to determine what the cursor should look like while the cursor moves over the control.*

Arguments
- *index*—an **Integer** that uniquely identifies a control in a control array. This argument is not present if the control is not part of a control array.
- *source*—a control object that is the control that is being dragged.

Tip

*You can access a property or method from the source control by using **source**.property or **source**.method. You can determine the type of object or control by using the **TypeOf** operator.*

- *x*—a **Single** that contains the horizontal location of the mouse pointer.
- *y*—a **Single** that contains the vertical location of the mouse pointer.

Private Sub *DriveListBoxControl*_DragOver([*index* As Integer ,] *source* As Control, *x* As Single, *y* As Single, *state* As Integer)

Usage   This event occurs while a drag operation is in progress and the cursor is moved over the control.

Tip

*When using drag-and-drop operations, use the **DragOver** event to determine what the cursor should look like while the cursor moves over the control. When **state** is 0, you can change the cursor to a No Drop (vbNoDrop) cursor or highlight the field that the cursor is near. When **state** is 1, you can undo the changes you made when the **state** was 0.*

Arguments
- *index*—an **Integer** that uniquely identifies a control in a control array. This argument is not present if the control is not part of a control array.
- *source*—a control object that is the control that is being dragged.

Tip

*You can access a property or method from the source control by using **source**.property or **source**.method. You can determine the type of object or control by using the **TypeOf** operator.*

- *x*—a **Single** that contains the horizontal location of the mouse pointer.
- *y*—a **Single** that contains the vertical location of the mouse pointer.
- *state*—an **Integer** value (see Table D-176) that indicates the state of the object being dragged.

state Name	Value	Description
vbEnter	0	The dragged object is entering range of the control.
vbLeave	1	The dragged object is leaving range of the control.
vbOver	2	The dragged object has moved from one position over the control to another.

Table D-176: state *values*.

Private Sub *DriveListBoxControl* _GotFocus ([*index* As Integer])

Usage   This event occurs when the control is given focus.

Tip

You can use this routine to display help or other information in a status bar.

Arguments   *index*—an **Integer** that uniquely identifies a control in a control array. This argument is not present if the control is not part of a control array.

Private Sub *DriveListBoxControl* _KeyDown ([*index* As Integer ,] *keycode* As Integer, *shift* As Single)

Usage   This event occurs when a key is pressed while the control has the focus.

Arguments
- *index*—an **Integer** that uniquely identifies a control in a control array. This argument is not present if the control is not part of a control array.
- *keycode*—an **Integer** that contains information about which key was pressed.
- *shift*—an **Integer** value (see Table D-177) that contains information about the Shift and Alt keys that were pushed when the mouse button was pressed. These values can be added together if more than one key was down. For instance, a value of 5 would mean that the Shift and Alt keys were both down when the mouse button was pressed.

shift Name	Value	Description
vbShiftMask	1	The Shift key was pressed.
vbCtrlMask	2	The Ctrl key was pressed.
vbAltMask	4	The Alt key was pressed.

Table D-177: shift *values*.

Private Sub *DriveListBoxControl*_KeyPress([*index* As Integer ,] *keychar* As Integer)

Usage   This event occurs whenever a key is pressed while the control has the focus.

Arguments
- *index*—an **Integer** that uniquely identifies a control in a control array. This argument is not present if the control is not part of a control array.
- *keychar*—an **Integer** that contains the ASCII character that was pressed.

Private Sub *ComoBoxControl*_KeyUp ([*index* As Integer ,] *keycode* As Integer, *shift* As Single)

Usage   This event occurs when a key is released while the control has the focus.

Arguments
- *index*—an **Integer** that uniquely identifies a control in a control array. This argument is not present if the control is not part of a control array.
- *keycode*—an **Integer** that contains information about which key was released.
- *shift*—an **Integer** value (see Table D-178) that contains information about the Shift and Alt keys that were pushed when the mouse button was pressed. These values can be added together if more than one key was down. For instance, a value of 5 would mean that the Shift and Alt keys were both down when the mouse button was pressed.

shift Name	Value	Description
vbShiftMask	1	The Shift key was pressed.
vbCtrlMask	2	The Ctrl key was pressed.
vbAltMask	4	The Alt key was pressed.

Table D-178: shift *values.*

Private Sub *DriveListBoxControl*_LostFocus ([*index* As Integer])

Usage   This event occurs when the control loses focus.

Tip

This routine is useful to performing data verification.

Arguments
- *index*—an **Integer** that uniquely identifies a control in a control array. This argument is not present if the control is not part of a control array.

Private Sub *DriveListBoxControl*_OLECompleteDrag ([*index* As Integer ,] *effect* As Long)

Usage — This event tells the source control the results of an OLE drag-and-drop operation. This is the final event to occur in the series of actions that make up an OLE drag-and-drop operation.

Arguments
- *index*—an **Integer** that uniquely identifies a control in a control array. This argument is not present if the control is not part of a control array.
- *effect*—a **Long** (see Table D-179) that returns the status of the OLE drag-and-drop operation.

effect Name	Value	Description
vbDropEffectNone	0	The operation was canceled or the target control can't accept the drop operation.
vbDropEffectCopy	1	The operation copied data from the source control to the target control. The original data is unchanged.
vbDropEffectMove	2	The operation results in a link from the original data to the target control.

Table D-179: effect *values*.

Private Sub *DriveListBoxControl*_OLEDragDrop([*index* As Integer ,] *data* As DataObject, *effect* As Long, *button* As Integer, *shift* As Single, *x* As Single, *y* As Single)

Usage — This event tells the source control the results of an OLE drag-and-drop operation. This is the final event to occur in the series of actions that make up an OLE drag-and-drop operation.

Arguments
- *index*—an **Integer** that uniquely identifies a control in a control array. This argument is not present if the control is not part of a control array.
- *data*—a **DataObject** that contains the formats that the source control will provide. If the data is not contained in the **DataObject**, then it can be retrieved with the **GetData** method.
- *effect*—a **Long** (see Table D-180) that returns the status of the OLE drag-and-drop operation.

effect Name	Value	Description
vbDropEffectNone	0	The operation was canceled or the target control can't accept the drop operation.
vbDropEffectCopy	1	The operation copied data from the source control to the target control. The original data is unchanged.
vbDropEffectMove	2	The operation results in a link from the original data to the target control.

Table D-180: effect *values*.

- *button*—an **Integer** value (see Table D-181) that contains information about the mouse buttons that were pressed. These values can be added together if more than one button was pushed. For instance, a value of 3 means that both the left and right buttons were pressed. A value of 0 means that no buttons were pressed.

button Name	Value	Description
vbLeftButton	1	The left button was pressed.
vbRightButton	2	The right button was pressed.
vbMiddleButton	4	The middle button was pressed.

Table D-181: button *values.*

- *shift*—an **Integer** value (see Table D-182) that contains information about the Shift and Alt keys that were pushed when the mouse button was released. These values can be added together if more than one key was down. For instance, a value of 5 would mean that the Shift and Alt keys were both down when the mouse button was released. A value of 0 means that none of these keys were pressed.

shift Name	Value	Description
vbShiftMask	1	The Shift key was pressed.
vbCtrlMask	2	The Ctrl key was pressed.
vbAltMask	4	The Alt key was pressed.

Table D-182: shift *values.*

- *x*—a **Single** that contains the horizontal location of the mouse pointer.
- *y*—a **Single** that contains the vertical location of the mouse pointer.

Private Sub *DriveListBoxControl* _OLEDragOver([*index* As Integer ,] *data* As DataObject, *effect* As Long, *button* As Integer, *shift* As Single, *x* As Single, *y* As Single, *state* As Integer)

Usage   This event happens when an OLE drag-and-drop operation is in progress.

Arguments
- *index*—an **Integer** that uniquely identifies a control in a control array. This argument is not present if the control is not part of a control array.
- *data*—a **DataObject** that contains the formats that the source control will provide. If the data is not contained in the **DataObject**, then it can be retrieved with the **GetData** method.
- *effect*—a **Long** (see Table D-183) that returns the status of the OLE drag-and-drop operation.

DriveListBox

effect Name	Value	Description
vbDropEffectNone	0	The operation was canceled or the target control can't accept the drop operation.
vbDropEffectCopy	1	The operation copied data from the source control to the target control. The original data is unchanged.
vbDropEffectMove	2	The operation results in a link from the original data to the target control.

Table D-183: effect values.

- *button*—an **Integer** value (see Table D-184) that contains information about the mouse buttons that were pressed. These values can be added together if more than one button was pushed. For instance, a value of 3 means that both the left and right buttons were pressed. A value of 0 means that no buttons were pressed.

button Name	Value	Description
vbLeftButton	1	The left button was pressed.
vbRightButton	2	The right button was pressed.
vbMiddleButton	4	The middle button was pressed.

Table D-184: button values.

- *shift*—an **Integer** value (see Table D-185) that contains information about the Shift and Alt keys that were pushed when the mouse button was released. These values can be added together if more than one key was down. For instance, a value of 5 would mean that the Shift and Alt keys were both down when the mouse button was released. A value of 0 means that none of these keys were pressed.

shift Name	Value	Description
vbShiftMask	1	The Shift key was pressed.
vbCtrlMask	2	The Ctrl key was pressed.
vbAltMask	4	The Alt key was pressed.

Table D-185: shift values.

- *x*—a **Single** that contains the horizontal location of the mouse pointer.
- *y*—a **Single** that contains the vertical location of the mouse pointer.
- *state*—an **Integer** value (see Table D-186) that indicates the state of the object being dragged.

state Name	Value	Description
vbEnter	0	The dragged object is entering range of the control.
vbLeave	1	The dragged object is leaving range of the control.
vbOver	2	The dragged object has moved from one position over the control to another.

Table D-186: state values.

Private Sub *DriveListBoxControl*_OLEGiveFeedback ([*index* As Integer ,] *effect* As Long)

Usage — This event tells the source control what is happening while the OLE drag-and-drop operation is in progress. This event occurs after the **OLEDragOver** event.

Tip

You may want to use this event to change the cursor to reflect what can happen in the remote object.

Arguments
- *index*—an **Integer** that uniquely identifies a control in a control array. This argument is not present if the control is not part of a control array.
- *effect*—a **Long** (see Table D-187) that returns the status of the OLE drag-and-drop operation.

effect Name	Value	Description
vbDropEffectNone	0	The operation was canceled or the target control can't accept the drop operation.
vbDropEffectCopy	1	The operation copied data from the source control to the target control. The original data is unchanged.
vbDropEffectMove	2	The operation results in a link from the original data to the target control.
vbDropEffectScroll	&H80000000	The target control is about to scroll or is scrolling. This value may be added to the other *effect* values.

Table D-187: effect *values.*

Private Sub *DriveListBoxControl*_OLESetData([*index* As Integer ,] *data* As DataObject, *DataFormat* As Integer)

Usage — This event happens in response to the target object performing a **GetData** method on *data*. This routine will respond by using the **SetData** method with the desired data using the **DataObject** *data*.

Arguments
- *index*—an **Integer** that uniquely identifies a control in a control array. This argument is not present if the control is not part of a control array.
- *data*—a **DataObject** that will contain the data to be returned to the target object.
- *format*—an **Integer** value (see Table D-188) that contains the format of the data.

format Name	Value	Description
vbCFText	1	Text (.TXT files)
vbCFBitmap	2	Bitmap (.BMP files)
vbCFMetafile	3	Metafile (.WMF files)
vbCFEDIB	8	Device independent bitmap (DIB)
vbCFPallette	9	Color palette
vbCFEMetafile	14	Enhanced metafile (.EMF files)
vbCFFiles	15	List of files
vbCFRTF	-16639	Rich Text Format (.RTF files)

Table D-188: format *values*.

Private Sub *DriveListBoxControl*_OLEStartDrag ([*index* As Integer ,] *data* As DataObject, *AllowedEffects* As Long)

Usage This event starts an OLE drag-and-drop operation.

Arguments
- *index*—an **Integer** that uniquely identifies a control in a control array. This argument is not present if the control is not part of a control array.
- *data*—a **DataObject** that will contain the formats that the source object is willing to provide to the target object. It may optionally contain the data to be transferred.
- *AllowedEffects*—a **Long** that contains the effects (see Table D-189) that the target object can request from the source object. The *AllowedEffects* can be added together if the source object supports more than one effect. Note that the target object can always use the *vbDropEffectNone* effect.

AllowedEffects Name	Value	Description
vbDropEffectNone	0	The target can't copy the data.
vbDropEffectCopy	1	The target can copy the data and the source will keep the data unchanged.
vbDropEffectMove	2	The target can copy the data and the source will delete the data.

Table D-189: AllowedEffects *values*.

Private Sub *DriveListBoxControl*_Scroll ([*index* As Integer])

Usage This event is called each time the scroll bar is repositioned in the drop-down box.

Arguments *index*—an **Integer** that uniquely identifies a control in a control array. This argument is not present if the control is not part of a control array.

Examples
```
Private Sub Command1_Click()
Dim i As Integer
Text2.Text = ""
For i = 0 To File1.ListCount--1
   If File1.Selected(i) Then
      Text2.Text = Text2.Text & File1.List(i) & vbCrLf
   End If
Next i
End Sub

Private Sub Dir1_Change()
File1.Path = Dir1.Path
File1.Refresh
End Sub

Private Sub Drive1_Change()
Dir1.Path = Drive1.Drive
Dir1.Refresh
End Sub

Private Sub Text1_Change()
File1.Pattern = Text1.Text
End Sub
```

This program will cascade changes from the **DriveListBox** to the **DirListBox** and then to the **DriveListBox**. Changing the information in Text1 **TextBox** will change the **Pattern** property in the **DriveListBox**. After the user selects the files in the **DriveListBox**, and presses the OK button, the list of selected files is copied to the Text2 **TextBbox**.

See Also **CommonDialog** (control), **Dir** (function), **DirListBox** (control), **FileListBox** (control)

End

STATEMENT

CCE, LE, PE, EE

Syntax   **End**

Usage   The **End** statement immediately terminates a program's execution without invoking the **Unload**, **QueryUnload**, or **Terminate** events. Any files opened with the **Open** statement will be closed, all objects created by the program will be destroyed, and all object references held by other programs will be invalidated.

> **Tip**
>
> The **Unload** statement doesn't bypass the **Unload**, **QueryUnload**, or **Terminate** events. One way to gain the benefits of the **End** statement without sacrificing these events is to include the **End** statement as the last statement in the **Terminate** event of the main form.

Examples

```
Private Sub Command1_Click()
    End
End Sub

Private Sub Command2_Click()
    Unload Me
End Sub
Private Sub Form_Terminate()
    MsgBox "In terminate"
End Sub
```

This program uses two command buttons to demonstrate the difference between the **End** statement and the **Unload** statement. Press the Command1 button to execute the **End** statement, and you will not see the message box from the **Terminate** event. Press the Command2 button to execute the **Unload** statement, and you will see the message box from the **Terminate** event.

See Also   **Open** (statement), **Stop** (statement), **Unload** (statement)

Enum

STATEMENT

CCE, LE, PE, EE

Syntax

```
[ Private | Public ] Enum EnumName
    name1 [ = value1 ]
    name2 [ = value2 ]
        .
        .
        .
    nameN [ = valueN ]
End Enum
```

Usage	The **Enum** statement defines a list of constants. **Private** means that the constants will be local to the module in which they are declared. **Public** means that you can reference the constants from anywhere in the program. If neither **Public** nor **Private** is specified, then **Public** will be assumed.
Arguments	• *EnumName*—a valid Visual Basic identifier that describes the collection of constants.
	• *name1*—a valid Visual Basic identifier that is associated with a particular constant.
	• *value1*—a **Long** value that can be any expression including using other constants and enum values. If this value is omitted, it will default to zero.
	• *name2*—a valid Visual Basic identifier that is associated with a particular constant.
	• *value2*—a **Long** value that can be any expression including using other constants and enum values. If this value is omitted, it will default to one or one more than the previous constant.
	• *nameN*—a valid Visual Basic identifier that is associated with a particular constant.
	• *valueN*—a **Long** value that can be any expression including using other constants and enum values. If this value is omitted, it will default to one more than the previous constant.

Examples
```
Public Enum MyBits
    bit1 = 2
    bit2 = 4
    Bit3 = 8
    bit4 = 16
    Bit5 = 32
    Bit6 = 64
    Bit7 = 128
End Enum

Private Sub Command1_Click()
MsgBox "The value of bit 1 in B is " & Format(Asc("B") Mod bit1)
End Sub
```

This program uses enumerated set of values MyBits to examine the lowest order bit of the character B. Since the ASCII value of B is 01000010 the answer will be zero.

See Also   **Const** (statement), **Dim** (statement)

Environ

FUNCTION

CCE, LE, PE, EE

Syntax   *Value* = **Environ** (*variable*)

Usage   The **Environ** function returns a single value from the environmental variable table. If *variable* is an **Integer**, then *Value* is of the form *var=value* where *var* is the name of the environmental variable and *value* is its value. If *variable* is a **String**, then *Value* contains only the variable's value. If the variable does not exist, then an empty string will be returned.

Environmental variables are one way to pass information to your program at run time. Another way is to use the **Command** function to return the list of arguments that were initially passed to the program.

> **Tip**
>
> *If you need to create a temporary file in your program, check for an environmental variable called TEMP or TMP to get the path where the user prefers to create temporary files.*

Arguments
- *Value*—a **String** that contains the corresponding value for an environmental variable.
- *variable*—a **String** or **Integer** that selects an environmental variable. The first **Integer** value in the table is 1.

Examples
```
Private Sub Command1_Click()
Dim i As Integer
Dim e As String
Text1.Text = ""
i = 1
s = Environ(i)
Do While Len(s) > 0
    Text1.Text = Text1.Text & s & vbCrLf
    i = i + 1
    s = Environ(i)
Loop
End Sub
```

This routine displays all of the environmental variables in a system. It starts by selecting the value of the first variable in the table and appends it to the Text1 text box. It continues this process until there are no more variables in the table.

See Also   **Command** (function)

EOF

FUNCTION

CCE, LE, PE, EE

Syntax   *BValue* = **EOF** (*filenum*)

Usage   The **EOF** function returns a single **Boolean** value that indicates whether there is more data in the file to be processed. For files opened as output, this function will always return **True**. When reading binary files and random files with the **Get** statement, this function will return **True** when the last **Get** doesn't read an entire record.

Arguments
- *BValue*—a **Boolean** value when **True** means that the file pointer is at or past the end of file marker. When **False**, there is more data to be processed in the file.
- *CharCode*—a **Long** value that contains the numeric character code value.

Examples
```
Private Sub Command1_Click()
Dim s As String
On Error Resume Next
Text2.Text = ""
Open Text1.Text For Input As #1
If Err.Number <> 0 Then
    MsgBox "Can't open the input file: " & Err.Description
Else
    Do While Not EOF(1)
       Input #1, s
       Text2.Text = Text2.Text & s & vbCrLf
    Loop
    Close #1
End If
End Sub
```

This routine opens the file specified in Text1.Text. It then reads each line of the file and appends it to the Text2 text box until the **EOF** is reached. Then it closes the file and ends the routine.

See Also **Close** (statement), **Get** (statement), **Input** (statement), **Open** (function), **String** (data type), **Variant** (data type)

Erase

STATEMENT

CCE, LE, PE, EE

Syntax **Erase** *name* [,*name*] . . .

Usage The **Erase** statement initializes a list of array names to the empty state. It will also release the space for any dynamic arrays. You will have to either use the **ReDim** statement or the **Array** function to reacquire the space before you can use the array.

In fixed size arrays, numeric elements are set to zero, variable length strings are set to empty, and fixed length strings are initialized with zeros for each character. In fixed size arrays of **Variant**, each element will be initialized to empty and fixed size arrays of objects will set each element to **Nothing**.

Arguments *name*—the Visual Basic identifier containing the name of an array. Can be of type **Byte**, **Boolean**, **Currency**, **Date**, **Double**, **Integer**, **Long**, **Single**, **String**, or **Variant**.

Examples
```
Private Sub Command1_Click()
Dim i As Integer
Dim x(10) As Integer
Text1.Text = ""
Text2.Text = ""
```

```
For i = 1 To 10
    x(i) = i
Next i
For i = 1 To 10
    Text1.Text = Text1.Text & Format(x(i)) & vbCrLf
Next i
Erase x
For i = 1 To 10
    Text2.Text = Text2.Text & Format(x(i)) & vbCrLf
Next i
End Sub
```

This program declares and initializes an integer array with nonzero values. It then displays the contents of the array in text box Text1. Then the array is initialized using the **Erase** statement, and the array is displayed again in Text2.

See Also **Array** (function), **Byte** (data type), **Boolean** (data type), **Currency** (data type), **Date** (data type), **Dim** (statement), **Double** (data type), **Integer** (data type), **Long** (data type), **ReDim** (statement), **Single** (data type), **String** (data type), **Variant** (data type)

Err

OBJECT

CCE, LE, PE, EE

Usage The **Err** object contains a set of properties and methods that can be used to determine information about the last error that occurred. Visual Basic errors occur in the range of 0 to 65,535. User errors are created by adding your own error code to the constant *vbObjectError*, which is a very large negative number. Thus all user errors will be less than zero, and the number can be extracted by subtracting *vbObjectError*.

Tip

*Use the **On Error** statement to trap errors that would normally kill your program. Using the **On Error Resume Next** statement will continue processing after the error occurs, which leaves you free to test for an error condition immediately after the statement where you expect an error. **On Error GoTo** allows you to transfer control to a different block of code in your subroutine whenever an error occurs.*

Warning

*If you use the **On Error Resume Next** statement, be sure to reset the **Err** object by using the **Clear** method before executing any code that could cause an error. If the executed code is successful, the **Err** object will not be changed. That means the **Err.Number** property could potentially contain the results of a previous error, so checking this property could lead you to believe an error had occurred when it really hadn't.*

Properties
- **Err.Description**—a **String** value that provides a short text description of the error. This property will be automatically set for Visual Basic errors. For user-defined errors, this property should be set at the same time the **Number** property is set.

> **Warning**
>
> *If you create your own error code that duplicates a number already used by Visual Basic and fail to set the **Description**, the corresponding description from the Visual Basic error code will be returned.*

- **Err.HelpContext**—a **String** that contains a help file context ID number which references an entry in the help file.

> **Tip**
>
> *A help file must be compiled using the Windows Help Compiler available in the Professional and Enterprise editions of Visual Basic.*

- **Err.HelpFile**—a **String** that contains the name of the help file.
- **Err.LastDLLError**—a **Long** containing an error code from a call to DLL routine. Since DLL calls do not generate Visual Basic error conditions, it is important to check this property after each DLL call.
- **Err.Number**—a **Long** containing the error code. This is the default property for this object. A value of zero means that no error has occurred.

> **Tip**
>
> *The Visual Basic developers were very clever when implementing this object. By making the **Number** the default property for the **Err** object, programs that were written in previous versions of Visual Basic continue to work the same way (i.e., testing **Err** for a nonzero value). However, you should take advantage of the new object oriented view of **Err** to help prevent future incompatibilities.*

- **Err.Source**—a **String** containing the name of the component that failed. In a class object, it will be in the form of *Project.Class*. For all other modules, it will be in the form of *Project*.

Methods **Err.Clear**

Usage   This method clears the **Err** object. The **Clear** method is used automatically whenever an **On Error**, a **Resume**, an **Exit Sub**, an **Exit Function**, or an **Exit Property** statement is executed.

Err.Raise *number* [, *source* [, *description* [, *helpfile* [, *helpcontex*]]]]

Usage This method generates a run-time error.

Arguments
- *number*—a **Long** value that indicates the error number. Visual Basic errors are in the range of 0 to 65,535. User errors are created by adding the user error code to *vbObjectError* which is a very large negative number.
- *format*—a **String** containing the information about the source of the error. In a class object, it will be in the form of *Project.Class*. For all other modules, it will be in the form of *Project*.
- *description*—a **String** containing a description of the error.
- *helpfile*—a **String** containing the name of the help file that contains additional information about the error.
- *helpcontext*—a **String** containing the help file context information about the error.

Examples
```
Private Sub Command1_Click()
Dim x As Integer
On Error Resume Next
x = 1 / 0
If Err.Number <> 0 Then
    MsgBox Err.Description, vbOKOnly + vbMsgBoxHelpButton, "Reply OK to continue",
    Err.HelpFile, Err.HelpContext
End If
End Sub
```

This routine tries to divide one by zero. This will raise a run-time error, "Division by zero." The **On Error Resume Next** statement prevents the error from occurring and allows a test of the **Err** object. Then the message box will be displayed with a help button and the help file and help context. This lets the user see the help file message about division by zero.

See Also **Error** (function), **On Error** (statement), **Raise** (statement)

Error

FUNCTION

CCE, LE, PE, EE

Syntax *SValue* = **Error[$]**(*ErrorCode*)

Usage The **Error** function returns a text string with the text description of a Visual Basic error code. This is similar to the **Description** property of the **Err** object. If the error code is not a valid Visual Basic error code, then it will return the string "Application-defined or object-defined error."

Arguments
SValue—a **Variant** that contains text description of *ErrorCode*. If the **Error$** is used instead of **Error**, *SValue* will be a **String**.

ErrorCode—a **Long** value that contains a Visual Basic error code.

Examples
```
Private Sub Command1_Click()
If IsNumeric(Text1.Text) Then
    Text2.Text = Error(CLng(Text1.Text))
End If
End Sub
```

This routine displays the error description for the specified error code.

See Also **Err** (object), **Description** (property)

Error

OBJECT

CCE, LE, PE, EE

Usage The **Error** object contains errors that are generated by the Data Access Objects (DAO). These objects are contained in the **Errors** collection.

> **Warning**
>
> Do not confuse this object with the **Err** object. The **Err** object contains information about Visual Basic errors, while the **Error** object contains information about the DAO object.

Properties
- **Error.Description**—a **String** value that provides a short text description of the error. This property will be automatically set for Visual Basic errors. For user-defined errors, this property should be set at the same time the **Number** property is set.
- **Error.HelpContext**—a **String** that contains a help file context ID number which references an entry in the help file.

> **Tip**
>
> A help file must be compiled using the Windows Help Compiler available in the Professional and Enterprise editions of Visual Basic.

- **Error.HelpFile**—a **String** that contains the name of the help file.
- **Error.Number**—a **Long** containing the error code. This is the default property for this object. A value of zero means that no error has occurred.
- **Error.Source**—a **String** containing the name of the component that failed. In a class object, it will be in the form of *Project.Class*. For all other modules, it will be in the form of *Project*.

See Also **Err** (object), **Error** (function), **Errors** (collection)

Error

STATEMENT

CCE, LE, PE, EE

Syntax
: **Error** *ErrorCode*

Usage
: The **Error** statement generates a run-time error. This statement is obsolete and exists primarily to maintain compatibility with previous versions of Visual Basic. It has been replaced with the **Err.Raise** method.

Arguments
: *ErrorCode*—a **Long** value that contains the error code.

Examples
:
```
Private Sub Command1_Click()
On Error Resume Next
If IsNumeric(Text1.Text) Then
    Error CLng(Text1.Text)
    Text2.Text = Format(Err.Number)
    Text3.Text = Err.Description
    Text4.Text = Err.HelpContext
    Text5.Text = Err.HelpFile
    Text6.Text = Err.LastDllError
    Text7.Text = Err.Source
End If
End Sub
```

This routine raises the error code found in the Text1 text box and then displays the information contained in the **Err** object.

See Also
: **Err** (object)

Errors

COLLECTION

CCE, LE, PE, EE

Usage
: The **Errors** collection contains the set of errors that may be generated by a single Data Access Object operation. The original error may trip other errors. The last error in the collection will be the one that is assigned to the **Err** object.

Properties
: **Errors**(*index*)—an **Array** of **Error** objects. The range of values for *index* range from 0 to **Errors.Count** - 1.
  Errors.Count—an **Integer** containing the number of **Error** objects in the collection.

Methods
: ## Errors.Refresh

  Usage
  : This method gets a current copy of the errors generated by a Data Access Object.

See Also
: **DBEngine** (object), **Err** (object), **Error** (object)

Event

STATEMENT

CCE, LE, PE, EE

Syntax [**Public**] **Event** *EName* ([*arg* [, *arg*] . . .])

Usage The **Event** statement defines a subroutine that a user control can call in a user program.

Arguments
- *EName*—a valid Visual Basic identifier that describes the name of the event.
- *arg*—a subroutine argument in the following format:

  [**ByVal** | **ByRef**] *AName* [( )] [**As** *type*]

ByVal	the argument is passed by value to the event. Thus, the event is free to change the contents of the argument, and the calling control will not see the changes.
ByRef	the argument is passed by reference to the event. Any changes to the argument in the calling control will be seen by the calling control.

> **Tip**
>
> *When developing your own ActiveX controls, you should define the arguments to the events to be **ByVal** unless you really want the event to be able to send information back to the control. Using **ByRef** leaves open the possibility that someone using the control could change the contents of the argument, and this could cause unpredictable results in your control.*

- *AName*—the formal argument being passed to the event.
- [( )]—if present, indicates that the argument is an array.
- *type*—a valid Visual Basic type: **Byte**, **Boolean**, **Currency**, **Date**, **Double**, **Integer**, **Long**, **Single**, **String**, or **Variant**.

Examples
```
' UserControl1
Public Event Zap(z As String)

Private Sub Command1_Click()
RaiseEvent Zap(Text1.Text)
End Sub
' Program that references UserControl1 as
' UserControl11

Private Sub UserControl11_Zap(z As String)
MsgBox z
End Sub
```

This example consists of a user control and a program that uses it. The user control has a text box and a command button. After you enter text into the text box, click the button to trigger the Command1_Click event inside the user control. This action will use the **RaiseEvent** statement to trigger the Zap event inside the program. Inside the program, the Zap event for UserControl11 simply displays the argument using a message box.

See Also **RaiseEvent** (statement), **UserControl** (object)

Exit

STATEMENT

CCE, LE, PE, EE

Syntax
```
Exit Do
Exit For
Exit Function
Exit Property
Exit Sub
```

Usage The **Exit** statement is used to leave a block before it reaches its normal end point. Execution will continue as if the block of code completed normally.

> **Warning**
>
> Don't confuse the **Exit** statement with the **End** statement which stops the program. Also don't confuse the **Exit** statement with the **End Function**, **End Property**, or the **End Sub** statement, which indicate the end of a function, property, or subroutine.

- **Exit Do** leaves a **Do** . . . **Loop** and resumes execution at the end of the loop.
- **Exit For** leaves a **For** . . . **Next** loop and resumes execution after the **Next** statement.
- **Exit Function**, **Exit Property**, and **Exit Sub** will leave the routine as if the **End Function**, **End Property**, or **End Sub** were executed.

Examples
```
Private Sub Command1_Click()
Dim i As Integer
For i = 1 To 10
    If i = 5 Then Exit For
Next i
MsgBox "i = " & Format(i)
End Sub
```

This routine starts a **For** . . . **Next** loop and leaves it when the value of i is 5. This is confirmed by displaying a message box.

See Also **Do** (statement), **End** (statement), **For** (statement), **Function** (statement), **Property** (statement), **Sub** (statement)

Exp

FUNCTION

CCE, LE, PE, EE

Syntax *RValue* = **Exp** (*Number*)

Usage The **Exp** function will return the value of e raised to the *Number* power. The value of e is approximately 2.71828182845905. This is the inverse function of the natural log function, **Log**.

Arguments
- *RValue*—a **Double** that contains the value of e raised to the *Number* power.
- *Number*—a **Double** expression that is passed to the Exp function.

288 • The Visual Basic 5 Programmer's Reference

Examples
```
Private Sub Command1_Click()
If IsNumeric(Text1.Text) Then
    MsgBox Format(Exp(Text1.Text))
End If
End Sub
```

This routine will compute the exp of the value in the Text1 text box and display the results in a message box.

See Also **Log** (function)

Extender

OBJECT

CCE, LE, PE, EE

Usage The **Extender** object accesses the properties of the object's container. Listed below are the properties that are always available via the **Extender** object. Other properties may be available depending on the specific container.

Properties
- **Extender.Cancel**—a **Boolean** when **True** means that the control is the default cancel button for the container. When **False** means that the control is not the default cancel button for the container.
- **Extender.Default**—a **Boolean** when **True** means that the control is the default button for the container. When **False** means that the control is not the cancel button for the container.
- **Extender.Name**—a **String** that contains the name of the control that will be used to reference the control in a Visual Basic program. This property is read only at run time.
- **Extender.Parent**—an object that contains a reference to the **Form**, **Frame,** or other container that contains the control.
- **Extender.Visible**—a **Boolean** value when **True** means that the control is visible. When **False** means that the control is not visible.

Examples
```
' From the main program

Private Sub Form_Load()
MyControl1.Tag = "This value was set in the main program."
End Sub
' This is from the MyControl UserControl

Private Sub Command1_Click()
Text1.Text = "UserControl.Name: " & UserControl.Name
Text1.Text = Text1.Text & vbCrLf & "UserControl.Extender.Name: " & _
    UserControl.Extender.Name
Text1.Text = Text1.Text & vbCrLf & "UserControl.Parent.Name: " & _
    UserControl.Parent.Name
Text1.Text = Text1.Text & vbCrLf & "UserControl.Tag: " & UserControl.Tag
```

```
Text1.Text = Text1.Text & vbCrLf & "UserControl.Extender.Tag: " & _
    UserControl.Extender.Tag
Text1.Text = Text1.Text & vbCrLf & "UserControl.Parent.Tag: " & _
    UserControl.Parent.Tag
End Sub

Private Sub UserControl_Initialize()
UserControl.Tag = "The value was set in the UserControl_Initialize event."
End Sub
```

This example consists of a main program and a user control. The main program sets the **Tag** property of the MyControl user control. In the MyControl user control, the **Tag** property of the **UserControl** was also set. Running the program and pressing the command button will display various tag values in the text box inside the control. This shows that the way to get the tag information set in the main program is to use the **Extender** property of the **UserControl** object.

See Also   **UserControl** (object)

Field

OBJECT

Usage The **Field** object contains information about a field in the database.

Properties
- *FieldObject*.**AllowZeroLength**—a **Boolean** when **True** means that a zero length string is permitted when the data type is *text* or *memo*. **False** means that zero length strings are not permitted.
- *FieldObject*.**Attributes**—an **Integer** containing one or more attributes for a column (see Table F-1).

Attributes Name	Description
dbAutoIncrColumn	The field contains a unique value that was automatically incremented and can't be changed.
dbDescending	The field is sorted in descending order.
dbFixedField	The field size is fixed.
dbHyperlinkField	The field contains a hyperlink.
dbSystemField	The field contains information for replication.
dbUpdatableField	The data in the field can be changed.
dbVariableField	The field size can vary.

Table F-1: Attributes values.

- *FieldObject*.**CollatingOrder**—a **Long** value describing the sort order and how strings are compared (see Table F-2).

CollatingOrder Name	Value	Description
dbSortArabic	1025	Arabic.
dbSortChineseSimplified	2052	Simplified Chinese.
dbSortChineseTraditional	1028	Traditional Chinese.
dbSortCyrillic	1049	Cyrillic.
dbSortCzech	1029	Czech.
dbSortDutch	1043	Dutch.
dbSortGeneral	1033	English, French, German, Portuguese, Italian, and Modern Spanish.
dbSortGreek	1032	Greek.
dbSortHebrew	1037	Hebrew.
dbSortHungarian	1038	Hungarian.
dbSortIcelandic	1039	Icelandic.
dbSortJapanese	1041	Japanese.
dbSortKorean	1042	Korean.
dbSortNeutral	1024	Neutral.
dbSortNorwDan	1030	Norwegian or Danish.
dbSortPDXIntl	1033	Paradox International.
dbSortPDXNor	1030	Paradox Norwegian.
dbSortPDXSwe	1053	Paradox Swedish.
dbSortPolish	1045	Polish.
dbSortSlovenian	1060	Slovenian.
dbSortSpanish	1034	Spanish.

CollatingOrder Name	Value	Description
dbSortSwedFin	1053	Swedish or Finnish.
dbSortThai	1054	Thai.
dbSortTurkish	1055	Turkish.
dbSortUndefined	-1	Undefined.

Table F-2: CollatingOrder *values.*

- *FieldObject*.**DataUpdatable**—a **Boolean** when **True** means that the data can be updated. **False** means that data can't be updated.
- *FieldObject*.**DefaultValue**—a **Variant** containing the value that will be used if no value is supplied for the field.
- *FieldObject*.**FieldSize**—a **Long** containing the maximum size of the field in bytes for a long binary field or characters for a memo field.
- *FieldObject*.**ForeignName**—a **String** containing the name of a **Field** object in a foreign table corresponding to this field. Their relationship can be one to one or one to many or many to many.
- *FieldObject*.**Name**—a **String** containing the name of the field.
- *FieldObject*.**OrdinalPosition**—an **Integer** containing the relative position of the **Field** object within the **Fields** collection. The first **Field** in the collection has an **OrdinalPosition** of 0.
- *FieldObject*.**OrdinalValue**—a **Variant** when containing the original value of a field from the database.
- *FieldObject*.**Required**—a **Boolean** when **True** means that a non-null value is required. **False** means that null values are permitted.
- *FieldObject*.**Size**—a **Long** containing the maximum size in bytes of the field.
- *FieldObject*.**SourceField**—a **String** containing the original name of the field in the database.
- *FieldObject*.**SourceTable**—a **String** containing the original name of the table containing the field in the database.
- *FieldObject*.**Type**—an **Integer** value describing the type of the value (see Table F-3).

Type Name	Description
dbBigInt	Big integer data type.
dbBinary	Fixed length binary data, up to 255 bytes long.
dbBoolean	Boolean data type.
DbByte	Integer value one byte wide.
DbChar	Fixed length character string.
DbCurrency	Currency data type.
DbDate	Date/time data type.
DbDecimal	Decimal data type.
DbDouble	Double precision floating point data type.
DbFloat	Floating point data type.
DbGUID	Globally Unique Identifier data type.
DbInteger	16 bit integer data type.
DbLong	32 bit integer data type.
DbLongBinary	Long binary data type.
DbMemo	Memo data type.

Type Name	Description
DbNumeric	Numeric data type.
DbSingle	Single precision floating point data type.
DbText	Field data type.
dbTime	Time data type.
DbTimeStamp	Time stamp data type.
DbVarBinary	Variable length binary, up to 255 bytes long.

Table F-3: Type *values*.

- *FieldObject*.**ValidateOnSet**—a **Boolean** when **True** means that field's **Value** is validated immediately. **False** means that the field will be validated when the record is updated.
- *FieldObject*.**ValidationRule**—a **String** value containing an SQL Where clause without the Where clause. If this clause returns **True** the field is considered valid, otherwise an error will occur.
- *FieldObject*.**ValidationText**—a **String** containing the text that will be displayed when a validation error occurs.
- *FieldObject*.**Value**—a **Variant** containing the data from the column.
- *FieldObject*.**VisibleValue**—a **Variant** containing the most current value of the field from the database, when performing an optimistic batch update.

Methods

FieldObject.**AppendChunk** *source*

Usage This method appends a chunk of data to the end of value of a *dbMemo* or *dbLongBinary* field.

Arguments
- *source*—an expression containing the data to be appended to field's current value.

property = *FieldObject*.**CreateProperty** ([*name*] [, [*type*] [, [*value*] [, DDL]]])

Usage This method is used to create a user defined **Property** object.

Arguments
- *property*—an object variable that will contain the new property object.
- *name*—a **String** containing the name of the property. Must begin with a letter and can be followed by letters, numbers or an underscore ("_").
- *type*—a value selected from Table F-4 below.

type Name	Description
dbBigInt	Big Integer.
dbBinary	Binary.
dbBoolean	Boolean.
dbByte	Byte.
dbChar	Character.
dbCurrency	Currency.
dbDate	Date.

type Name	Description
dbDecimal	Decimal.
dbDouble	Double.
dbFloat	Float.
dbGUID	Globally unique identifier.
dbInteger	Integer.
dbLong	Long.
dbLongBinary	Long binary.
DbMemo	Memo.
DbNumeric	Numeric.
DbSingle	Single.
DbText	Text.
DbTime	Time.
dbTimeStamp	Time stamp.
DbVarBinary	Variable length binary data (up to 255 bytes).

Table F-4: type values.

- *value*—a **Variant** containing the initial value for the property.
- *DDL*—a **Boolean** when **True** means that the user cannot change this property value without the *dbSecWriteDef* permission. When **False** this permission is not required to change the value.

value = *FieldObject*.GetChunk (*offset, number*)

Usage This method retrieves a block of data from a Memo or Long Binary field.

Arguments
- *value*—a **Variant** variable that will contain the result of the **GetChunk** method.
- *offset*—a **Long** containing the starting position of the data to be retrieved.
- *number*—a **Long** containing the number of bytes to be returned.

See Also **Fields** (collection)

Fields

COLLECTION

PE, EE

Usage The **Fields** collection is used by Data Access Objects (DAO) to contain information about the fields in a table or recordset object.

Properties
- *FieldsCollection*.**Count**—an **Integer** containing the number of **Field** objects in the collection.

Methods

FieldsCollection.Append *object*

Usage This method adds a **Field** object to the collection.

Arguments
- *object*—a reference to a **Field** object to be added to the collection.

FieldsCollection.Delete *objectname*

Usage This method removes a **Field** object from the collection.

Arguments *objectname*—a **String** containing the name of the **Field** object to be removed from the collection.

FieldsCollection.Refresh

Usage This method gets a current copy of the **Fields** contained in the collection. This is important in a multi-user environment where more than one user may be making changes in the **Databases** collection.

See Also **Database** (object), **Databases** (collection), **Field** (object), **Recordset** (object), **Recordsets** (collection), **Relation** (object), **Relations** (collection), **TableDef** (object), **TableDefs** (collection)

FileAttr

FUNCTION

CCE, LE, PE, EE

Syntax `AValue = FileAttr ( filenum , [ returninfo ] )`

Usage The **FileAttr** function returns the file mode value that was used with the file that was opened with the **Open** statement.

Arguments *AValue*—an **Integer** value containing the file's File Mode. Each bit in the File that Mode has a specific meaning as listed in Table F-5 below.

File Mode	Value
Input	1
Output	2
Random	4
Append	8
Binary	32

Table F-5: File Mode *values.*

filenum—an **Integer** value that contains the file number of the open file.

returninfo—an **Integer** value, when 1 will retrieve information about the file mode. When 2, will retrieve an operating system file handle on 16 bit systems only. If omitted, *returninfo* will default to 1.

Examples
```
Private Sub Command1_Click()
Dim i As Integer
On Error Resume Next
Check1.Value = 0
```

```
        Check2.Value = 0
        Check3.Value = 0
        Check4.Value = 0
        Check5.Value = 0
        Open Text1.Text For Input As #1
        If Err.Number = 0 Then
            i = FileAttr(1)
            If i And 1 Then Check1.Value = 1
            If i And 2 Then Check2.Value = 1
            If i And 4 Then Check3.Value = 1
            If i And 8 Then Check4.Value = 1
            If i And 32 Then Check5.Value = 1
        Else
            MsgBox Err.Description

        End If
        Close #1
    End Sub
```

This routine opens the file specified in the text box, Text1, and will display the file attributes in a series of check boxes.

See Also **FileDateTime** (function), **FileLen** (function), **Open** (statement)

FileCopy

STATEMENT

CCE, LE, PE, EE

Syntax **FileCopy** *fromfile* , *tofile*

Usage The **FileCopy** statement copies one file to another. This is similar to the MS-DOS copy command.

> **Warning**
>
> The **FileCopy** statement cannot copy files that are open. The **FileCopy** statement will replace the tofile *without any warnings.*

Arguments
- *fromfile*—a **String** expression containing the name of the source file.
- *tofile*—a **String** expression containing the name of the destination file.

Examples
```
Private Sub Command1_Click()
If Len(Dir(Text1.Text)) = 0 Then
    MsgBox "From file does not exist."
```

```
ElseIf Len(Dir(Text2.Text)) <> 0 Then
    MsgBox "To file exists."
Else
    FileCopy Text1.Text, Text2.Text
    MsgBox "Done."
End If
End Sub
```

This routine verifies that the *fromfile* exists and that the *tofile* doesn't exist and then performs the file copy.

See Also   **Dir** (statement), **Name** (statement)

FileDateTime   FUNCTION

CCE, LE, PE, EE

Syntax   `DValue = FileDateTime ( filename )`

Usage   The **FileDateTime** function returns the date and time the file was created or last modified.

Arguments
- *DValue*—a **Date** value containing the date and time the file was created or last modified.
- *filename*—a **String** value containing the name of the file.

Examples
```
Private Sub Command1_Click()
If Len(Dir(Text1.Text)) > 0 Then
    Text2.Text = Format(FileDateTime(Text1.Text))
Else
    Text2.Text = "File does not exist."
End If
End Sub
```

This routine verifies that the filename in the Text1 text box exists and then displays the date and time the file was created or last modified in the Text2 text box.

See Also   **FileAttr** (function), **FileLen** (function)

FileLen   FUNCTION

CCE, LE, PE, EE

Syntax   `LValue = FileLen ( filename )`

Usage   The **FileLen** function returns the size of the file.

Arguments
- *LValue*—a **Long** value containing the size of the file in bytes.
- *filename*—a **String** value containing the name of the file.

| Examples | ```
Private Sub Command1_Click()
If Len(Dir(Text1.Text)) > 0 Then
    Text2.Text = Format(FileLen(Text1.Text))
Else
    Text2.Text = "File does not exist."
End If
End Sub
``` |
|---|---|

This routine verifies that the filename in the Text1 text box exists and then displays the size of the file in the Text2 text box.

See Also **FileAttr** (function), **FileDateTime** (function)

FileListBox

CONTROL

CCE, LE, PE, EE

Usage
The **FileListBox** control is an intrinsic control that displays a list of files in the specified directory.

Properties
- *FileListControl*.**Appearance**—an **Integer** value (see Table F-6) that determines how the file list box will appear on the form.

AppearanceValue	Description
0	The file list box displays without the 3D effects.
1	The file list box displays with 3D effects (default value).

Table F-6: Appearance values.

- *FileListControl*.**Archive**—a **Boolean** when **True**, means that files with the archive bit set will be displayed (default). When **False**, no files with the archive bit will be displayed.
- *FileListControl*.**BackColor**—a **Long** that contains the suggested value for the background color of the control. The **BackColor** and **ForeColor** must both be solid to display text. If you choose a color that is dithered, it will be changed to the nearest solid color.
- *FileListControl*.**Container**—an object that sets or returns the container of the control at run time. This property cannot be set at design time.
- *FileListControl*.**DragIcon**—an object that contains the picture value of an icon. At design time, you can specify an icon file that has a file type of .ICO.

> **Tip**
>
> *This value can be created by copying the value from another control's **DragIcon** value, a form's icon, or by using the **LoadPicture** function.*
```

- *FileListControl*.**DragMode**—an **Integer** value (see Table F-7) specifying how the control will respond to a drag request.

> **Tip**
>
> Setting **DragMode** to vbAutomatic will automatically begin a drag operation when the user clicks on the control. However, the control will not respond to the usual mouse events (**Click, DblClick**).

DragMode Name	Value	Description
vbManual	0	The **Drag** method must be used to begin a drag-and-drop operation (default value).
vbAutomatic	1	The source control will automatically begin a drag-and-drop operation when the user clicks on the control.

Table F-7: **DragMode** values.

- *FileListControl*.**Enabled**—a **Boolean** value when **True** means that the control will respond to events. When **False**, the control will not respond to events.
- *FileListControl*.**FileName**—a **String** value that contains the name of the file selected from the list box. If no file is selected, a **FileName** will be set to an empty string. Setting **FileName** will also set the default drive and path information.
- *FileListControl*.**Font**—an object that contains information about the character font used by this object.

> **Tip**
>
> The **Font** object should be used in place of the other **Font** properties, since it offers more functionality than the individual properties.

- *FileListControl*.**FontBold**—a **Boolean** when **True**, means that the characters display in bold. **False** means that the characters display normally.
- *FileListControl*.**FontItalic**—a **Boolean** when **True**, means that the characters display in italics. **False** means that the characters display normally.
- *FileListControl*.**FontName**—a **String** that specifies the name of the font that should be used to display the characters in this control.
- *FileListControl*.**FontSize**—a **Single** that specifies the point size that should be used to display the characters in the control.
- *FileListControl*.**FontStrikethru**—a **Boolean** when **True**, means that the characters display with a line through the center. **False** means that the characters display normally.
- *FileListControl*.**FontUnderlined**—a **Boolean** when **True**, means that the characters display with a line beneath them. **False** means that the characters display normally.
- *FileListControl*.**Height**—a **Single** that contains the height of the control.
- *FileListControl*.**HelpContextID**—a **Long** that contains a help file context ID number which references an entry in the help file. When the user presses the F1 key while this control is active, the corresponding entry in the help file will automatically be displayed. A value of zero means that no context number was specified.

FileListBox • 299

> **Tip**
>
> *A help file must be compiled using the Windows Help Compiler available in the Professional and Enterprise editions of Visual Basic.*

- *FileListControl*.**Hidden**—a **Boolean** when **True**, means that files with the hidden bit set will be displayed. When **False**, no files with the hidden bit will be displayed (default).
- *FileListControl*.**hWnd**—a **Long** that contains a Windows handle to the control.

> **Tip**
>
> *The **hWnd** property is most useful when making calls to Windows API functions. Since this value can change during execution, do not save the value into a variable for later use.*

- *FileListControl*.**Index**—an **Integer** that uniquely identifies a control in a control array.
- *FileListControl*.**Left**—a **Single** that contains the distance measured in twips between the left edge of the control and the left edge of the control's container.
- *FileListControl*.**List**(*index*)—an array of **String** values displayed in the drop-down part of the **FileListBox**. The number of elements in this array can be found in the **ListCount** property.

> **Tip**
>
> *The first element of the **List** array is zero, while the last array element is **ListCount** -1.*

- *FileListControl*.**ListCount**—an **Integer** value containing the number of elements in the **List**.
- *FileListControl*.**ListIndex**—an **Integer** value containing the index of the selected item from the drop-down box. If no value was selected, **ListIndex** will be set to -1.
- *FileListControl*.**MouseIcon**—a picture object (a bitmap, icon, or metafile) that will be used as a cursor when the **MousePointer** property is set to 99. Note that Visual Basic does not support color cursors from a .CUR file. A color icon from a .ICO file should be used instead.
- *FileListControl*.**MousePointer**—an **Integer** value (see Table F-8) that contains the value of the cursor that should be displayed when the cursor is moved over this control. Use *vbCustom* to display the custom icon stored in the **MouseIcon** property.

Cursor Name	Value	Description
vbDefault	0	Shape determined by the object (default value)
vbArrow	1	Arrow
vbCrosshair	2	Crosshair
vbIbeam	3	I beam
vbIconPointer	4	Square inside a square
vbSizePointer	5	Four sided arrow (north, south, east, west)
vbSizeNESW	6	Two sided arrow (northeast, southwest)
vbSizeNS	7	Two sided arrow (north, south)
vbSizeNWSE	8	Two sided arrow (northwest, southeast)

Cursor Name	Value	Description
vbSizeWE	9	Two sided arrow (west, east)
vbUpArrow	10	Single sided arrow pointing north
vbHourglass	11	Hourglass
vbNoDrop	12	No Drop
vbArrowHourglass	13	An arrow and an Hourglass
vbArrowQuestion	14	An arrow and a question mark
vbSizeAll	15	Size all
vbCustom	99	Custom icon from the **MouseIcon** property of this control

Table F-8: **Cursor** values.

- *FileListControl*.**MultiSelect**—an **Integer** value (see Table F-9) that specifies how the file list box will appear on the form.

MultiSelectValue	Description
0	Multiple selections are not allowed.
1	Multiple items can be selected with either a mouse click or by pressing the space bar.
2	Multiple items can be selected by selecting one item with the mouse and then pressing the Shift key while selecting another item. All items between the two will be selected.

Table F-9: **MultiSelect** values.

- *FileListControl*.**Name**—a **String** that contains the name of the control that will be used to reference the control in a Visual Basic program. This property is read only at run-time.
- *FileListControl*.**Normal**—a **Boolean** when **True**, means that files with the normal bit set will be displayed (default). When **False**, no files with the normal bit will be displayed.
- *FileListControl*.**OLEDragMode**—an **Integer** value (see Table F-10) that describes how the control will respond to OLE drag operations.

> **Note**
>
> When the **DragMode** is **True**, the standard Visual Basic drag-and-drop functions will override the OLE drag-and-drop functions.

OLEDragMode Name	Value	Description
vbOLEDragManual	0	All drag requests will be handled by the programmer (default value).
vbOLEDragAutomatic	1	The control responds to all OLE drag request automatically.

Table F-10: **OLEDragMode** values.

- *FileListControl*.**OLEDropMode**—an **Integer** value (see Table F-11) that describes how the control will respond to OLE drop operations.

OLEDropMode Name	Value	Description
vbOLEDropNone	0	The control does not accept OLE drops. The cursor is changed to the No Drop cursor (default value).
vbOLEDropManual	1	The control responds to OLE drops under the program's control (manual).
vbOLEDropAutomatic	2	The control automatically accepts OLE drops if it recognizes the format of the data object.

Table F-11: **OLEDropMode** *values.*

- *FileListControl*.**Parent**—an object that contains a reference to the **Form**, **Frame,** or other container that contains this control.
- *FileListControl*.**Path**—a **String** containing the path to the directory to be displayed in the **FileListBox** control.

Tip

*This property can be set using the **DirListBox** and the **DriveListBox**.*

- *FileListControl*.**Pattern**—a **String** containing one or more directory wild cards separated by semicolons (i.e., "*.TXT;*.ME;*.1ST" could be used to select text files).
- *FileListControl*.**ReadOnly**—a **Boolean** when **True**, means that files with the read-only bit set will be displayed. When **False**, no files with the read-only bit will be displayed (default).
- *FileListControl*.**RightToLeft**—a **Boolean** value when **True** means that the text is displayed from right to left. When **False** means that the text is displayed from left to right. A bi-directional version of Windows is required to set this property to true.
- *FileListControl*.**Selected**(*index*)—a **Boolean** array containing one entry for each entry in the **List** property. When **True**, the file is selected. When **False**, the file is not selected.
- *FileListControl*.**System**—a **Boolean** when **True**, means that files with the system bit set will be displayed. When **False**, no files with the system bit will be displayed (default).
- *FileListControl*.**TabIndex**—an Integer that determines the order that a user will tab through the objects on a form.
- *FileListControl*.**TabStop**—a **Boolean** value when **True** means that the user can tab to this object. When **False**, means that this control will be skipped to the next control in the **TabIndex** order.
- *FileListControl*.**Tag**—a **String** that can hold programmer specific information. This property is not used by Visual Basic.
- *FileListControl*.**ToolTipText**—a **String** that holds a text value that can be displayed as a **ToolTip** box that is displayed whenever the cursor is held over the control for about one second.
- *FileListControl*.**Top**—a **Single** that contains the distance measured in twips between the top edge of the control and the top edge of the control's container.

- *FileListControl.***Visible**—a **Boolean** value when **True** means that the control is visible. When **False** means that the control is not visible.

> **Tip**
>
> *This property can be used to hide the control until the program is ready to display it.*

- *FileListControl.***WhatsThisHelpID**—a **Long** that contains a help file context ID number references an entry in the help file. This provides a What's This PopUp help display in response to the What's This button in the upper right corner of the window.
- *FileListControl.***Width**—a **Single** that contains the width of the control.

Methods

*FileListControl.*Drag [*DragAction*]

Usage   This method begins, ends, or cancels a drag operation.

Arguments   *DragAction*—an **Integer** that contains a value selected from Table F-12 below.

DragAction Name	Value	Description
vbCancel	0	Cancels any drag operation in progress.
vbBeginDrag	1	Begins a drag operation (default).
vbEndDrag	2	Ends a drag operation and drops *object*.

Table F-12: DragAction *values.*

*FileListControl.*Move *Left* [, *Top* [, *Width* [, *Height*]]]

Usage   This method changes the position and the size of the **CheckBox** control. The **ScaleMode** of the **Form** or other container object that holds the animation control will determine the units used to specify the coordinates.

Arguments
- *Left*—a **Single** that specifies the new position of the left edge of the control.
- *Top*—a **Single** that specifies the new position of the top edge of the control.
- *Width*—a **Single** that specifies the new width of the control.
- *Height*—a **Single** that specifies the new height of the control.

*FileListControl.*OLEDrag

Usage   This method begins an **OLEDrag** and drop operation. Invoking this method will trigger the **OLEStartDrag** event.

FileListControl.Refresh

Usage   This method redraws the contents of the control.

FileListControl.SetFocus

Usage   This method transfers the focus from the form or control that currently has the focus to this control. To receive the focus, this control must be enabled and visible.

FileListControl.ShowWhatsThis

Usage   This method displays the ShowWhatsThis help information for this control.

FileListControl.ZOrder [*position*]

Usage   This method specifies the position of the file list control relative to the other objects on the form.

> **Tip**
>
> *Note that there are three layers of objects on a form: the back layer is the drawing space which contains the results of the graphical methods, the middle layer contains graphical objects and* **Labels**, *and the top layer contains nongraphical controls such as the* **FileListControl**. *The* **ZOrder** *method only affects how the objects are arranged within a single layer.*

Arguments   • *position*—an **Integer** that specifies the relative position of this object. A value of 0 means that the control is positioned at the head of the list, a value of 1 means that the control will be placed at the end of the list.

Events   ### Private Sub *FileListControl*_Click([*index* As Integer])

Usage   This event occurs when the user clicks a mouse button to select an item in the drop-down list or selects an item from the drop-down list using the keyboard.

Arguments   • *index*—an **Integer** that uniquely identifies a control in a control array. This argument is not present if the control is not part of a control array.

Private Sub *FileListControl*_DblClick([*index* As Integer])

Usage   This event occurs when the user double-clicks a mouse button to select an item in the list or selects an item from the list using the keyboard.

Arguments   • *index*—an **Integer** that uniquely identifies a control in a control array. This argument is not present if the control is not part of a control array.

Private Sub *FileListControl*_DragDrop([*index* As Integer ,] *source* As Control, *x* As Single, *y* As Single)

Usage This event occurs when a drag-and-drop operation is completed by using the **Drag** method with an *DragAction* value of *vbEndDrag*.

> **Tip**
>
> When using drag-and-drop operations, use the **DragOver** event to determine what the cursor should look like while the cursor moves over the control.

Arguments
- *index*—an **Integer** that uniquely identifies a control in a control array. This argument is not present if the control is not part of a control array.
- *source*—a control object that is the control that is being dragged.

> **Tip**
>
> You can access a property or method from the source control by using *source.property* or *source.method*. You can determine the type of object or control by using the **TypeOf** operator.

- *x*—a **Single** that contains the horizontal location of the mouse pointer.
- *y*—a **Single** that contains the vertical location of the mouse pointer.

Private Sub *FileListControl*_DragOver([*index* As Integer ,] *source* As Control, *x* As Single, *y* As Single, *state* As Integer)

Usage This event occurs while a drag operation is in progress and the cursor is moved over the control.

> **Tip**
>
> When using drag-and-drop operations, use the **DragOver** event to determine what the cursor should look like while the cursor moves over the control. When **state** is 0, you can change the cursor to a No Drop (vbNoDrop) cursor or highlight the field that the cursor is near. When **state** is 1, you can undo the changes you made when the **state** was 0.

Arguments
- *index*—an **Integer** that uniquely identifies a control in a control array. This argument is not present if the control is not part of a control array.
- *source*—a control object that is the control that is being dragged.

> **Tip**
>
> You can access a property or method from the source control by using *source.property* or *source.method*. You can determine the type of object or control by using the **TypeOf** operator.

- *x*—a **Single** that contains the horizontal location of the mouse pointer.
- *y*—a **Single** that contains the vertical location of the mouse pointer.
- *state*—an **Integer** value (see Table F-13) that indicates the state of the object being dragged.

state Name	Value	Description
vbEnter	0	The dragged object is entering range of the control.
vbLeave	1	The dragged object is leaving range of the control.
vbOver	2	The dragged object has moved from one position over the control to another.

Table F-13: state values.

Private Sub *FileListControl_*GotFocus ([*index* As Integer])

Usage   This event occurs when the control is given focus.

Tip

You can use this routine to display help or other information in a status bar.

Arguments   *index*—an **Integer** that uniquely identifies a control in a control array. This argument is not present if the control is not part of a control array.

Private Sub *FileListControl_*KeyDown ([*index* As Integer ,] *keycode* As Integer, *shift* As Single)

Usage   This event occurs when a key is pressed while the control has the focus.

Arguments
- *index*—an **Integer** that uniquely identifies a control in a control array. This argument is not present if the control is not part of a control array.
- *keycode*—an **Integer** that contains information about which key was pressed.
- *shift*—an **Integer** value (see Table F-14) that contains information about the Shift and Alt keys that were pushed when the mouse button was pressed. These values can be added together if more than one key was down. For instance, a value of 5 would mean that the Shift and Alt keys were both down when the mouse button was pressed.

shift Name	Value	Description
vbShiftMask	1	The Shift key was pressed.
vbCtrlMask	2	The Ctrl key was pressed.
vbAltMask	4	The Alt key was pressed.

Table F-14: shift values.

Private Sub *FileListControl*_KeyPress([*index* As Integer ,] *keychar* As Integer)

Usage   This event occurs whenever a key is pressed while the control has the focus.

Arguments
- *index*—an **Integer** that uniquely identifies a control in a control array. This argument is not present if the control is not part of a control array.
- *keychar*—an **Integer** that contains the ASCII character that was pressed.

Private Sub *ComoBoxControl*_KeyUp ([*index* As Integer ,] *keycode* As Integer, *shift* As Single)

Usage   This event occurs when a key is released while the control has the focus.

Arguments
- *index*—an **Integer** that uniquely identifies a control in a control array. This argument is not present if the control is not part of a control array.
- *keycode*—an **Integer** that contains information about which key was released.
- *shift*—an **Integer** value (see Table F-15) that contains information about the Shift and Alt keys that were pushed when the mouse button was pressed. These values can be added together if more than one key was down. For instance, a value of 5 would mean that the Shift and Alt keys were both down when the mouse button was pressed.

shift Name	Value	Description
vbShiftMask	1	The Shift key was pressed.
vbCtrlMask	2	The Ctrl key was pressed.
vbAltMask	4	The Alt key was pressed.

Table F-15: *shift values.*

Private Sub *FileListControl*_LostFocus ([*index* As Integer])

Usage   This event occurs when the control loses focus.

Tip

This routine is useful in performing data verification.

Arguments
- *index*—an **Integer** that uniquely identifies a control in a control array. This argument is not present if the control is not part of a control array.

Private Sub *FileListControl_OLECompleteDrag*([*index* As Integer ,] *effect* As Long)

Usage
This event tells the source control the results of an OLE drag-and-drop operation. This is the final event to occur in the series of actions that make up an OLE drag-and-drop operation.

Arguments
- *index*—an **Integer** that uniquely identifies a control in a control array. This argument is not present if the control is not part of a control array.
- *effect*—a **Long** (see Table F-16) that returns the status of the OLE drag-and-drop operation.

effect Name	Value	Description
vbDropEffectNone	0	The operation was canceled or the target control can't accept the drop operation.
vbDropEffectCopy	1	The operation copied data from the source control to the target control. The original data is unchanged.
vbDropEffectMove	2	The operation results in a link from the original data to the target control.

Table F-16: effect *values*.

Private Sub *FileListControl_OLEDragDrop*([*index* As Integer ,] *data* As DataObject, *effect* As Long, *button* As Integer, *shift* As Single, *x* As Single, *y* As Single)

Usage
This event tells the source control the results of an OLE drag-and-drop operation. This is the final event to occur in the series of actions that make up an OLE drag-and-drop operation.

Arguments
- *index*—an **Integer** that uniquely identifies a control in a control array. This argument is not present if the control is not part of a control array.
- *data*—a **DataObject** that contains the formats that the source control will provide. If the data is not contained in the **DataObject**, then it can be retrieved with the **GetData** method.
- *effect*—a **Long** value (see Table F-17) that returns the status of the OLE drag-and-drop operation.

effect Name	Value	Description
vbDropEffectNone	0	The operation was canceled or the target control can't accept the drop operation.
vbDropEffectCopy	1	The operation copied data from the source control to the target control. The original data is unchanged.
vbDropEffectMove	2	The operation results in a link from the original data to the target control.

Table F-17: effect *values*.

- *button*—an **Integer** value (see Table F-18) that contains information about the mouse buttons that were pressed. These values can be added together if more than one button was pushed. For instance, a value of 3 means that both the left and right buttons were pressed. A value of 0 means that no buttons were pressed.

button Name	Value	Description
vbLeftButton	1	The left button was pressed.
vbRightButton	2	The right button was pressed.
vbMiddleButton	4	The middle button was pressed.

Table F-18: *button values.*

- *shift*—an **Integer** value (see Table F-19) that contains information about the Shift and Alt keys that were pushed when the mouse button was released. These values can be added together if more than one key was down. For instance, a value of 5 would mean that the Shift and Alt keys were both down when the mouse button was released. A value of 0 means that none of these keys were pressed.

shift Name	Value	Description
vbShiftMask	1	The Shift key was pressed.
vbCtrlMask	2	The Ctrl key was pressed.
vbAltMask	4	The Alt key was pressed.

Table F-19: *shift values.*

- *x*—a **Single** that contains the horizontal location of the mouse pointer.
- *y*—a **Single** that contains the vertical location of the mouse pointer.

Private Sub *FileListControl_OLEDragOver*([*index* As Integer ,] *data* As DataObject, *effect* As Long, *button* As Integer, *shift* As Single, *x* As Single, *y* As Single, *state* As Integer)

Usage   This event happens when an OLE drag-and-drop operation is in progress.

Arguments
- *index*—an **Integer** that uniquely identifies a control in a control array. This argument is not present if the control is not part of a control array.
- *data*—a **DataObject** that contains the formats that the source control will provide. If the data is not contained in the **DataObject**, then it can be retrieved with the **GetData** method.
- *effect*—a **Long** (see Table F-20) that returns the status of the OLE drag-and-drop operation.

effect Name	Value	Description
vbDropEffectNone	0	The operation was canceled or the target control can't accept the drop operation.
vbDropEffectCopy	1	The operation copied data from the source control to the target control. The original data is unchanged.
vbDropEffectMove	2	The operation results in a link from the original data to the target control.

Table F-20: effect values.

- *button*—an **Integer** value (see Table F-21) that contains information about the mouse buttons that were pressed. These values can be added together if more than one button was pushed. For instance, a value of 3 means that both the left and right buttons were pressed. A value of 0 means that no buttons were pressed.

button Name	Value	Description
vbLeftButton	1	The left button was pressed.
vbRightButton	2	The right button was pressed.
vbMiddleButton	4	The middle button was pressed.

Table F-21: button values.

- *shift*—an **Integer** value (see Table F-22) that contains information about the Shift and Alt keys that were pushed when the mouse button was released. These values can be added together if more than one key was down. For instance, a value of 5 would mean that the Shift and Alt keys were both down when the mouse button was released. A value of 0 means that none of these keys were pressed.

shift Name	Value	Description
vbShiftMask	1	The Shift key was pressed.
vbCtrlMask	2	The Ctrl key was pressed.
vbAltMask	4	The Alt key was pressed.

Table F-22: shift values.

- *x*—a **Single** that contains the horizontal location of the mouse pointer.
- *y*—a **Single** that contains the vertical location of the mouse pointer.
- *state*—an **Integer** value (see Table F-23) that indicates the state of the object being dragged.

state Name	Value	Description
vbEnter	0	The dragged object is entering range of the control.
vbLeave	1	The dragged object is leaving range of the control.
vbOver	2	The dragged object has moved from one position over the control to another.

Table F-23: state values.

Private Sub *FileListControl_OLEGiveFeedback* ([*index* As Integer ,] *effect* As Long)

Usage This event tells the source control what is happening while the OLE drag-and-drop operation is in progress. This event occurs after the **OLEDragOver** event.

> **Tip**
>
> *You may want to use this event to change the cursor to reflect what can happen in the remote object.*

Arguments
- *index*—an **Integer** that uniquely identifies a control in a control array. This argument is not present if the control is not part of a control array.
- *effect*—a **Long** (see Table F-24) that returns the status of the OLE drag-and-drop operation.

effect Name	Value	Description
vbDropEffectNone	0	The operation was canceled or the target control can't accept the drop operation.
vbDropEffectCopy	1	The operation copied data from the source control to the target control. The original data is unchanged.
vbDropEffectMove	2	The operation results in a link from the original data to the target control.
vbDropEffectScroll	&H80000000	The target control is about to scroll or is scrolling. This value may be added to the other *shift* values.

Table F-24: effect *values.*

Private Sub *FileListControl_OLESetData*([*index* As Integer ,] *data* As DataObject, *DataFormat* As Integer)

Usage This event happens in response to the target object performing a **GetData** method on *data*. This routine will respond by using the **SetData** method with the desired data using the **DataObject** *data*.

Arguments
- *index*—an **Integer** that uniquely identifies a control in a control array. This argument is not present if the control is not part of a control array.
- *data*—a **DataObject** that will contain the data to be returned to the target object.
- *format*—an **Integer** value (see Table F-25) that contains the format of the data.

format Name	Value	Description
vbCFText	1	Text (.TXT files)
vbCFBitmap	2	Bitmap (.BMP files)
vbCFMetafile	3	Metafile (.WMF files)
vbCFEDIB	8	Device independent bitmap (DIB)

format Name	Value	Description
vbCFPallette	9	Color palette
vbCFEMetafile	14	Enhanced metafile (.EMF files)
vbCFFiles	15	List of files
vbCFRTF	-16639	Rich Text Format (.RTF files)

Table F-25: format *values.*

Private Sub *FileListControl*_OLEStartDrag ([*index* As Integer ,] *data* As DataObject, *AllowedEffects* As Long)

Usage   This event starts an OLE drag-and-drop operation.

Arguments
- *index*—an **Integer** that uniquely identifies a control in a control array. This argument is not present if the control is not part of a control array.
- *data*—a **DataObject** that will contain the formats that the source object is willing to provide to the target object. It may optionally contain the data to be transferred.
- *AllowedEffects*—a **Long** (see Table F-26) that contains the effects that the target object can request from the source object. The *AllowedEffects* can be added together if the source object supports more than one effect. Note that the target object can always use the *vbDropEffectNone* effect.

AllowedEffects Name	Value	Description
vbDropEffectNone	0	The target can't copy the data.
vbDropEffectCopy	1	The target can copy the data and the source will keep the data unchanged.
vbDropEffectMove	2	The target can copy the data and the source will delete the data.

Table F-26: AllowedEffects *values.*

Private Sub *FileListControl*_PathChange([*index* As Integer])

Usage   This event occurs anytime the **Path** property is changed either directly or by changing the **FileName** property.

Arguments
- *index*—an **Integer** that uniquely identifies a control in a control array. This argument is not present if the control is not part of a control array.

Private Sub *FileListControl*_PatternChange ([*index* As Integer])

Usage   This event occurs anytime the **Pattern** property is changed, either directly or by changing the **FileName** property.

Arguments
- *index*—an **Integer** that uniquely identifies a control in a control array. This argument is not present if the control is not part of a control array.

Private Sub *FileListControl*_Scroll ([*index* As Integer])

Usage This event is called each time the scroll bar is repositioned in the drop-down box.

Arguments • *index*—an **Integer** that uniquely identifies a control in a control array. This argument is not present if the control is not part of a control array.

Examples
```
Private Sub Command1_Click()

Dim i As Integer

Text2.Text = ""

For i = 0 To File1.ListCount--1
    If File1.Selected(i) Then
        Text2.Text = Text2.Text & File1.List(i) & vbCrLf
    End If
Next i

End Sub

Private Sub Dir1_Change()

File1.Path = Dir1.Path
File1.Refresh

End Sub

Private Sub Drive1_Change()

Dir1.Path = Drive1.Drive
Dir1.Refresh

End Sub

Private Sub Text1_Change()

File1.Pattern = Text1.Text

End Sub
```

This program will cascade changes from the **DriveListBox** to the **DirListBox** and then to the **FileListBox**. Changing the information in Text1 text box will change the **Pattern** property in the **FileListBox**. After the user selects the files in the **FileListBox**, and presses the OK button, the list of selected files is copied to the Text2 text box.

See Also **CommonDialog** (control), **Dir** (function), **DirListBox** (control), **DriveListBox** (control)

Fill

OBJECT

PE, EE

Usage
: The **Fill** object is used by the **MSChart** control to hold information about the area behind a chart object.

Properties
: • *FillObject*.**Brush**—an object reference to a **Brush** object containing information about the fill type for the area beneath the chart.
: • *FillObject*.**Style**—an **Integer** containing a style constant from Table F-27 below.

AllowedEffects Name	Description
vtFillStyleNull	No fill is done.
vtFillStyleBrush	A solid color or a pattern fill.

Table F-27: AllowedEffects *values.*

Fix

FUNCTION

CCE, LE, PE, EE

Syntax
: *IValue* = **Fix** (*Number*)

Usage
: For positive numbers, the **Fix** function truncates any fractional parts of the number (i.e., **Fix** (8.9) will return 8). For negative numbers, the **Fix** function takes the absolute value of the number, truncates any fractional part, and then multiplies by -1 to restore the sign (i.e., **Fix** (-8.9) will return -8).

Arguments
: • *IValue*—the **Fix** value of **Number**.
: • *Number*—an **Integer**, **Long**, **Single**, or **Double**.

Examples
:
```
Private Sub Command1_Click()
If IsNumeric(Text1.Text) Then
    Text2.Text = Format(Fix(CDbl(Text1.Text)))
Else
    Text2.Text = "Illegal number."
End If
End Sub
```

This routine displays the **Fix** of the number in the Text1 text box.

See Also
: **Abs** (function), **Int** (function), **Sng** (function)

Font

OBJECT

CCE, LE, PE, EE

Usage The **Font** object contains a set of properties that describe a font.

> **Warning**
>
> You can't create a new instance of the **Font** object by using Dim f As New Font. You need to use the **StdFont** object, (Dim f As New StdFont).

Properties
- *FontObject*.**Bold**—a **Boolean** when **True**, means that the characters display in bold. **False** means that the characters display normally.
- *FontObject*.**Charset**—an **Integer** value (see Table F-28) containing how a particular column of information is arranged.

Charset Value	Description
0	The standard Windows character set.
2	The symbol character set.
128	Double-byte character set unique to the Japanese version of Windows.
255	Extended MS-DOS character set.

Table F-28: **CharSet** values.

- *FontObject*.**Italic**—a **Boolean** when **True**, means that the characters display in italics. **False** means that the characters display normally.
- *FontObject*.**Name**—a **String** that specifies the name of the font that should be used to display the characters in this control.
- *FontObject*.**Size**—a **Single** that specifies the point size that should be used to display the characters in the control.
- *FontObject*.**Strikethru**—a **Boolean** when **True**, means that the characters display with a line through the center. **False** means that the characters display normally.
- *FontObject*.**Underlined**—a **Boolean** when **True**, means that the characters display with a line beneath them. **False** means that the characters display normally.
- *FontObject*.**Weight**—an **Integer** containing the weight of the character font. Weight is limited to two values 400 and 700. Bold characters have a weight of 700. Nonbold characters have a weight of 400. If you specify a weight of 550 or less, it will be converted to 400. If you specify a weight of 551 or more, it will be converted to 700.

Examples
```
Private Sub Check1_Click()
If Check1.Value = 0 Then
    Label1.Font.Bold = False
Else
    Label1.Font.Bold = True
End If
End Sub
```

This routine changes the **Bold** property of the Label1 **Font** object each time the check box is checked.

See Also   **Label** (control), **TextBox** (control)

For . . . Next

STATEMENT

CCE, LE, PE, EE

Syntax
```
For Variable = InitialValue To FinalValue [ Step Increment ]
    [ list of statements ]
    [ Exit For ]
    [ list of statements ]
Next [ Variable ]
```

Usage   The **For . . . Next** statement allows you to build a loop with a variable that is automatically incremented at the end of each loop. When you begin to execute the **For . . . Next** loop, *Variable* is assigned the value from *InitialValue*. Then the statements between the **For** and **Next** are executed. When the **Next** statement is reached, the value of *Increment* is added to *Variable*. Then if the value of *Variable* is equal to or greater than *FinalValue*, the program will continue with the statement following the **Next** statement. Otherwise the loop will be repeated starting with the first statement following the **For** statement.

Executing the **Exit For** statement will cause the **For . . . Next** loop to finish, and execution will continue with the first statement after the **Next** statement.

If *Variable* is omitted from the **Next** statement, then the variable from the nearest, unmatched **For** statement will be used.

> **Tip**
>
> *The **For...Next** loop is very useful when you want to process an array or string one element at a time. Use an **Integer** or a **Long** variable for* Variable *for better performance.*

> **Warning**
>
> *You can nest one **For . . . Next** loop inside another; however, the inner loop must exist totally inside the outer. Also, you will need to use different variables for* Variable *to prevent problems.*

Arguments
- *Variable*—a **Date**, **Double**, **Integer**, **Long**, or **Single** variable.
- *InitialValue*—an expression that contains the initial value for *Variable*.
- *FinalValue*—an expression that contains the final value for *Variable*.
- *Increment*—the value that would be added to *Variable* after each loop.

Examples

```
Private Sub Command1_Click()
Dim i As Integer
Dim l As Integer
Dim c1 As Integer
l = Len(Text1.Text)
c1 = 0

For i = 1 To l
    If Mid(Text1.Text, i, 1) = Left(Text2.Text, 1) Then
        c1 = c1 + 1
    End If
Next i
Text3.Text = Format(c1)
End Sub
```

This routine counts the number of times a letter occurs in the big string. It uses a **For ... Next** loop to look at each character in the string and increments a counter each time one is found.

See Also

Do (statement), **While** (statement)

For Each ... Next   STATEMENT

CCE, LE, PE, EE

Syntax

```
For Each element In group
    [ list of statements ]
    [ Exit For ]
    [ list of statements ]
Next [ element ]
```

Usage

The **For Each ... Next** statement allows you to loop through each element in a collection or an array. The variable used for *element* will contain a pointer to an object in the group, which can be referenced just as if you had used a **Set** statement.

Executing the **Exit For** statement will cause the **For Each ... Next** loop to finish, and execution will continue with the first statement after the **Next** statement.

If *element* is omitted from the **Next** statement, then the variable from the nearest, unmatched **For** statement will be used.

Arguments

- *element*—a **Variant** or object variable that corresponds to the type in of the elements in *group*.
- *group*—the name of a collection or an array.

Examples
```
Private Sub Command1_Click()
Dim o As Control
For Each o In Form1.Controls
    MsgBox o.Name
Next o
End Sub
```

This routine loops through all of the controls in the form and displays their names in a message box.

See Also **Do** (statement), **For** (statement), **Set** (statement), **While** (statement)

Form

OBJECT

CCE, LE, PE, EE

Usage The **Form** object is the object that puts the visual in Visual Basic. A form is a window in which you can paint different controls and then attach some code to the various events to control how the controls operate.

Properties
- *FormObject*.**ActiveControl**—an object of type **Control** that contains a reference to the currently active control.

- *FormObject*.**Appearance**—an **Integer** value (see Table F-29) that specifies how the form will be drawn.

AppearanceValue	Description
0	The form is displayed without the 3D effects.
1	The form is displayed with 3D effects (default value).

Table F-29: **Appearance** *values.*

- *FormObject*.**AutoRedraw**—a **Boolean** value when **True** means that the graphics and text written directly to the form will be redrawn from a copy stored in memory. When **False**, the **Paint** event will be triggered to redraw the contents of the form.

> **Tip**
>
> *Setting* **AutoRedraw** *to* **True** *will slow down most operations involving the form. Most of the common controls (i.e., labels, text boxes, and command buttons) will automatically redraw themselves. If you display graphics directly on the form, then you may want to use* **AutoRedraw***.*

- *FormObject*.**BackColor**—a **Long** that contains the suggested value for the background color of the form. The **BackColor** and **ForeColor** must both be solid to display text. If you choose a color that is dithered, it will be changed to the nearest solid color.
- *FormObject*.**BorderStyle**—an **Integer** value (see Table F-30) specifying how the border will be drawn. These values indicate how the form can be resized, and are read only at run time.

BorderStyle Name	Value	Description
vbBSNone	0	No border, control box menu, title, bar, maximize and minimize buttons. Cannot be resized.
vbFixedSingle	1	Single line around the form. Form can only be resized by maximize and minimize buttons.
vbSizable	2	Normal Visual Basic window. Can be resized by dragging the border. Can include control menu box, title bar, maximize and minimize buttons (default).
vbFixedDouble	3	Fixed dialog window. Can't be resized. Can't include maximize and minimize buttons.
vbFixedToolWindow	4	Fixed tool window. Includes title bar and close button. Can't be resized. The caption is shown with reduced fonts.
vbSizableToolWindow	5	Sizable tool window. Includes title bar and Close button. The caption is shown with reduced fonts.

Table F-30: **BorderStyle** *values.*

- *FormObject*.**Caption**—a **String** value that displays inside the title bar. The leading text will also be displayed in the Window's taskbar.
- *FormObject*.**ClipControls**—a **Boolean** when **True** means that the graphic events repaint the entire form. When **False** means that graphic events only repaint the newly exposed parts of the form.
- *FormObject*.**ControlBox**—a **Boolean** when **True** means that the control menu box will be displayed on the form. When **False** means that the control menu box will not be displayed on the form.
- *FormObject*.**Controls**—an object that contains a collection of the controls on the form.
- *FormObject*.**Count**—an **Integer** containing the number of controls on the form.
- *FormObject*.**CurrentX**—a **Single** that specifies the horizontal coordinate measured from the form's left edge for the various drawing methods: **Circle**, **Cls**, **EndDoc**, **Line**, **NewPage**, **Print**, and **PSet**.
- *FormObject*.**CurrentY**—a **Single** that specifies the vertical coordinate measured from the form's top edge for the various drawing methods: **Circle**, **Cls**, **EndDoc**, **Line**, **NewPage**, **Print**, and **PSet**.
- *FormObject*.**DrawMode**—an **Integer** value (see Table F-31) specifying how the drawing methods: **Circle**, **Cls**, **EndDoc**, **Line**, **NewPage**, **Print**, and **PSet** will appear on the form.

DrawMode Name	Value	Description
vbBlackness	1	Blackness
vbNotMergePen	2	Inverse of *vbMergePen*
vbMaskNotPen	3	Combination of the colors common to the background color and the inverse of the pen
vbNotCopyPen	4	Inverse of *vbCopyPen*
vbMaskPenNot	5	Combination of the colors common to the pen and the inverse of the background
vbInvert	6	Inverse of the display color
vbXorPen	7	Combination of the colors in the display and pen, but not in both
vbNotMaskPen	8	Inverse setting of *vbMaskPen*
vbMaskPen	9	Combination of the colors common to the pen and display
vbNotXorPen	10	Inverse setting of *vbXorPen*
vbNop	11	Turns drawing off
vbMergeNotPen	12	Combination of the display and inverse of the pen color.
vbCopyPen	13	Color specified in the **ForeColor** property
vbMergePenNot	14	Combination of the pen color and the inverse of the display color
vbMergePen	15	Combination of the pen color and the display color
vbWhiteness	16	Whiteness

Table F-31: **DrawMode** *values*.

- *FormObject*.**DrawStyle**—an **Integer** value (see Table F-32) specifying how the drawing methods: **Circle**, **Cls**, **EndDoc**, **Line**, **NewPage**, **Print**, and **PSet** will appear on the form. If **DrawWidth** is greater than 1, then *vbDash*, *vbDot*, *vbDashDot*, and *vbDashDotDot* will draw a solid line.

DrawStyle Name	Value	Description
vbSolid	0	Solid line
vbDash	1	Dashed line
vbDot	2	Dotted line
vbDashDot	3	Dash followed by a dot
vbDashDotDot	4	Dash followed by two dots
vbInvisible	5	No displayed line
vbInsideSolid	6	Inside solid

Table F-32: **DrawStyle** *values*.

- *FormObject*.**DrawWidth**—an **Integer** specifying the width of the line in pixels that will be drawn and how the following methods: **Circle**, **Cls**, **EndDoc**, **Line**, **NewPage**, **Print**, and **PSet** will appear on the form. If **DrawWidth** is greater than 1, then the **DrawStyles** *vbDash*, *vbDot*, *vbDashDot*, and *vbDashDotDot* will draw a solid line.

- *FormObject*.**Enabled**—a **Boolean** value when **True** means that the control will respond to events. When **False**, the control will not respond to events.

- *FormObject*.**FillColor**—a **Long** that contains the color that will be used to fill in shapes created with the following graphical methods: **Circle**, **Cls**, **EndDoc**, **Line**, **NewPage**, **Print**, and **PSet**.
- *FormObject*.**FillStyle**—an **Integer** value (see Table F-33) specifying how the drawing methods: **Circle**, **Cls**, **EndDoc**, **Line**, **NewPage**, **Print**, and **PSet** will appear on the form. If **DrawWidth** is greater than 1, then *vbDash*, *vbDot*, *vbDashDot*, and *vbDashDotDot* will draw a solid line.

FillStyle Name	Value	Description
vbFSSolid	0	Solid
vbFSTransparent	1	Transparent
vbHorizontalLine	2	Horizontal line
vbVerticalLine	3	Vertical line
vbUpwardDiagonal	4	Diagonal line from lower left to upper right
vbDownwardDiagonal	5	Diagonal line from upper left to lower right
vbCross	6	Crosshatch with horizontal and vertical lines
vbDiagonalCross	7	Crosshatch with diagonal lines

Table F-33: **FillStyle** *values.*

- *FormObject*.**Font**—an object that contains information about the character font used by this object.

> **Tip**
>
> *Setting values for the **Font** object on the form at design time makes these values the default when other controls and objects are placed on the form.*

- *FormObject*.**FontBold**—a **Boolean** when **True**, means that the characters display in bold. **False** means that the characters are displayed normally.
- *FormObject*.**FontItalic**—a **Boolean** when **True**, means that the characters display in italics. **False** means that the characters display normally.
- *FormObject*.**FontName**—a **String** that specifies the name of the font that should be used to display the characters in this control.
- *FormObject*.**FontSize**—a **Single** that specifies the point size that should be used to display the characters in the control.
- *FormObject*.**FontStrikethru**—a **Boolean** when **True**, means that the characters display with a line through the center. **False** means that the characters display normally.
- *FormObject*.**FontTransparent**—a **Boolean** when **True**, means that the graphics and text behind the characters will be shown around the spaces of the character. **False** means that the graphics and text behind the character will be masked.
- *FormObject*.**FontUnderlined**—a **Boolean** when **True**, means that the characters display with a line beneath them. **False** means that the characters display normally.
- *FormObject*.**hDC**—a **Long** that contains a handle to the device context to the form.

- *FormObject*.**Height**—a **Single** that contains the height of the control.
- *FormObject*.**HelpContextID**—a **Long** that contains a help file context ID number which references an entry in the help file. When the user presses the F1 key while this control is active, the corresponding entry in the help file will automatically be displayed. A value of zero means that no context number was specified.

> **Tip**
>
> *A help file must be compiled using the Windows Help Compiler available in the Professional and Enterprise editions of Visual Basic.*

- *FormObject*.**hWnd**—a **Long** that contains a Windows handle to the control.

> **Tip**
>
> *The **hWnd** property is most useful when making calls to Windows API functions. Since this value can change during execution, do not save the value into a variable for later use.*

- *FormObject*.**Icon**—a picture object that contains the icon associated with this form. This icon will be displayed in the Windows taskbar.

> **Tip**
>
> *Visual Basic includes a lot of icons that you can use with your program. Check the graphics\icons directory for a list of the available icons.*

- *FormObject*.**Image**—a handle to a persistent graphic that is returned by the Windows environment. Available only at run time.
- *FormObject*.**KeyPreview**—a **Boolean** when **True** means that the form will receive keyboard events (**KeyDown**, **KeyUp**, and **KeyPress**) before any controls. When **False** means that the control will receive the keyboard events and the form will not.

> **Tip**
>
> *This function is useful to provide global key stroke handling at the form level for such keys as function keys and other control keys.*

- *FormObject*.**Left**—a **Single** that contains the distance measured in twips between the left edge of the control and the left edge of the control's container.
- *FormObject*.**LinkMode**—an **Integer** value (see Table F-34) that specifies how the form will act in a DDE conversation.

LinkMode Name	Value	Description
vbLinkNone	0	No DDE interaction. If initially specified at design time, it cannot be changed at run time.
vbLinkSource	1	DDE links permitted to labels, picture boxes, and text boxes. If initially specified at design time, it can be changed to *vbLinkNone* and back again.

Table F-34: **LinkMode** *values.*

- *FormObject*.**LinkTopic**—a **String** that contains a reference to a DDE application. While the actual format of the string is dependent on the exact application, strings will usually include an application, topic, and item. For example, in Excel a valid **LinkTopic** string is "Excel | Sheet1."
- *FormObject*.**MaxButton**—a **Boolean** when **True** means the maximize button will be displayed at the top of the form. When **False** the maximize button will not be displayed.

Note

To display the maximize button, **BorderStyle** *must be set to either* vbFixedSingle, vbSizable, *or* vbFixedDouble.

- *FormObject*.**MDIChild**—a **Boolean** when **True** means that the form is an MDI child form and displays inside a parent MDI form. When **False**, the form is not an MDI child form.
- *FormObject*.**MinButton**—a **Boolean** when **True** means the minimize button will be displayed at the top of the form. When **False** the minimize button will not be displayed.

Note

To display the minimize button, **BorderStyle** *must be set to either* vbFixedSingle, vbSizable, *or* vbFixedDouble.

- *FormObject*.**MouseIcon**—a picture object (a bitmap, icon, or metafile) that will be used as a cursor when the **MousePointer** property is set to 99. Note that Visual Basic does not support color cursors from a .CUR file. A color icon from a .ICO file should be used instead.
- *FormObject*.**MousePointer**—an **Integer** value (see Table F-35) that contains the value of the cursor that should be displayed when the cursor is moved over this control. Use *vbCustom* to display the custom icon stored in the **MouseIcon** property.

Cursor Name	Value	Description
vbDefault	0	Shape determined by the object (default value)
vbArrow	1	Arrow
vbCrosshair	2	Crosshair
vbIbeam	3	I beam
vbIconPointer	4	Square inside a square
vbSizePointer	5	Four sided arrow (north, south, east, west)

Cursor Name	Value	Description
vbSizeNESW	6	Two sided arrow (northeast, southwest)
vbSizeNS	7	Two sided arrow (north, south)
vbSizeNWSE	8	Two sided arrow (northwest, southeast)
vbSizeWE	9	Two sided arrow (west, east)
vbUpArrow	10	Single sided arrow pointing north
vbHourglass	11	Hourglass
vbNoDrop	12	No Drop
vbArrowHourglass	13	An arrow and an Hourglass
vbArrowQuestion	14	An arrow and a question mark
vbSizeAll	15	Size all
vbCustom	99	Custom icon from the **MouseIcon** property of this control

Table F-35: **Cursor** values.

- *FormObject*.**Moveable**—a **Boolean** when **True** means that the form can be moved. When **False** means that the form can't be moved.
- *FormObject*.**Name**—a **String** that contains the name of the control that will be used to reference the control in a Visual Basic program. This property is read only at run time.
- *FormObject*.**NegotiateMenus**—a **Boolean** when **True** means that the menu items from an MDI child form will be combined with the MDI parent's form. When **False**, the menu items will not be combined.
- *FormObject*.**OLEDropMode**—an **Integer** value (see Table F-36) that describes how the control will respond to OLE drop operations.

OLEDropMode Name	Value	Description
vbOLEDropNone	0	The form does not accept OLE drops. The cursor is changed to the No Drop cursor (default value).
vbOLEDropManual	1	The form responds to OLE drops under the program's control (manual).
vbOLEDropAutomatic	2	The form automatically accepts OLE drops if it recognizes the format of the data object.

Table F-36: **OLEDropMode** values.

- *FormObject*.**Palette**—a **Picture** object that contains a suggested palette for the control. This property is read only at run time.
- *FormObject*.**PaletteMode**—an **Integer** value (see Table F-37) that describes the palette that should be used with the form.

PaletteMode Name	Value	Description
vbPaletteModeHalfTone	0	The form uses the half tone palette (default).
vbPaletteModeUseZOrder	1	The form uses the palette from the control nearest the front of the **ZOrder** with a palette.
vbModeCustom	2	The form uses the palette specified in the **Palette** property.

Table F-37: **PaletteMode** values.

- *FormObject*.**Picture**—a picture object (a bitmap, icon, metafile, GIF, or JPEG) that will be displayed on the control. You can also use the **LoadPicture** function at run time to load a bitmap, icon, or metafile. Note that **Style** must be set to *vbButtonGraphical* for the image to be shown.
- *FormObject*.**RightToLeft**—a **Boolean** value when **True** means that the text is displayed from right to left. When **False** means that the text is displayed from left to right. A bi-directional version of Windows is required to set this property to true.
- *FormObject*.**ScaleHeight**—an **Integer** value that sets or returns the height of the object in the units specified by **ScaleMode**.
- *FormObject*.**ScaleLeft**—an **Integer** value that sets or returns the value of the X-coordinate of the left edge of the form.
- *FormObject*.**ScaleMode**—an **Integer** value (see Table F-38) that describes the unit of measurement used for the form.

> **Tip**
>
> When dealing with graphic images such as BMP or GIF files it is often useful to set **ScaleMode** to vbPixels to help set the proper relationships.

ScaleMode Name	Value	Description
vbUser	0	Measurements are custom defined, based on the values in **ScaleHeight**, **ScaleLeft**, **ScaleTop**, or **ScaleWidth** properties.
vbTwips	1	Measurements are in twips (1440 twips per inch).
vbPoints	2	Measurements are in points (72 per inch).
vbPixels	3	Measurements are in pixels (smallest unit of measure for a monitor or printer).
vbCharacters	4	Measurements are in characters (horizontal = 120 twips per character, vertical = 240 twips per character).
vbInches	5	Measurements are in inches.
vbMillimeters	6	Measurements are in millimeters.
vbCentimeters	7	Measurements are in centimeters.

Table F-38: **ScaleMode** *values.*

- *FormObject*.**ScaleTop**—an **Integer** value that sets or returns the value of the Y-coordinate of the top edge of the form.
- *FormObject*.**ScaleWidth**—an **Integer** value that sets or returns the width of the object in the units specified by **ScaleMode**.
- *FormObject*.**ShowInTaskbar**—a **Boolean** value when **True** means that the form will be displayed in the taskbar. When **False** means that the form will not be displayed.
- *FormObject*.**StartUpPosition**—an **Integer** value (see Table F-39) describing how the form will initially be shown on the screen.

StartUpPosition Name	Value	Description
vbStartUpManual	0	No position is specified.
vbStartUpOwner	1	The form will be centered on the owner's form.
vbStartUpScreen	2	The form will be centered on the screen.
vbStartUpWindowsDefault	3	Windows will choose where the form is initially displayed.

Table F-39: **StartUpPosition** *values.*

- *FormObject*.**Tag**—a **String** that can hold programmer specific information. This property is not used by Visual Basic.
- *FormObject*.**Top**—a **Single** that contains the distance measured in twips between the top edge of the control and the top edge of the control's container.
- *FormObject*.**Visible**—a **Boolean** value when **True** means that the control is visible. When **False** means that the control is not visible.
- *FormObject*.**WhatsThisHelpID**—a **Long** that contains a help file context ID number that references an entry in the help file. This provides a What's This PopUp help display in response to the What's This button in the upper right corner of the window.
- *FormObject*.**Width**—a **Single** containing the width of the form.
- *FormObject*.**WindowState**—an **Integer** value (see Table F-40) containing the state of the form when it is initially displayed.

WindowState Name	Value	Description
vbNormal	0	The form is initially displayed normally.
vbMinimized	1	The form is initially displayed minimized.
vbMaximized	2	The form is initially displayed maximized.

Table F-40: **WindowState** *values.*

Methods

FormObject.Circle [Step] (x , y), radius [, color [, start [, stop [, aspect]]]]

Usage This method draws a circle, ellipse or a curved line on the form. All coordinate information used is relative to the **ScaleMode**, **ScaleHeight**, **ScaleLeft**, **ScaleTop**, and **ScaleWidth**.

Arguments
- **Step**—a keyword that specifies that the coordinates are relative to the form's **CurrentX** and **CurrentY** properties.
- *x*—a **Single** specifying the X-coordinate of the center of the circle.
- *y*—a **Single** specifying the Y-coordinate of the center of the circle.
- *radius*—a **Single** specifying the radius of the circle.
- *color*—a **Long** containing the color of the line to be drawn. If omitted, it will default to the value in the **ForeColor** property.
- *start*—a **Single** specifying the starting angle for the circle in radians. If omitted, it will default to zero.

- *stop*—a **Single** specifying the ending angle for the circle in radians. It omitted, it will default to 2 times pi (approximately 6.28).
- *aspect*—a **Single** specifying the height to width ratio of the circle. The default is 1.0 which will yield a perfect circle.

> **Tip**
>
> To draw a half a circle, assign start *a value of 0,* stop *a value of pi (approximately 3.14), and choose values for the other parameters.*
>
> *To draw a vertical ellipse, assign a value greater than 1.0 to* aspect. *A horizontal ellipse would have an aspect ratio of less than 1.0.*

FormObject.Cls

Usage   This method clears all of the graphics and text from a form.

FormObject.Hide

Usage   This method removes a form from the screen, but does not unload it.

FormObject.Line [Step] (x1 , y1), [Step] (x2 , y2) [, B | BF]

Usage   This method draws lines or boxes on the form. All coordinate information used is relative to the **ScaleMode**, **ScaleHeight**, **ScaleLeft**, **ScaleTop**, and **ScaleWidth**.

Arguments
- **Step**—a keyword that specifies that the *x1* and *y1* coordinates are relative to the form's **CurrentX** and **CurrentY** properties.
- *x1*—a **Single** specifying the starting X-coordinate of the center of the line or box.
- *y1*—a **Single** specifying the starting Y-coordinate of the center of the line or box.
- **Step**—a keyword that specifies that the *x2* and *y2* coordinates are relative to the form's **CurrentX** and **CurrentY** properties.
- *x2*—a **Single** specifying the stopping X-coordinate of the center of the line or box.
- *y2*—a **Single** specifying the stopping Y-coordinate of the center of the line or box.
- *color*—a **Long** containing the color of the line to be drawn. If omitted, it will default to the value in the **ForeColor** property.
- **B**—draw a box with (*x1, y1*) and (*x2, y2*) specifying the opposite corners of the box. If omitted, a line will be drawn on the form.
- **BF**—draw a box with (*x1, y1*) and (*x2, y2*) specifying the opposite corners of the box and fill the interior with the color specified by **FillColor** and **FillStyle**. If omitted, a line will be drawn on the form.

FormObject.Move *Left* [, *Top* [, *Width* [, *Height*]]]

Usage　　This method changes the position and the size of the **Form object**. The **ScaleMode** of the **Form** or other container object that holds the animation control will determine the units used to specify the coordinates.

Arguments
- *Left*—a **Single** that specifies the new position of the left edge of the control.
- *Top*—a **Single** that specifies the new position of the top edge of the control.
- *Width*—a **Single** that specifies the new width of the control.
- *Height*—a **Single** that specifies the new height of the control.

FormObject.OLEDrag

Usage　　This method begins an **OLEDrag** and drop operation. Invoking this method will trigger the **OLEStartDrag** event.

FormObject.PaintPicture *picture, x1 , y1,* [*width1*] , [*height1*] , [*x2*] , [*y2*] , [*width2*] , [*height2*] , [*rasterop*]

Usage　　This method displays an image (.BMP, .DIB, .EMF, .ICO, or .WMF) on the form. All coordinate information used is relative to the **ScaleMode**, **ScaleHeight**, **ScaleLeft**, **ScaleTop**, and **ScaleWidth**.

Arguments
- *picture*—the image to be displayed on the form. It can come from the **Picture** property of a picture box or another form.
- *x1*—a **Single** specifying the starting X-coordinate of the picture.
- *y1*—a **Single** specifying the starting Y-coordinate of the picture.
- *width1*—a **Single** specifying the width of the image. If omitted, the width will default to the width of the image. If greater or less than the width of the image, the image will be stretched or shrunk to fit.
- *height1*—a **Single** specifying the height of the image. If omitted, the height will default to the height of the image. If greater or less than the height of the image, the image will be stretched or shrunk to fit.
- *x2*—a **Single** specifying the starting X-coordinate of a clipping region within the picture. If omitted, zero will be used.
- *y2*—a **Single** specifying the starting Y-coordinate of a clipping region within the picture. If omitted, zero will be used.
- *width2*—a **Single** specifying the width of the clipping region of the image. If omitted, the width will default to the width of the image. If greater or less than the width of the image, the image will be stretched or shrunk to fit.
- *height2*—a **Single** specifying the height of the clipping region of the image. If omitted, the height will default to the height of the image. If greater or less than the height of the image, the image will be stretched or shrunk to fit.

- *rasterop*—a **Long** containing a raster op code from Table F-41 below that will perform a bit-wise operation on the image as it is displayed. The default will be to display the image as is.

RasterOp Name	Value	Description
vbDstInvert	&H005A0049	Inverted the destination image.
vbMergeCopy	&H00C000CA	Combine the source and the pattern.
vbMergePaint	&H00BB0226	Combine inverted source image with destination image using OR.
vbNotSrcCopy	&H00330008	Copies inverted source image to the destination.
vbNotSrcErase	&H001100A6	Inverts the result of combining the source and destination images using OR.
vbPatCopy	&H00F00021	Copies the source pattern to the destination bitmap.
vbPatInvert	&H005A0049	Combines the inverted source pattern with the destination image using XOR.
vbPatPaint	&H00FB0A09	Combines the destination image with the source pattern.
vbScrAnd	&H008800C6	Combines the destination and source images using AND.
vbSrcCopy	&H00CC0020	Copies the source image to the destination bitmap.
vbSrcErase	&H00440328	Combines the inverted destination image with the source image by using AND.
vbSrcInvert	&H00660046	Combines the source and destination images using XOR.
vbSrcPaint	&H00EE0086	Combines the source and destination images using OR.

Table F-41: rasterop values.

color = FormObject.Point (x , y)

Usage   This method returns a **Long** containing the color at the point at location *x, y*. If the location is outside the form, then -1 will be returned. All coordinate information used is relative to the **ScaleMode**, **ScaleHeight**, **ScaleLeft**, **ScaleTop**, and **ScaleWidth**.

Arguments
- *color*—a **Long** containing the color at location *x, y*.
- *x*—a **Single** specifying the X-coordinate of the point.
- *y*—a **Single** specifying the Y-coordinate of the point.

FormObject.PopupMenu menu, flags, x, y, menuitem

Usage   This method will display a pop-up menu on the screen.

Tip

Set **Visible** to **False** for menu items to be displayed as pop-up menus to prevent them from being displayed in the menu bar.

Form • 329

Arguments
- *menu*—the name of a **Menu** object to be displayed. It must include at least one submenu item.
- *flags*—zero or more items from Table F-42 below. If omitted zero will be used. Multiple values can be selected by adding them together.

Menu Flags Name	Value	Description
vbPopupMenuLeftButton	0	The items on the menu can be selected by only the left mouse button.
vbPopupMenuLeftAlign	0	The left edge of the menu is located at *x*.
vbPopupMenuRightButton	2	The items on the menu can be selected by either mouse button.
vbPopupMenuCenterAlign	4	The center of the menu is located at *x*.
vbPopupMenuRightAlign	8	The right edge of the menu is located at *x*.

Table F-42: Menu Flags values.

- *x*—a **Single** specifying the X-coordinate of the menu. If omitted, it will default to the current X-coordinate of the mouse.
- *y*—a **Single** specifying the Y-coordinate of the menu. If omitted, it will default to the current Y-coordinate of the mouse.
- *menuitem*—the name of the submenu item that will be displayed in bold text. If omitted, no items will be displayed in bold.

FormObject.PrintForm

Usage This method sends a snapshot of all the objects on the form to the default system printer.

Tip

*Set **AutoRedraw** to **True** to include graphics and text drawn directly on the form.*

FormObject.Point [Step] (x , y), color

Usage This method sets the point at *x, y* to the color specified in *color*. All coordinate information used is relative to the **ScaleMode**, **ScaleHeight**, **ScaleLeft**, **ScaleTop**, and **ScaleWidth**.

Arguments
- **Step**—keyword that specifies that the *x* and *y* coordinates are relative to the form's **CurrentX** and **CurrentY** properties.
- *x*—a **Single** specifying the X-coordinate of the point.
- *y*—a **Single** specifying the Y-coordinate of the point.
- *color*—a **Long** containing the color to be displayed at location *x, y*. If omitted, this value will default to the value of **ForeColor**.

FormObject.Refresh

Usage This method redraws the contents of the form.

FormObject.Scale [(x1 , y1)—(x2 , y2)]

Usage This method will define the coordinate system used on the form and set the appropriate values in **ScaleMode**, **ScaleHeight**, **ScaleLeft**, **ScaleTop**, and **ScaleWidth**. If the **Scale** method is used without any arguments, the coordinate is reset to default.

Arguments
- *x1*—a **Single** specifying the X-coordinate of the left edge of the form.
- *y1*—a **Single** specifying the Y-coordinate of the top edge of the form.
- *x2*—a **Single** specifying the X-coordinate of the right edge of the form.
- *y2*—a **Single** specifying the Y-coordinate of the bottom edge of the form.

result = FormObject.ScaleX (width , fromscale , toscale)

Usage This method will compute a new value for *width* in a different scale.

Arguments
- *result*—a **Single** containing a new value for *width*.
- *fromscale*—an **Integer** specifying a **ScaleMode** value for the current *width*.
- *toscale*—an **Integer** value (see Table F-43) specifying the **ScaleMode** value for the new *width*.

ScaleMode Name	Value	Description
vbUser	0	Measurements are custom defined, based on the values in **ScaleHeight**, **ScaleLeft**, **ScaleTop**, or **ScaleWidth** properties.
vbTwips	1	Measurements are in twips (1440 twips per inch).
vbPoints	2	Measurements are in points (72 per inch).
vbPixels	3	Measurements are in pixels (smallest unit of measure for a monitor or printer).
vbCharacters	4	Measurements are in characters (horizontal = 120 twips per character, vertical = 240 twips per character).
vbInches	5	Measurements are in inches.
vbMillimeters	6	Measurements are in millimeters.
vbCentimeters	7	Measurements are in centimeters.
vbHimetric	8	Measurements are in himetrics.

Table F-43: ScaleMode values.

result = FormObject.ScaleY (height , fromscale , toscale)

Usage This method will compute a new value for *height* in a different scale.

Arguments
- *result*—a **Single** containing a new value for *height*.
- *fromscale*—an **Integer** specifying a **ScaleMode** value for the current *height*.

- *toscale*—an **Integer** value (see Table F-44) specifying the **ScaleMode** value for the new *height*.

ScaleMode Name	Value	Description
vbUser	0	Measurements are custom defined, based on the values in **ScaleHeight**, **ScaleLeft**, **ScaleTop**, or **ScaleWidth** properties.
vbTwips	1	Measurements are in twips (1440 twips per inch).
vbPoints	2	Measurements are in points (72 per inch).
vbPixels	3	Measurements are in pixels (smallest unit of measure for a monitor or printer).
vbCharacters	4	Measurements are in characters (horizontal = 120 twips per character, vertical = 240 twips per character).
vbInches	5	Measurements are in inches.
vbMillimeters	6	Measurements are in millimeters.
vbCentimeters	7	Measurements are in centimeters.
vbHimetric	8	Measurements are in himetrics.

Table F-44: *ScaleMode values.*

FormObject.SetFocus

Usage   This method transfers the focus from the form or control that currently has the focus to this form. To receive the focus, this form must be enabled and visible.

FormObject.Show [style [, owner]]

Usage   This method displays a form.

Arguments
- *style*—an **Integer** that specifies how the form will be displayed. When 0, the form will be displayed as modeless (i.e., other forms in the program can be used). When 1, the form will be displayed as modal (i.e., no other forms in the program can be used until this form is hidden or unloaded—forms in other applications are not affected).
- *owner*—a **Form** object or the keyword **Me** that specifies the owner of this form.

height = FormObject.TextHeight (string)

Usage   This method will compute the height of the string in the units specified by **ScaleMode**. The height is computed using the font information specified in the **Font** object. It will also include space at the top and the bottom of the characters, so that multiple lines of text can be placed next to each other. If *string* contains embedded carriage return linefeed pairs, then the total height of the block of text will be returned.

Arguments
- *height*—a **Single** that contains the height of *string*.
- *string*—a **String** that contains characters to be printed on the form.

width = FormObject.TextWidth (string)

Usage This method will compute the width of the string in the units specified by **ScaleMode**. The width is computed using the font information specified in the **Font** object. If *string* contains embedded carriage return linefeed pairs, then the length of the longest line will be returned.

Arguments
- *width*—a **Single** that contains the width of *string*.
- *string*—a **String** that contains characters to be printed on the form.

FormObject.WhatsThisMode

Usage This method places the mouse pointer into the "What's This?" mode. This is exactly the same thing as if the user clicked on the What's This button on the title bar.

FormObject.ZOrder [position]

Usage This method specifies the position of the form relative to the other forms on the screen.

Arguments *position*—an **Integer** that specifies the relative position of the form. A value of 0 means that the control is positioned at the front of the screen. A value of 1 means that the form will be placed at the back of the screen.

Events

Private Sub FormObject_Activate ( )

Usage This event occurs when the form becomes the active form. The form becomes active if either the **Show** or **SetFocus** methods were used or if the user takes some action such as clicking on the form.

Private Sub FormObject_Click( )

Usage This event occurs when the user clicks a mouse button while the cursor is positioned over a disabled control or blank area on the form.

> **Tip**
> *If you need to identify which mouse button was pressed, use the **MouseUp** and **MouseDown** events.*

Private Sub FormObject_DblClick( )

Usage This event occurs when the user double-clicks a mouse button while the cursor is positioned over a disabled control or blank area on the form.

> **Warning**
> *If there is code in the **Click** event, then the **DblClick** event will never occur.*

Private Sub *FormObject*_Deactivate ( )

> Usage   This event occurs when the form loses the focus and is no longer the active window.

Private Sub *FormObject*_DragDrop (*source* As Control, *x* As Single, *y* As Single)

> Usage   This event occurs when a drag-and-drop operation is completed by using the Drag method with a *DragAction* value of *vbEndDrag* (2).

Tip

*When using drag-and-drop operations, use the **DragOver** event to determine what the cursor should look like while the cursor moves over the control.*

> Arguments
> - *source*—a control object that is the control that is being dragged.

Tip

You can access a property or method from the source control by using source.*property or* source.*method. You can determine the type of object or control by using the **TypeOf** operator.*

> - *x*—a **Single** that contains the horizontal location of the mouse pointer.
> - *y*—a **Single** that contains the vertical location of the mouse pointer.

Private Sub *FormObject*_DragOver (*source* As Control, *x* As Single, *y* As Single, *state* As Integer)

> Usage   This event occurs while a drag operation is in progress and the cursor is moved over the control.

Tip

*When using drag-and-drop operations, use the **DragOver** event to determine what the cursor should look like while the cursor moves over the control. When* state *is 0, you can change the cursor to a No Drop (vbNoDrop) cursor or highlight the field that the cursor is near. When* state *is 1, you can undo the changes you made when the* state *was 0.*

> Arguments
> - *source*—a control object that is the control that is being dragged.

Tip

You can access a property or method from the source control by using source.*property or* source.*method. You can determine the type of object or control by using the **TypeOf** operator.*

- *x*—a **Single** that contains the horizontal location of the mouse pointer.
- *y*—a **Single** that contains the vertical location of the mouse pointer.
- *state*—an **Integer** value (see Table F-45) that indicates the state of the object being dragged.

state Name	Value	Description
vbEnter	0	The dragged object is entering range of the control.
vbLeave	1	The dragged object is leaving range of the control.
vbOver	2	The dragged object has moved from one position over the control to another.

Table F-45: state values.

Private Sub *FormObject*_GotFocus ( )

Usage   This event occurs when the form is given focus.

Warning

This event will only occur if all of the visible controls on the form are disabled.

Private Sub *FormObject*_Initialize ( )

Usage   This event occurs when the form is first created. This event will occur before the **Load** event.

Tip

*Since this event is triggered only when the form is created and the **Load** event is triggered when the form is created and when it is loaded, it makes sense to put your initialization code in the **Load** event, unless you have specific actions that need to be done only when the form is created.*

Private Sub *FormObject*_KeyDown (*keycode* As Integer, *shift* As Single)

Usage   This event occurs when a key is pressed. If the **KeyPreview** property is **True** this event will occur before the **KeyPress** event for control with the focus. Otherwise, the form will only see this event if it contains no visible and enabled controls.

Arguments
- *keycode*—an **Integer** that contains information about which key was pressed.
- *shift*—an **Integer** value (see Table F-46) that contains information about the Shift and Alt keys that were pushed when the mouse button was pressed. These values can be added together if more than one key was down. For instance, a value of 5 would mean that the Shift and Alt keys were both down when the mouse button was pressed.

shift Name	Value	Description
vbShiftMask	1	The Shift key was pressed.
vbCtrlMask	2	The Ctrl key was pressed.
vbAltMask	4	The Alt key was pressed.

Table F-46: shift *values*.

Private Sub *FormObject*_KeyPress (*keychar* As Integer)

Usage This event occurs when a key is pressed. If the **KeyPreview** property is **True,** this event will occur before the **KeyPress** event for control with the focus. Otherwise, the form will only see this event if it contains no visible and enabled controls.

Arguments • *keychar*—an **Integer** that contains the ASCII character that was pressed. Changing the value of *keychar* to zero will cancel the keystroke.

Private Sub *FormObject*_KeyUp (*keycode* As Integer, *shift* As Single)

Usage This event occurs when a key is pressed. If the **KeyPreview** property is **True,** this event will occur before the **KeyPress** event for control with the focus. Otherwise, the form will only see this event if it contains no visible and enabled controls.

Arguments • *keycode*—an **Integer** that contains information about which key was released.
• *shift*—an **Integer** value (see Table F-47) that contains information about the Shift and Alt keys that were pushed when the mouse button was pressed. These values can be added together if more than one key was down. For instance, a value of 5 would mean that the Shift and Alt keys were both down when the mouse button was pressed.

shift Name	Value	Description
vbShiftMask	1	The Shift key was pressed.
vbCtrlMask	2	The Ctrl key was pressed.
vbAltMask	4	The Alt key was pressed.

Table F-47: shift *values*.

Private Sub *FormObject*_LinkClose ( )

Usage This event occurs when a DDE link is closed.

Private Sub *FormObject*_LinkError (*errcode* As Integer)

Usage This event occurs when a DDE link error occurs.

Arguments • *errcode*—an **Integer** that contains an error code listed in Table F-48 below.

errcode Value	Description
1	The other application requested data in wrong format. This may occur more than once while Visual Basic attempts to find an acceptable format.
6	The other application attempted to continue the DDE conversation after **LinkMode** in this application was set to zero.
7	All 128 DDE links are in use.
8	Destination control: an automatic link or **LinkRequest** failed when communicating. Source forms: the other application was unable to poke data to a control.
11	Insufficient memory available for DDE.

Table F-48: DDE errcode values.

Private Sub *FormObject*_LinkExecute (*cmd* As String, *cancel* As Integer)

Usage   This event occurs when a destination application requests the source application to perform the function in *cmd*.

Note

*If there your program doesn't include a **LinkExecute** event, then all commands will be rejected.*

Arguments • *cmd*—a **String** containing a command for the source application to execute. The format string is application specific.
• *cancel*—an **Integer** when zero, means that the command was accepted. Any other value will inform the destination application that the command was rejected.

Private Sub *FormObject*_LinkOpen (*cancel* As Integer)

Usage   This event occurs when a DDE session is being set up.

Arguments • *cancel*—an **Integer** when zero, means that the command was accepted. Any other value will inform the destination application that the link will be refused.

Private Sub *FormObject*_Load ( )

Usage   This event occurs when a form is being loaded. This event occurs after the **Initialize** event.

Tip

This is a good spot to place any initialization code for the form.

Private Sub *FormObject*_LostFocus ( )

Usage This event occurs when the form loses focus.

Private Sub *FormObject*_MouseDown (*button* As Integer, *shift* As Single, *x* As Single, *y* As Single)

Usage This event occurs when a mouse button was pressed while the cursor is over any unoccupied part of the form.

Arguments
- *button*—an **Integer** value (see Table F-49) that contains information about the mouse buttons that were pressed. Only one button will be indicated when this event occurs.

button Name	Value	Description
vbLeftButton	1	The left button was pressed.
vbRightButton	2	The right button was pressed.
vbMiddleButton	4	The middle button was pressed.

Table F-49: button *values*.

- *shift*—an **Integer** value (see Table F-50) that contains information about the Shift and Alt keys that were pushed when the mouse button was pressed. These values can be added together if more than one key was down. For instance, a value of 5 would mean that the Shift and Alt keys were both down when the mouse button was pressed.

shift Name	Value	Description
vbShiftMask	1	The Shift key was pressed.
vbCtrlMask	2	The Ctrl key was pressed.
vbAltMask	4	The Alt key was pressed.

Table F-50: shift *values*.

- *x*—a **Single** that contains the horizontal location of the mouse pointer.
- *y*—a **Single** that contains the vertical location of the mouse pointer.

Private Sub *FormObject*_MouseMove (*button* As Integer, *shift* As Single, *x* As Single, *y* As Single)

Usage This event occurs while the cursor is moved over any unoccupied part of the form.

Arguments
- *button*—an **Integer** value (see Table F-51) that contains information about the mouse buttons that were pressed. These values can be added together if more than one button was pushed. For instance, a value of 3 means that both the left and right buttons were pressed. A value of 0 means that no buttons were pressed.

button Name	Value	Description
vbLeftButton	1	The left button was pressed.
vbRightButton	2	The right button was pressed.
vbMiddleButton	4	The middle button was pressed.

Table F-51: button *values*.

- *shift*—an **Integer** value (see Table F-52) that contains information about the Shift and Alt keys that were pushed when the mouse button was pressed. These values can be added together if more than one key was down. For instance, a value of 5 would mean that the Shift and Alt keys were both down when the mouse button was pressed. A value of 0 means that none of these keys were pressed.

shift Name	Value	Description
vbShiftMask	1	The Shift key was pressed.
vbCtrlMask	2	The Ctrl key was pressed.
vbAltMask	4	The Alt key was pressed.

Table F-52: shift *values*.

- *x*—a **Single** that contains the horizontal location of the mouse pointer.
- *y*—a **Single** that contains the vertical location of the mouse pointer.

Private Sub *FormObject*_MouseUp (*button* As Integer, *shift* As Single, *x* As Single, *y* As Single)

Usage   This event occurs when a mouse button is released while the cursor is over any unoccupied part of the form.

Arguments   - *button*—an **Integer** value (see Table F-53) that contains information about the mouse buttons that were released. Only one of these values will be present.

button Name	Value	Description
vbLeftButton	1	The left button was released.
vbRightButton	2	The right button was released.
vbMiddleButton	4	The middle button was released.

Table F-53: button *values*.

- *shift*—an **Integer** value (see Table F-54) that contains information about the Shift and Alt keys that were pushed when the mouse button was released. These values can be added together if more than one key was down. For instance, a value of 5 would mean that the Shift and Alt keys were both down when the mouse button was released. A value of 0 means that none of these keys were pressed.

shift Name	Value	Description
vbShiftMask	1	The Shift key was pressed.
vbCtrlMask	2	The Ctrl key was pressed.
vbAltMask	4	The Alt key was pressed.

Table F-54: shift *values*.

- *x*—a **Single** that contains the horizontal location of the mouse pointer.
- *y*—a **Single** that contains the vertical location of the mouse pointer.

Private Sub *FormObject*_OLECompleteDrag(*effect* As Long)

Usage   This event tells the source control the results of an OLE drag-and-drop operation. This is the final event to occur in the series of actions that make up an OLE drag-and-drop operation.

Arguments
- *effect*—a **Long** (see Table F-55) that returns the status of the OLE drag-and-drop operation.

effect Name	Value	Description
vbDropEffectNone	0	The operation was canceled or the target control can't accept the drop operation.
vbDropEffectCopy	1	The operation copied data from the source control to the target control. The original data is unchanged.
vbDropEffectMove	2	The operation results in a link from the original data to the target control.

Table F-55: effect *values*.

Private Sub *FormObject*_OLEDragDrop (*data* As DataObject, *effect* As Long, *button* As Integer, *shift* As Single, *x* As Single, *y* As Single)

Usage   This event tells the source control the results of an OLE drag-and-drop operation. This is the final event to occur in the series of actions that make up an OLE drag-and drop-operation.

Arguments
- *data*—a **DataObject** that contains the formats that the source control will provide. If the data is not contained in the **DataObject**, then it can be retrieved with the **GetData** method.
- *effect*—a **Long** (see Table F-56) that returns the status of the OLE drag-and-drop operation.

effect Name	Value	Description
vbDropEffectNone	0	The operation was canceled or the target control can't accept the drop operation.
vbDropEffectCopy	1	The operation copied data from the source control to the target control. The original data is unchanged.
vbDropEffectMove	2	The operation results in a link from the original data to the target control.

Table F-56: effect values.

- *button*—an **Integer** value (see Table F-57) that contains information about the mouse buttons that were pressed. These values can be added together if more than one button was pushed. For instance, a value of 3 means that both the left and right buttons were pressed. A value of 0 means that no buttons were pressed.

button Name	Value	Description
vbLeftButton	1	The left button was pressed.
vbRightButton	2	The right button was pressed.
vbMiddleButton	4	The middle button was pressed.

Table F-57: button values.

- *shift*—an **Integer** value (see Table F-58) that contains information about the Shift and Alt keys that were pushed when the mouse button was released. These values can be added together if more than one key was down. For instance, a value of 5 would mean that the Shift and Alt keys were both down when the mouse button was released. A value of 0 means that none of these keys were pressed.

shift Name	Value	Description
vbShiftMask	1	The Shift key was pressed.
vbCtrlMask	2	The Ctrl key was pressed.
vbAltMask	4	The Alt key was pressed.

Table F-58: shift values.

- *x*—a **Single** that contains the horizontal location of the mouse pointer.
- *y*—a **Single** that contains the vertical location of the mouse pointer.

Private Sub *FormObject*_OLEDragOver (*data* As DataObject, *effect* As Long, *button* As Integer, *shift* As Single, *x* As Single, *y* As Single, *state* As Integer)

Usage   This event happens when an OLE drag-and-drop operation is in progress.

Arguments
- *data*—a **DataObject** that contains the formats that the source control will provide. If the data is not contained in the **DataObject**, then it can be retrieved with the **GetData** method.

- *effect*—a **Long** (see Table F-59) that returns the status of the OLE drag-and-drop operation.

effect Name	Value	Description
vbDropEffectNone	0	The operation was canceled or the target control can't accept the drop operation.
vbDropEffectCopy	1	The operation copied data from the source control to the target control. The original data is unchanged.
vbDropEffectMove	2	The operation results in a link from the original data to the target control.

Table F-59: effect *values*.

- *button*—an **Integer** value (see Table F-60) that contains information about the mouse buttons that were pressed. These values can be added together if more than one button was pushed. For instance, a value of 3 means that both the left and right buttons were pressed. A value of 0 means that no buttons were pressed.

button Name	Value	Description
vbLeftButton	1	The left button was pressed.
vbRightButton	2	The right button was pressed.
vbMiddleButton	4	The middle button was pressed.

Table F-60: button *values*.

- *shift*—an **Integer** value (see Table F-61) that contains information about the Shift and Alt keys that were pushed when the mouse button was released. These values can be added together if more than one key was down. For instance, a value of 5 would mean that the Shift and Alt keys were both down when the mouse button was released. A value of 0 means that none of these keys were pressed.

shift Name	Value	Description
vbShiftMask	1	The Shift key was pressed.
vbCtrlMask	2	The Ctrl key was pressed.
vbAltMask	4	The Alt key was pressed.

Table F-61: shift *values*.

- *x*—a **Single** that contains the horizontal location of the mouse pointer.
- *y*—a **Single** that contains the vertical location of the mouse pointer.
- *state*—an **Integer** value (see Table F-62) that indicates the state of the object being dragged.

state Name	Value	Description
vbEnter	0	The dragged object is entering range of the control.
vbLeave	1	The dragged object is leaving range of the control.
vbOver	2	The dragged object has moved from one position over the control to another.

Table F-62: state *values*.

Private Sub *FormObject*_OLEGiveFeedback (*effect* As Long)

Usage This event tells the source control what is happening while the OLE drag-and-drop operation is in progress. This event occurs after the **OLEDragOver** event.

> **Tip**
> *You may want to use this event to change the cursor to reflect what can happen in the remote object.*

Arguments • *effect*—a **Long** (see Table F-63) that returns the status of the OLE drag-and-drop operation.

effect Name	Value	Description
vbDropEffectNone	0	The operation was canceled or the target control can't accept the drop operation.
vbDropEffectCopy	1	The operation copied data from the source control to the target control. The original data is unchanged.
vbDropEffectMove	2	The operation results in a link from the original data to the target control.
vbDropEffectScroll	&H80000000	The target control is about to scroll or is scrolling. This value may be added to the other *shift* values.

Table F-63: effect *values*.

Private Sub *FormObject*_OLESetData (*data* As DataObject, *DataFormat* As Integer)

Usage This event happens in response to the target object performing a **GetData** method on *data*. This routine will respond by using the **SetData** method with the desired data using the **DataObject** *data*.

Arguments • *data*—a **DataObject** that will contain the data to be returned to the target object.
• *format*—an **Integer** value (see Table F-64) that contains the format of the data.

format Name	Value	Description
vbCFText	1	Text (.TXT files)
vbCFBitmap	2	Bitmap (.BMPT files)
vbCFMetafile	3	Metafile (.WMF files)
vbCFEDIB	8	Device independent bitmap (DIB)
vbCFPallette	9	Color palette
vbCFEMetafile	14	Enhanced metafile (EMF files)
vbCFFiles	15	List of files
vbCFRTF	-16639	Rich Text Format (.RTF files)

Table F-64: format *values*.

Private Sub *FormObject*_OLEStartDrag (*data* As DataObject, *AllowedEffects* As Long)

Usage	This event starts an OLE drag-and-drop operation.
Arguments	*data*—a **DataObject** that will contain the formats that the source object is willing to provide to the target object. It may optionally contain the data to be transferred.
	AllowedEffects—a **Long** (see Table F-65) that contains the effects that the target object can request from the source object. The *AllowedEffects* can be added together if the source object supports more than one effect. Note that the target object can always use the *vbDropEffectNone* effect.

AllowedEffects Name	Value	Description
vbDropEffectNone	0	The target can't copy the data.
vbDropEffectCopy	1	The target can copy the data and the source will keep the data unchanged.
vbDropEffectMove	2	The target can copy the data and the source will delete the data.

Table F-65: AllowedEffects *values.*

Private Sub *FormObject*_Paint ( )

Usage	This event occurs when the form must redraw itself. This can happen because the form was previously covered and now is not, the size of the form has been changed, or if the form has been moved. A **Paint** event is necessary if you generate graphics or print text directly to the form and have set the **AutoRedraw** property to **False**.

Warning

Avoid moving the form, changing any variables that affect the form's size or appearance and using the **Refresh** *method. This can cause a cascading event where the event will trigger the same event over and over again until the system crashes.*

Private Sub *FormObject*_QueryUnload (*cancel* As Integer, *unloadmode* As Long)

Usage	This event is called before a form is unloaded. Depending on *unloadmode*, one or more forms will be closed. Before the first form is unloaded, all forms will see the **QueryUnload** event. If one form cancels the request, then no forms will be unloaded.

Arguments
- *cancel*—an **Integer** that when set to any value except zero will stop the unload process. Setting *cancel* to zero will let the process continue.
- *unloadmode*—an **Integer** value (see Table F-66) that indicates the origin of the unload request.

unloadmode Name	Value	Description
vbFormControlMenu	0	The Close command from the control menu issued the request.
vbFormCode	1	The program issued the request.
vbAppWindows	2	A Windows shutdown request was issued.
vbAppTaskManager	3	The Windows TaskManager is closing the application.
vbFormMDIForm	4	The MDI parent form is closing the MDI child form.

Table F-66: unloadmode values.

Private Sub *FormObject*_Resize ( )

Usage   This event occurs when the form is first displayed, when the value of **WindowState** changes, or when the form is resized. After the resize event occurs, the **Paint** event will be called (if **AutoResize** is **False**) to redraw the contents of the form.

Private Sub *FormObject*_Terminate ( )

Usage   This event occurs when the last instance of a form is ready to be removed from memory. It will not be called if for some reason (such as the **End** statement being executed) the program terminates abnormally.

Private Sub *FormObject*_Unload (*cancel* As Integer)

Usage   This event is called before a form is unloaded. While *cancel* can be set to keep the form from being unloaded, it will not stop processes like Windows from being shutdown. You should use the **QueryUnload** event instead.

Arguments
- *cancel*—an **Integer** that when set to any value except zero will stop the unload process. Setting *cancel* to zero will let the process continue.

Examples
```
Private Sub Form_Paint()
Dim i As Integer
Dim s As String
Debug.Print "Form_Paint"
s = ""
Form1.Cls
Form1.CurrentX = 0
Form1.CurrentY = 0
Form1.Font.Name = "Ariel"
```

```
For i = Asc("A") To Asc("z")
    s = s & Chr(i)
Next i
i = 3
Do While Form1.CurrentY < Form1.ScaleHeight
    i = i + 1
    Form1.Font.Size = i
    Form1.ForeColor = QBColor(i Mod 16)
    Form1.CurrentX = (Form1.ScaleWidth--Form1.TextWidth(s)) / 2
    Print s
Loop
End Sub
```

This routine repaints the display each time a form overlays it. First, I clear the form. Then, I build a string with the characters from uppercase A to lowercase z. Next, I start a loop that will fill the form with the string. Each time, I select the next larger font size, choose a new color for the string and then position the cursor so that the text will be centered on the screen. Finally, I print the string and start the loop again. I stop the loop when the cursor moves below the bottom of the screen.

See Also   **Forms** (collection), **MDIForm** (object)

Format

FUNCTION

CCE, LE, PE, EE

Syntax   *svalue* = **Format** (*expr* [, *format* [, *firstday* [, *firstweek*]]])

Usage   The **Format** function converts an expression to a string.

Arguments
- *expr*—an expression to be formatted. Can be any numeric, **Date,** or **String** expression.
- *format*—a **String** (see Tables F-67 through F-71) that contains a named format or series of characters that describe how to format *expr*.

Named Date Formats	Description
General Date	If date information is included in the expression, display the date as mm/dd/yy. If time information is included in the expression, display the time as hh:mm XM (ex: 5/15/97 2:37:00 PM).
Long Date	Display the date in your system's long date format (ex: Thursday, May 15, 1997).
Medium Date	Display the date in your system's medium date format (ex: 15-May-97).
Short Date	Display the date in your system's short date format (ex: 5/15/97).
Long Time	Display the time in your system's long time format (ex: 2:37:00 PM).
Medium Time	Display the time in your system's medium time format (ex: 02:37 PM).
Short Time	Display the time in your system's short time format (ex: 14:37).

Table F-67: Named Date formats.

Named Numeric Formats	Description
General Number	Display the number without thousands separator (ex: 123456.789).
Currency	Display the number with a leading dollar sign, thousands separators, and two decimal digits (ex: $123,456.79).
Fixed	Display the number with at least one digit to the left of the decimal point and two digits to the right. Do not use the thousands separator (ex: 123456.79).
Standard	Display the number with at least one digit to the left of the decimal point and two digits to the right. Use the thousands separator if needed (ex: 123,456.79).
Percent	Display the number multiplied by 100 and with two decimal places (ex: 12345678.90%).
Scientific	Display the number as a leading digit with two decimal places times 10 to the nth power (ex: 1.23E+05).
Yes/No	If the number is zero, display No otherwise display Yes (ex: Yes).
True/False	If the number is zero, display False otherwise display True (ex: True).
Yes/No	If the number is zero, display Off otherwise display On (ex: On).

Table F-68: Named Numeric formats.

Date Format Characters	Description
/	The system defined date separator will be displayed.
:	The system defined time separator will be displayed.
AM/PM	Display an uppercase AM for 00:00 to 11:59 and an uppercase PM for 12:00 to 23:59.
am/pm	Display a lowercase am for 00:00 to 11:59 and a lowercase pm for 12:00 to 23:59.
A/P	Display an uppercase A for 00:00 to 11:59 and an uppercase P for 12:00 to 23:59.
a/p	Display a lowercase a for 00:00 to 11:59 and a lowercase p for 12:00 to 23:59.
AMPM	Display an AM/PM indicator as defined by your system settings.
c	If date information is present, display it using the ddddd format. If time information is present, display it using the ttttt format.
d	Display the day of month without a leading zero (1-31).
dd	Display the day of month with a leading zero if necessary (01-31).
ddd	Display the day as a three character abbreviation (Sun, Mon, Tue, Wen, Thu, Fri, Sat).
dddd	Display the day with its full name (Sunday, Monday, Tuesday, Wednesday, Thursday, Friday, Saturday).
ddddd	Display the date using the short date format.
dddddd	Display the date using the long date format.
h	Display the hour without a leading zero (1-23).
hh	Display the hour with a leading zero if necessary (01-23).
m	Display the month without a leading zero (1-12). If m is preceded by an h or hh, then the minutes display without a leading zero (0-59).

Date Format Characters	Description
mm	Display the month with a leading zero if necessary (01-12). If mm is preceded by an h or hh then the minutes display with a leading zero (00-59).
mmm	Display the month as a three character abbreviation (Jan, Feb, Mar, Apr, May, Jun, Jul, Aug, Sep, Oct, Nov, Dec).
mmmm	Display the month with its full name (January, February, March, April, May, June, July, August, September, October, November, December).
n	Display the minutes without a leading zero (0-59).
nn	Display the minutes with a leading zero if necessary (00-59).
q	Display the quarter of the year (1-4).
s	Display the seconds without a leading zero (0-59).
ss	Display the seconds with a leading zero if necessary (00-59).
ttttt	Display the time in the long time format.
w	Display the day of the week as a number. The first day of the week is specified by *firstday*.
ww	Display the week of the year (1-54).
y	Display the day of year (1-366).
yy	Display the year as a two digit number (00-99).
yyyy	Display the year as a four digit number (0100-9999).

Table F-69: *Date Format characters.*

Numeric Format Characters	Description
none	Display the number without special formatting.
0	Display a digit of the number or zero. If there are more digits to the left of the decimal point than there are 0s, then display the additional digits without special formatting. If there are more digits to the right of the decimal point than there are 0s, the number will be rounded.
#	Display a digit or nothing.
.	Display a decimal point indicator as defined in Windows.
%	Multiply the value by 100 and insert percent sign.
,	Insert thousands separator as defined by Windows. Normally the thousands separator will be inserted between #s and 0s. If two thousands separators are next to each other or a thousand separator is next to a decimal point, then that means to scale the value by 1,000 or 1 million. Formatting 123,456,789 with the format string "#0,," would result in 123. Formatting 123,456,789 with the format string "#0,." would result in 123457. (including the period).
:	Display a time separator as defined in Windows.
/	Display a date separator as defined in Windows.
E- E+ e- e+	Display in scientific notation, with E or e inserted between the mantissa and the exponent.
- + $ ( )	Display this character.
\	Display the next character without formatting.
"xyz"	Display the string exactly.

Table F-70: *Numeric Format characters.*

String Format Characters	Description
@	Display the character or a space. This is a placeholder.
&	Display the character or nothing. This is a placeholder.
<	Display all characters in lowercase.
>	Display all characters in uppercase.
!	Fill placeholders from left to right, instead of right to left.
- + $ ( )	Display this character.
\	Display the next character without formatting.
"xyz"	Display the string exactly.

Table F-71: String Format characters.

- *firstday*—an **Integer** value (see Table F-72) describing the first day of the week. This is used primarily by the date format character "w."

firstday Name	Value	Description
vbUseSystem	0	Use the system default.
vbSunday	1	Use Sunday as the first day of the week.
vbMonday	2	Use Monday as the first day of the week.
vbTuesday	3	Use Tuesday as the first day of the week.
vbWednesday	4	Use Wednesday as the first day of the week.
vbThursday	5	Use Thursday as the first day of the week.
vbFriday	6	Use Friday as the first day of the week.
vbSaturday	7	Use Saturday as the first day of the week.

Table F-72: firstday values.

- *firstweek*—an **Integer** value (see Table F-73) describing the first week of the year. This is used primarily by the date format string "ww."

firstweek Name	Value	Description
vbUseSystem	0	Use the system default.
vbFirstJan1	1	Use the week where 1 January falls.
vbFirstFourDays	2	If the first week of the year has three or fewer days, then use the following week as the first week of the year.
vbFirstFullWeek	3	Start the year with the first full week.

Table F-73: firstweek values.

Examples
```
Private Sub Command1_Click()
If Option1.Value Then
    Text2.Text = Format(CDate(Text1.Text), Combo1.Text, CInt(Left(Combo4.Text,
    1)), CInt(Left(Combo5.Text, 1)))
```

```
    ElseIf Option2.Value Then
        Text2.Text = Format(CDbl(Text1.Text), Combo2.Text)
    Else
        Text2.Text = Format(Text1.Text, Combo3.Text)
    End If
End Sub
```

This routine converts a date, double, or string value using formatting strings supplied in combo1, combo2, and combo3 respectively.

See Also **CDate** (function), **CDbl** (function), **CStr** (function), **Date** (data type), **Double** (data type), **String** (data type)

Forms

COLLECTION

CCE, LE, PE, EE

Usage The **Forms** collection contains the set of all loaded forms in a running Visual Basic program.

Properties ■ **Forms.Count**—a **Long** value that contains the number of loaded forms in the collection.

Methods *formobject* = **Forms.Point** (*item*)

Usage This method returns a **Form** object from the **Forms** collection.

Arguments ■ *formobject*—a **Form** object.
■ *item*—an **Integer** specifying a form in the collection.

Examples
```
Private Sub Command1_Click()
Dim f As Form
For Each f In Forms
   MsgBox f.Name
   If f.Name = "Form3" Then
      Unload Form3
   ElseIf f.Name = "Form2" Then
      Unload Form2
   End If

Next f
End Sub
```

This program declares a variable as **Form** and then uses the **For Each** statement to display the names of all of the loaded forms.

See Also **For Each** (statement), **Form** (object)

Frame

CONTROL

CCE, LE, PE, EE

Usage The **Frame** control can be used to provide a container for a set of controls. It may also be used to create a more interesting user interface.

To use the **Frame** control, draw a frame on the form. Then draw the controls on top of the frame. The frame will then be a container for the controls.

> **Tip**
>
> When using the **OptionButton** only one can be selected at a time. However you can use multiple frames to group **OptionButtons** and allow more than one button to be selected at a time.

Properties
- *FrameControl*.**Appearance**—an **Integer** value (see Table F-74) that specifies how the form will be drawn.

AppearanceValue	Description
0	The frame is displayed without the 3D effects.
1	The frame is displayed with 3D effects (default value).

Table F-74: **Appearance** *values.*

- *FrameControl*.**BackColor**—a **Long** that contains the suggested value for the background color of the form. The **BackColor** and **ForeColor** must both be solid to display text. If you choose a color that is dithered, it will be changed to the nearest solid color.
- *FrameControl*.**BorderStyle**—an **Integer** value (see Table F-75) specifying how the border will be drawn. These values also indicate how the form can be resized, and are read only at run time.

BorderStyle Name	Value	Description
vbBSNone	0	No border.
vbFixedSingle	1	Single line around the frame.

Table F-75: **BorderStyle** *values.*

- *FrameControl*.**Caption**—a **String** value that is displayed inside the frame's border.
- *FrameControl*.**ClipControls**—a **Boolean** when **True** means that the graphic events repaint the entire frame. When **False** means that graphic events only repaint the newly exposed parts of the frame.
- *FrameControl*.**Container**—an object that can be used to set or return the container of the control at run time. This property cannot be set at design time.
- *FrameControl*.**DragIcon**—an object that contains the picture value of an icon. At design time, you can specify an icon file that has a file type of .ICO.

> **Tip**
>
> This value can be created by copying the value from another control's **DragIcon** value, a form's icon, or by using the **LoadPicture** function.

- *FrameControl*.**DragMode**—an **Integer** value (see Table F-76) specifying how the control will respond to a drag request.

> **Tip**
>
> Setting **DragMode** to vbAutomatic *will automatically begin a drag operation when the user clicks on the control. However, the control will not respond to the usual mouse events (****Click****, ****DblClick****).*

DragMode Name	Value	Description
vbManual	0	The **Drag** method must be used to begin a drag-and-drop operation (default value).
vbAutomatic	1	The source control will automatically begin a drag-and-drop operation when the user clicks on the control.

Table F-76: **DragMode** *values.*

- *FrameControl*.**Enabled**—a **Boolean** value when **True** means that the control will respond to events. When **False**, the control will not respond to events.
- *FrameControl*.**Font**—an object that contains information about the character font used by this object.

> **Tip**
>
> *Setting values for the* **Font** *object on the form at design time makes these values the default when other controls and objects are placed on the form.*

- *FrameControl*.**FontBold**—a **Boolean** when **True**, means that the characters display in bold. **False** means that the characters display normally.
- *FrameControl*.**FontItalic**—a **Boolean** when **True**, means that the characters display in italics. **False** means that the characters display normally.
- *FrameControl*.**FontName**—a **String** that specifies the name of the font that should be used to display the characters in this control.
- *FrameControl*.**FontSize**—a **Single** that specifies the point size that should be used to display the characters in the control.
- *FrameControl*.**FontStrikethru**—a **Boolean** when **True**, means that the characters display with a line through the center. **False** means that the characters display normally.
- *FrameControl*.**FontUnderlined**—a **Boolean** when **True**, means that the characters display with a line beneath them. **False** means that the characters display normally.
- *FrameControl*.**Height**—a **Single** that contains the height of the control.
- *FrameControl*.**HelpContextID**—a **Long** that contains a help file context ID number which references an entry in the help file. When the user presses the F1 key while this control is active, the corresponding entry in the help file will automatically be displayed. A value of zero means that no context number was specified.

> **Tip**
>
> *A help file must be compiled using the Windows Help Compiler available in the Professional and Enterprise editions of Visual Basic.*

- *FrameControl*.**hWnd**—a **Long** that contains a Windows handle to the control.

> **Tip**
>
> *The **hWnd** property is most useful when making calls to Windows API functions. Since this value can change during execution, do not save the value into a variable for later use.*

- *FrameControl*.**Index**—an **Integer** that uniquely identifies a control in a control array.
- *FrameControl*.**Left**—a **Single** that contains the distance measured in twips between the left edge of the control and the left edge of the control's container.
- *FrameControl*.**MouseIcon**—a picture object (a bitmap, icon, or metafile) that will be used as a cursor when the **MousePointer** property is set to 99. Note that Visual Basic does not support color cursors from a .CUR file. A color icon from a .ICO file should be used instead.
- *FrameControl*.**MousePointer**—an **Integer** value (see Table F-77) that contains the value of the cursor that should be displayed when the cursor is moved over this control. Use *vbCustom* to display the custom icon stored in the **MouseIcon** property.

Cursor Name	Value	Description
vbDefault	0	Shape determined by the object (default value)
vbArrow	1	Arrow
vbCrosshair	2	Crosshair
vbIbeam	3	I beam
vbIconPointer	4	Square inside a square
vbSizePointer	5	Four sided arrow (north, south, east, west)
vbSizeNESW	6	Two sided arrow (northeast, southwest)
vbSizeNS	7	Two sided arrow (north, south)
vbSizeNWSE	8	Two sided arrow (northwest, southeast)
vbSizeWE	9	Two sided arrow (west, east)
vbUpArrow	10	Single sided arrow pointing north
vbHourglass	11	Hourglass
vbNoDrop	12	No Drop
vbArrowHourglass	13	An arrow and an Hourglass
vbArrowQuestion	14	An arrow and a question mark
vbSizeAll	15	Size all
vbCustom	99	Custom icon from the **MouseIcon** property of this control

Table F-77: **Cursor** *values.*

- *FrameControl*.**Name**—a **String** that contains the name of the control that will be used to reference the control in a Visual Basic program. This property is read only at runtime.

- *FrameControl*.**OLEDropMode**—an **Integer** value (see Table F-78) that describes how the control will respond to OLE drop operations.

OLEDropMode Name	Value	Description
vbOLEDropNone	0	The form does not accept OLE drops. The cursor is changed to the No Drop cursor (default value).
vbOLEDropManual	1	The form responds to OLE drops under the program's control (manual).
vbOLEDropAutomatic	2	The form automatically accepts OLE drops if it recognizes the format of the data object.

Table F-78: **OLEDropMode** values.

- *FrameControl*.**Parent**—an object that contains a reference to the **Form**, **Frame**, or other container that contains this control.
- *FrameControl*.**RightToLeft**—a **Boolean** value when **True** means that the text is displayed from right to left. When **False** means that the text is displayed from left to right. A bi-directional version of Windows is required to set this property to **True**.
- *FrameControl*.**TabIndex**—an **Integer** that determines the order that a user will tab through the objects on a form.
- *FrameControl*.**Tag**—a **String** that can hold programmer specific information. This property is not used by Visual Basic.
- *FrameControl*.**Top**—a **Single** that contains the distance measured in twips between the top edge of the control and the top edge of the control's container.
- *FrameControl*.**ToolTipText**—a **String** that holds a text value that can be displayed as a **ToolTip** box that is displayed whenever the cursor is held over the control for about one second.
- *FrameControl*.**Visible**—a **Boolean** value when **True** means that the control is visible. When **False** means that the control is not visible.
- *FrameControl*.**WhatsThisHelpID**—a **Long** that contains a help file context ID number that references an entry in the help file. This provides a What's This PopUp help display in response to the What's This button in the upper right corner of the window.
- *FrameControl*.**Width**—a **Single** containing the width of the frame.

Methods

FrameControl.Drag [*DragAction*]

Usage This method begins, ends, or cancels a drag operation.

Arguments
- *DragAction*—an **Integer** that contains a value selected from Table F-79 below.

DragAction Name	Value	Description
vbCancel	0	Cancels any drag operation in progress.
vbBeginDrag	1	Begins a drag operation (default).
vbEndDrag	2	Ends a drag operation and drops *object*.

Table F-79: DragAction values.

FrameControl.Move Left [, Top [, Width [, Height]]]

> **Usage** This method changes the position and the size of the **Frame** control. The **ScaleMode** of the **Form** or other container object that holds the animation control will determine the units used to specify the coordinates.
>
> **Arguments**
> - *Left*—a **Single** that specifies the new position of the left edge of the control.
> - *Top*—a **Single** that specifies the new position of the top edge of the control.
> - *Width*—a **Single** that specifies the new width of the control.
> - *Height*—a **Single** that specifies the new height of the control.

FrameControl.OLEDrag

> **Usage** This method begins an **OLEDrag** and drop operation. Invoking this method will trigger the **OLEStartDrag** event.

FrameControl.Refresh

> **Usage** This method redraws the contents of the frame control.

FrameControl.ShowWhatsThis

> **Usage** This method displays the ShowWhatsThis help information for this control.

FrameControl.ZOrder [position]

> **Usage** This method specifies the position of the file list control relative to the other objects on the form.

> **Tip**
>
> *Note that there are three layers of objects on a form: the back layer is the drawing space which contains the results of the graphical methods, the middle layer contains graphical objects and **Labels**, and the top layer contains nongraphical controls such as the **FileListControl**. The ZOrder method only affects how the objects are arranged within a single layer.*

> **Arguments** *position*—an **Integer** that specifies the relative position of this object. A value of 0 means that the control is positioned at the head of the list, a value of 1 means that the control will be placed at the end of the list.

Events *Private Sub FrameControl_Click([index As Integer])*

> **Usage** This event occurs when the user clicks a mouse button to select an item in the drop-down list or selects an item from the drop-down list using the keyboard.
>
> **Arguments** *index*—an **Integer** that uniquely identifies a control in a control array. This argument is not present if the control is not part of a control array.

Private Sub *FrameControl*_DblClick([*index* As Integer])

- Usage — This event occurs when the user double-clicks a mouse button to select an item in the list or selects an item from the list using the keyboard.

- Arguments
  - *index*—an **Integer** that uniquely identifies a control in a control array. This argument is not present if the control is not part of a control array.

Private Sub *FrameControl*_DragDrop([*index* As Integer ,] *source* As Control, *x* As Single, *y* As Single)

- Usage — This event occurs when a drag-and-drop operation is completed by using the **Drag** method with an *DragAction* value of *vbEndDrag*.

> **Tip**
>
> *When using drag-and-drop operations, use the **DragOver** event to determine what the cursor should look like while the cursor moves over the control.*

- Arguments
  - *index*—an **Integer** that uniquely identifies a control in a control array. This argument is not present if the control is not part of a control array.
  - *source*—a control object that is the control that is being dragged.

> **Tip**
>
> *You can access a property or method from the source control by using* source.property *or* source.method. *You can determine the type of object or control by using the **TypeOf** operator.*

  - *x*—a **Single** that contains the horizontal location of the mouse pointer.
  - *y*—a **Single** that contains the vertical location of the mouse pointer.

Private Sub *FrameControl*_DragOver([*index* As Integer ,] *source* As Control, *x* As Single, *y* As Single, *state* As Integer)

- Usage — This event occurs while a drag operation is in progress and the cursor is moved over the control.

> **Tip**
>
> *When using drag-and-drop operations, use the **DragOver** event to determine what the cursor should look like while the cursor moves over the control. When* state *is 0, you can change the cursor to a No Drop (vbNoDrop) cursor or highlight the field that the cursor is near. When* state *is 1, you can undo the changes you made when the* state *was 0.*

Arguments
- *index*—an **Integer** that uniquely identifies a control in a control array. This argument is not present if the control is not part of a control array.
- *source*—a control object that is the control that is being dragged.

> **Tip**
> You can access a property or method from the source control by using source.*property* or source.*method*. You can determine the type of object or control by using the **TypeOf** operator.

- *x*—a **Single** that contains the horizontal location of the mouse pointer.
- *y*—a **Single** that contains the vertical location of the mouse pointer.
- *state*—an **Integer** value (see Table F-80) that indicates the state of the object being dragged.

state Name	Value	Description
vbEnter	0	The dragged object is entering range of the control.
vbLeave	1	The dragged object is leaving range of the control.
vbOver	2	The dragged object has moved from one position over the control to another.

Table F-80: state *values*.

Private Sub *FrameControl*_MouseDown([*index* As Integer ,] *button* As Integer, *shift* As Single, *x* As Single, *y* As Single)

Usage This event occurs when a mouse button was pressed while the cursor is over the control.

Arguments
- *index*—an **Integer** that uniquely identifies a control in a control array. This argument is not present if the control is not part of a control array.
- *button*—an **Integer** value (see Table F-81) that contains information about the mouse buttons that were pressed. Only one button will be indicated when this event occurs.

button Name	Value	Description
vbLeftButton	1	The left button was pressed.
vbRightButton	2	The right button was pressed.
vbMiddleButton	4	The middle button was pressed.

Table F-81: button *values*.

- *shift*—an **Integer** value (see Table F-82) that contains information about the Shift and Alt keys that were pushed when the mouse button was pressed. These values can be added together if more than one key was down. For instance, a value of 5 would mean that the Shift and Alt keys were both down when the mouse button was pressed.

shift Name	Value	Description
vbShiftMask	1	The Shift key was pressed.
vbCtrlMask	2	The Ctrl key was pressed.
vbAltMask	4	The Alt key was pressed.

Table F-82: shift *values*.

- *x*—a **Single** that contains the horizontal location of the mouse pointer.
- *y*—a **Single** that contains the vertical location of the mouse pointer.

Private Sub *FrameControl*_MouseMove ([*index* As Integer ,] *button* As Integer, *shift* As Single, *x* As Single, *y* As Single)

Usage — This event occurs while the cursor is moved over the control.

Arguments
- *index*—an **Integer** that uniquely identifies a control in a control array. This argument is not present if the control is not part of a control array.
- *button*—an **Integer** value (see Table F-83) that contains information about the mouse buttons that were pressed. These values can be added together if more than one button was pushed. For instance, a value of 3 means that both the left and right buttons were pressed. A value of 0 means that no buttons were pressed.

button Name	Value	Description
vbLeftButton	1	The left button was pressed.
vbRightButton	2	The right button was pressed.
vbMiddleButton	4	The middle button was pressed.

Table F-83: button *values*.

- *shift*—an **Integer** value (see Table F-84) that contains information about the Shift and Alt keys that were pushed when the mouse button was pressed. These values can be added together if more than one key was down. For instance, a value of 5 would mean that the Shift and Alt keys were both down when the mouse button was pressed. A value of 0 means that none of these keys were pressed.

shift Name	Value	Description
vbShiftMask	1	The Shift key was pressed.
vbCtrlMask	2	The Ctrl key was pressed.
vbAltMask	4	The Alt key was pressed.

Table F-84: shift *values*.

- *x*—a **Single** that contains the horizontal location of the mouse pointer.
- *y*—a **Single** that contains the vertical location of the mouse pointer.

Private Sub *FrameControl*_MouseUp([*index* As Integer ,] *button* As Integer, *shift* As Single, *x* As Single, *y* As Single)

Usage · This event occurs when a mouse button is released while the cursor is over the control.

Arguments
- *index*—an **Integer** that uniquely identifies a control in a control array. This argument is not present if the control is not part of a control array.
- *button*—an **Integer** value (see Table F-85) that contains information about the mouse buttons that were released. Only one of these values will be present.

button Name	Value	Description
vbLeftButton	1	The left button was released.
vbRightButton	2	The right button was released.
vbMiddleButton	4	The middle button was released.

Table F-85: button *values*.

- *shift*—an **Integer** value (see Table F-86) that contains information about the Shift and Alt keys that were pushed when the mouse button was released. These values can be added together if more than one key was down. For instance, a value of 5 would mean that the Shift and Alt keys were both down when the mouse button was released. A value of 0 means that none of these keys were pressed.

shift Name	Value	Description
vbShiftMask	1	The Shift key was pressed.
vbCtrlMask	2	The Ctrl key was pressed.
vbAltMask	4	The Alt key was pressed.

Table F-86: shift *values*.

- *x*—a **Single** that contains the horizontal location of the mouse pointer.
- *y*—a **Single** that contains the vertical location of the mouse pointer.

Private Sub *FrameControl*_OLECompleteDrag([*index* As Integer ,] *effect* As Long)

Usage · This event tells the source control the results of an OLE drag-and-drop operation. This is the final event to occur in the series of actions that make up an OLE drag-and-drop operation.

Arguments
- *index*—an **Integer** that uniquely identifies a control in a control array. This argument is not present if the control is not part of a control array.
- *effect*—a **Long** (see Table F-87) that returns the status of the OLE drag-and-drop operation.

effect Name	Value	Description
vbDropEffectNone	0	The operation was canceled or the target control can't accept the drop operation.
vbDropEffectCopy	1	The operation copied data from the source control to the target control. The original data is unchanged.
vbDropEffectMove	2	The operation results in a link from the original data to the target control.

Table F-87: effect *values.*

Private Sub *FrameControl*_OLEDragDrop([*index* As Integer ,] *data* As DataObject, *effect* As Long, *button* As Integer, *shift* As Single, *x* As Single, *y* As Single)

Usage
: This event tells the source control the results of an OLE drag-and-drop operation. This is the final event to occur in the series of actions that make up an OLE drag-and-drop operation.

Arguments
: - *index*—an **Integer** that uniquely identifies a control in a control array. This argument is not present if the control is not part of a control array.
  - *data*—a **DataObject** that contains the formats that the source control will provide. If the data is not contained in the **DataObject**, then it can be retrieved with the **GetData** method.
  - *effect*—a **Long** (see Table F-88) that returns the status of the OLE drag-and-drop operation.

effect Name	Value	Description
vbDropEffectNone	0	The operation was canceled or the target control can't accept the drop operation.
vbDropEffectCopy	1	The operation copied data from the source control to the target control. The original data is unchanged.
vbDropEffectMove	2	The operation results in a link from the original data to the target control.

Table F-88: effect *values.*

- *button*—an **Integer** value (see Table F-89) that contains information about the mouse buttons that were pressed. These values can be added together if more than one button was pushed. For instance, a value of 3 means that both the left and right buttons were pressed. A value of 0 means that no buttons were pressed.

button Name	Value	Description
vbLeftButton	1	The left button was pressed.
vbRightButton	2	The right button was pressed.
vbMiddleButton	4	The middle button was pressed.

Table F-89: button *values.*

- *shift*—an **Integer** value (see Table F-90) that contains information about the Shift and Alt keys that were pushed when the mouse button was released. These values can be added together if more than one key was down. For instance, a value of 5 would mean that the Shift and Alt keys were both down when the mouse button was released. A value of 0 means that none of these keys were pressed.

shift Name	Value	Description
vbShiftMask	1	The Shift key was pressed.
vbCtrlMask	2	The Ctrl key was pressed.
vbAltMask	4	The Alt key was pressed.

Table F-90: shift *values*.

- *x*—a **Single** that contains the horizontal location of the mouse pointer.
- *y*—a **Single** that contains the vertical location of the mouse pointer.

Private Sub *FrameControl*_OLEDragOver([*index* As Integer ,] *data* As DataObject, *effect* As Long, *button* As Integer, *shift* As Single, *x* As Single, *y* As Single, *state* As Integer)

Usage   This event happens when an OLE drag-and-drop operation is in progress.

Arguments
- *index*—an **Integer** that uniquely identifies a control in a control array. This argument is not present if the control is not part of a control array.
- *data*—a **DataObject** that contains the formats that the source control will provide. If the data is not contained in the **DataObject**, then it can be retrieved with the **GetData** method.
- *effect*—a **Long** that returns the status of the OLE drag-and-drop operation (see Table F-91).

effect Name	Value	Description
vbDropEffectNone	0	The operation was canceled or the target control can't accept the drop operation.
vbDropEffectCopy	1	The operation copied data from the source control to the target control. The original data is unchanged.
vbDropEffectMove	2	The operation results in a link from the original data to the target control.

Table F-91: effect *values*.

- *button*—an **Integer** value (see Table F-92) that contains information about the mouse buttons that were pressed. These values can be added together if more than one button was pushed. For instance, a value of 3 means that both the left and right buttons were pressed. A value of 0 means that no buttons were pressed.

button Name	Value	Description
vbLeftButton	1	The left button was pressed.
vbRightButton	2	The right button was pressed.
vbMiddleButton	4	The middle button was pressed.

Table F-92: button *values*.

- *shift*—an **Integer** value (see Table F-93) that contains information about the Shift and Alt keys that were pushed when the mouse button was released. These values can be added together if more than one key was down. For instance, a value of 5 would mean that the Shift and Alt keys were both down when the mouse button was released. A value of 0 means that none of these keys were pressed.

shift Name	Value	Description
vbShiftMask	1	The Shift key was pressed.
vbCtrlMask	2	The Ctrl key was pressed.
vbAltMask	4	The Alt key was pressed.

Table F-93: shift *values*.

- *x*—a **Single** that contains the horizontal location of the mouse pointer.
- *y*—a **Single** that contains the vertical location of the mouse pointer.
- *state*—an **Integer** value (see Table F-94) that indicates the state of the object being dragged.

state Name	Value	Description
vbEnter	0	The dragged object is entering range of the control.
vbLeave	1	The dragged object is leaving range of the control
vbOver	2	The dragged object has moved from one position over the control to another.

Table F-94: state *values*.

Private Sub *FrameControl*_OLEGiveFeedback ([*index* As Integer ,] *effect* As Long)

Usage   This event tells the source control what is happening while the OLE drag-and-drop operation is in progress. This event occurs after the **OLEDragOver** event.

Tip

You may want to use this event to change the cursor to reflect what can happen in the remote object.

Arguments
- *index*—an **Integer** that uniquely identifies a control in a control array. This argument is not present if the control is not part of a control array.
- *effect*—a **Long** (see Table F-95) that returns the status of the OLE drag-and-drop operation.

effect Name	Value	Description
vbDropEffectNone	0	The operation was canceled or the target control can't accept the drop operation.
vbDropEffectCopy	1	The operation copied data from the source control to the target control. The original data is unchanged.
vbDropEffectMove	2	The operation results in a link from the original data to the target control.
vbDropEffectScroll	&H80000000	The target control is about to scroll or is scrolling. This value may be added to the other *shift* values.

Table F-95: effect *values.*

Private Sub *FrameControl_OLESetData*([*index* As Integer ,] *data* As DataObject, *DataFormat* As Integer)

Usage This event happens in response to the target object performing a **GetData** method on *data*. This routine will respond by using the **SetData** method with the desired data using the **DataObject** *data*.

Arguments
- *index*—an **Integer** that uniquely identifies a control in a control array. This argument is not present if the control is not part of a control array.
- *data*—a **DataObject** that will contain the data to be returned to the target object.
- *format*—an **Integer** value (see Table F-96) that contains the format of the data.

format Name	Value	Description
vbCFText	1	Text (.TXT files)
vbCFBitmap	2	Bitmap (.BMP files).
vbCFMetafile	3	Metafile (.WMF files)
vbCFEDIB	8	Device independent bitmap (DIB)
vbCFPallette	9	Color palette
vbCFEMetafile	14	Enhanced metafile (.EMF files)
vbCFFiles	15	List of files
vbCFRTF	-16639	Rich Text Format (.RTF files)

Table F-96: format *values.*

Private Sub *FrameControl_OLEStartDrag* ([*index* As Integer ,] *data* As DataObject, *AllowedEffects* As Long)

Usage This event starts an OLE drag-and-drop operation.

Arguments
- *index*—an **Integer** that uniquely identifies a control in a control array. This argument is not present if the control is not part of a control array.
- *data*—a **DataObject** that will contain the formats that the source object is willing to provide to the target object. It may optionally contain the data to be transferred.
- *AllowedEffects*—a **Long** (see Table F-97) that contains the effects that the target object can request from the source object. The *AllowedEffects* can be added together if the source object supports more than one effect. Note that the target object can always use the *vbDropEffectNone* effect.

AllowedEffects Name	Value	Description
vbDropEffectNone	0	The target can't copy the data.
vbDropEffectCopy	1	The target can copy the data and the source will keep the data unchanged.
vbDropEffectMove	2	The target can copy the data and the source will delete the data.

Table F-97: AllowedEffects *values.*

See Also **OptionButton** (control)

FreeFile

FUNCTION

CCE, LE, PE, EE

Syntax *filenum =* **FreeFile** (*range*)

Usage The **FreeFile** function returns an unused file number.

Arguments
- *filenum*—an **Integer** value that contains the file number of the open file.
- *range*—an **Integer** value, when 0 will return a file number between 0 and 255. When 1, will return a file number between 256 and 511. If omitted, *range* will default to 0.

Examples
```
Private Sub Command1_Click()
Dim i As Integer
For i = 1 To 10
    Open CStr(i) & ".dat" For Random As i
Next i
MsgBox Format(FreeFile(0))
For i = 1 To 10
    Close #i
Next i
End Sub
```

This routine opens a series of files and then uses the **FreeFile** function to find an available file number. It cleans up by closing the files.

See Also **Open** (statement)

Function

STATEMENT

CCE, LE, PE, EE

Syntax
```
[ Public | Private | Friend ] [ Static ] Function name ( [ arg ] [, arg ] . . . [, arg ] ) As type
    [ list of statements ]
    [ Exit Function ]
    [ list of statements ]
End Function
```

Usage
The **Function** statement defines a routine that will return a value. The arguments are variables that will be passed to the function when it is called. The function name, *name*, is a special variable that is assigned the value that will be returned to the calling program. Therefore, it is important that you assign a value to *name* prior to ending the function.

The **Exit Function** statement can be used to leave the function at any time. The **End Function** statement marks the end of the function. Executing either statement will cause the function to return back to where it was called.

Arguments
- **Public**—an optional keyword indicating that the function can be called from any module in the program.
- **Private**—an optional keyword indicating that the function can be only called by other routines in the same module.
- **Friend**—an optional keyword indicating that the function can be called from any module in the program, but it can't be called by the controller of an instance of the object. This argument applies to class modules only.
- **Static**—an optional keyword indicating that the variables declared inside the function are preserved from one call to the next.
- *name*—a Visual Basic identifier that contains the name of the function.
- *arg*—an argument that is passed to the function:

`[ Optional ] [ ByVal | ByRef ] [ ParamArray ] AName [ () ] [ As type ] [ = value ]`

Optional	An optional keyword meaning that the argument is optional and need not be passed to the function. Once an argument is declared to be optional, all arguments that follow must be declared as optional.
ByVal	An optional keyword meaning that the argument is passed by value to the event. This event is free to change the contents of the argument and the calling object will not see the changes.
ByRef	An optional keyword meaning that the argument is passed by reference to the event. Any changes to the argument in the calling control will be seen by the calling object.

	ParamArray	An optional keyword meaning that the function can receive an unspecified number of arguments of type **Variant** starting at this position. This must be the last argument in the function declaration and can't be used with **Optional**, **ByVal**, or **ByRef**.
	AName	The formal argument being passed to the event.
	[( )]	If present, indicates that the argument is an array.
	type	A valid Visual Basic type: **Byte, Boolean, Currency, Date, Double, Integer, Long, Single, String, Object,** or **Variant**. If the argument is not **Optional**, then specific object types and user defined types may be used.
	value	Used to provide a default value for an argument that was marked as **Optional**. Arguments of type **Object** can only be assigned a value of **Nothing**.

- *type*—a valid Visual Basic type: **Byte, Boolean, Currency, Date, Double, Integer, Long, Single, String, Object,** or **Variant**.

Examples
```
Private Static Function CountIt(Optional Clear As Boolean = False) As Integer
Dim Counter As Integer
If Clear Then
   Counter = 0
Else
   Counter = Counter + 1
End If
CountIt = Counter
End Function

Private Sub Command1_Click()
Text1.Text = Format(CountIt())
End Sub

Private Sub Form_Load()
CountIt (True)
End Sub
```

This program has a **Static** function that counts the number of times the command1 command button was pressed. The CountIt **Function** has one optional parameter that initializes the counter to zero. The function is called twice, once in **Form_Load** to set the counter to zero, and once in the **Command1_** event to get the incremented counter.

See Also   **Sub** (statement)

FV

FUNCTION

CCE, LE, PE, EE

Syntax `fvalue = FV ( rate, nper [, pmt [, pv [, type ] ] ] )`

Usage The **FV** function returns the future value of fixed payment annuity. Cash paid out is represented by negative numbers. Cash received is represented by positive numbers.

Arguments
- *fvalue*—a **Double** value containing the future value of the annuity.
- *rate*—a **Double** value containing the interest rate per period.

> **Tip**
>
> To convert from APR to rate *divide the APR by 100 to get a percentage rate and then by the number of periods in a year to get a value for* rate.

- *nper*—an **Integer** value containing the number of periods in the annuity.
- *pmt*—a **Double** value containing the payment for each period.
- *pv*—a **Variant** value containing the present value of the annuity. If not specified, it will default to zero.
- *type*—a **Variant** value when 0 means that the payment is due at the end of the period. When 1, means that the payment is due at the beginning of the period. If not specified, it will default to 0.

Examples
```
Private Sub Command1_Click()
Text4.Text = Format(-FV(CDbl(Text1.Text), CInt(Text2.Text), CDbl(Text3.Text)),
   "currency")
End Sub
```

This routine computes the future value of a stream of payments.

See Also **DDB** (function), **IPmt** (function), **IRR** (function), **MIRR** (function), **NPer** (function), **NPV** (function), **PMT** (function), **PPmt** (function), **PV** (function), **Rate** (function), **SLN** (function), **SYD** (function)

Get

STATEMENT

CCE, LE, PE, EE

Syntax **Get** [#]*filenum*,[*recnum*], *vname*

Usage The **Get** statement reads data from a disk file into a variable. The first record has a record number of 1. If the *recnum* argument is omitted, then the next record will be read from the file, unless you use the **Seek** statement to change the pointer to the next record.

For files opened with the random option, the **Len** option of the **Open** statement determines the record size. Variable length **Strings** are stored with their length, so the length of the record must be at least two bytes longer than the length of the longest string. If you are reading **Variant** variables from disk, then two bytes are required to identify the **Variant's** type. (If the type is **String** then two more bytes are required.) Fixed-length arrays do not have any additional overhead, but variable length arrays require two bytes plus eight bytes for each dimension of the array (e.g., a two-dimensional array will require 2 bytes + 2 times 8 bytes for a total of 18 bytes of overhead storage).

For files opened with the binary option, the **Len** clause on the open statement has no effect. Variables are read from disk without any overhead bytes, including variable-length **Strings**. When variable-length **Strings** are read from disk, only the number of characters already in the string are read (e.g., if the length of the string before the **Get** was 80 characters, then the next 80 characters will be read).

> **Tip**
>
> Use the **Get** statement to read data written with the **Put** statement.

Arguments
- *filenum*—an open file number created by the **Open** statement.
- *recnum*—a **Long** that specifies the record number (random files) or byte number (binary files) of the file. If omitted, then the next record in the file will be read.
- *vname*—any valid Visual Basic variable. It can be of type **Byte, Boolean, Currency, Date, Double, Integer, Long, Single, String,** or **Variant.**

Examples
```
Private Sub Command1_Click()
Dim i As Integer
Open App.Path & "GetPut.Dat" For Binary Access Read As #1
Text1.Text = ""
Get #1, , i
Do While Not EOF(1)
    Text1.Text = Text1.Text & Format(i) & vbCrLf
    Get #1, , i
Loop
Close #1
End Sub
```

This routine opens a binary file and reads a series of integers and displays them in a text box.

See Also **Byte** (data type), **Boolean** (data type), **Close** (statement), **Currency** (data type), **Date** (data type), **Double** (data type), **Integer** (data type), **Long** (data type), **Open** (statement), **Put** (statement), **Single** (data type), **Seek** (statement), **Stop** (statement), **String** (data type), **Variant** (data type)

GetAllSettings

FUNCTION
CCE, LE, PE, EE

Syntax   `Value = GetAllSettings ( app , section )`

Usage   The **GetAllSettings** function returns a two-dimensional array that contains a series of keys and their values from the Windows Registry. Information is stored by application name. Within each application are one or more sections. Within each section are one or more key and value pairs. The format is the same as a standard .INI file. The only real difference is where the information is stored.

> **Tip**
>
> *This function and the related functions **GetSetting**, **SaveSetting**, and **DeleteSetting** are useful to save information about the state from one run to the next.*

Arguments
- *value*—a **Variant** that contains a two-dimensional array with a series of keys and their values from the Windows Registry that corresponds to the application specified in *app* and the section specified in *section*.
- *app*—a **String** that identifies the application.
- *section*—a **String** that identifies a section within the application.

Examples
```
Private Sub Command2_Click()
Dim v As Variant
Dim i As Integer
v = GetAllSettings("VBPR", "Settings")
If IsEmpty(v) Then
   Text1.Text = "No settings are available"
Else
   Text1.Text = ""
   For i = LBound(v, 1) To UBound(v, 1)
      Text1.Text = Text1.Text & v(i, 0) & ":" & v(i, 1) & vbCrLf
   Next i
End If
End Sub
```

This routine retrieves all of the settings made under the application "VBPR" and the section "Settings." Then they are displayed on the screen in the Text1 text box.

See Also   **DeleteSetting** (statement), **GetSetting** (function), **SaveSetting** (statement)

GetAttr

FUNCTION
CCE, LE, PE, EE

Syntax   *AValue* = **GetAttr** (*filename*)

Usage   The **GetAttr** function returns the file attributes for an unopened file.

Arguments
- *AValue*—an **Integer** value containing the attributes. Each bit has a specific meaning as listed in Table G-1.

Attribute Name	Value	Description
vbNormal	0	The file has no attributes set.
vbReadOnly	1	The file has the read only attribute set.
vbHidden	2	The file has the hidden attribute set.
vbSystem	4	The file has the system attribute set.
vbDirectory	16	The file is a directory.
vbArchive	32	The file has the archive attribute set.

Table G-1: Attribute values.

- *filename*—a **String** value that contains the name of a file, including any path information needed.

Examples
```
Private Sub Command1_Click()
Dim i As Integer
On Error Resume Next
i = GetAttr(Text1.Text)
If Err.Number = 0 Then
   Check1.Value = 0
   Check2.Value = 0
   Check3.Value = 0
   Check4.Value = 0
   Check5.Value = 0
   If i And vbReadOnly Then Check1.Value = 1
   If i And vbHidden Then Check2.Value = 1
   If i And vbsystemfile Then Check3.Value = 1
   If i And vbDirectory Then Check4.Value = 1
   If i And vbArchive Then Check5.Value = 1
Else
   MsgBox Err.Description
End If
End Sub
```

This routine gets the attributes for the file specified in the text1 text box and then sets the bits in a series of check boxes that indicate the various bits in the attributes.

See Also   **FileAttr** (function), **SetAttr** (statement)

GetObject

FUNCTION

CCE, LE, PE, EE

Syntax — `RValue = GetObject( [ filename ] [, class ])`

Usage — The **GetObject** will dynamically create an instance of an ActiveX object.

Arguments
- *filename*—a **String** containing the path and filename of an object to be retrieved. If omitted, *class* must be specified.
- *class*—a **String** containing the name of an application and an object type within the application. If omitted, *filename* must be specified.

Examples
```
Private Sub Command1_Click()
Dim myobj As Object
On Error Resume Next
Set myobj = GetObject(App.Path & "\book1.xls")
If Err.Number <> 0 Then
    MsgBox Err.Description
End If
myobj.application.Visible = True
myobj.Parent.Windows(1).Visible = True

End Sub
```

This routine declares a variable of type object and creates an instance of the book1.xls file. Then the application and the worksheet are made visible.

See Also — **CreateObject** (function)

GetSetting

FUNCTION

CCE, LE, PE, EE

Syntax — `Value = GetSetting (app , section , key [, default])`

Usage — The **GetSetting** function returns a single value for a given application, section, and key. You can also provide a default value that will be returned if the setting is not found in the Windows Registry.

> **Tip**
>
> *This function and the related functions **GetAllSettings**, **SaveSetting**, and **DeleteSetting** are useful to save information about the state from one run to the next.*

Arguments
- *value*—a **String** that contains a value associated with the *app*, *section*, and *key* arguments.
- *app*—a **String** that identifies the application.
- *section*—a **String** that identifies a section within the application.
- *key*—a **String** that identifies a keyword within the section.

default—a **String** that will be returned if the *app*, *section*, and *key* arguments can't be found in the Windows Registry.

Examples
```
Private Sub Command3_Click()
Text1.Text = GetSetting("VBPR", "Settings", Text2.Text, "No setting available")
End Sub
```

This routine retrieves a single setting from the Windows Registry.

```
Private Sub Command1_Click()

Unload Me
End Sub

Private Sub Form_Load()
Me.Show 0
Me.Top = GetSetting("VBPR", "GetSetting", "Top", Me.Top)
Me.Left = GetSetting("VBPR", "GetSetting", "Left", Me.Left)
Me.Height = GetSetting("VBPR", "GetSetting", "Height", Me.Height)
Me.Width = GetSetting("VBPR", "GetSetting", "Width", Me.Width)
End Sub

Private Sub Form_Unload(Cancel As Integer)
SaveSetting "VBPR", "GetSetting", "Top", Me.Top
SaveSetting "VBPR", "GetSetting", "Left", Me.Left
SaveSetting "VBPR", "GetSetting", "Height", Me.Height
SaveSetting "VBPR", "GetSetting", "Width", Me.Width
End Sub
```

In this example you see a more practical use of **GetSetting** and **SaveSetting**. Keeping form size and placement from the last time they were used is a desirable feature for the user. With these functions and just a few lines of code, this feature is almost trivial to implement.

In the form's **Load** routine, values for **Top**, **Left**, **Height**, and **Width** are set from values saved in the Windows Registry. If the values don't exist, then the values that the program was compiled with will be used. In the **Unload** routine, the same values are saved into the Registry. The command button exits the program by calling the **Unload** routine.

See Also **DeleteSetting** (statement), **GetAllSettings** (function), **SaveSetting** (statement)

GoSub

STATEMENT

CCE, LE, PE, EE

Syntax **GoSub** *label*

Usage The **GoSub** statement transfers control to a block of code within a procedure and returns back to the statement following the **GoSub** statement.

> **Tip**
>
> *Avoid using the **GoSub** statement. The **GoSub** statement is included in Visual Basic since it was part of the original BASIC language, where the concept of subroutines did not exist. A subroutine is much more flexible than what can be developed using **GoSub** and **Return** statements.*

Arguments *label*—a Visual Basic line label or line number.

Examples
```
Private Sub Command1_Click()
Dim i As Single
On Error Resume Next
i = 1 / 0
GoSub CheckErr
i = 2 / 0
GoSub CheckErr
Exit Sub
CheckErr:
    If Err.Number <> 0 Then
        MsgBox Err.Description
    End If

    Err.Clear

    Return
End Sub
```

This places a common block of code at the end of the subroutine after the CheckErr: line label. Then after each statement I do a **GoSub** to this routine to check for errors. Next, when I've finished executing the test statements, I exit the subroutine before I fall into it. Finally I code the CheckErr routine itself to check for an error, display the error if I find it, and clear the **Err** object before I return.

> **Tip**
>
> *If you want to use **GoSub** statements (something I don't recommend), place them at the end of the subroutine. Before the first **GoSub** routine, place an **Exit Sub** statement to ensure that you do not accidentally fall into one of the **GoSub** routines.*

See Also **Exit** (statement), **GoTo** (statement), **On GoSub** (statement), **On GoTo** (statement), **Return** (statement), **Sub** (statement)

GoTo

STATEMENT

CCE, LE, PE, EE

Syntax **GoTo** *label*

Usage The **GoTo** statement unconditionally transfers control to a block of code within a procedure.

> **Tip**
>
> *Avoid using the **GoTo** statement. The **GoTo** statement is included in Visual Basic since it was part of the original BASIC language. BASIC predates the concept of structured programming. Since structured programs are easier to develop and maintain, you should take advantage of **If Then Else** statements and subroutines and functions rather than using the **GoTo** statement.*

Arguments *label*—a Visual Basic line label or line number.

Examples
```
Private Sub Command1_Click()
Dim i As Integer
Dim j As Integer
i = 1
j = 2
If i <> j Then GoTo Step2
MsgBox "i = j"
GoTo Step4
Step2:
If i > j Then GoTo Step3
MsgBox "i < j"
GoTo Step4
Step3:
MsgBox "i > j"
Step4:
End Sub

Private Sub Command2_Click()
Dim i As Integer
Dim j As Integer
i = 1
j = 2
If i = j Then
    MsgBox "i = j"
ElseIf i < j Then
    MsgBox "i < j"
Else
    MsgBox "i > j"
End If
End Sub
```

This example consists of two subroutines. Both do the same thing. The first routine uses simple **If** statements and **GoTo** statements to determine if *i* is greater than, equal to, or less than *j*. The second routine uses **If Then Else** and **ElseIf** statements to accomplish the same thing.

See Also **Exit** (statement), **GoSub** (statement), **On GoSub** (statement), **On GoTo** (statement), **Return** (statement), **Sub** (statement)

Group

OBJECT

PE, EE

Usage The **Group** object contains information about a group of database users that have been assigned a common set of properties.

Properties
- *GroupObject*.**Name**—a **String** value containing the name of the group. It is limited to 20 characters.
- *GroupObject*.**PID**—a **String** value containing a Personal ID for the group. It can range in size from 4 to 20 characters and can contain only alphanumeric characters. This property is write-only for objects not yet appended to a new collection.
- *GroupObject*.**Properties**—an object reference to a collection of **Property** objects.
- *GroupObject*.**Users**—an object reference to a collection of **User** objects.

Methods **user = GroupObject.CreateUser (*name, pid, password*)**

Usage This method creates a new user in the group.

Arguments
- *user*—a reference to a **User** object containing the new user information.
- *name*—a **String** that uniquely names the new **User** object.
- *pid*—a **String** containing the Personal ID for the new user. It can contain from 4 to 20 alphanumeric characters.
- *password*—a **String** containing the password for the new user. It can be up to 14 characters long and may contain any ASCII character except for Null (ASCII 0).

See Also **DBEngine** (object), **Groups** (collection) , **User** (object), **Workspace** (object)

Groups

COLLECTION

PE, EE

Usage	The **Groups** collection contains a set of **Group** objects used by the **DBEngine** object.
Properties	*GroupsCollection*.**Count**—an **Integer** value that contains the number of items in the collection.

Methods **GroupsCollection.Append** *object*

Usage	This method is used to append a user object to the collection. The appended objects are persistent objects since they are kept in the database until they are explicitly deleted.
Arguments	*object*—a **User** object that was created by the **CreateUser** method of the **Group** object.

ListItemsCollection.Delete *name*

Usage	This method removed a **User** object from the collection.
Arguments	*name*—a **String** object containing the name of a **User** object to be deleted.

ListItemsCollection.Refresh

Usage	This method deletes an item specified by *index* from the collection.
See Also	**DBEngine** (object), **Group** (object), **User** (object), **Workspace** (object)

Hex

FUNCTION

CCE, LE, PE, EE

Syntax   *HValue* = **Hex[$]**(*HNumber*)

Usage   The **Hex** function returns a **String** with the hexadecimal equivalent of the passed number.

Arguments
- *HValue*—a **String** that contains the hexadecimal equivalent of *HNumber*. The largest hex value that will be returned is FFFFFFFF.
- *HNumber*—any numeric value or **String** that contains a number in the range of -2,147,483,648 to 2,147,483,647. Any number outside this range will cause an overflow and fractional values will be rounded to the nearest whole number.

Examples
```
Private Sub Command1_Click()
If IsNumeric(Text1.Text) Then
   Text2.Text = Hex(Text1.Text)
Else
   Text2.Text = "Invalid number"
End If
End Sub
```

This routine converts the value in the text1 text box into its hexadecimal equivalent and stores it in the text2 text box.

See Also   **Oct** (function)

Hour

FUNCTION

CCE, LE, PE, EE

Syntax   *HValue* = **Hour** (*Time*)

Usage   The **Hour** function returns the hour of day from a numeric, **Date**, or **String** variable containing a valid date or time. If only a date is supplied, this function will always return 0.

Arguments
- *HValue*—an **Integer** value in the range of 0 to 23, where 0 corresponds to midnight and 23 corresponds to 11:00 P.M.
- *Time*—a **Date**, **Long**, or **String** value that contains a valid time or date.

Examples
```
Private Sub Command1_Click()
If IsDate(Text1.Text) Then
   Text2.Text = Hour(Text1.Text)
Else
   Text2.Text = "Illegal time:"
End If
End Sub
```

This routine verifies that the date or time in the text1 text box is valid and then extracts the hour value from the text box.

See Also **CDate** (function), **Date** (data type), **Day** (function), **IsDate** (function), **Minute** (function), **Now** (function), **Second** (function), **Time** (function), **Time** (statement)

HScrollBar

CONTROL

CCE, LE, PE, EE

Usage The **HScrollBar** control is an intrinsic control that provides you with a tool to capture analog input from the user. The horizontal scroll bar consists of a short, wide box with arrows at each end. In between the arrows is another box that the user can position anywhere inside the box. **HScrollBar** will return a **Value** that represents the relative position of the scroll box inside the scroll bar.

Tip

If you position the scroll arrows next to each other, you have a spinner where you can increment or decrement a number. This may be useful where you wish to provide an alternate method to entering a number into a text box.

Properties
- *HScrollBarControl.***Container**—an object that you can use to set or return the container of the control at run time. You cannot set this property at design time.
- *HScrollBarControl.***DragIcon**—an object containing the picture value of an icon. At design time, you can specify an icon file that has a file type of .ICO.

Tip

*This value can be created by copying the value from another control's **DragIcon** value, a form's icon, or by using the **LoadPicture** function.*

- *HScrollBarControl.***DragMode**—an **Integer** value (see Table H-1) specifying how the control will respond to a drag request.

Tip

*Setting **DragMode** to vbAutomatic will automatically begin a drag operation when the user clicks on the control. However, the control will not respond to the usual mouse events (**Click**, **DblClick**).*

DragMode Name	Value	Description
vbManual	0	The **Drag** method must be used to begin a drag-and-drop operation (default value).
vbAutomatic	1	The source control will automatically begin a drag-and-drop operation when the user clicks on the control.

Table H-1: *DragMode values.*

- *HScrollBarControl*.**Enabled**—a **Boolean** value when **True** means that the control will respond to events. When **False**, the control will not respond to events.
- *HScrollBarControl*.**Height**—a **Single** that contains the height of the control.
- *HScrollBarControl*.**HelpContextID**—a **Long** that contains a help file context ID number which references an entry in the help file. When the user presses the F1 key while this control is active, the corresponding entry in the help file will automatically be displayed. A value of zero means that no context number was specified.

> **Tip**
>
> *A help file must be compiled using the Windows Help Compiler available in the Professional and Enterprise editions of Visual Basic.*

- *HScrollBarControl*.**hWnd**—a **Long** that contains a Windows handle to the control.

> **Tip**
>
> *The **hWnd** property is most useful when making calls to Windows API functions. Since this value can change during execution, do not save the value into a variable for later use.*

- *HScrollBarControl*.**Index**—an **Integer** that uniquely identifies a control in a control array.
- *HScrollBarControl*.**LargeChange**—the **Integer** value that is added or subtracted from the **Value** property each time the user clicks in the area between the scroll box and the scroll arrow.
- *HScrollBarControl*.**Left**—a **Single** that contains the distance measured in twips between the left edge of the control and the left edge of the control's container.
- *HScrollBarControl*.**Max**—the **Integer** value that is returned when the scroll box is at the extreme right position, next to the scroll right arrow. The default value is 32767.
- *HScrollBarControl*.**Min**—the **Integer** value that is returned when the scroll box is at the extreme left position, next to the scroll left arrow. The default value is 0.
- *HScrollBarControl*.**MouseIcon**—a picture object (a bitmap, icon, or metafile) that will be used as a cursor when the **MousePointer** property is set to 99. Note that Visual Basic does not support color cursors from a .CUR file. A color icon from an .ICO file should be used instead.
- *HScrollBarControl*.**MousePointer**—an **Integer** value (see Table H-2) that contains the value of the cursor that should be displayed when the cursor is moved over this control. Use *vbCustom* to display the custom icon stored in the **MouseIcon** property.

Cursor Name	Value	Description
vbDefault	0	Shape determined by the object (default value)
vbArrow	1	Arrow
vbCrosshair	2	Crosshair
vbIbeam	3	I beam
vbIconPointer	4	Square inside a square
vbSizePointer	5	Four-sided arrow (north, south, east, west)

Cursor Name	Value	Description
vbSizeNESW	6	Two-sided arrow (northeast, southwest)
vbSizeNS	7	Two-sided arrow (north, south)
vbSizeNWSE	8	Two-sided arrow (northwest, southeast)
vbSizeWE	9	Two-sided arrow (west, east)
vbUpArrow	10	Single-sided arrow pointing north
vbHourglass	11	Hourglass
vbNoDrop	12	No drop
vbArrowHourglass	13	An arrow and an hourglass
vbArrowQuestion	14	An arrow and a question mark
vbSizeAll	15	Size all
vbCustom	99	Custom icon from the **MouseIcon** property of this control

Table H-2: Cursor values.

- *HScrollBarControl*.**Name**—a **String** that contains the name of the control that will be used to reference the control in a Visual Basic program. This property is read only at run time.
- *HScrollBarControl*.**Parent**—an object that contains a reference to the **Form**, **Frame**, or other container that contains the **HScrollBar** control.
- *HScrollBarControl*.**RightToLeft**—a **Boolean** value when **True** means that the text is displayed from right to left. When **False** means that the text is displayed from left to right. A bi-directional version of Windows is required to set this property to **True**.
- *HScrollBarControl*.**SmallChange**—the **Integer** value that is added or subtracted from the **Value** property each time the user clicks on the scroll arrow.
- *HScrollBarControl*.**TabIndex**—an Integer that determines the order that a user will tab through the objects on a form.
- *HScrollBarControl*.**TabStop**—a **Boolean** value when **True** means that the user can tab to this object. When **False**, means that this control will be skipped to the next control in the **TabIndex** order.
- *HScrollBarControl*.**Tag**—a **String** that can hold programmer-specific information. This property is not used by Visual Basic.
- *HScrollBarControl*.**Top**—a **Single** that contains the distance measured in twips between the top edge of the control and the top edge of the control's container.
- *HScrollBarControl*.**Value**—an **Integer** that represents the relative position of the scroll box inside the **HScrollBar**. Changing the **Value** property in code will trigger the **Change** event.
- *HScrollBarControl*.**Visible**—a **Boolean** value when **True** means that the control is visible. When **False** means that the control is not visible.

Tip

You can hide the control until the program is ready to display it using this property.

- *HScrollBarControl*.**WhatsThisHelpID**—a **Long** that contains a help file context ID number that references an entry in the help file. This provides a What's This PopUp help display in response to the What's This button in the upper right corner of the window.
- *HScrollBarControl*.**Width**—a **Single** that contains the width of the control.

Methods

HScrollBarControl.Drag [DragAction]

Usage This method begins, ends, or cancels a drag operation.

Arguments *DragAction*—an **Integer** that contains a value selected from Table H-3 below.

DragAction Name	Value	Description
vbCancel	0	Cancels any drag operation in progress.
vbBeginDrag	1	Begins a drag operation (default).
vbEndDrag	2	Ends a drag operation and drops *object*.

Table H-3: DragAction values.

HScrollBarControl.Move Left [, Top [, Width [, Height]]]

Usage This method changes the position and the size of the **HScrollBar** control. The **ScaleMode** of the **Form** or other container object that holds the animation control will determine the units used to specify the coordinates.

Arguments
- *Left*—a **Single** that specifies the new position of the left edge of the control.
- *Top*—a **Single** that specifies the new position of the top edge of the control.
- *Width*—a **Single** that specifies the new width of the control.
- *Height*—a **Single** that specifies the new height of the control.

HScrollBarControl.Refresh

Usage This method redraws the contents of the control.

HScrollBarControl.SetFocus

Usage This method transfers the focus from the form or control that currently has the focus to this control. To receive the focus, this control must be enabled and visible.

HScrollBarControl.ShowWhatsThis

Usage This method displays the ShowWhatsThis help information for this control.

HScrollBarControl.ZOrder [position]

Usage This method specifies the position of the animation control relative to the other objects on the form.

> **Tip**
>
> Note that there are three layers of objects on a form; the back layer is the drawing space which contains the results of the graphical methods, the middle layer contains graphical objects such as the **HScrollBar** and **Labels**, and the top layer contains nongraphical controls such as the **CommandButton**. The **ZOrder** method only affects how the objects are arranged within a single layer.

HScrollBar • 381

Arguments
- *position*—an **Integer** that specifies the relative position of this object. A value of 0 means that the control is positioned at the head of the list, a value of 1 means that the control will be placed at the end of the list.

Events

Private Sub *HScrollBarControl*_Change([*index* As Integer])

Usage This event occurs when the text in the text box part of the control is changed.

> **Warning**
>
> *Changing the **Value** property in your program will cause the **Change** event to be triggered. While this normally won't cause a problem, changing the **Value** property inside the **Change** event could trigger an infinite recursion that could ultimately end in the program crashing.*

Arguments
- *index*—an **Integer** that uniquely identifies a control in a control array. This argument is not present if the control is not part of a control array.

Private Sub *HScrollBarControl*_DragDrop([*index* As Integer ,] *source* as Control, *x* as Single, *y* as Single)

Usage This event occurs when a drag-and-drop operation is completed using the Drag method with a *DragAction* value of *vbEndDrag*.

> **Tip**
>
> *When using drag-and-drop operations, use the **DragOver** event to determine what you want the cursor to look like while the cursor moves over the control.*

Arguments
- *index*—an **Integer** that uniquely identifies a control in a control array. This argument is not present if the control is not part of a control array.
- *source*—a control object that is the control that is being dragged.

> **Tip**
>
> *You can access a property or method from the source control by using source.property or source.method. You can determine the type of object or control by using the **TypeOf** operator.*

- *x*—a **Single** that contains the horizontal location of the mouse pointer.
- *y*—a **Single** that contains the vertical location of the mouse pointer.

Private Sub *HScrollBarControl*_DragOver([*index* As Integer ,] *source* as Control, *x* as Single, *y* as Single, *state* as Integer)

Usage This event occurs while a drag operation is in progress and the cursor is moved over the control.

> **Tip**
>
> When using drag-and-drop operations, use the **DragOver** event to determine what you want the cursor to look like while the cursor moves over the control. When state is 0, you can change the cursor to a no drop (vbNoDrop) cursor or highlight the field that the cursor is near. When state is 1, you can undo the changes you made when the state was 0.

Arguments
- *index*—an **Integer** that uniquely identifies a control in a control array. This argument is not present if the control is not part of a control array.
- *source*—a control object that is the control that is being dragged.

> **Tip**
>
> You can access a property or method from the source control by using source.property or source.method. You can determine the type of object or control by using the **TypeOf** operator.

- *x*—a **Single** that contains the horizontal location of the mouse pointer.
- *y*—a **Single** that contains the vertical location of the mouse pointer.
- *state*—an **Integer** value (see Table H-4) that indicates the state of the object being dragged.

state Name	Value	Description
vbEnter	0	The dragged object is entering range of the control.
vbLeave	1	The dragged object is leaving range of the control.
vbOver	2	The dragged object has moved from one position over the control to another.

Table H-4: state values.

Private Sub *HScrollBarControl* _GotFocus ([*index* As Integer])

Usage   This event occurs when the control is given focus.

> **Tip**
>
> You can use this routine to display help or other information in a status bar.

Arguments
- *index*—an **Integer** that uniquely identifies a control in a control array. This argument is not present if the control is not part of a control array.

Private Sub *HScrollBarControl* _KeyDown ([*index* As Integer ,] *keycode* as Integer, *shift* as Single)

Usage   This event occurs when a key is pressed while the control has the focus.

Arguments
- *index*—an **Integer** that uniquely identifies a control in a control array. This argument is not present if the control is not part of a control array.
- *keycode*—an **Integer** that contains information about which key was pressed.
- *shift*—an **Integer** value (see Table H-5) that contains information about the Shift and Alt keys that were pushed when the mouse button was pressed. These values can be added together if more than one key was down. For instance, a value of 5 means that the Shift and Alt keys were both down when the mouse button was pressed.

shift Name	Value	Description
vbShiftMask	1	The Shift key was pressed.
vbCtrlMask	2	The Ctrl key was pressed.
vbAltMask	4	The Alt key was pressed.

Table H-5: *shift values.*

Private Sub *HScrollBarControl* _KeyPress([*index* As Integer ,] *keychar* as Integer)

Usage This event occurs whenever a key is pressed while the control has the focus.

Arguments
- *index*—an **Integer** that uniquely identifies a control in a control array. This argument is not present if the control is not part of a control array.
- *keychar*—an **Integer** that contains the ASCII character that was pressed.

Private Sub *ComoBoxControl* _KeyUp ([*index* As Integer ,] *keycode* as Integer, *shift* as Single)

Usage This event occurs when a key is released while the control has the focus.

Arguments
- *index*—an **Integer** that uniquely identifies a control in a control array. This argument is not present if the control is not part of a control array.
- *keycode*—an **Integer** that contains information about which key was released.
- *shift*—an **Integer** value (see Table H-6) that contains information about the Shift and Alt keys that were pushed when the mouse button was pressed. These values can be added together if more than one key was down. For instance, a value of 5 means that the Shift and Alt keys were both down when the mouse button was pressed.

shift Name	Value	Description
vbShiftMask	1	The Shift key was pressed.
vbCtrlMask	2	The Ctrl key was pressed.
vbAltMask	4	The Alt key was pressed.

Table H-6: *shift values.*

Private Sub *HScrollBarControl*_LostFocus ([*index* As Integer])

Usage   This event occurs when the control loses focus.

Tip

This routine is useful in performing data verification.

Arguments   ▪ *index*—an **Integer** that uniquely identifies a control in a control array. This argument is not present if the control is not part of a control array.

Private Sub *HScrollBarControl*_Scroll ([*index* As Integer])

Usage   This event is called each time the scroll bar is repositioned in the drop-down box.

Arguments   ▪ *index*—an **Integer** that uniquely identifies a control in a control array. This argument is not present if the control is not part of a control array.

Examples
```
Private Sub Form_Load()

HScroll1.Min = 0
HScroll1.Max = 100
HScroll1.Value = 50
HScroll1.LargeChange = 5
HScroll1.SmallChange = 1

End Sub

Private Sub HScroll1_Change()

Text1.Text = Format(HScroll1.Value)

End Sub
```

This program initializes the horizontal scroll bar with values for **Min**, **Max**, **Value**, **LargeChange**, and **SmallChange**. Note that setting the **Value** property will trigger the **Change** event. The **Change** event will display the current **Value** in the text1 text box.

See Also   **VScrollBar** (control)

Hyperlink

OBJECT

CCE, LE, PE, EE

Usage The **Hyperlink** object is used to direct a hyperlink container object (like Microsoft Internet Explorer) to perform links to other locations.

Methods *HyperlinkObject.GoBack*

Usage This method is used to go back one level if the container supports OLE hyperlinking, otherwise a run-time error will occur.

HyperlinkObject.GoForward

Usage This method is used to go forward one level if the container supports OLE hyperlinking, otherwise a run-time error will occur.

HyperlinkObject.NavigateTo target [, location [, frame]]

Usage This method executes a hyperlink jump to the location specified in *target*.

Arguments
- *target*—a **String** value that specifies the location to which you want to navigate. It can be either a document or a Uniform Resource Locator (URL).
- *location*—a **String** value that specifies the location in the *target* to which you want to navigate. If omitted, the default document will be used.
- *frame*—a **String** value that specifies the name of the frame in the *target* to which you want to navigate. If omitted, the default frame will be used.

See Also **Form** (control), **Image** (control), **LoadPicture** (function), **PictureBox** (control), **RichTextBox** (control), **TextBox** (control)

If ... Then ... Else   STATEMENT

                                                    CCE LE PE EE

Syntax   If *expr* **Then** [list of statements] **Else** [list of statements]

              If *expr* **Then**
                    [list of statements]
              Elseif *expr* **Then**
                    [list of statements]
                        .
                        .
                        .
              Elseif *expr* **Then**
                    [list of statements]
              Else
                    [list of statements]
              End If

Usage   The **If ... Then ... Else** statement allows you to execute a list of statements based on the value of a **Boolean** expression. When the expression is **True** the list of statements immediately following **Then** will be executed, otherwise the list of statements following the **Else** will be executed. **Elseif ... Else** can be used in place of **Else** to execute another list of statements based on the value of another expression.

The **If** statement takes two forms. The first form is where everything is on a single line. Each statement in the list of statements must be separated by a colon (":").

The second form of the **If** statement spans multiple lines. This form more clearly shows the statements and how they are related to the **If** statement and also permits an **ElseIf** clause that was not present in the first form.

Arguments   *expr*—a **Boolean** expression.

Examples
```
Private Sub Command1_Click()
If Option1.Value Then
    Text1.Text = "Stop"
    Text1.BackColor = &H80FF80
Else
    Text1.Text = "Go"
    Text1.BackColor = &H80000005
End If
End Sub

§Private Sub Command2_Click()
If Option1.Value Then Text2.Text = "Stop": Text2.BackColor = &H8080FF Else
    Text2.Text = "Go": Text2.BackColor = &H80000005
End Sub
```

In these routines, an **If** statement evaluates Option1.Value to determine which statements to execute. For all practical purposes they are the same, differing only in how the **If** statement is arranged.

See Also   **IIf** (function) , **Select Case** (statement), **Switch** (function)

IIf

FUNCTION

CCE LE PE EE

Syntax
: `Value = IIf ( expr, val1, val2 )`

Usage
: This function is like an **If** statement for expressions, since a **Boolean** expression is evaluated (*expr*), letting you choose one value (*val1*) if it is **True** or another (*val2*) if it is **False**.

Arguments
: - *Value*—will contain *val1* if *expr* is **True**, otherwise it will contain *val2*.
  - *expr*—a **Boolean** expression.
  - *val1*—a **Variant** containing any string or numeric expression.
  - *val2*—a **Variant** containing any string or numeric expression.

Examples
: ```
Private Sub Command1_Click()
Text3.Text = IIf(Option1.Value, Text1.Text, Text2.Text)
End Sub
```

    This routine copies Text1.Text into Text3.Text if Option1.Value is **True**. Otherwise, Text2.Text is copied into Text3.Text.

See Also
: **If** (statement), **Select Case** (statement), **Switch** (function)

# Image

**CONTROL**

**CCE  LE  PE  EE**

Usage
: The **Image** control is an intrinsic control that can display an icon file (.ICO), metafile (.WMF), bitmap file (.BMP), a .GIF file, or a .JPG file.

> **Tip**
>
> The **Image** control is more efficient than the **PictureBox** control, while offering less functions. This makes it highly desirable for displaying graphic images. For more complex functions, the **PictureBox** control should be used.

Properties
: - *ImageControl*.**Appearance**—an **Integer** value (see Table I-1) that specifies how the combo box will appear on the form.

    | AppearanceValue | Description |
    | --- | --- |
    | 0 | The image box displays without the 3D effects. |
    | 1 | The image box displays with 3D effects (default value). |

    Table I-1: **Appearance** values.

  - *ImageControl*.**BackColor**—a **Long** that contains the suggested value for the background color of the control.
  - *FormObject*.**BorderStyle**—an **Integer** value (see Table I-2) specifying how the border will be drawn. These values also indicate how the form can be resized, and are read only at run time.
```

BorderStyle Name	Value	Description
vbBSNone	0	No border, control box menu, title, bar, maximize and minimize buttons. Cannot be resized.
vbFixedSingle	1	Single line around the form. Form can only be resized by maximize and minimize buttons.

Table I-2: **BorderStyle** *values.*

- *ImageControl*.**Container**—an object that sets or returns the container of the control at run time. This property cannot be set at design time.
- *ImageControl*.**DataChanged**—a **Boolean** that applies only to data bound controls. When **True**, means that the data contained in this control was changed either by the user or by some means other than retrieving data from the current record. When **False**, means the data in the control is unchanged from the current record. Simply reading the next record is not sufficient to set the **DataChanged** property to **True**.

   When the **Data** control moves to the next record, it will automatically invoke the **Edit** and **Update** methods to post the changes to the database.
- *ImageControl*.**DataField**—a **String** value that associates the control with a field in a **RecordSet** object in a **Data** control.
- *ImageControl*.**DataSource**—a **String** value that associates the control with a **Data** control.
- *ImageControl*.**DragIcon**—an object that contains the picture value of an icon. At design time, you can specify an icon file that has a file type of .ICO.

Tip

This value can be created by copying the value from another control's **DragIcon** *value, a form's icon, or by using the* **LoadPicture** *function.*

- *ImageControl*.**DragMode**—an **Integer** value (see Table I-3) specifying how the control will respond to a drag request.

Tip

Setting **DragMode** *to* vbAutomatic *will automatically begin a drag operation when the user clicks on the control. However, the control will not respond to the usual mouse events (***Click***,* ***DblClick***).*

DragMode Name	Value	Description
vbManual	0	The Drag method must be used to begin a drag-and-drop operation (default value).
vbAutomatic	1	The source control will automatically begin a drag-and-drop operation when the user clicks on the control.

Table I-3: **DragMode** *values.*

- *ImageControl*.**Enabled**—a **Boolean** value when **True** means that the control will respond to events. When **False**, the control will not respond to events.

- *ImageControl*.**Height**—a **Single** that contains the height of the control.
- *ImageControl*.**Index**—an **Integer** that uniquely identifies a control in a control array.
- *ImageControl*.**Left**—a **Single** that contains the distance measured in twips between the left edge of the control and the left edge of the control's container.
- *ImageControl*.**MouseIcon**—a picture object (a bitmap, icon, or metafile) that will be used as a cursor when the **MousePointer** property is set to 99. Note that Visual Basic does not support color cursors from a .CUR file. A color icon from an .ICO file should be used instead.
- *ImageControl*.**MousePointer**—an **Integer** value (see Table I-4) that contains the value of the cursor that should be displayed when the cursor is moved over this control. Use *vbCustom* to display the custom icon stored in the **MouseIcon** property.

Cursor Name	Value	Description
vbDefault	0	Shape determined by the object (default value)
vbArrow	1	Arrow
vbCrosshair	2	Crosshair
vbIbeam	3	I beam
vbIconPointer	4	Square inside a square
vbSizePointer	5	Four-sided arrow (north, south, east, west)
vbSizeNESW	6	Two-sided arrow (northeast, southwest)
vbSizeNS	7	Two-sided arrow (north, south)
vbSizeNWSE	8	Two-sided arrow (northwest, southeast)
vbSizeWE	9	Two-sided arrow (west, east)
vbUpArrow	10	Single-sided arrow pointing north
vbHourglass	11	Hourglass
vbNoDrop	12	No Drop
vbArrowHourglass	13	An arrow and an Hourglass
vbArrowQuestion	14	An arrow and a question mark
vbSizeAll	15	Size all
vbCustom	99	Custom icon from the **MouseIcon** property of this control

Table I-4: **Cursor** *values*.

- *ImageControl*.**Name**—a **String** that contains the name of the control that will be used to reference the control in a Visual Basic program. This property is read only at run time.
- *ImageControl*.**OLEDragMode**—an **Integer** value (see Table I-5) that describes how the control will respond to OLE drag operations.

> **Note**
>
> When the **DragMode** is *True*, the standard Visual Basic drag-and-drop functions will override the OLE drag-and-drop functions.

OLEDragMode Name	Value	Description
vbOLEDragManual	0	All drag requests will be handled by the programmer (default value).
vbOLEDrapAutomatic	1	The control responds to all OLE drag request automatically.

Table I-5: **OLEDragMode** *values*.

- *ImageControl*.**OLEDropMode**—an **Integer** value (see Table I-6) that describes how the control will respond to OLE drop operations.

OLEDropMode Name	Value	Description
vbOLEDropNone	0	The control does not accept OLE drops. The cursor is changed to the No Drop cursor (default value).
vbOLEDropManual	1	The control responds to OLE drops under the program's control (manual).
vbOLEDropAutomatic	2	The control automatically accepts OLE drops if it recognizes the format of the data object.

Table I-6: **OLEDropMode** values.

- *ImageControl*.**Parent**—an object that contains a reference to the **Form, Frame,** or other container that contains the **Image** control.
- *ImageControl*.**Picture**—a picture object (a bitmap, icon, metafile, GIF, or JPEG) that will be displayed on the control. You can also use the **LoadPicture** function at run time to load a bitmap, icon, or metafile.
- *ImageControl*.**Stretch**—a **Boolean** value when **True** means that the image will be resized to fit the control and when **False** means that the image will not be resized. Resizing the control will automatically resize the image if this control is set to **True**.
- *ImageControl*.**Tag**—a **String** that can hold programmer specific information. This property is not used by Visual Basic.
- *ImageControl*.**ToolTipText**—a **String** that holds a text value that can be displayed as a **ToolTip** box that displays whenever the cursor is held over the control for about one second.
- *ImageControl*.**Top**—a **Single** that contains the distance measured in twips between the top edge of the control and the top edge of the control's container.
- *ImageControl*.**Visible**—a **Boolean** value when **True** means that the control is visible. When **False** means that the control is not visible.

> **Tip**
>
> *This property can hide the control until the program is ready to display it.*

- *ImageControl*.**WhatsThisHelpID**—a **Long** that contains a help file context ID number which references an entry in the help file. This provides a What's This PopUp help display in response to the What's This button in the upper right corner of the window.
- *ImageControl*.**Width**—a **Single** that contains the width of the control.

Methods

ImageControl.Drag [*DragAction*]

Usage This method begins, ends, or cancels a drag operation.

Arguments
- *DragAction*—an **Integer** that contains a value selected from Table I-7 below.

DragAction Name	Value	Description
vbCancel	0	Cancels any drag operation in progress.
vbBeginDrag	1	Begins a drag operation (default).
vbEndDrag	2	Ends a drag operation and drops *object*.

Table I-7: DragAction *values.*

*ImageControl.*Move *Left* [, *Top* [, *Width* [, *Height*]]]

Usage   This method changes the position and the size of the **Image** control. The **ScaleMode** of the **Form** or other container object that holds the animation control will determine the units used to specify the coordinates.

Arguments
- *Left*—a **Single** that specifies the new position of the left edge of the control.
- *Top*—a **Single** that specifies the new position of the top edge of the control.
- *Width*—a **Single** that specifies the new width of the control.
- *Height*—a **Single** that specifies the new height of the control.

*ImageControl.*OLEDrag

Usage   This method begins an **OLEDrag** and drop operation. Invoking this method will trigger the **OLEStartDrag** event.

*ImageControl.*Refresh

Usage   This method redraws the contents of the control.

*ImageControl.*ShowWhatsThis

Usage   This method displays the ShowWhatsThis help information for this control.

*ImageControl.*ZOrder [*position*]

Usage   This method specifies the position of the **Image** control relative to the other objects on the form.

Tip

Note that there are three layers of objects on a form: the back layer is the drawing space which contains the results of the graphical methods, the middle layer contains graphical objects and **Labels***, and the top layer contains nongraphical controls such as the* **CommandButton***. The* **ZOrder** *method only affects how the objects are arranged within a single layer.*

Arguments
- *position*—an **Integer** that specifies the relative position of this object. A value of 0 means that the control is positioned at the head of the list, a value of 1 means that the control will be placed at the end of the list.

Events **Private Sub *ImageControl*_Click([*index* As Integer])**

> Usage   This event occurs when the user clicks a mouse button while the cursor is over the control.
>
> Arguments   ▪ *index*—an **Integer** that uniquely identifies a control in a control array. This argument is not present if the control is not part of a control array.

Private Sub *ImageControl*_DblClick([*index* As Integer])

> Usage   This event occurs when the user double-clicks a mouse button while over the control.
>
> Arguments   ▪ *index*—an **Integer** that uniquely identifies a control in a control array. This argument is not present if the control is not part of a control array.

Private Sub *ImageControl*_DragDrop([*index* As Integer ,] *source* Panel Control, *x* As Single, *y* As Single)

> Usage   This event occurs when a drag-and-drop operation is completed by using the Drag method with a *DragAction* value of *vbEndDrag*.

Tip

*When using drag-and-drop operations, use the **DragOver** event to determine what the cursor should look like while the cursor moves over the control.*

> Arguments   ▪ *index*—an **Integer** that uniquely identifies a control in a control array. This argument is not present if the control is not part of a control array.
>
> ▪ *source*—a control object that is the control that is being dragged.

Tip

You can access a property or method from the source control by using source.property *or* source.method. *You can determine the type of object or control by using the **TypeOf** operator.*

> ▪ *x*—a **Single** that contains the horizontal location of the mouse pointer.
> ▪ *y*—a **Single** that contains the vertical location of the mouse pointer.

Private Sub *ImageControl*_DragOver([*index* As Integer ,] *source* As Control, *x* As Single, *y* As Single, *state* As Integer)

> Usage   This event occurs while a drag operation is in progress and the cursor is moved over the control.

> **Tip**
>
> When using drag-and-drop operations, use the **DragOver** event to determine what the cursor should look like while the cursor moves over the control. When state is 0, you can change the cursor to a No Drop (vbNoDrop) cursor or highlight the field that the cursor is near. When state is 1, you can undo the changes you made when the state was 0.

Arguments
- *index*—an **Integer** that uniquely identifies a control in a control array. This argument is not present if the control is not part of a control array.
- *source*—a control object that is the control that is being dragged.

> **Tip**
>
> You can access a property or method from the source control by using source.property or source.method. You can determine the type of object or control by using the **TypeOf** operator.

- *x*—a **Single** that contains the horizontal location of the mouse pointer.
- *y*—a **Single** that contains the vertical location of the mouse pointer.
- *state*—an **Integer** value (see Table I-8) that indicates the state of the object being dragged.

state Name	Value	Description
vbEnter	0	The dragged object is entering range of the control.
vbLeave	1	The dragged object is leaving range of the control.
vbOver	2	The dragged object has moved from one position over the control to another.

Table I-8: state *values*.

Private Sub *ImageControl* _MouseDown([*index* As Integer ,] *button* As Integer, *shift* As Single, *x* As Single, *y* As Single)

Usage
This event occurs when a mouse button is pressed while the cursor is over the control.

Arguments
- *index*—an **Integer** that uniquely identifies a control in a control array. This argument is not present if the control is not part of a control array.
- *button*—an **Integer** value (see Table I-9) that contains information about the mouse buttons that were pressed. Only one button will be indicated when this event occurs.

button Name	Value	Description
vbLeftButton	1	The left button was pressed.
vbRightButton	2	The right button was pressed.
vbMiddleButton	4	The middle button was pressed.

Table I-9: button *values*.

- *shift*—an **Integer** value (see Table I-10) that contains information about the Shift and Alt keys that were pushed when the mouse button was pressed. These values can be added together if more than one key was down. For instance, a value of 5 would mean that the Shift and Alt keys were both down when the mouse button was pressed.

shift Name	Value	Description
vbShiftMask	1	The Shift key was pressed.
vbCtrlMask	2	The Ctrl key was pressed.
vbAltMask	4	The Alt key was pressed.

Table I-10: shift *values*.

- *x*—a **Single** that contains the horizontal location of the mouse pointer.
- *y*—a **Single** that contains the vertical location of the mouse pointer.

Private Sub *ImageControl*_MouseMove ([*index* As Integer ,] *button* As Integer, *shift* As Single, *x* As Single, *y* As Single)

Usage: This event occurs while the cursor is moved over the control.

Arguments:
- *index*—an **Integer** that uniquely identifies a control in a control array. This argument is not present if the control is not part of a control array.
- *button*—an **Integer** value (see Table I-11) that contains information about the mouse buttons that were pressed. These values can be added together if more than one button was pushed. For instance, a value of 3 means that both the left and right buttons were pressed. A value of 0 means that no buttons were pressed.

button Name	Value	Description
vbLeftButton	1	The left button was pressed.
vbRightButton	2	The right button was pressed.
vbMiddleButton	4	The middle button was pressed.

Table I-11: button *values*.

- *shift*—an **Integer** value (see Table I-12) that contains information about the Shift and Alt keys that were pushed when the mouse button was pressed. For instance, a value of 5 would mean that the Shift and Alt keys were both down when the mouse button was pressed. A value of 0 means that none of these keys were pressed.

shift Name	Value	Description
vbShiftMask	1	The Shift key was pressed.
vbCtrlMask	2	The Ctrl key was pressed.
vbAltMask	4	The Alt key was pressed.

Table I-12: shift *values*.

- *x*—a **Single** that contains the horizontal location of the mouse pointer.
- *y*—a **Single** that contains the vertical location of the mouse pointer.

Private Sub *ImageControl* _MouseUp([*index* As Integer ,] *button* As Integer, *shift* As Single, *x* As Single, *y* As Single)

Usage
: This event occurs when a mouse button is released while the cursor is over the control.

Arguments
: - *index*—an **Integer** that uniquely identifies a control in a control array. This argument is not present if the control is not part of a control array.
  - *button*—an **Integer** value (see Table I-13) that contains information about the mouse buttons that were released. Only one of these values will be present.

button Name	Value	Description
vbLeftButton	1	The left button was released.
vbRightButton	2	The right button was released.
vbMiddleButton	4	The middle button was released.

Table I-13: button *values*.

- *shift*—an **Integer** value (see Table I-14) that contains information about the Shift and Alt keys that were pushed when the mouse button was released. These values can be added together if more than one key was down. For instance, a value of 5 would mean that the Shift and Alt keys were both down when the mouse button was released. A value of 0 means that none of these keys were pressed.

shift Name	Value	Description
vbShiftMask	1	The Shift key was pressed.
vbCtrlMask	2	The Ctrl key was pressed.
vbAltMask	4	The Alt key was pressed.

Table I-14: shift *values*.

- *x*—a **Single** that contains the horizontal location of the mouse pointer.
- *y*—a **Single** that contains the vertical location of the mouse pointer.

Private Sub *ImageControl*_OLECompleteDrag([*index* As Integer ,] *effect* As Long)

Usage — This event tells the source control the results of an OLE drag-and-drop operation. This is the final event to occur in the series of actions that make up an OLE drag-and-drop operation.

Arguments
- *index*—an **Integer** that uniquely identifies a control in a control array. This argument is not present if the control is not part of a control array.
- *effect*—a **Long** (see Table I-15) that returns the status of the OLE drag-and-drop operation.

effect Name	Value	Description
vbDropEffectNone	0	The operation was canceled or the target control can't accept the drop operation.
vbDropEffectCopy	1	The operation copied data from the source control to the target control. The original data is unchanged.
vbDropEffectMove	2	The operation results in a link from the original data to the target control.

Table I-15: effect *values.*

Private Sub *ImageControl*_OLEDragDrop([*index* As Integer ,] *data* As DataObject, *effect* As Long, *button* As Integer, *shift* As Single, *x* As Single, *y* As Single)

Usage — This event tells the source control the results of an OLE drag-and-drop operation. This is the final event to occur in the series of actions that make up an OLE drag-and-drop operation.

Arguments
- *index*—an **Integer** that uniquely identifies a control in a control array. This argument is not present if the control is not part of a control array.
- *data*—a **DataObject** that contains the formats that the source control will provide. If the data is not contained in the **DataObject**, then it can be retrieved with the **GetData** method.
- *effect*—a **Long** (see Table I-16) that returns the status of the OLE drag-and-drop operation.

effect Name	Value	Description
vbDropEffectNone	0	The operation was canceled or the target control can't accept the drop operation.
vbDropEffectCopy	1	The operation copied data from the source control to the target control. The original data is unchanged.
vbDropEffectMove	2	The operation results in a link from the original data to the target control.

Table I-16: effect *values.*

- *button*—an **Integer** value (see Table I-17) that contains information about the mouse buttons that were pressed. These values can be added together if more than one button was pushed. For instance, a value of 3 means that both the left and right buttons were pressed. A value of 0 means that no buttons were pressed.

button Name	Value	Description
vbLeftButton	1	The left button was pressed.
vbRightButton	2	The right button was pressed.
vbMiddleButton	4	The middle button was pressed.

Table I-17: button *values.*

- *shift*—an **Integer** value (see Table I-18) that contains information about the Shift and Alt keys that were pushed when the mouse button was released. These values can be added together if more than one key was down. For instance, a value of 5 would mean that the Shift and Alt keys were both down when the mouse button was released. A value of 0 means that none of these keys were pressed.

shift Name	Value	Description
vbShiftMask	1	The Shift key was pressed.
vbCtrlMask	2	The Ctrl key was pressed.
vbAltMask	4	The Alt key was pressed.

Table I-18: shift *values.*

- *x*—a **Single** that contains the horizontal location of the mouse pointer.
- *y*—a **Single** that contains the vertical location of the mouse pointer.

Private Sub *ImageControl* _OLEDragOver([*index* As Integer ,] *data* As DataObject, *effect* As Long, *button* As Integer, *shift* As Single, *x* As Single, *y* As Single, *state* As Integer)

Usage — This event happens when an OLE drag-and-drop operation is in progress.

Arguments
- *index*—an **Integer** that uniquely identifies a control in a control array. This argument is not present if the control is not part of a control array.
- *data*—a **DataObject** that contains the formats that the source control will provide. If the data is not contained in the **DataObject**, then it can be retrieved with the **GetData** method.
- *effect*—a **Long** (see Table I-19) that returns the status of the OLE drag-and-drop operation.

effect Name	Value	Description
vbDropEffectNone	0	The operation was canceled or the target control can't accept the drop operation.
vbDropEffectCopy	1	The operation copied data from the source control to the target control. The original data is unchanged.
vbDropEffectMove	2	The operation results in a link from the original data to the target control.

Table I-19: effect *values*.

- *button*—an **Integer** value (see Table I-20) that contains information about the mouse buttons that were pressed. These values can be added together if more than one button was pushed. For instance, a value of 3 means that both the left and right buttons were pressed. A value of 0 means that no buttons were pressed.

button Name	Value	Description
vbLeftButton	1	The left button was pressed.
vbRightButton	2	The right button was pressed.
vbMiddleButton	4	The middle button was pressed.

Table I-20: button *values*.

- *shift*—an **Integer** value (see Table I-21) that contains information about the Shift and Alt keys that were pushed when the mouse button was released. These values can be added together if more than one key was down. For instance, a value of 5 would mean that the Shift and Alt keys were both down when the mouse button was released. A value of 0 means that none of these keys were pressed.

shift Name	Value	Description
vbShiftMask	1	The Shift key was pressed.
vbCtrlMask	2	The Ctrl key was pressed.
vbAltMask	4	The Alt key was pressed.

Table I-21: shift *values*.

- *x*—a **Single** that contains the horizontal location of the mouse pointer.
- *y*—a **Single** that contains the vertical location of the mouse pointer.
- *state*—an **Integer** value (see Table I-22) that indicates the state of the object being dragged.

state Name	Value	Description
vbEnter	0	The dragged object is entering range of the control.
vbLeave	1	The dragged object is leaving range of the control.
vbOver	2	The dragged object has moved from one position over the control to another.

Table I-22: state *values*.

Private Sub *ImageControl* _OLEGiveFeedback ([*index* As Integer ,] *effect* As Long)

Usage This event tells the source control what is happening while the OLE drag-and-drop operation is in progress. This event occurs after the **OLEDragOver** event.

Tip
You may want to use this event to change the cursor to reflect what can happen in the remote object.

Arguments
- *index*—an **Integer** that uniquely identifies a control in a control array. This argument is not present if the control is not part of a control array.
- *effect*—a **Long** (see Table I-23) that returns the status of the OLE drag-and-drop operation.

shift Name	Value	Description
vbDropEffectNone	0	The operation was canceled or the target control can't accept the drop operation.
vbDropEffectCopy	1	The operation copied data from the source control to the target control. The original data is unchanged.
vbDropEffectMove	2	The operation results in a link from the original data to the target control.
vbDropEffectScroll	&H80000000	The target control is about to scroll or is scrolling. This value may be added to the other *shift* values.

Table I-23: effect *values.*

Private Sub *ImageControl* _OLESetData([*index* As Integer ,] *data* As DataObject, *DataFormat* As Integer)

Usage This event happens in response to the target object performing a **GetData** method on *data*. This routine will respond by using the **SetData** method with the desired data using the **DataObject** *data*.

Arguments
- *index*—an **Integer** that uniquely identifies a control in a control array. This argument is not present if the control is not part of a control array.
- *data*—a **DataObject** that will contain the data to be returned to the target object.
- *format*—an **Integer** value (see Table I-24) that contains the format of the data.

format Name	Value	Description
vbCFText	1	Text (.TXT files)
vbCFBitmap	2	Bitmap (.BMP files)
vbCFMetafile	3	Metafile (.WMF files)
vbCFEDIB	8	Device independent bitmap (DIB)
vbCFPallette	9	Color palette
vbCFEMetafile	14	Enhanced metafile (.EMF files)
vbCFFiles	15	List of files
vbCFRTF	-16639	Rich Text Format (.RTF files)

Table I-24: format *values*.

Private Sub *ImageControl* _OLEStartDrag ([*index* As Integer ,] *data* As DataObject, *AllowedEffects* As Long)

Usage This event starts an OLE drag-and-drop operation.

Arguments
- *index*—an **Integer** that uniquely identifies a control in a control array. This argument is not present if the control is not part of a control array.
- *data*—a **DataObject** that will contain the formats that the source object is willing to provide to the target object. It may optionally contain the data to be transferred.
- *AllowedEffects*—a **Long** (see Table I-25) that contains the effects that the target object can request from the source object. The *AllowedEffects* can be added together if the source object supports more than one effect. Note that the target object can always use the *vbDropEffectNone* effect.

AllowedEffects Name	Value	Description
vbDropEffectNone	0	The target can't copy the data.
vbDropEffectCopy	1	The target can copy the data and the source will keep the data unchanged.
vbDropEffectMove	2	The target can copy the data and the source will delete the data.

Table I-25: AllowedEffects *values*.

Examples
```
Private Sub Command1_Click()
Image1.Picture = LoadPicture(App.Path & "\jpclogo1.gif")
End Sub
```

This routine uses the **LoadPicture** function to load a GIF image onto Image1.

See Also **LoadPicture** (function), **PictureBox** (control), **SavePicture** (statement)

ImageList

CONTROL

CCE LE PE EE

Usage The **ImageList** control is a control containing a collection of **ListImage** objects. It is found in the Microsoft Common Windows Controls 5.0 library. This control is designed to be a repository for other controls like **Toolbar** and **ListView**.

> **Warning**
>
> *All of the images stored in the control must be the same size. You can only change the size of the images (**ImageHeight** and **ImageWidth**) when there are no images in **ListImage**.*

Properties
- *ImageListControl*.**BackColor**—a **Long** that contains the suggested value for the background color of the control.
- *ImageListControl*.**hImageList**—a **Long** that contains a Windows handle to the control.
- *ImageListControl*.**ImageHeight**—an **Integer** that contains the height of the images in **ListImage** in pixels.
- *ImageListControl*.**ImageWidth**—an **Integer** that contains the width of the images in **ListImage** in pixels.
- *ImageListControl*.**ListImages**—returns a reference to the **ListImages** collection.
- *ImageListControl*.**Index**—an **Integer** that uniquely identifies a control in a control array.
- *ImageListControl*.**MaskColor**—a **Long** that identifies a color that will be used as a mask or transparent color for bitmaps displayed within the control. This is useful for bitmap images that do not specify transparency information like icons and metafiles. The **UseMaskColor** property must be **True** for this property to take effect.
- *ImageListControl*.**Name**—a **String** that contains the name of the control that will reference the control in a Visual Basic program. This property is read only at run time.
- *ImageListControl*.**Object**—an object that contains a reference to the *ImageListControl* object.
- *ImageListControl*.**Parent**—an object that contains a reference to the **Form**, **Frame**, or other container that contains the **Image** control.
- *ImageListControl*.**UseMaskColor**—a **Boolean** value when **True** means you should use the color specified in the **MaskColor** property to create a transparent background for the picture objects contained in the control. When **False**, the picture objects will not be displayed with a transparent background.

Methods *picture = ImageListControl.*Overlay *image1, image2*

Usage This method draws *image2* on top of *image1* and returns the result. The **MaskColor** property determines which color is transparent in *image2*.

Arguments
- *image1*—a **Single** that specifies the new position of the left edge of the control.
- *image2*—a **Single** that specifies the new position of the top edge of the control.

Examples

```
Private Sub Command1_Click()
Static Img As Integer
Img = (Img + 1) Mod 8
If Img = 0 Then Img = 1
Picture1.Picture = ImageList1.ListImages.Item(Img).Picture
End Sub
```

This routine displays the next image from the ImageList control.

See Also

ListImage (object), **ListImages** (collection), **ListView** (control), **TreeView** (control)

IMEStatus

FUNCTION

CCE LE PE EE

Syntax

IMEStat = **IMEStatus( )**

Usage

The **IMEStatus** function returns the current Input Method Editor (IME) available in Windows. The IME is available only in the Far East version of Windows.

Arguments

- *IMEStat*—an **Integer** value (see Tables I-26, I-27, and I-28) containing the IME status.

For Japanese locale:

IMEStat Name	Value	Description
vbIMENoOP	0	No IME is installed.
vbIMEOn	1	IME is on.
VbIMEOff	2	IME is off.
vbIMEDisable	3	IME is disabled.
VbIMEHiragana	4	Hiragana double byte characters.
vbIMEKatakanaDbl	5	Katakana double byte characters.
vbIMEKatakanaSng	6	Katakana single byte characters.
vbIMEAlphaDbl	7	Alphanumeric double byte characters.
vbIMEAlphaSng	8	Alphanumeric single byte characters.

Table I-26: IMEStat values.

For Chinese locale (traditional and simplified):

IMEStat Name	Value	Description
vbIMENoOP	0	No IME is installed.
vbIMEOn	1	IME is on.
VbIMEOff	2	IME is off.

Table I-27: IMEStat values.

For Korean locale, the first five bits of the return value are:

Bit	Value	Description
0	0	No IME is installed.
	1	IME is installed.
1	0	IME is disabled.
	1	IME is enabled.
2	0	IME English mode.
	1	IME Hangul mode.
3	0	IME Banja mode.
	1	IME Junja mode (double byte).
4	0	Normal mode.
	1	Hanja conversation mode.

Table I-28: IMEStat values.

Examples
```
Private Sub Command1_Click()
MsgBox Format(IMEStatus())
End Sub
```

This routine displays the IMEStatus.

Implements   STATEMENT
                                                             CCE   LE   PE   EE

Syntax **Implements** [*InterfaceName* | *Class*]

Usage The **Implements** statement identifies an interface or class that will be implemented in a class module.

Arguments
- *InterfaceName*—a valid interface name.
- *Class*—a valid class name.

See Also **Property Get** (statement), **Property Let** (statement), **Property Set** (statement)

Index   OBJECT
                                                                     PE   EE

Usage The **Index** object is used by the **TableDef** object to manage an index for a table.

Properties
- *IndexObject*.**Clustered**—a **Boolean** value when **True** means that this index is a clustered index. Microsoft Jet does not support clustered indexes and ODBC databases do not detect if an index is clustered, so both will return **False**.
- *IndexObject*.**DistanceCount**—a **Long** value containing the number of unique values in the index.

- *IndexObject*.**Foreign**—a **Boolean** value when **True** means that the index represents a foreign key in another table. Supported by Microsoft Jet databases only. The index must be part of a relationship that enforces referential integrity.
- *IndexObject*.**IgnoreNulls**—a **Boolean** value when **True** means that records with **Null** values are not added to the index. **False** means that records with **Null** values are added to the index.
- *IndexObject*.**Name**—a **String** value that contains the name of the index object.
- *IndexObject*.**Primary**—a **Boolean** value when **True** means that this index is the primary index for a table. This applies to Microsoft Jet database only.
- *IndexObject*.**Required**—a **Boolean** value when **True** means that all of the fields in an index may have **Null** values (this property overrides the **NullsAllowed** property).
- *IndexObject*.**Unique**—a **Boolean** value when **True** means that only one record in the table may have a particular index value.

Methods

field = IndexObject.CreateField ([name [, type [, size]]])

Usage This method creates a new field in the index.

Arguments
- *field*—a reference to a new **Field** object.
- *name*—a **String** containing the name of the new field.
- *type*—an **Integer** value describing the type of field.

Type Name	Description
dbBigInt	Big integer data type.
dbBinary	Fixed-length binary data, up to 255 bytes long.
dbBoolean	Boolean data type.
DbByte	Integer value one byte wide.
DbChar	Fixed-length character string.
DbCurrency	Currency data type.
DbDate	Date/time data type.
DbDecimal	Decimal data type.
DbDouble	Double precision floating point data type.
DbFloat	Floating point data type.
DbGUID	Globally Unique Identifier data type.
DbInteger	16-bit integer data type.
DbLong	32-bit integer data type.
DbLongBinary	Long binary data type.
DbMemo	Memo data type.
DbNumeric	Numeric data type.
DbSingle	Single precision floating point data type.
DbText	Field data type.
dbTime	Time data type.
DbTimeStamp	Time stamp data type.
DbVarBinary	Variable-length binary, up to 255 bytes long.

Table I-29: Type *values.*

- *size*—an **Integer** containing the size of the field.

property = **IndexObject.CreateProperty** ([*name*] [, [*type*] [, [*value*] [, *DDL*]]])

Usage	This method is used to create a user-defined **Property** object.
Arguments	▪ *property*—an object variable that will contain the new property object.
	▪ *name*—a **String** containing the name of the property. Must begin with a letter and can be followed by letters, numbers, or an underscore ("_").
	▪ *type*—a value selected from the table below.

Type Name	Description
dbBigInt	Big integer data type.
dbBinary	Fixed-length binary data, up to 255 bytes long.
dbBoolean	Boolean data type.
DbByte	Integer value one byte wide.
DbChar	Fixed-length character string.
DbCurrency	Currency data type.
DbDate	Date/time data type.
DbDecimal	Decimal data type.
DbDouble	Double precision floating point data type.
DbFloat	Floating point data type.
DbGUID	Globally Unique Identifier data type.
DbInteger	16-bit integer data type.
DbLong	32-bit integer data type.
DbLongBinary	Long binary data type.
DbMemo	Memo data type.
DbNumeric	Numeric data type.
DbSingle	Single precision floating point data type.
DbText	Field data type.
dbTime	Time data type.
DbTimeStamp	Time stamp data type.
DbVarBinary	Variable-length binary, up to 255 bytes long.

Table I-30: Type values.

	▪ *value*—a **Variant** containing the initial value for the property.
	▪ *DDL*—a **Boolean** when **True** means that the user cannot change this property value without the *dbSecWriteDef* permission. When **False,** this permission is not required to change the value.
See Also	**Database** (object), **Databases** (collection), **Field** (object), **Property** (object), **Properties** (collection), **Recordset** (object), **Recordsets** (collection), **Relation** (object), **Relations** (collection), **TableDef** (object), **TableDefs** (collection)

Indexes

COLLECTION

PE EE

Usage The **Indexes** collection is used by Data Access Objects (DAO) to contain information about the indexes associated with a table.

Properties • *IndexesCollection*.**Count**—an **Integer** containing the number of **Indexes** objects in the collection.

Methods

IndexesCollection.Append *object*

Usage This method adds an **Index** object to the collection.

Arguments • *object*—a reference to an **Index** object to be added to the collection.

IndexesCollection.Delete *objectname*

Usage This method removes an **Index** object from the collection.

Arguments • *objectname*—a **String** containing the name of the **Index** object to be removed from the collection.

IndexesCollection.Refresh

Usage This method gets a current copy of the **Indexes** contained in the collection. This is important in a multiuser environment where more than one user may be making changes in the **Databases** collection.

See Also **Index** (object)

Input

FUNCTION

CCE LE PE EE

Syntax *SValue* = **Input** (*count*, [#] *filenum*)

Usage The **Input** function reads characters from a file that was opened in **Input** or **Binary** mode.

> **Tip**
>
> This function differs from the **Input** statement in that this function will return every character it reads including carriage returns, line feeds, quotation marks, and leading spaces.

Arguments • *SValue*—a **String** value containing the data from the file.
• *count*—a numeric value containing the number of characters to read from the file.
• *filenum*—an **Integer** containing the file number from an **Open** statement.

Examples `Private Sub Command1_Click()`

```
Open "\config.sys" For Input As #1
Text1.Text = ""
Do While Not EOF(1)
    Text1.Text = Text1.Text & Input(1, #1)
Loop
Close #1
End Sub
```

This routine uses the **Input** function to read the config.sys file one character at a time and display it in the Text1 text box.

See Also   **Input** (statement), **InputB** (function), **Open** (statement)

Input

STATEMENT

CCE   LE   PE   EE

Syntax   **Input** #*filenum* , *var* [, *var*] [, *var*] . . . [, *var*]

Usage   The **Input** statement reads information from an open file.

> **Tip**
>
> Use the **Write** statement to write data to the file in the proper format to be read with the **Input** statement.

Arguments
- *filenum*—a numeric expression containing the file number.
- *var*—any variable, except for objects or arrays. Array elements are acceptable. A value of "#NULL#" assigns a **Null** value to a **Variant** variable. A value of "#ERROR number#" assigns an error value to a **Variant** variable. A value of "#TRUE#" or "#F ALSE#" assigns a value to a **Boolean** variable. The format "#yyyy-mm-dd hh:mm:ss# holds information for a **Date** variable.

Examples
```
Private Sub Command2_Click()
Dim s As String
Open App.Path & "\temp.dat" For Input As #1
Input #1, s
Close #1
Text1.Text = s
End Sub
```

This routine reads a string from a file and copies it to the Text1 text box.

See Also   **Close** (statement), **Open** (statement), **Write** (statement)

InputB

FUNCTION

CCE LE PE EE

Syntax   `BValue = InputB ( count, [#] filenum )`

Usage   The **InputB** function reads characters from a file that was opened in **Input** or **Binary** mode. It works similar to the **Input** function, except that it reads bytes instead of characters.

Arguments
- *BValue*—a **Byte Array** value containing the data from the file.
- *count*—a numeric value containing the number of characters to read from the file.
- *filenum*—an **Integer** containing the file number from an **Open** statement.

Examples
```
Private Sub Command1_Click()
Dim b() As Byte
Open "\config.sys" For Input As #1
ReDim b(LOF(1))
b = InputB(LOF(1), 1)
Close #1
MsgBox "Bytes read: " & Format(UBound(b))
End Sub
```

This routine uses the **InputB** function to read the entire config.sys file in one operation and then return the length of the byte array.

See Also   **Input** (function), **Input** (statement), **Open** (statement)

InputBox

FUNCTION

CCE LE PE EE

Syntax   `SValue = InputBox ( prompt [,title [, default [, x [, y [, helpfile [, contextid ] ] ] ] ] )`

Usage   The **InputBox** function displays a pop-up window with a label containing the prompt and a text box where the user can enter a response. Also displayed on the pop-up window are an OK button and a Cancel button. The user enters the information into the text box and presses either OK to accept the information or Cancel to reject the information.

Arguments
- *SValue*—a **String** value containing the user's input.
- *prompt*—a **String** containing a message to display to the user inside the input box.
- *title*—a **String** containing the title to display in the input box's title bar. If omitted, it will default to the application's name.
- *default*—a **String** containing the value to return if the user does not enter anything in the text box. If omitted, the routine will return an empty string.

- *x*—a numeric expression containing the distance in twips between the left edge of the screen and the left edge of the input box. If omitted, the input box will be centered horizontally on the screen.
- *y*—a numeric expression containing the distance in twips between the top edge of the screen and the top edge of the input box. If omitted, the input box will be centered vertically on the screen.
- *helpfile*—a **String** containing the name of a help file. This argument is required if you specify a *contextid*.
- *contextid*—a numeric expression containing the help context to display if the user presses F1. This argument is required if you specify a *helpfile*.

Examples
```
Private Sub Command1_Click()
MsgBox InputBox("Enter information.")
End Sub
```

This routine uses the **InputBox** control to get information from the user.

See Also   **MsgBox** (function)

InStr

FUNCTION

CCE   LE   PE   EE

Syntax   *VValue* = **InStr** ([*start* ,] *str1*, *str2*, [, *comp*])

Usage   The **InStr** function searches *str1* for *str2* and if a match is found, **InStr** returns a **Long** value containing the starting position of *str2* within *str1*.

> **Tip**
>
> *This is a fast, powerful tool for searching for strings inside other strings. It is much more efficient than writing your own code using a **For...Next** or **Do...Loop** statement.*

Arguments
- *VValue*—a **Variant** value is either a **Long** containing the starting position of *str2* within *str1* or **Null**.
- *start*—a **Variant** containing the starting position in *str1* for the search. If omitted, the search will start with the first character in *str1*.
- *str1*—a **String** or **Variant** containing a string of characters to search.
- *str2*—a **String** or **Variant** containing the search string.
- *comp*—an **Integer** value (see Table I-31) containing the type of comparison.

> **Tip**
>
> *Use the **Option Compare** statement to set the default value for* comp.

compValue	Name	Description
vbBinaryCompare	0	Perform a binary comparison. (Default value.)
vbTextCompare	1	Perform a non-case sensitive comparison.

Table I-31: *comp values.*

Examples
```
Private Sub Command1_Click()
Text4.Text = Format(InStr(Text1.Text, Text2.Text))
End Sub
```

This routine uses the **InStr** function to find the string in Text2.Text inside Text1.Text.

See Also   **InStrB** (function), **Mid** (function), **String** (data type), **Variant** (data type)

InStrB

FUNCTION

CCE   LE   PE   EE

Syntax   *VValue* = **InStrB** ([*start ,*] *str1, str2,* [, *comp*])

Usage   The **InStrB** function searches *str1* for *str2*. If a match is found, **InStrB** will return a **Long** value containing the starting position of *str2* within *str1*. This function is similar to **InStr**, except that **Byte** arrays are used in place of strings.

> **Tip**
>
> *This is a fast, powerful tool for searching for strings inside other strings. It is much more efficient than writing your own code using a **For...Next** or **Do...Loop** statement.*

Arguments
- *VValue*—a **Variant** value is either a **Long** containing the starting position of *str2* within *str1* or **Null**.
- *start*—a **Variant** containing the starting position in *str1* for the search. If omitted, the search will start with the first character in *str1*.
- *str1*—a **Byte Array** containing a string of characters to search.
- *str2*—a **Byte Array** containing the search string.
- *comp*—an **Integer** value (see Table I-32) containing the type of comparison.

> **Tip**
>
> Use the **Option Compare** statement to set the default value for *comp*.

compValue	Name	Description
vbBinaryCompare	0	Perform a binary comparison (default value).
vbTextCompare	1	Perform a non-case sensitive comparison.

Table I-32: *comp values.*

Examples
```
Private Sub Command1_Click()
Dim str1() As Byte
Dim str2() As Byte
ReDim str1(Len(Text1.Text))
str1 = Text1.Text
ReDim str2(Len(Text2.Text))
str2 = Text2.Text
Text4.Text = Format(InStrB(str1, str2))
End Sub
```

This routine converts Text1.Text and Text2.Text into **Byte** arrays and then uses the **InStr** function to find where str2 starts inside str1.

See Also   **Byte** (data type), **InStr** (function), **Mid** (function), **String** (data type), **Variant** (data type)

Int

FUNCTION

CCE   LE   PE   EE

Syntax   *IValue* = **Int** (*Number*)

Usage   The **Int** function truncates any fractional parts of the number (i.e., **Int** (8.9) will return 8).

Arguments
- *IValue*—the **Fix** value of **Number**.
- *Number*—an **Integer**, **Long**, **Single**, or **Double**.

Examples
```
Private Sub Command1_Click()
If IsNumeric(Text1.Text) Then
    Text2.Text = Format(Int(CDbl(Text1.Text)))
Else
    Text2.Text = "Illegal number."
End If
End Sub
```

This routine displays the **Fix** of the number in the Text1 text box.

See Also   **Abs** (function), **Fix** (function), **Sng** (function)

Integer

DATA TYPE

CCE   LE   PE   EE

Usage   The **Integer** data type holds integer values in the range from -32,768 to 32,767. A single **Integer** variable only occupies 16 bits of storage or 2 bytes.

See Also   **Byte** (data type), **CByte** (function), **CInt** (function), **CLng** (function), **CStr** (function), **Dim** (statement), **Format** (function), **IsNumeric** (function), **Long** (data type)

IPmt

FUNCTION

CCE LE PE EE

Syntax pmt = **IPmt**(rate, pper, nper, pv [, fv [, type]])

Usage The **IPmt** function returns the interest payment for a fixed rate, fixed-payment annuity. Cash paid out is represented by negative numbers. Cash received is represented by positive numbers.

Arguments
- *pmt*—a **Double** value containing the interest payment for the period specified by *pper*.
- *rate*—a **Double** value containing the interest rate per period.
- *pper*—a **Double** value containing the period for which the payment will be computed.
- *nper*—a **Double** value containing the number of periods in the annuity.
- *pv*—a **Double** value containing the present value of the annuity.
- *fv*—a **Variant** value containing the future value of the annuity. If omitted, 0 will be assumed.
- *type*—a **Variant** value when 0, means that the payment is due at the end of the period. When 1, means that the payment is due at the beginning of the period. If not specified, it will default to 0.

Examples
```
Private Sub Command1_Click()
Text5.Text = Format(IPmt(CDbl(Text1.Text), CDbl(Text2.Text), CDbl(Text3.Text),
    CDbl(Text4.Text)), "currency")
End Sub
```

This routine computes the interest payment for a particular period.

See Also **DDB** (function), **FV** (function), **IRR** (function), **MIRR** (function), **NPer** (function), **NPV** (function), **Pm** (function), **PPmt** (function), **PV** (function), **Rate** (function), **SLN** (function), **SYD** (function)

IRR

FUNCTION

CCE LE PE EE

Syntax DValue = **IRR** (vals() [, guess])

Usage The **IRR** function returns a **Double** value that contains the internal rate of return for a stream of payments and receipts.

Arguments
- *DValue*—a **Double** value containing the internal rate of return.
- *vals()*—an array of **Double** containing the cash flow. Cash receipts are represented by positive numbers and cash payments are represented by negative numbers.
- *guess*—a **Variant** that contains an initial guess for the interest rate. If omitted, it will default to 10% (.01).

Examples
```
Private Sub Command1_Click()
Dim v(12) As Double
v(0) = -1000
For i = 1 To 12
    v(i) = 100
Next i
MsgBox Format(IRR(v), "percent")
End Sub
```

This routine computes an internal rate of return based on a single cash payment of $1,000 followed by 12 receipts of $100.

See Also **DDB** (function), **FV** (function), **IPmt** (function), **MIRR** (function), **NPer** (function), **NPV** (function), **PMT** (function), **PPmt** (function), **PV** (function), **Rate** (function), **SLN** (function), **SYD** (function)

IsArray

FUNCTION

CCE LE PE EE

Syntax *BValue* = **IsArray** (*name*)

Usage The **IsArray** function returns **True** when *name* is an array and **False** otherwise.

Arguments
- *BValue*—a **Boolean** value that is **True** when *name* is an array and **False** otherwise.
- *name*—a Visual Basic identifier.

Examples
```
Private Sub Command1_Click()
Dim x As Variant
x = Array("Jill", "Chris", "Samantha")
If IsArray(x) Then
    MsgBox "x is an array"
Else
    MsgBox "x is not an array"
End If
End Sub
```

This routine uses the **Array** function to create an array in a **Variant** called x. Then, it uses the **IsArray** function to determine if x is an array.

See Also **Array** (function), **IsDate** (function), **IsEmpty** (function), **IsError** (function), **IsMissing** (function), **IsNull** (function), **IsNumeric** (function), **IsObject** (function), **TypeName** (function), **Variant** (data type), **VarType** (function)

IsDate

FUNCTION

CCE LE PE EE

Syntax *BValue* = **IsDate** (*name*)

Usage The **IsDate** function returns **True** when *name* contains a date value or is a date variable and **False** otherwise.

> **Tip**
>
> *This function is useful to verify that you have a valid date value before trying to convert it to a* **Date** *variable with the* **CDate** *function.*

Arguments
- *BValue*—a **Boolean** value that is **True** when *name* contains a date value or is a date variable and **False** otherwise.
- *name*—a Visual Basic identifier.

Examples
```
Private Sub Command1_Click()
Dim x As Variant
x = "15 May 1997"
If IsDate(x) Then
    MsgBox "x contains a date"
Else
    MsgBox "x does not contain a date"
End If
End Sub
```

This routine assigns a **String** value containing a date to a **Variant** called x. Then, it uses the **IsDate** function to determine if x contains a date.

See Also **CDate** (function), **IsArray** (function), **IsEmpty** (function), **IsError** (function), **IsMissing** (function), **IsNull** (function), **IsNumeric** (function), **IsObject** (function), **TypeName** (function), **Variant** (data type), **VarType** (function)

IsEmpty

FUNCTION

CCE LE PE EE

Syntax *BValue* = **IsEmpty** (*name*)

Usage The **IsEmpty** function returns **True** when *name* is a **Variant** variable that has been assigned a value and **False** otherwise.

Arguments
- *BValue*—a **Boolean** value that is **True** when *name* is a **Variant** variable that has been assigned a value and **False** otherwise.
- *name*—a Visual Basic identifier.

Examples
```
Private Sub Command1_Click()
Dim x As Variant
If IsEmpty(x) Then
    MsgBox "x is empty"
Else
    MsgBox "x is not empty"
End If
End Sub
```

This routine uses the **IsEmpty** function to determine if x has been assigned a value.

See Also   **IsArray** (function), **IsDate** (function), **IsError** (function), **IsMissing** (function), **IsNull** (function), **IsNumeric** (function), **IsObject** (function), **TypeName** (function), **Variant** (data type), **VarType** (function)

IsError

FUNCTION

CCE LE PE EE

Syntax   *BValue* = **IsError** (*name*)

Usage   The **IsError** function returns **True** when *name* is a **Variant** variable containing a **VarType** of *vbError*.

> **Tip**
>
> *Use the **CVErr** function to assign an error value to a **Variant** variable.*

Arguments
- *BValue*—a **Boolean** value that is **True** when *name* is a **Variant** variable containing a **VarType** of *vbError*.
- *name*—a Visual Basic identifier.

Examples
```
Private Sub Command1_Click()
Dim x As Variant
x = CVErr(100)
If IsError(x) Then
    MsgBox "x contains an error value"
Else
    MsgBox "x does not contain an error"
End If
End Sub
```

This routine uses the **IsError** function to determine if x has been assigned an **Error** value.

See Also   **CVErr** (function), **IsArray** (function), **IsDate** (function), **IsEmpty** (function), **IsMissing** (function), **IsNull** (function), **IsNumeric** (function), **IsObject** (function), **TypeName** (function), **Variant** (data type), **VarType** (function)

IsMissing

FUNCTION

CCE LE PE EE

Syntax *BValue* = **IsMissing** (*name*)

Usage The **IsMissing** function returns **True** when *name* is an **Optional** argument of type **Variant** in a subroutine and **False** otherwise. If the argument is of any other type, this routine will always return **False**.

Arguments
- *BValue*—a **Boolean** value that is **True** when *name* is an **Optional** argument of type **Variant** in a subroutine and **False** otherwise.
- *name*—a Visual Basic identifier.

Examples
```
Private Sub Sample(Optional a As Variant, Optional b As Variant)
If IsMissing(a) And IsMissing(b) Then
    MsgBox "a and b are missing. "
ElseIf IsMissing(b) Then
    MsgBox "b is missing."

ElseIf IsMissing(a) Then
   MsgBox "a is missing."

Else
    MsgBox "nothing is missing."
End If
End Sub

§Private Sub Command1_Click()
Call Sample
Call Sample(1)
Call Sample(, 1)
Call Sample(1, 1)
End Sub
```

The Sample subroutine takes two optional **Variant** arguments and displays messages indicating which arguments have values. Then the **Command1_Click** event calls Sample with all four combinations of values.

See Also **Function** (statement), **IsArray** (function), **IsDate** (function), **IsEmpty** (function), **IsError** (function), **IsNull** (function), **IsNumeric** (function), **IsObject** (function), **TypeName** (function), **Variant** (data type), **VarType** (function)

IsNull

FUNCTION

CCE LE PE EE

Syntax `BValue = IsNull ( name )`

Usage The **IsNull** function returns **True** when *name* is a **Variant** variable that has a value of **Null** and **False** otherwise.

Arguments
- *BValue*—a **Boolean** value that is **True** when *name* is a **Variant** variable that has a value of **Null** and **False** otherwise.
- *name*—a Visual Basic identifier.

Examples
```
Private Sub Command1_Click()
Dim x As Variant
x = Null
If IsNull(x) Then
    MsgBox "x is Null."
Else
    MsgBox "x is not Null."
End If
End Sub
```

This routine uses the **IsNull** function to determine if x has been assigned a **Null** value.

See Also **IsArray** (function), **IsDate** (function), **IsEmpty** (function), **IsError** (function), **IsMissing** (function), **IsNumeric** (function), **IsObject** (function), **TypeName** (function), **Variant** (data type), **VarType** (function).

IsNumeric

FUNCTION

CCE LE PE EE

Syntax `BValue = IsNumeric ( name )`

Usage The **IsNumeric** function returns **True** when *name* contains a valid numeric value and **False** otherwise.

Arguments
- *BValue*—a **Boolean** value that is **True** when *name* contains a valid numeric value and **False** otherwise.
- *name*—a Visual Basic identifier.

Examples
```
Private Sub Command1_Click()
Dim x As String
x = "-$123,456.789"
If IsNumeric(x) Then
    MsgBox "x is numeric."
Else
    MsgBox "x is not numeric."
End If
End Sub
```

This routine uses the **IsNumeric** function to determine if x has a numeric value.

See Also **CCur** (function), **CBbl** (function), **CDec** (function), **CInt** (function), **CLng** (function), **CSng** (function), **IsArray** (function), **IsDate** (function), **IsEmpty** (function), **IsError** (function), **IsMissing** (function), **IsNull** (function), **IsObject** (function), **TypeName** (function), **Variant** (data type), **VarType** (function)

IsObject   FUNCTION

CCE LE PE EE

Syntax   *BValue =* **IsObject** (*name*)

Usage   The **IsObject** function returns **True** when *name* is a type object or a **Variant** that contains an object and **False** otherwise.

Arguments
- *BValue*—a **Boolean** value that is **True** when *name* is a type object or a **Variant** that contains an object and **False** otherwise.
- *name*—a Visual Basic identifier.

Examples
```
Private Sub Command1_Click()
Dim x As Variant
Set x = Form1
If IsObject(x) Then
    MsgBox "x contains a reference to an object."
Else
    MsgBox "x does not contain a reference to an object."
End If
End Sub
```

This routine uses the **IsObject** function to determine if x contains a reference to an object.

See Also **IsArray** (function), **IsDate** (function), **IsEmpty** (function), **IsError** (function), **IsMissing** (function), **IsNull** (function), **IsObject** (function), **Set** (statement), **TypeName** (function), **Variant** (data type), **VarType** (function)

Kill

STATEMENT

CCE, LE, PE, EE

Syntax **Kill** *filename*

Usage The **Kill** statement deletes files from the system.

> **Warning**
>
> *If you try to delete an open file, an error will occur.*

Arguments
- *filename*—a **String** expression that contains the path and the name of the file to delete. You can use normal Windows wildcards ("*", "#") as part of the filename to delete more than one file.

Examples
```
Private Sub Command1_Click()
Open App.Path & "\temp.dat" For Output As #1
Print #1, "Testing"
Close #1
If Len(Dir(App.Path & "\temp.dat")) > 0 Then
   MsgBox "The file was created successfully."
   Kill App.Path & "\temp.dat"
   If Len(Dir(App.Path & "\temp.dat")) = 0 Then
      MsgBox "The Kill statement deleted the file."
   End If
End If
End Sub
```

This routine creates a junk file called temp.dat and then deletes it with the **Kill** statement.

See Also **Dir** (function), **Name** (statement), **RmDir** (statement)

Label

CONTROL

CCE, LE, PE, EE

Usage
The **Label** control displays information to a user that can't be changed. This is useful when identifying the contents of a text box or other element on a form.

Properties
- *LabelControl*.**Alignment**—an **Integer** value (see Table L-1) that describes the placement of the text within the control.

Alignment Name	Value	Description
vbLeftJustify	0	The text is left justified within the caption area (default value).
vbRightJustify	1	The text is right justified within the caption area.
vbCenter	2	The text is centered within the caption area.

Table L-1: Alignment *values.*

- *LabelControl*.**Appearance**—an **Integer** value (see Table L-2) that describes how the label will appear on the form.

Appearance Value	Description
0	The label displays without the 3D effects.
1	The label displays with 3D effects (default value).

Table L-2: Appearance *values.*

- *LabelControl*.**AutoSize**—a **Boolean** when **True** means that the label control is automatically resized to display all of its data. When **False** means the control will not be resized to fit the data and if it doesn't fit it will be truncated (default).
- *LabelControl*.**BackColor**—a **Long** that contains the suggested value for the background color of the control.
- *LabelControl*.**BackStyle**—an **Integer** value (see Table L-3) that describes how the background of the control displays.

BackStyle Value	Description
0	The label displays with a transparent background. Any objects behind the control can be seen.
1	The label displays with an opaque background. Any objects behind the control can't be seen (default value).

Table L-3: BackStyle *values.*

- *LabelObject*.**BorderStyle**—an **Integer** value (see Table L-4) specifying how the border will be drawn.

BorderStyle Name	Value	Description
vbBSNone	0	No border displays.
vbFixedSingle	1	A single line appears around the label.

Table L-4: **BorderStyle** *values.*

- *LabelControl.***Caption**—a **String** value that displays inside the label control. You can include an access key for this control by inserting an ampersand (&) in front of the character you want to use and then setting the **UseMnemonic** property to **True**. The selected character will then appear with an underline. Then, if the user presses the Alt key with the underlined character, the control will gain the focus.
- *LabelControl.***Container**—an object that sets or returns the container of the control at run time. This property cannot be set at design time.
- *LabelControl.***DataChanged**—a **Boolean** that applies only to data bound controls. When **True** means that the data contained in this control was changed either by the user or by some means other than retrieving data from the current record. When **False** means the data in the control is unchanged from the current record. Simply reading the next record is not sufficient to set the **DataChanged** property to **True**.

    When the **Data** control moves to the next record, it will automatically invoke the **Edit** and **Update** methods to post the changes to the database.
- *LabelControl.***DataField**—a **String** value that associates the control with a field in a **RecordSet** object in a **Data** control.
- *LabelControl.***DataSource**—a **String** value that associates the control with a **Data** control.
- *LabelControl.***DragIcon**—an object that contains the **Picture** value of an icon. At design time, you can specify an icon file that has a file type of .ICO.

Tip

This value can be created by copying the value from another control's **DragIcon** *value, a form's icon, or by using the* **LoadPicture** *function.*

- *LabelControl.***DragMode**—an **Integer** value (see Table L-5) specifying how the control will respond to a drag request.

Tip

Setting **DragMode** *to vbAutomatic will automatically begin a drag operation when the user clicks on the control. However, the control will not respond to the usual mouse events (***Click***,* **DblClick***).*

DragMode Name	Value	Description
vbManual	0	The Drag method must be used to begin a drag-and-drop operation (default value).
vbAutomatic	1	The source control will automatically begin a drag-and-drop operation when the user clicks on the control.

Table L-5: **DragMode** *values.*

- *LabelControl*.**Enabled**—a **Boolean** value when **True** means that the control will respond to events. When **False**, the control will not respond to events.
- *LabelControl*.**Font**—a reference to a **Font** object containing information about the character font used by this object.

> **Tip**
>
> The **Font** object should be used in place of the other **Font** properties, since it offers more functionality than the individual properties.

- *LabelControl*.**FontBold**—a **Boolean** when **True** means that the characters display in bold. **False** means that the characters display normally.
- *LabelControl*.**FontItalic**—a **Boolean** when **True** means that the characters display in italics. **False** means that the characters display normally.
- *LabelControl*.**FontName**—a **String** that specifies the name of the font that should be used to display the characters in this control.
- *LabelControl*.**FontSize**—a **Single** that specifies the point size that should be used to display the characters in the control.
- *LabelControl*.**FontStrikethru**—a **Boolean** when **True** means that the characters display with a line through the center. **False** means that the characters display normally.
- *LabelControl*.**FontUnderlined**—a **Boolean** when **True** means that the characters display with a line beneath them. **False** means that the characters display normally.
- *LabelControl*.**Height**—a **Single** that contains the height of the control.
- *LabelControl*.**Index**—an **Integer** that uniquely identifies a control in a control array.
- *LabelControl*.**Left**—a **Single** containing the distance measured in twips between the left edge of the control and the left edge of the control's container.
- *LabelControl*.**LinkItem**—a **String** containing data that is passed to a destination control in a DDE link. This property is the same as the item specification in a normal DDE specification.
- *LabelControl*.**LinkMode**—an **Integer** value (see Table L-6) that specifies how the form will act in a dynamic data exchange (DDE) conversation.

LinkMode Name	Value	Description
vbLinkNone	0	No DDE interaction.
vbLinkAutomatic	1	The destination control is updated each time the data is updated.
vbLinkManual	2	The destination control is updated only when the LinkRequest method is used.
vbLinkNotify	3	The **LinkNotify** event occurs each time the data is updated. Then the **LinkRequest** method can be used to refresh the linked data.

Table L-6: **LinkMode** values.

- *LabelControl*.**LinkTimeout**—an **Integer** containing the amount of time in tenths of seconds that the application will wait for a DDE message.

- *LabelControl*.**LinkTopic**—a **String** that contains a reference to a DDE application. The actual format of the string is dependent on the exact application, but strings will usually include an application, topic, and item. For example, in Microsoft Excel a valid **LinkTopic** string is "Excel|Sheet1".
- *LabelControl*.**MouseIcon**—a **Picture** object (a bitmap, icon, or metafile) that will be used as a cursor when the **MousePointer** property is set to 99. Note that Visual Basic does not support color cursors from a .CUR file. A color icon from an .ICO file should be used instead.
- *LabelControl*.**MousePointer**—an **Integer** that contains the value of the cursor (see Table L-7) to display when the cursor is moved over this control. Use *vbCustom* to display the custom icon stored in the **MouseIcon** property.

Cursor Name	Value	Description
vbDefault	0	Shape determined by the object (default value)
vbArrow	1	Arrow
vbCrosshair	2	Crosshair
vbIbeam	3	I beam
vbIconPointer	4	Square inside a square
vbSizePointer	5	Four sided arrow (north, south, east, west)
vbSizeNESW	6	Two sided arrow (northeast, southwest)
vbSizeNS	7	Two sided arrow (north, south)
vbSizeNWSE	8	Two sided arrow (northwest, southeast)
vbSizeWE	9	Two sided arrow (west, east)
vbUpArrow	10	Single sided arrow pointing north
vbHourglass	11	Hourglass
vbNoDrop	12	No Drop
vbArrowHourglass	13	An arrow and an hourglass
vbArrowQuestion	14	An arrow and a question mark
vbSizeAll	15	Size all
vbCustom	99	Custom icon from the MouseIcon property of this control

Table L-7: Cursor *values.*

- *LabelControl*.**Name**—a **String** that contains the name of the control that will be used to reference the control in a Visual Basic program. This property is read only at run time.
- *LabelControl*.**OLEDragMode**—an **Integer** value (see Table L-8) that describes how the control will respond to OLE drag operations.

> **Note**
>
> When the **DragMode** is *True*, the standard Visual Basic drag-and-drop functions will override the OLE drag-and-drop functions.

OLEDragMode Name	Value	Description
vbOLEDragManual	0	All drag requests will be handled by the programmer (default value).
vbOLEDragAutomatic	1	The control responds to all OLE drag-and-drop requests automatically.

Table L-8: OLEDragMode values.

- *LabelControl*.**OLEDropMode**—an **Integer** value (see Table L-9) that describes how the control will respond to OLE drop operations.

OLEDropMode Name	Value	Description
vbOLEDropNone	0	The control does not accept OLE drops. The cursor is changed to the No Drop cursor (default value).
vbOLEDropManual	1	The control responds to OLE drops under the program's control (manual).
vbOLEDropAutomatic	2	The control automatically accepts OLE drops if it recognizes the format of the data object.

Table L-9: OLEDropMode values.

- *LabelControl*.**Parent**—an object that contains a reference to the **Form**, **Frame**, or other container that contains the **Label** control
- *LabelControl*.**TabIndex**—an **Integer** that determines the order that a user will tab through the objects on a form.
- *LabelControl*.**Tag**—a **String** that can hold programmer specific information. This property is not used by Visual Basic.
- *LabelControl*.**ToolTipText**—a **String** that holds a text value that can be displayed as a **ToolTip** box that displays whenever the cursor is held over the control for about one second.
- *LabelControl*.**Top**—a **Single** that contains the distance measured in twips between the top edge of the control and the top edge of the control's container.
- *LabelControl*.**UseMnemonic**—a **Boolean** value when **True** means that the character following the ampersand ("&") in the caption is the access key. When **False** the access key is disabled for this control.
- *LabelControl*.**Visible**—a **Boolean** value when **True** means that the control is visible. When **False** means that the control is not visible.

> **Tip**
>
> *This property hides the control until the program is ready to display it.*

- *LabelControl*.**WhatsThisHelpID**—a **Long** that contains a help file context ID number references an entry in the help file. This provides a What's This PopUp help display in response to the What's This button in the upper right corner of the window.
- *LabelControl*.**Width**—a **Single** that contains the width of the control.
- *LabelControl*.**WordWrap**—a **Boolean** value used only with **AutoSize** is **True**. When **WordWrap** is **True** the height of the control will expand or contract to fit the text in the caption, while the width of the control is fixed. When **False**, the height and width of the control will be adjusted to fit the text (default).

Methods   ## LabelControl.Drag [DragAction]

Usage   This method begins, ends, or cancels a drag operation.

Arguments   *DragAction*—an **Integer** that contains a value selected from Table L-10 below.

DragAction Name	Value	Description
vbCancel	0	Cancels any drag operation in progress.
vbBeginDrag	1	Begins a drag operation (default).
vbEndDrag	2	Ends a drag operation and drops *object*.

Table L-10: DragAction *values.*

*LabelControl.*LinkExecute *command*

Usage   This method will send a command to the source application in a DDE link.

Arguments   *command*—a **String** containing the command.

*LabelControl.*LinkPoke

Usage   This method is used by the destination application in a DDE link to send the contents of the label's caption to the source application.

*LabelControl.*LinkRequest

Usage   This method is used by the destination application in a DDE link to send the request to the source application to refresh its contents.

*LabelControl.*LinkSend

Usage   This method sends the contents of a **Picture** control to the destination application in a DDE link.

*LabelControl.*Move *Left* [, *Top* [, *Width* [, *Height*]]]

Usage   This method changes the position and the size of the **Label** control. The **ScaleMode** of the **Form** or other container object that holds the **Label** control will determine the units used to specify the coordinates.

Arguments
- *Left*—a **Single** that specifies the new position of the left edge of the control.
- *Top*—a **Single** that specifies the new position of the top edge of the control.
- *Width*—a **Single** that specifies the new width of the control.
- *Height*—a **Single** that specifies the new height of the control.

LabelControl.OLEDrag

Usage This method begins an **OLEDrag** and drop operation. Invoking this method will trigger the **OLEStartDrag** event.

LabelControl.Refresh

Usage This method redraws the contents of the control.

LabelControl.ShowWhatsThis

Usage This method displays the ShowWhatsThis help information for this control.

LabelControl.ZOrder [position]

Usage This method specifies the position of the label control relative to the other objects on the form.

> **Tip**
>
> *Note that there are three layers of objects on a form: the back layer is the drawing space which contains the results of the graphical methods, the middle layer contains graphical objects and **Labels**, and the top layer contains nongraphical controls such as the **CommandButton**. The **ZOrder** method only affects how the objects are arranged within a single layer.*

Arguments *position*—an **Integer** that specifies the relative position of this object. A value of 0 means that the control is positioned at the head of the list, a value of 1 means that the control will be placed at the end of the list.

Events

Private Sub LabelControl_Change ([index As Integer])

Usage This event occurs whenever the contents of the label's caption is changed, either by the program changing the **Caption** property directly or by a DDE link.

Arguments *index*—an **Integer** that uniquely identifies a control in a control array. This argument is not present if the control is not part of a control array.

Private Sub LabelControl_Click([index As Integer])

Usage This event occurs then the user clicks a mouse button while the cursor is over the control.

Arguments *index*—an **Integer** that uniquely identifies a control in a control array. This argument is not present if the control is not part of a control array.

Private Sub *LabelControl*__DblClick([*index* As Integer])

> Usage   This event occurs when the user double-clicks a mouse button while over the control.
>
> Arguments
> - *index*—an **Integer** that uniquely identifies a control in a control array. This argument is not present if the control is not part of a control array.

Private Sub *LabelControl*__DragDrop([*index* As Integer ,] *source* As Control, *x* As Single, *y* As Single)

> Usage   This event occurs when a drag-and-drop operation is completed by using the **Drag** method with a *DragAction* value of *vbEndDrag*.

Tip

*When using drag-and-drop operations, use the **DragOver** event to determine what the cursor should look like while the cursor moves over the control.*

> Arguments
> - *index*—an **Integer** that uniquely identifies a control in a control array. This argument is not present if the control is not part of a control array.
> - *source*—a control object that is the control that is being dragged.

Tip

You can access a property or method from the source control by using source.property *or* source.method. *You can determine the type of object or control by using the **TypeOf** operator.*

> - *x*—a **Single** that contains the horizontal location of the mouse pointer.
> - *y*—a **Single** that contains the vertical location of the mouse pointer.

Private Sub *LabelControl*__DragOver([*index* As Integer ,] *source* As Control, *x* As Single, *y* As Single, *state* As Integer)

> Usage   This event occurs while a drag operation is in progress and the cursor is moved over the control.

Tip

*When using drag-and-drop operations, use the **DragOver** event to determine what the cursor should look like while the cursor moves over the control. When* state *is 0, you can change the cursor to a No Drop (vbNoDrop) cursor or highlight the field that the cursor is near. When* state *is 1, you can undo the changes you made when the* state *was 0.*

> Arguments
> - *index*—an **Integer** that uniquely identifies a control in a control array. This argument is not present if the control is not part of a control array.
> - *source*—a control object that is the control that is being dragged.

> **Tip**
>
> *You can access a property or method from the source control by using* source.property *or* source.method. *You can determine the type of object or control by using the* **TypeOf** *operator.*

- *x*—a **Single** that contains the horizontal location of the mouse pointer.
- *y*—a **Single** that contains the vertical location of the mouse pointer.
- *state*—an **Integer** value (see Table L-11) that indicates the state of the object being dragged.

state Name	Value	Description
vbEnter	0	The dragged object is entering range of the control.
vbLeave	1	The dragged object is leaving range of the control.
vbOver	2	The dragged object has moved from one position over the control to another.

Table L-11: state *values.*

Private Sub *LabelControl*_LinkClose ([*index* As Integer ,])

Usage This event occurs when a DDE link is closed.

Arguments - *index*—an **Integer** that uniquely identifies a control in a control array. This argument is not present if the control is not part of a control array.

Private Sub *LabelControl* _LinkError ([*index* As Integer ,] errcode As Integer)

Usage This event occurs when a DDE link error occurs.

Arguments - *index*—an **Integer** that uniquely identifies a control in a control array. This argument is not present if the control is not part of a control array.
- *errcode*—an **Integer** that contains an error code listed in Table L-12 below.

errcode Value	Description
1	The other application requested data in wrong format. This may occur more than once while Visual Basic attempts to find an acceptable format.
6	The other application attempted to continue the DDE conversation after LinkMode in this application was set to zero.
7	All 128 DDE links are in use.
8	Destination control: an automatic link or LinkRequest failed when communicating. Source forms: the other application was unable to poke data to a control.
11	Insufficient memory available for DDE.

Table L-12: *DDE errcode values.*

Private Sub *LabelControl*_LinkExecute ([*index* As Integer ,] *cmd* As String, *cancel* As Integer)

| Usage | This event occurs when a destination application requests the source application to perform the function in *cmd*. |

Note

*If your program doesn't include a **LinkExecute** event, then all commands will be rejected.*

Arguments	• *index*—an **Integer** that uniquely identifies a control in a control array. This argument is not present if the control is not part of a control array.
	• *cmd*—a **String** containing a command for the source application to execute. The format of the string is application-specific.
	• *cancel*—an **Integer** when zero means that the command was accepted. Any other value will inform the destination application that the command was rejected.

Private Sub *LabelControl*_LinkOpen ([*index* As Integer ,] *cancel* As Integer)

Usage	This event occurs when a DDE session is being set up.
Arguments	• *index*—an **Integer** that uniquely identifies a control in a control array. This argument is not present if the control is not part of a control array.
	• *cancel*—an **Integer** when zero means that the command was accepted. Any other value will inform the destination application that the link will be refused.

Private Sub *LabelControl*_MouseDown([*index* As Integer ,] *button* As Integer, *shift* As Single, *x* As Single, *y* As Single)

Usage	This event occurs when a mouse button was pressed while the cursor is over the control.
Arguments	• *index*—an **Integer** that uniquely identifies a control in a control array. This argument is not present if the control is not part of a control array.
	• *button*—an **Integer** value (see Table L-13) that contains information about the mouse buttons that were pressed. Only one button will be indicated when this event occurs.

button Name	Value	Description
vbLeftButton	1	The left button was pressed.
vbRightButton	2	The right button was pressed.
vbMiddleButton	4	The middle button was pressed.

Table L-13: button *values.*

- *shift*—an **Integer** value (see Table L-14) that contains information about the Shift and Alt keys that were pushed when the mouse button was pressed. These values can be added together if more than one key was down. For instance, a value of 5 would mean that the Shift and Alt keys were both down when the mouse button was pressed.

shift Name	Value	Description
vbShiftMask	1	The Shift key was pressed.
vbCtrlMask	2	The Ctrl key was pressed.
vbAltMask	4	The Alt key was pressed.

Table L-14: shift *values*.

- *x*—a **Single** that contains the horizontal location of the mouse pointer.
- *y*—a **Single** that contains the vertical location of the mouse pointer.

Private Sub *LabelControl*_MouseMove ([*index* As Integer ,] *button* As Integer, *shift* As Single, *x* As Single, *y* As Single)

Usage   This event occurs while the cursor is moved over the control.

Arguments
- *index*—an **Integer** that uniquely identifies a control in a control array. This argument is not present if the control is not part of a control array.
- *button*—an **Integer** value (see Table L-15) that contains information about the mouse buttons that were pressed. These values can be added together if more than one button was pushed. For instance, a value of 3 means that both the left and right buttons were pressed. A value of 0 means that no buttons were pressed.

button Name	Value	Description
vbLeftButton	1	The left button was pressed.
vbRightButton	2	The right button was pressed.
vbMiddleButton	4	The middle button was pressed.

Table L-15: button *values*.

- *shift*—an **Integer** value (see Table L-16) that contains information about the Shift and Alt keys that were pushed when the mouse button was pressed. For instance, a value of 5 would mean that the Shift and Alt keys were both down when the mouse button was pressed. A value of 0 means that none of these keys were pressed.

shift Name	Value	Description
vbShiftMask	1	The Shift key was pressed.
vbCtrlMask	2	The Ctrl key was pressed.
vbAltMask	4	The Alt key was pressed.

Table L-16: shift *values*.

- *x*—a **Single** that contains the horizontal location of the mouse pointer.
- *y*—a **Single** that contains the vertical location of the mouse pointer.

Private Sub *LabelControl*_MouseUp([*index* As Integer ,] *button* As Integer, *shift* As Single, *x* As Single, *y* As Single)

Usage
: This event occurs when a mouse button is released while the cursor is over the control.

Arguments
: - *index*—an **Integer** that uniquely identifies a control in a control array. This argument is not present if the control is not part of a control array.
  - *button*—an **Integer** value (see Table L-17) that contains information about the mouse buttons that were released. Only one of these values will be present.

button Name	Value	Description
vbLeftButton	1	The left button was released.
vbRightButton	2	The right button was released.
vbMiddleButton	4	The middle button was released.

Table L-17: button *values*.

- *shift*—an **Integer** value (see Table L-18) that contains information about the Shift and Alt keys that were pushed when the mouse button was released. These values can be added together if more than one key was down. For instance, a value of 5 would mean that the Shift and Alt keys were both down when the mouse button was released. A value of 0 means that none of these keys were pressed.

shift Name	Value	Description
vbShiftMask	1	The Shift key was pressed.
vbCtrlMask	2	The Ctrl key was pressed.
vbAltMask	4	The Alt key was pressed.

Table L-18: shift *values*.

- *x*—a **Single** that contains the horizontal location of the mouse pointer.
- *y*—a **Single** that contains the vertical location of the mouse pointer.

Private Sub *LabelControl*_OLECompleteDrag([*index* As Integer ,] *effect* As Long)

Usage
: This event tells the source control the results of an OLE drag-and-drop operation. This is the final event to occur in the series of actions that make up an OLE drag-and-drop operation.

Arguments
: - *index*—an **Integer** that uniquely identifies a control in a control array. This argument is not present if the control is not part of a control array.

- *effect*—a **Long** (see Table L-19) that returns the status of the OLE drag-and-drop operation.

effect Name	Value	Description
vbDropEffectNone	0	The operation was canceled or the target control can't accept the drop operation.
vbDropEffectCopy	1	The operation copied data from the source control to the target control. The original data is unchanged.
vbDropEffectMove	2	The operation results in a link from the original data to the target control.

Table L-19: effect *values.*

Private Sub *LabelControl*_OLEDragDrop([*index* As Integer ,] *data* As DataObject, *effect* As Long, *button* As Integer, *shift* As Single, *x* As Single, *y* As Single)

Usage This event tells the source control the results of an OLE drag-and-drop operation. This is the final event to occur in the series of actions that make up an OLE drag-and-drop operation.

Arguments
- *index*—an **Integer** that uniquely identifies a control in a control array. This argument is not present if the control is not part of a control array.
- *data*—a **DataObject** that contains the formats that the source control will provide. If the data is not contained in the **DataObject**, then it can be retrieved with the **GetData** method.
- *effect*—a **Long** (see Table L-20) that returns the status of the OLE drag-and-drop operation.

effect Name	Value	Description
vbDropEffectNone	0	The operation was canceled or the target control can't accept the drop operation.
vbDropEffectCopy	1	The operation copied data from the source control to the target control. The original data is unchanged.
vbDropEffectMove	2	The operation results in a link from the original data to the target control.

Table L-20: effect *values.*

- *button*—an **Integer** value (see Table L-21) that contains information about the mouse buttons that were pressed. These values can be added together if more than one button was pushed. For instance, a value of 3 means that both the left and right buttons were pressed. A value of 0 means that no buttons were pressed.

button Name	Value	Description
vbLeftButton	1	The left button was pressed.
vbRightButton	2	The right button was pressed.
vbMiddleButton	4	The middle button was pressed.

Table L-21: button *values.*

- *shift*—an **Integer** value (see Table L-22) that contains information about the Shift and Alt keys that were pushed when the mouse button was released. These values can be added together if more than one key was down. For instance, a value of 5 would mean that the Shift and Alt keys were both down when the mouse button was released. A value of 0 means that none of these keys were pressed.

shift Name	Value	Description
vbShiftMask	1	The Shift key was pressed.
vbCtrlMask	2	The Ctrl key was pressed.
vbAltMask	4	The Alt key was pressed.

Table L-22: shift *values.*

- *x*—a **Single** that contains the horizontal location of the mouse pointer.
- *y*—a **Single** that contains the vertical location of the mouse pointer.

Private Sub *LabelControl*_OLEDragOver([*index* As Integer ,] *data* As DataObject, *effect* As Long, *button* As Integer, *shift* As Single, *x* As Single, *y* As Single, *state* As Integer)

Usage   This event happens when an OLE drag-and-drop operation is in progress.

Arguments
- *index*—an **Integer** that uniquely identifies a control in a control array. This argument is not present if the control is not part of a control array.
- *data*—a **DataObject** that contains the formats that the source control will provide. If the data is not contained in the **DataObject**, then it can be retrieved with the **GetData** method.
- *effect*—a **Long** (see Table L-23) that returns the status of the OLE drag-and-drop operation.

effect Name	Value	Description
vbDropEffectNone	0	The operation was canceled or the target control can't accept the drop operation.
vbDropEffectCopy	1	The operation copied data from the source control to the target control. The original data is unchanged.
vbDropEffectMove	2	The operation results in a link from the original data to the target control.

Table L-23: effect *values.*

- *button*—an **Integer** value (see Table L-24) that contains information about the mouse buttons that were pressed. These values can be added together if more than one button was pushed. For instance, a value of 3 means that both the left and right buttons were pressed. A value of 0 means that no buttons were pressed.

button Name	Value	Description
vbLeftButton	1	The left button was pressed.
vbRightButton	2	The right button was pressed.
vbMiddleButton	4	The middle button was pressed.

Table L-24: button *values.*

- *shift*—an **Integer** value (see Table L-25) that contains information about the Shift and Alt keys that were pushed when the mouse button was released. These values can be added together if more than one key was down. For instance, a value of 5 would mean that the Shift and Alt keys were both down when the mouse button was released. A value of 0 means that none of these keys were pressed.

shift Name	Value	Description
vbShiftMask	1	The Shift key was pressed.
vbCtrlMask	2	The Ctrl key was pressed.
vbAltMask	4	The Alt key was pressed.

Table L-25: shift *values.*

- *x*—a **Single** that contains the horizontal location of the mouse pointer.
- *y*—a **Single** that contains the vertical location of the mouse pointer.
- *state*—an **Integer** value (see Table L-26) that indicates the state of the object being dragged.

state Name	Value	Description
vbEnter	0	The dragged object is entering range of the control.
vbLeave	1	The dragged object is leaving range of the control.
vbOver	2	The dragged object has moved from one position over the control to another.

Table L-26: state *values.*

Private Sub *LabelControl*_OLEGiveFeedback ([*index* As Integer ,] *effect* As Long)

Usage   This event tells the source control what is happening while the OLE drag-and-drop operation is in progress. This event occurs after the **OLEDragOver** event.

> **Tip**
> You may want to use this event to change the cursor to reflect what can happen in the remote object.

Arguments
- *index*—an **Integer** that uniquely identifies a control in a control array. This argument is not present if the control is not part of a control array.
- *effect*—a **Long** (see Table L-27) that returns the status of the OLE drag-and-drop operation.

effect Name	Value	Description
vbDropEffectNone	0	The operation was canceled or the target control can't accept the drop operation.
vbDropEffectCopy	1	The operation copied data from the source control to the target control. The original data is unchanged.
vbDropEffectMove	2	The operation results in a link from the original data to the target control.
vbDropEffectScroll	&H80000000	The target control is about to scroll or is scrolling. This value may be added to the other *effect* values.

Table L-27: effect *values*.

Private Sub *LabelControl*_OLESetData([*index* As Integer ,] *data* As DataObject, *DataFormat* As Integer)

Usage
This event happens in response to the target object performing a **GetData** method on *data*. This routine will respond by using the **SetData** method with the desired data using the **DataObject** *data*.

Arguments
- *index*—an **Integer** that uniquely identifies a control in a control array. This argument is not present if the control is not part of a control array.
- *data*—a **DataObject** that will contain the data to be returned to the target object.
- *format*—an **Integer** value (see Table L-28) that contains the format of the data.

format Name	Value	Description
vbCFText	1	Text (.TXT files)
vbCFBitmap	2	Bitmap (.BMP files)
vbCFMetafile	3	Metafile (.WMF files)
vbCFEDIB	8	Device independent bitmap (DIB)
vbCFPallette	9	Color palette
vbCFEMetafile	14	Enhanced metafile (.EMF files)
vbCFFiles	15	List of files
vbCFRTF	-16639	Rich Text Format (.RTF files)

Table L-28: format *values*.

Private Sub *LabelControl*_**OLEStartDrag** ([*index* **As Integer** ,] *data* **As DataObject**, *AllowedEffects* **As Long**)

Usage   This event starts an OLE drag-and-drop operation.

Arguments
- *index*—an **Integer** that uniquely identifies a control in a control array. This argument is not present if the control is not part of a control array.
- *data*—a **DataObject** that will contain the formats that the source object is willing to provide to the target object. It may optionally contain the data to transfer.
- *AllowedEffects*—a **Long** that contains the effects (see Table L-29) that the target object can request from the source object. The *AllowedEffects* can be added together if the source object supports more than one effect. Note that the target object can always use the *vbDropEffectNone* effect.

AllowedEffects Name	Value	Description
vbDropEffectNone	0	The target can't copy the data.
vbDropEffectCopy	1	The target can copy the data and the source will keep the data unchanged.
vbDropEffectMove	2	The target can copy the data and the source will delete the data.

Table L-29: AllowedEffects *values.*

Examples
```
Private Sub Text1_Change()
Label1.Caption = Text1.Text
End Sub
```

This routine changes the value of a label's caption each time someone enters something into a text box. By entering a long string of words, you can see the effect of the **AutoSize** and **WordWrap** properties.

See Also   **Font** (object), **Form** (object), **TextBox** (control)

Label

OBJECT

PE, EE

Usage   The **Label** object is part of the **MSChart** control containing information about a label on the chart.

Properties
- *LabelObject*.**Auto**—a **Boolean** when **True** means the labels are automatically rotated to improve the layout. **False** means that the label can't be rotated.
- *LabelObject*.**Backdrop**—a reference to a **Backdrop** object containing information about the pattern, shadow, or picture behind the label.
- *LabelObject*.**Font**—a reference to a **Font** object containing information about the character font used by this object.
- *LabelObject*.**Format**—a **String** containing the format information for the characters in the label.

- *LabelObject*.**FormatLength**—an **Integer** that contains the length of the format string. This property is read-only.
- *LabelObject*.**Standing**—a **Boolean** when **True** means the labels display vertically in the Y-plane. **False** means the labels display horizontally in the X-or Z-plane.
- *LabelObject*.**TextLayout**—a reference to a **TextLayout** object containing information about how the text inside the label displays.
- *LabelObject*.**VtFont**—a reference to a **VtFont** object containing font information.

See Also   **Labels** (collection), **MSChart** (control)

Labels

COLLECTION

PE, EE

Usage   The **Labels** collection contains a set of **Label** objects.

Properties
- *LabelsCollection*.**Count**—a **Long** value that contains the number of items in the collection.
- *LabelsCollection*.**Item**(*index*)—an array of **Label** objects.

See Also   **Label** (object), **MSChart** (control)

LBound

FUNCTION

CCE, LE, PE, EE

Syntax   *lower* = **LBound** (*array* [, *dimension*])

Usage   The **LBound** function returns the lower bound of an array. A compiler error will occur if *array* is not an array and a run-time error will occur if *dimension* does not exist in the array.

Arguments
- *lower*—a **Long** value containing the lower bound of the array.
- *array*—a Visual Basic identifier that has been defined as an array.
- *dimension*—a **Long** value containing the dimension for which the lower bound will be returned. If not specified, it will default to 1 (the first dimension).

Examples
```
Private Sub Command1_Click()
Dim MyArray(-1 To 1, 127, 1 To 99)
Dim i As Long
For i = 1 To 3
    MsgBox "The lower bound for dimension " & Format(i) & " is " &
    Format(LBound(MyArray, i))
Next i
End Sub
```

This routine displays the lower bound of each dimension of the array.

See Also   **Array** (function), **Dim** (statement), **ReDim** (statement), **UBound** (function)

LCase

FUNCTION

CCE, LE, PE, EE

Syntax   *lower* = **LCase[$]** (*string*)

Usage   The **LCase** function converts any uppercase characters to lowercase characters in the string.

Arguments
- *lower*—a **String** value containing the converted string.
- *string*—a **String** value to convert.

Examples
```
Private Sub Command1_Click()
Text2.Text = LCase(Text1.Text)
End Sub
```

This routine converts the contents of the Text1 text box to lowercase and returns the result in the Text2 text box.

See Also   **String** (data type), **UCase** (function)

LCoor

OBJECT

PE, EE

Usage   The **LCoor** object contains a pair of **Long** coordinate values.

Properties
- *LCoorObject*.**X**—a **Long** value that contains the X-coordinate.
- *LCoorObject*.**Y**—a **Long** value that contains the Y-coordinate

Methods   ***LCoorObject*.Set *xvalue, yvalue***

   Usage   This method assigns a value to the coordinates.

   Arguments
   - *xvalue*—a **Long** expression that contains the X-coordinate value.
   - *yvalue*—a **Long** expression that contains the Y-coordinate value.

See Also   **Coor** (object), **MSChart** (control)

Left

FUNCTION

CCE, LE, PE, EE

Syntax `result = Left[$] ( string , length )`

Usage The **Left** function returns the specified number of characters from *string* starting with the first character. The dollar sign ($) is optional and indicates that the return value is a **String** rather than a **Variant**.

Arguments
- *result*—a **String** value or a **Variant** containing a string value containing the result of the **Left** function.
- *string*—a **String** value from which to extract the characters.
- *Length*—a **Long** value containing the number of characters to return.

Examples
```
Private Sub Command1_Click()
Text2.Text = Left(Text1.Text, 5)
End Sub
```

This routine stores the first five characters from Text1.Text in Text2.Text.

See Also **Byte** (data type), **LeftB** (function), **Mid** (function), **MidB** (function), **Right** (function), **RightB** (function), **String** (data type)

LeftB

FUNCTION

CCE, LE, PE, EE

Syntax `result = LeftB[$] ( string , length )`

Usage The **LeftB** function returns the specified number of bytes from *string* starting with the first byte. The dollar sign ($) is optional and indicates that the return value is a **String** rather than a **Variant**.

Arguments
- *result*—a **String** value or a **Variant** containing a string value containing the result of the **LeftB** function.
- *string*—a **String** value from which to extract the bytes.
- *length*—a **Long** value containing the number of bytes to return.

See Also **Byte** (data type), **Left** (function) **Len** (function), **LenB** (function), **Mid** (function), **MidB** (function), **Right** (function), **RightB** (function), **String** (data type)

Legend

OBJECT

PE, EE

Usage
The **Legend** object is part of the **MSChart** control containing information about the legend on the chart.

Properties
- *LegendObject*.**Backdrop**—a reference to a **Backdrop** object containing information about the pattern, shadow, or picture behind the legend.
- *LegendObject*.**Font**—a reference to a **Font** object containing information about the character font used by this object.
- *LegendObject*.**Location**—a reference to a **Location** object containing information about the placement of the legend on the chart.
- *LegendObject*.**TextLayout**—a reference to a **TextLayout** object containing information about how the text inside the legend displays.
- *LegendObject*.**VtFont**—a reference to a **VtFont** object containing font information.

Methods
LegendObject.Select

Usage   This method selects the legend for the chart.

See Also   **MSChart** (control)

Len

FUNCTION

CCE, LE, PE, EE

Syntax   `result = Len ( string )`

Usage   The **Len** function returns the number of characters in *string*.

Arguments
- *result*—a **Long** value containing the number of characters in *string*.
- *string*—any valid **String** expression or variable name.

Examples
```
Private Sub Command1_Click()
MsgBox "Length in characters: " & Format(Len(Text1.Text)) & vbCrLf & "Length in
    bytes:" & Format(LenB(Text1.Text))
End Sub
```

This routine stores returns the length of the text box in characters and bytes.

See Also   **Byte** (data type), **Left** (function), **LeftB** (function), **Mid** (function), **MidB** (function), **Right** (function), **RightB** (function), **String** (data type)

LenB

FUNCTION

CCE, LE, PE, EE

Syntax   `result = LenB ( string )`

Usage   The **LenB** function returns the number of bytes in *string*.

Arguments
- *result*—a **Long** value containing the number of bytes in *string*.
- *string*—any valid **String** expression or variable name.

Examples
```
Private Sub Command1_Click()
MsgBox "Length in characters: " & Format(Len(Text1.Text)) & vbCrLf & "Length in
    bytes:" & Format(LenB(Text1.Text))
End Sub
```

This routine returns the length of the text box in characters and bytes.

See Also   **Byte** (data type), **LeftB** (function), **Len** (function), **Mid** (function), **MidB** (function), **Right** (function), **RightB** (function), **String** (data type)

Let

STATEMENT

CCE, LE, PE, EE

Syntax   `[ Let ] var = expr`

Usage   The **Let** statement assigns a value to a variable. The statement name is optional, so any statement that begins with a variable name is considered to be a **Let** statement. The expression can be nearly anything as long as it is compatible with the variable's type.

    Object variables should use the **Set** statement when assigning an object variable a reference to an object.

Arguments
- *var*—the name of a variable.
- *expr*—an expression compatible with the type of *var*.

Examples
```
Private Sub Command1_Click()
Dim i As Integer
Dim j As Integer
Let i = 1 + 1 + 1 + 1
j = 2 * 4 * 6 * 8
MsgBox "i = " & Format(i) & vbCrLf & "j = " & Format(j)
End Sub
```

This routine assigns values to two variables with the **Let** statement. The first statement shows how the statement name **Let** assigns a value to a variable. The second statement shows how to use the **Let** statement without the word let.

See Also   **Set** (statement)

Light

OBJECT

PE, EE

Usage The **Light** object contains the light source illuminating a three dimensional chart.

Properties
- *LightObject*.**AmbientIntensity**—a **Single** value ranging from zero to one, that contains the relative percents of ambient light illuminating a three dimensional chart.
- *LightObject*.**EdgeIntensity**—a **Single** value ranging from zero to one, that contains the relative percents of light illuminating the edge of a three dimensional chart. Zero means that the edges will not be illuminated, while one means that the edges fully illuminate.
- *LightObject*.**EdgeVisible**—a **Boolean** when **True** means they are visible on the chart. **False** means the edges do not display.
- *LightObject*.**LightSources**—a reference to a **LightSources** collection.

Methods *LightObject*.**Set** *xvalue, yvalue*

    Usage This method assigns a value to the coordinates.

    Arguments
- *xvalue*—a **Long** expression that contains the X-coordinate value.
- *yvalue*—a **Long** expression that contains the Y-coordinate value.

See Also **LCoor** (object), **LightSources** (collection), **MSChart** (control)

LightSource

OBJECT

PE, EE

Usage The **LightSource** object contains the position of the light source that is illuminating a three dimensional chart.

Properties
- *LightObject*.**Intensity**—a **Single** value ranging from zero to one, that contains the relative percents of the light source that is light illuminating a three dimensional chart.
- *LightObject*.**X**—a **Single** value that contains the X-location of the light source.
- *LightObject*.**Y**—a **Single** value that contains the Y-location of the light source.
- *LightObject*.**Z**—a **Single** value that contains the Z-location of the light source.

Methods *LightSourceObject*.**Set** *xvalue, yvalue, zvalue, intensity*

    Usage This method creates a light source at a specific location with a certain intensity.

    Arguments
- *xvalue*—a **Single** expression that contains the X-coordinate value.
- *yvalue*—a **Single** expression that contains the Y-coordinate value.

- *zvalue*—a **Single** expression that contains the Z-coordinate value.
- *intensity*—a **Single** expression that contains the intensity as a value ranging from zero to one.

See Also   **LightSources** (collection), **MSChart** (control)

LightSources

COLLECTION

PE, EE

Usage   The **LightSources** collection contains a set of **LightSource** objects for the **MSChart** control.

Properties
- *LightSources*.**Count**—a **Long** value that contains the number of items in the collection.
- *LightSources*.**Item**(*index*)—an array of **LightSource** objects.

Methods   **LightSourcesCollection.Add** *xvalue, yvalue, zvalue, intensity*

    Usage   This method creates a light source at a specific location with a certain intensity.

    Arguments
- *xvalue*—a **Single** expression that contains the X-coordinate value.
- *yvalue*—a **Single** expression that contains the Y-coordinate value.
- *zvalue*—a **Single** expression that contains the Z-coordinate value.
- *intensity*—a **Single** expression that contains the intensity as a value ranging from zero to one.

LightSourcesCollection.Remove *index*

    Usage   This method deletes an item specified by *index* from the collection specified by *CollectionObject*.

    Arguments
- *index*—an **Integer** value that contains the relative position of the light source in the collection.

See Also   **LightSource** (object), **MSChart** (control)

Line

CONTROL

CCE, LE, PE, EE

Usage   The **Line** control draws lines on a **Form** or **PictureBox** control.

Properties
- *LineControl*.**BorderColor**—a **Long** that contains the value for the color of the line.
- *LineControl*.**BorderStyle**—an **Integer** value (see Table L-30) specifying how the border will be drawn. This property also indicates how the form can be resized and is read only at run time.

BorderStyle Name	Value	Description
vbTransparent	0	The line is transparent.
vbBSSolid	1	The line is solid and the border is centered on the edge of the line (default).
vbBSDash	2	The line is a series of dashes.
vbBSDot	3	The line is a series of dots.
vbBSDashDot	4	The line is a series of dash dots.
vbBSDashDotDot	5	The line is a series of dash dot dots.
vbBSInsideSolid	6	The line is solid on the inside and is on the outer edge of the line.

Table L-30: **BorderStyle** *values.*

- *LineControl.***BorderWidth**—an **Integer** value describing how wide the line will be drawn.
- *LineControl.***Container**—an object that sets or returns the container of the control at run time. This property cannot be set at design time.
- *LineControl.***DrawMode**—an **Integer** value (see Table L-31) specifying how the line will appear on the form.

DrawMode Name	Value	Description
vbBlackness	1	Blackness
vbNotMergePen	2	Inverse of *vbMergePen*
vbMaskNotPen	3	Combination of the colors common to the background color and the inverse of the pen
vbNotCopyPen	4	Inverse of *vbCopyPen*
vbMaskPenNot	5	Combination of the colors common to the pen and the inverse of the background
vbInvert	6	Inverse of the display color
vbXorPen	7	Combination of the colors in the display and pen, but not in both
vbNotMaskPen	8	Inverse setting of *vbMaskPen*
vbMaskPen	9	Combination of the colors common to the pen and display
vbNotXorPen	10	Inverse setting of *vbXorPen*
vbNop	11	Turns drawing off
vbMergeNotPen	12	Combination of the display and inverse of the pen color.
vbCopyPen	13	Color specified in the ForeColor property
vbMergePenNot	14	Combination of the pen color and the inverse of the display color
vbMergePen	15	Combination of the pen color and the display color
vbWhiteness	16	Whiteness

Table L-31: **DrawMode** *values.*

- *LineControl.***Index**—an **Integer** that uniquely identifies a control in a control array.
- *LineControl.***Name**—a **String** that contains the name of the control that will be used to reference the control in a Visual Basic program. This property is read only at run time.
- *LineControl.***Parent**—an object that contains a reference to the **Form, Frame,** or other container that contains the **Label** control.
- *LineControl.***Tag**—a **String** that can hold programmer specific information. This property is not used by Visual Basic.
- *LineControl.***Visible**—a **Boolean** value when **True** means that the control is visible. When **False** means that the control is not visible.

> **Tip**
>
> *This property hides the control until the program is ready to display it.*

- *LineControl*.**X1**—a **Single** that contains the starting X-coordinate of the line.
- *LineControl*.**Y1**—a **Single** that contains the starting Y-coordinate of the line.
- *LineControl*.**X2**—a **Single** that contains the stopping X-coordinate of the line.
- *LineControl*.**Y2**—a **Single** that contains the stopping Y-coordinate of the line.

Methods *LineControl.***Refresh**

Usage   This method redraws the contents of the control.

*LineControl.***ZOrder** [*position*]

Usage   This method specifies the position of the line control relative to the other objects on the form.

> **Tip**
>
> *Note that there are three layers of objects on a form: the back layer is the drawing space which contains the results of the graphical methods, the middle layer contains graphical objects and **Labels**, and the back layer contains nongraphical controls such as the **Line** control. The **ZOrder** method only affects how the objects are arranged within a single layer.*

Arguments
- *position*—an **Integer** that specifies the relative position of this object. A value of 0 means that the control is positioned at the head of the list, a value of 1 means that the control will be placed at the end of the list.

See Also   **Form** (object), **PictureBox** (control)

Line Input

STATEMENT

CCE, LE, PE, EE

Syntax   `Line Input # fnum, var`

Usage   The **Line Input** statement reads a single line of information from a file into a string variable. The lines are delimited by either a carriage return or a carriage return line feed pair.

> **Tip**
>
> *Use the **Print #** statement to write to a file that will be read with the **Line Input #** statement.*

Arguments
- *expr*—an expression compatible with the type of *var*.
- *var*—the name of a **String** variable.

446 • The Visual Basic 5 Programmer's Reference

Examples
```
Private Sub Command1_Click()
Dim s As String
On Error Resume Next
Open Text2.Text For Input As #1
If Err.Number = 0 Then
   Text1.Text = ""
   Line Input #1, s
   Do While Not EOF(1)
      Text1.Text = Text1.Text & s & vbCrLf
      Line Input #1, s
   Loop
   Close #1
End If
End Sub
```

This routine opens the file listed in the Text2 text box. Then it reads the file one line at a time using the **Line Input #** statement and appends it to the end of the Text2 text box. Finally when there is no more data, the file is closed and the routine ends.

See Also   **Input** (statement)

ListBox

CONTROL

CCE, LE, PE, EE

Usage   The **ListBox** control let's a user chose one or more items from a list of items.

Properties
- *ListBoxControl*.**Appearance**—an **Integer** value (see Table L-32) that describes how the combo box will appear on the form.

Appearance Value	Description
0	The **ListBox** control displays without the 3D effects.
1	The **ListBox** control displays with 3D effects (default value.)

Table L-32: Appearance *values.*

- *ListBoxControl*.**BackColor**—a **Long** that contains the suggested value for the background color of the control. The **BackColor** and **ForeColor** must both be solid to display text. If you choose a color that is dithered, it will be changed to the nearest solid color.
- *ListBoxControl*.**Columns**—an **Integer** value when zero means that the contents of the list box display in a single column and scroll vertically. When a value greater than zero is specified the contents of the list box display in the number of columns specified and the scrolling is done horizontally.
- *ListBoxControl*.**Container**—an object that sets or returns the container of the control at run time. This property cannot be set at design time.

- *ListBoxControl*.**DataChanged**—a **Boolean** that applies only to data bound controls. When **True** means that the data contained in this control was changed either by the user or by some means other than retrieving data from the current record. When **False** means the data in the control is unchanged from the current record. Simply reading the next record is not sufficient to set the **DataChanged** property to **True**.
- *ListBoxControl*.**DataField**—a **String** value that associates the control with a field in a **RecordSet** object in a **Data** control.
- *ListBoxControl*.**DataSource**—a **String** containing the name of a **Data** control that will be updated once the selection is made.
- *ListBoxControl*.**DragIcon**—an object that contains the **Picture** value of an icon. At design time, you can specify an icon file that has a file type of .ICO.

> **Tip**
>
> *This value can be created by copying the value from another control's **DragIcon** value, a form's icon, or by using the **LoadPicture** function.*

- *ListBoxControl*.**DragMode**—an **Integer** value (see Table L-33) specifying how the control will respond to a drag request.

> **Tip**
>
> *Setting **DragMode** to vbAutomatic will automatically begin a drag operation when the user clicks on the control. However, the control will not respond to the usual mouse events (**Click**, **DblClick**, **MouseDown**, **MouseMove**, **MouseUp**).*

DragMode Name	Value	Description
vbManual	0	The Drag method must be used to begin a drag-and-drop operation (default value).
vbAutomatic	1	The source control will automatically begin a drag-and-drop operation when the user clicks on the control.

Table L-33: **DragMode** *values*.

- *ListBoxControl*.**Enabled**—a **Boolean** value when **True** means that the control will respond to events. When **False**, the control will not respond to events.
- *ListBoxControl*.**Font**—an object that contains information about the character font used by this object.

> **Tip**
>
> *The **Font** object should be used in place of the other **Font** properties, since it offers more functionality than the individual properties.*

- *ListBoxControl*.**FontBold**—a **Boolean** when **True** means that the characters display in bold. **False** means that the characters display normally.
- *ListBoxControl*.**FontItalic**—a **Boolean** when **True** means that the characters display in italics. **False** means that the characters display normally.
- *ListBoxControl*.**FontName**—a **String** that specifies the name of the font that should be used to display the characters in this control.
- *ListBoxControl*.**FontSize**—a **Single** that specifies the point size that should be used to display the characters in the control.
- *ListBoxControl*.**FontStrikethru**—a **Boolean** when **True** means that the characters display with a line through the center. **False** means that the characters display normally.
- *ListBoxControl*.**FontUnderlined**—a **Boolean** when **True** means that the characters display with a line beneath them. **False** means that the characters display normally.
- *ListBoxControl*.**ForeColor**—a **Long** that contains the suggested value for the foreground color of the contained control. This property is read only at run time.
- *ListBoxControl*.**Height**—a **Single** that contains the height of the control.
- *ListBoxControl*.**HelpContextID**—a **Long** that contains a help file context ID number which references an entry in the help file. When the user presses the F1 key while this control is active, the corresponding entry in the help file will automatically display. A value of zero means that no context number was specified.

> **Tip**
>
> *A help file must be compiled using the Windows Help Compiler available in the Professional and Enterprise editions of Visual Basic.*

- *ListBoxControl*.**hWnd**—a **Long** that contains a Windows handle to the control.

> **Tip**
>
> *The **hWnd** property is most useful when making calls to Windows API functions. Since this value can change during execution, do not save the value into a variable for later use.*

- *ListBoxControl*.**Index**—an **Integer** that uniquely identifies a control in a control array.
- *ListBoxControl*.**IntegralHeight**—a **Boolean** value when **True** means that drop-down list will resize itself so that it will only show complete items. When **False** the drop-down list will show partial items.
- *ListBoxControl*.**ItemData**(*index*)—an array of **Long** values where each value pointed to by *index* corresponds to the an entry in array of strings in the **List** property. The first element in this array has an index value of zero.
- *ListBoxControl*.**Left**—a **Single** that contains the distance measured in twips between the left edge of the control and the left edge of the control's container.
- *ListBoxControl*.**List**(*index*)—an array of **String** values display in the drop-down part of the **ListBox**. The number of elements in this array can be found in the **ListCount** property.

> **Tip**
>
> *The first element of the **List** array is zero, while the last array element is **ListCount** -1.*

- *ListBoxControl*.**ListCount**—an **Integer** value containing the number of elements in the **List**.
- *ListBoxControl*.**ListIndex**—an **Integer** value containing the index of the selected item from the drop-down box. If no value was selected, **ListIndex** will be set to -1.
- *ListBoxControl*.**MouseIcon**—a **Picture** object (a bitmap, icon, or metafile) that will be used as a cursor when the **MousePointer** property is set to 99. Note that Visual Basic does not support color cursors from a .CUR file. A color icon from an .ICO file should be used instead.
- *ListBoxControl*.**MousePointer**—an **Integer** value (see Table L-34) that contains the value of the cursor that should be displayed when the cursor is moved over this control. Use *vbCustom* to display the custom icon stored in the **MouseIcon** property.

Cursor Name	Value	Description
vbDefault	0	Shape determined by the object (default value)
vbArrow	1	Arrow
vbCrosshair	2	Crosshair
vbIbeam	3	I beam
vbIconPointer	4	Square inside a square
vbSizePointer	5	Four sided arrow (north, south, east, west)
vbSizeNESW	6	Two sided arrow (northeast, southwest)
vbSizeNS	7	Two sided arrow (north, south)
vbSizeNWSE	8	Two sided arrow (northwest, southeast)
vbSizeWE	9	Two sided arrow (west, east)
vbUpArrow	10	Single sided arrow pointing north
vbHourglass	11	Hourglass
vbNoDrop	12	No Drop
vbArrowHourglass	13	An arrow and an hourglass
vbArrowQuestion	14	An arrow and a question mark
vbSizeAll	15	Size all
vbCustom	99	Custom icon from the MouseIcon property of this control

Table L-34: Cursor *values.*

- *ListBoxControl*.**MultiSelect**—an **Integer** value (see Table L-35) that specifies how the file list box will appear on the form.

MultiSelectValue	Description
0	Multiple selections are not allowed.
1	Multiple items can be selected with either a mouse click or by pressing the space bar.
2	Multiple items can be selected by selecting one item with the mouse and then pressing the Shift key while selecting another item. All items between the two will be selected.

Table L-35: **MultiSelect** *values.*

- *ListBoxControl*.**Name**—a **String** that contains the name of the control that will be used to reference the control in a Visual Basic program. This property is read only at run time.
- *ListBoxControl*.**NewIndex**—an **Integer** value corresponding to the index of the last item added to the control. This property will have a value of -1 if there are no items in **List** or the most recent action was to delete an item from **List**.
- *ListBoxControl*.**OLEDragMode**—an **Integer** value (see Table L-36) that describes how the control will respond to OLE drag operations.

Note

When the **DragMode** is **True**, the standard Visual Basic drag-and-drop functions will override the OLE drag-and-drop functions.

OLEDragMode Name	Value	Description
vbOLEDragManual	0	All drag requests will be handled by the programmer (default value).
vbOLEDragAutomatic	1	The control responds to all OLE drag requests automatically.

Table L-36: OLEDragMode values.

- *ListBoxControl*.**OLEDropMode**—an **Integer** value (see Table L-37) that describes how the control will respond to OLE drop operations.

OLEDropMode Name	Value	Description
vbOLEDropNone	0	The control does not accept OLE drops. The cursor is changed to the No Drop cursor (default value).
vbOLEDropManual	1	The control responds to OLE drops under the program's control (manual).
vbOLEDropAutomatic	2	The control automatically accepts OLE drops if it recognizes the format of the data object.

Table L-37: OLEDropMode values.

- *ListBoxControl*.**Parent**—an object that contains a reference to the **Form**, **Frame**, or other container that contains this control.
- *ListBoxControl*.**RightToLeft**—a **Boolean** value when **True** means that the text displays from right to left. When **False** means that the text displays from left to right. A bi-directional version of Windows is required to set this property to **True**.
- *ListBoxControl*.**SelCount**—an **Integer** value containing the number of items selected.
- *ListBoxControl*.**Selected** (*index*)—an array of **Boolean** values corresponding to the elements **List** property. For a given value of *index*, if **Selected** (*index*) is **True** then the value in **List** (*index*) was selected. A value of **False** means that the item was not selected.

Tip

The first element of the **Selected** array is zero, while the last array element is **ListCount** -1.

- *ListBoxControl*.**Sorted**—a **Boolean** value when **True** means that the list is sorted by character code. When **False** means that list will not be sorted (default).
- *ListBoxControl*.**Style**—an **Integer** value (see Table L-38) describing how the list displays.

Style Name	Value	Description
vbListBoxStandard	0	The contents display as a simple list as in previous versions of Visual Basic (default value).
vbListBoxCheckbox	1	The contents display with a check box in front of each item in the list.

*Table L-38: **Style** values.*

- *ListBoxControl*.**TabIndex**—an Integer that determines the order that a user will tab through the objects on a form.
- *ListBoxControl*.**TabStop**—a **Boolean** value when **True** means that the user can tab to this object. When **False** means that this control will be skipped to the next control in the **TabIndex** order.
- *ListBoxControl*.**Tag**—a **String** that can hold programmer specific information. This property is not used by Visual Basic.
- *ListBoxControl*.**Text**—a **String** that sets or returns the value from the text box part of the control. This value can only be accessed at run time.
- *ListBoxControl*.**ToolTipText**—a **String** that holds a text value that can be displayed as a **ToolTip** box that displays whenever the cursor is held over the control for about one second.
- *ListBoxControl*.**Top**—a **Single** that contains the distance measured in twips between the top edge of the control and the top edge of the control's container.
- *ListBoxControl*.**TopIndex**—an **Integer** containing the first number visible in the list box. The default value is zero (the first item in the list).
- *ListBoxControl*.**Visible**—a **Boolean** value when **True** means that the control is visible. When **False** means that the control is not visible.

Tip

This property hides the control until the program is ready to display it.

- *ListBoxControl*.**WhatsThisHelpID**—a **Long** that contains a help file context ID number references an entry in the help file. This provides a What's This PopUp help display in response to the What's This button in the upper right corner of the window.
- *ListBoxControl*.**Width**—a **Single** that contains the width of the control.

Methods

ListBoxControl.AddItem *item* [, *index*]

Usage   This method inserts a new value into a **ListBox**.

Warning

*This method will not work if the control is bound to a **Data** control.*

Arguments
- *item*—a **String** that contains the value to be added to the drop-down list.
- *index*—an **Integer** that specifies the position in the drop-down list where the item will be added. This value must be in the range of zero to **ListCount**, where zero is the first item in the list and **ListCount** will add the item to the end of the list. If omitted, the item will be added to the end of the list.

> **Note**
>
> *Specifying a value for index, while the **Sorted** property is set to **True**, may cause unpredictable results.*

ListBoxControl.Clear

Usage   This method clears all of the items in the list box.

ListBoxControl.Drag [*DragAction*]

Usage   This method begins, ends, or cancels a drag operation.

Arguments   *DragAction*—an **Integer** that contains a value selected from Table L-39 below.

DragAction Name	Value	Description
vbCancel	0	Cancels any drag operation in progress.
vbBeginDrag	1	Begins a drag operation (default).
vbEndDrag	2	Ends a drag operation and drops *object*.

Table L-39: DragAction *values*.

ListBoxControl.Move Left [, Top [, Width [, Height]]]

Usage   This method changes the position and the size of the **ListBox** control. The **ScaleMode** of the **Form** or other container object that holds the **ListBox** control will determine the units used to specify the coordinates.

Arguments
- *Left*—a **Single** that specifies the new position of the left edge of the control.
- *Top*—a **Single** that specifies the new position of the top edge of the control.
- *Width*—a **Single** that specifies the new width of the control.
- *Height*—a **Single** that specifies the new height of the control.

ListBoxControl.OLEDrag

Usage   This method begins an **OLEDrag** and drop operation. Invoking this method will trigger the **OLEStartDrag** event.

ListBoxControl.Refresh

Usage This method redraws the contents of the control.

ListBoxControl.SetFocus

Usage This method transfers the focus from the form or control that currently has the focus to this control. To receive the focus, this control must be enabled and visible.

ListBoxControl.ShowWhatsThis

Usage This method displays the ShowWhatsThis help information for this control.

ListBoxControl.ZOrder [*position*]

Usage This method specifies the position of the **ListBox** control relative to the other objects on the form.

> **Tip**
>
> *Note that there are three layers of objects on a form: the back layer is the drawing space which contains the results of the graphical methods, the middle layer contains graphical objects and **Labels**, and the top layer contains nongraphical controls such as the **ListBox** control. The **ZOrder** method only affects how the objects are arranged within a single layer.*

Arguments *position*—an **Integer** that specifies the relative position of this object. A value of 0 means that the control is positioned at the head of the list, a value of 1 means that the control will be placed at the end of the list.

Events

Private Sub *ListBoxControl*_Click([*index* As Integer])

Usage This event occurs then the user clicks a mouse button to select an item in the drop-down list or selects an item from the drop-down list using the keyboard.

Arguments *index*—an **Integer** that uniquely identifies a control in a control array. This argument is not present if the control is not part of a control array.

Private Sub *ListBoxControl*_DblClick([*index* As Integer])

Usage This event occurs when the user double-clicks a mouse button to select an item in the drop-down list or selects an item from the drop-down list using the keyboard.

Arguments *index*—an **Integer** that uniquely identifies a control in a control array. This argument is not present if the control is not part of a control array.

Private Sub ListBoxControl_DragDrop([*index* As Integer ,] *source* As Control, *x* As Single, *y* As Single)

Usage This event occurs when a drag-and-drop operation is completed by using the **Drag** method with a *DragAction* value of *vbEndDrag*.

Tip

When using drag-and-drop operations, use the **DragOver** event to determine what the cursor should look like while the cursor moves over the control.

Arguments
- *index*—an **Integer** that uniquely identifies a control in a control array. This argument is not present if the control is not part of a control array.
- *source*—a control object that is the control that is being dragged.

Tip

You can access a property or method from the source control by using **source**.*property* or **source**.*method*. You can determine the type of object or control by using the **TypeOf** operator.

- *x*—a **Single** that contains the horizontal location of the mouse pointer.
- *y*—a **Single** that contains the vertical location of the mouse pointer.

Private Sub ListBoxControl_DragOver([*index* As Integer ,] *source* As Control, *x* As Single, *y* As Single, *state* As Integer)

Usage This event occurs while a drag operation is in progress and the cursor is moved over the control.

Tip

When using drag-and-drop operations, use the **DragOver** event to determine what the cursor should look like while the cursor moves over the control. When *state* is 0, you can change the cursor to a No Drop (vbNoDrop) cursor or highlight the field that the cursor is near. When *state* is 1, you can undo the changes you made when the *state* was 0.

Arguments
- *index*—an **Integer** that uniquely identifies a control in a control array. This argument is not present if the control is not part of a control array.
- *source*—a control object that is the control that is being dragged.

Tip

You can access a property or method from the source control by using **source**.*property* or **source**.*method*. You can determine the type of object or control by using the **TypeOf** operator.

- *x*—a **Single** that contains the horizontal location of the mouse pointer.
- *y*—a **Single** that contains the vertical location of the mouse pointer.
- *state*—an **Integer** value (see Table L-40) that indicates the state of the object being dragged.

state Name	Value	Description
vbEnter	0	The dragged object is entering range of the control.
vbLeave	1	The dragged object is leaving range of the control.
vbOver	2	The dragged object has moved from one position over the control to another.

Table L-40: state *values.*

Private Sub *ListBoxControl*_GotFocus ([*index* As Integer])

Usage   This event occurs when the control is given focus.

Tip

You can use this routine to display help or other information in a status bar.

Arguments
- *index*—an **Integer** that uniquely identifies a control in a control array. This argument is not present if the control is not part of a control array.

Private Sub *ListBoxControl*_KeyDown ([*index* As Integer ,] *keycode* As Integer, *shift* As Single)

Usage   This event occurs when a key is pressed while the control has the focus.

Arguments
- *index*—an **Integer** that uniquely identifies a control in a control array. This argument is not present if the control is not part of a control array.
- *keycode*—an **Integer** that contains information about which key was pressed.
- *shift*—an **Integer** value (see Table L-41) that contains information about the Shift and Alt keys that were pushed when the mouse button was pressed. These values can be added together if more than one key was down. For instance, a value of 5 would mean that the Shift and Alt keys were both down when the mouse button was pressed.

shift Name	Value	Description
vbShiftMask	1	The Shift key was pressed.
vbCtrlMask	2	The Ctrl key was pressed.
vbAltMask	4	The Alt key was pressed.

Table L-41: shift *values.*

Private Sub *ListBoxControl*_KeyPress([*index* As Integer ,] *keychar* As Integer)

Usage   This event occurs whenever a key is pressed while the control has the focus.

Arguments
- *index*—an **Integer** that uniquely identifies a control in a control array. This argument is not present if the control is not part of a control array.
- *keychar*—an **Integer** that contains the ASCII character that was pressed.

Private Sub *ListBoxControl*_KeyUp ([*index* As Integer ,] *keycode* As Integer, *shift* As Single)

Usage   This event occurs when a key is released while the control has the focus.

Arguments
- *index*—an **Integer** that uniquely identifies a control in a control array. This argument is not present if the control is not part of a control array.
- *keycode*—an **Integer** that contains information about which key was released.
- *shift*—an **Integer** value (see Table L-42) that contains information about the Shift and Alt keys that were pushed when the mouse button was pressed. These values can be added together if more than one key was down. For instance, a value of 5 would mean that the Shift and Alt keys were both down when the mouse button was pressed.

shift Name	Value	Description
vbShiftMask	1	The Shift key was pressed.
vbCtrlMask	2	The Ctrl key was pressed.
vbAltMask	4	The Alt key was pressed.

Table L-42: shift *values*.

Private Sub *ListBoxControl*_LostFocus ([*index* As Integer])

Usage   This event occurs when the control loses focus.

> **Tip**
>
> *This routine is useful to performing data verification.*

Arguments
- *index*—an **Integer** that uniquely identifies a control in a control array. This argument is not present if the control is not part of a control array.

Private Sub *ListBoxBoxControl*_MouseDown([*index* As Integer ,] *button* As Integer, *shift* As Single, *x* As Single, *y* As Single)

Usage   This event occurs when a mouse button was pressed while the cursor is over the control.

ListBox

Arguments	*index*—an **Integer** that uniquely identifies a control in a control array. This argument is not present if the control is not part of a control array.
	button—an **Integer** value (see Table L-43) that contains information about the mouse buttons that were pressed. Only one button will be indicated when this event occurs.

button Name	Value	Description
vbLeftButton	1	The left button was pressed.
vbRightButton	2	The right button was pressed.
vbMiddleButton	4	The middle button was pressed.

Table L-43: button *values.*

- *shift*—an **Integer** value (see Table L-44) that contains information about the Shift and Alt keys that were pushed when the mouse button was pressed. These values can be added together if more than one key was down. For instance, a value of 5 would mean that the Shift and Alt keys were both down when the mouse button was pressed.

shift Name	Value	Description
vbShiftMask	1	The Shift key was pressed.
vbCtrlMask	2	The Ctrl key was pressed.
vbAltMask	4	The Alt key was pressed.

Table L-44: shift *values.*

- *x*—a **Single** that contains the horizontal location of the mouse pointer.
- *y*—a **Single** that contains the vertical location of the mouse pointer.

Private Sub *ListBoxControl*_MouseMove ([*index* As Integer ,] *button* As Integer, *shift* As Single, *x* As Single, *y* As Single)

Usage	This event occurs while the cursor is moved over the control.
Arguments	*index*—an **Integer** that uniquely identifies a control in a control array. This argument is not present if the control is not part of a control array.
	button—an **Integer** value (see Table L-45) that contains information about the mouse buttons that were pressed. These values can be added together if more than one button was pushed. For instance, a value of 3 means that both the left and right buttons were pressed. A value of 0 means that no buttons were pressed.

button Name	Value	Description
vbLeftButton	1	The left button was pressed.
vbRightButton	2	The right button was pressed.
vbMiddleButton	4	The middle button was pressed.

Table L-45: button *values.*

- *shift*—an **Integer** value (see Table L-46) that contains information about the Shift and Alt keys that were pushed when the mouse button was pressed. For instance, a value of 5 would mean that the Shift and Alt keys were both down when the mouse button was pressed. A value of 0 means that none of these keys were pressed.

shift Name	Value	Description
vbShiftMask	1	The Shift key was pressed.
vbCtrlMask	2	The Ctrl key was pressed.
vbAltMask	4	The Alt key was pressed.

Table L-46: shift *values*.

- *x*—a **Single** that contains the horizontal location of the mouse pointer.
- *y*—a **Single** that contains the vertical location of the mouse pointer.

Private Sub *ListBoxBoxControl*_MouseUp([*index* As Integer ,] *button* As Integer, *shift* As Single, *x* As Single, *y* As Single)

Usage This event occurs when a mouse button is released while the cursor is over the control.

Arguments
- *index*—an **Integer** that uniquely identifies a control in a control array. This argument is not present if the control is not part of a control array.
- *button*—an **Integer** value (see Table L-47) that contains information about the mouse buttons that were released. Only one of these values will be present.

button Name	Value	Description
vbLeftButton	1	The left button was released.
vbRightButton	2	The right button was released.
vbMiddleButton	4	The middle button was released.

Table L-47: button *values*.

- *shift*—an **Integer** value (see Table L-48) that contains information about the Shift and Alt keys that were pushed when the mouse button was released. These values can be added together if more than one key was down. For instance, a value of 5 would mean that the Shift and Alt keys were both down when the mouse button was released. A value of 0 means that none of these keys were pressed.

shift Name	Value	Description
vbShiftMask	1	The Shift key was pressed.
vbCtrlMask	2	The Ctrl key was pressed.
vbAltMask	4	The Alt key was pressed.

Table L-48: shift *values*.

- *x*—a **Single** that contains the horizontal location of the mouse pointer.
- *y*—a **Single** that contains the vertical location of the mouse pointer.

Private Sub *ListBoxControl*_OLECompleteDrag([*index* As Integer ,] *effect* As Long)

Usage — This event tells the source control the results of an OLE drag-and-drop operation. This is the final event to occur in the series of actions that make up an OLE drag-and-drop operation.

Arguments
- *index*—an **Integer** that uniquely identifies a control in a control array. This argument is not present if the control is not part of a control array.
- *effect*—a **Long** (see Table L-49) that returns the status of the OLE drag-and-drop operation.

effect Name	Value	Description
vbDropEffectNone	0	The operation was canceled or the target control can't accept the drop operation.
vbDropEffectCopy	1	The operation copied data from the source control to the target control. The original data is unchanged.
vbDropEffectMove	2	The operation results in a link from the original data to the target control.

Table L-49: effect *values.*

Private Sub *ListBoxControl*_OLEDragDrop([*index* As Integer ,] *data* As DataObject, *effect* As Long, *button* As Integer, *shift* As Single, *x* As Single, *y* As Single)

Usage — This event tells the source control the results of an OLE drag-and-drop operation. This is the final event to occur in the series of actions that make up an OLE drag-and-drop operation.

Arguments
- *index*—an **Integer** that uniquely identifies a control in a control array. This argument is not present if the control is not part of a control array.
- *data*—a **DataObject** that contains the formats that the source control will provide. If the data is not contained in the **DataObject**, then it can be retrieved with the **GetData** method.
- *effect*—a **Long** (see Table L-50) that returns the status of the OLE drag-and-drop operation.

effect Name	Value	Description
vbDropEffectNone	0	The operation was canceled or the target control can't accept the drop operation.
vbDropEffectCopy	1	The operation copied data from the source control to the target control. The original data is unchanged.
vbDropEffectMove	2	The operation results in a link from the original data to the target control.

Table L-50: effect *values.*

- *button*—an **Integer** value (see Table L-51) that contains information about the mouse buttons that were pressed. These values can be added together if more than one button was pushed. For instance, a value of 3 means that both the left and right buttons were pressed. A value of 0 means that no buttons were pressed.

button Name	Value	Description
vbLeftButton	1	The left button was pressed.
vbRightButton	2	The right button was pressed.
vbMiddleButton	4	The middle button was pressed.

Table L-51: button *values*.

- *shift*—an **Integer** value (see Table L-52) that contains information about the Shift and Alt keys that were pushed when the mouse button was released. These values can be added together if more than one key was down. For instance, a value of 5 would mean that the Shift and Alt keys were both down when the mouse button was released. A value of 0 means that none of these keys were pressed.

shift Name	Value	Description
vbShiftMask	1	The Shift key was pressed.
vbCtrlMask	2	The Ctrl key was pressed.
vbAltMask	4	The Alt key was pressed.

Table L-52: shift *values*.

- *x*—a **Single** that contains the horizontal location of the mouse pointer.
- *y*—a **Single** that contains the vertical location of the mouse pointer.

Private Sub *ListBoxControl*_OLEDragOver([*index* As Integer ,] *data* As DataObject, *effect* As Long, *button* As Integer, *shift* As Single, *x* As Single, *y* As Single, *state* As Integer)

Usage — This event happens when an OLE drag-and-drop operation is in progress.

Arguments
- *index*—an **Integer** that uniquely identifies a control in a control array. This argument is not present if the control is not part of a control array.
- *data*—a **DataObject** that contains the formats that the source control will provide. If the data is not contained in the **DataObject**, then it can be retrieved with the **GetData** method.
- *effect*—a **Long** (see Table L-53) that returns the status of the OLE drag-and-drop operation.

effect Name	Value	Description
vbDropEffectNone	0	The operation was canceled or the target control can't accept the drop operation.
vbDropEffectCopy	1	The operation copied data from the source control to the target control. The original data is unchanged.
vbDropEffectMove	2	The operation results in a link from the original data to the target control.

Table L-53: effect *values.*

- *button*—an **Integer** value (see Table L-54) that contains information about the mouse buttons that were pressed. These values can be added together if more than one button was pushed. For instance, a value of 3 means that both the left and right buttons were pressed. A value of 0 means that no buttons were pressed.

button Name	Value	Description
vbLeftButton	1	The left button was pressed.
vbRightButton	2	The right button was pressed.
vbMiddleButton	4	The middle button was pressed.

Table L-54: button *values.*

- *shift*—an **Integer** value (see Table L-55) that contains information about the Shift and Alt keys that were pushed when the mouse button was released. These values can be added together if more than one key was down. For instance, a value of 5 would mean that the Shift and Alt keys were both down when the mouse button was released. A value of 0 means that none of these keys were pressed.

shift Name	Value	Description
vbShiftMask	1	The Shift key was pressed.
vbCtrlMask	2	The Ctrl key was pressed.
vbAltMask	4	The Alt key was pressed.

Table L-55: shift *values.*

- *x*—a **Single** that contains the horizontal location of the mouse pointer.
- *y*—a **Single** that contains the vertical location of the mouse pointer.
- *state*—an **Integer** value (see Table L-56) that indicates the state of the object being dragged.

state Name	Value	Description
vbEnter	0	The dragged object is entering range of the control.
vbLeave	1	The dragged object is leaving range of the control.
vbOver	2	The dragged object has moved from one position over the control to another.

Table L-56: state *values.*

Private Sub ListBoxControl_OLEGiveFeedback ([index As Integer ,] effect As Long)

Usage This event tells the source control what is happening while the OLE drag-and-drop operation is in progress. This event occurs after the **OLEDragOver** event.

Tip

You may want to use this event to change the cursor to reflect what can happen in the remote object.

Arguments
- *index*—an **Integer** that uniquely identifies a control in a control array. This argument is not present if the control is not part of a control array.
- *effect*—a **Long** (see Table L-57) that returns the status of the OLE drag-and-drop operation.

effect Name	Value	Description
vbDropEffectNone	0	The operation was canceled or the target control can't accept the drop operation.
vbDropEffectCopy	1	The operation copied data from the source control to the target control. The original data is unchanged.
vbDropEffectMove	2	The operation results in a link from the original data to the target control.
vbDropEffectScroll	&H80000000	The target control is about to scroll or is scrolling. This value may be added to the other *effect* values.

Table L-57: effect values.

Private Sub ListBoxControl_OLESetData([index As Integer ,] data As DataObject, DataFormat As Integer)

Usage This event happens in response to the target object performing a **GetData** method on *data*. This routine will respond by using the **SetData** method with the desired data using the **DataObject** *data*.

Arguments
- *index*—an **Integer** that uniquely identifies a control in a control array. This argument is not present if the control is not part of a control array.
- *data*—a **DataObject** that will contain the data to be returned to the target object.
- *format*—an **Integer** value (see Table L-58) that contains the format of the data.

format Name	Value	Description
vbCFText	1	Text (.TXT files)
vbCFBitmap	2	Bitmap (.BMP files)
vbCFMetafile	3	Metafile (.WMF files)
vbCFEDIB	8	Device independent bitmap (DIB)

ListBox

format Name	Value	Description
vbCFPallette	9	Color palette
vbCFEMetafile	14	Enhanced metafile (.EMF files)
vbCFFiles	15	List of files
vbCFRTF	-16639	Rich Text Format (.RTF files)

Table L-58: format *values.*

Private Sub *ListBoxControl*_OLEStartDrag ([*index* As Integer ,] *data* As DataObject, *AllowedEffects* As Long)

Usage This event starts an OLE drag-and-drop operation.

Arguments
- *index*—an **Integer** that uniquely identifies a control in a control array. This argument is not present if the control is not part of a control array.
- *data*—a **DataObject** that will contain the formats that the source object is willing to provide to the target object. It may optionally contain the data to transfer.
- *AllowedEffects*—a **Long** (see Table L-59) that contains the effects that the target object can request from the source object. The *AllowedEffects* can be added together if the source object supports more than one effect. Note that the target object can always use the *vbDropEffectNone* effect.

AllowedEffects Name	Value	Description
vbDropEffectNone	0	The target can't copy the data.
vbDropEffectCopy	1	The target can copy the data and the source will keep the data unchanged.
vbDropEffectMove	2	The target can copy the data and the source will delete the data.

Table L-59: AllowedEffects *values.*

Examples
```
Private Sub Form_Load()
List1.AddItem "One"
List1.AddItem "Two"
List1.AddItem "Three"
List1.AddItem "Four"
List1.AddItem "Five"
List1.AddItem "Six"
List1.AddItem "Seven"
List1.AddItem "Eight"
List1.AddItem "Nine"
List1.AddItem "Ten"
List1.AddItem "Eleven"
List1.AddItem "Twelve"
End Sub
```

```
Private Sub List1_Click()
MsgBox List1.List(List1.ListIndex)
End Sub
```

This program initializes a list box with a dozen values and then displays a message box whenever the user clicks on one of the items.

See Also   **DBComboBox** (control), **DBListBox** (control), **ComboBox** (control), **TextBox** (control)

ListImage

OBJECT

PE, EE

Usage   The **ListImage** object contains an image that is included in the **ImageList** control.

Properties
- *ListImageObject*.**Index**—an **Integer** value that uniquely identifies the image.
- *ListImageObject*.**Keyword**—a **String** value that uniquely identifies the image.
- *ListImageObject*.**Picture**—a **Picture** object (a bitmap, icon, metafile, GIF, or JPEG) that will be displayed on the control. You can also use the **LoadPicture** function at run time to load a bitmap, icon, or metafile.
- *ListImageObject*.**Tag**—a **String** that can hold programmer specific information. This property is not used by Visual Basic.

Methods   *ListImageObject*.**Draw** *hDC* [, *x*, *y* [, *style*]]

Usage   This method creates a light source at a specific location with a certain intensity.

Arguments
- *hDC*—a reference to a device context that will receive the image.
- *x*—a **Single** expression that contains the X-coordinate value of where the image will be drawn. If omitted, the image will be drawn at the device context's origin.
- *y*—a **Single** expression that contains the Y-coordinate value of where the image will be drawn. If omitted, the image will be drawn at the device context's origin.
- *style*—an **Integer** expression (see Table L-60) describing how the image is drawn.

style Name	Value	Description
imlNormal	0	The image is drawn without change (default).
imlTransparent	1	The image is drawn with the color specified in MaskColor treated as transparent.
imlSelected	2	The image is drawn by dithering the image with the system highlight color.
imlFocus	3	The image is drawn by dithering and striping the image with the system highlight color to show that the object represented by the image has the focus.

Table L-60: style *values.*

icon = ListImageObject.ExtractIcon

Usage This method creates an icon from the image.

Arguments • *icon*—a **Picture** object that will contain the extracted icon.

See Also **ListImages** (collection), **MSChart** (control), **TreeView** (control)

ListImages
COLLECTION

PE, EE

Usage The **ListImages** collection contains a set of **ListImage** objects for the **MSChart** control.

Properties • *ListImages*.**Count**—a **Long** value that contains the number of items in the collection.
• *ListImages*.**Item**(*index*)—an array of **ListImage** objects.

Methods ### ListImagesCollection.Add [index], [key], picture

Usage This method adds a picture to the collection.

Arguments • *index*—an **Integer** expression that contains the position where the image should be added. This value can range from 1 to **Count** +1. If omitted, it will default to **Count** +1.
• *key*—a **String** expression that contains a unique name for the image.
• *picture*—a **Picture** object that contains the image to add to the collection.

ListImagesCollection.Clear

Usage This method removes all of the objects in the collection.

ListImagesCollection.Remove index

Usage This method deletes an item specified by *index* from the collection.

Arguments • *index*—an **Integer** value that contains the relative position of image in the collection or a **String** value containing the **Keyword** value.

See Also **ListImage** (object), **MSChart** (control), **TreeView** (control)

ListItem

OBJECT

PE, EE

Usage The **ListItem** object contains information about an item that displays inside the **ListView** control.

Properties
- *ListItemObject*.**Ghosted**—a **Boolean** when **True** means that the **ListItem** object is unavailable to the user. **False** means that the item is available. When an item is **Ghosted**, the **ListView** control will show the item as dimmed.
- *ListItemObject*.**Height**—a **Single** that contains the height of the object.
- *ListItemObject*.**Icon**—an **Integer** value that specifies an index value of an icon object in a **ImageList** control.
- *ListItemObject*.**Index**—an **Integer** value that uniquely identifies the item.
- *ListItemObject*.**Key**—a **String** value that uniquely identifies the item.
- *ListItemObject*.**Left**—a **Single** that contains the distance measured in twips between the left edge of the object and the left edge of the object's container.
- *ListItemObject*.**Selected**—a **Boolean** when **True** means that the **ListItem** object is selected. **False** means that the item is not selected.
- *ListItemObject*.**SmallIcon**—an **Integer** value that specifies an index value of an icon object in an **ImageList** control.
- *ListItemObject*.**SubItems**(*index*)—an array of **Strings** that contain additional information about the item. Additional strings in this property can be added using the **Add** method of the **ColumnHeaders** collection.
- *ListItemObject*.**Tag**—a **String** that can hold programmer specific information. This property is not used by Visual Basic.
- *ListItemObject*.**Text**—a **String** value that is shown when the item is displayed.
- *ListItemObject*.**Top**—a **Single** that contains the distance measured in twips between the top edge of the object and the top edge of the object's container.
- *ListItemObject*.**Width**—a **Single** that contains the width of the control.

Methods *image* = **ListItemObject.CreateDragImage**

Usage This method creates an icon based on the item's image and text.

Tip

*Use this method to create an image for the **DragIcon** property when performing a drag-and-drop operation.*

Arguments *image*—a **Picture** object that can be used in drag-and-drop operations.

*BValue = ListItemObject.*EnsureVisible

Usage   This method ensures that the item is visible by scrolling a **ListView** control or expanding the nodes in a **TreeView** control.

Arguments   ▪ *BValue*—a **Boolean** value when **True** means that the item was not visible before the method was used. **False** means that the item was visible before the method was used.

See Also   **ListItems** (collection), **MSChart** (control), **TreeView** (control)

ListItems

COLLECTION

PE, EE

Usage   The **ListItems** collection contains a set of **ListItem** objects for the **ListView** control.

Properties   ▪ *ListItems*.**Count**—a **Long** value that contains the number of items in the collection.
▪ *ListItems*.**Item**(*index*)—an array of **ListItem** objects.

Methods   *ListItemsCollection.*Add [*index* [, *key* [, *text* [, *icon* [, *smallicon*]]]]

Usage   This method adds an item to the collection.

Arguments   ▪ *index*—an **Integer** expression containing the position where the image should be added. This value can range from 1 to **Count** +1. If omitted, it will default to **Count** +1.
▪ *key*—a **String** expression containing a unique name for the image.
▪ *text*—a **String** containing a value that will be assigned to the **Text** property. If omitted, it will default to an empty string.
▪ *icon*—an **Integer** containing a reference to an image in an **ImageList** control that will be displayed when the control is set to icon view.
▪ *smallicon*—an **Integer** containing a reference to an image in an **ImageList** control that will be displayed when the control is set to small icon view.

*ListItemsCollection.*Clear

Usage   This method removes all of the objects in the collection.

*ListItemsCollection.*Remove *index*

Usage   This method deletes an item specified by *index* from the collection.

Arguments   ▪ *index*—an **Integer** value that contains the relative position of image in the collection or a **String** value containing the **Keyword** value.

See Also   **ListItem** (object), **MSChart** (control), **TreeView** (control)

ListView

CONTROL
PE, EE

Usage The **ListView** control is an ActiveX control (part of the Microsoft Windows Common Controls 5.0) that provides four different ways to view a collection of objects: large icons, small icons, list, and report.

Properties
- *ListViewControl*.**Appearance**—an **Integer** value (see Table L-61) that describes how the combo box will appear on the form.

Appearance Value	Description
0	The ListView control displays without the 3D effects.
1	The **ListView** control displays with 3D effects (default value).

Table L-61: Appearance *values.*

- *ListViewControl*.**Arrange**—an **Integer** value (see Table L-62) that describes how the combo box will appear on the form.

Arrange Name	Value	Description
lvwNoArrange	0	Items are not automatically arranged on the control (default).
lvwAutoLeft	1	Items are automatically aligned on the left side of the control.
lvwAutoTop	2	Items are automatically aligned on the top of the control.

Table L-62: Arrange *values.*

- *ListViewControl*.**BackColor**—a **Long** that contains the suggested value for the background color of the control. The **BackColor** and **ForeColor** must both be solid to display text. If you choose a color that is dithered, it will be changed to the nearest solid color.
- *LabelObject*.**BorderStyle**—an **Integer** value (see Table L-63) specifying how the border will be drawn.

BorderStyle Name	Value	Description
vbBSNone	0	No border displays.
vbFixedSingle	1	Single line around the label.

Table L-63: **BorderStyle** *values.*

- *ListViewControl*.**ColumnHeaders**—a reference to a **ColumnHeaders** object, which contains information about the headings displayed in the report view.
- *ListViewControl*.**Container**—an object that sets or returns the container of the control at run time. This property cannot be set at design time.
- *ListViewControl*.**DragIcon**—an object that contains the **Picture** value of an icon. At design time, you can specify an icon file that has a file type of .ICO.

> **Tip**
>
> *This value can be created by copying the value from another control's **DragIcon** value, a form's icon, or by using the **LoadPicture** function.*

- *ListViewControl*.**DragMode**—an **Integer** value (see Table L-64) specifying how the control will respond to a drag request.

> **Tip**
>
> *Setting **DragMode** to vbAutomatic will automatically begin a drag operation when the user clicks on the control. However, the control will not respond to the usual mouse events (**Click**, **DblClick**, **MouseDown**, **MouseMove**, **MouseUp**).*

DragMode Name	Value	Description
vbManual	0	The Drag method must be used to begin a drag-and-drop operation (default value).
vbAutomatic	1	The source control will automatically begin a drag-and-drop operation when the user clicks on the control.

Table L-64: **DragMode** *values.*

- *ListViewControl*.**DropHighlight**—a reference to a **ListItem** object that will be highlighted in the system highlight color when the cursor passes over it.

> **Tip**
>
> *Use this property in conjunction with the **HitTest** method to determine the object that is under the cursor.*

- *ListViewControl*.**Enabled**—a **Boolean** value when **True** means that the control will respond to events. When **False**, the control will not respond to events.
- *ListViewControl*.**Font**—an object that contains information about the character font used by this object.
- *ListViewControl*.**ForeColor**—a **Long** that contains the suggested value for the foreground color of the contained control. This property is read only at run time.
- *ListViewControl*.**Height**—a **Single** that contains the height of the control.
- *ListViewControl*.**HelpContextID**—a **Long** that contains a help file context ID number which references an entry in the help file. When the user presses the F1 key while this control is active, the corresponding entry in the help file will automatically display. A value of zero means that no context number was specified.

> **Tip**
>
> *A help file must be compiled using the Windows Help Compiler available in the Professional and Enterprise editions of Visual Basic.*

- *ListViewControl*.**HideColumnHeaders**—a **Boolean** value when **True** means that the column headers will not be shown. **False** means that the column headers are visible (default).
- *ListViewControl*.**HideSelection**—a **Boolean** value when **True** means that the selected item will be hidden when the control loses focus. **False** means that the selected item will continue to be highlighted even if the control loses focus.
- *ListViewControl*.**hWnd**—a **Long** that contains a Windows handle to the control.

> **Tip**
>
> The **hWnd** *property is most useful when making calls to Windows API functions. Since this value can change during execution, do not save the value into a variable for later use.*

- *ListViewControl*.**Icons**—a reference to an **ImageList** object that contains the pictures that will be used for the large icon display.
- *ListViewControl*.**Index**—an **Integer** that uniquely identifies a control in a control array.
- *ListViewControl*.**LabelEdit**—an **Integer** value (see Table L-65) that determines if a user can change the contents of the label.

LabelEdit Name	Value	Description
lvwAutomatic	0	The BeforeLabelEdit event is always called when the user clicks on the label (default).
lvwManual	1	The user can only change the label if the **StartLabelEdit** method is called.

Table L-65: **LabelEdit** *values.*

- *ListViewControl*.**LabelWrap**—a **Boolean** value when **True** means that the text in the label will be wrapped to fit the display. When **False** the drop-down list will show partial items.
- *ListViewControl*.**Left**—a **Single** that contains the distance measured in twips between the left edge of the control and the left edge of the control's container.
- *ListViewControl*.**ListItems**—an object reference to a **ListItems** collection, which contains the items that will be displayed inside the control.
- *ListViewControl*.**MouseIcon**—a **Picture** object (a bitmap, icon, or metafile) that will be used as a cursor when the **MousePointer** property is set to 99. Note that Visual Basic does not support color cursors from a .CUR file. A color icon from an .ICO file should be used instead.
- *ListViewControl*.**MousePointer**—an **Integer** value (see Table L-66) that contains the value of the cursor that should be displayed when the cursor is moved over this control. Use *vbCustom* to display the custom icon stored in the **MouseIcon** property.

Cursor Name	Value	Description
vbDefault	0	Shape determined by the object (default value)
vbArrow	1	Arrow
vbCrosshair	2	Crosshair
vbIbeam	3	I beam
vbIconPointer	4	Square inside a square
vbSizePointer	5	Four sided arrow (north, south, east, west)

Cursor Name	Value	Description
vbSizeNESW	6	Two sided arrow (northeast, southwest)
vbSizeNS	7	Two sided arrow (north, south)
vbSizeNWSE	8	Two sided arrow (northwest, southeast)
vbSizeWE	9	Two sided arrow (west, east)
vbUpArrow	10	Single sided arrow pointing north
vbHourglass	11	Hourglass
vbNoDrop	12	No Drop
vbArrowHourglass	13	An arrow and an hourglass
vbArrowQuestion	14	An arrow and a question mark
vbSizeAll	15	Size all
vbCustom	99	Custom icon from the MouseIcon property of this control

Table L-66: Cursor *values*.

- *ListViewControl*.**MultiSelect**—a **Boolean** value when **True** means that the user may select multiple items. **False** means that only one item can be selected at a time (default).
- *ListViewControl*.**Name**—a **String** that contains the name of the control that will be used to reference the control in a Visual Basic program. This property is read only at run time.
- *ListViewControl*.**Object**—an object that contains a reference to the *ListViewControl* object.
- *ListViewControl*.**OLEDragMode**—an **Integer** value (see Table L-67) that describes how the control will respond to OLE drag operations.

Note

*When the **DragMode** is **True**, the standard Visual Basic drag-and-drop functions will override the OLE drag-and-drop functions.*

OLEDragMode Name	Value	Description
vbOLEDragManual	0	All drag requests will be handled by the programmer (default value).
vbOLEDragAutomatic	1	The control responds to all OLE drag requests automatically.

Table L-67: OLEDragMode values.

- *ListViewControl*.**OLEDropMode**—an **Integer** value (see Table L-68) that describes how the control will respond to OLE drop operations.

OLEDropMode Name	Value	Description
vbOLEDropNone	0	The control does not accept OLE drops. The cursor is changed to the No Drop cursor (default value).
vbOLEDropManual	1	The control responds to OLE drops under the program's control (manual).
vbOLEDropAutomatic	2	The control automatically accepts OLE drops if it recognizes the format of the data object.

Table L-68: OLEDropMode values.

- *ListViewControl*.**Parent**—an object that contains a reference to the **Form**, **Frame**, or other container that contains this control.
- *ListViewControl*.**SelectedItem**—a reference to the currently selected **ListItem** object.
- *ListViewControl*.**SmallIcons**—a reference to an **ImageList** object that contains the pictures that will be used for the small icon display.
- *ListViewControl*.**Sorted**—a **Boolean** value when **True** means that the items will be sorted by the column specified in **SortKey** and in the order specified by **SortOrder**. When **False** means that items will not be sorted (default).
- *ListViewControl*.**SortKey**—an **Integer** value the column uses in sorting the items. If **SortKey** is zero, the **Text** field of the **ListItem** object will be sorted. If **SortKey** is greater than zero, indicates the **SubItem** value that will be used in the sort.
- *ListViewControl*.**SortOrder**—an **Integer** value (see Table L-69) containing the sort direction.

SortOrder Name	Value	Description
lvwAscending	0	The items are sorted in ascending order (default value).
lvwDescending	1	The items are sorted in descending order.

Table L-69: **SortOrder** *values.*

- *ListViewControl*.**TabIndex**—an Integer that determines the order that a user will tab through the objects on a form.
- *ListViewControl*.**TabStop**—a **Boolean** value when **True** means that the user can tab to this object. When **False** means that this control will be skipped to the next control in the **TabIndex** order.
- *ListViewControl*.**Tag**—a **String** that can hold programmer specific information. This property is not used by Visual Basic.
- *ListViewControl*.**ToolTipText**—a **String** that holds a text value that can be displayed as a **ToolTip** box that displays whenever the cursor is held over the control for about one second.
- *ListViewControl*.**Top**—a **Single** that contains the distance measured in twips between the top edge of the control and the top edge of the control's container.
- *ListViewControl*.**View**—an **Integer** value (see Table L-70) containing the appearance of the control.

View Name	Value	Description
lvwIcon	0	Items display as normal icons with a text value below them (default value).
lvwSmallIcon	1	Items display as small icons with a text value beside them in a horizontal list.
lvwList	2	Items display as small icons with a text value beside them in a vertical list.
lvwReport	3	Items display in a series of rows with the information in the **SubItems** displayed in columns beside the icon and text information.

Table L-70: **View** *values.*

- *ListViewControl*.**WhatsThisHelpID**—a **Long** that contains a help file context ID number references an entry in the help file. This provides a What's This PopUp help display in response to the What's This button in the upper right corner of the window.
- *ListViewControl*.**Width**—a **Single** that contains the width of the control.

Methods

ListViewControl.**Drag** [*DragAction*]

Usage   This method begins, ends, or cancels a drag operation.

Arguments
- *DragAction*—an **Integer** that contains a value selected from Table L-71 below.

DragAction Name	Value	Description
vbCancel	0	Cancels any drag operation in progress.
vbBeginDrag	1	Begins a drag operation (default).
vbEndDrag	2	Ends a drag operation and drops *object*.

Table L-71: DragAction *values.*

result = *ListViewControl*.**FindItem** (*string* [, *where* [, *index* [, *match*]]])

Usage   This method searches the **ListItems** collection for the specified value and returns an object reference to the matching **ListItem**.

Arguments
- *result*—an object reference to the **ListItem** object found.
- *string*—a **String** value containing the search value.
- *where*—an **Integer** value (see Table L-72) specifying which properties to search in the **ListItem** object.

where Name	Value	Description
lvwText	0	The Text property is searched (default).
lvwSubitem	1	The SubItem property is searched.
lvwList	2	The Tag property is searched.

Table L-72: where *values.*

- *index*—an **Index** specifying the starting location in the **ListItems** collection. If omitted, this value will default to 1.
- *match*—an **Integer** value (see Table L-73) that specifies how *string* will be matched with the **Text** property, when *where* is zero. This value does not apply to the other values of *where*.

match Name	Value	Description
lvwWholeWord	0	*string* must match the whole value in Text (default).
lvwPartial	1	*string* can match any leading portion of the value in **Text**.

Table L-73: match *values.*

result = ListViewControl.GetFirstVisible

Usage This method returns an object reference to the first **ListItem** object visible in the control.

Arguments
- *result*—an object reference to the **ListItem** object.

result = ListViewControl.HitTest (x As Single, y As Single)

Usage This method returns an object reference to the **ListItem** object at coordinates *x* and *y*.

Arguments
- *result*—an object reference to the **ListItem** object.
- *x*—a **Single** containing the X-coordinate on the screen.
- *y*—a **Single** containing Y-coordinate on the screen.

ListViewControl.Move Left [, Top [, Width [, Height]]]

Usage This method changes the position and the size of the **ListView** control. The **ScaleMode** of the **Form** or other container object that holds the **ListView** control will determine the units used to specify the coordinates.

Arguments
- *Left*—a **Single** that specifies the new position of the left edge of the control.
- *Top*—a **Single** that specifies the new position of the top edge of the control.
- *Width*—a **Single** that specifies the new width of the control.
- *Height*—a **Single** that specifies the new height of the control.

ListViewControl.OLEDrag

Usage This method begins an **OLEDrag** and drop operation. Invoking this method will trigger the **OLEStartDrag** event.

ListViewControl.Refresh

Usage This method redraws the contents of the control.

ListViewControl.SetFocus

Usage This method transfers the focus from the form or control that currently has the focus to this control. To receive the focus, this control must be enabled and visible.

ListViewControl.ShowWhatsThis

Usage This method displays the ShowWhatsThis help information for this control.

ListViewControl.StartLabelEdit

Usage This method is required to let a user edit a label when the **LabelEdit** property is set to *lvwManual*. This will also cause the **BeforeLabelEdit** event to occur.

ListViewControl.ZOrder [*position*]

Usage This method specifies the position of the **ListView** control relative to the other objects on the form.

Tip

*Note that there are three layers of objects on a form: the back layer is the drawing space which contains the results of the graphical methods, the middle layer contains graphical objects and **Labels**, and the top layer contains nongraphical controls such as the **ListView** control. The **ZOrder** method only affects how the objects are arranged within a single layer.*

Arguments • *position*—an **Integer** that specifies the relative position of this object. A value of 0 means that the control is positioned at the head of the list, a value of 1 means that the control will be placed at the end of the list.

Events Private Sub *ListViewControl*_AfterLabelEdit([*index* As Integer ,] *cancel* As Integer, *NewString* As String)

Usage This event occurs after the user edits a label.

Tip

*Use the **SelectedItem** property to determine which item is being edited.*

Arguments • *index*—an **Integer** that uniquely identifies a control in a control array. This argument is not present if the control is not part of a control array.
• *cancel*—an **Integer** value when zero means that the edit is accepted. Any nonzero value means that the edit is canceled.
• *NewString*—a **String** containing the new value entered by the user or Null if the user canceled the operation.

Private Sub *ListViewControl*_BeforeLabelEdit([*index* As Integer ,] *cancel* As Integer)

Usage This event occurs before the user edits a label.

Tip

*Use the **SelectedItem** property to determine which item is being edited.*

Arguments
- *index*—an **Integer** that uniquely identifies a control in a control array. This argument is not present if the control is not part of a control array.
- *cancel*—an **Integer** value when zero means that the edit process can continue. Any nonzero value means that the edit is canceled.

Private Sub *ListViewControl*_Click([*index* As Integer])

Usage This event occurs when the user clicks a mouse button to select an item or selects an item using the keyboard.

Arguments
- *index*—an **Integer** that uniquely identifies a control in a control array. This argument is not present if the control is not part of a control array.

Private Sub *ListViewControl*_ColumnClick([*index* As Integer ,] *ColumnHeader* As ColumnHeader)

Usage This event occurs when the user clicks a mouse button on a column header while the control is in Report view.

Arguments
- *index*—an **Integer** that uniquely identifies a control in a control array. This argument is not present if the control is not part of a control array.
- *ColumnHeader*—an object reference to the column header that the user clicked.

Private Sub *ListViewControl*_DblClick([*index* As Integer])

Usage This event occurs when the user double-clicks a mouse button to select an item or selects an item using the keyboard.

Arguments
- *index*—an **Integer** that uniquely identifies a control in a control array. This argument is not present if the control is not part of a control array.

Private Sub *ListViewControl*_DragDrop([*index* As Integer ,] *source* As Control, *x* As Single, *y* As Single)

Usage This event occurs when a drag-and-drop operation is completed by using the **Drag** method with a *DragAction* value of *vbEndDrag*.

Tip

*When using drag-and-drop operations, use the **DragOver** event to determine what the cursor should look like while the cursor moves over the control.*

Arguments
- *index*—an **Integer** that uniquely identifies a control in a control array. This argument is not present if the control is not part of a control array.
- *source*—a control object that is the control that is being dragged.

> **Tip**
>
> *You can access a property or method from the source control by using* **source**.*property or* **source**.*method. You can determine the type of object or control by using the* **TypeOf** *operator.*

- *x*—a **Single** that contains the horizontal location of the mouse pointer.
- *y*—a **Single** that contains the vertical location of the mouse pointer.

Private Sub *ListViewControl*_DragOver([*index* As Integer ,] *source* As Control, *x* As Single, *y* As Single, *state* As Integer)

Usage   This event occurs while a drag operation is in progress and the cursor is moved over the control.

> **Tip**
>
> *When using drag-and-drop operations, use the* **DragOver** *event to determine what the cursor should look like while the cursor moves over the control. When* **state** *is 0, you can change the cursor to a No Drop (vbNoDrop) cursor or highlight the field that the cursor is near. When* **state** *is 1, you can undo the changes you made when the* **state** *was 0.*

Arguments
- *index*—an **Integer** that uniquely identifies a control in a control array. This argument is not present if the control is not part of a control array.
- *source*—a control object that is the control that is being dragged.

> **Tip**
>
> *You can access a property or method from the source control by using* **source**.*property or* **source**.*method. You can determine the type of object or control by using the* **TypeOf** *operator.*

- *x*—a **Single** that contains the horizontal location of the mouse pointer.
- *y*—a **Single** that contains the vertical location of the mouse pointer.
- *state*—an **Integer** value (see Table L-74) that indicates the state of the object being dragged.

state Name	Value	Description
vbEnter	0	The dragged object is entering range of the control.
vbLeave	1	The dragged object is leaving range of the control.
vbOver	2	The dragged object has moved from one position over the control to another.

Table L-74: state *values.*

Private Sub *ListViewControl*_GotFocus ([*index* As Integer])

Usage   This event occurs when the control is given focus.

Tip

You can use this routine to display help or other information in a status bar.

Arguments
- *index*—an **Integer** that uniquely identifies a control in a control array. This argument is not present if the control is not part of a control array.

Private Sub *ListViewControl*_ItemClick([*index* As Integer ,] *Item* As ListItem)

Usage   This event occurs when the user clicks a mouse button on an item or selects an item using the keyboard.

Arguments
- *index*—an **Integer** that uniquely identifies a control in a control array. This argument is not present if the control is not part of a control array.
- *Item*—an object reference to the **ListItem** object that the user selected.

Private Sub *ListViewControl*_KeyDown ([*index* As Integer ,] *keycode* As Integer, *shift* As Single)

Usage   This event occurs when a key is pressed while the control has the focus.

Arguments
- *index*—an **Integer** that uniquely identifies a control in a control array. This argument is not present if the control is not part of a control array.
- *keycode*—an **Integer** that contains information about which key was pressed.
- *shift*—an **Integer** value (see Table L-75) that contains information about the Shift and Alt keys that were pushed when the mouse button was pressed. These values can be added together if more than one key was down. For instance, a value of 5 would mean that the Shift and Alt keys were both down when the mouse button was pressed.

shift Name	Value	Description
vbShiftMask	1	The Shift key was pressed.
vbCtrlMask	2	The Ctrl key was pressed.
vbAltMask	4	The Alt key was pressed.

Table L-75: shift *values.*

Private Sub *ListViewControl*_KeyPress([*index* As Integer ,] *keychar* As Integer)

Usage This event occurs whenever a key is pressed while the control has the focus.

Arguments
- *index*—an **Integer** that uniquely identifies a control in a control array. This argument is not present if the control is not part of a control array.
- *keychar*—an **Integer** that contains the ASCII character that was pressed.

Private Sub *ListViewControl*_KeyUp ([*index* As Integer ,] *keycode* As Integer, *shift* As Single)

Usage This event occurs when a key is released while the control has the focus.

Arguments
- *index*—an **Integer** that uniquely identifies a control in a control array. This argument is not present if the control is not part of a control array.
- *keycode*—an **Integer** that contains information about which key was released.
- *shift*—an **Integer** value (see Table L-76) that contains information about the Shift and Alt keys that were pushed when the mouse button was pressed. These values can be added together if more than one key was down. For instance, a value of 5 would mean that the Shift and Alt keys were both down when the mouse button was pressed.

shift Name	Value	Description
vbShiftMask	1	The Shift key was pressed.
vbCtrlMask	2	The Ctrl key was pressed.
vbAltMask	4	The Alt key was pressed.

Table L-76: shift *values*.

Private Sub *ListViewControl*_LostFocus ([*index* As Integer])

Usage This event occurs when the control loses focus.

Tip

This routine is useful to performing data verification.

Arguments
- *index*—an **Integer** that uniquely identifies a control in a control array. This argument is not present if the control is not part of a control array.

Private Sub *ListViewBoxControl*_MouseDown([*index* As Integer ,] *button* As Integer, *shift* As Single, *x* As Single, *y* As Single)

Usage   This event occurs when a mouse button was pressed while the cursor is over the control.

Arguments
- *index*—an **Integer** that uniquely identifies a control in a control array. This argument is not present if the control is not part of a control array.
- *button*—an **Integer** value (see Table L-77) that contains information about the mouse buttons that were pressed. Only one button will be indicated when this event occurs.

button Name	Value	Description
vbLeftButton	1	The left button was pressed.
vbRightButton	2	The right button was pressed.
vbMiddleButton	4	The middle button was pressed.

Table L-77: button *values.*

- *shift*—an **Integer** value (see Table L-78) that contains information about the Shift and Alt keys that were pushed when the mouse button was pressed. These values can be added together if more than one key was down. For instance, a value of 5 would mean that the Shift and Alt keys were both down when the mouse button was pressed.

shift Name	Value	Description
vbShiftMask	1	The Shift key was pressed.
vbCtrlMask	2	The Ctrl key was pressed.
vbAltMask	4	The Alt key was pressed.

Table L-78: shift *values.*

- *x*—a **Single** that contains the horizontal location of the mouse pointer.
- *y*—a **Single** that contains the vertical location of the mouse pointer.

Private Sub *ListViewControl*_MouseMove ([*index* As Integer ,] *button* As Integer, *shift* As Single, *x* As Single, *y* As Single)

Usage   This event occurs while the cursor is moved over the control.

Arguments
- *index*—an **Integer** that uniquely identifies a control in a control array. This argument is not present if the control is not part of a control array.
- *button*—an **Integer** value (see Table L-79) that contains information about the mouse buttons that were pressed. These values can be added together if more than one button was pushed. For instance, a value of 3 means that both the left and right buttons were pressed. A value of 0 means that no buttons were pressed.

button Name	Value	Description
vbLeftButton	1	The left button was pressed.
vbRightButton	2	The right button was pressed.
vbMiddleButton	4	The middle button was pressed.

Table L-79: button *values*.

- *shift*—an **Integer** value (see Table L-80) that contains information about the Shift and Alt keys that were pushed when the mouse button was pressed. For instance, a value of 5 would mean that the Shift and Alt keys were both down when the mouse button was pressed. A value of 0 means that none of these keys were pressed.

shift Name	Value	Description
vbShiftMask	1	The Shift key was pressed.
vbCtrlMask	2	The Ctrl key was pressed.
vbAltMask	4	The Alt key was pressed.

Table L-80: shift *values*.

- *x*—a **Single** that contains the horizontal location of the mouse pointer.
- *y*—a **Single** that contains the vertical location of the mouse pointer.

Private Sub *ListViewBoxControl*_MouseUp([*index* As Integer ,] *button* As Integer, *shift* As Single, *x* As Single, *y* As Single)

Usage   This event occurs when a mouse button is released while the cursor is over the control.

Arguments
- *index*—an **Integer** that uniquely identifies a control in a control array. This argument is not present if the control is not part of a control array.
- *button*—an **Integer** value (see Table L-81) that contains information about the mouse buttons that were released. Only one of these values will be present.

button Name	Value	Description
vbLeftButton	1	The left button was released.
vbRightButton	2	The right button was released.
vbMiddleButton	4	The middle button was released.

Table L-81: button *values*.

- *shift*—an **Integer** value (see Table L-82) that contains information about the Shift and Alt keys that were pushed when the mouse button was released. These values can be added together if more than one key was down. For instance, a value of 5 would mean that the Shift and Alt keys were both down when the mouse button was released. A value of 0 means that none of these keys were pressed.

shift Name	Value	Description
vbShiftMask	1	The Shift key was pressed.
vbCtrlMask	2	The Ctrl key was pressed.
vbAltMask	4	The Alt key was pressed.

Table L-82: shift *values*.

- *x*—a **Single** that contains the horizontal location of the mouse pointer.
- *y*—a **Single** that contains the vertical location of the mouse pointer.

Private Sub *ListViewControl*_OLECompleteDrag([*index* As Integer ,] *effect* As Long)

Usage   This event tells the source control the results of an OLE drag-and-drop operation. This is the final event to occur in the series of actions that make up an OLE drag-and-drop operation.

Arguments
- *index*—an **Integer** that uniquely identifies a control in a control array. This argument is not present if the control is not part of a control array.
- *effect*—a **Long** (see Table L-83) that returns the status of the OLE drag-and-drop operation.

effect Name	Value	Description
vbDropEffectNone	0	The operation was canceled or the target control can't accept the drop operation.
vbDropEffectCopy	1	The operation copied data from the source control to the target control. The original data is unchanged.
vbDropEffectMove	2	The operation results in a link from the original data to the target control.

Table L-83: effect *values*.

Private Sub *ListViewControl*_OLEDragDrop([*index* As Integer ,] *data* As DataObject, *effect* As Long, *button* As Integer, *shift* As Single, *x* As Single, *y* As Single)

Usage   This event tells the source control the results of an OLE drag-and-drop operation. This is the final event to occur in the series of actions that make up an OLE drag-and-drop operation.

Arguments
- *index*—an **Integer** that uniquely identifies a control in a control array. This argument is not present if the control is not part of a control array.
- *data*—a **DataObject** that contains the formats that the source control will provide. If the data is not contained in the **DataObject**, then it can be retrieved with the **GetData** method.

- *effect*—a **Long** (see Table L-84) that returns the status of the OLE drag-and-drop operation.

effect Name	Value	Description
vbDropEffectNone	0	The operation was canceled or the target control can't accept the drop operation.
vbDropEffectCopy	1	The operation copied data from the source control to the target control. The original data is unchanged.
vbDropEffectMove	2	The operation results in a link from the original data to the target control.

Table L-84: effect values.

- *button*—an **Integer** value (see Table L-85) that contains information about the mouse buttons that were pressed. These values can be added together if more than one button was pushed. For instance, a value of 3 means that both the left and right buttons were pressed. A value of 0 means that no buttons were pressed.

button Name	Value	Description
vbLeftButton	1	The left button was pressed.
vbRightButton	2	The right button was pressed.
vbMiddleButton	4	The middle button was pressed.

Table L-85: button values.

- *shift*—an **Integer** value (see Table L-86) that contains information about the Shift and Alt keys that were pushed when the mouse button was released. These values can be added together if more than one key was down. For instance, a value of 5 would mean that the Shift and Alt keys were both down when the mouse button was released. A value of 0 means that none of these keys were pressed.

shift Name	Value	Description
vbShiftMask	1	The Shift key was pressed.
vbCtrlMask	2	The Ctrl key was pressed.
vbAltMask	4	The Alt key was pressed.

Table L-86: shift values.

- *x*—a **Single** that contains the horizontal location of the mouse pointer.
- *y*—a **Single** that contains the vertical location of the mouse pointer.

Private Sub *ListViewControl*_OLEDragOver([*index* As Integer ,] *data* As DataObject, *effect* As Long, *button* As Integer, *shift* As Single, *x* As Single, *y* As Single, *state* As Integer)

Usage   This event happens when an OLE drag-and-drop operation is in progress.

Arguments
- *index*—an **Integer** that uniquely identifies a control in a control array. This argument is not present if the control is not part of a control array.
- *data*—a **DataObject** that contains the formats that the source control will provide. If the data is not contained in the **DataObject**, then it can be retrieved with the **GetData** method.
- *effect*—a **Long** (see Table L-87) that returns the status of the OLE drag-and-drop operation.

effect Name	Value	Description
vbDropEffectNone	0	The operation was canceled or the target control can't accept the drop operation.
vbDropEffectCopy	1	The operation copied data from the source control to the target control. The original data is unchanged.
vbDropEffectMove	2	The operation results in a link from the original data to the target control.

Table L-87: effect *values*.

- *button*—an **Integer** value (see Table L-88) that contains information about the mouse buttons that were pressed. These values can be added together if more than one button was pushed. For instance, a value of 3 means that both the left and right buttons were pressed. A value of 0 means that no buttons were pressed.

button Name	Value	Description
vbLeftButton	1	The left button was pressed.
vbRightButton	2	The right button was pressed.
vbMiddleButton	4	The middle button was pressed.

Table L-88: button *values*.

- *shift*—an **Integer** value (see Table L-89) that contains information about the Shift and Alt keys that were pushed when the mouse button was released. These values can be added together if more than one key was down. For instance, a value of 5 would mean that the Shift and Alt keys were both down when the mouse button was released. A value of 0 means that none of these keys were pressed.

shift Name	Value	Description
vbShiftMask	1	The Shift key was pressed.
vbCtrlMask	2	The Ctrl key was pressed.
vbAltMask	4	The Alt key was pressed.

Table L-89: shift *values*.

- *x*—a **Single** that contains the horizontal location of the mouse pointer.
- *y*—a **Single** that contains the vertical location of the mouse pointer.
- *state*—an **Integer** value (see Table L-90) that indicates the state of the object being dragged.

state Name	Value	Description
vbEnter	0	The dragged object is entering range of the control.
vbLeave	1	The dragged object is leaving range of the control.
vbOver	2	The dragged object has moved from one position over the control to another.

Table L-90: state *values.*

Private Sub *ListViewControl*_OLEGiveFeedback ([*index* As Integer ,] *effect* As Long)

Usage   This event tells the source control what is happening while the OLE drag-and-drop operation is in progress. This event occurs after the **OLEDragOver** event.

Tip

You may want to use this event to change the cursor to reflect what can happen in the remote object.

Arguments
- *index*—an **Integer** that uniquely identifies a control in a control array. This argument is not present if the control is not part of a control array.
- *effect*—a **Long** (see Table L-91) that returns the status of the OLE drag-and-drop operation.

effect Name	Value	Description
vbDropEffectNone	0	The operation was canceled or the target control can't accept the drop operation.
vbDropEffectCopy	1	The operation copied data from the source control to the target control. The original data is unchanged.
vbDropEffectMove	2	The operation results in a link from the original data to the target control.
vbDropEffectScroll	&H80000000	The target control is about to scroll or is scrolling. This value may be added to the other *effect* values.

Table L-91: effect *values.*

Private Sub *ListViewControl*_OLESetData([*index* As Integer ,] *data* As DataObject, *DataFormat* As Integer)

Usage   This event happens in response to the target object performing a **GetData** method on *data*. This routine will respond by using the **SetData** method with the desired data using the **DataObject** *data*.

Arguments
- *index*—an **Integer** that uniquely identifies a control in a control array. This argument is not present if the control is not part of a control array.
- *data*—a **DataObject** that will contain the data to be returned to the target object.
- *format*—an **Integer** value (see Table L-92) that contains the format of the data.

format Name	Value	Description
vbCFText	1	Text (.TXT files)
vbCFBitmap	2	Bitmap (.BMP files)
vbCFMetafile	3	Metafile (.WMF files)
vbCFEDIB	8	Device independent bitmap (DIB)
vbCFPallette	9	Color palette
vbCFEMetafile	14	Enhanced metafile (.EMF files)
vbCFFiles	15	List of files
vbCFRTF	-16639	Rich Text Format (.RTF files)

Table L-92: format *values.*

Private Sub *ListViewControl_OLEStartDrag* ([*index* As Integer ,] *data* As DataObject, *AllowedEffects* As Long)

Usage — This event starts an OLE drag-and-drop operation.

Arguments
- *index*—an **Integer** that uniquely identifies a control in a control array. This argument is not present if the control is not part of a control array.
- *data*—a **DataObject** that will contain the formats that the source object is willing to provide to the target object. It may optionally contain the data to transfer.
- *AllowedEffects*—a **Long** (see Table L-93) that contains the effects that the target object can request from the source object. The *AllowedEffects* can be added together if the source object supports more than one effect. Note that the target object can always use the *vbDropEffectNone* effect.

AllowedEffects Name	Value	Description
vbDropEffectNone	0	The target can't copy the data.
vbDropEffectCopy	1	The target can copy the data, and the source will keep the data unchanged.
vbDropEffectMove	2	The target can copy the data, and the source will delete the data.

Table L-93: AllowedEffects *values.*

Examples
```
Private Sub Form_Load()
Dim x As Object
Set x = ListView1.ColumnHeaders.Add(, , "Words")
Set x = ListView1.ColumnHeaders.Add(, , "Letters")
Set x = ListView1.ColumnHeaders.Add(, , "Roman Numerals")
Set x = ListView1.ListItems.Add(, , "One", 1, 1)
x.SubItems(1) = "A"
x.SubItems(2) = "I"
Set x = ListView1.ListItems.Add(, , "Two", 2, 2)
x.SubItems(1) = "B"
```

```
x.SubItems(2) = "II"
Set x = ListView1.ListItems.Add(, , "Three", 3, 3)
x.SubItems(1) = "C"
x.SubItems(2) = "III"
Set x = ListView1.ListItems.Add(, , "Four", 4, 4)
x.SubItems(1) = "D"
x.SubItems(2) = "IV"
Set x = ListView1.ListItems.Add(, , "Five", 5, 5)
x.SubItems(1) = "E"
x.SubItems(2) = "V"
Set x = ListView1.ListItems.Add(, , "Six", 6, 6)
x.SubItems(1) = "F"
x.SubItems(2) = "VI"
Set x = ListView1.ListItems.Add(, , "Seven", 7, 7)
x.SubItems(1) = "G"
x.SubItems(2) = "VII"
Set x = ListView1.ListItems.Add(, , "Eight", 8, 8)
x.SubItems(1) = "H"
x.SubItems(2) = "VIII"
End Sub

Private Sub ListView1_Click()
MsgBox "You selected " & ListView1.SelectedItem.Text
End Sub

Private Sub ListView1_ColumnClick(ByVal ColumnHeader As ComctlLib.ColumnHeader)
If ListView1.SortKey = ColumnHeader.Index - 1 Then
   ListView1.Sorted = False
   ListView1.SortOrder = (ListView1.SortOrder + 1) Mod 2
   ListView1.Sorted = True
Else
   ListView1.Sorted = False
   ListView1.SortKey = ColumnHeader.Index - 1
   ListView1.Sorted = True
End If
End Sub

Private Sub Option1_Click(Index As Integer)
ListView1.View = Index
End Sub
```

This program initializes a **ListView** control with some values that can be displayed on any of the four basic views. Clicking on an object will display its name in a message box. Changing views is accomplished by selecting one of the **OptionButtons** on the form. While in the Report view, clicking on a column header will sort the data in ascending order. Clicking on it a second time will resort the data in descending order.

See Also **DBComboBox** (control), **DBList** (control), **ComboBox** (control), **TextBox** (control), **TreeView** (control)

Load

STATEMENT

CCE, LE, PE, EE

Syntax   **Load** *form*

Usage   The **Load** statement brings a form into memory without displaying it.

Arguments   *form*—the name of a form.

Examples
```
Private Sub Command1_Click()
Load Form2
End Sub

Private Sub Command2_Click()
Form2.Show
End Sub

Private Sub Command3_Click()
Unload Form2
Unload Form1
End Sub
```

This program consists of two forms. Form1 is the main form with three command buttons. The first button loads Form2. The Second button uses the Form2.Show method to display Form2. The third button unloads both forms and ends the program.

When the first button is pushed, Form2 is loaded and a message box displays saying that the form was loaded. At this point Form2 is not visible to the user. Pressing the second button will display the form and a message box will be displayed saying the form is activated.

See Also   **Hide** (method), **Show** (method), **Unload** (method)

LoadPicture

FUNCTION

CCE, LE, PE, EE

Syntax   *picture* = **LoadPicture** (*filename*)

Usage   The **LoadPicture** function returns a **Picture** object that was loaded from the specified filename. This function supports .BMP, .EMF, .GIF, .ICO, .JPG, .RLE, and .WMF files.

Arguments   *picture*—a **Picture** object containing the loaded picture.

filename—a **String** containing the name of the picture file to be loaded.

Examples
```
Private Sub Picture1_Click()
On Error Resume Next
CommonDialog1.filename = App.Path & "\jpglogo1.gif"
CommonDialog1.Flags = cdlOFNHideReadOnly
CommonDialog1.Filter = "All Files (*.*)|*.*|GIF Files (*.gif)|*.GIF|JPEG Files
    (*.jpg)|*.jpg"
```

```
CommonDialog1.FilterIndex = 2
CommonDialog1.ShowOpen
If Err.Number = 0 Then
    Picture1.Picture = LoadPicture(CommonDialog1.filename)
End If
End Sub
```

This routine displays a File Open dialog box to select a file to be loaded into the **Picture** control. Then it uses the **LoadPicture** function to load the picture file.

See Also   **Picture** (control), **SavePicture** (statement)

LoadResData

FUNCTION

CCE, LE, PE, EE

Syntax   *data* = **LoadResData**(*index, format*)

Usage   The **LoadResData** function returns a **Byte Array** containing the information from a resource (.RES) file.

> **Tip**
>
> *Use resource files to keep messages and other information independent of the program. This makes it easier to convert your application to multiple languages.*

Arguments
- *data*—a **Byte** array containing the resource data.
- *index*—an **Integer** or **String** value that references the data in the resource file.
- *format*—an **Integer** value (see Table L-94) specifying the type of data to retrieve from the resource file.

format Value	Description
1	Cursor resource
2	Bitmap resource
3	Icon resource
4	Menu resource
5	Dialog box resource
6	String resource
7	Font directory
8	Font resource
9	Accelerator resource
10	User-defined resource
12	Group cursor
14	Group icon

Table L-94: format *values.*

See Also   **LoadResPicture** (function), **LoadResString** (function)

LoadResPicture

FUNCTION

CCE, LE, PE, EE

Syntax   *data* = **LoadResPicture** (*index, format*)

Usage   The **LoadResPicture** function returns a **Picture** containing a bitmap, cursor, or icon from a resource (.RES) file.

> **Tip**
>
> *Use resource files to keep information independent of the program. This makes it easier to convert your application to multiple languages.*

Arguments
- *data*—a **Picture** object from the resource file.
- *index*—an **Integer** or **String** value that references the data in the resource file.
- *format*—an **Integer** value (see Table L-95) specifying the type of data to be retrieved from the resource file.

format Name	Value	Description
vbResBitmap	0	Bitmap resource
vbResIcon	1	Icon resource
vbResCursor	2	Cursor resource

Table L-95: format *values.*

See Also   **LoadResData** (function), **LoadResString** (function)

LoadResString

FUNCTION

CCE, LE, PE, EE

Syntax   *data* = **LoadResString** (*index*)

Usage   The **LoadResString** function returns a **String** from a resource (.RES) file.

> **Tip**
>
> *Use resource files to keep information independent of the program. This makes it easier to convert your application to multiple languages.*

Arguments
- *data*—a **String** containing information from the resource file.
- *index*—an **Integer** or **String** value that references the data in the resource file.

See Also   **LoadResData** (function), **LoadResPicture** (function)

Loc

FUNCTION

CCE, LE, PE, EE

Syntax *pos* = **Loc** (*fnum*)

Usage The **Loc** function returns the current position in the file. For random files the current record number will be returned. For sequential files, the current byte position divided by 128 will be returned. For binary files, the current byte position will be returned.

Arguments
- *pos*—a **Long** containing position in the file.
- *fnum*—an **Integer** containing the opened file.

Examples
```
Private Sub Command1_Click()
Dim l As Long
Dim s As String
On Error Resume Next
Open Text2.Text For Binary As #1
If Err.Number = 0 Then
    Text1.Text = ""
    l = Loc(1)
    Line Input #1, s
    Do While Not EOF(1)
        Text1.Text = Text1.Text & Format(l) & ":" & s & vbCrLf
        l = Loc(1)
        Line Input #1, s
    Loop
    Close #1

End If
End Sub
```

This routine opens the file specified in Text2.Text and displays it one line at a time in the Text1 text box. Each line is preceded by the byte location in the file which was obtained by using the **Loc** function.

See Also **LOF** (function), **Open** (statement)

Location

OBJECT

PE, EE

Usage The **Location** object is part of the **MSChart** ActiveX control containing information about a text object such as a title, legend, or footnote on the chart.

Properties
- *LocationObject*.**LocationType**—an **Integer** value (see Table L-96) containing the standard location of the object on the chart.

LocationType Name	Description
vtChLocationTypeTop	Top
vtChLocationTypeTopLeft	Top left
vtChLocationTypeTopRight	Top right
vtChLocationTypeLeft	Left
vtChLocationTypeRight	Right
vtChLocationTypeBottom	Bottom
vtChLocationTypeBottomLeft	Bottom left
vtChLocationTypeBottomRight	Bottom right
vtChLocationTypeCustom	Custom

Table L-96: LocationType values.

- *LocationObject*.**Rect**—a reference to a **Rect** object containing the location of the text information.
- *LocationObject*.**Visible**—a **Boolean** when **True** means the object displays. **False** means that the object is not displayed.

See Also   **Footnote** (object), **Legend** (object), **MSChart** (control), **Title** (object)

Lock

STATEMENT

CCE, LE, PE, EE

Syntax   Lock *fnum*

Lock *fnum, recnum*

Lock *fnum*, [*brecnum*] **To** *erecnum*

Usage   The **Lock** statement has three forms. The first form locks the entire file. The second form locks only the specified record. The third form locks the records from *brecnum* to *erecnum*.

Warning

Calls to **Lock** must be matched with a similar call to **Unlock**. Failure to do so may cause problems.

Arguments
- *fnum*—an **Integer** containing a valid file number from an **Open** statement.
- *recnum*—a **Long** value containing the record number (or byte offset in a binary file) to be locked.
- *brecnum*—a **Long** value containing the beginning record number (or byte offset in a binary file) in a range to be locked. If omitted, then it will default to the first record in the file.
- *erecnum*—a **Long** value containing the ending record number (or byte offset in a binary file) to be locked.

Examples
```
Private Sub Command2_Click()
Dim s As String
Open App.Path & "\temp.dat" For Random As #1 Len = 10
Lock #1, 2
Get #1, 2, s
Text1.Text = s
End Sub

Private Sub Command3_Click()
Dim s As String
On Error Resume Next
Open App.Path & "\temp.dat" For Random As #2 Len = 10
Get #2, 2, s
If Err.Number <> o Then
    MsgBox Err.Description
Else
    Text2.Text = s
End If
Close #2
End Sub
```

The first routine (Command2_Click) opens a file, places a lock on the second record, reads it, and displays it in Text1.Text. The second routine (Command3_Click) opens a new file and tries to read the second record. Since the first routine locks the record, a Permission Denied error will be returned.

See Also **Get** (statement), **Open** (statement), **Put** (statement), **Unlock** (statement)

LOF

FUNCTION

CCE, LE, PE, EE

Syntax *lvalue* = **LOF** (*fnum*)

Usage The **LOF** function returns the size of the file in bytes for an open file. For an unopened file, use the **FileLen** function.

Arguments
- *lvalue*—a **Long** value containing the size of the file in bytes.
- *fnum*—an **Integer** containing a valid file number from an **Open** statement.

Examples
```
Private Sub Command1_Click()
Open Text1.Text For Input As #1
If Err.Number = 0 Then
    MsgBox Format(LOF(1))
End If
End Sub
```

This routine opens a file specified in Text1.Text and displays the number of bytes in the file.

See Also **FileLen** (function), **Open** (statement)

Log

FUNCTION

CCE, LE, PE, EE

Syntax   *RValue* = **Log** (*Number*)

Usage   The **Log** function will return the natural log of a number. This is the inverse function of the exponential function, **Exp**.

Arguments
- *RValue*—a **Double** that contains the value of the natural log of *Number*.
- *Number*—a **Double** expression that is passed to the **Log** function.

Examples
```
Private Sub Command1_Click()
If IsNumeric(Text1.Text) Then
    MsgBox Format(Log(Text1.Text))
End If
End Sub
```

This routine will compute the natural log of the value in the Text1 text box and display the results in a message box.

See Also   **Exp** (function)

Long

DATA TYPE

CCE, LE, PE, EE

Usage
- The **Long** data type holds integer values in the range from -2,147,483,648 to 2,147,483,647. A single **Long** variable only occupies 32 bits of storage or 4 bytes.

See Also   **Byte** (data type), **CByte** (function), **CInt** (function), **CLng** (function), **CStr** (function), **Dim** (statement), **Format** (function), **Integer** (data type), **IsNumeric** (function)

LSet

STATEMENT

CCE, LE, PE, EE

Syntax   **LSet** *svar* = *sval*

Lset *uvar1* = *uvar2*

Usage   The **LSet** statement has two forms. The first form will left align a string value (*sval*) within a string variable (*svar*). The size of the string variable is unchanged and if the length of the value is less then the size of the string, then the string variable will be padded with spaces. The second form copies one user-defined variable to another.

> **Warning**
>
> *While it is possible to copy from one user-defined variable type to another, it is not recommended. A binary copy is used without regard for the user variable defined data structure, which could result in unpredictable results.*

Arguments
- *svar*—a **String** variable.
- *sval*—a **String** value containing the data to be left aligned in *svar*.
- *uvar1*—a user-defined variable.
- *uvar2*—a user-defined variable.

Examples
```
Private Sub Command1_Click()
Dim s As String
s = String(32, "*")
LSet s = Text1.Text
Text2.Text = ">>>" & s & "<<<"
End Sub
```

This routine fills a string variable with 32 asterisks. Then the contents of Text1.Text are left aligned into s. Finally I show the results of the **LSet** statement in the Text2 text box.

See Also **RSet** (statement), **Type** (statement)

LTrim

FUNCTION

CCE, LE, PE, EE

Syntax `svar = LTrim ( sval )`

Usage The **LTrim** function will delete any leading spaces from a string value.

Arguments
- *svar*—a **String** variable.
- *sval*—a **String** value that will have the leading spaces trimmed.

Examples
```
Private Sub Command1_Click()
Text2.Text = LTrim(Text1.Text)
End Sub
```

This routine trims the leading spaces from the value in the Text1 text box and saves the results in the Text2 text box.

See Also **RTrim** (function), **Trim** (function)

MAPIMessages

CONTROL

CCE, LE, PE, EE

Usage The **MAPIMessages** control works with the **MAPISession** control to send and receive electronic mail. The **MAPIMessages** control accesses existing in the inbox, compose and send messages, access attachments, and manage the address book.

> **Warning**
>
> MAPI requires that the 32-bit MAPI DLLs be installed. If they are not present, you may have to install them using your Windows installation disks.

Properties ■ *MAPIMessagesControl*.**Action**—an **Integer** value specifying the action to take. This property exists primarily to maintain compatibility with older versions of Visual Basic. To take advantages of the new features, use the methods listed in Table M-1 below.

Action Name	Description
ATTACHMENT_DELETE	Deletes the current attachment.
MESSAGE_COMPOSE	Begins a message compose dialog.
MESSAGE_COPY	The message is copied from the currently indexed message to the compose buffer.
MESSAGE_DELETE	The current message is deleted.
MESSAGE_FETCH	The message is retrieved from the server.
MESSAGE_FORWARD	The current message is forwarded to a new user.
MESSAGE_REPLY	Create a new message by replying to the sender of the current message.
MESSAGE_REPLYALL	Create a new message by replying to the all recipients of the current message.
MESSAGE_RESOLVENAME	Resolve the names in the current message.
MESSAGE_SAVEMSG	The message is saved.
MESSAGE_SEND	The message is sent.
MESSAGE_SENDDLG	The message is sent.
MESSAGE_SHOWADBOOK	The Address Book is displayed to the user.
MESSAGE_SHOWDETAILS	The details about the message are shown.
RECIPIENT_DELETE	The current recipient is deleted.

Table M-1: **Action** values.

■ *MAPIMessagesControl*.**AddressCaption**—a **String** value containing the caption that will appear at the top of the Address Book dialog box.

■ *MAPIMessagesControl*.**AddressEditFieldCount**—an **Integer** value (see Table M-2) describing which controls should be displayed when the Address Book is shown.

AddressEditFieldCount Value	Description
0	No edit controls are shown.
1	To edit controls are shown (default).
2	To and CC edit controls are shown.
3	To, CC, and BCC edit controls are shown.
4	Only the edit controls that the message system supports are shown.

Table M-2: **AddressEditFieldCount** *values*.

- *MAPIMessagesControl*.**AddressLabel**—a **String** containing the value that will be displayed on the To edit control when **AddressEditFieldCount** equals 1.
- *MAPIMessagesControl*.**AddressModifiable**—a **Boolean** value when **True** means that the user can modify their personal Address Book. **False** means that the Address Book is read-only (default).
- *MAPIMessagesControl*.**AddressResolveUI**—a **Boolean** value when **True** means that a dialog box will be displayed when the **ResolveName** method is used. **False** means that the dialog box will not be displayed (default).
- *MAPIMessagesControl*.**AttachmentCount**—a **Long** value containing the number of attachments to the current message. This property is read only at run time.
- *MAPIMessagesControl*.**AttachmentIndex**—a **Long** value containing the index of the current attachment. It can range in value from 1 to **AttachmentCount** –1. Changing this value will change the values in the **AttachmentName, AttachmentPathName, AttachmentPosition,** and **AttachmentType** properties.
- *MAPIMessagesControl*.**AttachmentName**—a **String** value containing the name of the attachment.
- *MAPIMessagesControl*.**AttachmentPathName**—a **String** value containing the path and filename of the current attachment.
- *MAPIMessagesControl*.**AttachmentType**—an **Integer** value (see Table M-3) containing the type of attachment.

AttachmentType Name	Value	Description
mapData	0	A data file is attached.
mapEOLE	1	An embedded OLE object is attached.
mapSOLE	2	A static OLE object is attached.

Table M-3: **AttachmentType** *values*.

- *MAPIMessagesControl*.**FetchMsgType**—a **String** value containing the type of messages to retrieve. An empty string means that an Interpersonal Message (IPM) is assumed. Other message types may be available depending on your mail system.
- *MAPIMessagesControl*.**FetchSorted**—a **Boolean** value when **True** means that the messages will be added in the order in which they were received. **False** means that messages will be added based on the sort order defined in the user's inbox (default).
- *MAPIMessagesControl*.**FetchUnreadOnly**—a **Boolean** value when **True** means that only unread messages will be retrieved (default). **False** means that all messages will be retrieved from the user's inbox.

- *MAPIMessagesControl*.**Index**—an **Integer** that uniquely identifies a control in a control array.
- *MAPIMessagesControl*.**MsgConversationID**—a **String** containing a value that is identical for all messages in a conversation.
- *MAPIMessagesControl*.**MsgCount**—a **Long** value containing the number of messages in the message set. This property is read only at run time.
- *MAPIMessagesControl*.**MsgDateReceived**—a **String** containing the date the message was received in the format: "YYYY/MM/DD HH:MM". This property is read only at run time.
- *MAPIMessagesControl*.**MsgID**—a **String** containing a value unique identifier for the message. This property is read only at run time.
- *MAPIMessagesControl*.**MsgIndex**—a **Long** value containing the index of the message. For existing messages, it can range in value from 0 to **MsgCount** –1. For new messages, it will have the value –1. Changing this value will change the values in the associated message and attachment properties.
- *MAPIMessagesControl*.**MsgNoteText**—a **String** containing the text of the message. This property is read-only unless **MsgIndex** equals –1. Paragraphs are separated by a carriage return and a line feed.
- *MAPIMessagesControl*.**MsgOrigAddress**—a **String** containing the address of the person who sent the message.
- *MAPIMessagesControl*.**MsgOrigDisplayName**—a **String** containing the name of the person who sent the message.
- *MAPIMessagesControl*.**MsgRead**—a **Boolean** value when **True** means that the message has been read by the user. **False** means that the message has not been read.
- *MAPIMessagesControl*.**MsgReceiptRequested**—a **Boolean** value when **True** means the person that sent the message has requested a return receipt when the message is read by the user. **False** means no return receipt was requested.
- *MAPIMessagesControl*.**MsgSent**—a **Boolean** value when **True** means that the message has been sent to the mail server for distribution to the recipients of the message. **False** means that the message has not been sent. This property is read only at run time.
- *MAPIMessagesControl*.**MsgRead**—a **String** value containing the subject of the message.
- *MAPIMessagesControl*.**MsgType**—a **String** value containing the type of message. An empty string means that an Interpersonal Message (IPM) is assumed. Other message types may be available depending on your mail system.
- *MAPIMessagesControl*.**Name**—a **String** that contains the name of the control that will be used to reference the control in a Visual Basic program. This property is read only at run time.
- *MAPIMessagesControl*.**Object**—an object that contains a reference to the *MAPIMessagesControl* object.
- *MAPIMessagesControl*.**Parent**—an object that contains a reference to the **Form, Frame,** or other container that contains this control.
- *MAPIMessagesControl*.**RecipAddress**—a **String** containing the address of the current recipient pointed by **RecipIndex**.
- *MAPIMessagesControl*.**RecipCount**—a **Long** value containing the number of recipients of the current message. This property is read only at run time.
- *MAPIMessagesControl*.**RecipDisplayName**—a **String** value containing the recipient's name.

- *MAPIMessagesControl*.**RecipIndex**—a **Long** value containing the index of the current attachment. It can range in value from 1 to **RecipCount** –1. Changing this value will change the values in the **RecipAddress, RecipDisplayName**, and **RecipType** properties.
- *MAPIMessagesControl*.**RecipType**—an **Integer** value (see Table M-4) containing the type of attachment.

RecipType Name	Value	Description
mapOrigList	0	The person sending the message
mapToList	1	A primary recipient
mapCcList	2	A secondary recipient
mapBccList	3	A secondary recipient receiving a blind copy of the message

Table M-4: **RecipType** *values*.

- *MAPIMessagesControl*.**SessionID**—a **Long** containing a handle to the current messaging session.
- *MAPIMessagesControl*.**Tag**—a **String** that can hold programmer specific information. This property is not used by Visual Basic.

Methods

MAPIMessagesControl.Compose

Usage — This method clears the compose buffers, sets **MsgIndex** to –1, and allows the user to compose a message.

MAPIMessagesControl.Copy

Usage — This method copies the messages pointed to by **MsgIndex** into the compose buffer.

MAPIMessagesControl.Delete object

Usage — This method deletes the specified object.

Arguments — *object*—an **Integer** value (see Table M-5) containing the object to be deleted.

object Name	Value	Description
mapMessageDelete	0	The message pointed to by MsgIndex is deleted. The MsgIndex value for all subsequent messages will be decremented.
mapRecipientDelete	1	The recipient pointed to by RecipIndex is deleted. The RecipIndex value for all subsequent recipients will be decremented.
mapAttachmentDelete	2	The attachment pointed to by AttachmentIndex is deleted. The AttachmentIndex value for all subsequent attachments will be decremented.

Table M-5: *object values*.

MAPIMessagesControl.Fetch

Usage   This method retrieves the messages from the server based on the criteria in the **FetchMsgType, FetchUnreadOnly,** and **FetchSorted** properties.

MAPIMessagesControl.Forward

Usage   This method copies the current message into the compose buffer as a forwarded note and puts "FW:" in front of the subject line. It also sets the **MsgIndex** to –1.

MAPIMessagesControl.Reply

Usage   This method copies the current message into the compose buffer as a replied note and puts "RE:" in front of the subject line. It also sets the **MsgIndex** to –1. This message is sent only to the person that originated the message.

MAPIMessagesControl.ReplyAll

Usage   This method copies the current message into the compose buffer as a replied note and puts "RE:" in front of the subject line. It also sets the **MsgIndex** to –1. This message is sent to the person that originated the message. All other people (except the BCC recipient) that received copies of the note will be added to the CC list.

MAPIMessagesControl.ResolveName

Usage   This method attempts to resolve the name of the currently indexed recipient. If no match is found, then an error is returned (**AddressResolveUI = False**) or a dialog box to resolve the address (**AddressResolveUI = True**).

MAPIMessagesControl.Save

Usage   This method saves the message in the compose buffer (**MsgIndex = –1**).

MAPIMessagesControl.Send *dialog*

Usage   This method sends the note in the compose buffer.

Arguments   *dialog*—a **Boolean** when **True** means that a dialog box will be displayed with all of the compose information. **False** means that the message will be sent without displaying the dialog box.

MAPIMessagesControl.Send [*details*]

Usage   This method displays the Address Book or details about the current recipient.

Arguments   • *dialog*—a **Boolean** when **True** means that a dialog box with the information about the currently indexed recipient. **False** displays the Address Book dialog box (default).

See Also   **MAPISession** (control)

MAPISession

CONTROL

CCE, LE, PE, EE

Usage   The **MAPISession** control establishes a session with a mail server. Once the session is established, the **MAPIMessages** control can be used to send and receive messages. This property exists primarily to maintain compatibility with older versions of Visual Basic. To take advantages of the new features, use the methods listed below.

> **Warning**
>
> *MAPI requires that the 32-bit MAPI DLLs be installed. If they are not present, you may have to install them using your Windows installation disks.*

Properties   • *MAPISessionControl*.**Action**—an **Integer** value (see Table M-6) specifying the action to be taken. This property exists primarily to maintain compatibility with older versions of Visual Basic. To take advantage of the new features, use the methods listed below.

Action Name	Description
mapSignOn	Sign onto the mail server.
mapSignOff	Sign off the mail server.

Table M-6: **Action** *values.*

• *MAPISessionControl*.**DownLoadMail**—a **Boolean** value when **True** means that all new messages are downloaded at signon time (default). **False** means that the messages are downloaded after the first time interval passes.

• *MAPISessionControl*.**Index**—an **Integer** that uniquely identifies a control in a control array.

• *MAPISessionControl*.**LogonUI**—a **Boolean** value when **True** means a dialog box will be displayed to prompt the user for their username and password (default). **False** means that no dialog box will be displayed and all the information will be used from the **UserName** and **Password** properties.

- *MAPISessionControl*.**Name**—a **String** containing the name of the control that will be used to reference the control in a Visual Basic program. This property is read only at run time.
- *MAPISessionControl*.**NewSession**—a **Boolean** value when **True** means a new messaging session will be established, whether or not there is already a messaging session. **False** means the current messaging session will be used (default).
- *MAPISessionControl*.**Object**—an object that contains a reference to the *MAPISessionControl* object.
- *MAPISessionControl*.**Parent**—an object that contains a reference to the **Form**, **Frame**, or other container that contains this control.
- *MAPISessionControl*.**Password**—a **String** containing the user's password to the mail server. If empty, then a dialog box will be displayed to prompt the user for the password.
- *MAPISessionControl*.**SessionID**—a **Long** value containing the handle to the messaging session; it is needed by the **MAPIMessages** control. This property is read only at run time.
- *MAPISessionControl*.**Tag**—a **String** that can hold programmer specific information. This property is not used by Visual Basic.
- *MAPISessionControl*.**UserName**—a **String** containing the user's name for the mail server. If empty and if the **LogonUI** is **True**, then a dialog box will be displayed to prompt the user for their name and password.

Methods

MAPISessionControl.SignOff

Usage This method terminates the current messaging session.

MAPISessionControl.SignOn

Usage This method signs onto the messaging server using the values in the **UserName** and **Password** properties or prompts the user for signon information if the **UserName** or **Password** properties are empty and if the **LogonUI** property is **True**.

See Also **MAPIMessages** (control)

Masked Edit

CONTROL

CCE, LE, PE, EE

Usage The **Masked Edit** control works like a text box but adds the ability to automatically validate whatever the user enters into the control.

Properties
- *MaskedEditControl*.**AllowPrompt**—a **Boolean** when **True** means that the prompt character is also acceptable as an input character (default). **False** means that the prompt character can't be typed by the user.
- *MaskedEditControl*.**Appearance**—an **Integer** value (see Table M-7) that describes how the combo box will appear on the form.

AppearanceValue	Description
0	The MaskedEdit control displays without the 3D effects.
1	The **MaskedEdit** control displays with 3D effects (default value).

Table M-7: Appearance *values*.

- *MaskedEditControl*.**AutoTab**—a **Boolean** when **True** means that focus will shift to the next control in the tab order when all of the characters required by the input mask are filled. **False** means that a **ValidationError** event will occur if the user types more characters than the input mask requires.
- *MaskedEditControl*.**BackColor**—a **Long** that contains the suggested value for the background color of the control. The **BackColor** and **ForeColor** must both be solid to display text. If you choose a color that is dithered, it will be changed to the nearest solid color.
- *MaskedEditControl*.**BorderStyle**—an **Integer** value (see Table M-8) specifying how the border will be drawn.

BorderStyle Name	Value	Description
vbBSNone	0	No border displays.
vbFixedSingle	1	Single line around the label.

Table M-8: **BorderStyle** *values*.

- *MaskedEditControl*.**ClipMode**—an **Integer** value (see Table M-9) specifying whether the border characters should be included in a cut or copy operation. This property applies only when the **Mask** property is not empty.

ClipMode Name	Value	Description
mskIncludeLiterals	0	Literals are included in a cut or copy operation.
mskExcludeLiterals	1	Literals are not included in a cut or copy operation.

Table M-9: *ClipMode values*.

- *MaskedEditControl*.**ClipText**—a **String** value similar to **SelText** except that all of the mask characters (if any), are excluded.
- *MaskedEditControl*.**Container**—an object that sets or returns the container of the control at run time. This property cannot be set at design time.
- *MaskedEditControl*.**DataBindings**—a reference to a **DataBindings** collection containing information about multiple properties that are bound to a database.
- *MaskedEditControl*.**DataChanged**—a **Boolean** that applies only to data bound controls. When **True** means that the data contained in this control was changed either by the user or by some means other than retrieving data from the current record. When **False** means the data in the control is unchanged from the current record. Simply reading the next record is not sufficient to set the **DataChanged** property to **True**.
- *MaskedEditControl*.**DataField**—a **String** value that associates the control with a field in a **RecordSet** object in a **Data** control.

- *MaskedEditControl*.**DragIcon**—an object that contains the picture value of an icon. At design time, you can specify an icon file that has a file type of .ICO.

> **Tip**
>
> *This value can be created by copying the value from another control's **DragIcon** value, a form's icon, or by using the **LoadPicture** function.*

- *MaskedEditControl*.**DragMode**—an **Integer** value (see Table M-10) specifying how the control will respond to a drag request.

> **Tip**
>
> *Setting **DragMode** to vbAutomatic will automatically begin a drag operation when the user clicks on the control. However, the control will not respond to the usual mouse events (**Click**, **DblClick**, **MouseDown**, **MouseMove**, **MouseUp**).*

DragMode Name	Value	Description
vbManual	0	The Drag method must be used to begin a drag-and-drop operation (default value).
vbAutomatic	1	The source control will automatically begin a drag-and-drop operation when the user clicks on the control.

Table M-10: **DragMode** *values.*

- *MaskedEditControl*.**Enabled**—a **Boolean** value when **True** means that the control will respond to events. When **False**, the control will not respond to events.
- *MaskedEditControl*.**Font**—an object that contains information about the character font used by this object.
- *MaskedEditControl*.**ForeColor**—a **Long** that contains the suggested value for the foreground color of the contained control. This property is read only at run time.
- *MaskedEditControl*.**Format**—a series of up to four strings separated by semicolons (";"). These strings contain format information as used in the **Format** function and will be used for displaying the information in the **MaskEdit** control. The first string contains the format for positive numbers. The second string contains the format for negative numbers. The third string contains the format for a number when it is zero. The fourth string contains the format for a Null value. If one of the formats is not specified, the first format will be used.
- *MaskedEditControl*.**FormattedText**—a **String** containing the value of the text after being formatted using the format strings in the **Format** property. This is the value that displays in the control when the control doesn't have the focus. This property is read only at run time.
- *MaskedEditControl*.**Height**—a **Single** that contains the height of the control.
- *MaskedEditControl*.**HelpContextID**—a **Long** that contains a help file context ID number which references an entry in the help file. When the user presses the F1 key while this control is active, the corresponding entry in the help file will automatically displays. A value of zero means that no context number was specified.

> **Tip**
>
> *A help file must be compiled using the Windows Help Compiler available in the Professional and Enterprise editions of Visual Basic.*

- *MaskedEditControl*.**HideSelection**—a **Boolean** value when **True** means that the selected text does not appear highlighted when the control loses focus. When **False**, the text will continue to be highlighted when the control loses focus.
- *MaskedEditControl*.**hWnd**—a **Long** that contains a Windows handle to the control.

> **Tip**
>
> *The **hWnd** property is most useful when making calls to Windows API functions. Since this value can change during execution, do not save the value into a variable for later use.*

- *MaskedEditControl*.**Index**—an **Integer** that uniquely identifies a control in a control array.
- *MaskedEditControl*.**Left**—a **Single** that contains the distance measured in twips between the left edge of the control and the left edge of the control's container.
- *MaskedEditControl*.**Mask**—a **String** value (see Table M-11) containing a series of input mask characters.

Mask Characters	Description
#	A required numeric character.
.	A decimal point indicator as defined in Windows. Treated as a literal.
,	A thousands separator as defined by Windows. Treated as a literal.
/	A date separator as defined in Windows. Treated as a literal.
:	A time separator as defined in Windows. Treated as a literal.
\	Treat the next character as a literal. Used to insert #, &, A, a, and ? as literals.
&	An ASCII character from 32 to 126 and 128 to 255.
>	Convert the following characters to uppercase.
<	Convert the following characters to lowercase.
A	A required alphanumeric character.
a	An optional alphanumeric character.
9	An optional numeric character.
C	Same as &. Ensures compatibility with Microsoft Access.
?	A required alphabetic character.
other	Any other character. Treated as a literal.

Table M-11: **Mask** *characters.*

- *MaskedEditControl*.**MaxLength**—an **Integer** value from 1 to 64 containing the maximum number of characters in the **Text** property.
- *MaskedEditControl*.**MouseIcon**—a **Picture** object (a bitmap, icon, or metafile) that will be used as a cursor when the **MousePointer** property is set to 99. Note that Visual Basic does not support color cursors from a .CUR file. A color icon from an .ICO file should be used instead.

- *MaskedEditControl*.**MousePointer**—an **Integer** value (see Table M-12) that contains the value of the cursor that should be displayed when the cursor is moved over this control. Use *vbCustom* to display the custom icon stored in the **MouseIcon** property.

Cursor Name	Value	Description
vbDefault	0	Shape determined by the object (default value)
vbArrow	1	Arrow
vbCrosshair	2	Crosshair
vbIbeam	3	I beam
vbIconPointer	4	Square inside a square
vbSizePointer	5	Four sided arrow (north, south, east, west)
vbSizeNESW	6	Two sided arrow (northeast, southwest)
vbSizeNS	7	Two sided arrow (north, south)
vbSizeNWSE	8	Two sided arrow (northwest, southeast)
vbSizeWE	9	Two sided arrow (west, east)
vbUpArrow	10	Single sided arrow pointing north
vbHourglass	11	Hourglass
vbNoDrop	12	No Drop
vbArrowHourglass	13	An arrow and an Hourglass
vbArrowQuestion	14	An arrow and a question mark
vbSizeAll	15	Size all
vbCustom	99	Custom icon from the **MouseIcon** property of this control

Table M-12: Cursor *values*.

- *MaskedEditControl*.**Name**—a **String** that contains the name of the control that will be used to reference the control in a Visual Basic program. This property is read only at run time.
- *MaskedEditControl*.**Object**—an object that contains a reference to the *MAPISessionControl* object.
- *MaskedEditControl*.**OLEDragMode**—an **Integer** value (see Table M-13) that describes how the control will respond to OLE drag operations.

> **Note**
>
> When the **DragMode** is **True**, the standard Visual Basic drag-and-drop functions will override the OLE drag-and-drop functions.

OLEDragMode Name	Value	Description
vbOLEDragManual	0	All drag requests will be handled by the programmer (default value).
vbOLEDragAutomatic	1	The control responds to all OLE drag requests automatically.

Table M-13: OLEDragMode *values*.

- *MaskedEditControl*.**OLEDropMode**—an **Integer** value (see Table M-14) that describes how the control will respond to OLE drop operations.

OLEDropMode Name	Value	Description
vbOLEDropNone	0	The control does not accept OLE drops. The cursor is changed to the No Drop cursor (default value).
vbOLEDropManual	1	The control responds to OLE drops under the program's control (manual).
vbOLEDropAutomatic	2	The control automatically accepts OLE drops if it recognizes the format of the data object.

Table M-14: OLEDropMode values.

- *MaskedEditControl*.**Parent**—an object that contains a reference to the **Form, Frame,** or other container that contains this control.
- *MaskedEditControl*.**PromptChar**—a **String** that can contain up to one character which will be to prompt the user for input. The **PromptInclude** must also be set to **True** to display the prompt character.
- *MaskedEditControl*.**PromptInclude**—a **Boolean** when **True** means that the prompt character is included in the **Text** property. **False** means that is it not included. For bound controls when **PromptInclude** is **True**, the **Text** property will be saved in the database. **False** means that the data from the **ClipText** property is saved.
- *MaskedEditControl*.**SelLength**—a **Long** value containing the length of the selected text. When **SelLength** is zero, then no text is selected.
- *MaskedEditControl*.**SelStart**—a **Long** value containing the starting position of the selected text.
- *MaskedEditControl*.**SelText**—a **String** value containing the selected text. When **SelText** is empty, then no text is selected.

> **Tip**
>
> *The **SelLength**, **SelStart**, and **SelText** properties are very powerful tools for inserting and deleting text inside the control. Setting **SelStart** to a position inside the **Text** string and assigning a value to **SelText** will insert text at that position. To change a block of text, simply set the **SelStart** and **SelLength** values and then change the value of **SelText**. The **Text** property will be updated accordingly. Assigning an empty string to **SelText** will delete the selected text.*

- *MaskedEditControl*.**TabIndex**—an Integer that determines the order that a user will tab through the objects on a form.
- *MaskedEditControl*.**TabStop**—a **Boolean** value when **True** means that the user can tab to this object. When **False** means that this control will be skipped to the next control in the **TabIndex** order.
- *MaskedEditControl*.**Tag**—a **String** that can hold programmer specific information. This property is not used by Visual Basic.
- *MaskedEditControl*.**Text**—a **String** that sets or returns the value from the text box part of the control. This value can only be accessed at run time.
- *MaskedEditControl*.**ToolTipText**—a **String** that holds a text value that can be displayed as a **ToolTip** box that displays whenever the cursor is held over the control for about one second.

- *MaskedEditControl*.**Top**—a **Single** that contains the distance measured in twips between the top edge of the control and the top edge of the control's container.
- *MaskedEditControl*.**TopIndex**—an **Integer** containing the first number visible in the list box. The default value is zero (the first item in the list).
- *MaskedEditControl*.**Visible**—a **Boolean** value when **True** means that the control is visible. When **False** means that the control is not visible.

> **Tip**
>
> *This property hides the control until the program is ready to display it.*

- *MaskedEditControl*.**WhatsThisHelpID**—a **Long** that contains a help file context ID number references an entry in the help file. This provides a What's This PopUp help display in response to the What's This button in the upper right corner of the window.
- *MaskedEditControl*.**Width**—a **Single** that contains the width of the control.

Methods

MaskedEditControl.Drag [DragAction]

Usage This method begins, ends, or cancels a drag operation.

Arguments • *DragAction*—an **Integer** that contains a value selected from Table M-15 below.

DragAction Name	Value	Description
vbCancel	0	Cancels any drag operation in progress.
vbBeginDrag	1	Begins a drag operation (default).
vbEndDrag	2	Ends a drag operation and drops *object*.

Table M-15: DragAction *values*.

MaskedEditControl.Move Left [, Top [, Width [, Height]]]

Usage This method changes the position and the size of the **MaskedEdit** control. The **ScaleMode** of the **Form** or other container object that holds the **MaskedEdit** control will determine the units used to specify the coordinates.

Arguments
- *Left*—a **Single** that specifies the new position of the left edge of the control.
- *Top*—a **Single** that specifies the new position of the top edge of the control.
- *Width*—a **Single** that specifies the new width of the control.
- *Height*—a **Single** that specifies the new height of the control.

MaskedEditControl.OLEDrag

Usage This method begins an **OLEDrag** and drop operation. Invoking this method will trigger the **OLEStartDrag** event.

MaskedEditControl.Refresh

Usage   This method redraws the contents of the control.

MaskedEditControl.SetFocus

Usage   This method transfers the focus from the form or control that currently has the focus to this control. To receive the focus, this control must be enabled and visible.

MaskedEditControl.ShowWhatsThis

Usage   This method displays the ShowWhatsThis help information for this control.

MaskedEditControl.ZOrder [*position*]

Usage   This method specifies the position of the **MaskedEdit** control relative to the other objects on the form.

Tip

*Note that there are three layers of objects on a form: the back layer is the drawing space which contains the results of the graphical methods, the middle layer contains graphical objects and **Labels**, and the top layer contains nongraphical controls such as the **MaskedEdit** control. The **ZOrder** method only affects how the objects are arranged within a single layer.*

Arguments   • *position*—an **Integer** that specifies the relative position of this object. A value of 0 means that the control is positioned at the head of the list, a value of 1 means that the control will be placed at the end of the list.

Events

Private Sub *MaskedEditControl*_Change ([*index* As Integer])

Usage   This event occurs whenever the contents of the label's caption are changed, either by the program changing the **Caption** property directly or by a DDE link.

Arguments   • *index*—an **Integer** that uniquely identifies a control in a control array. This argument is not present if the control is not part of a control array.

Private Sub *MaskedEditControl*_DragDrop([*index* As Integer ,] *source* As Control, *x* As Single, *y* As Single)

Usage   This event occurs when a drag-and-drop operation is completed by using the **Drag** method with a *DragAction* value of *vbEndDrag*.

Tip

*When using drag-and-drop operations, use the **DragOver** event to determine what the cursor should look like while the cursor moves over the control.*

Arguments
- *index*—an **Integer** that uniquely identifies a control in a control array. This argument is not present if the control is not part of a control array.
- *source*—a control object that is the control that is being dragged.

> **Tip**
>
> You can access a property or method from the source control by using **source**.*property* or **source**.*method*. You can determine the type of object or control by using the **TypeOf** operator.

- *x*—a **Single** that contains the horizontal location of the mouse pointer.
- *y*—a **Single** that contains the vertical location of the mouse pointer.

Private Sub *MaskedEditControl*_DragOver([*index* As Integer ,] *source* As Control, *x* As Single, *y* As Single, *state* As Integer)

Usage This event occurs while a drag operation is in progress and the cursor is moved over the control.

> **Tip**
>
> When using drag-and-drop operations, use the **DragOver** event to determine what the cursor should look like while the cursor moves over the control. When **state** is 0, you can change the cursor to a no drop (vbNoDrop) cursor or highlight the field that the cursor is near. When **state** is 1, you can undo the changes you made when the **state** was 0.

Arguments
- *index*—an **Integer** that uniquely identifies a control in a control array. This argument is not present if the control is not part of a control array.
- *source*—a control object that is the control that is being dragged.

> **Tip**
>
> You can access a property or method from the source control by using **source**.*property* or **source**.*method*. You can determine the type of object or control by using the **TypeOf** operator.

- *x*—a **Single** that contains the horizontal location of the mouse pointer.
- *y*—a **Single** that contains the vertical location of the mouse pointer.
- *state*—an **Integer** value (see Table M-16) that indicates the state of the object being dragged.

state Name	Value	Description
vbEnter	0	The dragged object is entering range of the control.
vbLeave	1	The dragged object is leaving range of the control.
vbOver	2	The dragged object has moved from one position over the control to another.

Table M-16: state values.

Private Sub *MaskedEditControl*_GotFocus ([*index* As Integer])

Usage   This event occurs when the control is given focus.

Tip

You can use this routine to display help or other information in a status bar.

Arguments
- *index*—an **Integer** that uniquely identifies a control in a control array. This argument is not present if the control is not part of a control array.

Private Sub *MaskedEditControl*_KeyDown ([*index* As Integer ,] *keycode* As Integer, *shift* As Single)

Usage   This event occurs when a key is pressed while the control has the focus.

Arguments
- *index*—an **Integer** that uniquely identifies a control in a control array. This argument is not present if the control is not part of a control array.
- *keycode*—an **Integer** that contains information about which key was pressed.
- *shift*—an **Integer** value (see Table M-17) that contains information about the Shift and Alt keys that were pushed when the mouse button was pressed. These values can be added together if more than one key was down. For instance, a value of 5 would mean that the Shift and Alt keys were both down when the mouse button was pressed.

shift Name	Value	Description
vbShiftMask	1	The Shift key was pressed.
vbCtrlMask	2	The Ctrl key was pressed.
vbAltMask	4	The Alt key was pressed.

Table M-17: shift values.

Private Sub *MaskedEditControl*_KeyPress([*index* As Integer ,] *keychar* As Integer)

Usage   This event occurs whenever a key is pressed while the control has the focus.

Arguments
- *index*—an **Integer** that uniquely identifies a control in a control array. This argument is not present if the control is not part of a control array.
- *keychar*—an **Integer** that contains the ASCII character that was pressed.

Private Sub *MaskedEditControl*_KeyUp ([*index* As Integer ,] *keycode* As Integer, *shift* As Single)

Usage   This event occurs when a key is released while the control has the focus.

Arguments
- *index*—an **Integer** that uniquely identifies a control in a control array. This argument is not present if the control is not part of a control array.
- *keycode*—an **Integer** that contains information about which key was released.
- *shift*—an **Integer** value (see Table M-18) that contains information about the Shift and Alt keys that were pushed when the mouse button was pressed. These values can be added together if more than one key was down. For instance, a value of 5 would mean that the Shift and Alt keys were both down when the mouse button was pressed.

shift Name	Value	Description
vbShiftMask	1	The Shift key was pressed.
vbCtrlMask	2	The Ctrl key was pressed.
vbAltMask	4	The Alt key was pressed.

Table M-18: shift *values.*

Private Sub *MaskedEditControl*_LostFocus ([*index* As Integer])

Usage This event occurs when the control loses focus.

Arguments
- *index*—an **Integer** that uniquely identifies a control in a control array. This argument is not present if the control is not part of a control array.

Private Sub *MaskedEditBoxControl*_MouseDown([*index* As Integer ,] *button* As Integer, *shift* As Single, *x* As Single, *y* As Single)

Usage This event occurs when a mouse button was pressed while the cursor is over the control.

Arguments
- *index*—an **Integer** that uniquely identifies a control in a control array. This argument is not present if the control is not part of a control array.
- *button*—an **Integer** value (see Table M-19) that contains information about the mouse buttons that were pressed. Only one button will be indicated when this event occurs.

button Name	Value	Description
vbLeftButton	1	The left button was pressed.
vbRightButton	2	The right button was pressed.
vbMiddleButton	4	The middle button was pressed.

Table M-19: button *values.*

- *shift*—an **Integer** value (see Table M-20) that contains information about the Shift and Alt keys that were pushed when the mouse button was pressed. These values can be added together if more than one key was down. For instance, a value of 5 would mean that the Shift and Alt keys were both down when the mouse button was pressed.

Masked Edit • 513

shift Name	Value	Description
vbShiftMask	1	The Shift key was pressed.
vbCtrlMask	2	The Ctrl key was pressed.
vbAltMask	4	The Alt key was pressed.

Table M-20: shift *values*.

- *x*—a **Single** that contains the horizontal location of the mouse pointer.
- *y*—a **Single** that contains the vertical location of the mouse pointer.

Private Sub *MaskedEditControl*_MouseMove ([*index* As Integer ,] *button* As Integer, *shift* As Single, *x* As Single, *y* As Single)

Usage: This event occurs while the cursor is moved over the control.

Arguments:
- *index*—an **Integer** that uniquely identifies a control in a control array. This argument is not present if the control is not part of a control array.
- *button*—an **Integer** value (see Table M-21) that contains information about the mouse buttons that were pressed. These values can be added together if more than one button was pushed. For instance, a value of 3 means that both the left and right buttons were pressed. A value of 0 means that no buttons were pressed.

button Name	Value	Description
vbLeftButton	1	The left button was pressed.
vbRightButton	2	The right button was pressed.
vbMiddleButton	4	The middle button was pressed.

Table M-21: button *values*.

- *shift*—an **Integer** value (see Table M-22) that contains information about the Shift and Alt keys that were pushed when the mouse button was pressed. For instance, a value of 5 would mean that the Shift and Alt keys were both down when the mouse button was pressed. A value of 0 means that none of these keys were pressed.

shift Name	Value	Description
vbShiftMask	1	The Shift key was pressed.
vbCtrlMask	2	The Ctrl key was pressed.
vbAltMask	4	The Alt key was pressed.

Table M-22: shift *values*.

- *x*—a **Single** that contains the horizontal location of the mouse pointer.
- *y*—a **Single** that contains the vertical location of the mouse pointer.

Private Sub *MaskedEditBoxControl_MouseUp*([*index* As Integer ,] *button* As Integer, *shift* As Single, *x* As Single, *y* As Single)

Usage This event occurs when a mouse button is released while the cursor is over the control.

Arguments
- *index*—an **Integer** that uniquely identifies a control in a control array. This argument is not present if the control is not part of a control array.
- *button*—an **Integer** value (see Table M-23) that contains information about the mouse buttons that were released. Only one of these values will be present.

button Name	Value	Description
vbLeftButton	1	The left button was released.
vbRightButton	2	The right button was released.
vbMiddleButton	4	The middle button was released.

Table M-23: button *values*.

- *shift*—an **Integer** value (see Table M-24) that contains information about the Shift and Alt keys that were pushed when the mouse button was released. These values can be added together if more than one key was down. For instance, a value of 5 would mean that the Shift and Alt keys were both down when the mouse button was released. A value of 0 means that none of these keys were pressed.

shift Name	Value	Description
vbShiftMask	1	The Shift key was pressed.
vbCtrlMask	2	The Ctrl key was pressed.
vbAltMask	4	The Alt key was pressed.

Table M-24: shift *values*.

- *x*—a **Single** that contains the horizontal location of the mouse pointer.
- *y*—a **Single** that contains the vertical location of the mouse pointer.

Private Sub *MaskedEditControl_OLECompleteDrag*([*index* As Integer ,] *effect* As Long)

Usage This event tells the source control the results of an OLE drag-and-drop operation. This is the final event to occur in the series of actions that make up an OLE drag-and-drop operation.

Arguments
- *index*—an **Integer** that uniquely identifies a control in a control array. This argument is not present if the control is not part of a control array.
- *effect*—a **Long** (see Table M-25) that returns the status of the OLE drag-and-drop operation.

Masked Edit

effect Name	Value	Description
vbDropEffectNone	0	The operation was canceled or the target control can't accept the drop operation.
vbDropEffectCopy	1	The operation copied data from the source control to the target control. The original data is unchanged.
vbDropEffectMove	2	The operation results in a link from the original data to the target control.

Table M-25: effect *values.*

Private Sub *MaskedEditControl*_OLEDragDrop([*index* As Integer ,] *data* As DataObject, *effect* As Long, *button* As Integer, *shift* As Single, *x* As Single, *y* As Single)

Usage This event tells the source control the results of an OLE drag-and-drop operation. This is the final event to occur in the series of actions that make up an OLE drag-and-drop operation.

Arguments
- *index*—an **Integer** that uniquely identifies a control in a control array. This argument is not present if the control is not part of a control array.
- *data*—a **DataObject** that contains the formats that the source control will provide. If the data is not contained in the **DataObject**, then it can be retrieved with the **GetData** method.
- *effect*—a **Long** (see Table M-26) that returns the status of the OLE drag-and-drop operation.

effect Name	Value	Description
vbDropEffectNone	0	The operation was canceled or the target control can't accept the drop operation.
vbDropEffectCopy	1	The operation copied data from the source control to the target control. The original data is unchanged.
vbDropEffectMove	2	The operation results in a link from the original data to the target control.

Table M-26: effect *values.*

- *button*—an **Integer** value (see Table M-27) that contains information about the mouse buttons that were pressed. These values can be added together if more than one button was pushed. For instance, a value of 3 means that both the left and right buttons were pressed. A value of 0 means that no buttons were pressed.

button Name	Value	Description
vbLeftButton	1	The left button was pressed.
vbRightButton	2	The right button was pressed.
vbMiddleButton	4	The middle button was pressed.

Table M-27: button *values.*

- *shift*—an **Integer** value (see Table M-28) that contains information about the Shift and Alt keys that were pushed when the mouse button was released. These values can be added together if more than one key was down. For instance, a value of 5 would mean that the Shift and Alt keys were both down when the mouse button was released. A value of 0 means that none of these keys were pressed.

shift Name	Value	Description
vbShiftMask	1	The Shift key was pressed.
vbCtrlMask	2	The Ctrl key was pressed.
vbAltMask	4	The Alt key was pressed.

Table M-28: shift *values*.

- *x*—a **Single** that contains the horizontal location of the mouse pointer.
- *y*—a **Single** that contains the vertical location of the mouse pointer.

Private Sub *MaskedEditControl*_OLEDragOver([*index* As Integer ,] *data* As DataObject, *effect* As Long, *button* As Integer, *shift* As Single, *x* As Single, *y* As Single, *state* As Integer)

Usage — This event happens when an OLE drag-and-drop operation is in progress.

Arguments
- *index*—an **Integer** that uniquely identifies a control in a control array. This argument is not present if the control is not part of a control array.
- *data*—a **DataObject** that contains the formats that the source control will provide. If the data is not contained in the **DataObject**, then it can be retrieved with the **GetData** method.
- *effect*—a **Long** (see Table M-29) that returns the status of the OLE drag-and-drop operation.

effect Name	Value	Description
vbDropEffectNone	0	The operation was canceled or the target control can't accept the drop operation.
vbDropEffectCopy	1	The operation copied data from the source control to the target control. The original data is unchanged.
vbDropEffectMove	2	The operation results in a link from the original data to the target control.

Table M-29: effect *values*.

- *button*—an **Integer** value (see Table M-30) that contains information about the mouse buttons that were pressed. These values can be added together if more than one button was pushed. For instance, a value of 3 means that both the left and right buttons were pressed. A value of 0 means that no buttons were pressed.

button Name	Value	Description
vbLeftButton	1	The left button was pressed.
vbRightButton	2	The right button was pressed.
vbMiddleButton	4	The middle button was pressed.

Table M-30: button *values*.

- *shift*—an **Integer** value (see Table M-31) that contains information about the Shift and Alt keys that were pushed when the mouse button was released. These values can be added together if more than one key was down. For instance, a value of 5 would mean that the Shift and Alt keys were both down when the mouse button was released. A value of 0 means that none of these keys were pressed.

shift Name	Value	Description
vbShiftMask	1	The Shift key was pressed.
vbCtrlMask	2	The Ctrl key was pressed.
vbAltMask	4	The Alt key was pressed.

Table M-31: shift *values*.

- *x*—a **Single** that contains the horizontal location of the mouse pointer.
- *y*—a **Single** that contains the vertical location of the mouse pointer.
- *state*—an **Integer** value (see Table M-32) that indicates the state of the object being dragged.

state Name	Value	Description
vbEnter	0	The dragged object is entering range of the control.
vbLeave	1	The dragged object is leaving range of the control.
vbOver	2	The dragged object has moved from one position over the control to another.

Table M-32: state *values*.

Private Sub *MaskedEditControl*_OLEGiveFeedback ([*index* As Integer ,] *effect* As Long)

Usage — This event tells the source control what is happening while the OLE drag-and-drop operation is in progress. This event occurs after the **OLEDragOver** event.

Tip

You may want to use this event to change the cursor to reflect what can happen in the remote object.

Arguments
- *index*—an **Integer** that uniquely identifies a control in a control array. This argument is not present if the control is not part of a control array.
- *effect*—a **Long** (see Table M-33) that returns the status of the OLE drag-and-drop operation.

effect Name	Value	Description
vbDropEffectNone	0	The operation was canceled or the target control can't accept the drop operation.
vbDropEffectCopy	1	The operation copied data from the source control to the target control. The original data is unchanged.
vbDropEffectMove	2	The operation results in a link from the original data to the target control.
vbDropEffectScroll	&H80000000	The target control is about to scroll or is scrolling. This value may be added to the other *effect* values.

Table M-33: effect *values*.

Private Sub *MaskedEditControl_OLESetData*([*index* As Integer ,] *data* As DataObject, *DataFormat* As Integer)

Usage
This event happens in response to the target object performing a **GetData** method on *data*. This routine will respond by using the **SetData** method with the desired data using the **DataObject** *data*.

Arguments
- *index*—an **Integer** that uniquely identifies a control in a control array. This argument is not present if the control is not part of a control array.
- *data*—a **DataObject** that will contain the data to be returned to the target object.
- *format*—an **Integer** value (see Table M-34) that contains the format of the data.

format Name	Value	Description
vbCFText	1	Text (.TXT files)
vbCFBitmap	2	Bitmap (.BMP files)
vbCFMetafile	3	Metafile (.WMF files)
vbCFEDIB	8	Device independent bitmap (DIB)
vbCFPallette	9	Color palette
vbCFEMetafile	14	Enhanced metafile (.EMF files)
vbCFFiles	15	List of files
vbCFRTF	-16639	Rich Text Format (.RTF files)

Table M-34: format *values*.

Private Sub *MaskedEditControl_OLEStartDrag* ([*index* As Integer ,] *data* As DataObject, *AllowedEffects* As Long)

Usage This event starts an OLE drag-and-drop operation.

Arguments
- *index*—an **Integer** that uniquely identifies a control in a control array. This argument is not present if the control is not part of a control array.
- *data*—a **DataObject** that will contain the formats that the source object is willing to provide to the target object. It may optionally contain the data to transfer.
- *AllowedEffects*—a **Long** (see Table M-35) that contains the effects that the target object can request from the source object. The *AllowedEffects* can be added together if the source object supports more than one effect. Note that the target object can always use the *vbDropEffectNone* effect.

AllowedEffects Name	Value	Description
vbDropEffectNone	0	The target can't copy the data.
vbDropEffectCopy	1	The target can copy the data, and the source will keep the data unchanged.
vbDropEffectMove	2	The target can copy the data, and the source will delete the data.

Table M-35: AllowedEffects *values.*

Examples
```
Private Sub Form_Load()
Combo1.AddItem "###,###"
Combo1.AddItem "(###) ###-####"
Combo1.AddItem "AAAAAA"
Combo1.AddItem ">aaaaaa"
Combo1.AddItem "<aaaaaa"
End Sub

Private Sub MaskEdBox1_ValidationError(InvalidText As String, StartPosition As
    Integer)
MsgBox "Validation Error!"
End Sub
```

This program initializes a combo box with some different edit masks. Changing the value in the combo box, changes the edit mask. Each time that a user enters an invalid character, the **ValidationError** event is invoked and a message displays.

See Also **TextBox** (control)

MDIForm

OBJECT

CCE, LE, PE, EE

Usage The **MDIForm** (Multiple Document Interface Form) object is similar to the **Form** object, however it permits you to have forms nested inside other forms, similar to products like Microsoft Word and Excel. The **MDIForm** consists of the parent form and one or more child forms. While the child forms are designed independently of the parent form, they display only inside the parent form while the application is active.

Properties
- *MDIFormObject*.**ActiveControl**—an object of type control that contains a reference to the currently active control.
- *MDIFormObject*.**ActiveForm**—an object of type **MDIForm** that contains a reference to the currently active form.
- *MDIFormObject*.**Appearance**—an **Integer** value (see Table M-36) that specifies how the form will be drawn. This property affects only the parent **MDIForm**. Child forms are controlled by their own **Appearance** properties.

AppearanceValue	Description
0	The form displays without the 3D effects.
1	The form displays with 3D effects (default value).

Table M-36: **Appearance** *values.*

- *MDIFormObject*.**AutoShowChildren**—a **Boolean** value when **True** means child forms are automatically shown when loaded (default). **False** means they are not shown when loaded.
- *MDIFormObject*.**BackColor**—a **Long** that contains the suggested value for the background color of the form. The **BackColor** and **ForeColor** must both be solid to display text. If you choose a color that is dithered, it will be changed to the nearest solid color.
- *MDIFormObject*.**Caption**—a **String** value that displays inside the title bar. The leading text will also display in the Window's taskbar.
- *MDIFormObject*.**Controls**—an object reference to the **Controls** collection which contains all of the controls on the parent and child forms.
- *MDIFormObject*.**Count**—an **Integer** containing the number of controls on the parent and child forms.
- *MDIFormObject*.**Enabled**—a **Boolean** value when **True** means that the control will respond to events. When **False**, the control will not respond to events.
- *MDIFormObject*.**Height**—a **Single** that contains the height of the control.
- *MDIFormObject*.**HelpContextID**—a **Long** that contains a help file context ID number which references an entry in the help file. When the user presses the F1 key while this control is active, the corresponding entry in the help file will automatically display. A value of zero means that no context number was specified.

> **Tip**
>
> *A help file must be compiled using the Windows Help Compiler available in the Professional and Enterprise editions of Visual Basic.*

- *MDIFormObject*.**Icon**—a **Picture** object that contains the icon associated with this form. This icon displays in the Windows taskbar.

> ### Tip
> *Visual Basic includes a lot of icons that you can use with your program. Check the graphics\icons directory for a list of the available icons.*

- *MDIFormObject*.**Left**—a **Single** that contains the distance measured in twips between the left edge of the control and the left edge of the control's container.
- *MDIFormObject*.**LinkMode**—an **Integer** value (see Table M-37) that specifies how the form will act in a DDE conversation.

LinkMode Name	Value	Description
vbLinkNone	0	No DDE interaction. If initially specified at design time, it cannot be changed at run time.
vbLinkSource	1	DDE links permitted to labels, picture boxes, and text boxes. If initially specified at design time, it can be changed to *vbLinkNone* and back again.

Table M-37: **LinkMode** *values.*

- *MDIFormObject*.**LinkTopic**—a **String** that contains a reference to a DDE application. While the actual format of the string is dependent on the exact application, strings will usually include an application, topic, and item. For example, in Microsoft Excel a valid **LinkTopic** string is "Excel | Sheet1."
- *MDIFormObject*.**MouseIcon**—a **Picture** object (a bitmap, icon, or metafile) that will be used as a cursor when the **MousePointer** property is set to 99. Note that Visual Basic does not support color cursors from a .CUR file. A color icon from an .ICO file should be used instead.
- *MDIFormObject*.**MousePointer**—an **Integer** value (see Table M-38) that contains the value of the cursor that should be displayed when the cursor is moved over this control. Use *vbCustom* to display the custom icon stored in the **MouseIcon** property.

Cursor Name	Value	Description
vbDefault	0	Shape determined by the object (default value)
vbArrow	1	Arrow
vbCrosshair	2	Crosshair
vbIbeam	3	I beam
vbIconPointer	4	Square inside a square
vbSizePointer	5	Four sided arrow (north, south, east, west)
vbSizeNESW	6	Two sided arrow (northeast, southwest)
vbSizeNS	7	Two sided arrow (north, south)
vbSizeNWSE	8	Two sided arrow (northwest, southeast)
vbSizeWE	9	Two sided arrow (west, east)
vbUpArrow	10	Single sided arrow pointing north

Cursor Name	Value	Description
vbHourglass	11	Hourglass
vbNoDrop	12	No Drop
vbArrowHourglass	13	An arrow and an Hourglass
vbArrowQuestion	14	An arrow and a question mark
vbSizeAll	15	Size all
vbCustom	99	Custom icon from the **MouseIcon** property of this control

Table M-38: **Cursor** values.

- MDIFormObject.**Moveable**—a **Boolean** when **True** means that the form can be moved. When **False** means that the form can't be moved.
- MDIFormObject.**Name**—a **String** that contains the name of the control that will be used to reference the control in a Visual Basic program. This property is read only at run time.
- MDIFormObject.**OLEDropMode**—an **Integer** value (see Table M-39) that describes how the control will respond to OLE drop operations.

OLEDropMode Name	Value	Description
vbOLEDropNone	0	The form does not accept OLE drops. The cursor is changed to the No Drop cursor (default value).
vbOLEDropManual	1	The form responds to OLE drops under the program's control (manual).
vbOLEDropAutomatic	2	The form automatically accepts OLE drops if it recognizes the format of the data object.

Table M-39: **OLEDropMode** values.

- MDIFormObject.**Picture**—a **Picture** object (a bitmap, icon, metafile, GIF, or JPEG) that displays on the control. You can also use the **LoadPicture** function at run time to load a bitmap, icon, or metafile. Note that **Style** must be set to *vbButtonGraphical* for the image to be shown.
- MDIFormObject.**RightToLeft**—a **Boolean** value when **True** means that the text displays from right to left. When **False** means that the text displays from left to right. A bi-directional version of Windows is required to set this property to **True**.
- MDIFormObject.**ScaleHeight**—an **Integer** value that sets or returns the height of the object in the units specified by **ScaleMode**. This property refers only to the area not covered by **PictureBox** controls and is not available at design time and is read only at run time.
- MDIFormObject.**ScaleWidth**—an **Integer** value that sets or returns the width of the object in the units specified by **ScaleMode**. This property refers only to the area not covered by **PictureBox** controls and is not available at design time and is read only at run time.
- MDIFormObject.**ScrollBars**—a **Boolean** value when **True** means that the form has both a horizontal and a vertical scroll bar. **False** means that no scroll bars display.
- MDIFormObject.**StartUpPosition**—an **Integer** value (see Table M-40) that describes how the control will respond to OLE drop operations.

OLEDropMode Name	Value	Description
vbOLEDropNone	0	The form does not accept OLE drops. The cursor is changed to the No Drop cursor (default value).
vbOLEDropManual	1	The form responds to OLE drops under the program's control (manual).
vbOLEDropAutomatic	2	The form automatically accepts OLE drops if it recognizes the format of the data object.

Table M-40: **OLEDropMode** values.

- *MDIFormObject*.**Tag**—a **String** that can hold programmer specific information. This property is not used by Visual Basic.
- *MDIFormObject*.**Top**—a **Single** that contains the distance measured in twips between the top edge of the control and the top edge of the control's container.
- *MDIFormObject*.**Visible**—a **Boolean** value when **True** means that the control is visible. When **False** means that the control is not visible.
- *MDIFormObject*.**WhatsThisHelpID**—a **Long** that contains a help file context ID number references an entry in the help file. This provides a What's This PopUp help display in response to the What's This button in the upper right corner of the window.
- *MDIFormObject*.**Width**—a **Single** containing the width of the form.
- *MDIFormObject*.**WindowState**—an **Integer** value (see Table M-41) containing the state of the form when it initially displays.

WindowState Name	Value	Description
vbNormal	0	The form initially displays normally.
vbMinimized	1	The form initially displays minimized.
vbMaximized	2	The form initially displays maximized.

Table M-41: **WindowState** values.

Methods

MDIFormObject.Arrange *arrange*

Usage This method arranges the MDI child windows and icons on the MDI parent window.

Arguments - *arrange*—an **Integer** value (see Table M-42) specifying how the windows and icons are to be arranged.

arrange Name	Value	Description
vbCascade	0	The nonminimized MDI child forms are cascaded.
vbTileHorizontal	1	The nonminimized MDI child forms are tiled horizontally.
vbTileVertical	2	The nonminimized MDI child forms are tiled vertically.
vbArrangeIcons	3	The minimized icons are arranged.

Table M-42: *arrange* values.

MDIFormObject.Hide

Usage   This method removes a form from the screen but does not unload it.

MDIFormObject.Move Left [, Top [, Width [, Height]]]

Usage   This method changes the position and the size of the parent **MDIForm object**.

Arguments
- *Left*—a **Single** that specifies the new position of the left edge of the control.
- *Top*—a **Single** that specifies the new position of the top edge of the control.
- *Width*—a **Single** that specifies the new width of the control.
- *Height*—a **Single** that specifies the new height of the control.

MDIFormObject.OLEDrag

Usage   This method begins an **OLEDrag** and drop operation. Invoking this method will trigger the **OLEStartDrag** event.

MDIFormObject.PopupMenu menu, flags, x, y, menuitem

Usage   This method will display a pop-up menu on the screen.

> **Tip**
>
> Set **Visible** to **False** for menu items to display as pop-up menus to prevent them from displaying in the menu bar.

Arguments
- *menu*—the name of a **Menu** object to display. It must include at least one submenu item.
- *flags*—zero or more items from Table M-43. If omitted zero will be used. Multiple values can be selected by adding them together.

Menu Flags Name	Value	Description
vbPopupMenuLeftButton	0	The items on the menu can be selected by only the left mouse button.
vbPopupMenuLeftAlign	0	The left edge of the menu is located at x.
vbPopupMenuRightButton	2	The items on the menu can be selected by either mouse button.
vbPopupMenuCenterAlign	4	The center of the menu is located at x.
vbPopupMenuRightAlign	8	The right edge of the menu is located at x.

Table M-43: Menu Flags values.

- *x*—a **Single** specifying the X-coordinate of the menu. If omitted, it will default to the current X-coordinate of the mouse.

- *y*—a **Single** specifying the Y-coordinate of the menu. If omitted, it will default to the current Y-coordinate of the mouse.
- *menuitem*—the name of the submenu item to display in bold text. If omitted, no items display in bold.

MDIFormObject.SetFocus

Usage This method transfers the focus from the form or control that currently has the focus to this form. To receive the focus, this form must be enabled and visible.

MDIFormObject.Show [*style* [, *owner*]]

Usage This method displays a form.

Arguments
- *style*—an **Integer** that specifies how the form will be displayed. **MDIForm** objects can only be shown as modeless forms, so the only acceptable value for *style* is 0.
- *owner*—a **Form** object or the keyword **Me** that specifies the owner of this form.

MDIFormObject.WhatsThisMode

Usage This method places the mouse pointer into the "What's This?" mode. This is exactly the same thing as if the user clicked on the What's This button on the title bar.

MDIFormObject.ZOrder [*position*]

Usage This method specifies the position of the form relative to the other forms on the screen.

Arguments
- *position*—an **Integer** that specifies the relative position of the form. A value of 0 means that the control is positioned at the front of the screen. A value of 1 means that the form will be placed at the back of the screen.

Events

Private Sub *MDIFormObject*_Activate ( )

Usage This event occurs when the form becomes the active form. The form becomes active if either the **Show** or **SetFocus** methods were used or if the user takes some action such as clicking on the form.

Private Sub *MDIFormObject*_Click( )

Usage This event occurs when the user clicks a mouse button while the cursor is positioned over a disabled control or blank area on the form.

> **Tip**
>
> *If you need to identify which mouse button was pressed, use the **MouseUp** and **MouseDown** events.*

Private Sub *MDIFormObject*_DblClick( )

Usage This event occurs when the user double-clicks a mouse button while the cursor is positioned over a disabled control or blank area on the form.

Warning

*If there is code in the **Click** event, then the **DblClick** event will never occur.*

Private Sub *MDIFormObject*_Deactivate ( )

Usage This event occurs when the form loses the focus and is no longer the active window.

Private Sub *MDIFormObject*_DragDrop (*source* As Control, *x* As Single, *y* As Single)

Usage This event occurs when a drag-and-drop operation is completed by using the **Drag** method with a *DragAction* value of *vbEndDrag* (2).

Tip

*When using drag-and-drop operations, use the **DragOver** event to determine what the cursor should look like while the cursor moves over the control.*

Arguments ■ *source*—a control object that is the control that is being dragged.

Tip

You can access a property or method from the source control by using source.property *or* source.method. *You can determine the type of object or control by using the **TypeOf** operator.*

- *x*—a **Single** that contains the horizontal location of the mouse pointer.
- *y*—a **Single** that contains the vertical location of the mouse pointer.

Private Sub *MDIFormObject*_DragOver (*source* As Control, *x* As Single, *y* As Single, *state* As Integer)

Usage This event occurs while a drag operation is in progress and the cursor is moved over the control.

Tip

*When using drag-and-drop operations, use the **DragOver** event to determine what the cursor should look like while the cursor moves over the control. When **state** is 0, you can change the cursor to a No Drop (vbNoDrop) cursor or highlight the field that the cursor is near. When **state** is 1, you can undo the changes you made when the **state** was 0.*

Arguments ▪ *source*—a control object that is the control that is being dragged.

Tip

*You can access a property or method from the source control by using source.property or source.method. You can determine the type of object or control by using the **TypeOf** operator.*

- *x*—a **Single** that contains the horizontal location of the mouse pointer.
- *y*—a **Single** that contains the vertical location of the mouse pointer.
- *state*—an **Integer** value (see Table M-44) that indicates the state of the object being dragged.

state Name	Value	Description
vbEnter	0	The dragged object is entering range of the control.
vbLeave	1	The dragged object is leaving range of the control.
vbOver	2	The dragged object has moved from one position over the control to another.

Table M-44: state *values.*

Private Sub *MDIFormObject*_Initialize ( )

Usage This event occurs when the form is first created. This event will occur before the **Load** event.

Tip

*Since this event is triggered only when the form is created, and the **Load** event is triggered when the form is created and when it is loaded, it makes sense to put your initialization code in the **Load** event, unless you have specific actions that need to be done only when the form is created.*

Private Sub *MDIFormObject*_LinkClose ( )

Usage This event occurs when a DDE link is closed.

Private Sub *MDIFormObject*_LinkError (*errcode* As Integer)

Usage   This event occurs when a DDE link error occurs.

Arguments   • *errcode*—an **Integer** that contains an error code listed in Table M-45 below.

errcode Value	Description
1	The other application requested data in wrong format. This may occur more than once while Visual Basic attempts to find an acceptable format.
6	The other application attempted to continue the DDE conversation after **LinkMode** in this application was set to zero.
7	All 128 DDE links are in use.
8	Destination control: an automatic link or **LinkRequest** failed when communicating. Source forms: the other application was unable to poke data to a control.
11	Insufficient memory available for DDE.

Table M-45: DDE errcode values.

Private Sub *MDIFormObject*_LinkExecute (*cmd* As String, *cancel* As Integer)

Usage   This event occurs when a destination application requests the source application to perform the function in *cmd*.

> **Note**
>
> *If your program doesn't include a **LinkExecute** event there, then all commands will be rejected.*

Arguments   • *cmd*—a **String** containing a command for the source application to execute. The format of the string is application specific.
• *cancel*—an **Integer** when zero means that the command was accepted. Any other value will inform the destination application that the command was rejected.

Private Sub *MDIFormObject*_LinkOpen (*cancel* As Integer)

Usage   This event occurs when a DDE session is being set up.

Arguments   • *cancel*—an **Integer** when zero means that the command was accepted. Any other value will inform the destination application that the link will be refused.

Private Sub *MDIFormObject*_Load ( )

Usage   This event occurs when a form is being loaded and after the **Initialize** event has finished.

> **Tip**
>
> *This is a good spot to place any initialization code for the form.*

Private Sub *MDIFormObject*_MouseDown (*button* As Integer, *shift* As Single, *x* As Single, *y* As Single)

Usage This event occurs when a mouse button was pressed while the cursor is over any unoccupied part of the form.

Arguments
- *button*—an **Integer** value (see Table M-46) that contains information about the mouse buttons that were pressed. Only one button will be indicated when this event occurs.

button Name	Value	Description
vbLeftButton	1	The left button was pressed.
vbRightButton	2	The right button was pressed.
vbMiddleButton	4	The middle button was pressed.

Table M-46: button *values.*

- *shift*—an **Integer** value (see Table M-47) that contains information about the Shift and Alt keys that were pushed when the mouse button was pressed. These values can be added together if more than one key was down. For instance, a value of 5 would mean that the Shift and Alt keys were both down when the mouse button was pressed.

shift Name	Value	Description
vbShiftMask	1	The Shift key was pressed.
vbCtrlMask	2	The Ctrl key was pressed.
vbAltMask	4	The Alt key was pressed.

Table M-47: shift *values.*

- *x*—a **Single** that contains the horizontal location of the mouse pointer.
- *y*—a **Single** that contains the vertical location of the mouse pointer.

Private Sub *MDIFormObject*_MouseMove (*button* As Integer, *shift* As Single, *x* As Single, *y* As Single)

Usage This event occurs while the cursor is moved over any unoccupied part of the form.

Arguments
- *button*—an **Integer** value (see Table M-48) that contains information about the mouse buttons that were pressed. These values can be added together if more than one button was pushed. For instance, a value of 3 means that both the left and right buttons were pressed. A value of 0 means that no buttons were pressed.

button Name	Value	Description
vbLeftButton	1	The left button was pressed.
vbRightButton	2	The right button was pressed.
vbMiddleButton	4	The middle button was pressed.

Table M-48: button *values*.

- *shift*—an **Integer** value (see Table M-49) that contains information about the Shift and Alt keys that were pushed when the mouse button was pressed. For instance, a value of 5 would mean that the Shift and Alt keys were both down when the mouse button was pressed. A value of 0 means that none of these keys were pressed.

shift Name	Value	Description
vbShiftMask	1	The Shift key was pressed.
vbCtrlMask	2	The Ctrl key was pressed.
vbAltMask	4	The Alt key was pressed.

Table M-49: shift *values*.

- *x*—a **Single** that contains the horizontal location of the mouse pointer.
- *y*—a **Single** that contains the vertical location of the mouse pointer.

Private Sub *MDIFormObject*_MouseUp (*button* As Integer, *shift* As Single, *x* As Single, *y* As Single)

Usage — This event occurs when a mouse button is released while the cursor is over any unoccupied part of the form.

Arguments
- *button*—an **Integer** value (see Table M-50) that contains information about the mouse buttons that were released. Only one of these values will be present.

button Name	Value	Description
vbLeftButton	1	The left button was released.
vbRightButton	2	The right button was released.
vbMiddleButton	4	The middle button was released.

Table M-50: button *values*.

- *shift*—an **Integer** value (see Table M-51) that contains information about the Shift and Alt keys that were pushed when the mouse button was released. These values can be added together if more than one key was down. For instance, a value of 5 would mean that the Shift and Alt keys were both down when the mouse button was released. A value of 0 means that none of these keys were pressed.

MDIForm • **531**

shift Name	Value	Description
vbShiftMask	1	The Shift key was pressed.
vbCtrlMask	2	The Ctrl key was pressed.
vbAltMask	4	The Alt key was pressed.

Table M-51: shift *values.*

- *x*—a **Single** that contains the horizontal location of the mouse pointer.
- *y*—a **Single** that contains the vertical location of the mouse pointer.

Private Sub *MDIFormObject*_OLECompleteDrag(*effect* As Long)

Usage: This event tells the source control the results of an OLE drag-and-drop operation. This is the final event to occur in the series of actions that make up an OLE drag-and-drop operation.

Arguments:
- *effect*—a **Long** (see Table M-52) that returns the status of the OLE drag-and-drop operation.

effect Name	Value	Description
vbDropEffectNone	0	The operation was canceled or the target control can't accept the drop operation.
vbDropEffectCopy	1	The operation copied data from the source control to the target control. The original data is unchanged.
vbDropEffectMove	2	The operation results in a link from the original data to the target control.

Table M-52: effect *values.*

Private Sub *MDIFormObject*_OLEDragDrop (*data* As DataObject, *effect* As Long, *button* As Integer, *shift* As Single, *x* As Single, *y* As Single)

Usage: This event tells the source control the results of an OLE drag-and-drop operation. This is the final event to occur in the series of actions that make up an OLE drag-and drop-operation.

Arguments:
- *data*—a **DataObject** that contains the formats that the source control will provide. If the data is not contained in the **DataObject**, then it can be retrieved with the **GetData** method.
- *effect*—a **Long** (see Table M-53) that returns the status of the OLE drag-and-drop operation.

effect Name	Value	Description
vbDropEffectNone	0	The operation was canceled or the target control can't accept the drop operation.
vbDropEffectCopy	1	The operation copied data from the source control to the target control. The original data is unchanged.
vbDropEffectMove	2	The operation results in a link from the original data to the target control.

Table M-53: effect *values*.

- *button*—an **Integer** value (see Table M-54) that contains information about the mouse buttons that were pressed. These values can be added together if more than one button was pushed. For instance, a value of 3 means that both the left and right buttons were pressed. A value of 0 means that no buttons were pressed.

button Name	Value	Description
vbLeftButton	1	The left button was pressed.
vbRightButton	2	The right button was pressed.
vbMiddleButton	4	The middle button was pressed.

Table M-54: button *values*.

- *shift*—an **Integer** value (see Table M-55) that contains information about the Shift and Alt keys that were pushed when the mouse button was released. These values can be added together if more than one key was down. For instance, a value of 5 would mean that the Shift and Alt keys were both down when the mouse button was released. A value of 0 means that none of these keys were pressed.

shift Name	Value	Description
vbShiftMask	1	The Shift key was pressed.
vbCtrlMask	2	The Ctrl key was pressed.
vbAltMask	4	The Alt key was pressed.

Table M-55: shift *values*.

- *x*—a **Single** that contains the horizontal location of the mouse pointer.
- *y*—a **Single** that contains the vertical location of the mouse pointer.

Private Sub *MDIFormObject*_OLEDragOver (*data* As DataObject, *effect* As Long, *button* As Integer, *shift* As Single, *x* As Single, *y* As Single, *state* As Integer)

Usage   This event happens when an OLE drag-and-drop operation is in progress.

Arguments
- *data*—a **DataObject** that contains the formats that the source control will provide. If the data is not contained in the **DataObject**, then it can be retrieved with the **GetData** method.
- *effect*—a **Long** (see Table M-56) that returns the status of the OLE drag-and-drop operation.

effect Name	Value	Description
vbDropEffectNone	0	The operation was canceled or the target control can't accept the drop operation.
vbDropEffectCopy	1	The operation copied data from the source control to the target control. The original data is unchanged.
vbDropEffectMove	2	The operation results in a link from the original data to the target control.

Table M-56: effect *values.*

- *button*—an **Integer** value (see Table M-57) that contains information about the mouse buttons that were pressed. These values can be added together if more than one button was pushed. For instance, a value of 3 means that both the left and right buttons were pressed. A value of 0 means that no buttons were pressed.

button Name	Value	Description
vbLeftButton	1	The left button was pressed.
vbRightButton	2	The right button was pressed.
vbMiddleButton	4	The middle button was pressed.

Table M-57: button *values.*

- *shift*—an **Integer** value (see Table M-58) that contains information about the Shift and Alt keys that were pushed when the mouse button was released. These values can be added together if more than one key was down. For instance, a value of 5 would mean that the Shift and Alt keys were both down when the mouse button was released. A value of 0 means that none of these keys were pressed.

shift Name	Value	Description
vbShiftMask	1	The Shift key was pressed.
vbCtrlMask	2	The Ctrl key was pressed.
vbAltMask	4	The Alt key was pressed.

Table M-58: shift *values.*

- *x*—a **Single** that contains the horizontal location of the mouse pointer.
- *y*—a **Single** that contains the vertical location of the mouse pointer.
- *state*—an **Integer** value (see Table M-59) that indicates the state of the object being dragged.

state Name	Value	Description
vbEnter	0	The dragged object is entering range of the control.
vbLeave	1	The dragged object is leaving range of the control.
vbOver	2	The dragged object has moved from one position over the control to another.

Table M-59: state *values.*

Private Sub *MDIFormObject*_OLEGiveFeedback (*effect* As Long)

Usage   This event tells the source control what is happening while the OLE drag-and-drop operation is in progress. This event occurs after the **OLEDragOver** event.

Tip

You may want to use this event to change the cursor to reflect what can happen in the remote object.

Arguments   ▪ *effect*—a **Long** (see Table M-60) that returns the status of the OLE drag-and-drop operation.

effect Name	Value	Description
vbDropEffectNone	0	The operation was canceled or the target control can't accept the drop operation.
vbDropEffectCopy	1	The operation copied data from the source control to the target control. The original data is unchanged.
vbDropEffectMove	2	The operation results in a link from the original data to the target control.
vbDropEffectScroll	&H80000000	The target control is about to scroll or is scrolling. This value may be added to the other *effect* values.

Table M-60: effect *values*.

Private Sub *MDIFormObject*_OLESetData (*data* As DataObject, *DataFormat* As Integer)

Usage   This event happens in response to the target object performing a **GetData** method on *data*. This routine will respond by using the **SetData** method with the desired data using the **DataObject** *data*.

Arguments   ▪ *data*—a **DataObject** that will contain the data to return to the target object.

              ▪ *format*—an **Integer** value (see TableM-61) that contains the format of the data.

format Name	Value	Description
vbCFText	1	Text (.TXT files)
vbCFBitmap	2	Bitmap (.BMP files)
vbCFMetafile	3	Metafile (.WMF files)
vbCFEDIB	8	Device independent bitmap (DIB)
vbCFPallette	9	Color palette
vbCFEMetafile	14	Enhanced metafile (.EMF files)
vbCFFiles	15	List of files
vbCFRTF	-16639	Rich Text Format (.RTF files)

Table M-61: format *values*.

Private Sub *MDIFormObject*_OLEStartDrag (*data* As DataObject, *AllowedEffects* As Long)

- Usage: This event starts an OLE drag-and-drop operation.

- Arguments:
  - *data*—a **DataObject** that will contain the formats that the source object is willing to provide to the target object. It may optionally contain the data to be transferred.
  - *AllowedEffects*—a **Long** (see Table M-62) that contains the effects that the target object can request from the source object. The *AllowedEffects* can be added together if the source object supports more than one effect. Note that the target object can always use the *vbDropEffectNone* effect.

AllowedEffects Name	Value	Description
vbDropEffectNone	0	The target can't copy the data.
vbDropEffectCopy	1	The target can copy the data and the source will keep the data unchanged.
vbDropEffectMove	2	The target can copy the data and the source will delete the data.

Table M-62: AllowedEffects *values.*

Private Sub *MDIFormObject*_QueryUnload (*cancel* As Integer, *unloadmode* As Long)

- Usage: This event is called before a form unloads. Depending on *unloadmode,* one or more forms will be closed. Before the first form unloads, all forms will see the **QueryUnload** event. If one form cancels the request, then no forms will unload.

- Arguments:
  - *cancel*—an **Integer** that when set to any value except zero will stop the unload process. Setting *cancel* to zero will let the process continue.
  - *unloadmode*—an **Integer** value (see Table M-63) that indicates the origin of the unload request.

unloadmode Name	Value	Description
vbFormControlMenu	0	The Close command from the control menu issued the request.
vbFormCode	1	The program issued the request.
vbAppWindows	2	A Windows shutdown request was issued.
vbAppTaskManager	3	The Windows TaskManager is closing the application.
vbFormMDIForm	4	The MDI parent form is closing the MDI child form.

Table M-63: unloadmode values.

Private Sub *MDIFormObject*_Resize ( )

Usage   This event occurs when the form first displays, when the value of **WindowState** changes, or when the form is resized. After the **Resize** event occurs, the **Paint** event will be called (if **AutoResize** is **False**) to redraw the contents of the form.

Private Sub *MDIFormObject*_Terminate ( )

Usage   This event occurs when the last instance of a form is ready to be removed from memory. It will not be called if for some reason (such as when the **End** statement executes) the program terminates abnormally.

Private Sub *MDIFormObject*_Unload (*cancel* As Integer)

Usage   This event is called before a form unloads. While *cancel* can be set to keep the form from unloading, it will not stop processes like Windows from shutting down. You should use the **QueryUnload** event instead.

Arguments   *cancel*—an **Integer** that when set to any value except zero will stop the unload process. Setting *cancel* to zero will let the process continue.

Examples
```
Global MyForms(127) As Object
Global MyFormsActive(127) As Boolean
Global MyFormCount As Integer

Private Sub MenuCascade_Click()
MDIForm1.Arrange vbCascade
End Sub

Private Sub MenuExit_Click()
Dim i As Integer
For i = 0 To MyFormCount
    If MyFormsActive(i) Then
        Unload MyForms(i)
    End If
Next i
End
End Sub

Private Sub MenuNew_Click()
If MyFormCount < 127 Then
    Set MyForms(MyFormCount) = New Form1
    MyForms(MyFormCount).Caption = "Form #" & Format(MyFormCount)
    MyForms(MyFormCount).Tag = Format(MyFormCount)
    MyForms(MyFormCount).Show
    MyFormsActive(MyFormCount) = True
    MyFormCount = MyFormCount + 1
End If
End Sub
```

```
Private Sub MenuClose_Click()
MyFormsActive(CInt(Me.Tag)) = False
Unload Me
End Sub
```

This program uses three global variables, MyForms, MyFormCount, and MyFormsActive, to track each of the MDI child forms created by the MDI parent form.

The **MenuNew_Click** event creates new instances of Form1 and saves a reference to the new object in the global variable MyForms using MyFormCount as a subscript. It also sets the caption for the new form to indicate the form number and saves the form number in the form's Tag property. Then it shows the form. Finally it sets, MyFormsActive to **True** using MyFormCount as a subscript and increments MyFormCount.

The **MenuCascade_Click** event arranges MDI child forms on the MDI parent form. **MenuClose_Click** marks that the form is no longer active in the MyFormsActive array and unloads the form. The **MenuExit_Click** event unloads all open MDI child forms and exits the program.

See Also   **Forms** (collection), **MDIForm** (object)

Menu

CONTROL

CCE, LE, PE, EE

Usage   The **Menu** control is an intrinsic control that displays menus at the top of a form. A menu can contain up to four levels of submenus. To create a **Menu** on a particular form, use the Tools | Menu Editor command from the Visual Basic development environment.

When developing menus for a Multiple Document Interface environment, note that the menu for the active MDI child form will replace the MDI parent form's menu.

> **Tip**
>
> *To create a separator bar in a menu, run the Menu Editor. Then enter a dash ("-") as the caption, and enter a dummy name for the **Click** event.*
>
> *To create a check box in the space between the left edge of the submenu and the caption, select the checked box.*

Properties
- *MenuControl*.**Caption**—a **String** value that displays the menu object name.
- *MenuControl*.**Checked**—a **Boolean** when **True** means that a checkmark displays in front of the menu object's caption. **False** means no checkmark will display.
- *MenuControl*.**Enabled**—a **Boolean** value when **True** means that the menu control will respond to events. When **False**, the control will not respond to events.
- *MenuControl*.**HelpContextID**—a **Long** that contains a help file context ID number which references an entry in the help file. When the user presses the F1 key while this control is active, the corresponding entry in the help file will automatically display. A value of zero means that no context number was specified.

> **Tip**
>
> *A help file must be compiled using the Windows Help Compiler available in the Professional and Enterprise editions of Visual Basic.*

- *MenuControl*.**Index**—an **Integer** that uniquely identifies a control in a control array.
- *MenuControl*.**Name**—a **String** that contains the name of the control that will reference the control in a Visual Basic program. This property is read only at run time.
- *MenuControl*.**NegotiatePosition**—an **Integer** value (see Table M-64) that determines how menus from active embedded or linked objects display on the form's top level menu bar.

NegotiatePosition Value	Description
0	The menu doesn't display when the object is active (default).
1	The menu displays on the left side of the menu bar.
2	The menu displays in the middle of the menu bar.
3	The menu displays on the right side of the menu bar.

Table M-64: **NegotiatePosition** *values.*

- *MenuControl*.**Parent**—an object that contains a reference to the **Form**, **Frame**, or other container that contains this control.
- *MenuControl*.**Tag**—a **String** that can hold programmer specific information. This property is not used by Visual Basic.
- *MenuControl*.**Visible**—a **Boolean** value when **True** means that the control is visible. When **False** means that the control is not visible.

> **Tip**
>
> *This property hides the control until the program is ready to display it.*

- *MenuControl*.**WindowList**—a **Boolean** value when **True** means that the menu object will display a list of open MDI child windows. Only one menu object may have this property set to **True**.

Events

Private Sub *MenuControl*_Click([*index* As Integer])

Usage This event occurs when the user clicks a mouse button on the menu object.

Arguments
- *index*—an **Integer** that uniquely identifies a control in a control array. This argument is not present if the control is not part of a control array.

Examples
```
Private Sub MenuExit_Click()
Unload Me
End Sub
```

This routine unloads the main form in response to a user selecting the **MenuExit** object.

See Also **Form** (object), **MDIForm** (object)

Microsoft Internet Transfer Control

CONTROL
CCE, LE, PE, EE

Usage
The **Microsoft Internet Transfer Control** provides the ability to send and receive documents on the Internet using HTTP and FTP protocols.

Tip

Testing Internet programs is always a challenge if you are connected via a 28.8k baud modem to the Internet. However if your system is configured for dial-up Internet access under Windows 95 or NT, you can also run Internet programs locally. All you need is Personal Web Server for Windows 95 or Peer-to-peer Web Server for Windows NT and you can test both FTP and HTTP programs without connecting to the rest of the Internet. Just use the magic address 127.0.0.1 (ex: HTTP://127.0.0.1) to refer to your machine.

Properties
- *INetControl.***AccessType**—an **Integer** value (see Table M-65) that identifies how to connect to the Internet.

AccessType Name	Value	Description
icUseDefault	0	Use the default value from the Windows Registry.
icDirect	1	Connect directly to the Internet.
icNamedProxy	2	Connect to the Internet through a proxy.

Table M-65: **AcessType** *values.*

- *INetControl.***Document**—a **String** value containing the path and filename of the local document used with the **Execute** method.
- *MaskedEditControl.***hInternet**—a **Long** that contains a Windows handle to the underlying WinINet API.

Tip

*The **hInternet** property is most useful when making calls to the WinINet API functions. Since this value can change during execution, do not save the value into a variable for later use.*

- *INetControl.***Index**—an **Integer** that uniquely identifies a control in a control array.
- *INetControl.***Name**—a **String** containing the name of the control that will be used to reference the control in a Visual Basic program. This property is read only at run time.
- *INetControl.***Object**—an object that contains a reference to the *INetControl* object.
- *INetControl.***Parent**—an object that contains a reference to the **Form, Frame,** or other container that contains this control.

- *INetControl*.**Password**—a **String** containing the user's password to the Internet server. If empty, then a dialog box will display to prompt the user for the password.
- *INetControl*.**Protocol**—an **Integer** value (see Table M-66) containing the Internet protocol to use for the transfer. Changing this property will also change the **URL** property.

Protocol Name	Value	Description
icUnknown	0	Unknown protocol
icDefault	1	Default protocol
icFTP	2	File Transfer Protocol
icReserved	3	Reserved for future use
icHTTP	4	HyperText Transfer Protocol
icHTTPS	5	Secure HTTP

Table M-66: **Protocol** *values.*

- *INetControl*.**Proxy**—a **String** containing the name of the proxy server, when the **AccessType** property is set to *icNamedProxy*.
- *INetControl*.**RemoteHost**—a **String** value containing the hostname or IP address of the remote computer. Changing this property will also change the **URL** property.
- *INetControl*.**RemotePort**—a **Long** value containing the remote port on the remote system. The default value for FTP is 21, and 80 for HTTP transfers.
- *INetControl*.**RequestTimeout**—a **Long** value containing the number of seconds allowed after a request was submitted and when a timeout will occur. If the **OpenURL** method was used, an error will occur. If the **Execute** method was used, the **StateChanged** event will occur.
- *INetControl*.**ResponseCode**—a **Long** value containing the response code from the remote host. This is viewed in the **StateChanged** event when *state* is *icError* (11).
- *INetControl*.**ResponseInfo**—a **String** value containing the text response from the remote host. This is viewed in the **StateChanged** event when *state* is *icError* (11).
- *INetControl*.**StillExecuting**—a **Boolean** value when **True** means that the control is busy performing an operation and is unable to process other requests.
- *INetControl*.**Tag**—a **String** that can hold programmer specific information. This property is not used by Visual Basic.
- *INetControl*.**URL**—a **String** value specifying the remote host, and remote directory or document to return.

> **Warning**
>
> Setting the **URL** property will set the **UserName** and **Password** properties to empty strings, so you will need to reset these properties each time you change URLs.

- *INetControl*.**UserName**—a **String** containing the user's name for the mail server. If empty and if the **LogonUI** is **True**, then a dialog box will display to prompt the user for their name and password.

Microsoft Internet Transfer Control

Methods   *INetControl.***Cancel**

> Usage   This method terminates any current processing and closes the connection to the remote system.

*INetControl.***Execute** [*url* [, *operation* [, *data* [, *headers*]]]]

> Usage   This method begins a transfer operation. The **StateChanged** event tracks the progress of the operation.
>
> Arguments
> - *url*—a **String** containing the URL value to use. If not specified, the value from the **URL** property will be used.
> - *operation*—a **String** (see Tables M-67 and M-68) containing the function to execute.

FTP operation	Comments
CD *dir*	Change current directory to *dir*.
CDUP	Change current directory to the parent directory.
CLOSE	End the FTP session.
DELETE *file*	Delete *file*.
DIR [*dir*]	Use **GetChunk** to retrieve files contained in *dir*. Wildcards are also permitted. If *dir* is omitted, the files in the current directory are returned.
GET *file1 file2*	Retrieve remote file *file1* as local file *file2*.
LS [*dir*]	Use **GetChunk** to retrieve files contained in *dir*. Wildcards are also permitted. If *dir* is omitted, the files in the current directory are returned.
MKDIR *dir*	Create a new remote directory called *dir*.
PUT *file1 file2*	Send local file *file1* to remote file *file2*.
PWD	Use **GetChunk** to retrieve the name of the current directory.
QUIT	End the FTP session.
RECV *file1 file2*	Save as GET.
RENAME *file1 file2*	Change the name of *file1* to *file2*.
RMDIR *dir*	Delete the remote directory called *dir*.
SEND *file1 file2*	Same as PUT.
SIZE *dir*	Returns the size of the remote directory *dir*.

Table M-67: FTP operation *values.*

HTTP operation	Comments
GET	Retrieve data from remote web server.
HEAD	Send the request headers.
POST	Posts data contained in *data* argument to the web server.
PUT	Put new web page to the web server. The name of the page to replace is contained in the *data* argument.

Table M-68: HTTP operation *values.*

- *data*—a **String** specifies data to use in various operations. The exact meaning depends on the operation performed.
- *headers*—a **String** specifies additional header values. This string consists of a series of standard Internet headers separated by a carriage return and line feed. Each header consists of a keyword, followed by a colon (":"), and its value.

value = INetControl.GetChunk size [, datatype]

Usage   This method returns data from the server when the **Execute** method is used.

Arguments
- *value*—a **Variant** (either a **String** or **Byte Array**) containing data retrieved from the server.
- *url*—a **String** containing the URL value to retrieve.
- *datatype*—an **Integer** value (see Table M-69) specifying the type of data to return.

datatype Name	Value	Description
icString	0	Return a String value (default).
icByteArray	1	Return a **Byte Array** value.

Table M-69: datatype values.

value = INetControl.GetHeader [header]

Usage   This method returns information for the requested header from a web server.

Arguments
- *value*—a **String** containing data retrieved from the server.
- *header*—a **String** value containing the name of the header to retrieve. If omitted, all headers will be retrieved.

value = INetControl.OpenURL url [, datatype]

Usage   This method performs an **Execute** and a **GetChunk** in a single function.

Arguments
- *value*—a **Variant** (either a **String** or **Byte Array**) containing data retrieved from the server.
- *size*—a **Long** value containing the number of bytes to retrieve.
- *datatype*—an **Integer** value (see Table M-70) specifying the type of data to return.

datatype Name	Value	Description
icString	0	Return a String value (default).
icByteArray	1	Return a Byte Array value.

Table M-70: datatype values.

Microsoft Internet Transfer Control • **543**

Events   **Private Sub *MaskedEditControl*_StateChanged ([*index* As Integer ,] ByVal *state* As Integer)**

Usage   This event is called whenever there is a change in the control's state.

Arguments
- *index*—an **Integer** that uniquely identifies a control in a control array. This argument is not present if the control is not part of a control array.
- *state*—an **Integer** value (see Table M-71) containing the current state of the control.

state Name	Value	Description
icNone	0	No state information.
icHostResolvingHost	1	Looking up the IP address for the specified remote server name.
icHostResolved	2	Found the IP address.
icConnecting	3	Connecting to the remote server.
icConnected	4	Connected to the remote server.
icRequesting	5	Requesting information from the remote server.
icRequestSent	6	The request was successfully sent to the remote server.
icReceivingResponse	7	Receiving a response from the remote server.
icResponseReceived	8	Received a response from the remote server.
icDisconnecting	9	Disconnecting from the host computer.
icDisconnected	10	Disconnected from the host computer.
icError	11	An error was detected.
icResponseCompleted	12	Request was completed, all data received.

Table M-71: *state values.*

Examples
```
Private Sub Command1_Click()
Text3.Text = Inet1.OpenURL(Text1.Text)
End Sub

Private Sub Inet1_StateChanged(ByVal State As Integer)
Text2.Text = Text2.Text & "Current status: " & Format(State) & vbCrLf
End Sub
```

This program uses the **OpenURL** method to retrieve the contents from the server specified by the URL in the Text1 text box. As the process is running, the **StateChanged** event records all of the various state changes in Text2 text box.

See Also   **MAPIMessages** (control), **MAPISession** (control)

Mid

FUNCTION

CCE, LE, PE, EE

Syntax   `result = Mid[$] ( string , start, [ length ] )`

Usage   The **Mid** function returns the specified number of characters from *string* starting with the character at location *start*. The dollar sign ($) is optional and indicates that the return value is a **String** rather than a **Variant**.

Arguments
- *result*—a **String** value or a **Variant** containing a **String** value containing the result of the **Mid** function.
- *string*—a **String** value from which the characters are to be extracted.
- *start*—a **Long** value containing the starting position within *string*.
- *length*—a **Long** value containing the number of characters to return. If omitted, the rest of the characters in the string will be copied.

Examples
```
Private Sub Command1_Click()
Dim s As String
s = "**************************"
Mid(s, 3, 3) = Mid(Text1.Text, 3, 3)
Text2.Text = s
End Sub
```

This routine extracts three characters, starting with the third character from the Text1 text box and places it into the string starting with s's third character. Then the s string is copied into the Text2 text box.

See Also   **Byte** (data type), **LeftB** (function), **Mid** (statement), **MidB** (function), **MidB** (statement), **Right** (function), **RightB** (function), **String** (data type)

Mid

STATEMENT

CCE, LE, PE, EE

Syntax   `Mid[$] ( string , start, [ length ] ) = value`

Usage   The **Mid** statement replaces the specified number of characters in *string* starting with the character at location *start*. The dollar sign ($) is optional and indicates that the return value is a **String** rather than a **Variant**.

Arguments
- *string*—a **String** variable into which the characters will be copied.
- *start*—a **Long** value containing the starting position within *string*.
- *length*—a **Long** value containing the number of characters to replace. If omitted, all of the characters in *value* will replace the characters in *string*.
- *value*—a **String** value or a **Variant** containing a **String** value containing the characters to copy into *string*.

Examples
```
Private Sub Command1_Click()
    Dim s As String
    s = "**************************"
    Mid(s, 3, 3) = Mid(Text1.Text, 3, 3)
    Text2.Text = s
End Sub
```

This routine extracts three characters, starting with the third character from the Text1 text box and places it into the string starting with s's third character. Then the s string is copied into the Text2 text box.

See Also **Byte** (data type), **LeftB** (function), **Mid** (function), **MidB** (function), **MidB** (statement), **Right** (function), **RightB** (function), **String** (data type)

MidB

FUNCTION

CCE, LE, PE, EE

Syntax *result* = **MidB[$]** (*string* , *start*, [*length*])

Usage The **MidB** function returns the specified number of bytes from *string* starting with the byte at location *start*. The dollar sign ($) is optional and indicates that the return value is a **String** rather than a **Variant**.

Arguments
- *result*—a **String** value or a **Variant** containing a **String** value containing the result of the **MidB** function.
- *string*—a **String** value from which the bytes are to be extracted.
- *start*—a **Long** value containing the starting position within *string*.
- *length*—a **Long** value containing the number of bytes to return. If omitted, the rest of the bytes in the string will be copied.

See Also **Byte** (data type), **LeftB** (function), **Mid** (function), **Mid** (statement), **MidB** (statement), **Right** (function), **RightB** (function), **String** (data type)

MidB

STATEMENT

CCE, LE, PE, EE

Syntax **MidB[$]** (*string* , *start*, [*length*]) = *value*

Usage The **MidB** statement replaces the specified number of bytes in *string* starting with the byte at location *start*. The dollar sign ($) is optional and indicates that the return value is a **String** rather than a **Variant**.

Arguments
- *string*—a **String** variable into which the bytes will be copied.
- *start*—a **Long** value containing the starting position within *string*.

- *length*—a **Long** value containing the number of bytes to replace. If omitted, all of the bytes in *value* will replace the corresponding bytes in *string*.
- *value*—a **String** value or a **Variant** containing a **String** value containing the bytes to copy into *string*.

See Also **Byte** (data type), **LeftB** (function), **Mid** (function), **Mid** (statement), **MidB** (function), **Right** (function), **RightB** (function), **String** (data type)

Minute   FUNCTION
CCE, LE, PE, EE

Syntax `MValue = Minute ( Time )`

Usage The **Minute** function returns the minute of the hour from a numeric, **Date**, or **String** variable containing a valid date or time. If only a date is supplied, this function will always return 0.

Arguments
- *MValue*—an **Integer** value in the range of 0 to 59.
- *Time*—a **Date**, **Long**, or **String** value that contains a valid time or date.

Examples
```
Private Sub Command1_Click()
If IsDate(Text1.Text) Then
    Text2.Text = Minute(Text1.Text)
Else
    Text2.Text = "Illegal time:"
End If
End Sub
```

This routine verifies that the date or time in the Text1 text box is valid and then extracts the minute value from the text box.

See Also **CDate** (function), **Date** (data type), **Day** (function), **Hour** (function), **IsDate** (function), **Now** (function), **Second** (function), **Time** (function), **Time** (statement)

MIRR   FUNCTION
CCE, LE, PE, EE

Syntax `DValue = MIRR ( vals() , FinanceRate, ReinvestRate )`

Usage The **MIRR** function returns a **Double** value that contains the modified internal rate of return for a stream of payments and receipts.

Arguments
- *DValue*—a **Double** value containing the modified internal rate of return.
- *vals()*—an array of **Double** containing the cash flow. Cash receipts are represented by positive numbers and cash payments are represented by negative numbers.
- *FinanceRate*—a **Double** containing the interest rate for cost of money.
- *ReinvestRate*—a **Double** containing the interest rate for cash reinvestment.

MkDir • 547

Examples
```
Private Sub Command1_Click()
Dim v(12) As Double
v(0) = -1000
For i = 1 To 12
    v(i) = 100
Next i
MsgBox Format(MIRR(v, 0.015, 0.005), "percent")
End Sub
```

This routine computes an internal rate of return based on a single cash payment of $1,000 followed by 12 receipts of $100. It assumes a cost of money rate of 18 percent/year (1.5%/month) and a cash reinvestment rate of 6 percent (.5%/month).

See Also DDB (function), FV (function), IPmt (function), IRR (function), NPer (function), NPV (function), PMT (function), PPmt (function), PV (function), Rate (function), SLN (function), SYD (function)

MkDir

STATEMENT

CCE, LE, PE, EE

Syntax **MkDir** *path*

Usage The **MkDir** statement creates a new directory.
If the directory path in *path* is not valid, a Run-time error '76' path not found will display.

> **Tip**
>
> *To prevent run-time errors, use the **On Error** statement to prevent the error from stopping the program, and test the **Err** object to see if an error occurred.*

Arguments *path*—a **String** expression that contains the new directory.

Examples
```
Private Sub Command1_Click()
On Error Resume Next
If Len(Text1.Text) > 0 Then
    MkDir Text1.Text
End If
If Err.Number = 0 Then
    Text2.Text = "Directory created"
Else
    Text2.Text = Err.Description
End If
End Sub
```

This routine uses the **MkDir** function to create a new directory as specified in Text1.Text. I then check the **Err** object to see if an error occurred and display either the error information or a message saying the new directory was created.

See Also **ChDir** (statement), **ChDrive** (function), **Common Dialog** (control), **CurDir** (function), **Dir** (function), **DirListBox** (control), **DriveListBox** (control), **FileListBox** (control), **RmDir** (statement)

Month

FUNCTION

CCE, LE, PE, EE

Syntax *MValue* = **Month** (*date*)

Usage The **Month** function returns the month of the year from a numeric, **Date**, or **String** variable containing a valid date or time. If only a time is supplied, this function will always return 12.

Arguments
- *MValue*—an **Integer** value in the range of 1 to 12.
- *date*—a **Date**, **Long**, or **String** value that contains a valid time or date.

Examples
```
Private Sub Command1_Click()
If IsDate(Text1.Text) Then
    Text2.Text = Month(Text1.Text)
Else
    Text2.Text = "Illegal date:"
End If
End Sub
```

This routine verifies that the date or time in the Text1 text box is valid and then extracts the month value from the text box.

See Also **CDate** (function), **Date** (data type), **Day** (function), **Hour** (function), **IsDate** (function), **Now** (function), **Second** (function), **Time** (function), **Time** (statement)

MSChart

CONTROL

CCE, LE, PE, EE

Usage The **MSChart** control includes the ability to display advanced charts in a Visual Basic program.

Properties
- *MSChartControl*.**ActiveSeriesCount**—an **Integer** containing the number of series on the chart.
- *MSChartControl*.**AllowDithering**—a **Boolean** value when **True** means that color dithering is permitted. **False** means that the control's color palette is used.
- *MSChartControl*.**AllowDynamicRotation**—a **Boolean** when **True** means that the user can rotate the chart interactively. **False** means that the user can't rotate the chart.
- *MSChartControl*.**AllowSelections**—a **Boolean** when **True** means that the user can select chart objects interactively. **False** means that the user can't select chart objects.
- *MSChartControl*.**AllowSeriesSelection**—a **Boolean** when **True** means that the user can select a series by clicking a data point. **False** means that clicking a data point, selects only the data point.
- *MSChartControl*.**Backdrop**—a reference to a **Backdrop** object containing the shadow, picture, or pattern displayed behind the chart.
- *MSChartControl*.**BorderStyle**—an **Integer** value (see Table M-72) specifying how the border will be drawn.

MSChart

BorderStyle Name	Value	Description
vbBSNone	0	No border displays.
vbFixedSingle	1	Single line around the control.

Table M-72: **BorderStyle** values.

- *MSChartControl*.**Chart3d**—a **Boolean** when **True** means that the chart will display as a three dimensional chart. **False** means that the chart will display as a two dimensional chart.
- *MSChartControl*.**ChartData**—a two dimensional **Variant** array containing the data to display as the chart.
- *MSChartControl*.**ChartType**—an **Integer** value (see Table M-73) that describes the type of chart displayed.

ChartType Name	Description
vtChChartType3dBar	Three dimensional bar chart
vtChChartType2dBar	Two dimensional bar chart
vtChChartType3dLine	Three dimensional line chart
vtChChartType2dLine	Two dimensional line chart
vtChChartType3dArea	Three dimensional area chart
vtChChartType2dArea	Two dimensional area chart
vtChChartType3dStep	Three dimensional step chart
vtChChartType2dStep	Two dimensional step chart
vtChChartType3dCombination	Three dimensional combination chart
vtChChartType2dCombination	Two dimensional combination chart
vtChChartType2dPie	Two dimensional pie chart
vtChChartType2dXY	Two dimensional XY chart

Table M-73: **ChartType** values.

- *MSChartControl*.**Column**—an **Integer** containing the current data column.
- *MSChartControl*.**ColumnCount**—an **Integer** containing the number of data columns.
- *MSChartControl*.**ColumnLabel**—a **String** containing the text displayed in a column label.
- *MSChartControl*.**ColumnLabelCount**—an **Integer** containing the number of column label levels. The bottom most level is 1, and levels are added or subtracted from the top.
- *MSChartControl*.**ColumnLabelIndex**—an **Integer** indicating the current column label displayed in the **ColumnLabel** property. This property can range in value from 1 to **ColumnLabelCount**.
- *MSChartControl*.**Container**—an object that sets or returns the container of the control at run time. This property cannot be set at design time.
- *MSChartControl*.**Data**—an **Integer** containing the current data point value.
- *MSChartControl*.**DataBindings**—a reference to a **DataBindings** collection containing information about multiple properties that are bound to a database.
- *MSChartControl*.**DataGrid**—a reference to a **DataGrid** object containing the data for the chart.
- *MSChartControl*.**DoSetCursor**—a **Boolean** value when **True** means that the application can control the mouse pointer appearance. **False** means that the application can't control the appearance of the mouse pointer.

- *MSChartControl.***DragIcon**—an object that contains the picture value of an icon. At design time, you can specify an icon file that has a file type of .ICO.

> **Tip**
>
> *This value can be created by copying the value from another control's* **DragIcon** *value, a form's icon, or by using the* **LoadPicture** *function.*

- *MSChartControl.***DragMode**—an **Integer** specifying how the control will respond to a drag request.

> **Tip**
>
> *Setting* **DragMode** *to vbAutomatic will automatically begin a drag operation when the user clicks on the control. However, the control will not respond to the usual mouse events (***Click***,* ***DblClick***,* ***MouseDown***,* ***MouseMove***,* ***MouseUp***).*

DragMode Name	Value	Description
vbManual	0	The Drag method must be used to begin a drag-and-drop operation (default value).
vbAutomatic	1	The source control will automatically begin a drag-and-drop operation when the user clicks on the control.

Table M-74: **DragMode** *values.*

- *MSChartControl.***DrawMode**—an **Integer** specifying how the chart is repainted (see Table M-75).

DrawMode Name	Value	Description
vtChDrawModeDraw	0	The control will draw directly to the display device.
vtChDrawModeBlit	1	The control will draw to an internal bitmap and then copy it to the display device.

Table M-75: **DrawMode** *values.*

- *MSChartControl.***Enabled**—a **Boolean** value when **True** means that the control will respond to events. When **False**, the control will not respond to events.
- *MSChartControl.***Footnote**—a reference to a **Footnote** object containing information about the display and placement of the footnote.
- *MSChartControl.***FootnoteText**—a **String** containing the text that will display in the footnote.
- *MSChartControl.***Height**—a **Single** that contains the height of the control.
- *MSChartControl.***HelpContextID**—a **Long** that contains a help file context ID number which references an entry in the help file. When the user presses the F1 key while this control is active, the corresponding entry in the help file will automatically display. A value of zero means that no context number was specified.

MSChart • 551

> **Tip**
>
> *A help file must be compiled using the Windows Help Compiler available in the Professional and Enterprise editions of Visual Basic.*

- *MSChartControl*.**hWnd**—a **Long** that contains a Windows handle to the control.

> **Tip**
>
> *The **hWnd** property is most useful when making calls to Windows API functions. Since this value can change during execution, do not save the value into a variable for later use.*

- *MSChartControl*.**Index**—an **Integer** that uniquely identifies a control in a control array.
- *MSChartControl*.**LabelLevelCount**—an **Integer** containing the number of levels of labels for an axis.
- *MSChartControl*.**Left**—a **Single** that contains the distance measured in twips between the left edge of the control and the left edge of the control's container.
- *MSChartControl*.**Legend**—a reference to a **Legend** object containing information about how the chart's legend is placed and displayed.
- *MSChartControl*.**MousePointer**—an **Integer** value (see Table M-76) that contains the value of the cursor that should display when the cursor is moved over this control. Use *vbCustom* to display the custom icon stored in the **MouseIcon** property.

MousePointer Name	Description
vtMousePointerArrow	Arrow
vtMousePointerArrowHourglass	An arrow and an Hourglass
vtMousePointerArrowQuestion	An arrow and a question mark
vtMousePointerCross	Crosshair
vtMousePointerDefault	Shape determined by the the **MSChart** control (default value)
vtMousePointerHourglass	Hourglass
vtMousePointerIbeam	I beam
vtMousePointerIcon	Square inside a square
vtMousePointerNoDrop	No Drop
vtMousePointerSize	Four sided arrow (north, south, east, west)
vtMousePointerSizeAll	Size all
vtMousePointerNESW	Two sided arrow (northeast, southwest)
vtMousePointerNS	Two sided arrow (north, south)
vtMousePointerNWSE	Two sided arrow (northwest, southeast)
vtMousePointerWE	Two sided arrow (west, east)
vtMousePointerUpArrow	Single sided arrow pointing north

Table M-76: MousePointer *values.*

- *MSChartControl*.**Name**—a **String** that contains the name of the control that will reference the control in a Visual Basic program. This property is read only at run time.
- *MSChartControl*.**Object**—an object that contains a reference to the **MSChart** control.

- *MSChartControl*.**Parent**—an object that contains a reference to the **Form, Frame,** or other container that contains this control.
- *MSChartControl*.**Plot**—an object reference to a **Plot** object containing information about the chart's display area.
- *MSChartControl*.**RamdomFill**—a **Boolean** value when **True** means that random data is generated to draw the chart. **False** means that the data is taken from the **DataGrid** object.

Tip

*Set **RandomFill** to **True** to display sample charts in different formats.*

- *MSChartControl*.**Repaint**—a **Boolean** value when **True** means that the chart is redrawn each time a change is made. **False** means that it is not redrawn each time a change is made.

Tip

*Set **Repaint** to **False** while making multiple changes to the chart to improve performance.*

- *MSChartControl*.**Row**—an **Integer** containing the current data row.
- *MSChartControl*.**RowCount**—an **Integer** containing the number of data rows.
- *MSChartControl*.**RowLabel**—a **String** containing the text displayed in a row label.
- *MSChartControl*.**RowLabelCount**—an **Integer** containing the number of column label levels. The bottom most level is 1, and levels are added or subtracted from the top.
- *MSChartControl*.**RowLabelIndex**—an **Integer** indicating the current column label displayed in the **RowLabel** property. This property can range in value from 1 to **RowLabelCount**.
- *MSChartControl*.**SeriesColumn**—an **Integer** containing the current column position for the current series. If two series have the same **SeriesColumn** position then the values will be stacked.
- *MSChartControl*.**SeriesType**—an **Integer** value (see Table M-77) containing the method to describe the current series as specified by the **Column** property.

SeriesType Name	Description
vtChSeriesType3dBar	Three dimensional bar chart
vtChSeriesType2dBar	Two dimensional bar chart
vtChSeriesType3dLine	Three dimensional line chart
vtChSeriesType2dLine	Two dimensional line chart
vtChSeriesType3dArea	Three dimensional area chart
vtChSeriesType2dArea	Two dimensional area chart
vtChSeriesType3dStep	Three dimensional step chart
vtChSeriesType2dStep	Two dimensional step chart
vtChSeriesType3dCombination	Three dimensional combination chart
vtChSeriesType2dCombination	Two dimensional combination chart
vtChSeriesType2dPie	Two dimensional pie chart
vtChSeriesType2dXY	Two dimensional XY chart

Table M-77: **SeriesType** *values.*

- *MSChartControl*.**ShowLegend**—a **Boolean** value when **True** means that the legend will be shown on the chart. **False** means that the legend will not be shown.
- *MSChartControl*.**Stacking**—a **Boolean** value when **True** means that all chart series will be stacked. **False** means that chart values will not be stacked.
- *MSChartControl*.**TabIndex**—an Integer that determines the order that a user will tab through the objects on a form.
- *MSChartControl*.**TabStop**—a **Boolean** value when **True** means that the user can tab to this object. When **False** means that this control will be skipped to the next control in the **TabIndex** order.
- *MSChartControl*.**Tag**—a **String** that can hold programmer specific information. This property is not used by Visual Basic.
- *MSChartControl*.**TextLengthType**—an **Integer** value (see Table M-78) describing how the text will appear on the chart.

TextLengthType Name	Description
vtTextLengthTypeVirtual	This value is optimized for printing. The text on the display may vary from what was requested and may not fit in the requested space. Some clipping of text may occur.
vtTextLengthTypeDevice	This value is optimized for screen display. The printed text size may vary from what was requested, and the text may appear in a slightly different space.

Table M-78: **TextLengthType** values.

- *MSChartControl*.**Title**—a reference to a **Title** object containing information about the layout and placement of the chart's title.
- *MSChartControl*.**TitleText**—a **String** containing the chart's title.
- *MSChartControl*.**ToolTipText**—a **String** that holds a text value that can be displayed as a **ToolTip** box that displays whenever the cursor is held over the control for about one second.
- *MSChartControl*.**Top**—a **Single** that contains the distance measured in twips between the top edge of the control and the top edge of the control's container.
- *MSChartControl*.**Visible**—a **Boolean** value when **True** means that the control is visible. When **False** means that the control is not visible.

Tip

This property hides the control until the program is ready to display it.

- *MSChartControl*.**WhatsThisHelpID**—a **Long** that contains a help file context ID number that references an entry in the help file. This provides a What's This PopUp help display in response to the What's This button in the upper right corner of the window.
- *MSChartControl*.**Width**—a **Single** that contains the width of the control.

Methods

MSChartControl.About

Usage This method displays an About Box for this control.

MSChartControl.Drag [DragAction]

Usage This method begins, ends, or cancels a drag operation.

Arguments - *DragAction*—an **Integer** that contains a value selected from Table M-79.

DragAction Name	Value	Description
vbCancel	0	Cancels any drag operation in progress.
vbBeginDrag	1	Begins a drag operation (default).
vbEndDrag	2	Ends a drag operation and drops *object*.

Table M-79: DragAction *values*.

MSChartControl.EditCopy

Usage This method copies the current chart to the Windows clipboard using the metafile format.

MSChartControl.EditPaste

Usage This method pastes the value from the Windows clipboard onto the currently selected chart element.

MSChartControl.GetSelectedPart *parttype, index1, index2, index3, index4*

Usage This method returns the currently selected part of the chart.

Arguments - *parttype*—an **Integer** value (see Table M-80) containing the part that was selected.

parttype Name	Description
vtChPartTypeChart	The entire chart was selected.
vtChPartTypeTitle	The chart's title was selected.
vtChParTypetFootnote	The chart's footnote was selected.
vtChPartTypeLegend	The chart's legend was selected.
vtChPartTypePlot	The chart's plot area was selected.
vtChPartTypeSeries	A data series was selected from the chart.
vtChPartTypePoint	A data point was selected from the chart.
vtChPartTypePointLabel	A data point label was selected from the chart.
vtChPartTypeAxis	An axis was selected from the chart.
vtChPartTypeAxisLabel	An axis label was selected from the chart.
vtChPartTypeAxisTitle	An axis title was selected from the chart.

Table M-80: parttype *values*.

- *index1*—an **Integer** that contains additional information about the selected part. If *parttype* is *vtChPartTypeSeries* or *vtChPartTypeDataPoint* then this value contains the series number. If *parttype* is *vtChPartTypeAxis* or *vtChPartTypeAxisLabel* then this value contains *vtChAxisIdX* (X-axis), *vtChAxisIdY* (Y-axis), *vtChAxisIdY2* (secondary Y-axis), or *vtChAxisIdZ* (Z-axis).
- *index2*—an **Integer** that contains additional information about the selected part. If *parttype* is *vtChPartTypeDataPoint* then this value contains the data point for the series identified in *index1*.
- *index3*—an **Integer** that contains additional information about the selected part of the chart. If *parttype* is *vtChPartTypeAxisLabel* then this value contains the level of the axis label.
- *index4*—an **Integer** that contains additional information about the selected part of the chart (currently unused).

MSChartControl.Layout

Usage — This method lays out a chart and recomputes any automatic values, such as the min and max values for each axis.

MSChartControl.Move *Left* [, *Top* [, *Width* [, *Height*]]]

Usage — This method changes the position and the size of the **MSChart** control. The **ScaleMode** of the **Form** or other container object that holds the **MSChart** control will determine the units used to specify the coordinates.

Arguments
- *Left*—a **Single** that specifies the new position of the left edge of the control.
- *Top*—a **Single** that specifies the new position of the top edge of the control.
- *Width*—a **Single** that specifies the new width of the control.
- *Height*—a **Single** that specifies the new height of the control.

MSChartControl.Refresh

Usage — This method redraws the contents of the control.

MSChartControl.SelectPart *parttype, index1, index2, index3, index4*

Usage — This method selects an element of the chart.

Arguments
- *parttype*—an **Integer** value (see Table M-81) containing the part that was selected.

parttype Name	Description
vtChPartTypeChart	The entire chart was selected.
vtChPartTypeTitle	The chart's title was selected.
vtChPartTypeFootnote	The chart's footnote was selected.
vtChPartTypeLegend	The chart's legend was selected.

parttype Name	Description
vtChPartTypePlot	The chart's plot area was selected.
vtChPartTypeSeries	A data series was selected from the chart.
vtChPartTypePoint	A data point was selected from the chart.
vtChPartTypePointLabel	A data point label was selected from the chart.
vtChPartTypeAxis	An axis was selected from the chart.
vtChPartTypeAxisLabel	An axis label was selected from the chart.
vtChPartTypeAxisTitle	An axis title was selected from the chart.

Table M-81: parttype values.

- *index1*—an **Integer** that contains additional information about the selected part. If *parttype* is *vtChPartTypeSeries* or *vtChPartTypeDataPoint* then this value contains the series number. If *parttype* is *vtChPartTypeAxis* or *vtChPartTypeAxisLabel* then this value contains *vtChAxisIdX* (X-axis), *vtChAxisIdY* (Y-axis), *vtChAxisIdY2* (secondary Y-axis), or *vtChAxisIdZ* (Z-axis).

- *index2*—an **Integer** that contains additional information about the selected part. If *parttype* is *vtChPartTypeDataPoint* then this value contains the data point for the series identified in *index1*.

- *index3*—an **Integer** that contains additional information about the selected part of the chart. If *parttype* is *vtChPartTypeAxisLabel* then this value contains the level of the axis label.

- *index4*—an **Integer** that contains additional information about the selected part of the chart (currently unused).

MSChartControl.SetFocus

Usage   This method transfers the focus from the form or control that currently has the focus to this control. To receive the focus, this control must be enabled and visible.

MSChartControl.ShowWhatsThis

Usage   This method displays the ShowWhatsThis help information for this control.

MSChartControl.ToDefaults

Usage   This method resets the chart to its default values.

MSChartControl.TwipsToChartPart x, y, parttype, index1, index2, index3, index4

Usage   This method identifies the part of the chart at location *x, y*.

Arguments
- *x*—a **Long** containing the X-location in twips.
- *y*—a **Long** containing the Y-location in twips.
- *parttype*—an **Integer** value (see Table M-82) containing the part that was selected.

parttype Name	Description
vtChPartTypeChart	The entire chart was selected.
vtChPartTypeTitle	The chart's title was selected.
vtChPartTypeFootnote	The chart's footnote was selected.
vtChPartTypeLegend	The chart's legend was selected.
vtChPartTypePlot	The chart's plot area was selected.
vtChPartTypeSeries	A data series was selected from the chart.
vtChPartTypePoint	A data point was selected from the chart.
vtChPartTypePointLabel	A data point label was selected from the chart.
vtChPartTypeAxis	An axis was selected from the chart.
vtChPartTypeAxisLabel	An axis label was selected from the chart.
vtChPartTypeAxisTitle	An axis title was selected from the chart.

Table M-82: parttype *values*.

- *index1*—an **Integer** that contains additional information about the selected part. If *parttype* is *vtChPartTypeSeries* or *vtChPartTypeDataPoint* then this value contains the series number. If *parttype* is *vtChPartTypeAxis* or *vtChPartTypeAxisLabel* then this value contains an *axisId*.
- *index2*—an **Integer** that contains additional information about the selected part. If *parttype* is *vtChPartTypeDataPoint* then this value contains the data point for the series identified in *index1*.
- *index3*—an **Integer** that contains additional information about the selected part of the chart. If *parttype* is *vtChPartTypeAxisLabel* then this value contains the level of the axis label.
- *index4*—an **Integer** that contains additional information about the selected part of the chart (currently unused).

MSChartControl.ZOrder [position]

Usage — This method specifies the position of the **MSChart** control relative to the other objects on the form.

Tip

*Note that there are three layers of objects on a form: the back layer is the drawing space which contains the results of the graphical methods, the middle layer contains graphical objects and **Labels**, and the top layer contains nongraphical controls such as the **MSChart** control. The **ZOrder** method only affects how the objects are arranged within a single layer.*

Arguments — *position*—an **Integer** that specifies the relative position of this object. A value of 0 means that the control is positioned at the head of the list, a value of 1 means that the control will be placed at the end of the list.

Events

Private Sub *MSChartControl*_AxisActivated ([*index* As Integer ,] *axisId* As Integer, *axisIndex* As Integer, *mouseFlag* As Integer, *cancel* As Integer)

Usage This event occurs when a user double-clicks on a chart axis.

Arguments
- *index*—an **Integer** that uniquely identifies a control in a control array. This argument is not present if the control is not part of a control array.
- *axisId*—an **Integer** value (see Table M-83) identifying an axis.

axisId Name	Description
vtChAxisIdX	X-axis
vtChAxisIdY	Y-axis
vtChAxisIdY2	Secondary Y-axis
vtChAxisIdZ	Z-axis

Table M-83: axisId values.

- *axisIndex*—an **Integer** reserved for future use.
- *mouseFlag*—an **Integer** value (see Table M-84) containing which keys were pressed when the user clicked on the axis.

mouseFlag Name	Description
vtChMouseFlagShiftKeyDown	The Shift key was pressed.
vtChMouseFlagControlKeyDown	The Ctrl key was pressed.

Table M-84: mouseFlag values.

- *cancel*—an **Integer** reserved for future use.

Private Sub *MSChartControl*_AxisLabelActivated ([*index* As Integer ,] *axisId* As Integer, *axisIndex* As Integer, *labelSetIndex* As Integer, *labelIndex* As Integer, *mouseFlag* As Integer, *cancel* As Integer)

Usage This event occurs when a user double-clicks on a chart axis label.

Arguments
- *index*—an **Integer** that uniquely identifies a control in a control array. This argument is not present if the control is not part of a control array.
- *axisId*—an **Integer** value (see Table M-85) identifying an axis.

axisId Name	Description
vtChAxisIdX	X-axis
vtChAxisIdY	Y-axis
vtChAxisIdY2	Secondary Y-axis
vtChAxisIdZ	Z-axis

Table M-85: axisId values.

- *axisIndex*—an **Integer** reserved for future use.
- *labelSetIndex*—an **Integer** containing the level of the labels on which the user clicked.
- *labelIndex*—an **Integer** reserved for future use.
- *mouseFlag*—an **Integer** value (see Table M-86) containing which keys were pressed when the user clicked on the axis label.

mouseFlag Name	Description
vtChMouseFlagShiftKeyDown	The Shift key was pressed.
vtChMouseFlagControlKeyDown	The Ctrl key was pressed.

Table M-86: mouseFlag values.

- *cancel*—an **Integer** reserved for future use.

Private Sub *MSChartControl*_AxisLabelSelected ([*index* As Integer ,] *axisId* As Integer, *axisIndex* As Integer, *labelSetIndex* As Integer, *labelIndex* As Integer, *mouseFlag* As Integer, *cancel* As Integer)

Usage   This event occurs when an axis label is selected.

Arguments
- *index*—an **Integer** that uniquely identifies a control in a control array. This argument is not present if the control is not part of a control array.
- *axisId*—an **Integer** value (see Table M-87) identifying an axis.

axisId Name	Description
vtChAxisIdX	X-axis
vtChAxisIdY	Y-axis
vtChAxisIdY2	Secondary Y-axis
vtChAxisIdZ	Z-axis

Table M-87: axisId values.

- *axisIndex*—an **Integer** reserved for future use.
- *labelSetIndex*—an **Integer** containing the level of the labels on which the user clicked.
- *labelIndex*—an **Integer** reserved for future use.
- *mouseFlag*—an **Integer** value (see Table M-88) containing which keys were pressed when the user clicked on the axis label.

mouseFlag Name	Description
vtChMouseFlagShiftKeyDown	The Shift key was pressed.
vtChMouseFlagControlKeyDown	The Ctrl key was pressed.

Table M-88: mouseFlag values.

- *cancel*—an **Integer** reserved for future use.

Private Sub *MSChartControl_AxisLabelUpdated* ([*index* As Integer ,] *axisId* As Integer, *axisIndex* As Integer, *labelSetIndex* As Integer, *labelIndex* As Integer, *updateFlag* As Integer)

Usage This event occurs when a chart axis label is changed.

Arguments
- *index*—an **Integer** that uniquely identifies a control in a control array. This argument is not present if the control is not part of a control array.
- *axisId*—an **Integer** value (see Table M-89) identifying an axis.

axisId Name	Description
vtChAxisIdX	X-axis
vtChAxisIdY	Y-axis
vtChAxisIdY2	Secondary Y-axis
vtChAxisIdZ	Z-axis

Table M-89: axisId values.

- *axisIndex*—an **Integer** reserved for future use.
- *labelSetIndex*—an **Integer** containing the level of the labels on which the user clicked.
- *labelIndex*—an **Integer** reserved for future use.
- *updateFlags*—an **Integer** value (see Table M-90) containing information about the update.

updateFlag Name	Description
vtChNoDisplay	The chart display is not changed.
vtChDisplayPlot	The chart plot will be repainted.
vtChLayoutPlot	The chart will be laid out.
vtChDisplayLegend	The chart legend will be repainted.
vtChLayoutLegend	The chart legend will be laid out.
vtChLayoutSeries	The chart series will be laid out.
vtChPositionSection	A chart section or position has been moved or resized.

Table M-90: updateFlag values.

Private Sub *MSChartControl_AxisSelected* ([*index* As Integer ,] *axisId* As Integer, *axisIndex* As Integer, *mouseFlag* As Integer, *cancel* As Integer)

Usage This event occurs when an axis is selected.

Arguments
- *index*—an **Integer** that uniquely identifies a control in a control array. This argument is not present if the control is not part of a control array.
- *axisId*—an **Integer** value (see Table M-91) identifying an axis.

MSChart • 561

axisId Name	Description
vtChAxisIdX	X-axis
vtChAxisIdY	Y-axis
vtChAxisIdY2	Secondary Y-axis
vtChAxisIdZ	Z-axis

Table M-91: axisId values.

- *axisIndex*—an **Integer** reserved for future use.
- *mouseFlag*—an **Integer** value (see Table M-92) containing which keys were pressed when the user clicked on the axis.

mouseFlag Name	Description
vtChMouseFlagShiftKeyDown	The Shift key was pressed.
vtChMouseFlagControlKeyDown	The Ctrl key was pressed.

Table M-92: mouseFlag values.

- *cancel*—an **Integer** reserved for future use.

Private Sub *MSChartControl*_AxisTitleActivated ([*index* As Integer ,] *axisId* As Integer, *axisIndex* As Integer, *mouseFlag* As Integer, *cancel* As Integer)

Usage This event occurs when a user double-clicks on an axis title.

Arguments
- *index*—an **Integer** that uniquely identifies a control in a control array. This argument is not present if the control is not part of a control array.
- *axisId*—an **Integer** value (see Table M-93) identifying an axis.

axisId Name	Description
vtChAxisIdX	X-axis
vtChAxisIdY	Y-axis
vtChAxisIdY2	Secondary Y-axis
vtChAxisIdZ	Z-axis

Table M-93: axisId values.

- *axisIndex*—an **Integer** reserved for future use.
- *mouseFlag*—an **Integer** value (see Table M-94) containing which keys were pressed when the user clicked on the axis title.

mouseFlag Name	Description
vtChMouseFlagShiftKeyDown	The Shift key was pressed.
vtChMouseFlagControlKeyDown	The Ctrl key was pressed.

Table M-94: mouseFlag values.

- *cancel*—an **Integer** reserved for future use.

Private Sub *MSChartControl_AxisTitleSelected* ([*index* As Integer ,] *axisId* As Integer, *axisIndex* As Integer, *mouseFlag* As Integer, *cancel* As Integer)

Usage   This event occurs when an axis title is selected.

Arguments
- *index*—an **Integer** that uniquely identifies a control in a control array. This argument is not present if the control is not part of a control array.
- *axisId*—an **Integer** value (see Table M-95) identifying an axis.

axisId Name	Description
vtChAxisIdX	X-axis
vtChAxisIdY	Y-axis.
vtChAxisIdY2	Secondary Y-axis
vtChAxisId	Z-axis

Table M-95: axisId values.

- *axisIndex*—an **Integer** reserved for future use.
- *mouseFlag*—an **Integer** value (see Table M-96) containing which keys were pressed when the user clicked on the axis title.

mouseFlag Name	Description
vtChMouseFlagShiftKeyDown	The Shift key was pressed.
vtChMouseFlagControlKeyDown	The Ctrl key was pressed.

Table M-96: mouseFlag values.

- *cancel*—an **Integer** reserved for future use.

Private Sub *MSChartControl_AxisTitleUpdated* ([*index* As Integer ,] *axisId* As Integer, *axisIndex* As Integer, *updateFlag* As Integer)

Usage   This event occurs when an axis title is updated.

Arguments
- *index*—an **Integer** that uniquely identifies a control in a control array. This argument is not present if the control is not part of a control array.
- *axisId*—an **Integer** value (see Table M-97) identifying an axis.

axisId Name	Description
vtChAxisIdX	X-axis
vtChAxisIdY	Y-axis
vtChAxisIdY2	Secondary Y-axis
vtChAxisIdZ	Z-axis

Table M-97: axisId values.

- *axisIndex*—an **Integer** reserved for future use.
- *updateFlags*—an **Integer** value (see Table M-98) containing information about the update.

updateFlag Name	Description
vtChNoDisplay	The chart display is not changed.
vtChDisplayPlot	The chart plot will be repainted.
vtChLayoutPlot	The chart will be laid out.
vtChDisplayLegend	The chart legend will be repainted.
vtChLayoutLegend	The chart legend will be laid out.
vtChLayoutSeries	The chart series will be laid out.
vtChPositionSection	A chart section or position has been moved or resized.

Table M-98: updateFlag values.

Private Sub *MSChartControl*_AxisUpdated ([*index* As Integer ,] *axisId* As Integer, *axisIndex* As Integer, *updateFlag* As Integer)

Usage   This event occurs when an axis is updated.

Arguments
- *index*—an **Integer** that uniquely identifies a control in a control array. This argument is not present if the control is not part of a control array.
- *axisId*—an **Integer** value (see Table M-99) identifying an axis.

axisId Name	Description
vtChAxisIdX	X-axis
vtChAxisIdY	Y-axis
vtChAxisIdY2	Secondary Y-axis
vtChAxisIdZ	Z-axis

Table M-99: axisId values.

- *axisIndex*—an **Integer** reserved for future use.
- *updateFlags*—an **Integer** value (see Table M-100) containing information about the update.

updateFlag Name	Description
vtChNoDisplay	The chart display is not changed.
vtChDisplayPlot	The chart plot will be repainted.
vtChLayoutPlot	The chart will be laid out.
vtChDisplayLegend	The chart legend will be repainted.
vtChLayoutLegend	The chart legend will be laid out.
vtChLayoutSeries	The chart series will be laid out.
vtChPositionSection	A chart section or position has been moved or resized.

Table M-100: updateFlag values.

Private Sub *MSChartControl*_ChartActivated ([*index* As Integer ,] *mouseFlag* As Integer, *cancel* As Integer)

Usage This event occurs when a user double-clicks on the chart but not on a specific part of the chart.

Arguments
- *index*—an **Integer** that uniquely identifies a control in a control array. This argument is not present if the control is not part of a control array.
- *mouseFlag*—an **Integer** value (see Table M-101) containing which keys were pressed when the user clicked on the chart.

mouseFlag Name	Description
vtChMouseFlagShiftKeyDown	The Shift key was pressed.
vtChMouseFlagControlKeyDown	The Ctrl key was pressed.

Table M-101: mouseFlag values.

- *cancel*—an **Integer** reserved for future use.

Private Sub *MSChartControl*_ChartSelected ([*index* As Integer ,] *cancel* As Integer)

Usage This event occurs when the chart is selected.

Arguments
- *index*—an **Integer** that uniquely identifies a control in a control array. This argument is not present if the control is not part of a control array.
- *mouseFlag*—an **Integer** value (see Table M-102) containing which keys were pressed when the user clicked on the chart.

mouseFlag Name	Description
vtChMouseFlagShiftKeyDown	The Shift key was pressed.
vtChMouseFlagControlKeyDown	The Ctrl key was pressed.

Table M-102: mouseFlag values.

- *cancel*—an **Integer** reserved for future use.

Private Sub *MSChartControl*_ChartUpdated ([*index* As Integer ,] *updateFlag* As Integer)

Usage This event occurs when a chart is updated.

Arguments
- *index*—an **Integer** that uniquely identifies a control in a control array. This argument is not present if the control is not part of a control array.
- *updateFlags*—an **Integer** value (see Table M-103) containing information about the update.

updateFlag Name	Description
vtChNoDisplay	The chart display is not changed.
vtChDisplayPlot	The chart plot will be repainted.
vtChLayoutPlot	The chart will be laid out.
vtChDisplayLegend	The chart legend will be repainted.
vtChLayoutLegend	The chart legend will be laid out.
vtChLayoutSeries	The chart series will be laid out.
vtChPositionSection	A chart section or position has been moved or resized.

Table M-103: updateFlag values.

Private Sub *MSChartControl*_Click([*index* As Integer])

Usage — This event occurs when the user clicks a mouse button to select an item in the drop-down list or selects an item from the drop-down list using the keyboard.

Arguments
- *index*—an **Integer** that uniquely identifies a control in a control array. This argument is not present if the control is not part of a control array.

Private Sub *MSChartControl*_DataUpdated ([*index* As Integer ,] *row* As Integer, *column* As Integer, *labelRow* As Integer, *labelColumn* As Integer, *labelSetIndex* As Integer, *updateFlag* As Integer)

Usage — This event occurs when the chart's data grid is updated.

Arguments
- *index*—an **Integer** that uniquely identifies a control in a control array. This argument is not present if the control is not part of a control array.
- *row*—an **Integer** containing the row where the update occurred.
- *column*—an **Integer** containing the column where the update occurred.
- *labelRow*—an **Integer** containing the index of the row's label.
- *labelColumn*—an **Integer** containing the index of the column's label.
- *labelSetIndex*—an **Integer** containing the level of the labels.
- *updateFlags*—an **Integer** value (see Table M-104) containing information about the update.

updateFlag Name	Description
vtChNoDisplay	The chart display is not changed.
vtChDisplayPlot	The chart plot will be repainted.
vtChLayoutPlot	The chart will be laid out.
vtChDisplayLegend	The chart legend will be repainted.
vtChLayoutLegend	The chart legend will be laid out.
vtChLayoutSeries	The chart series will be laid out.
vtChPositionSection	A chart section or position has been moved or resized.

Table M-104: updateFlag values.

Private Sub *MSChartControl*_DblClick([*index* As Integer])

Usage This event occurs when the user double-clicks a mouse button to select an item in the drop-down list or selects an item from the drop-down list using the keyboard.

Arguments
- *index*—an **Integer** that uniquely identifies a control in a control array. This argument is not present if the control is not part of a control array.

Private Sub *MSChartControl*_DonePainting ([*index* As Integer])

Usage This event occurs when the chart has finished painting.

Arguments
- *index*—an **Integer** that uniquely identifies a control in a control array. This argument is not present if the control is not part of a control array.

Private Sub *MSChartControl*_DragDrop([*index* As Integer ,] *source* As Control, *x* As Single, *y* As Single)

Usage This event occurs when a drag-and-drop operation is completed by using the **Drag** method with an *DragAction* value of *vbEndDrag*.

> **Tip**
>
> When using drag-and-drop operations, use the **DragOver** event to determine what the cursor should look like while the cursor moves over the control.

Arguments
- *index*—an **Integer** that uniquely identifies a control in a control array. This argument is not present if the control is not part of a control array.
- *source*—a control object that is the control that is being dragged.

> **Tip**
>
> You can access a property or method from the source control by using *source.property* or *source.method*. You can determine the type of object or control by using the **TypeOf** operator.

- *x*—a **Single** that contains the horizontal location of the mouse pointer.
- *y*—a **Single** that contains the vertical location of the mouse pointer.

Private Sub *MSChartControl*_DragOver([*index* As Integer ,] *source* As Control, *x* As Single, *y* As Single, *state* As Integer)

Usage This event occurs while a drag operation is in progress and the cursor is moved over the control.

Tip

When using drag-and-drop operations, use the **DragOver** event to determine what the cursor should look like while the cursor moves over the control. When **state** is **0**, you can change the cursor to a No Drop (vbNoDrop) cursor or highlight the field that the cursor is near. When **state** is **1**, you can undo the changes you made when the **state** was **0**.

Arguments
- *index*—an **Integer** that uniquely identifies a control in a control array. This argument is not present if the control is not part of a control array.
- *source*—a control object that is the control that is being dragged.

Tip

You can access a property or method from the source control by using source.*property* or source.*method*. You can determine the type of object or control by using the **TypeOf** operator.

- *x*—a **Single** that contains the horizontal location of the mouse pointer.
- *y*—a **Single** that contains the vertical location of the mouse pointer.
- *state*—an **Integer** value (see Table M-105) that indicates the state of the object being dragged.

state Name	Value	Description
vbEnter	0	The dragged object is entering range of the control.
vbLeave	1	The dragged object is leaving range of the control.
vbOver	2	The dragged object has moved from one position over the control to another.

Table M-105: state *values*.

Private Sub *MSChartControl*_FootnoteActivated ([*index* As Integer ,] *mouseFlag* As Integer, *cancel* As Integer)

Usage
This event occurs when a user double-clicks on a footnote.

Arguments
- *index*—an **Integer** that uniquely identifies a control in a control array. This argument is not present if the control is not part of a control array.
- *mouseFlag*—an **Integer** value (see Table M-106) containing which keys were pressed when the user clicked on the footnote.

mouseFlag Name	Description
vtChMouseFlagShiftKeyDown	The Shift key was pressed.
vtChMouseFlagControlKeyDown	The Ctrl key was pressed.

Table M-106: mouseFlag *values*.

- *cancel*—an **Integer** reserved for future use.

Private Sub *MSChartControl*_FootnoteSelected ([*index* As Integer ,] *mouseFlag* As Integer, *cancel* As Integer)

Usage This event occurs when a footnote is selected.

Arguments
- *index*—an **Integer** that uniquely identifies a control in a control array. This argument is not present if the control is not part of a control array.
- *mouseFlag*—an **Integer** value (see Table M-107) containing which keys were pressed when the user clicked on the footnote.

mouseFlag Name	Description
vtChMouseFlagShiftKeyDown	The Shift key was pressed.
vtChMouseFlagControlKeyDown	The Ctrl key was pressed.

Table M-107: mouseFlag values.

- *cancel*—an **Integer** reserved for future use.

Private Sub *MSChartControl*_FootnoteUpdated ([*index* As Integer ,] *updateFlag* As Integer)

Usage This event occurs when a footnote is updated.

Arguments
- *index*—an **Integer** that uniquely identifies a control in a control array. This argument is not present if the control is not part of a control array.
- *updateFlags*—an **Integer** value (see Table M-108) containing information about the update.

updateFlag Name	Description
vtChNoDisplay	The chart display is not changed.
vtChDisplayPlot	The chart plot will be repainted.
vtChLayoutPlot	The chart will be laid out.
vtChDisplayLegend	The chart legend will be repainted.
vtChLayoutLegend	The chart legend will be laid out.
vtChLayoutSeries	The chart series will be laid out.
vtChPositionSection	A chart section or position has been moved or resized.

Table M-108: updateFlag values.

Private Sub *MSChartControl*_GotFocus ([*index* As Integer])

Usage This event occurs when the control is given focus.

Tip

You can use this routine to display help or other information in a status bar.

Arguments
- *index*—an **Integer** that uniquely identifies a control in a control array. This argument is not present if the control is not part of a control array.

Private Sub *MSChartControl*_KeyDown ([*index* As Integer ,] *keycode* As Integer, *shift* As Single)

Usage   This event occurs when a key is pressed while the control has the focus.

Arguments
- *index*—an **Integer** that uniquely identifies a control in a control array. This argument is not present if the control is not part of a control array.
- *keycode*—an **Integer** that contains information about which key was pressed.
- *shift*—an **Integer** value (see Table M-109) that contains information about the Shift and Alt keys that were pushed when the mouse button was pressed. These values can be added together if more than one key was down. For instance, a value of **5** would mean that the Shift and Alt keys were both down when the mouse button was pressed.

shift Name	Value	Description
vbShiftMask	1	The Shift key was pressed.
vbCtrlMask	2	The Ctrl key was pressed.
vbAltMask	4	The Alt key was pressed.

Table M-109: shift *values.*

Private Sub *MSChartControl*_KeyPress([*index* As Integer ,] *keychar* As Integer)

Usage   This event occurs whenever a key is pressed while the control has the focus.

Arguments
- *index*—an **Integer** that uniquely identifies a control in a control array. This argument is not present if the control is not part of a control array.
- *keychar*—an **Integer** that contains the ASCII character that was pressed.

Private Sub *MSChartControl*_KeyUp ([*index* As Integer ,] *keycode* As Integer, *shift* As Single)

Usage   This event occurs when a key is released while the control has the focus.

Arguments
- *index*—an **Integer** that uniquely identifies a control in a control array. This argument is not present if the control is not part of a control array.
- *keycode*—an **Integer** that contains information about which key was released.
- *shift*—an **Integer** value (see Table M-110) that contains information about the Shift and Alt keys that were pushed when the mouse button was pressed. These values can be added together if more than one key was down. For instance, a value of **5** would mean that the Shift and Alt keys were both down when the mouse button was pressed.

shift Name	Value	Description
vbShiftMask	1	The Shift key was pressed.
vbCtrlMask	2	The Ctrl key was pressed.
vbAltMask	4	The Alt key was pressed.

Table M-110: shift *values*.

Private Sub *MSChartControl*_LegendActivated ([*index* As Integer ,] *mouseFlag* As Integer, *cancel* As Integer)

Usage   This event occurs when a user double-clicks on the legend.

Arguments
- *index*—an **Integer** that uniquely identifies a control in a control array. This argument is not present if the control is not part of a control array.
- *mouseFlag*—an **Integer** value (see Table M-111) containing which keys were pressed when the user clicked on the chart.

mouseFlag Name	Description
vtChMouseFlagShiftKeyDown	The Shift key was pressed.
vtChMouseFlagControlKeyDown	The Ctrl key was pressed.

Table M-111: *mouseFlag values*.

- *cancel*—an **Integer** reserved for future use.

Private Sub *MSChartControl*_LegendSelected ([*index* As Integer ,] *cancel* As Integer)

Usage   This event occurs when the legend is selected.

Arguments
- *index*—an **Integer** that uniquely identifies a control in a control array. This argument is not present if the control is not part of a control array.
- *mouseFlag*—an **Integer** value (see Table M-112) containing which keys were pressed when the user clicked on the chart.

mouseFlag Name	Description
vtChMouseFlagShiftKeyDown	The Shift key was pressed.
vtChMouseFlagControlKeyDown	The Ctrl key was pressed.

Table M-112: *mouseFlag values*.

- *cancel*—an **Integer** reserved for future use.

Private Sub *MSChartControl*_LegendUpdated ([*index* As Integer ,] *updateFlag* As Integer)

Usage — This event occurs when the legend is updated.

Arguments
- *index*—an **Integer** that uniquely identifies a control in a control array. This argument is not present if the control is not part of a control array.
- *updateFlags*—an **Integer** value (see Table M-113) containing information about the update.

updateFlag Name	Description
vtChNoDisplay	The chart display is not changed.
vtChDisplayPlot	The chart plot will be repainted.
vtChLayoutPlot	The chart will be laid out.
vtChDisplayLegend	The chart legend will be repainted.
vtChLayoutLegend	The chart legend will be laid out.
vtChLayoutSeries	The chart series will be laid out.
vtChPositionSection	A chart section or position has been moved or resized.

Table M-113: updateFlag values.

Private Sub *MSChartControl*_LostFocus ([*index* As Integer])

Usage — This event occurs when the control loses focus.

Tip

This routine is useful to performing data verification.

Arguments
- *index*—an **Integer** that uniquely identifies a control in a control array. This argument is not present if the control is not part of a control array.

Private Sub *MSChartBoxControl*_MouseDown([*index* As Integer ,] *button* As Integer, *shift* As Single, *x* As Single, *y* As Single)

Usage — This event occurs when a mouse button was pressed while the cursor is over the control.

Arguments
- *index*—an **Integer** that uniquely identifies a control in a control array. This argument is not present if the control is not part of a control array.
- *button*—an **Integer** value (see Table M-114) that contains information about the mouse buttons that were pressed. Only one button will be indicated when this event occurs.

button Name	Value	Description
vbLeftButton	1	The left button was pressed.
vbRightButton	2	The right button was pressed.
vbMiddleButton	4	The middle button was pressed.

Table M-114: button *values.*

- *shift*—an **Integer** value (see Table M-115) that contains information about the Shift and Alt keys that were pushed when the mouse button was pressed. These values can be added together if more than one key was down. For instance, a value of **5** would mean that the Shift and Alt keys were both down when the mouse button was pressed.

shift Name	Value	Description
vbShiftMask	1	The Shift key was pressed.
vbCtrlMask	2	The Ctrl key was pressed.
vbAltMask	4	The Alt key was pressed.

Table M-115: shift *values.*

- *x*—a **Single** that contains the horizontal location of the mouse pointer.
- *y*—a **Single** that contains the vertical location of the mouse pointer.

Private Sub *MSChartControl*_MouseMove ([*index* As Integer ,] *button* As Integer, *shift* As Single, *x* As Single, *y* As Single)

Usage   This event occurs while the cursor is moved over the control.

Arguments
- *index*—an **Integer** that uniquely identifies a control in a control array. This argument is not present if the control is not part of a control array.
- *button*—an **Integer** value (see Table M-116) that contains information about the mouse buttons that were pressed. These values can be added together if more than one button was pushed. For instance, a value of **3** means that both the left and right buttons were pressed. A value of **0** means that no buttons were pressed.

button Name	Value	Description
vbLeftButton	1	The left button was pressed.
vbRightButton	2	The right button was pressed.
vbMiddleButton	4	The middle button was pressed.

Table M-116: button *values.*

- *shift*—an **Integer** value (see Table M-117) that contains information about the Shift and Alt keys that were pushed when the mouse button was pressed. For instance, a value of **5** would mean that the Shift and Alt keys were both down when the mouse button was pressed. A value of **0** means that none of these keys were pressed.

shift Name	Value	Description
vbShiftMask	1	The Shift key was pressed.
vbCtrlMask	2	The Ctrl key was pressed.
vbAltMask	4	The Alt key was pressed.

Table M-117: shift *values*.

- *x*—a **Single** that contains the horizontal location of the mouse pointer.
- *y*—a **Single** that contains the vertical location of the mouse pointer.

Private Sub *MSChartBoxControl*_MouseUp([*index* As Integer ,] *button* As Integer, *shift* As Single, *x* As Single, *y* As Single)

Usage — This event occurs when a mouse button is released while the cursor is over the control.

Arguments
- *index*—an **Integer** that uniquely identifies a control in a control array. This argument is not present if the control is not part of a control array.
- *button*—an **Integer** value (see Table M-118) that contains information about the mouse buttons that were released. Only one of these values will be present.

button Name	Value	Description
vbLeftButton	1	The left button was released.
vbRightButton	2	The right button was released.
vbMiddleButton	4	The middle button was released.

Table M-118: button *values*.

- *shift*—an **Integer** value (see Table M-119) that contains information about the Shift and Alt keys that were pushed when the mouse button was released. These values can be added together if more than one key was down. For instance, a value of **5** would mean that the Shift and Alt keys were both down when the mouse button was released. A value of **0** means that none of these keys were pressed.

shift Name	Value	Description
vbShiftMask	1	The Shift key was pressed.
vbCtrlMask	2	The Ctrl key was pressed.
vbAltMask	4	The Alt key was pressed.

Table M-119: shift *values*.

- *x*—a **Single** that contains the horizontal location of the mouse pointer.
- *y*—a **Single** that contains the vertical location of the mouse pointer.

Private Sub *MSChartControl*_PlotActivated ([*index* As Integer ,] *mouseFlag* As Integer, *cancel* As Integer)

- **Usage** This event occurs when a user double-clicks on the plot area of the chart.

- **Arguments**
  - *index*—an **Integer** that uniquely identifies a control in a control array. This argument is not present if the control is not part of a control array.
  - *mouseFlag*—an **Integer** value (see Table M-120) containing which keys were pressed when the user clicked on the chart.

mouseFlag Name	Description
vtChMouseFlagShiftKeyDown	The Shift key was pressed.
vtChMouseFlagControlKeyDown	The Ctrl key was pressed.

    Table M-120: *mouseFlag values.*

  - *cancel*—an **Integer** reserved for future use.

Private Sub *MSChartControl*_PlotSelected ([*index* As Integer ,] *cancel* As Integer)

- **Usage** This event occurs when the plot area is selected.

- **Arguments**
  - *index*—an **Integer** that uniquely identifies a control in a control array. This argument is not present if the control is not part of a control array.
  - *mouseFlag*—an **Integer** value (see Table M-121) containing which keys were pressed when the user clicked on the chart.

mouseFlag Name	Description
vtChMouseFlagShiftKeyDown	The Shift key was pressed.
vtChMouseFlagControlKeyDown	The Ctrl key was pressed.

    Table M-121: *mouseFlag values.*

  - *cancel*—an **Integer** reserved for future use.

Private Sub *MSChartControl*_PlotUpdated ([*index* As Integer ,] *updateFlag* As Integer)

- **Usage** This event occurs when the plot area is updated.

- **Arguments**
  - *index*—an **Integer** that uniquely identifies a control in a control array. This argument is not present if the control is not part of a control array.
  - *updateFlags*—an **Integer** value (see Table M-122) containing information about the update.

updateFlag Name	Description
vtChNoDisplay	The chart display is not changed.
vtChDisplayPlot	The chart plot will be repainted.
vtChLayoutPlot	The chart will be laid out.
vtChDisplayLegend	The chart legend will be repainted.
vtChLayoutLegend	The chart legend will be laid out.
vtChLayoutSeries	The chart series will be laid out.
vtChPositionSection	A chart section or position has been moved or resized.

Table M-122: updateFlag values.

Private Sub *MSChartControl*_PointActivated ([*index* As Integer ,] *series* As Integer, *dataPoint* As Integer, *mouseFlag* As Integer, *cancel* As Integer)

Usage This event occurs when a user double-clicks on a data point.

Arguments
- *index*—an **Integer** that uniquely identifies a control in a control array. This argument is not present if the control is not part of a control array.
- *series*—an **Integer** that identifies the series containing the data point.
- *dataPoint*—an **Integer** that identifies the data point's position in the series.
- *mouseFlag*—an **Integer** value (see Table M-123) containing which keys were pressed when the user clicked on the chart.

mouseFlag Name	Description
vtChMouseFlagShiftKeyDown	The Shift key was pressed.
vtChMouseFlagControlKeyDown	The Ctrl key was pressed.

Table M-123: mouseFlag values.

- *cancel*—an **Integer** reserved for future use.

Private Sub *MSChartControl*_PointLabelActivated ([*index* As Integer ,] *series* As Integer, *dataPoint* As Integer, *mouseFlag* As Integer, *cancel* As Integer)

Usage This event occurs when a user double-clicks on a data point label.

Arguments
- *index*—an **Integer** that uniquely identifies a control in a control array. This argument is not present if the control is not part of a control array.
- *series*—an **Integer** that identifies the series containing the data point.
- *dataPoint*—an **Integer** that identifies the data point's position in the series.
- *mouseFlag*—an **Integer** value (see Table M-124) containing which keys were pressed when the user clicked on the chart.

mouseFlag Name	Description
vtChMouseFlagShiftKeyDown	The Shift key was pressed.
vtChMouseFlagControlKeyDown	The Ctrl key was pressed.

Table M-124: *mouseFlag values.*

- *cancel*—an **Integer** reserved for future use.

Private Sub *MSChartControl*_PointLabelSelected ([*index* As Integer ,] *series* As Integer, *dataPoint* As Integer, *cancel* As Integer)

Usage This event occurs when a data point label is selected.

Arguments
- *index*—an **Integer** that uniquely identifies a control in a control array. This argument is not present if the control is not part of a control array.
- *series*—an **Integer** that identifies the series containing the data point.
- *dataPoint*—an **Integer** that identifies the data point's position in the series.
- *mouseFlag*—an **Integer** value (see Table M-125) containing which keys were pressed when the user clicked on the chart.

mouseFlag Name	Description
vtChMouseFlagShiftKeyDown	The Shift key was pressed.
vtChMouseFlagControlKeyDown	The Ctrl key was pressed.

Table M-125: *mouseFlag values.*

- *cancel*—an **Integer** reserved for future use.

Private Sub *MSChartControl*_PointLabelUpdated ([*index* As Integer ,] *series* As Integer, *dataPoint* As Integer, *updateFlag* As Integer)

Usage This event occurs when a data point label is updated.

Arguments
- *index*—an **Integer** that uniquely identifies a control in a control array. This argument is not present if the control is not part of a control array.
- *series*—an **Integer** that identifies the series containing the data point.
- *dataPoint*—an **Integer** that identifies the data point's position in the series.
- *updateFlags*—an **Integer** value (see Table M-126) containing information about the update.

updateFlag Name	Description
vtChNoDisplay	The chart display is not changed.
vtChDisplayPlot	The chart plot will be repainted.
vtChLayoutPlot	The chart will be laid out.
vtChDisplayLegend	The chart legend will be repainted.
vtChLayoutLegend	The chart legend will be laid out.

updateFlag Name	Description
vtChLayoutSeries	The chart series will be laid out.
vtChPositionSection	A chart section or position has been moved or resized.

Table M-126: updateFlag values.

Private Sub *MSChartControl*_PointSelected ([*index* As Integer ,] *series* As Integer, *dataPoint* As Integer, *cancel* As Integer)

Usage — This event occurs when a data point is selected.

Arguments
- *index*—an **Integer** that uniquely identifies a control in a control array. This argument is not present if the control is not part of a control array.
- *series*—an **Integer** that identifies the series containing the data point.
- *dataPoint*—an **Integer** that identifies the data point's position in the series.
- *mouseFlag*—an **Integer** value (see Table M-127) containing which keys were pressed when the user clicked on the chart.

mouseFlag Name	Description
vtChMouseFlagShiftKeyDown	The Shift key was pressed.
vtChMouseFlagControlKeyDown	The Ctrl key was pressed.

Table M-127: mouseFlag values.

- *cancel*—an **Integer** reserved for future use.

Private Sub *MSChartControl*_PointUpdated ([*index* As Integer ,] *series* As Integer, *dataPoint* As Integer, *updateFlag* As Integer)

Usage — This event occurs when a data point is updated.

Arguments
- *index*—an **Integer** that uniquely identifies a control in a control array. This argument is not present if the control is not part of a control array.
- *series*—an **Integer** that identifies the series containing the data point.
- *dataPoint*—an **Integer** that identifies the data point's position in the series.
- *updateFlags*—an **Integer** value (see Table M-128) containing information about the update.

updateFlag Name	Description
vtChNoDisplay	The chart display is not changed.
vtChDisplayPlot	The chart plot will be repainted.
vtChLayoutPlot	The chart will be laid out.
vtChDisplayLegend	The chart legend will be repainted.
vtChLayoutLegend	The chart legend will be laid out.
vtChLayoutSeries	The chart series will be laid out.
vtChPositionSection	A chart section or position has been moved or resized.

Table M-128: updateFlag values.

Private Sub MSChartControl_SeriesActivated ([*index* As Integer ,] *series* As Integer, *mouseFlag* As Integer, *cancel* As Integer)

Usage This event occurs when a user double-clicks on a data series.

Arguments
- *index*—an **Integer** that uniquely identifies a control in a control array. This argument is not present if the control is not part of a control array.
- *series*—an **Integer** that identifies the series containing the data point.
- *mouseFlag*—an **Integer** value (see Table M-129) containing which keys were pressed when the user clicked on the chart.

mouseFlag Name2	Description
vtChMouseFlagShiftKeyDown	The Shift key was pressed.
vtChMouseFlagControlKeyDown	The Ctrl key was pressed.

Table M-129: mouseFlag values.

- *cancel*—an **Integer** reserved for future use.

Private Sub MSChartControl_SeriesSelected ([*index* As Integer ,] *series* As Integer, *dataPoint* As Integer, *cancel* As Integer)

Usage This event occurs when a data series is selected.

Arguments
- *index*—an **Integer** that uniquely identifies a control in a control array. This argument is not present if the control is not part of a control array.
- *series*—an **Integer** that identifies the series containing the data point.
- *mouseFlag*—an **Integer** value (see Table M-130) containing which keys were pressed when the user clicked on the chart.

mouseFlag Name	Description
vtChMouseFlagShiftKeyDown	The Shift key was pressed.
vtChMouseFlagControlKeyDown	The Ctrl key was pressed.

Table M-130: mouseFlag values.

- *cancel*—an **Integer** reserved for future use.

Private Sub MSChartControl_SeriesUpdated ([*index* As Integer ,] *series* As Integer, *dataPoint* As Integer, *updateFlag* As Integer)

Usage This event occurs when a data series is updated.

Arguments
- *index*—an **Integer** that uniquely identifies a control in a control array. This argument is not present if the control is not part of a control array.
- *series*—an **Integer** that identifies the series containing the data point.
- *updateFlags*—an **Integer** value (see Table M-131) containing information about the update.

updateFlag Name	Description
vtChNoDisplay	The chart display is not changed.
vtChDisplayPlot	The chart plot will be repainted.
vtChLayoutPlot	The chart will be laid out.
vtChDisplayLegend	The chart legend will be repainted.
vtChLayoutLegend	The chart legend will be laid out.
vtChLayoutSeries	The chart series will be laid out.
vtChPositionSection	A chart section or position has been moved or resized.

Table M-131: *updateFlag values.*

Private Sub *MSChartControl*_TitleActivated ([*index* As Integer ,] *mouseFlag* As Integer, *cancel* As Integer)

Usage This event occurs when a user double-clicks on the title of the chart.

Arguments
- *index*—an **Integer** that uniquely identifies a control in a control array. This argument is not present if the control is not part of a control array.
- *mouseFlag*—an **Integer** value (see Table M-132) containing which keys were pressed when the user clicked on the chart.

mouseFlag Name	Description
vtChMouseFlagShiftKeyDown	The Shift key was pressed.
vtChMouseFlagControlKeyDown	The Ctrl key was pressed.

Table M-132: *mouseFlag values.*

- *cancel*—an **Integer** reserved for future use.

Private Sub *MSChartControl*_TitleSelected ([*index* As Integer ,] *cancel* As Integer)

Usage This event occurs when the title is selected.

Arguments
- *index*—an **Integer** that uniquely identifies a control in a control array. This argument is not present if the control is not part of a control array.
- *mouseFlag*—an **Integer** value (see Table M-133) containing which keys were pressed when the user clicked on the chart.

mouseFlag Name	Description
vtChMouseFlagShiftKeyDown	The Shift key was pressed.
vtChMouseFlagControlKeyDown	The Ctrl key was pressed.

Table M-133: *mouseFlag values.*

- *cancel*—an **Integer** reserved for future use.

**Private Sub *MSChartControl*_TitleUpdated ([*index* As Integer ,]
updateFlag As Integer)**

Usage   This event occurs when the title is updated.

Arguments
- *index*—an **Integer** that uniquely identifies a control in a control array. This argument is not present if the control is not part of a control array.
- *updateFlags*—an **Integer** value (see Table M-134) containing information about the update.

updateFlag Name	Description
vtChNoDisplay	The chart display is not changed.
vtChDisplayPlot	The chart plot will be repainted.
vtChLayoutPlot	The chart will be laid out.
vtChDisplayLegend	The chart legend will be repainted.
vtChLayoutLegend	The chart legend will be laid out.
vtChLayoutSeries	The chart series will be laid out.
vtChPositionSection	A chart section or position has been moved or resized.

Table M-134: updateFlag values.

Examples
```
Private Sub Command1_Click()

Dim i As Integer
Dim j As Integer
mychart = mychart + 1
If mychart = 10 Then
    mychart = 14
ElseIf mychart = 15 Then
    mychart = 16
ElseIf mychart = 17 Then
    mychart = 1
End If

MSChart1.Repaint = False

MSChart1.chartType = mychart
MSChart1.ColumnCount = 4
MSChart1.RowCount = 12
For i = 1 To 4
    For j = 1 To 12
        MSChart1.Column = i
        MSChart1.Row = j
        MSChart1.Data = CInt(Rnd() * i)
    Next j
```

```
Next i
MSChart1.Repaint = True
End Sub
```

This routine displays a random chart each time the command button is pushed. It first chooses the next available chart type and disables the chart's refresh while changes are made. It then sets the number of rows and columns and generates some random data for display. Finally, it enables the chart's ability to repaint and the chart then displays to the user.

See Also   **DataGrid** (control)

MSComm

CONTROL

CCE, LE, PE, EE

Usage   The **MSComm** control permits a Visual Basic program to operate a serial communications port. This is useful when you want to access a nonstandard device such as a home security system or global positioning unit that communicates via an RS-232 connection.

Properties   ▪ *MSCommControl*.**Break**—a **Boolean** when **True** means that the com port will send a break signal to the remote computer.

> **Tip**
>
> *While a break signal is not an ASCII character, it may be received as a series of ASCII null characters.*

> **Warning**
>
> *Setting this property to **True** places the com port into a break state, during which no other characters may be sent. This property must be set to **False** after a short interval (about 500 milliseconds) to restore normal communications.*
>
> *Not all computer systems support the break signal.*

▪ *MSCommControl*.**CDHolding**—a **Boolean** when **True** means that the Carrier Detect line is high. This will set the **CommEvent** property to *comEventCDTO* and trigger the **OnComm** event.

▪ *MSCommControl*.**CommEvent**—an **Integer** value (see Table M-135) containing the current status of the control.

CommEvent Name	Value	Description
comEvSend	1	Fewer than SThreshold characters remain in the transmit buffer.
comEvReceive	2	**RThreshold** or more characters in the receive buffer.
comEvCTS	3	Clear To Send changed.
comEvDSR	4	Data Set Ready changed.
comEvCD	5	Carrier Detect line changed.
comEvRing	6	Ring detected (may not be supported in all devices).

CommEvent Name	Value	Description
comEvEOF	7	End of File (ASCII value 26) received.
comEventBreak	1001	A break signal was received.
comEventCTSTO	1002	Clear To Send time out.
comEventDSRTO	1003	Data Set Ready time out.
comEventFrame	1004	Framing error.
comEventOverrun	1006	A character was lost by the hardware.
comEventCDTO	1007	Carrier Detect time out.
comEventRxOver	1008	Receive buffer full.
comEventRxParity	1009	Parity error.
comEventTxFull	1010	Transmit buffer full.
comEventDCB	1011	Unexpected error retrieving Device Control Block.

Table M-135: **CommEvent** values.

- *MSCommControl*.**CommId**—a **Long** containing the handle for the communications port. It was created by the Windows API routine, CreateFile.
- *MSCommControl*.**CommPort**—an **Integer** containing the communications port. It can range from 1 to 16, though most computers do not have a communications port greater than 4. A run-time error 68 will be generated if the port is unavailable.

> **Warning**
>
> Set this property before setting the **PortOpen** property to open the port.

- *MSCommControl*.**CTSHolding**—a **Boolean** value when **True** means that the Clear To Send line is high. **False** means that the Clear To Send line is low.
- *MSCommControl*.**DSRHolding**—a **Boolean** value when **True** means that the Data Set Ready line is high. **False** means that the Data Set Ready line is low.
- *MSCommControl*.**DTREnable**—a **Boolean** value when **True** means that the Data Terminal Ready line should be set high. **False** means that the Data Terminal Ready line should be set low.
- *MSCommControl*.**EOFEnable**—a **Boolean** that when **True** means that the **CommEvent** property will be set to *comEvEOF* when the EOF character is found in the input stream. **False** means the data is not scanned for the EOF character.
- *MSCommControl*.**Handshaking**—an **Integer** value (see Table M-136) containing the handshaking protocol.

Handshaking Name	Value	Description
comNone	0	No handshaking (default value).
comXOnXOff	1	Use XOn/Xoff handshaking.
comRTS	2	Use Request To Send/Clear To Send handshaking.
comRTSXOnXOff	3	Use Request To Send/Clear To Send and XOn/Xoff handshaking.

Table M-136: **Handshaking** values.

MSComm • **583**

- *MSCommControl*.**InBufferCount**—an **Integer** value containing the number of characters in the input buffer.
- *MSCommControl*.**InBufferSize**—an **Integer** containing the size of the input buffer in bytes. The default buffer size is 1024.
- *MSCommControl*.**Index**—an **Integer** that uniquely identifies a control in a control array.
- *MSCommControl*.**Input**—a **Variant** value that will remove a stream of characters from the input buffer. The number of characters removed is determined by **InputLen** and the type of value returned is determined by **InputMode**.
- *MSCommControl*.**InputLen**—an **Integer** value containing the number of characters to be retrieved from the input buffer.
- *MSCommControl*.**InputMode**—an **Integer** value when *comInputModeText* (0) the data is returned as text. When *comInputModeBinary* (1) the data is returned as binary.
- *MSCommControl*.**Name**—a **String** that contains the name of the control that will be used to reference the control in a Visual Basic program. This property is read only at run time.
- *MSCommControl*.**NullDiscard**—a **Boolean** when **True** means that null (ASCII value 0) characters will be discarded. **False** means that null characters will not be discarded (default).
- *MSCommControl*.**Object**—an object that contains a reference to the **MSComm** control.
- *MSCommControl*.**OutBufferCount**—an **Integer** value containing the number of characters in the output buffer. The buffer can be cleared by setting this property to **0**.
- *MSCommControl*.**OutBufferSize**—an **Integer** containing the size of the output buffer in bytes. The default buffer size is 512.
- *MSCommControl*.**Output**—a **Variant** value that will add data to the output buffers. Binary data is added by using a **Byte Array,** and text data is added by using a **String**.
- *MSCommControl*.**Parent**—an object that contains a reference to the **Form**, **Frame,** or other container that contains this control.
- *MSCommControl*.**ParityReplace**—a **String** containing a single character that will replace a character received with a parity error. If this property contains an empty string, then the bad character will not be replaced. The default value is "?".
- *MSCommControl*.**PortOpen**—a **Boolean** when **True** means that the port is open. **False** means that the port is closed.

Tip

*Set all other properties before setting the **PortOpen** to **True** since setting **PortOpen** to **True** opens the connection.*

- *MSCommControl*.**Rthreshold**—an **Integer** containing the minimum number of characters in the input buffer required before the **CommEvent** property is set to *comEvReceive*. Setting this value to **0** disables setting the **CommEvent** property.
- *MSCommControl*.**RTSEnable**—a **Boolean** value when **True** means that the Request To Send line should be set high. **False** means that the Request To Send line should be set low.

- *MSCommControl*.**Settings**—a **String** value containing the settings for baud rate, parity, data bits, and stop bits using the following format: "b,p,d,s". (For example: "9600,N,8,1").

Values for baud rate:	110, 300, 600, 1200, 2400, 9600 (default), 14400, 19200, 28800, 38400 (reserved), 56000 (reserved), 128000 (reserved), and 256000 (reserved).
Values for parity:	E (even), M (mark), N (none, default), O (odd), and S (space).
Values for data bits:	4, 5, 6, 7, and 8 (default).
Values for stop bits:	1 (default), 1.5, and 2.

- *MSCommControl*.**Sthreshold**—an **Integer** containing the minimum number of characters in the output buffer required before the **CommEvent** property is set to *comEvSend*. Setting this value to **0** disables setting the **CommEvent** property.
- *MSCommControl*.**Tag**—a **String** that can hold programmer specific information. This property is not used by Visual Basic.

Events

Private Sub *MSCommControl*_OnComm ([*index* As Integer])

Usage This event occurs whenever the **CommEvent** property changes values, signaling either a communication or error event has occurred.

Arguments *index*—an **Integer** that uniquely identifies a control in a control array. This argument is not present if the control is not part of a control array.

Examples
```
Private Sub Command1_Click()
Dim i As Integer
If Not MSComm1.PortOpen Then
    MSComm1.CommPort = 3
    MSComm1.Settings = "9600,N,7,1"
    MSComm1.RThreshold = 1
    MSComm1.PortOpen = True
End If
MSComm1.Output = Text2.Text & vbCrLf
End Sub

Private Sub MSComm1_OnComm()
Text3.Text = Text3.Text & Format(MSComm1.CommEvent) & "/"
If MSComm1.CommEvent = 2 Then
    Text1.Text = Text1.Text & MSComm1.Input
End If
End Sub
```

The **Command1_Click** event will open the communications port if it is not already open and send the data in the Text1 text box to it. The **MSComm1_OnComm** event displays the CommEvent codes in the Text3 text box and any characters received from the other computer in the Text1 text box.

I used port 3 on my computer for testing since it has a modem connected and it is easy to use basic modem commands to receive input and respond with meaningful output.

See Also **Microsoft Internet Transfer Control** (control)

MSFlexGrid

CONTROL

PE, EE

Usage
The **MSFlexGrid** control is an ActiveX control that allows you to include a spreadsheet like grid in your program.

Properties
- *MSFlexGridControl*.**AllowBigSelection**—a **Boolean** when **True** means that clicking on a row or column header will select the entire row or column (default). **False** means that the row or column will not be selected.

  - *MSFlexGridControl*.**AllowUserResizing**—an **Integer** value (see Table M-137) describing what user resizing functions are permitted.

AllowUserResizing Name	Value	Description
flexResizeNone	0	No user resizing permitted (default).
flexResizeColumns	1	The user can resize columns.
flexResizeRows	2	The user can resize rows.
flexResizeBoth	3	The user can resize rows and columns.

    Table M-137: **AllowUserResizing** *values.*

  - *MSFlexGridControl*.**Appearance**—an **Integer** value (see Table M-138) that describes how the combo box will appear on the form.

AppearanceValue	Description
0	The MSFlexGrid control displays without the 3D effects.
1	The **MSFlexGrid** control displays with 3D effects (default value).

    Table M-138: Appearance *values.*

- *MSFlexGridControl*.**BackColor**—a **Long** that contains the suggested value for the background color of the nonfixed cells.
- *MSFlexGridControl*.**BackColorBkg**—a **Long** that contains the suggested value for the background color of the area not occupied by the grid.
- *MSFlexGridControl*.**BackColorFixed**—a **Long** that contains the suggested value for the background color of the fixed cells.
- *MSFlexGridControl*.**BackColorSel**—a **Long** that contains the suggested value for the background color of the selected cells.
- *MSFlexGridControl*.**BorderStyle**—an **Integer** value (see Table M-139) specifying how the border will be drawn. This property also indicates how the form can be resized and is read only at run time.

BorderStyle Name	Value	Description
vbBSNone	0	No border, control box menu, title bar, maximize and minimize buttons. Cannot be resized.
vbFixedSingle	1	Single line around the form. Form can only be resized by maximize and minimize buttons.

  Table M-139: **BorderStyle** *values.*

- *MSFlexGridControl*.**CellAlignment**—an **Integer** value (see Table M-140) specifying how the data inside the cell will be aligned.

CellAlignment Name	Value	Description
flexAlignLeftTop	0	Top aligned vertically, left aligned horizontally.
flexAlignLeftCenter	1	Centered vertically, left aligned horizontally (default for strings).
flexAlignLeftBottom	2	Bottom aligned vertically, left aligned horizontally.
flexAlignCenterTop	3	Top aligned vertically, centered horizontally.
flexAlignCenterCenter	4	Centered vertically, centered horizontally.
flexAlignCenterBottom	5	Bottom aligned vertically, centered horizontally.
flexAlignRightTop	6	Top aligned vertically, right aligned horizontally.
flexAlignRightCenter	7	Center aligned vertically, right aligned horizontally (default for numbers).
flexAlignRightBottom	8	Bottom aligned vertically, right aligned horizontally.
flexAlignGeneral	9	*flexAlignLeftCenter* for strings and *flexAlignRightCenter* for numbers.

Table M-140: **CellAlignment** *values*.

- *MSFlexGridControl*.**CellBackColor**—a **Long** that contains the suggested value for the background color of the cell. If this value is **0**, then the default color will display.

> **Tip**
>
> To display the color black in a cell, use a value of **1** rather than **0**.

- *MSFlexGridControl*.**CellForeColor**—a **Long** that contains the suggested value for the foreground color of the cell. If this value is **0**, then the default color will display.

> **Tip**
>
> To display the color black in a cell, use a value of **1** rather than **0**.

- *MSFlexGridControl*.**CellFontBold**—a **Boolean** when **True** means that the characters in the cell display in bold. **False** means that the characters display normally.
- *MSFlexGridControl*.**CellFontItalic**—a **Boolean** when **True** means that the characters in the cell display in italics. **False** means that the characters display normally.
- *MSFlexGridControl*.**CellFontName**—a **String** that specifies the name of the font that should be used to display the characters in the cell.
- *MSFlexGridControl*.**CellFontSize**—a **Single** that specifies the point size that should be used to display the characters in the cell.
- *MSFlexGridControl*.**CellFontStrikethrough**—a **Boolean** when **True** means that the characters in the cell display with a line through the center. **False** means that the characters display normally.
- *MSFlexGridControl*.**CellFontUnderlined**—a **Boolean** when **True** means that the characters in the cell display with a line beneath them. **False** means that the characters display normally.

- *MSFlexGridControl*.**CellFontWidth**—a **Single** that specifies the font width in points for the current cell.
- *MSFlexGridControl*.**CellHeight**—a **Single** containing the height of the cell in twips.
- *MSFlexGridControl*.**CellLeft**—a **Single** containing the distance from the left edge of the control to the left edge of the cell in twips.
- *MSFlexGridControl*.**CellPicture**—a **Picture** object containing an image to display in the cell. The picture can be a bitmap, icon, or metafile, or it can be loaded from another controls's **Picture** property.

> **Tip**
>
> Use the **LoadPicture** function to load a picture into this property.

- *MSFlexGridControl*.**CellPictureAlignment**—an **Integer** value (see Table M-141) specifying how the picture inside the cell will be aligned.

CellPictureAlignment Name	Value	Description
flexAlignLeftTop	0	Top aligned vertically, left aligned horizontally.
flexAlignLeftCenter	1	Centered vertically, left aligned horizontally (default for strings).
flexAlignLeftBottom	2	Bottom aligned vertically, left aligned horizontally.
flexAlignCenterTop	3	Top aligned vertically, centered horizontally.
flexAlignCenterCenter	4	Centered vertically, centered horizontally.
flexAlignCenterBottom	5	Bottom aligned vertically, centered horizontally.
flexAlignRightTop	6	Top aligned vertically, right aligned horizontally.
flexAlignRightCenter	7	Center aligned vertically, right aligned horizontally (default for numbers).
flexAlignRightBottom	8	Bottom aligned vertically, right aligned horizontally.

Table M-141: **CellPictureAlignment** *values.*

- *MSFlexGridControl*.**CellTextStyle**—an **Integer** value (see Table M-142) specifying how the data inside the cell will be aligned.

CellTextStyle Name	Value	Description
flexTextFlat	0	Normal text (default)
flexTextRaised	1	Raised text
flexTextInset	2	Inset text
flexTextRaisedLight	3	Raised light text
flexTextInsetLight	4	Inset light text

Table M-142: **CellTextStyle** *values.*

- *MSFlexGridControl*.**CellTop**—a **Single** containing the distance from the left edge of the control to the left edge of the cell in twips.
- *MSFlexGridControl*.**CellWidth**—a **Single** containing the width of the cell in twips.
- *MSFlexGridControl*.**Clip**—a **String** containing the text of the selected cells. Each cell is stored as a block of text separated by a tab character (*vbTab*). If more than one row is present, they will be separated by a carriage return (*vbCR*).

- *MSFlexGridControl*.**Col**—a **Long** containing the current column. This property can be used with the **Row** property to determine the current cell.
- *MSFlexGridControl*.**ColAlignment** (*col*)—an **Integer** value (see Table M-143) specifying how the data in the column specified by *col* will be aligned.

ColAlignment Name	Value	Description
flexAlignLeft	0	Left alignment
flexAlignRight	1	Right alignment
flexAlignCenter	2	Centered

Table M-143: **ColAlignment** values.

- *MSFlexGridControl*.**ColData** (*col*)—a **Long** value containing user defined information associated with the column specified by *col*.
- *MSFlexGridControl*.**ColIsVisible** (*col*)—a **Boolean** value when **True** means that the column specified by *col* is visible.
- *MSFlexGridControl*.**ColPos** (*col*)—a **Long** value containing the distance in twips between the left edge of the column specified by *col* and the left edge of the control.
- *MSFlexGridControl*.**ColPosition** (*col*)—a **Long** value containing the relative position of the column specified by *col* in the grid.

> **Tip**
>
> This property is useful to move a column from one position on the grid to another.

- *MSFlexGridControl*.**Cols**—a **Long** value containing the total number of columns in the grid.
- *MSFlexGridControl*.**ColSel**—a **Long** value when used with the **Col**, **Row**, and **RowSel** properties mark the selected area on the grid.
- *MSFlexGridControl*.**ColWidth** (*col*)—a **Long** value containing the width of the column in twips.
- *MSFlexGridControl*.**Container**—an object that sets or returns the container of the control at run time. This property cannot be set at design time.
- *MSFlexGridControl*.**DataBindings**—a reference to the **DataBindings** collection containing the bindable properties available.
- *MSFlexGridControl*.**DataSource**—a **String** containing the name of a **Data** control that will be updated once the selection is made.
- *MSFlexGridControl*.**DragIcon**—an object that contains the picture value of an icon. At design time, you can specify an icon file that has a file type of .ICO.

> **Tip**
>
> This value can be created by copying the value from another control's **DragIcon** value, a form's icon, or by using the **LoadPicture** function.

- *MSFlexGridControl*.**DragMode**—an **Integer** value (see Table M-144) specifying how the control will respond to a drag request.

> **Tip**
>
> Setting **DragMode** to vbAutomatic *will automatically begin a drag operation when the user clicks on the control. However, the control will not respond to the usual mouse events (**Click**, **DblClick**, **MouseDown**, **MouseMove**, **MouseUp**).*

DragMode Name	Value	Description
vbManual	0	The Drag method must be used to begin a drag-and-drop operation (default value).
vbAutomatic	1	The source control will automatically begin a drag-and-drop operation when the user clicks on the control.

Table M-144: **DragMode** *values.*

- *MSFlexGridControl*.**Enabled**—a **Boolean** value when **True** means that the control will respond to events. When **False**, the control will not respond to events.
- *MSFlexGridControl*.**FillStyle**—an **Integer** value when 1 means that setting the **Text** property for the current cell applies also to all selected cells. Zero means that the changes only apply to the current cell.
- *MSFlexGridControl*.**FirstRow**—a bookmark to the first visible row in the grid.
- *MSFlexGridControl*.**FixedAlignment** (*col*)—an **Integer** value (see Table M-145) specifying how the information in the fixed cells in the column specified by *col* will be aligned.

FixedAlignment Name	Value	Description
flexAlignLeftTop	0	Top aligned vertically, left aligned horizontally.
flexAlignLeftCenter	1	Centered vertically, left aligned horizontally (default for strings).
flexAlignLeftBottom	2	Bottom aligned vertically, left aligned horizontally.
flexAlignCenterTop	3	Top aligned vertically, centered horizontally.
flexAlignCenterCenter	4	Centered vertically, centered horizontally.
flexAlignCenterBottom	5	Bottom aligned vertically, centered horizontally.
flexAlignRightTop	6	Top aligned vertically, right aligned horizontally.
flexAlignRightCenter	7	Center aligned vertically, right aligned horizontally (default for numbers).
flexAlignRightBottom	8	Bottom aligned vertically, right aligned horizontally.

Table M-145: **FixedAlignment** *values.*

- *MSFlexGridControl*.**FixedCols**—a **Long** specifying the number of fixed columns in the grid. Fixed columns do not scroll.
- *MSFlexGridControl*.**FixedRows**—a **Long** specifying the number of fixed rows in the grid. Fixed rows do not scroll.

- *MSFlexGridControl*.**FocusRect**—an **Integer** value (see Table M-146) specifying how the current cell will display.

FocusRect Name	Value	Description
flexFocusNone	0	No focus rectangle displays.
flexFocusLight	1	A light focus rectangle displays.
flexFocusHeavy	2	A heavy focus rectangle displays.

Table M-146: **FocusRect** *values.*

- *MSFlexGridControl*.**Font**—an object that contains information about the default character font for this control.
- *MSFlexGridControl*.**FontWidth**—a **Single** containing the width of the font in points.

> **Tip**
>
> *This property is useful for overiding the default width of a character font to make the characters wider or narrower.*

- *MSFlexGridControl*.**ForeColor**—a **Long** that contains the suggested value for the foreground color of the nonfixed cells.
- *MSFlexGridControl*.**ForeColorFixed**—a **Long** that contains the suggested value for the foreground color of the fixed cells.
- *MSFlexGridControl*.**ForeColorSel**—a **Long** that contains the suggested value for the foreground color of the selected cells.
- *MSFlexGridControl*.**FormatString**—a **String** containing formatting information for the grid. The format string consists of a series of pipe ("|") characters defining each column. Inside each column is a text label. The less than ("<"), greater than (">"), and circumflex ("^") characters to left, right, or center justify the contents of the cell. A semicolon (";") ends the column information and begins row information. The width of each column is set by the width of the text in each format string.
  The **FormatString** begins with row 0, column 0 and continues as long as information exists. If more columns or rows are included in the format string than are in the grid, the grid is automatically expanded to accommodate the additional information. If more rows or columns are in the grid than the format string, then the remaining cells are just left empty.
- *MSFlexGridControl*.**GridColor**—a **Long** that contains the suggested value for the color of the lines between the nonfixed cells. This property is only used when the **GridLines** property is set to *flexGridFlat* (1).
- *MSFlexGridControl*.**GridColorFixed**—a **Long** that contains the suggested value for the color of the lines between the fixed cells. This property is only used when the **GridLinesFixed** property is set to *flexGridFlat* (1).
- *MSFlexGridControl*.**GridLines**—an **Integer** value (see Table M-147) that describes how the lines will be drawn between nonfixed cells.

GridLines Name	Value	Description
flexGridNone	0	No lines display between cells.
flexGridFlat	1	Normal lines display between cells (default).
flexGridInset	2	Inset lines are drawn between the cells.
flexGridRaised	3	Raised lines are drawn between cells.

Table M-147: **GridLines** values.

- *MSFlexGridControl*.**GridLinesFixed**—an **Integer** value (see Table M-148) that describes how the lines will be drawn between fixed cells.

GridLinesFixed Name	Value	Description
flexGridNone	0	No lines display between cells.
flexGridFlat	1	Normal lines display between cells.
flexGridInset	2	Inset lines are drawn between the cells (default).
flexGridRaised	3	Raised lines are drawn between cells.

Table M-148: **GridLinesFixed** values.

- *MSFlexGridControl*.**GridLineWidth**—an **Integer** containing the size of lines drawn between cells in pixels. It can range from 1 pixel (default) to 10 pixels.
- *MSFlexGridControl*.**Height**—a **Single** that contains the height of the control.
- *MSFlexGridControl*.**HelpContextID**—a **Long** that contains a help file context ID number which references an entry in the help file. When the user presses the F1 key while this control is active, the corresponding entry in the help file will automatically display. A value of **0** means that no context number was specified.

Tip

A help file must be compiled using the Windows Help Compiler available in the Professional and Enterprise editions of Visual Basic.

- *MSFlexGridControl*.**HighLight**—an **Integer** value (see Table M-149) describing how selected cells are indicated on the grid.

HighLight Name	Value	Description
flexHighlightNever	0	Selected cells are not highlighted.
flexHighlightAlways	1	Selected cells are always highlighted.
flexHighlightWithFocus	2	Selected cells are only highlighted with the control that has the focus.

Table M-149: **HighLight** values.

- *MSFlexGridControl*.**hWnd**—a **Long** that contains a Windows handle to the control.

Tip

*The **hWnd** property is most useful when making calls to Windows API functions. Since this value can change during execution, do not save the value into a variable for later use.*

- *MSFlexGridControl*.**Index**—an **Integer** that uniquely identifies a control in a control array.
- *MSFlexGridControl*.**Left**—a **Single** that contains the distance measured in twips between the left edge of the control and the left edge of the control's container.
- *MSFlexGridControl*.**LeftCol**—an **Integer** value containing the leftmost visible column.
- *MSFlexGridControl*.**MergeCells**—an **Integer** value (see Table M-150) specifying how cells can be merged to eliminate duplicate infomration in a grid.

MergeCells Name	Value	Description
flexMergeNever	0	Never group cells with the same contents (default).
flexMergeFree	1	Can merge any cell with the same content.
flexMergeRestrictRows	2	Can merge a cell only if there is a cell with the same content immediately above.
flexMergeRestrictColumns	3	Can merge a cell only if there is a cell with the same content immediately to the left.
flexMergeRestrictBoth	4	Can merge a cell only if there is a cell with the same content immediately above or to the left.

Table M-150: **MergeCells** *values.*

- *MSFlexGridControl*.**MergeCol** (*col*)—a **Boolean** value when **True** means that the data in the specified column is available to be merged.
- *MSFlexGridControl*.**MergeRow** (*row*)—a **Boolean** value when **True** means that the data in the specified row is available to be merged.
- *MSFlexGridControl*.**MouseCol**—a **Long** value containing the column pointed to by the mouse.
- *MSFlexGridListControl*.**MouseIcon**—a **Picture** object (a bitmap, icon, or metafile) that will be used as a cursor when the **MousePointer** property is set to 99. Note that Visual Basic does not support color cursors from a .CUR file. A color icon from an .ICO file should be used instead.
- *MSFlexGridControl*.**MousePointer**—an **Integer** value (see Table M-151) that contains the value of the cursor that should be displayed when the cursor is moved over this control. Use *vbCustom* to display the custom icon stored in the **MouseIcon** property.

Cursor Name	Value	Description
vbDefault	0	Shape determined by the object (default value)
vbArrow	1	Arrow
vbCrosshair	2	Crosshair
vbIbeam	3	I beam
vbIconPointer	4	Square inside a square
vbSizePointer	5	Four sided arrow (north, south, east, west)
vbSizeNESW	6	Two sided arrow (northeast, southwest)
vbSizeNS	7	Two sided arrow (north, south)
vbSizeNWSE	8	Two sided arrow (northwest, southeast)
vbSizeWE	9	Two sided arrow (west, east)
vbUpArrow	10	Single sided arrow pointing north
vbHourglass	11	Hourglass
vbNoDrop	12	No Drop
vbArrowHourglass	13	An arrow and an Hourglass

MSFlexGrid • 593

Cursor Name	Value	Description
vbArrowQuestion	14	An arrow and a question mark
vbSizeAll	15	Size all
vbCustom	99	Custom icon from the **MouseIcon** property of this control

Table M-151: **Cursor** *values.*

- *MSFlexGridControl*.**MouseRow**—a **Long** value containing the row pointed to by the mouse.
- *MSFlexGridControl*.**Name**—a **String** that contains the name of the control that will be used to reference the control in a Visual Basic program. This property is read only at run time.
- *MSFlexGridControl*.**Object**—an object that contains a reference to the *MSFlexGridControl* object.
- *MSFlexGridControl*.**OLEDropMode**—an **Integer** value (see Table M-152) that describes how the control will respond to OLE drop operations.

OLEDropMode Name	Value	Description
vbOLEDropNone	0	The control does not accept OLE drops. The cursor is changed to the No Drop cursor (default value).
vbOLEDropManual	1	The control responds to OLE drops under the program's control (manual).
vbOLEDropAutomatic	2	The control automatically accepts OLE drops if it recognizes the format of the data object.

Table M-152: **OLEDropMode** *values.*

- *MSFlexGridControl*.**Parent**—an object that contains a reference to the **Form**, **Frame**, or other container that contains the **MSFlexGrid** control.
- *MSFlexGridControl*.**Picture**—a picture object that contains a picture of the **MSFlexGrid** control that can be used for printing, saved to disk, or copied to the clipboard. Unlike the grid displayed on the screen, all rows and columns will be visible in the picture.

Warning

A large grid will return a large picture. Set the **PictureType** *property to flexPictureMonochrome (1) to save memory, or hide portions of the grid before taking the picture.*

- *MSFlexGridControl*.**PictureType**—an **Integer** value when *flexPictureColor* (0) means that the **Picture** property will return a color bitmap. When *flexPictureMonochrome* (1) means that a monochrome bitmap will be returned.
- *MSFlexGridControl*.**Redraw**—a **Boolean** value when **True** means that changes to the grid are immediately shown. **False** means that changes to the grid are not shown.

Tip

Use the property to freeze the display while making complex changes. Once the changes are finished, you can set **Redraw** *to* **True** *to show the most current image. This technique improves performance and reduces screen flicker.*

- *MSFlexGridControl*.**RightToLeft**—a **Boolean** value when **True** means that the text displays from right to left. When **False** means that the text displays from left to right. A bi-directional version of Windows is required to set this property to **True**.
- *MSFlexGridControl*.**Row**—a **Long** containing the current row. Can be used with the **Col** property to determine the current cell.
- *MSFlexGridControl*.**RowData** (*row*)—a **Long** value containing user defined information associated with the row specified by *row*.
- *MSFlexGridControl*.**RowHeight** (*row*)—a **Long** value containing the height of the row in twips.
- *MSFlexGridControl*.**RowHeightMin**—a **Long** value containing the minimum height of a row in twips.
- *MSFlexGridControl*.**RowIsVisible** (*row*)—a **Boolean** value when **True** means that the row specified by *row* is visible.
- *MSFlexGridControl*.**RowPos** (*row*)—a **Long** value containing the distance in twips between the top edge of the row specified by *row* and the top edge of the control.
- *MSFlexGridControl*.**RowPosition** (*row*)—a **Long** value containing the relative position of the row specified by *row* in the grid.

> **Tip**
>
> *This property is useful to move a row from one position on the grid to another.*

- *MSFlexGridControl*.**Rows**—a **Long** value containing the total number of rows in the grid.
- *MSFlexGridControl*.**RowSel**—a **Long** value when used with the **Col, Row,** and **ColSel** properties mark the selected area on the grid.
- *MSFlexGridControl*.**ScrollBars**—an **Integer** value (see Table M-153) containing the row divider style for the **MSFlexGrid** control.

ScrollBars Name	Value	Description
flexScrollNone	0	No scroll bars display (default).
flexScrollHorizontal	1	A horizontal scroll bar displays.
flexScrollVertical	2	A vertical scroll bar displays.
flexScrollBoth	3	Both scroll bars display.

Table M-153: ScrollBars *values.*

- *MSFlexGridControl*.**ScrollTrack**—a **Boolean** value when **True** means that the scroll box on the scroll bars will scroll the contents of the grid. **False** means that moving the scroll box will not scroll the grid. Note that the user can still click on either side of the scroll bar or use the scroll arrows to move around in the grid.

> **Tip**
>
> *Set this value to **False** to reduce screen flicker.*

- *MSFlexGridControl*.**SelectionMode**—an **Integer** value (see Table M-154) specifying how selections are done.

SelectionMode Name	Value	Description
flexSelectionFree	0	All selections are available (default).
flexSelectionByRow	1	Only complete rows can be selected.
flexSelectionByColumn	2	Only complete columns can be selected.

Table M-154: **SelectionMode** *values.*

- *MSFlexGridControl*.**Sort**—an **Integer** value (see Table M-155) specifying how rows are sorted. The sort keys are the contiguous cells beginning with **Col** and ending with **ColSel**.

Sort Name	Value	Description
flexSortNone	0	None.
flexSortGenericAscending	1	Sort ascending, guess whether text is a string or a number.
flexSortGenericDescending	2	Sort descending, guess whether text is a string or a number.
flexSortNumericAscending	3	Sort ascending, assume that text is a number.
flexSortNumericDescending	4	Sort descending, assume that text is a number.
flexSortStringNoCaseAscending	5	Sort ascending, case-insensitive.
flexSortNoCaseDescending	6	Sort descending, case-insensitive.
flexSortStringAscenging	7	Sort ascending, case-sensitive.
flexSortStringDescending	8	Sort descending, case-sensitive.
flexSortCustom	9	Custom. Use the **Compare** event.

Table M-155: **Sort** *values.*

> **Tip**
>
> *For a complex sort, create an invisible column with the sort key and sort on that column.*

- *MSFlexGridControl*.**TabIndex**—an Integer that determines the order that a user will tab through the objects on a form.
- *MSFlexGridControl*.**TabStop**—a **Boolean** value when **True** means that the user can tab to this object. When **False** means that this control will be skipped to the next control in the **TabIndex** order.
- *MSFlexGridControl*.**Tag**—a **String** that can hold programmer specific information. This property is not used by Visual Basic.
- *MSFlexGridControl*.**Text**—a **String** containing the value of the current cell. Setting this value will either change the contents of the current cell or the selected area depending on the value of the **FillStyle** property.
- *MSFlexGridControl*.**TextArray** (*index*)—a **String** containing the value of a cell in the grid. *Index* is computed by multiplying the cell's row by the number of columns in the grid and then adding the cell's column.

> **Tip**
>
> *Use the* **TextMatrix** *property for easier access to a cell.*

- *MSFlexGridControl*.**TextMatrix** (*row, col*)—a **String** containing the value of a cell in the grid, where *row* and *col* are the row and column of the desired cell.
- *MSFlexGridControl*.**TextStyle**—an **Integer** value (see Table M-156) specifying how the data inside a nonfixed cell will be aligned.

TextStyle Name	Value	Description
flexTextFlat	0	Normal text (default)
flexTextRaised	1	Raised text
flexTextInset	2	Inset text
flexTextRaisedLight	3	Raised light text
flexTextInsetLight	4	Inset light text

Table M-156: **TextStyle** *values.*

- *MSFlexGridControl*.**TextStyleFixed**—an **Integer** value (see Table M-157) specifying how the data inside a fixed cell will be aligned.

TextStyleFixed Name	Value	Description
flexTextFlat	0	Normal text (default)
flexTextRaised	1	Raised text
flexTextInset	2	Inset text
flexTextRaisedLight	3	Raised light text
flexTextInsetLight	4	Inset light text

Table M-157: **TextStyleFixed** *values.*

- *MSFlexGridControl*.**ToolTipText**—a **String** that holds a text value that can be displayed as a **ToolTip** box that displays whenever the cursor is held over the control for about one second.
- *MSFlexGridControl*.**Top**—a **Single** that contains the distance measured in twips between the top edge of the control and the top edge of the control's container.
- *MSFlexGridControl*.**TopRow**—an **Integer** value containing the topmost visible row.
- *MSFlexGridControl*.**Version**—an **Integer** value containing the version number of the **MSFlexGrid** control.
- *MSFlexGridControl*.**Visible**—a **Boolean** value when **True** means that the control is visible. When **False** means that the control is not visible.

Tip

This property hides the control until the program is ready to display it.

- *MSFlexGridControl*.**WhatsThisHelpID**—a **Long** that contains a help file context ID number references an entry in the help file. This provides a What's This PopUp help display in response to the What's This button in the upper right corner of the window.
- *MSFlexGridControl*.**Width**—a **Single** that contains the width of the control.
- *MSFlexGridControl*.**WordWrap**—a **Boolean** value when **True** means that if the text inside the cell does not fit, it will be wrapped on a word boundary so that the complete text will display. **False** means that text would truncate at the cell's edge.

Methods

MSFlexGridControl.AddItem *item*, [*row*]

Usage   This method adds a row to the grid.

Arguments
- *item*—a **String** containing a list of values (one for each column) to display in the grid separated by the tab (*vbTab*) character.
- *row*—a **Long** value specifying the position for the new row. If omitted, *row* will default to the last row in the grid.

MSFlexGridControl.Clear

Usage   This method clears the contents of the grid.

MSFlexGridControl.Drag [*DragAction*]

Usage   This method begins, ends, or cancels a drag operation.

Arguments
- *DragAction*—an **Integer** that contains a value selected from Table M-158 below.

DragAction Name	Value	Description
vbCancel	0	Cancels any drag operation in progress.
vbBeginDrag	1	Begins a drag operation (default).
vbEndDrag	2	Ends a drag operation and drops *object*.

Table M-158: DragAction *values*.

MSFlexGridControl.Move *Left* [, *Top* [, *Width* [, *Height*]]]

Usage   This method changes the position and the size of the **MSFlexGrid** control. The **ScaleMode** of the **Form** or other container object that holds the **MSFlexGrid** control will determine the units used to specify the coordinates.

Arguments
- *Left*—a **Single** that specifies the new position of the left edge of the control.
- *Top*—a **Single** that specifies the new position of the top edge of the control.
- *Width*—a **Single** that specifies the new width of the control.
- *Height*—a **Single** that specifies the new height of the control.

MSFlexGridControl.OLEDrag

Usage   This method begins an **OLEDrag** and drop operation. Invoking this method will trigger the **OLEStartDrag** event.

MSFlexGridControl.Refresh

Usage   This method redraws the contents of the control.

MSFlexGridControl.RemoveItem [rowvalue]

Usage   This method removes the specified row from the grid.

Arguments   ▪ *rowvalue*—a **Long** containing the row number to remove.

MSFlexGridControl.SetFocus

Usage   This method transfers the focus from the form or control that currently has the focus to this control. To receive the focus, this control must be enabled and visible.

MSFlexGridControl.ShowWhatsThis

Usage   This method displays the ShowWhatsThis help information for this control.

MSFlexGridControl.ZOrder [position]

Usage   This method specifies the position of the **MSFLexGrid** control relative to the other objects on the form.

> **Tip**
>
> *Note that there are three layers of objects on a form: the back layer is the drawing space which contains the results of the graphical methods, the middle layer contains graphical objects and **Labels**, and the top layer contains nongraphical controls such as the **MSFlexGrid** control. The **ZOrder** method only affects how the objects are arranged within a single layer.*

Arguments   ▪ *position*—an **Integer** that specifies the relative position of this object. A value of **0** means that the control is positioned at the head of the list; a value of **1** means that the control will be placed at the end of the list.

Events   Private Sub MSFlexGridControl_Click([index As Integer])

Usage   This event occurs when the user clicks a mouse button to select an item in the drop-down list or selects an item from the drop-down list using the keyboard.

Arguments   ▪ *index*—an **Integer** that uniquely identifies a control in a control array. This argument is not present if the control is not part of a control array.

Private Sub MSFlexGridControl_Compare ([index As Integer ,] row1 As Long, row2 As Long, comp As Integer)

Usage   This event occurs when the **Sort** property is set to custom sort.

Arguments   ▪ *index*—an **Integer** that uniquely identifies a control in a control array. This argument is not present if the control is not part of a control array.

▪ *row1*—a **Long** containing the first row to compare.

MSFlexGrid • 599

- *row2*—a **Long** containing the second row to compare.
- *comp*—an **Integer** value when –1 means that *row1* is less than *row2*. When 0 means that the two rows are equal. When 1 means that *row1* is greater than *row2*.

Private Sub *MSFlexGridControl*_DblClick([*index* As Integer])

Usage This event occurs when the user double-clicks a mouse button to select an item in the drop-down list or selects an item from the drop-down list using the keyboard. This applies only when **Style** is set to *vbComboSimple*.

Arguments • *index*—an **Integer** that uniquely identifies a control in a control array. This argument is not present if the control is not part of a control array.

Private Sub *MSFlexGridControl*_DragDrop([*index* As Integer ,] *source* As Control, *x* As Single, *y* As Single)

Usage This event occurs when a drag-and-drop operation is completed by using the **Drag** method with an *DragAction* value of *vbEndDrag*.

> **Tip**
>
> *When using drag-and-drop operations, use the **DragOver** event to determine what the cursor should look like while the cursor moves over the control.*

Arguments • *index*—an **Integer** that uniquely identifies a control in a control array. This argument is not present if the control is not part of a control array.
- *source*—a control object that is the control that is being dragged.

> **Tip**
>
> *You can access a property or method from the source control by using* source.property *or* source.method. *You can determine the type of object or control by using the **TypeOf** operator.*

- *x*—a **Single** that contains the horizontal location of the mouse pointer.
- *y*—a **Single** that contains the vertical location of the mouse pointer.

Private Sub *MSFlexGridControl*_DragOver([*index* As Integer ,] *source* As Control, *x* As Single, *y* As Single, *state* As Integer)

Usage This event occurs while a drag operation is in progress and the cursor is moved over the control.

> **Tip**
>
> *When using drag-and-drop operations, use the **DragOver** event to determine what the cursor should look like while the cursor moves over the control. When* state *is* **0***, you can change the cursor to a No Drop (vbNoDrop) cursor or highlight the field that the cursor is near. When* state *is* **1***, you can undo the changes you made when the* state *was* **0***.*

Arguments
- *index*—an **Integer** that uniquely identifies a control in a control array. This argument is not present if the control is not part of a control array.
- *source*—a control object that is the control that is being dragged.

> **Tip**
>
> *You can access a property or method from the source control by using* **source.**property *or* **source.**method. *You can determine the type of object or control by using the* **TypeOf** *operator.*

- *x*—a **Single** that contains the horizontal location of the mouse pointer.
- *y*—a **Single** that contains the vertical location of the mouse pointer.
- *state*—an **Integer** value (see Table M-159) that indicates the state of the object being dragged.

state Name	Value	Description
vbEnter	0	The dragged object is entering range of the control.
vbLeave	1	The dragged object is leaving range of the control.
vbOver	2	The dragged object has moved from one position over the control to another.

Table M-159: state *values*.

Private Sub *MSFlexGridControl*_EnterCell ([*index* As Integer])

Usage This event occurs when another cell is selected. First the **LeaveCell** event will occur, followed by the **EnterCell** event, and finally the **RowColChange** event.

Private Sub *MSFlexGridControl*_GotFocus ([*index* As Integer])

Usage This event occurs when the control is given focus.

> **Tip**
>
> *You can use this routine to display help or other information in a status bar.*

Arguments *index*—an **Integer** that uniquely identifies a control in a control array. This argument is not present if the control is not part of a control array.

Private Sub *MSFlexGridControl*_KeyDown ([*index* As Integer ,] *keycode* As Integer, *shift* As Single)

Usage This event occurs when a key is pressed while the control has the focus.

Arguments
- *index*—an **Integer** that uniquely identifies a control in a control array. This argument is not present if the control is not part of a control array.
- *keycode*—an **Integer** that contains information about which key was pressed.
- *shift*—an **Integer** value (see Table M-160) that contains information about the Shift and Alt keys that were pushed when the mouse button was pressed. These values can be added together if more than one key was down. For instance, a value of **5** would mean that the Shift and Alt keys were both down when the mouse button was pressed.

shift Name	Value	Description
vbShiftMask	1	The Shift key was pressed.
vbCtrlMask	2	The Ctrl key was pressed.
vbAltMask	4	The Alt key was pressed.

Table M-160: shift *values.*

Private Sub *MSFlexGridControl*_KeyPress([*index* As Integer ,] *keychar* As Integer)

Usage This event occurs whenever a key is pressed while the control has the focus.

Arguments
- *index*—an **Integer** that uniquely identifies a control in a control array. This argument is not present if the control is not part of a control array.
- *keychar*—an **Integer** that contains the ASCII character that was pressed.

Private Sub *MSFlexGridControl*_KeyUp ([*index* As Integer ,] *keycode* As Integer, *shift* As Single)

Usage This event occurs when a key is released while the control has the focus.

Arguments
- *index*—an **Integer** that uniquely identifies a control in a control array. This argument is not present if the control is not part of a control array.
- *keycode*—an **Integer** that contains information about which key was released.
- *shift*—an **Integer** value (see Table M-161) that contains information about the Shift and Alt keys that were pushed when the mouse button was pressed. These values can be added together if more than one key was down. For instance, a value of **5** would mean that the Shift and Alt keys were both down when the mouse button was pressed.

shift Name	Value	Description
vbShiftMask	1	The Shift key was pressed.
vbCtrlMask	2	The Ctrl key was pressed.
vbAltMask	4	The Alt key was pressed.

Table M-161: shift *values.*

Private Sub *MSFlexGridControl*_LeaveCell ([*index* As Integer])

Usage   This event occurs when another cell is selected. First the **LeaveCell** event will occur, followed by the **EnterCell** event and finally the **RowColChange** event.

Tip

This routine is useful to performing data verification for a particular cell.

Arguments
- *index*—an **Integer** that uniquely identifies a control in a control array. This argument is not present if the control is not part of a control array.

Private Sub *MSFlexGridControl*_LostFocus ([*index* As Integer])

Usage   This event occurs when the control loses focus.

Arguments
- *index*—an **Integer** that uniquely identifies a control in a control array. This argument is not present if the control is not part of a control array.

Private Sub *MSFlexGridBoxControl*_MouseDown([*index* As Integer ,] *button* As Integer, *shift* As Single, *x* As Single, *y* As Single)

Usage   This event occurs when a mouse button was pressed while the cursor is over the control.

Arguments
- *index*—an **Integer** that uniquely identifies a control in a control array. This argument is not present if the control is not part of a control array.
- *button*—an **Integer** value (see Table M-162) that contains information about the mouse buttons that were pressed. Only one button will be indicated when this event occurs.

button Name	Value	Description
vbLeftButton	1	The left button was pressed.
vbRightButton	2	The right button was pressed.
vbMiddleButton	4	The middle button was pressed.

Table M-162: button *values.*

- *shift*—an **Integer** value (see Table M-163) that contains information about the Shift and Alt keys that were pushed when the mouse button was pressed. These values can be added together if more than one key was down. For instance, a value of **5** would mean that the Shift and Alt keys were both down when the mouse button was pressed.

shift Name	Value	Description
vbShiftMask	1	The Shift key was pressed.
vbCtrlMask	2	The Ctrl key was pressed.
vbAltMask	4	The Alt key was pressed.

Table M-163: shift *values.*

- *x*—a **Single** that contains the horizontal location of the mouse pointer.
- *y*—a **Single** that contains the vertical location of the mouse pointer.

Private Sub *MSFlexGridControl*_MouseMove ([*index* As Integer ,] *button* As Integer, *shift* As Single, *x* As Single, *y* As Single)

Usage This event occurs while the cursor is moved over the control.

Arguments
- *index*—an **Integer** that uniquely identifies a control in a control array. This argument is not present if the control is not part of a control array.
- *button*—an **Integer** value (see Table M-164) that contains information about the mouse buttons that were pressed. These values can be added together if more than one button was pushed. For instance, a value of **3** means that both the left and right buttons were pressed. A value of **0** means that no buttons were pressed.

button Name	Value	Description
vbLeftButton	1	The left button was pressed.
vbRightButton	2	The right button was pressed.
vbMiddleButton	4	The middle button was pressed.

Table M-164: button *values.*

- *shift*—an **Integer** value (see Table M-165) that contains information about the Shift and Alt keys that were pushed when the mouse button was pressed. For instance, a value of **5** would mean that the Shift and Alt keys were both down when the mouse button was pressed. A value of **0** means that none of these keys were pressed.

shift Name	Value	Description
vbShiftMask	1	The Shift key was pressed.
vbCtrlMask	2	The Ctrl key was pressed.
vbAltMask	4	The Alt key was pressed.

Table M-165: shift *values.*

- *x*—a **Single** that contains the horizontal location of the mouse pointer.
- *y*—a **Single** that contains the vertical location of the mouse pointer.

Private Sub *MSFlexGridBoxControl*_MouseUp([*index* As Integer ,] *button* As Integer, *shift* As Single, *x* As Single, *y* As Single)

Usage   This event occurs when a mouse button is released while the cursor is over the control.

Arguments
- *index*—an **Integer** that uniquely identifies a control in a control array. This argument is not present if the control is not part of a control array.
- *button*—an **Integer** value (see Table M-166) that contains information about the mouse buttons that were released. Only one of these values will be present.

button Name	Value	Description
vbLeftButton	1	The left button was released.
vbRightButton	2	The right button was released.
vbMiddleButton	4	The middle button was released.

Table M-166: button *values*.

- *shift*—an **Integer** value (see Table M-167) that contains information about the Shift and Alt keys that were pushed when the mouse button was released. These values can be added together if more than one key was down. For instance, a value of **5** would mean that the Shift and Alt keys were both down when the mouse button was released. A value of **0** means that none of these keys were pressed.

shift Name	Value	Description
vbShiftMask	1	The Shift key was pressed.
vbCtrlMask	2	The Ctrl key was pressed.
vbAltMask	4	The Alt key was pressed.

Table M-167: shift *values*.

- *x*—a **Single** that contains the horizontal location of the mouse pointer.
- *y*—a **Single** that contains the vertical location of the mouse pointer.

Private Sub *MSFlexGridControl*_OLECompleteDrag(*effect* As Long)

Usage   This event tells the source control the results of an OLE drag-and-drop operation. This is the final event to occur in the series of actions that make up an OLE drag-and-drop operation.

Arguments
- *effect*—a **Long** (see Table M-168) that returns the status of the OLE drag-and-drop operation.

effect Name	Value	Description
vbDropEffectNone	0	The operation was canceled or the target control can't accept the drop operation.
vbDropEffectCopy	1	The operation copied data from the source control to the target control. The original data is unchanged.
vbDropEffectMove	2	The operation results in a link from the original data to the target control.

Table M-168: effect *values.*

Private Sub *MSFlexGridControl*_OLEDragDrop (*data* As DataObject, *effect* As Long, *button* As Integer, *shift* As Single, *x* As Single, *y* As Single)

Usage
: This event tells the source control the results of an OLE drag-and-drop operation. This is the final event to occur in the series of actions that make up an OLE drag-and drop-operation.

Arguments
: • *data*—a **DataObject** that contains the formats that the source control will provide. If the data is not contained in the **DataObject**, then it can be retrieved with the **GetData** method.
: • *effect*—a **Long** (see Table M-169) that returns the status of the OLE drag-and-drop operation.

effect Name	Value	Description
vbDropEffectNone	0	The operation was canceled or the target control can't accept the drop operation.
vbDropEffectCopy	1	The operation copied data from the source control to the target control. The original data is unchanged.
vbDropEffectMove	2	The operation results in a link from the original data to the target control.

Table M-169: effect *values.*

: • *button*—an **Integer** value (see Table M-170) that contains information about the mouse buttons that were pressed. These values can be added together if more than one button was pushed. For instance, a value of **3** means that both the left and right buttons were pressed. A value of **0** means that no buttons were pressed.

button Name	Value	Description
vbLeftButton	1	The left button was pressed.
vbRightButton	2	The right button was pressed.
vbMiddleButton	4	The middle button was pressed.

Table M-170: button *values.*

- *shift*—an **Integer** value (see Table M-171) that contains information about the Shift and Alt keys that were pushed when the mouse button was released. These values can be added together if more than one key was down. For instance, a value of **5** would mean that the Shift and Alt keys were both down when the mouse button was released. A value of **0** means that none of these keys were pressed.

shift Name	Value	Description
vbShiftMask	1	The Shift key was pressed.
vbCtrlMask	2	The Ctrl key was pressed.
vbAltMask	4	The Alt key was pressed.

Table M-171: shift *values*.

- *x*—a **Single** that contains the horizontal location of the mouse pointer.
- *y*—a **Single** that contains the vertical location of the mouse pointer.

Private Sub *MSFlexGridControl*_OLEDragOver (*data* As DataObject, *effect* As Long, *button* As Integer, *shift* As Single, *x* As Single, *y* As Single, *state* As Integer)

Usage This event happens when an OLE drag-and-drop operation is in progress.

Arguments
- *data*—a **DataObject** that contains the formats that the source control will provide. If the data is not contained in the **DataObject**, then it can be retrieved with the **GetData** method.
- *effect*—a **Long** (see Table M-172) that returns the status of the OLE drag-and-drop operation.

effect Name	Value	Description
vbDropEffectNone	0	The operation was canceled or the target control can't accept the drop operation.
vbDropEffectCopy	1	The operation copied data from the source control to the target control. The original data is unchanged.
vbDropEffectMove	2	The operation results in a link from the original data to the target control.

Table M-172: effect *values*.

- *button*—an **Integer** value (see Table M-173) that contains information about the mouse buttons that were pressed. These values can be added together if more than one button was pushed. For instance, a value of **3** means that both the left and right buttons were pressed. A value of **0** means that no buttons were pressed.

button Name	Value	Description
vbLeftButton	1	The left button was pressed.
vbRightButton	2	The right button was pressed.
vbMiddleButton	4	The middle button was pressed.

Table M-173: button *values*.

- *shift*—an **Integer** value (see Table M-174) that contains information about the Shift and Alt keys that were pushed when the mouse button was released. These values can be added together if more than one key was down. For instance, a value of **5** would mean that the Shift and Alt keys were both down when the mouse button was released. A value of **0** means that none of these keys were pressed.

shift Name	Value	Description
vbShiftMask	1	The Shift key was pressed.
vbCtrlMask	2	The Ctrl key was pressed.
vbAltMask	4	The Alt key was pressed.

Table M-174: shift *values*.

- *x*—a **Single** that contains the horizontal location of the mouse pointer.
- *y*—a **Single** that contains the vertical location of the mouse pointer.
- *state*—an **Integer** value (see Table M-175) that indicates the state of the object being dragged.

state Name	Value	Description
vbEnter	0	The dragged object is entering range of the control.
vbLeave	1	The dragged object is leaving range of the control.
vbOver	2	The dragged object has moved from one position over the control to another.

Table M-175: state *values*.

Private Sub *MSFlexGridControl_OLEGiveFeedback* (*effect* As Long)

Usage This event tells the source control what is happening while the OLE drag-and-drop operation is in progress. This event occurs after the **OLEDragOver** event.

Tip

You may want to use this event to change the cursor to reflect what can happen in the remote object.

Arguments
- *effect*—a **Long** (see Table M-176) that returns the status of the OLE drag-and-drop operation.

effect Name	Value	Description
vbDropEffectNone	0	The operation was canceled or the target control can't accept the drop operation.
vbDropEffectCopy	1	The operation copied data from the source control to the target control. The original data is unchanged.
vbDropEffectMove	2	The operation results in a link from the original data to the target control.
vbDropEffectScroll	&H80000000	The target control is about to scroll or is scrolling. This value may be added to the other *effect* values.

Table M-176: effect *values*.

Private Sub *MSFlexGridControl*_OLESetData (*data* As DataObject, *DataFormat* As Integer)

Usage This event happens in response to the target object performing a **GetData** method on *data*. This routine will respond by using the **SetData** method with the desired data using the **DataObject** *data*.

Arguments
- *data*—a **DataObject** that will contain the data to return to the target object.
- *format*—an **Integer** value (see Table M-177) that contains the format of the data.

format Name	Value	Description
vbCFText	1	Text (.TXT files)
vbCFBitmap	2	Bitmap (.BMP files)
vbCFMetafile	3	Metafile (.WMF files)
vbCFEDIB	8	Device independent bitmap (DIB)
vbCFPallette	9	Color palette
vbCFEMetafile	14	Enhanced metafile (.EMF files)
vbCFFiles	15	List of files
vbCFRTF	-16639	Rich Text Format (.RTF files)

Table M-177: format *values.*

Private Sub *MSFlexGridControl*_OLEStartDrag (*data* As DataObject, *AllowedEffects* As Long)

Usage This event starts an OLE drag-and-drop operation.

Arguments
- *data*—a **DataObject** that will contain the formats that the source object is willing to provide to the target object. It may optionally contain the data to transfer.
- *AllowedEffects*—a **Long** (see Table M-178) that contains the effects that the target object can request from the source object. The *AllowedEffects* can be added together if the source object supports more than one effect. Note that the target object can always use the *vbDropEffectNone* effect.

AllowedEffects Name	Value	Description
vbDropEffectNone	0	The target can't copy the data.
vbDropEffectCopy	1	The target can copy the data and the source will keep the data unchanged.
vbDropEffectMove	2	The target can copy the data and the source will delete the data.

Table M-178: AllowedEffects *values.*

Private Sub *MSFlexGridControl*_RowColChange ([*index* As Integer])

Usage This event occurs whenever the current cell is moved from one location to another. First the **LeaveCell** event will occur, followed by the **EnterCell** event, and finally the **RowColChange** event.

Arguments *index*—an **Integer** that uniquely identifies a control in a control array. This argument is not present if the control is not part of a control array.

Private Sub *MSFlexGridControl*_Scroll ([*index* As Integer])

Usage This event is called each time the scroll bar is repositioned in the drop-down box.

Arguments *index*—an **Integer** that uniquely identifies a control in a control array. This argument is not present if the control is not part of a control array.

Private Sub *MSFlexGridControl*_SelChange ([*index* As Integer])

Usage This event is called when the range of selected cells changes.

Arguments *index*—an **Integer** that uniquely identifies a control in a control array. This argument is not present if the control is not part of a control array.

Examples
```
Private Sub Form_Load()
MSFlexGrid1.Cols = 7
MSFlexGrid1.Rows = 20
MSFlexGrid1.FixedCols = 1
MSFlexGrid1.FixedRows = 1
For i = 1 To MSFlexGrid1.Cols - 1
   MSFlexGrid1.TextMatrix(0, i) = Chr(Asc("A") + i - 1)
Next i
For i = 1 To MSFlexGrid1.Rows - 1
   MSFlexGrid1.TextMatrix(i, 0) = Format(i)
Next i
End Sub

Private Sub MSFlexGrid1_KeyPress(KeyAscii As Integer)
MSFlexGrid1.Text = MSFlexGrid1.Text & Chr(KeyAscii)
End Sub

Private Sub MSFlexGrid1_KeyUp(KeyCode As Integer, Shift As Integer)
If KeyCode = vbKeyDown Then
   Row = IIf(Row + 1 > Rows, Rows, Row + 1)
ElseIf KeyCode = vbKeyUp Then
   Row = IIf(Row - 1 < 1, 1, Row - 1)
```

```
ElseIf KeyCode = vbKeyLeft Then
    Col = IIf(Col - 1 < 1, 1, Col - 1)
ElseIf KeyCode = vbKeyRight Then
    Col = IIf(Col + 1 > Cols, Cols, Col + 1)
End If
End Sub
```

This program shows how to set up an **MSFlexGrid** with 7 columns and 20 rows in the form's **Load** event. I also took the time to create a fixed column and a fixed row to apply the typical spreadsheet letter/number labels.

I included code in the grid's **KeyPress** event to capture characters for display and used the **KeyUp** event to let the user use the cursor keys to move around the grid.

See Also   **Data** (control), **MSFlexGrid** (control)

MsgBox

FUNCTION

CCE, LE, PE, EE

Syntax   `result = MsgBox ( msg [, graphics [, helpfile, context ] ] )`

Usage   The **MsgBox** function displays a message in a modal box on the screen and returns a value indicating which button was pushed. Because a modal box is used, the application is suspended while the box is displayed.

Tip

*The **MsgBox** function can be used as a statement to provide information when the user response is not important.*

Arguments
- *result*—an **Integer** value (see Table M-179) containing the button that was pushed.

result Name	Value	Description
vbOK	1	The OK button.
vbCancel	2	The Cancel button.
vbAbort	3	The Abort button.
vbRetry	4	The Retry button.
vbIgnore	5	The Ignore button.
vbYes	6	The Yes button.
vbNo	7	The No button.

Table M-179: result values.

- *msg*—a **String** value to display to the user. It is limited to about 1,024 characters. Multiple lines may be separated with embedded carriage return line feed pairs (*vbCrLf*).
- *graphics*—a **Long** value consisting of values from the *buttons, icons, defaults, modal,* and *otheroptions* in Tables M-180 through M-184. Only one value may be selected from each table except *otheroptions* may be selected. The *graphics* value is created by adding all of the selected options together.

buttons Name	Value	Description
vbOKOnly	0	The OK button
vbOKCancel	1	The OK and Cancel buttons
vbAbortRetryIgnore	2	The Abort, Retry, and Ignore buttons
vbYesNoCancel	3	The Yes, No, and Cancel buttons
vbYesNo	4	The Yes and No buttons
vbRetryCancel	5	The Retry and Cancel buttons

Table M-180: buttons values.

icons Name	Value	Description
vbCritical	16	The Critical message icon
vbQuestion	32	The Question mark icon
vbExclamation	48	The Exclamation icon
vbInformation	64	The Information icon

Table M-181: icons values.

defaults Name	Value	Description
vbDefaultButton1	0	Make the first button default.
vbDefaultButton2	256	Make the second button default.
vbDefaultButton3	512	Make the third button default.
vbDefaultButton4	768	Make the fouth button default.

Table M-182: defaults values.

modal Name	Value	Description
vbApplicationModal	0	Stop the current application from running until the user responds.
vbSystemModal	4096	Stop the system from running until the user responds.

Table M-183: modal values.

otheroptions Name	Value	Description
vbMsgBoxHelpButton	16384	Add the help button to the message box (requires values for *helpfile* and *context*).
vbMsgBoxSetForeground	65536	Make the message box the foreground window.
vbMsgBoxRight	524288	Display the message right aligned.
vbMsgBoxRtlReading	1048576	The message is read from right to left.

Table M-184: otheroptions values.

- *helpfile*—a **String** value containing the name of a help file. If specified, *context* must also be specified.
- *context*—a **Long** value containing the context number for the help text in the help file. If specified, *helpfile* must also be specified.

Examples

```
Dim mybutton As Long
Dim myicon As Long

Private Sub Command1_Click()
Dim result As Integer
Text1.Text = Format(MsgBox(Message.Text, mybutton + myicon))
End Sub

Private Sub Form_Load()
mybutton = 0
myicon = 0
Message.Text = ""
End Sub

Private Sub Option1_Click(Index As Integer)
mybutton = Index
End Sub

Private Sub Option2_Click(Index As Integer)
myicon = Index * 16
End Sub
```

This program shows how the various buttons and icons can be combined to create a message box. Each option control array consists of an **Option Button** for each button or icon value. Since the buttons range from 0 to 6, I use the value of the index to set the global variable mybutton. Since the icons range from 16 to 64 in jumps of 16, I added a none **Option Button** and assigned it a value of **0**. Each time the icon option button is clicked, I set the value of the global variable myicon to 16 times the value of the index.

The command button displays a message box using the value from the Message text box and the mybutton and myicon variables. The result from the function is formatted and then placed in the Text1 text box.

See Also   **InputBox** (function)

Multimedia MCI Control

CONTROL

PE, EE

Usage   The **Multimedia MCI Control** is an ActiveX control that allows you to manage recording and playback using Medial Control Interface devices. Such devices include, audio boards, MIDI sequencers, CD-ROM drives, audio CD players, videodisc players, and videotape recorders and players. This control also provides the ability to play .WAV sound files and to display Windows .AVI video files.

Properties
- *MMControl*.**AutoEnable**—a **Boolean** when **True** means the appropriate buttons will automatically be selected depending on the mode of the control. **False** means that the settings of the individual button enabled properties will be used.
- *MMControl*.**BackEnable**—a **Boolean** when **True** means the Back button will be enabled. **False** means that the Back button will be disabled.

Multimedia MCI Control • 613

- *MMControl.***BackVisible**—a **Boolean** when **True** means the Back button is visible. **False** means the Back button is hidden.
- *MMControl.***BorderStyle**—an **Integer** value (see Table M-185) specifying how the border will be drawn. This property also indicates how the form can be resized and is read only at run time.

BorderStyle Name	Value	Description
vbBSNone	0	No border, control box menu, title bar, maximize and minimize buttons. Cannot be resized.
vbFixedSingle	1	Single line around the form. Form can only be resized by maximize and minimize buttons.

Table M-185: **BorderStyle** *values.*

- *MMControl.***CanEject**—a **Boolean** when **True** means that the device can eject its media. This property is read only at run time.
- *MMControl.***CanPlay**—a **Boolean** when **True** means that the device can play. This property is read only at run time.
- *MMControl.***CanRecord**—a **Boolean** when **True** means that the device can record. This property is read only at run time.
- *MMControl.***CanStep**—a **Boolean** when **True** means that the device can move a video image forward or back one frame at a time. This property is read only at run time.
- *MMControl.***Command**—a **String** (see Table M-186) containing the command to execute.

Command Name	Description
Back	Step backward.
Close	Close the device.
Eject	Eject the media.
Next	Go to the next track.
Open	Open a device specified in **DeviceType**.
Pause	Pause the device if currently playing or recording. If paused, then resume the previous activity.
Play	Play a device.
Prev	Go back to the beginning of the current track. Will go back to the previous track within the first three seconds of the prior Prev command.
Record	Record.
Save	Save an open file.
Seek	Seek the new position. If playing continue playing from the new position.
Sound	Play a sound.
Step	Step forward.
Stop	Stop playing or recording.

Table M-186: **Command** *values.*

- *MMControl.***Container**—an object that sets or returns the container of the control at run time. This property cannot be set at design time.
- *MMControl.***DataBindings**—a reference to the **DataBindings** collection containing the bindable properties available.

- *MMControl*.**DeviceID**—an **Integer** containing the device for the open MCI device. If no device is open, this value will be **0**.
- *MMControl*.**DeviceType**—a **String** containing the type of device to open. Valid device types are: AVIVideo, CDAudio, DAT, DigitalVideo, MMMovie, Other, Overlay, Scanner, Sequencer, VCR, Videodisc, or WaveAudio.
- *MMControl*.**DragIcon**—an object that contains the picture value of an icon. At design time, you can specify an icon file that has a file type of .ICO.

> **Tip**
>
> This value can be created by copying the value from another control's **DragIcon** value, a form's icon, or by using the **LoadPicture** function.

- *MMControl*.**DragMode**—an **Integer** value (see Table M-187) specifying how the control will respond to a drag request.

> **Tip**
>
> Setting **DragMode** to vbAutomatic will automatically begin a drag operation when the user clicks on the control. However, the control will not respond to the usual mouse events (**Click**, **DblClick**, **MouseDown**, **MouseMove**, **MouseUp**).

DragMode Name	Value	Description
vbManual	0	The Drag method must be used to begin a drag-and-drop operation (default value).
vbAutomatic	1	The source control will automatically begin a drag-and-drop operation when the user clicks on the control.

Table M-187: **DragMode** values.

- *MMControl*.**EjectEnable**—a **Boolean** when **True** means the Eject button will be enabled. **False** means that the Eject button will be disabled.
- *MMControl*.**EjectVisible**—a **Boolean** when **True** means the Eject button is visible. **False** means the Eject button is hidden.
- *MMControl*.**Enabled**—a **Boolean** value when **True** means that the control will respond to events. When **False**, the control will not respond to events.
- *MMControl*.**Error**—an **Integer** value containing the error code returned from executing the last command. If no error occurred, then this value will be **0**. This property is read-only.
- *MMControl*.**ErrorMessage**—a **String** containing a description of the error code found in **Error**. This property is read-only.
- *MMControl*.**FileName**—a **String** specifying the file to be opened by the Open command or to be saved by the Save command. This property can't be changed after the Open command is used unless a Close command executes first.
- *MMControl*.**Frames**—a **Long** specifying the number of frames to move using the Step or Back commands.

Multimedia MCI Control • 615

- *MMControl*.**From**—a **Long** specifying the starting time location in units defined by the **TimeFormat** property which will be used by the next Play or Record command. Afterwards this property is ignored by all commands until it has been assigned a new value.
- *MMControl*.**Height**—a **Single** that contains the height of the control.
- *MMControl*.**HelpContextID**—a **Long** that contains a help file context ID number which references an entry in the help file. When the user presses the F1 key while this control is active, the corresponding entry in the help file will automatically display. A value of **0** means that no context number was specified.

> **Tip**
>
> *A help file must be compiled using the Windows Help Compiler available in the Professional and Enterprise editions of Visual Basic.*

- *MMControl*.**hWnd**—a **Long** that contains a Windows handle to the control.

> **Tip**
>
> *The **hWnd** property is most useful when making calls to Windows API functions. Since this value can change during execution, do not save the value into a variable for later use.*

- *MMControl*.**hWndDisplay**—a **Long** that contains a Windows handle to the display device used for MMMovie or Overlay devices.
- *MMControl*.**Index**—an **Integer** that uniquely identifies a control in a control array.
- *MMControl*.**Left**—a **Single** that contains the distance measured in twips between the left edge of the control and the left edge of the control's container.
- *MMControl*.**Length**—a **Long** value containing the length of the media in units defined by the **TimeFormat** property. This property is read only at run time.
- *MMControl*.**Mode**—a **Long** value (see Table M-188) containing the current mode of an MCI device.

Mode Name	Value	Description
mciModeNotOpen	524	The device is not open.
mciModeStop	525	The device is stopped.
mciModePlay	526	The device is playing.
mciModeRecord	527	The device is recording.
mciModeSeek	528	The device is seeking.
mciModePause	529	The device is paused.
mciModeReady	530	The device is ready.

Table M-188: **Mode** *values.*

- *MMListControl*.**MouseIcon**—a **Picture** object (a bitmap, icon, or metafile) that will be used as a cursor when the **MousePointer** property is set to 99. Note that Visual Basic does not support color cursors from a .CUR file. A color icon from an .ICO file should be used instead.

- *MMControl*.**MousePointer**—an **Integer** value (see Table M-189) that contains the value of the cursor that should display when the cursor is moved over this control. Use *vbCustom* to display the custom icon stored in the **MouseIcon** property.

Cursor Name	Value	Description
vbDefault	0	Shape determined by the object (default value)
vbArrow	1	Arrow
vbCrosshair	2	Crosshair
vbIbeam	3	I beam
vbIconPointer	4	Square inside a square
vbSizePointer	5	Four sided arrow (north, south, east, west)
vbSizeNESW	6	Two sided arrow (northeast, southwest)
vbSizeNS	7	Two sided arrow (north, south)
vbSizeNWSE	8	Two sided arrow (northwest, southeast)
vbSizeWE	9	Two sided arrow (west, east)
vbUpArrow	10	Single sided arrow pointing north
vbHourglass	11	Hourglass
vbNoDrop	12	No Drop
vbArrowHourglass	13	An arrow and an Hourglass
vbArrowQuestion	14	An arrow and a question mark
vbSizeAll	15	Size all
vbCustom	99	Custom icon from the **MouseIcon** property of this control

Table M-189: **Cursor** *values.*

- *MMControl*.**MouseRow**—a **Long** value containing the row pointed to by the mouse.
- *MMControl*.**Name**—a **String** that contains the name of the control that will reference the control in a Visual Basic program. This property is read only at run time.
- *MMControl*.**NextEnable**—a **Boolean** when **True** means the Next button will be enabled. **False** means that the Next button will be disabled.
- *MMControl*.**NextVisible**—a **Boolean** when **True** means the Next button is visible. **False** means the Next button is hidden.
- *MMControl*.**Notify**—a **Boolean** when **True** means that when each command completes, the corresponding event will be called. **False** means no events will be triggered.
- *MMControl*.**NotifyMessage**—a **String** that contains a text description of the code returned in a notify event.
- *MMControl*.**NotifyValue**—an **Integer** value (see Table M-190) containing the result of the last MCI command.

NotifyValue Name	Value	Description
mciNotifySuccessful	1	The command was successful.
mciNotifySuperseded	2	The command was superseded by a new command.
mciNotifyAborted	4	The command was aborted by the user.
mciNotifyFailure	8	The command failed.

Table M-190: *NotifyValue values.*

- *MMControl*.**Object**—an object that contains a reference to the *MMControl* object.
- *MMControl*.**Orientation**—an **Integer** value (see Table M-191) that describes how the control will respond to OLE drop operations.

Orientation Name	Value	Description
mciOrientHorz	0	The buttons are arranged horizontally.
mciOrientVert	1	The buttons are arranged vertically.

Table M-191: **Orientation** *values.*

- *MMControl*.**Parent**—an object that contains a reference to the **Form**, **Frame,** or other container that contains the **MMcontrol**.
- *MMControl*.**PauseEnable**—a **Boolean** when **True** means the Pause button will be enabled. **False** means that the Pause button will be disabled.
- *MMControl*.**PauseVisible**—a **Boolean** when **True** means the Pause button is visible. **False** means the Pause button is hidden.
- *MMControl*.**PlayEnable**—a **Boolean** when **True** means the Play button will be enabled. **False** means that the Play button will be disabled.
- *MMControl*.**PlayVisible**—a **Boolean** when **True** means the Play button is visible. **False** means the Play button is hidden.
- *MMControl*.**Position**—a **Long** value containing the current position of an open MCI device. This property is read only at run time.
- *MMControl*.**PrevEnable**—a **Boolean** when **True** means the Prev button will be enabled. **False** means that the Prev button will be disabled.
- *MMControl*.**PrevVisible**—a **Boolean** when **True** means the Prev button is visible. **False** means the Prev button is hidden.
- *MMControl*.**RecordEnable**—a **Boolean** when **True** means the Record button will be enabled. **False** means that the Record button will be disabled.
- *MMControl*.**RecordMode**—an **Integer** value (see Table M-192) containing the current recording mode.

RecordMode Name	Value	Description
mciRecordInsert	0	The newly recorded material will be inserted at Position (available for .WAV files only).
mciRecordOverwrite	1	The newly recorded material will overlay any other material in the file.

Table M-192: **RecordMode** *values.*

- *MMControl*.**RecordVisible**—a **Boolean** when **True** means the Record button is visible. **False** means the Record button is hidden.
- *MMControl*.**Sharable**—a **Boolean** when **True** means that multiple programs may share the device. **False** means that only one program at a time may use the device.
- *MMControl*.**Silent**—a **Boolean** when **True** means that the sound is disabled. **False** means that if sound is available it will play.

- **MMControl.Start**—a **Long** containing the starting position of the media in units specified by **TimeFormat**.
- **MMControl.Step**—a **Boolean** when **True** means the Step button will be enabled. **False** means that the Step button will be disabled.
- **MMControl.StepVisible**—a **Boolean** when **True** means the Step button is visible. **False** means the Step button is hidden.
- **MMControl.StopEnable**—a **Boolean** when **True** means the Stop button will be enabled. **False** means that the Stop button will be disabled.
- **MMControl.StopVisible**—a **Boolean** when **True** means the Stop button is visible. **False** means the Stop button is hidden.
- **MMControl.TabIndex**—an Integer that determines the order that a user will tab through the objects on a form.
- **MMControl.TabStop**—a **Boolean** value when **True** means that the user can tab to this object. When **False** means that this control will be skipped to the next control in the **TabIndex** order.
- **MMControl.Tag**—a **String** that can hold programmer specific information. This property is not used by Visual Basic.
- **MMControl.TimeFormat**—a **Long** (see Table M-193) containing the format used for the **From**, **Length**, **Position**, **Start**, **To**, **TrackLength**, and **TrackPosition** properties. Note that not all devices support all time formats.

TimeFormat Name	Value	Description
mciFormatMilliseconds	0	A Long containing the time in milliseconds.
mciFormatHms	1	A 4 byte value, where each byte contains a specific value—from least significant to most significant: hours, minutes, seconds, unused.
mciFormatMsf	2	A 4 byte value, where each byte contains a specific value—from least significant to most significant: minutes, seconds, frames, unused.
mciFrames	3	A **Long** containing the frame count.
mciFormatSmpte24	4	A 4 byte value, where each byte contains a specific value for the SMPTE-24 format—from least significant to most significant: hours, minutes, seconds, frames.
mciFormatSmpte25	5	A 4 byte value, where each byte contains a specific value for the SMPTE-25 format—from least significant to most significant: hours, minutes, seconds, frames.
mciFormatSmpte30	6	A 4 byte value, where each byte contains a specific value for the SMPTE-30 format—from least significant to most significant: hours, minutes, seconds, frames.
mciFormatSmpte30Drop	7	A 4 byte value, where each byte contains a specific value for the SMPTE-30 drop format—from least significant to most significant: hours, minutes, seconds, frames.
mciFormatBytes	8	A **Long** containing the number of bytes.
mciFormatSamples	9	A **Long** containing the number of samples.
mciFormatTmsf	10	A 4 byte value, where each byte contains a specific value—from least significant to most significant: tracks, minutes, seconds, frames.

Table M-193: **TimeFormat** *values.*

> **Tip**
>
> SMPTE stands for the Society of Motion Picture and Television Engineers. Their standard division types are 24, 25, and 30 frames per second.

- *MMControl*.**To**—a **Long** specifying the ending time location in units defined by the **TimeFormat** property which will be used by the next Play or Record command. Afterwards this property is ignored by all commands until it has been assigned a new value.
- *MMControl*.**ToolTipText**—a **String** that holds a text value that can be displayed as a **ToolTip** box that displays whenever the cursor is held over the control for about one second.
- *MMControl*.**Top**—a **Single** that contains the distance measured in twips between the top edge of the control and the top edge of the control's container.
- *MMControl*.**Track**—a **Long** value containing the track used by **TrackLength** and **TrackPosition**.
- *MMControl*.**TrackLength**—a **Long** containing the length in units defined by the **TimeFormat** property for the track specified by the **Track** property.
- *MMControl*.**TrackPosition**—a **Long** containing the starting time location in units defined by the **TimeFormat** property for the track specified by the **Track** property.
- *MMControl*.**Tracks**—a **Long** value containing the number of tracks on the current media.
- *MMControl*.**UpdateInterval**—an **Integer** containing the number of milliseconds between **Status** events.
- *MMControl*.**UsesWindows**—a **Boolean** when **True** means the current device uses a window for display information. Also, the **hWndDisplay** property will contain a valid handle. **False** means that no windows are needed by the device.
- *MMControl*.**Visible**—a **Boolean** value when **True** means that the control is visible. When **False** means that the control is not visible.

> **Tip**
>
> This property hides the control until the program is ready to display it.

- *MMControl*.**Wait**—a **Boolean** value when **True** means that the control will not return control back to the program until the current command is finished. **False** means that the program will not wait until the command is finished. Afterwards this property is ignored by all commands until it has been assigned a new value.
- *MMControl*.**WhatsThisHelpID**—a **Long** that contains a help file context ID number references an entry in the help file. This provides a What's This PopUp help display in response to the What's This button in the upper right corner of the window.
- *MMControl*.**Width**—a **Single** that contains the width of the control.

Methods

MMControl.Drag [*DragAction*]

Usage   This method begins, ends, or cancels a drag operation.

Arguments ■ *DragAction*—an **Integer** that contains a value selected from Table M-194 below.

DragAction Name	Value	Description
vbCancel	0	Cancels any drag operation in progress.
vbBeginDrag	1	Begins a drag operation (default).
vbEndDrag	2	Ends a drag operation and drops *object*.

Table M-194: DragAction *values.*

MMControl.Move Left [, Top [, Width [, Height]]]

Usage This method changes the position and the size of the **MMcontrol**. The **ScaleMode** of the **Form** or other container object that holds the **MMControl** control will determine the units used to specify the coordinates.

Arguments ■ *Left*—a **Single** that specifies the new position of the left edge of the control.
■ *Top*—a **Single** that specifies the new position of the top edge of the control.
■ *Width*—a **Single** that specifies the new width of the control.
■ *Height*—a **Single** that specifies the new height of the control.

MMControl.OLEDrag

Usage This method begins an **OLEDrag** and drop operation. Invoking this method will trigger the **OLEStartDrag** event.

MMControl.Refresh

Usage This method redraws the contents of the control.

MMControl.SetFocus

Usage This method transfers the focus from the form or control that currently has the focus to this control. To receive the focus, this control must be enabled and visible.

MMControl.ShowWhatsThis

Usage This method displays the ShowWhatsThis help information for this control.

MMControl.ZOrder [position]

Usage This method specifies the position of the **MMControl** control relative to the other objects on the form.

> **Tip**
>
> *Note that there are three layers of objects on a form: the back layer is the drawing space which contains the results of the graphical methods, the middle layer contains graphical objects and **Labels**, and the top layer contains nongraphical controls such as the **MMControl**. The **ZOrder** method only affects how the objects are arranged within a single layer.*

Arguments
- *position*—an **Integer** that specifies the relative position of this object. A value of **0** means that the control is positioned at the head of the list; a value of **1** means that the control will be placed at the end of the list.

Events

Private Sub *MMControl*_BackClick([*index* As Integer ,] *cancel* As Integer)

Usage This event occurs when the user clicks a mouse button on the Back button on the MCI control.

Arguments
- *index*—an **Integer** that uniquely identifies a control in a control array. This argument is not present if the control is not part of a control array.
- *cancel*—an **Integer** when **True** means that the user's request is canceled. **False** means that the requested command will be performed.

Private Sub *MMControl*_BackCompleted([*index* As Integer ,] *ErrorCode* As Long)

Usage This event occurs when the Back command has finished.

Arguments
- *index*—an **Integer** that uniquely identifies a control in a control array. This argument is not present if the control is not part of a control array.
- *ErrorCode*—a **Long** value when **0** means that the command finished successfully. A nonzero value is an error. The **ErrorMessage** property will contain a text description of the error.

Private Sub *MMControl*_BackGotFocus ([*index* As Integer])

Usage This event occurs when the Back button is given focus.

Arguments
- *index*—an **Integer** that uniquely identifies a control in a control array. This argument is not present if the control is not part of a control array.

Private Sub *MMControl*_BackLostFocus ([*index* As Integer])

Usage This event occurs when the Back button loses focus.

Arguments
- *index*—an **Integer** that uniquely identifies a control in a control array. This argument is not present if the control is not part of a control array.

Private Sub *MMControl*_Done ([*index* As Integer ,] *NotifyCode*)

Usage   This event occurs only when the **Notify** property is **True** and returns the status of the last command executed.

Arguments
- *index*—an **Integer** that uniquely identifies a control in a control array. This argument is not present if the control is not part of a control array.
- *NotifyCode*—an **Integer** value (see Table M-195) containing the result of the last MCI command.

NotifyCode Name	Value	Description
mciNotifySuccessful	1	The command was successful.
mciNotifySuperseded	2	The command was superseded by a new command.
mciNotifyAborted	4	The command was aborted by the user.
mciNotifyFailure	8	The command failed.

Table M-195: **NotifyCode** *values.*

Private Sub *MMControl*_DragDrop([*index* As Integer ,] *source* As Control, *x* As Single, *y* As Single)

Usage   This event occurs when a drag-and-drop operation is completed by using the **Drag** method with an *DragAction* value of *vbEndDrag*.

Tip

*When using drag-and-drop operations, use the **DragOver** event to determine what the cursor should look like while the cursor moves over the control.*

Arguments
- *index*—an **Integer** that uniquely identifies a control in a control array. This argument is not present if the control is not part of a control array.
- *source*—a control object that is the control that is being dragged.

Tip

You can access a property or method from the source control by using source.property *or* source.method. *You can determine the type of object or control by using the* **TypeOf** *operator.*

- *x*—a **Single** that contains the horizontal location of the mouse pointer.
- *y*—a **Single** that contains the vertical location of the mouse pointer.

Private Sub *MMControl*_DragOver([*index* As Integer ,] *source* As Control, *x* As Single, *y* As Single, *state* As Integer)

Usage This event occurs while a drag operation is in progress and the cursor is moved over the control.

Tip

*When using drag-and-drop operations, use the **DragOver** event to determine what the cursor should look like while the cursor moves over the control. When* state *is **0**, you can change the cursor to a No Drop (vbNoDrop) cursor or highlight the field that the cursor is near. When* state *is **1**, you can undo the changes you made when the* state *was **0**.*

Arguments
- *index*—an **Integer** that uniquely identifies a control in a control array. This argument is not present if the control is not part of a control array.
- *source*—a control object that is the control that is being dragged.

Tip

You can access a property or method from the source control by using source.property *or* source.method. *You can determine the type of object or control by using the **TypeOf** operator.*

- *x*—a **Single** that contains the horizontal location of the mouse pointer.
- *y*—a **Single** that contains the vertical location of the mouse pointer.
- *state*—an **Integer** value (see Table M-196) that indicates the state of the object being dragged.

state Name	Value	Description
vbEnter	0	The dragged object is entering range of the control.
vbLeave	1	The dragged object is leaving range of the control.
vbOver	2	The dragged object has moved from one position over the control to another.

Table M-196: state *values.*

Private Sub *MMControl*_EjectClick([*index* As Integer ,] *cancel* As Integer)

Usage This event occurs when the user clicks a mouse button on Eject button on the MCI control.

Arguments
- *index*—an **Integer** that uniquely identifies a control in a control array. This argument is not present if the control is not part of a control array.
- *cancel*—an **Integer** when **True** means that the user's request is canceled. **False** means that the requested command will be performed.

Private Sub *MMControl*_EjectCompleted([*index* As Integer ,] *ErrorCode* As Long)

Usage This event occurs when Eject command has finished.

Arguments
- *index*—an **Integer** that uniquely identifies a control in a control array. This argument is not present if the control is not part of a control array.
- *ErrorCode*—a **Long** value when **0** means that the command finished successfully. A nonzero value is an error. The **ErrorMessage** property will contain a text description of the error.

Private Sub *MMControl*_EjectGotFocus ([*index* As Integer])

Usage This event occurs when the Eject button is given focus.

Arguments *index*—an **Integer** that uniquely identifies a control in a control array. This argument is not present if the control is not part of a control array.

Private Sub *MMControl*_EjectLostFocus ([*index* As Integer])

Usage This event occurs when the Eject button loses focus.

Arguments *index*—an **Integer** that uniquely identifies a control in a control array. This argument is not present if the control is not part of a control array.

Private Sub *MMControl*_GotFocus ([*index* As Integer])

Usage This event occurs when the control is given focus.

> **Tip**
>
> *You can use this routine to display help or other information in a status bar.*

Arguments *index*—an **Integer** that uniquely identifies a control in a control array. This argument is not present if the control is not part of a control array.

Private Sub *MMControl*_LostFocus ([*index* As Integer])

Usage This event occurs when the control loses focus.

Arguments *index*—an **Integer** that uniquely identifies a control in a control array. This argument is not present if the control is not part of a control array.

Private Sub *MMControl*_NextClick([*index* As Integer ,] *cancel* As Integer)

Usage This event occurs when the user clicks a mouse button on Next button on the MCI control.

Multimedia MCI Control • 625

Arguments
- *index*—an **Integer** that uniquely identifies a control in a control array. This argument is not present if the control is not part of a control array.
- *cancel*—an **Integer** when **True** means that the user's request is canceled. **False** means that the requested command will be performed.

Private Sub *MMControl_NextCompleted* ([*index* As Integer ,] ErrorCode As Long)

Usage This event occurs when Next command has finished.

Arguments
- *index*—an **Integer** that uniquely identifies a control in a control array. This argument is not present if the control is not part of a control array.
- *ErrorCode*—a **Long** value when **0** means that the command finished successfully. A nonzero value is an error. The **ErrorMessage** property will contain a text description of the error.

Private Sub *MMControl_NextGotFocus* ([*index* As Integer])

Usage This event occurs when the Next button is given focus.

Arguments
- *index*—an **Integer** that uniquely identifies a control in a control array. This argument is not present if the control is not part of a control array.

Private Sub *MMControl_NextLostFocus* ([*index* As Integer])

Usage This event occurs when the Next button loses focus.

Arguments
- *index*—an **Integer** that uniquely identifies a control in a control array. This argument is not present if the control is not part of a control array.

Private Sub *MMControl_OLECompleteDrag*(*effect* As Long)

Usage This event tells the source control the results of an OLE drag-and-drop operation. This is the final event to occur in the series of actions that make up an OLE drag-and-drop operation.

Arguments
- *effect*—a **Long** (see Table M-197) that returns the status of the OLE drag-and-drop operation.

effect Name	Value	Description
vbDropEffectNone	0	The operation was canceled or the target control can't accept the drop operation.
vbDropEffectCopy	1	The operation copied data from the source control to the target control. The original data is unchanged.
vbDropEffectMove	2	The operation results in a link from the original data to the target control.

Table M-197: effect *values*.

Private Sub *MMControl_OLEDragDrop* (*data* As DataObject, *effect* As Long, *button* As Integer, *shift* As Single, *x* As Single, *y* As Single)

Usage
: This event tells the source control the results of an OLE drag-and-drop operation. This is the final event to occur in the series of actions that make up an OLE drag-and drop-operation.

Arguments
: - *data*—a **DataObject** that contains the formats that the source control will provide. If the data is not contained in the **DataObject**, then it can be retrieved with the **GetData** method.
  - *effect*—a **Long** (see Table M-198) that returns the status of the OLE drag-and-drop operation.

effect Name	Value	Description
vbDropEffectNone	0	The operation was canceled or the target control can't accept the drop operation.
vbDropEffectCopy	1	The operation copied data from the source control to the target control. The original data is unchanged.
vbDropEffectMove	2	The operation results in a link from the original data to the target control.

Table M-198: effect values.

- *button*—an **Integer** value (see Table M-199) that contains information about the mouse buttons that were pressed. These values can be added together if more than one button was pushed. For instance, a value of **3** means that both the left and right buttons were pressed. A value of **0** means that no buttons were pressed.

button Name	Value	Description
vbLeftButton	1	The left button was pressed.
vbRightButton	2	The right button was pressed.
vbMiddleButton	4	The middle button was pressed.

Table M-199: button values.

- *shift*—an **Integer** value (see Table M-200) that contains information about the Shift and Alt keys that were pushed when the mouse button was released. These values can be added together if more than one key was down. For instance, a value of **5** would mean that the Shift and Alt keys were both down when the mouse button was released. A value of **0** means that none of these keys were pressed.

shift Name	Value	Description
vbShiftMask	1	The Shift key was pressed.
vbCtrlMask	2	The Ctrl key was pressed.
vbAltMask	4	The Alt key was pressed.

Table M-200: shift values.

- *x*—a **Single** that contains the horizontal location of the mouse pointer.
- *y*—a **Single** that contains the vertical location of the mouse pointer.

Private Sub *MMControl*_OLEDragOver (*data* As DataObject, *effect* As Long, *button* As Integer, *shift* As Single, *x* As Single, *y* As Single, *state* As Integer)

Usage This event happens when an OLE drag-and-drop operation is in progress.

Arguments
- *data*—a **DataObject** that contains the formats that the source control will provide. If the data is not contained in the **DataObject**, then it can be retrieved with the **GetData** method.
- *effect*—a **Long** (see Table M-201) that returns the status of the OLE drag-and-drop operation.

effect Name	Value	Description
vbDropEffectNone	0	The operation was canceled or the target control can't accept the drop operation.
vbDropEffectCopy	1	The operation copied data from the source control to the target control. The original data is unchanged.
vbDropEffectMove	2	The operation results in a link from the original data to the target control.

Table M-201: effect values.

- *button*—an **Integer** value (see Table M-202) that contains information about the mouse buttons that were pressed. These values can be added together if more than one button was pushed. For instance, a value of **3** means that both the left and right buttons were pressed. A value of **0** means that no buttons were pressed.

button Name	Value	Description
vbLeftButton	1	The left button was pressed.
vbRightButton	2	The right button was pressed.
vbMiddleButton	4	The middle button was pressed.

Table M-202: button values.

- *shift*—an **Integer** value (see Table M-203) that contains information about the Shift and Alt keys that were pushed when the mouse button was released. These values can be added together if more than one key was down. For instance, a value of **5** would mean that the Shift and Alt keys were both down when the mouse button was released. A value of **0** means that none of these keys were pressed.

shift Name	Value	Description
vbShiftMask	1	The Shift key was pressed.
vbCtrlMask	2	The Ctrl key was pressed.
vbAltMask	4	The Alt key was pressed.

Table M-203: shift values.

- *x*—a **Single** that contains the horizontal location of the mouse pointer.

- *y*—a **Single** that contains the vertical location of the mouse pointer.
- *state*—an **Integer** value (see Table M-204) that indicates the state of the object being dragged.

state Name	Value	Description
vbEnter	0	The dragged object is entering range of the control.
vbLeave	1	The dragged object is leaving range of the control.
vbOver	2	The dragged object has moved from one position over the control to another.

Table M-204: state *values*.

Private Sub *MMControl_OLEGiveFeedback* (*effect* As Long)

Usage   This event tells the source control what is happening while the OLE drag-and-drop operation is in progress. This event occurs after the **OLEDragOver** event.

Tip

You may want to use this event to change the cursor to reflect what can happen in the remote object.

Arguments   - *effect*—a **Long** (see Table M-205) that returns the status of the OLE drag-and-drop operation.

effect Name	Value	Description
vbDropEffectNone	0	The operation was canceled or the target control can't accept the drop operation.
vbDropEffectCopy	1	The operation copied data from the source control to the target control. The original data is unchanged.
vbDropEffectMove	2	The operation results in a link from the original data to the target control.
vbDropEffectScroll	&H80000000	The target control is about to scroll or is scrolling. This value may be added to the other *effect* values.

Table M-205: effect *values*.

Private Sub *MMControl_OLESetData* (*data* As DataObject, *DataFormat* As Integer)

Usage   This event happens in response to the target object performing a **GetData** method on *data*. This routine will respond by using the **SetData** method with the desired data using the **DataObject** *data*.

Arguments   - *data*—a **DataObject** that will contain the data to return to the target object.
- *format*—an **Integer** value (see TableM-206) that contains the format of the data.

Multimedia MCI Control • 629

format Name	Value	Description
vbCFText	1	Text (.TXT files)
vbCFBitmap	2	Bitmap (.BMP files)
vbCFMetafile	3	Metafile (.WMF files)
vbCFEDIB	8	Device independent bitmap (DIB)
vbCFPallette	9	Color palette
vbCFEMetafile	14	Enhanced metafile (.EMF files)
vbCFFiles	15	List of files
vbCFRTF	-16639	Rich Text Format (.RTF files)

Table M-206: format *values*.

Private Sub *MMControl_OLEStartDrag* (*data* As DataObject, *AllowedEffects* As Long)

Usage This event starts an OLE drag-and-drop operation.

Arguments
- *data*—a **DataObject** that will contain the formats that the source object is willing to provide to the target object. It may optionally contain the data to transfer.
- *AllowedEffects*—a **Long** (see Table M-207) that contains the effects that the target object can request from the source object. The *AllowedEffects* can be added together if the source object supports more than one effect. Note that the target object can always use the *vbDropEffectNone* effect.

AllowedEffects Name	Value	Description
vbDropEffectNone	0	The target can't copy the data.
vbDropEffectCopy	1	The target can copy the data and the source will keep the data unchanged.
vbDropEffectMove	2	The target can copy the data and the source will delete the data.

Table M-207: AllowedEffects *values*.

Private Sub *MMControl_PauseClick*([*index* As Integer ,] *cancel* As Integer)

Usage This event occurs when the user clicks a mouse button on Pause button on the MCI control.

Arguments
- *index*—an **Integer** that uniquely identifies a control in a control array. This argument is not present if the control is not part of a control array.
- *cancel*—an **Integer** when **True** means that the user's request is canceled. **False** means that the requested command will be performed.

Private Sub *MMControl*_PauseCompleted([*index* As Integer ,] *ErrorCode* As Long)

Usage   This event occurs when Pause command has finished.

Arguments
- *index*—an **Integer** that uniquely identifies a control in a control array. This argument is not present if the control is not part of a control array.
- *ErrorCode*—a **Long** value when **0** means that the command finished successfully. A nonzero value is an error. The **ErrorMessage** property will contain a text description of the error.

Private Sub *MMControl*_PauseGotFocus ([*index* As Integer])

Usage   This event occurs when the Pause button is given focus.

Arguments
- *index*—an **Integer** that uniquely identifies a control in a control array. This argument is not present if the control is not part of a control array.

Private Sub *MMControl*_PauseLostFocus ([*index* As Integer])

Usage   This event occurs when the Pause button loses focus.

Arguments
- *index*—an **Integer** that uniquely identifies a control in a control array. This argument is not present if the control is not part of a control array.

Private Sub *MMControl*_PlayClick([*index* As Integer ,] *cancel* As Integer)

Usage   This event occurs when the user clicks a mouse button on Play button on the MCI control.

Arguments
- *index*—an **Integer** that uniquely identifies a control in a control array. This argument is not present if the control is not part of a control array.
- *cancel*—an **Integer** when **True** means that the user's request is canceled. **False** means that the requested command will be performed.

Private Sub *MMControl*_PlayCompleted([*index* As Integer ,] *ErrorCode* As Long)

Usage   This event occurs when Play command has finished.

Arguments
- *index*—an **Integer** that uniquely identifies a control in a control array. This argument is not present if the control is not part of a control array.
- *ErrorCode*—a **Long** value when **0** means that the command finished successfully. A nonzero value is an error. The **ErrorMessage** property will contain a text description of the error.

Private Sub *MMControl*_PlayGotFocus ([*index* As Integer])

Usage   This event occurs when the Play button is given focus.

Arguments   ▪ *index*—an **Integer** that uniquely identifies a control in a control array. This argument is not present if the control is not part of a control array.

Private Sub *MMControl*_PlayLostFocus ([*index* As Integer])

Usage   This event occurs when the Play button loses focus.

Arguments   ▪ *index*—an **Integer** that uniquely identifies a control in a control array. This argument is not present if the control is not part of a control array.

Private Sub *MMControl*_PrevClick([*index* As Integer ,] *cancel* As Integer)

Usage   This event occurs when the user clicks a mouse button on Prev button on the MCI control.

Arguments   ▪ *index*—an **Integer** that uniquely identifies a control in a control array. This argument is not present if the control is not part of a control array.

▪ *cancel*—an **Integer** when **True** means that the user's request is canceled. **False** means that the requested command will be performed.

Private Sub *MMControl*_PrevCompleted([*index* As Integer ,] *ErrorCode* As Long)

Usage   This event occurs when Prev command has finished.

Arguments   ▪ *index*—an **Integer** that uniquely identifies a control in a control array. This argument is not present if the control is not part of a control array.

▪ *ErrorCode*—a **Long** value when **0** means that the command finished successfully. A nonzero value is an error. The **ErrorMessage** property will contain a text description of the error.

Private Sub *MMControl*_PrevGotFocus ([*index* As Integer])

Usage   This event occurs when the Prev button is given focus.

Arguments   ▪ *index*—an **Integer** that uniquely identifies a control in a control array. This argument is not present if the control is not part of a control array.

Private Sub *MMControl*_PrevLostFocus ([*index* As Integer])

Usage   This event occurs when the Prev button loses focus.

Arguments   ▪ *index*—an **Integer** that uniquely identifies a control in a control array. This argument is not present if the control is not part of a control array.

Private Sub *MMControl*_RecordClick([*index* As Integer ,] *cancel* As Integer)

Usage   This event occurs when the user clicks a mouse button on Record button on the MCI control.

Arguments
- *index*—an **Integer** that uniquely identifies a control in a control array. This argument is not present if the control is not part of a control array.
- *cancel*—an **Integer** when **True** means that the user's request is canceled. **False** means that the requested command will be performed.

Private Sub *MMControl*_RecordCompleted([*index* As Integer ,] *ErrorCode* As Long)

Usage   This event occurs when Record command has finished.

Arguments
- *index*—an **Integer** that uniquely identifies a control in a control array. This argument is not present if the control is not part of a control array.
- *ErrorCode*—a **Long** value when **0** means that the command finished successfully. A nonzero value is an error. The **ErrorMessage** property will contain a text description of the error.

Private Sub *MMControl*_RecordGotFocus ([*index* As Integer])

Usage   This event occurs when the Record button is given focus.

Arguments
- *index*—an **Integer** that uniquely identifies a control in a control array. This argument is not present if the control is not part of a control array.

Private Sub *MMControl*_RecordLostFocus ([*index* As Integer])

Usage   This event occurs when the Record button loses focus.

Arguments
- *index*—an **Integer** that uniquely identifies a control in a control array. This argument is not present if the control is not part of a control array.

Private Sub *MMControl*_StatusUpdate ([*index* As Integer])

Usage   This event occurs every **UpdateInterval**.

Arguments
- *index*—an **Integer** that uniquely identifies a control in a control array. This argument is not present if the control is not part of a control array.

Private Sub *MMControl*_StepClick([*index* As Integer ,] *cancel* As Integer)

Usage This event occurs when the user clicks a mouse button on the Step button on the MCI control.

Arguments
- *index*—an **Integer** that uniquely identifies a control in a control array. This argument is not present if the control is not part of a control array.
- *cancel*—an **Integer** when **True** means that the user's request is canceled. **False** means that the requested command will be performed.

Private Sub *MMControl*_StepCompleted([*index* As Integer ,] *ErrorCode* As Long)

Usage This event occurs when the Step command has finished.

Arguments
- *index*—an **Integer** that uniquely identifies a control in a control array. This argument is not present if the control is not part of a control array.
- *ErrorCode*—a **Long** value when **0** means that the command finished successfully. A nonzero value is an error. The **ErrorMessage** property will contain a text description of the error.

Private Sub *MMControl*_StepGotFocus ([*index* As Integer])

Usage This event occurs when the Step button is given focus.

Arguments
- *index*—an **Integer** that uniquely identifies a control in a control array. This argument is not present if the control is not part of a control array.

Private Sub *MMControl*_StepLostFocus ([*index* As Integer])

Usage This event occurs when the Step button loses focus.

Arguments
- *index*—an **Integer** that uniquely identifies a control in a control array. This argument is not present if the control is not part of a control array.

Private Sub *MMControl*_StopClick([*index* As Integer ,] *cancel* As Integer)

Usage This event occurs when the user clicks a mouse button on the Stop button on the MCI control.

Arguments
- *index*—an **Integer** that uniquely identifies a control in a control array. This argument is not present if the control is not part of a control array.
- *cancel*—an **Integer** when **True** means that the user's request is canceled. **False** means that the requested command will be performed.

Private Sub MMControl_StopCompleted([index As Integer ,] ErrorCode As Long)

Usage   This event occurs when the Stop command has finished.

Arguments
- *index*—an **Integer** that uniquely identifies a control in a control array. This argument is not present if the control is not part of a control array.
- *ErrorCode*—a **Long** value when **0** means that the command finished successfully. A nonzero value is an error. The **ErrorMessage** property will contain a text description of the error.

Private Sub MMControl_StopGotFocus ([index As Integer])

Usage   This event occurs when the Stop button is given focus.

Arguments
- *index*—an **Integer** that uniquely identifies a control in a control array. This argument is not present if the control is not part of a control array.

Private Sub MMControl_StopLostFocus ([index As Integer])

Usage   This event occurs when the Stop button loses focus.

Arguments
- *index*—an **Integer** that uniquely identifies a control in a control array. This argument is not present if the control is not part of a control array.

Examples
```
Private Sub Command1_Click()
MMControl1.filename = Text1.Text
MMControl1.Command = "Open"
MMControl1.Wait = True
MMControl1.Command = "Play"
MMControl1.Command = "Close"
End Sub
```

This routine loads the name of a .WAV file from the Text1 text box into the multimedia control's filename. Next it opens the file using the Open command. Then it sets the **Wait** property **True** so that the program will wait until the Play command has finished. Finally it executes the Close command to close the device.

See Also   **Beep** (statement)

Name

STATEMENT

CCE, LE, PE, EE

Syntax **Name** *oldfilename* **As** *newfilename*

Usage The **Name** statement renames a file or directory. Wildcards are not permitted, and the file must remain on the same drive.

> **Warning**
>
> *If you try to rename an open file, an error will occur.*
> *The* oldfilename *must exist and* newfilename *must not exist or an error will occur.*

Arguments
- *oldfilename*—a **String** expression that contains the path and the name of the file to rename.
- *newfilename*—a **String** expression that contains the new name of the file.

Examples
```
Open App.Path & "\temp.dat" For Output As #1
Print #1, "Testing"
Close #1
If Len(Dir(App.Path & "\temp.dat")) > 0 Then
    MsgBox "The file was created successfully."
    If Len(Dir(App.Path & "\temp1.dat")) > 0 Then
        Kill App.Path & "\temp1.dat"
    End If
    Name App.Path & "\temp.dat" As App.Path & "\temp1.dat"
    If (Len(Dir(App.Path & "\temp.dat")) = 0) And (Len(Dir(App.Path & "\temp1.dat")) > 0) Then
        MsgBox "The file was renamed successfully."
    End If
End If
End Sub
```

This routine creates a junk file called temp.dat and then checks to delete temp1.dat with the **Kill** statement, if it exists. Finally, it renames the file using the **Name** statement.

See Also **Dir** (function), **Kill** (statement), **RmDir** (statement)

Node

OBJECT

CCE, LE, PE, EE

Usage The **Node** object contains a set of properties that describe a font.

Properties
- *NodeObject*.**Child**—an object reference to the first node in the nodes collection.
- *NodeObject*.**Children**—an **Integer** value containing the number of nodes in the collection.

- *NodeObject*.**Expanded**—a **Boolean** when **True** means that the node object in the **TreeView** control is expanded. **False** means that node object is not expanded.
- *NodeObject*.**ExpandedImage**—a **Variant** that either the index number or key value of a **ListImage** object that will display when the node is expanded.
- *NodeObject*.**FirstSibling**—an object reference to the first sibling of a node.
- *NodeObject*.**FullPath**—a **String** containing the full path of the node, based on the **Text** property of this node and its predecessors, each one separated by a **PathSeparator**.
- *NodeObject*.**Image**—a **Variant** that either the index number or key value of a **ListImage** object that will display for this node, unless the node is expanded and the **ExpandedImage** property is set.
- *NodeObject*.**Index**—an **Integer** that uniquely identifies a node in the **Nodes** collection. The first node in the collection will always have a value of **1**.

> **Warning**
>
> The values of **Index** may change over time as nodes are sorted, so you should use the **Key** property to reference a particular node.

- *NodeObject*.**Key**—a **String** containing a unique name for the node.
- *NodeObject*.**LastSibling**—an object reference to the last sibling of a node.
- *NodeObject*.**Next**—an object reference to the next node at this level in the hierarchy.
- *NodeObject*.**Parent**—an object reference to the node's parent.
- *NodeObject*.**Previous**—an object reference to the previous node at this level in the hierarchy.
- *NodeObject*.**Root**—an object reference to the first node in the collection.
- *NodeObject*.**Selected**—a **Boolean** when **True** means that the node object in the **TreeView** control is selected. **False** means that node object is not selected.
- *NodeObject*.**SelectedImage**—a **Variant** that either the index number or key value of a **ListImage** object that will display when the node is selected.
- *NodeObject*.**Sorted**—a **Boolean** when **True** means that the nodes in the **TreeView** control are sorted by name. When **False** means that the nodes are unsorted.
- *NodeControl*.**Tag**—a **String** that can hold programmer specific information. This property is not used by Visual Basic.
- *NodeControl*.**Text**—a **String** that sets or returns the value from the text box part of the control.
- *NodeControl*.**Visible**—a **Boolean** value when **True** means that the control is visible. When **False** it means that the control is not visible.

Methods

image = *NodeObject*.**CreateDragImage**

Usage This method returns a dithered version of the node's image that is suitable for drag-and-drop operations.

Arguments
- *image*—an image object that can be assigned to the **DragIcon** property of most controls.

bvalue = *NodeObject*.**EnsureVisible**

- **Usage** This method will automatically scroll and/or expand a **TreeView** display to ensure that the node is visible.

- **Arguments** *bvalue*—a **Boolean** when **True** means that the **TreeView** control had to scroll or expand to make the node visible. **False** means that no scrolling or expansion was required.

See Also **Nodes** (collection), **TreeView** (control)

Nodes

COLLECTION

CCE, LE, PE, EE

Usage The **Nodes** collection contains a set of properties and methods to store and retrieve nodes for the **TreeView** control.

Properties *NodesCollection*.**Count**—a **Long** value that contains the number of items in the collection.

Methods ### *NodesCollection*.**Add** *item, key,* [*before* | *, after*]

- **Usage** This method adds an item to the collection specified by *CollectionObject*.

- **Arguments** *item*—an expression that contains an object to add to the collection.
  - *key*—a **String** that contains a unique value that references the value of *item*.
  - *before*—either a numeric value that represents the relative position or a **String** value that contains the key value of the object that will immediately precede this object in the collection. This argument cannot be used if a value for *after* is specified.
  - *after*—either a numeric value that represents the relative position or a **String** value that contains a key value of the object that will immediately follow this object in the collection. This argument cannot be used if a value for *before* is specified.

NodesCollection.**Clear**

- **Usage** This method removes all of the objects in the nodes collection.

NodesCollection.**Remove** *index*

- **Usage** This method deletes an item specified by *index* from the nodes collection.

- **Arguments** *index*—either a numeric value that represents the relative position or a **String** value that contains the key value of the node object to delete from the collection.

See Also **For Each** (statement), **TreeView** (control)

Now

FUNCTION

CCE, LE, PE, EE

Syntax *DValue* = **Now**

Usage The **Now** function returns the current date and time.

Arguments
- *DValue*—a **Date** value containing the current date and time.

Examples
```
Private Sub Command1_Click()
Dim d As Date
d = Now
MsgBox "The current date is: " & Format(d)
End Sub
```

This routine saves the current date and time from the **Now** function into a local variable and displays it using a message box.

See Also **CDate** (function), **Date** (data type), **Date** (function), **Date** (statement), **Time** (function), **Time** (statement)

NPer

FUNCTION

CCE, LE, PE, EE

Syntax *periods* = **NPer**(*rate, pmt, pv* [, *fv* [, *type*]])

Usage The **NPer** function returns the number of periods required for an annuity based on a fixed interest rate and fixed payments.

> **Tip**
>
> *Periods of loans can be confusing until you realize that the period is the interval of time in which you make a payment. Thus a 5-year car loan that is paid monthly will have 60 periods.*

Arguments
- *periods*—a **Double** value containing the number of periods in the annuity.
  - *rate*—a **Double** value containing the interest rate per period. A 12 percent annual interest rate with monthly payments would correspond to a *rate* of 0.01.
  - *pmt*—a **Double** value containing the fixed, periodic payment. Cash receipts are represented by positive numbers, and cash payments are represented by negative numbers.
  - *pv*—an **Double** value specifying the present value of the annuity.
  - *fv*—a **Variant** value specifying the future value of the annuity. If not specified, it will default to **0**.

- *type*—a **Variant** value specifying when the payment is due. A value of **0** indicates the payments are due at the end of the period (default). A value of **1** indicates that the payments are due at the beginning of the period.

Examples
```
Private Sub Command1_Click()
    If IsNumeric(Text1.Text) And IsNumeric(Text2.Text) And IsNumeric(Text3.Text) Then
        Text4.Text = Format(NPer(CDbl(Text1.Text), CDbl(Text2.Text),
          CDbl(Text3.Text)))
    End If
End Sub
```

This routine verifies that the values are numeric and then computes the number of periods required for the annuity.

See Also **FV** (function), **IPmt** (function), **IRR** (function), **MIRR** (function), **NPV** (function), **PMT** (function), **PPmt** (function), **PV** (function), **Rate** (function), **SLN** (function), **SYD** (function)

NPV

FUNCTION

CCE, LE, PE, EE

Syntax *DValue* = **NPV** (*rate*, *vals* ( ))

Usage The **NPV** function returns a **Double** value that contains the net present value for a stream of payments and receipts.

Arguments
- *DValue*—a **Double** value containing the net present value.
- *rate*—a **Double** that contains a discount rate.
- *vals()*—an array of **Double** containing the cash flow. Cash receipts are represented by positive numbers, and cash payments are represented by negative numbers.

Examples
```
Private Sub Command1_Click()
Dim v(12) As Double
For i = 0 To 11
    v(i) = -100
Next i
MsgBox Format(NPV(0.01, v), "Currency")
End Sub
```

This routine computes the net present value based on 12 payments of $1,000 and a discount rate of 12 percent per year (or 1 percent per month).

See Also **DDB** (function), **FV** (function), **IPmt** (function), **IRR** (function), **MIRR** (function), **NPer** (function), **PMT** (function), **PPmt** (function), **PV** (function), **Rate** (function), **SLN** (function), **SYD** (function)

Object

DATA TYPE

CCE, LE, PE, EE

Usage The **Object** data type holds a pointer to the object. Unlike other data types, an object variable contains a pointer or reference to the object rather than actually holding the information itself. For this reason, you can't use a **Let** statement when using object variables. The **Set** statement is used to copy object references from one variable to another. Note that this will not copy the actual object. The object is created by using the **New** keyword in a **Dim** statement or in a **Set** statement. A single **Object** variable occupies 32 bits of storage or 4 bytes.

Object variables can be declared either as **Object**, as **Variant**, or as a specific object class. Variables declared as **Object** or **Variant** are bound at run-time. An object variable that has been defined as a specific object class will be bound at compile-time.

See Also **Dim** (statement), **IsObject** (function), **Variant** (data type)

Oct

FUNCTION

CCE, LE, PE, EE

Syntax `OValue = Oct[$]( ONumber )`

Usage The **Oct** function returns a **String** with the octal equivalent of the passed number.

Arguments
- *OValue*—a **String** that contains the octal equivalent of *ONumber*. The largest octal value that will be returned is 37777777777.
- *ONumber*—any numeric value or **String** that contains a number in the range of -2,147,483,648 to 2,147,483,647. Any number outside this range will cause an overflow, and fractional values will be rounded to the nearest whole number.

Examples
```
Private Sub Command1_Click()
If IsNumeric(Text1.Text) Then
    Text2.Text = Oct(Text1.Text)
Else
    Text2.Text = "Invalid number"
End If
End Sub
```

This routine converts the value in the text1 text box into its octal equivalent and stores it in the text2 text box.

See Also **Hex** (function)

OLE Container

CONTROL
CCE, LE, PE, EE

Usage The **OLE Container** control is an intrinsic control that provides you with the ability to embed OLE-capable applications in your applications. You can determine the type of object embedded at design time by selecting the object from a dialog, or you can wait until run time to determine the actual object.

Properties
- *OLEContainerControl*.**Action**—an **Integer** value (see Table O-1) that determines an action. This property exists primarily to maintain compatibility with previous versions of Visual Basic. You should use the new methods, shown in the table, for more functionality. This property is not available at design time.

Action Value	New Method	Description
0	**CreateEmbed**	Creates an embedded object.
1	**CreateLink**	Creates a linked object.
4	**Copy**	Copies the object to the clipboard.
5	**Paste**	Copies the data from the clipboard to the control.
6	**Update**	Retrieves the data from the source and display it as a picture in the control.
7	**DoVerb**	Opens the specified object.
9	**Close**	Closes the specified object.
10	**Delete**	Deletes the specified object.
11	**SaveToFile**	Saves the specified object to a file.
12	**ReadFromFile**	Reads the specified from a file.
14	**InsertObjectDlg**	Displays the Insert Object dialog box.
15	**PasteSpecialDlg**	Displays the Paste Special dialog box.
17	**FetchVerbs**	Updates the list of verbs that the object supports.
18	**SaveToOle1File**	Saves the specified object in the OLE version 1.0 file format.

Table O-1: Action *values.*

- *OLEContainerControl*.**Appearance**—an **Integer** value (see Table O-2) that describes how the OLE container will appear on the form:

Appearance Value	Description
0	The OLE container is displayed without the 3D effects.
1	The OLE container is displayed with 3D effects (default value).

Table O-2: Appearance *values.*

- *OLEContainerControl*.**AppIsRunning**—a **Boolean** when **True** means the application that generated the object in the OLE container control is running. **False** means that it is not running.

> **Tip**
>
> *Set the value of* **AppIsRunning** *to* **True** *to start the application so that objects are activated more quickly.*

- *OLEContainerControl*.**AutoActivate**—an **Integer** describing how the object's application is activated (see Table O-3).

AutoActivate Name	Value	Description
vbOLEActivateManual	0	The object isn't automatically activated. You must explicitly activate the object using the DoVerb method.
vbOLEActivateGetFocus	1	The object is activated when the control gets focus.
vbOLEActivateDoubleclick	2	The object is activated when the user double clicks on the object.
vbOLEActivateAuto	3	The object is activated when the object gets focus or the user double clicks the object.

Table O-3: *AutoActivate* values.

- *OLEContainerControl*.**AutoVerbMenu**—a **Boolean** when **True** means that the control will display a pop-up menu with the object's commands. **False** means that the pop-up will not be displayed.
- *OLEContainerControl*.**BackColor**—a **Long** that contains the suggested value for the background color of the control. The **BackColor** and **ForeColor** must both be solid to display text. If you choose a color that is dithered, it will be changed to the nearest solid color.
- *OLEContainerControl*.**BackStyle**—an **Integer** value that describes how the background of the control is displayed (see Table O-4).

BackStyle	Description
0	The control is displayed with a transparent background. Any objects behind the control can be seen.
1	The control is displayed with an opaque background. Any objects behind the control can't be seen. (Default value.)

Table O-4: *BackStyle* values.

OLEContainerControl.**BorderStyle**—an **Integer** specifying how the border will be drawn (see Table O-5).

BorderStyle Name	Value	Description
vbBSNone	0	No border is displayed.
vbFixedSingle	1	Single line around the label.

Table O-5: *BorderStyle* values.

- *OLEContainerControl*.**Class**—a **String** value containing the class name of an embedded object.
- *OLEContainerControl*.**Container**—an object that can be used to set or return the container of the control at run time. This property cannot be set at design time.
- *OLEContainerControl*.**Data**—a handle to a memory object or a Graphical Device Interface (GDI) containing the data. The **Format** must be set prior to using this property.

OLE Container • 643

- *OLEContainerControl*.**DataChanged**—a **Boolean** that applies only to data-bound controls. When **True**, it means that the data contained in this control was changed either by the user or by some means other than retrieving data from the current record. When **False**, it means the data in the control is unchanged from the current record. Simply reading the next record is not sufficient to set the **DataChanged** property to **True**.

    When the **Data** control moves to the next record, it will automatically invoke the **Edit** and **Update** methods to post the changes to the database.

- *OLEContainerControl*.**DataField**—a **String** value that associates the control with a field in a **RecordSet** object in a **Data** control.
- *OLEContainerControl*.**DataText**—a **String** value that is sent or received from the object.
- *OLEContainerControl*.**DisplayType**—an **Integer** value that describes how the control will look when it contains an object (see Table O-6).

DisplayType Name	Value	Description
vbOLEDisplayContent	0	Displays the object's data.
vbOLEDisplayIcon	1	Displays the object's icon.

Table O-6: DisplayType *values.*

- *OLEContainerControl*.**DragIcon**—an object that contains the picture value of an icon. At design time, you can specify an icon file that has a file type of .ICO.

Tip

*This value can be created by copying the value from another control's **DragIcon** value or from a form's icon, or by using the **LoadPicture** function.*

- *OLEContainerControl*.**DragMode**—an **Integer** value (see Table O-7) specifying how the control will respond to a drag request.

Tip

*Setting **DragMode** to vbAutomatic will automatically begin a drag operation when the user clicks on the control. However, the control will not respond to the usual mouse events (**Click**, **DblClick**, **MouseDown**, **MouseMove**, **MouseUp**).*

DragMode Name	Value	Description
vbManual	0	The Drag method must be used to begin a drag-and-drop operation (default value).
vbAutomatic	1	The source control will automatically begin a drag-and-drop operation when the user clicks on the control.

Table O-7: DragMode *values.*

- *OLEContainerControl*.**Enabled**—a **Boolean** value when **True** means that the control will respond to events. When **False**, the control will not respond to events.
- *OLEContainerControl*.**FileNumber**—an **Integer** containing the file number used when saving and reading OLE objects with files using **Actions**: 11, 12, and 18.
- *OLEContainerControl*.**Format**—a **String** that contains the format used with the **Data** and **DataText** properties.
- *OLEContainerControl*.**Height**—a **Single** that contains the height of the control.
- *OLEContainerControl*.**HelpContextID**—a **Long** that contains a help file context ID number that references an entry in the help file. When the user presses the F1 key while this control is active, the corresponding entry in the help file will automatically be displayed. A value of zero means that no context number was specified.

> **Tip**
>
> *A help file must be compiled using the Windows Help Compiler available in the Professional and Enterprise editions of Visual Basic.*

- *OLEContainerControl*.**HostName**—a **String** containing the host name to be displayed in the object's title window. This value may not be used by all objects.
- *OLEContainerControl*.**hWnd**—a **Long** that contains a Windows handle to the control.

> **Tip**
>
> *The **hWnd** property is most useful when making calls to Windows API functions. Since this value can change during execution, do not save the value into a variable for later use.*

- *OLEContainerControl*.**Index**—an **Integer** that uniquely identifies a control in a control array.
- *OLEContainerControl*.**Left**—a **Single** that contains the distance, measured in twips, between the left edge of the control and the left edge of the control's container.
- *OLEContainerControl*.**LpOleObject**—a **Long** containing the address of the object. This property would typically be used when calling ActiveX DLLs.
- *OLEContainerControl*.**MiscFlags**—an **Integer** containing flags that determine how the object behaves (see Table O-8).

MiscFlags Name	Value	Description
vbOLEMiscFlagMemStorage	1	Uses memory instead of a temporary disk file to store the object.
vbOLEMiscFlagDisableInPlace	2	Allows in-place activation for objects that support it.

Table O-8: MiscFlags *values*.

- *OLEContainerControl*.**MouseIcon**—a picture object (a bitmap, icon, or metafile) that will be used as a cursor when the **MousePointer** property is set to 99. Note that Visual Basic does not support color cursors from a .CUR file. A color icon from an .ICO file should be used instead.

OLE Container • 645

- *OLEContainerControl*.**MousePointer**—an **Integer** value (see Table O-9) that contains the value of the cursor that should be displayed when the cursor is moved over this control. Use *vbCustom* to display the custom icon stored in the **MouseIcon** property.

Cursor Name	Value	Description
vbDefault	0	Shape determined by the object (default value).
vbArrow	1	Arrow.
vbCrosshair	2	Crosshair.
vbIbeam	3	I beam.
vbIconPointer	4	Square inside a square.
vbSizePointer	5	Four-sided arrow (north, south, east, west).
vbSizeNESW	6	Two-sided arrow (northeast, southwest).
vbSizeNS	7	Two-sided arrow (north, south).
vbSizeNWSE	8	Two-sided arrow (northwest, southeast).
vbSizeWE	9	Two-sided arrow (west, east).
vbUpArrow	10	Single-sided arrow pointing north.
vbHourglass	11	Hourglass.
vbNoDrop	12	No Drop.
vbArrowHourglass	13	An arrow and an hourglass.
vbArrowQuestion	14	An arrow and a question mark.
vbSizeAll	15	Size all.
vbCustom	99	Custom icon from the **MouseIcon** property of this control.

Table O-9: Cursor *values.*

- *OLEContainerControl*.**Name**—a **String** that contains the name of the control that will be used to reference the control in a Visual Basic program. This property is read only at run time.
- *OLEContainerControl*.**Object**—an object that contains a reference to the object.
- *OLEContainerControl*.**ObjectAcceptFormats** (*index*)—a **String** array containing a list of the formats the object will accept. *Index* can range from zero to **ObjectAcceptFormatsCount** -1.
- *OLEContainerControl*.**ObjectAcceptFormatsCount**—an **Integer** containing the number of accept formats supported by the object.
- *OLEContainerControl*.**ObjectGetFormats** (*index*)—a **String** array containing a list of the formats the object can provide. *Index* can range from zero to **ObjectGetFormatsCount** -1.
- *OLEContainerControl*.**ObjectGetFormatsCount**—an **Integer** containing the number of get formats supported by the object.
- *OLEContainerControl*.**ObjectVerbFlags** (*index*)—an **Integer** array containing the menu flags associated with the **ObjectVerb** array (see Table O-10). *Index* can range from zero to **ObjectVerbsCount** -1.

ObjectVerbFlags Name	Value	Description
vbOLEFlagChecked	&H0008	The item is checked.
vbOLEFlagDisabled	&H0002	The item is disabled.
vbOLEFlagEnabled	&H0000	The item is enabled.
vbOLEFlagGrayed	&H0001	The item is dimmed.
vbOLEFlagSeparator	&H0800	The item is a separator.

Table O-10: ObjectVerbFlags *values.*

- *OLEContainerControl.***ObjectVerbs** (*index*)—an **Integer** array containing the verbs supported by an object. Most OLE applications support the verbs listed in Table O-11. Other verbs may be included in the array. The exact meaning of each verb is dependent on the application. Index can range from zero to **ObjectVerbsCount** -1.

ObjectVerbs Name	Value	Description
vbOLEPrimary	0	Takes the default action for the object.
vbOLEShow	-1	Opens the object within the OLE container if the object supports in-place activation.
vbOLEOpen	-2	Opens the object in a separate application window.
vbOLEHide	-3	Hides the application that created the object.
vbOLEInPlaceUIActivate	-4	Opens the object within the OLE container and shows the user interface tools, if the object supports in-place activation.
vbOLEInPlaceActivate	-5	Opens the object in a separate application window when the container gets the focus.
vbOLEDiscardUndoState	-6	Discards all undo information for an active object.

Table O-11: ObjectVerbs *values*.

- *OLEContainerControl.***OLEDropAllowed**—a **Boolean** when **True** means that an object can be dropped on the control. Dropping has the same effect as a copy-and-paste operation. **False** means the No Drop icon will be shown when the mouse pointer passes over the control.
- *OLEContainerControl.***OLEType**—an **Integer** containing the status of the object (see Table O-12).

OLEType Name	Value	Description
vbOLELinked	0	The OLE container has a linked object.
vbOLEEmbedded	1	The OLE container has an embedded object.
vbOLENone	3	The OLE container does not have any objects.

Table O-12: OLEType *values*.

- *OLEContainerControl.***OLETypeAllowed**—an **Integer** containing the status of the object (see Table O-13).

OLETypeAllowed Name	Value	Description
vbOLELinked	0	The OLE container can have a linked object.
vbOLEEmbedded	1	The OLE container can have an embedded object.
vbOLEEither	2	The OLE container can have either type of object.

Table O-13: OLETypeAllowed *values*.

- *OLEContainerControl.***Parent**—an object that contains a reference to the **Form**, **Frame**, or other container that contains the control.

OLE Container

- *OLEContainerControl*.**PasteOK**—a **Boolean** when **True** means that data from the system clipboard may be pasted into the object. **False** means that you can't paste into the object from the system clipboard.
- *OLEContainerControl*.**Picture**—a picture object (a bitmap, icon, metafile, GIF, or JPEG) that will be displayed on the control. You can also use the **LoadPicture** function at run time to load a bitmap, icon, or metafile. Note that **Style** must be set to *vbButtonGraphical* for the image to be shown.
- *OLEContainerControl*.**SizeMode**—an **Integer** value (see Table O-14) describing how the **OLE Container** is resized or how its image is displayed.

SizeMode Name	Value	Description
vbOLESizeClip	0	The object is displayed in full size and, if larger, it will be clipped (default value).
vbOLESizeStretch	1	The object is stretched to fit the size of the container, even if the proportions have to be adjusted.
vbOLESizeAutoSize	2	The container is resized to fit the entire object.
vbOLESizeZoom	3	The object is resized to fit the container, while maintaining the object's original proportions.

Table O-14: SizeMode values.

- *OLEContainerControl*.**SourceDoc**—a **String** containing the file to be linked to the control. This property is used with the **SourceItem** to identify the data to be linked.
- *OLEContainerControl*.**SourceItem**—a **String** containing the data within the file to be linked. This property is used with the **SourceDoc** property.
- *OLEContainerControl*.**TabIndex**—an **Integer** that determines the order that a user will tab through the objects on a form.
- *OLEContainerControl*.**TabStop**—a **Boolean** value when **True** means that the user can tab to this object. When **False**, means that this control will be skipped to the next control in the **TabIndex** order.
- *OLEContainerControl*.**Tag**—a **String** that can hold programmer-specific information. This property is not used by Visual Basic.
- *OLEContainerControl*.**Top**—a **Single** that contains the distance, measured in twips, between the top edge of the control and the top edge of the control's container.
- *OLEContainerControl*.**UpdateOptions**—an **Integer** containing how updates should be handled (see Table O-15).

UpdateOptions Name	Value	Description
vbOLEAutomatic	0	Updates are done automatically (default).
vbOLEFrozen	1	The object is updated when the user saves the data in the application.
vbOLEManual	2	The object is updated only when the **Update** method is used.

Table O-15: UpdateOptions values.

- *OLEContainerControl*.**Verb**—an **Integer** value that points to an entry in the **ObjectVerbs** array containing the operation to be executed. Setting the **Action** property to 2 will begin the operation. This property has been superseded by the **DoVerb** method.
- *OLEContainerControl*.**Visible**—a **Boolean** value when **True** means that the control is visible. When **False,** the control is not visible.

> **Tip**
>
> *This property can hide the control until the program is ready to display it.*

- *OLEContainerControl*.**WhatsThisHelpID**—a **Long** that contains a help file context ID number that references an entry in the help file. This provides a What's This PopUp help display in response to the What's This button in the upper-right corner of the window.
- *OLEContainerControl*.**Width**—a **Single** that contains the width of the control.

Methods

OLEContainerControl.Close

Usage This method closes the object and terminates the connection to the application. This method corresponds to **Action** property number 9.

OLEContainerControl.Copy

Usage This method copies the object to the clipboard. This method corresponds to **Action** property number 4.

OLEContainerControl.CreateEmbed *sourcedoc,* [*class*]

Usage This method creates an embedded object. This method corresponds to **Action** property number 0.

Arguments
- *sourcedoc*—a **String** containing the filename of the document to be embedded, or an empty string if you don't want to use a source document.
- *class*—a **String** containing the class of the embedded object.

OLEContainerControl.CreateLink *sourcedoc,* [*sourceitem*]

Usage This method creates an embedded object. This method corresponds to **Action** property number 1.

Arguments
- *sourcedoc*—a **String** containing the filename of the document to be linked.
- *sourceitem*—a **String** containing the data within the file to be linked.

OLEContainerControl.Delete

Usage This method deletes the object and frees its resources. This method corresponds to **Action** property number 10.

OLEContainerControl.DoVerb verb

Usage   This method sends a request to the object to perform a specific function, such as open the object for editing.

Arguments   *verb*—an **Integer** containing the request to be performed (see Table O-16).

Verb Name	Value	Description
vbOLEPrimary	0	Takes the default action for the object.
vbOLEShow	-1	Opens the object within the OLE container if the object supports in-place activation.
vbOLEOpen	-2	Opens the object in a separate application window.
vbOLEHide	-3	Hides the application that created the object.
vbOLEInPlaceUIActivate	-4	Opens the object within the OLE container and shows the user interface tools, if the object supports in-place activation.
vbOLEInPlaceActivate	-5	Opens the object in a separate application window when the container gets the focus.
vbOLEDiscardUndoState	-6	Discards all undo information for an active object.

Table O-16: Verb *values.*

OLEContainerControl.Drag [DragAction]

Usage   This method begins, ends, or cancels a drag operation.

Arguments   *DragAction*—an **Integer** that contains a value selected from Table O-17 below.

DragAction Name	Value	Description
vbCancel	0	Cancels any drag operation in progress.
vbBeginDrag	1	Begins a drag operation (default).
vbEndDrag	2	Ends a drag operation and drops *object*.

Table O-17: DragAction *values.*

OLEContainerControl.FetchVerbs

Usage   This method refreshes the list of verbs in the **ObjectVerbs** property. This method corresponds to **Action** property number 17.

OLEContainerControl.InsertObjDlg

Usage   This method displays a dialog box at run time that lets the user select the type of object. This method corresponds to **Action** property number 14.

OLEContainerControl.Move Left [, Top [, Width [, Height]]]

Usage This method changes the position and the size of the **OLEContainer** control. The **ScaleMode** of the **Form** or other container object that holds this control will determine the units used to specify the coordinates.

Arguments
- *Left*—a **Single** that specifies the new position of the left edge of the control.
- *Top*—a **Single** that specifies the new position of the top edge of the control.
- *Width*—a **Single** that specifies the new width of the control.
- *Height*—a **Single** that specifies the new height of the control.

OLEContainerControl.Paste

Usage This method copies data from the clipboard to the object. This method corresponds to **Action** property number 5.

OLEContainerControl.PasteSpecialDlg

Usage This method displays the Paste Special dialog box. This method corresponds to **Action** property number 15.

OLEContainerControl.ReadFromFile *filenum*

Usage This method reads an object from a data file. This method corresponds to **Action** property number 12.

Arguments *filenum*—an **Integer** that contains the file number of an open binary file with the object to be read.

OLEContainerControl.Refresh

Usage This method redraws the contents of the control.

OLEContainerControl.SaveToFile *filenum*

Usage This method copies the object to the clipboard. This method corresponds to **Action** property number 11.

Arguments *filenum*—an **Integer** that contains the file number of an open binary file where the object will be saved.

OLEContainerControl.SaveToOle1File *filenum*

Usage This method copies the object to the clipboard. This method corresponds to **Action** property number 18.

Arguments *filenum*—an **Integer** that contains the file number of an open binary file where the object will be saved.

OLEContainerControl.SetFocus

Usage This method transfers the focus from the form or control that currently has the focus to this control. To receive the focus, this control must be enabled and visible.

OLEContainerControl.ShowWhatsThis

Usage This method displays the ShowWhatsThis help information for this control.

OLEContainerControl.Update

Usage This method gets a picture of the current application and displays it. This method corresponds to **Action** property number 6.

OLEContainerControl.ZOrder [*position*]

Usage This method specifies the position of the animation control relative to the other objects on the form.

> **Tip**
>
> *Note that there are three layers of objects on a form: The back layer is the drawing space that contains the results of the graphical methods, the middle layer contains graphical objects and* **Labels***, and the top layer contains nongraphical controls such as the* **CommandButton***. The* **ZOrder** *method only affects how the objects are arranged within a single layer.*

Arguments *position*—an **Integer** that specifies the relative position of this object. A value of 0 means that the control is positioned at the head of the list, a value of 1 means that the control will be placed at the end of the list.

Events

Private Sub OLEContainerControl_Click([*index* As Integer])

Usage This event occurs when the user clicks a mouse button while the cursor is positioned over this control.

> **Tip**
>
> *If you need to identify which mouse button was pressed, use the* **MouseUp** *and* **MouseDown** *events.*

Arguments *index*—an **Integer** that uniquely identifies a control in a control array. This argument is not present if the control is not part of a control array.

Private Sub OLEContainerControl_DblClick([*index* As Integer])

Usage   This event occurs when the user double-clicks a mouse button to select an item in the drop-down list or selects an item from the drop-down list using the keyboard. This applies only when **Style** is set to *vbComboSimple*.

Arguments   • *index*—an **Integer** that uniquely identifies a control in a control array. This argument is not present if the control is not part of a control array.

Private Sub OLEContainerControl_DragDrop([*index* As Integer,] *source* As Control, *x* As Single, *y* As Single)

Usage   This event occurs when a drag-and-drop operation is completed by using the **Drag** method with a *DragAction* value of *vbEndDrag* (2).

Tip

*When using drag-and-drop operations, use the **DragOver** event to determine what the cursor should look like while the cursor moves over the control.*

Arguments   • *index*—an **Integer** that uniquely identifies a control in a control array. This argument is not present if the control is not part of a control array.
• *source*—a control object that is the control that is being dragged.

Tip

You can access a property or method from the source control by using source.property *or* source.method. *You can determine the type of object or control by using the **TypeOf** operator.*

• *x*—a **Single** that contains the horizontal location of the mouse pointer.
• *y*—a **Single** that contains the vertical location of the mouse pointer.

Private Sub OLEContainerControl_DragOver([*index* As Integer,] *source* As Control, *x* As Single, *y* As Single, *state* As Integer)

Usage   This event occurs while a drag operation is in progress and the cursor is moved over the control.

Tip

*When using drag-and-drop operations, use the **DragOver** event to determine what the cursor should look like while the cursor moves over the control. When* state *is 0, you can change the cursor to a No Drop (vbNoDrop) cursor or highlight the field that the cursor is near. When* state *is 1, you can undo the changes you made when the* state *was 0.*

OLE Container

Arguments
- *index*—an **Integer** that uniquely identifies a control in a control array. This argument is not present if the control is not part of a control array.
- *source*—a control object that is the control that is being dragged.

Tip
You can access a property or method from the source control by using source.property *or* source.method. *You can determine the type of object or control by using the* **TypeOf** *operator.*

- *x*—a **Single** that contains the horizontal location of the mouse pointer.
- *y*—a **Single** that contains the vertical location of the mouse pointer.
- *state*—an **Integer** value (see Table O-18) that indicates the state of the object being dragged.

state Name	Value	Description
vbEnter	0	The dragged object is entering range of the control.
vbLeave	1	The dragged object is leaving range of the control.
vbOver	2	The dragged object has moved from one position over the control to another.

Table O-18: State values.

Private Sub *OLEContainerControl*_GotFocus ([*index* As Integer])

Usage This event occurs when the control is given focus.

Tip
You can use this routine to display help or other information in a status bar.

Arguments
- *index*—an **Integer** that uniquely identifies a control in a control array. This argument is not present if the control is not part of a control array.

Private Sub *OLEContainerControl*_KeyDown ([*index* As Integer,] *keycode* As Integer, *shift* As Single)

Usage This event occurs when a key is pressed while the control has the focus.

Arguments
- *index*—an **Integer** that uniquely identifies a control in a control array. This argument is not present if the control is not part of a control array.
- *keycode*—an **Integer** that contains information about which key was pressed.

- *shift*—an **Integer** value (see Table O-19) that contains information about the Shift and Alt keys that were pressed when the mouse button was pressed. These values can be added together if more than one key was down. For instance, a value of 5 would mean that the Shift and Alt keys were both down when the mouse button was pressed.

shift Name	Value	Description
vbShiftMask	1	The Shift key was pressed.
vbCtrlMask	2	The Ctrl key was pressed.
vbAltMask	4	The Alt key was pressed.

Table O-19: Shift *values*.

Private Sub *OLEContainerControl*_KeyPress([*index* As Integer,] *keychar* As Integer)

Usage   This event occurs whenever a key is pressed while the control has the focus.

Arguments
- *index*—an **Integer** that uniquely identifies a control in a control array. This argument is not present if the control is not part of a control array.
- *keychar*—an **Integer** that contains the ASCII character that was pressed.

Private Sub *OLEContainerControl*_KeyUp ([*index* As Integer,] *keycode* As Integer, *shift* As Single)

Usage   This event occurs when a key is released while the control has the focus.

Arguments
- *index*—an **Integer** that uniquely identifies a control in a control array. This argument is not present if the control is not part of a control array.
- *keycode*—an **Integer** that contains information about which key was released.
- *shift*—an **Integer** value (see Table O-20) that contains information about the Shift and Alt keys that were pressed when the mouse button was pressed. These values can be added together if more than one key was down. For instance, a value of 5 would mean that the Shift and Alt keys were both down when the mouse button was pressed.

shift Name	Value	Description
vbShiftMask	1	The Shift key was pressed.
vbCtrlMask	2	The Ctrl key was pressed.
vbAltMask	4	The Alt key was pressed.

Table O-20: Shift *values*.

Private Sub *OLEContainerControl*_LostFocus ([*index* As Integer])

Usage   This event occurs when the control loses focus.

Tip

This routine is useful in performing data verification.

Arguments
- *index*—an **Integer** that uniquely identifies a control in a control array. This argument is not present if the control is not part of a control array.

Private Sub *OLEContainerControl*_MouseDown([*index* As Integer,] *button* As Integer, *shift* As Single, *x* As Single, *y* As Single)

Usage   This event occurs when a mouse button is pressed while the cursor is over the control.

Arguments
- *index*—an **Integer** that uniquely identifies a control in a control array. This argument is not present if the control is not part of a control array.
- *button*—an **Integer** value (see Table O-21) that contains information about the mouse buttons that were pressed. Only one button will be indicated when this event occurs.

button Name	Value	Description
vbLeftButton	1	The left button was pressed.
vbRightButton	2	The right button was pressed.
vbMiddleButton	4	The middle button was pressed.

Table O-21: Button *values.*

- *shift*—an **Integer** value (see Table O-22) that contains information about the Shift and Alt keys that were pushed when the mouse button was pressed. These values can be added together if more than one key was down. For instance, a value of 5 would mean that the Shift and Alt keys were both down when the mouse button was pressed.

shift Name	Value	Description
vbShiftMask	1	The Shift key was pressed.
vbCtrlMask	2	The Ctrl key was pressed.
vbAltMask	4	The Alt key was pressed.

Table O-22: Shift *values.*

- *x*—a **Single** that contains the horizontal location of the mouse pointer.
- *y*—a **Single** that contains the vertical location of the mouse pointer.

Private Sub *OLEContainerControl*_MouseMove ([*index* As Integer,] *button* As Integer, *shift* As Single, *x* As Single, *y* As Single)

Usage   This event occurs while the cursor is moved over the control.

Arguments
- *index*—an **Integer** that uniquely identifies a control in a control array. This argument is not present if the control is not part of a control array.
- *button*—an **Integer** value (see Table O-23) that contains information about the mouse buttons that were pressed. These values can be added together if more than one button was pressed. For instance, a value of 3 means that both the left and right buttons were pressed. A value of 0 means that no buttons were pressed.

button Name	Value	Description
vbLeftButton	1	The left button was pressed.
vbRightButton	2	The right button was pressed.
vbMiddleButton	4	The middle button was pressed.

Table O-23: Button *values*.

- *shift*—an **Integer** value (see Table O-24) that contains information about the Shift and Alt keys that were pressed when the mouse button was pressed. For instance, a value of 5 would mean that the Shift and Alt keys were both down when the mouse button was pressed. A value of 0 means that none of these keys were pressed.

shift Name	Value	Description
vbShiftMask	1	The Shift key was pressed.
vbCtrlMask	2	The Ctrl key was pressed.
vbAltMask	4	The Alt key was pressed.

Table O-24: Shift *values*.

- *x*—a **Single** that contains the horizontal location of the mouse pointer.
- *y*—a **Single** that contains the vertical location of the mouse pointer.

Private Sub *OLEContainerControl*_MouseUp([*index* As Integer,] *button* As Integer, *shift* As Single, *x* As Single, *y* As Single)

Usage   This event occurs when a mouse button is released while the cursor is over the control.

Arguments
- *index*—an **Integer** that uniquely identifies a control in a control array. This argument is not present if the control is not part of a control array.
- *button*—an **Integer** value (see Table O-25) that contains information about the mouse buttons that were released. Only one of these values will be present.

button Name	Value	Description
vbLeftButton	1	The left button was released.
vbRightButton	2	The right button was released.
vbMiddleButton	4	The middle button was released.

Table O-25: Button *values*.

- *shift*—an **Integer** value (see Table O-26) that contains information about the Shift and Alt keys that were pressed when the mouse button was released. These values can be added together if more than one key was down. For instance, a value of 5 would mean that the Shift and Alt keys were both down when the mouse button was released. A value of 0 means that none of these keys were pressed.

shift Name	Value	Description
vbShiftMask	1	The Shift key was pressed.
vbCtrlMask	2	The Ctrl key was pressed.
vbAltMask	4	The Alt key was pressed.

Table O-26: Shift *values*.

- *x*—a **Single** that contains the horizontal location of the mouse pointer.
- *y*—a **Single** that contains the vertical location of the mouse pointer.

Private Sub *OLEContainerControl*_ObjectMove ([*index* As Integer,] *left* As Single, *top* As Single, *width* As Single, *height* As Single)

Usage This event occurs when an active object inside the control is moved or resized.

Arguments
- *index*—an **Integer** that uniquely identifies a control in a control array. This argument is not present if the control is not part of a control array.
- *left*—a **Single** value containing the distance between the container and the left edge of the object.
- *top*—a **Single** value containing the distance between the container and the top edge of the object.
- *width*—a **Single** value containing the width of the object.
- *height*—a **Single** value containing the height of the object.

Private Sub *OLEContainerControl*_Resize ([*index* As Integer,] *width* As Single, *height* As Single)

Usage This event occurs when the control is resized.

Arguments
- *index*—an **Integer** that uniquely identifies a control in a control array. This argument is not present if the control is not part of a control array.
- *width*—a **Single** value containing the width of the control.
- *height*—a **Single** value containing the height of the control.

Private Sub *OLEContainerControl*_Updated ([*index* **As Integer**,] *code* **As Integer**)

Usage   This event occurs when the object's data has been changed.

Arguments
- *index*—an **Integer** that uniquely identifies a control in a control array. This argument is not present if the control is not part of a control array.
- *code*—an **Integer** value (see Table O-27) that contains information about the mouse buttons that were pressed. These values can be added together if more than one button was pressed. For instance, a value of 3 means that both the left and right buttons were pressed. A value of 0 means that no buttons were pressed.

code Name	Value	Description
vbOLEChanged	0	The object's data was changed.
vbOLESaved	1	The object's data was saved.
vbOLEClosed	2	The file containing the linked object's data was closed.
vbOLERenamed	3	The file containing the linked object's data was renamed.

Table O-27: Code values.

Examples
```
Private Sub Check1_Click()
MsgBox "The value of the OLEContainer is " & Format(Check1.Value)
End Sub
```

This routine will display the value of the OLE container each time it is clicked.

See Also   **Data** (control), **LoadPicture** (function), **OptionButton** (control)

On Error

STATEMENT
CCE, LE, PE, EE

Syntax   `On Error GoTo label`

`On Error Resume Next`

`On Error GoTo 0`

Usage   The **On Error** statement traps error conditions that would normally result in a run-time error. There are three forms of the **On Error** statement. In the first form, control is transferred to the code at the specified label value. In the second form, control continues with the next statement. The third form is used to cancel the effects of the other two forms.

Note that *label* must refer to a label within the current routine or a compile-time error will occur.

On GoSub • 659

> **Tip**
>
> Use the **On Error Resume Next** statement with the **Err** object to avoid using **GoTo** statements.

Arguments
- *label*—a Visual Basic line label or line number.

Examples
```
Private Sub Command1_Click()
On Error Resume Next
Open "this file doesn't exist" For Input As #1
If Err.Number <> 0 Then
    MsgBox "Error " & Format(Err.Number) & ": " & Err.Description
End If
End Sub
```

This example begins by using the **On Error** statement to trap any run-time errors and save the error in the **Err** object. Then I force an error by trying to open a file that doesn't exist. Finally I check the **Err** object and display a message if the **Err.Number** property is not zero.

See Also   **Err** (object)

On GoSub

STATEMENT

CCE, LE, PE, EE

Syntax   **On** *expr* **GoSub** *label1* [, *label2*] . . . [, *labelN*]

Usage   The **On GoSub** statement will execute a **GoSub** statement depending on the value of *expr*. If *expr* is 1, then a **GoSub** to *label1* will be executed. If *expr* is 2, then a **GoSub** to *label2* will be executed. This continues until the value of *expr* is N, when a **GoSub** to *labelN* will be executed.

Note that each label must refer to a label within the current routine or a compile-time error will occur. A run-time error will occur when *expr* has a value less than one or greater than the number of labels on the list.

> **Tip**
>
> The **OnGoSub** statement exists primarily to maintain compatibility with older versions of Basic. Use the **Select Case** instead of the **On GoSub** statement for more flexible code.

Arguments
- *label1*—a Visual Basic line label or line number.
- *label2*—another Visual Basic line label or line number.
- *labelN*—another Visual Basic line label or line number.

Examples

```
Private Sub Command1_Click()
On Error Resume Next
On CInt(Text1.Text) GoSub One, Two, Three
If Err.Number <> 0 Then
    MsgBox "Error " & Format(Err.Number) & ": " & Err.Description
End If
Exit Sub
One:
    Text2.Text = "One"
    Return
Two:
    Text2.Text = "Two"
    Return
Three:
    Text2.Text = "Three"
    Return
End Sub
```

This example uses the **On GoSub** statement to execute one of three different GoSub routines based on a user-supplied value. It uses the **On Error** statement to trap run-time errors caused by bad input data.

See Also   **Select Case** (statement)

On GoTo

STATEMENT

CCE, LE, PE, EE

Syntax   **On** *expr* **GoSub** *label1* [, *label2*] . . . [, *labelN*]

Usage   The **On GoTo** statement will execute a **GoTo** statement depending on the value of *expr*. If *expr* is 1, then a **GoTo** to *label1* will be executed. If *expr* is 2, then a **GoTo** to *label2* will be executed. This continues until the value of *expr* is N, when a **GoTo** to *labelN* will be executed.

Note that each label must refer to a label within the current routine or a compile-time error will occur. A run-time error will occur when *expr* has a value less than one or greater than the number of labels on the list.

> **Tip**
>
> *The **OnGoTo** statement exists primarily to maintain compatibility with older versions of Basic. Use the **Select Case** instead of the **On GoTo** statement for more flexible code.*

Arguments
- *label1*—a Visual Basic line label or line number.
- *label2*—another Visual Basic line label or line number.
- *labelN*—another Visual Basic line label or line number.

Examples
```
Private Sub Command1_Click()
On Error Resume Next
On CInt(Text1.Text) GoTo One, Two, Three
If Err.Number <> 0 Then
    MsgBox "Error " & Format(Err.Number) & ": " & Err.Description
End If
Exit Sub
One:
    Text2.Text = "One"
    Exit Sub
Two:
    Text2.Text = "Two"
    Exit Sub
Three:
    Text2.Text = "Three"
    Exit Sub
End Sub
```

This example uses the **On GoTo** statement to execute one of three different blocks of code. It uses the **On Error** statement to trap run-time errors caused by bad input data.

See Also **Select Case** (statement)

Open   STATEMENT

CCE, LE, PE, EE

Syntax **Open** *filename* **For** *mode* [**Access** *access*] [*lock*] **As** [#] *filenum* [**Len** = *reclen*]

Usage The **Open** statement provides access to the data in a file.

Arguments
- *filename*—a **String** value containing the path and filename of a file.
- *mode*—a keyword describing how the file is opened: **Append**, **Binary**, **Input**, **Output**, and **Random**.
- *access*—a keyword describing the operations permitted against the file: **Read**, **Write**, and **Read Write**.
- *lock*—describes how the file is shared: **Shared**, **Lock Read**, **Lock Write**, and **Lock Read Write**.
- *filenum*—an **Integer** in the range of 0 to 511 that is not currently assigned to an open file.

> **Tip**
>
> Use **FreeFile** to determine the next available, unused file number.

- *reclen*—an **Integer** value containing the size of a record. It can range in size from 1 to 32,767 bytes. In **Random** files, this is the size of the record. In all other files, it is the amount of data buffered.

Examples
```
Private Sub Command1_Click()
Dim s As String
On Error Resume Next
Text2.Text = ""
Open Text1.Text For Input As #1
If Err.Number <> 0 Then
    MsgBox "Can't open the input file: " & Err.Description
Else
    Do While Not EOF(1)
        Input #1, s
        Text2.Text = Text2.Text & s & vbCrLf
    Loop
    Close #1
End If
End Sub
```

This routine opens the file specified in Text1.Text, displays the contents in Text2.Text, and then closes the file.

See Also **Close** (statement), **Eof** (function), **FreeFile** (function), **Line Input** (statement), **On Error** (statement), **Read** (statement), **Print** (statement), **Write** (statement)

Operators

CCE, LE, PE, EE

Usage   Operators are used to build expressions, which are used in statements such as the **Let** statement, **If** statement and many other statements. Operators fall into three major groups: Arithmetic Operators (see Table O-28), Comparison Operators (see Table O-29), Logical Operators (see Table O-30), and Miscellaneous Operators (see Table O-31).

Arithmetic Operators

Arithmetic Operator	Description
nexpr ^ nexpr	Exponentiation.
- nexpr	Negation.
nexpr * nexpr	Multiplication.
nexpr / nexpr	Division.
nexpr \ nexpr	Integer division.
nexpr **Mod** nexpr	Modulus.
nexpr + nexpr	Addition.
nexpr—nexpr	Subtraction.
string & string	String concatenation.

Table O-28: Arithmetic Operators.

Comparison Operators

Comparison Operator	Description
expr = expr	Equality.
expr <> expr	Inequality.
expr < expr	Less than.
expr > expr	Greater than.
expr <= expr	Less than or equal to.
expr >= expr	Greater than or equal to.
string **Like** pattern	String concatenation.

Table O-29: Comparison Operators.

Logical Operators

Logical Operator	Description
Not expr	Logical not.
expr **And** expr	Logical and.
expr **Or** expr	Logical or.
expr **Xor** expr	Logical xor.
expr **Eqv** expr	Logical equivalence.
expr **Imp** expr	Logical implication.

Table O-30: Logical Operators.

Miscellaneous Operators

Miscellaneous Operator	Description
AddressOf procedure	Memory address of a procedure.
TypeOf variable	Type of variable.
function [(argument list)]	Function call.

Table O-31: Miscellaneous Operators.

Arguments
- *argument list*—a list of arguments that are passed to a function.
- *expr*—a numeric value or an expression resulting in a numeric value.
- *function*—the name of a Visual Basic function or object property.
- *nexpr*—a numeric (**Double**, **Integer**, **Long**, or **Single**) value or constant or an expression resulting in a numeric value.
- *pattern*—a **String** value containing values from the Table O-32 below. In *list of chars* a hyphen ("-") can be used to specify a range of characters.

Pattern Characters	Description
?	Matches any single character.
*	Matches zero or more characters.
#	Matches any single digit.
[list of chars]	Matches any character in the list.
[! list of chars]	Matches any character not in the list.

Table O-32: Pattern Characters.

- *procedure*—the name of a function or subroutine.
- *string*—a **String** variable or string expression.
- *variable*—a Visual Basic identifier.

See Also   **If** (statement), **Let** (statement)

Option Base

STATEMENT

CCE, LE, PE, EE

Syntax   `Option Base { 0 | 1 }`

Usage   The **Option Base** statement determines the default lower bound for arrays. This statement has no effect on arrays created with the **ParamArray** keyword or the **Array** function. The only valid default values for lower bound are 0 and 1.

See Also   **Dim** (statement), **LBound** (function), **Private** (statement), **Public** (statement), **ReDim** (statement)

Option Compare

STATEMENT

CCE, LE, PE, EE

Syntax   `Option Compare { Binary | Database | Text }`

Usage   The **Option Compare** statement determines how strings are compared. **Binary** means that string comparisons are done using the binary value of each character. **Database** is used only with Microsoft Access programs and uses locale information from the database to determine the sort order. **Text** means that the characters are compared based on the system's locale setting. Both **Database** and **Text** comparisons are case insensitive.

See Also   **String** (data type)

Option Explicit

STATEMENT
CCE, LE, PE, EE

Syntax   `Option Explicit`

Usage   The **Option Explicit** statement requires that all variables must be declared before they are used.

> **Tip**
>
> *I strongly encourage using this statement in your programs since it prevents Visual Basic from creating a new variable when you simply typed the wrong name.*

See Also   **Dim** (statement), **Private** (statement), **Public** (statement), **ReDim** (statement)

Option Private

STATEMENT
CCE, LE, PE, EE

Syntax   `Option Private Module`

Usage   The **Option Private Module** statement is used to limit the scope of references to a single module in applications that permit references between multiple projects, such as Visual Basic for Applications. This statement is not needed in Visual Basic Control Creation Edition, Learning Edition, Professional Edition, or Enterprise Edition.

See Also   **Option Base** (statement), **Option Compare** (statement), **Option Explicit** (statement)

OptionButton

CONTROL
CCE, LE, PE, EE

Usage   The **OptionButton** control is an intrinsic control that provides the user with a Yes/No choice. Text can be displayed next to the box by using the **Caption** property. The value of the control can be checked by using the **Value** property.

An **OptionButton** control is similar to a **CheckBox** control in that it allows a user to make a Yes/No choice. However an **OptionButton** only allows one choice in a group to be Yes or **True**, the rest of the buttons must be **False**. A **CheckBox** control does not have this restriction.

Properties   ▪ *OptionButtonControl.***Alignment**—an **Integer** value (see Table O-33) that describes the placement of the Option Button and the caption within the space occupied by the control.

Alignment Name	Value	Description
vbLeftJustify	0	The Option Button is shown on the left side of the control, while the caption is shown to the right of the Option Button (default value).
vbRightJustify	1	The Option Button is shown on the right side of the control, while the caption is shown to the left of the Option Button.

Table O-33: *Alignment values.*

- *OptionButtonControl*.**Appearance**—an **Integer** value (see Table O-34) that describes how the Option Button will appear on the form:

AppearanceValue	Description
0	The Option Button is displayed without the 3D effects.
1	The Option Button is displayed with 3D effects (default value).

Table O-34: Appearance *values*.

- *OptionButtonControl*.**BackColor**—a **Long** that contains the suggested value for the background color of the control. The **BackColor** and **ForeColor** must both be solid to display text. If you choose a color that is dithered, it will be changed to the nearest solid color.
- *OptionButtonControl*.**Caption**—a **String** value that is displayed next to the Option Button. You can include an access key for this control by inserting an ampersand (&) in front of the character you want to use. The selected character will then appear with an underline. Then if the user presses the Alt key with the underlined character the control will gain the focus.
- *OptionButtonControl*.**Container**—an object that can be used to set or return the container of the control at run time. This property cannot be set at design time.
- *OptionButtonControl*.**DisabledPicture**—a picture object (a bitmap, icon, or metafile) that will be shown on top of the control when the control's **Enabled** property is **False** and the **Style** property is set to *vbButtonGraphical*.

Tip

This value can be created using the **LoadPicture** *function.*

- *OptionButtonControl*.**DownPicture**—a picture object (a bitmap, icon, or metafile) that will be displayed on top of the control when the control is pressed. This will replace the standard picture displayed when the control is not pressed. This feature requires that the **Style** property be set to *vbButtonGraphical*.

Tip

This value can be created using the **LoadPicture** *function.*

- *OptionButtonControl*.**DragIcon**—an object that contains the picture value of an icon. At design time, you can specify an icon file that has a file type of .ICO.

Tip

This value can be created by copying the value from another control's **DragIcon** *value, by copying a form's icon, or by using the* **LoadPicture** *function.*

- *OptionButtonControl*.**DragMode**—an **Integer** value (see Table O-35) specifying how the control will respond to a drag request.

> **Tip**
>
> Setting **DragMode** to vbAutomatic *will automatically begin a drag operation when the user clicks on the control. However, the control will not respond to the usual mouse events (**Click**, **DblClick**, **MouseDown**, **MouseMove**, **MouseUp**).*

DragMode Name	Value	Description
vbManual	0	The **Drag** method must be used to begin a drag-and-drop operation (default value).
vbAutomatic	1	The source control will automatically begin a drag-and-drop operation when the user clicks on the control.

Table O-35: DragMode *values*.

- *OptionButtonControl*.**Enabled**—a **Boolean** value when **True** means that the control will respond to events. When **False**, the control will not respond to events.
- *OptionButtonControl*.**Font**—an object that contains information about the character font used by this object.

> **Tip**
>
> *The **Font** object should be used in place of the other **Font** properties, since it offers more functionality than the individual properties.*

- *OptionButtonControl*.**FontBold**—a **Boolean,** when **True**, means that the characters display in bold. **False** means that the characters display normally.
- *OptionButtonControl*.**FontItalic**—a **Boolean,** when **True**, means that the characters display in italics. **False** means that the characters display normally.
- *OptionButtonControl*.**FontName**—a **String** that specifies the name of the font that should be used to display the characters in this control.
- *OptionButtonControl*.**FontSize**—a **Single** that specifies the point size that should be used to display the characters in the control.
- *OptionButtonControl*.**FontStrikethru**—a **Boolean,** when **True**, means that the characters display with a line through the center. **False** means that the characters display normally.
- *OptionButtonControl*.**FontUnderlined**—a **Boolean,** when **True**, means that the characters display with a line beneath them. **False** means that the characters display normally.
- *OptionButtonControl*.**ForeColor**—a **Long** that contains the suggested value for the foreground color of the contained control. This property is read only at run time.
- *OptionButtonControl*.**Height**—a **Single** that contains the height of the control.

- *OptionButtonControl*.**HelpContextID**—a **Long** that contains a help file context ID number that references an entry in the help file. When the user presses the F1 key while this control is active, the corresponding entry in the help file will automatically be displayed. A value of zero means that no context number was specified.

> **Tip**
>
> *A help file must be compiled using the Windows Help Compiler available in the Professional and Enterprise editions of Visual Basic.*

- *OptionButtonControl*.**hWnd**—a **Long** that contains a Windows handle to the control.

> **Tip**
>
> *The **hWnd** property is most useful when making calls to Windows API functions. Since this value can change during execution, do not save the value into a variable for later use.*

- *OptionButtonControl*.**Index**—an **Integer** that uniquely identifies a control in a control array.
- *OptionButtonControl*.**Left**—a **Single** that contains the distance, measured in twips between the left edge of the control and the left edge of the control's container.
- *OptionButtonControl*.**MaskColor**—a **Long** that identifies a color that will be used as a mask or transparent color for bitmaps displayed within the control. This is useful for bitmap images, that do not specify a transparency information. The **UseMaskColor** property must be **True** for this property to take effect.
- *OptionButtonControl*.**MouseIcon**—a picture object (a bitmap, icon, or metafile) that will be used as a cursor when the **MousePointer** property is set to 99. Note that Visual Basic does not support color cursors from a .CUR file. A color icon from an .ICO file should be used instead.
- *OptionButtonControl*.**MousePointer**—an **Integer** value (see Table O-36) that contains the value of the cursor that should be displayed when the cursor is moved over this control. Use *vbCustom* to display the custom icon stored in the **MouseIcon** property.

Cursor Name	Value	Description
vbDefault	0	Shape determined by the object (default value).
vbArrow	1	Arrow.
vbCrosshair	2	Crosshair.
vbIbeam	3	I beam.
vbIconPointer	4	Square inside a square.
vbSizePointer	5	Four-sided arrow (north, south, east, west).
vbSizeNESW	6	Two-sided arrow (northeast, southwest).
vbSizeNS	7	Two-sided arrow (north, south).
vbSizeNWSE	8	Two-sided arrow (northwest, southeast).
vbSizeWE	9	Two-sided arrow (west, east).
vbUpArrow	10	Single-sided arrow pointing north.
vbHourglass	11	Hourglass.

OptionButton • 669

Cursor Name	Value	Description
vbNoDrop	12	No Drop.
vbArrowHourglass	13	An arrow and an hourglass.
vbArrowQuestion	14	An arrow and a question mark.
vbSizeAll	15	Size all.
vbCustom	99	Custom icon from the **MouseIcon** property of this control.

Table O-36: Cursor *values.*

- *OptionButtonControl.***Name**—a **String** that contains the name of the control that will be used to reference the control in a Visual Basic program. This property is read only at run time.
- *OptionButtonControl.***OLEDropMode**—an **Integer** value (see Table O-37) that describes how the control will respond to OLE drop operations.

OLEDropMode Name	Value	Description
vbOLEDropNone	0	The control does not accept OLE drops. The cursor is changed to the No Drop cursor (default value).
vbOLEDropManual	1	The control responds to OLE drops under the program's control (manual).
vbOLEDropAutomatic	2	The control automatically accepts OLE drops if it recognizes the format of the data object.

Table O-37: OLEDropMode *values.*

- *OptionButtonControl.***Parent**—an object that contains a reference to the **Form**, **Frame**, or other container that contains the **Animation** control.
- *OptionButtonControl.***Picture**—a picture object (a bitmap, icon, metafile, GIF, or JPEG) that will be displayed on the control. You can also use the **LoadPicture** function at run time to load a bitmap, icon, or metafile. Note that **Style** must be set to *vbButtonGraphical* for the image to be shown.
- *OptionButtonControl.***RightToLeft**—a **Boolean** value when **True** means that the text is displayed from right to left. **False** means that the text is displayed from left to right. A bi-directional version of Windows is required to set this property to **True**.
- *OptionButtonControl.***Style**—an **Integer** value (see Table O-38) that contains the style used to display the control.

Style Name	Value	Description
vbButtonStandard	0	The control is displayed as an Option Button next to a caption (default value).
vbButtonGraphic	1	The control is displayed like a command button, which can be toggled on and off.

Table O-38: Style *values.*

- *OptionButtonControl.***TabIndex**—an Integer that determines the order that a user will tab through the objects on a form.

- *OptionButtonControl*.**TabStop**—a **Boolean** value when **True** means that the user can tab to this object. **False** means that this control will be skipped to the next control in the **TabIndex** order.
- *OptionButtonControl*.**Tag**—a **String** that can hold programmer-specific information. This property is not used by Visual Basic.
- *OptionButtonControl*.**ToolTipText**—a **String** that holds a text value that can be displayed as a **ToolTip** box that is displayed whenever the cursor is held over the control for about one second.
- *OptionButtonControl*.**Top**—a **Single** that contains the distance, measured in twips, between the top edge of the control and the top edge of the control's container.
- *OptionButtonControl*.**UseMaskColor**—a **Boolean** value when **True** means you should use the color specified in the **MaskColor** property to create a transparent background for the picture objects contained in the control. When **False**, the picture objects will not be displayed with a transparent background.
- *OptionButtonControl*.**Value**—a **Boolean** value when **True** means the option button is pushed. **False** means that the option button is not pushed.

Tip

Only one option button in a container can be pushed at a time. If you want to have multiple groups of option buttons, you should place them in a container such as a frame or tab control.

- *OptionButtonControl*.**Visible**—a **Boolean** value when **True** means that the control is visible. **False** means that the control is not visible.

Tip

This property can hide the control until the program is ready to display it.

- *OptionButtonControl*.**WhatsThisHelpID**—a **Long** that contains a help file context ID number that references an entry in the help file. This provides a What's This PopUp help display in response to the What's This button in the upper-right corner of the window.
- *OptionButtonControl*.**Width**—a **Single** that contains the width of the control.

Methods

OptionButtonControl.Drag [DragAction]

Usage This method begins, ends, or cancels a drag operation.

Arguments - *DragAction*—an **Integer** that contains a value selected from Table O-39 below.

DragAction Name	Value	Description
vbCancel	0	Cancels any drag operation in progress.
vbBeginDrag	1	Begins a drag operation (default).
vbEndDrag	2	Ends a drag operation and drops *object*.

Table O-39: DragAction values.

OptionButtonControl.Move Left [, Top [, Width [, Height]]]

Usage This method changes the position and the size of the **OptionButton** control. The **ScaleMode** of the **Form** or other container object that holds the **OptionButton** control will determine the units used to specify the coordinates.

Arguments
- *Left*—a **Single** that specifies the new position of the left edge of the control.
- *Top*—a **Single** that specifies the new position of the top edge of the control.
- *Width*—a **Single** that specifies the new width of the control.
- *Height*—a **Single** that specifies the new height of the control.

OptionButtonControl.OLEDrag

Usage This method begins an **OLE** drag-and-drop operation. Invoking this method will trigger the **OLEStartDrag** event.

OptionButtonControl.Refresh

Usage This method redraws the contents of the control.

OptionButtonControl.SetFocus

Usage This method transfers the focus from the form or control that currently has the focus to this control. To receive the focus, this control must be enabled and visible.

OptionButtonControl.ShowWhatsThis

Usage This method displays the ShowWhatsThis help information for this control.

OptionButtonControl.ZOrder [position]

Usage This method specifies the position of the animation control relative to the other objects on the form.

> **Tip**
>
> *Note that there are three layers of objects on a form: The back layer is the drawing space that contains the results of the graphical methods, the middle layer contains graphical objects and **Labels**, and the top layer contains nongraphical controls such as the **OptionButton**. The **ZOrder** method only affects how the objects are arranged within a single layer.*

Arguments
- *position*—an **Integer** that specifies the relative position of this object. A value of 0 means that the control is positioned at the head of the list, a value of 1 means that the control will be placed at the end of the list.

Events — **Private Sub *OptionButtonControl*_Click([*index* As Integer])**

Usage — This event occurs when the user clicks a mouse button while the cursor is positioned over this control.

> **Tip**
>
> *If you need to identify which mouse button was pressed, use the **MouseUp** and **MouseDown** events.*

Arguments — *index*—an **Integer** that uniquely identifies a control in a control array. This argument is not present if the control is not part of a control array.

Private Sub *OptionButtonControl*_DragDrop([*index* As Integer,] *source* As Control, *x* As Single, *y* As Single)

Usage — This event occurs when a drag-and-drop operation is completed by using the **Drag** method with a *DragAction* value of *vbEndDrag* (2).

> **Tip**
>
> *When using drag-and-drop operations, use the **DragOver** event to determine what the cursor should look like while the cursor moves over the control.*

Arguments — *index*—an **Integer** that uniquely identifies a control in a control array. This argument is not present if the control is not part of a control array.

- *source*—a control object that is the control that is being dragged.

> **Tip**
>
> *You can access a property or method from the source control by using source.property or source.method. You can determine the type of object or control by using the **TypeOf** operator.*

- *x*—a **Single** that contains the horizontal location of the mouse pointer.
- *y*—a **Single** that contains the vertical location of the mouse pointer.

Private Sub *OptionButtonControl*_DragOver([*index* As Integer,] *source* As Control, *x* As Single, *y* As Single, *state* As Integer)

Usage — This event occurs while a drag operation is in progress and the cursor is moved over the control.

> **Tip**
>
> When using drag-and-drop operations, use the **DragOver** event to determine what the cursor should look like while the cursor moves over the control. When **state** is 0, you can change the cursor to a No Drop (vbNoDrop) cursor or highlight the field that the cursor is near. When **state** is 1, you can undo the changes you made when the **state** was 0.

Arguments
- *index*—an **Integer** that uniquely identifies a control in a control array. This argument is not present if the control is not part of a control array.
- *source*—a control object that is the control that is being dragged.

> **Tip**
>
> You can access a property or method from the source control by using source.*property* or source.*method*. You can determine the type of object or control by using the **TypeOf** operator.

- *x*—a **Single** that contains the horizontal location of the mouse pointer.
- *y*—a **Single** that contains the vertical location of the mouse pointer.
- *state*—an **Integer** value (see Table O-40) that indicates the state of the object being dragged.

state Name	Value	Description
vbEnter	0	The dragged object is entering range of the control.
vbLeave	1	The dragged object is leaving range of the control.
vbOver	2	The dragged object has moved from one position over the control to another.

Table O-40: State values.

Private Sub *OptionButtonControl*_GotFocus ([*index* As Integer])

Usage This event occurs when the control is given focus.

> **Tip**
>
> You can use this routine to display help or other information in a status bar.

Arguments
- *index*—an **Integer** that uniquely identifies a control in a control array. This argument is not present if the control is not part of a control array.

Private Sub *OptionButtonControl*_KeyDown ([*index* As Integer,] *keycode* As Integer, *shift* As Single)

Usage   This event occurs when a key is pressed while the control has the focus.

Arguments
- *index*—an **Integer** that uniquely identifies a control in a control array. This argument is not present if the control is not part of a control array.
- *keycode*—an **Integer** that contains information about which key was pressed.
- *shift*—an **Integer** value (see Table O-41) that contains information about the Shift and Alt keys that were pressed when the mouse button was pressed. These values can be added together if more than one key was down. For instance, a value of 5 would mean that the Shift and Alt keys were both down when the mouse button was pressed.

shift Name	Value	Description
vbShiftMask	1	The Shift key was pressed.
vbCtrlMask	2	The Ctrl key was pressed.
vbAltMask	4	The Alt key was pressed.

Table O-41: Shift values.

Private Sub *OptionButtonControl*_KeyPress([*index* As Integer,] *keychar* As Integer)

Usage   This event occurs whenever a key is pressed while the control has the focus.

Arguments
- *index*—an **Integer** that uniquely identifies a control in a control array. This argument is not present if the control is not part of a control array.
- *keychar*—an **Integer** that contains the ASCII character that was pressed.

Private Sub *OptionButtonControl*_KeyUp ([*index* As Integer,] *keycode* As Integer, *shift* As Single)

Usage   This event occurs when a key is released while the control has the focus.

Arguments
- *index*—an **Integer** that uniquely identifies a control in a control array. This argument is not present if the control is not part of a control array.
- *keycode*—an **Integer** that contains information about which key was released.
- *shift*—an **Integer** value (see Table O-42) that contains information about the Shift and Alt keys that were pressed when the mouse button was pressed. These values can be added together if more than one key was down. For instance, a value of 5 would mean that the Shift and Alt keys were both down when the mouse button was pressed.

shift Name	Value	Description
vbShiftMask	1	The Shift key was pressed.
vbCtrlMask	2	The Ctrl key was pressed.
vbAltMask	4	The Alt key was pressed.

Table O-42: Shift values.

Private Sub *OptionButtonControl*_LostFocus ([*index* As Integer])

Usage   This event occurs when the control loses focus.

Tip

This routine is useful in performing data verification.

Arguments
- *index*—an **Integer** that uniquely identifies a control in a control array. This argument is not present if the control is not part of a control array.

Private Sub *OptionButtonControl*_MouseDown([*index* As Integer,] *button* As Integer, *shift* As Single, *x* As Single, *y* As Single)

Usage   This event occurs when a mouse button is pressed while the cursor is over the control.

Arguments
- *index*—an **Integer** that uniquely identifies a control in a control array. This argument is not present if the control is not part of a control array.
- *button*—an **Integer** value (see Table O-43) that contains information about the mouse buttons that were pressed. Only one button will be indicated when this event occurs.

button Name	Value	Description
vbLeftButton	1	The left button was pressed.
vbRightButton	2	The right button was pressed.
vbMiddleButton	4	The middle button was pressed.

Table O-43: Button values.

- *shift*—an **Integer** value (see Table O-44) that contains information about the Shift and Alt keys that were pressed when the mouse button was pressed. These values can be added together if more than one key was down. For instance, a value of 5 would mean that the Shift and Alt keys were both down when the mouse button was pressed.

shift Name	Value	Description
vbShiftMask	1	The Shift key was pressed.
vbCtrlMask	2	The Ctrl key was pressed.
vbAltMask	4	The Alt key was pressed.

Table O-44: *Shift values.*

- *x*—a **Single** that contains the horizontal location of the mouse pointer.
- *y*—a **Single** that contains the vertical location of the mouse pointer.

Private Sub *OptionButtonControl*_MouseMove ([*index* As Integer,] *button* As Integer, *shift* As Single, *x* As Single, *y* As Single)

Usage — This event occurs while the cursor is moved over the control.

Arguments
- *index*—an **Integer** that uniquely identifies a control in a control array. This argument is not present if the control is not part of a control array.
- *button*—an **Integer** value (see Table O-45) that contains information about the mouse buttons that were pressed. These values can be added together if more than one button was pressed. For instance, a value of 3 means that both the left and right buttons were pressed. A value of 0 means that no buttons were pressed.

button Name	Value	Description
vbLeftButton	1	The left button was pressed.
vbRightButton	2	The right button was pressed.
vbMiddleButton	4	The middle button was pressed.

Table O-45: *Button values.*

- *shift*—an **Integer** value (see Table O-46) that contains information about the Shift and Alt keys that were pressed when the mouse button was pressed. For instance, a value of 5 would mean that the Shift and Alt keys were both down when the mouse button was pressed. A value of 0 means that none of these keys were pressed.

shift Name	Value	Description
vbShiftMask	1	The Shift key was pressed.
vbCtrlMask	2	The Ctrl key was pressed.
vbAltMask	4	The Alt key was pressed.

Table O-46: *Shift values.*

- *x*—a **Single** that contains the horizontal location of the mouse pointer.
- *y*—a **Single** that contains the vertical location of the mouse pointer.

Private Sub *OptionButtonControl*_MouseUp([*index* As Integer,] *button* As Integer, *shift* As Single, *x* As Single, *y* As Single)

Usage — This event occurs when a mouse button is released while the cursor is over the control.

Arguments
- *index*—an **Integer** that uniquely identifies a control in a control array. This argument is not present if the control is not part of a control array.
- *button*—an **Integer** value (see Table O-47) that contains information about the mouse buttons that were released. Only one of these values will be present.

button Name	Value	Description
vbLeftButton	1	The left button was released.
vbRightButton	2	The right button was released.
vbMiddleButton	4	The middle button was released.

Table O-47: Button *values*.

- *shift*—an **Integer** value (see Table O-48) that contains information about the Shift and Alt keys that were pressed when the mouse button was released. These values can be added together if more than one key was down. For instance, a value of 5 would mean that the Shift and Alt keys were both down when the mouse button was released. A value of 0 means that none of these keys were pressed.

shift Name	Value	Description
vbShiftMask	1	The Shift key was pressed.
vbCtrlMask	2	The Ctrl key was pressed.
vbAltMask	4	The Alt key was pressed.

Table O-48: Shift *values*.

- *x*—a **Single** that contains the horizontal location of the mouse pointer.
- *y*—a **Single** that contains the vertical location of the mouse pointer.

Private Sub *OptionButtonControl*_OLECompleteDrag([*index* As Integer,] *effect* As Long)

Usage — This event tells the source control the results of an OLE drag-and-drop operation. This is the final event to occur in the series of actions that make up an OLE drag-and-drop operation.

Arguments
- *index*—an **Integer** that uniquely identifies a control in a control array. This argument is not present if the control is not part of a control array.
- *effect*—a **Long** (see Table O-49) that returns the status of the OLE drag-and-drop operation.

effect Name	Value	Description
vbDropEffectNone	0	The operation was canceled or the target control can't accept the drop operation.
vbDropEffectCopy	1	The operation copied data from the source control to the target control. The original data is unchanged.
vbDropEffectMove	2	The operation results in a link from the original data to the target control.

Table O-49: Effect *values*.

Private Sub OptionButtonControl_OLEDragDrop([*index* As Integer,] *data* As DataObject, *effect* As Long, *button* As Integer, *shift* As Single, *x* As Single, *y* As Single)

Usage — This event tells the source control the results of an OLE drag and drop operation. This is the final event to occur in the series of actions that make up an OLE drag-and-drop operation.

Arguments
- *index*—an **Integer** that uniquely identifies a control in a control array. This argument is not present if the control is not part of a control array.
- *data*—a **DataObject** that contains the formats that the source control will provide. If the data is not contained in the **DataObject**, then it can be retrieved with the **GetData** method.
- *effect*—a **Long** (see Table O-50) that returns the status of the OLE drag-and-drop operation.

effect Name	Value	Description
vbDropEffectNone	0	The operation was canceled or the target control can't accept the drop operation.
vbDropEffectCopy	1	The operation copied data from the source control to the target control. The original data is unchanged.
vbDropEffectMove	2	The operation results in a link from the original data to the target control.

Table O-50: Effect *values*.

- *button*—an **Integer** value (see Table O-51) that contains information about the mouse buttons that were pressed. These values can be added together if more than one button was pressed. For instance, a value of 3 means that both the left and right buttons were pressed. A value of 0 means that no buttons were pressed.

button Name	Value	Description
vbLeftButton	1	The left button was pressed.
vbRightButton	2	The right button was pressed.
vbMiddleButton	4	The middle button was pressed.

Table O-51: Button *values*.

- *shift*—an **Integer** value (see Table O-52) that contains information about the Shift and Alt keys that were pressed when the mouse button was released. These values can be added together if more than one key was down. For instance, a value of 5 would mean that the Shift and Alt keys were both down when the mouse button was released. A value of 0 means that none of these keys were pressed.

shift Name	Value	Description
vbShiftMask	1	The Shift key was pressed.
vbCtrlMask	2	The Ctrl key was pressed.
vbAltMask	4	The Alt key was pressed.

Table O-52: Shift values.

- *x*—a **Single** that contains the horizontal location of the mouse pointer.
- *y*—a **Single** that contains the vertical location of the mouse pointer.

Private Sub *OptionButtonControl*_OLEDragOver([*index* As Integer,] *data* As DataObject, *effect* As Long, *button* As Integer, *shift* As Single, *x* As Single, *y* As Single, *state* As Integer)

Usage — This event happens when an OLE drag-and-drop operation is in progress.

Arguments
- *index*—an **Integer** that uniquely identifies a control in a control array. This argument is not present if the control is not part of a control array.
- *data*—a **DataObject** that contains the formats that the source control will provide. If the data is not contained in the **DataObject**, then it can be retrieved with the **GetData** method.
- *effect*—a **Long** (see Table O-53) that returns the status of the OLE drag-and-drop operation.

effect Name	Value	Description
vbDropEffectNone	0	The operation was canceled or the target control can't accept the drop operation.
vbDropEffectCopy	1	The operation copied data from the source control to the target control. The original data is unchanged.
vbDropEffectMove	2	The operation results in a link from the original data to the target control.

Table O-53: Effect values.

- *button*—an **Integer** value (see Table O-54) that contains information about the mouse buttons that were pressed. These values can be added together if more than one button was pressed. For instance, a value of 3 means that both the left and right buttons were pressed. A value of 0 means that no buttons were pressed.

button Name	Value	Description
vbLeftButton	1	The left button was pressed.
vbRightButton	2	The right button was pressed.
vbMiddleButton	4	The middle button was pressed.

Table O-54: Button *values*.

- *shift*—an **Integer** value (see Table O-55) that contains information about the Shift and Alt keys that were pressed when the mouse button was released. These values can be added together if more than one key was down. For instance, a value of 5 would mean that the Shift and Alt keys were both down when the mouse button was released. A value of 0 means that none of these keys were pressed.

shift Name	Value	Description
vbShiftMask	1	The Shift key was pressed.
vbCtrlMask	2	The Ctrl key was pressed.
vbAltMask	4	The Alt key was pressed.

Table O-55: Shift *values*.

- *x*—a **Single** that contains the horizontal location of the mouse pointer.
- *y*—a **Single** that contains the vertical location of the mouse pointer.
- *state*—an **Integer** value (see Table O-56) that indicates the state of the objecting being dragged.

state Name	Value	Description
vbEnter	0	The dragged object is entering range of the control.
vbLeave	1	The dragged object is leaving range of the control
vbOver	2	The dragged object has moved from one position over the control to another.

Table O-56: State *values*.

Private Sub *OptionButtonControl_OLEGiveFeedback* ([*index* As Integer,] *effect* As Long)

Usage   This event tells the source control what is happening while the OLE drag-and-drop operation is in progress. This event occurs after the **OLEDragOver** event.

Tip

You may want to use this event to change the cursor to reflect what can happen in the remote object.

Arguments
- *index*—an **Integer** that uniquely identifies a control in a control array. This argument is not present if the control is not part of a control array.
- *effect*—a **Long** (see Table O-57) that returns the status of the OLE drag-and-drop operation.

effect Name	Value	Description
vbDropEffectNone	0	The operation was canceled or the target control can't accept the drop operation.
vbDropEffectCopy	1	The operation copied data from the source control to the target control. The original data is unchanged.
vbDropEffectMove	2	The operation results in a link from the original data to the target control.
vbDropEffectScroll	&H80000000	The target control is about to scroll or is scrolling. This value may be added to the other *shift* values.

Table O-57: Effect values.

Private Sub *OptionButtonControl*_OLESetData([*index* As Integer,] *data* As DataObject, *DataFormat* As Integer)

Usage — This event happens in response to the target object performing a **GetData** method on *data*. This routine will respond by using the **SetData** method with the desired data using the **DataObject** *data*.

Arguments
- *index*—an **Integer** that uniquely identifies a control in a control array. This argument is not present if the control is not part of a control array.
- *data*—a **DataObject** that will contain the data to be returned to the target object.
- *format*—an **Integer** value (see Table O-58) that contains the format of the data.

format Name	Value	Description
vbCFText	1	Text (.TXT files).
vbCFBitmap	2	Bitmap (.BMP files).
vbCFMetafile	3	Metafile (.WMF files).
vbCFEDIB	8	Device independent bitmap (DIB).
vbCFPallette	9	Color palette.
vbCFEMetafile	14	Enhanced metafile (.EMF files).
vbCFFiles	15	List of files.
vbCFRTF	-16639	Rich Text Format (.RTF files).

Table O-58: Format values.

Private Sub *OptionButtonControl*_OLEStartDrag ([*index* As Integer,] *data* As DataObject, *AllowedEffects* As Long)

Usage This event starts an OLE drag-and-drop operation.

Arguments
- *index*—an **Integer** that uniquely identifies a control in a control array. This argument is not present if the control is not part of a control array.
- *data*—a **DataObject** that will contain the formats that the source object is willing to provide to the target object. It may optionally contain the data to be transferred.
- *AllowedEffects*—a **Long** value (see Table O-59) that contains the effects that the target object can request from the source object. The *AllowedEffects* can be added together if the source object supports more than one effect. Note that the target object can always use the *vbDropEffectNone* effect.

AllowedEffects Name	Value	Description
vbDropEffectNone	0	The target can't copy the data.
vbDropEffectCopy	1	The target can copy the data and the source will keep the data unchanged.
vbDropEffectMove	2	The target can copy the data and the source will delete the data.

Table O-59: AllowedEffects *values.*

See Also **Data** (control), **LoadPicture** (function), **CheckButton** (control)

Panel

OBJECT

PE, EE

Usage The **Panel** object is used by the **StatusBar** control to hold information about an individual item in the status bar.

Properties *PanelObject*.**Alignment**—an **Integer** value describing how the text appears in the panel.

alignment Name	Value	Description
sbrLeft	0	Text is left justified and to the right of the bitmap (default).
sbrCenter	1	Text is centered and to the right of the bitmap.
sbrRight	2	Text is right justified and to the left of the bitmap.

Table P-1: Alignment *values.*

PanelObject.**AutoSize**—an **Integer** value describing how the size of the panel is adjusted.

AutoSize Name	Value	Description
sbrNoAutoSize	0	No autosizing occurs (default).
sbrSpring	1	The panel size is adjusted as the parent form's size is adjusted, however the size does not fall below **MinWidth**.
sbrContents	2	The panel size is adjusted as the size of the contents changes, however the size does not fall below **MinWidth**.

Table P-2: Autosize *values.*

PanelObject.**Bevel**—an **Integer** value describing how the panel is displayed in the **StatusBar**.

Bevel Name	Value	Description
sbrNoBevel	0	No bevel is displayed.
sbrInset	1	The panel is inset (default).
sbrRaised	2	The panel is raised.

Table P-3: Bevel *values.*

PanelObject.**Enabled**—a **Boolean** value when **True** means that the panel will be displayed in the **StatusBar**. **False** means that the panel will not be displayed.

PanelObject.**Index**—an **Integer** value containing a unique value to identify the panel in the **Panels** collection.

PanelObject.**Key**—a **String** value containing a unique value to identify the panel in the **Panels** collection.

> **Tip**
>
> *Use the **Key** property to identify a value rather than **Index** since the value of **Index** can easily be changed, while the value of **Key** can't.*

- *PanelObject*.**Left**—a **Single** that contains the distance, measured in twips, between the left edge of the control and the left edge of the control's container.
- *PanelObject*.**MinWidth**—a **Single** that contains the minimum width of the panel.
- *PanelObject*.**Picture**—a picture object containing the icon or bitmap that will be displayed in the panel.
- *PanelObject*.**Style**—an **Integer** value describing what will be displayed in the panel.

Style Name	Value	Description
sbrText	0	Display text from Text and/or bitmap from Picture (default).
sbrCaps	1	Display CAPS when Caps Lock is enabled.
sbrNum	2	Display NUM when Num Lock is enabled.
SbrIns	3	Display INS when in Insert mode.
SbrScrl	4	Display SCRL when Scroll Lock is enabled.
SbrTime	5	Display the current time.
SbrDate	6	Display the current date.
SbrKana	7	Display KANA when Scroll Lock is enabled.

Table P-4: Style *values*.

- *PanelObject*.**Tag**—a **String** that can hold programmer-specific information. This property is not used by Visual Basic.
- *PanelObject*.**Text**—a **String** value containing the text that will be displayed in the panel.
- *PanelObject*.**ToolTipText**—a **String** that holds a text value that can be displayed as a **ToolTip** box that is displayed whenever the cursor is held over the panel for about one second.
- *PanelObject*.**Visible**—a **Boolean** value when **True** means that the panel is visible. When **False**, the control is not visible.
- *PanelObject*.**Width**—a **Single** containing the width of the panel. This value can't be smaller than the **MinWidth** property.

See Also   **Panels** (collection), **StatusBar** (control)

Panels

COLLECTION

PE, EE

Usage   The **Panels** collection contains a set of methods to store and retrieve items in a set. The items need not be of the same data type. Items can be retrieved by specifying their relative position within the collection or by a unique key value.

> **Tip**
>
> To loop through each item in the collection, use the **For Each** statement.

Properties
- *PanelsCollection*.**Count**—a **Long** value that contains the number of items in the collection.
- *PanelsCollection*.**Item** (*index*)—a reference to a **Panel** object in the collection. *Index* is either a numeric value that represents the relative position of the item in the collection or a **String** value that contains the key value of the object.

Parameter • **685**

Methods | *panel = **PanelsCollection**.**Add** ([index [, key [, text [, style [, picture]]]])*

Usage | This method is used to add an item to the **Panels** collection.

Arguments
- *panel*—a reference to the newly created **Panel** object.
- *index*—an **Integer** containing the position where the new panel will be inserted. If omitted, the panel will be inserted at the end of the collection. This value will be saved in the **Index** property of the new **Panel** object.
- *key*—a **String** that contains a unique value that can be used to reference the newly created panel object. This value will be saved in the **Key** property of the new **Panel** object.
- *text*—a **String** value that will be put into the **Text** property of the **Panel** object.
- *style*—an **Integer** value that will be put into the **Style** property of the new **Panel** object.
- *picture*—a picture object that will be put into the **Picture** property of the new **Panel** object.

PanelsObject.**Clear**

Usage | This method is used to remove all of the objects in the panels collection.

PanelsObject.**Remove** *index*

Usage | This method is used to delete from the collection an item specified by *index*.

Arguments
- *index*—either a numeric value that represents the relative position or a **String** value that contains the key value of the panel to be deleted from the collection.

See Also | **Panel** (object), **StatusBar** (control)

Parameter

OBJECT

PE, EE

Usage | The **Parameter** object is used with a **QueryDef** object to hold parameters associated with an ODBC query.

Properties
- *ParameterObject*.**Direction**—an **Integer** value describing how the parameter information is passed to and from the query.

Direction Name	Value	Description
dbParamInput	0	The parameter is passed to the query (default).
dbParamInputOutput	1	The parameter is passed to the query and also returned as an output parameter from the query.
dbParamOutput	2	The parameter is returned as an output parameter from the query.
dbParamReturnValue	3	The parameter is returned as the return value from the query.

Table P-5: Direction *values.*

- *ParameterObject*.**Name**—a **String** value containing the name of the parameter.
- *ParameterObject*.**Properties**—an object reference to a **Properties** collection.
- *ParameterObject*.**Type**—an **Integer** value describing the type of the value.

Type Name	Description
dbBigInt	Big integer data type.
dbBinary	Fixed-length binary data, up to 255 bytes long.
dbBoolean	Boolean data type.
DbByte	Integer value one byte wide.
DbChar	Fixed-length character string.
DbCurrency	Currency data type.
DbDate	Date/time data type.
DbDecimal	Decimal data type.
DbDouble	Double precision floating point data type.
DbFloat	Floating point data type.
DbGUID	Globally Unique Identifier data type.
DbInteger	16 bit integer data type.
DbLong	32 bit integer data type.
DbLongBinary	Long binary data type.
DbMemo	Memo data type.
DbNumeric	Numeric data type.
DbSingle	Single precision floating point data type.
DbText	Field data type.
dbTime	Time data type.
DbTimeStamp	Time stamp data type.
DbVarBinary	Variable-length binary, up to 255 bytes long.

Table P-6: Type *values*.

- *ParameterObject*.**Value**—a **Variant** containing the parameter's value.

See Also **Panels** (collection), **StatusBar** (control)

Parameters

COLLECTION

PE, EE

Usage The **Parameters** collection contains the parameters associated with a **QueryDef** object.

> **Tip**
>
> To loop through each item in the collection, use the **For Each** statement.

Properties
- *ParametersCollection*.**Count**—an **Integer** value that contains the number of items in the collection.

Methods	**ParametersCollection.Refresh**
Usage	This method gets a current copy of the **QueryDefs** contained in the collection. This is important in a multi-user environment where more than one user may be making changes in the **Databases** collection.
See Also	**Parameter** (object), **QueryDef** (object)

Pen

OBJECT

PE, EE

Usage The **Pen** object is used by the **MSChart** control to hold information about the color and patterns used for lines or edges in a chart.

Properties
- *PenObject*.**Cap**—an **Integer** value describing how line endings are displayed.

PenCap Name	Description
vtPenCapButt	The line is squared off at the end.
vtPenCapRound	The line ends with a semicircle the width of the line.
vtPenCapSquare	The line ends one-half the width of the line beyond the end point and is squared off at the end.

Table P-7: PenCap *values.*

- *PenObject*.**Join**—an **Integer** value describing how line segments are connected.

PenJoin Name	Description
vtPenJoinMiter	The outer edges of the line are extended until they meet.
vtPenJoinRound	An arc is drawn around the point where the lines are joined.
vtPenJoinBevel	The notch between the two lines is filled.

Table P-8: PenJoin *values.*

- *PenObject*.**Limit**—a **Single** value describing the joint limit in terms of multiples of the line widths. If the distance from the inner joint point to the outer joint point exceeds this value, the joint is changed to a bevel joint.
- *PenObject*.**Style**—an **Integer** value describing how line segments are connected.

PenStyle Name	Description
vtPenStyleNull	No pen is used.
vtPenStyleSolid	Solid line.
vtPenStyleDashed	Dashed line.
vtPenStyleDotted	Dotted line.

PenStyle Name	Description
vtPenStyleDashDot	Dash followed by a dot.
vtPenStyleDashDotDot	Dash followed by two dots.
vtPenStyleDitted	Ditted line.
vtPenStyleDashDit	Dash followed by a dit.
vtPenStyleDashDitDit	Dash followed by two dits.

Table P-9: PenStyle *values*.

- *PenObject*.**VtColor**—a reference to a **VtColor** object containing the color of the pen.
- *PenObject*.**Width**—a **Single** value containing the width of the pen in points.

See Also **MSChart** (control), **VtColor** (object)

Picture

OBJECT

LE, CCE, PE, EE

Usage The **Picture** object holds a bitmap, enhanced metafile, icon, or regular metafile. It can also hold a JPEG or GIF image. This object is used in a number of controls and objects, such as the **PictureBox** control and the **ImageList** control.

Properties
- *PictureObject*.**Handle**—a handle to the picture object. The exact type of handle depends on the **Type** property.

> **Tip**
>
> The **Handle** *property is most useful when making calls to Windows API functions. Since this value can change during execution, do not save the value into a variable for later use.*

- *PictureObject*.**Height**—a **Single** containing the height of the picture in himetrics.

> **Tip**
>
> *Use the* **ScaleX** *and* **ScaleY** *methods of the container object to convert the himetric values into a more useable scale.*

- *PictureObject*.**hPal**—a handle to the palette used by the picture object.

> **Tip**
>
> The **hPal** *property is most useful when making calls to Windows API functions. Since this value can change during execution, do not save the value into a variable for later use.*

- *PictureObject*.**Type**—an **Integer** value describing the graphic format of the picture object.

Type Name	Value	Description
vbPicTypeNone	0	The picture is empty.
vbPicTypeBitmap	1	The picture is a bitmap (or a GIF or a JPEG).
vbPicTypeMetafile	2	The picture is a metafile.
vbPicTypeIcon	3	The picture is an icon.
vbPicTypeEMetafile	4	The picture is an enhanced metafile.

Table P-10: Type values.

- *PictureObject*.**Width**—a **Single** containing the height of the picture in himetrics.

> **Tip**
>
> Use the **ScaleX** and **ScaleY** methods of the container object to convert the himetric values into a more useable scale.

Methods

PictureObject.Render *hdc, xdest, ydest, destwidth, destheight, xsrc, ysrc, srcwidth, srcheight, wbounds*

Usage   This method draws all or part of an image to another object.

> **Tip**
>
> Use the **PaintPicture** method of a **Form** object, a **Printer** object, or a **PictureBox** control to paint part of a graphic.

Arguments
- *hdc*—a handle to the destination's device context.
- *xdest*—the x coordinate of the upper left corner of the destination object using the destination object's scale units.
- *ydest*—the y coordinate of the upper left corner of the destination object using the destination object's scale units.
- *destwidth*—the width of the destination object using the destination object's scale units.
- *destheight*—the height of the destination object using the destination object's scale units.
- *xsrc*—the x coordinate of the upper left corner of the source object using himetric units.
- *ysrc*—the y coordinate of the upper left corner of the source object using himetric units.
- *srcwidth*—the width of the source object using himetric units.
- *srcheight*—the height of the source object using himetric units.
- *wbounds*—the world bounds for a metafile object. All other objects should pass a value of Null.

See Also   **PictureBox** (control)

PictureBox

CONTROL
CCE, LE, PE, EE

Usage   The **PictureBox** control is an intrinsic control that can display an icon file (.ICO), metafile (.WMF), bitmap file (.BMP), a .GIF file, or a .JPG file.

> **Tip**
>
> The **Image** control is more efficient than the **PictureBox** control, while offering less functions. This makes it highly desirable for displaying graphic images. For more complex functions, the **PictureBox** control should be used.

Properties   • *PictureBoxControl*.**Align**—an **Integer** value that describes the placement of the control.

Align Name	Value	Description
vbAlignNone	0	The control's position is set at design time or by the program (default value for objects on a non-MDI Form).
vbAlignTop	1	The control is placed at the top of the form and its width is set to **ScaleWidth**. It will automatically be resized when the form is resized (default value for objects on an MDI Form).
vbAlignBottom	2	The control is placed at the bottom of the form and its width is set to **ScaleWidth**. It will automatically be resized when the form is resized.
vbAlignLeft	3	The control is placed at the left edge of the form and its width is set to **ScaleWidth**. It is not resized when the form is resized.
vbAlignRight	4	The control is placed at the right edge of the form and its width is set to **ScaleWidth**. It is not resized when the form is resized.

Table P-11: *Align* values.

• *PictureBoxControl*.**Appearance**—an **Integer** value (see Table P-12) that specifies how the combo box will appear on the form.

AppearanceValue	Description
0	The picture box displays without the 3D effects.
1	The picture box displays with 3D effects (default value).

Table P-12: Appearance *values*.

• *PictureBoxControl*.**AutoRedraw**—a **Boolean** value when **True** means that the graphics and text written directly to the form will be redrawn from a copy stored in memory. When **False**, the **Paint** event will be triggered to redraw the contents of the form.

> **Tip**
>
> Setting **AutoRedraw** to **True** will slow down most operations involving the form. Most of the common controls (i.e., labels, text boxes, and command buttons) will automatically redraw themselves. If you display graphics directly on the form, then you may want to use **AutoRedraw**.

- *PictureBoxControl.***AutoSize**—a **Boolean,** when **True**, means that the label control is automatically resized to display all of its data. When **False**, the control will not be resized to fit the data and if it doesn't fit it will be truncated (default).
- *PictureBoxControl.***BackColor**—a **Long** that contains the suggested value for the background color of the control.
- *PictureBoxControl.***BorderStyle**—an **Integer** value (see Table P-13) specifying how the border will be drawn. These values also indicate how the form can be resized, and are read only at run time.

BorderStyle Name	Value	Description
vbBSNone	0	No border, control box menu, title bar, or maximize and minimize buttons. Cannot be resized.
vbFixedSingle	1	Single line around the form. Form can only be resized by maximize and minimize buttons.

Table P-13: BorderStyle *values.*

- *PictureBoxControl.***ClipControls**—a **Boolean** when **True** means that the graphic events repaint the entire picture. **False** means that graphic events only repaint the newly exposed parts of the picture.
- *PictureBoxControl.***Container**—an object that sets or returns the container of the control at run time. This property cannot be set at design time.
- *PictureBoxControl.***CurrentX**—a **Single** that specifies the horizontal coordinate measured from the form's left edge for the various drawing methods: **Circle**, **Cls**, **EndDoc**, **Line**, **NewPage**, **Print**, and **PSet**.
- *PictureBoxControl.***CurrentY**—a **Single** that specifies the vertical coordinate measured from the form's top edge for the various drawing methods: **Circle**, **Cls**, **EndDoc**, **Line**, **NewPage**, **Print**, and **PSet**.
- *PictureBoxControl.***DataChanged**—a **Boolean** that applies only to data bound controls. When **True**, means that the data contained in this control was changed either by the user or by some means other than retrieving data from the current record. **False** means the data in the control is unchanged from the current record.

  Simply reading the next record is not sufficient to set the **DataChanged** property to **True**. When the **Data** control moves to the next record, it will automatically invoke the **Edit** and **Update** methods to post the changes to the database.
- *PictureBoxControl.***DataField**—a **String** value that associates the control with a field in a **RecordSet** object in a **Data** control.
- *PictureBoxControl.***DataSource**—a **String** value that associates the control with a **Data** control.
- *PictureBoxControl.***DragIcon**—an object that contains the picture value of an icon. At design time, you can specify an icon file that has a file type of .ICO.

> **Tip**
>
> *This value can be created by copying the value from another control's* **DragIcon** *value or copying a form's icon, or by using the* **LoadPicture** *function.*

- *PictureBoxControl*.**DragMode**—an **Integer** value (see Table P-14) specifying how the control will respond to a drag request.

> **Tip**
>
> Setting **DragMode** to vbAutomatic *will automatically begin a drag operation when the user clicks on the control. However, the control will not respond to the usual mouse events* (**Click, DblClick**).

DragMode Name	Value	Description
vbManual	0	The Drag method must be used to begin a drag-and-drop operation (default value).
vbAutomatic	1	The source control will automatically begin a drag-and-drop operation when the user clicks on the control.

Table P-14: DragMode *values.*

- *PictureBoxControl*.**DrawMode**—an **Integer** specifying how the drawing methods **Circle, Cls, EndDoc, Line, NewPage, Print,** and **PSet** will appear on the form.

DrawMode Name	Value	Description
vbBlackness	1	Blackness.
vbNotMergePen	2	Inverse of *vbMergePen*.
vbMaskNotPen	3	Combination of the colors common to the background color and the inverse of the pen.
vbNotCopyPen	4	Inverse of *vbCopyPen*.
vbMaskPenNot	5	Combination of the colors common to the pen and the inverse of the background.
vbInvert	6	Inverse of the display color.
vbXorPen	7	Combination of the colors in the display and pen, but not in both.
vbNotMaskPen	8	Inverse setting of *vbMaskPen*.
vbMaskPen	9	Combination of the colors common to the pen and display.
vbNotXorPen	10	Inverse setting of *vbXorPen*.
vbNop	11	Turns drawing off.
vbMergeNotPen	12	Combination of the display and inverse of the pen color.
vbCopyPen	13	Color specified in the **ForeColor** property.
vbMergePenNot	14	Combination of the pen color and the inverse of the display color.
vbMergePen	15	Combination of the pen color and the display color.
vbWhiteness	16	Whiteness.

Table P-15: DrawMode *values.*

- *PictureBoxControl*.**DrawStyle**—an **Integer** specifying how the drawing methods **Circle, Cls, EndDoc, Line, NewPage, Print,** and **PSet** will appear on the form. If **DrawWidth** is greater than 1, then *vbDash, vbDot, vbDashDot,* and *vbDashDotDot* will draw a solid line.

DrawStyle Name	Value	Description
vbSolid	0	Solid line.
vbDash	1	Dashed line.
vbDot	2	Dotted line.
vbDashDot	3	Dash followed by a dot.
vbDashDotDot	4	Dash followed by two dots.
vbInvisible	5	No displayed line.
vbInsideSolid	6	Inside is solid.

Table P-16: **DrawStyle** values.

- *PictureClipControl*.**DrawWidth**—an **Integer** specifying the width of the line, in pixels, that will be drawn by the following methods: **Circle**, **Cls**, **EndDoc**, **Line**, **NewPage**, **Print**, and **PSet**.
  If **DrawWidth** is greater than 1, then the **DrawStyles** *vbDash*, *vbDot*, *vbDashDot*, and *vbDashDotDot* will draw a solid line.
- *PictureBoxControl*.**Enabled**—a **Boolean** value when **True** means that the control will respond to events. When **False**, the control will not respond to events.
- *PictureBoxControl*.**FillColor**—a **Long** that contains the color that will be used to fill in shapes created with the following graphical methods: **Circle**, **Cls**, **EndDoc**, **Line**, **NewPage**, **Print**, and **PSet**.
- *PictureBoxControl*.**FillStyle**—an **Integer** specifying how the drawing methods **Circle**, **Cls**, **EndDoc**, **Line**, **NewPage**, **Print**, and **PSet** will appear on the form. If **DrawWidth** is greater than 1, then *vbDash*, *vbDot*, *vbDashDot*, and *vbDashDotDot* will draw a solid line.

FillStyle Name	Value	Description
vbFSSolid	0	Solid.
vbFSTransparent	1	Transparent.
vbHorizontalLine	2	Horizontal line.
vbVerticalLine	3	Vertical line.
vbUpwardDiagonal	4	Upward diagonal.
vbDownwardDiagonal	5	Downward diagonal.
vbCross	6	Cross.
vbDiagonalCross	7	Diagonal cross.

Table P-17: FillStyle values.

- *PictureBoxControl*.**Font**—an object that contains information about the character font used by this object.

Tip

*Setting values for the **Font** object on the form at design time makes these values the default when other controls and objects are placed on the form.*

- *PictureBoxControl*.**FontBold**—a **Boolean,** when **True**, means that the characters are displayed in bold. **False** means that the characters are displayed normally.
- *PictureBoxControl*.**FontItalic**—a **Boolean,** when **True**, means that the characters are displayed in italics. **False** means that the characters are displayed normally.
- *PictureBoxControl*.**FontName**—a **String** that specifies the name of the font that should be used to display the characters in this control.
- *PictureBoxControl*.**FontSize**—a **Single** that is used to specify the point size that should be used to display the characters in the control.
- *PictureBoxControl*.**FontStrikethru**—a **Boolean,** when **True**, means that the characters are displayed with a line through the center. **False** means that the characters are displayed normally.
- *PictureBoxControl*.**FontUnderlined**—a **Boolean,** when **True**, means that the characters are displayed with a line beneath them. **False** means that the characters are displayed normally.
- *PictureBoxControl*.**ForeColor**—a **Long** that contains the suggested value for the foreground color of the contained control. This property is read only at run time.
- *PictureBoxControl*.**hDC**—a **Long** that contains a handle to the device context to the form.
- *PictureBoxControl*.**Height**—a **Single** that contains the height of the control.
- *PictureBoxControl*.**HelpContextID**—a **Long** that contains a help file context ID number that references an entry in the help file. When the user presses the F1 key while this control is active, the corresponding entry in the help file will automatically be displayed. A value of zero means that no context number was specified.

Tip

A help file must be compiled using the Windows Help Compiler available in the Professional and Enterprise editions of Visual Basic.

- *PictureBoxControl*.**hWnd**—a **Long** that contains a Windows handle to the control.

Tip

*The **hWnd** property is most useful when making calls to Windows API functions. Since this value can change during execution, do not save the value into a variable for later use.*

- *PictureBoxControl*.**Image**—a handle to a persistent graphic that is returned by the Windows environment. Available only at run time.
- *PictureBoxControl*.**Index**—an **Integer** that uniquely identifies a control in a control array.
- *PictureBoxControl*.**Left**—a **Single** that contains the distance, measured in twips between the left edge of the control and the left edge of the control's container.
- *PictureBoxControl*.**LinkItem**—a **String** containing data that is passed to a destination control in a DDE link. This property is the same as the item specification in a normal DDE specification.

- *PictureBoxControl*.**LinkMode**—an **Integer** that specifies how the form will act in a DDE conversation.

LinkMode Name	Value	Description
vbLinkNone	0	No DDE interaction.
vbLinkAutomatic	1	The destination control is updated each time the data is updated.
vbLinkManual	2	The destination control is updated only when the **LinkRequest** method is used.
vbLinkNotify	3	The **LinkNotify** event occurs each time the data is updated. Then the **LinkRequest** method can be used to refresh the linked data.

Table P-18: LinkMode *values.*

- *PictureBoxControl*.**LinkTimeout**—an **Integer** containing the amount of time, in tenths of seconds, that the application will wait for a DDE message.
- *PictureBoxControl*.**LinkTopic**—a **String** that contains a reference to a DDE application. The actual format of the string is dependent on the exact application, but strings will usually include an application, topic, and item. For example, in Excel a valid **LinkTopic** string is "Excel|Sheet1."
- *PictureBoxControl*.**MouseIcon**—a picture object (a bitmap, icon, or metafile) that will be used as a cursor when the **MousePointer** property is set to 99. Note that Visual Basic does not support color cursors from a .CUR file. A color icon from an .ICO file should be used instead.
- *PictureBoxControl*.**MousePointer**—an **Integer** value (see Table P-19) that contains the value of the cursor that should be displayed when the cursor is moved over this control. Use *vbCustom* to display the custom icon stored in the **MouseIcon** property.

Cursor Name	Value	Description
vbDefault	0	Shape determined by the object (default value).
vbArrow	1	Arrow.
vbCrosshair	2	Crosshair.
vbIbeam	3	I beam.
vbIconPointer	4	Square inside a square.
vbSizePointer	5	Four-sided arrow (north, south, east, west).
vbSizeNESW	6	Two-sided arrow (northeast, southwest).
vbSizeNS	7	Two-sided arrow (north, south).
vbSizeNWSE	8	Two-sided arrow (northwest, southeast).
vbSizeWE	9	Two-sided arrow (west, east).
vbUpArrow	10	Single-sided arrow pointing north.
vbHourglass	11	Hourglass.
vbNoDrop	12	No Drop.
vbArrowHourglass	13	An arrow and an hourglass.
vbArrowQuestion	14	An arrow and a question mark.
vbSizeAll	15	Size all.
vbCustom	99	Custom icon from the **MouseIcon** property of this control.

Table P-19: Cursor *values.*

- *PictureBoxControl*.**Name**—a **String** that contains the name of the control that will be used to reference the control in a Visual Basic program. This property is read only at run time.
- *PictureBoxControl*.**OLEDragMode**—an **Integer** value (see Table P-20) that describes how the control will respond to OLE drag operations.

> **Tip**
>
> When the **DragMode** is **True**, the standard Visual Basic drag-and-drop functions will override the OLE drag-and-drop functions.

OLEDragMode Name	Value	Description
vbOLEDragManual	0	All drag requests will be handled by the programmer (default value).
vbOLEDragAutomatic	1	The control responds to all OLE drag requests automatically.

Table P-20: **OLEDragMode** values.

- *PictureBoxControl*.**OLEDropMode**—an **Integer** value (see Table P-21) that describes how the control will respond to OLE drop operations.

OLEDropMode Name	Value	Description
vbOLEDropNone	0	The control does not accept OLE drops. The cursor is changed to the No Drop cursor (default value).
vbOLEDropManual	1	The control responds to OLE drops under the program's control (manual).
vbOLEDropAutomatic	2	The control automatically accepts OLE drops if it recognizes the format of the data object.

Table P-21: OLEDropMode values.

- *PictureBoxControl*.**Parent**—an object that contains a reference to the **Form,** **Frame,** or other container that contains the **Image** control.
- *PictureBoxControl*.**Picture**—a picture object (a bitmap, icon, metafile, GIF, or JPEG) that will be displayed on the control. You can also use the **LoadPicture** function at run time to load a bitmap, icon, or metafile.
- *PictureBoxControl*.**RightToLeft**—a **Boolean** value when **True** means that the text is displayed from right to left. **False** means that the text is displayed from left to right. A bi-directional version of Windows is required to set this property to true.
- *PictureBoxControl*.**ScaleHeight**—an **Integer** value that sets or returns the height of the object in the units specified by **ScaleMode**.
- *PictureBoxControl*.**ScaleLeft**—an **Integer** value that sets or returns the value of the X-coordinate of the left edge of the form.
- *PictureBoxControl*.**ScaleMode**—an **Integer** value (see Table P-22) that describes the unit of measurement used for the form.

> **Tip**
>
> When dealing with graphic images such as BMP or GIF files it is often useful to set **ScaleMode** to vbPixels *to help set the proper relationships.*

ScaleMode Name	Value	Description
vbUser	0	Measurements are custom defined, based on the values in ScaleHeight, ScaleLeft, ScaleTop, or ScaleWidth properties.
vbTwips	1	Measurements are in twips (1440 twips per inch).
vbPoints	2	Measurements are in points (72 per inch).
vbPixels	3	Measurements are in pixels (smallest unit of measure for a monitor or printer).
vbCharacters	4	Measurements are in characters (horizontal = 120 twips per character, vertical = 240 twips per character).
vbInches	5	Measurements are in inches.
vbMillimeters	6	Measurements are in millimeters.
vbCentimeters	7	Measurements are in centimeters.

Table P-22: ScaleMode *values.*

- *PictureBoxControl.***ScaleTop**—an **Integer** value that sets or returns the value of the Y-coordinate of the top edge of the form.
- *PictureBoxControl.***ScaleWidth**—an **Integer** value that sets or returns the width of the object in the units specified by **ScaleMode**.
- *PictureBoxControl.***TabIndex**—an **Integer** value that is used to determine the order that a user will tab through the objects on a form.
- *PictureBoxControl.***TabStop**—a **Boolean** value when **True** means that the user can tab to this object. **False** means that this control will be skipped to the next control in the **TabIndex** order.
- *PictureBoxControl.***Tag**—a **String** that can hold programmer-specific information. This property is not used by Visual Basic.
- *PictureBoxControl.***ToolTipText**—a **String** that holds a text value that can be displayed as a **ToolTip** box that displays whenever the cursor is held over the control for about one second.
- *PictureBoxControl.***Top**—a **Single** that contains the distance, measured in twips, between the top edge of the control and the top edge of the control's container.
- *PictureBoxControl.***Visible**—a **Boolean** value when **True** means that the control is visible. **False** means that the control is not visible.

> **Tip**
>
> *This property can hide the control until the program is ready to display it.*

- *PictureBoxControl.***WhatsThisHelpID**—a **Long** that contains a help file context ID number that references an entry in the help file. This provides a What's This PopUp help display in response to the What's This button in the upper right corner of the window.
- *PictureBoxControl.***Width**—a **Single** that contains the width of the control.

Methods

PictureBoxControl.Circle [Step] (x , y), radius [, color [, start [, stop [, aspect]]]]

Usage This method draws a circle, an ellipse, or a curved line on the control. All coordinate information used is relative to the **ScaleMode, ScaleHeight, ScaleLeft, ScaleTop,** and **ScaleWidth**.

Arguments
- **Step**—a keyword that specifies that the coordinates are relative to the control's **CurrentX** and **CurrentY** properties.
- *x*—a **Single** specifying the X-coordinate of the center of the circle.
- *y*—a **Single** specifying the Y-coordinate of the center of the circle.
- *radius*—a **Single** specifying the radius of the circle.
- *color*—a **Long** containing the color of the line to be drawn. If omitted, it will default to the value in the **ForeColor** property.
- *start*—a **Single** specifying the starting angle for the circle, in radians. If omitted, it will default to zero.
- *stop*—a **Single** specifying the ending angle for the circle, in radians. If omitted, it will default to 2 times pi (approximately 6.28).
- *aspect*—a **Single** specifying the height-to-width ratio of the circle. The default is 1.0, which will yield a perfect circle.

Tip

To draw a half-circle, assign **start** *a value of 0 and* **stop** *a value of pi (approximately 3.14), and choose values for the other parameters.*

To draw a vertical ellipse, assign a value greater than 1.0 to aspect. *A horizontal ellipse would have an aspect ratio of less than 1.0.*

PictureBoxControl.Cls

Usage This method clears all of the graphics and text from a form.

PictureBoxControl.Drag [DragAction]

Usage This method begins, ends, or cancels a drag operation.

Arguments *DragAction*—an **Integer** that contains a value selected from Table P-23 below.

DragAction Name	Value	Description
vbCancel	0	Cancels any drag operation in progress.
vbBeginDrag	1	Begins a drag operation (default).
vbEndDrag	2	Ends a drag operation and drops *object*.

Table P-23: DragAction *values.*

PictureBoxControl.Line [Step] (x1 , y1), [Step] (x2 , y2) [, B | BF]

Usage   This method draws lines or boxes on the form. All coordinate information used is relative to the **ScaleMode, ScaleHeight, ScaleLeft, ScaleTop,** and **ScaleWidth.**

Arguments
- **Step**—a keyword that specifies that the *x1* and *y1* coordinates are relative to the form's **CurrentX** and **CurrentY** properties.
- *x1*—a **Single** specifying the starting X-coordinate of the center of the line or box.
- *y1*—a **Single** specifying the starting Y-coordinate of the center of the line or box.
- **Step**—a keyword that specifies that the *x2* and *y2* coordinates are relative to the form's **CurrentX** and **CurrentY** properties.
- *x2*—a **Single** specifying the stopping X-coordinate of the center of the line or box.
- *y2*—a **Single** specifying the stopping Y-coordinate of the center of the line or box.
- *color*—a **Long** containing the color of the line to be drawn. If omitted, it will default to the value in the **ForeColor** property.
- **B**—draw a box with (*x1*, *y1*) and (*x2*, *y2*) specifying the opposite corners of the box. If omitted, a line will be drawn on the form.
- **BF**—draw a box with (*x1*, *y1*) and (*x2*, *y2*) specifying the opposite corners of the box and fill the interior with the color specified by **FillColor** and **FillStyle**. If omitted, a line will be drawn on the form.

PictureBoxControl.LinkExecute command

Usage   This method will send a command to the source application in a DDE link.

Arguments   *command*—a **String** containing the command.

PictureBoxControl.LinkPoke

Usage   This method is used by the destination application in a DDE link to send the contents of the label's caption to the source application.

PictureBoxControl.LinkRequest

Usage   This method is used by the destination application in a DDE link to send a request to the source application to refresh its contents.

PictureBoxControl.LinkSend

Usage   This method sends the contents of a **Picture** control to the destination application in a DDE link.

PictureBoxControl.Move Left [, Top [, Width [, Height]]]

Usage   This method changes the position and the size of the **PictureBox** control. The **ScaleMode** of the **Form** or other container object that holds the **PictureBox** control will determine the units used to specify the coordinates.

Arguments
- *Left*—a **Single** that specifies the new position of the left edge of the control.
- *Top*—a **Single** that specifies the new position of the top edge of the control.
- *Width*—a **Single** that specifies the new width of the control.
- *Height*—a **Single** that specifies the new height of the control.

PictureBoxControl.OLEDrag

Usage   This method begins an **OLEDrag** and drop operation. Invoking this method will trigger the **OLEStartDrag** event.

PictureBoxControl.PaintPicture *picture, x1 , y1, [width1] , [height1] ,[x2] , [y2] , [width2] , [height2] , [rasterop]*

Usage   This method displays an image (.BMP, .DIB, .EMF, .ICO, or .WMF) on the form. All coordinate information used is relative to the **ScaleMode, ScaleHeight, ScaleLeft, ScaleTop,** and **ScaleWidth.**

Arguments
- *picture*—the image to be displayed on the form. It can come from the **Picture** property of a picture box or another form.
- *x1*—a **Single** specifying the starting X-coordinate of the picture.
- *y1*—a **Single** specifying the starting Y-coordinate of the picture.
- *width1*—a **Single** specifying the width of the image. If omitted, the width will default to the width of the image. If greater or less than the width of the image, the image will be stretched or shrunk to fit.
- *height1*—a **Single** specifying the height of the image. If omitted, the height will default to the height of the image. If greater or less than the height of the image, the image will be stretched or shrunk to fit.
- *x2*—a **Single** specifying the starting X-coordinate of a clipping region within the picture. If omitted, zero will be used.
- *y2*—a **Single** specifying the starting Y-coordinate of a clipping region within the picture. If omitted, zero will be used.
- *width2*—a **Single** specifying the width of the clipping region of the image. If omitted, the width will default to the width of the image. If greater or less than the width of the image, the image will be stretched or shrunk to fit.
- *height2*—a **Single** specifying the height of the clipping region of the image. If omitted, the height will default to the height of the image. If greater or less than the height of the image, the image will be stretched or shrunk to fit.
- *rasterop*—a **Long** containing a raster op code from Table P-24 below that will perform a bit-wise operation on the image as it is displayed. The default will be to display the image as is.

PictureBox • **701**

RasterOp Name	Value	Description
vbDstInvert	&H005A0049	Inverts the destination image.
vbMergeCopy	&H00C000CA	Combines the source and the pattern.
vbMergePaint	&H00BB0226	Combines inverted source image with destination image using OR.
vbNotSrcCopy	&H00330008	Copies inverted source image to the destination.
vbNotSrcErase	&H001100A6	Inverts the result of combining the source and destination images using OR.
vbPatCopy	&H00F00021	Copies the source pattern to the destination bitmap.
vbPatInvert	&H005A0049	Combines the inverted source pattern with the destination image using XOR.
vbPatPaint	&H00FB0A09	Combines the destination image with the source pattern.
vbScrAnd	&H008800C6	Combines the destination and source images using AND.
vbSrcCopy	&H00CC0020	Copies the source image to the destination bitmap.
vbSrcErase	&H00440328	Combines the inverted destination image with the source image by using AND.
vbSrcInvert	&H00660046	Combines the source and destination images using XOR.
vbSrcPaint	&H00EE0086	Combines the source and destination images using OR.

Table P-24: RasterOp *values.*

color = PictureBoxControl.Point (x , y)

Usage — This method returns a **Long** containing the color at the point at location *x, y*. If the location is outside the form, then -1 will be returned. All coordinate information used is relative to the **ScaleMode**, **ScaleHeight**, **ScaleLeft**, **ScaleTop,** and **ScaleWidth**.

Arguments
- *color*—a **Long** containing the color at location *x, y*.
- *x*—a **Single** specifying the X-coordinate of the point.
- *y*—a **Single** specifying the Y-coordinate of the point.

PictureBoxControl.PSet [Step] (x , y), [color]

Usage — This method sets the point at *x, y* to the color specified in *color*. All coordinate information used is relative to the **ScaleMode**, **ScaleHeight**, **ScaleLeft**, **ScaleTop,** and **ScaleWidth**.

Arguments
- **Step**—keyword that specifies that the *x* and *y* coordinates are relative to the form's **CurrentX** and **CurrentY** properties.
- *x*—a **Single** specifying the X-coordinate of the point.
- *y*—a **Single** specifying the Y-coordinate of the point.
- *color*—a **Long** containing the color to be displayed at location *x, y*. If omitted, this value will default to the value of **ForeColor**.

PictureBoxControl.Refresh

Usage   This method redraws the contents of the control.

PictureBoxControl.Scale [(x1 , y1)—(x2 , y2)]

Usage   This method will define the coordinate system used on the form and set the appropriate values in **ScaleMode**, **ScaleHeight**, **ScaleLeft**, **ScaleTop**, and **ScaleWidth**. If the **Scale** method is used without any arguments, the coordinate is reset to default.

Arguments
- *x1*—a **Single** specifying the X-coordinate of the left edge of the form.
- *y1*—a **Single** specifying the Y-coordinate of the top edge of the form.
- *x2*—a **Single** specifying the X-coordinate of the right edge of the form.
- *y2*—a **Single** specifying the Y-coordinate of the bottom edge of the form.

result = PictureBoxControl.ScaleX (width , fromscale , toscale)

Usage   This method will compute a new value for *width* in a different scale.

Arguments
- *result*—a **Single** containing a new value for *width*.
- *fromscale*—an **Integer** specifying a **ScaleMode** value for the current *width*.
- *toscale*—an **Integer** value (see Table P-25) specifying the **ScaleMode** value for the new *width*.

ScaleMode Name	Value	Description
vbUser	0	Measurements are custom defined, based on the values in ScaleHeight, ScaleLeft, ScaleTop, or ScaleWidth properties.
vbTwips	1	Measurements are in twips (1440 twips per inch).
vbPoints	2	Measurements are in points (72 per inch).
vbPixels	3	Measurements are in pixels (smallest unit of measure for a monitor or printer).
vbCharacters	4	Measurements are in characters (horizontal = 120 twips per character, vertical = 240 twips per character).
vbInches	5	Measurements are in inches.
vbMillimeters	6	Measurements are in millimeters.
vbCentimeters	7	Measurements are in centimeters.
vbHimetric	8	Measurements are in himetrics.

Table P-25: ScaleMode values.

result = PictureBoxControl.ScaleY (height , fromscale , toscale)

Usage   This method will compute a new value for *height* in a different scale.

Arguments
- *result*—a **Single** containing a new value for *height*.
- *fromscale*—an **Integer** specifying a **ScaleMode** value for the current *height*.

- *toscale*—an **Integer** value (see Table P-26) specifying the **ScaleMode** value for the new *height*.

ScaleMode Name	Value	Description
vbUser	0	Measurements are custom defined, based on the values in ScaleHeight, ScaleLeft, ScaleTop, or ScaleWidth properties.
vbTwips	1	Measurements are in twips (1440 twips per inch).
vbPoints	2	Measurements are in points (72 per inch).
vbPixels	3	Measurements are in pixels (smallest unit of measure for a monitor or printer).
vbCharacters	4	Measurements are in characters (horizontal = 120 twips per character, vertical = 240 twips per character).
vbInches	5	Measurements are in inches.
vbMillimeters	6	Measurements are in millimeters.
vbCentimeters	7	Measurements are in centimeters.
vbHimetric	8	Measurements are in himetrics.

Table P-26: ScaleMode *values.*

PictureBoxControl.SetFocus

Usage   This method transfers the focus from the form or control that currently has the focus to this form. To receive the focus, this form must be enabled and visible.

PictureBoxControl.ShowWhatsThis

Usage   This method displays the ShowWhatsThis help information for this control.

height = PictureBoxControl.TextHeight (string)

Usage   This method will compute the height of the string in the units specified by **ScaleMode**. The height is computed using the font information specified in the **Font** object. It will also include space at the top and the bottom of the characters, so that multiple lines of text can be placed next to each other. If *string* contains embedded carriage return linefeed pairs, then the total height of the block of text will be returned.

Arguments
- *height*—a **Single** that contains the height of *string*.
- *string*—a **String** that contains characters to be printed on the form.

width = PictureBoxControl.TextWidth (string)

Usage   This method will compute the width of the string in the units specified by **ScaleMode**. The width is computed using the font information specified in the **Font** object. If *string* contains embedded carriage return linefeed pairs, then the length of the longest line will be returned.

Arguments
- *width*—a **Single** that contains the width of *string*.
- *string*—a **String** that contains characters to be printed on the form.

PictureBoxControl.ZOrder [position]

Usage This method specifies the position of the **PictureBox** control relative to the other objects on the form.

> **Tip**
> Note that there are three layers of objects on a form: The back layer is the drawing space that contains the results of the graphical methods, the middle layer contains graphical objects and **PictureBox,** and the top layer contains nongraphical controls such as the **CommandButton**. The **ZOrder** method only affects how the objects are arranged within a single layer.

Arguments *position*—an **Integer** that specifies the relative position of this object. A value of 0 means that the control is positioned at the head of the list, a value of 1 means that the control will be placed at the end of the list.

Events

Private Sub *PictureBoxControl*__Change ([*index* As Integer])

Usage This event occurs whenever the contents of the label's caption are changed, either by the program changing the **Caption** property directly or by a DDE link.

Arguments *index*—an **Integer** that is used to uniquely identify a control in a control array. This argument is not present if the control is not part of a control array.

Private Sub *PictureBoxControl*__Click([*index* As Integer])

Usage This event occurs when the user clicks a mouse button while the cursor is over the control.

Arguments *index*—an **Integer** that uniquely identifies a control in a control array. This argument is not present if the control is not part of a control array.

Private Sub *PictureBoxControl*_DblClick([*index* As Integer])

Usage This event occurs when the user double-clicks a mouse button while over the control.

Arguments *index*—an **Integer** that uniquely identifies a control in a control array. This argument is not present if the control is not part of a control array.

Private Sub *PictureBoxControl*_DragDrop([*index* As Integer ,] *source* Panel Control, *x* As Single, *y* As Single)

Usage — This event occurs when a drag-and-drop operation is completed by using the Drag method with a *DragAction* value of *vbEndDrag*.

Tip

*When using drag-and-drop operations, use the **DragOver** event to determine what the cursor should look like while the cursor moves over the control.*

Arguments
- *index*—an **Integer** that uniquely identifies a control in a control array. This argument is not present if the control is not part of a control array.
- *source*—a control object that is the control that is being dragged.

Tip

You can access a property or method from the source control by using source.*property or* source.*method. You can determine the type of object or control by using the **TypeOf** operator.*

- *x*—a **Single** that contains the horizontal location of the mouse pointer.
- *y*—a **Single** that contains the vertical location of the mouse pointer.

Private Sub *PictureBoxControl*_DragOver([*index* As Integer ,] *source* As Control, *x* As Single, *y* As Single, *state* As Integer)

Usage — This event occurs while a drag operation is in progress and the cursor is moved over the control.

Tip

*When using drag-and-drop operations, use the **DragOver** event to determine what the cursor should look like while the cursor moves over the control. When* state *is 0, you can change the cursor to a No Drop (vbNoDrop) cursor or highlight the field that the cursor is near. When* state *is 1, you can undo the changes you made when the* state *was 0.*

Arguments
- *index*—an **Integer** that uniquely identifies a control in a control array. This argument is not present if the control is not part of a control array.
- *source*—a control object that is the control that is being dragged.

Tip

You can access a property or method from the source control by using source.*property or* source.*method. You can determine the type of object or control by using the **TypeOf** operator.*

- *x*—a **Single** that contains the horizontal location of the mouse pointer.
- *y*—a **Single** that contains the vertical location of the mouse pointer.
- *state*—an **Integer** value (see Table P-27) that indicates the state of the object being dragged.

state Name	Value	Description
vbEnter	0	The dragged object is entering range of the control.
vbLeave	1	The dragged object is leaving range of the control.
vbOver	2	The dragged object has moved from one position over the control to another.

Table P-27: State *values*.

Private Sub *PicturetBoxControl*_GotFocus ([*index* As Integer])

Usage   This event occurs when the control is given focus.

Tip

You can use this routine to display help or other information in a status bar.

Arguments   *index*—an **Integer** that is used to uniquely identify a control in a control array. This argument is not present if the control is not part of a control array.

Private Sub *PictureBoxControl*_KeyDown ([*index* As Integer ,] *keycode* As Integer, *shift* As Single)

Usage   This event occurs when a key is pressed while the control has the focus.

Arguments   *index*—an **Integer** that is used to uniquely identify a control in a control array. This argument is not present if the control is not part of a control array.

- *keycode*—an **Integer** that contains information about which key was pressed.
- *shift*—an **Integer** that contains information about the Shift and Alt keys that were pressed when the mouse button was pressed. These values can be added together if more than one key was down. For instance, a value of 5 would mean that the Shift and Alt keys were both down when the mouse button was pressed.

shift Name	Value	Description
vbShiftMask	1	The Shift key was pressed.
vbCtrlMask	2	The Ctrl key was pressed.
vbAltMask	4	The Alt key was pressed.

Table P-28: Shift *values*.

Private Sub *PictureBoxControl*_KeyPress([*index* As Integer ,] *keychar* As Integer)

- Usage This event occurs whenever a key is pressed while the control has the focus.

- Arguments
  - *index*—an **Integer** that is used to uniquely identify a control in a control array. This argument is not present if the control is not part of a control array.
  - *keychar*—an **Integer** that contains the ASCII character that was pressed.

Private Sub *PictureBoxControl*_KeyUp ([*index* As Integer ,] *keycode* As Integer, *shift* As Single)

- Usage This event occurs when a key is released while the control has the focus.

- Arguments
  - *index*—an **Integer** that is used to uniquely identify a control in a control array. This argument is not present if the control is not part of a control array.
  - *keycode*—an **Integer** that contains information about which key was released.
  - *shift*—an **Integer** that contains information about the Shift and Alt keys that were pressed when the mouse button was pressed. These values can be added together if more than one key was down. For instance, a value of 5 would mean that the Shift and Alt keys were both down when the mouse button was pressed.

shift Name	Value	Description
vbShiftMask	1	The Shift key was pressed.
vbCtrlMask	2	The Ctrl key was pressed.
vbAltMask	4	The Alt key was pressed.

Table P-29: Shift *values.*

Private Sub *PictureBoxControl*_LinkClose ([*index* As Integer ,])

- Usage This event occurs when a DDE link is closed.

- Arguments
  - *index*—an **Integer** that is used to uniquely identify a control in a control array. This argument is not present if the control is not part of a control array.

Private Sub *PictureBoxControl*_LinkError ([*index* As Integer ,] *errcode* As Integer)

- Usage This event occurs when a DDE link error occurs.

- Arguments
  - *index*—an **Integer** that is used to uniquely identify a control in a control array. This argument is not present if the control is not part of a control array.
  - *errcode*—an **Integer** that contains an error code listed in Table P-30.

errcode Value	Description
1	The other application requested data in wrong format. This may occur more than once while Visual Basic attempts to find an acceptable format.
6	The other application attempted to continue the DDE conversation after **LinkMode** in this application was set to zero.
7	All 128 DDE links are in use.
8	Destination control: An automatic link or **LinkRequest** failed when communicating. Source forms: The other application was unable to poke data to a control.
11	Insufficient memory available for DDE.

Table P-30: DDE errcode *values*.

Private Sub *PictureBoxControl*_LinkNotify ([*index* As Integer])

Usage   This event occurs when **LinkMode** is set to *vbLinkNotify* (3) and the source has changed the data in the DDE link.

Arguments
- *index*—an **Integer** that is used to uniquely identify a control in a control array. This argument is not present if the control is not part of a control array.

Private Sub *PictureBoxControl* _LinkOpen ([*index* As Integer ,] *cancel* As Integer)

Usage   This event occurs when a DDE session is being set up.

Arguments
- *index*—an **Integer** that is used to uniquely identify a control in a control array. This argument is not present if the control is not part of a control array.
- *cancel*—an **Integer,** when zero, means that the command was accepted. Any other value will inform the destination application that the link will be refused.

Private Sub *PictureBoxControl*_LostFocus ([*index* As Integer])

Usage   This event occurs when the control loses focus.

Tip

This routine is useful in performing data verification.

Arguments
- *index*—an **Integer** that is used to uniquely identify a control in a control array. This argument is not present if the control is not part of a control array.

Private Sub *PictureBoxControl*_MouseDown([*index* As Integer ,] *button* As Integer, *shift* As Single, *x* As Single, *y* As Single)

Usage   This event occurs when a mouse button was pressed while the cursor was over the control.

Arguments
- *index*—an **Integer** that uniquely identifies a control in a control array. This argument is not present if the control is not part of a control array.
- *button*—an **Integer** value (see Table P-31) that contains information about the mouse buttons that were pressed. Only one button will be indicated when this event occurs.

button Name	Value	Description
vbLeftButton	1	The left button was pressed.
vbRightButton	2	The right button was pressed.
vbMiddleButton	4	The middle button was pressed.

Table P-31: Button *values*.

- *shift*—an **Integer** value (see Table P-32) that contains information about the Shift and Alt keys that were pressed when the mouse button was pressed. These values can be added together if more than one key was down. For instance, a value of 5 would mean that the Shift and Alt keys were both down when the mouse button was pressed.

shift Name	Value	Description
vbShiftMask	1	The Shift key was pressed.
vbCtrlMask	2	The Ctrl key was pressed.
vbAltMask	4	The Alt key was pressed.

Table P-32: Shift *values*.

- *x*—a **Single** that contains the horizontal location of the mouse pointer.
- *y*—a **Single** that contains the vertical location of the mouse pointer.

Private Sub *PictureBoxControl*_MouseMove ([*index* As Integer ,] *button* As Integer, *shift* As Single, *x* As Single, *y* As Single)

Usage — This event occurs while the cursor is moved over the control.

Arguments
- *index*—an **Integer** that uniquely identifies a control in a control array. This argument is not present if the control is not part of a control array.
- *button*—an **Integer** value (see Table P-33) that contains information about the mouse buttons that were pressed. These values can be added together if more than one button was pressed. For instance, a value of 3 means that both the left and right buttons were pressed. A value of 0 means that no buttons were pressed.

button Name	Value	Description
vbLeftButton	1	The left button was pressed.
vbRightButton	2	The right button was pressed.
vbMiddleButton	4	The middle button was pressed.

Table P-33: Button *values*.

- *shift*—an **Integer** value (see Table P-34) that contains information about the Shift and Alt keys that were pressed when the mouse button was pressed. For instance, a value of 5 would mean that the Shift and Alt keys were both down when the mouse button was pressed. A value of 0 means that none of these keys were pressed.

shift Name	Value	Description
vbShiftMask	1	The Shift key was pressed.
vbCtrlMask	2	The Ctrl key was pressed.
vbAltMask	4	The Alt key was pressed.

Table P-34: Shift *values*.

- *x*—a **Single** that contains the horizontal location of the mouse pointer.
- *y*—a **Single** that contains the vertical location of the mouse pointer.

Private Sub *PictureBoxControl*_MouseUp([*index* As Integer ,] *button* As Integer, *shift* As Single, *x* As Single, *y* As Single)

Usage   This event occurs when a mouse button is released while the cursor is over the control.

Arguments
- *index*—an **Integer** that uniquely identifies a control in a control array. This argument is not present if the control is not part of a control array.
- *button*—an **Integer** value (see Table P-35) that contains information about the mouse buttons that were released. Only one of these values will be present.

button Name	Value	Description
vbLeftButton	1	The left button was released.
vbRightButton	2	The right button was released.
vbMiddleButton	4	The middle button was released.

Table P-35: Button *values*.

- *shift*—an **Integer** value (see Table P-36) that contains information about the Shift and Alt keys that were pressed when the mouse button was released. These values can be added together if more than one key was down. For instance, a value of 5 would mean that the Shift and Alt keys were both down when the mouse button was released. A value of 0 means that none of these keys were pressed.

shift Name	Value	Description
vbShiftMask	1	The Shift key was pressed.
vbCtrlMask	2	The Ctrl key was pressed.
vbAltMask	4	The Alt key was pressed.

Table P-36: Shift *values*.

- *x*—a **Single** that contains the horizontal location of the mouse pointer.
- *y*—a **Single** that contains the vertical location of the mouse pointer.

Private Sub *PictureBoxControl*_OLECompleteDrag([*index* As Integer ,] *effect* As Long)

Usage — This event tells the source control the results of an OLE drag-and-drop operation. This is the final event to occur in the series of actions that make up an OLE drag-and-drop operation.

Arguments
- *index*—an **Integer** that uniquely identifies a control in a control array. This argument is not present if the control is not part of a control array.
- *effect*—a **Long** (see Table P-37) that returns the status of the OLE drag-and-drop operation.

effect Name	Value	Description
vbDropEffectNone	0	The operation was canceled or the target control can't accept the drop operation.
vbDropEffectCopy	1	The operation copies data from the source control to the target control. The original data is unchanged.
vbDropEffectMove	2	The operation results in a link from the original data to the target control.

Table P-37: Effect *values*.

Private Sub *PictureBoxControl*_OLEDragDrop([*index* As Integer ,] *data* As DataObject, *effect* As Long, *button* As Integer, *shift* As Single, *x* As Single, *y* As Single)

Usage — This event tells the source control the results of an OLE drag-and-drop operation. This is the final event to occur in the series of actions that make up an OLE drag-and-drop operation.

Arguments
- *index*—an **Integer** that uniquely identifies a control in a control array. This argument is not present if the control is not part of a control array.
- *data*—a **DataObject** that contains the formats that the source control will provide. If the data is not contained in the **DataObject**, then it can be retrieved with the **GetData** method.
- *effect*—a **Long** (see Table P-38) that returns the status of the OLE drag-and-drop operation.

effect Name	Value	Description
vbDropEffectNone	0	The operation was canceled or the target control can't accept the drop operation.
vbDropEffectCopy	1	The operation copies data from the source control to the target control. The original data is unchanged.
vbDropEffectMove	2	The operation results in a link from the original data to the target control.

Table P-38: Effect *values*.

- *button*—an **Integer** value (see Table P-39) that contains information about the mouse buttons that were pressed. These values can be added together if more than one button was pressed. For instance, a value of 3 means that both the left and right buttons were pressed. A value of 0 means that no buttons were pressed.

button Name	Value	Description
vbLeftButton	1	The left button was pressed.
vbRightButton	2	The right button was pressed.
vbMiddleButton	4	The middle button was pressed.

Table P-39: Button *values.*

- *shift*—an **Integer** value (see Table P-40) that contains information about the Shift and Alt keys that were pressed when the mouse button was released. These values can be added together if more than one key was down. For instance, a value of 5 would mean that the Shift and Alt keys were both down when the mouse button was released. A value of 0 means that none of these keys were pressed.

shift Name	Value	Description
vbShiftMask	1	The Shift key was pressed.
vbCtrlMask	2	The Ctrl key was pressed.
vbAltMask	4	The Alt key was pressed.

Table P-40: Shift *values.*

- *x*—a **Single** that contains the horizontal location of the mouse pointer.
- *y*—a **Single** that contains the vertical location of the mouse pointer.

Private Sub *PictureBoxControl*_OLEDragOver([*index* As Integer ,] *data* As DataObject, *effect* As Long, *button* As Integer, *shift* As Single, *x* As Single, *y* As Single, *state* As Integer)

Usage: This event happens when an OLE drag-and-drop operation is in progress.

Arguments:
- *index*—an **Integer** that uniquely identifies a control in a control array. This argument is not present if the control is not part of a control array.
- *data*—a **DataObject** that contains the formats that the source control will provide. If the data is not contained in the **DataObject**, then it can be retrieved with the **GetData** method.
- *effect*—a **Long** (see Table P-41) that returns the status of the OLE drag-and-drop operation.

effect Name	Value	Description
vbDropEffectNone	0	The operation was canceled or the target control can't accept the drop operation.
vbDropEffectCopy	1	The operation copies data from the source control to the target control. The original data is unchanged.
vbDropEffectMove	2	The operation results in a link from the original data to the target control.

Table P-41: Effect *values*.

- *button*—an **Integer** value (see Table P-42) that contains information about the mouse buttons that were pressed. These values can be added together if more than one button was pressed. For instance, a value of 3 means that both the left and right buttons were pressed. A value of 0 means that no buttons were pressed.

button Name	Value	Description
vbLeftButton	1	The left button was pressed.
vbRightButton	2	The right button was pressed.
vbMiddleButton	4	The middle button was pressed.

Table P-42: Button *values*.

- *shift*—an **Integer** value (see Table P-43) that contains information about the Shift and Alt keys that were pressed when the mouse button was released. These values can be added together if more than one key was down. For instance, a value of 5 would mean that the Shift and Alt keys were both down when the mouse button was released. A value of 0 means that none of these keys were pressed.

shift Name	Value	Description
vbShiftMask	1	The Shift key was pressed.
vbCtrlMask	2	The Ctrl key was pressed.
vbAltMask	4	The Alt key was pressed.

Table P-43: Shift *values*.

- *x*—a **Single** that contains the horizontal location of the mouse pointer.
- *y*—a **Single** that contains the vertical location of the mouse pointer.
- *state*—an **Integer** value (see Table P-44) that indicates the state of the object being dragged.

state Name	Value	Description
vbEnter	0	The dragged object is entering range of the control.
vbLeave	1	The dragged object is leaving range of the control.
vbOver	2	The dragged object has moved from one position over the control to another.

Table P-44: State *values*.

Private Sub *PictureBoxControl*_OLEGiveFeedback ([*index* As Integer ,] *effect* As Long)

Usage This event tells the source control what is happening while the OLE drag-and-drop operation is in progress. This event occurs after the **OLEDragOver** event.

Tip

You may want to use this event to change the cursor to reflect what can happen in the remote object.

Arguments
- *index*—an **Integer** that uniquely identifies a control in a control array. This argument is not present if the control is not part of a control array.
- *effect*—a **Long** (see Table P-45) that returns the status of the OLE drag-and-drop operation.

effect Name	Value	Description
vbDropEffectNone	0	The operation was canceled or the target control can't accept the drop operation.
vbDropEffectCopy	1	The operation copies data from the source control to the target control. The original data is unchanged.
vbDropEffectMove	2	The operation results in a link from the original data to the target control.
vbDropEffectScroll	&H80000000	The target control is about to scroll or is scrolling. This value may be added to the other *shift* values.

Table P-45: Effect values.

Private Sub *PictureBoxControl*_OLESetData([*index* As Integer ,] *data* As DataObject, *DataFormat* As Integer)

Usage This event happens in response to the target object performing a **GetData** method on *data*. This routine will respond by using the **SetData** method with the desired data using the **DataObject** *data*.

Arguments
- *index*—an **Integer** that uniquely identifies a control in a control array. This argument is not present if the control is not part of a control array.
- *data*—a **DataObject** that will contain the data to be returned to the target object.
- *format*—an **Integer** value (see Table P-46) that contains the format of the data.

format Name	Value	Description
vbCFText	1	Text (.TXT files)
vbCFBitmap	2	Bitmap (.BMP files)
vbCFMetafile	3	Metafile (.WMF files)
vbCFEDIB	8	Device independent bitmap (DIB)
vbCFPallette	9	Color palette

format Name	Value	Description
vbCFEMetafile	14	Enhanced metafile (.EMF files)
vbCFFiles	15	List of files
vbCFRTF	-16639	Rich Text Format (.RTF files)

Table P-46: *Format values.*

Private Sub *PictureBoxControl*_OLEStartDrag ([*index* As Integer ,] *data* As DataObject, *AllowedEffects* As Long)

Usage   This event starts an OLE drag-and-drop operation.

Arguments
- *index*—an **Integer** that uniquely identifies a control in a control array. This argument is not present if the control is not part of a control array.
- *data*—a **DataObject** that will contain the formats that the source object is willing to provide to the target object. It may optionally contain the data to be transferred.
- *AllowedEffects*—a **Long** (see Table P-47) that contains the effects that the target object can request from the source object. The *AllowedEffects* can be added together if the source object supports more than one effect. Note that the target object can always use the *vbDropEffectNone* effect.

AllowedEffects Name	Value	Description
vbDropEffectNone	0	The target can't copy the data.
vbDropEffectCopy	1	The target can copy the data, and the source will keep the data unchanged.
vbDropEffectMove	2	The target can copy the data, and the source will delete the data.

Table P-47: AllowedEffects *values.*

Private Sub *PictureBoxControl*_Paint ([*index* As Integer])

Usage   This event occurs when the control must redraw itself. This can happen because the control's container was previously covered and now is not, because the size of the control has been changed, or if the control has been moved. A **Paint** event is necessary if you generate graphics or print text directly to the form and have set the **AutoRedraw** property to **False**.

Arguments
- *index*—an **Integer** that uniquely identifies a control in a control array. This argument is not present if the control is not part of a control array.

Warning

*Avoid moving the control, changing any variables that affect the controls size or appearance, and using the **Refresh** method. This can cause a cascading event where the **Move** event will trigger another **Paint** event, which in turn triggers the **Move** event again. Without safeguards, this process will continue until the program crashes or your system crashes.*

Private Sub *PictureBoxControl*_Resize ([*index* As Integer])

Usage This event occurs when the form is first displayed, when the value of **WindowState** changes, or when the form is resized. After the resize event occurs, the **Paint** event will be called (if **AutoResize** is **False**) to redraw the contents of the form.

Arguments *index*—an **Integer** that uniquely identifies a control in a control array. This argument is not present if the control is not part of a control array.

Examples
```
Private Sub Command1_Click()
Picture1.Picture = LoadPicture(App.Path & "\" & Text1.Text)
End Sub
```
This routine uses the **LoadPicture** function to load a GIF image onto the picture box.

See Also **Image** (control), **LoadPicture** (function), **SavePicture** (statement)

PictureClip

CONTROL
PE, EE

Usage The **PictureClip** control is an ActiveX control that allows you to clip parts of an image for use with other functions. It is more efficient to store one large bitmap containing a number of smaller images and clip out the needed images rather than storing the individual images.

The clipping process works in one of two different ways. First you can divide the image into a series of rows and columns. Then you can easily extract pieces using the **GraphicCell** property. The second approach uses the **ClipX**, **ClipY**, **ClipHeight**, and **ClipWidth** to define a rectangle on the image and then copy the rectangle using the **Clip** property.

> **Tip**
>
> *Set the container's **ScaleMode** property to vbPixels (3) to ensure proper scaling between the PictureClip control and the destination control.*

Properties
- *PictureClipControl*.**CellHeight**—an **Integer** value containing the height of each cell, in pixels, within the control.
- *PictureClipControl*.**CellWidth**—an **Integer** value containing the width of each cell, in pixels, within the control.
- *PictureClipControl*.**Clip**—a bitmap extracted from the **Picture** using the starting coordinate **ClipX** and **ClipY** and the height and width, **ClipHeight** and **ClipWidth**.
- *PictureClipControl*.**ClipHeight**—an **Integer** value containing the height of the clip area, in pixels, within the control.
- *PictureClipControl*.**ClipWidth**—an **Integer** value containing the width of the clip area cell, in pixels, within the control.

- *PictureClipControl*.**ClipX**—an **Integer** value containing the x coordinate, in pixels, of the upper-left corner of the area to be clipped.
- *PictureClipControl*.**ClipY**—an **Integer** value containing the Y coordinate, in pixels, of the upper-left corner of the area to be clipped.
- *PictureClipControl*.**Cols**—an **Integer** value containing the number of columns in the image. Setting this property will adjust the **CellWidth** property based on the total width of the image.
- *PictureClipControl*.**GraphicCell** (*index*)—a bitmap value containing the image at location *index*. Index can be computed from the desired value for row and column by the following formula:

```
index = PC1.Cols * row + col
```

where PC1.Cols is the number of columns in the image and row and col are the desired row and column from the grid. Rows and columns both begin with zero, so the cell at location 0,0 has an *index* value of zero.

- *PictureClipControl*.**Height**—an **Integer** value containing the height of the bitmap area in pixels. This property is read only at run time.
- *PictureClipControl*.**hWnd**—a **Long** that contains a Windows handle to the control.

> **Tip**
>
> The **hWnd** property is most useful when making calls to Windows API functions. Since this value can change during execution, do not save the value into a variable for later use.

- *PictureClipControl*.**Index**—an **Integer** that is used to uniquely identify a control in a control array.
- *PictureClipControl*.**Name**—a **String** that contains the name of the control that will be used to reference the control in a Visual Basic program. This property is read-only at run time.
- *PictureClipControl*.**Object**—an object that contains a reference to the *ListViewControl* object.
- *PictureClipControl*.**Parent**—an object that contains a reference to the **Form, Frame,** or other container that contains the **Image** control.
- *PictureClipControl*.**Picture**—a picture object (only a bitmap is directly supported) that will be displayed on the control. You can also use the **LoadPicture** function at run time to load a bitmap, icon, or metafile.
- *PictureClipControl*.**Rows**—an **Integer** value containing the number of rows in the image. Setting this property will adjust the **CellHeight** property based on the total height of the image.
- *PictureClipControl*.**StretchX**—an **Integer** value containing the size of the target image in pixels. The image in the picture clip will be either stretched or shrunk to fit the size.
- *PictureClipControl*.**StretchY**—an **Integer** value containing the size of the target image in pixels. The image in the picture clip will be either stretched or shrunk to fit the size.
- *PictureClipControl*.**Tag**—a **String** that can hold programmer-specific information. This property is not used by Visual Basic.
- *PictureClipControl*.**Width**—an **Integer** value containing the width of the bitmap area in pixels. This property is read only at run time.

| Examples | ``` 
Private Sub Command1_Click(Index As Integer)
   Picture1.Picture = PictureClip1.GraphicCell(Index)
End Sub
``` |

This program has three command buttons with the same name that is used to create a **CommandButton** array, a **PictureBox** control, and a **PictureClip** control. The **PictureClip** control is used to hold a bitmap with three different colored squares. Pressing any of the command buttons will display a different colored square in the **PictureBox** control.

See Also	**Image** (control), **PictureBox** (control), **LoadPicture** (function), **SavePicture** (statement)

Plot

OBJECT

PE, EE

Usage	The **Plot** object is used by the **MSChart** control to hold information about the chart's plot area.
Properties	▪ *PlotObject*.**AngleUnits**—an **Integer** value containing the units used to measure the angles.

AngleUnits Name	Description
vtAngleUnitsDegrees	Angles are measured in degrees.
vtAngleUnitsRadians	Angles are measured in radians.
vtAngleUnitsGrad	Angles are measured in gradients.

Table P-48: AngleUnits *values*.

▪ *PlotObject*.**AutoLayout**—a **Boolean** value when **True** means that the plot object automatically determines the size and location of the plot elements. **False** means that you will need to set the values.

▪ *PlotObject*.**Backdrop**—an object reference to a **Backdrop** object that describes the elements shown behind the chart.

▪ *PlotObject*.**BarGap**—a **Single** value that determines the gap between the bars in a bar chart. It ranges from a value of 0 (meaning that the bars are touching) to a value of 100 (meaning that the gaps are the same size as the bars).

▪ *PlotObject*.**Clockwise**—a **Boolean** value when **True** means that pie charts are drawn clockwise. **False** means that pie charts are drawn counterclockwise.

▪ *PlotObject*.**DataSeriesInRow**—a **Boolean** value when **True** means that the data for a series is read from a row in the data grid. **False** means that the data is read from a column in the data grid.

▪ *PlotObject*.**DefaultPercentBasis**—an **Integer** value containing the default axis starting percentage.

▪ *PlotObject*.**DepthToHeightRatio**—an **Integer** value containing the percentage of chart height to depth.

▪ *PlotObject*.**Light**—an object reference to a **Light** object that illuminates a three-dimensional chart.
```

- *PlotObject*.**LocationRect**—an object reference to a **Rect** object that specifies the location of the plot area.
- *PlotObject*.**PlotBase**—an object reference to a **PlotBase** object that describes the area beneath the chart.
- *PlotObject*.**Projection**—an **Integer** value containing the type of projection that will be used to display the chart.

Projection Name	Description
vtProjectionTypePerspective	A three-dimensional appearance. Objects that are further away from you converge to a vanishing point.
vtProjectionTypeOblique	A 2.5-dimensional appearance. While the chart has depth, the xy plane remains constant when the chart is rotated or elevated.
vtProjectionTypeOrthogonal	No perspective. Vertical lines are parallel.

Table P-49: Projection *values*.

- *PlotObject*.**Sort**—object reference to a **SeriesCollection** containing information about the data that generates the chart.
- *PlotObject*.**Sort**—an **Integer** value containing the sort order used for pie charts.

Sort Name	Description
vtSortTypeNone	The pie slices are drawn in the order of the data.
vtSortTypeAscending	The pie slices are drawn from the smallest to the largest.
vtSortTypeDescending	The pie slices are drawn from the largest to the smallest.

Table P-50: Sort *values*.

- *PlotObject*.**StartingAngle**—a **Single** containing the starting position of a pie chart that measures in **AngleUnits** in the direction of the **Clockwise** property. A value of zero degrees is pointing due east. A value of 90 degrees is a point due north if **Clockwise** is **True**, otherwise it is pointing 90 degrees due south.
- *PlotObject*.**SubPlotLabelPosition**—an **Integer** value containing the position of the labels on a pie chart.

SubPlotLabelPosition Name	Description
vtSubPlotLabelLocationTypeNone	The subplot label is not displayed.
vtSubPlotLabelLocationTypeAbove	The subplot label is displayed above the pie.
vtSubPlotLabelLocationTypeBelow	The subplot label is displayed below the pie.
vtSubPlotLabelLocationTypeCenter	The subplot label is displayed on the pie.

Table P-51: SubPlotLabelPosition *values*.

- *PlotObject*.**UniformAxis**—a **Boolean** value when **True** means that the unit scale will be the same for all axes. **False** means that the **AutoLayout** and **LocationRect** properties will determine the unit scale.

- *PlotObject*.**View3D**—an object reference to a **View3D** object describing the view of a three-dimensional chart.
- *PlotObject*.**Wall**—an object reference to a **Wall** object describing the planar area for the y axis on a three-dimensional chart.
- *PlotObject*.**Weighting**—an object reference to a **Weighting** object that describes the size of a pie relative to the size of other pies in the chart.
- *PlotObject*.**WidthToHeightRatio**—an **Integer** value containing the percentage of chart height to width.
- *PlotObject*.**XGap**—a **Single** value that determines the spacing of bars between divisions on the x axis. A value of 0 means that the bars are touching.
- *PlotObject*.**YGap**—a **Single** value that determines the spacing of bars between divisions on the y axis. A value of 0 means that the bars are touching.

See Also **MSChart** (control)

PlotBase

OBJECT

PE, EE

Usage The **PlotBase** object is used by the **Plot** object of the **MSChart** control to hold information about the area beneath a chart.

Properties
- *PlotBaseObject*.**BaseHeight**—a **Single** value containing the height in points of the three-dimensional chart base.
- *PlotBaseObject*.**Brush**—an object reference to a **Brush** object containing information about the fill type for the area beneath the chart.
- *PlotBaseObject*.**Pen**—an object reference to a **Pen** object that describes the lines and colors of the edges shown behind the chart.

Pmt

FUNCTION

CCE, LE, PE, EE

Syntax pmt = **Pmt**(rate, nper, pv [, fv [, type]])

Usage The **Pmt** function returns the total payment (interest and principal) for a fixed-rate, fixed-payment annuity. Cash paid out is represented by negative numbers. Cash received is represented by positive numbers.

Arguments
- *pmt*—a **Double** value containing the interest payment for the period specified by *pper*.
- *rate*—a **Double** value containing the interest rate per period.
- *nper*—a **Double** value containing the number of periods in the annuity.
- *pv*—a **Double** value containing the present value of the annuity.

- *fv*—a **Variant** value containing the future value of the annuity. If omitted, 0 will be assumed.
- *type*—a **Variant** value, when 0, means that the payment is due at the end of the period. When 1, means that the payment is due at the beginning of the period. If not specified, it will default to 0.

Examples
```
Private Sub Command1_Click()
Text5.Text = Format(Pmt(CDbl(Text1.Text), CDbl(Text2.Text), CDbl(Text3.Text),
    CDbl(Text4.Text)), "currency")
End Sub
```

This routine computes the interest payment for a particular period.

See Also **DDB** (function), **FV** (function), **IPmt** (function), **IRR** (function), **MIRR** (function), **NPer** (function), **NPV** (function), **PPmt** (function), **PV** (function), **Rate** (function), **SLN** (function), **SYD** (function).

PPmt

FUNCTION

CCE, LE, PE, EE

Syntax *pmt* = **PPmt**(*rate, pper, nper, pv* [, *fv* [, *type*]])

Usage The **PPmt** function returns the principal payment for a fixed-rate, fixed-payment annuity. Cash paid out is represented by negative numbers. Cash received is represented by positive numbers.

Arguments
- *pmt*—a **Double** value containing the interest payment for the period specified by *pper*.
- *rate*—a **Double** value containing the interest rate per period.
- *pper*—a **Double** value containing the period for which the payment will be computed.
- *nper*—a **Double** value containing the number of periods in the annuity.
- *pv*—a **Double** value containing the present value of the annuity.
- *fv*—a **Variant** value containing the future value of the annuity. If omitted, 0 will be assumed.
- *type*—a **Variant** value, when 0, means that the payment is due at the end of the period. When 1, means that the payment is due at the beginning of the period. If not specified, it will default to 0.

Examples
```
Private Sub Command1_Click()
Text5.Text = Format(PPmt(CDbl(Text1.Text), CDbl(Text2.Text), CDbl(Text3.Text),
    CDbl(Text4.Text)), "currency")
End Sub
```

This routine computes the principal payment for a particular period.

See Also **DDB** (function), **FV** (function), **IPmt** (function), **IRR** (function), **MIRR** (function), **NPer** (function), **NPV** (function), **Pmt** (function), **PV** (function), **Rate** (function), **SLN** (function), **SYD** (function).

Print
STATEMENT

CCE, LE, PE, EE

Syntax   **Print #** *filenum*, [*printexpr* [{ **,** | **;** } *printexpr*] . . .] [{ **,** | **;** }]

Usage   The **Print #** statement is used to write formatted data to a file.

> **Tip**
>
> Use the **Input #** or **Line Input #** statement to read data written with the **Print #** statement.

Arguments
- *filenum*—any open file number that was assigned in an **Open** statement.
- *printexpr*—any **Boolean**, numeric, or s**String** expression, plus the functions listed below. If *printexpr* is omitted, then a blank line will be printed. A comma (",") is used to position the print cursor at the next print zone. A semicolon (";") is used to position the print cursor immediately after the expression that was just printed. Each print zone is 14 characters wide and begins with column 1. Note that the print zones are characters and not inches, so you may experience problems when using proportional character fonts.
- **Spc**(*chars*)—prints the specified number of spaces.
- **Tab** [(*col*)]—positions the print cursor at the specified print column. If the print column is less than the current position of the cursor, then the print cursor will be moved to the next line. If no argument is specified, the cursor will be positioned at the beginning of the next print zone.

Examples
```
Private Sub Command2_Click()
Open App.Path & "\testfile.dat" For Output As #1
Print #1, Text1.Text
Close #1
End Sub
```

This routine writes the information contained in the Text1 text box to the file testfile.dat.

See Also   **Close** (statement), **Input** (statement), **Line Input** (statement), **Open** (statement)

Printer
OBJECT

CCE, LE, PE, EE

Usage   The **Printer** object provides information necessary to access a system printer. You can query and set various properties to configure the printer to your application's needs and then use the supplied methods to output text and graphics to the printer.

> **Tip**
>
> Many of the properties and methods are highly dependent on the printer and printer driver used. See the printer and the printer driver's documentation for more information.

Properties
- *PrinterObject*.**ColorMode**—an **Integer** value (see Table P-52) showing whether a color printer should generate monochrome or color output. This property is ignored if the printer can't print in color.

ColorMode Name	Value	Description
vbPRCMMonochrome	1	Output will be in black and white.
vbPRCMColor	2	Output will be in color.

Table P-52: ColorMode *values.*

- *PrinterObject*.**Copies**—an **Integer** value containing the number of copies of the output to be printed. The actual effect of this value will be determined by the printer driver.
- *PrinterObject*.**CurrentX**—a **Single** that specifies the horizontal coordinate measured from the printer's left edge for these various drawing methods: **Circle**, **Cls**, **EndDoc**, **Line**, **NewPage**, **Print**, and **PSet**.
- *PrinterObject*.**CurrentY**—a **Single** that specifies the vertical coordinate measured from the printer's top edge for these various drawing methods: **Circle**, **Cls**, **EndDoc**, **Line**, **NewPage**, **Print**, and **PSet**.
- *PrinterObject*.**DeviceName**—a **String** containing the name of the printer, as defined in the printer's device driver.
- *PrinterObject*.**DrawMode**—an **Integer** specifying how the drawing methods: **Circle**, **Cls**, **EndDoc**, **Line**, **NewPage**, **Print**, and **PSet**.

DrawMode Name	Value	Description
vbBlackness	1	Blackness.
vbNotMergePen	2	Inverse of *vbMergePen*.
vbMaskNotPen	3	Combination of the colors common to the background color and the inverse of the pen.
vbNotCopyPen	4	Inverse of *vbCopyPen*.
vbMaskPenNot	5	Combination of the colors common to the pen and the inverse of the background.
vbInvert	6	Inverse of the display color.
vbXorPen	7	Combination of the colors in the display and the pen, but not in both.
vbNotMaskPen	8	Inverse setting of *vbMaskPen*.
vbMaskPen	9	Combination of the colors common to the pen and the display.
vbNotXorPen	10	Inverse setting of *vbXorPen*.
vbNop	11	Turns drawing off.
vbMergeNotPen	12	Combination of the display and inverse of the pen color.
vbCopyPen	13	Color specified in the **ForeColor** property.
vbMergePenNot	14	Combination of the pen color and the inverse of the display color.
vbMergePen	15	Combination of the pen color and the display color.
vbWhiteness	16	Whiteness.

Table P-53: DrawMode *values.*

- *PrinterObject*.**DrawStyle**—an **Integer** specifying how the drawing methods **Circle**, **Cls**, **EndDoc**, **Line**, **NewPage**, **Print**, and **PSet** will appear on the form. If **DrawWidth** is greater than 1, then *vbDash*, *vbDot*, *vbDashDot*, and *vbDashDotDot* will draw a solid line.

DrawStyle Name	Value	Description
vbSolid	0	Solid line.
vbDash	1	Dashed line.
vbDot	2	Dotted line.
vbDashDot	3	Dash followed by a dot.
vbDashDotDot	4	Dash followed by two dots.
vbInvisible	5	No displayed line.
vbInsideSolid	6	Inside is solid.

Table P-54: DrawStyle *values*.

- *PrinterObject*.**DrawWidth**—an **Integer** specifying the width of the line, in pixels, that will be drawn by the following methods: **Circle**, **Cls**, **EndDoc**, **Line**, **NewPage**, **Print**, and **PSet**. If **DrawWidth** is greater than 1, then the **DrawStyles** *vbDash*, *vbDot*, *vbDashDot*, and *vbDashDotDot* will draw a solid line.
- *PrinterObject*.**DriverName**—a **String** value containing the name of the device driver.
- *PrinterObject*.**Duplex**—an **Integer** value (see Table P-55) describing how the output will be generated, assuming that the printer is capable of duplex printing.

Duplex Name	Value	Description
vbPRDPSimplex	1	Single-sided printing.
vbPRDPHorizontal	2	Double-sided printing, using a horizontal page turn.
vbPRDPVertical	3	Double-sided printing, using a vertical page turn.

Table P-55: Duplex *values*.

- *PrinterObject*.**FillColor**—a **Long** that contains the color that will be used to fill in shapes created with the following graphical methods: **Circle**, **Cls**, **EndDoc**, **Line**, **NewPage**, **Print**, and **PSet**.
- *PrinterObject*.**FillStyle**—an **Integer** specifying how the drawing methods **Circle**, **Cls**, **EndDoc**, **Line**, **NewPage**, **Print**, and **PSet** will appear on the form. If **DrawWidth** is greater than 1, then *vbDash*, *vbDot*, *vbDashDot*, and *vbDashDotDot* will draw a solid line.

FillStyle Name	Value	Description
vbFSSolid	0	Solid.
vbFSTransparent	1	Transparent.
vbHorizontalLine	2	Horizontal line.
vbVerticalLine	3	Vertical line.
vbUpwardDiagonal	4	Upward diagonal.
vbDownwardDiagonal	5	Downward diagonal.
vbCross	6	Cross.
vbDiagonalCross	7	Diagonal cross.

Table P-56: FillStyle *values*.

- *PrinterObject*.**Font**—an object that contains information about the character font used by this object.

> **Tip**
>
> *Setting values for the **Font** object on the form at design time makes these values the default when other controls and objects are placed on the form.*

- *PrinterObject*.**FontBold**—a **Boolean,** when **True**, means that the characters are displayed in bold. **False** means that the characters are displayed normally.
- *PrinterObject*.**FontCount**—an **Integer** containing the number of fonts available in the **Fonts** property.
- *PrinterObject*.**FontItalic**—a **Boolean,** when **True**, means that the characters are displayed in italics. **False** means that the characters are displayed normally.
- *PrinterObject*.**FontName**—a **String** that specifies the name of the font that should be used to display the characters in this control.
- *PrinterObject*.**Fonts** (*index*)—an array of **Strings** containing the available font names for the printer. *Index* can range in value from zero to **FontCount** -1.
- *PrinterObject*.**FontSize**—a **Single** that is used to specify the point size that should be used to display the characters in the control.
- *PrinterObject*.**FontStrikethru**—a **Boolean,** when **True**, means that the characters are displayed with a line through the center. **False** means that the characters are displayed normally.
- *PrinterObject*.**FontTransparent**—a **Boolean,** when **True,** means that the background graphics and text will show through the open spaces in a character (default). **False** means that the background will not show through.
- *PrinterObject*.**FontUnderlined**—a **Boolean,** when **True**, means that the characters are displayed with a line beneath them. **False** means that the characters are displayed normally.
- *PrinterObject*.**ForeColor**—a **Long** that contains the suggested value for the foreground color of the contained control. This property is read only at run time.
- *PrinterObject*.**hDC**—a **Long** that contains a handle to the device context to the form.
- *PrinterObject*.**Height**—a **Single** that contains the height of the page.
- *PrinterObject*.**Orientation**—an **Integer** that specifies how the paper will be oriented in the printer.

Orientation Name	Value	Description
vbPRORPortrait	1	The paper is taller than wide.
vbPRORLandscape	2	The paper is wider than tall.

Table P-57: Orientation *values.*

- *PrinterObject*.**Page**—an **Integer** containing the current page number.
- *PrinterObject*.**PaperBin**—an **Integer** that specifies which bin should be used to feed paper to the printer.

PaperBin Name	Value	Description
vbPRBNUpper	1	Use the upper bin.
vbPRBNLower	2	Use the lower bin.
vbPRBNMiddle	3	Use the middle bin.
vbPRBNManual	4	Use manual feed.
vbPRBNEnvelope	5	Use the envelope feeder.
vbPRBNEnvManual	6	Manually feed envelopes.
vbPRBNAuto	7	Use the current default bin.
vbPRBNTractor	8	Use tractor feeder.
vbPRBNSmallFmt	9	Use the small paper feeder.
vbPRBNLargeFmt	10	Use the large paper feeder.
vbPRBNLargeCapacity	11	Use the large capacity feeder.
vbPRBNCassette	12	Use the paper from the attached cassette.

Table P-58: PaperBin *values.*

- **PrinterObject.PaperSize**—an **Integer** that specifies the paper size. If you specify either the **Height** or **Width** properties, the **PaperSize** will be set to *vbPRPSUser*.

PaperSize Name	Value	Description
vbPRPSLetter	1	Letter: 8.5 x 11 in.
vbPRPSLetterSmall	2	Letter Small: 8.5 x 11 in.
vbPRPSTabloid	3	Tabloid: 11 x 17 in.
vbPRPSLedger	4	Ledger: 17 x 11 in.
vbPRPSLegal	5	Legal: 8.5 x 14 in.
vbPRPSStatement	6	Statement: 5.5 x 8 1/2 in.
vbPRPSExecutive	7	Executive: 7.5 x 10 1/2 in.
vbPRPSA3	8	A3: 297 x 420 mm
vbPRPSA4	9	A4: 210 x 297 mm
vbPRPSA4Small	10	A4 Small: 210 x 297 mm
vbPRPSA5	11	A5: 148 x 210 mm
vbPRPSB4	12	B4: 250 x 354 mm
vbPRPSB5	13	B5: 182 x 257 mm
vbPRPSFolio	14	Folio: 8.5 x 13 in.
vbPRPSQuarto	15	Quarto: 215 x 275 mm
vbPRPS10x14	16	10 x 14 in.
vbPRPS11x17	17	11 x 17 in.
vbPRPSNote	18	Note: 8 1/2 x 11 in.
vbPRPSEnv9	19	Envelope #9: 3 7/8 x 8 7/8 in.
vbPRPSEnv10	20	Envelope #10: 4 1/8 x 9 1/2 in.
vbPRPSEnv11	21	Envelope #11: 4 1/2 x 10 3/8 in.
vbPRPSEnv12	22	Envelope #12: 4 1/2 x 11 in.
vbPRPSEnv14	23	Envelope #14: 5 x 11 1/2 in.
vbPRPSCSheet	24	C size sheet
vbPRPSDSheet	25	D size sheet

Printer • 727

PaperSize Name	Value	Description
vbPRPSESheet	26	E size sheet
vbPRPSEnvDL	27	Envelope DL: 110 x 220 mm
vbPRPSEnvC3	29	Envelope C3: 324 x 458 mm
vbPRPSEnvC4	30	Envelope C4: 229 x 324 mm
vbPRPSEnvC5	28	Envelope C5: 162 x 229 mm
vbPRPSEnvC6	31	Envelope C6: 114 x 162 mm
vbPRPSEnvC65	32	Envelope C65: 114 x 229 mm
vbPRPSEnvB4	33	Envelope B4: 250 x 353 mm
vbPRPSEnvB5	34	Envelope B5: 176 x 250 mm
vbPRPSEnvB6	35	Envelope B6: 176 x 125 mm
vbPRPSEnvItaly	36	Envelope: 110 x 230 mm
vbPRPSEnvMonarch	37	Envelope Monarch: 3 7/8 x 7 1/2 in.
vbPRPSEnvPersonal	38	Envelope: 3 5/8 x 6 1/2 in.
vbPRPSFanfoldUS	39	U.S. Standard Fanfold: 14 7/8 x 11 in.
vbPRPSFanfoldStdGerman	40	German Standard Fanfold: 8 1/2 x 12 in.
vbPRPSFanfoldLglGerman	41	German Legal Fanfold: 8 1/2 x 13 in.
vbPRPSUser	256	User-defined

Table P-59: PaperSize *values.*

- *PrinterObject*.**Port**—a **String** that contains the name of the port to which the printer is attached.
- *PrinterObject*.**PrintQuality**—an **Integer** value (see Table P-60) that describes the print quality. In addition to the constants, you can set this property to the number of dots per inch (i.e., 300) desired.

PrintQuality Name	Value	Description
vbPRPQDraft	-1	Draft quality.
vbPRPQLow	-2	Low resolution.
vbPRPQMedium	-3	Medium resolution.
vbPRPQHigh	-4	High resolution.

Table P-60: PrintQuality *values.*

- *PrinterObject*.**ScaleHeight**—an **Integer** value that sets or returns the height of the object in the units specified by **ScaleMode**.
- *PrinterObject*.**ScaleLeft**—an **Integer** value that sets or returns the value of the X-coordinate of the left edge of the page.
- *PrinterObject*.**ScaleMode**—an **Integer** value (see Table P-61) that describes the unit of measurement used for the printer.

Tip

When dealing with graphic images such as BMP or GIF files it is often useful to set **ScaleMode** *to* vbPixels *to help set the proper relationships.*

ScaleMode Name	Value	Description
vbUser	0	Measurements are custom defined, based on the values in ScaleHeight, ScaleLeft, ScaleTop, or ScaleWidth properties.
vbTwips	1	Measurements are in twips (1440 twips per inch).
vbPoints	2	Measurements are in points (72 per inch).
vbPixels	3	Measurements are in pixels (smallest unit of measure for a monitor or printer).
vbCharacters	4	Measurements are in characters (horizontal = 120 twips per character, vertical = 240 twips per character).
vbInches	5	Measurements are in inches.
vbMillimeters	6	Measurements are in millimeters.
vbCentimeters	7	Measurements are in centimeters.

Table P-61: ScaleMode values.

- *PrinterObject*.**ScaleTop**—an **Integer** value that sets or returns the value of the Y-coordinate of the top edge of the page.
- *PrinterObject*.**ScaleWidth**—an **Integer** value that sets or returns the width of the object in the units specified by **ScaleMode**.
- *PrinterObject*.**TrackDefault**—a **Boolean** value when **True** means that **Printer** object will change when the default system printer changes. **False** means that the **Printer** object will continue to point to the same printer, even if the default system printer changes.
- *PrinterObject*.**Tag**—a **String** that can hold programmer-specific information. This property is not used by Visual Basic.
- *PrinterObject*.**TwipsPerPixelX**—a **Single** containing the number of twips occupied by a single pixel horizontally. This value is useful for converting pixels into twips without setting the **ScaleMode** property.
- *PrinterObject*.**TwipsPerPixelY**—a **Single** containing the number of twips occupied by a single pixel vertically. This value is useful for converting pixels into twips without setting the **ScaleMode** property.
- *PrinterObject*.**Width**—a **Single** that contains the width of the page.
- *PrinterObject*.**Zoom**—a **Single** containing the percentage of which the print is scaled up or down. A value of 50 means that an 8.5 x 11 page can hold the same content as a 17 x 22 page.

Methods

PrinterObject.Circle [Step] (x , y), radius [, color [, start [, stop [, aspect]]]]

Usage: This method draws a circle, an ellipse, or a curved line on the page. All coordinate information used is relative to the **ScaleMode, ScaleHeight, ScaleLeft, ScaleTop,** and **ScaleWidth**.

Arguments:
- **Step**—a keyword that specifies that the coordinates are relative to the page's **CurrentX** and **CurrentY** properties.
- *x*—a **Single** specifying the X-coordinate of the center of the circle.

- *y*—a **Single** specifying the Y-coordinate of the center of the circle.
- *radius*—a **Single** specifying the radius of the circle.
- *color*—a **Long** containing the color of the line to be drawn. If omitted, it will default to the value in the **ForeColor** property.
- *start*—a **Single** specifying the starting angle for the circle, in radians. If omitted, it will default to zero.
- *stop*—a **Single** specifying the ending angle for the circle, in radians. It omitted, it will default to 2 times pi (approximately 6.28).
- *aspect*—a **Single** specifying the height-to-width ratio of the circle. The default is 1.0, which will yield a perfect circle.

Tip

To draw a half-circle, assign start *a value of 0 and* stop *a value of pi (approximately 3.14), and choose values for the other parameters.*

To draw a vertical ellipse, assign a value greater than 1.0 to aspect. *A horizontal ellipse would have an aspect ratio of less than 1.0.*

PrinterObject.EndDoc

Usage — This method finishes the print operation and releases the output to the print spooler or printer.

PrinterObject.KillDoc

Usage — This method finishes the print operation and instructs **PrintManager** to kill the spool file. If **PrintManager** is not controlling the printer, then some output may have been produced. This method will reset the printer as soon as possible to prevent any other output from printing.

PrinterObject.Line [Step] (x1 , y1), [Step] (x2 , y2) [, B | BF]

Usage — This method draws lines or boxes on the form. All coordinate information used is relative to the **ScaleMode**, **ScaleHeight**, **ScaleLeft**, **ScaleTop**, and **ScaleWidth**.

Arguments
- **Step**—a keyword that specifies that the *x1* and *y1* coordinates are relative to the form's **CurrentX** and **CurrentY** properties.
  - *x1*—a **Single** specifying the starting X-coordinate of the center of the line or box.
  - *y1*—a **Single** specifying the starting Y-coordinate of the center of the line or box.
  - **Step**—a keyword that specifies that the *x2* and *y2* coordinates are relative to the form's **CurrentX** and **CurrentY** properties.
  - *x2*—a **Single** specifying the stopping X-coordinate of the center of the line or box.
  - *y2*—a **Single** specifying the stopping Y-coordinate of the center of the line or box.

- *color*—a **Long** containing the color of the line to be drawn. If omitted, it will default to the value in the **ForeColor** property.
- *B*—draw a box with (*x1*, *y1*) and (*x2*, *y2*) specifying the opposite corners of the box. If omitted, a line will be drawn on the form.
- *BF*—draw a box with (*x1*, *y1*) and (*x2*, *y2*) specifying the opposite corners of the box and fill the interior with the color specified by **FillColor** and **FillStyle**. If omitted, a line will be drawn on the form.

PrinterObject.NewPage

Usage   This method will eject the current page and begin a new page. The **Page** property will also be incremented.

PrinterObject.PaintPicture *picture, x1 , y1,* [*width1*] , [*height1*] ,[*x2*] , [*y2*] , [*width2*] , [*height2*] , [*rasterop*]

Usage   This method displays an image (.BMP, .DIB, .EMF, .ICO, or .WMF) on the form. All coordinate information used is relative to the **ScaleMode**, **ScaleHeight**, **ScaleLeft**, **ScaleTop**, and **ScaleWidth**.

Arguments
- *picture*—the image to be displayed on the form. It can come from the **Picture** property of a picture box or another form.
- *x1*—a **Single** specifying the starting X-coordinate of the picture.
- *y1*—a **Single** specifying the starting Y-coordinate of the picture.
- *width1*—a **Single** specifying the width of the image. If omitted, the width will default to the width of the image. If greater or less than the width of the image, the image will be stretched or shrunk to fit.
- *height1*—a **Single** specifying the height of the image. If omitted, the height will default to the height of the image. If greater or less than the height of the image, the image will be stretched or shrunk to fit.
- *x2*—a **Single** specifying the starting X-coordinate of a clipping region within the picture. If omitted, zero will be used.
- *y2*—a **Single** specifying the starting Y-coordinate of a clipping region within the picture. If omitted, zero will be used.
- *width2*—a **Single** specifying the width of the clipping region of the image. If omitted, the width will default to the width of the image. If greater or less than the width of the image, the image will be stretched or shrunk to fit.
- *height2*—a **Single** specifying the height of the clipping region of the image. If omitted, the height will default to the height of the image. If greater or less than the height of the image, the image will be stretched or shrunk to fit.
- *rasterop*—a **Long** containing a raster op code from Table P-62 below that will perform a bit-wise operation on the image as it is displayed. The default will be to display the image as is.

Printer • **731**

RasterOp Name	Value	Description
vbDstInvert	&H005A0049	Inverts the destination image.
vbMergeCopy	&H00C000CA	Combines the source and the pattern.
vbMergePaint	&H00BB0226	Combines the inverted source image with the destination image using OR.
vbNotSrcCopy	&H00330008	Copies inverted source image to the destination.
vbNotSrcErase	&H001100A6	Inverts the result of combining the source and destination images using OR.
vbPatCopy	&H00F00021	Copies the source pattern to the destination bitmap.
vbPatInvert	&H005A0049	Combines the inverted source pattern with the destination image using XOR.
vbPatPaint	&H00FB0A09	Combines the destination image with the source pattern.
vbScrAnd	&H008800C6	Combines the destination and source images using AND.
vbSrcCopy	&H00CC0020	Copies the source image to the destination bitmap.
vbSrcErase	&H00440328	Combines the inverted destination image with the source image by using AND.
vbSrcInvert	&H00660046	Combines the source and destination images using XOR.
vbSrcPaint	&H00EE0086	Combines the source and destination images using OR.

Table P-62: RasterOp values.

PrinterObject.PSet [Step] (*x* , *y*), [*color*]

Usage — This method sets the point at *x*, *y* to the color specified in *color*. All coordinate information used is relative to the **ScaleMode, ScaleHeight, ScaleLeft, ScaleTop,** and **ScaleWidth.**

Arguments
- **Step**—keyword that specifies that the *x* and *y* coordinates are relative to the form's **CurrentX** and **CurrentY** properties.
- *x*—a **Single** specifying the X-coordinate of the point.
- *y*—a **Single** specifying the Y-coordinate of the point.
- *color*—a **Long** containing the color to be displayed at location *x*, *y*. If omitted, this value will default to the value of **ForeColor.**

PrinterObject.Scale [(*x1* , *y1*) - (*x2* , *y2*)]

Usage — This method will define the coordinate system used on the form and set the appropriate values in **ScaleMode, ScaleHeight, ScaleLeft, ScaleTop,** and **ScaleWidth**. If the **Scale** method is used without any arguments, the coordinate is reset to default.

Arguments
- *x1*—a **Single** specifying the X-coordinate of the left edge of the form.
- *y1*—a **Single** specifying the Y-coordinate of the top edge of the form.
- *x2*—a **Single** specifying the X-coordinate of the right edge of the form.
- *y2*—a **Single** specifying the Y-coordinate of the bottom edge of the form.

result = PrinterObject.ScaleX (width , fromscale , toscale)

Usage   This method will compute a new value for *width* in a different scale.

Arguments
- *result*—a **Single** containing a new value for *width*.
- *fromscale*—an **Integer** specifying a **ScaleMode** value for the current *width*.
- *toscale*—an **Integer** value (see Table P-63) specifying the **ScaleMode** value for the new *width*.

ScaleMode Name	Value	Description
vbUser	0	Measurements are custom defined, based on the values in ScaleHeight, ScaleLeft, ScaleTop, or ScaleWidth properties.
vbTwips	1	Measurements are in twips (1440 twips per inch).
vbPoints	2	Measurements are in points (72 per inch).
vbPixels	3	Measurements are in pixels (smallest unit of measure for a monitor or printer).
vbCharacters	4	Measurements are in characters (horizontal = 120 twips per character, vertical = 240 twips per character).
vbInches	5	Measurements are in inches.
vbMillimeters	6	Measurements are in millimeters.
vbCentimeters	7	Measurements are in centimeters.
vbHimetric	8	Measurements are in himetrics.

Table P-63: ScaleMode *values.*

result = PrinterObject.ScaleY (height , fromscale , toscale)

Usage   This method will compute a new value for *height* in a different scale.

Arguments
- *result*—a **Single** containing a new value for *height*.
- *fromscale*—an **Integer** specifying a **ScaleMode** value for the current *height*.
- *toscale*—an **Integer** value (see Table P-64) specifying the **ScaleMode** value for the new *height*.

ScaleMode Name	Value	Description
vbUser	0	Measurements are custom defined, based on the values in ScaleHeight, ScaleLeft, ScaleTop, or ScaleWidth properties.
vbTwips	1	Measurements are in twips (1440 twips per inch).
vbPoints	2	Measurements are in points (72 per inch).

ScaleMode Name	Value	Description
vbPixels	3	Measurements are in pixels (smallest unit of measure for a monitor or printer).
vbCharacters	4	Measurements are in characters (horizontal = 120 twips per character, vertical = 240 twips per character).
vbInches	5	Measurements are in inches.
vbMillimeters	6	Measurements are in millimeters.
vbCentimeters	7	Measurements are in centimeters.
vbHimetric	8	Measurements are in himetrics.

Table P-64: ScaleMode *values.*

height = PrinterObject.TextHeight (string)

Usage This method will compute the height of the string in the units specified by **ScaleMode**. The height is computed using the font information specified in the **Font** object. It will also include space at the top and the bottom of the characters, so that multiple lines of text can be placed next to each other. If *string* contains embedded carriage return linefeed pairs, then the total height of the block of text will be returned.

Arguments
- *height*—a **Single** that contains the height of *string*.
- *string*—a **String** that contains characters to be printed on the form.

width = PrinterObject.TextWidth (string)

Usage This method will compute the width of the string in the units specified by **ScaleMode**. The width is computed using the font information specified in the **Font** object. If *string* contains embedded carriage return linefeed pairs, then the length of the longest line will be returned.

Arguments
- *width*—a **Single** that contains the width of *string*.
- *string*—a **String** that contains characters to be printed on the form.

Examples

```
Private Sub Command1_Click()
MsgBox Printer.DeviceName
End Sub
```

This routine displays the name of the default printer.

See Also **Printers** (collection)

Printers

COLLECTION

PE, EE

Usage
: The **Printers** collection contains a set of **Printer** objects.

> **Caution**
>
> While the Microsoft documentation states that you can access a specific printer value using the form **Printers** (index), this syntax is not accepted by Visual Basic. I suggest that you use the **CommonDialog** control to select a printer.

> **Tip**
>
> To loop through each item in the collection, use the **For Each** statement.

Properties
: *PrintersCollection*.**Count**—a **Long** value that contains the number of items in the collection.

Examples
:
```
Private Sub Form_Load()
Dim p As Printer
For Each p In Printers
    Combo1.AddItem p.DeviceName
Next p
End Sub
```

This routine displays a list of available printers in a combo box.

See Also
: **CommonDialog** (control), **Printer** (object)

Private

STATEMENT

CCE, LE, PE, EE

Syntax
: **Private** [**WithEvents**] *identifier*[*typechar*] [*arrayinfo*] [**As** [**New**] *type*]
, [[**WithEvents**] *identifier*[*typechar*] [*arrayinfo*] [**As** [**New**] *type*]
] . . .

Usage
: The **Private** statement is used to declare the variables at the module level, outside any procedure. These variables will be available to all of the routines in the module, but can't be accessed from outside the module.

   If **Option Explicit** is included in a module, then all of the variables used in your program must be declared before they can be used.

> **Tip**
>
> Use **Option Explicit** in all modules, because this will force you to declare all variables before you use them. This will help you avoid the situation where you think you have one variable, but Visual Basic thinks you have two because you used two different spellings.

Arguments
- **WithEvents**—an optional keyword used only in class modules that means *Variable* is used to respond to events triggered by an ActiveX object.
- *identifier*—the Visual Basic identifier that will be used to reference this particular variable. It must begin with a letter, which can be followed by any number of letters or numbers or the underscore character ("_"). Identifiers are not case sensitive, though the case will be preserved for easier reading.
- *typechar*—one of the following characters can be included as the last character of a variable name to declare its type: "@" for **Currency**, "#" for **Double**, "%" for **Integer**, "&" for **Long**, "!" for **Single**, or "$" for **String**. The default type for variables without a typechar is **Variant** unless the type is specified using the **As** clause or by using one of the **Deftype** statements.
- *arrayinfo*—optionally indicates an array. It can have zero or more dimensions. An array can have no more than 60 dimensions. If no dimensions are specified, then the variable is considered a dynamic array and the subscripts must be set with the **ReDim** statement before it can be used. The subscripts are defined as:

([*ubound* | *lbound* **To** *ubound*] [, *ubound* | , *lbound* **To** *ubound*]
   . . .)]

ubound	the upper bound for an array.
lbound	the lower bound for an array's subscript. If omitted, the value from **Option Base** will be used. If there is no **Option Base** statement in the module, zero is assumed.

- **New**—an optional keyword that means that a new instance of the object is automatically created the first time it is used. It can't be used with either the **WithEvents** keyword or with a non-object type.
- *type*—a valid Visual Basic type: **Byte**, **Boolean**, **Currency**, **Date**, **Double**, **Integer**, **Long**, **Single**, **String**, **Object**, or **Variant**. Specific objects can also be used, as well as user-defined types defined with the **Type** statement.

Examples
```
Private MyCount As Integer
Option Explicit

Private Sub Command1_Click()
MyCount = MyCount + 1
Text1.Text = Format(MyCount)
End Sub
```

```
Private Sub Command2_Click()
MyCount = MyCount--1
Text1.Text = Format(MyCount)
End Sub

Private Sub Form_Load()
MyCount = 0
Text1.Text = Format(MyCount)
End Sub
```

This demonstrates how a module level variable can keep a value that is independent of any one routine.

See Also **Byte** (data type), **Boolean** (data type), **Currency** (data type), **Date** (data type), **Dim** (statement), **Double** (data type), **Integer** (data type), **Long** (data type), **Object** (data type), **Option Base** (statement), **Option Explicit** (statement), **Public** (statement), **ReDim** (statement), **Single** (data type), **String** (data type), **Static** (statement), **Type** (statement), **TypeName** (function), **Variant** (data type)

ProgressBar

CONTROL

PE, EE

Usage The **ProgressBar** control is an ActiveX control that can be used to display the progress of a long running operation.

Properties *ProgressBarControl*.**Align**—an **Integer** value that describes the placement of the control.

Align Name	Value	Description
vbAlignNone	0	The control's position is set at design time or by the program (default value for objects on a non-MDI Form).
vbAlignTop	1	The control is placed at the top of the form and its width is set to **ScaleWidth**. It will automatically be resized when the form is resized (default value for objects on a MDI Form).
vbAlignBottom	2	The control is placed at the bottom of the form and its width is set to **ScaleWidth**. It will automatically be resized when the form is resized.
vbAlignLeft	3	The control is placed at the left edge of the form and its width is set to **ScaleWidth**. It is not resized when the form is resized.
vbAlignLeft	4	The control is placed at the right edge of the form and its width is set to **ScaleWidth**. It is not resized when the form is resized.

Table P-65: Align *values.*

- *ProgressBarControl.***Appearance**—an **Integer** value that specifies how the label will appear on the form.

Appearance Value	Description
0	The label is displayed without the 3D effects.
1	The label is displayed with 3D effects (default value.)

Table P-66: Appearance *values.*

- *ProgressBarControl.***BorderStyle**—an **Integer** specifying how the border will be drawn.

BorderStyle Name	Value	Description
vbBSNone	0	No border is displayed.
vbFixedSingle	1	Single line around the label.

Table P-67: BorderStyle *values.*

- *ProgressBarControl.***Container**—an object that can be used to set or return the container of the control at run time. This property cannot be set at design time.
- *ProgressBarControl.***DragIcon**—an object that contains the picture value of an icon. At design time, you can specify an icon file that has a file type of .ico.

Tip

*This value can be created by copying the value from another control's **DragIcon** value, by copying a form's icon, or by using the **LoadPicture** function.*

- *ProgressBarControl.***DragMode**—an **Integer** specifying how the control will respond to a drag request.

Tip

*Setting **DragMode** to* vbAutomatic *will automatically begin a drag operation when the user clicks on the control. However, the control will not respond to the usual mouse events (**Click**, **DblClick**).*

DragMode Name	Value	Description
vbManual	0	The Drag method must be used to begin a drag-and-drop operation (default value).
vbAutomatic	1	The source control will automatically begin a drag-and-drop operation when the user clicks on the control.

Table P-68: DragMode *values.*

- *ProgressBarControl*.**Enabled**—a **Boolean** value when **True** means that the control will respond to events. When **False**, the control will not respond to events.
- *ProgressBarControl*.**Height**—a **Single** that contains the height of the control.
- *ProgressBarControl*.**hWnd**—a **Long** that contains a Windows handle to the control.

> **Tip**
>
> *The **hWnd** property is most useful when making calls to Windows API functions. This value can change during execution, so do not save the value into a variable for later use.*

- *ProgressBarControl*.**Index**—an **Integer** that uniquely identifies a control in a control array.
- *ProgressBarControl*.**Left**—a **Single** containing the distance, measured in twips, between the left edge of the control and the left edge of the control's container.
- *ProgressBarControl*.**Max**—an **Integer** containing the maximum value for the progress bar. If not specified, this value defaults to 32,767.
- *ProgressBarControl*.**Min**—an **Integer** containing the minimum value for the progress bar. If not specified, this value defaults to 0.
- *ProgressBarControl*.**MouseIcon**—a picture object (a bitmap, icon, or metafile) that will be used as a cursor when the **MousePointer** property is set to 99. Note that Visual Basic does not support color cursors from a .cur file. A color icon from an .ico file should be used instead.
- *ProgressBarControl*.**MousePointer**—an **Integer** that contains the value of the cursor that should be displayed when the cursor is moved over this control. Use *vbCustom* to display the custom icon stored in the **MouseIcon** property.

Cursor Name	Value	Description
vbDefault	0	Shape determined by the object (default value).
vbArrow	1	Arrow.
vbCrosshair	2	Crosshair.
vbIbeam	3	I beam.
vbIconPointer	4	Square inside a square.
vbSizePointer	5	Four-sided arrow (north, south, east, west).
vbSizeNESW	6	Two-sided arrow (northeast, southwest).
vbSizeNS	7	Two-sided arrow (north, south).
vbSizeNWSE	8	Two-sided arrow (northwest, southeast).
vbSizeWE	9	Two-sided arrow (west, east).
vbUpArrow	10	Single-sided arrow pointing north.
vbHourglass	11	Hourglass.
vbNoDrop	12	No drop.
vbArrowHourglass	13	An arrow and an hourglass.
vbArrowQuestion	14	An arrow and a question mark.
vbSizeAll	15	Size all.
vbCustom	99	Custom icon from the MouseIcon property of this control.

Table P-69: Cursor *values.*

- *ProgressBarControl*.**Name**—a **String** that contains the name of the control that will be used to reference the control in a Visual Basic program. This property is read only at run time.
- *ProgressBarControl*.**Object**—an object that contains a reference to the *ListViewControl* object.
- *ProgressBarControl*.**OLEDropMode**—an **Integer** value (see Table P-70) that describes how the control will respond to OLE drop operations.

OLEDropMode Name	Value	Description
vbOLEDropNone	0	The control does not accept OLE drops. The cursor is changed to the No Drop cursor (default value).
vbOLEDropManual	1	The control responds to OLE drops under the program's control (manual).
vbOLEDropAutomatic	2	The control automatically accepts OLE drops if it recognizes the format of the data object.

Table P-70: OLEDropMode *values.*

- *ProgressBarControl*.**Parent**—an object that contains a reference to the **Form**, **Frame,** or other container that contains the **Label** control.
- *ProgressBarControl*.**TabIndex**—an **Integer** that is used to determine the order that a user will tab through the objects on a form.
- *ProgressBarControl*.**Tag**—a **String** that can hold programmer-specific information. This property is not used by Visual Basic.
- *ProgressBarControl*.**ToolTipText**—a **String** that holds a text value that can be displayed as a **ToolTip** box that is displayed whenever the cursor is held over the control for about one second.
- *ProgressBarControl*.**Top**—a **Single** that contains the distance, measured in twips, between the top edge of the control and the top edge of the control's container.
- *ProgressBarControl*.**Value**—an **Integer** containing the current value of the progress bar. This value, with the **Min** and **Max** controls the amount of progress bar that is displayed.
- *ProgressBarControl*.**Visible**—a **Boolean** value when **True** means that the control is visible. When **False** means that the control is not visible.

> **Tip**
>
> *This property can be used to hide the control until the program is ready to display it.*

- *ProgressBarControl*.**WhatsThisHelpID**—a **Long** that contains a help file context ID number that references an entry in the help file. This is used to provide a What's This PopUp help display in response to the What's This button in the upper-right corner of the window.
- *ProgressBarControl*.**Width**—a **Single** that contains the width of the control.

Methods

ProgressBarControl.Drag [DragAction]

Usage This method is used to begin, end, or cancel a drag operation.

Arguments • *DragAction*—an **Integer** that contains a value selected from Table P-71 below.

DragAction Name	Value	Description
vbCancel	0	Cancels any drag operation in progress.
vbBeginDrag	1	Begins a drag operation (default value).
vbEndDrag	2	Ends a drag operation and drops *object*.

Table P-71: DragAction values.

ProgressBarControl.Move Left [, Top [, Width [, Height]]]

Usage This method is used to change the position and the size of the **ProgressBar** control. The **ScaleMode** of the **Form** or other container object that holds the **ProgressBar** control will determine the units used to specify the coordinates.

Arguments
- *Left*—a **Single** that specifies the new position of the left edge of the control.
- *Top*—a **Single** that specifies the new position of the top edge of the control.
- *Width*—a **Single** that specifies the new width of the control.
- *Height*—a **Single** that specifies the new height of the control.

ProgressBarControl.OLEDrag

Usage This method is used to begin an **OLEDrag**-and-drop operation. Invoking this method will trigger the **OLEStartDrag** event.

ProgressBarControl.ShowWhatsThis

Usage This method displays the ShowWhatsThis help information for this control.

ProgressBarControl.ZOrder [position]

Usage This method is used to specify the position of the label control relative to the other objects on the form.

Tip

*Note that there are three layers of objects on a form: The back layer is the drawing space that contains the results of the graphical methods, the middle layer contains graphical objects and **Labels**, and the top layer contains non-graphical controls such as the **ProgressBar**. The **ZOrder** method only affects how the objects are arranged within a single layer.*

ProgressBar • 741

Arguments
- *position*—an **Integer** that specifies the relative position of this object. A value of 0 means that the control is positioned at the head of the list, a value of 1 means that the control will be placed at the end of the list.

Events

Private Sub *ProgressBarControl*_Click([*index* As Integer])

Usage — This event occurs when the user clicks a mouse button while the cursor is over the control.

Arguments
- *index*—an **Integer** that is used to uniquely identify a control in a control array. This argument is not present if the control is not part of a control array.

Private Sub *ProgressBarControl*_DragDrop([*index* As Integer ,] *source* As Control, *x* As Single, *y* As Single)

Usage — This event occurs when a drag-and-drop operation is completed by using the Drag method with a *DragAction* value of *vbEndDrag*.

Tip

*When using drag-and-drop operations, use the **DragOver** event to determine what the cursor should look like while the cursor moves over the control.*

Arguments
- *index*—an **Integer** that is used to uniquely identify a control in a control array. This argument is not present if the control is not part of a control array.
- *source*—a control object that is the control that is being dragged.

Tip

You can access a property or method from the source control by using source.property *or* source.method. *You can determine the type of object or control by using the **TypeOf** operator.*

- *x*—a **Single** that contains the horizontal location of the mouse pointer.
- *y*—a **Single** that contains the vertical location of the mouse pointer.

Private Sub *ProgressBarControl*_DragOver([*index* As Integer ,] *source* As Control, *x* As Single, *y* As Single, *state* As Integer)

Usage — This event occurs while a drag operation is in progress and the cursor is moved over the control.

Tip

*When using drag-and-drop operations, use the **DragOver** event to determine what the cursor should look like while the cursor moves over the control. When* state *is 0, you can change the cursor to a no drop (vbNoDrop) cursor or highlight the field that the cursor is near. When* state *is 1, you can undo the changes you made when the* state *was 0.*

Arguments
- *index*—an **Integer** that is used to uniquely identify a control in a control array. This argument is not present if the control is not part of a control array.
- *source*—a control object that is the control that is being dragged.

> **Tip**
>
> You can access a property or method from the source control by using source.*property* or source.*method*. You can determine the type of object or control by using the **TypeOf** operator.

- *x*—a **Single** that contains the horizontal location of the mouse pointer.
- *y*—a **Single** that contains the vertical location of the mouse pointer.
- *state*—an **Integer** that indicates the state of the object being dragged.

state Name	Value	Description
vbEnter	0	The dragged object is entering range of the control.
vbLeave	1	The dragged object is leaving range of the control.
vbOver	2	The dragged object has moved from one position over the control to another.

Table P-72: State *values.*

Private Sub *ProgressBarControl*_MouseDown([*index* As Integer ,] *button* As Integer, *shift* As Single, *x* As Single, *y* As Single)

Usage
This event occurs when a mouse button was pressed while the cursor was over the control.

Arguments
- *index*—an **Integer** that is used to uniquely identify a control in a control array. This argument is not present if the control is not part of a control array.
- *button*—an **Integer** that contains information about the mouse buttons that were pressed. Only one button will be indicated when this event occurs.

button Name	Value	Description
vbLeftButton	1	The left button was pressed.
vbRightButton	2	The right button was pressed.
vbMiddleButton	4	The middle button was pressed.

Table P-73: Button *values.*

- *shift*—an **Integer** that contains information about the Shift and Alt keys that were pressed when the mouse button was pressed. These values can be added together if more than one key was down. For instance, a value of 5 would mean that the Shift and Alt keys were both down when the mouse button was pressed.

shift Name	Value	Description
vbShiftMask	1	The Shift key was pressed.
vbCtrlMask	2	The Ctrl key was pressed.
vbAltMask	4	The Alt key was pressed.

Table P-74: Shift *values*.

- *x*—a **Single** that contains the horizontal location of the mouse pointer.
- *y*—a **Single** that contains the vertical location of the mouse pointer.

Private Sub *ProgressBarControl*_MouseMove ([*index* As Integer ,] *button* As Integer, *shift* As Single, *x* As Single, *y* As Single)

Usage This event occurs while the cursor is moved over the control.

Arguments
- *index*—an **Integer** that is used to uniquely identify a control in a control array. This argument is not present if the control is not part of a control array.
- *button*—an **Integer** that contains information about the mouse buttons that were pressed. These values can be added together if more than one button was pressed. For instance, a value of 3 means that both the left and right buttons were pressed. A value of 0 means that no buttons were pressed.

button Name	Value	Description
vbLeftButton	1	The left button was pressed.
vbRightButton	2	The right button was pressed.
vbMiddleButton	4	The middle button was pressed.

Table P-75: Button *values*.

- *shift*—an **Integer** that contains information about the Shift and Alt keys that were pressed when the mouse button was pressed. For instance, a value of 5 would mean that the Shift and Alt keys were both down when the mouse button was pressed. A value of 0 means that none of these keys were pressed.

shift Name	Value	Description
vbShiftMask	1	The Shift key was pressed.
vbCtrlMask	2	The Ctrl key was pressed.
vbAltMask	4	The Alt key was pressed.

Table P-76: Shift *values*.

- *x*—a **Single** that contains the horizontal location of the mouse pointer.
- *y*—a **Single** that contains the vertical location of the mouse pointer.

Private Sub *ProgressBarControl*_MouseUp([*index* As Integer ,] *button* As Integer, *shift* As Single, *x* As Single, *y* As Single)

Usage This event occurs when a mouse button is released while the cursor is over the control.

Arguments
- *index*—an **Integer** that is used to uniquely identify a control in a control array. This argument is not present if the control is not part of a control array.
- *button*—an **Integer** that contains information about the mouse buttons that were released. Only one of these values will be present.

button Name	Value	Description
vbLeftButton	1	The left button was released.
vbRightButton	2	The right button was released.
vbMiddleButton	4	The middle button was released.

Table P-77: Button *values.*

- *shift*—an **Integer** that contains information about the Shift and Alt keys that were pressed when the mouse button was released. These values can be added together if more than one key was down. For instance, a value of 5 would mean that the Shift and Alt keys were both down when the mouse button was released. A value of 0 means that none of these keys were pressed.

shift Name	Value	Description
vbShiftMask	1	The Shift key was pressed.
vbCtrlMask	2	The Ctrl key was pressed.
vbAltMask	4	The Alt key was pressed.

Table P-78: Shift *values.*

- *x*—a **Single** that contains the horizontal location of the mouse pointer.
- *y*—a **Single** that contains the vertical location of the mouse pointer.

Private Sub *ProgressBarControl*_OLECompleteDrag([*index* As Integer ,] *effect* As Long)

Usage This event is used to tell the source control the results of an OLE drag-and-drop operation. This is the final event to occur in the series of actions that make up an OLE drag-and-drop operation.

Arguments
- *index*—an **Integer** that is used to uniquely identify a control in a control array. This argument is not present if the control is not part of a control array.
- *effect*—a **Long** that returns the status of the OLE drag-and-drop operation.

ProgressBar • 745

effect Name	Value	Description
vbDropEffectNone	0	The operation was canceled or the target control can't accept the drop operation.
vbDropEffectCopy	1	The operation copies data from the source control to the target control. The original data is unchanged.
vbDropEffectMove	2	The operation results in a link from the original data to the target control.

Table P-79: Effect *values*.

Private Sub *ProgressBarControl*_OLEDragDrop([*index* As Integer ,] *data* As DataObject, *effect* As Long, *button* As Integer, *shift* As Single, *x* As Single, *y* As Single)

Usage — This event is used to tell the source control the results of an OLE drag-and-drop operation. This is the final event to occur in the series of actions that make up an OLE drag-and-drop operation.

Arguments
- *index*—an **Integer** that is used to uniquely identify a control in a control array. This argument is not present if the control is not part of a control array.
- *data*—a **DataObject** that contains the formats that the source control will provide. If the data is not contained in the **DataObject**, then it can be retrieved with the **GetData** method.
- *effect*—a **Long** that returns the status of the OLE drag-and-drop operation.

effect Name	Value	Description
vbDropEffectNone	0	The operation was canceled or the target control can't accept the drop operation.
vbDropEffectCopy	1	The operation copies data from the source control to the target control. The original data is unchanged.
vbDropEffectMove	2	The operation results in a link from the original data to the target control.

Table P-80: Effect *values*.

- *button*—an **Integer** that contains information about the mouse buttons that were pressed. These values can be added together if more than one button was pressed. For instance, a value of 3 means that both the left and right buttons were pressed. A value of 0 means that no buttons were pressed.

button Name	Value	Description
vbLeftButton	1	The left button was pressed.
vbRightButton	2	The right button was pressed.
vbMiddleButton	4	The middle button was pressed.

Table P-81: Button *values*.

- *shift*—an **Integer** that contains information about the Shift and Alt keys that were pressed when the mouse button was released. These values can be added together if more than one key was down. For instance, a value of 5 would mean that the Shift and Alt keys were both down when the mouse button was released. A value of 0 means that none of these keys were pressed.

shift Name	Value	Description
vbShiftMask	1	The Shift key was pressed.
vbCtrlMask	2	The Ctrl key was pressed.
vbAltMask	4	The Alt key was pressed.

Table P-82: Shift *values*.

- *x*—a **Single** that contains the horizontal location of the mouse pointer.
- *y*—a **Single** that contains the vertical location of the mouse pointer.

Private Sub *ProgressBarControl_OLEDragOver*([*index* As Integer ,] *data* As DataObject, *effect* As Long, *button* As Integer, *shift* As Single, *x* As Single, *y* As Single, *state* As Integer)

Usage   This event happens when an OLE drag-and-drop operation is in progress.

Arguments
- *index*—an **Integer** that is used to uniquely identify a control in a control array. This argument is not present if the control is not part of a control array.
- *data*—a **DataObject** that contains the formats that the source control will provide. If the data is not contained in the **DataObject**, then it can be retrieved with the **GetData** method.
- *effect*—a **Long** that returns the status of the OLE drag-and-drop operation.

effect Name	Value	Description
vbDropEffectNone	0	The operation was canceled or the target control can't accept the drop operation.
vbDropEffectCopy	1	The operation copies data from the source control to the target control. The original data is unchanged.
vbDropEffectMove	2	The operation results in a link from the original data to the target control.

Table P-83: Effect *values*.

- *button*—an **Integer** that contains information about the mouse buttons that were pressed. These values can be added together if more than one button was pressed. For instance, a value of 3 means that both the left and right buttons were pressed. A value of 0 means that no buttons were pressed.

button Name	Value	Description
vbLeftButton	1	The left button was pressed.
vbRightButton	2	The right button was pressed.
vbMiddleButton	4	The middle button was pressed.

Table P-84: Button *values*.

- *shift*—an **Integer** that contains information about the Shift and Alt keys that were pressed when the mouse button was released. These values can be added together if more than one key was down. For instance, a value of 5 would mean that the Shift and Alt keys were both down when the mouse button was released. A value of 0 means that none of these keys were pressed.

shift Name	Value	Description
vbShiftMask	1	The Shift key was pressed.
vbCtrlMask	2	The Ctrl key was pressed.
vbAltMask	4	The Alt key was pressed.

Table P-85: Shift *values*.

- *x*—a **Single** that contains the horizontal location of the mouse pointer.
- *y*—a **Single** that contains the vertical location of the mouse pointer.
- *state*—an **Integer** that indicates the state of the object being dragged.

state Name	Value	Description
vbEnter	0	The dragged object is entering range of the control.
vbLeave	1	The dragged object is leaving range of the control.
vbOver	2	The dragged object has moved from one position over the control to another.

Table P-86: State *values*.

Private Sub *ProgressBarControl*_OLEGiveFeedback ([*index* As Integer ,] *effect* As Long)

Usage   This event is used to tell the source control what is happening while the OLE drag-and-drop operation is in progress. This event occurs after the OLEDragOver event.

Tip

You may want to use this event to change the cursor to reflect what can happen in the remote object.

Arguments
- *index*—an **Integer** that is used to uniquely identify a control in a control array. This argument is not present if the control is not part of a control array.
- *effect*—a **Long** that returns the status of the OLE drag-and-drop operation.

effect Name	Value	Description
vbDropEffectNone	0	The operation was canceled or the target control can't accept the drop operation.
vbDropEffectCopy	1	The operation copies data from the source control to the target control. The original data is unchanged.
vbDropEffectMove	2	The operation results in a link from the original data to the target control.
vbDropEffectScroll	&H80000000	The target control is about to scroll or is scrolling. This value may be added to the other *shift* values.

Table P-87: Effect values.

Private Sub *ProgressBarControl_OLESetData*([*index* As Integer ,] *data* As DataObject, *DataFormat* As Integer)

Usage — This event happens in response to the target object performing a **GetData** method on *data*. This routine will respond by using the **SetData** method with the desired data using the **DataObject** *data*.

Arguments
- *index*—an **Integer** that is used to uniquely identify a control in a control array. This argument is not present if the control is not part of a control array.
- *data*—a **DataObject** that will contain the data to be returned to the target object.
- *format*—an **Integer** that contains the format of the data.

format Name	Value	Description
vbCFText	1	Text (.txt files).
vbCFBitmap	2	Bitmap (.bmp files).
vbCFMetafile	3	Metafile (.wmf files).
vbCFEDIB	8	Device-independent bitmap (DIB).
vbCFPallette	9	Color palette
vbCFEMetafile	14	Enhanced metafile (.emf files).
vbCFFiles	15	List of files.
vbCFRTF	-16639	Rich Text Format (.RTF files).

Table P-88: Format values.

Private Sub *ProgressBarControl*_OLEStartDrag ([*index* As Integer ,] *data* As DataObject, *AllowedEffects* As Long)

Usage   This event is used to start an OLE drag-and-drop operation.

Arguments
- *index*—an **Integer** that is used to uniquely identify a control in a control array. This argument is not present if the control is not part of a control array.
- *data*—a **DataObject** that will contain the formats that the source object is willing to provide to the target object. It may optionally contain the data to be transferred.
- *AllowedEffects*—a **Long** that contains the effects that the target object can request from the source object. The *AllowedEffects* can be added together if the source object supports more than one effect. Note that the target object can always use the *vbDropEffectNone* effect.

AllowedEffects Name	Value	Description
vbDropEffectNone	0	The target can't copy the data.
vbDropEffectCopy	1	The target can copy the data, and the source will keep the data unchanged.
vbDropEffectMove	2	The target can copy the data, and the source will delete the data.

Table P-89: AllowedEffects *values.*

Examples
```
Private Sub Command1_Click()
    If ProgressBar1.Value <> ProgressBar1.Max Then
        ProgressBar1.Value = ProgressBar1.Value + 1
    Else
        ProgressBar1.Value = 0
    End If
End Sub

Private Sub Form_Load()
ProgressBar1.Min = 0
ProgressBar1.Max = 10
ProgressBar1.Value = 0
End Sub
```

This program moves the progress bar by clicking on the Command1 command button. After ten clicks, the progress bar will reach the end. One more click will reset the bar to zero.

See Also   **StatusBar** (control)

Properties

COLLECTION

PE, EE

Usage The **Properties** collection is used by Data Access Objects (DAO) to contain information about user-defined properties that are created with the **CreateProperty** method.

Properties • *PropertiesCollection*.**Count**—an **Integer** containing the number of **Property** objects in the collection.

Methods *PropertiesCollection*.**Append** *object*

> **Usage** This method adds a **Property** object to the collection.
>
> **Arguments** • *object*—a reference to a **Property** object to be added to the collection.

PropertiesCollection.**Delete** *objectname*

> **Usage** This method removes a **Property** object from the collection.
>
> **Arguments** • *objectname*—a **String** containing the name of the **Property** object to be removed from the collection.

PropertiesCollection.**Refresh**

> **Usage** This method gets a current copy of the **Properties** contained in the collection. This is important in a multi-user environment where more than one user may be making changes in the **Databases** collection.

See Also **Database** (object), **Databases** (collection), **Field** (object), **Property** (object), **Recordset** (object), **Recordsets** (collection), **Relation** (object), **Relations** (collection), **TableDef** (object), **TableDefs** (collection)

Property

OBJECT

PE, EE

Usage The **Property** object is used by Data Access Objects (DAO) to contain information about a user-defined property that was created with the **CreateProperty** method.

Properties • *PropertyObject*.**Inherited**—a **Boolean** value when **True** means that the property was inherited from another object. **False** means that this property was not inherited from another object. For example, when creating a new **Recordset** object from a **QueryDef** object, all of the user-defined properties will be available in the new object.

• *PropertyObject*.**Name**—a **String** value that contains the name of the property object.

• *PropertyObject*.**Type**—an **Integer** value describing the type of the value.

Type Name	Description
dbBigInt	Big integer data type.
dbBinary	Fixed-length binary data, up to 255 bytes long.
dbBoolean	Boolean data type.
DbByte	Integer value one byte wide.
DbChar	Fixed-length character string.
DbCurrency	Currency data type.
DbDate	Date/time data type.
DbDecimal	Decimal data type.
DbDouble	Double precision floating point data type.
DbFloat	Floating point data type.
DbGUID	Globally Unique Identifier data type.
DbInteger	16 bit integer data type.
DbLong	32 bit integer data type.
DbLongBinary	Long binary data type.
DbMemo	Memo data type.
DbNumeric	Numeric data type.
DbSingle	Single precision floating point data type.
DbText	Field data type.
dbTime	Time data type.
DbTimeStamp	Time stamp data type.
DbVarBinary	Variable-length binary, up to 255 bytes long.

Table P-90: Type *values.*

- *PropertyObject*.**Value**—a **Variant** containing the parameter's value.

See Also **Database** (object), **Databases** (collection), **Field** (object), **Properties** (collection), **QueryDef** (object), **QueryDefs** (collection), **Recordset** (object), **Recordsets** (collection), **Relation** (object), **Relations** (collection), **TableDef** (object), **TableDefs** (collection)

Property Get

STATEMENT

CCE, LE, PE, EE

Syntax
```
[ Public | Private | Friend ] [ Static ] Property Get name ( [ arg ] [, arg ]
   . . . [, arg ] ) As type
      [ list of statements ]
      [ Exit Property ]
      [ list of statements ]
End Property
```

Usage The **Property Get** statement defines a routine that will return a property value from an object. This routine is identical to a function for all practical purposes. However, while a property can use parameters, it is relatively uncommon.

The arguments are variables that will be passed to the property routine when it is called. The property name, *name,* is a special variable that is assigned the value that will be returned to the calling program. Therefore, it is important that you assign a value to *name* prior to ending the property routine.

Note that this statement is used to define a read-only property. If you want to assign a value to the property, then the appropriate **Property Let** or **Property Set** must be coded using the same value for *name*.

The **Exit Property** statement can be used to leave the routine at any time. The **End Property** statement marks the end of the routine. Executing either statement will cause the routine to return back to where it was called.

Arguments
- **Public**—an optional keyword indicating that the routine can be called from any module in the program.
- **Private**—an optional keyword indicating that the routine can only be called by other routines in the same module.
- **Friend**—an optional keyword indicating that the function can be called from any module in the program, but it can't be called by the controller of an instance of the object. This argument applies to class modules only.
- **Static**—an optional keyword indicating that the variables declared inside the routine are preserved from one call to the next.
- *name*—a Visual Basic identifier that contains the name of the property.
- *arg*—an argument that is passed to the routine:

  [Optional] [ByVal | ByRef] [ParamArray] AName [()] [As type] [= value]

Optional	an optional keyword meaning that the argument is optional and need not be passed to the routine. Once an argument is declared to be optional, all arguments that follow must be declared as optional.
ByVal	an optional keyword meaning that the argument is passed by value to the routine. This event is free to change the contents of the argument and the calling object will not see the changes.
ByRef	an optional keyword meaning that the argument is passed by reference to the routine. Any changes to the argument in the calling control will be seen by the calling object.
ParamArray	an optional keyword meaning that the routine can receive an unspecified number of arguments of type **Variant** starting at this position. This must be the last argument in the routine declaration and can't be used with **Optional**, **ByVal**, or **ByRef**.
AName	the formal argument being passed to the routine.
[()]	if present, indicates that the argument is an array.
type	a valid Visual Basic type: **Byte, Boolean, Currency, Date, Double, Integer, Long, Single, String, Object,** or **Variant**. If the argument is not **Optional**, then specific object types and user-defined types may be used.

> *value* — used to provide a default value for an argument that was marked as **Optional**. Arguments of type **Object** can only be assigned a value of **Nothing**.
>
> *type* — a valid Visual Basic type: **Byte**, **Boolean**, **Currency**, **Date**, **Double**, **Integer**, **Long**, **Single**, **String**, **Object**, or **Variant**.

Examples

```
' ActiveX control - MyObject
Private myValue As String
Public Event Error(ErrorString As String)
Public Property Get Value() As String
Value = myValue
End Property
Public Property Let Value(s As String)
If Len(s) > 0 Then
   myValue = s
Else
   RaiseEvent Error("Illegal Value for the Value property")
End If
End Property
```

This is a short ActiveX control that demonstrates how to use the **Property Get** and **Property Let** statements to access a property value. First a private variable called myValue is defined to hold the property's data. The **Property Let** routine verifies that the length of the value to be assigned to the property is not empty before saving it. If the value is empty, then the error event is raised. The **Property Get** routine merely returns the current value of the property.

```
' Main Program
Private Sub Command1_Click()
MyObject1.Value = Text1.Text
End Sub

Private Sub Command2_Click()
Text2.Text = MyObject1.Value
End Sub

Private Sub MyObject1_Error(ErrorString As String)
MsgBox ErrorString
End Sub
```

The main program consists of two command buttons, one that will set the value of the control's property and the other to return the value of the property. The ActiveX control's error event is coded here to handle any invalid data.

See Also **Event** (statement), **Property Let** (statement), **Property Set** (statement), **RaiseEvent** (statement).

Property Let

STATEMENT

CCE, LE, PE, EE

Syntax
```
[ Public | Private | Friend ] [ Static ] Property Let name ( [ arg ] [, arg ]
    . . . [, newvalue ] ) As type
      [ list of statements ]
      [ Exit Property ]
      [ list of statements ]
End Property
```

Usage

The **Property Let** statement defines a routine that will assign a value to a property value. This routine is identical to a subroutine for all practical purposes.

The arguments are variables that will be passed to the property routine when it is called. The last argument is the new value for the property.

Note that this statement is used to define a write-only property for normal variables. If you wish to save an object value, then you will need to code a **Property Set** routine. If you want to retrieve a value from the property, then a **Property Get** must be coded using the same value for *name*.

The **Exit Property** statement can be used to leave the routine at any time. The **End Property** statement marks the end of the routine. Executing either statement will cause the routine to return back to where it was called.

Arguments

- **Public**—an optional keyword indicating that the routine can be called from any module in the program.
- **Private**—an optional keyword indicating that the routine can only be called by other routines in the same module.
- **Friend**—an optional keyword indicating that the function can be called from any module in the program, but it can't be called by the controller of an instance of the object. This argument applies to class modules only.
- **Static**—an optional keyword indicating that the variables declared inside the routine are preserved from one call to the next.
- *name*—a Visual Basic identifier that contains the name of the property.
- *arg*—an argument that is passed to the routine:

```
[ Optional ] [ ByVal | ByRef ] [ ParamArray ] AName [ () ] [ As type ] [ = value
]
```

    Optional — an optional keyword meaning that the argument is optional and need not be passed to the routine. Once an argument is declared to be optional, all arguments that follow must be declared as optional.

    ByVal — an optional keyword meaning that the argument is passed by value to the routine. This event is free to change the contents of the argument and the calling object will not see the changes.

    ByRef — an optional keyword meaning that the argument is passed by reference to the routine. Any changes to the argument in the calling control will be seen by the calling object.

    ParamArray — an optional keyword meaning that the routine can receive an unspecified number of arguments of type **Variant** starting at this position. This must be the last argument in the routine declaration and can't be used with **Optional, ByVal,** or **ByRef**.

AName	the formal argument being passed to the routine.
[( )]	if present, indicates that the argument is an array.
type	a valid Visual Basic type: **Byte**, **Boolean**, **Currency**, **Date**, **Double**, **Integer**, **Long**, **Single**, **String**, **Object**, or **Variant**. If the argument is not **Optional**, then specific object types and user-defined types may be used.
value	used to provide a default value for an argument that was marked as **Optional**. Arguments of type **Object** can only be assigned a value of **Nothing**.

- *newvalue*—a value that will be assigned to the property. This is always the last value in the sequence.

Examples

```
' ActiveX control - MyObject
Private myValue As String
Public Event Error(ErrorString As String)
Public Property Get Value() As String
Value = myValue
End Property
Public Property Let Value(s As String)
If Len(s) > 0 Then
   myValue = s
Else
    RaiseEvent Error("Illegal Value for the Value property")
End If
End Property
```

This is a short ActiveX control that demonstrates how to use the **Property Get** and **Property Let** statements to access a property value. First a private variable called myValue is defined to hold the property's data. The **Property Let** routine verifies that the length of the value to be assigned to the property is not empty before saving it. If the value is empty, then the error event is raised. The **Property Get** routine merely returns the current value of the property.

```
' Main Program
Private Sub Command1_Click()
MyObject1.Value = Text1.Text
End Sub

Private Sub Command2_Click()
Text2.Text = MyObject1.Value
End Sub

Private Sub MyObject1_Error(ErrorString As String)
MsgBox ErrorString
End Sub
```

The main program consists of two command buttons, one that will set the value of the control's property and the other to return the value of the property. The ActiveX control's error event is coded here to handle any invalid data.

See Also **Event** (statement), **Property Get** (statement), **Property Set** (statement), **RaiseEvent** (statement)

Property Set

STATEMENT

CCE, LE, PE, EE

Syntax
```
[ Public | Private | Friend ] [ Static ] Property Set name ( [ arg ] [, arg ]
    . . . [, newvalue ] ) As type
      [ list of statements ]
      [ Exit Property ]
      [ list of statements ]
End Property
```

Usage

The **Property Set** statement defines a routine that will assign an object reference to a property value. This routine is identical to a subroutine for all practical purposes.

The arguments are variables that will be passed to the property routine when it is called. The last argument is the new value for the property.

Note that this statement is used to define a write-only property for object references. If you wish to save a regular variable, then you will need to code a **Property Let** routine. If you want to retrieve a value from the property, then a **Property Get** must be coded using the same value for *name*.

The **Exit Property** statement can be used to leave the routine at any time. The **End Property** statement marks the end of the routine. Executing either statement will cause the routine to return back to where it was called.

Arguments

- **Public**—an optional keyword indicating that the routine can be called from any module in the program.

- **Private**—an optional keyword indicating that the routine can only be called by other routines in the same module.

- **Friend**—an optional keyword indicating that the function can be called from any module in the program, but it can't be called by the controller of an instance of the object. This argument applies to class modules only.

- **Static**—an optional keyword indicating that the variables declared inside the routine are preserved from one call to the next.

- *name*—a Visual Basic identifier that contains the name of the property.

- *arg*—an argument that is passed to the routine:

  `[ Optional ] [ ByVal | ByRef ] [ ParamArray ] AName [ () ] [ As type ] [ = value ]`

Optional	an optional keyword meaning that the argument is optional and need not be passed to the routine. Once an argument is declared to be optional, all arguments that follow must be declared as optional.
ByVal	an optional keyword meaning that the argument is passed by value to the routine. This event is free to change the contents of the argument, and the calling object will not see the changes.
ByRef	an optional keyword meaning that the argument is passed by reference to the routine. Any changes to the argument in the calling control will be seen by the calling object.
ParamArray	an optional keyword meaning that the routine can receive an unspecified number of arguments of type **Variant** starting at this position. This must be the last argument in the routine declaration and can't be used with **Optional, ByVal,** or **ByRef**.

AName	the formal argument being passed to the routine.
[()]	if present, indicates that the argument is an array.
type	a valid Visual Basic type: **Byte**, **Boolean**, **Currency**, **Date**, **Double**, **Integer**, **Long**, **Single**, **String**, **Object**, or **Variant**. If the argument is not **Optional**, then specific object types and user defined types may be used.
value	used to provide a default value for an argument that was marked as **Optional**. Arguments of type **Object** can only be assigned a value of **Nothing**.

- *newvalue*—a value that will be assigned to the property. This is always the last value in the sequence.

See Also **Event** (statement), **Property Get** (statement), **Property Let** (statement), **RaiseEvent** (statement)

PropertyBag

OBJECT

CCE, LE, PE, EE

Usage The **PropertyBag** object holds information keyed by name. This object is a parameter to the **ReadProperties** and **WriteProperties** events of the **UserControl** object.

> **Tip**
>
> *To improve efficiency, include a value for* default *when saving an item into the property bag. Data will only be saved to a file if it is different from the default value.*

Methods *value* = **PropertyBag.ReadProperty** *name,* [, *default*]

Usage This method saves a value into the property bag.

Arguments
- *name*—a **String** containing the name associated with the value to be returned.
- *value*—a variable that will contain the value associated with *name*.
- *default*—an optional value that will be returned if *name* is not found in the bag.

PropertBag.WriteProperty *name, value* [, *default*]

Usage This method saves a value into a property bag.

Arguments
- *name*—a **String** containing the name associated with the value to be saved.
- *value*—a value to be saved in the bag that is associated with *name*.
- *default*—an optional value that be saved in the property bag.

See Also **UserControl** (object)

PropertyPage

OBJECT

CCE, LE, PE, EE

Usage The **PropertyPage** object is the object that provides an alternate method of setting property values in a **UserControl**. A key part to this object is a form that contains all of the properties for viewing purposes.

Properties
- *PropertyPageObject*.**ActiveControl**—an object of type control that contains a reference to the currently active control.
- *PropertyPageObject*.**Appearance**—an **Integer** value (see Table P-91) that specifies how the form will be drawn.

Appearance Value	Description
0	The form is displayed without the 3D effects.
1	The form is displayed with 3D effects (default value).

Table P-91: Appearance values.

- *PropertyPageObject*.**AutoRedraw**—a **Boolean** value when **True** means that the graphics and text written directly to the form will be redrawn from a copy stored in memory. When **False**, the **Paint** event will be triggered to redraw the contents of the form.

> **Tip**
>
> Setting **AutoRedraw** to **True** will slow down most operations involving the form. Most of the common controls (i.e., labels, text boxes, and command buttons) will automatically redraw themselves. If you display graphics directly on the form, then you may want to use **AutoRedraw**.

- *PropertyPageObject*.**BackColor**—a **Long** that contains the suggested value for the background color of the form. The **BackColor** and **ForeColor** must both be solid to display text. If you choose a color that is dithered, it will be changed to the nearest solid color.
- *PropertyPageObject*.**Caption**—a **String** value that displays inside the title bar. The leading text will also be displayed in the Window's taskbar.
- *PropertyPageObject*.**Changed**—a **Boolean,** when **True,** means that at least one property on the form has been changed. **False** means no properties have been changed.
- *PropertyPageObject*.**ClipControls**—a **Boolean,** when **True,** means that the graphic events repaint the entire form. **False** means that graphic events only repaint the newly exposed parts of the form.
- *PropertyPageObject*.**Controls**—an object that contains a collection of the controls on the form.
- *PropertyPageObject*.**Count**—an **Integer** containing the number of controls on the form.
- *PropertyPageObject*.**CurrentX**—a **Single** that specifies the horizontal coordinate measured from the form's left edge for the various drawing methods: **Circle, Cls, EndDoc, Line, NewPage, Print,** and **PSet.**
- *PropertyPageObject*.**CurrentY**—a **Single** that specifies the vertical coordinate measured from the form's top edge for the various drawing methods: **Circle, Cls, EndDoc, Line, NewPage, Print,** and **PSet.**

PropertyPage • 759

- *PropertyPageObject*.**DrawMode**—an **Integer** value (see Table P-92) specifying how the drawing methods **Circle**, **Cls**, **EndDoc**, **Line**, **NewPage**, **Print**, and **PSet** will appear on the form.

DrawMode Name	Value	Description
vbBlackness	1	Blackness.
vbNotMergePen	2	Inverse of *vbMergePen*.
vbMaskNotPen	3	Combination of the colors common to the background color and the inverse of the pen.
vbNotCopyPen	4	Inverse of *vbCopyPen*.
vbMaskPenNot	5	Combination of the colors common to the pen and the inverse of the background.
vbInvert	6	Inverse of the display color.
vbXorPen	7	Combination of the colors in the display and pen, but not in both.
vbNotMaskPen	8	Inverse setting of *vbMaskPen*.
vbMaskPen	9	Combination of the colors common to the pen and display.
vbNotXorPen	10	Inverse setting of *vbXorPen*.
vbNop	11	Turns drawing off.
vbMergeNotPen	12	Combination of the display and inverse of the pen color.
vbCopyPen	13	Color specified in the **ForeColor** property.
vbMergePenNot	14	Combination of the pen color and the inverse of the display color.
vbMergePen	15	Combination of the pen color and the display color.
vbWhiteness	16	Whiteness.

Table P-92: DrawMode *values.*

- *PropertyPageObject*.**DrawStyle**—an **Integer** value (see Table P-93) specifying how the drawing methods **Circle**, **Cls**, **EndDoc**, **Line**, **NewPage**, **Print**, and **PSet** will appear on the form. If **DrawWidth** is greater than 1, then *vbDash*, *vbDot*, *vbDashDot*, and *vbDashDotDot* will draw a solid line.

DrawStyle Name	Value	Description
vbSolid	0	Solid line.
vbDash	1	Dashed line.
vbDot	2	Dotted line.
vbDashDot	3	Dash followed by a dot.
vbDashDotDot	4	Dash followed by two dots.
vbInvisible	5	No displayed line.
vbInsideSolid	6	Inside solid.

Table P-93: DrawStyle *values.*

- *PropertyPageObject*.**DrawWidth**—an **Integer** specifying the width of the line in pixels that will be drawn and how the following methods: **Circle**, **Cls**, **EndDoc**, **Line**, **NewPage**, **Print**, and **PSet** will appear on the form. If **DrawWidth** is greater than 1, then the **DrawStyles** *vbDash*, *vbDot*, *vbDashDot*, and *vbDashDotDot* will draw a solid line.

- *PropertyPageObject*.**FillColor**—a **Long** that contains the color that will be used to fill in shapes created with the following graphical methods: **Circle**, **Cls**, **EndDoc**, **Line**, **NewPage**, **Print**, and **PSet**.

- *PropertyPageObject*.**FillStyle**—an **Integer** value (see Table P-94) specifying how the drawing methods **Circle**, **Cls**, **EndDoc**, **Line**, **NewPage**, **Print**, and **PSet** will appear on the form. If **DrawWidth** is greater than 1, then *vbDash*, *vbDot*, *vbDashDot*, and *vbDashDotDot* will draw a solid line.

FillStyle Name	Value	Description
vbFSSolid	0	Solid.
vbFSTransparent	1	Transparent.
vbHorizontalLine	2	Horizontal line.
vbVerticalLine	3	Vertical line.
vbUpwardDiagonal	4	Diagonal lines going from the bottom left to the upper right.
vbDownwardDiagonal	5	Diagonal lines going from the top left to the bottom right.
vbCross	6	Cross.
vbDiagonalCross	7	Diagonal cross.

Table P-94: FillStyle *values*.

- *PropertyPageObject*.**Font**—an object that contains information about the character font used by this object.

> **Tip**
>
> Setting values for the **Font** object on the form at design time makes these values the default when other controls and objects are placed on the form.

- *PropertyPageObject*.**FontBold**—a **Boolean**, when **True**, means that the characters display in bold. **False** means that the characters are displayed normally.
- *PropertyPageObject*.**FontItalic**—a **Boolean**, when **True**, means that the characters display in italics. **False** means that the characters display normally.
- *PropertyPageObject*.**FontName**—a **String** that specifies the name of the font that should be used to display the characters in this control.
- *PropertyPageObject*.**FontSize**—a **Single** that specifies the point size that should be used to display the characters in the control.
- *PropertyPageObject*.**FontStrikethru**—a **Boolean**, when **True**, means that the characters display with a line through the center. **False** means that the characters display normally.
- *PropertyPageObject*.**FontUnderlined**—a **Boolean**, when **True**, means that the characters display with a line beneath them. **False** means that the characters display normally.
- *PropertyPageObject*.**ForeColor**—a **Long** that contains the suggested value for the foreground color of the contained control. This property is read only at run time.
- *PropertyPageObject*.**hDC**—a **Long** that contains a handle to the device context to the form.
- *PropertyPageObject*.**Height**—a **Single** that contains the height of the control.
- *PropertyPageObject*.**HelpContextID**—a **Long** that contains a help file context ID number that references an entry in the help file. When the user presses the F1 key while this control is active, the corresponding entry in the help file will automatically be displayed. A value of zero means that no context number was specified.

PropertyPage • 761

> **Tip**
>
> *A help file must be compiled using the Windows Help Compiler available in the Professional and Enterprise editions of Visual Basic.*

- *PropertyPageObject*.**hWnd**—a **Long** that contains a Windows handle to the control.

> **Tip**
>
> *The **hWnd** property is most useful when making calls to Windows API functions. Since this value can change during execution, do not save the value into a variable for later use.*

- *PropertyPageObject*.**Image**—a handle to a persistent graphic that is returned by the Windows environment. Available only at run time.
- *PropertyPageObject*.**KeyPreview**—a **Boolean,** when **True,** means that the form will receive keyboard events (**KeyDown**, **KeyUp**, and **KeyPress**) before any controls. **False** means that the control will receive the keyboard events and the form will not.

> **Tip**
>
> *This function is useful in providing global keystroke handling at the form level for such keys as function keys and other control keys.*

- *PropertyPageObject*.**Left**—a **Single** that contains the distance, measured in twips, between the left edge of the control and the left edge of the control's container.
- *PropertyPageObject*.**MouseIcon**—a picture object (a bitmap, icon, or metafile) that will be used as a cursor when the **MousePointer** property is set to 99. Note that Visual Basic does not support color cursors from a .CUR file. A color icon from an .ICO file should be used instead.
- *PropertyPageObject*.**MousePointer**—an **Integer** value (see Table P-95) that contains the value of the cursor that should be displayed when the cursor is moved over this control. Use *vbCustom* to display the custom icon stored in the **MouseIcon** property.

Cursor Name	Value	Description
vbDefault	0	Shape determined by the object (default value).
vbArrow	1	Arrow.
vbCrosshair	2	Crosshair.
vbIbeam	3	I beam.
vbIconPointer	4	Square inside a square.
vbSizePointer	5	Four-sided arrow (north, south, east, west).
vbSizeNESW	6	Two-sided arrow (northeast, southwest).
vbSizeNS	7	Two-sided arrow (north, south).
vbSizeNWSE	8	Two-sided arrow (northwest, southeast).
vbSizeWE	9	Two-sided arrow (west, east).
vbUpArrow	10	Single-sided arrow pointing north.

Cursor Name	Value	Description
vbHourglass	11	Hourglass.
vbNoDrop	12	No Drop.
vbArrowHourglass	13	An arrow and an hourglass.
vbArrowQuestion	14	An arrow and a question mark.
vbSizeAll	15	Size all.
vbCustom	99	Custom icon from the **MouseIcon** property of this control.

Table P-95: Cursor *values*.

- *PropertyPageObject*.**Name**—a **String** that contains the name of the control that will be used to reference the control in a Visual Basic program. This property is read only at run time.
- *PropertyPageObject*.**OLEDropMode**—an **Integer** value (see Table P-96) that describes how the control will respond to OLE drop operations.

OLEDropMode Name	Value	Description
vbOLEDropNone	0	The form does not accept OLE drops. The cursor is changed to the No Drop cursor (default value).
vbOLEDropManual	1	The form responds to OLE drops under the program's control (manual).
vbOLEDropAutomatic	2	The form automatically accepts OLE drops if it recognizes the format of the data object.

Table P-96: OLEDropMode *values*.

- *PropertyPageObject*.**Palette**—a **Picture** object that contains a suggested palette for the control. This property is read only at run time.
- *PropertyPageObject*.**PaletteMode**—an **Integer** value (see Table P-97) that describes the palette that should be used with the form.

PaletteMode Name	Value	Description
vbPaletteModeHalfTone	0	The form uses the half tone palette (default).
vbPaletteModeUseZOrder	1	The form uses the palette from the control nearest the front of the **ZOrder** with a palette.
vbModeCustom	2	The form uses the palette specified in the **Palette** property.

Table P-97: PaletteMode *values*.

- *PropertyPageObject*.**Picture**—a picture object (a bitmap, icon, metafile, GIF, or JPEG) that will be displayed on the control. You can also use the **LoadPicture** function at run time to load a bitmap, icon, or metafile. Note that **Style** must be set to *vbButtonGraphical* for the image to be shown.
- *PropertyPageObject*.**ScaleHeight**—an **Integer** value that sets or returns the height of the object in the units specified by **ScaleMode**.
- *PropertyPageObject*.**ScaleLeft**—an **Integer** value that sets or returns the value of the X-coordinate of the left edge of the form.
- *PropertyPageObject*.**ScaleMode**—an **Integer** value (see Table P-98) that describes the unit of measurement used for the form.

PropertyPage

> **Tip**
>
> *When dealing with graphic images such as BMP or GIF files it is often useful to set* **ScaleMode** *to* vbPixels *to help set the proper relationships.*

ScaleMode Name	Value	Description
vbUser	0	Measurements are custom defined, based on the values in ScaleHeight, ScaleLeft, ScaleTop, or ScaleWidth properties.
vbTwips	1	Measurements are in twips (1440 twips per inch).
vbPoints	2	Measurements are in points (72 per inch).
vbPixels	3	Measurements are in pixels (smallest unit of measure for a monitor or printer).
vbCharacters	4	Measurements are in characters (horizontal = 120 twips per character, vertical = 240 twips per character).
vbInches	5	Measurements are in inches.
vbMillimeters	6	Measurements are in millimeters.
vbCentimeters	7	Measurements are in centimeters.

Table P-98: ScaleMode *values.*

- *PropertyPageObject.***ScaleTop**—an **Integer** value that sets or returns the value of the Y-coordinate of the top edge of the form.
- *PropertyPageObject.***ScaleWidth**—an **Integer** value that sets or returns the width of the object in the units specified by **ScaleMode**.
- *PropertyPageObject.***SelectedControls**—an object reference to a collection containing all of the currently selected controls on the form.
- *PropertyPageObject.***StandardSize**—an **Integer** value (see Table P-99) that sets the property page to a standard size.

StandardSize Name	Value	Description
Custom	0	The size is determined by the Height and Width properties.
Small	1	The size is 101 by 375 pixels.
Large	2	The size is 197 by 375 pixels.

Table P-99: StandardSize *values.*

- *PropertyPageObject.***Tag**—a **String** that can hold programmer-specific information. This property is not used by Visual Basic.

Methods

PropertyPageObject.Circle [Step] (x , y), radius [, color [, start [, stop [, aspect]]]]

Usage   This method draws a circle, an ellipse, or a curved line on the form. All coordinate information used is relative to the **ScaleMode**, **ScaleHeight**, **ScaleLeft**, **ScaleTop**, and **ScaleWidth**.

Arguments
- **Step**—a keyword that specifies that the coordinates are relative to the form's **CurrentX** and **CurrentY** properties.
- *x*—a **Single** specifying the X-coordinate of the center of the circle.
- *y*—a **Single** specifying the Y-coordinate of the center of the circle.
- *radius*—a **Single** specifying the radius of the circle.
- *color*—a **Long** containing the color of the line to be drawn. If omitted, it will default to the value in the **ForeColor** property.
- *start*—a **Single** specifying the starting angle for the circle, in radians. If omitted, it will default to zero.
- *stop*—a **Single** specifying the ending angle for the circle, in radians. It omitted, it will default to 2 times pi (approximately 6.28).
- *aspect*—a **Single** specifying the height-to-width ratio of the circle. The default is 1.0, which will yield a perfect circle.

Tip

To draw a half-circle, assign start *a value of 0 and* stop *a value of pi (approximately 3.14), and choose values for the other parameters.*

To draw a vertical ellipse, assign a value greater than 1.0 to aspect. *A horizontal ellipse would have an aspect ratio of less than 1.0.*

PropertyPageObject.Cls

Usage   This method clears all of the graphics and text from a form.

PropertyPageObject.Line [Step] (x1 , y1), [Step] (x2 , y2) [, B | BF]

Usage   This method draws lines or boxes on the form. All coordinate information used is relative to the **ScaleMode**, **ScaleHeight**, **ScaleLeft**, **ScaleTop**, and **ScaleWidth**.

Arguments
- **Step**—a keyword that specifies that the *x1* and *y1* coordinates are relative to the form's **CurrentX** and **CurrentY** properties.
- *x1*—a **Single** specifying the starting X-coordinate of the center of the line or box.
- *y1*—a **Single** specifying the starting Y-coordinate of the center of the line or box.
- **Step**—a keyword that specifies that the *x2* and *y2* coordinates are relative to the form's **CurrentX** and **CurrentY** properties.
- *x2*—a **Single** specifying the stopping X-coordinate of the center of the line or box.
- *y2*—a **Single** specifying the stopping Y-coordinate of the center of the line or box.
- *color*—a **Long** containing the color of the line to be drawn. If omitted, it will default to the value in the **ForeColor** property.

- **B**—draw a box with (*x1, y1*) and (*x2, y2*) specifying the opposite corners of the box. If omitted, a line will be drawn on the form.
- **BF**—draw a box with (*x1, y1*) and (*x2, y2*) specifying the opposite corners of the box and fill the interior with the color specified by **FillColor** and **FillStyle**. If omitted, a line will be drawn on the form.

PropertyPageObject.OLEDrag

Usage — This method begins an **OLEDrag**-and-drop operation. Invoking this method will trigger the **OLEStartDrag** event.

PropertyPageObject.PaintPicture *picture, x1 , y1,* [*width1*] *,* [*height1*] *,*[*x2*] *,* [*y2*] *,* [*width2*] *,* [*height2*] *,* [*rasterop*]

Usage — This method displays an image (.BMP, .DIB, .EMF, .ICO, or .WMF) on the form. All coordinate information used is relative to the **ScaleMode**, **ScaleHeight**, **ScaleLeft**, **ScaleTop**, and **ScaleWidth**.

Arguments
- *picture*—the image to be displayed on the form. It can come from the **Picture** property of a picture box or another form.
- *x1*—a **Single** specifying the starting X-coordinate of the picture
- *y1*—a **Single** specifying the starting Y-coordinate of the picture.
- *width1*—a **Single** specifying the width of the image. If omitted, the width will default to the width of the image. If greater or less than the width of the image, the image will be stretched or shrunk to fit.
- *height1*—a **Single** specifying the height of the image. If omitted, the height will default to the height of the image. If greater or less than the height of the image, the image will be stretched or shrunk to fit.
- *x2*—a **Single** specifying the starting X-coordinate of a clipping region within the picture. If omitted, zero will be used.
- *y2*—a **Single** specifying the starting Y-coordinate of a clipping region within the picture. If omitted, zero will be used.
- *width2*—a **Single** specifying the width of the clipping region of the image. If omitted, the width will default to the width of the image. If greater or less than the width of the image, the image will be stretched or shrunk to fit.
- *height2*—a **Single** specifying the height of the clipping region of the image. If omitted, the height will default to the height of the image. If greater or less than the height of the image, the image will be stretched or shrunk to fit.
- *rasterop*—a **Long** containing a raster op code from Table P-100 below that will perform a bit-wise operation on the image as it is displayed. The default will be to display the image as is.

RasterOp Name	Value	Description
vbDstInvert	&H005A0049	Inverts the destination image.
vbMergeCopy	&H00C000CA	Combines the source and the pattern.
vbMergePaint	&H00BB0226	Combines inverted source image with destination image using OR.
vbNotSrcCopy	&H00330008	Copies inverted source image to the destination.
vbNotSrcErase	&H001100A6	Inverts the result of combining the source and destination images using OR.
vbPatCopy	&H00F00021	Copies the source pattern to the destination bitmap.
vbPatInvert	&H005A0049	Combines the inverted source pattern with the destination image using XOR.
vbPatPaint	&H00FB0A09	Combines the destination image with the source pattern.
vbScrAnd	&H008800C6	Combines the destination and source images using AND.
vbSrcCopy	&H00CC0020	Copies the source image to the destination bitmap.
vbSrcErase	&H00440328	Combines the inverted destination image with the source image using AND.
vbSrcInvert	&H00660046	Combines the source and destination images using XOR.
vbSrcPaint	&H00EE0086	Combines the source and destination images using OR.

Table P-100: RasterOp values.

color = PropertyPageObject.Point (x , y)

Usage   This method returns a **Long** containing the color at the point at location *x, y*. If the location is outside the form, then -1 will be returned. All coordinate information used is relative to the **ScaleMode**, **ScaleHeight**, **ScaleLeft**, **ScaleTop**, and **ScaleWidth**.

Arguments
- *color*—a **Long** containing the color at location *x, y*.
- *x*—a **Single** specifying the X-coordinate of the point.
- *y*—a **Single** specifying the Y-coordinate of the point.

PropertyPageObject.PopupMenu menu, flags, x, y, menuitem

Usage   This method will display a pop-up menu on the screen.

Tip

Set **Visible** to **False** for menu items to be displayed as pop-up menus to prevent them from being displayed in the menu bar.

PropertyPage

Arguments
- *menu*—the name of a **Menu** object to be displayed. It must include at least one submenu item.
- *flags*—zero or more items from Table P-101 below. If omitted, zero will be used. Multiple values can be selected by adding them together.

Menu Flags Name	Value	Description
vbPopupMenuLeftButton	0	The items on the menu can be selected by only the left mouse button.
vbPopupMenuLeftAlign	0	The left edge of the menu is located at *x*.
vbPopupMenuRightButton	2	The items on the menu can be selected by either mouse button.
vbPopupMenuCenterAlign	4	The center of the menu is located at *x*.
vbPopupMenuRightAlign	8	The right edge of the menu is located at *x*.

Table P-101: Menu Flags values.

- *x*—a **Single** specifying the X-coordinate of the menu. If omitted, it will default to the current X-coordinate of the mouse.
- *y*—a **Single** specifying the Y-coordinate of the menu. If omitted, it will default to the current Y-coordinate of the mouse.
- *menuitem*—the name of the submenu item that will be displayed in bold text. If omitted, no items will be displayed in bold.

PropertyPageObject.PSet [Step] (*x* , *y*), [*color*]

Usage
This method sets the point at *x*, *y* to the color specified in *color*. All coordinate information used is relative to the **ScaleMode**, **ScaleHeight**, **ScaleLeft**, **ScaleTop,** and **ScaleWidth**.

Arguments
- **Step**—keyword that specifies that the *x* and *y* coordinates are relative to the form's **CurrentX** and **CurrentY** properties.
- *x*—a **Single** specifying the X-coordinate of the point.
- *y*—a **Single** specifying the Y-coordinate of the point.
- *color*—a **Long** containing the color to be displayed at location *x*, *y*. If omitted, this value will default to the value of **ForeColor**.

PropertyPageObject.Refresh

Usage
This method redraws the contents of the form.

PropertyPageObject.Scale [(*x1* , *y1*)—(*x2* , *y2*)]

Usage
This method will define the coordinate system used on the form and set the appropriate values in **ScaleMode**, **ScaleHeight**, **ScaleLeft**, **ScaleTop,** and **ScaleWidth**. If the **Scale** method is used without any arguments, the coordinate is reset to default.

Arguments
- *x1*—a **Single** specifying the X-coordinate of the left edge of the form.
- *y1*—a **Single** specifying the Y-coordinate of the top edge of the form.
- *x2*—a **Single** specifying the X-coordinate of the right edge of the form.
- *y2*—a **Single** specifying the Y-coordinate of the bottom edge of the form.

result = PropertyPageObject.ScaleX (width , fromscale , toscale)

Usage   This method will compute a new value for *width* in a different scale.

Arguments
- *result*—a **Single** containing a new value for *width*.
- *fromscale*—an **Integer** specifying a **ScaleMode** value for the current *width*.
- *toscale*—an **Integer** value (see Table P-102) specifying the **ScaleMode** value for the new *width*.

ScaleMode Name	Value	Description
vbUser	0	Measurements are custom defined, based on the values in ScaleHeight, ScaleLeft, ScaleTop, or ScaleWidth properties.
vbTwips	1	Measurements are in twips (1440 twips per inch).
vbPoints	2	Measurements are in points (72 per inch).
vbPixels	3	Measurements are in pixels (smallest unit of measure for a monitor or printer).
vbCharacters	4	Measurements are in characters (horizontal = 120 twips per character, vertical = 240 twips per character).
vbInches	5	Measurements are in inches.
vbMillimeters	6	Measurements are in millimeters.
vbCentimeters	7	Measurements are in centimeters.
vbHimetric	8	Measurements are in himetrics.

Table P-102: ScaleMode *values.*

result = PropertyPageObject.ScaleY (height , fromscale , toscale)

Usage   This method will compute a new value for *height* in a different scale.

Arguments
- *result*—a **Single** containing a new value for *height*.
- *fromscale*—an **Integer** specifying a **ScaleMode** value for the current *height*.
- *toscale*—an **Integer** value (see Table P-103) specifying the **ScaleMode** value for the new *height*.

ScaleMode Name	Value	Description
vbUser	0	Measurements are custom defined, based on the values in ScaleHeight, ScaleLeft, ScaleTop, or ScaleWidth properties.
vbTwips	1	Measurements are in twips (1440 twips per inch).
vbPoints	2	Measurements are in points (72 per inch).
vbPixels	3	Measurements are in pixels (smallest unit of measure for a monitor or printer).
vbCharacters	4	Measurements are in characters (horizontal = 120 twips per character, vertical = 240 twips per character).
vbInches	5	Measurements are in inches.
vbMillimeters	6	Measurements are in millimeters.
vbCentimeters	7	Measurements are in centimeters.
vbHimetric	8	Measurements are in himetrics.

Table P-103: ScaleMode *values.*

*PropertyPageObject.*SetFocus

Usage This method transfers the focus from the form or control that currently has the focus to this form. To receive the focus, this form must be enabled and visible.

*height = PropertyPageObject.*TextHeight (*string*)

Usage This method will compute the height of the string in the units specified by **ScaleMode**. The height is computed using the font information specified in the **Font** object. If *string* contains embedded carriage return linefeed pairs, then the length of the longest line will be returned.

Arguments
- *height*—a **Single** that contains the height of *string*.
- *string*—a **String** that contains characters to be printed on the form.

*width = PropertyPageObject.*TextWidth (*string*)

Usage This method will compute the width of the string in the units specified by **ScaleMode**. The width is computed using the font information specified in the **Font** object. If *string* contains embedded carriage return linefeed pairs, then the length of the longest line will be returned.

Arguments
- *width*—a **Single** that contains the width of *string*.
- *string*—a **String** that contains characters to be printed on the form.

Events

Private Sub *PropertyPage*_Activate ( )

Usage This event occurs when the form becomes the active form. The form becomes active if either the **Show** or **SetFocus** method is used or if the user takes some action such as clicking on the form.

Private Sub *PropertyPage*_ApplyChanges ( )

Usage This event occurs when the user presses the OK button or the Apply button on the form.

Private Sub *PropertyPageObject*_Click( )

Usage This event occurs when the user clicks a mouse button while the cursor is positioned over a disabled control or blank area on the form.

Tip

*If you need to identify which mouse button was pressed, use the **MouseUp** and **MouseDown** events.*

Private Sub *PropertyPageObject*_DblClick( )

Usage This event occurs when the user double-clicks a mouse button while the cursor is positioned over a disabled control or blank area on the form.

Warning

*If there is code in the **Click** event, then the **DblClick** event will never occur.*

Private Sub *PropertyPageObject*_Deactivate ( )

Usage This event occurs when the form loses the focus and is no longer the active window.

Private Sub *PropertyPageObject*_DragDrop (*source* As Control, *x* As Single, *y* As Single)

Usage This event occurs when a drag-and-drop operation is completed by using the **Drag** method with a *DragAction* value of *vbEndDrag* (2).

Tip

*When using drag-and-drop operations, use the **DragOver** event to determine what the cursor should look like while the cursor moves over the control.*

Arguments
- *source*—a control object that is the control that is being dragged.

Tip

You can access a property or method from the source control by using **source**.*property or* **source**.*method. You can determine the type of object or control by using the* **TypeOf** *operator.*

- *x*—a **Single** that contains the horizontal location of the mouse pointer.
- *y*—a **Single** that contains the vertical location of the mouse pointer.

Private Sub *PropertyPageObject*_DragOver (*source* As Control, *x* As Single, *y* As Single, *state* As Integer)

Usage This event occurs while a drag operation is in progress and the cursor is moved over the control.

Tip

When using drag-and-drop operations, use the **DragOver** *event to determine what the cursor should look like while the cursor moves over the control. When* **state** *is 0, you can change the cursor to a No Drop (vbNoDrop) cursor or highlight the field that the cursor is near. When* **state** *is 1, you can undo the changes you made when the* **state** *was 0.*

Arguments
- *source*—a control object that is the control that is being dragged.

Tip

You can access a property or method from the source control by using **source**.*property or* **source**.*method. You can determine the type of object or control by using the* **TypeOf** *operator.*

- *x*—a **Single** that contains the horizontal location of the mouse pointer.
- *y*—a **Single** that contains the vertical location of the mouse pointer.
- *state*—an **Integer** value (see Table P-104) that indicates the state of the object being dragged.

state Name	Value	Description
vbEnter	0	The dragged object is entering range of the control.
vbLeave	1	The dragged object is leaving range of the control.
vbOver	2	The dragged object has moved from one position over the control to another.

Table P-104: State *values.*

Private Sub *PropertyPageObject*_EditProperty (*name* As String)

Usage   This event occurs when a user presses on an ellipsis button to change a property in the normal property window.

Tip

Use the routine to open the property page and place the cursor on the property selected by the user.

Arguments   ▪ *name*—the name of the property selected by the user.

Private Sub *PropertyPageObject*_GotFocus ( )

Usage   This event occurs when the form is given focus.

Tip

This event will only occur if all of the visible controls on the form are disabled.

Private Sub *PropertyPageObject*_Initialize ( )

Usage   This event occurs when the form is first created. This event will occur before the **Load** event.

Tip

*Since this event is triggered only when the form is created (and the **Load** event is triggered when the form is created and when it is loaded), it makes sense to put your initialization code in the **Load** event, unless you have specific actions that need to be done only when the form is created.*

Private Sub *PropertyPageObject*_KeyDown (*keycode* As Integer, *shift* As Single)

Usage   This event occurs when a key is pressed. If the **KeyPreview** property is **True,** this event will occur before the **KeyPress** event for control with the focus. Otherwise, the form will only see this event if it contains no visible and enabled controls.

Arguments   ▪ *keycode*—an **Integer** that contains information about which key was pressed.
▪ *shift*—an **Integer** value (see Table P-105) that contains information about the Shift and Alt keys that were pressed when the mouse button was pressed. These values can be added together if more than one key was down. For instance, a value of 5 would mean that the Shift and Alt keys were both down when the mouse button was pressed.

shift Name	Value	Description
vbShiftMask	1	The Shift key was pressed.
vbCtrlMask	2	The Ctrl key was pressed.
vbAltMask	4	The Alt key was pressed.

Table P-105: Shift *values.*

Private Sub *PropertyPageObject*_KeyPress (*keychar* As Integer)

Usage   This event occurs when a key is pressed. If the **KeyPreview** property is **True,** this event will occur before the **KeyPress** event for control with the focus. Otherwise, the form will only see this event if it contains no visible and enabled controls.

Arguments   • *keychar*—an **Integer** that contains the ASCII character that was pressed. Changing the value of *keychar* to zero will cancel the keystroke.

Private Sub *PropertyPageObject*_KeyUp (*keycode* As Integer, *shift* As Single)

Usage   This event occurs when a key is pressed. If the **KeyPreview** property is **True,** this event will occur before the **KeyPress** event for control with the focus. Otherwise, the form will only see this event if it contains no visible and enabled controls.

Arguments   • *keycode*—an **Integer** that contains information about which key was released.

• *shift*—an **Integer** value (see Table P-106) that contains information about the Shift and Alt keys that were pressed when the mouse button was pressed. These values can be added together if more than one key was down. For instance, a value of 5 would mean that the Shift and Alt keys were both down when the mouse button was pressed.

shift Name	Value	Description
vbShiftMask	1	The Shift key was pressed.
vbCtrlMask	2	The Ctrl key was pressed.
vbAltMask	4	The Alt key was pressed.

Table P-106: Shift *values.*

Private Sub *PropertyPageObject*_Load ( )

Usage   This event occurs when a form is being loaded and occurs after the **Initialize** event.

Tip

This is a good spot to place any initialization code for the form.

Private Sub *PropertyPageObject*_LostFocus ( )

Usage   This event occurs when the form loses focus.

Private Sub *PropertyPageObject*_MouseDown (*button* As Integer, *shift* As Single, *x* As Single, *y* As Single)

Usage   This event occurs when a mouse button is pressed while the cursor is over any unoccupied part of the form.

Arguments
- *button*—an **Integer** value (see Table P-107) that contains information about the mouse buttons that were pressed. Only one button will be indicated when this event occurs.

button Name	Value	Description
vbLeftButton	1	The left button was pressed.
vbRightButton	2	The right button was pressed.
vbMiddleButton	4	The middle button was pressed.

Table P-107: Button *values*.

- *shift*—an **Integer** value (see Table P-108) that contains information about the Shift and Alt keys that were pressed when the mouse button was pressed. These values can be added together if more than one key was down. For instance, a value of 5 would mean that the Shift and Alt keys were both down when the mouse button was pressed.

shift Name	Value	Description
vbShiftMask	1	The Shift key was pressed.
vbCtrlMask	2	The Ctrl key was pressed.
vbAltMask	4	The Alt key was pressed.

Table P-108: Shift *values*.

- *x*—a **Single** that contains the horizontal location of the mouse pointer.
- *y*—a **Single** that contains the vertical location of the mouse pointer.

Private Sub *PropertyPageObject*_MouseMove (*button* As Integer, *shift* As Single, *x* As Single, *y* As Single)

Usage   This event occurs while the cursor is moved over any unoccupied part of the form.

Arguments
- *button*—an **Integer** value (see Table P-109) that contains information about the mouse buttons that were pressed. These values can be added together if more than one button was pressed. For instance, a value of 3 means that both the left and right buttons were pressed. A value of 0 means that no buttons were pressed.

button Name	Value	Description
vbLeftButton	1	The left button was pressed.
vbRightButton	2	The right button was pressed.
vbMiddleButton	4	The middle button was pressed.

Table P-109: Button *values*.

- *shift*—an **Integer** value (see Table P-110) that contains information about the Shift and Alt keys that were pressed when the mouse button was pressed. For instance, a value of 5 would mean that the Shift and Alt keys were both down when the mouse button was pressed. A value of 0 means that none of these keys were pressed.

shift Name	Value	Description
vbShiftMask	1	The Shift key was pressed.
vbCtrlMask	2	The Ctrl key was pressed.
vbAltMask	4	The Alt key was pressed.

Table P-110: Shift *values*.

- *x*—a **Single** that contains the horizontal location of the mouse pointer.
- *y*—a **Single** that contains the vertical location of the mouse pointer.

Private Sub *PropertyPageObject*_MouseUp (*button* As Integer, *shift* As Single, *x* As Single, *y* As Single)

Usage This event occurs when a mouse button is released while the cursor is over any unoccupied part of the form.

Arguments
- *button*—an **Integer** value (see Table P-111) that contains information about the mouse buttons that were released. Only one of these values will be present.

button Name	Value	Description
vbLeftButton	1	The left button was released.
vbRightButton	2	The right button was released.
vbMiddleButton	4	The middle button was released.

Table P-111: Button *values*.

- *shift*—an **Integer** value (see Table P-112) that contains information about the Shift and Alt keys that were pressed when the mouse button was released. These values can be added together if more than one key was down. For instance, a value of 5 would mean that the Shift and Alt keys were both down when the mouse button was released. A value of 0 means that none of these keys were pressed.

shift Name	Value	Description
vbShiftMask	1	The Shift key was pressed.
vbCtrlMask	2	The Ctrl key was pressed.
vbAltMask	4	The Alt key was pressed.

Table P-112: Shift *values*.

- *x*—a **Single** that contains the horizontal location of the mouse pointer.
- *y*—a **Single** that contains the vertical location of the mouse pointer.

Private Sub *PropertyPageObject*_OLECompleteDrag(*effect* As Long)

Usage   This event tells the source control the results of an OLE drag-and-drop operation. This is the final event to occur in the series of actions that make up an OLE drag-and-drop operation.

Arguments
- *effect*—a **Long** (see Table P-113) that returns the status of the OLE drag-and-drop operation.

effect Name	Value	Description
vbDropEffectNone	0	The operation was canceled or the target control can't accept the drop operation.
vbDropEffectCopy	1	The operation copies data from the source control to the target control. The original data is unchanged.
vbDropEffectMove	2	The operation results in a link from the original data to the target control.

Table P-113: *Effect* values.

Private Sub *PropertyPageObject*_OLEDragDrop (*data* As DataObject, *effect* As Long, *button* As Integer, *shift* As Single, *x* As Single, *y* As Single)

Usage   This event tells the source control the results of an OLE drag-and-drop operation. This is the final event to occur in the series of actions that make up an OLE drag- and drop-operation.

Arguments
- *data*—a **DataObject** that contains the formats that the source control will provide. If the data is not contained in the **DataObject**, then it can be retrieved with the **GetData** method.
- *effect*—a **Long** (see Table P-114) that returns the status of the OLE drag-and-drop operation.

effect Name	Value	Description
vbDropEffectNone	0	The operation was canceled or the target control can't accept the drop operation.
vbDropEffectCopy	1	The operation copies data from the source control to the target control. The original data is unchanged.
vbDropEffectMove	2	The operation results in a link from the original data to the target control.

Table P-114: *Effect* values.

- *button*—an **Integer** value (see Table P-115) that contains information about the mouse buttons that were pressed. These values can be added together if more than one button was pressed. For instance, a value of 3 means that both the left and right buttons were pressed. A value of 0 means that no buttons were pressed.

button Name	Value	Description
vbLeftButton	1	The left button was pressed.
vbRightButton	2	The right button was pressed.
vbMiddleButton	4	The middle button was pressed.

Table P-115: Button *values*.

- *shift*—an **Integer** value (see Table P-116) that contains information about the Shift and Alt keys that were pressed when the mouse button was released. These values can be added together if more than one key was down. For instance, a value of 5 would mean that the Shift and Alt keys were both down when the mouse button was released. A value of 0 means that none of these keys were pressed.

shift Name	Value	Description
vbShiftMask	1	The Shift key was pressed.
vbCtrlMask	2	The Ctrl key was pressed.
vbAltMask	4	The Alt key was pressed.

Table P-116: Shift *values*.

- *x*—a **Single** that contains the horizontal location of the mouse pointer.
- *y*—a **Single** that contains the vertical location of the mouse pointer.

Private Sub *PropertyPageObject_OLEDragOver* (*data* **As** DataObject, *effect* **As Long,** *button* **As Integer,** *shift* **As Single,** *x* **As Single,** *y* **As Single,** *state* **As Integer**)

Usage   This event happens when an OLE drag-and-drop operation is in progress.

Arguments
- *data*—a **DataObject** that contains the formats that the source control will provide. If the data is not contained in the **DataObject**, then it can be retrieved with the **GetData** method.
- *effect*—a **Long** (see Table P-117) that returns the status of the OLE drag-and-drop operation.

shift Name	Value	Description
vbDropEffectNone	0	The operation was canceled or the target control can't accept the drop operation.
vbDropEffectCopy	1	The operation copies data from the source control to the target control. The original data is unchanged.
vbDropEffectMove	2	The operation results in a link from the original data to the target control.

Table P-117: Effect *values*.

- *button*—an **Integer** value (see Table P-118) that contains information about the mouse buttons that were pressed. These values can be added together if more than one button was pressed. For instance, a value of 3 means that both the left and right buttons were pressed. A value of 0 means that no buttons were pressed.

button Name	Value	Description
vbLeftButton	1	The left button was pressed.
vbRightButton	2	The right button was pressed.
vbMiddleButton	4	The middle button was pressed.

Table P-118: Button *values*.

- *shift*—an **Integer** value (see Table P-119) that contains information about the Shift and Alt keys that were pressed when the mouse button was released. These values can be added together if more than one key was down. For instance, a value of 5 would mean that the Shift and Alt keys were both down when the mouse button was released. A value of 0 means that none of these keys were pressed.

shift Name	Value	Description
vbShiftMask	1	The Shift key was pressed.
vbCtrlMask	2	The Ctrl key was pressed.
vbAltMask	4	The Alt key was pressed.

Table P-119: Shift *values*.

- *x*—a **Single** that contains the horizontal location of the mouse pointer.
- *y*—a **Single** that contains the vertical location of the mouse pointer.
- *state*—an **Integer** value (see Table P-120) that indicates the state of the object being dragged.

state Name	Value	Description
vbEnter	0	The dragged object is entering range of the control.
vbLeave	1	The dragged object is leaving range of the control.
vbOver	2	The dragged object has moved from one position over the control to another.

Table P-120: State values.

Private Sub *PropertyPageObject*_OLEGiveFeedback (*effect* As Long)

Usage This event tells the source control what is happening while the OLE drag-and-drop operation is in progress. This event occurs after the **OLEDragOver** event.

Tip

You may want to use this event to change the cursor to reflect what can happen in the remote object.

Arguments *effect*—a **Long** (see Table P-121) that returns the status of the OLE drag-and-drop operation.

effect Name	Value	Description
vbDropEffectNone	0	The operation was canceled or the target control can't accept the drop operation.
vbDropEffectCopy	1	The operation copies data from the source control to the target control. The original data is unchanged.
vbDropEffectMove	2	The operation results in a link from the original data to the target control.
vbDropEffectScroll	&H80000000	The target control is about to scroll or is scrolling. This value may be added to the other *shift* values.

Table P-121: Effect values.

Private Sub *PropertyPageObject*_OLESetData (*data* As DataObject, *DataFormat* As Integer)

Usage This event happens in response to the target object performing a **GetData** method on *data*. This routine will respond by using the **SetData** method with the desired data using the **DataObject** *data*.

Arguments • *data*—a **DataObject** that will contain the data to be returned to the target object.
• *format*—an **Integer** value (see Table P-122) that contains the format of the data.

format Name	Value	Description
vbCFText	1	Text (.TXT files).
vbCFBitmap	2	Bitmap (.BMP files).
vbCFMetafile	3	Metafile (.WMF files).
vbCFEDIB	8	Device independent bitmap (DIB).
vbCFPallette	9	Color palette.
vbCFEMetafile	14	Enhanced metafile (.EMF files).
vbCFFiles	15	List of files.
vbCFRTF	-16639	Rich Text Format (.RTF files).

Table P-122: Format *values.*

Private Sub *PropertyPageObject*_OLEStartDrag (*data* As DataObject, *AllowedEffects* As Long)

Usage This event starts an OLE drag-and-drop operation.

Arguments • *data*—a **DataObject** that will contain the formats that the source object is willing to provide to the target object. It may optionally contain the data to be transferred.

• *AllowedEffects*—a **Long** (see Table P-123) that contains the effects that the target object can request from the source object. The *AllowedEffects* can be added together if the source object supports more than one effect. Note that the target object can always use the *vbDropEffectNone* effect.

AllowedEffects Name	Value	Description
vbDropEffectNone	0	The target can't copy the data.
vbDropEffectCopy	1	The target can copy the data, and the source will keep the data unchanged.
vbDropEffectMove	2	The target can copy the data, and the source will delete the data.

Table P-123: AllowedEffects *values.*

Private Sub *PropertyPageObject*_Paint ( )

Usage This event occurs when the form must redraw itself. This can happen because the form was previously covered and now is not, the size of the form has been changed, or the form has been moved. A **Paint** event is necessary if you generate graphics or print text directly to the form and have set the **AutoRedraw** property to **False**.

> **Tip**
>
> *Avoid moving the form, changing any variables that affect the form's size or appearance, and using the **Refresh** method. This can cause a cascading event where the **Move** event will trigger another **Paint** event, which in turn triggers the **Move** event again. Without safeguards, this process will continue until the program crashes or your system crashes.*

Private Sub *PropertyPageObject*_SelectionChanged ( )

Usage   This event occurs when the selection of controls on the form changes.

Private Sub *PropertyPageObject*_Terminate ( )

Usage   This event occurs when the last instance of a form is ready to be removed from memory. It will not be called if for some reason (such as that the **End** statement is executed) the program terminates abnormally.

Private Sub *PropertyPageObject*_Unload (*cancel* As Integer)

Usage   This event is called before a form is unloaded. While *cancel* can be set to keep the form from being unloaded, it will not stop processes like Windows from being shut down. You should use the **QueryUnload** event instead.

Arguments   ▪ *cancel*—an **Integer** that, when set to any value except zero, will stop the unload process. Setting *cancel* to zero will let the process continue.

See Also   **UserControl** (object)

Public

STATEMENT

CCE, LE, PE, EE

Syntax   `Public [ WithEvents ] identifier[typechar] [ arrayinfo ] [ As [ New ] type ] , [ [ WithEvents ] identifier[typechar] [ arrayinfo ] [ As [ New ] type ] ] . . .`

Usage   The **Public** statement is used to declare the variables at the module level, outside any procedure. These variables will be available to all of the routines in the module and all other modules.

If **Option Explicit** is included in a module, then all of the variables used in your program must be declared before they can be used.

> **Tip**
>
> *Use **Option Explicit** in all modules, because this will force you to declare all variables before you use them. This will help you avoid the situation where you think you have one variable, but Visual Basic thinks you have two because you used two different spellings.*

Arguments
- **WithEvents**—an optional keyword, used only in class modules, that means *Variable* is used to respond to events triggered by an ActiveX object.
- *identifier*—the Visual Basic identifier that will be used to reference this particular variable. It must begin with a letter, which can be followed by any number of letters or numbers or the underscore character ("_"). Identifiers are not case sensitive, though the case will be preserved for easier reading.
- *typechar*—one of the following characters can be included as the last character of a variable name to declare its type: "@" for **Currency**, "#" for **Double**, "%" for **Integer**, "&" for **Long**, "!" for **Single**, or "$" for **String**. The default type for variables without a typechar is **Variant** unless the type is specified using the **As** clause or one of the **Deftype** statements.
- *arrayinfo*—optionally indicates an array. It can have zero or more dimensions. An array can have no more than 60 dimensions. If no dimensions are specified, then the variable is considered a dynamic array and the subscripts must be set with the **ReDim** statement before it can be used. The subscripts are defined as:

  ([ubound | lbound **To** ubound] [, ubound | , lbound **To** ubound] . . .)]

ubound	the upper bound for an array.
lbound	the lower bound for an array's subscript. If omitted, the value from **Option Base** will be used. If there is no **Option Base** statement in the module, a value of zero will be assumed.

- **New**—an optional keyword that means that a new instance of the object is automatically created the first time it is used. It can't be used either with the **WithEvents** keyword or with a non-object type.
- *type*—a valid Visual Basic type: **Byte**, **Boolean**, **Currency**, **Date**, **Double**, **Integer**, **Long**, **Single**, **String**, **Object**, or **Variant**. Specific objects can also be used, as well as user-defined types defined, with the **Type** statement.

See Also
Byte (data type), **Boolean** (data type), **Currency** (data type), **Date** (data type), **Dim** (statement), **Double** (data type), **Integer** (data type), **Long** (data type), **Object** (data type), **Option Base** (statement), **Option Explicit** (statement), **Public** (statement), **ReDim** (statement), **Single** (data type), **String** (data type), **Static** (statement), **Type** (statement), **TypeName** (function), **Variant** (data type)

Put

STATEMENT

CCE, LE, PE, EE

Syntax   `Put [#]`*filenum* `,[` *recnum* `] ,` *vname*

Usage   The **Get** statement reads data from a disk file into a variable. The first record has a record number of 1. If the *recnum* argument is omitted, then the next record will be read from the file, unless you use the **Seek** statement to change the pointer to the next record.

For files opened with the random option, the **Len** option of the **Open** statement determines the record size. Variable-length **Strings** are stored with their length, so the length of the record must be at least two bytes longer than the length of the longest string. If you are reading **Variant** variables from disk, then two bytes are required to identify the **Variant's** type. (If the type is **String,** then two more bytes are required.) Fixed-length arrays do not have any additional overhead, but variable-length arrays require two bytes plus eight bytes for each dimension of the array (e.g., a two-dimensional array will require 2 bytes + 2 times 8 bytes for a total of 18 bytes of overhead storage).

For files opened with the binary option, the **Len** clause on the open statement has no effect. Variables are read from disk without any overhead bytes, including variable-length **Strings**. When variable-length **Strings** are read from disk, only the number of characters already in the string are read (e.g., if the length of the string before the **Get** was 80 characters, then the next 80 characters will be read).

> **Tip**
>
> Use the **Put** statement to write data that will be read with the **Get** statement.

Arguments
- *filenum*—an open file number created by the **Open** statement.
- *recnum*—a **Long** that specifies the record number (random files) or byte number (binary files) of the file. If omitted, then the next record in the file will be read.
- *vname*—any valid Visual Basic variable. It can be of type **Byte, Boolean, Currency, Date, Double, Integer, Long, Single, String,** or **Variant**.

Examples
```
Private Sub Command2_Click()
Dim i As Integer
Open App.Path & "\GetPut.Dat" For Binary Access Write As #1
i = 1
Do While i <= 16
   Put #1, , i
   i = i + 1
Loop
Close #1
End Sub
```

This routine opens a binary file and writes a series of integers to it.

See Also   **Byte** (data type), **Boolean** (data type), **Close** (statement), **Currency** (data type), **Date** (data type), **Double** (data type), **Get** (statement), **Integer** (data type), **Long** (data type), **Open** (statement), **Single** (data type), **Seek** (statement), **Stop** (statement), **String** (data type), **Variant** (data type)

PV

FUNCTION

CCE, LE, PE, EE

Syntax `pvalue = PV ( rate, nper [, pmt [, fv [, type ] ] ] )`

Usage The **PV** function returns the present value of a fixed-payment annuity. Cash paid out is represented by negative numbers. Cash received is represented by positive numbers.

Arguments
- *pvalue*—a **Double** value containing the future value of the annuity.
- *rate*—a **Double** value containing the interest rate per period.

> **Tip**
>
> To convert from APR to rate *divide the APR by 100 to get a percentage rate and then by the number of periods in a year to get a value for* rate.

- *nper*—an **Integer** value containing the number of periods in the annuity.
- *pmt*—a **Double** value containing the payment for each period.
- *fv*—a **Variant** value containing the future value of the annuity. If not specified, it will default to zero.
- *type*—a **Variant** value, when 0, means that the payment is due at the end of the period. When 1, means that the payment is due at the beginning of the period. If not specified, it will default to 0.

Examples
```
Private Sub Command1_Click()
Text4.Text = Format(-PV(CDbl(Text1.Text), CInt(Text2.Text), CDbl(Text3.Text)),
    "currency")
End Sub
```

This routine computes the future value of a stream of payments.

See Also **DDB** (function), **FV** (function), **IPmt** (function), **IRR** (function), **MIRR** (function), **NPer** (function), **NPV** (function), **PMT** (function), **PPmt** (function), **Rate** (function), **SLN** (function), **SYD** (function)

QBColor

FUNCTION

CCE, LE, PE, EE

Syntax `LValue = QBColor ( color )`

Usage The **QBColor** function returns a 24 bit RGB (Red Green Blue) color value based on a color code from earlier versions of Visual Basic (such as Quick Basic).

Arguments
- *LValue*—a **Long** value containing the 24 bit RGB color.
- *color*—an **Integer** value from zero to fifteen corresponding to the following colors: black, blue, green, cyan, red, magenta, yellow, white, gray, light blue, light green, light cyan, light red, light magenta, light yellow, and bright white.

Examples
```
Private Sub Command1_Click()
mycolor = (mycolor + 1) Mod 16
Text1.BackColor = QBColor(mycolor)
End Sub
```

This routine changes the background color of the Text1 text box each time the button is pressed.

See Also **RGB** (function)

QueryDef

OBJECT

PE, EE

Usage The **QueryDef** object is used to access the Microsoft Jet database engine directly or to access other database systems using ODBC.

Properties
- *QueryDefObject*.**CacheSize**—a **Long** value containing the number of records retrieved from an ODBC source that will be kept locally. This property can range in size from 5 to 1,200, but it may be limited by available memory. A value of 100 is typical and a value of zero will disable caching.
- *QueryDefObject*.**Connect**—a **String** value containing the type of database and any necessary connection information.
- *QueryDefObject*.**DateCreated**—a **Variant** containing the date and time the object was created.
- *QueryDefObject*.**Containers**—an object containing the collection of **Container** objects defined in the database object.
- *QueryDefObject*.**KeepLocal**—a **String** value that, when it contains a "T," keeps the query definition local when it would normally be replicated.
- *QueryDefObject*.**LastUpdated**—a **Variant** containing the date and time the object was last updated.
- *QueryDefObject*.**LogMessages**—a **Boolean** value that, when **True,** means messages will be returned from a Microsoft Jet connected to an ODBC database that will be kept in a log. The **LogMessages** property must be created using the **CreateProperty** method before it is used. When **False** the messages will not be kept.

- *QueryDefObject*.**MaxRecords**—a **Long** containing the maximum number of records that can be retrieved in a query. A value of zero means that an unlimited number of records will be retrieved.
- *QueryDefObject*.**Name**—a **String** value containing the name of the **Querydef** object.
- *QueryDefObject*.**ODBCTimeout**—a **Long** value containing the number of seconds before a timeout will occur while running a query on an ODBC database. A value of zero will disable timeouts, and a value of -1 will set this property to the value specified in the **QueryTimeout** in the **Connection** object.
- *QueryDefObject*.**Prepare**—an **Integer** value containing either the constant *dbQPrepare* (the query is prepared on the ODBC server as a temporary stored procedure—default) or *dbQUnprepare* (the query is not prepared and executed directly).
- *QueryDefObject*.**RecordsAffected**—a **Long** value containing the number of records affected by the last **Execute** method.
- *QueryDefObject*.**Replicable**—an object created by using the **CreateProperty** method that, when "T," means that the database can be replicated. When "F," the database can't be replicated. Once this value is set to "T," it can't be changed.
- *QueryDefObject*.**ReturnsRecords**—a **Boolean** value that, when **True,** means a pass-through query (executed totally on the ODBC server) may return records. **False** means that no records will be returned.
- *QueryDefObject*.**SQL**—a **String** containing the SQL statement associated with the **QueryDef**.
- *QueryDefObject*.**Type**—an **Integer** value containing a value from Table Q-1 below.
- *QueryDefObject*.**Updatable**—a **Boolean** value when **True** means that the object can be updated. When **False** means that the object can't be updated.

type Name	Description
dbQAction	A query that copies or changes data, but doesn't return records.
dbQAppend	A query that appends rows to a table (doesn't return any records).
dbQCompound	Multiple queries are stored in the **SQL** property separated by a semicolon (";").
dbQCrosstab	A query that performs a crosstab operation.
dbQDDL	A query containing only data-definition language statements.
dbQDelete	A query that will delete rows from a table.
dbQMakeTable	A query that creates a new table based on the data contained in a **Recordset**.
dbQProcedure	A stored procedure query executed on an ODBC database server.
dbQSelect	A query that returns records as part of a **Recordset** object that may be updated.
dbQSetOperation	A query that returns a snapshot **Recordset** consisting of two or more tables with the duplicate records removed.
dbQSPTBulk	An SQL pass-through query using a Microsoft Jet database to access an ODBC database server that doesn't return any records.
dbQSQLPassThrough	A query that executes on a remote ODBC server.
dbQUpdate	An update query that changes records, but doesn't return any records.

Table Q-1: Type *values.*

Methods **QueryDefObject.Cancel**

Usage   This method is used to terminate an asynchronous query that was started with the **Execute** method.

QueryDefObject.Close

Usage   This method is used to close an open query. If the query is already closed, then a run-time error will occur.

property = **QueryDefObject.CreateProperty** ([*name*] [, [*type*] [, [*value*] [, *DDL*]]])

Usage   This method is used to create a user-defined **Property** object.

Arguments
- *property*—an object variable containing the new property object.
- *name*—a **String** containing the name of the property. Must begin with a letter and can be followed by letters, numbers, or an underscore ("_").
- *type*—a value selected from the Table Q-2.
- *value*—a **Variant** containing the initial value for the property.
- *DDL*—a **Boolean** when **True** means that the user cannot change this property value without the *dbSecWriteDef* permission. When **False** this permission is not required to change the value.

type Name	Description
dbQAction	A query that copies or changes data, but doesn't return records.
dbQAppend	A query that appends rows to a table (doesn't return any records).
dbQCompound	Multiple queries are stored in the SQL property separated by a semicolon (";").
dbQCrosstab	A query that performs a crosstab operation.
dbQDDL	A query containing only data-definition language statements.
dbQDelete	A query that deletes rows from a table.
dbQMakeTable	A query that creates a new table based on the data contained in a Recordset.
dbQProcedure	A stored procedure query that executes on an ODBC database server.
dbQSelect	A query that returns records as part of a Recordset object that may be updated.
dbQSetOperation	A query that returns a snapshot Recordset consisting of two or more tables with the duplicate records removed.
dbQSPTBulk	An SQL pass-through query using a Microsoft Jet database to access an ODBC database server that doesn't return any records.
dbQSQLPassThrough	A query that executes on a remote ODBC server.
dbQUpdate	An update query that changes records, but doesn't return any records.

Table Q-2: Type values.

QueryDefObject.Execute *source* [, *options*]

Usage   This method is used to run an SQL statement on a database object.

Arguments
- *source*—a **String** containing the name of a **QueryDef** object or an SQL query statement.
- *options*—a **Long** containing one or more of the attributes in Table Q-3.

options Name	Description
dbDenyWrite	Write access is denied to other users.
dbInconsistent	Allow inconsistent updates in Microsoft Jet databases.
dbConsistent	Allow only consistent updates in Microsoft Jet databases.
dbSQLPassThrough	Pass SQL query through Microsoft Jet workspace to remote ODBC database.
dbFileOnError	Perform a rollback if an error is encountered.
dbSeeChanges	Return error if another user is updating data you are using.

Table Q-3: Options values.

recordset = QueryDefObject.OpenRecordset (*type* [, *options*] [, *lockedits*]])

Usage   This method is used to create a new **RecordSet** object and append it to the **RecordSets** collection.

Arguments
- *recordset*—an object variable containing the new **TableDef** object.
- *type*—a constant from Table Q-4.

type Name	Description
dbOpenTable	Table type recordset.
dbOpenDynamic	Open a dynamic-type recordset (ODBC databases only).
dbOpenDynaset	Open a dynaset-type recordset.
dbOpenSnapshot	Open a snapshot-type recordset.
dbOpenForwardOnly	Open a forward-only type recordset.

Table Q-4: Type *values*.

- *options*—a **Long** containing one or more of the options in Table Q-5.

options Name	Description
dbAppendOnly	Add new records, but can't delete or edit existing records.
dbConsistent	Allow only consistent updates in Microsoft Jet databases. (Can't be used with *dbInconsistent*.)
dbDenyRead	Read access is denied to other users.
dbDenyWrite	Write access is denied to other users.
dbExecDirect	Skip SQLPrepare and run SQLExecDirect for ODBC queries only.

QueryDefs • **789**

options Name	Description
dbInconsistent	Allow inconsistent updates in Microsoft Jet databases. (Can't be used with dbConsistent.)
dbReadOnly	User can't change records in the database. (Can't be used if dbReadOnly is specified in lockedits.)
dbRunAsync	Run ODBC query asynchronously.
dbSeeChanges	Return error if another user is updating data you are using.
dbSQLPassThrough	Pass SQL query through Microsoft Jet workspace to remote ODBC database.

Table Q-5: Options *values*.

- *lockedits*—a **Long** containing one or more of the attributes in the Table Q-6.

lockedits Name	Description
dbOptimistic	Lock the page containing the record you are editing when you use the Update method.
dbOptimisticBatch	Enable batch optimistic updating.
dbOptimisticValue	Enable optimistic updating based on row values.
dbPessimistic	Lock the page containing the record you are editing as soon you use the **Edit** method.
dbReadOnly	User can't change records in the database. (Can't be used if dbReadOnly is specified in options.)

Table Q-6: Lockedits *values*.

See Also **Database** (object), **Databases** (collection), **Property** (object), **Properties** (collection), **Recordset** (object), **Recordsets** (collection), **Relation** (object), **Relations** (collection), **TableDef** (object), **TableDefs** (collection)

QueryDefs

COLLECTION

PE, EE

Usage   The **QueryDefs** collection is used by Data Access Objects (DAO) to contain information about a query.

Properties - *QueryDefsCollection*.**Count**—an **Integer** containing the number of **QueryDef** objects in the collection.

Methods ### QueryDefsCollection.Append *object*

Usage   This method adds a **QueryDef** object to the collection.

Arguments - *object*—a reference to a **QueryDef** object to be added to the collection.

QueryDefsCollection.Delete *objectname*

Usage This method removes a **QueryDef** object from the collection.

Arguments *objectname*—a **String** containing the name of the **QueryDef** object to be removed from the collection.

QueryDefsCollection.Refresh

Usage This method gets a current copy of the **QueryDefs** contained in the collection. This is important in a multi-user environment where more than one user may be making changes in the **Databases** collection.

See Also **QueryDef** (object)

RaiseEvent

STATEMENT

CCE, LE, PE, EE

Syntax `RaiseEvent` *event* ([*expr* [, *expr* . . . [, *expr*]]])

Usage The **RaiseEvent** statement is used inside a class, form, or document to fire an event declared at the module level.

Arguments
- *event*—the name of the event declared using the **Event** statement in the class, form or document.
- *expr*—any expression to pass to the event.

Examples
```
Public Event Zap(z As String)

Private Sub Command1_Click()
RaiseEvent Zap(Text1.Text)
End Sub
```

This routine triggers the **Zap** event, passing Text1.Text to the user's subroutine.

See Also **Event** (statement)

Randomize

STATEMENT

CCE, LE, PE, EE

Syntax `Randomize` [*expr*]

Usage The **Randomize** statement initializes the random number generator.

Arguments
- *expr*—a numeric value used as a seed for the random number generator. If not specified, a seed based on the system timer will be used.

Examples
```
Private Sub Command1_Click()
Dim i As Integer
Randomize
For i = 1 To 5
   Form1.Print Format(Rnd, "#.#####"),
Next i
Form1.Print
End Sub
```

This routine uses the **Randomize** statement to provide a seed for the random number generator. Then five random numbers will display on a single line.

See Also **Rnd** (function)

Rate

FUNCTION

CCE, LE, PE, EE

Syntax rvalue = **Rate** (nper, pmt, pv [, fv [, type [, guess]]])

Usage The **Rate** function returns the interest rate per period.

Arguments
- *rate*—a **Double** value containing the interest rate per period.

> **Tip**
>
> *To convert from APR to rate, divide the APR by 100 to get a percentage rate and then by the number of periods in a year to get a value for rate.*

- *nper*—an **Integer** value containing the number of periods in the annuity.
- *pmt*—a **Double** value containing the payment for each period.

> **Tip**
>
> *If a pmt is greater than zero, the pv will be negative or vice versa to indicate the proper direction of cash flow.*

- *pv*—a **Double** value containing the present value of the annuity.
- *fv*—a **Variant** value containing the future value of the annuity. If not specified, it will default to 0.
- *type*—a **Variant** value when 0 means that the payment is due at the end of the period. When 1 means that the payment is due at the beginning of the period. If not specified, it will default to 0.
- *guess*—a **Variant** value that contains the initial value that will be used to compute the interest rate.

Examples
```
Private Sub Command1_Click()
Text4.Text = Format(Rate(CDbl(Text1.Text), CInt(Text2.Text), CDbl(Text3.Text)),
   "percent")
End Sub
```

This routine computes the interest rate for a given number of periods, the payment, and the present value.

See Also **DDB** (function), **FV** (function), **IPmt** (function), **IRR** (function), **MIRR** (function), **NPer** (function), **NPV** (function), **PMT** (function), **PPmt** (function), **PV** (function), **SLN** (function), **SYD** (function)

rdoColumn

OBJECT
EE

Usage The **rdoColumn** object contains information about a field in the database.

Properties
- *rdoColumnObject*.**AllowZeroLength**—a **Boolean** when **True** means that a zero length string is permitted when the data type is *rdTypeCHAR*, *rdTypeVARCHAR*, or *rdTypeLONGVARCHAR*. **False** means that a zero length string is not permitted.

- *rdoColumnObject*.**Attributes**—an **Integer** containing one or more attributes for a column (see Table R-1).

Attributes Name	Value	Description
rdFixedColumn	1	The column size is fixed.
rdVariableColumn	2	The column size can vary.
rdAutoIncrColumn	16	The column contains a unique value that was automatically incremented and can't be changed.
rdUpdatable	32	The data in the column can be changed.
rdTimeStampColumn	64	The column contains a time stamp value.

Table R-1: Attributes values.

- *rdoColumnObject*.**BatchConflictValue**—a **Variant** containing the most current value of the column on the database server. This property is used only when using a batch update cursor and covers the situation where a second update process updates the data in the column in the time between when the data was retrieved and when it was updated.

- *rdoColumnObject*.**ChunkRequired**—a **Boolean** when **True** means that the data must be accessed with the **GetChunk** method. **False** means that the data doesn't require the **GetChunk** method.

- *rdoColumnObject*.**KeyColumn**—a **Boolean** when **True** means that this column is part of the primary key. **False** means that this column is not part of the primary key.

- *rdoColumnObject*.**Name**—a **String** containing the name of the column.

- *rdoColumnObject*.**OrdinalPosition**—an **Integer** containing the relative position of the column object within the columns collection. The first column in the collection has an **OrdinalPosition** of 1.

- *rdoColumnObject*.**OrdinalValue**—a **Variant** when containing the original value of a column from the database server. This property determines update conflicts with the **BatchConflictValue**.

- *rdoColumnObject*.**Required**—a **Boolean** when **True** means that a non-null value is required. **False** means that null values are permitted.

- *rdoColumnObject*.**Size**—a **Long** containing the maximum size of the column in bytes for character oriented types and the number of elements in the array for all other types.

- *rdoColumnObject*.**SourceColumn**—a **String** containing the original name of the column in the remote database.

- *rdoColumnObject*.**SourceTable**—a **String** containing the original name of the table containing the column in the remote database.
- *rdoColumnObject*.**Status**—an **Integer** containing the current status of the row containing the column with optimistic batch updates (see Table R-2).

Status Name	Value	Description
rdRowUnmodified	0	The row hasn't been changed.
rdRowModified	1	The row has been changed, but it hasn't been updated in the database.
rdRowNew	2	The row was created with the **AddNew** method, but it hasn't been inserted in the database.
rdUpdatable	3	The row has been deleted, but it hasn't been deleted in the database.
rdRowDBDeleted	4	The row has been deleted locally and on the database.

Table R-2: Status values.

- *rdoColumnObject*.**Type**—an **Integer** containing the type of data of the column (see Table R-3).

Type Name	Value	Description
rdTypeCHAR	1	A fixed length character string of length Size.
rdTypeNUMERIC	2	A signed exact numeric value.
rdTypeDECIMAL	3	A signed exact numeric value.
rdTypeINTEGER	4	A 32-bit integer.
rdTypeSMALLINT	5	A 16-bit integer.
rdTypeFLOAT	6	A double precision floating point number.
rdTypeREAL	7	A single precision floating point number.
rdTypeDOUBLE	8	A double precision floating point number.
rdTypeDATE	9	A date value. The exact format depends on the source of data.
rdTypeTIME	10	A time value. The exact format depends on the source of data.
rdTypeTIMESTAMP	11	A date-time value. The exact format depends on the source of data.
rdTypeVARCHAR	12	A variable length character string with a max length of 255.
rdTypeLONGVARCHAR	-1	A variable length character string. The max length depends on the source of the data.
rdTypeBINARY	-2	A fixed length binary data with a max length of 255.
rdTypeVARBINARY	-3	A variable length binary data with a max length of 255.
rdTypeLONGVARBINARY	-4	A variable length binary data. The max length depends on the source of the data.
rdTypeBIGINT	-5	A 64-bit integer.
rdTypeTINYINT	-6	A 1 byte integer.
rdTypeBIT	-7	A single binary digit.

Table R-3: Type values.

- *rdoColumnObject*.**Updatable**—a **Boolean** when **True** means that the data can be updated. **False** means that data can't be updated.
- *rdoColumnObject*.**Value**—a **Variant** containing the data from the column.

Methods

rdoColumnObject.AppendChunk *source*

Usage This method appends a chunk of data to the end of the value of an *rdTypeLONGVARBINARY* or *rdTypeLONGVARCHAR* column.

Arguments *source*—an expression containing the data to append to column's current value.

size = *rdoColumnObject*.ColumnSize ( )

Usage This method returns the size of the *rdTypeLONGVARBINARY* or *rdTypeLONGVARCHAR* column or -1 if the size information is not available.

value = *rdoColumnObject*.GetChunk (*number*)

Usage This method returns a chunk of data to the end of the value of an *rdTypeLONGVARBINARY* or *rdTypeLONGVARCHAR* column.

Arguments
- *value*—a **Variant** variable that will contain the result of the **GetChunk** method.
- *number*—a **Long** containing the number of bytes to return.

Events

Private Sub *rdoColumnObject*.DataChanged ( )

Usage This event occurs whenever the column's value changes.

Private Sub *rdoColumnObject*.WillChangeData (*NewValue* As Variant, *Cancel* As Boolean)

Usage This event occurs before the data changes in the column.

Arguments
- *NewValue*—an expression containing the updated data.
- *Cancel*—a **Boolean** when **True** means that the change will be aborted. **False** means that the change is permitted (default).

See Also **rdoColumns** (collection)

rdoColumns

COLLECTION

EE

Usage Remote Data Objects (RDO) uses the **rdoColumns** collection to hold information about a set of columns in an **rdoTable** or **rdoResultSet**.

Properties
- *rdoColumnsCollection*.**Count**—an **Integer** containing the number of **rdoColumn** objects in the collection.
- *rdoColumnsCollection*.**Item** (*index*)—an array of **rdoColumn** objects indexed by *index*. Index can range from 1 to **Count**.

Methods   **rdoColumnsCollection.Refresh**

Usage   This method gets a current copy of the objects in the collection. This is important in a multi-user environment where more than one user may be making changes in the database.

See Also   **rdoColumn** (object), **rdoResultSet** (object), **rdoTable** (object)

rdoConnection

OBJECT

EE

Usage   The **rdoConnection** object contains information about an open connection to a remote database.

Properties
- *rdoConnectionObject*.**AsyncCheckInterval**—a **Long** containing the number of milliseconds between checks to see if an asynchronous query has completed. It defaults to 1000 milliseconds.
- *rdoConnectionObject*.**Connect**—a **String** containing the Open Database Connectivity (ODBC) connection to a series of parameters separated by a semicolons (";"). Some common parameters are shown in Table R-4.

Connect Parameter	Description
DSN	Access registered ODBC data source (ex: DSN=Datasource;).
UID	User id for the database (ex: UID=Wayne;).
PWD	Password associated with the database (ex: PWD=Chris&Sam;).
DRIVER	ODBC driver name for the database (ex: DRIVER={SQL Server};).
DATABASE	Once connected, this database is the default (ex: DATABASE=mydatabase;).
SERVER	Use this database server (ex: DBSERV;).
WSID	Workstation id (ex: WSID=Jillion;).
APP	Application name (ex: APP=myprog;).

Table R-4: Connect values.

- *rdoConnectionObject*.**CursorDriver**—an **Integer** containing the type of cursor that will be used (see Table R-5).

CursorDriver Name	Value	Description
rdUseIfNeeded	0	The ODBC driver chooses the most appropriate cursor (default).
rdUseODBC	1	Use the ODBC cursor library. Better performance for small tables, but poorer performance on large tables.
rdUseServer	2	Use server side cursors. Better performance for large sets at the expense of higher network traffic.
rdUseClientBatch	3	Use the batch cursor library.
rdUseNone	4	Do not use a cursor. This results in a read-only result that can be read in a forward direction only. It has faster performance than the other options.

Table R-5: CursorDriver values.

- *rdoConnectionObject*.**hDbc**—a reference to an ODBC connection handle.
- *rdoConnectionObject*.**LastQueryResults**—a reference to an **rdoResultset** object containing the results of the last query executed or **Nothing** if there wasn't a last query.
- *rdoConnectionObject*.**LoginTimeout**—a **Long** containing the number of seconds a login will be attempted before returning an error.
- *rdoConnectionObject*.**Name**—a **String** containing the name of the connection.
- *rdoConnectionObject*.**QueryTimeout**—a **Long** containing the number of seconds to wait for a query to complete before returning an error.
- *rdoConnectionObject*.**rdoQueries**—an object reference to an **rdoQueries** collection.
- *rdoConnectionObject*.**rdoResultsets**—an object reference to an **rdoResultsets** collection.
- *rdoConnectionObject*.**rdoTables**—an object reference to an **rdoTables** collection.
- *rdoConnectionObject*.**RowsAffected**—a **Long** containing the number of rows affected by the most recent **Execute** method. A value of zero means that no records were affected.
- *rdoConnectionObject*.**StillConnecting**—a **Boolean** when **True** means the initial connection has been made but is not yet completely established. **False** means that the connection is fully established.
- *rdoConnectionObject*.**StillExecuting**—a **Boolean** when **True** means the query is still executing. **False** means that the query is ready to return the results.
- *rdoConnectionObject*.**Transactions**—a **Boolean** when **True** means that the remote system supports transactions (i.e., using the **BeginTrans**, **CommitTrans**, and **RollbackTrans** methods). **False** means that transactions are not supported.
- *rdoConnectionObject*.**UpdateOperation**—an **Integer** describing how an optimistic batch update will perform (see Table R-6).

UpdateOperation Name	Value	Description
rdOperationUpdate	0	An Update statement will be used for each row.
rdOperationDelIns	1	A Delete followed by an Insert will be used for each row.

Table R-6: **UpdateOperation** values.

- *rdoConnectionObject*.**Version**—a **String** value containing the version number of the data source.

Methods

rdoConnectionObject.BeginTrans

Usage   This method marks the beginning of a transaction.

rdoConnectionObject.Cancel

Usage   This method requests the remote data source to cancel an asynchronous query or cancel any pending results.

rdoConnectionObject.Close

Usage   This method closes an open remote database environment.

rdoConnectionObject.CommitTrans

Usage: This method marks the end of a transaction and saves the data into the database. After the commit has finished, the transaction can't be undone using the **RollBack** method.

rdoConnectionObject.CreateQuery name [, SQLQuery]

Usage: This method creates a new **rdoQuery** object.

Arguments:
- *connection*—a **String** containing the name of the new **rdoQuery** object.
- *SQLQuery*—a **String** containing the SQL query for the new **rdoQuery** object. If omitted, you must specify the query in the object itself.

rdoConnectionObject.EstablishConnection [prompt [, readonly [, options]]]

Usage: This method establishes a physical connection to the ODBC server.

Arguments:
- *prompt*—an **Integer** value containing the options for the connection process (see Table R-7).

prompt Name	Value	Description
rdDriverPrompt	0	The ODBC driver takes the information supplied in Name and Connect and displays it in the ODBC Data Sources dialog box.
rdDriverPrompt	1	Name and connect provide the necessary information to connect to the database. If sufficient information is not present, an error will occur.
rdDriverComplete	2	The ODBC driver uses the information supplied in **Name** and **Connect** to connect to the database. If there is insufficient information, the ODBC Data Sources dialog box will display (default).
rdDriverCompleteRequired	3	This is similar to the *dbDriverComplete* option, but information supplied in **Name** and **Connect** can't be changed.

Table R-7: prompt *values*.

- *readonly*—a **Boolean** value which is **True** for a read-only connection and **False** for a read/write connection (default).
- *options*—a **Variant** containing either 0 or *rdRunAsync* (connect to the database asynchronously).

rdoConnectionObject.Execute *source* [, *options*]

Usage — This method executes a query on the remote data source.

Arguments
- *source*—a **String** value either the name of an **rdoQuery** object or an SQL statement.
- *options*—an **Integer** value containing the options that execute the query (see Table R-8). These options can be added together if more than one option is desired.

options Name	Value	Description
rdAsyncEnable	32	Run the query asynchronously.
rdExecDirect	64	Don't create a stored procedure when executing the query. This is useful for queries that don't return any rows.

Table R-8: options *values.*

results = *rdoConnectionObject*.OpenResultset (*name* [, *type* [, *locktype* [, *options*]]])

Usage — This method creates a new **rdoResultset** object.

Arguments
- *results*—an **rdoResultset** object containing the results of a query.
- *name*—a **String** value containing the source of the rows. This can be the name of an **rdoTable** object, the name of an **rdoQuery** object, or an SQL statement.
- *type*—an **Integer** value containing the type of cursor that manages the **rdoResultset** object (see Table R-9).

type Name	Value	Description
rdOpenForwardOnly	0	Opens a forward only rdoResultset object (default).
rdOpenKeyset	1	Opens a keyset type **rdoResultset** object.
rdOpenDynamic	2	Opens a dynamic type **rdoResultset** object.
rdOpenStatic	3	Opens a static type **rdoResultset** object.

Table R-9: type *values.*

- *locktype*—an **Integer** value containing the type of locking to use (see Table R-10).

locktype Name	Value	Description
rdConcurReadOnly	1	Read-only (default)
rdConcurLock	2	Pessimistic concurrency
rdConcurRowVer	3	Optimistic concurrency based on row id
rdConcurValues	4	Optimistic concurrency based on row values
rdConcurBatch	5	Optimistic concurrency using batch update mode

Table R-10: locktype *values.*

- *options*—an **Integer** value containing the options used to execute the query (see Table R-11). These options can be added together if more than one option is desired.

options Name	Value	Description
rdAsyncEnable	32	Run the query asynchronously.
rdExecDirect	64	Don't create a stored procedure when executing the query. This is useful for queries that don't return any rows.

Table R-11: options *values.*

rdoConnectionObject.RollbackTrans

Usage — This method abandons all of the changes you may have made to the database. This leaves the database in the same state as it was when the **BeginTrans** method was used.

Events

Private Sub *rdoConnectionObject*.BeforeConnect (*ConnectString* As String, *Prompt* As Variant)

Usage — This event occurs before connecting to the remote database.

Arguments
- *ConnectString*—a **String** expression containing the ODBC connection parameters.
- *prompt*—an **Integer** value containing the options for the connection process (see Table R-12).

prompt Name	Value	Description
rdDriverPrompt	0	The ODBC driver takes the information supplied in Name and Connect and displays it in the ODBC Data Sources dialog box.
rdDriverPrompt	1	The connection information in **Name** and **Connect** connects to the database. If sufficient information is not present, an error will occur.
rdDriverComplete	2	The ODBC driver uses the information supplied in **Name** and **Connect** to connect to the database. If there is insufficient information, the ODBC Data Sources dialog box will display (default).
rdDriverCompleteRequired	3	This is similar to the *dbDriverComplete* option, but information supplied in **Name** and **Connect** can't be changed.

Table R-12: prompt *values.*

Private Sub *rdoConnectionObject*. **Connect (*ErrorOccured* As Boolean)**

Usage   This event occurs after a connection is made to the remote server.

Arguments   *ErrorOccured*—a **Boolean** value when **True** means that the connection failed. **False** means that the connection succeeded.

Private Sub *rdoConnectionObject*. **Disconnect ( )**

Usage   This event occurs after the connection to the remote database server has been closed.

Private Sub *rdoConnectionObject*. **QueryComplete (*Query* As rdoQuery, *ErrorOccured* As Boolean)**

Usage   This event occurs after a query has completed.

> **Tip**
>
> *Use this event rather than polling the **StillExecuting** property to determine when the query has finished.*

Arguments   *Query*—an object reference to the **rdoQuery** object that has just finished executing.

ErrorOccured—a **Boolean** value when **True** means that an error occurred while processing the query. **False** means that the query executed without errors.

rdoConnectionObject.**QueryTimeout (*Query* As rdoQuery, *Cancel* As Boolean)**

Usage   This event occurs when an executing query has not completed in the amount of time allowed by the **QueryTimeout** property.

Arguments   *Query*—an object reference to the **rdoQuery** object that is executing.

Cancel—a **Boolean** when **True** means that the query will be aborted. **False** means that the query can continue for another query time out period (default).

rdoConnectionObject.**WillExecute (*Query* As rdoQuery, *Cancel* As Boolean)**

Usage   This event occurs before a query executes.

Arguments   *Query*—an object reference to the **rdoQuery** object that is about to execute.

Cancel—a **Boolean** when **True** means that the query will be aborted. **False** means that the query can execute (default).

See Also   **rdoConnections** (collection)

rdoConnections

COLLECTION

EE

Usage Remote Data Objects (RDO) uses the **rdoConnections** collection to hold information about a set of active **rdoConnection** objects.

Properties
- *rdoConnectionsCollection*.**Count**—an **Integer** containing the number of **rdoConnection** objects in the collection.
- *rdoConnectionsCollection*.**Item** (*index*)—an array of **rdoConnection** objects indexed by *index*. Index can range from 1 to **Count**.

Methods *rdoConnectionsCollection*.**Add** *connection*

    Usage This method adds an **rdoConnection** object to the collection.

    Arguments *connection*—an object reference to the **rdoConnection** object to add to the collection.

rdoConnectionsCollection.**Remove** *connection*

    Usage This method removes an **rdoConnection** object from the collection.

    Arguments *connection*—a **Variant** containing the name of the **rdoConnection** object to remove from the collection.

See Also **rdoConnection** (object), **rdoEngine** (object)

rdoEngine

OBJECT

EE

Usage The **rdoEngine** object is the highest level object in the Remote Data Access Object model. It directly accesses the remote ODBC database.

Properties
- *rdoEngine*.**rdoDefaultCursorDriver**—an **Integer** containing the type of ODBC cursor used (see Table R-13).

DefaultCursorDriver Name	Value	Description
rdUseIfNeeded	0	The rdoEngine chooses the most appropriate cursor (default).
rdUseODBC	1	Use the ODBC cursor library. Better performance for small tables, but poorer performance on large tables.
rdUseServer	2	Use server side cursors. Better performance for large sets at the expense of higher network traffic.
rdUseClientBatch	3	Use the batch cursor library.
rdUseNone	4	Do not use a cursor. This results in a read-only result that can be read in a forward direction only. It has faster performance than the other options.

Table R-13: DefaultCursorDriver values.

- **rdoEngine.rdoDefaultErrorThreshold**—a **Long** containing the default error threshold for **RDO** objects. This property exists for compatibility with version 1.0 of the **RDO** library. Use the **InfoMessage** event instead.
- **rdoEngine.rdoDefaultLoginTimeout**—a **Long** containing the number of seconds a login will be attempted before returning an error.
- **rdoEngine.rdoDefaultPassword**—a **String** containing the password associated with **rdoDefaultUser**.
- **rdoEngine.rdoDefaultUser**—a **String** containing the username used to create the **rdoEnvironment**.
- **rdoEngine.rdoEnvironments**—an object reference to an **rdoEnvironments** collection.
- **rdoEngine.rdoErrors**—an object reference to an **rdoErrors** collection.
- **rdoEngine.rdoLocaleID**—an **Integer** describing the language in which the error messages will be returned (see Table R-14). The default value will be determined based on the Windows systems locale.

rdoLocaleID Name	Value	Description
rdLocaleSystem	0	The system default (default)
rdLocaleEnglish	1	English
rdLocaleFrench	2	French
rdLocaleGerman	3	German
rdLocaleItalian	4	Italian
rdLocaleJapanese	5	Japanese
rdLocaleSpanish	6	Spanish
rdLocaleChinese	7	Chinese
rdLocaleSimplifiedChinese	8	Simplified Chinese
rdLocaleKorean	9	Korean

Table R-14: rdoLocaleID values.

- **rdoEngine.Version**—a **String** value containing the version number of the RDO database engine.

Methods

environ = rdoEngine.rdoCreateEnvironment (name, user, password)

Usage This method creates a new environment.

Arguments
- *name*—a **String** value containing the name of the new environment.
- *user*—a **String** containing the username associated with the environment.
- *password*—a **String** containing the password for the environment.

rdoEngine.RegisterDataSource name, driver, silent, attributes

Usage This method enters connection information to a remote database into the Windows Registry.

804 • The Visual Basic 5 Programmer's Reference

Arguments
- *name*—a **String** value containing ODBC connection information.
- *driver*—a **String** containing the name of the ODBC driver.
- *silent*—a **Boolean** value when **True** means the ODBC driver dialog boxes will not display when connecting to a remote data source. All information must be contained in the definitions. **False** means that the dialog box will display.
- *attributes*—a **String** containing a list of keywords in a carriage return delimited string that will be added to the ODBC.INI file.

Events **Private Sub rdoEngine_InfoMessage ( )**

    Usage   This event occurs when the ODBC server returns a SQL_SUCCESS_WITH_INFO message. You can then examine the **rdoErrors** to determine the meaning of the messages.

See Also **rdoEnvironment** (object)

rdoEnvironment OBJECT

PE, EE

Usage The **rdoEnvironment** object contains information about a connection to an ODBC database.

Properties
- *rdoEnvironmentObject*.**CursorDriver**—an **Integer** containing the type of cursor to use (see Table R-15).

CursorDriver Name	Value	Description
rdUseIfNeeded	0	The rdoEngine chooses the most appropriate cursor (default).
rdUseODBC	1	Use the ODBC cursor library. Better performance for small tables, but poorer performance on large tables.
rdUseServer	2	Use server side cursors. Better performance for large sets at the expense of higher network traffic.
rdUseClientBatch	3	Use the batch cursor library.
rdUseNone	4	Do not use a cursor. This results in a read-only result that can be read in a forward direction only. It has faster performance than the other options.

Table R-15: CursorDriver values.

- *rdoEnvironmentObject*.**hEnv**—a reference to an ODBC environment handle.
- *rdoEnvironmentObject*.**LoginTimeout**—a **Long** containing the number of seconds a login will be attempted before returning an error.
- *rdoEnvironmentObject*.**Name**—a **String** containing the name of the environment.
- *rdoEnvironmentObject*.**Password**—a **String** containing the password associated with the object.
- *rdoEnvironmentObject*.**rdoConnections**—an object reference to an **rdoConnections** collection.
- *rdoEnvironmentObject*.**UserName**—a **String** containing the username associated with the object.

Methods

rdoEnvironmentObject.BeginTrans

Usage This method marks the beginning of a transaction.

rdoEnvironmentObject.Close

Usage This method closes an open remote database environment.

rdoEnvironmentObject.CommitTrans

Usage This method marks the end of a transaction and saves the data into the database. After the commit has finished, the transaction can't be undone using the **RollBack** method.

connection = rdoEnvironmentObject.OpenConnection (dsname [, prompt [, readonly [, connect [, options]]]])

Usage This method opens a connection to an ODBC database system.

Arguments
- *connection*—an **rdoConnection** object containing the opened connection.
- *dsname*—a **String** value containing the name of an ODBC data source from the Windows Registry.
- *prompt*—an **Integer** value containing the options for the connection process (see Table R-16).

prompt Name	Value	Description
rdDriverPrompt	0	The ODBC driver takes the information supplied in Name and Connect and displays it in the ODBC Data Sources dialog box.
rdDriverPrompt	1	The connection information in **Name** and **Connect** connects to the database. If sufficient information is not present, an error will occur.
rdDriverComplete	2	The ODBC driver uses the information supplied in **Name** and **Connect** to connect to the database. If there is insufficient information, the ODBC Data Sources dialog box will display (default).
rdDriverCompleteRequired	3	This is similar to the *dbDriverComplete* option, but information supplied in **Name** and **Connect** can't be changed.

Table R-16: prompt *values.*

- *readonly*—a **Boolean** value which is **True** for a read-only connection and **False** for a read/write connection (default).
- *connect*—a **String** value containing ODBC connection information.
- *options*—a **Variant** containing either 0 or *rdRunAsync* (connect to the database asynchronously).

rdoEnvironmentObject.RollbackTrans

Usage This method abandons all of the changes to the database returning the database to the same state as it was when the **BeginTrans** method was used.

Events **Private Sub** *rdoEnvironment*_**BeginTrans** ( )

Usage This event occurs after the **BeginTrans** method has completed.

Private Sub *rdoEnvironment*_**CommitTrans** ( )

Usage This event occurs after the **CommitTrans** method has completed.

Private Sub *rdoEnvironment*_**RollbackTrans** ( )

Usage This event occurs after the **RollbackTrans** method has completed.

See Also **rdoConnection** (object), **rdoEngine** (object)

rdoEnvironments   COLLECTION
EE

Usage Remote Data Objects (RDO) uses the **rdoEnvironments** collection to hold information about a set of active **rdoEnvironments** objects.

Properties • *rdoEnvironmentsCollection*.**Count**—an **Integer** containing the number of **rdoEnvironment** objects in the collection.

• *rdoEnvironmentsCollection*.**Item** (*index*)—an array of **rdoEnvironment** objects indexed by *index*. *Index* can range from 1 to **Count**.

Methods *rdoEnvironmentsCollection*.**Add** *environment*

Usage This method adds an **rdoEnvironment** object to the collection.

Arguments • *environment*—an object reference to the **rdoEnvironment** object to add to the collection.

rdoEnvironmentsCollection.**Remove** *connection*

Usage This method removes an **rdoEnvironment** object from the collection.

Arguments • *environment*—a **Variant** containing the name of the **rdoConnection** object to remove from the collection.

See Also **rdoEnvironment** (object), **rdoEngine** (object)

rdoError

OBJECT
EE

Usage The **rdoError** object contains errors that are generated by the Remote Data Objects (RDO).

Properties
- *rdoError*.**Description**—a **String** value that provides a short text description of the error.
- *rdoError*.**HelpContext**—a **String** that contains a help file context ID number which references an entry in the help file.
- *rdoError*.**HelpFile**—a **String** that contains the name of the help file.
- *rdoError*.**Number**—a **Long** containing the error code. This is the default property for this object. A value of 0 means that no error has occurred.
- *rdoError*.**Source**—a **String** containing the name of the component that failed.
- *rdoError*.**SQLRetCode**—a **Long** containing the ODBC error code from the most recent operation (see Table R-17).

SQLRetCode Name	Value	Description
rdSQLSuccess	0	The operation was successful.
rdSQLSuccessWithInfo	1	The operation was successful, and additional information is available in **SQLState**.
rdSQLNoDataFound	100	No data is available.
rdSQLError	-1	An error occurred while performing an operation.
rdSQLInvalidHandle	-2	An invalid handle was supplied.

Table R-17: SQLRetCode *values.*

- *rdoError*.**SQLState**—a **String** containing a five character return code. The first two characters contain the class and the remaining three characters contain the subclass. A class of "01" means that the operation was successful with additional information contained in the subclass. The class "IM" indicates an ODBC error. All other classes indicate an ANSI SQL-92 return code.

See Also **Err** (object), **rdoEngine** (object), **rdoErrors** (collection)

rdoErrors

COLLECTION
EE

Usage Remote Data Objects (RDO) uses the **rdoErrors** collection to hold the **rdoError** objects generated by a single RDO operation.

Properties
- *rdoErrorsCollection*.**Count**—an **Integer** containing the number of **rdoError** objects in the collection.
- *rdoErrorsCollection*.**Item** (*index*)—an array of **rdoError** objects indexed by *index*. *Index* can range from 1 to **Count**.

Methods rdoErrorsCollection.Clear

Usage This method removes all of the **rdoError** objects from collection.

See Also **rdoError** (object), **rdoEngine** (object)

rdoParameter   OBJECT
EE

Usage The **rdoParameter** object contains a parameter associated with an **rdoQuery** object.

Properties
- *rdoParameter*.**Direction**—an **Integer** value describing how the parameter is used (see Table R-18).

Direction Name	Value	Description
rdParamInput	0	The parameter is passed to the procedure.
rdParamInputOutput	1	The parameter is passed to and returned from the procedure.
rdParamOutput	2	The parameter is returned from the procedure.
rdParamReturnValue	3	The parameter contains a return status value from the procedure.

Table R-18: Direction *values*.

- *rdoParameterObject*.**Name**—a **String** containing the name of the parameter.
- *rdoParameterObject*.**Type**—an **Integer** containing the type of data of the column (see Table R-19).

Type Name	Value	Description
rdTypeCHAR	1	A fixed length character string of length Size.
rdTypeNUMERIC	2	A signed exact numeric value.
rdTypeDECIMAL	3	A signed exact numeric value.
rdTypeINTEGER	4	A 32-bit integer.
rdTypeSMALLINT	5	A 16-bit integer.
rdTypeFLOAT	6	A double precision floating point number.
rdTypeREAL	7	A single precision floating point number.
rdTypeDOUBLE	8	A double precision floating point number.
rdTypeDATE	9	A date value. The exact format depends on the source of data.
rdTypeTIME	10	A time value. The exact format depends on the source of data.
rdTypeTIMESTAMP	11	A date-time value. The exact format depends on the source of data.
rdTypeVARCHAR	12	A variable length character string with a max length of 255.
rdTypeLONGVARCHAR	-1	A variable length character string. The max length depends on the source of the data.
rdTypeBINARY	-2	A fixed length binary data with a max length of 255.
rdTypeVARBINARY	-3	A variable length binary data with a max length of 255.
rdTypeLONGVARBINARY	-4	A variable length binary data. The max length depends on the source of the data.

Type Name	Value	Description
rdTypeBIGINT	-5	A 64-bit integer.
rdTypeTINYINT	-6	A 1 byte integer.
rdTypeBIT	-7	A single binary digit.

Table R-19: Type values.

- *rdoParameterObject*.**Value**—a **Variant** containing the data for the parameter.

Methods

rdoColumnObject.**AppendChunk** *source*

Usage This method appends a chunk of data to the end of the value of an *rdTypeLONGVARBINARY* or *rdTypeLONGVARCHAR* parameter.

Arguments
- *source*—an expression containing the data to append to parameter's current value.

See Also **rdoParameters** (collection), **rdoQuery** (object)

rdoParameters   COLLECTION
EE

Usage Remote Data Objects (RDO) uses the **rdoParameters** collection to hold the **rdoParameter** objects associated with an **rdoQuery** object.

Properties
- *rdoParametersCollection*.**Count**—an **Integer** containing the number of **rdoError** objects in the collection.
- *rdoParametersCollection*.**Item** (*index*)—an array of **rdoParameter** objects indexed by *index*. *Index* can range from 1 to **Count**.

See Also **rdoParameter** (object), **rdoQuery** (object)

rdoQuery   OBJECT
EE

Usage The **rdoQuery** object contains information about a query.

Properties
- *rdoQueryObject*.**ActiveConnection**—an object reference to the **rdoConnection** object used by the query.
- *rdoQueryObject*.**BindThreshold**—a **Long** value containing the size of the largest column that will be automatically bound under ODBC.

- *rdoQueryObject*.**CursorType**—an **Integer** value containing the type of cursor that manages the query (see Table R-20).

CursorType Name	Value	Description
rdOpenForwardOnly	0	Opens a forward only rdoResultset object (default).
rdOpenKeyset	1	Opens a keyset type **rdoResultset** object.
rdOpenDynamic	2	Opens a dynamic type **rdoResultset** object.
rdOpenStatic	3	Opens a static type **rdoResultset** object.

Table R-20: *CursorType values.*

- *rdoQueryObject*.**hStmt**—a reference to an ODBC statement handle.
- *rdoQueryObject*.**KeysetSize**—a **Long** containing the number of rows in the keyset buffer. This value must be greater than or equal to the **RowsetSize** property.
- *rdoQueryObject*.**LockType**—a **Long** containing the locking method (see Table R-21).

LockType Name	Value	Description
rdConcurReadOnly	1	Read-only (default)
rdConcurLock	2	Pessimistic concurrency
rdConcurRowVer	3	Optimistic concurrency based on row id
rdConcurValues	4	Optimistic concurrency based on row values
rdConcurBatch	5	Optimistic concurrency using batch update mode

Table R-21: *LockType values.*

- *rdoQueryObject*.**LogMessages**—a **String** containing the path and filename where log messages are to be written. If this property contains an empty string, no logging will occur.

Tip

Using this property will adversely affect performance, so use it with care.

- *rdoQueryObject*.**Maxrows**—a **Long** containing the maximum number of rows to return or change.

Tip

This property is useful to limit the effect of an SQL statement when testing. Only the specified number of rows will be retrieved, updated, deleted, or inserted.

- *rdoQueryObject*.**Name**—a **String** containing the name of the prepared statement.
- *rdoQueryObject*.**Prepared**—a **Boolean** when **True** means that the user should be prepared using the **SQLPrepare** API function. **False** means that the query should not be prepared and executed directly using the **SQLExecDirect** API function.

- *rdoQueryObject*.**QueryTimeout**—a **Long** containing the number of seconds to wait for a query to complete before returning an error.
- *rdoQueryObject*.**rdoColumns**—an object reference to the **rdoColumns** collection used by the query.
- *rdoQueryObject*.**RowsAffected**—a **Long** containing the number of rows affected by the most recently executed query.
- *rdoQueryObject*.**SQL**—a **String** containing a valid SQL statement, "Execute" followed by the name of a stored procedure, the name of an **rdoQuery** object, the name of an **rdoResultset** object, or the name of an **rdoTable** object.
- *rdoQueryObject*.**StillExecuting**—a **Boolean** when **True** means that the query is still active. **False** means that the query has completed and is ready to return the result set.
- *rdoQueryObject*.**Type**—an **Integer** containing the type of data of the column (see Table R-22).

Type Name	Value	Description
rdTypeCHAR	1	A fixed length character string of length Size.
rdTypeNUMERIC	2	A signed exact numeric value.
rdTypeDECIMAL	3	A signed exact numeric value.
rdTypeINTEGER	4	A 32-bit integer.
rdTypeSMALLINT	5	A 16-bit integer.
rdTypeFLOAT	6	A double precision floating point number.
rdTypeREAL	7	A single precision floating point number.
rdTypeDOUBLE	8	A double precision floating point number.
rdTypeDATE	9	A date value. The exact format depends on the source of data.
rdTypeTIME	10	A time value. The exact format depends on the source of data.
rdTypeTIMESTAMP	11	A date-time value. The exact format depends on the source of data.
rdTypeVARCHAR	12	A variable length character string with a max length of 255.
rdTypeLONGVARCHAR	-1	A variable length character string. The max length depends on the source of the data.
rdTypeBINARY	-2	A fixed length binary data with a max length of 255.
rdTypeVARBINARY	-3	A variable length binary data with a max length of 255.
rdTypeLONGVARBINARY	-4	A variable length binary data. The max length depends on the source of the data.
rdTypeBIGINT	-5	A 64-bit integer.
rdTypeTINYINT	-6	A 1 byte integer.
rdTypeBIT	-7	A single binary digit.

Table R-22: Type values.

Methods

rdoQueryObject.Cancel

Usage   This method cancels a query running in asynchronous mode.

rdoQueryObject.Close

Usage   This method closes an open remote data object.

rdoQueryObject.Execute source [, options]

Usage This method executes a query on the remote data source.

Arguments
- *source*—a **String** value made up of either the name of an **rdoQuery** object or an SQL statement.
- *options*—an **Integer** value containing the options used to execute the query (see Table R-23). These options can be added together if more than one option is desired.

options Name	Value	Description
rdAsyncEnable	32	Run the query asynchronously.
rdExecDirect	64	Don't create a stored procedure when executing the query. This is useful for queries that don't return any rows.

Table R-23: options *values*.

results = rdoConnectionObject.OpenResultset ([, type [, locktype [, options]]])

Usage This method creates a new **rdoResultset** object.

Arguments
- *results*—an **rdoResultset** object containing the results of a query.
- *type*—an **Integer** value containing the type of cursor used to manage the **rdoResultset** object (see Table R-24).

type Name	Value	Description
rdOpenForwardOnly	0	Opens a forward only rdoResultset object (default).
rdOpenKeyset	1	Opens a keyset type **rdoResultset** object.
rdOpenDynamic	2	Opens a dynamic type **rdoResultset** object.
rdOpenStatic	3	Opens a static type **rdoResultset** object.

Table R-24: type *values*.

- *locktype*—an **Integer** value containing the type of locking to use (see Table R-25).

locktype Name	Value	Description
rdConcurReadOnly	1	Read-only (default)
rdConcurLock	2	Pessimistic concurrency
rdConcurRowVer	3	Optimistic concurrency based on row id
rdConcurValues	4	Optimistic concurrency based on row values
rdConcurBatch	5	Optimistic concurrency using batch update mode

Table R-25: locktype *values*.

- *options*—an **Integer** value containing the options used to execute the query (see Table R-26). These options can be added together if more than one option is desired.

options Name	Value	Description
rdAsyncEnable	32	Run the query asynchronously.
rdExecDirect	64	Don't create a stored procedure when executing the query. This is useful for queries that don't return any rows.

Table R-26: options values.

See Also   **rdoConnection** (object), **rdoQueries** (collection)

rdoResultset   OBJECT
EE

Usage   The **rdoResultset** object contains the results of a query.

Properties
- *rdoResultsetObject*.**AbsolutePosition**—a **Long** containing the absolute row number of an **rdoResultset** object. A value of -1 means that there isn't a current record or there are no rows are in the result set. The **AbsolutePosition** of the first record is 1.

> **Tip**
>
> *The absolute row number is not guaranteed to remain constant. You should use bookmarks instead.*

- *rdoResultsetObject*.**ActiveConnection**—an object reference to the **rdoConnection** object used by the result set.
- *rdoResultsetObject*.**BatchCollisionCount**—a **Long** containing the number of rows that were not updated in the last batch update.
- *rdoResultsetObject*.**BatchCollisionRows**—an array of bookmarks for each row that were not updated in the last batch update. This array is updated each time the **BatchUpdate** method is used.

> **Tip**
>
> *After resetting the values for each failed row, you can use the **BatchUpdate** method again to post the changes.*

- *rdoResultsetObject*.**BatchSize**—a **Long** value containing the number of statements sent to the server when performing an optimistic batch update. If not specified, a default value of 15 is assumed.

- *rdoResultsetObject*.**BOF**—a **Boolean** when **True** means that the current row position is before the first row. **False** means that the current row position is on or after the first row.
- *rdoResultsetObject*.**Bookmark**—a **Variant** containing a stable reference to the current row. This property is only valid when the **Bookmarkable** property is **True**.

> **Tip**
>
> *You can use this value to save a reference to the current row for later use.*

- *rdoResultsetObject*.**Bookmarkable**—a **Boolean** when **True** means that this result set supports bookmarks. **False** means that this result set doesn't support bookmarks.
- *rdoResultsetObject*.**EditMode**—an **Integer** value containing the type of cursor that manages the query (see Table R-27).

CursorType Name	Value	Description
rdEditNone	0	No editing operations are active (default).
rdEditInProgress	1	The **Edit** method was used and the current row is in the copy buffer.
rdEditAdd	2	The **AddNew** method was used and the current row in the copy buffer has not been saved to the database.

Table R-27: CursorType values.

- *rdoResultsetObject*.**EOF**—a **Boolean** when **True** means that the current row position is after the last row. **False** means that the current row position is on or before the last row.
- *RdoResultsetObject*.**hStmt**—a reference to an ODBC statement handle.
- *rdoResultsetObject*.**LastModified**—a **Long** containing the **Bookmark** of the most recently modified or added row.
- *rdoResultsetObject*.**LockEdits**—a **Boolean** when **True** means that pessimistic locking is in effect. **False** means that optimistic locking is in effect (default).
- *rdoResultsetObject*.**LockType**—a **Long** containing the locking method (see Table R-28).

LockType Name	Value	Description
rdConcurReadOnly	1	Read-only (default)
rdConcurLock	2	Pessimistic concurrency
rdConcurRowVer	3	Optimistic concurrency based on row id
rdConcurValues	4	Optimistic concurrency based on row values
rdConcurBatch	5	Optimistic concurrency using batch update mode

Table R-28: LockType values.

- *rdoResultsetObject*.**Name**—a **String** containing the name of the result set.
- *rdoResultsetObject*.**PercentPosition**—a **Single** containing the relative position of the row within the result set. Values range from 0.0 to 100.0.

rdoResultset • 815

> **Tip**
>
> *Use this value with a **ProgressBar** to display how many records were processed.*

- *rdoResultsetObject*.**rdoColumns**—an object reference to the **rdoColumns** collection used by the result set.
- *rdoResultsetObject*.**Restartable**—a **Boolean** when **True** means the **rdoResultset** can be restarted via the **Requery** method. **False** means **Requery** method can't be used.
- *rdoResultsetObject*.**RowCount**—a **Long** containing the number of rows accessed in the **rdoResultset**. Once all rows have been accessed (through a **MoveLast** method for example), this value will reflect the number of rows in the **rdoResultset**.
- *rdoResultsetObject*.**Status**—an **Integer** containing the current status of the row containing the column with optimistic batch updates (see Table R-29).

Status Name	Value	Description
rdRowUnmodified	0	The row hasn't been changed.
rdRowModified	1	The row has been changed, but it hasn't been updated in the database.
rdRowNew	2	The row was created with the **AddNew** method, but it hasn't been inserted in the database.
rdUpdatable	3	The row has been deleted, but it hasn't been deleted in the database.
rdRowDBDeleted	4	The row has been deleted locally and on the database.

Table R-29: Status values.

- *rdoResultsetObject*.**StillExecuting**—a **Boolean** when **True** means that the query is still active. **False** means that the query has completed and is ready to return the result set.
- *rdoResultsetObject*.**Transactions**—a **Boolean** when **True** means that the object supports transactions. **False** means that the object doesn't support transactions.
- *rdoResultsetObject*.**Type**—an **Integer** containing the type of data of the column (see Table R-30). Not all databases support all types.

Type Name	Value	Description
rdOpenForwardOnly	0	A forward-only fixed set
rdOpenKeyset	1	An updateable fixed set
rdOpenDynamic	2	An updateable dynamic set
rdOpenStatic	3	A read-only fixed set

Table R-30: Type values.

- *rdoResultsetObject*.**Updatable**—a **Boolean** when **True** means that the rows in the result set can be updated. **False** means that the rows in the result set can't be updated.
- *rdoResultsetObject*.**UpdateCriteria**—an **Integer** describing how the Where clause is built for an optimistic batch update (see Table R-31).

UpdateCriteria Name	Value	Description
rdCriteriaKey	0	Use the key columns in the Where clause (default).
rdCriteriaAllCols	1	Use the key columns and all updated columns.
rdCriteriaUpdCols	2	Use the key columns and all columns.
rdCriteriaTimeStamp	3	Use the time stamp column.

Table R-31: *UpdateCriteria values.*

- rdoResultsetObject.**UpdateOperation**—an **Integer** describing how an optimistic batch update performs (see Table R-32).

UpdateOperation Name	Value	Description
rdOperationUpdate	0	Use an Update statement for each row in an optimistic batch update (default).
rdOperationDelIns	1	Use a Delete statement and an Insert statement for each row in an optimistic batch update.

Table R-32: *UpdateOperation values.*

Methods

rdoResultsetObject.AddNew

Usage This method creates a new row in the result set's copy buffer. Enter information into each column and then use the **Update** method to add the data to the database. The **EditMode** property will be set to *rdEditAdd*.

Tip

If you don't save your changes with the Update method before you move to another row, those changes will be lost.

rdoResultsetObject.BatchUpdate [*singlerow* [, *force*]]

Usage This method performs an optimistic batch update.

Arguments
- *singlerow*—a **Boolean** value when **True** means that the update is done only for the current row. **False** means that the entire batch is updated (default).
- *force*—a **Boolean** value when **True** means that the update will overwrite existing rows even if they will cause collisions. **False** means that collisions will be saved in the **BatchCollisionRows.** You need to check each row and redo the changes if necessary (default).

rdoResultsetObject.Cancel

Usage This method cancels any pending database activity and releases any held resources.

rdoResultsetObject.CancelBatch

Usage This method cancels all uncommitted changes in the batch.

rdoResultsetObject.CancelUpdate

Usage This method cancels any pending database changes, flushes the copy buffer, and resets the **EditMode** property to *rdEditNone*.

rdoResultsetObject.Close

Usage This method closes an open remote data object.

rdoResultsetObject.Delete

Usage This method deletes the current row if the result set is updateable. If there is no current row, the result set is not updateable, or another user has locked the row, and an error will occur. After the row has been deleted, the deleted row remains the current row until the cursor has been moved.

rdoResultsetObject.Edit

Usage This method allows you to change values in the current row. It first creates a copy of the row in the copy buffer and then allows you to make changes. The **Update** method is used after the changes are complete to post the information to the database. The **EditMode** property will be set to *rdEditMode*. The **CancelUpdate** method will cancel the changes.

rows = rdoResultsetObject.GetClipString (*NumRows* [, *ColumnDelim* [, *RowDelim* [, *NullExp*]]])

Usage This method returns a delimited string containing the specified number of rows from the result set. Each row is separated by a *rowdelim*. Each column inside each row is separated by a *columndelim*.

> **Tip**
>
> *This method is useful for retrieving a number of rows to paste into another application like Microsoft Excel.*

Arguments
- *rows*—a **String** value containing the rows from the result set.
- *NumRows*—a **Long** value containing the number of rows to retrieve from the result set.
- *ColumnDelim*—a **String** containing the characters that separate columns. If omitted, it will default to *vtTab*.

- *RowDelim*—a **String** containing the characters that separate rows. If omitted, it will default to *vtCr*.
- *NullExpr*—a **String** containing the characters used in place of a Null value. If omitted, it will default to an empty string.

rows = rdoResultsetObject.GetRows (NumRows)

Usage This method returns an array containing a two-dimensional array of columns and rows. If a column requires you to use the **GetChunk** method, the ODBC S-Code will be returned in place of its value.

Arguments
- *rows*—a **Variant** variable that that will contain a two-dimensional array of columns and rows. The first subscript contains the column number ranging from 0 to number of columns -1. The second subscript contains the row number, ranging from 0 to the number of rows -1.
- *NumRows*—a **Long** value containing the number of rows to retrieve from the result set.

Return = rdoResultsetObject.MoreResults

Usage This method clears the current result set and returns a value indicating if one or more result sets are available.

Arguments *Return*—a **Boolean** value when **True** means that there is at least one more result set to process. **False** means no more result sets are available.

rdoResultsetObject.Move rows [, start]

Usage This method repositions the current row pointer and discards any changes in the copy buffer.

Arguments
- *rows*—a **Long** value containing the number of rows to move forward (positive values) or backward (negative values). A value of 0 will discard any changes made to the current row and fetch a new copy from the result set.
- *force*—a **Variant** value containing the bookmark of the row that will be used as the starting position. If not specified, the movement will be relative to the current row.

rdoResultsetObject.MoveFirst

Usage This method repositions the current row pointer to the first row in the result set and discards any changes in the copy buffer.

rdoResultsetObject.MoveLast [option]

Usage This method repositions the current row pointer to the last row in the result set and discards any changes in the copy buffer.

Arguments ▪ *option*—an **Integer** value containing a value of *rdAsyncEnable* to perform the operation asynchronously or 0 to wait for it to complete. If not specified, a value of 0 is assumed.

*rdoResultsetObject.*MoveNext

Usage   This method repositions the current row pointer to the next row in the result set and discards any changes in the copy buffer.

*rdoResultsetObject.*MovePrevious

Usage   This method repositions the current row pointer to the previous row in the result set and discards any changes in the copy buffer.

*rdoResultsetObject.*Requery [*option*]

Usage   This method refreshes the data in the result set by executing the query that generated this result set again.

Tip

Since the actual query is rerun to generate the result set, any saved bookmarks will be invalid.

Arguments ▪ *option*—an **Integer** value containing a value of *rdAsyncEnable* to perform the operation asynchronously or 0 to wait for it to complete. If not specified, a value of 0 is assumed.

*rdoResultsetObject.*Update

Usage   This method saves the copy buffer to the result set and resets the copy buffer.

Tip

*Use the **Update** method before repositioning the current row pointer. You can use **Edit** or **AddNew**, or close the result set if you have made any changes to the current row; otherwise the changes will be lost.*

Private Sub *rdoResultsetObject.*Associate ( )

Usage   This event occurs after a new connection is associated with the result set.

Private Sub *rdoResultsetObject.*Dissociate ( )

Usage   This event occurs after the **ActiveConnection** is set to **Nothing**.

Private Sub rdoResultsetObject.ResultsChanged ( )

Usage   This event occurs when a new result set is available after using the **MoreResults** method. If no more result sets are available, this event will still occur and the **BOF** and **EOF** properties will both be **True**.

Private Sub rdoResultsetObject.RowCurrentyChange ( )

Usage   This event occurs after the current row pointer has been changed.

> **Tip**
>
> *This event is useful for updating a **ProgressBar** with the **PercentPosition** information. Also, you can use this event to perform another query using values from the current row.*

Private Sub rdoResultsetObject.RowStatusChanged ( )

Usage   This event occurs after the **Status** of the current row changes.

Private Sub rdoResultsetObject.WillAssociate (connection As rdoConnection, Cancel As Boolean)

Usage   This event occurs before a new connection is associated with the record set.

Arguments
- *connection*—an **rdoConnection** object containing the new connection object to be associated with the record set.
- *Cancel*—a **Boolean** when **True** means that the association will not occur. **False** means that the association may be established (default).

Private Sub rdoResultsetObject.WillDissociate (Cancel As Boolean)

Usage   This event occurs before **ActiveConnection** is set to **Nothing**.

Arguments
- *Cancel*—a **Boolean** when **True** means that the association will not occur. **False** means that the association may be established (default).

Private Sub rdoResultsetObject.WillUpdateRows (returncode As Long)

Usage   This event occurs before any updates are made to the record set.

Arguments
- *returncode*—a **Long** describing how the update was handled (see Table R-33).

returncode Name	Description
rdUpdateSuccessful	Your code handled the update which was successful.
rdUpdateWithCollisions	Your code handled the update which resulted in some collisions while performing a batch update.
rdUpdateFailed	Your code attempted to handle the update, but encountered some errors.
RdUpdateNotHandled	Your code did not handle the update. RDO will notify any other clients and if none will handle the update RDO will perform the update itself.

Table R-33: returncode values.

See Also   **rdoConnection** (object), **rdoResultsets** (collection)

rdoResultsets   COLLECTION

Usage   Remote Data Objects (RDO) uses the **rdoResultsets** collection to hold the **rdoResultset** objects for a single **rdoConnection**.

Properties
- *rdoResultsetsCollection*.**Count**—an **Integer** containing the number of **rdoResultset** objects in the collection.
- *rdoResultsetsCollection*.**Item** (*index*)—an array of **rdoResultset** objects indexed by *index*. Index can range from 1 to **Count**.

See Also   **rdoConnection** (object), **rdoResultset** (object)

rdoTable   OBJECT

Usage   The **rdoTable** object contains the definition of a base table or an SQL view from the database.

> **Tip**
>
> *This object is obsolete; use the **rdoResultset** object instead.*

Properties
- *rdoTableObject*.**Name**—a **String** containing the name of the prepared statement.
- *rdoTableObject*.**rdoColumns**—an object reference to the **rdoColumns** collection used by the Table.
- *rdoTableObject*.**RowCount**—a **Long** containing the number of rows accessed in the **rdoTable**. Once all rows have been accessed (through a **MoveLast** method for example), this value will reflect the number of rows in the **rdoTable**.

- **rdoTableObject.Type**—a **String** containing the type table or view. This value depends on the type of the data source. Some typical values are "TABLE," "VIEW," "SYSTEM TABLE," "ALIAS," or "SYNONYM."
- **rdoTableObject.Updatable**—a **Boolean** when **True** means that row in the table can be updated. **False** means that the rows in the table can't be updated.

Methods

results = **rdoTableObject.OpenResultset** ([, *type* [, *locktype* [, *options*]]])

Usage This method creates a new **rdoResultset** object.

Arguments
- *results*—an **rdoResultset** object containing the results of a query.
- *type*—an **Integer** value containing the type of cursor that manages the **rdoResultset** object (see Table R-34).

type Name	Value	Description
rdOpenForwardOnly	0	Opens a forward only rdoResultset object (default).
rdOpenKeyset	1	Opens a keyset type **rdoResultset** object.
rdOpenDynamic	2	Opens a dynamic type **rdoResultset** object.
rdOpenStatic	3	Opens a static type **rdoResultset** object.

Table R-34: *type values.*

- *locktype*—an **Integer** value containing the type of locking to use (see Table R-35).

locktype Name	Value	Description
rdConcurReadOnly	1	Read-only (default)
rdConcurLock	2	Pessimistic concurrency
rdConcurRowVer	3	Optimistic concurrency based on row id
rdConcurValues	4	Optimistic concurrency based on row values
rdConcurBatch	5	Optimistic concurrency using batch update mode

Table R-35: locktype *values.*

- *options*—an **Integer** value containing the options that execute the query (see Table R-36). These options can be added together if more than one option is desired.

options Name	Value	Description
rdAsyncEnable	32	Run the query asynchronously.
rdExecDirect	64	Don't create a stored procedure when executing the query. This is useful for queries that don't return any rows.

Table R-36: options *values.*

See Also **rdoConnection** (object), **rdoTables** (collection)

rdoTables

COLLECTION

EE

Usage
Remote Data Objects (RDO) uses the **rdoTables** collection to hold information about a set of tables.

> **Tip**
>
> Use the **Refresh** method to initially populate the collection.

Properties
- *rdoTablesCollection*.**Count**—an **Integer** containing the number of **rdoTable** objects in the collection.
- *rdoTablesCollection*.**Item** (*index*)—an array of **rdoTable** objects indexed by *index*. *Index* can range from 1 to **Count**.

Methods
rdoTablesCollection.**Refresh**

Usage
This method gets a copy of all of the tables available from the data source. Until this method is used or each table is referenced by ordinal number, the information will not be available in the **rdoTables** collection.

See Also
rdoConnection (object), **rdoResultset** (object), **rdoTable** (object)

Recordset

OBJECT

PE, EE

Usage
The **Recordset** provides access to the records in a base table or the results of a query. There are five basic types of record sets: Dynamic, Dynaset, Forward-only, Snapshot, and Table.

Properties
- *RecordsetObject*.**AbsolutePosition**—a **Long** containing the absolute row number of a **Recordset** object. A value of -1 means that there isn't a current record or that there are no rows in the record set. The **AbsolutePosition** of the first record is 0. This property applies only to the Dynamic, Dynaset, and Snapshot record sets.

> **Tip**
>
> The absolute row number is not guaranteed to remain constant. You should use bookmarks instead.

- *RecordsetObject*.**BatchCollisionCount**—a **Long** containing the number of rows that were not updated in the last batch update. This property applies only to the Dynamic, Dynaset, Forward-only, and Snapshot record sets for ODBC type databases only.

- *RecordsetObject*.**BatchCollisions**—an array of bookmarks for each row that were not updated in the last batch update. This array is updated each time the **BatchUpdate** method is used. This property applies only to the Dynamic, Dynaset, Forward-only, and Snapshot record sets for ODBC type databases only.

> **Tip**
>
> *After resetting the values for each failed row, you can use the **Update** method again to post the changes.*

- *RecordsetObject*.**BatchSize**—a **Long** value containing the number of statements sent to the server when performing an optimistic batch update. If not specified, a default value of 15 is assumed. This property applies only to the Dynamic, Dynaset, Forward-only, and Snapshot record sets for ODBC type databases only.
- *RecordsetObject*.**BOF**—a **Boolean** when **True** means that the current row position is before the first row. **False** means that the current row position is on or after the first row.
- *RecordsetObject*.**Bookmark**—a **Variant** containing a stable reference to the current row. This property is only valid when the **Bookmarkable** property is **True**. This property applies to all types of record sets except for Forward-only.

> **Tip**
>
> *You can use this value to save a reference to the current row for later use.*

- *RecordsetObject*.**Bookmarkable**—a **Boolean** when **True** means that this record set supports bookmarks. **False** means that this record set doesn't support bookmarks. This property applies to all types of record sets except for Forward-only.
- *RecordsetObject*.**CacheSize**—a **Long** containing the number of ODBC records kept in a local cache. This value must be between 5 and 1200, or 0 to disable caching. This property applies to Dynamic, Dynaset, and Snapshot record sets.
- *RecordsetObject*.**CacheStart**—a **String** containing a bookmark with the starting location of the first record to cache in a Dynaset record set connected to an ODBC database.
- *RecordsetObject*.**Connection**—an object reference to the **Connection** object that owns the record set. This property applies only to the Dynamic, Dynaset, Forward-only, and Snapshot record sets for ODBC type databases only.
- *RecordsetObject*.**DateCreated**—a **Date** value containing the date and time a table was created. This property applies only to a Table type record set.
- *RecordsetObject*.**EditMode**—an **Integer** value containing the type of cursor that manages the query (see Table R-37).

CursorType Name	Value	Description
dbEditNone	0	No editing operations are active (default).
dbEditInProgress	1	The **Edit** method was used and the current row is in the copy buffer.
dbEditAdd	2	The **AddNew** method was used and the current row in the copy buffer has not been saved to the database.

Table R-37: CursorType values.

- *RecordsetObject*.**EOF**—a **Boolean** when **True** means that the current row position is after the last row. **False** means that the current row position is on or before the last row.
- *RecordsetObject*.**Fields**—an object reference to a **Fields** collection containing the fields in the record set.
- *RecordsetObject*.**Filter**—a **String** containing a Where clause without the Where that excludes records from the current record set. This property applies to Dynaset, Forward-only, and Snapshot record sets for Microsoft Jet databases only.

Tip

In many cases it is faster to simply use a new query rather than filter an existing query.

- *RecordsetObject*.**Index**—a **String** containing the name of the current Index object. This property applies to Table record sets only.
- *RecordsetObject*.**LastModified**—a **String** containing the **Bookmark** of the most recently modified or added row.
- *RecordsetObject*.**LastUpdated**—a **Date** value containing the date and time a table was most recently changed. This property applies only to a Table type record set.
- *RecordsetObject*.**LockEdits**—a **Boolean** when **True** means that pessimistic locking is in effect. The page is locked as soon as the **Edit** method executes. **False** means that optimistic locking is in effect (default). The page is locked only when the **Update** method executes. This property applies to all record set types except for Forward-only.
- *RecordsetObject*.**Name**—a **String** containing the name of the record set.
- *RecordsetObject*.**NoMatch**—a **Boolean** when **True** means the **Seek** or one of the **Find** methods were successful. **False** means that the desired record was not found. This property applies to Dynaset, Snapshot, and Table record sets using Microsoft Jet databases only.
- *RecordsetObject*.**PercentPosition**—a **Single** containing the relative position of the row within the result set. Values range from 0.0 to 100.0. This property applies to all record set types except for Forward-only.

Tip

*Use this value with a **ProgressBar** to display how many records were processed.*

- *RecordsetObject*.**Properties**—an object reference to a **Properties** collection.
- *RecordsetObject*.**RecordCount**—a **Long** containing the number of rows accessed in the **Recordset**. Once all rows have been accessed (through a **MoveLast** method for example), this value will reflect the number of rows in the **Recordset**.
- *RecordsetObject*.**RecordStatus**—an **Integer** containing the current status of the row containing the column with optimistic batch updates (see Table R-38). This property applies to all record set types except for Table and only to ODBC databases.

Status Name	Value	Description
dbRecordUnmodified	0	The row hasn't been changed.
dbRecordModified	1	The row has been changed, but it hasn't been updated in the database.
dbRecordNew	2	The row was created with the **AddNew** method, but it hasn't been inserted in the database.
dbUpdatable	3	The row has been deleted, but it hasn't been deleted in the database.
dbRecordDBDeleted	4	The row has been deleted locally and on the database.

Table R-38: Status values.

- *RecordsetObject*.**Restartable**—a **Boolean** when **True** means the **Recordset** can be restarted via the **Requery** method. **False** means **Requery** method can't be used.

- *RecordsetObject*.**Sort**—a **String** containing the Order By clause of an SQL query without the words Order By. This will sort the data of a Dynaset or Snapshot record set from a Microsoft Jet database.

- *RecordsetObject*.**StillExecuting**—a **Boolean** when **True** means that the query is still active. **False** means that the query has completed and is ready to return the record set. This property applies to all record sets except for Tables.

- *RecordsetObject*.**Transactions**—a **Boolean** when **True** means that object supports transactions. **False** means that the object doesn't support transactions. This property applies to all record sets except for Dynamic used with the Microsoft Jet database.

- *RecordsetObject*.**Type**—an **Integer** containing the type of data of the column (see Table R-39). Not all databases support all types.

Type Name	Description
dbOpenTable	A Table (Microsoft Jet databases only)
dbOpenForwardOnly	A Forward-only fixed set
dbOpenDynaset	A Dynaset
dbOpenDynamic	An updateable Dynamic set (ODBC database only)
dbOpenSnapshot	A read-only Snapshot

Table R-39: Type values.

- *RecordsetObject*.**Updatable**—a **Boolean** when **True** means that the rows in the record set can be updated. **False** means that the rows in the result set can't be updated.

- *RecordsetObject*.**UpdateOptions**—an **Integer** describing how the Where clause is built for an optimistic batch update (see Table R-40).

UpdateOptions Name	Description
dbCriteriaKey	Use the key columns in the Where clause (default).
dbCriteriaModValues	Use the key columns and all the updated columns.
dbCriteriaAllCols	Use the key columns and all columns.

UpdateOptions Name	Description
dbCriteriaTimeStamp	Use the time stamp column.
dbCriteriaDeleteInsert	Use a set of Delete and Insert statements will be used to make the change. This value can be added to any of the above values.
dbCriteriaUpdate	Use an Update statement to make the change (default).

Table R-40: *UpdateOptions values.*

- *RecordsetObject*.**ValidationRule**—a **String** containing a Where clause without the word Where that when **True** means that the record passes the validation text. **False** means that the record failed and the **ValidationText** will be displayed to the user.
- *RecordsetObject*.**ValidationText**—a **String** containing the text to display when a validation error occurs. This property applies to all record sets generated by the Microsoft Jet database.

Methods

RecordsetObject.AddNew

Usage   This method creates a new row in the record set's copy buffer. Enter information into each column and then use the **Update** method to add the data to the database. The **EditMode** property will be set to *dbEditAdd*. This method applies to all record sets except for Snapshot. Snapshot record sets may use this method if the ODBC driver supports updateable snapshots.

Tip

*If you don't save your changes with the **Update** method before you move to another row, those changes will be lost.*

RecordsetObject.Cancel

Usage   This method cancels any pending database activity and releases any held resources. This method is supported for all record sets except for Table.

RecordsetObject.CancelUpdate

Usage   This method cancels any pending database changes, flushes the copy buffer, and resets the **EditMode** property to *dbEditNone*.

RecordsetObject.Close

Usage   This method closes an open record set.

querydef = *RecordsetObject*.CopyQueryDef

Usage   This method creates a duplicate copy of the **QueryDef** object that created this record set. If a **QueryDef** wasn't used to create the record set, an error will occur.

Arguments
- *querydef*—a **Variant** variable that will contain a reference to the new **QueryDef** object.

rdoRecordsetObject.Delete

Usage This method deletes the current row if the record set is updateable. If there is no current row, the record set is not updateable, or another user has locked the row, an error will occur. After the row has been deleted, the deleted row remains the current row until the cursor has been moved. This method applies to all record sets except for Snapshot. Snapshot record sets may use this method if the ODBC driver supports updateable snapshots.

RecordsetObject.Edit

Usage This method allows you to change values in the current row. It first creates a copy of the row in the copy buffer and then allows you to make changes. The **Update** method is used after the changes are complete to post the information to the database. The **EditMode** property will be set to *dbEditMode*. The **CancelUpdate** method will cancel the changes. This method applies to all record sets except for Snapshot. Snapshot record sets may use this method if the ODBC driver supports updateable snapshots.

RecordsetObject.FillCache [rows] [, start]

Usage This method will load records into the local cache for a Microsoft Jet connected ODBC database. This method applies only Dynaset record sets.

Arguments
- *rows*—a **Long** containing the number of ODBC records to load. This value must be between 5 and 1200. If omitted, it will default to the current value of **CacheSize**.
- *start*—a **String** containing a bookmark with the starting location of the first record to be cached. If omitted, it will default to the current value of **CacheStart**.

RecordsetObject.FindFirst [criteria]

Usage This method finds the first occurrence of the specified criteria in a Microsoft Jet database by starting with the first record in the record set and searching to the end of the record set. Check the **NoMatch** property to determine the status of this method.

Tip

Don't use this method on a Microsoft Jet connected ODBC database, because it is very inefficient when compared with a properly designed query.

Arguments *criteria*—a **String** containing an SQL Where clause without the word Where that locates the record.

RecordsetObject.FindLast [*criteria*]

Usage This method finds the last occurrence of the specified criteria in a Microsoft Jet database by starting with the last record in the record set and searching to the beginning of the record set. Check the **NoMatch** property to determine the status of this method.

> **Tip**
>
> *Don't use this method on a Microsoft Jet connected ODBC database, because it is very inefficient when compared with a properly designed query.*

Arguments
- *criteria*—a **String** containing an SQL Where clause without the word Where that locates the record.

RecordsetObject.FindNext [*criteria*]

Usage This method finds the next occurrence of the specified criteria in a Microsoft Jet database by starting with the current record in the record set and searching to the end of the record set. Check the **NoMatch** property to determine the status of this method.

Arguments
- *criteria*—a **String** containing an SQL Where clause without the word Where that locates the record.

RecordsetObject.FindPrevious [*criteria*]

Usage This method finds the previous occurrence of the specified criteria in a Microsoft Jet database by starting with the current record in the record set and searching to the beginning of the record set. Check the **NoMatch** property to determine the status of this method.

Arguments
- *criteria*—a **String** containing an SQL Where clause without the word Where that locates the record.

rows = RecordsetObject.GetRows (*NumRows*)

Usage This method returns an array containing a two-dimensional array of columns and rows.

Arguments
- *rows*—a **Variant** variable that that will contain a two-dimensional array of columns and rows. The first subscript contains the column number ranging from 0 to the number of columns -1. The second subscript contains the row number, ranging from 0 to the number of rows -1.
- *NumRows*—a **Long** value containing the number of rows to retrieve from the record set.

RecordsetObject.Move rows [, start]

Usage This method repositions the current row pointer and discards any changes in the copy buffer.

Arguments
- *rows*—a **Long** value containing the number of rows to move forward (positive values) or backward (negative values). A value of 0 will discard any changes made to the current row and fetch a new copy from the record set. This value can't be negative in a Forward-only record set.
- *force*—a **Variant** value containing the bookmark of the row that will be used as the starting position. If not specified, the movement will be relative to the current row.

RecordsetObject.MoveFirst

Usage This method repositions the current row pointer to the first row in the record set and discards any changes in the copy buffer. This method is not available in a Forward-only record set.

RecordsetObject.MoveLast [option]

Usage This method repositions the current row pointer to the last row in the record set and discards any changes in the copy buffer. This method is not available in a Forward-only record set.

Arguments
- *option*—an **Integer** value containing a value of *dbRunAsync* to perform the operation asynchronously or 0 to wait for it to complete. If not specified, a value of 0 is assumed.

RecordsetObject.MoveNext

Usage This method repositions the current row pointer to the next row in the record set and discards any changes in the copy buffer.

RecordsetObject.MovePrevious

Usage This method repositions the current row pointer to the previous row in the record set and discards any changes in the copy buffer. This method is not available in a Forward-only record set.

Return = rdoRecordsetObject.NextRecordset

Usage This method clears the current record set and returns a value indicating if one or more record sets are available. This method applies to ODBC connected record sets only.

Arguments
- *Return*—a **Boolean** value when **True** means that there is at least one more record set to process. **False** means no more record sets are available.

results = RecordsetObject.OpenRecordset ([type [, options [, locktype]]])

Usage This method creates a new **Recordset** object.

Arguments
- *results*—a **Recordset** object containing the results of a query.
- *type*—an **Integer** value containing the type of cursor that manages the **Recordset** object (see Table R-41).

type Name	Description
dbOpenTable	A Table (Microsoft Jet databases only)
dbOpenForwardOnly	A Forward-only fixed set
dbOpenDynaset	A Dynaset
dbOpenDynamic	An updateable Dynamic set (ODBC database only)
dbOpenSnapshot	A read-only Snapshot

Table R-41: Type values.

- *options*—an **Integer** value containing the options that execute the query (see Table R-42). These options can be added together if more than one option is desired.

options Name	Description
dbAppendOnly	Allow the user to only add new records to the record set, but not modify or delete them.
dbSQLPassThrough	Pass an SQL statement through a Microsoft Jet database to an ODBC data source.
dbSeeChanges	Generate a run-time error when another user is editing the same record in a Microsoft Jet Dynaset type record set.
dbDenyWrite	Prevent other users from modifying and adding records.
dbDenyRead	Prevent other users from reading records.
dbRunAsync	Run the query asynchronously with an ODBC data source.
dbExecDirect	Don't create a stored procedure when executing the query. This is useful for queries that don't return any rows.
dbInconsistent	Allow inconsistent updates (mutually exclusive with *dbConsistent*).
dbConsistent	Allow consistent updates (mutually exclusive with *dbConsistent*).

Table R-42: options values.

> **Tip**
>
> *Inconsistent updates happen when you join two tables to create the record set and the two tables have a one-to-many relationship. If you change the data in such a way that you have an entry in the many table without the corresponding entry in the one table, an inconsistent update will result.*

- *locktype*—an **Integer** value containing the type of locking to use (see Table R-43).

locktype Name	Description
dbReadOnly	Read-only (default)
dbPessimistic	Pessimistic concurrency
dbOptimistic	Optimistic concurrency based on row id
dbOptimisticValue	Optimistic concurrency based on row values
dbOptimisticBatch	Optimistic concurrency using batch update mode

Table R-43: locktype *values.*

RecordsetObject.Requery [*option*]

Usage This method refreshes the data in the recordset by executing the query that generated this record set again.

Tip

Since the actual query is rerun to generate the record set, any saved bookmarks will be invalid.

Arguments *option*—an **Integer** value containing a value of *dbRunAsync* to perform the operation asynchronously or 0 to wait for it to complete. If not specified, a value of 0 is assumed.

RecordsetObject.Seek *comparison* [, *key* [, *key* . . . [, *key*]]])

Usage This method finds a record in a record set based on its primary key value. Since a primary key can span multiple fields, one value is permitted for each field. If less values are specified than the number of fields in the key, then you can't use the "=" relational operator, since there may not be an exact match with the default **Null** values in the unspecified parts of the key.
  The ">", and ">=" will start the search from the beginning of the index, while the "<" and "<=" will start at the end of the index.
  This method only works with record sets from a Microsoft Jet database.

Arguments *comparison*—a **String** containing one of the following comparison operators: "=," "<>," "<," ">," "<=," or ">=."

key—a series of values corresponding to the fields in the record set's key. Up to 13 values may be specified. If omitted, the value will default to **Null**. The type of each key value must be the same as the type of the corresponding key field.

RecordsetObject.Update [type] [, force]

Usage This method saves the copy buffer to an updateable record set and resets the copy buffer.

Arguments
- *type*—an **Integer** indicating how the update will be applied to the record set (see Table R-44).

type Name	Description
dbUpdateRegular	Write changes to disk immediately (default).
dbUpdateBatch	Write all pending changes in cache to disk.
dbUpdateCurrentRecord	Write all pending changed in cache to disk for the current record only.

Table R-44: type *values*.

- *force*—a **Boolean** value when **True** means that the update will be made even if someone has changed the record since the **AddNew**, **Delete**, or **EditMode** method was executed. **False** means that an error will be returned, except for optimistic batch updates which will add the failed update to the **BatchCollisions** property (default).

See Also **Recordsets** (collection)

Recordsets
COLLECTION

EE

Usage Data Access Objects (DAO) use the **Recordsets** collection to hold information about a set of record sets associated with a **Database** or **Connection** object.

Properties
- *RecordsetsCollection*.**Count**—an **Integer** containing the number of **Recordset** objects in the collection.

Methods *RecordsetsCollection*.**Refresh**

Usage This method gets a current copy of the objects in the collection. This is important in a multi-user environment where more than one user may be making changes in the database.

See Also **Connection** (object), **Database** (object), **Recordset** (object)

Rect

OBJECT

PE, EE

Usage
The **Rect** object defines the coordinate location for a rectangle.

Properties
- *RectObject*.**Max**—an object reference to a **Coor** object containing the ending coordinate of the rectangle.
- *RectObject*.**Min**—an object reference to a **Coor** object containing the beginning coordinate of the rectangle.

See Also
Coor (object), **MSChart** (control)

ReDim

STATEMENT

CCE, LE, PE, EE

Syntax
```
ReDim [ Preserve ] identifier[typechar] [ arrayinfo ] [ As type ] , [
    identifier[typechar] [ arrayinfo ] [ As type ] ] . . .
```

Usage
The **ReDim** statement reallocates storage for an array that was originally declared with no dimensions.

Arguments
- *Preserve*—an optional keyword that preserves the contents of an array. Using this keyword means that you can only change the size of the last dimension, and you can't change the number of dimensions in the array. Reducing the size of the last dimension will discard the eliminated data.
  - *identifier*—the Visual Basic identifier that will be used to reference this particular variable. It must begin with a letter which can be followed by any number of letters or numbers or the underscore character ("_"). Identifiers are not case-sensitive, though the case will be preserved for easier reading.
  - *typechar*—one of the following characters can be included as the last character of a variable name to declare its type: "@" for **Currency**, "#" for **Double**, "%" for **Integer**, "&" for **Long**, "!" for **Single**, or "$" for **String**.
  - *arrayinfo*—indicates the size of an array. It can have zero to 60 dimensions. The subscripts are defined as the following:
    ([ubound | lbound **To** ubound] [, ubound | , lbound **To** ubound]
        . . .)]
    - *ubound*   the upper bound for an array.
    - *lbound*   the lower bound for an array's subscript. If omitted, the value from **Option Base** will be used. If there is no **Option Base** statement in the module.
- *type*—a valid Visual Basic type: **Byte**, **Boolean**, **Currency**, **Date**, **Double**, **Integer**, **Long**, **Single**, **String**, **Object**, or **Variant**. Specific objects can also be used as well as user-defined types defined with the **Type** statement.

Examples
```
Private Sub Command1_Click()
Dim x() As Integer
ReDim x(10)
MsgBox "The upper bound of x is " & Format(UBound(x))
ReDim Preserve x(20)
MsgBox "The upper bound of x is " & Format(UBound(x))
End Sub
```

This routine declares an array with zero dimensions and then uses the **ReDim** statement to change it to a one-dimensional array with 10 elements. Then I change the array to a one-dimensional array with 20 elements and preserve the contents of the array.

See Also **Byte** (data type), **Boolean** (data type), **Currency** (data type), **Date** (data type), **Double** (data type), **Integer** (data type), **Long** (data type), **Object** (data type), **Option Base** (statement), **Option Explicit** (statement), **Private** (statement), **Public** (statement), **ReDim** (statement), **Single** (data type), **String** (data type), **Static** (statement), **Type** (statement), **TypeName** (function), **Variant** (data type)

Relation

OBJECT

PE, EE

Usage The **Relation** object describes the relationship between a primary table and a foreign table.

Properties
- *RelationObject*.**Attributes**—an **Integer** value containing one or more of the attributes listed in Table R-45.

Attributes Name	Description
dbRelationUnique	The relationship is one-to-one.
dbRelationDontEnforce	No referential integrity.
dbRelationInherited	The relationship exists in a non-current that contains two linked tables.
dbRelationUpdateCascade	Updates will cascade.
dbRelationDeleteCascade	Deletes will cascade.

Table R-45: Attributes *values*.

- *RelationObject*.**ForeignTable**—a **String** value containing the name of the foreign table that uses an item from this table as a key.
- *RelationObject*.**Name**—a **String** value that contains the name of the relation object.
- *RelationObject*.**PartialReplica**—a **Boolean** value when **True** means that the relation will be enforced when making a partial replica from a full replica. **False** means that records may be replicated even though all of the needed records for the relationship aren't available.
- *RelationObject*.**Table**—a **String** value containing the name of the primary table.

Methods **field = RelationObject.CreateField ([name [, type [, size]]])**

Usage This method creates a new field in the relation object.

Arguments
- *field*—a reference to a new **Field** object.
- *name*—a **String** containing the name of the new field.
- *type*—an **Integer** value describing the type of the field (see Table R-46).

Type Name	Description
dbBigInt	Big integer data type
dbBinary	Fixed length binary data, up to 255 bytes long
dbBoolean	Boolean data type
dbByte	Integer value one byte wide
dbChar	Fixed length character string
dbCurrency	Currency data type
dbDate	Date/time data type
dbDecimal	Decimal data type
dbDouble	Double precision floating point data type
dbFloat	Floating point data type
dbGUID	Globally Unique Identifier data type
dbInteger	16-bit integer data type
dbLong	32-bit integer data type
dbLongBinary	Long binary data type
dbMemo	Memo data type
dbNumeric	Numeric data type
dbSingle	Single precision floating point data type
dbText	Field data type
dbTime	Time data type
dbTimeStamp	Time stamp data type
dbVarBinary	Variable length binary, up to 255 bytes long

Table R-46: Type *values*.

- *size*—an **Integer** containing the size of the field.

See Also **Database** (object), **Databases** (collection), **Field** (object), **Property** (object), **Properties** (collection), **Recordset** (object), **Recordsets** (collection), **Relations** (collection), **TableDef** (object), **TableDefs** (collection)

Relations

COLLECTION

PE, EE

Usage Data Access Objects (DAO) uses the **Relations** collection to hold information about the relationships associated with a table.

Properties
- *RelationsCollection*.**Count**—an **Integer** containing the number of **Relation** objects in the collection.

Methods	**RelationsCollection.Append** *object*
Usage	This method adds a **Relation** object to the collection.
Arguments	*object*—a reference to a **Relation** object to add to the collection.

	RelationsCollection.Delete *objectname*
Usage	This method removes a **Relation** object from the collection.
Arguments	*objectname*—a **String** containing the name of the **Relation** object to remove from the collection.

	RelationsCollection.Refresh
Usage	This method gets a current copy of the **Relation** contained in the collection. This is important in a multi-user environment where more than one user may be making changes in the **Databases** collection.
See Also	**Relation** (object)

Rem

STATEMENT

CCE, LE, PE, EE

Syntax	**Rem** [*text*] [*statement*] ' [*text*]
Usage	The **Rem** statement allows you to add comments to your program. In the first form, the characters **Rem** must begin the statement, and the statement ends at the end of the line. In the second form, the apostrophe (') begins the comment and can follow any statement. Like the **Rem** form, the statement ends at the end of the line.

> **Tip**
>
> *Use an apostrophe in front of a statement to disable it without actually deleting the text. This is useful when debugging a program and you want to disable individual statements to observe the effects of the rest.*
>
> *Also use this statement after a **Function** or **Sub** statement to describe what the routine is and how it works.*

Arguments	*text*—a string of characters.
	statement—another Visual Basic statement.

Examples
```
Private Sub Command1_Click()
' This routine computes the sum of the numbers
' from 1 to 10 using a For Next loop.
Dim i As Integer
Dim j As Integer
j = 0
For i = 1 To 10
   j = j + i
'  The following statement is useful for debugging
'  Form1.Print "i = " & Format(i) & " j = " & Format(j)
Next i
MsgBox "Sum of the numbers 1 to 10 is " & Format(j)
End Sub
```

This routine shows how to use an apostrophe to disable a statement that is used for debugging.

See Also **Function** (statement), **Sub** (statement)

RemoteData

CONTROL
EE

Usage The **RemoteData** control is an intrinsic control that provides access to ODBC databases. This control includes facilities for inserting new records into the database, and updating and deleting existing records. It also provides you with the ability to move through the database and have other, data aware controls (like the **CheckBox**, **ComboBox**, **Image**, **Label**, **ListBox**, **MaskedEdit**, **Picture**, **RichTextBox**, and **TextBox** controls) automatically update the information they display. Other controls like **DBCombo**, **DBGrid**, **DBList**, and **MSFlexGrid** will also work with the **RemoteData** control to provide access to a database. This control is very similar to the **Data** control, except it uses the Remote Data Objects instead of the Data Access Objects.

Properties ▪ *RemoteDataControl*.**Align**—an **Integer** value (see Table R-47) that describes the placement of the **RemoteData** control.

Align Name	Value	Description
vbAlignNone	0	The Data control's position is set at design time or by the program (default value for objects on a non-MDIForm).
vbAlignTop	1	The **Data** control is placed at the top of the form and its width is set to **ScaleWidth**. It will automatically be resized when the form is resized (default value for objects on an MDI Form).
vbAlignBottom	2	The **Data** control is placed at the bottom of the form and its width is set to **ScaleWidth**. It will automatically be resized when the form is resized.

Align Name	Value	Description
vbAlignLeft	3	The **Data** control is placed at the left edge of the form and its width is set to **ScaleWidth**. It is not resized when the form is resized.
vbAlignRight	4	The **Data** control is placed at the right edge of the form and its width is set to **ScaleWidth**. It is not resized when the form is resized.

Table R-47: Align *values.*

- *RemoteDataControl.***Appearance**—an **Integer** value (see Table R-48) that specifies how the **Data** control will appear on the form.

AppearanceValue	Description
0	The RemoteData control displays without the 3D effects.
1	The **RemoteData** control displays with 3D effects (default value).

Table R-48: Appearance *values.*

- *RemoteDataControl.***BackColor**—a **Long** that contains the suggested value for the background color of the control. The **BackColor** and **ForeColor** must both be solid to display text. If you choose a color that is dithered, it will change to the nearest solid color.
- *RemoteDataControl.***BatchCollisionCount**—a **Long** containing the number of rows that were not updated in the last batch update.
- *RemoteDataControl.***BatchCollisionRows**—an array of bookmarks for each row that were not updated in the last batch update. This array is updated each time the **BatchUpdate** method is used.

Tip

After resetting the values for each failed row, you can use the **BatchUpdate** *method again to post the changes.*

- *RemoteDataControl.***BatchSize**—a **Long** value containing the number of statements sent to the server when performing an optimistic batch update. If not specified, a default value of 15 is assumed.
- *RemoteDataControl.***BOFAction**—an **Integer** value (see Table R-49) containing the action to take when the beginning of file is encountered.

BOFAction Name	Value	Description
rdMoveFirst	0	The first record is kept as the current record.
rdBOF	1	Encountering the BOF will trigger the **Validate** event, followed by a **Reposition** event. The Move Previous button on the control will be disabled.

Table R-49: BOFAction *values.*

- *RemoteDataControl*.**Caption**—a **String** value that displays inside data control. You can include an access key for this control by inserting an ampersand (&) in front of the character you want to use. The selected character will then appear with an underline. Then, if the user presses the Alt key with the underlined character, the control will gain the focus.
- *RemoteDataControl*.**Connect**—a **String** value containing the type of database and any necessary connection information.
- *RemoteDataControl*.**Connection**—an object reference to an **rdoConnection** object containing the underlying connection to the remote database.
- *RemoteDataControl*.**Container**—an object that can set or return the container of the control at run time. This property cannot be set at design time.
- *RemoteDataControl*.**CursorDriver**—an **Integer** containing the type of cursor to use (see Table R-50).

CursorDriver Name	Value	Description
rdUseIfNeeded	0	The rdoEngine chooses the most appropriate cursor (default).
rdUseODBC	1	Use the ODBC cursor library. Better performance for small tables, but poorer performance on large tables.
rdUseServer	2	Use server side cursors. Better performance for large sets at the expense of higher network traffic.
rdUseClientBatch	3	Use the batch cursor library.
rdUseNone	4	Do not use a cursor. This results in a read-only result that can be read in a forward direction only. It has faster performance than the other options.

Table R-50: *CursorDriver values.*

- *RemoteDataControl*.**DatabaseSourceName**—a **String** value containing the name of the registered remote data source as stored in the Windows Registry.
- *RemoteDataControl*.**DragIcon**—an object that contains the **Picture** value of an icon. At design time, you can specify an icon file that has a file type of .ICO.

> **Tip**
>
> This value can be created by copying the value from another control's **DragIcon** value, a form's icon, or by using the **LoadPicture** function.

- *RemoteDataControl*.**DragMode**—an **Integer** value (see Table R-51) specifying how the control will respond to a drag request.

> **Tip**
>
> Setting **DragMode** to vbAutomatic *will automatically begin a drag operation when the user clicks on the control. However, the control will not respond to the usual mouse events (***Click***, ***DblClick***, ***MouseDown***, ***MouseMove***, ***MouseUp***).*

DragMode Name	Value	Description
vbManual	0	The Drag method must be used to begin a drag-and-drop operation (default value).
vbAutomatic	1	The source control will automatically begin a drag-and-drop operation when the user clicks on the control.

Table R-51: **DragMode** *values.*

- *RemoteDataControl*.**EditMode**—an **Integer** value containing the type of cursor that manages the query (see Table R-52).

CursorType Name	Value	Description
dbEditNone	0	No editing operations are active (default).
dbEditInProgress	1	The **Edit** method was used and the current row is in the copy buffer.
dbEditAdd	2	The **AddNew** method was used and the current row in the copy buffer has not been saved to the database.

Table R-52: *CursorType values.*

- *RemoteDataControl*.**Enabled**—a **Boolean** value when **True** means that the control will respond to events. When **False**, the control will not respond to events.
- *RemoteDataControl*.**Environment**—an object reference to an **rdoEnvironment** object containing the properties and methods to help manage the transaction environment.
- *RemoteDataControl*.**EOFAction**—an **Integer** value (see Table R-53) containing the action to take when the end of file is encountered.

EOFAction Name	Value	Description
rdMoveLast	0	The last record is kept as the current record.
rdEOF	1	Encountering the EOF will trigger the **Validate** event, followed by a **Reposition** event. The Move Next button on the control will be disabled
rdAddNew	2	Encountering the EOF will trigger the **Validate** event on the current record, followed by an **AddNew**, followed by a **Reposition** event.

Table R-53: EOFAction *values.*

- *RemoteDataControl*.**ErrorThreshold**—a **Long** that contains the severity level which will determine a fatal error.
- *RemoteDataControl*.**Font**—an object that contains information about the character font used by this object.
- *RemoteDataControl*.**ForeColor**—a **Long** that contains the suggested value for the foreground color of the contained control. This property is read only at run time.
- *RemoteDataControl*.**Height**—a **Single** that contains the height of the control.
- *RemoteDataControl*.**Index**—an **Integer** that uniquely identifies a control in a control array.

- *RemoteDataControl*.**KeysetSize**—a **Long** containing the number of rows in the keyset buffer. This value must be greater than or equal to the **RowsetSize** property.
- *RemoteDataControl*.**Left**—a **Single** that contains the distance measured in twips between the left edge of the control and the left edge of the control's container.
- *RemoteDataControl*.**LockType**—a **Long** containing the locking method (see Table R-54).

LockType Name	Value	Description
rdConcurReadOnly	1	Read-only (default)
rdConcurLock	2	Pessimistic concurrency
rdConcurRowVer	3	Optimistic concurrency based on row id
rdConcurValues	4	Optimistic concurrency based on row values
rdConcurBatch	5	Optimistic concurrency using batch update mode

Table R-54: LockType values.

- *RemoteDataControl*.**LoginTimeout**—a **Long** containing the number of seconds a login will be attempted before returning an error.
- *RemoteDataControl*.**LogMessages**—a **String** containing the path and filename where log messages are to be written. If this property contains an empty string, no logging will occur.

Tip

Using this property will adversely affect performance, so use it with care.

- *RemoteDataControl*.**Maxrows**—a **Long** containing the maximum number of rows to return or change.

Tip

This property is useful to limit the effect of an SQL statement when testing. Only the specified number of rows will be retrieved, updated, deleted, or inserted.

- *RemoteDataControl*.**Name**—a **String** that contains the name of the control that will reference the control in a Visual Basic program. This property is read only at run time. The default value for this property is "MSRDC1."
- *RemoteDataControl*.**OLEDropMode**—an **Integer** value (see Table R-55) that describes how the control will respond to OLE drop operations.

OLEDropMode Name	Value	Description
vbOLEDropNone	0	The control does not accept OLE drops. The cursor is changed to the No Drop cursor (default value).
vbOLEDropManual	1	The control responds to OLE drops under the program's control (manual).
vbOLEDropAutomatic	2	The control automatically accepts OLE drops if it recognizes the format of the data object.

Table R-55: OLEDropMode values.

- *RemoteDataControl.***Object**—an object that contains a reference to the **MSComm** control.
- *RemoteDataControl.***Options**—an **Integer** value (see Table R-56) containing options that apply to the **Recordset**. To specify multiple options, simply add them together.

Options Name	Value	Description
rdAsyncEnable	32	Run the query asynchronously.
rdExecDirect	64	Don't create a stored procedure when executing the query. This is useful for queries that don't return any rows.

Table R-56: Options values.

- *RemoteDataControl.***Parent**—an object that contains a reference to the **Form, Frame,** or other container that contains the **Data** control.
- *RemoteDataControl.***Password**—a **String** value containing the password associated with the **rdoEnvironment** object.
- *RemoteDataControl.***Prompt**—an **Integer** value containing the options for the connection process (see Table R-57).

prompt Name	Value	Description
rdDriverPrompt	0	The ODBC driver takes the information supplied in Name and Connect and displays it in the ODBC Data Sources dialog box.
rdDriverPrompt	1	The connection information in **Name** and **Connect** connects to the database. If sufficient information is not present, an error will occur.
rdDriverComplete	2	The ODBC driver uses the information supplied in **Name** and **Connect** to connect to the database. If there is insufficient information, the ODBC Data Sources dialog box will display (default).
rdDriverCompleteRequired	3	This is similar to the *dbDriverComplete* option, but information supplied in **Name** and **Connect** can't be changed.

Table R-57: prompt values.

- *RemoteDataControl.***QueryTimeout**—a **Long** containing the number of seconds to wait for a query to complete before returning an error.
- *RemoteDataControl.***ReadOnly**—a **Boolean** value when **True** means that the **rdoConnection** object is opened in read-only mode. **False** means that the **rdoConnection** object is opened with full read/write access.
- *RemoteDataControl.***Resultset**—returns or sets a reference to the **Recordset** object used by the **RemoteData** control.
- *RemoteDataControl.***ResultsetType**—an **Integer** value (see Table R-58) that contains the type of record set.

RecordsetType Name	Value	Description
vbRSTypeTable	0	Table type record set
vbRSTypeDynaset	1	Dynaset type record set (default)
vbRSTypeSnapshot	2	Snapshot type record set

Table R-58: RecordsetType values.

- *RemoteDataControl*.**RowsetSize**—a **Long** value containing the number of rows in an **rdoResultset** cursor. If not specified, this property will default to 100.
- *RemoteDataControl*.**SQL**—a **String** value containing the SQL query.
- *RemoteDataControl*.**Tag**—a **String** that can hold programmer specific information. This property is not used by Visual Basic.
- *RemoteDataControl*.**ToolTipText**—a **String** that holds a text value that can be displayed as a **ToolTip** box that displays whenever the cursor is held over the control for about one second.
- *RemoteDataControl*.**Top**—a **Single** that contains the distance measured in twips between the top edge of the control and the top edge of the control's container.
- *RemoteDataControl*.**UpdateCriteria**—an **Integer** describing how the Where clause is built for an optimistic batch update (see Table R-59).

UpdateCriteria Name	Value	Description
rdCriteriaKey	0	Use the key columns in the Where clause (default).
rdCriteriaAllCols	1	Use the key columns and all updated columns.
rdCriteriaUpdCols	2	Use the key columns and all columns.
rdCriteriaTimeStamp	3	Use the time stamp column.

Table R-59: UpdateCriteria values.

- *RemoteDataControl*.**UpdateOperation**—an **Integer** describing how an optimistic batch update is performed (see Table R-60).

UpdateOperation Name	Value	Description
rdOperationUpdate	0	Use an Update statement for each row in an optimistic batch update (default).
rdOperationDelIns	1	Use a Delete statement and an Insert statement for each row in an optimistic batch update.

Table R-60: UpdateOperation values.

- *RemoteDataControl*.**UserName**—a **String** containing the username associated with the object.
- *RemoteDataControl*.**Version**—a **String** value containing the version number of the data source.
- *RemoteDataControl*.**Visible**—a **Boolean** value when **True** means that the control is visible. When **False** means that the control is not visible.

> **Tip**
>
> This property hides the control until the program is ready to display it.

- *RemoteDataControl*.**WhatsThisHelpID**—a **Long** that contains a help file context ID number that references an entry in the help file. This provides a What's This PopUp help display in response to the What's This button in the upper right corner of the window.
- *RemoteDataControl*.**Width**—a **Single** that contains the width of the control.

Methods

RemoteDataControl.BeginTrans

Usage This method marks the beginning of a transaction.

RemoteDataControl.Cancel

Usage This method requests the remote data source to cancel an asynchronous query or cancel any pending results.

RemoteDataControl.CommitTrans

Usage This method marks the end of a transaction and saves the data into the database. After the commit has finished, the transaction can't be undone using the **RollBack** method.

RemoteDataControl.Drag [*DragAction*]

Usage This method begins, ends, or cancels a drag operation.

Arguments • *DragAction*—an **Integer** that contains a value selected from Table R-61.

DragAction Name	Value	Description
vbCancel	0	Cancels any drag operation in progress.
vbBeginDrag	1	Begins a drag operation (default).
vbEndDrag	2	Ends a drag operation and drops *object*.

Table R-61: DragAction *values.*

RemoteDataControl.Move *Left* [, *Top* [, *Width* [, *Height*]]]

Usage This method changes the position and the size of the **Data** control. The **ScaleMode** of the **Form** or other container object that holds the control will determine the units used to specify the coordinates.

Arguments
- *Left*—a **Single** that specifies the new position of the left edge of the control.
- *Top*—a **Single** that specifies the new position of the top edge of the control.
- *Width*—a **Single** that specifies the new width of the control.
- *Height*—a **Single** that specifies the new height of the control.

RemoteDataControl.Refresh

Usage This method gets a fresh copy of the data in the record set.

rdoEnvironmentObject.RollbackTrans

Usage   This method abandons all of the changes made to the database, returning the database to the same state as it was when the **BeginTrans** method was used.

RemoteDataControl.ShowWhatsThis

Usage   This method displays the ShowWhatsThis help information for this control.

RemoteDataControl.UpdateControls

Usage   This method retrieves the current record from the record set object and updates the fields in the bound data controls.

Tip

When the user wants to cancel their changes to the bound data controls, use this method to restore the old values from the database. It has the added advantage of not triggering any events.

RemoteDataControl.UpdateRow

Usage   This method updates the database with the current values of the data bound controls.

Tip

When the user wants to save their changes to the bound data controls, use this method to save the changes. It has the added advantage of not triggering any events.

RemoteDataControl.ZOrder [*position*]

Usage   This method specifies the position of the control relative to the other objects on the form.

Tip

*Note that there are three layers of objects on a form: the back layer is the drawing space which contains the results of the graphical methods, the middle layer contains graphical objects and **Labels**, and the top layer contains nongraphical controls such as the **RemoteData** control. The **ZOrder** method only affects how the objects are arranged within a single layer.*

Arguments   ▪ *position*—an **Integer** that specifies the relative position of this object. A value of 0 means that the control is positioned at the head of the list, a value of 1 means that the control will be placed at the end of the list.

RemoteData

Events

Private Sub *RemoteDataControl*_DragDrop([*index* As Integer ,] *source* As Control, *x* As Single, *y* As Single)

Usage   This event occurs when a drag-and-drop operation is completed by using the **Drag** method with a *DragAction* value of *vbEndDrag* (2).

Tip

When using drag-and-drop operations, use the **DragOver** event to determine what the cursor will look like while the cursor moves over the control.

Arguments
- *index*—an **Integer** that uniquely identifies a control in a control array. This argument is not present if the control is not part of a control array.
- *source*—a control object that is the control that is being dragged.

Tip

You can access a property or method from the source control by using source.*property* or source.*method*. You can determine the type of object or control by using the **TypeOf** operator.

- *x*—a **Single** that contains the horizontal location of the mouse pointer.
- *y*—a **Single** that contains the vertical location of the mouse pointer.

Private Sub *RemoteDataControl*_DragOver([*index* As Integer ,] *source* As Control, *x* As Single, *y* As Single, *state* As Integer)

Usage   This event occurs while a drag operation is in progress and the cursor is moved over the control.

Tip

When using drag-and-drop operations, use the **DragOver** event to determine what the cursor will look like while the cursor moves over the control. When **state** is 0, you can change the cursor to a No Drop (vbNoDrop) cursor or highlight the field that the cursor is near. When **state** is 1, you can undo the changes you made when the **state** was 0.

Arguments
- *index*—an **Integer** that uniquely identifies a control in a control array. This argument is not present if the control is not part of a control array.
- *source*—a control object that is the control that is being dragged.

Tip

You can access a property or method from the source control by using source.*property* or source.*method*. You can determine the type of object or control by using the **TypeOf** operator.

- *x*—a **Single** that contains the horizontal location of the mouse pointer.
- *y*—a **Single** that contains the vertical location of the mouse pointer.
- *state*—an **Integer** value (see Table R-62) that indicates the state of the object being dragged.

state Name	Value	Description
vbEnter	0	The dragged object is entering the range of the control.
vbLeave	1	The dragged object is leaving the range of the control.
vbOver	2	The dragged object has moved from one position over the control to another.

Table R-62: state *values*.

Private Sub *RemoteDataControl*_Error ([*index* As Integer ,] *number* As Integer, *description* As String, *scode* As Long, *source* As String, *helpfile* As String, *helpcontext* As Long, *resp* As Single)

Usage This event occurs when a data error occurs while your code is not running. This could happen because a user clicked the **Data** control, the **Data** control automatically loaded a record set after Form_Load occurred, or if a custom control performed a **MoveNext**, **AddNew**, or a **Delete**.

Arguments
- *number*—an **Integer** containing the error code.
- *description*—a **String** containing a description of the error.
- *scode*—a **Long** containing the ODBC error code.
- *source*—a **String** containing the source of the error.
- *helpfile*—a **String** containing the path and filename of the help file containing information about the error.
- *helpcontext*—a **Long** containing the help file context number.
- *cancel*—an **Integer** value (see Table R-63) that contains the program's response to the error.

cancel Name	Value	Description
rdDataErrContinue	0	Continue processing
rdDataErrDisplay	1	Display error message (default)

Table R-63: cancel *values*.

Private Sub *RemoteDataControl*_MouseDown([*index* As Integer ,] *button* As Integer, *shift* As Single, *x* As Single, *y* As Single)

Usage This event occurs when a mouse button is pressed while the cursor is over the control.

RemoteData

Arguments
- *index*—an **Integer** that uniquely identifies a control in a control array. This argument is not present if the control is not part of a control array.
- *button*—an **Integer** value (see Table R-64) that contains information about the mouse buttons that were pressed. Only one button will be indicated when this event occurs.

button Name	Value	Description
vbLeftButton	1	The left button was pressed.
vbRightButton	2	The right button was pressed.
vbMiddleButton	4	The middle button was pressed.

Table R-64: button *values*.

- *shift*—an **Integer** value (see Table R-65) that contains information about the Shift and Alt keys that were pushed when the mouse button was pressed. These values can be added together if more than one key was down. For instance, a value of 5 would mean that the Shift and Alt keys were both down when the mouse button was pressed.

shift Name	Value	Description
vbShiftMask	1	The Shift key was pressed.
vbCtrlMask	2	The Ctrl key was pressed.
vbAltMask	4	The Alt key was pressed.

Table R-65: shift *values*.

- *x*—a **Single** that contains the horizontal location of the mouse pointer.
- *y*—a **Single** that contains the vertical location of the mouse pointer.

Private Sub *CheckBoxControl*_MouseMove ([*index* As Integer ,] *button* As Integer, *shift* As Single, *x* As Single, *y* As Single)

Usage
This event occurs while the cursor is moved over the control.

Arguments
- *index*—an **Integer** that uniquely identifies a control in a control array. This argument is not present if the control is not part of a control array.
- *button*—an **Integer** value (see Table R-66) that contains information about the mouse buttons that were pressed. These values can be added together if more than one button was pushed. For instance, a value of 3 means that both the left and right buttons were pressed. A value of 0 means that no buttons were pressed.

button Name	Value	Description
vbLeftButton	1	The left button was pressed.
vbRightButton	2	The right button was pressed.
vbMiddleButton	4	The middle button was pressed.

Table R-66: button *values*.

- *shift*—an **Integer** value (see Table R-67) that contains information about the Shift and Alt keys that were pushed when the mouse button was pressed. For instance, a value of 5 would mean that the Shift and Alt keys were both down when the mouse button was pressed. A value of 0 means that none of these keys were pressed.

shift Name	Value	Description
vbShiftMask	1	The Shift key was pressed.
vbCtrlMask	2	The Ctrl key was pressed.
vbAltMask	4	The Alt key was pressed.

Table R-67: shift *values*.

- *x*—a **Single** that contains the horizontal location of the mouse pointer.
- *y*—a **Single** that contains the vertical location of the mouse pointer.

Private Sub *RemoteDataControl*_MouseUp([*index* As Integer ,] *button* As Integer, *shift* As Single, *x* As Single, *y* As Single)

Usage — This event occurs when a mouse button is released while the cursor is over the control.

Arguments
- *index*—an **Integer** that uniquely identifies a control in a control array. This argument is not present if the control is not part of a control array.
- *button*—an **Integer** value (see Table R-68) that contains information about the mouse buttons that were released. Only one of these values will be present.

button Name	Value	Description
vbLeftButton	1	The left button was released.
vbRightButton	2	The right button was released.
vbMiddleButton	4	The middle button was released.

Table R-68: button *values*.

- *shift*—an **Integer** value (see Table R-69) that contains information about the Shift and Alt keys that were pushed when the mouse button was released. These values can be added together if more than one key was down. For instance, a value of 5 would mean that the Shift and Alt keys were both down when the mouse button was released. A value of 0 means that none of these keys were pressed.

shift Name	Value	Description
vbShiftMask	1	The Shift key was pressed.
vbCtrlMask	2	The Ctrl key was pressed.
vbAltMask	4	The Alt key was pressed.

Table R-69: shift *values*.

- *x*—a **Single** that contains the horizontal location of the mouse pointer.
- *y*—a **Single** that contains the vertical location of the mouse pointer.

Private Sub *RemoteDataControl*_QueryCompleted ([*index* As Integer])

Usage This event occurs after the **rdoResultset** generated by the **RemoteData** control produces its first result set.

Arguments • *index*—an **Integer** that uniquely identifies a control in a control array. This argument is not present if the control is not part of a control array.

Private Sub *RemoteDataControl*_Reposition ([*index* As Integer])

Usage This event occurs after a new record becomes the current record.

Tip

Use this event to perform any processing that may be required after a new record becomes the current record but before it is made available to the user.

Arguments • *index*—an **Integer** that uniquely identifies a control in a control array. This argument is not present if the control is not part of a control array.

Private Sub *RemoteDataControl*_Resize ([*index* As Integer])

Usage This event occurs whenever the form is resized.

Tip

*This event isn't particularly useful, since you can resize the control whenever the form is resized, in the form's **Resize** event.*

Arguments • *index*—an **Integer** that uniquely identifies a control in a control array. This argument is not present if the control is not part of a control array.

Private Sub *RemoteDataControl*_Validate ([*index* As Integer ,] *action* As Integer, *save* As Integer)

Usage This event occurs before a new record becomes the current record, before the **Update** method (but not the **UpdateRecord** method), before a **Delete**, **Unload**, or **Close** operation.

Arguments • *action*—an **Integer** value (see Table R-70) containing the action that triggers the event and the action to take when the **Validate** event finishes.

action Name	Value	Description
rdActionCancel	0	Cancel the command that triggers the Validate event.
rdActionMoveFirst	1	Move to the first record.
rdActionMovePrevious	2	Move to the previous record.
rdActionMoveNext	3	Move to the next record.
rdActionMoveLast	4	Move to the last record.

action Name	Value	Description
rdActionAddNew	5	Add a new record.
rdActionUpdate	6	Update the current record. (This is not the same as **UpdateRecord**.)
rdActionDelete	7	Delete the current record.
rdActionFind	8	Find a new record.
rdActionBookmark	9	Bookmark the current record.
rdActionClose	10	Close the record set.
rdActionUnload	11	Unload the form with the **RemoteData** control.
rdActionUpdateAddNew	12	A new row was inserted into the result set.
rdActionUpdateModified	13	The current row was changed.
rdActionRefresh	14	The **Refresh** method was executed.
rdActionCancelUpdate	15	The update was canceled.
rdActionBeginTransact	16	The **BeginTrans** method was used.
rdActionCommitTransact	17	The **CommitTrans** method was used.
rdActionRollbackTransact	18	The **RollbackTrans** method was used.
rdActionNewParameters	19	A change was made in the parameters or the columns or rows were reordered.
rdActionNewSQL	20	The SQL statement was changed.

Table R-70: action values.

- *save*—a **Boolean** when **True** means that the data has changed and will be saved. When **False** means that the data has not changed and will not be saved.

See Also   **CheckBox** (control), **ComboBox** (control), **DBCombo** (control), **DBGrid** (control), **DBList** (control), **Image** (control), **Label** (control), **ListBox** (control), **MSFlexGrid** (control), **Picture** (control), **rdoEngine** (object), **rdoResultset** (object), **TextBox** (control)

Reset

STATEMENT

CCE, LE, PE, EE

Syntax   Reset

Usage   The **Reset** statement closes all files that were opened with the **Open** statement and posts all file buffers to disk.

Examples
```
Private Sub Command1_Click()
Open App.Path & "\test1.dat" For Output As 1
Open App.Path & "\test2.dat" For Output As 2
Print #1, "testing"
Print #2, "testing"
Reset
End Sub
```

This routine opens two test files, writes some data to them, and then closes both files at the same time with the **Reset** statement.

See Also   **Close** (statement), **Open** (statement)

Resume

STATEMENT

CCE, LE, PE, EE

Syntax
Resume
Resume Next
Resume *label*

Usage The **Resume** statement is used in an error handling routine to continue execution after the error was handled. There are three forms of the **Resume** statement. The **Resume** statement will continue execution beginning with the statement that failed. The **Resume Next** statement continues execution with the statement following the statement that failed. The **Resume** *label* statement resumes execution at the specified label.

Arguments *label*—the name of a label in the routine.

Examples
```
Private Sub Command1_Click()
Dim i As Integer
i = 0
On Error GoTo GotErr:
MsgBox "Testing division: " & Format(1 / i)
Exit Sub
GotErr:
MsgBox "Error: " & Format(Err.Number) & " '" & Err.Description & "'"
If Err.Number = 11 Then
    i = 1
    Resume
End If
End Sub
```

This routine declares a variable called i and assigns it a value of 0 to force a divide by 0 runtime error. When the error occurs, the control is transferred to GotErr. GotErr assigns the variable a value of 1 and resumes execution with the same statement that failed.

See Also **On Error** (statement)

RGB

FUNCTION

CCE, LE, PE, EE

Syntax *LValue* = **RGB** (*red, green, blue*)

Usage The **RGB** function returns a 24-bit RGB (red-green-blue) color value based on values for red, green, and blue.

Arguments
- *LValue*—a **Long** value containing the 24-bit RGB color.
- *red*—an **Integer** value ranging from 0 to 255 describing the amount of red in the color.
- *green*—an **Integer** value ranging from 0 to 255 describing the amount of green in the color.
- *blue*—an **Integer** value ranging from 0 to 255 describing the amount of blue in the color.

Examples
```
Private Sub Command1_Click()
    Form1.BackColor = RGB(CInt(Text1.Text), CInt(Text2.Text), CInt(Text3))
End Sub
```

This routine changes the background color of the form based on the values in the Text1, Text2, and Text3 text boxes.

See Also   **QBColor** (function)

RichTextBox

CONTROL

PE, EE

Usage   The **RichTextBox** control is similar to the **TextBox** control, but it includes to the ability to load, edit, and save rich text documents. These documents may include multiple character fonts, sizes, and colors.

Properties
- *RichTextBoxControl*.**Appearance**—an **Integer** value that determines how the combo box will appear on the form (see Table R-71).

AppearanceValue	Description
0	The **RichTextBox** control displays without the 3D effects.
1	The **RichTextBox** control displays with 3D effects (default value).

Table R-71: Appearance values.

- *RichTextBoxControl*.**AutoVerbMenu**—a **Boolean** when **True** means that a pop-up menu will display when the user right clicks on the control. **False** means that no pop-up menu will display. The **Click** and **MouseDown** events will not happen when this property is **True**.
- *RichTextBoxControl*.**BackColor**—a **Long** that contains the suggested value for the background color of the control. The **BackColor** and **ForeColor** must both be solid to display text. If you choose a color that is dithered, it will be changed to the nearest solid color.
- *RichTextBoxControl*.**BorderStyle**—an **Integer** specifying how the border will be drawn (see Table R-72).

BorderStyle Name	Value	Description
vbBSNone	0	No border displays.
vbFixedSingle	1	Single line around the label.

Table R-72: BorderStyle values.

- *RichTextBoxControl*.**BulletIndent**—an **Integer** containing the amount of indent used when **SetBullet** is **True**.
- *RichTextBoxControl*.**Container**—an object that can set or return the container of the control at run time. This property cannot be set at design time.

- *RichTextBoxControl*.**DataBindings**—a reference to the **DataBindings** collection containing the bindable properties available.
- *RichTextBoxControl*.**DataChanged**—a **Boolean** that applies only to data bound controls. When **True** means that the data contained in this control was changed either by the user or by some means other than retrieving data from the current record. When **False** means the data in the control is unchanged from the current record. Simply reading the next record is not sufficient to set the **DataChanged** property to **True**.
- *RichTextBoxControl*.**DataField**—a **String** value that associates the control with a field in a **RecordSet** object in a **Data** control.
- *RichTextBoxControl*.**DisableNoScroll**—a **Boolean** value when **True** disables the scroll bars when the text fits on the screen. **False** means the scroll bars remain active on the screen (default). This property is active only when the **ScrollBars** property is greater than 0.
- *RichTextBoxControl*.**DragIcon**—an object that contains the **Picture** value of an icon. At design time, you can specify an icon file that has a file type of .ICO.

> **Tip**
>
> This value can be created by copying the value from another control's **DragIcon** value, a form's icon, or by using the **LoadPicture** function.

- *RichTextBoxControl*.**DragMode**—an **Integer** specifying how the control will respond to a drag request (see Table R-73).

> **Tip**
>
> Setting **DragMode** to vbAutomatic will automatically begin a drag operation when the user clicks on the control. However, the control will not respond to the usual mouse events (**Click**, **DblClick**, **MouseDown**, **MouseMove**, **MouseUp**).

DragMode Name	Value	Description
vbManual	0	The Drag method must be used to begin a drag-and-drop operation (default value).
vbAutomatic	1	The source control will automatically begin a drag-and-drop operation when the user clicks on the control.

Table R-73: DragMode values.

- *RichTextBoxControl*.**Enabled**—a **Boolean** value when **True** means that the control will respond to events. When **False**, the control will not respond to events.
- *RichTextBoxControl*.**FileName**—a **String** containing the path and filename of the file to load at design time. The file must either contain plain text or be in proper Rich Text Format.
- *RichTextBoxControl*.**Font**—an object that contains information about the character font used by this object.
- *RichTextBoxControl*.**Height**—a **Single** that contains the height of the control.

- *RichTextBoxControl*.**HelpContextID**—a **Long** that contains a help file context ID number that references an entry in the help file. When the user presses the F1 key while this control is active, the corresponding entry in the help file will automatically display. A value of 0 means that no context number was specified.

> **Tip**
>
> *A help file must be compiled using the Windows Help Compiler available in the Professional and Enterprise editions of Visual Basic.*

- *RichTextBoxControl*.**HideSelection**—a **Boolean** value when **True** means that the selected text does not appear as highlighted when the control loses focus. When **False**, the text will continue to be highlighted when the control loses focus.
- *RichTextBoxControl*.**hWnd**—a **Long** that contains a Windows handle to the control.

> **Tip**
>
> *The hWnd property is most useful when making calls to Windows API functions. Since this value can change during execution, do not save the value into a variable for later use.*

- *RichTextBoxControl*.**Index**—an **Integer** that uniquely identifies a control in a control array.
- *RichTextBoxControl*.**Left**—a **Single** that contains the distance, measured in twips, between the left edge of the control and the left edge of the control's container.
- *RichTextBoxControl*.**Locked**—a **Boolean** when **True** means that the text can't be changed in the control. **False** means that the text can be changed (default).
- *RichTextBoxControl*.**MaxLength**—an **Integer** value containing the maximum number of characters that the control will hold.
- *RichTextBoxControl*.**MouseIcon**—a **Picture** object (a bitmap, icon, or metafile) that will be used as a cursor when the **MousePointer** property is set to 99. Note that Visual Basic does not support color cursors from a .CUR file. A color icon from an .ICO file will be used instead.
- *RichTextBoxControl*.**MousePointer**—an **Integer** that contains the value of the cursor that will display when the cursor is moved over this control (see Table R-74). Use *vbCustom* to display the custom icon stored in the **MouseIcon** property.

Cursor Name	Value	Description
vbDefault	0	Shape determined by the object (default value)
vbArrow	1	Arrow
vbCrosshair	2	Crosshair
vbIbeam	3	I beam
vbIconPointer	4	Square inside a square
vbSizePointer	5	Four-sided arrow (north, south, east, west)
vbSizeNESW	6	Two-sided arrow (northeast, southwest)
vbSizeNS	7	Two-sided arrow (north, south)
vbSizeNWSE	8	Two-sided arrow (northwest, southeast)
vbSizeWE	9	Two-sided arrow (west, east)

Cursor Name	Value	Description
vbUpArrow	10	Single-sided arrow pointing north
vbHourglass	11	Hourglass
vbNoDrop	12	No Drop
vbArrowHourglass	13	An arrow and an hourglass
vbArrowQuestion	14	An arrow and a question mark
vbSizeAll	15	Size all
vbCustom	99	Custom icon from the **MouseIcon** property of this control

Table R-74: Cursor values.

- *RichTextBoxControl*.**MultiLine**—a **Boolean,** when **True** means that the text box will display multiple lines of text, with each line separated by a carriage return linefeed (*vbCrLf*). **False** means that the rich text box will only display a single line of text.
- *RichTextBoxControl*.**Name**—a **String** that contains the name of the control that will reference the control in a Visual Basic program. This property is read only at run time.
- *RichTextBoxControl*.**Object**—an object that contains a reference to the *RichTextBoxControl* object.
- *RichTextBoxControl*.**OLEDragMode**—an **Integer** value (see Table R-75) that describes how the control will respond to OLE drag operations.

> **Note**
>
> When the **DragMode** is **True**, the standard Visual Basic drag-and-drop functions will override the OLE drag-and-drop functions.

OLEDragMode Name	Value	Description
vbOLEDragManual	0	All drag requests will be handled by the programmer (default value).
vbOLEDragAutomatic	1	The control responds to all OLE drag request automatically.

Table R-75: OLEDragMode values.

- *RichTextBoxControl*.**OLEDropMode**—an **Integer** value (see Table R-76) that describes how the control will respond to OLE drop operations.

OLEDropMode Name	Value	Description
vbOLEDropNone	0	The control does not accept OLE drops. The cursor is changed to the No Drop cursor (default value).
vbOLEDropManual	1	The control responds to OLE drops under the program's control (manual).
vbOLEDropAutomatic	2	The control automatically accepts OLE drops if it recognizes the format of the data object.

Table R-76: OLEDropMode values.

- *RichTextBoxControl*.**OLEObjects**—an object reference to the **OLEObjects** collection containing OLE objects that are contained within the document.
- *RichTextBoxControl*.**Parent**—an object that contains a reference to the **Form, Frame,** or other container that holds this control.
- *RichTextBoxControl*.**RightMargin**—a **Single** containing the position of the right margin in twips.
- *DBGridControl*.**ScrollBars**—an **Integer** containing the row divider style for the **DBGrid** control (see Table R-77).

ScrollBars Name	Value	Description
vbSBNone	0	No scroll bars display (default).
vbHorizontal	1	A horizontal scroll bar displays.
vbVertical	2	A vertical scroll bar displays.
vbBoth	3	Both scroll bars display.

Table R-77: ScrollBars values.

- *RichTextBoxControl*.**SelAlignment**—a **Variant** value containing the paragraph alignment (see Table R-78) for the selected text.

SelAlignment Name	Value	Description
	Null	The selected text spans more than one paragraph with different alignments.
rtfLeft	0	The paragraph is aligned against the left margin.
rtfRight	1	The paragraph is aligned against the right margin.
rtfCenter	2	The paragraph is centered.

Table R-78: SelAlignment values.

- *RichTextBoxControl*.**SelBold**—a **Variant** value when **True** means that the selected text is bold. **False** means that the selected text is not bold. **Null** means that the selected text contains both bold and nonbold characters.
- *RichTextBoxControl*.**SelBullet**—a **Variant** value when **True** means that the selected text contains bulleted text. **False** means that the selected text does not contain bulleted text. **Null** means that the selected text contains both bulleted and nonbulleted text.
- *RichTextBoxControl*.**SelCharOffset**—a **Variant** value when 0 means that the characters display on the normal baseline. When greater than 0 means that the characters display the specified number of twips above the line (superscripts). When less than 0 means that the characters display the specified number of twips below the line (subscripts). **Null** means that the selected text contains multiple offsets from the baseline.
- *RichTextBoxControl*.**SelColor**—a **Variant** value containing the color of the selected text. **Null** means that the selected text has more than one color.
- *RichTextBoxControl*.**SelFontName**—a **Variant** value containing the name of the font for the selected text. **Null** means that the selected text contains more than one character font.
- *RichTextBoxControl*.**SelFontSize**—a **Variant** value containing the size in points for the font for the selected text. **Null** means that the selected text contains more than one font size.

- *RichTextBoxControl*.**SelHangingIndent**—an **Integer** value containing the number of twips between the left margin and the first character in the first line of a paragraph. Zero means that the selected text contains more than one value for hanging indent.
- *RichTextBoxControl*.**SelIndent**—an **Integer** value containing the number of twips between the left margin and the first character of each line in a paragraph. Zero means that the selected text contains more than one value for the indent.
- *RichTextBoxControl*.**SelItalic**—a **Variant** value when **True** means that the selected text is in italics. **False** means that the selected text is not in italics. **Null** means that the selected text contains characters in italics and not in italics.
- *RichTextBoxControl*.**SelLength**—a **Long** value containing the length of the selected text. When **SelLength** is 0, no text is selected.
- *RichTextBoxControl*.**SelProtected**—a **Variant** value when **True** means that the selected text is protected. **False** means that the selected text is not protected. **Null** means that the selected text contains both protected and unprotected text.
- *RichTextBoxControl*.**SelRightIndent**—an **Integer** value containing the number of twips between the right margin and the last character of each line in a paragraph. Zero means that the selected text contains more than one value for the indent.
- *RichTextBoxControl*.**SelRTF**—a **String** value containing the selected text in Rich Text Format.
- *RichTextBoxControl*.**SelStart**—a **Long** value containing the starting position of the selected text.
- *RichTextBoxControl*.**SelStrikethru**—a **Variant** value when **True** means that the selected text has a line through the center. **False** means that the selected text does not have a line through the center. **Null** means that the selected text contains characters with strikeouts and characters without strikeouts.
- *RichTextBoxControl*.**SelTabCount**—an **Integer** value containing the number of tab positions in the selected text.
- *RichTextBoxControl*.**SelTabs** (*index*)—a **Variant** value containing the location of the tab selected by *index*. *Index* can range in value from 0 to **SelTabCount** -1.
- *RichTextBoxControl*.**SelText**—a **String** value containing the selected text. When **SelText** is empty, no text is selected.

> **Tip**
>
> The **SelLength**, **SelStart**, and **SelText** properties are very powerful tools for inserting and deleting text inside the control. By setting **SelStart** to a position inside the **Text** string and assigning a value to **SelText**, you will insert text at that position. To change a block of text, simply set the **SelStart** and **SelLength** values and then change the value of **SelText**. The **Text** property will be updated accordingly. Assigning an empty string to **SelText** will delete the selected text.

- *RichTextBoxControl*.**SelUnderline**—a **Variant** value when **True** means that the selected text is underlined. **False** means that the selected text is not underlined. **Null** means that the selected text contains both underlined and not underlined characters.
- *RichTextBoxControl*.**TabIndex**—an Integer that determines the order that a user will tab through the objects on a form.

- *RichTextBoxControl*.**TabStop**—a **Boolean** value when **True** means that the user can tab to this object. **False** means that this control will be skipped to the next control in the **TabIndex** order.
- *RichTextBoxControl*.**Tag**—a **String** that can hold programmer specific information. This property is not used by Visual Basic.
- *RichTextBoxControl*.**Text**—a **String** that sets or returns the value from the text box part of the control.
- *RichTextBoxControl*.**TextRTF**—a **String** that sets or returns the value from the text box part of the control in Rich Text Format.
- *RichTextBoxControl*.**ToolTipText**—a **String** that holds a text value that can display as a **ToolTip** box whenever the cursor is held over the control for about one second.
- *RichTextBoxControl*.**Top**—a **Single** that contains the distance, measured in twips, between the top edge of the control and the top edge of the control's container.
- *RichTextBoxControl*.**Visible**—a **Boolean** value when **True** means that the control is visible. **False** means that the control is not visible.

> **Tip**
>
> *This property can hide the **RichTextBox** control until the program is ready to display it.*

- *RichTextBoxControl*.**WhatsThisHelpID**—a **Long** that contains a help file context ID number that references an entry in the help file. This provides a What's This PopUp help display in response to the What's This button in the upper right corner of the window.
- *RichTextBoxControl*.**Width**—a **Single** that contains the width of the control.

Methods

RichTextBoxControl.Drag [DragAction]

Usage This method begins, ends, or cancels a drag operation.

Arguments *DragAction*—an **Integer** that contains a value selected from Table R-79 below.

DragAction Name	Value	Description
vbCancel	0	Cancels any drag operation in progress.
vbBeginDrag	1	Begins a drag operation (default).
vbEndDrag	2	Ends a drag operation and drops *object*.

Table R-79: DragAction values.

return = RichTextBoxControl.Find (string [, start [, stop [, options]]])

Usage This method searches through the text in the rich text box.

Arguments *return*—a **Variant** containing the position of the string in the text. A value of -1 means that the string was not found.

- *string*—a **String** containing the desired characters.
- *start*—a **Long** containing the starting location for the search. If omitted, the search will start from the current insertion point if a value for *stop* is specified, or the start of the selected text or the beginning of the text if no text is selected.
- *stop*—a **Long** containing the ending location for the search. If omitted, the search will stop at the end of text if a value for *start* is specified, or the end of the selected text or the end of the text if no text is selected.
- *options*—an **Integer** containing zero or more of the options listed in Table R-80.

options Name	Value	Description
rtfWholeWord	2	If specified, only whole words will be found.
rtfMatchCase	4	If specified, the case must be the same as the search text.
rtfNoHighlight	8	If specified, the text will not be highlighted.

Table R-80: *options* values.

return = RichTextBoxControl.GetLineFromChar (*position*)

Usage This method returns the line number for any given character position.

Arguments
- *return*—a **Long** containing the line number.
- *position*—a **Long** containing the position of the desired character.

RichTextBoxControl.LoadFile *fname, ftype*

Usage This method loads the contents of the file into the control. The previous contents of the control are replaced.

Arguments
- *fname*—a **String** containing the path and filename of the file to load.
- *ftype*—an **Integer** containing the type of file to load (see Table R-81).

ftype Name	Value	Description
rtfRTF	0	The file is in Rich Text Format (.RTF) (default).
rtfText	1	The file is in text format.

Table R-81: *ftype* values.

RichTextBoxControl.Move *Left* [, *Top* [, *Width* [, *Height*]]]

Usage This method changes the position and the size of the **RichTextBox** control. The **ScaleMode** of the **Form** or other container object that holds the **RichTextBox** control will determine the units used to specify the coordinates.

Arguments
- *Left*—a **Single** that specifies the new position of the left edge of the control.
- *Top*—a **Single** that specifies the new position of the top edge of the control.
- *Width*—a **Single** that specifies the new width of the control.
- *Height*—a **Single** that specifies the new height of the control.

RichTextBoxControl.OLEDrag

Usage   This method begins an **OLEDrag** and drop operation. Invoking this method will trigger the **OLEStartDrag** event.

RichTextBoxControl.Refresh

Usage   This method redraws the contents of the control.

RichTextBoxControl.SaveFile fname, ftype

Usage   This method saves the contents of the control into a file.

Arguments
- *fname*—a **String** containing the path and filename of the file to save.
- *ftype*—an **Integer** containing the type of file to save (see Table R-82).

ftype Name	Value	Description
rtfRTF	0	The file is in Rich Text Format (.RTF) (default).
rtfText	1	The file is in text format.

Table R-82: ftype values.

RichTextBoxControl.SelPrint hdc

Usage   This method sends the selected text to a printer device context. The text will retain all of its special fonts and formatting.

Tip

*Initialize the **Printer** object's device context by printing a zero length string before using this method.*

Arguments
- *hdc*—a printer device context.

RichTextBoxControl.SetFocus

Usage   This method transfers the focus from the form or control that currently has the focus to this control. To receive the focus, this control must be enabled and visible.

RichTextBoxControl.ShowWhatsThis

Usage This method displays the ShowWhatsThis help information for this control.

RichTextBoxControl.Span *charset, forward, negate*

Usage This method highlights the text starting at the current insertion point until the first character specified in *charset* is found (*negate* is **True**) or while the text contains the specified *charset* (*negate* is **False**).

Arguments
- *charset*—a **String** containing a set of characters.
- *forward*—a **Boolean** when **True** means that the text is searched from the current insertion point to the end of the text. **False** means that the text is searched from the current insertion point to the beginning of text.
- *negate*—a **Boolean** when **True** means that the **Span** will end when the first character not in *charset* is found. **False** means that the **Span** will end with the first character found in *charset*.

RichTextBoxControl.Upto *charset, forward, negate*

Usage This method moves the insertion point to the first character specified in *charset* (when *negate* is **True**) the first character not in *charset* (when *negate* is **False**).

Arguments
- *charset*—a **String** containing a set of characters.
- *forward*—a **Boolean** when **True** means that the text is searched from the current insertion point to the end of the text. **False** means that the text is searched from the current insertion point to the beginning of text.
- *negate*—a **Boolean** when **True** means that the **Upto** will end when the first character not in *charset* is found. **False** means that the **Upto** will end when the first character found in *charset*.

RichTextBoxControl.ZOrder [*position*]

Usage This method specifies the position of the **RichTextBox** control relative to the other objects on the form.

> **Tip**
>
> *Note that there are three layers of objects on a form: the back layer is the drawing space that contains the results of the graphical methods, the middle layer contains graphical objects and **Labels**, and the top layer contains nongraphical controls such as the **RichTextBox** control. The **ZOrder** method only affects how the objects are arranged within a single layer.*

Arguments
- *position*—an **Integer** that specifies the relative position of this object. A value of 0 means that the control is positioned at the head of the list, a value of 1 means that the control will be placed at the end of the list.

Events

Private Sub *RichTextBoxControl*_Change ([*index* As Integer])

Usage
: This event occurs whenever the contents of the text box are changed, either by the program changing the **Text** property directly or by a DDE link.

Arguments
: - *index*—an **Integer** that uniquely identifies a control in a control array. This argument is not present if the control is not part of a control array.

Private Sub *RichTextBoxControl*_Click([*index* As Integer])

Usage
: This event occurs when the user clicks a mouse button while the cursor is over the control.

Arguments
: - *index*—an **Integer** that uniquely identifies a control in a control array. This argument is not present if the control is not part of a control array.

Private Sub *RichTextBoxControl*_DblClick([*index* As Integer])

Usage
: This event occurs when the user double-clicks a mouse button while the cursor is over the control.

Arguments
: - *index*—an **Integer** that uniquely identifies a control in a control array. This argument is not present if the control is not part of a control array.

Private Sub *RichTextBoxControl*_DragDrop([*index* As Integer ,] *source* As Control, *x* As Single, *y* As Single)

Usage
: This event occurs when a drag-and-drop operation is completed by using the **Drag** method with a *DragAction* value of *vbEndDrag*.

> **Tip**
>
> When using drag-and-drop operations, use the **DragOver** event to determine what the cursor will look like while the cursor moves over the control.

Arguments
: - *index*—an **Integer** that uniquely identifies a control in a control array. This argument is not present if the control is not part of a control array.
  - *source*—a control object that is the control that is being dragged.

> **Tip**
>
> You can access a property or method from the source control by using source.*property* or source.*method*. You can determine the type of object or control by using the **TypeOf** operator.

  - *x*—a **Single** that contains the horizontal location of the mouse pointer.
  - *y*—a **Single** that contains the vertical location of the mouse pointer.

Private Sub *RichTextBoxControl*_DragOver([*index* As Integer ,] *source* As Control, *x* As Single, *y* As Single, *state* As Integer)

Usage   This event occurs while a drag operation is in progress and the cursor is moved over the control.

Tip

*When using drag-and-drop operations, use the **DragOver** event to determine what the cursor will look like while the cursor moves over the control. When* state *is 0, you can change the cursor to a No Drop (vbNoDrop) cursor or highlight the field that the cursor is near. When* state *is 1, you can undo the changes you made when the* state *was 0.*

Arguments
- *index*—an **Integer** that uniquely identifies a control in a control array. This argument is not present if the control is not part of a control array.
- *source*—a control object that is the control that is being dragged.

Tip

You can access a property or method from the source control by using source.*property or* source.*method. You can determine the type of object or control by using the **TypeOf** operator.*

- *x*—a **Single** that contains the horizontal location of the mouse pointer.
- *y*—a **Single** that contains the vertical location of the mouse pointer.
- *state*—an **Integer** that indicates the state of the object being dragged (see Table R-83).

state Name	Value	Description
vbEnter	0	The dragged object is entering range of the control.
vbLeave	1	The dragged object is leaving range of the control.
vbOver	2	The dragged object has moved from one position over the control to another.

Table R-83: state values.

Private Sub *RichTextBoxControl*_GotFocus ([*index* As Integer])

Usage   This event occurs when the control is given focus.

Tip

You can use this routine to display help or other information in a status bar.

Arguments
- *index*—an **Integer** that uniquely identifies a control in a control array. This argument is not present if the control is not part of a control array.

Private Sub *RichTextBoxControl_KeyDown* ([*index* As Integer ,] *keycode* As Integer, *shift* As Single)

Usage   This event occurs when a key is pressed while the control has the focus.

Arguments
- *index*—an **Integer** that uniquely identifies a control in a control array. This argument is not present if the control is not part of a control array.
- *keycode*—an **Integer** that contains information about which key was pressed.
- *shift*—an **Integer** that contains information about the Shift and Alt keys that were pressed when the mouse button was pressed (see Table R-84). These values can be added together if more than one key was down. For instance, a value of 5 would mean that the Shift and Alt keys were both down when the mouse button was pressed.

shift Name	Value	Description
vbShiftMask	1	The Shift key was pressed.
vbCtrlMask	2	The Ctrl key was pressed.
vbAltMask	4	The Alt key was pressed.

Table R-84: shift values.

Private Sub *RichTextBoxControl_KeyPress*([*index* As Integer ,] *keychar* As Integer)

Usage   This event occurs whenever a key is pressed while the control has the focus.

Arguments
- *index*—an **Integer** that uniquely identifies a control in a control array. This argument is not present if the control is not part of a control array.
- *keychar*—an **Integer** that contains the ASCII character that was pressed.

Private Sub *RichTextBoxControl_KeyUp* ([*index* As Integer ,] *keycode* As Integer, *shift* As Single)

Usage   This event occurs when a key is released while the control has the focus.

Arguments
- *index*—an **Integer** that uniquely identifies a control in a control array. This argument is not present if the control is not part of a control array.
- *keycode*—an **Integer** that contains information about which key was released.
- *shift*—an **Integer** that contains information about the Shift and Alt keys that were pressed when the mouse button was pressed (see Table R-85). These values can be added together if more than one key was down. For instance, a value of 5 would mean that the Shift and Alt keys were both down when the mouse button was pressed.

shift Name	Value	Description
vbShiftMask	1	The Shift key was pressed.
vbCtrlMask	2	The Ctrl key was pressed.
vbAltMask	4	The Alt key was pressed.

Table R-85: *shift values.*

Private Sub *RichTextBoxControl*_LostFocus ([*index* As Integer])

Usage   This event occurs when the control loses focus.

Arguments
- *index*—an **Integer** that uniquely identifies a control in a control array. This argument is not present if the control is not part of a control array.

Private Sub *RichTextBoxBoxControl*_MouseDown([*index* As Integer ,] *button* As Integer, *shift* As Single, *x* As Single, *y* As Single)

Usage   This event occurs when a mouse button is pressed while the cursor is over the control.

Arguments
- *index*—an **Integer** that uniquely identifies a control in a control array. This argument is not present if the control is not part of a control array.
- *button*—an **Integer** that contains information about the mouse buttons that were pressed (see Table R-86). Only one of these values will be present.

button Name	Value	Description
vbLeftButton	1	The left button was pressed.
vbRightButton	2	The right button was pressed.
vbMiddleButton	4	The middle button was pressed.

Table R-86: *button values.*

- *shift*—an **Integer** that contains information about the Shift and Alt keys that were pressed when the mouse button was pressed (see Table R-87). These values can be added together if more than one key was down. For instance, a value of 5 would mean that the Shift and Alt keys were both down when the mouse button was pressed.

shift Name	Value	Description
vbShiftMask	1	The Shift key was pressed.
vbCtrlMask	2	The Ctrl key was pressed.
vbAltMask	4	The Alt key was pressed.

Table R-87: *shift values.*

- *x*—a **Single** that contains the horizontal location of the mouse pointer.
- *y*—a **Single** that contains the vertical location of the mouse pointer.

Private Sub *RichTextBoxControl_MouseMove* ([*index* As Integer ,] *button* As Integer, *shift* As Single, *x* As Single, *y* As Single)

Usage   This event occurs while the cursor is moved over the control.

Arguments
- *index*—an **Integer** that uniquely identifies a control in a control array. This argument is not present if the control is not part of a control array.
- *button*—an **Integer** that contains information about the mouse buttons that were pressed (see Table R-88). These values can be added together if more than one button was pressed. For instance, a value of 3 means that both the left and right buttons were pressed. A value of 0 means that no buttons were pressed.

button Name	Value	Description
vbLeftButton	1	The left button was pressed.
vbRightButton	2	The right button was pressed.
vbMiddleButton	4	The middle button was pressed.

Table R-88: *button values.*

- *shift*—an **Integer** that contains information about the Shift and Alt keys that were pressed when the mouse button was pressed (see Table R-89). For instance, a value of 5 would mean that the Shift and Alt keys were both down when the mouse button was pressed. A value of 0 means that none of these keys were pressed.

shift Name	Value	Description
vbShiftMask	1	The Shift key was pressed.
vbCtrlMask	2	The Ctrl key was pressed.
vbAltMask	4	The Alt key was pressed.

Table R-89: *shift values.*

- *x*—a **Single** that contains the horizontal location of the mouse pointer.
- *y*—a **Single** that contains the vertical location of the mouse pointer.

Private Sub *RichTextBoxBoxControl_MouseUp*([*index* As Integer ,] *button* As Integer, *shift* As Single, *x* As Single, *y* As Single)

Usage   This event occurs when a mouse button is released while the cursor is over the control.

Arguments
- *index*—an **Integer** that uniquely identifies a control in a control array. This argument is not present if the control is not part of a control array.
- *button*—an **Integer** that contains information about the mouse buttons that were released (see Table R-90). Only one of these values will be present.

button Name	Value	Description
vbLeftButton	1	The left button was released.
vbRightButton	2	The right button was released.
vbMiddleButton	4	The middle button was released.

Table R-90: button values.

- *shift*—an **Integer** that contains information about the Shift and Alt keys that were pressed when the mouse button was released (see Table R-91). These values can be added together if more than one key was down. For instance, a value of 5 would mean that the Shift and Alt keys were both down when the mouse button was released. A value of 0 means that none of these keys were pressed.

shift Name	Value	Description
vbShiftMask	1	The Shift key was pressed.
vbCtrlMask	2	The Ctrl key was pressed.
vbAltMask	4	The Alt key was pressed.

Table R-91: shift values.

- *x*—a **Single** that contains the horizontal location of the mouse pointer.
- *y*—a **Single** that contains the vertical location of the mouse pointer.

Private Sub *RichTextBoxControl*_OLECompleteDrag([*index* As Integer ,] *effect* As Long)

Usage
: This event tells the source control the results of an OLE drag-and-drop operation. This is the final event to occur in the series of actions that make up an OLE drag-and-drop operation.

Arguments
: - *index*—an **Integer** that uniquely identifies a control in a control array. This argument is not present if the control is not part of a control array.
- *effect*—a **Long** that returns the status of the OLE drag-and-drop operation (see Table R-92).

effect Name	Value	Description
vbDropEffectNone	0	The operation is canceled or the target control can't accept the drop operation.
vbDropEffectCopy	1	The operation copies data from the source control to the target control. The original data is unchanged.
vbDropEffectMove	2	The operation results in a link from the original data to the target control.

Table R-92: effect values.

Private Sub *RichTextBoxControl*_OLEDragDrop([*index* As Integer ,] *data* As DataObject, *effect* As Long, *button* As Integer, *shift* As Single, *x* As Single, *y* As Single)

Usage — This event tells the source control the results of an OLE drag-and-drop operation. This is the final event to occur in the series of actions that make up an OLE drag-and-drop operation.

Arguments
- *index*—an **Integer** that uniquely identifies a control in a control array. This argument is not present if the control is not part of a control array.
- *data*—a **DataObject** that contains the formats that the source control will provide. If the data is not contained in the **DataObject**, then it can be retrieved with the **GetData** method.
- *effect*—a **Long** that returns the status of the OLE drag-and-drop operation (see Table R-93).

effect Name	Value	Description
vbDropEffectNone	0	The operation is canceled or the target control can't accept the drop operation.
vbDropEffectCopy	1	The operation copies data from the source control to the target control. The original data is unchanged.
vbDropEffectMove	2	The operation results in a link from the original data to the target control.

Table R-93: *effect* values.

- *button*—an **Integer** that contains information about the mouse buttons that were pressed (see Table R-94). These values can be added together if more than one button was pressed. For instance, a value of 3 means that both the left and right buttons were pressed. A value of 0 means that no buttons were pressed.

button Name	Value	Description
vbLeftButton	1	The left button was pressed.
vbRightButton	2	The right button was pressed.
vbMiddleButton	4	The middle button was pressed.

Table R-94: *button* values.

- *shift*—an **Integer** that contains information about the Shift and Alt keys that were pressed when the mouse button was released (see Table R-95). These values can be added together if more than one key was down. For instance, a value of 5 would mean that the Shift and Alt keys were both down when the mouse button was released. A value of 0 means that none of these keys were pressed.

shift Name	Value	Description
vbShiftMask	1	The Shift key was pressed.
vbCtrlMask	2	The Ctrl key was pressed.
vbAltMask	4	The Alt key was pressed.

Table R-95: shift values.

- *x*—a **Single** that contains the horizontal location of the mouse pointer.
- *y*—a **Single** that contains the vertical location of the mouse pointer.

Private Sub *RichTextBoxControl*_**OLEDragOver**([*index* **As** Integer ,] *data* **As** DataObject, *effect* **As** Long, *button* **As** Integer, *shift* **As** Single, *x* **As** Single, *y* **As** Single, *state* **As** Integer)

Usage | This event happens when an OLE drag-and-drop operation is in progress.

Arguments
- *index*—an **Integer** that uniquely identifies a control in a control array. This argument is not present if the control is not part of a control array.
- *data*—a **DataObject** that contains the formats that the source control will provide. If the data is not contained in the **DataObject**, then it can be retrieved with the **GetData** method.
- *effect*—a **Long** that returns the status of the OLE drag-and-drop operation (see Table R-96).

effect Name	Value	Description
vbDropEffectNone	0	The operation is canceled or the target control can't accept the drop operation.
vbDropEffectCopy	1	The operation copies data from the source control to the target control. The original data is unchanged.
vbDropEffectMove	2	The operation results in a link from the original data to the target control.

Table R-96: effect values.

- *button*—an **Integer** that contains information about the mouse buttons that were pressed (see Table R-97). These values can be added together if more than one button was pressed. For instance, a value of 3 means that both the left and right buttons were pressed. A value of 0 means that no buttons were pressed.

button Name	Value	Description
vbLeftButton	1	The left button was pressed.
vbRightButton	2	The right button was pressed.
vbMiddleButton	4	The middle button was pressed.

Table R-97: button values.

- *shift*—an **Integer** that contains information about the Shift and Alt keys that were pressed when the mouse button was released (see Table R-98). These values can be added together if more than one key was down. For instance, a value of 5 would mean that the Shift and Alt keys were both down when the mouse button was released. A value of 0 means that none of these keys were pressed.

shift Name	Value	Description
vbShiftMask	1	The Shift key was pressed.
vbCtrlMask	2	The Ctrl key was pressed.
vbAltMask	4	The Alt key was pressed.

Table R-98: *shift values.*

- *x*—a **Single** that contains the horizontal location of the mouse pointer.
- *y*—a **Single** that contains the vertical location of the mouse pointer.
- *state*—an **Integer** that indicates the state of the object being dragged (see Table R-99).

state Name	Value	Description
vbEnter	0	The dragged object is entering range of the control.
vbLeave	1	The dragged object is leaving range of the control.
vbOver	2	The dragged object has moved from one position over the control to another.

Table R-99: *state values.*

Private Sub *RichTextBoxControl*_OLEGiveFeedback ([*index* As Integer ,] *effect* As Long)

Usage　This event tells the source control what is happening while the OLE drag-and-drop operation is in progress. This event occurs after the **OLEDragOver** event.

Tip

You may want to use this event to change the cursor to reflect what can happen in the remote object.

Arguments
- *index*—an **Integer** that uniquely identifies a control in a control array. This argument is not present if the control is not part of a control array.
- *effect*—a **Long** that returns the status of the OLE drag-and-drop operation (see Table R-100).

effect Name	Value	Description
vbDropEffectNone	0	The operation is canceled or the target control can't accept the drop operation.
vbDropEffectCopy	1	The operation copies data from the source control to the target control. The original data is unchanged.
vbDropEffectMove	2	The operation results in a link from the original data to the target control.
vbDropEffectScroll	&H80000000	The target control is about to scroll or is scrolling. This value may be added to the other *effect* values.

Table R-100: effect values.

Private Sub *RichTextBoxControl_OLESetData*([*index* As Integer ,] *data* As DataObject, *DataFormat* As Integer)

Usage
: This event happens in response to the target object performing a **GetData** method on *data*. This routine will respond by using the **SetData** method with the desired data using the **DataObject** *data*.

Arguments
: *index*—an **Integer** that uniquely identifies a control in a control array. This argument is not present if the control is not part of a control array.
: *data*—a **DataObject** that will contain the data to return to the target object.
: *format*—an **Integer** that contains the format of the data (see Table R-101).

format Name	Value	Description
vbCFText	1	Text (.TXT files)
vbCFBitmap	2	Bitmap (.BMP files)
vbCFMetafile	3	Metafile (.WMF files)
vbCFEDIB	8	Device independent bitmap (DIB)
vbCFPallette	9	Color palette
vbCFEMetafile	14	Enhanced metafile (.EMF files)
vbCFFiles	15	List of files
vbCFRTF	-16639	Rich Text Format (.RTF files)

Table R-101: format values.

Private Sub *RichTextBoxControl_OLEStartDrag* ([*index* As Integer ,] *data* As DataObject, *AllowedEffects* As Long)

Usage
: This event starts an OLE drag-and-drop operation.

Arguments
: *index*—an **Integer** that uniquely identifies a control in a control array. This argument is not present if the control is not part of a control array.
: *data*—a **DataObject** that will contain the formats that the source object is willing to provide to the target object. It may optionally contain the data to transfer.

- *AllowedEffects*—a **Long** that contains the effects that the target object can request from the source object (see Table R-102). The *AllowedEffects* can be added together if the source object supports more than one effect. Note that the target object can always use the *vbDropEffectNone* effect.

AllowedEffects Name	Value	Description
vbDropEffectNone	0	The target can't copy the data.
vbDropEffectCopy	1	The target can copy the data, and the source will keep the data unchanged.
vbDropEffectMove	2	The target can copy the data, and the source will delete the data.

Table R-102: AllowedEffects values.

Private Sub *RichTextBoxControl*_OLEStartDrag ([*index* As Integer ,] *data* As DataObject, *AllowedEffects* As Long)

Usage   This event occurs when the insertion point moves or the current selection is changed.

See Also   **Label** (control), **Masked Edit** (control), **TextBox** (control)

Right

FUNCTION

CCE, LE, PE, EE

Syntax   result = **Right[$]** (*string* , *length*)

Usage   The **Right** function returns the specified number of characters from *string* starting with the last character. The dollar sign ($) is optional and indicates that the return value is a **String** rather than a **Variant**.

Arguments
- *result*—a **String** value or a **Variant** containing a string value containing the result of the **Right** function.
- *string*—a **String** value from which to extract the characters.
- *length*—a **Long** value containing the number of characters to return.

Examples
```
Private Sub Command1_Click()
Text2.Text = Right(Text1.Text, 5)
End Sub
```

This routine displays the last five characters from Text1.Text in Text2.Text.

See Also   **Byte** (data type), **Left** (function), **LeftB** (function), **Mid** (function), **MidB** (function), **RightB** (function), **String** (data type)

RightB

FUNCTION

CCE, LE, PE, EE

Syntax   `result = RightB[$] ( string , length )`

Usage   The **RightB** function returns the specified number of bytes from *string* starting with the last byte. The dollar sign ($) is optional and indicates that the return value is a **String** rather than a **Variant**.

Arguments
- *result*—a **String** value or a **Variant** containing a string value containing the result of the **RightB** function.
- *string*—a **String** value from which to extract the bytes.
- *length*—a **Long** value containing the number of bytes to return.

See Also   **Byte** (data type), **Left** (function), **LeftB** (function), **Len** (function), **LenB** (function), **Mid** (function), **MidB** (function), **Right** (function), **String** (data type)

RmDir

STATEMENT

CCE, LE, PE, EE

Syntax   `RmDir path`

Usage   The **RmDir** statement deletes an existing directory.

If the directory path in *path* is not valid, a Run-time error '76' path not found will display. An error will also occur if the directory contains any files, including files with the hidden or system attributes.

> **Tip**
>
> To prevent run-time errors, use the **On Error** statement to prevent the error from stopping the program, and test the **Err** object to see if an error occurred.

Arguments   *path*—a **String** expression that contains the directory to delete.

Examples
```
Private Sub Command2_Click()
On Error Resume Next
If Len(Text1.Text) > 0 Then
    RmDir Text1.Text
End If
If Err.Number = 0 Then
    Text2.Text = "Directory destroyed"
Else
    Text2.Text = Err.Description
End If
End Sub
```

This routine uses the **RmDir** function to delete the directory as specified in Text1.Text. I then check the **Err** object to see if an error occurred and display either the error information or a message saying the directory was destroyed.

See Also **ChDir** (statement), **ChDrive** (function), **Common Dialog** (control), **CurDir** (function), **Dir** (function), **DirListBox** (control), **DriveListBox** (control), **FileListBox** (control), **MkDir** (statement)

Rnd

FUNCTION

CCE, LE, PE, EE

Syntax `rvalue = Rnd [( expr )]`

Usage The **Rnd** statement generates random numbers between 0 and 1.

Arguments
- *rvalue*—a **Single** containing a random number greater than or equal to 0 and less than 1.
- *expr*—a **Single** value when less than 0 will a random number based on *expr*. When equal to 0, the last random number generated will be returned. When greater than 0, the next random number in the series will be returned. If *expr* is omitted, the next random number in the series will be returned.

Examples
```
Private Sub Command1_Click()
If Len(Text1.Text) = 0 Then
    Form1.Print Format(Rnd, "#.#####")
ElseIf IsNumeric(Text1.Text) Then
    Form1.Print Format(Rnd(CDbl(Text1.Text)), "#.#####")
End If
End Sub
```

This routine displays a random number on the form based on the number in the text box.

See Also **Randomize** (statement)

RowBuffer

OBJECT

PE, EE

Usage The **RowBuffer** object is used by the **DBGrid** control to contain one or more rows of data for transfer between your application and an unbound **DBGrid** control.

Properties
- *RowBufferObject*.**Bookmark** (*index*)—a **Variant** array value containing bookmarks for the specified row. *Index* can range from 0 to **RowCount** -1.
- *RowBufferObject*.**ColumnCount**—an **Integer** containing the number of columns in the each row.
- *RowBufferObject*.**ColumnName** (*index*)—a **String** array containing the names of each column in the row. *Index* can range from 0 to **ColumnCount** -1.
- *RowBufferObject*.**RowCount**—a **Long** containing the number of rows in the object.

- *RowBufferObject*.**Value** (*row*, *column*)—a **Variant** containing the value for a specific row and column. *Row* can range from 0 to **RowCount** -1. *Column* can range from 0 to **ColumnCount** -1.

See Also   **DBGrid** (control)

RSet

STATEMENT

CCE, LE, PE, EE

Syntax   **RSet** *svar* = *sval*

Usage   The **RSet** statement will right align a string value (*sval*) within a string variable (*svar*). The size of the string variable is unchanged, and if the length of the value is less than the size of the string, then the string variable will be filled with leading spaces.

Arguments
- *svar*—a **String** variable.
- *sval*—a **String** value containing the data to be right aligned in *svar*.

Examples
```
Private Sub Command1_Click()
Dim s As String
s = String(32, "*")
RSet s = Text1.Text
Text2.Text = ">>>" & s & "<<<"
End Sub
```

This routine fills a string variable with 32 asterisks. Then the contents of Text1.Text are right aligned into s. Finally I show the results of the **RSet** statement in the Text2 text box.

See Also   **LSet** (statement), **Type** (statement)

RTrim

FUNCTION

CCE, LE, PE, EE

Syntax   *svar* = **RTrim** (*sval*)

Usage   The **RTrim** function will delete any trailing spaces from a string value.

Arguments
- *svar*—a **String** variable.
- *sval*—a **String** value that will have the trailing spaces trimmed.

Examples
```
Private Sub Command1_Click()
Text2.Text = RTrim(Text1.Text)
End Sub
```

This routine trims the trailing spaces from the value in the Text1 text box and saves the results in the Text2 text box.

See Also   **LTrim** (function), **Trim** (function)

SavePicture

STATEMENT

CCE, LE, PE, EE

Syntax **SavePicture** *picture, filename*

Usage The **SavePicture** statement saves a **Picture** object to disk in the specified filename. This function supports .BMP, .EMF, .ICO, .RLE, and .WMF files. It will save the file using its original file type, except for .GIF and .JPG files which are saved as .BMP files.

Arguments
- *picture*—a **Picture** object containing the loaded picture.
- *filename*—a **String** containing the name of the picture file to load.

Examples
```
Private Sub Command2_Click()
On Error Resume Next
CommonDialog1.filename = App.Path & "\jpglogo1.bmp"
CommonDialog1.Flags = cdlOFNHideReadOnly
CommonDialog1.Filter = "All Files (*.*)|*.*|BMP Files (*.bmp)|*.BMP"
CommonDialog1.FilterIndex = 2
CommonDialog1.ShowSave
If Err.Number = 0 Then
    SavePicture Picture1.Picture, CommonDialog1.filename
End If
End Sub
```

This routine displays a File Save dialog box to select the file that will contain the image in the **Picture** control. The **SavePicture** statement is then used to save the picture file.

See Also **LoadPicture** (function), **Picture** (control)

SaveSetting

STATEMENT

CCE, LE, PE, EE

Syntax **SaveSetting** *app , section , key , value*

Usage The **SaveSetting** statement stores a single value for a given application, section, and key in the Windows Registry.

> **Tip**
>
> *This function and the related functions* **GetAllSettings**, **GetSetting**, *and* **DeleteSetting** *are useful to save information about the state from one run to the next.*

Arguments
- *app*—a **String** that identifies the application.
- *section*—a **String** that identifies a section within the application.
- *key*—a **String** that identifies a keyword within the section.
- *value*—a **String** that contains a value associated with the *app*, *section*, and *key* arguments.

Examples
```
Private Sub Command3_Click()
Text1.Text = GetSetting("VBPR", "Settings", Text2.Text, "No setting available")
End Sub
```

This routine retrieves a single setting from the Windows Registry.
```
Private Sub Command1_Click()
Unload Me
End Sub

Private Sub Form_Load()
Me.Show 0
Me.Top = GetSetting("VBPR", "GetSetting", "Top", Me.Top)
Me.Left = GetSetting("VBPR", "GetSetting", "Left", Me.Left)
Me.Height = GetSetting("VBPR", "GetSetting", "Height", Me.Height)
Me.Width = GetSetting("VBPR", "GetSetting", "Width", Me.Width)
End Sub

Private Sub Form_Unload(Cancel As Integer)
SaveSetting "VBPR", "GetSetting", "Top", Me.Top
SaveSetting "VBPR", "GetSetting", "Left", Me.Left
SaveSetting "VBPR", "GetSetting", "Height", Me.Height
SaveSetting "VBPR", "GetSetting", "Width", Me.Width
End Sub
```

In this example you see a more practical use of **GetSetting** and **SaveSetting**. Keeping form size and placement from the last time they were used is a desirable feature for the user. With these functions and just a few lines of code, this feature is almost trivial to implement.

In the form's **Load** routine, values for **Top**, **Left**, **Height**, and **Width** are set from values saved in the Windows Registry. If the values don't exist, then the values that the program was compiled with will be used. In the **Unload** routine, the same values are saved into the Registry. The command button exits the program by calling the **Unload** routine.

See Also   **DeleteSetting** (statement), **GetAllSettings** (function), **GetSetting** (statement)

Screen

OBJECT

CCE, LE, PE, EE

Usage   The **Screen** object provides information about the current display environment.

Properties
- **Screen.ActiveControl**—an object of type **Control** that contains a reference to the currently active control. This property is not available at design time and is read only at run time.
- **Screen.ActiveForm**—an object of type **Form** that contains a reference to the currently active control. This property is not available at design time and is read only at run time.
- **Screen.FontCount**—an **Integer** containing the number of fonts available in the **Fonts** property. This property is not available at design time and is read only at run time.
- **Screen.Fonts** (*index*)—an array of **Strings** containing the available font names for the printer. *Index* can range in value from **0** to **FontCount -1**.

- **Screen.Height**—a **Single** that contains the height of the screen in twips. This property is not available at design time and is read only at run time.
- **Screen.MouseIcon**—a **Picture** object (a bitmap, icon, or metafile) that will be used as a cursor when the **MousePointer** property is set to **99**. Note that Visual Basic does not support color cursors from a .CUR file. A color icon from an .ICO file should be used instead.
- **Screen.MousePointer**—an **Integer** value (see Table S-1) that contains the value of the cursor that should display when the cursor is moved over this control. Use *vbCustom* to display the custom icon stored in the **MouseIcon** property.

Cursor Name	Value	Description
vbDefault	0	Shape determined by the object (default value)
vbArrow	1	Arrow
vbCrosshair	2	Crosshair
vbIbeam	3	I beam
vbIconPointer	4	Square inside a square
vbSizePointer	5	Four sided arrow (north, south, east, west)
vbSizeNESW	6	Two sided arrow (northeast, southwest)
vbSizeNS	7	Two sided arrow (north, south)
vbSizeNWSE	8	Two sided arrow (northwest, southeast)
vbSizeWE	9	Two sided arrow (west, east)
vbUpArrow	10	Single sided arrow pointing north
vbHourglass	11	hourglass
vbNoDrop	12	No Drop
vbArrowHourglass	13	An arrow and an Hourglass
vbArrowQuestion	14	An arrow and a question mark
vbSizeAll	15	Size all
vbCustom	99	Custom icon from the **MouseIcon** property of this control

Table S-1: *Cursor* values.

- **Screen.TwipsPerPixelX**—a **Single** containing the number of twips occupied by a single pixel horizontally. This value is useful for converting pixels into twips without setting the **ScaleMode** property.
- **Screen.TwipsPerPixelY**—a **Single** containing the number of twips occupied by a single pixel vertically. This value is useful for converting pixels into twips without setting the **ScaleMode** property.
- **Screen.Width**—a **Single** that contains the width of the screen in twips. This property is not available at design time and is read only at run time.

Examples
```
Private Sub Command1_Click()
MsgBox "The screen is " & Format(Screen.Width / Screen.TwipsPerPixelX) & " pixels
    high and " & Format(Screen.Height / Screen.TwipsPerPixelY) & " pixels wide."
End Sub
```

This routine returns the screen width and height in pixels, by using the **Screen.Height** and **Width** properties with the **Screen.TwipsPerPixelY** and **TwipsPerPixelX** properties.

See Also **Printer** (object), **Printers** (collection)

Second

FUNCTION

CCE, LE, PE, EE

Syntax   *SValue* = **Second** (*Time*)

Usage   The **Second** function returns the second of a minute from a numeric, **Date**, or **String** variable containing a valid date or time. If only a date is supplied, this function will always return **0**.

Arguments
- *SValue*—an **Integer** value in the range of **0** to **59**.
- *Time*—a **Date**, **Long**, or **String** value that contains a valid time or date.

Examples
```
Private Sub Command1_Click()
If IsDate(Text1.Text) Then
    Text2.Text = Second (Text1.Text)
Else
    Text2.Text = "Illegal time:"
End If
End Sub
```

This routine verifies that the date or time in the Text1 text box is valid and then extracts the second value from the text box.

See Also   **CDate** (function), **Date** (data type), **Day** (function), **Hour** (function), **IsDate** (function), **Minute** (function), **Now** (function), **Time** (function), **Time** (statement)

Seek

FUNCTION

CCE, LE, PE, EE

Syntax   *pos* = **Seek** (*fnum*)

Usage   The **Seek** function returns the current position in the file. For random files the current record number will be returned. For all other files, the current byte position will be returned.

Arguments
- *pos*—a **Long** containing position in the file.
- *fnum*—an **Integer** containing the opened file.

Examples
```
Private Sub Command5_Click()
Dim a As MyRecord
If FileIsOpen Then
    a.name = Text1.Text
    a.address = Text2.Text
    Put #1, , a
    Text3.Text = Format(Seek(1))
```

```
    Else
        MsgBox "File is not open"
    End If
End Sub
```

This routine verifies that a file is opened and then builds a record of someone's name and address and puts it to the file. Then the current record number is retrieved using the **Seek** function and displayed to the user.

See Also   LOF (function), **Open** (statement), **Seek** (statement)

Seek

STATEMENT

CCE, LE, PE, EE

Syntax   **Seek** [#]*fnum*, *pos*

Usage   The **Seek** function sets the file pointer. For random files, *pos* contains the desired record number. For all other files, *pos* contains the desired byte position.

Arguments
- *pos*—a **Long** containing position in the file.
- *fnum*—an **Integer** containing the opened file.

Examples

```
Private Sub Command2_click()
Dim a As MyRecord
If FileIsOpen Then
    If IsNumeric(Text3.Text) Then
        Seek #1, CLng(Text3.Text)
        Get #1, , a
        Text1.Text = a.name
        Text2.Text = a.address
    End If
Else

    MsgBox "Open file before making getting a record"
End If
End Sub
```

This routine verifies that a file is opened and then verifies that the user supplied a numeric record number. Then it uses the **Seek** statement to access that record, retrieve a record from the file, and display it to the user.

See Also   LOF (function), **Open** (statement), **Seek** (function)

SelBookmarks

COLLECTION

CCE, LE, PE, EE

Usage The **SelBookmarks** collection contains the set of selected **Bookmark** objects available in a **DBGrid** control.

Properties
- *SelBookmarksCollection*.**Count**—an **Integer** containing the number of **DataBinding** objects in the collection.
- *SelBookmarksCollection*.**Item** (*index*)—returns a specific member of the collection specified by *index*.

> **Tip**
> *The first element of the collection is **0**, while the last element is **Count -1**.*

Methods *SelBookmarksCollection*.**Add** *bookmark*

    Usage This method adds a new bookmark to the collection.

    Arguments *bookmark*—a **Bookmark** containing the location of the record to display as selected in the **DBGrid**.

SelBookmarksCollection.**Clear**

    Usage This method removes all of the objects from the collection.

SelBookmarksCollection.**Remove** *index*

    Usage This method removes the specified object from the collection.

    Arguments *index*—an **Integer** value specifying the item to remove from the collection.

See Also **DBGrid** (object)

Select Case

STATEMENT

CCE, LE, PE, EE

Syntax
```
Select Case expr
    [Case exprlist
        [ list of statements ]]
        .
        .
        .
    [Case Else
        [ list of statements ]]
    End Select
```

Usage The **Select Case** statement is a good alternative to the **If** statement when you have multiple **ElseIf** clauses. The value from *expr* compared to each expression in *exprlist*. When a match is found, the list of statements following the **Case** clause executes. If no match is found in any **Case** clause, the statements following **Case Else** will execute.

Arguments
- *expr*—a **String** or numeric expression.
- *exprlist*—a list of expressions separated by commas. In addition to normal expressions, two additional forms are permitted. The **To** operator specifies a range of values (ex: "A" **To** "E" is **True** for any string that begins "A," "B," "C," "D," or "E"). The **Is** keyword is used with the normal relational operators (=, <>, >, <, >=, and <=).

Examples
```
Private Sub Command1_Click()
Select Case Text1.Text
Case "a" To "z", "A" To "Z"
    MsgBox "The first character is a letter"
Case "0" To "9"
    MsgBox "The first character is a number"
Case Is <= " "
    MsgBox "The first character is a space or less"
Case Else
    MsgBox "The is a special character"
End Select
End Sub
```

In this routine, I examine the string in Text1.Text and display a message describing the first character in the string.

See Also **If** (statement), **IIf** (function) , **Switch** (function)

SendKeys

STATEMENT
CCE, LE, PE, EE

Syntax **SendKeys** *string* [,*wait*]

Usage The **SendKeys** statement sends one or more characters to the currently active application window. The Plus ("+"), caret ("^"), and percent ("%") keys represent the Shift, Ctrl, and Alt keys and are used to modify the next character (ex: Alt-K is represented by the string "%k"). Parentheses represent multiple keys being pressed at the same time (ex: pressing the a and b keys at the same time would be represented by the string "(ab)"). Braces contain special characters that can't be specified by a character (ex: the F1 key is represented by "{F1}"). You can also specify the number of times a character is repeated inside the braces (ex: {TAB 6} will send six tab characters).

> **Note**
> The **SendKeys** statement works only with Windows programs.

Arguments • *string*—a **String** containing one or more characters to send to the currently active application. See Table S-2 for the code to use for characters that can't be used directly.

Key Name	Code
+	{+}
^	{^}
%	{%}
~	{~}
(	{(}
)	{)}
[	{[}
]	{]}
{	{{}
}	{}}
Backspace	{BACKSPACE}, {BS}, {BKSP}
Break	{BREAK}
Caps Lock	{CAPSLOCK}
Delete or Del	{DELETE}, {DEL}
Down Arrow	{DOWN}
End	{END}
Enter	{ENTER}, ~
Esc	{ESC}
Fx (Function key x)	{Fx}
Help	{HELP}
Home	{HOME}
Insert or Ins	{INSERT}, {INS}

Key Name	Code
Left Arrow	{LEFT}
Num Lock	{NUMLOCK}
Page Down	{PGDN}
Page Up	{PGUP}
Print Screen	{PRTSC}
Right Arrow	{RIGHT}
Scroll Lock	{SCROLLLOCK}
Tab	{TAB}
Up Arrow	{UP}

Table S-2: *Key* values.

- *wait*—a **Boolean** when **True** means that the program will wait until the characters are processed. **False** means that control will return immediately.

Examples

```
Private Sub Command1_Click()
Dim AppId As Double
AppId = Shell("NotePad.Exe", vbNormalNoFocus)
AppActivate AppId
SendKeys "%Fo\config.sys~"
End Sub
```

In this routine, I launch the NotePad applet without giving it the focus. Then I activate it and use the **SendKeys** statement to send an Alt-F and an "o" to start the File Open dialog box. Then I send "\config.sys" followed by a carriage return.

See Also   **AppActivate** (statement), **Shell** (statement)

Series

OBJECT

PE, EE

Usage   The **Series** object contains information about a series of data points on the chart.

Properties
- *SeriesObject*.**DataPoints**—a reference to a **DataPoints** collection containing the data used in this series.
- *SeriesObject*.**GuidelinePen**—a reference to a **Pen** object that describes how guidelines display. Setting this property will set **ShowGuidelines** to **True**.
- *SeriesObject*.**LegendText**—a **String** containing the text that will display as the series legend.
- *SeriesObject*.**Pen**—a reference to a **Pen** object describing how the series is drawn.
- *SeriesObject*.**Position**—a reference to a **SeriesPosition** object containing how this series is related to the other series in the chart.

- *SeriesObject*.**SecondaryAxis**—a **Boolean** value when **True** means that this series is charted on the secondary axis.
- *SeriesObject*.**SeriesMarker**—a reference to a **SeriesMarker** object containing a marker identifying all data points in the series.
- *SeriesObject*.**SeriesType**—an **Integer** describing the type of series (see Table S-3).

SeriesType Name	Description
vtChSeriesType3dBar	3D bar
vtChSeriesType2dBar	2D bar
vtChSeriesType3dLine	3D line
vtChSeriesType2dLine	2D line
vtChSeriesType3dArea	3D area
vtChSeriesType2dArea	2D area
vtChSeriesType3dStep	3D step
vtChSeriesType2dStep	2D step
vtChSeriesType3dXY	XY
vtChSeriesType2dPie	2D pie

Table S-3: *SeriesType* values.

- *SeriesObject*.**ShowGuideline**—a **Boolean** when **True** will display a guideline between each data point in a series.
- *SeriesObject*.**ShowLine**—a **Boolean** when **True** will display a line between each data point in a series.
- *SeriesObject*.**StatLine**—a reference to a **StatLine** object describing how statistic lines are drawn.
- *SeriesObject*.**TypeByChartType** (*ChartType*)—an **Integer** containing the series type (see Table S-4) for a specific chart type (see Table S-5).

SeriesType Name	Description
vtChSeriesType3dBar	3D bar
vtChSeriesType2dBar	2D bar
vtChSeriesType3dLine	3D line
vtChSeriesType2dLine	2D line
vtChSeriesType3dArea	3D area
vtChSeriesType2dArea	2D area
vtChSeriesType3dStep	3D step
vtChSeriesType2dStep	2D step
vtChSeriesType2dXY	XY
vtChSeriesType2dPie	2D pie

Table S-4: *SeriesType* values.

ChartType Name	Description
vtChChartType3dBar	3D bar
vtChChartType2dBar	2D bar
vtChChartType3dLine	3D line
vtChChartType2dLine	2D line
vtChChartType3dArea	3D area
vtChChartType2dArea	2D area
vtChChartType3dStep	3D step
vtChChartType2dStep	2D step
vtChChartType3dCombination	3D combination
vtChChartType2dCombination	2D combination
vtChChartType2dXY	XY
vtChChartType2dPie	2D pie

Table S-5: ChartType values.

Methods ### SeriesObject.Select

Usage   This method selects the chart element.

See Also   MSChart (control), SeriesCollection (collection), SeriesMarker (object), SeriesPosition (object), StatLine (object)

SeriesCollection

COLLECTION

PE, EE

Usage   The **SeriesCollection** collection contains a set of **Series** objects for the **MSChart** control.

Properties   ▪ *SeriesCollection*.**Item**(*index*)—an array of **Series** objects.

Methods ### count = SeriesCollection.Count

Usage   This method returns the number of objects in the collection.

Arguments   ▪ *count*—a **Long** value containing the number of objects in the collection.

See Also   MSChart (control), Series (object)

SeriesMarker

OBJECT

PE, EE

Usage   The **SeriesMarker** object contains information about a series of data points on the chart.

Properties
- *SeriesMarkerObject*.**Auto**—a **Boolean** value when **True** means that the **SeriesMarker** object assigns the next available marker for the series. **False** means that you can assign your own marker. This property will be set to **False** if the **Marker** property of the **DataPoint** object is set.
- *SeriesMarkerObject*.**Show**—a **Boolean** value when **True** means that the series markers display. **False** means that the series markers do not display.

See Also **DataPoint** (object), **MSChart** (control), **Series** (object)

SeriesPosition

OBJECT

PE, EE

Usage The **SeriesPosition** object contains information about where a series is drawn in relation to the other series.

Properties
- *SeriesPositionObject*.**Excluded**—a **Boolean** value when **True** means that the chart is drawn without the series. **False** means that the chart is drawn with the series. Note, however, that the series may not be visible because it is **Hidden**.
- *SeriesPositionObject*.**Hidden**—a **Boolean** value when **True** means that the series draws the chart but does not display it. **False** means that the chart does display.
- *SeriesPositionObject*.**Order**—an **Integer** containing the order of the series in the chart. If the same value is used for two or more series, then those series will be stacked on the chart.
- *SeriesPositionObject*.**StackOrder**—an **Integer** containing the order of the series in a stack. The stack is arranged starting at the bottom with the lowest **StackOrder** value.

See Also **MSChart** (control), **Series** (object)

Set

FUNCTION

CCE, LE, PE, EE

Syntax
```
Set var = objectexpr
Set var = New objectexpr
Set var = Nothing
```

Usage The **Set** statement has three basic forms. The first form saves a reference to an object in the variable. The second form creates a new object and saves a reference to the newly created object in the variable. The third form releases the reference to the object and assigns a value of **Nothing** to the variable. If the variable was the last one containing a reference to the object, then the resources owned by the object are released and the object is deleted from memory.

> **Tip**
>
> *Unlike other variables in Visual Basic, object variables do not contain a value or data. Object variables merely contain a pointer or reference to an object. Thus, it is possible to have many object variables refer to the same object. Changing an object's property using one object variable changes the property for all object variables.*

Arguments

- *var*—a Visual Basic identifier of type **Variant**, **Object**, or a specific object type that will contain a reference to the object. If an object is defined to be a specific object type, then only references to objects of the same or compatible type may be assigned to this variable.
- *objectexpr*—an object variable, function, property, or method that contains a reference to an object.

Examples

```
Private Sub Command1_Click()
Dim f As Form
Set f = New Form1
f.Caption = "Started by " & Me.Caption
f.Left = Me.Left + 100
f.Top = Me.Top + 100
f.Show
End Sub
```

This routine creates a new instance of the object Form1 using the **Set** statement. After assigning a value to the new form's caption and setting new values for the forms position, I show the form.

See Also **Object** (data type)

SetAttr

FUNCTION

CCE, LE, PE, EE

Syntax `SetAttr filename, AValue`

Usage The **SetAttr** statement sets the file attributes for an unopened file.

Arguments

- *filename*—a **String** value that contains the name of a file, including any path information needed.
- *AValue*—an **Integer** value containing the attributes. Each bit has a specific meaning as listed in Table S-6 below.

Attribute Name	Value	Description
vbNormal	0	The file has no attributes set.
vbReadOnly	1	The file has the read-only attribute set.
vbHidden	2	The file has the hidden attribute set.
vbSystem	4	The file has the system attribute set.
vbArchive	32	The file has the archive attribute set.

Table S-6: *Attribute* values.

Examples
```
Private Sub Command2_Click()
Dim i As Integer
On Error Resume Next
i = 0
If Check1.Value = 1 Then i = i + 1
If Check2.Value = 1 Then i = i + 2
If Check3.Value = 1 Then i = i + 4
If Check5.Value = 1 Then i = i + 32
SetAttr Text1.Text, i
If Err.Number <> 0 Then
    MsgBox Err.Description
End If
End Sub
```

This routine sets the attributes for the file specified in the Text1 text box.

See Also   **FileAttr** (function), **GetAttr** (statement)

Sgn

FUNCTION

CCE, LE, PE, EE

Syntax   *SValue* = **Sgn** (*expr*)

Usage   The **Sgn** function returns **-1**, if the value of *expr* is less than zero. It returns **0** if the value of *expr* is zero. It returns **1**, if the value of *expr* is greater than zero.

Arguments
- *SValue*—an **Integer** value of **-1, 0, 1** depending on the value of *expr*.
- *expr*—a numeric expression.

Examples
```
Private Sub Command1_Click()
If IsNumeric(Text1.Text) Then
    MsgBox "Sgn(" & Text1.Text & ")=" & Format(Sgn(CDbl(Text1.Text)))
End If
End Sub
```

This routine verifies that a numeric value was entered in the Text1 text box and then displays a message box with the sign of the value.

See Also   **Abs** (function), **IsNumeric** (function)

Shadow

OBJECT

PE, EE

Usage
: The **Shadow** object holds information about the shadow to be drawn for a particular chart element.

Properties
: - *ShadowObject*.**Brush**—an object reference to a **Brush** object containing information about the fill type for the area on the Y-axis of a three dimensional chart.
  - *ShadowObject*.**Offset**—an object reference to a **Coor** object containing the X-and Y-location of the offset.
  - *ShadowObject*.**Style**—an **Integer** value containing the style of the shadow (see Table S-7).

Style Name	Description
vbShadowStyleNull	No shadow displays.
vbShadowStyleDrop	A drop shadow displays.

Table S-7: *Style* values.

See Also
: **Coor** (object), **MSChart** (control)

Shape

CONTROL

CCE, LE, PE, EE

Usage
: The **Shape** control draws squares, rectangles, ovals, and circles on a form or a container control.

Properties
: - *ShapeControl*.**BackColor**—a **Long** that contains the suggested value for the background color of the control.
  - *ShapeControl*.**BackStyle**—an **Integer** value that describes how the background of the control displays (see Table S-8).

BackStyle	Description
0	The shape displays with a transparent background. Any objects behind the control can be seen.
1	The shape displays with an opaque background. Any objects behind the control can't be seen (default value).

Table S-8: *BackStyle* values.

- *ShapeControl*.**BorderColor**—a **Long** that contains the value for the color of the line.
- *ShapeControl*.**BorderStyle**—an **Integer** specifying how the border will be drawn (see Table S-9). This property also indicates how the form can be resized and is read only at run time.

BorderStyle Name	Value	Description
vbTransparent	0	The line is transparent.
vbBSSolid	1	The line is solid and the border is centered on the edge of the line (default).
vbBSDash	2	The line is a series of dashes.
vbBSDot	3	The line is a series of dots.
vbBSDashDot	4	The line is a series of dash dots.
vbBSDashDotDot	5	The line is a series of dash dot dots.
VbBSInsideSolid	6	The line is solid on the inside and is on the outer edge of the line.

Table S-9: *BorderStyle* values.

- *ShapeControl*.**BorderWidth**—an **Integer** value describing how wide the line will be drawn.
- *ShapeControl*.**Container**—an object that sets or returns the container of the control at run time. This property cannot be set at design time.
- *ShapeControl*.**DrawMode**—an **Integer** value (see Table S-10) specifying how a line will appear on the form.

DrawMode Name	Value	Description
vbBlackness	1	Blackness
vbNotMergePen	2	Inverse of *vbMergePen*
vbMaskNotPen	3	Combination of the colors common to the background color and the inverse of the pen
vbNotCopyPen	4	Inverse of *vbCopyPen*
vbMaskPenNot	5	Combination of the colors common to the pen and the inverse of the background
vbInvert	6	Inverse of the display color
vbXorPen	7	Combination of the colors in the display and pen, but not in both
vbNotMaskPen	8	Inverse setting of *vbMaskPen*
vbMaskPen	9	Combination of the colors common to the pen and display
vbNotXorPen	10	Inverse setting of *vbXorPen*
vbNop	11	Turns drawing off
vbMergeNotPen	12	Combination of the display and inverse of the pen color
vbCopyPen	13	Color specified in the **ForeColor** property
vbMergePenNot	14	Combination of the pen color and the inverse of the display color
vbMergePen	15	Combination of the pen color and the display color
vbWhiteness	16	Whiteness

Table S-10: *DrawMode* values.

- *ShapeControl*.**FillColor**—a **Long** that will be used to fill in shapes created with the following graphical methods: **Circle**, **Cls**, **EndDoc**, **Line**, **NewPage**, **Print**, and **PSet**.
- *ShapeControl*.**FillStyle**—an **Integer** specifying how the drawing methods: **Circle**, **Cls**, **EndDoc**, **Line**, **NewPage**, **Print**, and **PSet** will appear on the form (see Table S-11). If **DrawWidth** is greater than **1**, then *vbDash*, *vbDot*, *vbDashDot*, and *vbDashDotDot* will draw a solid line.

FillStyle Name	Value	Description
vbFSSolid	0	Solid
vbFSTransparent	1	Transparent
vbHorizontalLine	2	Horizontal line
vbVerticalLine	3	Vertical line
vbUpwardDiagonal	4	Upward diagonal
vbDownwardDiagonal	5	Downward diagonal
vbCross	6	Cross
vbDiagonalCross	7	Diagonal cross

Table S-11: *FillStyle* values.

- **ShapeControl.Height**—a **Single** that contains the height of the control.
- **ShapeControl.Index**—an **Integer** that uniquely identifies a control in a control array.
- **ShapeControl.Left**—a **Single** that contains the distance measured in twips between the left edge of the control and the left edge of the control's container.
- **ShapeControl.Name**—a **String** that contains the name of the control that will reference the control in a Visual Basic program. This property is read only at run time.
- **ShapeControl.Parent**—an object that contains a reference to the **Form, Frame,** or other container that contains the **Shape** control.
- **ShapeControl.Shape**—an **Integer** value (see Table S-12) containing the appearance of the **Shape** control.

Shape Name	Value	Description
vbShapeRectangle	0	Rectangle
vbShapeSquare	1	Square
vbShapeOval	2	Oval
vbShapeCircle	3	Circle
vbShapeRoundedRectangle	4	Rounded Rectangle
vbShapeRoundedSquare	5	Rounded Square

Table S-12: *Shape* values.

- **ShapeControl.Tag**—a **String** that can hold programmer specific information. This property is not used by Visual Basic.
- **ShapeControl.Top**—a **Single** that contains the distance measured in twips between the top edge of the control and the top edge of the control's container.
- **ShapeControl.Visible**—a **Boolean** value when **True** means that the control is visible. When **False** means that the control is not visible.

> **Tip**
>
> *This property hides the control until the program is ready to display it.*

- **ShapeControl.Width**—a **Single** that contains the width of the control.

Methods

ShapeControl.Move *Left* [, *Top* [, *Width* [, *Height*]]]

Usage This method changes the position and the size of the **Shape** control. The **ScaleMode** of the **Form** or other container object that holds the control will determine the units used to specify the coordinates.

Arguments
- *Left*—a **Single** that specifies the new position of the left edge of the control.
- *Top*—a **Single** that specifies the new position of the top edge of the control.
- *Width*—a **Single** that specifies the new width of the control.
- *Height*—a **Single** that specifies the new height of the control.

ShapeControl.Refresh

Usage This method redraws the contents of the control.

ShapeControl.ZOrder [*position*]

Usage This method specifies the position of the line control relative to the other objects on the form.

> **Tip**
>
> *Note that there are three layers of objects on a form: the back layer is the drawing space which contains the results of the graphical methods, the middle layer contains graphical objects and **Labels**, and the back layer contains nongraphical controls such as the **Line** control. The **ZOrder** method only affects how the objects are arranged within a single layer.*

Arguments *position*—an **Integer** that specifies the relative position of this object. A value of **0** means that the control is positioned at the head of the list, a value of **1** means that the control will be placed at the end of the list.

See Also **Form** (object), **Line** (control), **PictureBox** (control)

Shell

STATEMENT

CCE, LE, PE, EE

Syntax `TaskId = Shell ( program, windowstyle )`

Usage The **Shell** function launches an executable program and optionally is given the focus. If the new program is not given the focus, the **AppActivate** statement transfers the focus to the new program.

Arguments
- *TaskId*—a **Double** containing the task id of the new process. A value of **0** means that the program didn't start.

- *program*—a **String** containing the path and filename of a program to run.
- *windowstyle*—an **Integer** containing the initial window style that the program will use when it is started (see Table S-13).

windowstyle Name	Value	Description
vbHide	0	Window is hidden and given the focus.
vbNormalFocus	1	Window is started with its normal size and is given the focus.
vbMinimizedFocus	2	Window is started minimized and is given the focus (default).
vbMaximizedFocus	3	Window is started maximized and is given the focus.
vbNormalNoFocus	4	Window is started with its normal size, and the currently active remains active.
vbMinimizedNoFocus	6	Window is started minimized, and the currently active remains active.

Table S-13: *windowstyle* values.

Examples
```
Private Sub Command1_Click()
Dim TaskID As Variant
TaskID = Shell("C:\Program Files\MSOffice\WINWORD\WINWORD.EXE", vbNormalNoFocus)
MsgBox "Ready to activate Word?"
AppActivate TaskID
End Sub
```

This routine launches Microsoft Word and activates it when the user responds to the message box.

See Also   **AppActivate** (statement), **SendKeys** (statement)

Sin

FUNCTION

CCE, LE, PE, EE

Syntax   *RValue* = **Sin** (*Number*)

Usage   The **Sin** function will return the sine of *Number* specified in radians.

> **Tip**
>
> There are two pi radians in a circle, and there are 360 degrees in a circle. Pi is approximately equal to 3.1415926535897932384. To convert radians to degrees, multiply by 180/pi. To convert degrees to radians, multiply by pi/180.

Arguments
- *RValue*—a **Double** that contains the sine of *Number*.
- *Number*—a **Double** expression that is passed to the **Sin** function. This value is specified in radians.

Examples
```
Private Sub Command1_Click()
If IsNumeric(Text1.Text) Then
    Text2.Text = Format(Sin(CDbl(Text1.Text)))
End If
End Sub
```

This routine will compute the sine of the value in the Text1 text box and display the results in the Text2 text box.

See Also   **Atn** (function), **Cos** (function), **Tan** (function)

Single

DATA TYPE

CCE, LE, PE, EE

Usage   The **Single** data type holds integer values in the range from -3.402823E38 to -1.401298E-45 for negative values and from 1.401298E-45 to 3.402823E38 for positive values. A **Single** variable only occupies 32 bits of storage or 4 bytes.

See Also   **Byte** (data type), **CByte** (function), **CInt** (function), **CLng** (function), **CStr** (function), **Dim** (statement), **Double** (data type), **Format** (function), **Integer** (data type), **IsNumeric** (function), **Long** (data type), **Variant** (data type)

Slider

CONTROL

PE, EE

Usage   The **Slider** control is an ActiveX control in the Windows Common Controls that provides graphical slide control that returns a value.

Properties   *SliderControl*.**BorderStyle**—an **Integer** specifying how the border will be drawn (see Table S-14).

BorderStyle Name	Value	Description
vbBSNone	0	No border displays.
vbFixedSingle	1	Single line around the label.

Table S-14: *BorderStyle* values.

- *SliderControl*.**Container**—an object that sets or returns the container of the control at run time. This property cannot be set at design time.
- *SliderControl*.**DataBindings**—a reference to the **DataBindings** collection containing the bindable properties available.
- *SliderControl*.**DragIcon**—an object that contains the picture value of an icon. At design time, you can specify an icon file that has a file type of .ICO.

> **Tip**
>
> *This value can be created by copying the value from another control's **DragIcon** value, a form's icon, or by using the **LoadPicture** function.*

- *SliderControl*.**DragMode**—an **Integer** specifying how the control will respond to a drag request (see Table S-15).

> **Tip**
>
> *Setting **DragMode** to vbAutomatic will automatically begin a drag operation when the user clicks on the control. However, the control will not respond to the usual mouse events (**Click**, **DblClick**).*

DragMode Name	Value	Description
vbManual	0	The Drag method must be used to begin a drag-and-drop operation (default value).
vbAutomatic	1	The source control will automatically begin a drag-and-drop operation when the user clicks on the control.

Table S-15: *DragMode* values.

- *SliderControl*.**Enabled**—a **Boolean** value when **True** means that the control will respond to events. When **False**, the control will not respond to events.
- *SliderControl*.**GetNumTicks**—a **Long** containing the number of ticks displayed on the control.
- *SliderControl*.**Height**—a **Single** that contains the height of the control.
- *SliderControl*.**HelpContextID**—a **Long** that contains a help file context ID number which references an entry in the help file. When the user presses the F1 key while this control is active, the corresponding entry in the help file will automatically display. A value of **0** means that no context number was specified.

> **Tip**
>
> *A help file must be compiled using the Windows Help Compiler available in the Professional and Enterprise editions of Visual Basic.*

- *SliderControl*.**hWnd**—a **Long** that contains a Windows handle to the control.

> **Tip**
>
> *The **hWnd** property is most useful when making calls to Windows API functions. Since this value can change during execution, do not save the value into a variable for later use.*

- *SliderControl*.**Index**—an **Integer** that uniquely identifies a control in a control array.
- *SliderControl*.**LargeChange**—a **Long** containing the number of ticks the slider will move when the user presses the PgUp or PgDn key or clicks on the area to the right or left of the slider. The default value is **5**.
- *SliderControl*.**Left**—a **Single** containing the distance measured in twips between the left edge of the control and the left edge of the control's container.
- *SliderControl*.**Max**—an **Integer** containing the maximum value for the progress bar. If not specified, this value defaults to **32,767**.
- *SliderControl*.**Min**—an **Integer** containing the minimum value for the progress bar. If not specified, this value defaults to **0**.
- *SliderControl*.**MouseIcon**—a **Picture** object (a bitmap, icon, or metafile) that will be used as a cursor when the **MousePointer** property is set to **99**. Note that Visual Basic does not support color cursors from a .CUR file. A color icon from an .ICO file should be used instead.
- *SliderControl*.**MousePointer**—an **Integer** that contains the value of the cursor that should display when the cursor is moved over this control (see Table S-16). Use *vbCustom* to display the custom icon stored in the **MouseIcon** property.

Cursor Name	Value	Description
vbDefault	0	Shape determined by the object (default value)
vbArrow	1	Arrow
vbCrosshair	2	Crosshair
vbIbeam	3	I beam
vbIconPointer	4	Square inside a square
vbSizePointer	5	Four sided arrow (north, south, east, west)
vbSizeNESW	6	Two sided arrow (northeast, southwest)
vbSizeNS	7	Two sided arrow (north, south)
vbSizeNWSE	8	Two sided arrow (northwest, southeast)
vbSizeWE	9	Two sided arrow (west, east)
vbUpArrow	10	Single sided arrow pointing north
vbHourglass	11	hourglass
vbNoDrop	12	No Drop
vbArrowHourglass	13	An arrow and an Hourglass
vbArrowQuestion	14	An arrow and a question mark
vbSizeAll	15	Size all
vbCustom	99	Custom icon from the **MouseIcon** property of this control

Table S-16: *Cursor* values.

- *SliderControl*.**Name**—a **String** that contains the name of the control that will reference the control in a Visual Basic program. This property is read only at run time.
- *SliderControl*.**Object**—an object that contains a reference to the *ListViewControl* object.
- *SliderControl*.**OLEDropMode**—an **Integer** value (see Table S-17) that describes how the control will respond to OLE drop operations.

OLEDropMode Name	Value	Description
vbOLEDropNone	0	The control does not accept OLE drops. The cursor is changed to the No Drop cursor (default value).
vbOLEDropManual	1	The control responds to OLE drops under the program's control (manual).
vbOLEDropAutomatic	2	The control automatically accepts OLE drops if it recognizes the format of the data object.

Table S-17: *OLEDropMode values.*

- *SliderControl.***Orientation**—an **Integer** value (see Table S-18) describing how the control is positioned.

Orientation Name	Value	Description
sldHorizontal	0	The control is positioned horizontally (default value).
sldVertical	1	The control is positioned vertically.

Table S-18: *Orientation values.*

- *SliderControl.***Parent**—an object that contains a reference to the **Form, Frame,** or other container that contains the **Label** control.
- *SliderControl.***SelectRange**—a **Boolean** when **True** means that the **Slider** can have a selected range.
- *SliderControl.***SelLength**—a **Long** containing the length of the selected area.
- *SliderControl.***SelStart**—a **Long** containing the starting position of the selected area.

> **Tip**
>
> The *SelectRange, SelLength,* and *SelStart* properties and the *ClearSel* method work together to display a select area next to the slider. You can use this area to do a number of things. If you program the *MouseUp* and *MouseDown* events to check for the Shift key the user can select a range of values. The program can also display a range of values and check in the *Change* event to ensure that the user has stayed inside the valid range.

- *SliderControl.***SmallChange**—a **Long** containing the number of ticks the slider will move when the user presses the left or right arrow keys. The default value is **1**.
- *SliderControl.***TabIndex**—an **Integer** that determines the order that a user will tab through the objects on a form.
- *SliderControl.***TabStop**—a **Boolean** value when **True** means that the user can tab to this object. When **False** means that this control will be skipped to the next control in the **TabIndex** order.
- *SliderControl.***Tag**—a **String** that can hold programmer specific information. This property is not used by Visual Basic.
- *SliderControl.***TickFrequency**—a **Long** containing the number of units between each tick mark.
- *SliderControl.***TickStyle**—an **Integer** value (see Table S-19) describing the tick marks are displayed.

TickStyle Name	Value	Description
sldBottomRight	0	The ticks display along the bottom of the slider when horizontal and the right when vertical (default value).
sldTopLeft	1	The ticks display along the top of the slider when horizontal and the left when vertical.
sldBoth	2	The ticks display on the top and bottom of the slider when horizontal and the right and left when vertical.
SldNoTicks	3	No ticks display.

Table S-19: TickStyle values.

- *SliderControl*.**ToolTipText**—a **String** that holds a text value that can be displayed as a **ToolTip** box that displays whenever the cursor is held over the control for about one second.
- *SliderControl*.**Top**—a **Single** that contains the distance measured in twips between the top edge of the control and the top edge of the control's container.
- *SliderControl*.**Value**—an **Integer** containing the current value of the progress bar. This value must be between the **Min** and **Max** values.
- *SliderControl*.**Visible**—a **Boolean** value when **True** means that the control is visible. When **False** means that the control is not visible.

Tip

This property hides the control until the program is ready to display it.

- *SliderControl*.**WhatsThisHelpID**—a **Long** that contains a help file context ID number that references an entry in the help file. This provides a What's This PopUp help display in response to the What's This button in the upper right corner of the window.
- *SliderControl*.**Width**—a **Single** that contains the width of the control.

Methods

SliderControl.ClearSel

Usage   This method sets **SelLength** to **0**.

SliderControl.Drag [DragAction]

Usage   This method begins, ends, or cancels a drag operation.

Arguments   *DragAction*—an **Integer** that contains a value selected from Table S-20 below.

DragAction Name	Value	Description
vbCancel	0	Cancels any drag operation in progress.
vbBeginDrag	1	Begins a drag operation (default).
vbEndDrag	2	Ends a drag operation and drops *object*.

Table S-20: *DragAction* values.

SliderControl.Move Left [, Top [, Width [, Height]]]

Usage This method changes the position and the size of the **Label** control. The **ScaleMode** of the **Form** or other container object that holds the slider control will determine the units used to specify the coordinates.

Arguments
- *Left*—a **Single** that specifies the new position of the left edge of the control.
- *Top*—a **Single** that specifies the new position of the top edge of the control.
- *Width*—a **Single** that specifies the new width of the control.
- *Height*—a **Single** that specifies the new height of the control.

SliderControl.OLEDrag

Usage This method begins an **OLEDrag** and drop operation. Invoking this method will trigger the **OLEStartDrag** event.

SliderControl.Refresh

Usage This method redraws the contents of the control.

SliderControl.SetFocus

Usage This method transfers the focus from the form or control that currently has the focus to this control. To receive the focus, this control must be enabled and visible.

SliderControl.ShowWhatsThis

Usage This method displays the ShowWhatsThis help information for this control.

SliderControl.ZOrder [position]

Usage This method specifies the position of the label control relative to the other objects on the form.

> **Tip**
>
> *Note that there are three layers of objects on a form: the back layer is the drawing space which contains the results of the graphical methods, the middle layer contains graphical objects and **Labels**, and the top layer contains nongraphical controls such as the **CommandButton**. The **ZOrder** method only affects how the objects are arranged within a single layer.*

Arguments *position*—an **Integer** that specifies the relative position of this object. A value of **0** means that the control is positioned at the head of the list, a value of **1** means that the control will be placed at the end of the list.

Events **Private Sub *SliderControl*_Change ([*index* As Integer])**

> Usage   This event occurs whenever the value of the slider changes.
>
> Arguments ▪ *index*—an **Integer** that uniquely identifies a control in a control array. This argument is not present if the control is not part of a control array.

Private Sub *SliderControl*_Click([*index* As Integer])

> Usage   This event occurs when the user clicks a mouse button while the cursor is over the control.
>
> Arguments ▪ *index*—an **Integer** that uniquely identifies a control in a control array. This argument is not present if the control is not part of a control array.

Private Sub *SliderControl*_DragDrop([*index* As Integer ,] *source* As Control, *x* As Single, *y* As Single)

> Usage   This event occurs when a drag-and-drop operation is completed by using the **Drag** method with a *DragAction* value of *vbEndDrag*.

> **Tip**
>
> When using drag-and-drop operations, use the **DragOver** event to determine what the cursor should look like while the cursor moves over the control.

> Arguments ▪ *index*—an **Integer** that uniquely identifies a control in a control array. This argument is not present if the control is not part of a control array.
> ▪ *source*—a control object that is the control that is being dragged.

> **Tip**
>
> You can access a property or method from the source control by using source.*property* or source.*method*. You can determine the type of object or control by using the **TypeOf** operator.

> ▪ *x*—a **Single** that contains the horizontal location of the mouse pointer.
> ▪ *y*—a **Single** that contains the vertical location of the mouse pointer.

Private Sub *SliderControl*_DragOver([*index* As Integer ,] *source* As Control, *x* As Single, *y* As Single, *state* As Integer)

> Usage   This event occurs while a drag operation is in progress and the cursor is moved over the control.

Tip

*When using drag-and-drop operations, use the **DragOver** event to determine what the cursor should look like while the cursor moves over the control. When state is **0**, you can change the cursor to a No Drop (vbNoDrop) cursor or highlight the field that the cursor is near. When state is **1**, you can undo the changes you made when the state was **0**.*

Arguments
- *index*—an **Integer** that uniquely identifies a control in a control array. This argument is not present if the control is not part of a control array.
- *source*—a control object that is the control that is being dragged.

Tip

*You can access a property or method from the source control by using source.property or source.method. You can determine the type of object or control by using the **TypeOf** operator.*

- *x*—a **Single** that contains the horizontal location of the mouse pointer.
- *y*—a **Single** that contains the vertical location of the mouse pointer.
- *state*—an **Integer** that indicates the state of the object being dragged (see Table S-21).

state Name	Value	Description
vbEnter	0	The dragged object is entering range of the control.
vbLeave	1	The dragged object is leaving range of the control.
vbOver	2	The dragged object has moved from one position over the control to another.

Table S-21: *state* values.

Private Sub *SliderControl*_GotFocus ([*index* As Integer])

Usage   This event occurs when the control is given focus.

Tip

You can use this routine to display help or other information in a status bar.

Arguments   *index*—an **Integer** that uniquely identifies a control in a control array. This argument is not present if the control is not part of a control array.

Private Sub *SliderControl*_KeyDown ([*index* As Integer ,] *keycode* As Integer, *shift* As Single)

Usage   This event occurs when a key is pressed while the control has the focus.

Slider

Arguments
- *index*—an **Integer** that uniquely identifies a control in a control array. This argument is not present if the control is not part of a control array.
- *keycode*—an **Integer** that contains information about which key was pressed.
- *shift*—an **Integer** that contains information about the Shift and Alt keys that were pushed when the mouse button was pressed (see Table S-22). These values can be added together if more than one key was down. For instance, a value of **5** would mean that the Shift and Alt keys were both down when the mouse button was pressed.

shift Name	Value	Description
vbShiftMask	1	The Shift key was pressed.
vbCtrlMask	2	The Ctrl key was pressed.
vbAltMask	4	The Alt key was pressed.

Table S-22: *shift* values.

Private Sub *SliderControl*_KeyPress([*index* As Integer ,] *keychar* As Integer)

Usage This event occurs whenever a key is pressed while the control has the focus.

Arguments
- *index*—an **Integer** that uniquely identifies a control in a control array. This argument is not present if the control is not part of a control array.
- *keychar*—an **Integer** that contains the ASCII character that was pressed.

Private Sub *SliderControl*_KeyUp ([*index* As Integer ,] *keycode* As Integer, *shift* As Single)

Usage This event occurs when a key is released while the control has the focus.

Arguments
- *index*—an **Integer** that uniquely identifies a control in a control array. This argument is not present if the control is not part of a control array.
- *keycode*—an **Integer** that contains information about which key was released.
- *shift*—an **Integer** that contains information about the Shift and Alt keys that were pushed when the mouse button was pressed (see Table S-23). These values can be added together if more than one key was down. For instance, a value of **5** would mean that the Shift and Alt keys were both down when the mouse button was pressed.

shift Name	Value	Description
vbShiftMask	1	The Shift key was pressed.
vbCtrlMask	2	The Ctrl key was pressed.
vbAltMask	4	The Alt key was pressed.

Table S-23: *shift* values.

Private Sub *SliderControl_MouseDown*([*index* As Integer ,] *button* As Integer, *shift* As Single, *x* As Single, *y* As Single)

Usage This event occurs when a mouse button was pressed while the cursor is over the control.

Arguments
- *index*—an **Integer** that uniquely identifies a control in a control array. This argument is not present if the control is not part of a control array.
- *button*—an **Integer** that contains information about the mouse buttons that were pressed (see Table S-24). Only one button will be indicated when this event occurs.

button Name	Value	Description
vbLeftButton	1	The left button was pressed.
vbRightButton	2	The right button was pressed.
vbMiddleButton	4	The middle button was pressed.

Table S-24: *button* values.

- *shift*—an **Integer** that contains information about the Shift and Alt keys that were pushed when the mouse button was pressed (see Table S-25). These values can be added together if more than one key was down. For instance, a value of **5** would mean that the Shift and Alt keys were both down when the mouse button was pressed.

shift Name	Value	Description
vbShiftMask	1	The Shift key was pressed.
vbCtrlMask	2	The Ctrl key was pressed.
vbAltMask	4	The Alt key was pressed.

Table S-25: *shift* values.

- *x*—a **Single** that contains the horizontal location of the mouse pointer.
- *y*—a **Single** that contains the vertical location of the mouse pointer.

Private Sub *SliderControl_MouseMove* ([*index* As Integer ,] *button* As Integer, *shift* As Single, *x* As Single, *y* As Single)

Usage This event occurs while the cursor is moved over the control.

Arguments
- *index*—an **Integer** that uniquely identifies a control in a control array. This argument is not present if the control is not part of a control array.
- *button*—an **Integer** that contains information about the mouse buttons that were pressed (see Table S-26). These values can be added together if more than one button was pushed. For instance, a value of **3** means that both the left and right buttons were pressed. A value of **0** means that no buttons were pressed.

button Name	Value	Description
vbLeftButton	1	The left button was pressed.
vbRightButton	2	The right button was pressed.
vbMiddleButton	4	The middle button was pressed.

Table S-26: *button* values.

- *shift*—an **Integer** that contains information about the Shift and Alt keys that were pushed when the mouse button was pressed (see Table S-27). For instance, a value of **5** would mean that the Shift and Alt keys were both down when the mouse button was pressed. A value of **0** means that none of these keys were pressed.

shift Name	Value	Description
vbShiftMask	1	The Shift key was pressed.
vbCtrlMask	2	The Ctrl key was pressed.
vbAltMask	4	The Alt key was pressed.

Table S-27: *shift* values.

- *x*—a **Single** that contains the horizontal location of the mouse pointer.
- *y*—a **Single** that contains the vertical location of the mouse pointer.

Private Sub *SliderControl*_MouseUp([*index* As Integer ,] *button* As Integer, *shift* As Single, *x* As Single, *y* As Single)

Usage
This event occurs when a mouse button is released while the cursor is over the control.

Arguments
- *index*—an **Integer** that uniquely identifies a control in a control array. This argument is not present if the control is not part of a control array.
- *button*—an **Integer** that contains information about the mouse buttons that were released (see Table S-28). Only one of these values will be present.

button Name	Value	Description
vbLeftButton	1	The left button was released.
vbRightButton	2	The right button was released.
vbMiddleButton	4	The middle button was released.

Table S-28: *button* values.

- *shift*—an **Integer** that contains information about the Shift and Alt keys that were pushed when the mouse button was released (see Table S-29). These values can be added together if more than one key was down. For instance, a value of **5** would mean that the Shift and Alt keys were both down when the mouse button was released. A value of **0** means that none of these keys were pressed.

shift Name	Value	Description
vbShiftMask	1	The Shift key was pressed.
vbCtrlMask	2	The Ctrl key was pressed.
vbAltMask	4	The Alt key was pressed.

Table S-29: *shift* values.

- *x*—a **Single** that contains the horizontal location of the mouse pointer.
- *y*—a **Single** that contains the vertical location of the mouse pointer.

Private Sub *SliderControl_OLECompleteDrag*([*index* As Integer ,] *effect* As Long)

Usage This event tells the source control the results of an OLE drag-and-drop operation. This is the final event to occur in the series of actions that make up an OLE drag-and-drop operation.

Arguments
- *index*—an **Integer** that uniquely identifies a control in a control array. This argument is not present if the control is not part of a control array.
- *effect*—a **Long** that returns the status of the OLE drag-and-drop operation (see Table S-30).

effect Name	Value	Description
vbDropEffectNone	0	The operation was canceled or the target control can't accept the drop operation.
vbDropEffectCopy	1	The operation copied data from the source control to the target control. The original data is unchanged.
vbDropEffectMove	2	The operation results in a link from the original data to the target control.

Table S-30: *effect* values.

Private Sub *SliderControl_OLEDragDrop*([*index* As Integer ,] *data* As DataObject, *effect* As Long, *button* As Integer, *shift* As Single, *x* As Single, *y* As Single)

Usage This event tells the source control the results of an OLE drag-and-drop operation. This is the final event to occur in the series of actions that make up an OLE drag-and-drop operation.

Arguments
- *index*—an **Integer** that uniquely identifies a control in a control array. This argument is not present if the control is not part of a control array.
- *data*—a **DataObject** that contains the formats that the source control will provide. If the data is not contained in the **DataObject**, then it can be retrieved with the **GetData** method.

- *effect*—a **Long** that returns the status of the OLE drag-and-drop operation (see Table S-31).

effect Name	Value	Description
vbDropEffectNone	0	The operation was canceled or the target control can't accept the drop operation.
vbDropEffectCopy	1	The operation copied data from the source control to the target control. The original data is unchanged.
vbDropEffectMove	2	The operation results in a link from the original data to the target control.

Table S-31: *effect* values.

- *button*—an **Integer** that contains information about the mouse buttons that were pressed (see Table S-32). These values can be added together if more than one button was pushed. For instance, a value of **3** means that both the left and right buttons were pressed. A value of **0** means that no buttons were pressed.

button Name	Value	Description
vbLeftButton	1	The left button was pressed.
vbRightButton	2	The right button was pressed.
vbMiddleButton	4	The middle button was pressed.

Table S-32: *button* values.

- *shift*—an **Integer** that contains information about the Shift and Alt keys that were pushed when the mouse button was released (see Table S-33). These values can be added together if more than one key was down. For instance, a value of **5** would mean that the Shift and Alt keys were both down when the mouse button was released. A value of **0** means that none of these keys were pressed.

shift Name	Value	Description
vbShiftMask	1	The Shift key was pressed.
vbCtrlMask	2	The Ctrl key was pressed.
vbAltMask	4	The Alt key was pressed.

Table S-33: *shift* values.

- *x*—a **Single** that contains the horizontal location of the mouse pointer.
- *y*—a **Single** that contains the vertical location of the mouse pointer.

Private Sub *SliderControl*_OLEDragOver([*index* As Integer ,] *data* As DataObject, *effect* As Long, *button* As Integer, *shift* As Single, *x* As Single, *y* As Single, *state* As Integer)

Usage   This event happens when an OLE drag-and-drop operation is in progress.

Arguments
- *index*—an **Integer** that uniquely identifies a control in a control array. This argument is not present if the control is not part of a control array.
- *data*—a **DataObject** that contains the formats that the source control will provide. If the data is not contained in the **DataObject**, then it can be retrieved with the **GetData** method.
- *effect*—a **Long** that returns the status of the OLE drag-and-drop operation (see Table S-34).

effect Name	Value	Description
vbDropEffectNone	0	The operation was canceled or the target control can't accept the drop operation.
vbDropEffectCopy	1	The operation copied data from the source control to the target control. The original data is unchanged.
vbDropEffectMove	2	The operation results in a link from the original data to the target control.

Table S-34: *effect* values.

- *button*—an **Integer** that contains information about the mouse buttons that were pressed (see Table S-35). These values can be added together if more than one button was pushed. For instance, a value of **3** means that both the left and right buttons were pressed. A value of **0** means that no buttons were pressed.

button Name	Value	Description
vbLeftButton	1	The left button was pressed.
vbRightButton	2	The right button was pressed.
vbMiddleButton	4	The middle button was pressed.

Table S-35: *button* values.

- *shift*—an **Integer** that contains information about the Shift and Alt keys that were pushed when the mouse button was released (see Table S-36). These values can be added together if more than one key was down. For instance, a value of **5** would mean that the Shift and Alt keys were both down when the mouse button was released. A value of **0** means that none of these keys were pressed.

shift Name	Value	Description
vbShiftMask	1	The Shift key was pressed.
vbCtrlMask	2	The Ctrl key was pressed.
vbAltMask	4	The Alt key was pressed.

Table S-36: *shift* values.

- *x*—a **Single** that contains the horizontal location of the mouse pointer.
- *y*—a **Single** that contains the vertical location of the mouse pointer.
- *state*—an **Integer** that indicates the state of the object being dragged (see Table S-37).

state Name	Value	Description
vbEnter	0	The dragged object is entering range of the control.
vbLeave	1	The dragged object is leaving range of the control.
vbOver	2	The dragged object has moved from one position over the control to another.

Table S-37: *state* values.

Private Sub *SliderControl*_OLEGiveFeedback ([*index* As Integer ,] *effect* As Long)

Usage   This event tells the source control what is happening while the OLE drag-and-drop operation is in progress. This event occurs after the **OLEDragOver** event.

Tip

You may want to use this event to change the cursor to reflect what can happen in the remote object.

Arguments
- *index*—an **Integer** that uniquely identifies a control in a control array. This argument is not present if the control is not part of a control array.
- *effect*—a **Long** that returns the status of the OLE drag-and-drop operation (see Table S-38).

effect Name	Value	Description
vbDropEffectNone	0	The operation was canceled or the target control can't accept the drop operation.
vbDropEffectCopy	1	The operation copied data from the source control to the target control. The original data is unchanged.
vbDropEffectMove	2	The operation results in a link from the original data to the target control.
vbDropEffectScroll	&H80000000	The target control is about to scroll or is scrolling. This value may be added to the other *effect* values.

Table S-38: *effect* values.

Private Sub *SliderControl*_OLESetData([*index* As Integer ,] *data* As DataObject, *DataFormat* As Integer)

Usage   This event happens in response to the target object performing a **GetData** method on *data*. This routine will respond by using the **SetData** method with the desired data using the **DataObject** *data*.

Arguments
- *index*—an **Integer** that uniquely identifies a control in a control array. This argument is not present if the control is not part of a control array.

- *data*—a **DataObject** that will contain the data to return to the target object.
- *format*—an **Integer** that contains the format of the data (see Table S-39).

format Name	Value	Description
vbCFText	1	Text (.TXT files)
vbCFBitmap	2	Bitmap (.BMP files)
vbCFMetafile	3	Metafile (.WMF files)
vbCFEDIB	8	Device independent bitmap (DIB)
vbCFPallette	9	Color palette
vbCFEMetafile	14	Enhanced metafile (.EMF files)
vbCFFiles	15	List of files
vbCFRTF	-16639	Rich Text Format (.RTF files)

Table S-39: *format* values.

Private Sub *SliderControl_OLEStartDrag* ([*index* As Integer ,] *data* As DataObject, *AllowedEffects* As Long)

Usage   This event starts an OLE drag-and-drop operation.

Arguments
- *index*—an **Integer** that uniquely identifies a control in a control array. This argument is not present if the control is not part of a control array.
- *data*—a **DataObject** that will contain the formats that the source object is willing to provide to the target object. It may optionally contain the data to transfer.
- *AllowedEffects*—a **Long** that contains the effects that the target object can request from the source object (see Table S-40). The *AllowedEffects* can be added together if the source object supports more than one effect. Note that the target object can always use the *vbDropEffectNone* effect.

AllowedEffects Name	Value	Description
vbDropEffectNone	0	The target can't copy the data.
vbDropEffectCopy	1	The target can copy the data and the source will keep the data unchanged.
vbDropEffectMove	2	The target can copy the data and the source will delete the data.

Table S-40: *AllowedEffects* values.

Private Sub *SliderControl_Scroll* ([*index* As Integer])

Usage   This event occurs while the user is moving the slider.

> **Tip**
>
> *This event receives a large number of calls. Use the event when you want to perform something continuously. Use the **Change** event instead of this event when you only need to process something once.*

Arguments
: *index*—an **Integer** that uniquely identifies a control in a control array. This argument is not present if the control is not part of a control array.

Examples
```
Private Sub Slider1_Change()
ProgressBar1.Value = Slider1.Value
End Sub
```

This routine updates the progress bar each time the value of the slider is changed.

See Also
: **ProgressBar** (control)

SLN

FUNCTION

CCE, LE, PE, EE

Syntax
: *depreciation* = **SLN**(*cost, salvage, life*)

Usage
: The **SLN** function returns the straight line depreciation for an asset.

Arguments
: - *depreciation*—a **Double** value containing the depreciation.
  - *cost*—a **Double** value containing the initial cost of the asset.
  - *salvage*—a **Double** value containing the salvage value of the asset.
  - *life*—an **Double** value specifying the useful life of the asset.

Examples
```
Private Sub Command1_Click()
If IsNumeric(Text1.Text) And IsNumeric(Text2.Text) And IsNumeric(Text3.Text) Then
    Text4.Text = Format(SLN(CDbl(Text1.Text), CDbl(Text2.Text), CDbl(Text3.Text)))
Else
    MsgBox "Invalid value"
End If
End Sub
```

This routine computes the straight line depreciation for an asset with values specified in the Text1, Text2, and Text3 text boxes and displays the result in the Text4 text box.

See Also
: **DDB** (function), **FV** (function), **IPmt** (function), **IRR** (function), **MIRR** (function), **NPer** (function), **NPV** (function), **PMT** (function), **PPmt** (function), **PV** (function), **Rate** (function), **SYD** (function)

Space

FUNCTION

CCE, LE, PE, EE

Syntax `svar = Space[$]( number )`

Usage The **Space** function returns a string with the specified number of spaces.

> **Tip**
>
> A more general form of this function is **String**, which will return the specified number of an arbitrary character.

Arguments
- *svar*—a **String** variable.
- *number*—a **Long** value containing the number of spaces to return.

Examples
```
Private Sub Command1_Click()
Dim s As String
s = Space(128)
MsgBox "The length of s is " & Format(Len(s))
End Sub
```

This routine creates a string of 128 spaces and saves it in the variable *s*. Then it displays the length of *s* in a message box.

See Also **String** (function)

Split

OBJECT

PE, EE

Usage The **Split** object contains information about a split in a **DBGrid** control. A split displays a view of the information in the database and consists of a group of columns of data that will scroll together. By default, the **DBGrid** contains one split.

Properties
- *SplitObject*.**AllowFocus**—a **Boolean** value when **True** the user will be allowed to give the focus to the split. When **False** the user will not be permitted to access the split interactively.
- *SplitObject*.**AllowRowSizing**—a **Boolean** value when **True** the user will be allowed to resize rows in the grid. When **False** the user will not be allowed to resize rows in the grid.
- *SplitObject*.**AllowSizing**—a **Boolean** value when **True** the user will be allowed resize splits. When **False** the user will not be allowed to resize splits (default).
- *SplitObject*.**Columns**—returns a **Columns** collection.
- *SplitObject*.**CurrentCellVisible**—a **Boolean** value when **True** the current cell is visible. When **False** the current cell is not visible.
- *SplitObject*.**FirstRow**—a bookmark to the first visible row in the grid.

- *SplitObject*.**Index**—an **Integer** that uniquely identifies a split in a **DBGrid** control.
- *SplitObject*.**LeftCol**—an **Integer** value containing the leftmost visible column.
- *SplitObject*.**Locked**—a **Boolean** value when **True** the user can't make changes in any cells.
- *SplitObject*.**MarqueeStyle**—an **Integer** containing the Marquee style (see Table S-41) for the **DBGrid** or split object.

MarqueeStyle Name	Value	Description
dbgDottedCellBorder	0	The current cell will be highlighted by drawing a dotted border around the cell.
dbgSolidCellBorder	1	The current cell will be highlighted by drawing a solid line around the cell.
dbgHighlightCell	2	The current cell will be highlighted.
dbgHighlightRow	3	The current row will be highlighted by inverting the colors within the row.
dbgHighlightRowRaiseCell	4	The current row will be highlighted and the current cell will be raised.
dbgNoMarquee	5	No highlighting will be used.
dbgFloatingEditor	6	The current cell will be highlighted by a floating editor window (default).

Table S-41: *MarqueeStyle* values.

- *SplitObject*.**RecordSelectors**—a **Boolean** value when **True** the record selectors display. When **False** the record selectors do not display.
- *SplitObject*.**ScrollBars**—an **Integer** value (see Table S-42) containing the row divider style for the **DBGrid** control.

ScrollBars Name	Value	Description
vbSBNone	0	No scroll bars display (default).
vbHorizontal	1	A horizontal scroll bar displays.
vbVertical	2	A vertical scroll bar displays.
vbBoth	3	Both scroll bars display.

Table S-42: *ScrollBars* values.

- *SplitObject*.**ScrollGroup**—an **Integer** value containing the scrolling group. All splits with the same **ScrollGroup** value will automatically scroll together. Newly created splits will have a value of **1**.
- *SplitObject*.**SelEndCol**—an **Integer** value containing the ending column when a range of rows and columns is selected.
- *SplitObject*.**SelStartCol**—an **Integer** value containing the starting column when a range of rows and columns is selected.
- *SplitObject*.**Size**—a **Variant** value containing information for the specified value of **SizeMode**.
- *SplitObject*.**SizeMode**—an **Integer** value containing a value as specified in Table S-43. Setting this property will return information in the **Size** property.

SizeMode Name	Value	Description
dbgScalable	0	Return the size of the split relative to the total of all splits (default). Values of 1, 2 and 3 for three splits would mean that the first split would occupy $1/6$ of the display, the second $1/3$ and the third $1/2$.
dbgExact	1	Return the size of the split in units specified by **ScaleMode** of the container.
dbgNumberOfColumns	2	Return the number of columns displayed in the split.

Table S-43: *SizeMode* values.

Methods *SplitObject.ClearSelCols*

Usage This method deselects all columns in a split that were selected using the **SelStartCol** and **SelEndCol** properties.

See Also **DBGrid** (control), **Printers** (collection)

Splits

COLLECTION

PE, EE

Usage The **Splits** collection contains the set of splits in the **DBGrid** control.

Properties ▪ SplitsCollection.**Count**—an **Integer** containing the number of **Split** objects in the collection.

Methods *split = SplitsCollection.Add index*

Usage This method adds a new split to the collection.

Arguments ▪ *split*—a reference to the new **Split** object.
▪ *index*—an **Integer** containing where the split is to be added to the collection.

Tip

Use the **Count** property to add a new split object to the end of the collection.

split = SplitsCollection.Item (index)

Usage This method returns a split object.

Arguments ▪ *split*—a reference to a **Split** object.
▪ *index*—an **Integer** containing the index value of the desired split.

Tip

The first element of the collection is **0**, while the last element is **Count -1**.

SplitsCollection.Remove *index*

Usage This method removes the specified object from the collection.

Arguments ▪ *index*—an **Integer** value specifying the item to be removed from the collection.

See Also **DBGrid** (object), **Split** (object)

Sqr
FUNCTION

CCE, LE, PE, EE

Syntax `value = Sqr( number )`

Usage The **Sqr** function returns the square root of *number*.

Arguments ▪ *value*—a **Double** value containing the square root.

▪ *number*—a numeric value.

Examples
```
Private Sub Command1_Click()
If IsNumeric(Text1.Text) Then
    Text2.Text = Format(Sqr(CDbl(Text1.Text)))
Else
    MsgBox "Invalid value"
End If
End Sub
```

This routine computes the square root for the value in the Text1 text boxes and displays the result in the Text2 text box.

See Also **Exp** (function), **Log** (function)

SSTab
CONTROL

PE, EE

Usage The **SSTab** control is an ActiveX control that provides a set of tabbed pages. Unlike the **TabStrip** control, the **SSTab** control will hide the controls on each tab form when the user selects another tab. However, you still have to provide a frame or other container on the tab form to restrict the scope of **OptionButtons** and similar controls, since the **SSTab** control does not act as a container.

Properties ▪ *SSTabControl*.**BackColor**—a **Long** that contains the suggested value for the background color of the control.

▪ *SSTabControl*.**Caption**—a **String** value containing the caption for the current tab.

▪ *SSTabControl*.**Container**—an object that sets or returns the container of the control at run time. This property cannot be set at design time.

▪ *SliderControl*.**DataBindings**—a reference to the **DataBindings** collection containing the bindable properties available.

- *SSTabControl*.**DragIcon**—an object that contains the picture value of an icon. At design time, you can specify an icon file that has a file type of .ICO.

> **Tip**
>
> *This value can be created by copying the value from another control's **DragIcon** value, a form's icon, or by using the **LoadPicture** function.*

- *SSTabControl*.**DragMode**—an **Integer** specifying how the control will respond to a drag request (see Table S-44).

> **Tip**
>
> *Setting **DragMode** to vbAutomatic will automatically begin a drag operation when the user clicks on the control. However, the control will not respond to the usual mouse events (**Click**, **DblClick**, **MouseDown**, **MouseMove**, **MouseUp**).*

DragMode Name	Value	Description
vbManual	0	The Drag method must be used to begin a drag-and-drop operation (default value).
vbAutomatic	1	The source control will automatically begin a drag-and-drop operation when the user clicks on the control.

Table S-44: *DragMode* values.

- *SSTabControl*.**Enabled**—a **Boolean** value when **True** means that the control will respond to events. When **False**, the control will not respond to events.
- *SSTabControl*.**Font**—an object that contains information about the character font used by this object.
- *SSTabControl*.**ForeColor**—a **Long** that contains the suggested value for the foreground color of the contained control. This property is read only at run time.
- *SSTabControl*.**Height**—a **Single** that contains the height of the control.
- *SSTabControl*.**HelpContextID**—a **Long** that contains a help file context ID number which references an entry in the help file. When the user presses the F1 key while this control is active, the corresponding entry in the help file will automatically display. A value of **0** means that no context number was specified.

> **Tip**
>
> *A help file must be compiled using the Windows Help Compiler available in the Professional and Enterprise editions of Visual Basic.*

- *SSTabControl*.**hWnd**—a **Long** that contains a Windows handle to the control.

> **Tip**
>
> The **hWnd** property is most useful when making calls to Windows API functions. Since this value can change during execution, do not save the value into a variable for later use.

- *SSTabControl*.**Index**—an **Integer** that uniquely identifies a control in a control array.
- *SSTabControl*.**Left**—a **Single** that contains the distance measured in twips between the left edge of the control and the left edge of the control's container.
- *SSTabControl*.**MouseIcon**—a **Picture** object (a bitmap, icon, or metafile) that will be used as a cursor when the **MousePointer** property is set to **99**. Note that Visual Basic does not support color cursors from a .CUR file. A color icon from an .ICO file should be used instead.
- *SSTabControl*.**MousePointer**—an **Integer** that contains the value of the cursor that should display when the cursor is moved over this control (see Table S-45). Use *vbCustom* to display the custom icon stored in the **MouseIcon** property.

Cursor Name	Value	Description
vbDefault	0	Shape determined by the object (default value)
vbArrow	1	Arrow
vbCrosshair	2	Crosshair
vbIbeam	3	I beam
vbIconPointer	4	Square inside a square
vbSizePointer	5	Four sided arrow (north, south, east, west)
vbSizeNESW	6	Two sided arrow (northeast, southwest)
vbSizeNS	7	Two sided arrow (north, south)
vbSizeNWSE	8	Two sided arrow (northwest, southeast)
vbSizeWE	9	Two sided arrow (west, east)
vbUpArrow	10	Single sided arrow pointing north
vbHourglass	11	Hourglass
vbNoDrop	12	No Drop
vbArrowHourglass	13	An arrow and an Hourglass
vbArrowQuestion	14	An arrow and a question mark
vbSizeAll	15	Size all
vbCustom	99	Custom icon from the **MouseIcon** property of this control

Table S-45: *Cursor* values.

- *SSTabControl*.**Name**—a **String** that contains the name of the control that will reference the control in a Visual Basic program. This property is read only at run time.
- *SSTabControl*.**Object**—an object that contains a reference to the *SSTabControl* object.
- *SSTabControl*.**OLEDropMode**—an **Integer** value (see Table S-46) that describes how the control will respond to OLE drop operations.

OLEDropMode Name	Value	Description
vbOLEDropNone	0	The control does not accept OLE drops. The cursor is changed to the No Drop cursor (default value).
vbOLEDropManual	1	The control responds to OLE drops under the program's control (manual).
vbOLEDropAutomatic	2	The control automatically accepts OLE drops if it recognizes the format of the data object.

Table S-46: OLEDropMode values.

- *SSTabControl*.**Parent**—an object that contains a reference to the **Form**, **Frame**, or other container that contains this control.
- *SSTabControl*.**Picture**—a **Picture** object (a bitmap, icon or metafile) displayed on the current tab. You can also use the **LoadPicture** function at run time to load a bitmap, icon, or metafile.
- *SSTabControl*.**Rows**—an **Integer** containing the number of rows of tabs.
- *SSTabControl*.**ShowFocusRect**—a **Boolean** value when **True** a rectangle will be drawn around the caption on a tab when the tab has the focus.
- *SSTabControl*.**Style**—an **Integer** value describing how the tabs display (see Table S-47).

Style Name	Value	Description
ssStyleTabbedDialog	0	The tabs appear with rounded corners (default value).
ssStylePropertyPage	1	The tabs appear with square corners similar to the property page tabs in Windows 95.

Table S-47: Style values.

- *SSTabControl*.**Tab**—an **Integer** value containing the number of the active tabs.
- *SSTabControl*.**TabCaption** (*index*)—a **String** array containing the caption of each tab. *Index* ranges from **0** to **Tabs-1**. You can include an access key for this control by inserting an ampersand (&) in front of the character you want to. The selected character will then appear with an underline. Then if the user presses the Alt key with the underlined character the control will gain the focus.
- *SSTabControl*.**TabEnabled** (*index*)—a **Boolean** array when **True** the tab corresponding to *index* is enabled. *Index* ranges from **0** to **Tabs-1**.
- *SSTabControl*.**TabHeight**—a **Single** value containing the height of a tab.
- *SSTabControl*.**TabIndex**—an **Integer** that determines the order that a user will tab through the objects on a form.
- *SSTabControl*.**TabMaxWidth**—a **Single** value containing the maximum width of a tab.
- *SSTabControl*.**TabOrientation**—an **Integer** value describing how the tabs display (see Table S-48).

Style Name	Value	Description
ssTabOrientationTop	0	The tabs appear on the top the control (default value).
ssTabOrientationBottom	1	The tabs appear on the bottom of the control.
ssTabOrientationLeft	2	The tabs appear on the left side of the control.
ssTabOrientationRight	3	The tabs appear on the right side of the control.

Table S-48: Style values.

- *SSTabControl*.**TabPicture** (*index*)—a **Picture** object (a bitmap, icon or metafile) displayed on the tab corresponding to *index* is enabled. *Index* ranges from **0** to **Tabs-1**. You can also use the **LoadPicture** function at run time to load a bitmap, icon, or metafile.
- *SSTabControl*.**Tabs**—an **Integer** value containing the number of tabs on the control.
- *SSTabControl*.**TabsPerRow**—an **Integer** value containing the maximum number of tabs that can display in a single row.
- *SSTabControl*.**TabStop**—a **Boolean** value when **True** means that the user can tab to this object. When **False** means that this control will be skipped to the next control in the **TabIndex** order.
- *SSTabControl*.**TabVisible** (*index*)—a **Boolean** array when **True** the tab corresponding to *index* is visible. *Index* ranges from **0** to **Tabs-1**.
- *SSTabControl*.**Tag**—a **String** that can hold programmer specific information. This property is not used by Visual Basic.
- *SSTabControl*.**ToolTipText**—a **String** that holds a text value that can be displayed as a **ToolTip** box that displays whenever the cursor is held over the control for about one second.
- *SSTabControl*.**Top**—a **Single** that contains the distance measured in twips between the top edge of the control and the top edge of the control's container.
- *SSTabControl*.**Visible**—a **Boolean** value when **True** means that the control is visible. When **False** means that the control is not visible.

> **Tip**
>
> *This property hides the control until the program is ready to display it.*

- *SSTabControl*.**WhatsThisHelpID**—a **Long** that contains a help file context ID number that references an entry in the help file. This provides a What's This PopUp help display in response to the What's This button in the upper right corner of the window.
- *SSTabControl*.**Width**—a **Single** that contains the width of the control.
- *SSTabControl*.**WordWrap**—a **Boolean** value when **True** the text in the caption of each tab will wrap to another line on the tab if it does not fit within the space available.

Methods

*SSTabControl.*Drag [*DragAction*]

Usage   This method begins, ends, or cancels a drag operation.

Arguments   *DragAction*—an **Integer** that contains a value selected from Table S-49 below.

DragAction Name	Value	Description
vbCancel	0	Cancels any drag operation in progress.
vbBeginDrag	1	Begins a drag operation (default).
vbEndDrag	2	Ends a drag operation and drops *object*.

Table S-49: *DragAction* values.

SSTabControl.Move Left [, Top [, Width [, Height]]]

Usage This method changes the position and the size of the **TextBox** control. The **ScaleMode** of the **Form** or other container object that holds the SSTab control will determine the units used to specify the coordinates.

Arguments
- *Left*—a **Single** that specifies the new position of the left edge of the control.
- *Top*—a **Single** that specifies the new position of the top edge of the control.
- *Width*—a **Single** that specifies the new width of the control.
- *Height*—a **Single** that specifies the new height of the control.

SSTabControl.OLEDrag

Usage This method begins an **OLEDrag** and drop operation. Invoking this method will trigger the **OLEStartDrag** event.

SSTabControl.SetFocus

Usage This method transfers the focus from the form or control that currently has the focus to this control. To receive the focus, this control must be enabled and visible.

SSTabControl.ShowWhatsThis

Usage This method displays the ShowWhatsThis help information for this control.

SSTabControl.ZOrder [position]

Usage This method specifies the position of the SSTab control relative to the other objects on the form.

> **Tip**
>
> *Note that there are three layers of objects on a form: the back layer is the drawing space which contains the results of the graphical methods, the middle layer contains graphical objects and **Labels**, and the top layer contains nongraphical controls such as the **TextBox** control. The **ZOrder** method only affects how the objects are arranged within a single layer.*

Arguments *position*—an **Integer** that specifies the relative position of this object. A value of **0** means that the control is positioned at the head of the list, a value of **1** means that the control will be placed at the end of the list.

Events **Private Sub SSTabControl_Click([index As Integer ,] oldtab As Integer)**

Usage This event occurs when the user clicks a mouse button while the cursor is over a tab. The new tab becomes the current tab.

Arguments
- *index*—an **Integer** that uniquely identifies a control in a control array. This argument is not present if the control is not part of a control array.
- *oldtab*—an **Integer** containing the index of the previous tab.

Private Sub *SSTabControl*_DblClick([*index* As Integer])

Usage   This event occurs when the user double-clicks a mouse button while over the control.

Arguments
- *index*—an **Integer** that uniquely identifies a control in a control array. This argument is not present if the control is not part of a control array.

Private Sub *SSTabControl*_DragDrop([*index* As Integer ,] *source* As Control, *x* As Single, *y* As Single)

Usage   This event occurs when a drag-and-drop operation is completed by using the **Drag** method with a *DragAction* value of *vbEndDrag*.

Tip

*When using drag-and-drop operations, use the **DragOver** event to determine what the cursor should look like while the cursor moves over the control.*

Arguments
- *index*—an **Integer** that uniquely identifies a control in a control array. This argument is not present if the control is not part of a control array.
- *source*—a control object that is the control that is being dragged.

Tip

You can access a property or method from the source control by using source.property *or* source.method. *You can determine the type of object or control by using the **TypeOf** operator.*

- *x*—a **Single** that contains the horizontal location of the mouse pointer.
- *y*—a **Single** that contains the vertical location of the mouse pointer.

Private Sub *SSTabControl*_DragOver([*index* As Integer ,] *source* As Control, *x* As Single, *y* As Single, *state* As Integer)

Usage   This event occurs while a drag operation is in progress and the cursor is moved over the control.

Tip

*When using drag-and-drop operations, use the **DragOver** event to determine what the cursor should look like while the cursor moves over the control. When* state *is* **0**, *you can change the cursor to a No Drop (vbNoDrop) cursor or highlight the field that the cursor is near. When* state *is* **1**, *you can undo the changes you made when the* state *was* **0**.

Arguments
- *index*—an **Integer** that uniquely identifies a control in a control array. This argument is not present if the control is not part of a control array.
- *source*—a control object that is the control that is being dragged.

> **Tip**
>
> You can access a property or method from the source control by using *source.property* or *source.method*. You can determine the type of object or control by using the **TypeOf** operator.

- *x*—a **Single** that contains the horizontal location of the mouse pointer.
- *y*—a **Single** that contains the vertical location of the mouse pointer.
- *state*—an **Integer** that indicates the state of the object being dragged (see Table S-50).

state Name	Value	Description
vbEnter	0	The dragged object is entering range of the control.
vbLeave	1	The dragged object is leaving range of the control.
vbOver	2	The dragged object has moved from one position over the control to another.

Table S-50: *state* values.

Private Sub SSTabControl_GotFocus ([*index* As Integer])

Usage   This event occurs when the control is given focus.

> **Tip**
>
> You can use this routine to display help or other information in a status bar.

Arguments   *index*—an **Integer** that uniquely identifies a control in a control array. This argument is not present if the control is not part of a control array.

Private Sub SSTabControl_KeyDown ([*index* As Integer ,] *keycode* As Integer, *shift* As Single)

Usage   This event occurs when a key is pressed while the control has the focus.

Arguments
- *index*—an **Integer** that uniquely identifies a control in a control array. This argument is not present if the control is not part of a control array.
- *keycode*—an **Integer** that contains information about which key was pressed.
- *shift*—an **Integer** that contains information about the Shift and Alt keys that were pushed when the mouse button was pressed (see Table S-51). These values can be added together if more than one key was down. For instance, a value of **5** would mean that the Shift and Alt keys were both down when the mouse button was pressed.

shift Name	Value	Description
vbShiftMask	1	The Shift key was pressed.
vbCtrlMask	2	The Ctrl key was pressed.
vbAltMask	4	The Alt key was pressed.

Table S-51: *shift* values.

Private Sub *SSTabControl*_KeyPress([*index* As Integer ,] *keychar* As Integer)

Usage — This event occurs whenever a key is pressed while the control has the focus.

Arguments
- *index*—an **Integer** that uniquely identifies a control in a control array. This argument is not present if the control is not part of a control array.
- *keychar*—an **Integer** that contains the ASCII character that was pressed.

Private Sub *SSTabControl*_KeyUp ([*index* As Integer ,] *keycode* As Integer, *shift* As Single)

Usage — This event occurs when a key is released while the control has the focus.

Arguments
- *index*—an **Integer** that uniquely identifies a control in a control array. This argument is not present if the control is not part of a control array.
- *keycode*—an **Integer** that contains information about which key was released.
- *shift*—an **Integer** that contains information about the Shift and Alt keys that were pushed when the mouse button was pressed (see Table S-52). These values can be added together if more than one key was down. For instance, a value of **5** would mean that the Shift and Alt keys were both down when the mouse button was pressed.

shift Name	Value	Description
vbShiftMask	1	The Shift key was pressed.
vbCtrlMask	2	The Ctrl key was pressed.
vbAltMask	4	The Alt key was pressed.

Table S-52: *shift* values.

Private Sub *SSTabControl*_LostFocus ([*index* As Integer])

Usage — This event occurs when the control loses focus.

Arguments
- *index*—an **Integer** that uniquely identifies a control in a control array. This argument is not present if the control is not part of a control array.

Private Sub *TextBoxBoxControl*_MouseDown([*index* As Integer ,] *button* As Integer, *shift* As Single, *x* As Single, *y* As Single)

Usage   This event occurs when a mouse button was pressed while the cursor is over the control.

Arguments
- *index*—an **Integer** that uniquely identifies a control in a control array. This argument is not present if the control is not part of a control array.
- *button*—an **Integer** that contains information about the mouse buttons that were pressed (see Table S-53). Only one button will be indicated when this event occurs.

button Name	Value	Description
vbLeftButton	1	The left button was pressed.
vbRightButton	2	The right button was pressed.
vbMiddleButton	4	The middle button was pressed.

Table S-53: *button* values.

- *shift*—an **Integer** that contains information about the Shift and Alt keys that were pushed when the mouse button was pressed (see Table S-54). These values can be added together if more than one key was down. For instance, a value of **5** would mean that the Shift and Alt keys were both down when the mouse button was pressed.

shift Name	Value	Description
vbShiftMask	1	The Shift key was pressed.
vbCtrlMask	2	The Ctrl key was pressed.
vbAltMask	4	The Alt key was pressed.

Table S-54: *shift* values.

- *x*—a **Single** that contains the horizontal location of the mouse pointer.
- *y*—a **Single** that contains the vertical location of the mouse pointer.

Private Sub *SSTabControl*_MouseMove ([*index* As Integer ,] *button* As Integer, *shift* As Single, *x* As Single, *y* As Single)

Usage   This event occurs while the cursor is moved over the control.

Arguments
- *index*—an **Integer** that uniquely identifies a control in a control array. This argument is not present if the control is not part of a control array.
- *button*—an **Integer** that contains information about the mouse buttons that were pressed (see Table S-55). These values can be added together if more than one button was pushed. For instance, a value of **3** means that both the left and right buttons were pressed. A value of **0** means that no buttons were pressed.

button Name	Value	Description
vbLeftButton	1	The left button was pressed.
vbRightButton	2	The right button was pressed.
vbMiddleButton	4	The middle button was pressed.

Table S-55: *button* values.

- *shift*—an **Integer** that contains information about the Shift and Alt keys that were pushed when the mouse button was pressed (see Table S-56). For instance, a value of **5** would mean that the Shift and Alt keys were both down when the mouse button was pressed. A value of **0** means that none of these keys were pressed.

shift Name	Value	Description
vbShiftMask	1	The Shift key was pressed.
vbCtrlMask	2	The Ctrl key was pressed.
vbAltMask	4	The Alt key was pressed.

Table S-56: *shift* values.

- *x*—a **Single** that contains the horizontal location of the mouse pointer.
- *y*—a **Single** that contains the vertical location of the mouse pointer.

Private Sub *TextBoxBoxControl*_MouseUp([*index* As Integer ,] *button* As Integer, *shift* As Single, *x* As Single, *y* As Single)

Usage   This event occurs when a mouse button is released while the cursor is over the control.

Arguments
- *index*—an **Integer** that uniquely identifies a control in a control array. This argument is not present if the control is not part of a control array.
- *button*—an **Integer** that contains information about the mouse buttons that were released (see Table S-57). Only one of these values will be present.

button Name	Value	Description
vbLeftButton	1	The left button was released.
vbRightButton	2	The right button was released.
vbMiddleButton	4	The middle button was released.

Table S-57: *button* values.

- *shift*—an **Integer** that contains information about the Shift and Alt keys that were pushed when the mouse button was released (see Table S-58). These values can be added together if more than one key was down. For instance, a value of **5** would mean that the Shift and Alt keys were both down when the mouse button was released. A value of **0** means that none of these keys were pressed.

shift Name	Value	Description
vbShiftMask	1	The Shift key was pressed.
vbCtrlMask	2	The Ctrl key was pressed.
vbAltMask	4	The Alt key was pressed.

Table S-58: *shift* values.

- *x*—a **Single** that contains the horizontal location of the mouse pointer.
- *y*—a **Single** that contains the vertical location of the mouse pointer.

Private Sub *SSTabControl_OLECompleteDrag*([*index* As Integer ,] *effect* As Long)

Usage   This event tells the source control the results of an OLE drag-and-drop operation. This is the final event to occur in the series of actions that make up an OLE drag-and-drop operation.

Arguments
- *index*—an **Integer** that uniquely identifies a control in a control array. This argument is not present if the control is not part of a control array.
- *effect*—a **Long** that returns the status of the OLE drag-and-drop operation (see Table S-59).

effect Name	Value	Description
vbDropEffectNone	0	The operation was canceled or the target control can't accept the drop operation.
vbDropEffectCopy	1	The operation copied data from the source control to the target control. The original data is unchanged.
vbDropEffectMove	2	The operation results in a link from the original data to the target control.

Table S-59: *effect* values.

Private Sub *SSTabControl_OLEDragDrop*([*index* As Integer ,] *data* As DataObject, *effect* As Long, *button* As Integer, *shift* As Single, *x* As Single, *y* As Single)

Usage   This event tells the source control the results of an OLE drag-and-drop operation. This is the final event to occur in the series of actions that make up an OLE drag-and-drop operation.

Arguments
- *index*—an **Integer** that uniquely identifies a control in a control array. This argument is not present if the control is not part of a control array.
- *data*—a **DataObject** that contains the formats that the source control will provide. If the data is not contained in the **DataObject**, then it can be retrieved with the **GetData** method.
- *effect*—a **Long** that returns the status of the OLE drag-and-drop operation (see Table S-60).

effect Name	Value	Description
vbDropEffectNone	0	The operation was canceled or the target control can't accept the drop operation.
vbDropEffectCopy	1	The operation copied data from the source control to the target control. The original data is unchanged.
vbDropEffectMove	2	The operation results in a link from the original data to the target control.

Table S-60: *effect* values.

- *button*—an **Integer** that contains information about the mouse buttons that were pressed (see Table S-61). These values can be added together if more than one button was pushed. For instance, a value of **3** means that both the left and right buttons were pressed. A value of **0** means that no buttons were pressed.

button Name	Value	Description
vbLeftButton	1	The left button was pressed.
vbRightButton	2	The right button was pressed.
vbMiddleButton	4	The middle button was pressed.

Table S-61: *button* values.

- *shift*—an **Integer** that contains information about the Shift and Alt keys that were pushed when the mouse button was released (see Table S-62). These values can be added together if more than one key was down. For instance, a value of **5** would mean that the Shift and Alt keys were both down when the mouse button was released. A value of **0** means that none of these keys were pressed.

shift Name	Value	Description
vbShiftMask	1	The Shift key was pressed.
vbCtrlMask	2	The Ctrl key was pressed.
vbAltMask	4	The Alt key was pressed.

Table S-62: *shift* values.

- *x*—a **Single** that contains the horizontal location of the mouse pointer.
- *y*—a **Single** that contains the vertical location of the mouse pointer.

Private Sub *SSTabControl*_OLEDragOver([*index* As Integer ,] *data* As DataObject, *effect* As Long, *button* As Integer, *shift* As Single, *x* As Single, *y* As Single, *state* As Integer)

Usage: This event happens when an OLE drag-and-drop operation is in progress.

Arguments:
- *index*—an **Integer** that uniquely identifies a control in a control array. This argument is not present if the control is not part of a control array.
- *data*—a **DataObject** that contains the formats that the source control will provide. If the data is not contained in the **DataObject**, then it can be retrieved with the **GetData** method.

- *effect*—a **Long** that returns the status of the OLE drag-and-drop operation (see Table S-63).

effect Name	Value	Description
vbDropEffectNone	0	The operation was canceled or the target control can't accept the drop operation.
vbDropEffectCopy	1	The operation copied data from the source control to the target control. The original data is unchanged.
vbDropEffectMove	2	The operation results in a link from the original data to the target control.

Table S-63: *effect* values.

- *button*—an **Integer** that contains information about the mouse buttons that were pressed (see Table S-64). These values can be added together if more than one button was pushed. For instance, a value of **3** means that both the left and right buttons were pressed. A value of **0** means that no buttons were pressed.

button Name	Value	Description
vbLeftButton	1	The left button was pressed.
vbRightButton	2	The right button was pressed.
vbMiddleButton	4	The middle button was pressed.

Table S-64: *button* values.

- *shift*—an **Integer** that contains information about the Shift and Alt keys that were pushed when the mouse button was released (see Table S-65). These values can be added together if more than one key was down. For instance, a value of **5** would mean that the Shift and Alt keys were both down when the mouse button was released. A value of **0** means that none of these keys were pressed.

shift Name	Value	Description
vbShiftMask	1	The Shift key was pressed.
vbCtrlMask	2	The Ctrl key was pressed.
vbAltMask	4	The Alt key was pressed.

Table S-65: *shift* values.

- *x*—a **Single** that contains the horizontal location of the mouse pointer.
- *y*—a **Single** that contains the vertical location of the mouse pointer.
- *state*—an **Integer** that indicates the state of the object being dragged (see Table S-66).

state Name	Value	Description
vbEnter	0	The dragged object is entering range of the control.
vbLeave	1	The dragged object is leaving range of the control.
vbOver	2	The dragged object has moved from one position over the control to another.

Table S-66: *state* values.

Private Sub *SSTabControl_OLEGiveFeedback* ([*index* As Integer ,] *effect* As Long)

Usage — This event tells the source control what is happening while the OLE drag-and-drop operation is in progress. This event occurs after the **OLEDragOver** event.

Tip

You may want to use this event to change the cursor to reflect what can happen in the remote object.

Arguments
- *index*—an **Integer** that uniquely identifies a control in a control array. This argument is not present if the control is not part of a control array.
- *effect*—a **Long** that returns the status of the OLE drag-and-drop operation (see Table S-67).

effect Name	Value	Description
vbDropEffectNone	0	The operation was canceled or the target control can't accept the drop operation.
vbDropEffectCopy	1	The operation copied data from the source control to the target control. The original data is unchanged.
vbDropEffectMove	2	The operation results in a link from the original data to the target control.
vbDropEffectScroll	&H80000000	The target control is about to scroll or is scrolling. This value may be added to the other *effect* values.

Table S-67: *effect* values.

Private Sub *SSTabControl_OLESetData*([*index* As Integer ,] *data* As DataObject, *DataFormat* As Integer)

Usage — This event happens in response to the target object performing a **GetData** method on *data*. This routine will respond by using the **SetData** method with the desired data using the **DataObject** *data*.

Arguments
- *index*—an **Integer** that uniquely identifies a control in a control array. This argument is not present if the control is not part of a control array.
- *data*—a **DataObject** that will contain the data to be returned to the target object.
- *format*—an **Integer** that contains the format of the data (see Table S-68).

format Name	Value	Description
vbCFText	1	Text (.TXT files)
vbCFBitmap	2	Bitmap (.BMP files)
vbCFMetafile	3	Metafile (.WMF files)
vbCFEDIB	8	Device independent bitmap (DIB)

format Name	Value	Description
vbCFPallette	9	Color palette
vbCFEMetafile	14	Enhanced metafile (.EMF files)
vbCFFiles	15	List of files
vbCFRTF	-16639	Rich Text Format (.RTF files)

Table S-68: *format* values.

Private Sub *SSTabControl_OLEStartDrag* ([*index* As Integer ,] *data* As DataObject, *AllowedEffects* As Long)

Usage   This event starts an OLE drag-and-drop operation.

Arguments
- *index*—an **Integer** that uniquely identifies a control in a control array. This argument is not present if the control is not part of a control array.
- *data*—a **DataObject** that will contain the formats that the source object is willing to provide to the target object. It may optionally contain the data to transfer.
- *AllowedEffects*—a **Long** that contains the effects that the target object can request from the source object (see Table S-69). The *AllowedEffects* can be added together if the source object supports more than one effect. Note that the target object can always use the *vbDropEffectNone* effect.

AllowedEffects Name	Value	Description
vbDropEffectNone	0	The target can't copy the data.
vbDropEffectCopy	1	The target can copy the data and the source will keep the data unchanged.
vbDropEffectMove	2	The target can copy the data and the source will delete the data.

Table S-69: *AllowedEffects* values.

See Also   **TabStrip** (control)

Static

STATEMENT

CCE, LE, PE, EE

Syntax
```
Static identifier[typechar] [ arrayinfo ] [ As [ New ] type ] , [
    identifier[typechar] [ arrayinfo ] [ As [ New ] type ] ] . . .
```

Usage   The **Static** statement declares the variables inside a subroutine or function. These variables are only available inside the routine and other routines in the module can't access them.

Any values assigned to a static variable will remain unchanged between calls to the subroutine. This provides a good alternative to using variables declared at the module level and has the added benefit of ensuring that no other routines can access information contained in the static variable.

If **Option Explicit** is included in a module, then you must declare all of the variables used in your program before you can use them.

> **Tip**
>
> Use **Option Explicit** in all modules, because this will force you to declare all variables before you use them. This will help you avoid the situation where you think you have one variable, but Visual Basic thinks you have two because you used two different spellings.

Arguments
- *identifier*—the Visual Basic identifier that will reference this particular variable. It must begin with a letter which can be followed by any number of letters or numbers or the underscore character ("_"). Identifiers are not case-sensitive, though the case will be preserved for easier reading.
- *typechar*—one of the following characters can be included as the last character of a variable name to declare its type: "@" for **Currency**, "#" for **Double**, "%" for **Integer**, "&" for **Long**, "!" for **Single**, or "$" for **String**. The default type for variables without a typechar is **Variant** unless the type is specified using the **As** clause or by using one of the **Deftype** statements.
- *arrayinfo*—optionally indicates an array. It can have zero or more dimensions. An array can have no more than 60 dimensions. If no dimensions are specified, then the variable is considered a dynamic array and the subscripts must be set with the **ReDim** statement before it can be used. The subscripts are defined as the following:

([ubound | lbound **To** ubound] [, ubound | , lbound **To** ubound] . . .)]

| ubound | the upper bound for an array. |
| lbound | the lower bound for an array's subscript. If omitted, the value from **Option Base** will be used. If there is no **Option Base** statement in the module. |

- **New**—an optional keyword that means that a new instance of the object is automatically created the first time it is used.
- *type*—a valid Visual Basic type: **Byte**, **Boolean**, **Currency**, **Date**, **Double**, **Integer**, **Long**, **Single**, **String**, **Object**, or **Variant**. Specific objects can also be used, as well as, user-defined types defined with the **Type** statement.

Examples
```
Private Sub Command1_Click()
Static mycount As Integer
mycount = mycount + 1
Text1.Text = Format(mycount)
End Sub
```

This routine declares a static variable that it uses as a counter. Each time the user clicks on the Command1 command button, the counter is incremented and displays in the Text1 text box.

See Also
Byte (data type), **Boolean** (data type), **Currency** (data type), **Date** (data type), **Dim** (statement), **Double** (data type), **Integer** (data type), **Long** (data type), **Object** (data type), **Option Base** (statement), **Option Explicit** (statement), **Private** (statement), **Public** (statement), **ReDim** (statement), **Single** (data type), **String** (data type), **Type** (statement), **TypeName** (function), **Variant** (data type)

StatLine

OBJECT

PE, EE

Usage The **StatLine** object contains information about how statistic lines display on an **MSChart**.

Properties • *StatLineObject*.**Flag**—an **Integer** containing which statistic lines display on the chart (see Table S-70). Multiple statistic lines may be displayed by adding their values together.

Flag Name	Description
vtChStatsMinimum	Show the minimum value in a series.
VtChStatsMaximum	Show the maximum value in a series.
VtChStatsMean	Show the mean value in a series.
VtChStatsStddev	Show the standard deviation of the values in a series.
VtChStatsRegession	Show a regression line based on the values in a series.

Table S-70: *Flag* values.

• *StatLineObject*.**Style**—an **Integer** value (see Table S-71) describing how the statistic line is drawn.

Style Name	Description
vtPenStyleNull	No pen
vtPenStyleSolid	Solid line
vtPenStyleDashed	Dashed line
vtPenStyleDotted	Dotted line
vtPenStyleDashDot	Dash followed by a dot
vtPenStyleDashDotDot	Dash followed by two dots
vtPenStyleDitted	Ditted line
vtPenStyleDashDit	Dash followed by a dit
vtPenStyleDashDitDit	Dash followed by two dits

Table S-71: Style values.

• *StatLineObject*.**VtColor**—a reference to a **VtColor** object containing the color of the pen.
• *StatLineObject*.**Width**—a **Single** value containing the width of the pen in points.

See Also **MSChart** (control), **VtColor** (object)

StatusBar

CONTROL

PE, EE

Usage The **StatusBar** control is an ActiveX control that is part of the Microsoft Windows Common Controls 5.0 and contains a series of panels that is useful for displaying status information for an application. You can define up to sixteen panels.

StatusBar

Properties
- *StatusBarControl*.**Align**—an **Integer** value that describes the placement of the control (see Table S-72).

Align Name	Value	Description
vbAlignNone	0	The control's position is set at design time or by the program (default value for objects on a non-MDI Form).
vbAlignTop	1	The control is placed at the top of the form and its width is set to **ScaleWidth**. It will automatically be resized when the form is resized (default value for objects on an MDI Form).
vbAlignBottom	2	The control is placed at the bottom of the form and its width is set to ScaleWidth. It will automatically be resized when the form is resized.
vbAlignLeft	3	The control is placed at the left edge of the form and its width is set to ScaleWidth. It is not resized when the form is resized.
vbAlignRight	4	The control is placed at the right edge of the form and its width is set to **ScaleWidth**. It is not resized when the form is resized.

Table S-72: *Align* values.

- *StatusBarControl*.**Container**—an object that set or return the container of the control at run time. This property cannot be set at design time.
- *StatusBarControl*.**DragIcon**—an object that contains the picture value of an icon. At design time, you can specify an icon file that has a file type of .ICO.

Tip

*This value can be created by copying the value from another control's **DragIcon** value, a form's icon, or by using the **LoadPicture** function.*

- *StatusBarControl*.**DragMode**—an **Integer** specifying how the control will respond to a drag request (see Table S-73).

Tip

*Setting **DragMode** to vbAutomatic will automatically begin a drag operation when the user clicks on the control. However, the control will not respond to the usual mouse events (**Click**, **DblClick**, **MouseDown**, **MouseMove**, **MouseUp**).*

DragMode Name	Value	Description
vbManual	0	The Drag method must be used to begin a drag-and-drop operation (default value).
vbAutomatic	1	The source control will automatically begin a drag-and-drop operation when the user clicks on the control.

Table S-73: *DragMode* values.

- *StatusBarControl*.**Enabled**—a **Boolean** value when **True** means that the control will respond to events. When **False**, the control will not respond to events.

- *StatusBarControl*.**Font**—a reference to a **Font** object containing information about the character font used by this control.
- *StatusBarControl*.**Height**—a **Single** that contains the height of the control.
- *StatusBarControl*.**hWnd**—a **Long** that contains a Windows handle to the control.

> **Tip**
>
> *The **hWnd** property is most useful when making calls to Windows API functions. Since this value can change during execution, do not save the value into a variable for later use.*

- *StatusBarControl*.**Index**—an **Integer** that uniquely identifies a control in a control array.
- *StatusBarControl*.**Left**—a **Single** that contains the distance measured in twips between the left edge of the control and the left edge of the control's container.
- *StatusBarControl*.**MouseIcon**—a **Picture** object (a bitmap, icon, or metafile) that will be used as a cursor when the **MousePointer** property is set to **99**. Note that Visual Basic does not support color cursors from a .CUR file. A color icon from an .ICO file should be used instead.
- *StatusBarControl*.**MousePointer**—an **Integer** that contains the value of the cursor that should display when the cursor is moved over this control (see Table S-74). Use *vbCustom* to display the custom icon stored in the **MouseIcon** property.

Cursor Name	Value	Description
vbDefault	0	Shape determined by the object (default value)
vbArrow	1	Arrow
vbCrosshair	2	Crosshair
vbIbeam	3	I beam
vbIconPointer	4	Square inside a square
vbSizePointer	5	Four sided arrow (north, south, east, west)
vbSizeNESW	6	Two sided arrow (northeast, southwest)
vbSizeNS	7	Two sided arrow (north, south)
vbSizeNWSE	8	Two sided arrow (northwest, southeast)
vbSizeWE	9	Two sided arrow (west, east)
vbUpArrow	10	Single sided arrow pointing north
vbHourglass	11	hourglass
vbNoDrop	12	No Drop
vbArrowHourglass	13	An arrow and an Hourglass
vbArrowQuestion	14	An arrow and a question mark
vbSizeAll	15	Size all
vbCustom	99	Custom icon from the **MouseIcon** property of this control

Table S-74: *Cursor* values.

- *StatusBarControl*.**Name**—a **String** that contains the name of the control that will reference the control in a Visual Basic program. This property is read only at run time.
- *StatusBarControl*.**Object**—an object that contains a reference to the *StatusBarControl* object.
- *StatusBarControl*.**OLEDropMode**—an **Integer** value (see Table S-75) that describes how the control will respond to OLE drop operations.

OLEDropMode Name	Value	Description
vbOLEDropNone	0	The control does not accept OLE drops. The cursor is changed to the No Drop cursor (default value).
vbOLEDropManual	1	The control responds to OLE drops under the program's control (manual).
vbOLEDropAutomatic	2	The control automatically accepts OLE drops if it recognizes the format of the data object.

Table S-75: OLEDropMode values.

- *StatusBarControl*.**Panels**—an object reference to a **Panels** collection containing information about what displays in each panel.
- *StatusBarControl*.**Parent**—an object that contains a reference to the **Form**, **Frame,** or other container that contains this control.
- *StatusBarControl*.**ShowTips**—a **Boolean** when **True** means that the objects in the control may show tool tips. **False** means that the objects can't display tool tips.
- *StatusBarControl*.**SimpleText**—a **String** holding the text that will display in the status bar when the **Style** property is set to *sbrSimple*.
- *StatusBarControl*.**Style**—an **Integer** value (see Table S-76) that describes how the control will respond to OLE drop operations.

style Name	Value	Description
sbrNormal	0	The control displays the panels from the Panels collection (default value).
sbrSimple	1	The control displays the contents of **SimpleText** in a single box on the **StatusBar**.

Table S-76: Style values.

- *StatusBarControl*.**TabIndex**—an Integer that determines the order that a user will tab through the objects on a form.
- *StatusBarControl*.**Tag**—a **String** that can hold programmer specific information. This property is not used by Visual Basic.
- *StatusBarControl*.**ToolTipText**—a **String** that holds a text value that can be displayed as a **ToolTip** box that displays whenever the cursor is held over the control for about one second.
- *StatusBarControl*.**Top**—a **Single** that contains the distance measured in twips between the top edge of the control and the top edge of the control's container.
- *StatusBarControl*.**Visible**—a **Boolean** value when **True** means that the control is visible. When **False** means that the control is not visible.

> **Tip**
>
> *This property hides the control until the program is ready to display it.*

- *StatusBarControl*.**WhatsThisHelpID**—a **Long** that contains a help file context ID number that references an entry in the help file. This provides a What's This PopUp help display in response to the What's This button in the upper right corner of the window.
- *StatusBarControl*.**Width**—a **Single** that contains the width of the control.

Methods

StatusBarControl.Drag [DragAction]

Usage This method begins, ends, or cancels a drag operation.

Arguments *DragAction*—an **Integer** that contains a value selected from Table S-77 below.

DragAction Name	Value	Description
vbCancel	0	Cancels any drag operation in progress.
vbBeginDrag	1	Begins a drag operation (default).
vbEndDrag	2	Ends a drag operation and drops *object*.

Table S-77: *DragAction* values.

StatusBarControl.Move Left [, Top [, Width [, Height]]]

Usage This method changes the position and the size of the **StatusBar** control. The **ScaleMode** of the **Form** or other container object that holds the StatusBar control will determine the units used to specify the coordinates.

Arguments
- *Left*—a **Single** that specifies the new position of the left edge of the control.
- *Top*—a **Single** that specifies the new position of the top edge of the control.
- *Width*—a **Single** that specifies the new width of the control.
- *Height*—a **Single** that specifies the new height of the control.

StatusBarControl.OLEDrag

Usage This method begins an **OLEDrag** and drop operation. Invoking this method will trigger the **OLEStartDrag** event.

StatusBarControl.Refresh

Usage This method redraws the contents of the control.

StatusBarControl.ShowWhatsThis

Usage This method displays the ShowWhatsThis help information for this control.

StatusBarControl.ZOrder [position]

Usage This method specifies the position of the StatusBar control relative to the other objects on the form.

> **Tip**
>
> Note that there are three layers of objects on a form: the back layer is the drawing space which contains the results of the graphical methods, the middle layer contains graphical objects and **Labels**, and the top layer contains nongraphical controls such as the **StatusBar** control. The **ZOrder** method only affects how the objects are arranged within a single layer.

Arguments
- *position*—an **Integer** that specifies the relative position of this object. A value of **0** means that the control is positioned at the head of the list, a value of **1** means that the control will be placed at the end of the list.

Events

Private Sub *StatusBarControl*_Click([*index* As Integer])

Usage
This event occurs when the user clicks a mouse button while the cursor is over the status bar, but not over any panel.

Arguments
- *index*—an **Integer** that uniquely identifies a control in a control array. This argument is not present if the control is not part of a control array.

Private Sub *StatusBarControl*_DblClick([*index* As Integer])

Usage
This event occurs when the user double-clicks a mouse button while the cursor is over the status bar, but not over any panel.

Arguments
- *index*—an **Integer** that uniquely identifies a control in a control array. This argument is not present if the control is not part of a control array.

Private Sub *StatusBarControl*_DragDrop([*index* As Integer ,] *source* As Control, *x* As Single, *y* As Single)

Usage
This event occurs when a drag-and-drop operation is completed by using the **Drag** method with a *DragAction* value of *vbEndDrag*.

> **Tip**
>
> When using drag-and-drop operations, use the **DragOver** event to determine what the cursor should look like while the cursor moves over the control.

Arguments
- *index*—an **Integer** that uniquely identifies a control in a control array. This argument is not present if the control is not part of a control array.
- *source*—a control object that is the control that is being dragged.

> **Tip**
>
> You can access a property or method from the source control by using source.*property* or source.*method*. You can determine the type of object or control by using the **TypeOf** operator.

- *x*—a **Single** that contains the horizontal location of the mouse pointer.
- *y*—a **Single** that contains the vertical location of the mouse pointer.

Private Sub *StatusBarControl*_DragOver([*index* As Integer ,] *source* As Control, *x* As Single, *y* As Single, *state* As Integer)

Usage   This event occurs while a drag operation is in progress and the cursor is moved over the control.

Tip

*When using drag-and-drop operations, use the **DragOver** event to determine what the cursor should look like while the cursor moves over the control. When **state** is **0**, you can change the cursor to a No Drop (vbNoDrop) cursor or highlight the field that the cursor is near. When **state** is **1**, you can undo the changes you made when the **state** was **0**.*

Arguments
- *index*—an **Integer** that uniquely identifies a control in a control array. This argument is not present if the control is not part of a control array.
- *source*—a control object that is the control that is being dragged.

Tip

*You can access a property or method from the source control by using **source**.property or **source**.method. You can determine the type of object or control by using the **TypeOf** operator.*

- *x*—a **Single** that contains the horizontal location of the mouse pointer.
- *y*—a **Single** that contains the vertical location of the mouse pointer.
- *state*—an **Integer** that indicates the state of the object being dragged (see Table S-78).

state Name	Value	Description
vbEnter	0	The dragged object is entering range of the control.
vbLeave	1	The dragged object is leaving range of the control.
vbOver	2	The dragged object has moved from one position over the control to another.

Table S-78: *state* values.

Private Sub *StatusBarBoxControl*_MouseDown([*index* As Integer ,] *button* As Integer, *shift* As Single, *x* As Single, *y* As Single)

Usage   This event occurs when a mouse button was pressed while the cursor is over the control.

Arguments
- *index*—an **Integer** that uniquely identifies a control in a control array (see Table S-79). This argument is not present if the control is not part of a control array.

- *button*—an **Integer** that contains information about the mouse buttons that were pressed. Only one button will be indicated when this event occurs.

button Name	Value	Description
vbLeftButton	1	The left button was pressed.
vbRightButton	2	The right button was pressed.
vbMiddleButton	4	The middle button was pressed.

Table S-79: *button* values.

- *shift*—an **Integer** that contains information about the Shift and Alt keys that were pushed when the mouse button was pressed (see Table S-80). These values can be added together if more than one key was down. For instance, a value of **5** would mean that the Shift and Alt keys were both down when the mouse button was pressed.

shift Name	Value	Description
vbShiftMask	1	The Shift key was pressed.
vbCtrlMask	2	The Ctrl key was pressed.
vbAltMask	4	The Alt key was pressed.

Table S-80: *shift* values.

- *x*—a **Single** that contains the horizontal location of the mouse pointer.
- *y*—a **Single** that contains the vertical location of the mouse pointer.

Private Sub *StatusBarControl*_MouseMove ([*index* As Integer ,] *button* As Integer, *shift* As Single, *x* As Single, *y* As Single)

Usage — This event occurs while the cursor is moved over the control.

Arguments
- *index*—an **Integer** that uniquely identifies a control in a control array. This argument is not present if the control is not part of a control array.
- *button*—an **Integer** that contains information about the mouse buttons that were pressed (see Table S-81). These values can be added together if more than one button was pushed. For instance, a value of **3** means that both the left and right buttons were pressed. A value of **0** means that no buttons were pressed.

button Name	Value	Description
vbLeftButton	1	The left button was pressed.
vbRightButton	2	The right button was pressed.
vbMiddleButton	4	The middle button was pressed.

Table S-81: *button* values.

- *shift*—an **Integer** that contains information about the Shift and Alt keys that were pushed when the mouse button was pressed (see Table S-82). For instance, a value of **5** would mean that the Shift and Alt keys were both down when the mouse button was pressed. A value of **0** means that none of these keys were pressed.

shift Name	Value	Description
vbShiftMask	1	The Shift key was pressed.
vbCtrlMask	2	The Ctrl key was pressed.
vbAltMask	4	The Alt key was pressed.

Table S-82: *shift* values.

- *x*—a **Single** that contains the horizontal location of the mouse pointer.
- *y*—a **Single** that contains the vertical location of the mouse pointer.

Private Sub *StatusBarBoxControl*_MouseUp([*index* As Integer ,] *button* As Integer, *shift* As Single, *x* As Single, *y* As Single)

Usage   This event occurs when a mouse button is released while the cursor is over the control.

Arguments
- *index*—an **Integer** that uniquely identify a control in a control array. This argument is not present if the control is not part of a control array.
- *button*—an **Integer** that contains information about the mouse buttons that were released (see Table S-83). Only one of these values will be present.

button Name	Value	Description
vbLeftButton	1	The left button was released.
vbRightButton	2	The right button was released.
vbMiddleButton	4	The middle button was released.

Table S-83: *button* values.

- *shift*—an **Integer** that contains information about the Shift and Alt keys that were pushed when the mouse button was released (see Table S-84). These values can be added together if more than one key was down. For instance, a value of **5** would mean that the Shift and Alt keys were both down when the mouse button was released. A value of **0** means that none of these keys were pressed.

shift Name	Value	Description
vbShiftMask	1	The Shift key was pressed.
vbCtrlMask	2	The Ctrl key was pressed.
vbAltMask	4	The Alt key was pressed.

Table S-84: *shift* values.

- *x*—a **Single** that contains the horizontal location of the mouse pointer.
- *y*—a **Single** that contains the vertical location of the mouse pointer.

Private Sub *StatusBarControl_OLECompleteDrag*([*index* As Integer ,] *effect* As Long)

Usage — This event tells the source control the results of an OLE drag-and-drop operation. This is the final event to occur in the series of actions that make up an OLE drag-and-drop operation.

Arguments
- *index*—an **Integer** that uniquely identifies a control in a control array. This argument is not present if the control is not part of a control array.
- *effect*—a **Long** that returns the status of the OLE drag-and-drop operation (see Table S-85).

effect Name	Value	Description
vbDropEffectNone	0	The operation was canceled or the target control can't accept the drop operation.
vbDropEffectCopy	1	The operation copied data from the source control to the target control. The original data is unchanged.
vbDropEffectMove	2	The operation results in a link from the original data to the target control.

Table S-85: *effect* values.

Private Sub *StatusBarControl_OLEDragDrop*([*index* As Integer ,] *data* As DataObject, *effect* As Long, *button* As Integer, *shift* As Single, *x* As Single, *y* As Single)

Usage — This event tells the source control the results of an OLE drag-and-drop operation. This is the final event to occur in the series of actions that make up an OLE drag-and-drop operation.

Arguments
- *index*—an **Integer** that uniquely identifies a control in a control array. This argument is not present if the control is not part of a control array.
- *data*—a **DataObject** that contains the formats that the source control will provide. If the data is not contained in the **DataObject**, then it can be retrieved with the **GetData** method.
- *effect*—a **Long** that returns the status of the OLE drag-and-drop operation (see Table S-86).

effect Name	Value	Description
vbDropEffectNone	0	The operation was canceled or the target control can't accept the drop operation.
vbDropEffectCopy	1	The operation copied data from the source control to the target control. The original data is unchanged.
vbDropEffectMove	2	The operation results in a link from the original data to the target control.

Table S-86: *effect* values.

- *button*—an **Integer** that contains information about the mouse buttons that were pressed (see Table S-87). These values can be added together if more than one button was pushed. For instance, a value of **3** means that both the left and right buttons were pressed. A value of **0** means that no buttons were pressed.

button Name	Value	Description
vbLeftButton	1	The left button was pressed.
vbRightButton	2	The right button was pressed.
vbMiddleButton	4	The middle button was pressed.

Table S-87: *button* values.

- *shift*—an **Integer** that contains information about the Shift and Alt keys that were pushed when the mouse button was released (see Table S-88). These values can be added together if more than one key was down. For instance, a value of **5** would mean that the Shift and Alt keys were both down when the mouse button was released. A value of **0** means that none of these keys were pressed.

shift Name	Value	Description
vbShiftMask	1	The Shift key was pressed.
vbCtrlMask	2	The Ctrl key was pressed.
vbAltMask	4	The Alt key was pressed.

Table S-88: *shift* values.

- *x*—a **Single** that contains the horizontal location of the mouse pointer.
- *y*—a **Single** that contains the vertical location of the mouse pointer.

Private Sub *StatusBarControl_OLEDragOver*([*index* As Integer ,] *data* As DataObject, *effect* As Long, *button* As Integer, *shift* As Single, *x* As Single, *y* As Single, *state* As Integer)

Usage — This event happens when an OLE drag-and-drop operation is in progress.

Arguments
- *index*—an **Integer** that uniquely identifies a control in a control array. This argument is not present if the control is not part of a control array.
- *data*—a **DataObject** that contains the formats that the source control will provide. If the data is not contained in the **DataObject**, then it can be retrieved with the **GetData** method.
- *effect*—a **Long** that returns the status of the OLE drag-and-drop operation (see Table S-89).

effect Name	Value	Description
vbDropEffectNone	0	The operation was canceled or the target control can't accept the drop operation.
vbDropEffectCopy	1	The operation copied data from the source control to the target control. The original data is unchanged.
vbDropEffectMove	2	The operation results in a link from the original data to the target control.

Table S-89: *effect* values.

- *button*—an **Integer** that contains information about the mouse buttons that were pressed (see Table S-90). These values can be added together if more than one button was pushed. For instance, a value of **3** means that both the left and right buttons were pressed. A value of **0** means that no buttons were pressed.

button Name	Value	Description
vbLeftButton	1	The left button was pressed.
vbRightButton	2	The right button was pressed.
vbMiddleButton	4	The middle button was pressed.

Table S-90: *button* values.

- *shift*—an **Integer** that contains information about the Shift and Alt keys that were pushed when the mouse button was released (see Table S-91). These values can be added together if more than one key was down. For instance, a value of **5** would mean that the Shift and Alt keys were both down when the mouse button was released. A value of **0** means that none of these keys were pressed.

shift Name	Value	Description
vbShiftMask	1	The Shift key was pressed.
vbCtrlMask	2	The Ctrl key was pressed.
vbAltMask	4	The Alt key was pressed.

Table S-91: *shift* values.

- *x*—a **Single** that contains the horizontal location of the mouse pointer.
- *y*—a **Single** that contains the vertical location of the mouse pointer.
- *state*—an **Integer** that indicates the state of the object being dragged (see Table S-92).

state Name	Value	Description
vbEnter	0	The dragged object is entering range of the control.
vbLeave	1	The dragged object is leaving range of the control.
vbOver	2	The dragged object has moved from one position over the control to another.

Table S-92: *state* values.

Private Sub *StatusBarControl*_OLEGiveFeedback ([*index* As Integer ,] *effect* As Long)

Usage This event tells the source control what is happening while the OLE drag-and-drop operation is in progress. This event occurs after the **OLEDragOver** event.

Tip

You may want to use this event to change the cursor to reflect what can happen in the remote object.

Arguments
- *index*—an **Integer** that uniquely identifies a control in a control array. This argument is not present if the control is not part of a control array.
- *effect*—a **Long** that returns the status of the OLE drag-and-drop operation (see Table S-93).

effect Name	Value	Description
vbDropEffectNone	0	The operation was canceled or the target control can't accept the drop operation.
vbDropEffectCopy	1	The operation copied data from the source control to the target control. The original data is unchanged.
vbDropEffectMove	2	The operation results in a link from the original data to the target control.
vbDropEffectScroll	&H80000000	The target control is about to scroll or is scrolling. This value may be added to the other *effect* values.

Table S-93: *effect* values.

Private Sub *StatusBarControl*_OLESetData([*index* As Integer ,] *data* As DataObject, *DataFormat* As Integer)

Usage This event happens in response to the target object performing a **GetData** method on *data*. This routine will respond by using the **SetData** method with the desired data using the **DataObject** *data*.

Arguments
- *index*—an **Integer** that uniquely identifies a control in a control array. This argument is not present if the control is not part of a control array.
- *data*—a **DataObject** that will contain the data to return to the target object.
- *format*—an **Integer** that contains the format of the data (see Table S-94).

format Name	Value	Description
vbCFText	1	Text (.TXT files)
vbCFBitmap	2	Bitmap (.BMP files)
vbCFMetafile	3	Metafile (.WMF files)
vbCFEDIB	8	Device independent bitmap (DIB)
vbCFPallette	9	Color palette
vbCFEMetafile	14	Enhanced metafile (.EMF files)
vbCFFiles	15	List of files
vbCFRTF	-16639	Rich Text Format (.RTF files)

Table S-94: *format* values.

Private Sub *StatusBarControl*_OLEStartDrag ([*index* As Integer ,] *data* As DataObject, *AllowedEffects* As Long)

Usage   This event start an OLE drag-and-drop operation.

Arguments
- *index*—an **Integer** that uniquely identifies a control in a control array. This argument is not present if the control is not part of a control array.
- *data*—a **DataObject** that will contain the formats that the source object is willing to provide to the target object. It may optionally contain the data to transfer.
- *AllowedEffects*—a **Long** that contains the effects that the target object can request from the source object (see Table S-95). The *AllowedEffects* can be added together if the source object supports more than one effect. Note that the target object can always use the *vbDropEffectNone* effect.

AllowedEffects Name	Value	Description
vbDropEffectNone	0	The target can't copy the data.
vbDropEffectCopy	1	The target can copy the data, and the source will keep the data unchanged.
vbDropEffectMove	2	The target can copy the data, and the source will delete the data.

Table S-95: *AllowedEffects* values.

Private Sub *StatusBarControl*_PanelClick([*index* As Integer ,] ByVal *panel* As Panel)

Usage   This event occurs when the user clicks a mouse button while the cursor is over a panel object on the status bar.

Arguments
- *index*—an **Integer** that uniquely identifies a control in a control array. This argument is not present if the control is not part of a control array.
- *panel*—an object reference to the **Panel** object the user clicked.

Private Sub *StatusBarControl*_PanelDblClick([*index* As Integer ,] ByVal *panel* As Panel)

Usage This event occurs when the user double-clicks a mouse button while the cursor is over a panel object on the status bar.

Arguments
- *index*—an **Integer** that uniquely identifies a control in a control array. This argument is not present if the control is not part of a control array.
- *panel*—an object reference to the **Panel** object the user clicked.

Examples
```
Private Sub Text1_MouseMove(Button As Integer, Shift As Integer, X As Single, Y As Single)
If StatusBar1.Panels(1).Text <> Text1.Text Then
    StatusBar1.Panels(1).Text = Text1.Text
End If
End Sub
```

This routine displays the contents of the text box in the status bar's first panel whenever the mouse passes over the text box.

See Also **Toolbar** (control)

Stop

STATEMENT

CCE, LE, PE, EE

Syntax **Stop**

Usage The **Stop** statement suspends the execution of the program. This is similar to a breakpoint. You can resume execution while running in the Visual Basic development environment. In a complied program, the **Stop** statement will halt execution.

Examples
```
Private Sub Command1_Click()
Stop
MsgBox "Execution resuming..."
End Sub
```

This program uses the **Stop** statement to suspend executing when the command button is pressed. When execution resumes, a message box will display.

See Also **End** (statement)

Str

FUNCTION

CCE, LE, PE, EE

Syntax `svar = Str[$]( number )`

Usage The **Str** function converts the specified number into a string.

> **Tip**
>
> Use the **Format** function for more functionality.

Arguments
- *svar*—a **String** variable.
- *number*—a numeric value containing the value to convert.

Examples
```
Private Sub Command1_Click()
Text2.Text = Str(CDbl(Text1.Text))
End Sub
```

This routine converts the value in the Text1.Text text box and displays the result in the Text2.Text text box.

See Also **Format** (function)

StrComp

FUNCTION

CCE, LE, PE, EE

Syntax `return = StrComp ( string1, string2 [, type ] )`

Usage The **StrComp** function compares one string to another.

Arguments
- *return*—an **Integer** variable containing the result of the comparison (see Table S-96).

return Value	Description
-1	string1 is less than string2
0	string1 is equal to string2
1	string1 is greater than string2
Null	string1 or string2 is Null.

Table S-96: *return* values.

- *string1*—a **String** value.
- *string2*—a **String** value.
- *type*—an **Integer** containing the type of comparison (see Table S-97). If omitted, the value used will default to the **Option Compare** statement, if specified.

type Name	Value	Description
vbBinaryCompare	0	Binary comparison (default).
vbTextCompare	1	Textual comparison.
VbDatabaseCompare	2	Comparison based on information in your database. Applies to Microsoft Access only.

Table S-97: *type* values.

Examples
```
Private Sub Command1_Click()
Select Case StrComp(Text1.Text, Text2.Text, vbTextCompare)
Case -1
   MsgBox "String 1 is less than string 2"
Case 0
   MsgBox "The strings are equal"

Case 1
   MsgBox "String 1 is greater than string 2"
End Select
End Sub
```

This routine compares the value of Text1.Text with Text2.Text and displays the result as a message box.

See Also   **StrConv** (function), **String** (data type)

StrConv

FUNCTION

CCE, LE, PE, EE

Syntax   *svar* = **StrConv**(*value, type*)

Usage   The **StrConv** function converts a string from one form to another.

Arguments
- *svar*—a **String** variable.
- *value*—a **String** value to convert.
- *type*—an **Integer** containing the type of conversion (see Table S-98). Values may be combined where appropriate to do a more complex conversion.

type Name	Value	Description
vbUpperCase	1	Converts all characters in *value* to uppercase.
vbLowerCase	2	Converts all characters in *value* to lowercase.
vbProperCase	3	Converts the first character in each word in *value* to uppercase, the rest are converted to lowercase.
vbWide	4	Converts single byte characters in *value* to double byte characters (Far East locales).
vbNarrow	8	Converts double byte characters in *value* to single byte characters (Far East locales).
vbKatakana	16	Converts Hiragana characters to Katakana (Japan).
vbHiragana	32	Converts Katakana characters to Hiragana (Japan).
vbUnicode	64	Converts all characters to Unicode.
vbFromUnicode	128	Converts all characters from Unicode.

Table S-98: *type* values.

Examples
```
Private Sub Command1_Click()
Text2.Text = StrConv(Text1.Text, vbProperCase)
End Sub
```

This routine converts the value of Text1.Text into the proper case and saves the result in Text2.Text.

See Also   **StrComp** (function), **String** (data type)

Single

DATA TYPE

CCE, LE, PE, EE

Usage   The **String** data type holds character values. There are two types of strings, those declared with a fixed length and those declared to have a variable length.

A fixed-length **String** occupies the number of bytes of storage specified in the declaration. The maximum size of a fixed-length string is about 65,400 characters.

A variable-length **String** variable occupies 10 bytes of storage plus the number of characters in the string. The maximum length of a string is approximately 2 billion characters.

See Also   **Byte** (data type), **CByte** (function), **CInt** (function), **CLng** (function), **CStr** (function), **Dim** (statement), **Double** (data type), **Format** (function), **Integer** (data type), **IsNumeric** (function), **Long** (data type), **Variant** (data type)

String

FUNCTION

CCE, LE, PE, EE

Syntax svar = **String** [$](number, character)

Usage The **String** function returns a string with the specified number of the specified character.

Arguments
- *svar*—a **String** variable.
- *number*—a **Long** value containing the number of the characters to return.
- *character*—a **Variant** containing the character to repeat. If the integer value of the character is greater than 255, then the value *character* **Mod** 256 will be used.

Examples
```
Private Sub Command1_Click()
Dim s As String
s = String(128, "@")
MsgBox "The length of s is " & Format(Len(s))
End Sub
```

This routine creates a string of 128 at signs (@) and saves it in the variable *s*. Then it displays the length of *s* in a message box.

See Also **Space** (function)

Sub

STATEMENT

CCE, LE, PE, EE

Syntax
```
[ Public | Private | Friend ] [ Static ] Sub name ( [ arg ] [, arg ] . . . [, arg ] )
    [ list of statements ]
    [ Exit Sub ]
    [ list of statements ]
End Sub
```

Usage The **Sub** statement defines a subroutine that performs a task and returns to the caller. The arguments are variables that will be passed to the subroutine when it is called.

The **Exit Sub** statement can leave the function at any time. The **End Sub** statement marks the end of the function. Executing either statement will cause the function to return back to where it was called.

Events in Visual Basic use the **Sub** statement to define the arguments that will be passed to the main program.

Arguments
- **Public**—an optional keyword indicating that the function can be called from any module in the program.
- **Private**—an optional keyword indicating that the function can be only called by other routines in the same module.
- **Friend**—an optional keyword indicating that the function can be called from any module in the program, but it can't be called by the controller of an instance of the object. This argument applies to class modules only.
- **Static**—an optional keyword indicating that the variables declared inside the function are preserved from one call to the next.
- *name*—a Visual Basic identifier that contains the name of the function.
- *arg*—an argument that is passed to the function:

  ```
  [ Optional ] [ ByVal | ByRef ] [ ParamArray ] AName [ () ] [ As type ] [ = value ]
  ```

Optional	an optional keyword meaning that the argument is optional and need not be passed to the function. Once an argument is declared to be optional, all arguments that follow must be declared as optional.
ByVal	an optional keyword meaning that the argument is passed by value to the event. This event is free to change the contents of the argument and the calling object will not see the changes.
ByRef	an optional keyword meaning that the argument is passed by reference to the event. Any changes to the argument in the calling control will be seen by the calling object.
ParamArray	an optional keyword meaning that the function can receive an unspecified number of arguments of type **Variant** starting at this position. This must be the last argument in the function declaration and can't be used with **Optional**, **ByVal**, or **ByRef**.
AName	the formal argument being passed to the event.
[()]	if present, indicates that the argument is an array.
type	a valid Visual Basic type: **Byte, Boolean, Currency, Date, Double, Integer, Long, Single, String, Object,** or **Variant**. If the argument is not **Optional**, then specific object types and user-defined types may be used.
value	provides a default value for an argument that was marked as **Optional**. Arguments of type **Object** can only be assigned a value of **Nothing**.

- *type*—a valid Visual Basic type: **Byte, Boolean, Currency, Date, Double, Integer, Long, Single, String, Object,** or **Variant**.

See Also Function (statement)

Switch

FUNCTION

CCE, LE, PE, EE

Syntax `var = Switch ( expr, value [,expr, value ] . . .)`

Usage The **Switch** function contains a series of expression and value pairs. The value corresponding to the first **True** expression is returned. If no **True** values are found for *expr*, a **Null** value is returned.

> **Tip**
>
> To prevent this function from returning a **Null** value, use **True** as the last expression.

Arguments
- *var*—a **Variant** variable.
- *expr*—a **Variant** value that is either **True** or **False**. A value of **0** is considered **False** while a non-zero value is considered **True**.
- *value*—a **Variant** containing a value to return if *expr* is **True**.

Examples
```
Private Sub Command1_Click()
Dim d As Double
If IsNumeric(Text1.Text) Then
    d = CDbl(Text1.Text)
    MsgBox Switch(d < 0, "Value is negative", d < 100, "Value is less than 100",
    True, "Value is greater than 100")
End If
End Sub
```

This routine verifies that the contents of Text1.Text is numeric and then displays a message box describing the value. Note that while the last expression is **True**, its corresponding value will be returned if all of the other expressions are **False**.

See Also IIF (function)

SYD

FUNCTION

CCE, LE, PE, EE

Syntax `depreciation = SYD ( cost, salvage, life, period )`

Usage The **SYD** function returns the sum of years' digits depreciation for an asset.

Arguments
- *depreciation*—a **Double** value containing the depreciation.
- *cost*—a **Double** value containing the initial cost of the asset.
- *salvage*—a **Double** value containing the salvage value of the asset.
- *life*—an **Double** value specifying the useful life of the asset.
- *period*—a **Double** value specifying the period for which the depreciation is to be computed.

Examples

```
Private Sub Command1_Click()
Dim period As Double
Dim sum As Double
Dim temp As Double
Form1.Cls
Form1.Print
Form1.Print "Cost is", Format(1000, "currency")
Form1.Print "Salvage value is ", Format(100, "currency")
Form1.Print "Useful life is", Format(5); " years"
Form1.Print
For period = 1 To 5
    temp = SYD(1000, 100, 5, period)
    sum = sum + temp
    Form1.Print "Year "; period; " depreciation is ", Format(temp, "currency")
Next period
Form1.Print
Form1.Print "Total depreciation is ", Format(sum, "currency")
End Sub
```

This routine computes the sum of years' digits depreciation for an asset that cost $1,000 with a salvage value of $100 over a five year period. I use Form1's Print method to display this information and then start a For Next loop for each year of the asset's useful life. Inside the loop, I display the depreciation for each year and add the depreciation to the sum. After the loop finishes, I display the total depreciation.

See Also DDB (function) FV (function), IPmt (function), IRR (function), MIRR (function), NPer (function), NPV (function), PMT (function), PPmt (function), PV (function), Rate (function), SLN (function)

SysInfo

CONTROL

PE, EE

Usage The **SysInfo** control is an ActiveX control that provides a set of properties and events to interact with the operating system.

Properties
- *SysInfoControl*.**ACStatus**—a **Long** that contains the suggested value for the background color of the control (see Table S-99).

ACStatus Value	Description
0	The system is using battery power.
1	The system is using AC power.
255	The power status in unknown.

Table S-99: ACStatus values.

- *SysInfoControl*.**BatteryFullTime**—a **Long** value containing the number of seconds that a battery should last on a full charge. A value of **-1** means that the information is not available.

- *SysInfoControl*.**BatteryLifePercentFull**—an **Integer** value containing the percentage of charge in remaining in the battery. This value can range from **0** to **100** percent. A value of **255** means that the information is not available.
- *SysInfoControl*.**BatteryLifeTime**—a **Long** value containing the number of seconds remaining in the life of the battery. A value of **-1** means that the information is not available.
- *SysInfoControl*.**BatteryStatus**—an **Integer** containing the battery's status (see Table S-100).

BatteryStatus Value	Description
1	Battery charge is high.
2	Battery charge is low.
4	Battery charge is critical.
8	Battery is charging.
128	The system doesn't have a battery.
255	Battery information is not available.

Table S-100: BatteryStatus values.

- *SysInfoControl*.**Index**—an **Integer** that uniquely identifies a control in a control array.
- *SysInfoControl*.**Name**—a **String** that contains the name of the control that will reference the control in a Visual Basic program. This property is read only at run time.
- *SysInfoControl*.**Object**—an object that contains a reference to the *SysInfoControl* object.
- *SysInfoControl*.**OSBuild**—an **Integer** containing the operating system build level.
- *SysInfoControl*.**OSPlatform**—an **Integer** containing the operating system (see Table S-101).

OSPlatform Value	Description
0	Win32s
1	Windows 95
2	Windows NT

Table S-101: OSPlatform values.

- *SysInfoControl*.**Parent**—an object that contains a reference to the **Form**, **Frame,** or other container that contains this control.
- *SysInfoControl*.**ScrollBarSize**—a **Single** value containing the width of a scroll bar in twips.
- *SysInfoControl*.**Tag**—a **String** that can hold programmer specific information. This property is not used by Visual Basic.
- *SysInfoControl*.**WorkAreaHeight**—a **Single** containing the height of the screen in twips after adjusting for the Windows Taskbar.
- *SysInfoControl*.**WorkAreaLeft**—a **Single** containing the left edge of the screen in twips after adjusting for the Windows Taskbar.
- *SysInfoControl*.**WorkAreaTop**—a **Single** containing the top edge of the screen in twips after adjusting for the Windows Taskbar.
- *SysInfoControl*.**WorkAreaWidth**—a **Single** containing the width of the screen in twips after adjusting for the Windows Taskbar.

SysInfo • **957**

Events **Private Sub *SysInfoControl*_ConfigChangeCancelled ([*index* As Integer])**

Usage This event occurs when the operating system cancels a proposed configuration change. The original request was made through the **QueryChangeConfig** event.

Arguments
- *index*—an **Integer** that uniquely identifies a control in a control array. This argument is not present if the control is not part of a control array.

Private Sub *SysInfoControl*_ConfigChanged ([*index* As Integer ,] ByVal *oldconfignum* As Long, ByVal *newconfignum* As Long)

Usage This event occurs when the hardware profile has been changed on the system.

Arguments
- *index*—an **Integer** that uniquely identifies a control in a control array. This argument is not present if the control is not part of a control array.
- *oldconfignum*—a **Long** value containing the key in the Windows Registry for the old configuration.
- *newconfignum*—a **Long** value containing the key in the Windows Registry for the new configuration.

Private Sub *SysInfoControl*_DeviceArrival ([*index* As Integer ,] ByVal *devicetype* As Long, ByVal *deviceid* As Long, ByVal *devicetype* As Long, ByVal *devicename* As String, ByVal *devicedata* As Long)

Usage This event occurs when a new device is added to the system.

Arguments
- *index*—an **Integer** that uniquely identifies a control in a control array. This argument is not present if the control is not part of a control array.
- *devicetype*—a **Long** value containing the type of device added to the system (see Table S-102).

devicetype Name	Value	Description
DeviceTypeOEM	0	OEM-defined device type
DeviceTypeDevNode	1	Devnode number (Windows 95)
DeviceTypeVolume	2	Logical disk volume
DeviceTypePort	3	Serial or parallel port
DeviceTypeNet	4	Network resource

Table S-102: *devicetype values.*

- *deviceid*—a **Long** value identifying the device (see Table S-103).

devicetype Setting	deviceid Setting
DeviceTypeOEM	dbco_identifier
DeviceTypeDevNode	dbcd_devnode
DeviceTypeVolume	dbcv_unitmask
DeviceTypePort	**Null**
DeviceTypeNet	dbcn_resource

Table S-103: *deviceid values.*

- *devicename*—a **String** containing the name of the device (see Table S-104).

devicetype Setting	devicename Setting
DeviceTypeOEM	Null
DeviceTypeDevNode	**Null**
DeviceTypeVolume	Null
DeviceTypePort	dbcp_name
DeviceTypeNet	**Null**

Table S-104: *devicename values.*

- *devicedata*—a **Long** value with additional information for the device (see Table S-105).

devicetype Setting	devicedata Setting
DeviceTypeOEM	dbco_suppfunc
DeviceTypeDevNode	**Null**
DeviceTypeVolume	dbcv_flags
DeviceTypePort	**Null**
DeviceTypeNet	dbcn_flags

Table S-105: *devicedata values.*

Private Sub *SysInfoControl*_DeviceOtherEvent ([*index* As Integer ,] ByVal *devicetype* As Long, ByVal *eventname* As String, ByVal *datapointer* As Long)

Usage — This event occurs when an event occurs that is not covered by the standard events.

Arguments
- *index*—an **Integer** that uniquely identifies a control in a control array. This argument is not present if the control is not part of a control array.
  - *devicetype*—a **Long** value containing the type of device added to the system (see Table S-106).

SysInfo • 959

devicetype Name	Value	Description
DeviceTypeOEM	0	OEM-defined device type
DeviceTypeDevNode	1	Devnode number (Windows 95)
DeviceTypeVolume	2	Logical disk volume
DeviceTypePort	3	Serial or parallel port
DeviceTypeNet	4	Network resource

Table S-106: *devicetype values.*

- *eventname*—a **String** value containing the name of the event.
- *datapointer*—a **Long** containing a pointer to additional device specific information.

Private Sub *SysInfoControl*_**DeviceQueryRemove** ([*index* **As Integer** ,] **ByVal** *devicetype* **As Long, ByVal** *deviceid* **As Long, ByVal** *devicetype* **As Long, ByVal** *devicename* **As String, ByVal** *devicedata* **As Long,** *cancel* **As Boolean**)

Usage   This event occurs when a device is about to be removed from the system. You can cancel the removal by setting *cancel* to **True**.

Note

This event only occurs if the process removing the device sends a notification.

Arguments
- *index*—an **Integer** that uniquely identifies a control in a control array. This argument is not present if the control is not part of a control array.
- *devicetype*—a **Long** value containing the type of device added to the system (see Table S-107).

devicetype Name	Value	Description
DeviceTypeOEM	0	OEM-defined device type
DeviceTypeDevNode	1	Devnode number (Windows 95)
DeviceTypeVolume	2	Logical disk volume
DeviceTypePort	3	Serial or parallel port
DeviceTypeNet	4	Network resource

Table S-107: *devicetype values.*

- *deviceid*—a **Long** value identifying the device (see Table S-108).

devicetype Setting	deviceid Setting
DeviceTypeOEM	dbco_identifier
DeviceTypeDevNode	dbcd_devnode
DeviceTypeVolume	dbcv_unitmask
DeviceTypePort	**Null**
DeviceTypeNet	dbcn_resource

Table S-108: *deviceid values.*

- *devicename*—a **String** containing the name of the device (see Table S-109).

devicetype Setting	*devicename* Setting
DeviceTypeOEM	Null
DeviceTypeDevNode	**Null**
DeviceTypeVolume	Null
DeviceTypePort	dbcp_name
DeviceTypeNet	**Null**

Table S-109: *devicename values.*

- *devicedata*—a **Long** value with additional information for the device (see Table S-110).

devicetype Setting	*devicedata* Setting
DeviceTypeOEM	dbco_suppfunc
DeviceTypeDevNode	**Null**
DeviceTypeVolume	dbcv_flags
DeviceTypePort	**Null**
DeviceTypeNet	dbcn_flags

Table S-110: *devicedata values.*

- *cancel*—a **Boolean** value when set to **True** means that the device shouldn't be removed from the system. **False** means that the device can be removed (default).

Private Sub *SysInfoControl*_DeviceQueryRemoveFailed ([*index* As Integer ,] ByVal *devicetype* As Long, ByVal *deviceid* As Long, ByVal *devicetype* As Long, ByVal *devicename* As String, ByVal *devicedata* As Long)

Usage — This event occurs when a program responds to the **DeviceQueryRemoveFailed** with *cancel* = **True**.

Arguments
- *index*—an **Integer** that uniquely identifies a control in a control array. This argument is not present if the control is not part of a control array.
- *devicetype*—a **Long** value containing the type of device added to the system (see Table S-111).

devicetype Name	Value	Description
DeviceTypeOEM	0	OEM-defined device type
DeviceTypeDevNode	1	Devnode number (Windows 95)
DeviceTypeVolume	2	Logical disk volume
DeviceTypePort	3	Serial or parallel port
DeviceTypeNet	4	Network resource

Table S-111: *devicetype values.*

- *deviceid*—a **Long** value identifying the device (see Table S-112).

devicetype Setting	*deviceid* Setting
DeviceTypeOEM	dbco_identifier
DeviceTypeDevNode	dbcd_devnode
DeviceTypeVolume	dbcv_unitmask
DeviceTypePort	**Null**
DeviceTypeNet	dbcn_resource

Table S-112: deviceid values.

- *devicename*—a **String** containing the name of the device (see Table S-113).

devicetype Setting	*devicename* Setting
DeviceTypeOEM	Null
DeviceTypeDevNode	**Null**
DeviceTypeVolume	Null
DeviceTypePort	dbcp_name
DeviceTypeNet	**Null**

Table S-113: devicename values.

- *devicedata*—a **Long** value with additional information for the device (see Table S-114).

devicetype Setting	*devicedata* Setting
DeviceTypeOEM	dbco_suppfunc
DeviceTypeDevNode	**Null**
DeviceTypeVolume	dbcv_flags
DeviceTypePort	**Null**
DeviceTypeNet	dbcn_flags

Table S-114: devicedata values.

Private Sub *SysInfoControl*_DeviceRemoveComplete ([*index* As Integer ,] ByVal *devicetype* As Long, ByVal *deviceid* As Long, ByVal *devicetype* As Long, ByVal *devicename* As String, ByVal *devicedata* As Long)

Usage This event occurs after a device has been removed.

Arguments
- *index*—an **Integer** that uniquely identifies a control in a control array. This argument is not present if the control is not part of a control array.
- *devicetype*—a **Long** value containing the type of device added to the system (see Table S-115).

devicetype Name	Value	Description
DeviceTypeOEM	0	OEM-defined device type
DeviceTypeDevNode	1	Devnode number (Windows 95)
DeviceTypeVolume	2	Logical disk volume
DeviceTypePort	3	Serial or parallel port
DeviceTypeNet	4	Network resource

Table S-115: *devicetype values*.

- *deviceid*—a **Long** value identifying the device (see Table S-116).

devicetype Setting	*deviceid* Setting
DeviceTypeOEM	dbco_identifier
DeviceTypeDevNode	dbcd_devnode
DeviceTypeVolume	dbcv_unitmask
DeviceTypePort	**Null**
DeviceTypeNet	dbcn_resource

Table S-116: *deviceid values*.

- *devicename*—a **String** containing the name of the device (see Table S-117).

devicetype Setting	*devicename* Setting
DeviceTypeOEM	Null
DeviceTypeDevNode	**Null**
DeviceTypeVolume	Null
DeviceTypePort	dbcp_name
DeviceTypeNet	**Null**

Table S-117: *devicename values*.

- *devicedata*—a **Long** value with additional information for the device (see Table S-118).

devicetype Setting	*devicedata* Setting
DeviceTypeOEM	dbco_suppfunc
DeviceTypeDevNode	**Null**
DeviceTypeVolume	dbcv_flags
DeviceTypePort	**Null**
DeviceTypeNet	dbcn_flags

Table S-118: *devicedata values*.

Private Sub *SysInfoControl*_DeviceRemovePending ([*index* As Integer ,] ByVal *devicetype* As Long, ByVal *deviceid* As Long, ByVal *devicetype* As Long, ByVal *devicename* As String, ByVal *devicedata* As Long)

Usage
: This event occurs after all programs have given permission to remove a device via the **DeviceQueryRemove** event and before the device is removed.

Arguments
: - *index*—an **Integer** that uniquely identifies a control in a control array. This argument is not present if the control is not part of a control array.
  - *devicetype*—a **Long** value containing the type of device added to the system (see Table S-119).

devicetype Name	Value	Description
DeviceTypeOEM	0	OEM-defined device type
DeviceTypeDevNode	1	Devnode number (Windows 95)
DeviceTypeVolume	2	Logical disk volume
DeviceTypePort	3	Serial or parallel port
DeviceTypeNet	4	Network resource

Table S-119: *devicetype values.*

- *deviceid*—a **Long** value identifying the device (see Table S-120).

devicetype Setting	*deviceid* Setting
DeviceTypeOEM	dbco_identifier
DeviceTypeDevNode	dbcd_devnode
DeviceTypeVolume	dbcv_unitmask
DeviceTypePort	**Null**
DeviceTypeNet	dbcn_resource

Table S-120: *deviceid values.*

- *devicename*—a **String** containing the name of the device (see Table S-121).

devicetype Setting	*devicename* Setting
DeviceTypeOEM	Null
DeviceTypeDevNode	**Null**
DeviceTypeVolume	Null
DeviceTypePort	dbcp_name
DeviceTypeNet	**Null**

Table S-121: *devicename values.*

- *devicedata*—a **Long** value with additional information for the device (see Table S-122).

devicetype Setting	devicedata Setting
DeviceTypeOEM	dbco_suppfunc
DeviceTypeDevNode	**Null**
DeviceTypeVolume	dbcv_flags
DeviceTypePort	**Null**
DeviceTypeNet	dbcn_flags

Table S-122: *devicedata values.*

Private Sub SysInfoControl_DevModeChange ([*index* As Integer ,] ByVal *devicename* As String)

Usage This event occurs when the user changes device mode settings.

Arguments • *index*—an **Integer** that uniquely identifies a control in a control array. This argument is not present if the control is not part of a control array.

• *devicename*—a **String** containing a device name from the Windows Registry.

Private Sub SysInfoControl_DisplayChanged ([*index* As Integer])

Usage This event occurs when the screen resolution is changed.

Arguments • *index*—an **Integer** that uniquely identifies a control in a control array. This argument is not present if the control is not part of a control array.

Private Sub SysInfoControl_PowerQuerySuspend ([*index* As Integer ,] *cancel* As Boolean)

Usage This event occurs when the user wants to enter the suspend state and hold all processing.

Arguments • *index*—an **Integer** that uniquely identifies a control in a control array. This argument is not present if the control is not part of a control array.

• *cancel*—a **Boolean** value when set to **True** means that the system shouldn't enter a suspended state, because your program may be adversely affected. **False** means that the system can enter a suspended state (default).

Private Sub SysInfoControl_PowerResume ([*index* As Integer])

Usage This event occurs when the system comes out of the suspend state and resumes normal processing.

Arguments • *index*—an **Integer** that uniquely identifies a control in a control array. This argument is not present if the control is not part of a control array.

Private Sub SysInfoControl_PowerStatusChanged ([*index* As Integer])

Usage This event occurs when the battery is running low, the power was switched from battery to AC or vice versa, or the battery has completed recharging.

Arguments • *index*—an **Integer** that uniquely identifies a control in a control array. This argument is not present if the control is not part of a control array.

Private Sub SysInfoControl_PowerSuspend ([*index* As Integer])

Usage This event occurs just before the system enters a suspended state.

Arguments • *index*—an **Integer** that uniquely identifies a control in a control array. This argument is not present if the control is not part of a control array.

Private Sub SysInfoControl_QueryChangeConfig ([*index* As Integer ,] *cancel* As Boolean)

Usage This event occurs when the current hardware profile is about to be changed.

Arguments • *index*—an **Integer** that uniquely identifies a control in a control array. This argument is not present if the control is not part of a control array.

• *cancel*—a **Boolean** value when set to **True** means that the system shouldn't change the system configuration, because your program may be adversely affected. **False** means that the system will change the system configuration (default).

Private Sub SysInfoControl_SettingChanged ([*index* As Integer ,] ByVal *item* As Integer)

Usage This event occurs when an application changes a system wide parameter, such as moving or resizing the Windows Taskbar.

Arguments • *index*—an **Integer** that uniquely identifies a control in a control array. This argument is not present if the control is not part of a control array.

• *item*—an **Integer** containing the system parameter information that was changed. This value is the WPARAM from the WM_SETTINGCHANGE and corresponds to a parameter for the Win32 API routine.

Private Sub SysInfoControl_SysColorsChanged ([*index* As Integer])

Usage This event occurs when the system color setting changes.

Arguments • *index*—an **Integer** that uniquely identifies a control in a control array. This argument is not present if the control is not part of a control array.

Private Sub *SysInfoControl*_TimeChanged ([*index* As Integer])

Usage This event occurs whenever the time is changed on the computer. This is useful to determine situations such as when Windows automatically changes to and from daylight savings time.

Arguments *index*—an **Integer** that uniquely identifies a control in a control array. This argument is not present if the control is not part of a control array.

Examples
```
Sub Form_Load()
If SysInfo1.OSPlatform = 0 Then
    Text1.Text = "Running Win32s version " & Format(SysInfo1.OSVersion)
ElseIf SysInfo1.OSPlatform = 1 Then
    Text1.Text = "Running Windows 95 version " & Format(SysInfo1.OSVersion)
ElseIf SysInfo1.OSPlatform = 2 Then
    Text1.Text = "Running Windows NT version " & Format(SysInfo1.OSVersion)
End If
End Sub
```

This routine determines the operating system and the operating system's version by using the **SysInfo** control.

See Also **Screen** (control)

Tab

OBJECT

PE, EE

Usage The **Tab** object is used by the **TabStrip** control to hold information about an individual tab.

Properties
- *TabObject*.**Caption**—a **String** value containing the text to be displayed on the tab button.
- *TabObject*.**Height**—a **Single** that contains the height of the tab.
- *TabObject*.**Image**—a **Variant** that either contains the index number or key value of a **ListImage** object that will be displayed for this tab.
- *TabObject*.**Index**—an **Integer** value containing a unique value to identify the Tab in the **Tabs** collection.
- *TabObject*.**Key**—a **String** value containing a unique value to identify the Tab in the **Tabs** collection.

> **Tip**
>
> Use the **Key** property to identify a value rather than **Index** since the value of **Index** can easily be changed, while the value of **Key** can't.

- *TabObject*.**Left**—a **Single** that contains the distance, measured in twips, between the left edge of the control and the left edge of the control's container.
- *TabObject*.**Selected**—a **Boolean,** when **True**, means that the node object in the **TreeView** control is selected. **False** means that node object is not selected.
- *TabObject*.**Tag**—a **String** that can hold programmer-specific information. This property is not used by Visual Basic.
- *TabObject*.**Top**—a **Single** that contains the distance, measured in twips, between the top edge of the tab and the top edge of the tab's container.
- *TabObject*.**ToolTipText**—a **String** that holds a text value that can be displayed as a **ToolTip** box whenever the cursor is held over the Tab for about one second.
- *TabObject*.**Width**—a **Single** containing the width of the Tab.

See Also **ImageList** (control), **Tabs** (collection), **TabStrip** (control)

TableDef

OBJECT

PE, EE

Usage The **TableDef** object is used by the Microsoft Jet database to hold information about a table.

Properties
- *TableDefObject*.**Attributes**—a **Long** value containing zero or more of the listed attributes in Table T-1.

Attributes Name	Description
dbAttachExclusive	The table is a linked table and is opened for exclusive access.
dbAttachSavePWD	The table is a linked table, and the user id and password will be saved with the connection information.
dbSystemObject	The table is a system table.
dbHiddenObject	The table is hidden.
dbAttachedTable	The table is a linked table from a non-ODBC source.
dbAttachedODBC	The table is a linked table from an ODBC server.

Table T-1: Attributes *values*.

- *TableDefObject*.**ConflictTable**—a **String** value containing the name of the table that will hold conflicts when two replica tables are synchronized.
- *TableDefObject*.**Connect**—a **String** value containing the type of database and any necessary connection information.
- *TableDefObject*. **DateCreated**—a **Date** value containing the date and time the object was created.
- *TableDefObject*.**KeepLocal**—an object created by using the **CreateProperty** method that sets or returns a value that will not be copied when the database is replicated. Opposite of **Replicable**.
- *TableDefObject*.**LastUpdated**—a **Date** value containing the date and time the object was last updated.
- *TableDefObject*.**Name**—a **String** value containing the name of the table. It can be up to 64 characters in length.
- *TableDefObject*.**RecordCount**—a **Long** value containing the number of records in the table. A linked table will have a **RecordCount** of -1.
- *TableDefObject*.**Replicable**—an object created by using the **CreateProperty** method that sets or returns a value that will be copied when the database is replicated. Opposite of **KeepLocal**.
- *TableDefObject*.**ReplicaFilter**—a **Variant** that either contains a **String** containing the criteria for selecting replica records from the full replica table (similar to an SQL Where clause) or a **Boolean** that when **True** means that all records are replicated and when **False** means that no records are replicated.
- *TableDefObject*.**SourceTableName**—a **String** containing the name of the linked table or an empty string for a base table.
- *TableDefObject*.**Updatable**—a **Boolean** value when **True** means that the object can be updated. **False** means that the object can't be updated.
- *TableDefObject*.**ValidationRule**—a **String** containing the criteria (similar to an SQL Where clause) used to validate the data in a record.
- *TableDefObject*.**ValidationText**—a **String** containing the message that will be returned when a validation error occurs.

Methods **field = TableDefObject.CreateField ([name [, type [, size]]])**

Usage This method creates a new field in the index.

Arguments
- *field*—a reference to a new **Field** object.
- *name*—a **String** containing the name of the new field.
- *type*—an **Integer** value describing the type of the field (see Table T-2).

Type Name	Description
dbBigInt	Big integer data type.
dbBinary	Fixed length binary data, up to 255 bytes long.
dbBoolean	Boolean data type.
dbByte	Integer value one byte wide.
dbChar	Fixed-length character string.
dbCurrency	Currency data type.
dbDate	Date/time data type.
dbDecimal	Decimal data type.
dbDouble	Double precision floating point data type.
dbFloat	Floating point data type.
dbGUID	Globally Unique Identifier data type.
dbInteger	16 bit integer data type.
dbLong	32 bit integer data type.
dbLongBinary	Long binary data type.
dbMemo	Memo data type.
dbNumeric	Numeric data type.
dbSingle	Single precision floating point data type.
dbText	Field data type.
dbTime	Time data type.
dbTimeStamp	Time stamp data type.
dbVarBinary	Variable length binary, up to 255 bytes long.

Table T-2: Type *values*.

- *size*—an **Integer** containing the size of the field.

index = TableDefObject.CreateIndex ([name])

Usage This method is used to create a new **Index** object.

Arguments
- *index*—an object variable that will contain the new index object.
- *name*—a **String** containing the name of the index.

property = TableDefObject.CreateProperty ([name] [, [type] [, [value] [, DDL]]])

Usage This method is used to create a user-defined **Property** object.

Arguments
- *property*—an object variable that will contain the new property object.
- *name*—a **String** containing the name of the property. Must begin with a letter and can be followed by letters, numbers, or an underscore ("_").
- *type*—a value selected from Table T-3 below.

Type Name	Description
dbBigInt	Big integer data type.
dbBinary	Fixed length binary data, up to 255 bytes long.
dbBoolean	Boolean data type.
dbByte	Integer value one byte wide.
dbChar	Fixed-length character string.
dbCurrency	Currency data type.
dbDate	Date/time data type.
dbDecimal	Decimal data type.
dbDouble	Double precision floating point data type.
dbFloat	Floating point data type.
dbGUID	Globally Unique Identifier data type.
dbInteger	16 bit integer data type.
dbLong	32 bit integer data type.
dbLongBinary	Long binary data type.
dbMemo	Memo data type.
dbNumeric	Numeric data type.
dbSingle	Single precision floating point data type.
dbText	Field data type.
dbTime	Time data type.
dbTimeStamp	Time stamp data type.
dbVarBinary	Variable-length binary, up to 255 bytes long.

Table T-3: Type *values.*

- *value*—a **Variant** containing the initial value for the property.
- *DDL*—a **Boolean**, when **True**, means that the user cannot change this property value without the *dbSecWriteDef* permission. **False** means that this permission is not required to change the value.

recordset = TableDefObject.OpenRecordset (type [, options] [, lockedits])

Usage This method is used to create a new **RecordSet** object and append it to the **RecordSets** collection.

Arguments
- *recordset*—an object variable that will contain the new **RecordSet** object.
- *type*—a constant from Table T-4 below.

type Name	Description
dbOpenTable	Table type recordset.
dbOpenDynamic	Open a dynamic type recordset (ODBC databases only).
dbOpenDynaset	Open a dynaset type recordset.
dbOpenSnapshot	Open a snapshot type recordset.
dbOpenForwardOnly	Open a forward-only type recordset.

Table T-4: Type *values.*

- *options*—a **Long** containing one or more of the options in Table T-5 below.

options Name	Description
dbAppendOnly	Add new records, but can't delete or edit existing records.
dbConsistent	Allow only consistent updates in Microsoft Jet databases. (Can't be used with *dbInconsistent*).
dbDenyRead	Read access is denied to other users.
dbDenyWrite	Write access is denied to other users.
dbExecDirect	Skip SQLPrepare and run SQLExecDirect for ODBC queries only.
dbInconsistent	Allow inconsistent updates in Microsoft Jet databases. (Can't be used with *dbConsistent*).
dbReadOnly	User can't change records in the database. (Can't be used if *dbReadOnly* is specified in *lockedits*).
dbRunAsync	Run ODBC query asynchronously.
dbSeeChanges	Return error if another user is updating data you are using.
dbSQLPassThrough	Pass SQL query through Microsoft Jet workspace to remote ODBC database.

Table T-5: Options *values.*

- *lockedits*—a **Long** containing one or more of the attributes in Table T-6 below.

lockedits Name	Description
dbOptimistic	Lock the page containing the record you are editing when you use the Update method.
dbOptimisticBatch	Enable batch optimistic updating.
dbOptimisticValue	Enable optimistic updating based on row values.
dbPessimistic	Lock the page containing the record you are editing as soon you use the **Edit** method.
dbReadOnly	User can't change records in the database. (Can't be used if *dbReadOnly* is specified in *options*.)

Table T-6: Lockedits *values.*

TableDefObject.RefreshLink

Usage This method is used to update connection information for a linked table.

See Also **Database** (object), **TableDefs** (collection)

TableDefs

COLLECTION

PE, EE

Usage The **TableDefs** collection is used by Data Access Objects (DAO) to contain information about multiple tables.

Properties ▪ *TableDefsCollection*.**Count**—an **Integer** containing the number of **TableDef** objects in the collection.

Methods *TableDefsCollection*.**Append** *object*

    Usage This method adds a **TableDef** object to the collection.

    Arguments ▪ *object*—a reference to a **TableDef** object to be added to the collection.

TableDefsCollection.**Delete** *objectname*

    Usage This method removes a **TableDef** object from the collection.

    Arguments ▪ *objectname*—a **String** containing the name of the **TableDef** object to be removed from the collection.

TableDefsCollection.**Refresh**

    Usage This method gets a current copy of the **TableDefs** contained in the collection. This is important in a multi-user environment where more than one user may be making changes in the **Databases** collection.

See Also **TableDef** (object)

Tabs

COLLECTION

PE, EE

Usage The **Tabs** collection contains a set of methods to store and retrieve items in a set. The items need not be of the same data type. Items can be retrieved by specifying their relative position within the collection or by a unique key value.

> **Tip**
>
> *To loop through each item in the collection, use the **For Each** statement.*

Properties ▪ *TabsCollection*.**Count**—a **Long** value that contains the number of items in the collection.

▪ *TabsCollection*.**Item** (*index*)—a reference to a **Tab** object in the collection. *Index* is either a numeric value that represents the relative position of the item in the collection or a **String** value that contains the key value of the object.

Methods *Tab = TabsCollection.Add ([index [, key [, caption [, image]]])*

Usage   This method is used to add an item to the **Tabs** collection.

Arguments
- *Tab*—a reference to the newly created **Tab** object.
- *index*—an **Integer** containing the position where the new Tab will be inserted. If omitted, the Tab will be inserted at the end of the collection. This value will be saved in the **Index** property of the new **Tab** object.
- *key*—a **String** that contains a unique value that can be used to reference the newly created Tab object. This value will be saved in the **Key** property of the new **Tab** object.
- *caption*—a **String** value that will be put into the **Caption** property of the **Tab** object.
- *image*—a **Variant** that contains either the index number or key value of a **ListImage** object that will be displayed for this tab.

*TabsCollection.***Clear**

Usage   This method is used to remove all of the objects in the Tabs collection.

*TabsCollection.***Remove** *index*

Usage   This method is used to delete an item specified by *index* from the collection.

Arguments
- *index*—either a numeric value that represents the relative position or a **String** value that contains the key value of the Tab to be deleted from the collection.

See Also   **Tab** (object), **TabStrip** (control)

TabStrip

CONTROL

PE, EE

Usage   The **TabStrip** control is an ActiveX control (part of the Microsoft Windows Common Controls 5.0) that provides a set of tabbed pages. However, the **TabStrip** control can't act as a container.

> **Tip**
>
> Use a Frame control for each tab to act as a container. Set **Visible** to **False** for all frames except for the one associated with the active tab. You can set the **BorderStyle** property to none or **Caption** to an empty string to make it look better.

Properties
- *TabStripControl.***ClientHeight**—a **Single** containing the height of the client area of the control.
- *TabStripControl.***ClientLeft**—a **Single** containing the left coordinate of the client area of the control.
- *TabStripControl.***ClientTop**—a **Single** containing the top coordinate of the client area of the control.

- *TabStripControl*.**ClientWidth**—a **Single** containing the width of the client area of the control.
- *TabStripControl*.**Container**—an object that can be used to set or return the container of the control at run time. This property cannot be set at design time.
- *TabStripControl*.**DataBindings**—a reference to the **DataBindings** collection containing the bindable properties available.
- *TabStripControl*.**DragIcon**—an object that contains the picture value of an icon. At design time, you can specify an icon file that has a file type of .ICO.

> **Tip**
>
> *This value can be created by copying the value from another control's **DragIcon** value, a form's icon, or by using the **LoadPicture** function.*

- *TabStripControl*.**DragMode**—an **Integer** specifying how the control will respond to a drag request (see Table T-7).

> **Tip**
>
> *Setting **DragMode** to vbAutomatic will automatically begin a drag operation when the user clicks on the control. However, the control will not respond to the usual mouse events (**Click**, **DblClick**, **MouseDown**, **MouseMove**, **MouseUp**).*

DragMode Name	Value	Description
vbManual	0	The Drag method must be used to begin a drag drop operation (default value).
vbAutomatic	1	The source control will automatically begin a drag drop operation when the user clicks on the control.

Table T-7: DragMode *values.*

- *TabStripControl*.**Enabled**—a **Boolean** value when **True** means that the control will respond to events. When **False**, the control will not respond to events.
- *TabStripControl*.**Font**—an object that contains information about the character font used by this object.
- *TabStripControl*.**ForeColor**—a **Long** that contains the suggested value for the foreground color of the contained control. This property is read only at run time.
- *TabStripControl*.**Height**—a **Single** that contains the height of the control.
- *TabStripControl*.**HelpContextID**—a **Long** that contains a help file context ID number which references an entry in the help file. When the user presses the F1 key while this control is active, the corresponding entry in the help file will automatically be displayed. A value of zero means that no context number was specified.

> **Tip**
>
> *A help file must be compiled using the Windows Help Compiler available in the Professional and Enterprise editions of Visual Basic.*

- *TabStripControl*.**hWnd**—a **Long** that contains a Windows handle to the control.

> **Tip**
>
> The **hWnd** property is most useful when making calls to Windows API functions. Since this value can change during execution, do not save the value into a variable for later use.

- *TabStripControl*.**ImageList**—a reference to an **ImageList** object that contains the pictures that will be used for the large icon display.
- *TabStripControl*.**Index**—an **Integer** that is used to uniquely identify a control in a control array.
- *TabStripControl*.**Left**—a **Single** that contains the distance, measured in twips, between the left edge of the control and the left edge of the control's container.
- *TabStripControl*.**MouseIcon**—a picture object (a bitmap, icon, or metafile) that will be used as a cursor when the **MousePointer** property is set to 99. Note that Visual Basic does not support color cursors from a .CUR file. A color icon from an .ICO file should be used instead.
- *TabStripControl*.**MousePointer**—an **Integer** that contains the value of the cursor that should be displayed when the cursor is moved over this control (see Table T-8). Use *vbCustom* to display the custom icon stored in the **MouseIcon** property.

Cursor Name	Value	Description
vbDefault	0	Shape determined by the object (default value).
vbArrow	1	Arrow.
vbCrosshair	2	Crosshair.
vbIbeam	3	I beam.
vbIconPointer	4	Square inside a square.
vbSizePointer	5	Four-sided arrow (north, south, east, west).
vbSizeNESW	6	Two-sided arrow (northeast, southwest).
vbSizeNS	7	Two-sided arrow (north, south).
vbSizeNWSE	8	Two-sided arrow (northwest, southeast).
vbSizeWE	9	Two-sided arrow (west, east).
vbUpArrow	10	Single-sided arrow pointing north.
vbHourglass	11	Hourglass.
vbNoDrop	12	No drop.
vbArrowHourglass	13	An arrow and an hourglass.
vbArrowQuestion	14	An arrow and a question mark.
vbSizeAll	15	Size all.
vbCustom	99	Custom icon from the MouseIcon property of this control.

Table T-8: Cursor values.

- *TabStripControl*.**MultiRow**—a **Boolean** value when **True** means that the tab strip may contain more than one row of tabs. **False** means that only one row of tabs is allowed (default).
- *TabStripControl*.**Name**—a **String** that contains the name of the control that will be used to reference the control in a Visual Basic program. This property is read only at run time.
- *TabStripControl*.**Object**—an object that contains a reference to the *TabStripControl* object.
- *TabStripControl*.**OLEDropMode**—an **Integer** value (see Table T-9) that describes how the control will respond to OLE drop operations.

OLEDropMode Name	Value	Description
vbOLEDropNone	0	The control does not accept OLE drops. The cursor is changed to the No Drop cursor (default value).
vbOLEDropManual	1	The control responds to OLE drops under the program's control (manual).
vbOLEDropAutomatic	2	The control automatically accepts OLE drops if it recognizes the format of the data object.

Table T-9: OLEDropMode *values.*

- *TabStripControl.***Parent**—an object that contains a reference to the **Form**, **Frame**, or other container that contains this control.
- *TabStripControl.***SelectedItem**—a reference to the currently selected **Tab** object.
- *TabStripControl.***ShowTips**—a **Boolean**, when **True**, means that the objects in the control may show tool tips. **False** means that the objects can't display tool tips.
- *TabStripControl.***Style**—an **Integer** value containing the style used to draw the tabs (see Table T-10).

Style Name	Value	Description
tabTabs	0	The tabs appear as notebook tabs, and the client area has a three-dimensional border around it (default value).
tabButtons	1	The tabs appear as buttons, and the client area has no border around it.

Table T-10: Style *values.*

- *TabStripControl.***TabFixedHeight**—a **Single** containing the height of each tab in units specified by **ScaleMode**.
- *TabStripControl.***TabFixedWidth**—a **Single** containing the width of each tab in units specified by **ScaleMode** when **TabWidthStyle** is set to *tabFixed*.
- *TabStripControl.***Tabs**—a reference to a **Tabs** collection containing the information to be displayed on each tab.
- *TabStripControl.***TabIndex**—an Integer that is used to determine the order that a user will tab through the objects on a form.
- *TabStripControl.***TabStop**—a **Boolean** value when **True** means that the user can tab to this object. When **False**, this control will be skipped to the next control in the **TabIndex** order.
- *TabStripControl.***TabWidthStyle**—an **Integer** value (see Table T-11) describing how the tabs are displayed.

TabWidthStyle Name	Value	Description
tabJustified	0	Each tab is wide enough to contain its caption. Then the width of all tabs are adjusted so that the row of tabs span the width of the control (default value).
tabNonJustified	1	Each tab is wide enough to contain its caption.
tabFixed	2	Each tab is a fixed width, specified in **TabFixedWidth**.

Table T-11: TabWidthStyle *values.*

- *TabStripControl*.**Tag**—a **String** that can hold programmer-specific information. This property is not used by Visual Basic.
- *TabStripControl*.**ToolTipText**—a **String** that holds a text value that can be displayed as a **ToolTip** box whenever the cursor is held over the control for about one second.
- *TabStripControl*.**Top**—a **Single** that contains the distance, measured in twips, between the top edge of the control and the top edge of the control's container.
- *TabStripControl*.**Visible**—a **Boolean,** when **True**, means that the object is displayed. **False** means that the object is not displayed.
- *TabStripControl*.**WhatsThisHelpID**—a **Long** that contains a help file context ID number that references an entry in the help file. This is used to provide a What's This PopUp help display in response to the What's This button in the upper right corner of the window.
- *TabStripControl*.**Width**—a **Single** that contains the width of the control.

Methods

TabStripControl.**Drag** [*DragAction*]

Usage This method is used to begin, end, or cancel a drag operation.

Arguments
- *DragAction*—an **Integer** that contains a value selected from Table T-12 below.

DragAction Name	Value	Description
vbCancel	0	Cancels any drag operation in progress.
vbBeginDrag	1	Begins a drag operation (default).
vbEndDrag	2	Ends a drag operation and drops *object*.

Table T-12: DragAction *values.*

TabStripControl.**Move** *Left* [, *Top* [, *Width* [, *Height*]]]

Usage This method is used to change the position and the size of the **TabStrip** control. The **ScaleMode** of the **Form** or other container object that holds the **TabStrip** control will determine the units used to specify the coordinates.

Arguments
- *Left*—a **Single** that specifies the new position of the left edge of the control.
- *Top*—a **Single** that specifies the new position of the top edge of the control.
- *Width*—a **Single** that specifies the new width of the control.
- *Height*—a **Single** that specifies the new height of the control.

TabStripControl.**OLEDrag**

Usage This method is used to begin an **OLEDrag** and drop operation. Invoking this method will trigger the **OLEStartDrag** event.

TabStripControl.**Refresh**

Usage This method is used to redraw the contents of the control.

TabStripControl.SetFocus

Usage This method transfers the focus from the form or control that currently has the focus to this control. In order to receive the focus, this control must be enabled and visible.

TabStripControl.ShowWhatsThis

Usage This method displays the ShowWhatsThis help information for this control.

TabStripControl.ZOrder [position]

Usage This method is used to specify the position of the **TabStrip** control relative to the other objects on the form.

Tip

*Note that there are three layers of objects on a form. The back layer is the drawing space that contains the results of the graphical methods, and the middle layer contains graphical objects and **Labels**. The top layer contains non-graphical controls such as the **TabStrip** control. The **ZOrder** method only affects how the objects are arranged within a single layer.*

Arguments
- *position*—an **Integer** that specifies the relative position of this object. A value of 0 means that the control is positioned at the head of the list, a value of 1 means that the control will be placed at the end of the list.

Events

Private Sub TabStripControl_BeforeClick ([index As Integer ,] cancel As Integer)

Usage This event occurs when a new **Tab** object is clicked and before the focus is transferred to the new object.

Tip

Use this event to verify data in one tab's client area before another tab becomes visible.

Arguments
- *index*—an **Integer** that is used to uniquely identify a control in a control array. This argument is not present if the control is not part of a control array.
- *cancel*—an **Integer** value when zero means that the edit is accepted. Any non-zero value means that the edit is canceled.

Private Sub TabStripControl_Click([index As Integer])

Usage This event occurs when the user clicks a mouse button to select an item or selects an item using the keyboard.

Arguments
- *index*—an **Integer** that is used to uniquely identify a control in a control array. This argument is not present if the control is not part of a control array.

Private Sub *TabStripControl*_DragDrop([*index* As Integer ,] *source* As Control, *x* As Single, *y* As Single)

Usage   This event occurs when a drag-and-drop operation is completed by using the Drag method with a *DragAction* value of *vbEndDrag*.

Tip

*When using drag-and-drop operations, use the **DragOver** event to determine what the cursor should look like while the cursor moves over the control.*

Arguments
- *index*—an **Integer** that is used to uniquely identify a control in a control array. This argument is not present if the control is not part of a control array.
- *source*—a control object that is the control that is being dragged.

Tip

You can access a property or method from the source control by using source.*property or* source.*method. You can determine the type of object or control by using the **TypeOf** operator.*

- *x*—a **Single** that contains the horizontal location of the mouse pointer.
- *y*—a **Single** that contains the vertical location of the mouse pointer.

Private Sub *TabStripControl*_DragOver([*index* As Integer ,] *source* As Control, *x* As Single, *y* As Single, *state* As Integer)

Usage   This event occurs while a drag operation is in progress and the cursor is moved over the control.

Tip

*When using drag-and-drop operations, use the **DragOver** event to determine what the cursor should look like while the cursor moves over the control. When* **state** *is 0, you can change the cursor to a no drop (vbNoDrop) cursor or highlight the field that the cursor is near. When* **state** *is 1, you can undo the changes you made when the* **state** *was 0.*

Arguments
- *index*—an **Integer** that is used to uniquely identify a control in a control array. This argument is not present if the control is not part of a control array.
- *source*—a control object that is the control that is being dragged.

Tip

You can access a property or method from the source control by using source.*property or* source.*method. You can determine the type of object or control by using the **TypeOf** operator.*

- *x*—a **Single** that contains the horizontal location of the mouse pointer.
- *y*—a **Single** that contains the vertical location of the mouse pointer.
- *state*—an **Integer** that indicates the state of the object being dragged (see Table T-13).

state Name	Value	Description
vbEnter	0	The dragged object is entering range of the control.
vbLeave	1	The dragged object is leaving range of the control.
vbOver	2	The dragged object has moved from one position over the control to another.

Table T-13: State *values*.

Private Sub *TabStripControl*_GotFocus ([*index* As Integer])

Usage   This event occurs when the control is given focus.

> **Tip**
>
> *You can use this routine to display help or other information in a status bar.*

Arguments   *index*—an **Integer** that is used to uniquely identify a control in a control array. This argument is not present if the control is not part of a control array.

Private Sub *TabStripControl*_KeyDown ([*index* As Integer ,] *keycode* As Integer, *shift* As Single)

Usage   This event occurs when a key is pressed while the control has the focus.

Arguments
- *index*—an **Integer** that is used to uniquely identify a control in a control array. This argument is not present if the control is not part of a control array.
- *keycode*—an **Integer** that contains information about which key was pressed.
- *shift*—an **Integer** that contains information about the Shift and Alt keys that were pressed when the mouse button was pressed (see Table T-14). These values can be added together if more than one key was down. For instance, a value of 5 would mean that the Shift and Alt keys were both down when the mouse button was pressed.

shift Name	Value	Description
vbShiftMask	1	The Shift key was pressed.
vbCtrlMask	2	The Ctrl key was pressed.
vbAltMask	4	The Alt key was pressed.

Table T-14: Shift *values*.

Private Sub *TabStripControl*_KeyPress([*index* As Integer ,] *keychar* As Integer)

Usage This event occurs whenever a key is pressed while the control has the focus.

Arguments
- *index*—an **Integer** that is used to uniquely identify a control in a control array. This argument is not present if the control is not part of a control array.
- *keychar*—an **Integer** that contains the ASCII character that was pressed.

Private Sub *TabStripControl*_KeyUp ([*index* As Integer ,] *keycode* As Integer, *shift* As Single)

Usage This event occurs when a key is released while the control has the focus.

Arguments
- *index*—an **Integer** that is used to uniquely identify a control in a control array. This argument is not present if the control is not part of a control array.
- *keycode*—an **Integer** that contains information about which key was released.
- *shift*—an **Integer** that contains information about the Shift and Alt keys that were pressed when the mouse button was pressed (see Table T-15). These values can be added together if more than one key was down. For instance, a value of 5 would mean that the Shift and Alt keys were both down when the mouse button was pressed.

shift Name	Value	Description
vbShiftMask	1	The Shift key was pressed.
vbCtrlMask	2	The Ctrl key was pressed.
vbAltMask	4	The Alt key was pressed.

Table T-15: Shift *values.*

Private Sub *TabStripControl*_LostFocus ([*index* As Integer])

Usage This event occurs when the control loses focus.

Tip

This routine is useful when performing data verification.

Arguments
- *index*—an **Integer** that is used to uniquely identify a control in a control array. This argument is not present if the control is not part of a control array.

Private Sub *TabStripBoxControl*_MouseDown([*index* As Integer ,] *button* As Integer, *shift* As Single, *x* As Single, *y* As Single)

Usage This event occurs when a mouse button was pressed while the cursor is over the control.

Arguments
- *index*—an **Integer** that is used to uniquely identify a control in a control array. This argument is not present if the control is not part of a control array.
- *button*—an **Integer** that contains information about the mouse buttons that were pressed (see Table T-16). Only one button will be indicated when this event occurs.

button Name	Value	Description
vbLeftButton	1	The left button was pressed.
vbRightButton	2	The right button was pressed.
vbMiddleButton	4	The middle button was pressed.

Table T-16: Button *values*.

- *shift*—an **Integer** that contains information about the Shift and Alt keys that were pressed when the mouse button was pressed (see Table T-17). These values can be added together if more than one key was down. For instance, a value of 5 would mean that the Shift and Alt keys were both down when the mouse button was pressed.

shift Name	Value	Description
vbShiftMask	1	The Shift key was pressed.
vbCtrlMask	2	The Ctrl key was pressed.
vbAltMask	4	The Alt key was pressed.

Table T-17: Shift *values*.

- *x*—a **Single** that contains the horizontal location of the mouse pointer.
- *y*—a **Single** that contains the vertical location of the mouse pointer.

Private Sub *TabStripControl*_MouseMove ([*index* As Integer ,] *button* As Integer, *shift* As Single, *x* As Single, *y* As Single)

Usage
This event occurs while the cursor is moved over the control.

Arguments
- *index*—an **Integer** that is used to uniquely identify a control in a control array. This argument is not present if the control is not part of a control array.
- *button*—an **Integer** that contains information about the mouse buttons that were pressed (see Table T-18). These values can be added together if more than one button was pressed. For instance, a value of 3 means that both the left and right buttons were pressed. A value of 0 means that no buttons were pressed.

button Name	Value	Description
vbLeftButton	1	The left button was pressed.
vbRightButton	2	The right button was pressed.
vbMiddleButton	4	The middle button was pressed.

Table T-18: Button *values*.

- *shift*—an **Integer** that contains information about the Shift and Alt keys that were pressed when the mouse button was pressed (see Table T-19). These values can be addes together if more than one key was down. For instance, a value of 5 would mean that the Shift and Alt keys were both down when the mouse button was pressed. A value of 0 means that none of these keys were pressed.

shift Name	Value	Description
vbShiftMask	1	The Shift key was pressed.
vbCtrlMask	2	The Ctrl key was pressed.
vbAltMask	4	The Alt key was pressed.

Table T-19: Shift *values.*

- *x*—a **Single** that contains the horizontal location of the mouse pointer.
- *y*—a **Single** that contains the vertical location of the mouse pointer.

Private Sub *TabStripBoxControl*_MouseUp([*index* As Integer ,] *button* As Integer, *shift* As Single, *x* As Single, *y* As Single)

Usage | This event occurs when a mouse button is released while the cursor is over the control.

Arguments
- *index*—an **Integer** that is used to uniquely identify a control in a control array. This argument is not present if the control is not part of a control array.
- *button*—an **Integer** that contains information about the mouse buttons that were released (see Table T-20). Only one of these values will be present.

button Name	Value	Description
vbLeftButton	1	The left button was released.
vbRightButton	2	The right button was released.
vbMiddleButton	4	The middle button was released.

Table T-20: Button *values.*

- *shift*—an **Integer** that contains information about the Shift and Alt keys that were pressed when the mouse button was released (see Table T-21). These values can be added together if more than one key was down. For instance, a value of 5 would mean that the Shift and Alt keys were both down when the mouse button was released. A value of 0 means that none of these keys were pressed.

shift Name	Value	Description
vbShiftMask	1	The Shift key was pressed.
vbCtrlMask	2	The Ctrl key was pressed.
vbAltMask	4	The Alt key was pressed.

Table T-21: Shift *values.*

- *x*—a **Single** that contains the horizontal location of the mouse pointer.
- *y*—a **Single** that contains the vertical location of the mouse pointer.

Private Sub *TabStripControl*_OLECompleteDrag([*index* As Integer ,] *effect* As Long)

Usage This event is used to tell the source control the results of an OLE drag-and-drop operation. This is the final event to occur in the series of actions that make up an OLE drag-and-drop operation.

Arguments
- *index*—an **Integer** that is used to uniquely identify a control in a control array. This argument is not present if the control is not part of a control array.
- *effect*—a **Long** that returns the status of the OLE drag-and-drop operation (see Table T-22).

effect Name	Value	Description
vbDropEffectNone	0	The operation is canceled or the target control can't accept the drop operation.
vbDropEffectCopy	1	The operation copies data from the source control to the target control. The original data is unchanged.
vbDropEffectMove	2	The operation results in a link from the original data to the target control.

Table T-22: Effect values.

Private Sub *TabStripControl*_OLEDragDrop([*index* As Integer ,] *data* As DataObject, *effect* As Long, *button* As Integer, *shift* As Single, *x* As Single, *y* As Single)

Usage This event is used to tell the source control the results of an OLE drag-and-drop operation. This is the final event to occur in the series of actions that make up an OLE drag-and-drop operation.

Arguments
- *index*—an **Integer** that is used to uniquely identify a control in a control array. This argument is not present if the control is not part of a control array.
- *data*—a **DataObject** that contains the formats that the source control will provide. If the data is not contained in the **DataObject**, then it can be retrieved with the **GetData** method.
- *effect*—a **Long** that returns the status of the OLE drag-and-drop operation (see Table T-23).

effect Name	Value	Description
vbDropEffectNone	0	The operation is canceled or the target control can't accept the drop operation.
vbDropEffectCopy	1	The operation copies data from the source control to the target control. The original data is unchanged.
vbDropEffectMove	2	The operation results in a link from the original data to the target control.

Table T-23: Effect values.

- *button*—an **Integer** that contains information about the mouse buttons that were pressed (see Table T-24). These values can be added together if more than one button was pressed. For instance, a value of 3 means that both the left and right buttons were pressed. A value of 0 means that no buttons were pressed.

button Name	Value	Description
vbLeftButton	1	The left button was pressed.
vbRightButton	2	The right button was pressed.
vbMiddleButton	4	The middle button was pressed.

Table T-24: Button *values*.

- *shift*—an **Integer** that contains information about the Shift and Alt keys that were pressed when the mouse button was released (see Table T-25). These values can be added together if more than one key was down. For instance, a value of 5 would mean that the Shift and Alt keys were both down when the mouse button was released. A value of 0 means that none of these keys were pressed.

shift Name	Value	Description
vbShiftMask	1	The Shift key was pressed.
vbCtrlMask	2	The Ctrl key was pressed.
vbAltMask	4	The Alt key was pressed.

Table T-25: Shift *values*.

- *x*—a **Single** that contains the horizontal location of the mouse pointer.
- *y*—a **Single** that contains the vertical location of the mouse pointer.

Private Sub *TabStripControl*_OLEDragOver([*index* As Integer ,] *data* As DataObject, *effect* As Long, *button* As Integer, *shift* As Single, *x* As Single, *y* As Single, *state* As Integer)

Usage   This event happens when an OLE drag-and-drop operation is in progress.

Arguments
- *index*—an **Integer** that is used to uniquely identify a control in a control array. This argument is not present if the control is not part of a control array.
- *data*—a **DataObject** that contains the formats that the source control will provide. If the data is not contained in the **DataObject**, then it can be retrieved with the **GetData** method.
- *effect*—a **Long** that returns the status of the OLE drag-and-drop operation (see Table T-26).

effect Name	Value	Description
vbDropEffectNone	0	The operation is canceled or the target control can't accept the drop operation.
vbDropEffectCopy	1	The operation copies data from the source control to the target control. The original data is unchanged.
vbDropEffectMove	2	The operation results in a link from the original data to the target control.

Table T-26: Effect *values.*

- *button*—an **Integer** that contains information about the mouse buttons that were pressed (see Table T-27). These values can be added together if more than one button was pressed. For instance, a value of 3 means that both the left and right buttons were pressed. A value of 0 means that no buttons were pressed.

button Name	Value	Description
vbLeftButton	1	The left button was pressed.
vbRightButton	2	The right button was pressed.
vbMiddleButton	4	The middle button was pressed.

Table T-27: Button *values.*

- *shift*—an **Integer** that contains information about the Shift and Alt keys that were pressed when the mouse button was released (see Table T-28). These values can be added together if more than one key was down. For instance, a value of 5 would mean that the Shift and Alt keys were both down when the mouse button was released. A value of 0 means that none of these keys were pressed.

shift Name	Value	Description
vbShiftMask	1	The Shift key was pressed.
vbCtrlMask	2	The Ctrl key was pressed.
vbAltMask	4	The Alt key was pressed.

Table T-28: Shift *values.*

- *x*—a **Single** that contains the horizontal location of the mouse pointer.
- *y*—a **Single** that contains the vertical location of the mouse pointer.
- *state*—an **Integer** that indicates the state of the object being dragged (see Table T-29).

state Name	Value	Description
vbEnter	0	The dragged object is entering range of the control.
vbLeave	1	The dragged object is leaving range of the control.
vbOver	2	The dragged object has moved from one position over the control to another.

Table T-29: State *values.*

Private Sub *TabStripControl_OLEGiveFeedback* ([*index* As Integer ,] *effect* As Long)

Usage — This event is used to tell the source control what is happening while the OLE drag-and-drop operation is in progress. This event occurs after the OLEDragOver event.

Tip

You may want to use this event to change the cursor to reflect what can happen in the remote object.

Arguments
- *index*—an **Integer** that is used to uniquely identify a control in a control array. This argument is not present if the control is not part of a control array.
- *effect*—a **Long** that returns the status of the OLE drag-and-drop operation (see Table T-30).

effect Name	Value	Description
vbDropEffectNone	0	The operation is canceled or the target control can't accept the drop operation.
vbDropEffectCopy	1	The operation copies data from the source control to the target control. The original data is unchanged.
vbDropEffectMove	2	The operation results in a link from the original data to the target control.
vbDropEffectScroll	&H80000000	The target control is about to scroll or is scrolling. This value may be added to the other *shift* values.

Table T-30: Effect *values.*

Private Sub *TabStripControl_OLESetData*([*index* As Integer ,] *data* As DataObject, *DataFormat* As Integer)

Usage — This event happens in response to the target object performing a **GetData** method on *data*. This routine will respond by using the **SetData** method with the desired data using the **DataObject** *data*.

Arguments
- *index*—an **Integer** that is used to uniquely identify a control in a control array. This argument is not present if the control is not part of a control array.
- *data*—a **DataObject** that will contain the data to be returned to the target object.
- *format*—an **Integer** that contains the format of the data (see Table T-31).

format Name	Value	Description
vbCFText	1	Text (.TXT files).
vbCFBitmap	2	Bitmap (.BMP files).
vbCFMetafile	3	Metafile (.WMF files).
vbCFEDIB	8	Device-independent bitmap (DIB).
vbCFPallette	9	Color palette.
vbCFEMetafile	14	Enhanced metafile (.EMF files).
vbCFFiles	15	List of files.
vbCFRTF	-16639	Rich Text Format (.RTF files).

Table T-31: Format *values.*

Private Sub *TabStripControl*_OLEStartDrag ([*index* As Integer ,] *data* As DataObject, *AllowedEffects* As Long)

Usage   This event is used to start an OLE drag-and-drop operation.

Arguments
- *index*—an **Integer** that is used to uniquely identify a control in a control array. This argument is not present if the control is not part of a control array.
- *data*—a **DataObject** that will contain the formats that the source object is willing to provide to the target object. It may optionally contain the data to be transferred.
- *AllowedEffects*—a **Long** that contains the effects that the target object can request from the source object. The *AllowedEffects* can be added together if the source object supports more than one effect. Note that the target object can always use the *vbDropEffectNone* effect (see Table T-32).

AllowedEffects Name	Value	Description
vbDropEffectNone	0	The target can't copy the data.
vbDropEffectCopy	1	The target can copy the data, and the source will keep the data unchanged.
vbDropEffectMove	2	The target can copy the data, and the source will delete the data.

Table T-32: AllowedEffects *values.*

See Also   **Frame** (control), **Tab** (object), **Tabs** (collection)

Tan

FUNCTION

CCE, LE, PE, EE

Syntax *RValue* = **Tan** (*Number*)

Usage The **Tan** function will return the tangent of *Number* specified in radians.

> **Tip**
>
> *There are two pi radians in a circle, and there are 360 degrees in a circle. Pi is approximately equal to 3.14159. To convert radians to degrees, multiply by 180/pi. To convert degrees to radians, multiply by pi/180.*

Arguments
- *RValue*—a **Double** that contains the cosine of *Number*.
- *Number*—a **Double** expression that is passed to the tangent function. This value is specified in radians.

Examples
```
Private Sub Command1_Click()
If IsNumeric(Text1.Text) Then
    Text2.Text = Format(Tan(CDbl(Text1.Text)))
End If
End Sub
```

This routine will compute the tangent of the value in the Text1 text box and display the results in the Text2 text box.

See Also **Atn** (function), **Cos** (function), **Sin** (function)

TextBox

CONTROL

CCE, LE, PE, EE

Usage The **TextBox** control accepts user input and displays it.

Properties
- *TextBoxControl*.**Alignment**—an **Integer** value that describes the placement of the text within the control (see Table T-33).

Alignment Name	Value	Description
vbLeftJustify	0	The text is left justified within the caption area (default value).
vbRightJustify	1	The text is right justified within the caption area.
vbCenter	2	The text is centered within the caption area.

Table T-33: Alignment *values.*

- *TextBoxControl*.**Appearance**—an **Integer** value that determines how the text box will appear on the form (see Table T-34).

Appearance Value	Description
0	The TextBox control is displayed without the 3D effects.
1	The **TextBox** control is displayed with 3D effects (default value).

Table T-34: Appearance *values.*

- *TextBoxControl.***BackColor**—a **Long** that contains the suggested value for the background color of the control. The **BackColor** and **ForeColor** must both be solid to display text. If you choose a color that is dithered, it will be changed to the nearest solid color.
- *TextBoxControl.***BorderStyle**—an **Integer** specifying how the border will be drawn (see Table T-35).

BorderStyle Name	Value	Description
vbBSNone	0	No border is displayed.
vbFixedSingle	1	Single line around the label.

Table T-35: BorderStyle *values.*

- *TextBoxControl.***Container**—an object that can be used to set or return the container of the control at run time. This property cannot be set at design time.
- *TextBoxControl.***DataChanged**—a **Boolean** that applies only to data bound controls. When **True**, means that the data contained in this control was changed either by the user or by some means other than retrieving data from the current record. When **False**, means the data in the control is unchanged from the current record. Simply reading the next record is not sufficient to set the **DataChanged** property to **True**.
- *TextBoxControl.***DataField**—a **String** value that is used to associate the control with a field in a **RecordSet** object in a **Data** control.
- *TextBoxControl.***DataSource**—a **String** value that is used to associate the control with a **Data** control.
- *TextBoxControl.***DragIcon**—an object that contains the picture value of an icon. At design time, you can specify an icon file that has a file type of .ICO.

Tip

*This value can be created by copying the value from another control's **DragIcon** value or a form's icon, or by using the **LoadPicture** function.*

- *TextBoxControl.***DragMode**—an **Integer** specifying how the control will respond to a drag request (see Table T-36).

Tip

*Setting **DragMode** to vbAutomatic will automatically begin a drag operation when the user clicks on the control. However, the control will not respond to the usual mouse events (**Click**, **DblClick**, **MouseDown**, **MouseMove**, **MouseUp**).*

DragMode Name	Value	Description
vbManual	0	The Drag method must be used to begin a drag-and-drop operation (default value).
vbAutomatic	1	The source control will automatically begin a drag-and-drop operation when the user clicks on the control.

Table T-36: DragMode *values.*

- *TextBoxControl.***Enabled**—a **Boolean** value when **True** means that the control will respond to events. When **False**, the control will not respond to events.
- *TextBoxControl.***Font**—an object that contains information about the character font used by this object.
- *TextBoxControl.***FontBold**—a **Boolean,** when **True**, means that the characters are displayed in bold. **False** means that the characters are displayed normally.
- *TextBoxControl.***FontItalic**—a **Boolean,** when **True**, means that the characters are displayed in italics. **False** means that the characters are displayed normally.
- *TextBoxControl.***FontName**—a **String** that specifies the name of the font that should be used to display the characters in this control.
- *TextBoxControl.***FontSize**—a **Single** that is used to specify the point size that should be used to display the characters in the control.
- *TextBoxControl.***FontStrikethru**—a **Boolean,** when **True**, means that the characters are displayed with a line through the center. **False** means that the characters are displayed normally.
- *TextBoxControl.***FontUnderlined**—a **Boolean,** when **True**, means that the characters are displayed with a line beneath them. **False** means that the characters are displayed normally.
- *TextBoxControl.***ForeColor**—a **Long** that contains the suggested value for the foreground color of the contained control. This property is read only at run time.
- *TextBoxControl.***Height**—a **Single** that contains the height of the control.
- *TextBoxControl.***HelpContextID**—a **Long** that contains a help file context ID number that references an entry in the help file. When the user presses the F1 key while this control is active, the corresponding entry in the help file will automatically be displayed. A value of zero means that no context number was specified.

Tip

A help file must be compiled using the Windows Help Compiler available in the Professional and Enterprise editions of Visual Basic.

- *TextBoxControl.***HideSelection**—a **Boolean** value when **True** means that the selected text does not appear as highlighted when the control loses focus. When **False**, the text will continue to be highlighted when the control loses focus.
- *TextBoxControl.***hWnd**—a **Long** that contains a Windows handle to the control.

> **Tip**
>
> *The **hWnd** property is most useful when making calls to Windows API functions. Since this value can change during execution, do not save the value into a variable for later use.*

- *TextBoxControl*.**Index**—an **Integer** that is used to uniquely identify a control in a control array.
- *TextBoxControl*.**Left**—a **Single** that contains the distance, measured in twips, between the left edge of the control and the left edge of the control's container.
- *TextBoxControl*.**LinkItem**—a **String** containing data that is passed to a destination control in a DDE link. This property is the same as the item specification in a normal DDE specification.
- *TextBoxControl*.**LinkMode**—an **Integer** that specifies how the form will act in a DDE conversation (see Table T-37).

LinkMode Name	Value	Description
vbLinkNone	0	No DDE interaction.
vbLinkAutomatic	1	The destination control is updated each time the data is updated.
vbLinkManual	2	The destination control is updated only when the **LinkRequest** method is used.
vbLinkNotify	3	The **LinkNotify** event occurs each time the data is updated. Then the **LinkRequest** method can be used to refresh the linked data.

Table T-37: LinkMode *values.*

- *TextBoxControl*.**LinkTimeout**—an **Integer** containing the amount of time, in tenths of seconds, that the application will wait for a DDE message.
- *TextBoxControl*.**LinkTopic**—a **String** that contains a reference to a DDE application. The actual format of the string is dependent on the exact application, but strings will usually include an application, topic, and item. For example, in Excel a valid **LinkTopic** string is "Excel|Sheet1."
- *TextBoxControl*.**Locked**—a **Boolean** when **True** means that the text can't be changed in the control. **False** means that the text can be changed (default).
- *TextBoxControl*.**MaxLength**—an **Integer** value containing the maximum number of characters in the **Text** property.
- *TextBoxControl*.**MouseIcon**—a picture object (a bitmap, icon, or metafile) that will be used as a cursor when the **MousePointer** property is set to 99. Note that Visual Basic does not support color cursors from a .CUR file. A color icon from an .ICO file should be used instead.
- *TextBoxControl*.**MousePointer**—an **Integer** that contains the value of the cursor that should be displayed when the cursor is moved over this control (see Table T-38). Use *vbCustom* to display the custom icon stored in the **MouseIcon** property.

Cursor Name	Value	Description
vbDefault	0	Shape determined by the object (default value).
vbArrow	1	Arrow.
vbCrosshair	2	Crosshair.
vbIbeam	3	I beam.
vbIconPointer	4	Square inside a square.
vbSizePointer	5	Four-sided arrow (north, south, east, west).
vbSizeNESW	6	Two-sided arrow (northeast, southwest).
vbSizeNS	7	Two-sided arrow (north, south).
vbSizeNWSE	8	Two-sided arrow (northwest, southeast).
vbSizeWE	9	Two-sided arrow (west, east).
vbUpArrow	10	Single-sided arrow pointing north.
vbHourglass	11	Hourglass.
vbNoDrop	12	No drop.
vbArrowHourglass	13	An arrow and an hourglass.
vbArrowQuestion	14	An arrow and a question mark.
vbSizeAll	15	Size all.
vbCustom	99	Custom icon from the MouseIcon property of this control.

Table T-38: Cursor *values.*

- *TextBoxControl.***MultiLine**—a **Boolean,** when **True**, means that the text box will display multiple lines of text, with each line separated by a carriage return linefeed (*vbCrLf*). **False** means that the text box will only display a single line of text.
- *TextBoxControl.***Name**—a **String** that contains the name of the control that will be used to reference the control in a Visual Basic program. This property is read only at run time.
- *TextBoxControl.***OLEDragMode**—an **Integer** value (see Table T-39) that describes how the control will respond to OLE drag operations.

> **Note**
>
> When the **DragMode** is **True**, *the standard Visual Basic drag-and-drop functions will override the OLE drag-and-drop functions.*

OLEDragMode Name	Value	Description
vbOLEDragManual	0	All drag requests will be handled by the programmer (default value).
vbOLEDragAutomatic	1	The control responds to all OLE drag request automatically.

Table T-39: OLEDragMode *values.*

- *TextBoxControl.***OLEDropMode**—an **Integer** value (see Table T-40) that describes how the control will respond to OLE drop operations.

OLEDropMode Name	Value	Description
vbOLEDropNone	0	The control does not accept OLE drops. The cursor is changed to the No Drop cursor (default value).
vbOLEDropManual	1	The control responds to OLE drops under the program's control (manual).
vbOLEDropAutomatic	2	The control automatically accepts OLE drops if it recognizes the format of the data object.

Table T-40: OLEDropMode *values*.

- *TextBoxControl*.**Parent**—an object that contains a reference to the **Form, Frame,** or other container that holds this control.
- *TextBoxControl*.**PasswordChar**—a **String** that can contain up to one character, which is displayed in place of the characters in the text box. This conceals the characters typed by the user. If the string is empty, the characters typed are the characters displayed. This property has no effect if **MultiLine** is **True**.
- *DBGridControl*.**ScrollBars**—an **Integer** containing the row divider style for the **DBGrid** control (see Table T-41).

ScrollBars Name	Value	Description
vbSBNone	0	No scroll bars are displayed (default).
vbHorizontal	1	A horizontal scroll bar is displayed.
vbVertical	2	A vertical scroll bar is displayed.
vbBoth	3	Both scroll bars are displayed.

Table T-41: ScrollBars *values*.

- *TextBoxControl*.**SelLength**—a **Long** value containing the length of the selected text. When **SelLength** is zero, no text is selected.
- *TextBoxControl*.**SelStart**—a **Long** value containing the starting position of the selected text.
- *TextBoxControl*.**SelText**—a **String** value containing the selected text. When **SelText** is empty, no text is selected.

Tip

*The **SelLength**, **SelStart**, and **SelText** properties are very powerful tools for inserting and deleting text inside the control. By setting **SelStart** to a position inside the **Text** string and assigning a value to **SelText**, you will insert text at that position. To change a block of text, simply set the **SelStart** and **SelLength** values and then change the value of **SelText**. The **Text** property will be updated accordingly. Assigning an empty string to **SelText** will delete the selected text.*

- *TextBoxControl*.**TabIndex**—an **Integer** that is used to determine the order that a user will tab through the objects on a form.
- *TextBoxControl*.**TabStop**—a **Boolean** value when **True** means that the user can tab to this object. **False** means that this control will be skipped to the next control in the **TabIndex** order.
- *TextBoxControl*.**Tag**—a **String** that can hold programmer-specific information. This property is not used by Visual Basic.

- *TextBoxControl*.**Text**—a **String** that sets or returns the value from the text box part of the control.
- *TextBoxControl*.**ToolTipText**—a **String** that holds a text value that can be displayed as a **ToolTip** box whenever the cursor is held over the control for about one second.
- *TextBoxControl*.**Top**—a **Single** that contains the distance, measured in twips, between the top edge of the control and the top edge of the control's container.
- *TextBoxControl*.**Visible**—a **Boolean** value when **True** means that the control is visible. **False** means that the control is not visible.

> **Tip**
>
> *This property can be used to hide the **TextBox** control until the program is ready to display it.*

- *TextBoxControl*.**WhatsThisHelpID**—a **Long** that contains a help file context ID number that references an entry in the help file. This is used to provide a What's This PopUp help display in response to the What's This button in the upper right hand corner of the window.
- *TextBoxControl*.**Width**—a **Single** that contains the width of the control.

Methods

TextBoxControl.Drag [*DragAction*]

Usage This method is used to begin, end, or cancel a drag operation.

Arguments *DragAction*—an **Integer** that contains a value selected from Table T-42 below.

DragAction Name	Value	Description
vbCancel	0	Cancels any drag operation in progress.
vbBeginDrag	1	Begins a drag operation (default).
vbEndDrag	2	Ends a drag operation and drops *object*.

Table T-42: DragAction *values*.

TextBoxControl.LinkExecute *command*

Usage This method will send a command to the source application in a DDE link.

Arguments *command*—a **String** containing the command.

TextBoxControl.LinkPoke

Usage This method is used by the destination application in a DDE link to send the contents of the label's caption to the source application.

TextBoxControl.LinkRequest

Usage This method is used by the destination application in a DDE link to send a request to the source application to refresh its contents.

TextBoxControl.LinkSend

Usage This method sends the contents of a **Picture** control to the destination application in a DDE link.

TextBoxControl.Move Left [, Top [, Width [, Height]]]

Usage This method is used to change the position and the size of the **TextBox** control. The **ScaleMode** of the **Form** or other container object that holds the **TextBox** control will determine the units used to specify the coordinates.

Arguments
- *Left*—a **Single** that specifies the new position of the left edge of the control.
- *Top*—a **Single** that specifies the new position of the top edge of the control.
- *Width*—a **Single** that specifies the new width of the control.
- *Height*—a **Single** that specifies the new height of the control.

TextBoxControl.OLEDrag

Usage This method is used to begin an **OLEDrag** and drop operation. Invoking this method will trigger the **OLEStartDrag** event.

TextBoxControl.Refresh

Usage This method is used to redraw the contents of the control.

TextBoxControl.SetFocus

Usage This method transfers the focus from the form or control that currently has the focus to this control. In order to receive the focus, this control must be enabled and visible.

TextBoxControl.ShowWhatsThis

Usage This method displays the ShowWhatsThis help information for this control.

TextBoxControl.ZOrder [position]

Usage This method is used to specify the position of the **TextBox** control relative to the other objects on the form.

TextBox • 997

> **Tip**
>
> *Note that there are three layers of objects on a form. The back layer is the drawing space that contains the results of the graphical methods, and the middle layer contains graphical objects and **Labels**. The top layer contains non-graphical controls such as the **TextBox** control. The **ZOrder** method only affects how the objects are arranged within a single layer.*

Arguments
- *position*—an **Integer** that specifies the relative position of this object. A value of 0 means that the control is positioned at the head of the list, a value of 1 means that the control will be placed at the end of the list.

Events

Private Sub *TextBoxControl*_Change ([*index* As Integer])

Usage This event occurs whenever the contents of the text box are changed, either by the program changing the **Text** property directly or by a DDE link.

Arguments
- *index*—an **Integer** that is used to uniquely identify a control in a control array. This argument is not present if the control is not part of a control array.

Private Sub *TextBoxControl*_Click([*index* As Integer])

Usage This event occurs when the user clicks a mouse button while the cursor is over the control.

Arguments
- *index*—an **Integer** that is used to uniquely identify a control in a control array. This argument is not present if the control is not part of a control array.

Private Sub *TextBoxControl*_DblClick([*index* As Integer])

Usage This event occurs when the user double-clicks a mouse button while the cursor is over the control.

Arguments
- *index*—an **Integer** that is used to uniquely identify a control in a control array. This argument is not present if the control is not part of a control array.

Private Sub *TextBoxControl*_DragDrop([*index* As Integer ,] *source* As Control, *x* As Single, *y* As Single)

Usage This event occurs when a drag-and-drop operation is completed by using the Drag method with a *DragAction* value of *vbEndDrag*.

> **Tip**
>
> *When using drag-and-drop operations, use the **DragOver** event to determine what the cursor should look like while the cursor moves over the control.*

Arguments
- *index*—an **Integer** that is used to uniquely identify a control in a control array. This argument is not present if the control is not part of a control array.
- *source*—a control object that is the control that is being dragged.

> **Tip**
>
> You can access a property or method from the source control by using **source.property** or **source.method**. You can determine the type of object or control by using the **TypeOf** operator.

- *x*—a **Single** that contains the horizontal location of the mouse pointer.
- *y*—a **Single** that contains the vertical location of the mouse pointer.

Private Sub *TextBoxControl*_DragOver([*index* As Integer ,] *source* As Control, *x* As Single, *y* As Single, *state* As Integer)

Usage   This event occurs while a drag operation is in progress and the cursor is moved over the control.

> **Tip**
>
> When using drag-and-drop operations, use the **DragOver** event to determine what the cursor should look like while the cursor moves over the control. When **state** is 0, you can change the cursor to a no drop (vbNoDrop) cursor or highlight the field that the cursor is near. When **state** is 1, you can undo the changes you made when the **state** was 0.

Arguments
- *index*—an **Integer** that is used to uniquely identify a control in a control array. This argument is not present if the control is not part of a control array.
- *source*—a control object that is the control that is being dragged.

> **Tip**
>
> You can access a property or method from the source control by using **source.property** or **source.method**. You can determine the type of object or control by using the **TypeOf** operator.

- *x*—a **Single** that contains the horizontal location of the mouse pointer.
- *y*—a **Single** that contains the vertical location of the mouse pointer.
- *state*—an **Integer** that indicates the state of the object being dragged (see Table T-43).

state Name	Value	Description
vbEnter	0	The dragged object is entering range of the control.
vbLeave	1	The dragged object is leaving range of the control.
vbOver	2	The dragged object has moved from one position over the control to another.

Table T-43: State *values*.

Private Sub *TextBoxControl*_GotFocus ([*index* As Integer])

Usage   This event occurs when the control is given focus.

> **Tip**
>
> *You can use this routine to display help or other information in a status bar.*

Arguments
- *index*—an **Integer** that is used to uniquely identify a control in a control array. This argument is not present if the control is not part of a control array.

Private Sub *TextBoxControl*_KeyDown ([*index* As Integer ,] *keycode* As Integer, *shift* As Single)

Usage This event occurs when a key is pressed while the control has the focus.

Arguments
- *index*—an **Integer** that is used to uniquely identify a control in a control array. This argument is not present if the control is not part of a control array.
- *keycode*—an **Integer** that contains information about which key was pressed.
- *shift*—an **Integer** that contains information about the Shift and Alt keys that were pressed when the mouse button was pressed (see Table T-44). These values can be added together if more than one key was down. For instance, a value of 5 would mean that the Shift and Alt keys were both down when the mouse button was pressed.

shift Name	Value	Description
vbShiftMask	1	The Shift key was pressed.
vbCtrlMask	2	The Ctrl key was pressed.
vbAltMask	4	The Alt key was pressed.

Table T-44: Shift values.

Private Sub *TextBoxControl*_KeyPress([*index* As Integer ,] *keychar* As Integer)

Usage This event occurs whenever a key is pressed while the control has the focus.

Arguments
- *index*—an **Integer** that is used to uniquely identify a control in a control array. This argument is not present if the control is not part of a control array.
- *keychar*—an **Integer** that contains the ASCII character that was pressed.

Private Sub *TextBoxControl*_KeyUp ([*index* As Integer ,] *keycode* As Integer, *shift* As Single)

Usage This event occurs when a key is released while the control has the focus.

Arguments
- *index*—an **Integer** that is used to uniquely identify a control in a control array. This argument is not present if the control is not part of a control array.
- *keycode*—an **Integer** that contains information about which key was released.

- *shift*—an **Integer** that contains information about the Shift and Alt keys that were pressed when the mouse button was pressed (see Table T-45). These values can be added together if more than one key was down. For instance, a value of 5 would mean that the Shift and Alt keys were both down when the mouse button was pressed.

shift Name	Value	Description
vbShiftMask	1	The Shift key was pressed.
vbCtrlMask	2	The Ctrl key was pressed.
vbAltMask	4	The Alt key was pressed.

Table T-45: Shift *values*.

Private Sub *TextBoxControl*_LinkClose ([*index* As Integer ,])

Usage   This event occurs when a DDE link is closed.

Arguments   • *index*—an **Integer** that is used to uniquely identify a control in a control array. This argument is not present if the control is not part of a control array.

Private Sub *TextBoxControl*_LinkError ([*index* As Integer ,] *errcode* As Integer)

Usage   This event occurs when a DDE link error occurs.

Arguments   • *index*—an **Integer** that is used to uniquely identify a control in a control array. This argument is not present if the control is not part of a control array.

• *errcode*—an **Integer** that contains an error code listed in Table T-46 below.

errcode Value	Description
1	The other application requested data in wrong format. This may occur more than once while Visual Basic attempts to find an acceptable format.
6	The other application attempted to continue the DDE conversation after **LinkMode** in this application was set to zero.
7	All 128 DDE links are in use.
8	Destination control: An automatic link or **LinkRequest** failed when communicating. Source forms: The other application was unable to poke data to a control.
11	Insufficient memory available for DDE.

Table T-46: DDE errcode *values*.

Private Sub *TextBoxControl*_LinkExecute ([*index* As Integer ,] *cmd* As String, *cancel* As Integer)

Usage   This event occurs when a destination application requests the source application to perform the function in *cmd*.

> **Note**
>
> *If your program doesn't include a **LinkExecute** event, then all commands will be rejected.*

    Arguments
- *index*—an **Integer** that is used to uniquely identify a control in a control array. This argument is not present if the control is not part of a control array.
- *cmd*—a **String** containing a command for the source application to execute. The format of the string is application specific.
- *cancel*—an **Integer** of zero means that the command was accepted. Any other value will inform the destination application that the command was rejected.

Private Sub *TextBoxControl*_LinkOpen ([*index* As Integer ,] *cancel* As Integer)

    Usage   This event occurs when a DDE session is being set up.

    Arguments
- *index*—an **Integer** that is used to uniquely identify a control in a control array. This argument is not present if the control is not part of a control array.
- *cancel*—an **Integer** of zero means that the command was accepted. Any other value will inform the destination application that the link will be refused.

Private Sub *TextBoxControl*_LostFocus ([*index* As Integer])

    Usage   This event occurs when the control loses focus.

    Arguments
- *index*—an **Integer** that is used to uniquely identify a control in a control array. This argument is not present if the control is not part of a control array.

Private Sub *TextBoxBoxControl*_MouseDown([*index* As Integer ,] *button* As Integer, *shift* As Single, *x* As Single, *y* As Single)

    Usage   This event occurs when a mouse button is pressed while the cursor is over the control.

    Arguments
- *index*—an **Integer** that is used to uniquely identify a control in a control array. This argument is not present if the control is not part of a control array.
- *button*—an **Integer** that contains information about the mouse buttons that were pressed (see Table T-47). Only one of these values will be present.

button Name	Value	Description
vbLeftButton	1	The left button was pressed.
vbRightButton	2	The right button was pressed.
vbMiddleButton	4	The middle button was pressed.

Table T-47: Button *values.*

- *shift*—an **Integer** that contains information about the Shift and Alt keys that were pressed when the mouse button was pressed (see Table T-48). These values can be added together if more than one key was down. For instance, a value of 5 would mean that the Shift and Alt keys were both down when the mouse button was pressed.

shift Name	Value	Description
vbShiftMask	1	The Shift key was pressed.
vbCtrlMask	2	The Ctrl key was pressed.
vbAltMask	4	The Alt key was pressed.

Table T-48: Shift *values.*

- *x*—a **Single** that contains the horizontal location of the mouse pointer.
- *y*—a **Single** that contains the vertical location of the mouse pointer.

Private Sub *TextBoxControl*_MouseMove ([*index* As Integer ,] *button* As Integer, *shift* As Single, *x* As Single, *y* As Single)

Usage   This event occurs while the cursor is moved over the control.

Arguments
- *index*—an **Integer** that is used to uniquely identify a control in a control array. This argument is not present if the control is not part of a control array.
- *button*—an **Integer** that contains information about the mouse buttons that were pressed (see Table T-49). These values can be added together if more than one button was pressed. For instance, a value of 3 means that both the left and right buttons were pressed. A value of 0 means that no buttons were pressed.

button Name	Value	Description
vbLeftButton	1	The left button was pressed.
vbRightButton	2	The right button was pressed.
vbMiddleButton	4	The middle button was pressed.

Table T-49: Button *values.*

- *shift*—an **Integer** that contains information about the Shift and Alt keys that were pressed when the mouse button was pressed (see Table T-50). These values can be added together if more than one key was down. For instance, a value of 5 would mean that the Shift and Alt keys were both down when the mouse button was pressed. A value of 0 means that none of these keys were pressed.

shift Name	Value	Description
vbShiftMask	1	The Shift key was pressed.
vbCtrlMask	2	The Ctrl key was pressed.
vbAltMask	4	The Alt key was pressed.

Table T-50: Shift *values.*

- *x*—a **Single** that contains the horizontal location of the mouse pointer.
- *y*—a **Single** that contains the vertical location of the mouse pointer.

Private Sub *TextBoxBoxControl*_MouseUp([*index* As Integer ,] *button* As Integer, *shift* As Single, *x* As Single, *y* As Single)

Usage — This event occurs when a mouse button is released while the cursor is over the control.

Arguments
- *index*—an **Integer** that is used to uniquely identify a control in a control array. This argument is not present if the control is not part of a control array.
- *button*—an **Integer** that contains information about the mouse buttons that were released (see Table T-51). Only one of these values will be present.

button Name	Value	Description
vbLeftButton	1	The left button was released.
vbRightButton	2	The right button was released.
vbMiddleButton	4	The middle button was released.

Table T-51: Button *values*.

- *shift*—an **Integer** that contains information about the Shift and Alt keys that were pressed when the mouse button was released (see Table T-52). These values can be added together if more than one key was down. For instance, a value of 5 would mean that the Shift and Alt keys were both down when the mouse button was released. A value of 0 means that none of these keys were pressed.

shift Name	Value	Description
vbShiftMask	1	The Shift key was pressed.
vbCtrlMask	2	The Ctrl key was pressed.
vbAltMask	4	The Alt key was pressed.

Table T-52: Shift *Values*.

- *x*—a **Single** that contains the horizontal location of the mouse pointer.
- *y*—a **Single** that contains the vertical location of the mouse pointer.

Private Sub *TextBoxControl*_OLECompleteDrag([*index* As Integer ,] *effect* As Long)

Usage — This event is used to tell the source control the results of an OLE drag-and-drop operation. This is the final event to occur in the series of actions that make up an OLE drag-and-drop operation.

Arguments
- *index*—an **Integer** that is used to uniquely identify a control in a control array. This argument is not present if the control is not part of a control array.
- *effect*—a **Long** that returns the status of the OLE drag-and-drop operation (see Table T-53).

effect Name	Value	Description
vbDropEffectNone	0	The operation is canceled or the target control can't accept the drop operation.
vbDropEffectCopy	1	The operation copies data from the source control to the target control. The original data is unchanged.
vbDropEffectMove	2	The operation results in a link from the original data to the target control.

Table T-53: Effect *values*.

Private Sub TextBoxControl_OLEDragDrop([*index* As Integer ,] *data* As DataObject, *effect* As Long, *button* As Integer, *shift* As Single, *x* As Single, *y* As Single)

Usage
: This event tells the source control the results of an OLE drag-and-drop operation. This is the final event to occur in the series of actions that make up an OLE drag-and-drop operation.

Arguments
: - *index*—an **Integer** that is used to uniquely identify a control in a control array. This argument is not present if the control is not part of a control array.
  - *data*—a **DataObject** that contains the formats that the source control will provide. If the data is not contained in the **DataObject**, then it can be retrieved with the **GetData** method.
  - *effect*—a **Long** that returns the status of the OLE drag-and-drop operation (see Table T-54).

effect Name	Value	Description
vbDropEffectNone	0	The operation is canceled or the target control can't accept the drop operation.
vbDropEffectCopy	1	The operation copies data from the source control to the target control. The original data is unchanged.
vbDropEffectMove	2	The operation results in a link from the original data to the target control.

Table T-54: Effect *values*.

- *button*—an **Integer** that contains information about the mouse buttons that were pressed (see Table T-55). These values can be added together if more than one button was pressed. For instance, a value of 3 means that both the left and right buttons were pressed. A value of 0 means that no buttons were pressed.

button Name	Value	Description
vbLeftButton	1	The left button was pressed.
vbRightButton	2	The right button was pressed.
vbMiddleButton	4	The middle button was pressed.

Table T-55: Button *values*.

- *shift*—an **Integer** that contains information about the Shift and Alt keys that were pressed when the mouse button was released (see Table T-56). These values can be added together if more than one key was down. For instance, a value of 5 would mean that the Shift and Alt keys were both down when the mouse button was released. A value of 0 means that none of these keys were pressed.

shift Name	Value	Description
vbShiftMask	1	The Shift key was pressed.
vbCtrlMask	2	The Ctrl key was pressed.
vbAltMask	4	The Alt key was pressed.

Table T-56: Shift *values*.

- *x*—a **Single** that contains the horizontal location of the mouse pointer.
- *y*—a **Single** that contains the vertical location of the mouse pointer.

Private Sub *TextBoxControl*_OLEDragOver([*index* As Integer ,] *data* As DataObject, *effect* As Long, *button* As Integer, *shift* As Single, *x* As Single, *y* As Single, *state* As Integer)

Usage — This event happens when an OLE drag-and-drop operation is in progress.

Arguments
- *index*—an **Integer** that is used to uniquely identify a control in a control array. This argument is not present if the control is not part of a control array.
- *data*—a **DataObject** that contains the formats that the source control will provide. If the data is not contained in the **DataObject**, then it can be retrieved with the **GetData** method.
- *effect*—a **Long** that returns the status of the OLE drag-and-drop operation (see Table T-57).

effect Name	Value	Description
vbDropEffectNone	0	The operation is canceled or the target control can't accept the drop operation.
vbDropEffectCopy	1	The operation copies data from the source control to the target control. The original data is unchanged.
vbDropEffectMove	2	The operation results in a link from the original data to the target control.

Table T-57: Effect *values*.

- *button*—an **Integer** that contains information about the mouse buttons that were pressed (see Table T-58). These values can be added together if more than one button was pressed. For instance, a value of 3 means that both the left and right buttons were pressed. A value of 0 means that no buttons were pressed.

button Name	Value	Description
vbLeftButton	1	The left button was pressed.
vbRightButton	2	The right button was pressed.
vbMiddleButton	4	The middle button was pressed.

Table T-58: Button *values.*

- *shift*—an **Integer** that contains information about the Shift and Alt keys that were pressed when the mouse button was released (see Table T-59). These values can be added together if more than one key was down. For instance, a value of 5 would mean that the Shift and Alt keys were both down when the mouse button was released. A value of 0 means that none of these keys were pressed.

shift Name	Value	Description
vbShiftMask	1	The Shift key was pressed.
vbCtrlMask	2	The Ctrl key was pressed.
vbAltMask	4	The Alt key was pressed.

Table T-59: Shift *values.*

- *x*—a **Single** that contains the horizontal location of the mouse pointer.
- *y*—a **Single** that contains the vertical location of the mouse pointer.
- *state*—an **Integer** that indicates the state of the object being dragged (see Table T-60).

state Name	Value	Description
vbEnter	0	The dragged object is entering range of the control.
vbLeave	1	The dragged object is leaving range of the control.
vbOver	2	The dragged object has moved from one position over the control to another.

Table T-60: State *values.*

Private Sub *TextBoxControl*_OLEGiveFeedback ([*index* As Integer ,] *effect* As Long)

Usage   This event is used to tell the source control what is happening while the OLE drag-and-drop operation is in progress. This event occurs after the OLEDragOver event.

Tip

You may want to use this event to change the cursor to reflect what can happen in the remote object.

Arguments
- *index*—an **Integer** that is used to uniquely identify a control in a control array. This argument is not present if the control is not part of a control array.
- *effect*—a **Long** that returns the status of the OLE drag-and-drop operation (see Table T-61).

effect Name	Value	Description
vbDropEffectNone	0	The operation is canceled or the target control can't accept the drop operation.
vbDropEffectCopy	1	The operation copies data from the source control to the target control. The original data is unchanged.
vbDropEffectMove	2	The operation results in a link from the original data to the target control.
vbDropEffectScroll	&H80000000	The target control is about to scroll or is scrolling. This value may be added to the other *shift* values.

Table T-61: Effect *values.*

Private Sub *TextBoxControl_OLESetData*([*index* As Integer ,] *data* As DataObject, *DataFormat* As Integer)

Usage   This event happens in response to the target object performing a **GetData** method on *data*. This routine will respond by using the **SetData** method with the desired data using the **DataObject** *data*.

Arguments   ▪ *index*—an **Integer** that is used to uniquely identify a control in a control array. This argument is not present if the control is not part of a control array.

▪ *data*—a **DataObject** that will contain the data to be returned to the target object.

▪ *format*—an **Integer** that contains the format of the data (see Table T-62).

format Name	Value	Description
vbCFText	1	Text (.TXT files).
vbCFBitmap	2	Bitmap (.BMP files).
vbCFMetafile	3	Metafile (.WMF files).
vbCFEDIB	8	Device-independent bitmap (DIB).
vbCFPallette	9	Color palette.
vbCFEMetafile	14	Enhanced metafile (.EMF files).
vbCFFiles	15	List of files.
vbCFRTF	-16639	Rich Text Format (.RTF files).

Table T-62: Format *values.*

Private Sub *TextBoxControl_OLEStartDrag* ([*index* As Integer ,] *data* As DataObject, *AllowedEffects* As Long)

Usage   This event is used to start an OLE drag-and-drop operation.

Arguments   ▪ *index*—an **Integer** that is used to uniquely identify a control in a control array. This argument is not present if the control is not part of a control array.

▪ *data*—a **DataObject** that will contain the formats that the source object is willing to provide to the target object. It may optionally contain the data to be transferred.

1008 • The Visual Basic 5 Programmer's Reference

- *AllowedEffects*—a **Long** that contains the effects that the target object can request from the source object (see Table T-63). The *AllowedEffects* can be added together if the source object supports more than one effect. Note that the target object can always use the *vbDropEffectNone* effect.

AllowedEffects Name	Value	Description
vbDropEffectNone	0	The target can't copy the data.
vbDropEffectCopy	1	The target can copy the data, and the source will keep the data unchanged.
vbDropEffectMove	2	The target can copy the data, and the source will delete the data.

Table T-63: AllowedEffects *values*.

See Also **Label** (control), **Masked Edit** (control)

TextLayout

OBJECT

PE, EE

Usage The **TextLayout** object is part of the **MSChart** control containing information about how text is displayed on the chart.

Properties
- *TextLayoutObject*.**HorzAlignment**—an **Integer** containing the method used to horizontally align text (see Table T-64).

HorzAlignment Name	Value	Description
vtHorizontalAlignmentLeft	0	Text is left aligned.
vtHorizontalAlignmentRight	2	Text is right aligned.
vtHorizontalAlignmentCenter	1	Text is centered.

Table T-64: HorzAlignment *values*.

- *TextLayoutObject*.**Orientation**—an **Integer** describing how the text is displayed (see Table T-65).

Orientation Name	Value	Description
vtOrientationHorizontal	0	Text is displayed horizontally.
vtOrientationVertical	1	Text is displayed vertically with each character displayed on top of the next.
vtOrientationUp	2	Text is rotated to read from bottom to top.
vtOrientationDown	3	Text is rotated to read from top to bottom.

Table T-65: Orientation *values*.

- *TextLayoutObject*.**VertAlignment**—an **Integer** containing the method used to vertically align text (see Table T-66).

VertAlignment Name	Value	Description
vtVerticalAlignmentTop	0	Text is top aligned.
vtVerticalAlignmentBottom	2	Text is bottom aligned.
vtVerticalAlignmentCenter	1	Text is centered.

Table T-66: VertAlignment *values.*

- *TextLayoutObject*.**WordWrap**—a **Boolean,** when **True**, means the text is wrapped onto the next line. **False** means the text is not wrapped.

See Also   **MSChart** (control)

Tick

OBJECT

PE, EE

Usage   The **Tick** object is part of the **MSChart** control containing information about a marker along a chart axis.

Properties
- *TickObject*.**Length**—an **Integer** containing the length of a tick mark in points.
- *TextLayoutlObject*.**Style**—an **Integer** describing how the tick marks are displayed (see Table T-67).

Style Name	Value	Description
vtChAxisTickStyleNone	0	No tick marks are displayed.
vtChAxisTickStyleCenter	2	Tick marks are displayed centered on the axis.
vtAxisTickStyleInside	1	Tick marks are displayed inside the axis.
vtAxisTickStyleOutside	2	Tick marks are displayed outside the axis.

Table T-67: Style *values.*

See Also   **MSChart** (control)

Time

FUNCTION

CCE, LE, PE, EE

Syntax   `DValue = Time`

Usage   The **Time** function returns the current time as a **Date** variable.

Arguments	▪ *DValue*—a **Date** value containing the current time.
| Examples | ```
Private Sub Command1_Click()
Dim d As Date
d = Time
MsgBox "The current time is: " & Format(d)
Time = CDate("00:00:00")
MsgBox "The new time is: " & Format(Time)
Time = d
MsgBox "The time has been restored to: " & Format(Time)
End Sub
``` |

This routine saves the current time into a local variable and displays it. Then it changes the current time to midnight using the **Time** statement. Next the **Time** function is used to verify the new time. Finally it restores the original time using the **Time** statement and the **Time** function is again used to verify it.

See Also	**CDate** (function), **Date** (data type), **Date** (function), **Date** (statement), **Now** (function), **Time** (statement)

Time

STATEMENT

CCE, LE, PE, EE

Syntax	**Time** = *DValue*
Usage	The **Time** statement is used to set the computer's current date.
Arguments	▪ *DValue*—a **Date** value containing the current date.
| Examples | ```
Private Sub Command1_Click()
Dim d As Date
d = Time
MsgBox "The current time is: " & Format(d)
Time = CDate("00:00:00")
MsgBox "The new time is: " & Format(Time)
Time = d
MsgBox "The time has been restored to: " & Format(Time)
End Sub
``` |

This routine saves the current time into a local variable and displays it. Then it changes the current time to midnight using the **Time** statement. Next the **Time** function is used to verify the new time. Finally it restores the original time using the **Time** statement and the **Time** function is again used to verify it.

See Also	**CDate** (function), **Date** (data type), **Date** (function), **Date** (statement), **Now** (function), **Time** (function)

Timer

CONTROL
PE, EE

Usage The **Timer** control is an intrinsic control that invokes an event at periodic intervals.

> **Tip**
>
> *Unlike previous versions of Visual Basic, there is essentially no limit to the number of timers available when running under Windows 95 and Windows NT 4.0.*

Properties
- *TimerControl*.**Enabled**—a **Boolean** value when **True** means that the control will respond to events. When **False**, the control will not respond to events.
- *TimerControl*.**Index**—an **Integer** that is used to uniquely identify a control in a control array.
- *TimerControl*.**Interval**—a **Long** containing the number of milliseconds between calls to the **Timer** event. A value of zero will disable the timer. Legal values range from 1 to 65,535, or about 65 seconds.

> **Note**
>
> *The resolution of the timer is about 55 milliseconds. Thus an **Interval** of less than 55 milliseconds will be rounded to 55 milliseconds. A value between 56 and 110 milliseconds will be rounded to 110. While this doesn't cause problems for **Intervals** of a tenth of a second or greater, this can be a real problem if you need really fine timer values. To solve this problem, you have to use the Windows API directly or purchase a third party timer control.*

- *TimerControl*.**Left**—a **Single** that contains the distance, measured in twips, between the left edge of the control and the left edge of the control's container.
- *TimerControl*.**Name**—a **String** that contains the name of the control that will be used to reference the control in a Visual Basic program. This property is read only at run time.
- *TimerControl*.**Parent**—an object that contains a reference to the **Form**, **Frame**, or other container that contains this control.
- *TimerControl*.**Tag**—a **String** that can hold programmer-specific information. This property is not used by Visual Basic.

Events **Private Sub** *TimerControl*_**Timer** ([*index* **As Integer**])

Usage This event occurs every **Interval**.

Arguments
- *index*—an **Integer** that is used to uniquely identify a control in a control array. This argument is not present if the control is not part of a control array.

Examples
```
Dim CountDown As Integer

Private Sub Command1_Click()
CountDown = 10
Timer1.Interval = 1000
End Sub
```

```
Private Sub Timer1_Timer()
If CountDown = 0 Then
   Timer1.Interval = 0
   Text1.Text = "BOOM!"
Else
   Text1.Text = Format(CountDown)
   CountDown = CountDown--1
End If
End Sub
```

This starts the timer by setting the interval to 1000 milliseconds and sets the CountDown variable to 10 when the user presses the command button. In the **Timer** event, either the variable CountDown is displayed and decremented or the timer is disabled and BOOM is displayed in the text box.

See Also   **Time** (function), **Timer** (function)

Timer

FUNCTION

CCE, LE, PE, EE

Syntax   *Value* = **Timer**

Usage   The **Timer** function returns the number of seconds since midnight.

Arguments   • *Value*—a **Single** value containing the number of seconds since midnight.

Examples
```
Private Sub Command1_Click()
MsgBox Format(Timer) & " seconds since midnight."
End Sub
```

This routine displays the number of seconds since midnight.

See Also   **Time** (function)

TimeValue

FUNCTION

CCE, LE, PE, EE

Syntax   *DValue* = **TimeValue** (*hour, minute, seconds*)

Usage   The **TimeValue** function returns a date value for given values for hour, minute, and second. If a value for a given minute or second is outside its normal range, then that value is adjusted to be in the normal range and the other values will be adjusted accordingly. For example, assume an hour of 12, a minute of 30, and a second of -45. This would convert to the value 12:29:15.

Arguments   • *DValue*—a **Date** value including the hour, minute, and second.
   • *hour*—an **Integer** value containing the hour.
   • *minute*—an **Integer** value containing the minute.
   • *seconds*—an **Integer** value containing the seconds.

Examples
```
Private Sub Command1_Click()
Text4.Text = TimeSerial(CInt(Text1.Text), CInt(Text2.Text), CInt(Text3.Text))
End Sub
```

This routine takes the values from the text1, text2, and text3 text boxes to compute a time that displays in the text4 text box.

See Also **CDate** (function), **Date** (data type), **Hour** (function), **IsDate** (function), **Minute** (function), **Now** (function), **Second** (function), **Time** (function), **Time** (statement), **TimeSerial** (function), **TimeValue** (function)

TimeValue

FUNCTION

CCE, LE, PE, EE

Syntax *DValue* = **TimeValue** (*Value*)

Usage The **TimeValue** function converts a **String** value into a **Date** value. While any date information is ignored, an invalid date will cause a run-time error.

Arguments
- *DValue*—a **Date** value containing a valid time.
- *Value*—a **String** value containing the time.

Examples
```
Private Sub Command1_Click()
If IsDate(Text1.Text) Then
    Text2.Text = Format(TimeValue(Text1.Text))
Else
    Text2.Text = "Illegal date."
End If
End Sub
```

This routine verifies that a valid date and time value is in the Text1 text box and then converts it to a **Date** value.

See Also **CDate** (function), **Date** (data type), **Hour** (function), **IsDate** (function), **Minute** (function), **Now** (function), **Second** (function), **Time** (function), **Time** (statement), **TimeSerial** (function), **TimeValue** (function)

Title

OBJECT

PE, EE

Usage The **Title** object is used by the **MSChart** control to contain information about the chart's title.

Properties
- *TitleObject*.**Backdrop**—an object reference to a **Backdrop** object containing information about the appearance of the backdrop.
- *TitleObject*.**Font**—an object reference to a **Font** object containing the font used to display the title's text.

- *TitleObject*.**Location**—an object reference to a **Location** object describing where the title is placed on the chart.
- *TitleObject*.**Text**—a **String** containing the title to be displayed on the chart.
- *TitleObject*.**TextLayout**—an object reference to a **TextLayout** object describing how the text is oriented and positioned.
- *TitleObject*.**TextLength**—an **Integer** containing the number of characters in the **Text** property.
- *TitleObject*.**VtFont**—an object reference to a **VtFont** object containing information about the font used to display the title's text.

Methods **TitleObject.Select**

  Usage This method selects the title for the chart.

See Also **Backdrop** (object), **Font** (object), **Location** (object), **MSChart** (control), **TextLayout** (object), **VtFont** (object).

Toolbar

CONTROL

PE, EE

Usage The **Toolbar** control contains a series of buttons that provide quick and easy access for a user to perform functions.

Properties
- *ToolbarControl*.**Align**—an **Integer** value that describes the placement of the control (see Table T-68).

Align Name	Value	Description
vbAlignNone	0	The control's position is set at design time or by the program (default value for objects on a non-MDI Form).
vbAlignTop	1	The control is placed at the top of the form and its width is set to **ScaleWidth**. It will automatically be resized when the form is resized (default value for objects on an MDI Form).
vbAlignBottom	2	The control is placed at the bottom of the form and its width is set to **ScaleWidth**. It will automatically be resized when the form is resized.
vbAlignLeft	3	The control is placed at the left edge of the form and its width is set to **ScaleWidth**. It is not resized when the form is resized.
vbAlignRight	4	The control is placed at the right edge of the form and its width is set to **ScaleWidth**. It is not resized when the form is resized.

Table T-68: Align *values.*

- *ToolbarControl*.**AllowCustomize**—a **Boolean** value when **True** means that the user may customize the toolbar using the customize toolbar dialog box. **False** means that the user can't customize the toolbar.
- *ToolbarControl*.**Appearance**—an **Integer** value that determines how the combo box will appear on the form (see Table T-69).

Appearance Value	Description
0	The Toolbar control is displayed without the 3D effects.
1	The **Toolbar** control is displayed with 3D effects (default value).

Table T-69: Appearance values.

- *ToolbarControl.***BorderStyle**—an **Integer** specifying how the border will be drawn (see Table T-70).

BorderStyle Name	Value	Description
vbBSNone	0	No border is displayed.
vbFixedSingle	1	Single line around the label.

Table T-70: BorderStyle values.

- *ToolbarControl.***ButtonHeight**—a **Single** that contains the height of a button.
- *ToolbarControl.***ButtonWidth**—a **Single** that contains the width of a button.
- *ToolbarControl.***Buttons**—a reference to the **Buttons** collection containing information about the buttons on the toolbar.
- *ToolbarControl.***Container**—an object that can be used to set or return the container of the control at run time. This property cannot be set at design time.
- *ToolbarControl.***Controls**—a reference to a **Controls** collection that contains all of the controls placed on the toolbar. Note that the buttons on the toolbar are not considered controls, so they are not included in this collection.
- *ToolbarControl.***DataBindings**—a reference to the **DataBindings** collection containing the bindable properties available.
- *ToolbarControl.***DragIcon**—an object that contains the picture value of an icon. At design time, you can specify an icon file that has a file type of .ICO.

> **Tip**
>
> *This value can be created by copying the value from another control's **DragIcon** value, a form's icon, or by using the **LoadPicture** function.*

- *ToolbarControl.***DragMode**—an **Integer** specifying how the control will respond to a drag request (see Table T-71).

> **Tip**
>
> *Setting **DragMode** to vbAutomatic will automatically begin a drag operation when the user clicks on the control. However, the control will not respond to the usual mouse events (**Click**, **DblClick**, **MouseDown**, **MouseMove**, **MouseUp**).*

DragMode Name	Value	Description
vbManual	0	The Drag method must be used to begin a drag-and-drop operation (default value).
vbAutomatic	1	The source control will automatically begin a drag-and-drop operation when the user clicks on the control.

Table T-71: DragMode values.

- *ToolbarControl.***Enabled**—a **Boolean** value when **True** means that the control will respond to events. When **False**, the control will not respond to events.
- *ToolbarControl.***Height**—a **Single** that contains the height of the control.
- *ToolbarControl.***HelpContextID**—a **Long** that contains a help file context ID number that references an entry in the help file. When the user presses the F1 key while this control is active, the corresponding entry in the help file will automatically be displayed. A value of zero means that no context number was specified.

Tip

A help file must be compiled using the Windows Help Compiler available in the Professional and Enterprise editions of Visual Basic.

- *ToolbarControl.***HelpFile**—a **String** containing the path and name of a help file where the **HelpContextID** is located.
- *ToolbarControl.***hWnd**—a **Long** that contains a Windows handle to the control.

Tip

*The **hWnd** property is most useful when making calls to Windows API functions. Since this value can change during execution, do not save the value into a variable for later use.*

- *ToolbarControl.***ImageList**—a reference to an **ImageList** object that contains the pictures that will be used for the large icon display.
- *ToolbarControl.***Index**—an **Integer** that is used to uniquely identify a control in a control array.
- *ToolbarControl.***Left**—a **Single** that contains the distance, measured in twips, between the left edge of the control and the left edge of the control's container.
- *ToolbarControl.***MouseIcon**—a picture object (a bitmap, icon, or metafile) that will be used as a cursor when the **MousePointer** property is set to 99. Note that Visual Basic does not support color cursors from a .CUR file. A color icon from an .ICO file should be used instead.
- *ToolbarControl.***MousePointer**—an **Integer** that contains the value of the cursor that should be displayed when the cursor is moved over this control (see Table T-72). Use *vbCustom* to display the custom icon stored in the **MouseIcon** property.

Cursor Name	Value	Description
vbDefault	0	Shape determined by the object (default value).
vbArrow	1	Arrow.
vbCrosshair	2	Crosshair.
vbIbeam	3	I beam.
vbIconPointer	4	Square inside a square.
vbSizePointer	5	Four-sided arrow (north, south, east, west).
vbSizeNESW	6	Two-sided arrow (northeast, southwest).
vbSizeNS	7	Two-sided arrow (north, south).
vbSizeNWSE	8	Two-sided arrow (northwest, southeast).
vbSizeWE	9	Two-sided arrow (west, east).
vbUpArrow	10	Single-sided arrow pointing north.
vbHourglass	11	Hourglass.
vbNoDrop	12	No drop.
vbArrowHourglass	13	An arrow and an hourglass.
vbArrowQuestion	14	An arrow and a question mark.
vbSizeAll	15	Size all.
vbCustom	99	Custom icon from the MouseIcon property of this control.

Table T-72: Cursor *values.*

- *ToolbarControl.***Name**—a **String** that contains the name of the control that will be used to reference the control in a Visual Basic program. This property is read only at run time.
- *ToolbarControl.***Object**—an object that contains a reference to the *ToolbarControl* object.
- *ToolbarControl.***OLEDropMode**—an **Integer** value (see Table T-73) that describes how the control will respond to OLE drop operations.

OLEDropMode Name	Value	Description
vbOLEDropNone	0	The control does not accept OLE drops. The cursor is changed to the No Drop cursor (default value).
vbOLEDropManual	1	The control responds to OLE drops under the program's control (manual).
vbOLEDropAutomatic	2	The control automatically accepts OLE drops if it recognizes the format of the data object.

Table T-73: OLEDropMode *values.*

- *ToolbarControl.***Parent**—an object that contains a reference to the **Form**, **Frame**, or other container that holds this control.
- *ToolbarControl.***ShowTips**—a **Boolean**, when **True**, means that the objects in the control may show tool tips. **False** means that the objects can't display tool tips.
- *ToolbarControl.***TabIndex**—an Integer that is used to determine the order that a user will tab through the objects on a form.
- *ToolbarControl.***Tag**—a **String** that can hold programmer-specific information. This property is not used by Visual Basic.
- *ToolbarControl.***ToolTipText**—a **String** that holds a text value that can be displayed as a **ToolTip** box that is displayed whenever the cursor is held over the control for about one second.

- *ToolbarControl*.**Top**—a **Single** that contains the distance, measured in twips, between the top edge of the control and the top edge of the control's container.
- *ToolbarControl*.**Visible**—a **Boolean** value when **True** means that the control is visible. **False** means that the control is not visible.

> **Tip**
>
> *This property can be used to hide the control until the program is ready to display it.*

- *ToolbarControl*.**WhatsThisHelpID**—a **Long** that contains a help file context ID number that references an entry in the help file. This is used to provide a What's This PopUp help display in response to the What's This button in the upper right corner of the window.
- *ToolbarControl*.**Width**—a **Single** that contains the width of the control.
- *ToolbarObject*.**Wrappable**—a **Boolean,** when **True**, means the buttons will be wrapped if the form is resized. **False** means the buttons will not be wrapped.

Methods

ToolbarControl.Customize

Usage — This method invokes the Customize Toolbar dialog box to allow the user to customize the toolbar.

ToolbarControl.Drag [DragAction]

Usage — This method is used to begin, end, or cancel a drag operation.

Arguments
- *DragAction*—an **Integer** that contains a value selected from Table T-74 below.

DragAction Name	Value	Description
vbCancel	0	Cancels any drag operation in progress.
vbBeginDrag	1	Begins a drag operation (default).
vbEndDrag	2	Ends a drag operation and drops *object*.

Table T-74: DragAction *values*.

ToolbarControl.Move Left [, Top [, Width [, Height]]]

Usage — This method is used to change the position and the size of the **Toolbar** control. The **ScaleMode** of the **Form** or other container object that holds the **Toolbar** control will determine the units used to specify the coordinates.

Arguments
- *Left*—a **Single** that specifies the new position of the left edge of the control.
- *Top*—a **Single** that specifies the new position of the top edge of the control.
- *Width*—a **Single** that specifies the new width of the control.
- *Height*—a **Single** that specifies the new height of the control.

ToolbarControl.OLEDrag

Usage   This method is used to begin an **OLEDrag** and drop operation. Invoking this method will trigger the **OLEStartDrag** event.

ToolbarControl.Refresh

Usage   This method is used to redraw the contents of the control.

ToolbarControl.RestoreToolbar *key, subkey, value*

Usage   This method restores the toolbar from a value saved in the Windows registry. Note that the toolbar information has to have been previously saved using the **SaveToolbar** method.

Arguments
- *key*—a **String** containing a Windows registry key where the toolbar will be restored from.
- *subkey*—a **String** containing a Windows registry subkey where the toolbar will be restored from.
- *value*—a **String** that specifies the new width of the control.

ToolbarControl.SaveToolbar *key, subkey, value*

Usage   This method saves the toolbar information into the Windows registry.

Tip

*Use this method in the **Change** event to save the changes so that they may be restored the next time the program runs.*

Arguments
- *key*—a **String** containing a Windows registry key where the toolbar will be restored from.
- *subkey*—a **String** containing a Windows registry subkey where the toolbar will be restored from.
- *value*—a **String** that specifies the new width of the control.

ToolbarControl.ShowWhatsThis

Usage   This method displays the ShowWhatsThis help information for this control.

ToolbarControl.ZOrder [*position*]

Usage   This method is used to specify the position of the **Toolbar** control relative to the other objects on the form.

> **Tip**
>
> *Note that there are three layers of objects on a form. The back layer is the drawing space that contains the results of the graphical methods, and the middle layer contains graphical objects and **Labels**. The top layer contains non-graphical controls such as the **Toolbar** control. The **ZOrder** method only affects how the objects are arranged within a single layer.*

- Arguments
  - *position*—an **Integer** that specifies the relative position of this object. A value of 0 means that the control is positioned at the head of the list; a value of 1 means that the control will be placed at the end of the list.

Events

Private Sub *ToolbarControl*_ButtonClick([*index* As Integer ,] ByVal *button* As Button)

- Usage: This event occurs when the user clicks a toolbar button.
- Arguments
  - *index*—an **Integer** that is used to uniquely identify a control in a control array. This argument is not present if the control is not part of a control array.
  - *button*—a **Button** object containing information about the button that was pressed.

Private Sub *ToolbarControl*_Change ([*index* As Integer])

- Usage: This event occurs whenever the user has finished customizing the toolbar using the Customize Toolbar dialog box.
- Arguments
  - *index*—an **Integer** that is used to uniquely identify a control in a control array. This argument is not present if the control is not part of a control array.

Private Sub *ToolbarControl*_Click([*index* As Integer])

- Usage: This event occurs when the user clicks a mouse button while the cursor is over the toolbar, but not over any button.
- Arguments
  - *index*—an **Integer** that is used to uniquely identify a control in a control array. This argument is not present if the control is not part of a control array.

Private Sub *ToolbarControl*_DblClick([*index* As Integer])

- Usage: This event occurs when the user double-clicks a mouse button while the cursor is over the toolbar, but not over any button.
- Arguments
  - *index*—an **Integer** that is used to uniquely identify a control in a control array. This argument is not present if the control is not part of a control array.

Private Sub *ToolbarControl*_DragDrop([*index* As Integer ,] *source* As Control, *x* As Single, *y* As Single)

> Usage   This event occurs when a drag-and-drop operation is completed by using the Drag method with a *DragAction* value of *vbEndDrag*.

Tip

*When using drag-and-drop operations, use the **DragOver** event to determine what the cursor should look like while the cursor moves over the control.*

> Arguments
> - *index*—an **Integer** that is used to uniquely identify a control in a control array. This argument is not present if the control is not part of a control array.
> - *source*—a control object that is the control that is being dragged.

Tip

You can access a property or method from the source control by using source.property *or* source.method. *You can determine the type of object or control by using the **TypeOf** operator.*

> - *x*—a **Single** that contains the horizontal location of the mouse pointer.
> - *y*—a **Single** that contains the vertical location of the mouse pointer.

Private Sub *ToolbarControl*_DragOver([*index* As Integer ,] *source* As Control, *x* As Single, *y* As Single, *state* As Integer)

> Usage   This event occurs while a drag operation is in progress and the cursor is moved over the control.

Tip

*When using drag-and-drop operations, use the **DragOver** event to determine what the cursor should look like while the cursor moves over the control. When* state *is 0, you can change the cursor to a no drop (vbNoDrop) cursor or highlight the field that the cursor is near. When* state *is 1, you can undo the changes you made when the* state *was 0.*

> Arguments
> - *index*—an **Integer** that is used to uniquely identify a control in a control array. This argument is not present if the control is not part of a control array.
> - *source*—a control object that is the control that is being dragged.

Tip

You can access a property or method from the source control by using source.property *or* source.method. *You can determine the type of object or control by using the **TypeOf** operator.*

- *x*—a **Single** that contains the horizontal location of the mouse pointer.
- *y*—a **Single** that contains the vertical location of the mouse pointer.
- *state*—an **Integer** that indicates the state of the object being dragged (see Table T-75).

state Name	Value	Description
vbEnter	0	The dragged object is entering range of the control.
vbLeave	1	The dragged object is leaving range of the control.
vbOver	2	The dragged object has moved from one position over the control to another.

Table T-75: State *values*.

Private Sub *ToolbarBoxControl*_MouseDown([*index* As Integer ,] *button* As Integer, *shift* As Single, *x* As Single, *y* As Single)

Usage — This event occurs when a mouse button is pressed while the cursor is over the control.

Arguments
- *index*—an **Integer** that is used to uniquely identify a control in a control array. This argument is not present if the control is not part of a control array.
- *button*—an **Integer** that contains information about the mouse buttons that were pressed (see Table T-76). Only one button will be indicated when this event occurs.

button Name	Value	Description
vbLeftButton	1	The left button was pressed.
vbRightButton	2	The right button was pressed.
vbMiddleButton	4	The middle button was pressed.

Table T-76: Button *values*.

- *shift*—an **Integer** that contains information about the Shift and Alt keys that were pressed when the mouse button was pressed (see Table T-77). These values can be added together if more than one key was down. For instance, a value of 5 would mean that the Shift and Alt keys were both down when the mouse button was pressed.

shift Name	Value	Description
vbShiftMask	1	The Shift key was pressed.
vbCtrlMask	2	The Ctrl key was pressed.
vbAltMask	4	The Alt key was pressed.

Table T-77: Shift *values*.

- *x*—a **Single** that contains the horizontal location of the mouse pointer.
- *y*—a **Single** that contains the vertical location of the mouse pointer.

Private Sub *ToolbarControl*_MouseMove ([*index* As Integer ,] *button* As Integer, *shift* As Single, *x* As Single, *y* As Single)

Usage This event occurs while the cursor is moved over the control.

Arguments
- *index*—an **Integer** that is used to uniquely identify a control in a control array. This argument is not present if the control is not part of a control array.
- *button*—an **Integer** that contains information about the mouse buttons that were pressed (see Table T-78). These values can be added together if more than one button was pressed. For instance, a value of 3 means that both the left and right buttons were pressed. A value of 0 means that no buttons were pressed.

button Name	Value	Description
vbLeftButton	1	The left button was pressed.
vbRightButton	2	The right button was pressed.
vbMiddleButton	4	The middle button was pressed.

Table T-78: Button *values*.

- *shift*—an **Integer** that contains information about the Shift and Alt keys that were pressed when the mouse button was pressed (see Table T-79). These values can be added together if more than one key was down. For instance, a value of 5 would mean that the Shift and Alt keys were both down when the mouse button was pressed. A value of 0 means that none of these keys were pressed.

shift Name	Value	Description
vbShiftMask	1	The Shift key was pressed.
vbCtrlMask	2	The Ctrl key was pressed.
vbAltMask	4	The Alt key was pressed.

Table T-79: Shift *values*.

- *x*—a **Single** that contains the horizontal location of the mouse pointer.
- *y*—a **Single** that contains the vertical location of the mouse pointer.

Private Sub *ToolbarBoxControl*_MouseUp([*index* As Integer ,] *button* As Integer, *shift* As Single, *x* As Single, *y* As Single)

Usage This event occurs when a mouse button is released while the cursor is over the control.

Arguments
- *index*—an **Integer** that is used to uniquely identify a control in a control array. This argument is not present if the control is not part of a control array.
- *button*—an **Integer** that contains information about the mouse buttons that were released (see Table T-80). Only one of these values will be present.

button Name	Value	Description
vbLeftButton	1	The left button was released.
vbRightButton	2	The right button was released.
vbMiddleButton	4	The middle button was released.

Table T-80: Button *values*.

- *shift*—an **Integer** that contains information about the Shift and Alt keys that were pressed when the mouse button was released (see Table T-81). These values can be added together if more than one key was down. For instance, a value of 5 would mean that the Shift and Alt keys were both down when the mouse button was released. A value of 0 means that none of these keys were pressed.

shift Name	Value	Description
vbShiftMask	1	The Shift key was pressed.
vbCtrlMask	2	The Ctrl key was pressed.
vbAltMask	4	The Alt key was pressed.

Table T-81: Shift *values*.

- *x*—a **Single** that contains the horizontal location of the mouse pointer.
- *y*—a **Single** that contains the vertical location of the mouse pointer.

Private Sub *ToolbarControl*_OLECompleteDrag([*index* As Integer ,] *effect* As Long)

Usage | This event is used to tell the source control the results of an OLE drag-and-drop operation. This is the final event to occur in the series of actions that make up an OLE drag-and-drop operation.

Arguments
- *index*—an **Integer** that is used to uniquely identify a control in a control array. This argument is not present if the control is not part of a control array.
- *effect*—a **Long** that returns the status of the OLE drag-and-drop operation (see Table T-82).

effect Name	Value	Description
vbDropEffectNone	0	The operation is canceled or the target control can't accept the drop operation.
vbDropEffectCopy	1	The operation copies data from the source control to the target control. The original data is unchanged.
vbDropEffectMove	2	The operation results in a link from the original data to the target control.

Table T-82: Effect *values*.

Private Sub *ToolbarControl*_OLEDragDrop([*index* As Integer ,] *data* As DataObject, *effect* As Long, *button* As Integer, *shift* As Single, *x* As Single, *y* As Single)

Usage This event is used to tell the source control the results of an OLE drag-and-drop operation. This is the final event to occur in the series of actions that make up an OLE drag-and-drop operation.

Arguments
- *index*—an **Integer** that is used to uniquely identify a control in a control array. This argument is not present if the control is not part of a control array.
- *data*—a **DataObject** that contains the formats that the source control will provide. If the data is not contained in the **DataObject**, then it can be retrieved with the **GetData** method.
- *effect*—a **Long** that returns the status of the OLE drag-and-drop operation (see Table T-83).

effect Name	Value	Description
vbDropEffectNone	0	The operation is canceled or the target control can't accept the drop operation.
vbDropEffectCopy	1	The operation copies data from the source control to the target control. The original data is unchanged.
vbDropEffectMove	2	The operation results in a link from the original data to the target control.

Table T-83: Effect *values*.

- *button*—an **Integer** that contains information about the mouse buttons that were pressed (see Table T-84). These values can be added together if more than one button was pressed. For instance, a value of 3 means that both the left and right buttons were pressed. A value of 0 means that no buttons were pressed.

button Name	Value	Description
vbLeftButton	1	The left button was pressed.
vbRightButton	2	The right button was pressed.
vbMiddleButton	4	The middle button was pressed.

Table T-84: Button *values*.

- *shift*—an **Integer** that contains information about the Shift and Alt keys that were pressed when the mouse button was released (see Table T-85). These values can be added together if more than one key was down. For instance, a value of 5 would mean that the Shift and Alt keys were both down when the mouse button was released. A value of 0 means that none of these keys were pressed.

shift Name	Value	Description
vbShiftMask	1	The Shift key was pressed.
vbCtrlMask	2	The Ctrl key was pressed.
vbAltMask	4	The Alt key was pressed.

Table T-85: Shift *values*.

- *x*—a **Single** that contains the horizontal location of the mouse pointer.
- *y*—a **Single** that contains the vertical location of the mouse pointer.

Private Sub *ToolbarControl*_OLEDragOver([*index* As Integer ,] *data* As DataObject, *effect* As Long, *button* As Integer, *shift* As Single, *x* As Single, *y* As Single, *state* As Integer)

Usage   This event happens when an OLE drag-and-drop operation is in progress.

Arguments
- *index*—an **Integer** that is used to uniquely identify a control in a control array. This argument is not present if the control is not part of a control array.
- *data*—a **DataObject** that contains the formats that the source control will provide. If the data is not contained in the **DataObject**, then it can be retrieved with the **GetData** method.
- *effect*—a **Long** that returns the status of the OLE drag-and-drop operation (see Table T-86).

effect Name	Value	Description
vbDropEffectNone	0	The operation is canceled or the target control can't accept the drop operation.
vbDropEffectCopy	1	The operation copies data from the source control to the target control. The original data is unchanged.
vbDropEffectMove	2	The operation results in a link from the original data to the target control.

Table T-86: Effect *values*.

- *button*—an **Integer** that contains information about the mouse buttons that were pressed (see Table T-87). These values can be added together if more than one button was pressed. For instance, a value of 3 means that both the left and right buttons were pressed. A value of 0 means that no buttons were pressed.

button Name	Value	Description
vbLeftButton	1	The left button was pressed.
vbRightButton	2	The right button was pressed.
vbMiddleButton	4	The middle button was pressed.

Table T-87: Button *values*.

- *shift*—an **Integer** that contains information about the Shift and Alt keys that were pressed when the mouse button was released (see Table T-88). These values can be added together if more than one key was down. For instance, a value of 5 would mean that the Shift and Alt keys were both down when the mouse button was released. A value of 0 means that none of these keys were pressed.

shift Name	Value	Description
vbShiftMask	1	The Shift key was pressed.
vbCtrlMask	2	The Ctrl key was pressed.
vbAltMask	4	The Alt key was pressed.

Table T-88: Shift *values.*

- *x*—a **Single** that contains the horizontal location of the mouse pointer.
- *y*—a **Single** that contains the vertical location of the mouse pointer.
- *state*—an **Integer** that indicates the state of the object being dragged (see Table T-89).

state Name	Value	Description
vbEnter	0	The dragged object is entering range of the control.
vbLeave	1	The dragged object is leaving range of the control.
vbOver	2	The dragged object has moved from one position over the control to another.

Table T-89: State *values.*

Private Sub *ToolbarControl*_OLEGiveFeedback ([*index* As Integer ,] *effect* As Long)

Usage   This event is used to tell the source control what is happening while the OLE drag-and-drop operation is in progress. This event occurs after the OLEDragOver event.

Tip

You may want to use this event to change the cursor to reflect what can happen in the remote object.

Arguments
- *index*—an **Integer** that is used to uniquely identify a control in a control array. This argument is not present if the control is not part of a control array.
- *effect*—a **Long** that returns the status of the OLE drag-and-drop operation (see Table T-90).

effect Name	Value	Description
vbDropEffectNone	0	The operation is canceled or the target control can't accept the drop operation.
vbDropEffectCopy	1	The operation copies data from the source control to the target control. The original data is unchanged.
vbDropEffectMove	2	The operation results in a link from the original data to the target control.
vbDropEffectScroll	&H80000000	The target control is about to scroll or is scrolling. This value may be added to the other *shift* values.

Table T-90: Effect *values.*

Private Sub *ToolbarControl*_OLESetData([*index* As Integer ,] *data* As DataObject, *DataFormat* As Integer)

Usage   This event happens in response to the target object performing a **GetData** method on *data*. This routine will respond by using the **SetData** method with the desired data using the **DataObject** *data*.

Arguments
- *index*—an **Integer** that is used to uniquely identify a control in a control array. This argument is not present if the control is not part of a control array.
- *data*—a **DataObject** that will contain the data to be returned to the target object.
- *format*—an **Integer** that contains the format of the data (see Table T-91).

format Name	Value	Description
vbCFText	1	Text (.TXT files).
vbCFBitmap	2	Bitmap (.BMP files).
vbCFMetafile	3	Metafile (.WMF files).
vbCFEDIB	8	Device-independent bitmap (DIB).
vbCFPallette	9	Color palette.
vbCFEMetafile	14	Enhanced metafile (.EMF files).
vbCFFiles	15	List of files.
vbCFRTF	-16639	Rich Text Format (.RTF files).

Table T-91: Format *values.*

Private Sub *ToolbarControl*_OLEStartDrag ([*index* As Integer ,] *data* As DataObject, *AllowedEffects* As Long)

Usage   This event is used to start an OLE drag-and-drop operation.

Arguments
- *index*—an **Integer** that is used to uniquely identify a control in a control array. This argument is not present if the control is not part of a control array.
- *data*—a **DataObject** that will contain the formats that the source object is willing to provide to the target object. It may optionally contain the data to be transferred.

- *AllowedEffects*—a **Long** that contains the effects that the target object can request from the source object (see Table T-92). The *AllowedEffects* can be added together if the source object supports more than one effect. Note that the target object can always use the *vbDropEffectNone* effect.

AllowedEffects Name	Value	Description
vbDropEffectNone	0	The target can't copy the data.
vbDropEffectCopy	1	The target can copy the data, and the source will keep the data unchanged.
vbDropEffectMove	2	The target can copy the data, and the source will delete the data.

Table T-92: AllowedEffects *values*.

See Also StatusBar (control)

TreeView

CONTROL

PE, EE

Usage The **TreeView** control is an ActiveX control (part of the Microsoft Windows Common Controls 5.0) that provides a hierarchical list of objects.

Properties
- *TreeViewControl*.**Appearance**—an **Integer** value that determines how the combo box will appear on the form (see Table T-93).

Appearance Value	Description
0	The TreeView control is displayed without the 3D effects.
1	The **TreeView** control is displayed with 3D effects (default value).

Table T-93: Appearance *values*.

- *TreeViewControl*.**BorderStyle**—an **Integer** specifying how the border will be drawn (see Table T-94).

BorderStyle Name	Value	Description
vbBSNone	0	No border is displayed.
vbFixedSingle	1	Single line around the label.

Table T-94: BorderStyle *values*.

- *TreeViewControl*.**Container**—an object that can be used to set or return the container of the control at run time. This property cannot be set at design time.
- *TreeViewControl*.**DragIcon**—an object that contains the picture value of an icon. At design time, you can specify an icon file that has a file type of .ICO.

> **Tip**
>
> This value can be created by copying the value from another control's **DragIcon** value or a form's icon, or by using the **LoadPicture** function.

- *TreeViewControl*.**DragMode**—an **Integer** specifying how the control will respond to a drag request (see Table T-95).

> **Tip**
>
> Setting **DragMode** to vbAutomatic will automatically begin a drag operation when the user clicks on the control. However, the control will not respond to the usual mouse events (**Click**, **DblClick**, **MouseDown**, **MouseMove**, **MouseUp**).

DragMode Name	Value	Description
vbManual	0	The Drag method must be used to begin a drag-and-drop operation (default value).
vbAutomatic	1	The source control will automatically begin a drag-and-drop operation when the user clicks on the control.

Table T-95: DragMode values.

- *TreeViewControl*.**DropHighlight**—a reference to a **Node** object that will be highlighted in the system highlight color when the cursor is passed over it.

> **Tip**
>
> Use this property in conjunction with the **HitTest** method to determine the object that is under the cursor.

- *TreeViewControl*.**Enabled**—a **Boolean** value when **True** means that the control will respond to events. **False** means that the control will not respond to events.
- *TreeViewControl*.**Font**—an object that contains information about the character font used by this object.
- *TreeViewControl*.**Height**—a **Single** that contains the height of the control.
- *TreeViewControl*.**HelpContextID**—a **Long** that contains a help file context ID number that references an entry in the help file. When the user presses the F1 key while this control is active, the corresponding entry in the help file will automatically be displayed. A value of zero means that no context number was specified.

> **Tip**
>
> A help file must be compiled using the Windows Help Compiler available in the Professional and Enterprise editions of Visual Basic.

- *TreeViewControl*.**HideColumnHeaders**—a **Boolean** value when **True** means that the column headers will not be shown. **False** means that the column headers are visible (default).
- *TreeViewControl*.**HideSelection**—a **Boolean** value when **True** means that the selected item will be hidden when the control loses focus. **False** means that the selected item will continue to be highlighted even if the control loses focus.
- *TreeViewControl*.**hWnd**—a **Long** that contains a Windows handle to the control.

> **Tip**
>
> *The **hWnd** property is most useful when making calls to Windows API functions. Since this value can change during execution, do not save the value into a variable for later use.*

- *TreeViewControl*.**ImageList**—a reference to an **ImageList** object that contains the pictures that will be used for the large icon display.
- *TreeViewControl*.**Indentation**—a **Single** that contains the amount that each node will be indented from its parent. This value must be greater than zero.
- *TreeViewControl*.**Index**—an **Integer** that is used to uniquely identify a control in a control array.
- *TreeViewControl*.**LabelEdit**—an **Integer** value that determines if a user can change the contents of the label (see Table T-96).

LabelEdit Name	Value	Description
lwwAutomatic	0	The BeforeLabelEdit event is always called when the user clicks on the label (default).
lwwManual	1	The user can only change the label if the **StartLabelEdit** method is called.

Table T-96: LabelEdit *values.*

- *TreeViewControl*.**Left**—a **Single** that contains the distance, measured in twips, between the left edge of the control and the left edge of the control's container.
- *TreeViewControl*.**LineStyle**—an **Integer** value that determines the style of lines used between nodes (see Table T-97).

LineStyle Name	Value	Description
tvwTreeLines	0	Lines are drawn between a node and its parent node (default).
tvwRootLines	1	Lines are drawn between a node and its parent node, and lines are also drawn between root nodes.

Table T-97: LineStyle *values.*

- *TreeViewControl*.**MouseIcon**—a picture object (a bitmap, icon, or metafile) that will be used as a cursor when the **MousePointer** property is set to 99. Note that Visual Basic does not support color cursors from a .CUR file. A color icon from an .ICO file should be used instead.
- *TreeViewControl*.**MousePointer**—an **Integer** that contains the value of the cursor that should be displayed when the cursor is moved over this control (see Table T-98). Use *vbCustom* to display the custom icon stored in the **MouseIcon** property.

Cursor Name	Value	Description
vbDefault	0	Shape determined by the object (default value).
vbArrow	1	Arrow.
vbCrosshair	2	Crosshair.
vbIbeam	3	I beam.
vbIconPointer	4	Square inside a square.
vbSizePointer	5	Four-sided arrow (north, south, east, west).
vbSizeNESW	6	Two-sided arrow (northeast, southwest).
vbSizeNS	7	Two-sided arrow (north, south).
vbSizeNWSE	8	Two-sided arrow (northwest, southeast).
vbSizeWE	9	Two-sided arrow (west, east).
vbUpArrow	10	Single-sided arrow pointing north.
vbHourglass	11	Hourglass.
vbNoDrop	12	No drop.
vbArrowHourglass	13	An arrow and an hourglass.
vbArrowQuestion	14	An arrow and a question mark.
vbSizeAll	15	Size all.
vbCustom	99	Custom icon from the MouseIcon property of this control.

Table T-98: Cursor *values.*

- *TreeViewControl.***Name**—a **String** that contains the name of the control that will be used to reference the control in a Visual Basic program. This property is read only at run time.
- *TreeViewControl.***Nodes**—an object reference to a node's collection, which contains the information displayed in the **TreeView** control.
- *TreeViewControl.***Object**—an object that contains a reference to the *TreeViewControl* object.
- *TreeViewControl.***OLEDragMode**—an **Integer** value (see Table T-99) that describes how the control will respond to OLE drag operations.

> **Note**
>
> When the **DragMode** is **True**, the standard Visual Basic drag-and-drop functions will override the OLE drag and drop functions.

OLEDragMode Name	Value	Description
vbOLEDragManual	0	All drag requests will be handled by the programmer (default value).
vbOLEDragAutomatic	1	The control responds to all OLE drag requests automatically.

Table T-99: OLEDragMode *values.*

- *TreeViewControl.***OLEDropMode**—an **Integer** value (see Table T-100) that describes how the control will respond to OLE drop operations.

OLEDropMode Name	Value	Description
vbOLEDropNone	0	The control does not accept OLE drops. The cursor is changed to the No Drop cursor (default value).
vbOLEDropManual	1	The control responds to OLE drops under the program's control (manual).
vbOLEDropAutomatic	2	The control automatically accepts OLE drops if it recognizes the format of the data object.

Table T-100: OLEDropMode *values*.

- *TreeViewControl*.**Parent**—an object that contains a reference to the **Form**, **Frame**, or other container that contains this control.
- *TreeViewControl*.**PathSeparator**—a **String** object containing the character that will be used to return the **FullPath** in a **Node** object. The default value is the backslash character ("\").
- *TreeViewControl*.**SelectedItem**—a reference to the currently selected **Node** object.
- *TreeViewControl*.**Sorted**—a **Boolean** value when **True** means that the items will be sorted alphabetically. **False** means that items will not be sorted (default).
- *TreeViewControl*.**Style**—an **Integer** value (see Table T-101) describing how the information in the control is displayed.

Style Name	Value	Description
tvwTextOnly	0	Display text only.
tvwPictureText	1	Display text with an image.
tvwPlusMinusText	2	Display text with plus/minus signs.
tvwPlusPictureText	3	Display text with an image and plus/minus signs.
tvwTreelinesText	4	Display text with lines per **LineStyle**.
tvwTreelinesPictureText	5	Display text with lines per **LineStyle**, and an image.
tvwTreelinesPlusMinusText	6	Display text with lines per **LineStyle**, with plus/minus signs.
tvwTreelinesPlusMinusPicture	7	Display text with lines per **LineStyle**, with an image and plus/minus signs.

Table T-101: Style *values*.

- *TreeViewControl*.**TabIndex**—an Integer that is used to determine the order that a user will tab through the objects on a form.
- *TreeViewControl*.**TabStop**—a **Boolean** value when **True** means that the user can tab to this object. **False** means that this control will be skipped to the next control in the **TabIndex** order.
- *TreeViewControl*.**Tag**—a **String** that can hold programmer-specific information. This property is not used by Visual Basic.
- *TreeViewControl*.**ToolTipText**—a **String** that holds a text value that can be displayed as a **ToolTip** box whenever the cursor is held over the control for about one second.
- *TreeViewControl*.**Top**—a **Single** that contains the distance, measured in twips, between the top edge of the control and the top edge of the control's container.
- *TreeViewControl*.**WhatsThisHelpID**—a **Long** that contains a help file context ID number that references an entry in the help file. This is used to provide a What's This PopUp help display in response to the What's This button in the upper right corner of the window.
- *TreeViewControl*.**Width**—a **Single** that contains the width of the control.

Methods

TreeViewControl.Drag [DragAction]

Usage This method is used to begin, end, or cancel a drag operation.

Arguments • *DragAction*—an **Integer** that contains a value selected from Table T-102 below.

DragAction Name	Value	Description
vbCancel	0	Cancels any drag operation in progress.
vbBeginDrag	1	Begins a drag operation (default).
vbEndDrag	2	Ends a drag operation and drops *object*.

Table T-102: DragAction *values*.

result = TreeViewControl.GetVisibleCount

Usage This method searches the **ListItems** collection for the specified value and returns an object reference to the matching **ListItem**.

Arguments • *result*—an object reference to the **ListItem** object found.

result = TreeViewControl.GetFirstVisible

Usage This method returns the number of nodes that are visible in a tree view control.

Arguments • *result*—a **Long** value containing the number of **Node** objects that fit in the display area of the **TreeView** control.

result = TreeViewControl.HitTest (x As Single, y As Single)

Usage This method returns an object reference to the **Node** object at coordinates *x* and *y*.

Arguments • *result*—an object reference to the **Node** object.
• *x*—a **Single** containing the x coordinate on the screen.
• *y*—a **Single** containing the y coordinate on the screen.

TreeViewControl.Move Left [, Top [, Width [, Height]]]

Usage This method is used to change the position and the size of the **TreeView** control. The **ScaleMode** of the **Form** or other container object that holds the **TreeView** control will determine the units used to specify the coordinates.

Arguments • *Left*—a **Single** that specifies the new position of the left edge of the control.
• *Top*—a **Single** that specifies the new position of the top edge of the control.
• *Width*—a **Single** that specifies the new width of the control.
• *Height*—a **Single** that specifies the new height of the control.

TreeViewControl.OLEDrag

Usage This method is used to begin an **OLEDrag** and drop operation. Invoking this method will trigger the **OLEStartDrag** event.

TreeViewControl.Refresh

Usage This method is used to redraw the contents of the control.

TreeViewControl.SetFocus

Usage This method transfers the focus from the form or control that currently has the focus to this control. In order to receive the focus, this control must be enabled and visible.

TreeViewControl.ShowWhatsThis

Usage This method displays the ShowWhatsThis help information for this control.

TreeViewControl.StartLabelEdit

Usage This method is required to let a user edit a label when the **LabelEdit** property is set to *tvwManual*. This will also cause the **BeforeLabelEdit** event to occur.

TreeViewControl.ZOrder [*position*]

Usage This method is used to specify the position of the **TreeView** control relative to the other objects on the form.

> **Tip**
>
> *Note that there are three layers of objects on a form. The back layer is the drawing space that contains the results of the graphical methods, and the middle layer contains graphical objects and **Labels**. The top layer contains non-graphical controls such as the **TreeView** control. The ZOrder method only affects how the objects are arranged within a single layer.*

Arguments • *position*—an **Integer** that specifies the relative position of this object. A value of 0 means that the control is positioned at the head of the list; a value of 1 means that the control will be placed at the end of the list.

Events

Private Sub TreeViewControl_AfterLabelEdit([*index* As Integer ,] *cancel* As Integer, *NewString* As String)

Usage This event occurs after the user edits a label.

> **Tip**
>
> Use the **SelectedItem** property to determine which item is being edited.

Arguments
- *index*—an **Integer** that is used to uniquely identify a control in a control array. This argument is not present if the control is not part of a control array.
- *cancel*—an **Integer** value when zero means that the edit is accepted. Any non-zero value means that the edit is canceled.
- *NewString*—a **String** containing the new value entered by the user or Null if the user canceled the operation.

Private Sub *TreeViewControl*_BeforeLabelEdit([*index* As Integer ,] *cancel* As Integer)

Usage   This event occurs before the user edits a label.

> **Tip**
>
> Use the **SelectedItem** property to determine which item is being edited.

Arguments
- *index*—an **Integer** that is used to uniquely identify a control in a control array. This argument is not present if the control is not part of a control array.
- *cancel*—an **Integer** value when zero means that the edit process can continue. Any non-zero value means that the edit is canceled.

Private Sub *TreeViewControl*_Click([*index* As Integer])

Usage   This event occurs when the user clicks a mouse button to select an item or selects an item using the keyboard.

Arguments
- *index*—an **Integer** that is used to uniquely identify a control in a control array. This argument is not present if the control is not part of a control array.

Private Sub *TreeViewControl*_Collapse ([*index* As Integer ,] ByVal *node* As Node)

Usage   This event occurs when an expanded **Node** object is collapsed and before the **Click** event.

Arguments
- *index*—an **Integer** that is used to uniquely identify a control in a control array. This argument is not present if the control is not part of a control array.
- *node*—the **Node** object to be collapsed.

Private Sub *TreeViewControl*_DblClick([*index* As Integer])

Usage This event occurs when the user double-clicks a mouse button to select an item or selects an item using the keyboard.

Arguments ▪ *index*—an **Integer** that is used to uniquely identify a control in a control array. This argument is not present if the control is not part of a control array.

Private Sub *TreeViewControl*_DragDrop([*index* As Integer ,] *source* As Control, *x* As Single, *y* As Single)

Usage This event occurs when a drag-and-drop operation is completed by using the Drag method with a *DragAction* value of *vbEndDrag*.

Tip

*When using drag-and-drop operations, use the **DragOver** event to determine what the cursor should look like while the cursor moves over the control.*

Arguments ▪ *index*—an **Integer** that is used to uniquely identify a control in a control array. This argument is not present if the control is not part of a control array.

▪ *source*—a control object that is the control that is being dragged.

Tip

You can access a property or method from the source control by using source.*property or* source.*method. You can determine the type of object or control by using the **TypeOf** operator.*

▪ *x*—a **Single** that contains the horizontal location of the mouse pointer.

▪ *y*—a **Single** that contains the vertical location of the mouse pointer.

Private Sub *TreeViewControl*_DragOver([*index* As Integer ,] *source* As Control, *x* As Single, *y* As Single, *state* As Integer)

Usage This event occurs while a drag operation is in progress and the cursor is moved over the control.

Tip

*When using drag-and-drop operations, use the **DragOver** event to determine what the cursor should look like while the cursor moves over the control. When* state *is 0, you can change the cursor to a no drop (vbNoDrop) cursor or highlight the field that the cursor is near. When* state *is 1, you can undo the changes you made when the* state *was 0.*

Arguments
- *index*—an **Integer** that is used to uniquely identify a control in a control array. This argument is not present if the control is not part of a control array.
- *source*—a control object that is the control that is being dragged.

> **Tip**
> You can access a property or method from the source control by using *source.property* or *source.method*. You can determine the type of object or control by using the **TypeOf** operator.

- *x*—a **Single** that contains the horizontal location of the mouse pointer.
- *y*—a **Single** that contains the vertical location of the mouse pointer.
- *state*—an **Integer** that indicates the state of the object being dragged (see Table T-103).

state Name	Value	Description
vbEnter	0	The dragged object is entering range of the control.
vbLeave	1	The dragged object is leaving range of the control.
vbOver	2	The dragged object has moved from one position over the control to another.

Table T-103: State *values.*

Private Sub *TreeViewControl*_Expand([*index* As Integer ,] ByVal *node* As Node)

Usage This event occurs when a collapsed **Node** object is expanded and after the **Click** and **DblClick** events have occurred.

Arguments
- *index*—an **Integer** that is used to uniquely identify a control in a control array. This argument is not present if the control is not part of a control array.
- *node*—the **Node** object to be expanded.

Private Sub *TreeViewControl*_GotFocus ([*index* As Integer])

Usage This event occurs when the control is given focus.

> **Tip**
> You can use this routine to display help or other information in a status bar.

Arguments
- *index*—an **Integer** that is used to uniquely identify a control in a control array. This argument is not present if the control is not part of a control array.

Private Sub *TreeViewControl*_KeyDown ([*index* As Integer ,] *keycode* As Integer, *shift* As Single)

Usage   This event occurs when a key is pressed while the control has the focus.

Arguments
- *index*—an **Integer** that is used to uniquely identify a control in a control array. This argument is not present if the control is not part of a control array.
- *keycode*—an **Integer** that contains information about which key was pressed.
- *shift*—an **Integer** that contains information about the Shift and Alt keys that were pressed when the mouse button was pressed (see Table T-104). These values can be added together if more than one key was down. For instance, a value of 5 would mean that the Shift and Alt keys were both down when the mouse button was pressed.

shift Name	Value	Description
vbShiftMask	1	The Shift key was pressed.
vbCtrlMask	2	The Ctrl key was pressed.
vbAltMask	4	The Alt key was pressed.

Table T-104: Shift *values.*

Private Sub *TreeViewControl*_KeyPress([*index* As Integer ,] *keychar* As Integer)

Usage   This event occurs whenever a key is pressed while the control has the focus.

Arguments
- *index*—an **Integer** that is used to uniquely identify a control in a control array. This argument is not present if the control is not part of a control array.
- *keychar*—an **Integer** that contains the ASCII character that was pressed.

Private Sub *TreeViewControl*_KeyUp ([*index* As Integer ,] *keycode* As Integer, *shift* As Single)

Usage   This event occurs when a key is released while the control has the focus.

Arguments
- *index*—an **Integer** that is used to uniquely identify a control in a control array. This argument is not present if the control is not part of a control array.
- *keycode*—an **Integer** that contains information about which key was released.
- *shift*—an **Integer** that contains information about the Shift and Alt keys that were pressed when the mouse button was pressed (see Table T-105). These values can be added together if more than one key was down. For instance, a value of 5 would mean that the Shift and Alt keys were both down when the mouse button was pressed.

shift Name	Value	Description
vbShiftMask	1	The Shift key was pressed.
vbCtrlMask	2	The Ctrl key was pressed.
vbAltMask	4	The Alt key was pressed.

Table T-105: Shift *values*.

Private Sub *TreeViewControl*_LostFocus ([*index* As Integer])

Usage   This event occurs when the control loses focus.

Tip

This routine is useful when performing data verification.

Arguments
- *index*—an **Integer** that is used to uniquely identify a control in a control array. This argument is not present if the control is not part of a control array.

Private Sub *TreeViewBoxControl*_MouseDown([*index* As Integer ,] *button* As Integer, *shift* As Single, *x* As Single, *y* As Single)

Usage   This event occurs when a mouse button is pressed while the cursor is over the control.

Arguments
- *index*—an **Integer** that is used to uniquely identify a control in a control array. This argument is not present if the control is not part of a control array.
- *button*—an **Integer** that contains information about the mouse buttons that were pressed (see Table T-106). Only one button will be indicated when this event occurs.

button Name	Value	Description
vbLeftButton	1	The left button was pressed.
vbRightButton	2	The right button was pressed.
vbMiddleButton	4	The middle button was pressed.

Table T-106: Button *values*.

- *shift*—an **Integer** that contains information about the Shift and Alt keys that were pressed when the mouse button was pressed (see Table T-107). These values can be added together if more than one key was down. For instance, a value of 5 would mean that the Shift and Alt keys were both down when the mouse button was pressed.

shift Name	Value	Description
vbShiftMask	1	The Shift key was pressed.
vbCtrlMask	2	The Ctrl key was pressed.
vbAltMask	4	The Alt key was pressed.

Table T-107: Shift *values*.

- *x*—a **Single** that contains the horizontal location of the mouse pointer.
- *y*—a **Single** that contains the vertical location of the mouse pointer.

Private Sub *TreeViewControl*_MouseMove ([*index* As Integer ,] *button* As Integer, *shift* As Single, *x* As Single, *y* As Single)

Usage This event occurs while the cursor is moved over the control.

Arguments
- *index*—an **Integer** that is used to uniquely identify a control in a control array. This argument is not present if the control is not part of a control array.
- *button*—an **Integer** that contains information about the mouse buttons that were pressed (see Table T-108). These values can be added together if more than one button was pressed. For instance, a value of 3 means that both the left and right buttons were pressed. A value of 0 means that no buttons were pressed.

button Name	Value	Description
vbLeftButton	1	The left button was pressed.
vbRightButton	2	The right button was pressed.
vbMiddleButton	4	The middle button was pressed.

Table T-108: Button *values*.

- *shift*—an **Integer** that contains information about the Shift and Alt keys that were pressed when the mouse button was pressed (see Table T-109). These values can be added together if more than one key was down. For instance, a value of 5 would mean that the Shift and Alt keys were both down when the mouse button was pressed. A value of 0 means that none of these keys were pressed.

shift Name	Value	Description
vbShiftMask	1	The Shift key was pressed.
vbCtrlMask	2	The Ctrl key was pressed.
vbAltMask	4	The Alt key was pressed.

Table T-109: Shift *values*.

- *x*—a **Single** that contains the horizontal location of the mouse pointer.
- *y*—a **Single** that contains the vertical location of the mouse pointer.

Private Sub *TreeViewBoxControl*_MouseUp([*index* As Integer ,] *button* As Integer, *shift* As Single, *x* As Single, *y* As Single)

Usage — This event occurs when a mouse button is released while the cursor is over the control.

Arguments
- *index*—an **Integer** that is used to uniquely identify a control in a control array. This argument is not present if the control is not part of a control array.
- *button*—an **Integer** that contains information about the mouse buttons that were released (see Table T-110). Only one of these values will be present.

button Name	Value	Description
vbLeftButton	1	The left button was released.
vbRightButton	2	The right button was released.
vbMiddleButton	4	The middle button was released.

Table T-110: Button *values*.

- *shift*—an **Integer** that contains information about the Shift and Alt keys that were pressed when the mouse button was released (see Table T-111). These values can be added together if more than one key was down. For instance, a value of 5 would mean that the Shift and Alt keys were both down when the mouse button was released. A value of 0 means that none of these keys were pressed.

shift Name	Value	Description
vbShiftMask	1	The Shift key was pressed.
vbCtrlMask	2	The Ctrl key was pressed.
vbAltMask	4	The Alt key was pressed.

Table T-111: Shift *values*.

- *x*—a **Single** that contains the horizontal location of the mouse pointer.
- *y*—a **Single** that contains the vertical location of the mouse pointer.

Private Sub *TreeViewControl*_NodeClick([*index* As Integer ,] ByVal *node* As Node)

Usage — This event occurs when the user clicks on a **Node** object.

Arguments
- *index*—an **Integer** that is used to uniquely identify a control in a control array. This argument is not present if the control is not part of a control array.
- *node*—the **Node** object that was clicked.

Private Sub *TreeViewControl_OLECompleteDrag*([*index* As Integer ,] *effect* As Long)

Usage   This event is used to tell the source control the results of an OLE drag-and-drop operation. This is the final event to occur in the series of actions that make up an OLE drag-and-drop operation.

Arguments
- *index*—an **Integer** that is used to uniquely identify a control in a control array. This argument is not present if the control is not part of a control array.
- *effect*—a **Long** that returns the status of the OLE drag-and-drop operation (see Table T-112).

effect Name	Value	Description
vbDropEffectNone	0	The operation is canceled or the target control can't accept the drop operation.
vbDropEffectCopy	1	The operation copies data from the source control to the target control. The original data is unchanged.
vbDropEffectMove	2	The operation results in a link from the original data to the target control.

Table T-112: Effect *values.*

Private Sub *TreeViewControl_OLEDragDrop*([*index* As Integer ,] *data* As DataObject, *effect* As Long, *button* As Integer, *shift* As Single, *x* As Single, *y* As Single)

Usage   This event is used to tell the source control the results of an OLE drag-and-drop operation. This is the final event to occur in the series of actions that make up an OLE drag-and-drop operation.

Arguments
- *index*—an **Integer** that is used to uniquely identify a control in a control array. This argument is not present if the control is not part of a control array.
- *data*—a **DataObject** that contains the formats that the source control will provide. If the data is not contained in the **DataObject**, then it can be retrieved with the **GetData** method.
- *effect*—a **Long** that returns the status of the OLE drag-and-drop operation (see Table T-113).

effect Name	Value	Description
vbDropEffectNone	0	The operation is canceled or the target control can't accept the drop operation.
vbDropEffectCopy	1	The operation copies data from the source control to the target control. The original data is unchanged.
vbDropEffectMove	2	The operation results in a link from the original data to the target control.

Table T-113: Effect *values.*

- *button*—an **Integer** that contains information about the mouse buttons that were pressed (see Table T-114). These values can be added together if more than one button was pressed. For instance, a value of 3 means that both the left and right buttons were pressed. A value of 0 means that no buttons were pressed.

button Name	Value	Description
vbLeftButton	1	The left button was pressed.
vbRightButton	2	The right button was pressed.
vbMiddleButton	4	The middle button was pressed.

Table T-114: Button *values.*

- *shift*—an **Integer** that contains information about the Shift and Alt keys that were pressed when the mouse button was released (see Table T-115). These values can be added together if more than one key was down. For instance, a value of 5 would mean that the Shift and Alt keys were both down when the mouse button was released. A value of 0 means that none of these keys were pressed.

shift Name	Value	Description
vbShiftMask	1	The Shift key was pressed.
vbCtrlMask	2	The Ctrl key was pressed.
vbAltMask	4	The Alt key was pressed.

Table T-115: Shift *values.*

- *x*—a **Single** that contains the horizontal location of the mouse pointer.
- *y*—a **Single** that contains the vertical location of the mouse pointer.

Private Sub *TreeViewControl*_OLEDragOver([*index* As Integer ,] *data* As DataObject, *effect* As Long, *button* As Integer, *shift* As Single, *x* As Single, *y* As Single, *state* As Integer)

Usage This event happens when an OLE drag-and-drop operation is in progress.

Arguments
- *index*—an **Integer** that is used to uniquely identify a control in a control array. This argument is not present if the control is not part of a control array.
- *data*—a **DataObject** that contains the formats that the source control will provide. If the data is not contained in the **DataObject**, then it can be retrieved with the **GetData** method.
- *effect*—a **Long** that returns the status of the OLE drag-and-drop operation (see Table T-116).

effect Name	Value	Description
vbDropEffectNone	0	The operation is canceled or the target control can't accept the drop operation.
vbDropEffectCopy	1	The operation copies data from the source control to the target control. The original data is unchanged.
vbDropEffectMove	2	The operation results in a link from the original data to the target control.

Table T-116: Effect *values.*

- *button*—an **Integer** that contains information about the mouse buttons that were pressed (see Table T-117). These values can be added together if more than one button was pressed. For instance, a value of 3 means that both the left and right buttons were pressed. A value of 0 means that no buttons were pressed.

button Name	Value	Description
vbLeftButton	1	The left button was pressed.
vbRightButton	2	The right button was pressed.
vbMiddleButton	4	The middle button was pressed.

Table T-117: Button *values.*

- *shift*—an **Integer** that contains information about the Shift and Alt keys that were pressed when the mouse button was released (see Table T-118). These values can be added together if more than one key was down. For instance, a value of 5 would mean that the Shift and Alt keys were both down when the mouse button was released. A value of 0 means that none of these keys were pressed.

shift Name	Value	Description
vbShiftMask	1	The Shift key was pressed.
vbCtrlMask	2	The Ctrl key was pressed.
vbAltMask	4	The Alt key was pressed.

Table T-118: Shift *values.*

- *x*—a **Single** that contains the horizontal location of the mouse pointer.
- *y*—a **Single** that contains the vertical location of the mouse pointer.
- *state*—an **Integer** that indicates the state of the object being dragged (see Table T-119).

state Name	Value	Description
vbEnter	0	The dragged object is entering range of the control.
vbLeave	1	The dragged object is leaving range of the control.
vbOver	2	The dragged object has moved from one position over the control to another.

Table T-119: State *values.*

Private Sub TreeViewControl_OLEGiveFeedback ([*index* As Integer ,] *effect* As Long)

Usage This event is used to tell the source control what is happening while the OLE drag-and-drop operation is in progress. This event occurs after the OLEDragOver event.

Tip

You may want to use this event to change the cursor to reflect what can happen in the remote object.

Arguments
- *index*—an **Integer** that is used to uniquely identify a control in a control array. This argument is not present if the control is not part of a control array.
- *effect*—a **Long** that returns the status of the OLE drag-and-drop operation (see Table T-120).

effect Name	Value	Description
vbDropEffectNone	0	The operation is canceled or the target control can't accept the drop operation.
vbDropEffectCopy	1	The operation copies data from the source control to the target control. The original data is unchanged.
vbDropEffectMove	2	The operation results in a link from the original data to the target control.
vbDropEffectScroll	&H80000000	The target control is about to scroll or is scrolling. This value may be added to the other *shift* values.

Table T-120: Effect *values*.

Private Sub TreeViewControl_OLESetData([*index* As Integer ,] *data* As DataObject, *DataFormat* As Integer)

Usage This event happens in response to the target object performing a **GetData** method on *data*. This routine will respond by using the **SetData** method with the desired data using the **DataObject** *data*.

Arguments
- *index*—an **Integer** that is used to uniquely identify a control in a control array. This argument is not present if the control is not part of a control array.
- *data*—a **DataObject** that will contain the data to be returned to the target object.
- *format*—an **Integer** that contains the format of the data (see Table T-121).

format Name	Value	Description
vbCFText	1	Text (.TXT files).
vbCFBitmap	2	Bitmap (.BMP files).
vbCFMetafile	3	Metafile (.WMF files).
vbCFEDIB	8	Device-independent bitmap (DIB).
vbCFPallette	9	Color palette.
vbCFEMetafile	14	Enhanced metafile (.EMF files).
vbCFFiles	15	List of files.
vbCFRTF	-16639	Rich Text Format (.RTF files).

Table T-121: Format *values.*

Private Sub *TreeViewControl*_OLEStartDrag ([*index* As Integer ,] *data* As DataObject, *AllowedEffects* As Long)

Usage   This event is used to start an OLE drag-and-drop operation.

Arguments
- *index*—an **Integer** that is used to uniquely identify a control in a control array. This argument is not present if the control is not part of a control array.
- *data*—a **DataObject** that will contain the formats that the source object is willing to provide to the target object. It may optionally contain the data to be transferred.
- *AllowedEffects*—a **Long** that contains the effects that the target object can request from the source object (see Table T-122). The *AllowedEffects* can be added together if the source object supports more than one effect. Note that the target object can always use the *vbDropEffectNone* effect.

AllowedEffects Name	Value	Description
vbDropEffectNone	0	The target can't copy the data.
vbDropEffectCopy	1	The target can copy the data, and the source will keep the data unchanged.
vbDropEffectMove	2	The target can copy the data, and the source will delete the data.

Table T-122: AllowedEffects *values.*

Examples
```
Private Sub Form_Load()

Dim x As Object

Set x = TreeView1.ColumnHeaders.Add(, , "Words")
Set x = TreeView1.ColumnHeaders.Add(, , "Letters")
Set x = TreeView1.ColumnHeaders.Add(, , "Roman Numerals")
```

```
    Set x = TreeView1.ListItems.Add(, , "One", 1, 1)
    x.SubItems(1) = "A"
    x.SubItems(2) = "I"
    Set x = TreeView1.ListItems.Add(, , "Two", 2, 2)
    x.SubItems(1) = "B"
    x.SubItems(2) = "II"
    Set x = TreeView1.ListItems.Add(, , "Three", 3, 3)
    x.SubItems(1) = "C"
    x.SubItems(2) = "III"
    Set x = TreeView1.ListItems.Add(, , "Four", 4, 4)
    x.SubItems(1) = "D"
    x.SubItems(2) = "IV"
    Set x = TreeView1.ListItems.Add(, , "Five", 5, 5)
    x.SubItems(1) = "E"
    x.SubItems(2) = "V"
    Set x = TreeView1.ListItems.Add(, , "Six", 6, 6)
    x.SubItems(1) = "F"
    x.SubItems(2) = "VI"
    Set x = TreeView1.ListItems.Add(, , "Seven", 7, 7)
    x.SubItems(1) = "G"
    x.SubItems(2) = "VII"
    Set x = TreeView1.ListItems.Add(, , "Eight", 8, 8)
    x.SubItems(1) = "H"
    x.SubItems(2) = "VIII"
End Sub

Private Sub TreeView1_Click()
MsgBox "You selected " & TreeView1.SelectedItem.Text
End Sub

Private Sub TreeView1_ColumnClick(ByVal ColumnHeader As ComctlLib.ColumnHeader)
If TreeView1.SortKey = ColumnHeader.Index--1 Then
    TreeView1.Sorted = False
    TreeView1.SortOrder = (TreeView1.SortOrder + 1) Mod 2
    TreeView1.Sorted = True
Else
    TreeView1.Sorted = False
    TreeView1.SortKey = ColumnHeader.Index--1
    TreeView1.Sorted = True
End If
End Sub

Private Sub Option1_Click(Index As Integer)
TreeView1.View = Index
End Sub
```

This program initializes a **TreeView** control with some values that can be displayed on any of the four basic views. Clicking on an object will display its name in a message box. Changing views is accomplished by selecting one of the **OptionButtons** on the form. While in the Report view, clicking on a column header will sort the data in ascending order. Clicking on it a second time will re-sort the data in descending order.

See Also   **DBComboBox** (control), **DBList** (control), **ComboBox** (control), **ListView** (control)

Trim

FUNCTION

CCE, LE, PE, EE

Syntax   `svar = Trim ( sval )`

Usage   The **Trim** function will delete any leading and trailing spaces from a string value.

Arguments
- *svar*—a **String** variable.
- *sval*—a **String** value with the leading spaces trimmed.

Examples
```
Private Sub Command1_Click()
Text2.Text = Trim(Text1.Text)
End Sub
```

This routine trims the leading and trailing spaces from the value in the text1 text box and saves the results in the text2 text box.

See Also   **LTrim** (function), **RTrim** (function)

Type

STATEMENT

CCE, LE, PE, EE

Syntax
```
[ Private | Public ] Type typename
    identifier [ arrayinfo ] As type
    [ identifier [ arrayinfo ] As type ]
    .
    .
    .
    End Type
```

Usage   The **Type** statement is used to declare user-defined types with multiple elements inside. **Public** is assumed for standard modules, while all **Types** declared in class modules must be **Private**.

Arguments
- *identifier*—the Visual Basic identifier that will be used to reference this particular variable. It must begin with a letter, which can be followed by any number of letters or numbers or the underscore character (_). Identifiers are not case sensitive, though the case will be preserved for easier reading.

- *arrayinfo*—optionally indicates an array. It can have zero or more dimensions. An array can have no more than 60 dimensions. The subscripts are defined as:

  ([ubound | lbound **To** ubound] [, ubound | , lbound **To** ubound] . . .)

ubound	the upper bound for an array.
lbound	the lower bound for an array's subscript. If omitted, the value from **Option Base** will be used. If there is no **Option Base** statement in the module, zero will be used for the lower bound.

- *type*—a valid Visual Basic type: **Byte, Boolean, Currency, Date, Double, Integer, Long, Single, String, Object,** or **Variant**. Specific objects can also be used; user-defined types defined with the **Type** statement may also be used.

Examples

```
Private Type MyType
    Name As String
    Address As String
End Type

Private Sub Command1_Click()
Dim a As MyType
Dim b As MyType
a.Name = "Wayne S. Freeze"
b = a
MsgBox b.Name
End Sub
```

This declares a type called MyType that is private to this module. It also contains two subroutines: Name and Address. In Command1_Click, I declare two instances of MyType, a and b. Then I assign a value to a.Name and copy the contents of a into b. Then I use a message box to display b.Name.

See Also **Byte** (data type), **Boolean** (data type), **Currency** (data type), **Date** (data type), **Dim** (statement), **Double** (data type), **Integer** (data type), **Long** (data type), **Object** (data type), **Option Base** (statement), **Option Explicit** (statement), **Private** (statement), **Public** (statement), **Single** (data type), **String** (data type), **Static** (statement), **TypeName** (function), **Variant** (data type)

TypeName

FUNCTION

CCE, LE, PE, EE

Syntax `type = TypeName ( variable )`

Usage The **TypeName** function returns a **String** value containing the type of the variable specified.

Arguments
- *type*—a **String** containing the type of the Visual Basic identifier (see Table T-123). Arrays will have "()" appended to the end of the value.

type Name	Description
object type	The specific name of an object.
Boolean	Boolean.
Byte	Byte.
Currency	Currency value.
Date	Date and time value.
Decimal	Decimal value.
Double	Double-precision floating point number.
Empty	Uninitialized variant.
Error	A variant with an error value.
Integer	Integer.
Long	Long Integer.
Nothing	An object variable that doesn't refer to an object.
Null	A variant with no valid data.
Object	Object.
Single	Single-precision floating point number.
String	String.
Unknown	Unknown.

Table T-123: Type *values*.

- *variable*—a Visual Basic identifier.

Examples
```
Private Sub Command1_Click()
Dim x(10) As Integer
MsgBox TypeName(x)
End Sub
```

This routine displays a message box with the value "Integer()" indicating that the variable x is both an array and an **Integer**.

See Also **VarType** (function)

UBound

FUNCTION

CCE, LE, PE, EE

Syntax `upper = UBound ( array [, dimension ] )`

Usage The **UBound** function returns the upper bound of an array. A compiler error will occur if *array* is not an array, and a run-time error will occur if *dimension* does not exist in the array.

Arguments
- *upper*—a **Long** value containing the upper bound of the array.
- *array*—a Visual Basic identifier that has been defined as an array.
- *dimension*—a **Long** value containing the dimension for which the lower bound will be returned. If not specified, it will default to 1 (the first dimension).

Examples
```
Private Sub Command1_Click()
Dim MyArray(-1 To 1, 127, 1 To 99)
Dim i As Long
For i = 1 To 3
   MsgBox "The upper bound for dimension " & Format(i) & " is " & 
   Format(UBound(MyArray, i))
Next i
End Sub
```

This routine verifies that the values are numeric and then computes the number of periods required for the annuity.

See Also **Array** (function), **Dim** (statement), **LBound** (function), **ReDim** (statement)

UCase

FUNCTION

CCE, LE, PE, EE

Syntax `upper = UCase[$] ( string )`

Usage The **UCase** function converts any lowercase characters to uppercase characters in the string.

Arguments
- *upper*—a **String** value containing the converted string.
- *string*—a **String** value to be converted.

Examples
```
Private Sub Command1_Click()
Text2.Text = UCase(Text1.Text)
End Sub
```

This routine converts the contents of the Text1 text box to lowercase and returns the result in the Text2 text box.

See Also **UCase** (function), **String** (data type)

Unload

STATEMENT

CCE, LE, PE, EE

Syntax **Unload** *object*

Usage The **Unload** statement removes a form or control from memory.

Arguments ▪ *object*—the name of a form or control.

Examples
```
Private Sub Command1_Click()
Load Form2
End Sub

§Private Sub Command2_Click()
Form2.Show
End Sub

§Private Sub Command3_Click()
Unload Form2
Unload Form1
End Sub
```

 This program consists of two forms. Form1 is the main form with three command buttons. The first button loads Form2. The Second button uses the Form2.Show method to display Form2. The third button unloads both forms and ends the program.

 When the first button is pressed, Form2 is loaded and a message box is displayed saying that the form was loaded. At this point Form2 is not visible to the user. Pressing the second button will display the form and a message box will be displayed saying the form is activated.

See Also **Hide** (method), **Load** (method), **Show** (method)

Unlock

STATEMENT

CCE, LE, PE, EE

Syntax **Unlock** [#] *fnum*

 Unlock [#] *fnum*, *recnum*

 Unlock [#] *fnum*, [*brecnum*] **To** *erecnum*

Usage The **Unlock** statement has three forms. The first form unlocks the entire file. The second form unlocks only the specified record. The third form unlocks the records from *brecnum* to *erecnum*.

> **Warning**
>
> *Calls to **Unlock** must be matched with a similar call to **Lock**. Failure to do so may cause problems.*

Arguments
- *fnum*—an **Integer** containing a valid file number from an **Open** statement.
- *recnum*—a **Long** value containing the record number (or byte offset in a binary file) to be locked.
- *brecnum*—a **Long** value containing the beginning record number (or byte offset in a binary file) in a range to be locked. If omitted, then it will default to the first record in the file.
- *erecnum*—a **Long** value containing the ending record number (or byte offset in a binary file) to be locked.

Examples
```
Private Sub Command2_Click()
Dim s As String
Open App.Path & "\temp.dat" For Random As #1 Len = 10
Lock #1, 2
Get #1, 2, s
Text1.Text = s
End Sub

§Private Sub Command3_Click()
Dim s As String
On Error Resume Next
Open App.Path & "\temp.dat" For Random As #2 Len = 10
Get #2, 2, s
If Err.Number <> 0 Then
    MsgBox Err.Description
Else
    Text2.Text = s
End If
Close #2
End Sub
```

The first routine (Command2_Click) opens a file, places a lock on the second record, reads it, and displays it in Text1.Text. The second routine (Command3_Click) opens a new file and tries to read the second record. Since the first routine locks the record, a Permission Denied error is returned.

See Also   **Get** (statement), **Lock** (statement), **Open** (statement), **Put** (statement)

UpDown

CONTROL

CCE, LE, PE, EE

Usage
The **UpDown** control consists of a pair of buttons and a link to another control known as the buddy control that will be incremented or decremented as the user presses the up button or down button. This control is part of the Windows Common Controls 2 and is found in the COMCT232.OCX file.

> **Tip**
>
> *This control provides a better alternative to using the **VScrollBar** control to increment a counter.*

UpDown • 1055

Properties
- *UpDownControl.***Appearance**—an **Integer** value that determines how the control will appear on the form (see Table U-1).

Appearance Name	Value	Description
cc2alignmentLeft	0	The UpDown control is placed to left of the buddy control.
cc2alignmentRight	1	The **UpDown** control is placed to right of the buddy control (default value).

Table U-1: Appearance values.

- *UpDownControl.***AutoBuddy**—a **Boolean** value that, when **True,** means the previous control in the **TabIndex** will be used as the buddy control. If the previous control can't be used, the rest of the controls will be searched for a suitable control, starting backwards toward the first control in the tab index, and then starting with the next control until the last one is reached. **False** means that the control specified in **BuddyControl** will be used.
- *UpDownControl.***BuddyControl**—an object reference to another control to be used as the buddy control.
- *UpDownControl.***BuddyProperty**—an object reference to the buddy control's property that will be synchronized with the **UpDown** control. The **BuddyControl** property must be set before this property is set.
- *UpDownControl.***Container**—an object that you can use to set or return the container of the control at run time. You cannot set this property at design time.
- *UpDownControl.***DragIcon**—an object containing the picture value of an icon. At design time, you can specify an icon file that has a file type of .ICO.

> **Tip**
>
> *This value can be created by copying the value from another control's **DragIcon** value or from a form's icon, or by using the **LoadPicture** function.*

- *UpDownControl.***DragMode**—an **Integer** value (see Table U-2) specifying how the control will respond to a drag request.

> **Tip**
>
> *Setting **DragMode** to vbAutomatic automatically begins a drag operation when the user clicks on the control. However, the control will not respond to the usual mouse events (**Click, DblClick**).*

DragMode Name	Value	Description
vbManual	0	The Drag method must be used to begin a drag-and-drop operation (default value).
vbAutomatic	1	The source control will automatically begin a drag-and-drop operation when the user clicks on the control.

Table U-2: DragMode values.

- *UpDownControl*.**Enabled**—a **Boolean** value when **True** means that the control will respond to events. When **False**, the control will not respond to events.
- *UpDownControl*.**Height**—a **Single** that contains the height of the control.
- *UpDownControl*.**HelpContextID**—a **Long** containing a help file context ID number that references an entry in the help file. When the user presses the F1 key while this control is active, the corresponding entry in the help file will automatically display. A value of zero means that no context number was specified.

Tip

A help file must be compiled using the Windows Help Compiler available in the Professional and Enterprise editions of Visual Basic.

- *UpDownControl*.**hWnd**—a **Long** containing a Windows handle to the control.

Tip

*The **hWnd** property is most useful when making calls to Windows API functions. Since this value can change during execution, do not save the value into a variable for later use.*

- *UpDownControl*.**Increment**—a **Long** containing the value that will be added or subtracted from **Value** when the up or down button is pressed.
- *UpDownControl*.**Index**—an **Integer** that uniquely identifies a control in a control array.
- *UpDownControl*.**Left**—a **Single** containing the distance measured in twips between the left edge of the control and the left edge of the control's container.
- *UpDownControl*.**Max**—a **Long** value containing the largest number the **Value** property can reach.
- *UpDownControl*.**Min**—a **Long** value containing the smallest number the **Value** property can reach.
- *UpDownControl*.**Name**—a **String** containing the name of the control that will be used to reference the control in a Visual Basic program. This property is read only at run time.
- *UpDownControl*.**Object**—an object containing a reference to the *UpDownControl* object.
- *UpDownControl*.**OLEDropMode**—an **Integer** value (see Table U-3) that describes how the control will respond to OLE drop operations.

OLEDropMode Name	Value	Description
vbOLEDropNone	0	The control does not accept OLE drops. The cursor is changed to the No Drop cursor (default value).
vbOLEDropManual	1	The control responds to OLE drops under the program's control (manual).
vbOLEDropAutomatic	2	The control automatically accepts OLE drops if it recognizes the format of the data object.

Table U-3: OLEDropMode values.

- *UpDownControl*.**Orientation**—an **Integer** value (see Table U-4) that describes how the control will respond to OLE drop operations.

Orientation Name	Value	Description
cc2orientationVertical	0	The arrow buttons are vertical (default).
cc2orientationHorizontal	1	The arrow buttons are horizontal.

Table U-4: Orientation values.

- *UpDownControl*.**Parent**—an object containing a reference to the **Form**, **Frame**, or other container that contains the **UpDown** control.
- *UpDownControl*.**SyncBuddy**—a **Boolean** value when **True** means that the **UpDown** control will synchronize the **Value** property with the buddy control's property specified in the **BuddyProperty**. **False** means that the values are not synchronized.
- *UpDownControl*.**TabIndex**—an Integer that determines the order a user will tab through the objects on a form.
- *UpDownControl*.**TabStop**—a **Boolean** value when **True** means that the user can tab to this object. **False** means that this control will be skipped to the next control in the **TabIndex** order.
- *UpDownControl*.**Tag**—a **String** that can hold programmer-specific information. This property is not used by Visual Basic..
- *UpDownControl*.**Top**—a **Single** containing the distance measured in twips between the top edge of the control and the top edge of the control's container.
- *UpDownControl*.**ToolTipText**—a **String** that holds a text value that can be displayed as a **ToolTip** box whenever the cursor is held over the control for about one second.
- *UpDownControl*.**Value**—a **Long** containing the current value of the **UpDown** control.
- *UpDownControl*.**Visible**—a **Boolean** value when **True** means that the control is visible. **False** means that the control is not visible.

> **Tip**
>
> *You can hide the control until the program is ready to display it using this property.*

- *UpDownControl*.**WhatsThisHelpID**—a **Long** containing a help file context ID number that references an entry in the help file. This provides a What's This PopUp help display in response to the What's This button in the upper-right corner of the window.
- *UpDownControl*.**Width**—a **Single** containing the width of the control.
- *UpDownControl*.**Wrap**—a **Boolean** value when **True** means that when the user clicks the up button while **Value** is **Max**, or clicks the down button while **Value** is **Min**, the control will automatically wrap to **Min** or **Max** respectively. **False** means that no wrapping will occur.

Methods

UpDownControl.Drag [DragAction]

Usage   This method begins, ends, or cancels a drag operation.

Arguments   *DragAction*—an **Integer** containing a value selected from Table U-5.

DragAction Name	Value	Description
vbCancel	0	Cancels any drag operation in progress.
vbBeginDrag	1	Begins a drag operation (default).
vbEndDrag	2	Ends a drag operation and drops *object*.

Table U-5: DragAction values.

UpDownControl.Move Left [, Top [, Width [, Height]]]

Usage   This method changes the position and the size of the **UpDown** control. The **ScaleMode** of the **Form** or other container object that holds the animation control will determine the units used to specify the coordinates.

Arguments
- *Left*—a **Single** that specifies the new position of the left edge of the control.
- *Top*—a **Single** that specifies the new position of the top edge of the control.
- *Width*—a **Single** that specifies the new width of the control.
- *Height*—a **Single** that specifies the new height of the control.

UpDownControl.OLEDrag

Usage   This method is used to begin an OLE drag-and-drop operation. Invoking this method will trigger the **OLEStartDrag** event.

UpDownControl.SetFocus

Usage   This method transfers the focus from the form or control that currently has the focus to this control. To receive the focus, this control must be enabled and visible.

UpDownControl.ShowWhatsThis

Usage   This method displays the ShowWhatsThis help information for this control.

UpDownControl.ZOrder [position]

Usage   This method specifies the position of the animation control relative to the other objects on the form.

Tip

*Note that there are three layers of objects on a form: The back layer is the drawing space that contains the results of the graphical methods, the middle layer contains graphical objects such as the **UpDown** and **Labels**, and the top layer contains nongraphical controls such as the **UpDown**. The **ZOrder** method only affects how the objects are arranged within a single layer.*

Arguments *position*—an **Integer** that specifies the relative position of this object. A value of 0 means that the control is positioned at the head of the list, a value of 1 means that the control will be placed at the end of the list.

Events

Private Sub *UpDownControl* _Change([*index* As Integer])

Usage This event occurs when the **Value** property changes.

Warning

*Changing the **Value** property in your program will trigger the **Change** event. While this normally won't cause a problem, changing the **Value** property inside the **Change** event could trigger an infinite recursion that could ultimately end in the program crashing.*

Arguments *index*—an **Integer** that uniquely identifies a control in a control array. This argument is not present if the control is not part of a control array.

Private Sub *UpDownControl* _DownClick ([*index* As Integer])

Usage This event occurs when the user clicks the down button. This event will occur after the **Change** event.

Arguments *index*—an **Integer** that uniquely identifies a control in a control array. This argument is not present if the control is not part of a control array.

Private Sub *UpDownControl* _DragDrop([*index* As Integer,] *source* As Control, *x* As Single, *y* As Single)

Usage This event occurs when a drag-and-drop operation is completed using the Drag method with a *DragAction* value of *vbEndDrag*.

Tip

*When using drag-and-drop operations, use the **DragOver** event to determine what you want the cursor to look like when it moves over the control.*

Arguments
- *index*—an **Integer** that uniquely identifies a control in a control array. This argument is not present if the control is not part of a control array.
- *source*—a control object that is the control that is being dragged.

> **Tip**
>
> You can access a property or method from the source control by using **source**.*property* or **source**.*method*. You can determine the type of object or control by using the **TypeOf** operator.

- *x*—a **Single** containing the horizontal location of the mouse pointer.
- *y*—a **Single** containing the vertical location of the mouse pointer.

Private Sub UpDownControl_DragOver([*index* As Integer,] *source* As Control, *x* As Single, *y* As Single, *state* As Integer)

Usage   This event occurs while a drag operation is in progress and the cursor is moved over the control.

> **Tip**
>
> When using drag-and-drop operations, use the **DragOver** event to determine what you want the cursor to look like when it moves over the control. When **state** is 0, you can change the cursor to a no drop (vbNoDrop) cursor or highlight the field that the cursor is near. When **state** is 1, you can undo the changes you made when the **state** was 0.

Arguments
- *index*—an **Integer** that uniquely identifies a control in a control array. This argument is not present if the control is not part of a control array.
- *source*—a control object that is the control that is being dragged.

> **Tip**
>
> You can access a property or method from the source control by using **source**.*property* or **source**.*method*. You can determine the type of object or control by using the **TypeOf** operator.

- *x*—a **Single** that contains the horizontal location of the mouse pointer.
- *y*—a **Single** that contains the vertical location of the mouse pointer.
- *state*—an **Integer** value (see Table U-6) that indicates the state of the object being dragged.

state Name	Value	Description
vbEnter	0	The dragged object is entering range of the control.
vbLeave	1	The dragged object is leaving range of the control.
vbOver	2	The dragged object has moved from one position over the control to another.

Table U-6: State values.

Private Sub *UpDownControl*_GotFocus ([*index* As Integer])

Usage   This event occurs when the control is given focus.

Tip

You can use this routine to display help or other information in a status bar.

Arguments
- *index*—an **Integer** that uniquely identifies a control in a control array. This argument is not present if the control is not part of a control array.

Private Sub *UpDownControl*_LostFocus ([*index* As Integer])

Usage   This event occurs when the control loses focus.

Tip

This routine is useful in performing data verification.

Arguments
- *index*—an **Integer** that uniquely identifies a control in a control array. This argument is not present if the control is not part of a control array.

Private Sub *UpDownControl*_OLEDragDrop([*index* As Integer,] *data* As DataObject, *effect* As Long, *button* As Integer, *shift* As Single, *x* As Single, *y* As Single)

Usage   This event is used to tell the source control the results of an OLE drag-and-drop operation. This is the final event to occur in the series of actions that make up an OLE drag-and-drop operation.

Arguments
- *index*—an **Integer** that is used to uniquely identify a control in a control array. This argument is not present if the control is not part of a control array.
- *data*—a **DataObject** containing the formats that the source control will provide. If the data is not contained in the **DataObject**, then it can be retrieved with the **GetData** method.
- *effect*—a **Long** that returns the status of the OLE drag-and-drop operation (see Table U-7).

effect Name	Value	Description
vbDropEffectNone	0	The operation was canceled or the target control can't accept the drop operation.
vbDropEffectCopy	1	The operation copied data from the source control to the target control. The original data is unchanged.
vbDropEffectMove	2	The operation results in a link from the original data to the target control.

Table U-7: Effect values.

- *button*—an **Integer** containing information about the mouse buttons that were pressed (see Table U-8). These values can be added together if more than one button was pressed. For instance, a value of 3 means that both the left and right buttons were pressed. A value of 0 means that no buttons were pressed.

button Name	Value	Description
vbLeftButton	1	The left button was pressed.
vbRightButton	2	The right button was pressed.
vbMiddleButton	4	The middle button was pressed.

Table U-8: Button values.

- *shift*—an **Integer** containing information about the Shift and Alt keys that were pressed when the mouse button was released (see Table U-9). These values can be added together if more than one key was down. For instance, a value of 5 means that the Shift and Alt keys were both down when the mouse button was released. A value of 0 means that none of these keys were pressed.

shift Name	Value	Description
vbShiftMask	1	The Shift key was pressed.
vbCtrlMask	2	The Ctrl key was pressed.
vbAltMask	4	The Alt key was pressed.

Table U-9: Shift values.

- *x*—a **Single** that contains the horizontal location of the mouse pointer.
- *y*—a **Single** that contains the vertical location of the mouse pointer.

Private Sub *LabelControl*_OLEDragDrop([*index* As Integer,] *data* As DataObject, *effect* As Long, *button* As Integer, *shift* As Single, *x* As Single, *y* As Single)

Usage — This event is used to tell the source control the results of an OLE drag-and-drop operation. This is the final event to occur in the series of actions that make up an OLE drag-and-drop operation.

Arguments
- *index*—an **Integer** used to uniquely identify a control in a control array. This argument is not present if the control is not part of a control array.
- *data*—a **DataObject** containing the formats that the source control will provide. If the data is not contained in the **DataObject**, then it can be retrieved with the **GetData** method.
- *effect*—a **Long** that returns the status of the OLE drag-and-drop operation (see Table U-10).

effect Name	Value	Description
vbDropEffectNone	0	The operation was canceled or the target control can't accept the drop operation.
vbDropEffectCopy	1	The operation copied data from the source control to the target control. The original data is unchanged.
vbDropEffectMove	2	The operation results in a link from the original data to the target control.

Table U-10: Effect values.

- *button*—an **Integer** containing information about the mouse buttons that were pressed (see Table U-11). These values can be added together if more than one button was pressed. For instance, a value of 3 means that both the left and right buttons were pressed. A value of 0 means that no buttons were pressed.

button Name	Value	Description
vbLeftButton	1	The left button was pressed.
vbRightButton	2	The right button was pressed.
vbMiddleButton	4	The middle button was pressed.

Table U-11: Button values.

- *shift*—an **Integer** containing information about the Shift and Alt keys that were pressed when the mouse button was released (see Table U-12). These values can be added together if more than one key was down. For instance, a value of 5 means that the Shift and Alt keys were both down when the mouse button was released. A value of 0 means that none of these keys were pressed.

shift Name	Value	Description
vbShiftMask	1	The Shift key was pressed.
vbCtrlMask	2	The Ctrl key was pressed.
vbAltMask	4	The Alt key was pressed.

Table U-12: Shift values.

- *x*—a **Single** that contains the horizontal location of the mouse pointer.
- *y*—a **Single** that contains the vertical location of the mouse pointer.

Private Sub *LabelControl*_OLEDragOver([*index* As Integer,] *data* As DataObject, *effect* As Long, *button* As Integer, *shift* As Single, *x* As Single, *y* As Single, *state* As Integer)

Usage: This event happens when an OLE drag-and-drop operation is in progress.

Arguments:
- *index*—an **Integer** that is used to uniquely identify a control in a control array. This argument is not present if the control is not part of a control array.

- *data*—a **DataObject** containing the formats that the source control will provide. If the data is not contained in the **DataObject**, then it can be retrieved with the **GetData** method.
- *effect*—a **Long** that returns the status of the OLE drag-and-drop operation (see Table U-13).

effect Name	Value	Description
vbDropEffectNone	0	The operation was canceled or the target control can't accept the drop operation.
vbDropEffectCopy	1	The operation copied data from the source control to the target control. The original data is unchanged.
vbDropEffectMove	2	The operation results in a link from the original data to the target control.

Table U-13: Effect values.

- *button*—an **Integer** containing information about the mouse buttons that were pressed (see Table U-14). These values can be added together if more than one button was pressed. For instance, a value of 3 means that both the left and right buttons were pressed. A value of 0 means that no buttons were pressed.

button Name	Value	Description
vbLeftButton	1	The left button was pressed.
vbRightButton	2	The right button was pressed.
vbMiddleButton	4	The middle button was pressed.

Table U-14: Button values.

- *shift*—an **Integer** containing information about the Shift and Alt keys that were pressed when the mouse button was released (see Table U-15). These values can be added together if more than one key was down. For instance, a value of 5 means that the Shift and Alt keys were both down when the mouse button was released. A value of 0 means that none of these keys were pressed.

shift Name	Value	Description
vbShiftMask	1	The Shift key was pressed.
vbCtrlMask	2	The Ctrl key was pressed.
vbAltMask	4	The Alt key was pressed.

Table U-15: Shift values.

- *x*—a **Single** containing the horizontal location of the mouse pointer.
- *y*—a **Single** containing the vertical location of the mouse pointer.
- *state*—an **Integer** that indicates the state of the object being dragged (see Table U-16).

state Name	Value	Description
vbEnter	0	The dragged object is entering range of the control.
vbLeave	1	The dragged object is leaving range of the control.
vbOver	2	The dragged object has moved from one position over the control to another.

Table U-16: State values.

Private Sub *LabelControl*_OLEGiveFeedback ([*index* As Integer,] *effect* As Long)

Usage This event is used to tell the source control what is happening while the OLE drag-and-drop operation is in progress. This event occurs after the OLEDragOver event.

Tip

You may want to use this event to change the cursor to reflect what can happen in the remote object.

Arguments
- *index*—an **Integer** that is used to uniquely identify a control in a control array. This argument is not present if the control is not part of a control array.
- *effect*—a **Long** that returns the status of the OLE drag-and-drop operation (see Table U-17).

effect Name	Value	Description
vbDropEffectNone	0	The operation was canceled or the target control can't accept the drop operation.
vbDropEffectCopy	1	The operation copied data from the source control to the target control. The original data is unchanged.
vbDropEffectMove	2	The operation results in a link from the original data to the target control.
vbDropEffectScroll	&H80000000	The target control is about to scroll or is scrolling. This value may be added to the other *shift* values.

Table U-17: Effect values.

Private Sub *LabelControl*_OLESetData([*index* As Integer,] *data* As DataObject, *DataFormat* As Integer)

Usage This event happens in response to the target object performing a **GetData** method on *data*. This routine will respond by using the **SetData** method with the desired data using the **DataObject** *data*.

Arguments
- *index*—an **Integer** that is used to uniquely identify a control in a control array. This argument is not present if the control is not part of a control array.
- *data*—a **DataObject** that will contain the data to be returned to the target object.
- *format*—an **Integer** containing the format of the data (see Table U-18).

format Name	Value	Description
vbCFText	1	Text (.TXT files).
vbCFBitmap	2	Bitmap (.BMP files).
vbCFMetafile	3	Metafile (.WMF files).
vbCFEDIB	8	Device-independent bitmap (DIB).
vbCFPallette	9	Color palette.
vbCFEMetafile	14	Enhanced metafile (.EMF files).
vbCFFiles	15	List of files.
vbCFRTF	-16639	Rich text format (.RTF files).

Table U-18: Format values.

Private Sub *LabelControl*_OLEStartDrag ([*index* As Integer,] *data* As DataObject, *AllowedEffects* As Long)

Usage This event is used to start an OLE drag-and-drop operation.

Arguments
- *index*—an **Integer** that is used to uniquely identify a control in a control array. This argument is not present if the control is not part of a control array.
- *data*—a **DataObject** that will contain the formats that the source object is willing to provide to the target object. It may optionally contain the data to be transferred.
- *AllowedEffects*—a **Long** containing the effects that the target object can request from the source object (see Table U-19). The *AllowedEffects* can be added together if the source object supports more than one effect. Note that the target object can always use the *vbDropEffectNone* effect.

AllowedEffects Name	Value	Description
vbDropEffectNone	0	The target can't copy the data.
vbDropEffectCopy	1	The target can copy the data and the source will keep the data unchanged.
vbDropEffectMove	2	The target can copy the data and the source will delete the data.

Table U-19: AllowedEffects values.

Private Sub *UpDownControl*_UpClick ([*index* As Integer])

Usage This event occurs when the user clicks the down button. This event will occur after the **Change** event.

Arguments   *index*—an **Integer** that uniquely identifies a control in a control array. This argument is not present if the control is not part of a control array.

See Also   **VScrollBar** (control)

User

OBJECT

PE, EE

Usage   The **User** object is used by Data Access Objects (DAO) to permit someone to access a Microsoft Jet database.

Properties
- *UserObject*.**Groups**—an object reference to a **Groups** collection containing the groups of which the user is a member.
- *UserObject*.**Name**—a **String** value containing the name of the user. It can be up to 20 characters in length.
- *UserObject*.**Password**—a **String** containing the password for the user. This value can range from 0 to 14 characters in length.
- *UserObject*.**PID**—a **String** value containing a Personal Identifier for the user. It can range in size from 4 to 20 characters and can contain only alphanumeric characters. This property is write-only for objects not yet appended to a new collection.
- *UserObject*.**Properties**—an object reference to a collection of **Property** objects.

Methods   *Group = UserObject*.**CreateGroup** ([*name*] [, *pid*])

Usage   This method is used to create a new group.

Arguments
- *Group*—a **Group** object containing the new group.
- *name*—a **String** value containing the name of the User. It must begin with a letter and can contain any combination of letters, numbers or underscore characters ("_"). The length of the name can be up to 20 characters long.
- *pid*—a **String** containing the personal identifier associated with the group. It can be up to 20 characters long, but must be at least 4 characters long.

UserObject.**NewPassword** *oldpass, newpass*

Usage   This method is used to change a user's password.

Arguments
- *oldpassword*—a **String** containing the current password for the User.
- *newpassword*—a **String** containing the new password for the User. It can be up to 14 characters long and contain any ASCII character except for the null character (ASCII value of 0).

See Also   **Group** (object), **Groups** (collection), **Users** (collection)

Users

COLLECTION

PE, EE

Usage The **Users** collection is used by Data Access Objects (DAO) to contain information about the users that can access a database.

Properties ▪ *UsersCollection*.**Count**—an **Integer** containing the number of **User** objects in the collection.

Methods **UsersCollection.Append** *object*

Usage This method is used to append a **User** object to the collection.

Arguments ▪ *object*—a **User** object that was created by the **CreateUser** method of the **DBEngine** object.

UsersCollection.Delete *name*

Usage This method removes a **User** object from the collection.

Arguments ▪ *name*—a **String** object containing the name of the **User** object to be deleted.

UsersCollection.Refresh

Usage This method gets a current copy of the **Users** in the collection. This is important in a multi-user environment where more than one person may be making changes in the **Users** collection.

See Also **DBEngine** (object), **Group** (object), **User** (object)

UserControl

OBJECT

CCE, LE, PE, EE

Usage The **UserControl** object allows you to build ActiveX controls. You can place constituent controls on the user control just like you would place controls on a form.

Properties ▪ *UserControlObject*.**AccessKeys**—a **String** containing the set of access keys that the user can press to transfer focus to the user control. Access keys for the controls contained in the user control are implicitly included.

▪ *UserControlObject*.**ActiveControl**—an object of type **Control** that contains the currently active control.

▪ *UserControlObject*.**Ambient**—an object of type **AmbientProperties** that contains the ambient properties of the user control's container.

- *UserControlObject*.**Appearance**—an **Integer** value (see Table U-20) that specifies how the user control will be drawn.

Appearance Value	Description
0	The user control is displayed without the 3D effects.
1	The user control is displayed with 3D effects (default value).

Table U-20: Appearance values.

- *UserControlObject*.**AutoRedraw**—a **Boolean** value when **True** means that the graphics and text written directly to the user control will be redrawn from a copy stored in memory. When **False**, the **Paint** event will be triggered to redraw the contents of the user control.

Tip

*Setting **AutoRedraw** to **True** will slow down most operations involving the user control. Most of the common controls (i.e., labels, text boxes, and command buttons) will automatically redraw themselves. If you display graphics directly on the user control, then you may want to use **AutoRedraw**.*

- *UserControlObject*.**BackColor**—a **Long** containing the suggested value for the background color of the user control. The **BackColor** and **ForeColor** must both be solid to display text. If you choose a color that is dithered, it will be changed to the nearest solid color.
- *UserControlObject*.**BackStyle**—an **Integer** value (see Table U-21) specifying how the user control's background will appear. This property is read-only at run time.

BackStyle Value	Description
0	The background will be transparent. You can't draw or paint in the area between the constituent controls. Mouse events in the transparent area are passed to the user control's container.
1	The background will be opaque (default).
2	The background will be transparent. You can draw or paint in the area between the constituent controls. Mouse events in the transparent area are passed to the user control.

Table U-21: BackStyle values.

- *UserControlObject*.**BorderStyle**—an **Integer** value (see Table U-22) specifying how the border will be drawn.

BorderStyle Name	Value	Description
vbBSNone	0	No border is drawn around the control.
vbFixedSingle	1	Single line around the user control.

Table U-22: BorderStyle values.

- *UserControlObject*.**Caption**—a **String** value that displays inside the title bar. The leading text will also display in the Window's taskbar.
- *UserControlObject*.**ClipControls**—a **Boolean** when **True** means that the graphic events repaint the entire user control. When **False**, it means that graphic events only repaint the newly exposed parts of the user control.
- *UserControlObject*.**ContainedControls**—an object reference to the **ContainedControls** collection that contains the set of controls on the user control.
- *UserControlObject*.**Controls**—an object containing a collection of the controls on the form on which the user control was placed.
- *UserControlObject*.**Count**—an **Integer** containing the number of controls on the user control.
- *UserControlObject*.**CurrentX**—a **Single** specifying the horizontal coordinate measured from the user control's left edge for the various drawing methods: **Circle**, **Cls**, **EndDoc**, **Line**, **NewPage**, **Print**, and **PSet**.
- *UserControlObject*.**CurrentY**—a **Single** specifying the vertical coordinate measured from the user control's top edge for the various drawing methods: **Circle**, **Cls**, **EndDoc**, **Line**, **NewPage**, **Print**, and **PSet**.
- *UserControlObject*.**DrawMode**—an **Integer** value (see Table U-23) specifying how the drawing methods **Circle**, **Cls**, **EndDoc**, **Line**, **NewPage**, **Print**, and **PSet** will appear on the user control.

DrawMode Name	Value	Description
vbBlackness	1	Blackness.
vbNotMergePen	2	Inverse of *vbMergePen*.
vbMaskNotPen	3	Combination of the colors common to the background color and the inverse of the pen.
vbNotCopyPen	4	Inverse of *vbCopyPen*.
vbMaskPenNot	5	Combination of the colors common to the pen and the inverse of the background.
vbInvert	6	Inverse of the display color.
vbXorPen	7	Combination of the colors in the display and pen, but not in both.
vbNotMaskPen	8	Inverse setting of *vbMaskPen*.
vbMaskPen	9	Combination of the colors common to the pen and display.
vbNotXorPen	10	Inverse setting of *vbXorPen*.
vbNop	11	Turns drawing off.
vbMergeNotPen	12	Combination of the display and inverse of the pen color.
vbCopyPen	13	Color specified in the **ForeColor** property.
vbMergePenNot	14	Combination of the pen color and the inverse of the display color.
vbMergePen	15	Combination of the pen color and the display color.
vbWhiteness	16	Whiteness.

Table U-23: DrawMode values.

- *UserControlObject*.**DrawStyle**—an **Integer** value (see Table U-24) specifying how the drawing methods **Circle**, **Cls**, **EndDoc**, **Line**, **NewPage**, **Print**, and **PSet** will appear on the user control. If **DrawWidth** is greater than 1, then *vbDash*, *vbDot*, *vbDashDot*, and *vbDashDotDot* will draw a solid line.

UserControl • 1071

DrawStyle Name	Value	Description
vbSolid	0	Solid line.
vbDash	1	Dashed line.
vbDot	2	Dotted line.
vbDashDot	3	Dash followed by a dot.
vbDashDotDot	4	Dash followed by two dots.
vbInvisible	5	No displayed line.
vbInsideSolid	6	Inside solid.

Table U-24: DrawStyle values.

- *UserControlObject*.**DrawWidth**—an **Integer** specifying the width, in pixels, of the line that will be drawn and how the following methods: **Circle**, **Cls**, **EndDoc**, **Line**, **NewPage**, **Print**, and **PSet** will appear on the user control. If **DrawWidth** is greater than 1, then the **DrawStyles** *vbDash*, *vbDot*, *vbDashDot*, and *vbDashDotDot* will draw a solid line.
- *UserControlObject*.**Enabled**—a **Boolean** value when **True** means that the control will respond to events. When **False**, the control will not respond to events.
- *UserControlObject*.**EventsFrozen**—a **Boolean** value when **True** means that the user control's container will not respond to events raised by the user control. When **False**, the user control's container will respond normally to events.

Tip

If the events raised by the user control can't be lost, they must be queued until **EventsFrozen** *becomes* **False**.

- *UserControlObject*.**Extender**—an object reference to the **Extender** object that contains the collection of properties on the user control, which are actually controlled by the user control's container.
- *UserControlObject*.**FillColor**—a **Long** containing the color that will be used to fill in shapes created with the following graphical methods: **Circle**, **Cls**, **EndDoc**, **Line**, **NewPage**, **Print**, and **PSet**.
- *UserControlObject*.**FillStyle**—an **Integer** value (see Table U-25) specifying how the drawing methods **Circle**, **Cls**, **EndDoc**, **Line**, **NewPage**, **Print**, and **PSet** will appear on the user control. If **DrawWidth** is greater than 1, then *vbDash*, *vbDot*, *vbDashDot*, and *vbDashDotDot* will draw a solid line.

FillStyle Name	Value	Description
vbFSSolid	0	Solid.
vbFSTransparent	1	Transparent.
vbHorizontalLine	2	Horizontal line.
vbVerticalLine	3	Vertical line.
vbUpwardDiagonal	4	Diagonal line from lower left to upper right.
vbDownwardDiagonal	5	Diagonal line from upper left to lower right.
vbCross	6	Crosshatch with horizontal and vertical lines.
vbDiagonalCross	7	Crosshatch with diagonal lines.

Table U-25: FillStyle values.

- *UserControlObject*.**Font**—an object containing information about the character font used by this object.

> **Tip**
>
> *Setting values for the **Font** object on the user control at design time makes these values the default when other controls and objects are placed on the user control.*

- *UserControlObject*.**FontBold**—a **Boolean** value when **True** means that the characters display in bold. **False** means that the characters display normally.
- *UserControlObject*.**FontItalic**—a **Boolean** value when **True** means that the characters display in italics. **False** means that the characters display normally.
- *UserControlObject*.**FontName**—a **String** specifying the name of the font that should be used to display the characters in this control.
- *UserControlObject*.**FontSize**—a **Single** specifying the point size that should be used to display the characters in the control.
- *UserControlObject*.**FontStrikethru**—a **Boolean** value when **True** means that the characters display with a line through the center. **False** means that the characters display normally.
- *UserControlObject*.**FontTransparent**—a **Boolean** when **True** means that the graphics and text behind the characters will be shown around the spaces of the character. **False** means that the graphics and text behind the character will be masked.
- *UserControlObject*.**FontUnderline**—a **Boolean** when **True** means that the characters display with a line beneath them. **False** means that the characters display normally.
- *UserControlObject*.**ForeColor**—a **Long** containing the suggested value for the foreground color of the user control. The **BackColor** and **ForeColor** must both be solid to display text. If you choose a color that is dithered, it will change to the nearest solid color.
- *UserControlObject*.**hDC**—a **Long** containing a handle to the device context of the user control.
- *UserControlObject*.**Height**—a **Single** containing the height of the control.
- *UserControlObject*.**hWnd**—a **Long** containing a Windows handle to the control.

> **Tip**
>
> *The **hWnd** property is most useful when making calls to Windows API functions. Since this value can change during execution, do not save the value into a variable for later use.*

- *UserControlObject*.**Hyperlink**—a reference to a **Hyperlink** object that can request a hyperlink aware container (such as Microsoft Internet Explorer) to go to the specified URL.
- *UserControlObject*.**Image**—a handle to a persistent graphic that is returned by the Windows environment. Available only at run time.
- *UserControlObject*.**KeyPreview**—a **Boolean** when **True** means that the user control will receive keyboard events (**KeyDown**, **KeyUp**, and **KeyPress**) before any controls. **False** means that the control will receive the keyboard events and the user control will not.

Tip

This function is useful to provide global keystroke handling at the user control level for such keys as function keys and other control keys.

- *UserControlObject*.**Left**—a **Single** containing the distance measured in twips between the left edge of the control and the left edge of the control's container.
- *UserControlObject*.**MaskColor**—a **Long** value containing the color in the **MaskPicture** image that should be treated as transparent.
- *UserControlObject*.**MaskPicture**—an image-type bitmap (i.e., .BMP, .DIB, .GIF, or .JPEG) that will determine the transparent regions of the user control.
- *UserControlObject*.**MouseIcon**—a picture object (a bitmap, icon, or metafile) that will be used as a cursor when the **MousePointer** property is set to 99. Note that Visual Basic does not support color cursors from a .CUR file. A color icon from an .ICO file should be used instead.
- *UserControlObject*.**MousePointer**—an **Integer** value (see Table U-26) containing the value of the cursor that should display when the cursor is moved over this control. Use *vbCustom* to display the custom icon stored in the **MouseIcon** property.

Cursor Name	Value	Description
vbDefault	0	Shape determined by the object (default value).
vbArrow	1	Arrow.
vbCrosshair	2	Crosshair.
vbIbeam	3	I beam.
vbIconPointer	4	Square inside a square.
vbSizePointer	5	Four-sided arrow (north, south, east, west).
vbSizeNESW	6	Two-sided arrow (northeast, southwest).
vbSizeNS	7	Two-sided arrow (north, south).
vbSizeNWSE	8	Two-sided arrow (northwest, southeast).
vbSizeWE	9	Two-sided arrow (west, east).
vbUpArrow	10	Single-sided arrow pointing north.
vbHourglass	11	Hourglass.
vbNoDrop	12	No Drop.
vbArrowHourglass	13	An arrow and an Hourglass.
vbArrowQuestion	14	An arrow and a question mark.
vbSizeAll	15	Size all.
vbCustom	99	Custom icon from the **MouseIcon** property of this control.

Table U-26: Cursor values.

- *UserControlObject*.**Name**—a **String** containing the name of the control that will be used to reference the control in a Visual Basic program. This property is read only at run time.
- *UserControlObject*.**OLEDragMode**—an **Integer** value (see Table U-27) that describes how the user control will respond to OLE drag operations.

Tip

*When the **DragMode** is **True**, the standard Visual Basic drag-and-drop functions will override the OLE drag-and-drop functions.*

OLEDragMode Name	Value	Description
vbManual	0	All drag requests will be handled by the programmer (default value).
vbOLEDragAutomatic	1	The control responds to all OLE drag requests automatically.

Table U-27: OLEDragMode values.

- *UserControlObject*.**Palette**—a **Picture** object containing a suggested palette for the control. This property is read only at run time.
- *UserControlObject*.**PaletteMode**—an **Integer** value (see Table U-28) describing the palette that should be used with the user control.

PaletteMode Name	Value	Description
vbPaletteModeHalfTone	0	The user control uses the half tone palette (default).
vbPaletteModeUseZOrder	1	The user control uses the palette from the control nearest the front of the **ZOrder** with a palette.
vbModeCustom	2	The user control uses the palette specified in the **Palette** property.

Table U-28: PaletteMode values.

- *UserControlObject*.**Parent**—an object reference to the container of the user control. In Visual Basic, this will usually be a **Form** object; however, other environments will return different objects. Excel will return a workbook. Word will return a document, and Internet Explorer will return an object whose **Script** property returns the **IOmWindow** object.
- *UserControlObject*.**ParentControls**—an object containing a collection of the controls on the user control's parent container.
- *UserControlObject*.**Picture**—a picture object (a bitmap, icon, metafile, GIF, or JPEG) that will be displayed on the control. You can also use the **LoadPicture** function at run time to load a bitmap, icon, or metafile. Note that **Style** must be set to *vbButtonGraphical* for the image to be shown.
- *UserControlObject*.**PropertyPages** (*index*)—a string array containing the name of the property pages. A new property page may be added by assigning a value to the last element of the array, which will always be empty. The order of the elements in the array dictates the order in which they appear in the property page dialog box.
- *UserControlObject*.**RightToLeft**—a **Boolean** value when **True** means that the text is displayed from right to left. **False** means that the text is displayed from left to right. A bi-directional version of Windows is required to set this property to true.
- *UserControlObject*.**ScaleHeight**—an **Integer** value that sets or returns the height of the object in the units specified by **ScaleMode**.
- *UserControlObject*.**ScaleLeft**—an **Integer** value that sets or returns the value of the X-coordinate of the left edge of the user control.
- *UserControlObject*.**ScaleMode**—an **Integer** value (see Table U-29) describing the unit of measurement used for the user control.

Tip

When dealing with graphic images such as BMP or GIF files it is often useful to set **ScaleMode** *to* vbPixels *to help set the proper relationships.*

UserControl • 1075

ScaleMode Name	Value	Description
vbUser	0	Measurements are custom defined, based on the values in ScaleHeight, ScaleLeft, ScaleTop, or ScaleWidth properties.
vbTwips	1	Measurements are in twips (1440 twips per inch).
vbPoints	2	Measurements are in points (72 per inch).
vbPixels	3	Measurements are in pixels (smallest unit of measure for a monitor or printer).
vbCharacters	4	Measurements are in characters (horizontal = 120 twips per character, vertical = 240 twips per character).
vbInches	5	Measurements are in inches.
vbMillimeters	6	Measurements are in millimeters.
vbCentimeters	7	Measurements are in centimeters.

Table U-29: ScaleMode values.

- *UserControlObject*.**ScaleTop**—an **Integer** value that sets or returns the value of the Y-coordinate of the top edge of the user control.
- *UserControlObject*.**ScaleWidth**—an **Integer** value that sets or returns the width of the object in the units specified by **ScaleMode**.
- *UserControlObject*.**Tag**—a **String** that can hold programmer-specific information. This property is not used by Visual Basic.
- *UserControlObject*.**Width**—a **Single** containing the width of the user control.

Methods

UserControlObject.**AsyncRead** *target, type,* [*propertyname*]

Usage This method begins the process to read data from a file or URL. When the process is complete, the **AsyncReadComplete** event will be triggered.

Arguments
- *target*—a **String** containing a URL or the name of a file where the data will be read.
- *type*—an **Integer** containing the type of data to be read (see Table U-30).
- *propertyname*—a **String** containing a name that will be associated with the read request.

type Name	Description
vbAsyncTypeFile	The data is in a file created by Visual Basic.
vbAsyncTypeByteArray	The data is in a Byte Array.
vbAsyncTypePicture	The data is in a Picture object.

Table U-30: type values.

Tip

This value is useful when determining which asynchronous read process to complete in the **AsyncReadComplete** *event or which to cancel with the* **CancelAsyncRead** *method.*

UserControlObject.CancelAsyncRead [propertyname]

Usage This method cancels an asynchronous read request.

Arguments • *propertyname*—a **String** containing a name that is associated with the asynchronous read request. If omitted, the last asynchronous read request will be canceled.

status = UserControlObject.CanPropertyChange (propertyname)

Usage This method checks with the control's container to see if the specified property that is bound to a data source can be updated.

Arguments • *status*—a **Boolean** when **True** means that property can be changed. **False** means that it can't be changed.

• *propertyname*—a **String** containing the name of a property that is bound to a data source.

UserControlObject.Circle [Step] (x, y), radius [, color [, start [, stop [, aspect]]]]

Usage This method draws a circle, ellipse, or curved line on the user control. All coordinate information used is relative to the **ScaleMode**, **ScaleHeight**, **ScaleLeft**, **ScaleTop**, and **ScaleWidth**.

Arguments • **Step**—a keyword specifying that the coordinates are relative to the user control's **CurrentX** and **CurrentY** properties.

• *x*—a **Single** specifying the X-coordinate of the center of the circle.

• *y*—a **Single** specifying the Y-coordinate of the center of the circle.

• *radius*—a **Single** specifying the radius of the circle.

• *color*—a **Long** containing the color of the line to be drawn. If omitted, it will default to the value in the **ForeColor** property.

• *start*—a **Single** specifying the starting angle for the circle in radians. If omitted, it will default to zero.

• *stop*—a **Single** specifying the ending angle for the circle in radians. It omitted, it will default to 2 times pi (approximately 6.28).

• *aspect*—a **Single** specifying the height-to-width ratio of the circle. The default is 1.0, which will yield a perfect circle.

Tip

To draw a half a circle, assign *start* a value of 0, assign *stop* a value of pi (approximately 3.14), and choose values for the other parameters. To draw a vertical ellipse, assign a value greater than 1.0 to *aspect*. A horizontal ellipse would have an aspect ratio of less than 1.0.

UserControlObject.Cls

Usage This method clears all of the graphics and text from a user control.

UserControlObject.Line [Step] (x1, y1), [Step] (x2, y2) [, B | BF]

Usage This method draws lines or boxes on the user control. All coordinate information used is relative to the **ScaleMode**, **ScaleHeight**, **ScaleLeft**, **ScaleTop**, and **ScaleWidth**.

Arguments
- **Step**—a keyword specifying that the *x1* and *y1* coordinates are relative to the user control's **CurrentX** and **CurrentY** properties.
- *x1*—a **Single** specifying the starting X-coordinate of the center of the line or box.
- *y1*—a **Single** specifying the starting Y-coordinate of the center of the line or box.
- **Step**—a keyword specifying that the *x2* and *y2* coordinates are relative to the user control's **CurrentX** and **CurrentY** properties.
- *x2*—a **Single** specifying the stopping X-coordinate of the center of the line or box.
- *y2*—a **Single** specifying the stopping Y-coordinate of the center of the line or box.
- *color*—a **Long** containing the color of the line to be drawn. If omitted, it will default to the value in the **ForeColor** property.
- **B**—draw a box with (*x1*, *y1*) and (*x2*, *y2*) specifying the opposite corners of the box. If omitted, a line will be drawn on the user control.
- **BF**—draw a box with (*x1*, *y1*) and (*x2*, *y2*) specifying the opposite corners of the box and fill the interior with the color specified by **FillColor** and **FillStyle**. If omitted, a line will be drawn on the user control.

UserControlObject.OLEDrag

Usage This method begins an OLE drag-and-drop operation. Invoking this method will trigger the **OLEStartDrag** event.

UserControlObject.PaintPicture picture, x1, y1, [width1], [height1], [x2], [y2], [width2], [height2], [rasterop]

Usage This method displays an image (.BMP, .DIB, .EMF, .ICO, or .WMF) on the user control. All coordinate information used is relative to the **ScaleMode**, **ScaleHeight**, **ScaleLeft**, **ScaleTop**, and **ScaleWidth**.

Arguments
- *picture*—the image to be displayed on the user control. It can come from the **Picture** property of a picture box or another user control.
- *x1*—a **Single** specifying the starting X-coordinate of the picture.
- *y1*—a **Single** specifying the starting Y-coordinate of the picture.
- *width1*—a **Single** specifying the width of the image. If omitted, the width will default to the width of the image. If greater or less than the width of the image, the image will be stretched or shrunk to fit.

- *height1*—a **Single** specifying the height of the image. If omitted, the height will default to the height of the image. If greater or less than the height of the image, the image will be stretched or shrunk to fit.
- *x2*—a **Single** specifying the starting X-coordinate of a clipping region within the picture. If omitted, zero will be used.
- *y2*—a **Single** specifying the starting Y-coordinate of a clipping region within the picture. If omitted, zero will be used.
- *width2*—a **Single** specifying the width of the clipping region of the image. If omitted, the width will default to the width of the image. If greater or less than the width of the image, the image will be stretched or shrunk to fit.
- *height2*—a **Single** specifying the height of the clipping region of the image. If omitted, the height will default to the height of the image. If greater or less than the height of the image, the image will be stretched or shrunk to fit.
- *rasterop*—a **Long** containing a raster op code from Table U-31 that will perform a bit-wise operation on the image as it is displayed. The default will be to display the image as is.

RasterOp Name	Value	Description
vbDstInvert	&H005A0049	Inverts the destination image.
vbMergeCopy	&H00C000CA	Combines the source and the pattern.
vbMergePaint	&H00BB0226	Combines inverted source image with destination image using OR.
vbNotSrcCopy	&H00330008	Copies inverted source image to the destination.
vbNotSrcErase	&H001100A6	Inverts the result of combining the source and destination images using OR.
vbPatCopy	&H00F00021	Copies the source pattern to the destination bitmap.
vbPatInvert	&H005A0049	Combines the inverted source pattern with the destination image using XOR.
vbPatPaint	&H00FB0A09	Combines the destination image with the source pattern.
vbScrAnd	&H008800C6	Combines the destination and source images using AND.
vbSrcCopy	&H00CC0020	Copies the source image to the destination bitmap.
vbSrcErase	&H00440328	Combines the inverted destination image with the source image by using AND.
vbSrcInvert	&H00660046	Combines the source and destination images using XOR.
vbSrcPaint	&H00EE0086	Combines the source and destination images using OR.

Table U-31: RasterOp values.

color = UserControlObject.Point (x, y)

Usage   This method returns a **Long** containing the color at the point at location x, y. If the location is outside the user control, then -1 is returned. All coordinate information used is relative to the **ScaleMode**, **ScaleHeight**, **ScaleLeft**, **ScaleTop**, and **ScaleWidth**.

Arguments
- *color*—a **Long** containing the color at location *x*, *y*.
- *x*—a **Single** specifying the X-coordinate of the point.
- *y*—a **Single** specifying the Y-coordinate of the point.

UserControlObject.**PopupMenu** *menu, flags, x, y, menuitem*

Usage   This method displays a pop-up menu on the screen.

Tip

*Set **Visible** to **False** for menu items to be displayed as pop-up menus to prevent them from displaying in the menu bar.*

Arguments
- *menu*—the name of a **Menu** object to be displayed. It must include at least one submenu item.
- *flags*—zero or more items from Table U-32 below. If omitted, zero will be used. Multiple values can be selected by adding them together.

Menu Flags Name	Value	Description
vbPopupMenuLeftButton	0	The items on the menu can be selected by only the left mouse button.
vbPopupMenuLeftAlign	0	The left edge of the menu is located at *x*.
vbPopupMenuRightButton	2	The items on the menu can be selected by either mouse button.
vbPopupMenuCenterAlign	4	The center of the menu is located at *x*.
vbPopupMenuRightAlign	8	The right edge of the menu is located at *x*.

Table U-32: Menu Flags values.

- *x*—a **Single** specifying the X-coordinate of the menu. If omitted, it will default to the current X-coordinate of the mouse.
- *y*—a **Single** specifying the Y-coordinate of the menu. If omitted, it will default to the current Y-coordinate of the mouse.
- *menuitem*—the name of the submenu item that will be displayed in bold text. If omitted, no items will be displayed in bold.

UserControlObject.**PropertyChanged** *propertyname*

Usage   This method notifies the control's container when a property has been changed. This allows the container to synchronize its property window with the new value.

Arguments   *propertyname*—a **String** containing the name of a property that has changed.

UserControlObject.PSet [Step] (x, y), color

Usage This method sets the point at *x, y* to the color specified in *color*. All coordinate information used is relative to the **ScaleMode, ScaleHeight, ScaleLeft, ScaleTop,** and **ScaleWidth**.

Arguments
- **Step**—keyword specifying that the *x* and *y* coordinates are relative to the user control's **CurrentX** and **CurrentY** properties.
- *x*—a **Single** specifying the X-coordinate of the point.
- *y*—a **Single** specifying the Y-coordinate of the point.
- *color*—a **Long** containing the color to be displayed at location *x, y*. If omitted, this value will default to the value of **ForeColor**.

UserControlObject.Refresh

Usage This method redraws the contents of the user control.

UserControlObject.Scale [(x1, y1)—(x2, y2)]

Usage This method defines the coordinate system used on the user control and sets the appropriate values in **ScaleMode, ScaleHeight, ScaleLeft, ScaleTop,** and **ScaleWidth**. If the **Scale** method is used without any arguments, the coordinate is reset to default.

Arguments
- *x1*—a **Single** specifying the X-coordinate of the left edge of the user control.
- *y1*—a **Single** specifying the Y-coordinate of the top edge of the user control.
- *x2*—a **Single** specifying the X-coordinate of the right edge of the user control.
- *y2*—a **Single** specifying the Y-coordinate of the bottom edge of the user control.

result = UserControlObject.ScaleX (width, fromscale, toscale)

Usage This method computes a new value for *width* in a different scale.

Arguments
- *result*—a **Single** containing a new value for *width*.
- *fromscale*—an **Integer** specifying a **ScaleMode** value for the current *width*.
- *toscale*—an **Integer** value (see Table U-33) specifying the **ScaleMode** value for the new *width*.

ScaleMode Name	Value	Description
vbUser	0	Measurements are custom defined, based on the values in ScaleHeight, ScaleLeft, ScaleTop, or ScaleWidth properties.
vbTwips	1	Measurements are in twips (1440 twips per inch).
vbPoints	2	Measurements are in points (72 per inch).
vbPixels	3	Measurements are in pixels (smallest unit of measure for a monitor or printer).
vbCharacters	4	Measurements are in characters (horizontal = 120 twips per character, vertical = 240 twips per character).

ScaleMode Name	Value	Description
vbInches	5	Measurements are in inches.
vbMillimeters	6	Measurements are in millimeters.
vbCentimeters	7	Measurements are in centimeters.
vbHimetric	8	Measurements are in himetrics.

Table U-33: ScaleMode values.

result = UserControlObject.ScaleY (height, fromscale, toscale)

Usage This method computes a new value for *height* in a different scale.

Arguments
- *result*—a **Single** containing a new value for *height*.
- *fromscale*—an **Integer** specifying a **ScaleMode** value for the current *height*.
- *toscale*—an **Integer** value (see Table U-34) specifying the **ScaleMode** value for the new *height*.

ScaleMode Name	Value	Description
vbUser	0	Measurements are custom defined, based on the values in ScaleHeight, ScaleLeft, ScaleTop, or ScaleWidth properties.
vbTwips	1	Measurements are in twips (1440 twips per inch).
vbPoints	2	Measurements are in points (72 per inch).
vbPixels	3	Measurements are in pixels (smallest unit of measure for a monitor or printer).
vbCharacters	4	Measurements are in characters (horizontal = 120 twips per character, vertical = 240 twips per character).
vbInches	5	Measurements are in inches.
vbMillimeters	6	Measurements are in millimeters.
vbCentimeters	7	Measurements are in centimeters.
vbHimetric	8	Measurements are in himetrics.

Table U-34: ScaleMode values.

UserControlObject.SetFocus

Usage This method transfers the focus from the user control or control that currently has the focus to this user control. To receive the focus, this user control must be enabled and visible.

UserControlObject.Size width, height

Usage This method changes the size of the control.

Arguments
- *width*—a **Single** containing the new width of the control in twips.
- *height*—a **Single** containing the new height of the control in twips.

height = UserControlObject.TextHeight (*string*)

Usage This method computes the height of the string in the units specified by **ScaleMode**. The height is computed using the font information specified in the **Font** object. It will also include space at the top and the bottom of the characters, so that multiple lines of text can be placed next to each other. If *string* contains embedded carriage return linefeed pairs, then the total height of the block of text will be returned.

Arguments
- *height*—a **Single** containing the height of *string*.
- *string*—a **String** containing characters to be printed on the user control.

width = UserControlObject.TextWidth (*string*)

Usage This method will compute the width of the string in the units specified by **ScaleMode**. The width is computed using the font information specified in the **Font** object. If *string* contains embedded carriage return linefeed pairs, then the length of the longest line will be returned.

Arguments
- *width*—a **Single** containing the width of *string*.
- *string*—a **String** containing characters to be printed on the user control.

Events

Private Sub UserControlObject_AccessKeyPress (*keychar* As Integer)

Usage This event occurs when an access key is pressed.

Arguments *keychar*—an **Integer** containing the ASCII character that was pressed, without the Alt key.

Private Sub UserControlObject_AmbientChanged (*propertyname* As String)

Usage This event occurs when an ambient property changes.

Arguments *propertyname*—a **String** containing the name of the property that has changed.

Private Sub UserControlObject_AsyncReadComplete (*propertyvalue* As AsyncProperty)

Usage This event occurs when an asynchronous read request completes.

Arguments *propertyvalue*—an **AsyncProperty** object containing information about the read request.

Private Sub *UserControlObject*_Click( )

Usage   This event occurs when the user clicks a mouse button while the cursor is positioned over the user control.

> **Tip**
>
> *If you need to identify which mouse button was pressed, use the **MouseUp** and **MouseDown** events.*

Private Sub *UserControlObject*_DblClick( )

Usage   This event occurs when the user double-clicks a mouse button while the cursor is positioned over the user control.

> **Tip**
>
> *If there is code in the **Click** event, then the **DblClick** event will never occur.*

Private Sub *UserControlObject*_DragDrop (*source* As Control, *x* As Single, *y* As Single)

Usage   This event occurs when a drag-and-drop operation is completed by using the Drag method with a *DragAction* value of *vbEndDrag* (2).

> **Tip**
>
> *When using drag-and-drop operations, use the **DragOver** event to determine what the cursor should look like while the cursor moves over the control.*

Arguments   ▪ *source*—a control object that is the control that is being dragged.

> **Tip**
>
> *You can access a property or method from the source control by using* source.*property or* source.*method. You can determine the type of object or control by using the **TypeOf** operator.*

- *x*—a **Single** containing the horizontal location of the mouse pointer.
- *y*—a **Single** containing the vertical location of the mouse pointer.

Private Sub *UserControlObject*_DragOver (*source* As Control, *x* As Single, *y* As Single, *state* As Integer)

Usage   This event occurs while a drag operation is in progress and the cursor is moved over the control.

Tip

*When using drag-and-drop operations, use the **DragOver** event to determine what the cursor should look like while the cursor moves over the control. When* state *is 0, you can change the cursor to a No Drop (vbNoDrop) cursor or highlight the field that the cursor is near. When* state *is 1, you can undo the changes you made when the* state *was 0.*

Arguments   ▪ *source*—a control object that is the control that is being dragged.

Tip

You can access a property or method from the source control by using source.*property or* source.*method. You can determine the type of object or control by using the **TypeOf** operator.*

▪ *x*—a **Single** containing the horizontal location of the mouse pointer.
▪ *y*—a **Single** containing the vertical location of the mouse pointer.
▪ *state*—an **Integer** value (see Table U-35) that indicates the state of the object being dragged.

state Name	Value	Description
vbEnter	0	The dragged object is entering range of the control.
vbLeave	1	The dragged object is leaving range of the control.
vbOver	2	The dragged object has moved from one position over the control to another.

Table U-35: State values.

Private Sub *UserControlObject*_EnterFocus ( )

Usage   This event occurs when the user control or a constituent control is about to receive control. This event occurs before any **GotFocus** events occur. After this event occurs, only the **GotFocus** event associated with the constituent control or the user control will be triggered.

Private Sub *UserControlObject*_ExitFocus ( )

Usage This event occurs when the user control or a constituent control has lost focus. This event occurs after any **LostFocus** events occur.

Private Sub *UserControlObject*_GotFocus ( )

Usage This event occurs when the user control is given focus, and the mouse is not over any of the constituent controls.

> **Tip**
>
> *Do not raise the **GotFocus** extender event from within this event.*

Private Sub *UserControlObject*_Hide ( )

Usage This event occurs when the user control's **Visible** property becomes **False**.

Private Sub *UserControlObject* _Initialize ( )

Usage This event occurs when the user control is first created. This event will occur before the **Load** event.

> **Tip**
>
> *Since this event is triggered only when the user control is created (and the **Load** event is triggered when the user control is created and when it is loaded), it makes sense to put your initialization code in the **Load** event, unless you have specific actions that need to be done only when the user control is created.*

Private Sub *UserControlObject* _InitProperties ( )

Usage This event occurs when a new instance of the user control is created.

Private Sub *UserControlObject* _KeyDown (*keycode* As Integer, *shift* As Single)

Usage This event occurs when a key is pressed. If the **KeyPreview** property is **True**, this event will occur before the **KeyPress** event for control with the focus. Otherwise, the user control will only see this event if it contains no visible and enabled controls.

Arguments
- *keycode*—an **Integer** containing information about which key was pressed.
- *shift*—an **Integer** value (see Table U-36) containing information about the Shift and Alt keys that were pressed when the mouse button was pressed. These values can be added together if more than one key was down. For instance, a value of 5 means that the Shift and Alt keys were both down when the mouse button was pressed.

shift Name	Value	Description
vbShiftMask	1	The Shift key was pressed.
vbCtrlMask	2	The Ctrl key was pressed.
vbAltMask	4	The Alt key was pressed.

Table U-36: Shift values.

Private Sub *UserControlObject*_KeyPress (*keychar* As Integer)

Usage   This event occurs when a key is pressed. If the **KeyPreview** property is **True**, this event will occur before the **KeyPress** event for control with the focus. Otherwise, the user control will only see this event if it contains no visible and enabled controls.

Arguments
- *keychar*—an **Integer** containing the ASCII character that was pressed. Changing the value of *keychar* to zero will cancel the keystroke.

Private Sub *UserControlObject*_KeyUp (*keycode* As Integer, *shift* As Single)

Usage   This event occurs when a key is pressed. If the **KeyPreview** property is **True**, this event will occur before the **KeyPress** event for control with the focus. Otherwise, the user control will only see this event if it contains no visible and enabled controls.

Arguments
- *keycode*—an **Integer** containing information about which key was released.
- *shift*—an **Integer** value (see Table U-37) containing information about the Shift and Alt keys that were pressed when the mouse button was pressed. These values can be added together if more than one key was down. For instance, a value of 5 means that the Shift and Alt keys were both down when the mouse button was pressed.

shift Name	Value	Description
vbShiftMask	1	The Shift key was pressed.
vbCtrlMask	2	The Ctrl key was pressed.
vbAltMask	4	The Alt key was pressed.

Table U-37: Shift values.

Private Sub *UserControlObject* _LostFocus ( )

Usage   This event occurs when the user control loses focus.

Private Sub *UserControlObject* _MouseDown (*button* As Integer, *shift* As Single, *x* As Single, *y* As Single)

Usage   This event occurs when a mouse button is pressed while the cursor is over any unoccupied part of the user control.

Arguments
- *button*—an **Integer** value (see Table U-38) containing information about the mouse buttons that were pressed. Only one button will be indicated when this event occurs.

button Name	Value	Description
vbLeftButton	1	The left button was pressed.
vbRightButton	2	The right button was pressed.
vbMiddleButton	4	The middle button was pressed.

Table U-38: Button values.

- *shift*—an **Integer** value (see Table U-39) containing information about the Shift and Alt keys that were pressed when the mouse button was pressed. These values can be added together if more than one key was down. For instance, a value of 5 means that the Shift and Alt keys were both down when the mouse button was pressed.

shift Name	Value	Description
vbShiftMask	1	The Shift key was pressed.
vbCtrlMask	2	The Ctrl key was pressed.
vbAltMask	4	The Alt key was pressed.

Table U-39: Shift values.

- *x*—a **Single** containing the horizontal location of the mouse pointer.
- *y*—a **Single** containing the vertical location of the mouse pointer.

Private Sub *UserControlObject* _MouseMove (*button* As Integer, *shift* As Single, *x* As Single, *y* As Single)

Usage   This event occurs while the cursor is moved over any unoccupied part of the user control.

Arguments • *button*—an **Integer** value (see Table U-40) containing information about the mouse buttons that were pressed. These values can be added together if more than one button was pressed. For instance, a value of 3 means that both the left and right buttons were pressed. A value of 0 means that no buttons were pressed.

button Name	Value	Description
vbLeftButton	1	The left button was pressed.
vbRightButton	2	The right button was pressed.
vbMiddleButton	4	The middle button was pressed.

Table U-40: Button values.

• *shift*—an **Integer** value (see Table U-41) containing information about the Shift and Alt keys that were pressed when the mouse button was pressed. These values can be added together if more than one key was down. For instance, a value of 5 means that the Shift and Alt keys were both down when the mouse button was pressed. A value of 0 means that none of these keys were pressed.

shift Name	Value	Description
vbShiftMask	1	The Shift key was pressed.
vbCtrlMask	2	The Ctrl key was pressed.
vbAltMask	4	The Alt key was pressed.

Table U-41: Shift values.

• *x*—a **Single** containing the horizontal location of the mouse pointer.
• *y*—a **Single** containing the vertical location of the mouse pointer.

Private Sub *UserControlObject* _MouseUp (*button* As Integer, *shift* As Single, *x* As Single, *y* As Single)

Usage This event occurs when a mouse button is released while the cursor is over any unoccupied part of the user control.

Arguments • *button*—an **Integer** value (see Table U-42) containing information about the mouse buttons that were released. Only one of these values will be present.

button Name	Value	Description
vbLeftButton	1	The left button was released.
vbRightButton	2	The right button was released.
vbMiddleButton	4	The middle button was released.

Table U-42: Button values.

- *shift*—an **Integer** value (see Table U-43) containing information about the Shift and Alt keys that were pressed when the mouse button was released. These values can be added together if more than one key was down. For instance, a value of 5 means that the Shift and Alt keys were both down when the mouse button was released. A value of 0 means that none of these keys were pressed.

shift Name	Value	Description
vbShiftMask	1	The Shift key was pressed.
vbCtrlMask	2	The Ctrl key was pressed.
vbAltMask	4	The Alt key was pressed.

Table U-43: *Shift values.*

- *x*—a **Single** containing the horizontal location of the mouse pointer.
- *y*—a **Single** containing the vertical location of the mouse pointer.

Private Sub *UserControlObject*_OLECompleteDrag (*effect* As Long)

Usage — This event tells the source control the results of an OLE drag-and-drop operation. This is the final event to occur in the series of actions that make up an OLE drag-and-drop operation.

Arguments
- *effect*—a **Long** (see Table U-44) that returns the status of the OLE drag-and-drop operation.

effect Name	Value	Description
vbDropEffectNone	0	The operation was canceled or the target control can't accept the drop operation.
vbDropEffectCopy	1	The operation copied data from the source control to the target control. The original data is unchanged.
vbDropEffectMove	2	The operation results in a link from the original data to the target control.

Table U-44: *Effect values.*

Private Sub *UserControlObject*_OLEDragDrop (*data* As DataObject, *effect* As Long, *button* As Integer, *shift* As Single, *x* As Single, *y* As Single)

Usage — This event tells the source control the results of an OLE drag-and-drop operation. This is the final event to occur in the series of actions that make up an OLE drag-and-drop operation.

Arguments
- *data*—a **DataObject** containing the formats that the source control will provide. If the data is not contained in the **DataObject**, then it can be retrieved with the **GetData** method.
- *effect*—a **Long** (see Table U-45) that returns the status of the OLE drag-and-drop operation.

effect Name	Value	Description
vbDropEffectNone	0	The operation was canceled or the target control can't accept the drop operation.
vbDropEffectCopy	1	The operation copied data from the source control to the target control. The original data is unchanged.
vbDropEffectMove	2	The operation results in a link from the original data to the target control.

Table U-45: Effect values.

- *button*—an **Integer** value (see Table U-46) containing information about the mouse buttons that were pressed. These values can be added together if more than one button was pressed. For instance, a value of 3 means that both the left and right buttons were pressed. A value of 0 means that no buttons were pressed.

button Name	Value	Description
vbLeftButton	1	The left button was pressed.
vbRightButton	2	The right button was pressed.
vbMiddleButton	4	The middle button was pressed.

Table U-46: Button values.

- *shift*—an **Integer** value (see Table U-47) containing information about the Shift and Alt keys that were pressed when the mouse button was released. These values can be added together if more than one key was down. For instance, a value of 5 means that the Shift and Alt keys were both down when the mouse button was released. A value of 0 means that none of these keys were pressed.

shift Name	Value	Description
vbShiftMask	1	The Shift key was pressed.
vbCtrlMask	2	The Ctrl key was pressed.
vbAltMask	4	The Alt key was pressed.

Table U-47: Shift values.

- *x*—a **Single** containing the horizontal location of the mouse pointer.
- *y*—a **Single** containing the vertical location of the mouse pointer.

UserControl

Private Sub *UserControlObject*_**OLEDragOver** (*data* **As DataObject,** *effect* **As Long,** *button* **As Integer,** *shift* **As Single,** *x* **As Single,** *y* **As Single,** *state* **As Integer**)

Usage   This event happens when an OLE drag-and-drop operation is in progress.

Arguments
- *data*—a **DataObject** containing the formats that the source control will provide. If the data is not contained in the **DataObject**, then it can be retrieved with the **GetData** method.
- *effect*—a **Long** (see Table U-48) that returns the status of the OLE drag-and-drop operation.

effect Name	Value	Description
vbDropEffectNone	0	The operation was canceled or the target control can't accept the drop operation.
vbDropEffectCopy	1	The operation copied data from the source control to the target control. The original data is unchanged.
vbDropEffectMove	2	The operation results in a link from the original data to the target control.

Table U-48: Effect values.

- *button*—an **Integer** value (see Table U-49) containing information about the mouse buttons that were pressed. These values can be added together if more than one button was pressed. For instance, a value of 3 means that both the left and right buttons were pressed. A value of 0 means that no buttons were pressed.

button Name	Value	Description
vbLeftButton	1	The left button was pressed.
vbRightButton	2	The right button was pressed.
vbMiddleButton	4	The middle button was pressed.

Table U-49: Button values.

- *shift*—an **Integer** value (see Table U-50) containing information about the Shift and Alt keys that were pressed when the mouse button was released. These values can be added together if more than one key was down. For instance, a value of 5 means that the Shift and Alt keys were both down when the mouse button was released. A value of 0 means that none of these keys were pressed.

shift Name	Value	Description
vbShiftMask	1	The Shift key was pressed.
vbCtrlMask	2	The Ctrl key was pressed.
vbAltMask	4	The Alt key was pressed.

Table U-50: Shift values.

- *x*—a **Single** containing the horizontal location of the mouse pointer.
- *y*—a **Single** containing the vertical location of the mouse pointer.
- *state*—an **Integer** value (see Table U-51) that indicates the state of the object being dragged.

state Name	Value	Description
vbEnter	0	The dragged object is entering range of the control.
vbLeave	1	The dragged object is leaving range of the control.
vbOver	2	The dragged object has moved from one position over the control to another.

Table U-51: State values.

Private Sub UserControlObject_OLEGiveFeedback (*effect* As Long)

Usage This event tells the source control what is happening while the OLE drag-and-drop operation is in progress. This event occurs after the **OLEDragOver** event.

Tip

You may want to use this event to change the cursor to reflect what can happen in the remote object.

Arguments *effect*—a **Long** (see Table U-52) that returns the status of the OLE drag-and-drop operation.

effect Name	Value	Description
vbDropEffectNone	0	The operation was canceled or the target control can't accept the drop operation.
vbDropEffectCopy	1	The operation copied data from the source control to the target control. The original data is unchanged.
vbDropEffectMove	2	The operation results in a link from the original data to the target control.
vbDropEffectScroll	&H80000000	The target control is about to scroll or is scrolling. This value may be added to the other *shift* values.

Table U-52: Effect values.

Private Sub UserControlObject_OLESetData (*data* As DataObject, *DataFormat* As Integer)

Usage This event happens in response to the target object performing a **GetData** method on *data*. This routine responds by using the **SetData** method with the desired data using the **DataObject** *data*.

Arguments
- *data*—a **DataObject** that will contain the data to be returned to the target object.
- *format*—an **Integer** value (see Table U-53) containing the format of the data.

format Name	Value	Description
vbCFText	1	Text (.TXT files).
vbCFBitmap	2	Bitmap (.BMP files).
vbCFMetafile	3	Metafile (.WMF files).
vbCFEDIB	8	Device independent bitmap (DIB).
vbCFPallette	9	Color palette.
vbCFEMetafile	14	Enhanced metafile (EMF files).
vbCFFiles	15	List of files.
vbCFRTF	-16639	Rich Text Format (.RTF files).

Table U-53: Format values.

Private Sub *UserControlObject*_OLEStartDrag (*data* As DataObject, *AllowedEffects* As Long)

Usage　This event starts an OLE drag-and-drop operation.

Arguments
- *data*—a **DataObject** containing the formats that the source object is willing to provide to the target object. It may optionally contain the data to be transferred.
- *AllowedEffects*—a **Long** (see Table U-54) containing the effects that the target object can request from the source object. The *AllowedEffects* can be added together if the source object supports more than one effect. Note that the target object can always use the *vbDropEffectNone* effect.

AllowedEffects Name	Value	Description
vbDropEffectNone	0	The target can't copy the data.
vbDropEffectCopy	1	The target can copy the data and the source will keep the data unchanged.
vbDropEffectMove	2	The target can copy the data and the source will delete the data.

Table U-54: AllowedEffects values.

Private Sub *UserControlObject*_Paint ( )

Usage　This event occurs when the user control must redraw itself. This can happen if the user control was previously covered and now is not, the size of the user control has been changed, or the user control has been moved. A **Paint** event is necessary if you generate graphics or print text directly to the user control and have set the **AutoRedraw** property to **False**.

> **Tip**
>
> *Avoid moving the user control, changing any variables that affect the user control's size or appearance, and using the **Refresh** method. This can cause a cascading event where the event will trigger the same event over and over again until the system crashes.*

Private Sub *UserControlObject*_ReadProperties (*pb* As PropertyBag)

Usage This event is called when an old instance of an object with a saved state is loaded.

Arguments *pb*—a reference to a **PropertyBag** object containing the saved data to be loaded.

Private Sub *UserControlObject*_Resize ( )

Usage This event occurs when the user control is first displayed, when the value of **WindowState** changes, or when the user control is resized. After the resize event occurs, the **Paint** event will be called (if **AutoResize** is **False**) to redraw the contents of the user control.

Private Sub *UserControlObject*_Show ( )

Usage This event occurs when the user control's **Visible** property is set to **True**.

Private Sub *UserControlObject*_Terminate ( )

Usage This event occurs when the last instance of a user control is ready to be removed from memory. It will not be called if for some reason (such as the **End** statement being executed) the program terminates abnormally.

Private Sub *UserControlObject*_WriteProperties (*pb* As PropertyBag)

Usage This event is called when an instance of an object needs to be saved. It can be restored when the **ReadProperties** event is triggered.

Arguments *pb*—a reference to a **PropertyBag** object containing the saved data to be saved. Use the **WriteProperty** method in the **PropertyBag** to save the data.

See Also **Forms** (collection), **MDIForm** (object), **UserDocument** (object)

UserDocument

OBJECT

CCE, LE, PE, EE

Usage The **UserDocument** object allows you to build ActiveX documents. You can place constituent controls on the user control just like you would place controls on a form; however, you can't use an embedded object like an Excel spreadsheet or a Word document or an **OLE Container** control.

Properties
- *UserDocumentObject*.**ActiveControl**—an object of type control that contains a reference to the currently active control.
- *UserDocumentObject*.**Appearance**—an **Integer** value (see Table U-55) that specifies how the user document will be drawn.

Appearance Value	Description
0	The user document is displayed without the 3D effects.
1	The user document is displayed with 3D effects (default value).

Table U-55: Appearance values.

- *UserDocumentObject*.**AutoRedraw**—a **Boolean** value when **True** means that the graphics and text written directly to the user document will be redrawn from a copy stored in memory. When **False**, the **Paint** event will be triggered to redraw the contents of the user document.

Tip

*Setting **AutoRedraw** to **True** will slow down most operations involving the user document. Most of the common controls (i.e., labels, text boxes, and command buttons) will automatically redraw themselves. If you display graphics directly on the user document, then you may want to use **AutoRedraw**.*

- *UserDocumentObject*.**BackColor**—a **Long** containing the suggested value for the background color of the user document. The **BackColor** and **ForeColor** must both be solid to display text. If you choose a color that is dithered, it will be changed to the nearest solid color.
- *UserDocumentObject*.**ClipControls**—a **Boolean** when **True** means that the graphic events repaint the entire user document. When **False** means that graphic events only repaint the newly exposed parts of the user document.
- *UserDocumentObject*.**ContinuousScroll**—a **Boolean** when **True** means that the user document redraws the document continuously. **False** means that the document is only redrawn when the user releases the mouse button.
- *UserDocumentObject*.**Controls**—an object containing a collection of the controls on the form on which the user document was placed.
- *UserDocumentObject*.**Count**—an **Integer** containing the number of controls on the user document.
- *UserDocumentObject*.**CurrentX**—a **Single** specifying the horizontal coordinate measured from the user document's left edge for the various drawing methods: **Circle**, **Cls**, **EndDoc**, **Line**, **NewPage**, **Print**, and **PSet**.
- *UserDocumentObject*.**CurrentY**—a **Single** specifying the vertical coordinate measured from the user document's top edge for the various drawing methods: **Circle**, **Cls**, **EndDoc**, **Line**, **NewPage**, **Print**, and **PSet**.
- *UserDocumentObject*.**DrawMode**—an **Integer** value (see Table U-56) specifying how the drawing methods **Circle**, **Cls**, **EndDoc**, **Line**, **NewPage**, **Print**, and **PSet** will appear on the user document.

DrawMode Name	Value	Description
vbBlackness	1	Blackness.
vbNotMergePen	2	Inverse of *vbMergePen*.
vbMaskNotPen	3	Combination of the colors common to the background color and the inverse of the pen.

DrawMode Name	Value	Description
vbNotCopyPen	4	Inverse of *vbCopyPen*.
vbMaskPenNot	5	Combination of the colors common to the pen and the inverse of the background.
vbInvert	6	Inverse of the display color.
vbXorPen	7	Combination of the colors in the display and pen, but not in both.
vbNotMaskPen	8	Inverse setting of *vbMaskPen*.
vbMaskPen	9	Combination of the colors common to the pen and display.
vbNotXorPen	10	Inverse setting of *vbXorPen*.
vbNop	11	Turns drawing off.
vbMergeNotPen	12	Combination of the display and inverse of the pen color.
vbCopyPen	13	Color specified in the **ForeColor** property.
vbMergePenNot	14	Combination of the pen color and the inverse of the display color.
vbMergePen	15	Combination of the pen color and the display color.
vbWhiteness	16	Whiteness.

Table U-56: *DrawMode values*.

- *UserDocumentObject*.**DrawStyle**—an **Integer** value (see Table U-57) specifying how the drawing methods **Circle**, **Cls**, **EndDoc**, **Line**, **NewPage**, **Print**, and **PSet** will appear on the user document. If **DrawWidth** is greater than 1, then *vbDash*, *vbDot*, *vbDashDot*, and *vbDashDotDot* will draw a solid line.

DrawStyle Name	Value	Description
vbSolid	0	Solid line.
vbDash	1	Dashed line.
vbDot	2	Dotted line.
vbDashDot	3	Dash followed by a dot.
vbDashDotDot	4	Dash followed by two dots.
vbInvisible	5	No displayed line.
vbInsideSolid	6	Inside solid.

Table U-57: *DrawStyle values*.

- *UserDocumentObject*.**DrawWidth**—an **Integer** specifying the width of the line in pixels that will be drawn and how the following methods: **Circle**, **Cls**, **EndDoc**, **Line**, **NewPage**, **Print**, and **PSet** will appear on the user document. If **DrawWidth** is greater than 1, then the **DrawStyles** *vbDash*, *vbDot*, *vbDashDot*, and *vbDashDotDot* will draw a solid line.

- *UserDocumentObject*.**FillColor**—a **Long** containing the color that will be used to fill in shapes created with the following graphical methods: **Circle**, **Cls**, **EndDoc**, **Line**, **NewPage**, **Print**, and **PSet**.

- *UserDocumentObject*.**FillStyle**—an **Integer** value (see Table U-58) specifying how the drawing methods **Circle**, **Cls**, **EndDoc**, **Line**, **NewPage**, **Print**, and **PSet** will appear on the user document. If **DrawWidth** is greater than 1, then *vbDash*, *vbDot*, *vbDashDot*, and *vbDashDotDot* will draw a solid line.

FillStyle Name	Value	Description
vbFSSolid	0	Solid.
vbFSTransparent	1	Transparent.
vbHorizontalLine	2	Horizontal line.
vbVerticalLine	3	Vertical line.
vbUpwardDiagonal	4	Diagonal line from lower left to upper right.
vbDownwardDiagonal	5	Diagonal line from upper left to lower right.
vbCross	6	Crosshatch with horizontal and vertical lines.
vbDiagonalCross	7	Crosshatch with diagonal lines.

Table U-58: FillStyle values.

- *UserDocumentObject*.**Font**—an object containing information about the character font used by this object.

> **Tip**
>
> *Setting values for the **Font** object on the user document at design time makes these values the default when other controls and objects are placed on the user document.*

- *UserDocumentObject*.**FontBold**—a **Boolean** when **True** means that the characters display in bold. **False** means that the characters display normally.
- *UserDocumentObject*.**FontItalic**—a **Boolean** when **True** means that the characters display in italics. **False** means that the characters display normally.
- *UserDocumentObject*.**FontName**—a **String** specifying the name of the font that should be used to display the characters in this control.
- *UserDocumentObject*.**FontSize**—a **Single** specifying the point size that should be used to display the characters in the control.
- *UserDocumentObject*.**FontStrikethru**—a **Boolean** when **True** means that the characters display with a line through the center. **False** means that the characters display normally.
- *UserDocumentObject*.**FontTransparent**—a **Boolean** when **True** means that the graphics and text behind the characters will be shown around the spaces of the character. **False** means that the graphics and text behind the character will be masked.
- *UserDocumentObject*.**FontUnderline**—a **Boolean** when **True** means that the characters display with a line beneath them. **False** means that the characters display normally.
- *UserDocumentObject*.**ForeColor**—a **Long** containing the suggested value for the foreground color of the user document. The **BackColor** and **ForeColor** must both be solid to display text. If you choose a color that is dithered, it will be changed to the nearest solid color.
- *UserDocumentObject*.**hDC**—a **Long** containing a handle to the device context of the user document.
- *UserDocumentObject*.**Height**—a **Single** containing the height of the control.
- *UserDocumentObject*.**HScrollSmallChange**—a **Single** containing the height of the control.
- *UserDocumentObject*.**hWnd**—a **Long** containing a Windows handle to the control.

> **Tip**
>
> The **hWnd** property is most useful when making calls to Windows API functions. Since this value can change during execution, do not save the value into a variable for later use.

- *UserDocumentObject*.**Hyperlink**—a reference to a **Hyperlink** object that can request a hyperlink-aware container (such as Microsoft Internet Explorer) to go to the specified URL.
- *UserDocumentObject*.**Image**—a handle to a persistent graphic that is returned by the Windows environment. Available only at run time.
- *UserDocumentObject*.**KeyPreview**—a **Boolean** when **True** means that the user document will receive keyboard events (**KeyDown**, **KeyUp**, and **KeyPress**) before any controls. **False** means that the control will receive the keyboard events and the user document will not.

> **Tip**
>
> This function is useful to provide global keystroke handling at the user document level for such keys as function keys and other control keys.

- *UserDocumentObject*.**MinHeight**—a **Single** containing the minimum height of the user document.
- *UserDocumentObject*.**MinWidth**—a **Single** containing the minimum width of the user document.
- *UserDocumentObject*.**MouseIcon**—a picture object (a bitmap, icon, or metafile) that will be used as a cursor when the **MousePointer** property is set to 99. Note that Visual Basic does not support color cursors from a .CUR file. A color icon from an .ICO file should be used instead.
- *UserDocumentObject*.**MousePointer**—an **Integer** value (see Table U-59) containing the value of the cursor that should be displayed when the cursor is moved over this control. Use *vbCustom* to display the custom icon stored in the **MouseIcon** property.

Cursor Name	Value	Description
vbDefault	0	Shape determined by the object (default value).
vbArrow	1	Arrow.
vbCrosshair	2	Crosshair.
vbIbeam	3	I beam.
vbIconPointer	4	Square inside a square.
vbSizePointer	5	Four-sided arrow (north, south, east, west).
vbSizeNESW	6	Two-sided arrow (northeast, southwest).
vbSizeNS	7	Two-sided arrow (north, south).
vbSizeNWSE	8	Two-sided arrow (northwest, southeast).
vbSizeWE	9	Two-sided arrow (west, east).
vbUpArrow	10	Single-sided arrow pointing north.
vbHourglass	11	Hourglass.
vbNoDrop	12	No Drop.
vbArrowHourglass	13	An arrow and an Hourglass.

Cursor Name	Value	Description
vbArrowQuestion	14	An arrow and a question mark.
vbSizeAll	15	Size all.
vbCustom	99	Custom icon from the **MouseIcon** property of this control.

Table U-59: Cursor values.

- *UserDocumentObject*.**Name**—a **String** containing the name of the control that will be used to reference the control in a Visual Basic program. This property is read-only at run time.
- *UserDocumentObject*.**OLEDropMode**—an **Integer** value (see Table U-60) that describes how the control will respond to OLE drop operations.

OLEDropMode Name	Value	Description
vbOLEDropNone	0	The form does not accept OLE drops. The cursor is changed to the No Drop cursor (default value).
vbOLEDropManual	1	The form responds to OLE drops under the program's control (manual).
vbOLEDropAutomatic	2	The form automatically accepts OLE drops if it recognizes the format of the data object.

Table U-60: OLEDropMode values.

- *UserDocumentObject*.**Palette**—a **Picture** object containing a suggested palette for the control. This property is read-only at run time.
- *UserDocumentObject*.**PaletteMode**—an **Integer** value (see Table U-61) that describes the palette that should be used with the user document.

PaletteMode Name	Value	Description
vbPaletteModeHalfTone	0	The user document uses the half tone palette (default).
vbPaletteModeUseZOrder	1	The user document uses the palette from the control nearest the front of the **ZOrder** with a palette.
vbModeCustom	2	The user document uses the palette specified in the **Palette** property.

Table U-61: PaletteMode values.

- *UserDocumentObject*.**Parent**—an object reference to the container of the user document. In Visual Basic, this will usually be a **Form** object; however, other environments will return different objects. Excel will return a workbook. Word will return a document, and Internet Explorer will return an object whose **Script** property returns the **IOmWindow** object.
- *UserDocumentObject*.**Picture**—a picture object (a bitmap, icon, metafile, GIF, or JPEG) that will be displayed on the control. You can also use the **LoadPicture** function at run time to load a bitmap, icon, or metafile. Note that **Style** must be set to *vbButtonGraphical* for the image to be shown.
- *UserDocumentObject*.**RightToLeft**—a **Boolean** value when **True** means that the text is displayed from right to left. When **False** means that the text is displayed from left to right. A bi-directional version of Windows is required to set this property to true.

- *UserDocumentObject*.**ScaleHeight**—an **Integer** value that sets or returns the height of the object in the units specified by **ScaleMode**.
- *UserDocumentObject*.**ScaleLeft**—an **Integer** value that sets or returns the value of the X-coordinate of the left edge of the user document.
- *UserDocumentObject*.**ScaleMode**—an **Integer** value (see Table U-62) that describes the unit of measurement used for the user document.

> **Tip**
>
> When dealing with graphic images such as BMP or GIF files, it is often useful to set **ScaleMode** to vbPixels to help set the proper relationships.

ScaleMode Name	Value	Description
vbUser	0	Measurements are custom defined, based on the values in ScaleHeight, ScaleLeft, ScaleTop, or ScaleWidth properties.
vbTwips	1	Measurements are in twips (1440 twips per inch).
vbPoints	2	Measurements are in points (72 per inch).
vbPixels	3	Measurements are in pixels (smallest unit of measure for a monitor or printer).
vbCharacters	4	Measurements are in characters (horizontal = 120 twips per character, vertical = 240 twips per character).
vbInches	5	Measurements are in inches.
vbMillimeters	6	Measurements are in millimeters.
vbCentimeters	7	Measurements are in centimeters.

Table U-62: ScaleMode values.

- *UserDocumentObject*.**ScaleTop**—an **Integer** value that sets or returns the value of the Y-coordinate of the top edge of the user document.
- *UserDocumentObject*.**ScaleWidth**—an **Integer** value that sets or returns the width of the object in the units specified by **ScaleMode**.
- *UserDocumentObject*.**ScrollBars**—an **Integer** describing which scroll bars are displayed (see Table U-63).

ScrollBars Name	Value	Description
vbSBNone	0	No scroll bars are displayed (default).
vbHorizontal	1	A horizontal scroll bar is displayed.
vbVertical	2	A vertical scroll bar is displayed.
vbBoth	3	Both scroll bars are displayed.

Table U-63: ScrollBars values.

- *UserDocumentObject*.**Tag**—a **String** that can hold programmer-specific information. This property is not used by Visual Basic.

- *UserDocumentObject*.**ViewportHeight**—a **Single** containing the current value of the viewport's height.
- *UserDocumentObject*.**ViewportLeft**—a **Single** containing the current value of the viewport's left position.
- *UserDocumentObject*.**ViewportTop**—a **Single** containing the current value of the viewport's top position.
- *UserDocumentObject*.**ViewportWidth**—a **Single** containing the current value of the viewport's width.
- *UserDocumentObject*.**Width**—a **Single** containing the width of the user document.

Methods

UserDocumentObject.AsyncRead *target, type,* [*propertyname*]

Usage This method begins the process to read data from a file or URL. When the process is complete, the **AsyncReadComplete** event will be triggered.

Arguments
- *target*—a **String** containing a URL or the name of a file where the data will be read.
- *type*—an **Integer** containing the type of data to be read (see Table U-64).

type Name	Description
vbAsyncTypeFile	The data is in a file created by Visual Basic.
vbAsyncTypeByteArray	The data is in a Byte Array.
vbAsyncTypePicture	The data is in a Picture object.

Table U-64: *type values.*

- *propertyname*—a **String** containing a name that will be associated with the read request.

Tip

This value is useful when determining which asynchronous read process completed the **AsyncReadComplete** *event or is to be canceled with the* **CancelAsyncRead** *method.*

UserDocumentObject.CancelAsyncRead [*propertyname*]

Usage This method cancels an asynchronous read request.

Arguments
- *propertyname*—a **String** containing a name that is associated with the asynchronous read request. If omitted, the last asynchronous read request will be canceled.

UserDocumentObject.Circle [Step] (x, y), radius [, color [, start [, stop [, aspect]]]]

Usage This method draws a circle, an ellipse, or a curved line on the user document. All coordinate information used is relative to the **ScaleMode**, **ScaleHeight**, **ScaleLeft**, **ScaleTop**, and **ScaleWidth**.

Arguments
- **Step**—a keyword specifying that the coordinates are relative to the user document's **CurrentX** and **CurrentY** properties.
- *x*—a **Single** specifying the X-coordinate of the center of the circle.
- *y*—a **Single** specifying the Y-coordinate of the center of the circle.
- *radius*—a **Single** specifying the radius of the circle.
- *color*—a **Long** containing the color of the line to be drawn. If omitted, it will default to the value in the **ForeColor** property.
- *start*—a **Single** specifying the starting angle for the circle in radians. If omitted, it will default to zero.
- *stop*—a **Single** specifying the ending angle for the circle in radians. It omitted, it will default to 2 times pi (approximately 6.28).
- *aspect*—a **Single** specifying the height-to-width ratio of the circle. The default is 1.0, which will yield a perfect circle.

Tip
To draw a half a circle, assign start *a value of 0 and* stop *a value of pi (approximately 3.14), and choose values for the other parameters. To draw a vertical ellipse, assign a value greater than 1.0 to* aspect. *A horizontal ellipse would have an aspect ratio of less than 1.0.*

UserDocumentObject.Cls

Usage This method clears all of the graphics and text from a user document.

UserDocumentObject.Line [Step] (x1, y1), [Step] (x2, y2) [, B|BF]

Usage This method draws lines or boxes on the user document. All coordinate information used is relative to the **ScaleMode**, **ScaleHeight**, **ScaleLeft**, **ScaleTop**, and **ScaleWidth**.

Arguments
- **Step**—a keyword specifying that the *x1* and *y1* coordinates are relative to the user document's **CurrentX** and **CurrentY** properties.
- *x1*—a **Single** specifying the starting X-coordinate of the center of the line or box.
- *y1*—a **Single** specifying the starting Y-coordinate of the center of the line or box.
- **Step**—a keyword that specifies that the *x2* and *y2* coordinates are relative to the user document's **CurrentX** and **CurrentY** properties.

- *x2*—a **Single** specifying the stopping X-coordinate of the center of the line or box.
- *y2*—a **Single** specifying the stopping Y-coordinate of the center of the line or box.
- *color*—a **Long** containing the color of the line to be drawn. If omitted, it will default to the value in the **ForeColor** property.
- **B**—draw a box with (*x1*, *y1*) and (*x2*, *y2*) specifying the opposite corners of the box. If omitted, a line will be drawn on the user document.
- **BF**—draw a box with (*x1*, *y1*) and (*x2*, *y2*) specifying the opposite corners of the box, and fill the interior with the color specified by **FillColor** and **FillStyle**. If omitted, a line will be drawn on the user document.

UserDocumentObject.OLEDrag

Usage   This method begins an **OLE drag-and-drop** operation. Invoking this method triggers the **OLEStartDrag** event.

UserDocumentObject.PaintPicture picture, x1, y1, [width1], [height1], [x2], [y2], [width2], [height2], [rasterop]

Usage   This method displays an image (.BMP, .DIB, .EMF, .ICO, or .WMF) on the user document. All coordinate information used is relative to the **ScaleMode**, **ScaleHeight**, **ScaleLeft**, **ScaleTop**, and **ScaleWidth**.

Arguments
- *picture*—the image to be displayed on the user document. It can come from the **Picture** property of a picture box or another user document.
- *x1*—a **Single** specifying the starting X-coordinate of the picture.
- *y1*—a **Single** specifying the starting Y-coordinate of the picture.
- *width1*—a **Single** specifying the width of the image. If omitted, the width will default to the width of the image. If greater or less than the width of the image, the image will be stretched or shrunk to fit.
- *height1*—a **Single** specifying the height of the image. If omitted, the height will default to the height of the image. If greater or less than the height of the image, the image will be stretched or shrunk to fit.
- *x2*—a **Single** specifying the starting X-coordinate of a clipping region within the picture. If omitted, zero will be used.
- *y2*—a **Single** specifying the starting Y-coordinate of a clipping region within the picture. If omitted, zero will be used.
- *width2*—a **Single** specifying the width of the clipping region of the image. If omitted, the width will default to the width of the image. If greater or less than the width of the image, the image will be stretched or shrunk to fit.
- *height2*—a **Single** specifying the height of the clipping region of the image. If omitted, the height will default to the height of the image. If greater or less than the height of the image, the image will be stretched or shrunk to fit.

1104 • The Visual Basic 5 Programmer's Reference

- *rasterop*—a **Long** containing a raster op code from Table U-65 below that will perform a bit-wise operation on the image as it is displayed. The default displays the image as is.

RasterOp Name	Value	Description
vbDstInvert	&H005A0049	Inverts the destination image.
vbMergeCopy	&H00C000CA	Combines the source and the pattern.
vbMergePaint	&H00BB0226	Combines inverted source image with destination image using OR.
vbNotSrcCopy	&H00330008	Copies inverted source image to the destination.
vbNotSrcErase	&H001100A6	Inverts the result of combining the source and destination images using OR.
vbPatCopy	&H00F00021	Copies the source pattern to the destination bitmap.
vbPatInvert	&H005A0049	Combines the inverted source pattern with the destination image using XOR.
vbPatPaint	&H00FB0A09	Combines the destination image with the source pattern.
vbSrcAnd	&H008800C6	Combines the destination and source images using AND.
vbSrcCopy	&H00CC0020	Copies the source image to the destination bitmap.
vbSrcErase	&H00440328	Combines the inverted destination image with the source image by using AND.
vbSrcInvert	&H00660046	Combines the source and destination images using XOR.
vbSrcPaint	&H00EE0086	Combines the source and destination images using OR.

Table U-65: RasterOp values.

color = UserDocumentObject.Point (x, y)

Usage   This method returns a **Long** containing the color at the point at location *x, y*. If the location is outside the user document, then -1 will be returned. All coordinate information used is relative to the **ScaleMode, ScaleHeight, ScaleLeft, ScaleTop,** and **ScaleWidth**.

Arguments
- *color*—a **Long** containing the color at location *x, y*.
- *x*—a **Single** specifying the X-coordinate of the point.
- *y*—a **Single** specifying the Y-coordinate of the point.

UserDocumentObject.PopupMenu menu, flags, x, y, menuitem

Usage   This method displays a pop-up menu on the screen.

Tip

Set **Visible** to **False** *for menu items to be displayed as pop-up menus to prevent them from being displayed in the menu bar.*

UserDocument • 1105

Arguments
- *menu*—the name of a **Menu** object to be displayed. It must include at least one submenu item.
- *flags*—zero or more items from Table U-66 below. If omitted, zero will be used. Multiple values can be selected by adding them together.

Menu Flags Name	Value	Description
vbPopupMenuLeftButton	0	The items on the menu can be selected by only the left mouse button.
vbPopupMenuLeftAlign	0	The left edge of the menu is located at x.
vbPopupMenuRightButton	2	The items on the menu can be selected by either mouse button.
vbPopupMenuCenterAlign	4	The center of the menu is located at x.
vbPopupMenuRightAlign	8	The right edge of the menu is located at x.

Table U-66: Menu Flags values.

- *x*—a **Single** specifying the X-coordinate of the menu. If omitted, it will default to the current X-coordinate of the mouse.
- *y*—a **Single** specifying the Y-coordinate of the menu. If omitted, it will default to the current Y-coordinate of the mouse.
- *menuitem*—the name of the submenu item that will be displayed in bold text. If omitted, no items will be displayed in bold.

UserDocumentObject.PrintForm

Usage This method sends a snapshot of all the objects on the user document to the default system printer.

Tip

*Set **AutoRedraw** to **True** to include graphics and text drawn directly on the user document.*

UserDocumentObject.PropertyChanged propertyname

Usage This method notifies the control's container when a property has been changed. This allows the container to synchronize its property window with the new value.

Arguments *propertyname*—a **String** containing the name of a property that has changed.

UserDocumentObject.PSet [Step] (x, y), color

Usage This method sets the point at *x, y* to the color specified in *color*. All coordinate information used is relative to the **ScaleMode**, **ScaleHeight**, **ScaleLeft**, **ScaleTop**, and **ScaleWidth**.

Arguments
- **Step**—keyword specifying that the X- and Y- coordinates are relative to the user document's **CurrentX** and **CurrentY** properties.
- *x*—a **Single** specifying the X-coordinate of the point.
- *y*—a **Single** specifying the Y-coordinate of the point.
- *color*—a **Long** containing the color to be displayed at location *x*, *y*. If omitted, this value will default to the value of **ForeColor**.

UserDocumentObject.Refresh

Usage   This method redraws the contents of the user document.

UserDocumentObject.Scale [(x1, y1)—(x2, y2)]

Usage   This method defines the coordinate system used on the user document and sets the appropriate values in **ScaleMode, ScaleHeight, ScaleLeft, ScaleTop,** and **ScaleWidth**. If the **Scale** method is used without any arguments, the coordinate is reset to default.

Arguments
- *x1*—a **Single** specifying the X-coordinate of the left edge of the user document.
- *y1*—a **Single** specifying the Y-coordinate of the top edge of the user document.
- *x2*—a **Single** specifying the X-coordinate of the right edge of the user document.
- *y2*—a **Single** specifying the Y-coordinate of the bottom edge of the user document.

result = UserDocumentObject.ScaleX (width, fromscale, toscale)

Usage   This method computes a new value for *width* in a different scale.

Arguments
- *result*—a **Single** containing a new value for *width*.
- *fromscale*—an **Integer** specifying a **ScaleMode** value for the current *width*.
- *toscale*—an **Integer** value (see Table U-67) specifying the **ScaleMode** value for the new *width*.

ScaleMode Name	Value	Description
vbUser	0	Measurements are custom defined, based on the values in ScaleHeight, ScaleLeft, ScaleTop, or ScaleWidth properties.
vbTwips	1	Measurements are in twips (1440 twips per inch).
vbPoints	2	Measurements are in points (72 per inch).
vbPixels	3	Measurements are in pixels (smallest unit of measure for a monitor or printer).
vbCharacters	4	Measurements are in characters (horizontal = 120 twips per character, vertical = 240 twips per character).
vbInches	5	Measurements are in inches.
vbMillimeters	6	Measurements are in millimeters.
vbCentimeters	7	Measurements are in centimeters.
vbHimetric	8	Measurements are in himetrics.

Table U-67: ScaleMode values.

result = UserDocumentObject.ScaleY (height, fromscale, toscale)

Usage — This method computes a new value for *height* in a different scale.

Arguments
- *result*—a **Single** containing a new value for *height*.
- *fromscale*—an **Integer** specifying a **ScaleMode** value for the current *height*.
- *toscale*—an **Integer** value (see Table U-68) specifying the **ScaleMode** value for the new *height*.

ScaleMode Name	Value	Description
vbUser	0	Measurements are custom defined, based on the values in ScaleHeight, ScaleLeft, ScaleTop, or ScaleWidth properties.
vbTwips	1	Measurements are in twips (1440 twips per inch).
vbPoints	2	Measurements are in points (72 per inch).
vbPixels	3	Measurements are in pixels (smallest unit of measure for a monitor or printer).
vbCharacters	4	Measurements are in characters (horizontal = 120 twips per character, vertical = 240 twips per character).
vbInches	5	Measurements are in inches.
vbMillimeters	6	Measurements are in millimeters.
vbCentimeters	7	Measurements are in centimeters.
vbHimetric	8	Measurements are in himetrics.

Table U-68: ScaleMode values.

UserDocumentObject.SetFocus

Usage — This method transfers the focus from the user document or control that currently has the focus to this user document. To receive the focus, this user document must be enabled and visible.

UserDocumentObject.SetViewport *left, top*

Usage — This method sets the size of the viewport.

Arguments
- *left*—a **Single** containing the left coordinate of the viewport.
- *top*—a **Single** containing the top coordinate of the viewport.

height = UserDocumentObject.TextHeight (string)

Usage — This method computes the height of the string in the units specified by **ScaleMode**. The height is computed using the font information specified in the **Font** object. It will also include space at the top and the bottom of the characters, so that multiple lines of text can be placed next to each other. If *string* contains embedded carriage return linefeed pairs, then the total height of the block of text will be returned.

Arguments
- *height*—a **Single** containing the height of *string*.
- *string*—a **String** containing characters to be printed on the user document.

width = UserDocumentObject.TextWidth (*string*)

Usage This method will compute the width of the string in the units specified by **ScaleMode**. The width is computed using the font information specified in the **Font** object. If *string* contains embedded carriage return linefeed pairs, then the length of the longest line will be returned.

Arguments
- *width*—a **Single** containing the width of *string*.
- *string*—a **String** containing characters to be printed on the user document.

Events

Private Sub *UserDocumentObject*_AsyncReadComplete (*propertyvalue* As AsyncProperty)

Usage This event occurs when an asynchronous read request completes.

Arguments
- *propertyvalue*—an **AsyncProperty** object containing information about the read request.

Private Sub *UserDocumentObject*_Click( )

Usage This event occurs when the user clicks a mouse button while the cursor is positioned over the user document.

> **Tip**
>
> *If you need to identify which mouse button was pressed, use the **MouseUp** and **MouseDown** events.*

Private Sub *UserDocumentObject*_DblClick( )

Usage This event occurs when the user double-clicks a mouse button while the cursor is positioned over the user document.

> **Tip**
>
> *If there is code in the **Click** event, then the **DblClick** event will never occur.*

Private Sub *UserDocumentObject*_DragDrop (*source* As Control, *x* As Single, *y* As Single)

Usage This event occurs when a drag-and-drop operation is completed by using the Drag method with a *DragAction* value of *vbEndDrag* (2).

> **Tip**
>
> *When using drag-and-drop operations, use the **DragOver** event to determine what the cursor should look like while the cursor moves over the control.*

Arguments • *source*—a control object that is the control that is being dragged.

> **Tip**
>
> *You can access a property or method from the source control by using* **source**.*property or* **source**.*method. You can determine the type of object or control by using the* **TypeOf** *operator.*

• *x*—a **Single** containing the horizontal location of the mouse pointer.
• *y*—a **Single** containing the vertical location of the mouse pointer.

Private Sub *UserDocumentObject*_DragOver (*source* As Control, *x* As Single, *y* As Single, *state* As Integer)

Usage This event occurs while a drag operation is in progress and the cursor is moved over the control.

> **Tip**
>
> *When using drag-and-drop operations, use the* **DragOver** *event to determine what the cursor should look like while the cursor moves over the control. When* **state** *is 0, you can change the cursor to a No Drop (vbNoDrop) cursor or highlight the field that the cursor is near. When* **state** *is 1, you can undo the changes you made when the* **state** *was 0.*

Arguments • *source*—a control object that is the control that is being dragged.

> **Tip**
>
> *You can access a property or method from the source control by using* **source**.*property or* **source**.*method. You can determine the type of object or control by using the* **TypeOf** *operator.*

• *x*—a **Single** containing the horizontal location of the mouse pointer.
• *y*—a **Single** containing the vertical location of the mouse pointer.
• *state*—an **Integer** value (see Table U-69) that indicates the state of the object being dragged.

state Name	Value	Description
vbEnter	0	The dragged object is entering range of the control.
vbLeave	1	The dragged object is leaving range of the control.
vbOver	2	The dragged object has moved from one position over the control to another.

Table U-69: State values.

Private Sub *UserDocumentObject*_EnterFocus ( )

Usage This event occurs when the user document or a constituent control is about to receive control. This event occurs before any **GotFocus** events occur. After this event occurs, only the **GotFocus** event associated with the constituent control or the user document is triggered.

Private Sub *UserDocumentObject*_ExitFocus ( )

Usage This event occurs when the user document or a constituent control has lost focus. This event occurs after any **LostFocus** events occur.

Private Sub *UserDocumentObject*_GotFocus ( )

Usage This event occurs when the user document is given focus, and the mouse is not over any of the constituent controls.

Tip

*Do not raise the **GotFocus** extender event from within this event.*

Private Sub *UserDocumentObject*_Hide ( )

Usage This event occurs when the user document's **Visible** property becomes **False**.

Private Sub *UserDocumentObject*_Initialize ( )

Usage This event occurs when the user document is first created. This event will occur before the **Load** event.

Tip

*Since this event is triggered only when the user document is created (and the **Load** event is triggered when the user document is created and when it is loaded), it makes sense to put your initialization code in the **Load** event, unless you have specific actions that need to be done only when the user document is created.*

Private Sub *UserDocumentObject*_InitProperties ( )

Usage This event occurs when a new instance of the user document is created.

Private Sub *UserDocumentObject*_KeyDown (*keycode* As Integer, *shift* As Single)

Usage This event occurs when a key is pressed. If the **KeyPreview** property is **True**, this event will occur before the **KeyPress** event for control with the focus. Otherwise, the user document will only see this event if it contains no visible and enabled controls.

UserDocument

Arguments
- *keycode*—an **Integer** containing information about which key was pressed.
- *shift*—an **Integer** value (see Table U-70) containing information about the Shift and Alt keys that were pressed when the mouse button was pressed. These values can be added together if more than one key was down. For instance, a value of 5 means that the Shift and Alt keys were both down when the mouse button was pressed.

shift Name	Value	Description
vbShiftMask	1	The Shift key was pressed.
vbCtrlMask	2	The Ctrl key was pressed.
vbAltMask	4	The Alt key was pressed.

Table U-70: Shift values.

Private Sub *UserDocumentObject*_KeyPress (*keychar* As Integer)

Usage This event occurs when a key is pressed. If the **KeyPreview** property is **True**, this event will occur before the **KeyPress** event for control with the focus. Otherwise, the user document will only see this event if it contains no visible and enabled controls.

Arguments
- *keychar*—an **Integer** containing the ASCII character that was pressed. Changing the value of *keychar* to zero will cancel the keystroke.

Private Sub *UserDocumentObject*_KeyUp (*keycode* As Integer, *shift* As Single)

Usage This event occurs when a key is pressed. If the **KeyPreview** property is **True**, this event will occur before the **KeyPress** event for control with the focus. Otherwise, the user document will only see this event if it contains no visible and enabled controls.

Arguments
- *keycode*—an **Integer** containing information about which key was released.
- *shift*—an **Integer** value (see Table U-71) containing information about the Shift and Alt keys that were pressed when the mouse button was pressed. These values can be added together if more than one key was down. For instance, a value of 5 means that the Shift and Alt keys were both down when the mouse button was pressed.

shift Name	Value	Description
vbShiftMask	1	The Shift key was pressed.
vbCtrlMask	2	The Ctrl key was pressed.
vbAltMask	4	The Alt key was pressed.

Table U-71: Shift values.

Private Sub UserDocumentObject_LostFocus ( )

Usage This event occurs when the user document loses focus.

Private Sub UserDocumentObject _MouseDown (button As Integer, shift As Single, x As Single, y As Single)

Usage This event occurs when a mouse button is pressed while the cursor is over any unoccupied part of the user document.

Arguments *button*—an **Integer** value (see Table U-72) containing information about the mouse buttons that were pressed. Only one button will be indicated when this event occurs.

button Name	Value	Description
vbLeftButton	1	The left button was pressed.
vbRightButton	2	The right button was pressed.
vbMiddleButton	4	The middle button was pressed.

Table U-72: Button values.

shift—an **Integer** value (see Table U-73) containing information about the Shift and Alt keys that were pressed when the mouse button was pressed. These values can be added together if more than one key was down. For instance, a value of 5 means that the Shift and Alt keys were both down when the mouse button was pressed.

shift Name	Value	Description
vbShiftMask	1	The Shift key was pressed.
vbCtrlMask	2	The Ctrl key was pressed.
vbAltMask	4	The Alt key was pressed.

Table U-73: Shift values.

x—a **Single** containing the horizontal location of the mouse pointer.

y—a **Single** containing the vertical location of the mouse pointer.

Private Sub UserDocumentObject_MouseMove (button As Integer, shift As Single, x As Single, y As Single)

Usage This event occurs while the cursor is moved over any unoccupied part of the user document.

Arguments
- *button*—an **Integer** value (see Table U-74) containing information about the mouse buttons that were pressed. These values can be added together if more than one button was pressed. For instance, a value of 3 means that both the left and right buttons were pressed. A value of 0 means that no buttons were pressed.

button Name	Value	Description
vbLeftButton	1	The left button was pressed.
vbRightButton	2	The right button was pressed.
vbMiddleButton	4	The middle button was pressed.

Table U-74: Button values.

- *shift*—an **Integer** value (see Table U-75) containing information about the Shift and Alt keys that were pressed when the mouse button was pressed. These values can be added together if more than one key was down. For instance, a value of 5 means that the Shift and Alt keys were both down when the mouse button was pressed. A value of 0 means that none of these keys were pressed.

shift Name	Value	Description
vbShiftMask	1	The Shift key was pressed.
vbCtrlMask	2	The Ctrl key was pressed.
vbAltMask	4	The Alt key was pressed.

Table U-75: Shift values.

- *x*—a **Single** containing the horizontal location of the mouse pointer.
- *y*—a **Single** containing the vertical location of the mouse pointer.

Private Sub *UserDocumentObject*_MouseUp (*button* As Integer, *shift* As Single, *x* As Single, *y* As Single)

Usage
This event occurs when a mouse button is released while the cursor is over any unoccupied part of the user document.

Arguments
- *button*—an **Integer** value (see Table U-76) containing information about the mouse buttons that were released. Only one of these values will be present.

button Name	Value	Description
vbLeftButton	1	The left button was released.
vbRightButton	2	The right button was released.
vbMiddleButton	4	The middle button was released.

Table U-76: Button values.

- *shift*—an **Integer** value (see Table U-77) containing information about the Shift and Alt keys that were pressed when the mouse button was released. These values can be added together if more than one key was down. For instance, a value of 5 means that the Shift and Alt keys were both down when the mouse button was released. A value of 0 means that none of these keys were pressed.

shift Name	Value	Description
vbShiftMask	1	The Shift key was pressed.
vbCtrlMask	2	The Ctrl key was pressed.
vbAltMask	4	The Alt key was pressed.

Table U-77: Shift values.

- *x*—a **Single** containing the horizontal location of the mouse pointer.
- *y*—a **Single** containing the vertical location of the mouse pointer.

Private Sub *UserDocumentObject*_OLECompleteDrag (*effect* As Long)

Usage — This event tells the source control the results of an OLE drag-and-drop operation. This is the final event to occur in the series of actions that make up an OLE drag-and-drop operation.

Arguments — *effect*—a **Long** (see Table U-78) that returns the status of the OLE drag-and-drop operation.

effect Name	Value	Description
vbDropEffectNone	0	The operation was canceled or the target control can't accept the drop operation.
vbDropEffectCopy	1	The operation copied data from the source control to the target control. The original data is unchanged.
vbDropEffectMove	2	The operation results in a link from the original data to the target control.

Table U-78: Effect values.

Private Sub *UserDocumentObject*_OLEDragDrop (*data* As DataObject, *effect* As Long, *button* As Integer, *shift* As Single, *x* As Single, *y* As Single)

Usage — This event tells the source control the results of an OLE drag-and-drop operation. This is the final event to occur in the series of actions that make up an OLE drag-and-drop operation.

UserDocument • 1115

Arguments
- *data*—a **DataObject** containing the formats that the source control will provide. If the data is not contained in the **DataObject**, then it can be retrieved with the **GetData** method.
- *effect*—a **Long** (see Table U-79) that returns the status of the OLE drag-and-drop operation.

effect Name	Value	Description
vbDropEffectNone	0	The operation was canceled or the target control can't accept the drop operation.
vbDropEffectCopy	1	The operation copied data from the source control to the target control. The original data is unchanged.
vbDropEffectMove	2	The operation results in a link from the original data to the target control.

Table U-79: Effect values.

- *button*—an **Integer** value (see Table U-80) containing information about the mouse buttons that were pressed. These values can be added together if more than one button was pressed. For instance, a value of 3 means that both the left and right buttons were pressed. A value of 0 means that no buttons were pressed.

button Name	Value	Description
vbLeftButton	1	The left button was pressed.
vbRightButton	2	The right button was pressed.
vbMiddleButton	4	The middle button was pressed.

Table U-80: Button values.

- *shift*—an **Integer** value (see Table U-81) containing information about the Shift and Alt keys that were pressed when the mouse button was released. These values can be added together if more than one key was down. For instance, a value of 5 means that the Shift and Alt keys were both down when the mouse button was released. A value of 0 means that none of these keys were pressed.

shift Name	Value	Description
vbShiftMask	1	The Shift key was pressed.
vbCtrlMask	2	The Ctrl key was pressed.
vbAltMask	4	The Alt key was pressed.

Table U-81: Shift values.

- *x*—a **Single** containing the horizontal location of the mouse pointer.
- *y*—a **Single** containing the vertical location of the mouse pointer.

Private Sub *UserDocumentObject*_**OLEDragOver** (*data* **As DataObject**, *effect* **As Long**, *button* **As Integer**, *shift* **As Single**, *x* **As Single**, *y* **As Single**, *state* **As Integer**)

Usage   This event happens when an OLE drag-and-drop operation is in progress.

Arguments
- *data*—a **DataObject** containing the formats that the source control will provide. If the data is not contained in the **DataObject**, then it can be retrieved with the **GetData** method.
- *effect*—a **Long** (see Table U-82) that returns the status of the OLE drag-and-drop operation.

effect Name	Value	Description
vbDropEffectNone	0	The operation was canceled or the target control can't accept the drop operation.
vbDropEffectCopy	1	The operation copied data from the source control to the target control. The original data is unchanged.
vbDropEffectMove	2	The operation results in a link from the original data to the target control.

Table U-82: Effect values.

- *button*—an **Integer** value (see Table U-83) containing information about the mouse buttons that were pressed. These values can be added together if more than one button was pressed. For instance, a value of 3 means that both the left and right buttons were pressed. A value of 0 means that no buttons were pressed.

button Name	Value	Description
vbLeftButton	1	The left button was pressed.
vbRightButton	2	The right button was pressed.
vbMiddleButton	4	The middle button was pressed.

Table U-83: Button values.

- *shift*—an **Integer** value (see Table U-84) containing information about the Shift and Alt keys that were pressed when the mouse button was released. These values can be added together if more than one key was down. For instance, a value of 5 means that the Shift and Alt keys were both down when the mouse button was released. A value of 0 means that none of these keys were pressed.

shift Name	Value	Description
vbShiftMask	1	The Shift key was pressed.
vbCtrlMask	2	The Ctrl key was pressed.
vbAltMask	4	The Alt key was pressed.

Table U-84: Shift values.

- *x*—a **Single** containing the horizontal location of the mouse pointer.
- *y*—a **Single** containing the vertical location of the mouse pointer.
- *state*—an **Integer** value (see Table U-85) that indicates the state of the object being dragged.

state Name	Value	Description
vbEnter	0	The dragged object is entering range of the control.
vbLeave	1	The dragged object is leaving range of the control.
vbOver	2	The dragged object has moved from one position over the control to another.

Table U-85: State values.

Private Sub *UserDocumentObject*_OLEGiveFeedback (*effect* As Long)

Usage — This event tells the source control what is happening while the OLE drag-and-drop operation is in progress. This event occurs after the **OLEDragOver** event.

Tip

You may want to use this event to change the cursor to reflect what can happen in the remote object.

Arguments
- *effect*—a **Long** (see Table U-86) that returns the status of the OLE drag-and-drop operation.

effect Name	Value	Description
vbDropEffectNone	0	The operation was canceled or the target control can't accept the drop operation.
vbDropEffectCopy	1	The operation copied data from the source control to the target control. The original data is unchanged.
vbDropEffectMove	2	The operation results in a link from the original data to the target control.
vbDropEffectScroll	&H80000000	The target control is about to scroll or is scrolling. This value may be added to the other *shift* values.

Table U-86: Effect values.

Private Sub *UserDocumentObject*_OLESetData (*data* As DataObject, *DataFormat* As Integer)

Usage — This event happens in response to the target object performing a **GetData** method on *data*. This routine will respond by using the **SetData** method with the desired data using the **DataObject** *data*.

Arguments
- *data*—a **DataObject** containing the data to be returned to the target object.
- *format*—an **Integer** value (see Table U-87) containing the format of the data.

format Name	Value	Description
vbCFText	1	Text (.TXT files)
vbCFBitmap	2	Bitmap (.BMP files)
vbCFMetafile	3	Metafile (.WMF files)
vbCFEDIB	8	Device independent bitmap (DIB)
vbCFPallette	9	Color palette
vbCFEMetafile	14	Enhanced metafile (.EMF files)
vbCFFiles	15	List of files
vbCFRTF	-16639	Rich Text Format (.RTF files)

Table U-87: Format values.

Private Sub *UserDocumentObject*_OLEStartDrag (*data* As DataObject, *AllowedEffects* As Long)

Usage This event starts an OLE drag-and-drop operation.

Arguments
- *data*—a **DataObject** containing the formats that the source object is willing to provide to the target object. It may optionally contain the data to be transferred.
- *AllowedEffects*—a **Long** (see Table U-88) containing the effects that the target object can request from the source object. The *AllowedEffects* can be added together if the source object supports more than one effect. Note that the target object can always use the *vbDropEffectNone* effect.

AllowedEffects Name	Value	Description
vbDropEffectNone	0	The target can't copy the data.
vbDropEffectCopy	1	The target can copy the data and the source will keep the data unchanged.
vbDropEffectMove	2	The target can copy the data and the source will delete the data.

Table U-88: AllowedEffects values.

Private Sub *UserDocumentObject*_Paint ( )

Usage This event occurs when the user document must redraw itself. This can happen because the user document was previously covered and now is not, the size of the user document has changed, or the user document has been moved. A **Paint** event is necessary if you generate graphics or print text directly to the user document and have set the **AutoRedraw** property to **False**.

> **Tip**
>
> *Avoid moving the user document, changing any variables that affect the user document's size or appearance, and using the **Refresh** method. These can cause a cascading event in which the event will trigger the same event over and over again until the system crashes.*

Private Sub *UserDocumentObject*_ReadProperties (*pb* As PropertyBag)

Usage This event is called when an old instance of an object with a saved state is loaded.

Arguments *pb*—a reference to a **PropertyBag** object containing the saved data to be loaded.

Private Sub *UserDocumentObject*_Resize ( )

Usage This event occurs when the user document is first displayed, when the value of **WindowState** changes, or when the user document is resized. After the resize event occurs, the **Paint** event is called (if **AutoResize** is **False**) to redraw the contents of the user document.

Private Sub *UserDocumentObject*_Scroll ( )

Usage This event occurs when the user clicks or moves either the horizontal or vertical scroll bar.

Private Sub *UserDocumentObject*_Show ( )

Usage This event occurs when the user document's **Visible** property is set to **True**.

Private Sub *UserDocumentObject*_Terminate ( )

Usage This event occurs when the last instance of a user document is ready to be removed from memory. It will not be called if for some reason (such as the **End** statement being executed) the program terminates abnormally.

Private Sub *UserDocumentObject*_WriteProperties (*pb* As PropertyBag)

Usage This event is called when an instance of an object needs to be saved. It can be restored when the **ReadProperties** event is triggered.

Arguments *pb*—a reference to a **PropertyBag** object containing the data to be saved. Use the **WriteProperty** method in the **PropertyBag** to save the data.

See Also **Forms** (collection), **MDIForm** (object), **UserControl** (object)

Val

FUNCTION

CCE, LE, PE, EE

Syntax   *Value* = **Val** (*String*)

Usage   The **Val** function converts a **String** value to a number. It will ignore all blanks, tabs, and linefeed characters, while building a collection of digits. The first non-numeric value (like a letter, dollar sign, or even a dash) marks the end of the digits. The resulting collection of digits is then converted to a number.

> **Tip**
>
> *Use the **CDbl**, **CInt**, **CLng**, or **CSng** function to perform this function. These functions are more flexible than the **Val** function.*

Any **String** value that does not contain a valid numeric value will generate a run-time error '13' Type mismatch. Any value that is outside the range of acceptable values will generate a run-time error '6' Overflow.

> **Tip**
>
> *To prevent run-time errors, use the **On Error** statement to prevent the error from stopping the program. Then test the **Err** object to see if an error occurred. Also, using the **IsNumeric** function will help to prevent conversion errors.*

Arguments
- *Value*—a variable that contains the result of converting *value* to a numeric value.
- *String*—a numeric or string value to be converted to a **Double** value.

Examples
```
Private Sub Command1_Click()
On Error Resume Next
Text2.Text = Format(Val (Text1.Text))
If Err.Number > 0 Then
    Text2.Text = Err.Description
End If
End Sub
```

This routine converts the value in Text1.Text to a numeric value and then uses the **Format** function to convert the value into a form that can be shown in a **Text Box**. Note that I checked the **Err** object to insure that the conversion process worked properly.

See Also   **CDbl** (function), **CInt** (function), **CLng** (function), **CSng** (function), **Error** (object), **Format** (function), **IsNumeric** (function), **On Error** (statement)

ValueScale

OBJECT

PE, EE

Usage — The **ValueScale** object is used by the **Axis** object of the **MSChart** control to hold the information scale used to display a value.

Properties
- *ValueScaleObject*.**Auto**—a **Boolean** value when **True** means that the scale is automatically set based on the data. When **False**, the values will be determined by the contents of the **MajorDivision**, **Maximum**, **Minimum**, and **MinorDivision** properties.
- *ValueScaleObject*.**MajorDivision**—an **Integer** value that contains the number of major divisions displayed on the axis.
- *ValueScaleObject*.**Maximum**—a **Double** value that contains the largest data value displayed on the axis.
- *ValueScaleObject*.**Minimum**—a **Double** value that contains the smallest data value displayed on the axis.
- *ValueScaleObject*.**MinorDivision**—an **Integer** value that contains the number of minor divisions displayed on the axis.

See Also — **Axis** (object), **MSChart** (control)

Variant

DATA TYPE

CCE, LE, PE, EE

Usage — The **Variant** data type holds nearly any type of data. It is the default data type for a variable that is not explicitly defined. A variant variable can handle any of the standard data types (**Byte**, **Date**, **Double**, **Integer**, **Long**, **Single**, and **String**), **Objects**, and the special values **Empty**, **Error**, **Nothing,** and **Null**.

Empty means that the variant variable doesn't contain a value. **Error** contains a Visual Basic error value. **Nothing** means that the variable doesn't contain a reference to a valid object. **Null** means that the variable contains no valid data.

See Also — **Byte** (data type), **Date** (data type), **Double** (data type), **Integer** (data type), **Long** (data type), **Object** (data type), **Single** (data type), **String** (data type)

VarType

FUNCTION

CCE, LE, PE, EE

Syntax   type = **VarType** (variable)

Usage   The **VarType** function returns a value that contains the type of the variable specified.

Arguments
- *type*—the type of the Visual Basic identifier (see Table V-1). For instance an **Integer** array would have a value of 8194.
- *variable*—a Visual Basic identifier.

type Name	Value	Description
vbEmpty	0	Uninitialized.
vbNull	1	No valid data.
vbInteger	2	Integer value.
vbLong	3	Long integer value.
vbSingle	4	Single precision floating point number.
vbDouble	5	Double precision floating point number.
vbCurrency	6	Currency value.
vbDate	7	Date value.
vbString	8	String value.
vbObject	9	Object reference.
vbError	10	Error value.
vbBoolean	11	Boolean value.
vbVariant	12	Variant.
vbDataObject	13	Data access object.
vbDecimal	14	Decimal value.
vbByte	17	Byte value.
vbArray	8192	Array of other object. (Always used with one of the above values.)

Table V-1: Type values.

Examples
```
Private Sub Command1_Click()
Dim x(10) As Integer
MsgBox Format(VarType(x))
End Sub
```

This routine displays a message box with the value 8194, indicating that the variable x is both an array (8192) and an **Integer** (2).

See Also   **CDbl** (function), **CInt** (function), **CLng** (function), **CSng** (function), **Error** (object), **Format** (function), **IsNumeric** (function), **On Error** (statement)

View3D

OBJECT

PE, EE

Usage The **View3D** object is used by the **Plot** object of the **MSChart** control to describe physical orientation of a three-dimensional chart. By default both properties use degrees for measurements; however, they will use the settings of the **AngleUnits** property.

Properties
- *View3DObject*.**Elevation**—a **Single** that describes the elevation of the object. The elevation can range from zero to 90 degrees. If not specified, elevation will default to 30 degrees.
- *View3DObject*.**Rotation**—a **Single** that describes the rotation of the object. The rotation can range from zero to 360 degrees.

Methods **View3DObject.Set elevation, rotation**

Usage This method sets the elevation and rotation for a three-dimensional view of a chart.

Arguments
- *elevation*—a **Single** that describes the elevation of the object. The elevation can range from zero to 90 degrees. If not specified, elevation will default to 30 degrees.
- *rotation*—a **Single** that describes the rotation of the object. The rotation can range from zero to 360 degrees.

See Also **MSChart** (control), **Plot** (object)

VScrollBar

CONTROL

CCE, LE, PE, EE

Usage The **VScrollBar** control is an intrinsic control that provides you with a tool to capture analog input from the user. The vertical scroll bar consists of a short, wide box with arrows at each end. In between the arrows is another box that the user can position anywhere inside the box. **VScrollBar** will return a **Value** that represents the relative position of the scroll box inside the scroll bar.

> **Tip**
>
> *If you position the scroll arrows next to each other, you have a spinner where you can increment or decrement a number. This may be useful when you wish to provide an alternate method to entering a number into a text box.*

Properties
- *VScrollBarControl*.**Container**—an object that you can use to set or return the container of the control at run time. You cannot set this property at design time.

- *VScrollBarControl*.**DragIcon**—an object that contains the picture value of an icon. At design time, you can specify an icon file that has a file type of .ICO.

> **Tip**
>
> *This value can be created by copying the value from another control's **DragIcon** value or from a form's icon, or by using the **LoadPicture** function.*

- *VScrollBarControl*.**DragMode**—an **Integer** value (see Table V-2) that specifies how the control will respond to a drag request.

> **Tip**
>
> *Setting **DragMode** to vbAutomatic will automatically begin a drag operation when the user clicks on the control. However, the control will not respond to the usual mouse events (**Click**, **DblClick**).*

DragMode Name	Value	Description
vbManual	0	The Drag method must be used to begin a drag-and-drop operation (default value).
vbAutomatic	1	The source control will automatically begin a drag drop operation when the user clicks on the control.

Table V-2: DragMode values.

- *VScrollBarControl*.**Enabled**—a **Boolean** value when **True** means that the control will respond to events. When **False**, the control will not respond to events.
- *VScrollBarControl*.**Height**—a **Single** that contains the height of the control.
- *VScrollBarControl*.**HelpContextID**—a **Long** that contains a help file context ID number that references an entry in the help file. When the user presses the F1 key while this control is active, the corresponding entry in the help file is automatically displayed. A value of zero means that no context number was specified.

> **Tip**
>
> *A help file must be compiled using the Windows Help Compiler available in the Professional and Enterprise editions of Visual Basic.*

- *VScrollBarControl*.**hWnd**—a **Long** that contains a Windows handle to the control.

> **Tip**
>
> *The **hWnd** property is most useful when making calls to Windows API functions. Since this value can change during execution, do not save the value into a variable for later use.*

- *VScrollBarControl*.**Index**—an **Integer** that uniquely identifies a control in a control array.
- *VScrollBarControl*.**LargeChange**—the **Integer** value that is added or subtracted from the **Value** property each time the user clicks in the area between the scroll box and the scroll arrow.

- *VScrollBarControl.***Left**—a **Single** that contains the distance measured in twips between the left edge of the control and the left edge of the control's container.
- *VScrollBarControl.***Max**—the **Integer** value that returns when the scroll box is at the extreme right position, next to the scroll right arrow. The default value is 32767.
- *VScrollBarControl.***Min**—the **Integer** value that returns when the scroll box is at the extreme left position, next to the scroll left arrow. The default value is 0.
- *VScrollBarControl.***MouseIcon**—a picture object (a bitmap, icon, or metafile) that will be used as a cursor when the **MousePointer** property is set to 99. Note that Visual Basic does not support color cursors from a .CUR file. A color icon from a .ICO file should be used instead.
- *VScrollBarControl.***MousePointer**—an **Integer** value (see Table V-3) that contains the value of the cursor that should be displayed when the cursor is moved over this control. Use *vbCustom* to display the custom icon stored in the **MouseIcon** property.

Cursor Name	Value	Description
vbDefault	0	Shape determined by the object (default value).
vbArrow	1	Arrow.
vbCrosshair	2	Crosshair.
vbIbeam	3	I beam.
vbIconPointer	4	Square inside a square.
vbSizePointer	5	Four-sided arrow (north, south, east, west).
vbSizeNESW	6	Two-sided arrow (northeast, southwest).
vbSizeNS	7	Two-sided arrow (north, south).
vbSizeNWSE	8	Two-sided arrow (northwest, southeast).
vbSizeWE	9	Two-sided arrow (west, east).
vbUpArrow	10	Single-sided arrow pointing north.
vbHourglass	11	Hourglass.
vbNoDrop	12	No drop.
vbArrowHourglass	13	An arrow and an hourglass.
vbArrowQuestion	14	An arrow and a question mark.
vbSizeAll	15	Size all.
vbCustom	99	Custom icon from the **MouseIcon** property of this control.

Table V-3: Cursor values.

- *VScrollBarControl.***Name**—a **String** that contains the name of the control that will be used to reference the control in a Visual Basic program. This property is read only at run time.
- *VScrollBarControl.***Parent**—an object that contains a reference to the **Form, Frame,** or other container that contains the **VScrollBar** control.
- *VScrollBarControl.***RightToLeft**—a **Boolean** value when **True** means that the text is displayed from right to left. When **False,** the text is displayed from left to right. A bi-directional version of Windows is required to set this property to **True.**
- *VScrollBarControl.***SmallChange**—the **Integer** value that is added or subtracted from the **Value** property each time the user clicks on the scroll arrow.
- *VScrollBarControl.***TabIndex**—an Integer that determines the order that a user will tab through the objects on a form.
- *VScrollBarControl.***TabStop**—a **Boolean** value when **True** means that the user can tab to this object. When **False,** this control will be skipped to the next control in the **TabIndex** order.

- *VScrollBarControl.***Tag**—a **String** that can hold programmer-specific information. This property is not used by Visual Basic.
- *VScrollBarControl.***Top**—a **Single** that contains the distance measured in twips between the top edge of the control and the top edge of the control's container.
- *VScrollBarControl.***Value**—an **Integer** that represents the relative position of the scroll box inside the **VScrollBar**. Changing the **Value** property in code will trigger the **Change** event.
- *VScrollBarControl.***Visible**—a **Boolean** value when **True** means that the control is visible. When **False,** the control is not visible.

> **Tip**
>
> *You can hide the control until the program is ready to display it using this property.*

- *VScrollBarControl.***WhatsThisHelpID**—a **Long** that contains a help file context ID number that references an entry in the help file. This provides a What's This PopUp help display in response to the What's This button in the upper right corner of the window.
- *VScrollBarControl.***Width**—a **Single** that contains the width of the control.

Methods

*VScrollBarControl.*Drag [*DragAction*]

Usage This method begins, ends, or cancels a drag operation.

Arguments *DragAction*—an **Integer** that contains a value selected from Table V-4.

DragAction Name	Value	Description
vbCancel	0	Cancels any drag operation in progress.
vbBeginDrag	1	Begins a drag operation (default).
vbEndDrag	2	Ends a drag operation and drops *object.*

Table V-4: DragAction values.

*VScrollBarControl.*Move *Left* [, *Top* [, *Width* [, *Height*]]]

Usage This method changes the position and the size of the **VScrollBar** control. The **ScaleMode** of the **Form** or other container object that holds the animation control determines the units used to specify the coordinates.

Arguments
- *Left*—a **Single** that specifies the new position of the left edge of the control.
- *Top*—a **Single** that specifies the new position of the top edge of the control.
- *Width*—a **Single** that specifies the new width of the control.
- *Height*—a **Single** that specifies the new height of the control.

VScrollBarControl.Refresh

Usage   This method redraws the contents of the control.

VScrollBarControl.SetFocus

Usage   This method transfers the focus from the form or control that currently has the focus to this control. To receive the focus, this control must be enabled and visible.

VScrollBarControl.ShowWhatsThis

Usage   This method displays the ShowWhatsThis help information for this control.

VScrollBarControl.ZOrder [*position*]

Usage   This method specifies the position of the animation control relative to the other objects on the form.

> **Tip**
>
> *Note that there are three layers of objects on a form: the back layer is the drawing space that contains the results of the graphical methods, the middle layer contains graphical objects such as the **VScrollBar** and **Labels**, and the top layer contains nongraphical controls such as the **VScrollBar**. The **ZOrder** method only affects how the objects are arranged within a single layer.*

Arguments   *position*—an **Integer** that specifies the relative position of this object. A value of 0 means that the control is positioned at the head of the list, a value of 1 means that the control will be placed at the end of the list.

Events

Private Sub *VScrollBarControl*_Change([*index* As Integer])

Usage   This event occurs when the text in the text box part of the control is changed.

> **Warning**
>
> *Changing the **Value** property in your program will trigger the **Change** event. While this normally won't cause a problem, changing the **Value** property inside the **Change** event could trigger an infinite recursion that could ultimately crash the program.*

Arguments   *index*—an **Integer** that uniquely identifies a control in a control array. This argument is not present if the control is not part of a control array.

Private Sub *VScrollBarControl*_DragDrop([*index* As Integer ,] *source* As Control, *x* As Single, *y* As Single)

Usage This event occurs when a drag-and-drop operation is completed using the Drag method with a *DragAction* value of *vbEndDrag*.

Tip

When using drag-and-drop operations, use the **DragOver** event to determine what you want the cursor to look like when the cursor moves over the control.

Arguments
- *index*—an **Integer** that uniquely identifies a control in a control array. This argument is not present if the control is not part of a control array.
- *source*—a control object that is the control being dragged.

Tip

You can access a property or method from the source control by using source.*property* or source.*method*. You can determine the type of object or control by using the **TypeOf** operator.

- *x*—a **Single** that contains the horizontal location of the mouse pointer.
- *y*—a **Single** that contains the vertical location of the mouse pointer.

Private Sub *VScrollBarControl*_DragOver([*index* As Integer ,] *source* As Control, *x* As Single, *y* As Single, *state* As Integer)

Usage This event occurs while a drag operation is in progress and the cursor is moved over the control.

Tip

When using drag-and-drop operations, use the **DragOver** event to determine what you want the cursor to look like when the cursor moves over the control. When **state** is 0, you can change the cursor to a no drop (vbNoDrop) cursor or highlight the field that the cursor is near. When the **state** is 1, you can undo the changes you made when the **state** was 0.

Arguments
- *index*—an **Integer** that uniquely identifies a control in a control array. This argument is not present if the control is not part of a control array.
- *source*—a control object that is the control being dragged.

Tip

You can access a property or method from the source control by using source.*property* or source.*method*. You can determine the type of object or control by using the **TypeOf** operator.

- *x*—a **Single** that contains the horizontal location of the mouse pointer.
- *y*—a **Single** that contains the vertical location of the mouse pointer.
- *state*—an **Integer** value (see Table V-5) that indicates the state of the object being dragged.

state Name	Value	Description
vbEnter	0	The dragged object is entering range of the control.
vbLeave	1	The dragged object is leaving range of the control.
vbOver	2	The dragged object has moved from one position over the control to another.

Table V-5: State values.

Private Sub *VScrollBarControl*_GotFocus ([*index* As Integer])

Usage   This event occurs when the control is given focus.

Tip

You can use this routine to display help or other information in a status bar.

Arguments   *index*—an **Integer** that uniquely identifies a control in a control array. This argument is not present if the control is not part of a control array.

Private Sub *VScrollBarControl*_KeyDown ([*index* As Integer ,] *keycode* As Integer, *shift* As Single)

Usage   This event occurs when a key is pressed while the control has the focus.

Arguments
- *index*—an **Integer** that uniquely identifies a control in a control array. This argument is not present if the control is not part of a control array.
- *keycode*—an **Integer** that contains information about which key was pressed.
- *shift*—an **Integer** value (see Table V-6) that contains information about the Shift and Alt keys that were pressed when the mouse button was pressed. These values can be added together if more than one key was down. For instance, a value of 5 means that the Shift and Alt keys were both down when the mouse button was pressed.

shift Name	Value	Description
vbShiftMask	1	The Shift key was pressed.
vbCtrlMask	2	The Ctrl key was pressed.
vbAltMask	4	The Alt key was pressed.

Table V-6: Shift values.

Private Sub *VScrollBarControl*_KeyPress([*index* As Integer ,] *keychar* As Integer)

Usage   This event occurs whenever a key is pressed while the control has the focus.

Arguments
- *index*—an **Integer** that uniquely identifies a control in a control array. This argument is not present if the control is not part of a control array.
- *keychar*—an **Integer** that contains the ASCII character that was pressed.

Private Sub *ComoBoxControl*_KeyUp ([*index* As Integer ,] *keycode* As Integer, *shift* As Single)

Usage   This event occurs when a key is released while the control has the focus.

Arguments
- *index*—an **Integer** that uniquely identifies a control in a control array. This argument is not present if the control is not part of a control array.
- *keycode*—an **Integer** that contains information about which key was released.
- *shift*—an **Integer** value (see Table V-7) that contains information about the Shift and Alt keys that were pressed when the mouse button was pressed. These values can be added together if more than one key was down. For instance, a value of 5 means that the Shift and Alt keys were both down when the mouse button was pressed.

shift Name	Value	Description
vbShiftMask	1	The Shift key was pressed.
vbCtrlMask	2	The Ctrl key was pressed.
vbAltMask	4	The Alt key was pressed.

Table V-7: Shift values.

Private Sub *VScrollBarControl*_LostFocus ([*index* As Integer])

Usage   This event occurs when the control loses focus.

Tip

This routine is useful to performing data verification.

Arguments   *index*—an **Integer** that uniquely identifies a control in a control array. This argument is not present if the control is not part of a control array.

Private Sub *VScrollBarControl*_Scroll ([*index* As Integer])

Usage This event is called each time the scroll bar is repositioned in the drop-down box.

Arguments *index*—an **Integer** that uniquely identifies a control in a control array. This argument is not present if the control is not part of a control array.

Examples
```
Private Sub Form_Load()
VScroll1.Min = 0
VScroll1.Max = 100
VScroll1.Value = 50
VScroll1.LargeChange = 5
VScroll1.SmallChange = 1
End Sub

Private Sub VScroll1_Change()
Text1.Text = Format(VScroll1.Value)
End Sub
```

This program initializes the vertical scroll bar with values for **Min, Max, Value, LargeChange,** and **SmallChange**. Note that setting the **Value** property will trigger the **Change** event. The **Change** event will display the current **Value** in the text1 text box.

See Also **HScrollBar** (control)

VtColor
OBJECT

PE, EE

Usage The **VtColor** object is used by the **MSChart** control to describe an RGB (red, green, blue) color.

Properties
- *VtColorObject*.**Automatic**—a **Boolean** when **True** means that the color is automatically determined by the object. When **False,** the color will be determined by the contents of the **Blue, Green,** and **Red** properties.
  - *VtColorObject*.**Blue**—an **Integer** that describes the amount of blue in the color. It can range from 0 to 255. Any value larger than 255 will set the value to 255.
  - *VtColorObject*.**Green**—an **Integer** that describes the amount of green in the color. It can range from 0 to 255. Any value larger than 255 will set the value to 255.
  - *VtColorObject*.**Red**—an **Integer** that describes the amount of red in the color. It can range from 0 to 255. Any value larger than 255 will set the value to 255.

Methods

VtColorObject.Set red, green, blue

Usage: This method sets the color for a part of a chart.

Arguments:
- *red*—an **Integer** that describes the amount of red in the color. It can range from 0 to 255. Any value larger than 255 will set the value to 255.
- *green*—an **Integer** that describes the amount of green in the color. It can range from 0 to 255. Any value larger than 255 will set the value to 255.
- *blue*—an **Integer** that describes the amount of blue in the color. It can range from 0 to 255. Any value larger than 255 will set the value to 255.

See Also: **MSChart** (control)

VtFont

OBJECT

PE, EE

Usage: The **VtFont** object is used by the **MSChart** control to describe the font used to display text information.

Properties:
- *VtFontObject*.**Effect**— an **Integer** that describes if the displayed text is underlined or has a line through the center (see Table V-8).

Effect Name	Description
vtFontEffectStrikeThough	The text will be displayed with a line through the center.
vbFontEffectUnderline	The text will be displayed with a line underneath.

Table V-8: Effect values.

- *VtFontObject*.**Name**—a **String** that contains the name of the font to be used.
- *VtFontObject*.**Size**—a **Single** that contains the point size of the text.
- *VtFontObject*.**Style**—an **Integer** that describes the font style (see Table V-9).
- *VtFontObject*.**VtColor**—a reference to the **VtColor** object that contains the color of the text.

Style Name	Description
vtFontStyleBold	The text will be displayed in bold.
vtFontStyleOutline	The text will be displayed in italic.
vtFontStyleOutline	The text will be displayed with an outline.

Table V-9: Style values.

See Also: **MSChart** (control)

Wall

OBJECT

PE, EE

Usage
The **Wall** object is used by the **Plot** object of the **MSChart** control to hold information about the y axis on a three-dimensional chart.

Properties
- *WallObject*.**Brush**—an object reference to a **Brush** object containing information about the fill type for the area on the y axis of a three-dimensional chart.
- *WallObject*.**Pen**—an object reference to a **Pen** object describing the lines and colors of the edges shown on the y axis of a three-dimensional chart.
- *WallObject*.**Width**—a **Single** value containing the width of the pen in points.

See Also
MSChart (control)

Weekday

FUNCTION

CCE, LE, PE, EE

Syntax
`value = Weekday ( date [, firstday ] )`

Usage
The **Weekday** function returns an **Integer** value that contains the day of the week. One will be returned if the day of the week falls on the *firstday*, Two will be returned if the day of the week falls on the day after *firstday*. This continues until seven is returned for the day before *firstday*.

Arguments
- *value*—an **Integer** containing the number of the day of week.
- *date*—a **Date**, **String**, or numeric expression corresponding to a date value.
- *firstday*—an **Integer** (see Table W-1) containing the first day of the week. If omitted, will default to *vbSunday*.

firstday Name	Value	Description
vbUseSystem	0	Use the system default.
vbSunday	1	Use Sunday as the first day of the week.
vbMonday	2	Use Monday as the first day of the week.
vbTuesday	3	Use Tuesday as the first day of the week.
vbWednesday	4	Use Wednesday as the first day of the week.
vbThursday	5	Use Thursday as the first day of the week.
vbFriday	6	Use Friday as the first day of the week.
vbSaturday	7	Use Saturday as the first day of the week.

Table W-1: Firstday *values.*

Examples
```
Private Sub Command1_Click()
    If IsDate(Text1.Text) Then
        Text2.Text = WeekDay(CDate(Text1.Text), CInt(Left(Combo1.Text, 1)))
    Else
        Text2.Text = "Illegal date"
    End If
End Sub
```

This routine verifies that the contents of the Text1 text box is a valid date. If the date is valid, the weekday value will be computed based on the date and the first day of week value selected in the Combo1 combo box.

See Also   **CDate** (function), **Date** (data type), **Date** (function), **Day** (function), **Format** (function), **Month** (function), **Year** (function)

Weighting

OBJECT

PE, EE

Usage   The **Weighting** object is used by the **Plot** object of the **MSChart** control to describe the size of a pie in relation to other pies in the same chart.

Properties
- *WeightingObject*.**Basis**—an **Integer** describing the method used to determine the relative pie size (see Table W-2).

Basis Name	Description
vtChPieWeighBasisNone	All pies are the same size.
vtChPieWeightBasisTotal	The values in each pie are summed. The size of each pie is determined by the ratio of its total value to the largest total value.
vtChPieWeightBasisSeries	The size of each pie is determined by its value in the first data column relative to the pie with the largest value in the first data column.

Table W-2: Basis *values*.

- *WeightingObject*.**Style**—an **Integer** describing how the pies will be displayed (see Table W-3).

Style Name	Description
vtChPieWeighStyleArea	The area of the pie changes based on its weighting factor.
vtChPieWeightStyleDiameter	The diameter of the pie changes based on its weighting factor.

Table W-3: Style *values*.

Methods **WeightingObject.Set** *basis, style*

Usage This method sets the basis and style used for the weighting object.

Arguments
- *basis*—an **Integer** describing the method used to determine the relative pie size (see Table W-4).

Basis Name	Description
vtChPieWeighBasisNone	All pies are the same size.
vtChPieWeightBasisTotal	The values in each pie are summed. The size of each pie is determined by the ratio of its total value to the largest total value.
vtChPieWeightBasisSeries	The size of each pie is determined by its value in the first data column relative to the pie with the largest value in the first data column.

Table W-4: Basis values.

- *style*—an **Integer** describing how the pies will be displayed (see Table W-5).

Style Name	Description
vtChPieWeighStyleArea	The area of the pie changes based on its weighting factor.
vtChPieWeightStyleDiameter	The diameter of the pie changes based on its weighting factor.

Table W-5: Style values.

See Also **MSChart** (control)

While

STATEMENT

CCE, LE, PE, EE

Syntax
```
While condition
      [ list of statements ]
Wend
```

Usage The **While** statement executes a list of statements repeatedly until *condition* is **False**.

> **Tip**
>
> Use the **Do** statement for more function and flexibility.

Arguments
- *condition*—an expression resulting in a **True** or **False** value.

Examples
```
Private Sub Command1_Click()
Dim i As Integer
Text1.Text = ""
i = 0
While i < 100
   Text1.Text = Text1.Text & "*"
   i = i + 1
Wend
End Sub
```

This routine uses a **While** loop to put 100 asterisks in the Text1 text box.

See Also **Do** (statement), **For** (statement)

Width

STATEMENT

CCE, LE, PE, EE

Syntax **Width #** *filenum*, *width*

Usage The **Width** statement sets the number of characters in a single line of an output file.

Arguments
- *filenum*—an **Integer** expression containing the file number from the **Open** statement.
- *width*—an **Integer** value containing the maximum number of characters in a line before a new line is started. *Width* must be in the range of 0 to 255, with a value of 0 meaning that any number of characters can be on a single line.

See Also **Open** (statement), **Print** (statement)

Winsock

CONTROL

CCE, LE, PE, EE

Usage The **Winsock** control provides high-level access to the Winsock API. This makes it easier for you to develop Internet programs.

> **Tip**
>
> *Testing Internet programs is always a challenge if you are connected to the Internet via a 28.8k baud modem. However, if your system is configured for dial-up Internet access under Windows 95 or NT, you can run Internet programs locally. All you need is Personal Web Server for Windows 95 or Peer-to-peer Web Server for Windows NT and you can test both FTP and HTTP programs without connecting to the rest of the Internet. Just use the magic address 127.0.0.1 (ex: HTTP://127.0.0.1) to refer to your machine.*

Properties
- *WinsockControl*.**BytesReceived**—a **Long** value containing number of bytes received.
- *WinsockControl*.**Index**—an **Integer** that uniquely identifies a control in a control array.
- *WinsockControl*.**LocalHostName**—a **String** containing the local machine name. This property is read-only and is not available at design time.
- *WinsockControl*.**LocalIP**—a **String** containing the local IP address formatted as ###.###.###.###. This pr operty is read-only and is not available at design time.
- *WinsockControl*.**LocalPort**—a **Long** containing the port number. Specifying port 0 for a client program means that the system will assign a random port number when connecting to another system. Specifying port 0 for a server program means that the system will assign a random port when the **Listen** method is executed.
- *WinsockControl*.**Name**—a **String** containing the name of the control that will be used to reference the control in a Visual Basic program. This property is read-only at run time.
- *WinsockControl*.**Object**—an object containing a reference to the *WinsockControl* object.
- *WinsockControl*.**Parent**—an object containing a reference to the **Form, Frame,** or other container that contains this control.
- *WinsockControl*.**Protocol**—an **Integer** value containing the protocol used (see Table W-6). To change protocols, you must use the **Close** method first.

Protocol Name	Value	Description
sckTCPPotocol	0	Use TCP (default).
sckUDPPotocol	1	Use UDP.

Table W-6: Protocol *values.*

- *WinsockControl*.**RemoteHostName**—a **String** containing the name of the remote machine.
- *WinsockControl*.**RemoteIP**—a **String** containing the IP address of the remote machine formatted as ###.###.###.###. This pr operty is automatically set for client applications after the **Connect** method is used and for server programs after the **ConnectRequest** event (TCP) or **DataArrival** (UDP).
- *WinsockControl*.**RemotePort**—a **Long** containing the remote port number on the remote system. FTP uses port 21, and HTTP uses port 80.
- *WinsockControl*.**SocketHandle**—a **Long** containing the socket handle that is used by the Winsock APIs.
- *WinsockControl*.**State**—an **Integer** value containing the state of the control (see Table W-7).
- *WinsockControl*.**Tag**—a **String** that can hold programmer-specific information. This property is not used by Visual Basic.

State Name	Value	Description
sckClosed	0	Socket is closed (default).
sckOpen	1	Socket is open.
sckListening	2	Socket is listening.
sckConnectionPending	3	Connection is pending.
sckResolvingHost	4	Translating host name to IP address.

State Name	Value	Description
sckHostResolve	5	Host name has been translated.
sckConnecting	6	Connecting to a remote computer.
sckConnected	7	Connected to a remote computer.
sckClosing	8	Peer computer is closing the connection.
sckError	9	An error occurred.

Table W-7: State *values.*

Methods

WinsockControl.Accept *requestid*

Usage This method accepts an incoming connection in the **ConnectionRequest** event. This method applies to TCP server applications only.

Arguments • *requestid*—a **Long** containing the requestid.

WinsockControl.Bind *localport, localip*

Usage This method specifies the local port number and the local IP address used for TCP connections. This method is used to select the desired adapter when the system has multiple adapters.

Arguments • *localport*—a **Long** containing the local port number desired.
• *localip*—a **String** containing the local IP address desired.

WinsockControl.Close

Usage This method closes the listening socket or a TCP connection.

WinsockControl.GetData *data* [, *datatype* [, *len*]]

Usage This method retrieves data from the receive buffer.

> **Tip**
>
> Use this method inside the **DataArrival** event with the **totalbytes** argument.

Arguments • *data*—a **Variant** containing data from the retrieve buffer. If there isn't sufficient information to be returned, *data* will be set to Empty.
• *datatype*—an **Integer** value containing the type of data to be retrieved (see Table W-8).
• *len*—a **Long** containing number of bytes to be returned. Applies only when retrieving **Byte Arrays** and **Strings**. If omitted for **Byte Arrays** and **Strings** all available data will be retrieved.

datatype Name	Description
vbByte	Return a Byte value.
vbInteger	Return an Integer value.
vbLong	Return a Long value.
vbSingle	Return a Single value.
vbDouble	Return a Double value.
vbCurrency	Return a Currency value.
vbDate	Return a Date value.
vbBoolean	Return a Boolean value.
vbError	Return an error code.
VbString	Return a String value.
vbArray + vbByte	Return a Byte Array.

Table W-8: Datatype values.

WinsockControl.Listen

Usage This method creates a socket and listens for a connection request. It is used by TCP connections only. When a connection request is received, the **ConnectionRequest** event will occur.

WinsockControl.PeekData data [, datatype [, len]]

Usage This method retrieves and examines data from the receive buffer, but does not remove it from the buffer. Otherwise this method is identical to the **GetData** method.

Arguments
- *data*—a **Variant** containing data from the retrieve buffer. If there isn't sufficient information to be returned, *data* will be set to Empty.
- *datatype*—an **Integer** value containing the type of data to be retrieved (see Table W-9).
- *len*—a **Long** containing number of bytes to be returned. Applies only when retrieving **Byte Arrays** and **Strings**. If omitted for **Byte Arrays** and **Strings,** all available data will be retrieved.

datatype Name	Description
vbByte	Return a Byte value.
vbInteger	Return an Integer value.
vbLong	Return a Long value.
vbSingle	Return a Single value.
vbDouble	Return a Double value.
vbCurrency	Return a Currency value.
vbDate	Return a Date value.
vbBoolean	Return a Boolean value.
vbError	Return an error code.
VbString	Return a String value.
vbArray + vbByte	Return a Byte Array.

Table W-9: Datatype values.

WinsockControl.SendData *data*

Usage This method sends data to the remote computer.

Arguments • *data*—a variable containing the data to be sent. Binary data should be sent using a **Byte Array**.

Events

Private Sub *WinsockControl*_Close ([*index* As Integer])

Usage This event is called when the remote computer closes a TCP connection.

Arguments • *index*—an **Integer** that uniquely identifies a control in a control array. This argument is not present if the control is not part of a control array.

Private Sub *WinsockControl*_Connect ([*index* As Integer])

Usage This event is called when a connection has been made.

Arguments • *index*—an **Integer** that uniquely identifies a control in a control array. This argument is not present if the control is not part of a control array.

Private Sub *WinsockControl*_ConnectionRequest ([*index* As Integer ,] *requestid* As Long)

Usage This event is called whenever a connection is requested.

Arguments • *index*—an **Integer** that uniquely identifies a control in a control array. This argument is not present if the control is not part of a control array.
• *requestid*—a **Long** containing the requestid. This value is passed to the **Accept** method.

Private Sub *WinsockControl*_DataArrival ([*index* As Integer ,] *bytestotal* As Long)

Usage This event is called whenever new data arrives from the remote computer.

Arguments • *index*—an **Integer** that uniquely identifies a control in a control array. This argument is not present if the control is not part of a control array.
• *bytestotal*—a **Long** containing the total amount of data that can be retrieved.

Private Sub *WinsockControl*_Error ([*index* As Integer ,] *number* As Integer, *description* As String, *scode* As Long, *source* As String, *HelpFile* As String, *HelpContext* As Long, *CancelDisplay* As Boolean)

Usage This event is called whenever an error occurs.

Arguments
- *index*—an **Integer** that uniquely identifies a control in a control array. This argument is not present if the control is not part of a control array.
- *number*—an **Integer** containing the error code (see Table W-10).

Error Number Name	Value	Description
sckOutOfMemory	7	Out of memory.
sckInvalidPropertyValue	380	The property value is invalid.
sckSetNotSupported	383	The property is read-only.
sckGetNotSupported	394	The property is write-only.
sckOpCancled	1004	The operation was canceled.
sckInvalidAgument	10014	The requested address is a broadcast address, but the flag was not set.
sckWouldBlock	10035	The operation would block a non-blocking socket.
sckInProgress	10036	A blocking operation is in progress.
sckAlreadyComplete	10037	The operation is complete. No blocking operation in progress.
sckNotSocket	10038	The descriptor is not a socket.
sckMsgTooBig	10040	The datagram was truncated.
sckPortNotSupported	10043	The specified port is not supported.
sckAddressInUse	10048	The address is in use.
sckAddressNotAvailable	10049	The address is not on the local machine.
sckNetworkSubsystemFailed	10050	The network subsystem failed.
sckNetworkUnreachable	10051	The network can't be reached from the host.
sckNetReset	10052	The connection timed out when the SO_KEEPALIVE was set.
sckConnectAborted	10053	The connection was aborted.
sckConnectionReset	10054	The connection was reset by the remote system.
sckNoBufferSpace	10055	No buffer space is available.
sckAlreadyConnected	10056	The socket is already connected.
sckNotConnected	10057	The socket is not connected.
sckSocketShutdown	10058	The socket has been shut down.
sckTimedout	10060	The socket has timed out.
sckConnectionRefused	10061	The connection is refused.
sckNotInitialized	10093	The WinsockInit should be called first.
sckHostNotFound	11001	The host system was not found.
sckHostNotFoundTryAgain	11002	The host system was not found, but you should try again.
sckNonRecoverableError	11003	A non-recoverable error occurred.
sckNoData	11004	No data of the requested type was available.
sckBadState	40006	The wrong protocol or connection state.
sckInvalidAg	40014	The argument is outside the proper range or in the wrong format.
sckSuccess	40017	The request was completed successfully.
sckUnsupported	40018	An unsupported data type was used.
sckInvalidOp	40020	Invalid operation.
sckOutOfRange	40021	The argument is out of range.
sckWrongProtocol	40026	The wrong protocol was used.

Table W-10: Error Number values.

- *description*—a **String** containing a text description of the error code.
- *source*—a **String** containing the source of the error.
- *HelpFile*—a **String** containing the filename and path of the help file.
- *HelpContext*—a **Long** containing the help file reference.
- *CancelDisplay*—a **Boolean** when **True** means that no message box containing the error is displayed. **False** means that a message box describing the error is displayed (default).

Private Sub *WinsockControl*_SendComplete ([*index* As Integer])

Usage   This event is called after data sent in the **SendData** method has been sent and received.

Arguments
- *index*—an **Integer** that uniquely identifies a control in a control array. This argument is not present if the control is not part of a control array.

Private Sub *WinsockControl*_SendProgress ([*index* As Integer ,] *BytesSent* As Long, *BytesRemaining* As Long)

Usage   This event is called periodically while data is being sent to another computer.

Arguments
- *index*—an **Integer** that uniquely identifies a control in a control array. This argument is not present if the control is not part of a control array.
- *BytesSent*—an **Integer** containing the number of bytes sent.
- *BytesRemaining*—an **Integer** containing the number of bytes remaining in the output buffer to be sent.

Examples
```
Private Sub Command1_Click()
Text3.Text = Inet1.OpenURL(Text1.Text)
End Sub

Private Sub Inet1_StateChanged(ByVal State As Integer)
Text2.Text = Text2.Text & "Current status: " & Format(State) & vbCrLf
End Sub
```

This program uses the **OpenURL** method to retrieve the contents from the server specified by the URL in the Text1 text box. As the process is running, the **StateChanged** event records all of the various state changes in Text2 text box.

See Also   **Microsoft Internet Transfer Control** (control)

With

STATEMENT

CCE, LE, PE, EE

Syntax
```
With object
     [ list of statements ]
End With
```

Usage The **With** statement is used to qualify a single object or user-defined type. Properties of the qualified object may omit the object name and begin with a period (".").

Arguments *object*—the name of the object to be qualified.

Examples
```
Private Sub Command1_Click()
With Text1
   .Text = "Testing the with statement."
   .Font.Size = 36
   .Font.Bold = True
End With
End Sub
```

This routine uses a **With** statement to simplify assigning values to Text1 text box object.

See Also **Object** (data type)

Workspace

OBJECT

PE, EE

Usage The **Workspace** object is used by Data Access Objects (DAO) to provide a session for database access.

Properties *WorkspaceObject*.**DefaultCursor**—a **Long** containing the default cursor created by the **OpenConnection** and **OpenDatabase** methods for ODBC workspaces only (see Table W-11).

DefaultCursor Name	Description
dbUseDefaultCursor	Use a server side cursor if available, otherwise the ODBC cursor library will be used.
dbUseODBCCursor	Always use the ODBC cursor library. Good for small amounts of data.
dbUseServerCursor	Always use server side cursors. Good for large amounts of data.
dbUseClientBatchCursor	Always use the batch cursor library. This option is required for batch updates.
dbUseNoCursor	Use forward-only type of cursor, read-only and with a rowset size of 1.

Table W-11: DefaultCursor *values*.

- *WorkspaceObject*.**IsolateODBCTrans**—a **Boolean** when **True** means that multiple transactions using the same ODBC connection are isolated. **False** means that multiple transactions can use the same ODBC connection.
- *WorkspaceObject*.**LoginTimeout**—an **Integer** value containing the number of seconds that must pass before an error is returned during the login attempt to an ODBC database. The default value is 20 seconds.
- *WorkspaceObject*.**Name**—a **String** value containing the name of the object. It can be up to 20 characters in length.
- *WorkspaceObject*.**Type**—an **Integer** containing the type of workspace (see Table W-12).
- *WorkspaceObject*.**UserName**—a **String** value containing the name of a user associated with the workspace.

Type Name	Description
dbUseJet	The workspace is connected to a Microsoft Jet database engine.
dbUseODBC	The workspace is connected to an ODBC database server.

Table W-12: Type *values.*

Methods

WorkspaceObject.BeginTrans

Usage   This method marks the beginning of a transaction.

WorkspaceObject.Close

Usage   This method closes a workspace. If there are any open **Recordset** objects, they will be closed before the **Workspace** object is closed.

WorkspaceObject.CommitTrans [dbFlushOSCacheWrites]

Usage   This method marks the end of a transaction and saves the data into the database. After the commit has finished, the transaction can't be undone using the **RollBack** method.

Arguments   ▪ *dbFlushOSCacheWrites*—a **Long** value when present instructs the Microsoft Jet database engine to ensure that the operating system disk cache is flushed before returning to the user. This ensures that the transaction is posted to disk at a cost of slowing down the transaction a small amount.

Database = WorkspaceObject.CreateDatabase (dbname, locale, options)

Usage   This method is used to create a new database.

Arguments   ▪ *Dalubuse*—a **Database** object containing the new database.

- *dbname*—a **String** value containing the filename and path of the new database file.
- *locale*—a **String** value containing the language of the new database (see Table W-13), the password for the new database, or both. To specify the password, use the string ";pwd=password" where password is the new password. To specify both, concatenate the two strings together like, *dbLangNorwDan* & ";pwd=password".

Language Name	Description
dbLangArabic	Arabic.
dbLangChineseSimplified	Simplified Chinese.
dbLangChineseTraditional	Traditional Chinese.
dbLangCyrillic	Cyrillic.
dbLangCzech	Czech.
dbLangDutch	Dutch.
dbLangGeneral	English, French, German, Portuguese, Italian, and Modern Spanish.
dbLangGreek	Greek.
dbLangHebrew	Hebrew.
dbLangHungarian	Hungarian.
dbLangIcelandic	Icelandic.
dbLangJapanese	Japanese.
dbLangKorean	Korean.
DbLangNordic	Nordic (Jet version 1.0 only).
dbLangNorwDan	Norwegian or Danish.
dbLangPolish	Polish.
dbLangSlovenian	Slovenian.
dbLangSpanish	Spanish.
dbLangSwedFin	Swedish or Finnish.
dbLangThai	Thai.
dbLangTurkish	Turkish.

Table W-13: Language values.

- *options*—a **Variant** value containing the sum of the selected constants from Table W-14. If omitted, this argument will default to the values in the *olddb*.

options Name	Description
dbEncrypt	Encrypt the database.
dbDecrypt	Decrypt the database.
dbVersion10	Create a Version 1.0 compatible database.
dbVersion11	Create a Version 1.1 compatible database.
dbVersion20	Create a Version 2.0/2.5 compatible database.
dbVersion30	Create a Version 3.0/3.5 compatible database.

Table W-14: Options values.

Group = WorkspaceObject.CreateGroup ([name] [, pid])

Usage This method is used to create a new group.

Arguments
- *Group*—a **Group** object containing the new group.
  - *name*—a **String** value containing the name of the workspace. It must begin with a letter and can contain any combination of letters, numbers, or underscore characters ("_"). The length of the name can be up to 20 characters.
  - *pid*—a **String** containing the personal identifier associated with the group. It can be up to 20 characters long, but must be at least 4 characters long.

User = WorkspaceObject.CreateUser ([name] [, [pid] [,password]])

Usage This method is used to create a new user.

Arguments
- *User*—a **User** object containing the new user.
  - *name*—a **String** value containing the name of the workspace. It must begin with a letter and can contain any combination of letters, numbers, or underscore characters ("_"). The length of the name can be up to 20 characters.
  - *pid*—a **String** containing the personal identifier associated with the group. It can be up to 20 characters long, but must be at least 4 characters long.
  - *password*—a **String** containing the password for the workspace. It can be up to 14 characters long and contain any ASCII character except for the null character (ASCII value of 0).

connection = WorkspaceObject.OpenConnection name [, options [, readonly [, connect]]]

Usage This method is used to open a connection to an ODBC database system.

Arguments
- *connection*—a connection object containing the opened connection.
  - *name*—a **String** value containing the name of the group.
  - *options*—an **Integer** value containing the options for the connection process.

database = WorkspaceObject.OpenDatabase name [, options [, readonly [, connect]]]

Usage This method is used to open a Microsoft Jet database.

Arguments
- *database*—a database object containing the opened database.
  - *name*—a **String** value containing the filename and path of the Jet database or the ODBC data source.
  - *options*—an **Integer** value containing options for the database (see Table W-15).

options Name	Description
dbDriverNoPrompt	The connection information in *name* and *connect* are used to connect to the database. If sufficient information is not present, an error will occur.
dbDriverPrompt	The ODBC driver takes the information supplied in *name* and *connect* and displays it in the ODBC Data Sources dialog box.
dbDriverComplete	The ODBC driver uses the information supplied in *name* and *connect* to connect to the database. If there is insufficient information, the ODBC Data Sources dialog box will be displayed (default).
dbDriverCompleteRequired	This is similar to the *dbDriverComplete* option, but information supplied in *name* and *connect* can't be changed.

Table W-15: *Options values.*

- *readonly*—a **Boolean** value which is true for a read-only connection and **False** for a read/write connection (default).
- *connect*—a **String** value containing connection information including passwords.

WorkspaceObject.RollBack

Usage This method abandons all of the changes to the database, so the database is at the same state as it was when the **BeginTrans** method was used.

Arguments ■ *name*—a **String** containing the name of the property. Must begin with a letter and can be followed by letters, numbers, or an underscore ("_").

See Also **DBEngine** (object), **Workspaces** (collection)

Workspaces

COLLECTION

PE, EE

Usage The **Workspaces** collection is used by Data Access Objects (DAO) to contain information about the active workspaces in a program.

Properties ■ *WorkspacesCollection*.**Count**—an **Integer** containing the number of **Workspace** objects in the collection.

Methods *WorkspacesCollection*.**Append** *object*

Usage This method is used to append a workspace object to the collection.

Arguments ■ *object*—a **Workspace** object created by the **CreateWorkspace** method of the **DBEngine** object.

WorkspacesCollection.Delete *name*

Usage This method removes a **Workspace** object from the collection.

Arguments ▪ *name*—a **String** object containing the name of the **Workspace** object to be deleted.

WorkspacesCollection.Refresh

Usage This method gets a current copy of the workspaces in the collection. This is important in a multi-user environment where more than one user may be making changes in the **Workspaces** collection.

See Also **DBEngine** (object), **Workspace** (object)

Write

STATEMENT

CCE, LE, PE, EE

Syntax `Write # filenum, [expr ] [, expr ]. . . [, expr ]`

Usage The **Write #** statement is used to write data to a file. Expressions in a single **Write** statement are separated by commas. After the last expression is written, a carriage return linefeed pair (*vbCrLf*) will be written to the file.

> **Tip**
>
> Use the **Input** statement to read data written with the **Write** statement.

Arguments ▪ *filenum*—any open file number that was assigned in an **Open** statement.

▪ *expr*—any Boolean, numeric, or string expression. Each expression is formatted as listed in Table W-16.

expr Type	Description
Boolean	Written to disk as #TRUE# or #FALSE#.
Date	Written to disk as #yyyy-mm-dd, hh:mm:ss#, #yyyy-mm-dd#, or #hh:mm:ss#.
Double	Written to disk with a series of numbers with a decimal point.
Error (Variant)	Written to disk as #ERROR errornumber#.
Integer	Written to disk as a series of numbers.
Long	Written to disk as a series of numbers.
Null	Written to disk as #NULL#.
Single	Written to disk as a series of numbers with a decimal point.
String	Written to disk as a quote, followed by the characters in the string, followed by another quote. The string can contain embedded characters like carriage return and line feed.

Table W-16: Expr values.

Examples

```
Private Sub Command2_Click()
Open App.Path & "\testfile.dat" For Output As #1
Write #1, Text1.Text
Close #1
End Sub
```

This routine writes the information contained in the Text1 text box to the file testfile.dat.

See Also **Close** (statement), **Input** (statement), **Open** (statement)

Year

FUNCTION

CCE, LE, PE, EE

Syntax   *DValue* = **Year** (*year*)

Usage   The **Year** function returns the year from a numeric, **Date,** or **String** variable containing a valid date or time.

Arguments
- *DValue*—an **Integer** value that contains the year.
- *dime*—a **Date**, **Long,** or **String** value that contains a valid time or date.

Examples
```
Private Sub Command1_Click()
If IsDate(Text1.Text) Then
   Text2.Text = Year(Text1.Text)
Else
   Text2.Text = "Illegal date."
End If
End Sub
```

This routine verifies that the date or time in the Text1 text box is valid and then extracts the year from the date value in the text box.

See Also   **CDate** (function), **Date** (data type), **Day** (function), **IsDate** (function), **Month** (function), **Now** (function), **Time** (function)

Appendix A
About the Companion CD-ROM

The Companion CD-ROM included with your copy of *The Visual Basic 5 Programmer's Reference* contains the entire contents of the book, in hypertext format.

Navigating the CD-ROM

To find out more about the CD-ROM and its contents, please open the "README.HTM" file in your favorite browser. You will see a small menu offering several links, including a link to learn more about Ventana, and a link to view the contents of the book.

Technical Support

Technical support is available for installation-related problems only. The technical support office is open from 8:00 A.M. to 6:00 P.M. Monday through Friday and can be reached via the following methods:

- Phone: (919) 544-9404 extension 81
- Faxback Answer System: (919) 544-9404 extension 85
- E-mail: help@vmedia.com
- Fax: (919) 544-9472
- World Wide Web: **http://www.vmedia.com/support**
- America Online: keyword *Ventana*

Limits of Liability & Disclaimer of Warranty

The author and publisher of this book have used their best efforts in preparing the CD-ROM and the programs contained in it. These efforts include the development, research, and testing of the theories and programs to determine their effectiveness. The author and publisher make no warranty of any kind expressed or implied, with regard to these programs or the documentation contained in this book.

The author and publisher shall not be liable in the event of incidental or consequential damages in connection with, or arising out of, the furnishing, performance, or use of the programs, associated instructions, and/or claims of productivity gains.

VENTANA

http://www.vmedia.com

VENTANA

Official Netscape Enterprise Server 3 Book

Richard Cravens
$49.99, 480 pages, part #: 1-56604-664-5

- Detailed examination of web-site security issues and benefits.
- Complete coverage of installation, configuration and maintenance, along with troubleshooting tips.
- Shows how to enrich web sites with multimedia and interactivity.

CD-ROM contains sample HTML editors, HTML references, current Netscape plug-ins.

For Windows NT & UNIX • Intermediate to Advanced

Official Netscape Technologies Developer's Guide

Luke Duncan, Sean Michaels
$39.99, 352 pages, part #: 1-56604-749-8

- Guide to the most critical ONE SDKs and APIs—CORBA/IIOP, IFC, plug-ins and server-side JavaScript.
- Overview of Internet/intranet application development with IFC.
- Example plug-in project to integrate multiple aspects of Netscape ONE.

All Platforms • Intermediate to Advanced

VENTANA

Net Security: Your Digital Doberman

$29.99, 312 pages, illustrated, part #: 1-56604-506-1

Doing business on the Internet can be safe . . . if you know the risks and take appropriate steps. This thorough overview helps you put a virtual Web watchdog on the job—to protect both your company and your customers from hackers, electronic shoplifters and disgruntled employees. Easy-to-follow explanations help you understand complex security technologies, with proven technologies for safe Net transactions. Tips, checklists and action plans cover digital dollars, pilfer-proof "storefronts," protecting privacy and handling breaches.

Intranet Firewalls

$34.99, 360 pages, illustrated, part #: 1-56604-506-1

Protect your network by controlling access—inside and outside your company—to proprietary files. This practical, hands-on guide takes you from intranet and firewall basics through creating and launching your firewall. Professional advice helps you assess your security needs and choose the best system for you. Includes tips for avoiding costly mistakes, firewall technologies, in-depth reviews and uses for popular firewall software, advanced theory of firewall design strategies and implementation, and more.

VENTANA

Java Programming for the Internet

$49.95, 816 pages, illustrated, part #: 1-56604-355-7

Master the programming language of choice for Internet applications. Expand the scope of your online development with this comprehensive, step-by-step guide to creating Java applets. The CD-ROM features Java Developers Kit, source code for all the applets, samples and programs from the book, and much more.

The Visual Basic Programmer's Guide to Java

$39.99, 450 pages, part #: 1-56604-527-4

At last—a Java book that speaks your language! Use your understanding of Visual Basic as a foundation for learning Java and object-oriented programming. This unique guide not only relates Java features to what you already know—it also highlights the areas in which Java excels over Visual Basic, to build an understanding of its appropriate use. The CD-ROM features comparative examples written in Java & Visual Basic, code for projects created in the book and more

VENTANA

Principles of Object-Oriented Programming in Java

$39.99, 400 pages, illustrated, part #: 1-56604-530-4

Move from writing programs to designing solutions—with dramatic results! Take a step beyond syntax to discover the true art of software design, with Java as your paintbrush and objects on your palette. This in-depth discussion of how, when and why to use objects enables you to create programs—using Java or any other object-oriented language that not only work smoothly, but are easy to maintain and upgrade. The CD-ROM features the Java SDK, code samples and more.

The Comprehensive Guide to Visual J++

$49.99, 792 pages, illustrated, part #: 1-56604-533-9

Learn to integrate the Java language and ActiveX in one development solution! Master the Visual J++ environment using real-world coding techniques and project examples. Includes executable J++ sample projects plus undocumented tips and tricks. The CD-ROM features all code examples, sample ActiveX COM objects, Java documentation and an ActiveX component library.

VENTANA

Java 1.1 Programmer's Reference

Daniel I. Joshi, Pavel Vorobiev
$49.99, 1000 pages, illustrated, part #: 1-56604-687-4

The ultimate resource for Java professionals! And the perfect supplement to the JDK documentation. Whether you need a day-to-day reference for Java classes, an explanation of new APIs, a guide to common programming techniques, or all three, you've got it—all in an encyclopedic format that's convenient to refer to again and again. Covers new Java 1.1 features, including the AWT, JARs, Java Security API, the JDBC, JavaBeans, and more, with complete descriptions that include syntax, usage and code samples. **CD-ROM:** Complete, hyperlinked version of the book.
For all platforms • Intermediate to Advanced

Migrating From Java 1.0 to Java 1.1

Daniel I. Joshi, Pavel Vorobiev
$39.99, 600 pages, illustrated, part #: 1-56604-686-6

Your expertise with Java 1.0 provides the perfect springboard to rapid mastery of Java 1.1 and the new tools in the JDK 1.1. Viewing what's new from the perspective of what you already know gets you up to speed quickly. And you'll learn not only what's changed, but why—gaining deeper understanding of the evolution of Java and how to exploit its power for your projects. **CD-ROM:** All the sample Java 1.1 programs, plus extended examples.
For Windows NT/95, Macintosh, UNIX, Solaris
Intermediate to Advanced

The Comprehensive Guide to the JDBC SQL API

Daniel I. Joshi, Rodney Runolfson
$49.99, 456 pages, illustrated, part#: 1-56604-637-8

Develop high-powered database solutions for your Internet/intranet site! Covers the basics of Java and SQL, interface design with AWT and instructions for building an Internet-based search engine. **CD-ROM:** OpenLink Server-side JDBC driver, SQL databases and tables from the book, sample code, JDBC API specification and example sites.
For Windows 95/NT • Intermediate to Advanced

VENTANA

TO ORDER ANY VENTANA TITLE, COMPLETE THIS ORDER FORM AND MAIL OR FAX IT TO US, WITH PAYMENT, FOR QUICK SHIPMENT.

TITLE	PART #	QTY	PRICE	TOTAL

SHIPPING

For orders shipping within the United States, please add $4.95 for the first book, $1.50 for each additional book.
For "two-day air," add $7.95 for the first book, $3.00 for each additional book.
Email: vorders@kdc.com for exact shipping charges.
Note: Please include your local sales tax.

SUBTOTAL = $ _____
SHIPPING = $ _____
TAX = $ _____
TOTAL = $ _____

Mail to: International Thomson Publishing • 7625 Empire Drive • Florence, KY 41042
☎ US orders 800/332-7450 • fax 606/283-0718
☎ International orders 606/282-5786 • Canadian orders 800/268-2222

Name _____
E-mail _____ Daytime phone _____
Company _____
Address (No PO Box) _____
City _____ State _____ Zip _____
Payment enclosed ___ VISA ___ MC ___ Acc't # _____ Exp. date _____
Signature _____ Exact name on card _____

Check your local bookstore or software retailer for these and other bestselling titles, or call toll free:

800/332-7450
8:00 am - 6:00 pm EST